CARIBBEAN WRITERS

A Bio-Bibliographical-Critical Encyclopedia

Editor: Donald E. Herdeck

Associate Editors:

Maurice A. Lubin
John Figueroa
Dorothy Alexander Figueroa
José Alcántara Almánzar

General Editor: Margaret Laniak-Herdeck

THREE CONTINENTS PRESS, INC.
WASHINGTON, D. C.

3CP

Drawings (Frank Collymore, Louise Bennett and Derek Walcott) by Tom Gladden
Drawings of Dominican writers by Nick Clapp

ISBN: 0-914478-74-5

LC No: 77-3841

Three Continents Press, Inc., 1346 Connecticut Avenue, N. W., Washington, D. C. 20036

Mi wan' opodron
Lek friman borgu.

Kondre,
Dat' ede
M' e dorfu tide.

I want the drumming in the open
like a citizen who is free.

People!
For this
do I dare today

(from Johanna Schouten-Elsenhout's
Sranen-Tongo poem "Kodyo")

ACKNOWLEDGMENTS

Many persons over the past four years have helped make the shaping and the writing of this volume: foremost have been my associates Maurice Lubin, Dorothy Alexander Figueroa and John Figueroa and José Alcántara Almánzar, who wrote major sections or commented on and augmented the work already done. J.R.R. Casimir of Dominica, José Miguel Gómez of Santo Domingo, Clifford Sealy of Trinidad, and Paul Thompson, biographer of Bertène Juminer of Cayenne, have also contributed important material to us, as have Thomas Hale and Robert D. Hamner who provided most of our large entries respectively on Césaire and V. S. Naipaul. And special thanks are due my colleague, Margaret.

Dr. Christiaan J. Engels, poet, painter and long editor of *De Stoep* was very helpful to me during and since my visit to Curacao; Cola Debrot, former governor of the Netherlands Antilles, whose study of the literature of Curacao, Aruba and Bonaire has been very useful, and his kind letters have guided me in various particulars. Also helpful in that area were the staff of the Stichting Wettenschappelijke Bibliteek of Willemsted, Curacao, and especially Ms. Maritza Eustacia, head librarian. Mr. Eddy Pieters Heyliger, himself an important Papiamento author, also was helpful to me during my stay in Curacao.

In Trinidad, Mrs. Irma Goldstraw and Mrs. Wilma Primus, head librarians of the library at the St. Augustine campus of the University of the West Indies gave me desk space and every assistance for my study of their shelves and clipping archives, and Professor Keith Warner was a hospitable guide during my stay in Port of Spain.

In Guadeloupe, Roger Fortuné, Director of the Tourist Office, and Edward Dupland, long resident in Guadeloupe and student of the island's writers, were very helpful. In Martinique I was helped mightily by the Chief Librarian of La Bibliothèque Schoelcher, M. Rafael Henri, who brought me the books I wanted to see and discussed the island's literary scene in his old office in the dusky center of the great 19th century building he has occupied so long.

In Jamaica, Ms. Alvona Alleyn, Librarian of the West Indies and Special Collections of the Mona campus of the U.W.I. was helpful in furnishing files and information on the local writers as she had earlier been with the Figueroas.

• • • • •

At home I owe a word of special thanks to Brian Weinstein who first alerted me to the cultural world of the Caribbean. The libraries of Howard University, and my home library of Georgetown University provided me with many texts of creative works and background studies and the members of the staff of the Library of Congress made the work easier.

The National Endowment for the Humanities which awarded me a grant and the School of Foreign Service at Georgetown University which let me spend my sabbatical on this project were instrumental too.

Special thanks to Paul Bloch and Liz Maynard for editorial assistance on the Spanish section and to Magda George for help on the Anglophone section. Nick Clapp, a fine artist and enthusiastic friend, executed the line drawings of many of the Spanish writers. Acknowledgment is also made to the authors who have helped provide photographs of themselves and colleagues along with details of their lives and works which helped strengthen the information presented.

I especially wish to remember one scholar who can no longer hear or see these words: René de Rooy (1917-1974). René became a good friend and collaborator by correspondence until his sudden death in Mexico deprived this work of his own experience and scholarship.

D.E.H.

INTRODUCTION

Reasons for the Work

Only belatedly have the newly emerging political and cultural entities of the Caribbean islands and the three culturally connected South American areas of Guyana, Surinam and Guyane come into the world's consciousness. Admittedly, the land-areas concerned are minor when compared to the adjacent continental land masses, and the populations, too, are modest except for the heavily populated Cuba. But Haiti, for one instance and independent for 170 years, has produced hundreds of writers. Every area is increasingly literate and its artists expressing the complex racial, cultural, and political lives of the Caribbean.

The question for those of us interested in literature is then, *not* why should the literature of any one island state or group of states be considered, but rather, why should the areas of the Caribbean from Cuba south be grouped in one study of the sort we offer here. (For purposes of completeness, we have included a few authors from islands to the north of Cuba and from Belize [British Honduras]. The reasons—or the answers—come quickly to hand:

1. The Caribbean represents a significant cultural sub-section of the Western World, taking its European strain from the voyages of Columbus and his successors.

2. Almost everywhere people of African origin are either in the majority or at the least are highly visible and creative elements in the new states. And, in some cases, the vestigial African qualities are still relatively dynamic and unchanged from those of mother Africa, as in Haiti and Surinam. In these areas the Caribbean-African is particularly free to work out his own political, economic and cultural destiny in the Caribbean setting.

3. Into this area has also come the East Indian, the Chinese, the Javanese, the Syrian, and, here and there, native Amer-indian stocks and their cultures remain. Nowhere in the world do the races of mankind so mingle and struggle as in the tropical and sub-tropical latitudes of these sea-washed states and territories.

4. Even in non-Marxist terms, the peoples of this area must be seen as farmers and workers only now taking the reins of power from the few remaining Europeans and their créole allies. These mostly poor people, to a greater or lesser degree Europeanized, must now forge nativist and life-enhancing institutions of government, communication and intellectual values. Even the Balkanized Africans

in Africa seeking to establish new states have had an easier time, for they could fall back upon their own still-living socio-religious systems and life patterns inside relatively well-recognized territories or homelands. The Caribbean peoples, in contrast, must awaken from the long nightmare of slavery and reorganize the fragile economies and pluri-valued societies they have now inherited. From the sorrowful and heterogeneous past these peoples must construct their fresh, compound identities.

5. By definition the peoples of the Caribbean world are sealocked. They cannot escape each other in vast hinterlands or shut out the outer, more powerful world. The United States and the other great powers sail easily to their shores and draw into vast economic vortices the resources of these small states. So, whether the Caribbeans wish it or not, they all share much of the same history, geography and ecology; and the same problems of poverty, ignorance, crowding and weakness stare at them all.

Accordingly, the area cries for a united treatment. Where the ignorant North American or European might dismiss the culture and the writers of "little" Jamaica, of exotic Guyane, or of "carnalvalesque" Trinidad, it is harder to dismiss the thoughts and feelings of people, some fifty millions of them, spread over thousands of miles, speaking rich dialects of four of Europe's languages, and reflecting the glories and agonies of centuries of inter-racial, social and cultural experiences. For the Caribbeans, the world's growing inter-relatedness is a daily and even ancient reality.

The islands present a plethora of contrasts, vocabularies, religious and familial rites and habits. What a rich sea to fish for the creative writer. The Caribbean literatures can and do tell us much of what colonialism was and meant and still *is* to those who suffered it. And Caribbean literature speaks of the new man and woman of the new states. And Caribbean literature has the pathos, and often the tragedy which any literature needs to grow, parasite that it is of the human heart. Humor, too, comes when people confront other values and begin to reflect on their own—something "monocolore" cultures usually badly lack. And much Caribbean writing offers tones and rhythmical patterns—and verbal spontaneities—that make the native Caribbean eye light up and the non-Caribbean ear and heart take joy of.

Real people live in those palm-studded isles. They are often noisy and restless, full of talk and full of themselves. It is time enough we let them talk also to us, directly, not as servants in the hotels or as picturesque sugar-cane cutters, but as men and women living in the confusing but exciting world of freedom. Though some of them are still entrapped in colonial empires which refuse to die, they all know the fury of hurricanes, remember the wrath of alien masters, and the beauty of the Atlantean tropics. Many of the Caribbean peoples do not read, cannot read, but their writers speak for their spirit and their lives. We are the poorer if we any longer fail to hear them, or, if hearing, refuse to listen.

Some of the Problems Involved in Studying Caribbean Literature

As any student of a new field or discipline is only too aware, the plethora of background studies (the more or less definitive bibliographies, the mass of biographies and social-literary studies, handbooks and encyclopedias) and other aids to quick and even full understanding available to the scholar in older fields is not at all the case in the Caribbean area. Even such literatures as African, a veritable phenomenon since the 1940's, have quickly obtained much sound critical, bibliographical and biographical back-up material and more is coming out all the time.

Though recently publishers in the United States and elsewhere have slackened off from their commendable zeal to bring out anything written well by an African, there are literally thousands of African works available, most of them in paperback editions as well, to the serious student. In stark contrast, to those interested in Caribbean books, only a few partial bibliographies exist in readily available form in English and only a handful of bookstores are prepared to market Caribbean literature. Lacking is a compendium of information concerning all relevant writers. Here we attempt to offer details of the works of hundreds of writers from each of the several linguistic areas along with biographical and critical information.

When this project began over five years ago it seemed it would be easier to do than my *African Authors* just put to press. After all, the Caribbean area is closer, the languages all European, and the time span far briefer. But the contrasts are these (and they have made the struggle a hard one): where African authors by and large published first (and often still do) in the former colonial press, most Caribbean writers, it was soon found, had brought out their works at home in small, often quickly forgotten or poorly recorded editions. Where African writing of the contemporary sort was born in the full light of interest in things African (at long last), most early Caribbean books howled their birth into the deep night of slavery or the vast parochialism of the becalmed islands of the past centuries and got buried dead or alive, fetal cord and all. Where even the most Europeanized African writer was proud of his own culture and knew its forms and language and values, the Caribbean often fretted over his mixed heritage or hid it altogether. And being Black meant until recently one had only the worst experience of Europe and often only the debased and scorned remnants of Africa.

Since many if not all of the top cream of the Caribbean society once looked back to Europe for culture, the colonial ignorance of the local scene was nigh total—and literature fails badly, it seems, when few can write and fewer care to buy a local book, the complaint of every early editor or brazen poetic voice. But still works there were, and as the years passed more men and women turned their realities and visions into the written word and fortunately much of their work survives.

Though it was often difficult to identify the authors, to learn about their works and to give any account of them that would fit them into a reasonably accurate context, sociologically and literarily, there was no dearth of material. The task was how to come at it and clarify it.

Even with the books published since independence, however, there are problems. Many books are issued by miniscule presses, as stated above, or by the mimeograph machines of a school system or benevolent employer. In many places, too, there are few if any commercial publishers. Perforce, each author or a circle of friends must publish his or her work. Since libraries are few and educated readership still tiny, editions are expensive and often acts of artistic egotism at best and bravado at worst. Moreover, since such works rarely are sent to the newly designated depositories, they quickly disappear unless the author makes his way to the top and his early book sees a second edition in more imposing dress and carrying a more impressive address. (Who would not like to have a copy of the original edition of Derek Walcott's first poems, or of Aimé Césaire's?)

What resources were most helpful then in recovering the clouded record? For the Spanish and French language authors, and particularly for the Dominican, Cuban, and the Haitian, the splendor was that literary historians, born into or adopted by the wealthier humanistic class, had access to fine private libraries and often surprisingly good records in old newspapers and early periodicals. Their literary studies and anthologies were usually well supported with biographical and bibliographical details so our work was the easier.

For English language writers, we have found few such old testaments to the early days and indeed there seems to have been much less writing in the West Indies than elsewhere until recently. Our success has been to have a co-editor who himself is a force in the literature and a leading critic and commentator. He and his scholar-wife have been able to exploit not only the usual library and other resources but their own personal experiences and friendships to bring our readers a close-up of a wide range of contemporary writers.

Information on Dutch, Papiamento and Surinam-Sranen writing has been even more difficult to obtain than that of the West Indies, and accordingly the few available studies were heavily leaned upon.

Scope and Objectives

This volume contains biographical information on some 2000 creative writers and bibliographic detail on upwards of 15,000 works. Though the great majority of the titles dealt with are of works created in English, Dutch, French, or Spanish, many of the volumes of verse and prose here discussed or listed have been written in one of the "creole" languages which have sprung up from the mixing of African, Indian and European word-stocks, grammars and experiences.

Our efforts have been to provide a wide survey of as many Caribbean authors as possible, supported by detailed bibliographies on each, and extensive lists of the works written in each linguistic cultural area. Finally, lists of authors by country, by language used, by socio-political entity, are provided.

Moreover, this work seeks to offer information in a relaxed narrative manner to both the scholar and the casual student/reader. We hope to present the writer as a warm sentient personality—avoiding the impersonal aridity and "shorthand" of the usual biographic register but still offering as complete a "record" as possible. Accordingly, we have avoided abbreviations and other eliptical expressions and have attempted generally to provide definitions of any literary movement mentioned in each entry even though the term might be a fairly common one. The aim was to make each essay self-sustaining.

The capsule biography offers the briefest possible summary of the author's career. The dating of birth is given as fully as we can and where there are several dates we try to assign one where most authorities, or a major authority, lead(s) the way. Where we really have no authority we arbitrarily assign a year 30 years prior to the first published work of any consequence. The term "ca" (circa) is our code word for such an assignment. In a few cases we do have clues of the birth year; these too are indicated by the use of "ca." Regarding names, we have normally employed the family name, but in a few cases chose to list an author under his more commonly known pen-name. In any event, we have made cross-references. Spanish names have been particulary difficult, but we have tried to use names as they appear in standard reference works, accepting the indexes of the various literary histories of Max Henríquez-Ureña as the ultimate authority.

The entries conclude with what we believe are reasonably definitive lists of the cited author's own work published in separate volumes and where relevant, of the more important periodical literature. Likewise we have sought to provide relatively complete bibliographies of useful studies of the subject author, though in some cases, as with José Martí or Saint-John Perse, a complete bibliography of the studies of the author in a work of the sort we have projected would bulk disproportionately large and be of value only to the most determined and specialized scholar. In general we have sought to list such works beginning with the most recent—and with separate volumes before periodical articles.

We trust we have covered all the major authors and a satisfying number of all others, including a few of the very recent. Since this work is not a pure bibliography we may have had to ignore a few authors who might have published one or more interesting works but of whose lives we had no information. We have also tried to be as balanced as we could in each linguistic-cultural area. Hopefully any second volume will add hundreds of new authors and new works in print by authors already covered for each linguistic area.

Obviously, there is space for reasonably full discussion of only the major authors and of a handful of seminal works in such a work as this.

Each of the major sections are introduced by an informal essay seeking to set out the general socio-linguistic history of the areas and peoples concerned. Then the major literary movements or events are referred to, including some of the clubs and journals which may have for a period voiced the new concerns and subjects of a rising generation. The extensive bibliographies cite works where comprehensive studies are available.

The goal in the introductory essays has been to offer a brief survey of major themes, authors and developments. By reading a dozen or so of the entries of the authors cited in our tour of the literature concerned, the beginning student will hopefully be on his way to a broader voyage of his own making in the rich and newest major literature. For too long even broad and deep scholars in other areas of literature have scanted Caribbean writing—for them too we offer a modest compass to a rewarding first visit to undiscovered lands.

Although the senior editor has seen the project through from its original conception and has done much of the work in many of the sections, he hereby proudly calls attention to the particular valiant and useful labors of his major co-editors: Maurice Lubin (long a major Haitian critic and bibliographer), for the Francophone section; John Figueroa and Dorothy Alexander Figueroa for the West Indies; and José Alcántara Almánzar for the writers of the Dominican Republic. Dr. Christian Engels and Cola DeBrot were most helpful in the work of the Netherlands Antilles, an almost perfect "terra incognita" to the student in the United States and possibly elsewhere. Others who helped in greater or lesser degree are sincerely thanked in the formal acknowledgments page. All of the editors, all these others, and all the anthologists, scholars, journalists and, most importantly of course, the writers themselves, made this work possible. It was a task taking five years from start to finish and wisely might have been granted another five before we dared to bundle up the manuscript. Things left out or mistakenly put in no doubt may be cited to haunt our arrogance in trying to do the job at all. But that something like what we have here tried to do has long been overdue seems beyond dispute.

As was asserted at the conclusion of another volume of mine, *African Authors 1300-1973*, any good scholarship should excite the attention that will result in its being improved upon. We invite corrections and augmentations. This volume can be a bench-mark of where we all were in 1978. Who any longer will dare to ask: "Is there a Caribbean literature?"

Donald E. Herdeck

August 23, 1978

N.B. This book was set in ITEK Souvenir type fonts which did not accommodate the acute accent over the Spanish "i". The lack of a clear accent sign is not the fault of the editors, but a shortcoming of the typeface used.

Table of Contents

Volume I

Anglophone Literature from the Caribbean

ESSAY ON WEST INDIAN WRITING

From the letters and private journals of European adventurers and travelers in the 17th century to the sophisticated and world-conscious prose and verse of such writers as St. Lucia's Derek Walcott, Trinidad's controversial V.S. Naipaul, and Jamaica's John Hearne, Roger Mais, Neville Dawes and Andrew Salkey, is a long voyage. For the moment, disregarding what remains of the Amerindian culture in the Caribbean, one can say that in all the islands (not just those formerly occupied by the British), European culture, life-style, literary forms and preoccupations have bulked large from the beginning and still do. Particularly in the West Indies, only here or there in a random poem or essay did an original "Caribbean" note obtrude before the 20th century. The darkness that was slavery and the one-crop economies were exploited, if at all, only as the "romantic" background to the genteel European writing in all the islands and the three Guianas.

In Haiti (independent since 1804), in Cuba (the big island always full of itself and always vivid), and from time to time in Guadeloupe and Martinique, genuine writers did increasingly address themselves to expressing their realities, though couching their ideas in European modes. In the West Indies it takes an act of imagination to summon up a vision of busy (and rewarded) writers engaged in creating an imaginative literature in the earlier centuries.

Any colonial community has by definition suffered the trauma of displacement. The settlement of the Caribbean was triply a bath of forgetfulness and psychic loss: preceded and accompanied by conquest and genocide, it led to the importation of alien and enchattled human beings, and the creation of the grossest sort of absentee landlordism and control. By the mid-20th century, the Caribbean nations were akin to badly-overpopulated rafts drifting in a Sargasso Sea of abandonment and economic malaise. Only spottily, if at all, had education of any sort been provided. Each people lived in its own green-blue pool of stagnation and ignorance. But the world-movements of revolt and reform (revolutionary or evolutionary does not matter here), and the inevitable if painful movement upward of the formerly despised Africans and the other non-European elements of the population, would gradually coalesce into new prideful and cultural self-identification.

Perhaps the problems for the English-speaking Caribbeans were more difficult than those of their neighbors because of English racial attitudes of superiority to everyone, including the Latins, or because the British had bigger fish to fry in their great empire and so mostly ignored their outposts of progress south of Cuba. Close tutelage, coddling "parents," can be obstacles to self development, too, however, and today's West Indians may be the more reliant, more idiosyncratic, possibly even more creative for all the long years of neglect, than the still tightly embraced French Antilles or the Hispanic-oriented peoples.

One must recall Tom Redcam's two novels: *Becka's Buckra Baby* (1903) and *One Brown Girl And . . .* (1909); H. G. De Lisser's eleven novels, including *Jane's Career* and *The White Witch of Rosehall* (1929), and *Morgan's Daughter* (1953). These were relatively timid works and cut along white lines. Only Claude McKay of Jamaica (1890-1948) of the earlier group in his verse and fiction, wrote genuinely of the African component of the West Indian experience, but others began to follow his lead, including his near contemporary Eric Walrond whose stories in *Tropic Death* (1926) are still of vivid interest.

More fundamental, perhaps, was the the need for journals and the rise of thoughtful persons concerned with literature and island culture. Critical reviews and magazines carrying the stories of new writers had to be founded and somehow kept going so that these new voices could reach out to a public and speak across the waters to each other and those "others" in the rest of the world. In this area the work of Albert Gomes, Alfred H. Mendes, C.L.R. James, and their like, struggled to light a torch in the almost primieval 1930's with their magazines *Trinidad* (1929) and *Beacon* (1931-33). W.T. Barnes and Frank Collymore and their still living BIM; and the A.J. Seymour group around *Kyk-over-al* in Guyana; Mrs. Manley's *Focus* and the new editors of *Caribbean Quarterly, Black Images, Herambee Speaks, Kaie, Kairi, New Beacon Reviews* and *New World* of the past several decades have permitted new gleams and old ones to appear.

The BBC's Caribbean Programmes under Henry Swanzy during the second World War and early post-war years also can be credited with dramatizing the "facts" and names of the new writing. Complicated as the Afro-Caribbean scene was, the triple conflict of the Indian-Pakistani-Chinese peoples of Trinidad for instance added even more elements to the mix which had to be attacked by the writers. Here V.S. Naipaul and Sam Selvon led the way in wry portrayals of people always alive but often confused about just what roles were to be played. The very need to play "a role" bespoke an unsureness, but of course such a condition has always provided the satirist with his finest opportunities.

With all these new developments a career at home as a writer was more thinkable. Certainly the Jamaican dialect poems of Louise Bennett (b. 1919) are high points for this acceptance, nay, enthusiastic exploitation, of the local scene seen daily. George Lamming and V.S. Naipaul in their very different ways have also focussed much of their work on being part of the complicated cultural-racial world of the West Indies, and today literally hundreds of writers are engaged in picturing the realities of their Caribbean home.

Many of the new writers, however, could not make a go of it at home, or so they thought. So, they migrated to London and Leeds, to New York and Toronto;

a few went to Africa. University men and women, some of them, others just out of grammar school, they often held low-skilled jobs. But they wrote and began to establish reputations. Few were as assiduous as Mittelholzer of Guyana who wrote on the London tube the hours of journey to and from his jobs and did a novel almost every year, did plays, did stories, and finally, inexplicably a suicide in a field in southern England; he was the author of the longest list of published works of any Caribbean artist, all but a handful of them written abroad. But in England, or elsewhere, the world of the soul could not be denied and the more these men and women sojourned in colder worlds the brighter and warmer appeared the lives of home. This is an exile literature in earnest, the product more of poverty and isolation than the tyranny of the state, but the yearning qualities and freshness of memory make many of these writings of universal appeal.

And at home or abroad, such writers as Dominica's Jean Rhys or Guyana's Wilson Harris (who is extremely occupied by Indian culture) began to work with myth to explain the present to the past. A special aspect of the crucial need to deal with Africa has been the search for the minds of the slaves in the verse trilogy of Edward Brathwaite: *Islands, Masks,* and *Rights of Passage,* or, in a classical genre of the long hunt, in Jan Carew's novel, *The Leopard,* set in Kenya. Derek Walcott's many plays and verse collections, augmented by his very patterned, richly imaged "autobiography" in verse, *Another Life* (1973), is possibly the culmination of the effort to organize and to turn into a plastic form the total experience of the Caribbean.

• • • • •

Possibly central to any consideration of Caribbean literature must be insularity or smallness or "being way out there." Even denizens of Jamaica, that "giant" of West Indian islands, is but a "speck of dust" to borrow De Gaulle's slighting reference to Martinique and the other French Antilles. To get out seems terribly important, but going home too is a strongly felt hunger. Somehow, Caribbean man or woman must find a stage big enough to allow their characters or emotions flights beyond claustrophobia—yet not so wide as to dwarf them back into insignificant islanders all over again.

And here the re-discovery, or first discovery, of the other islands with their several richnesses, the re-collecting of the Indian past, and the identification by the artist with the simple farmer or fisherman, or city worker, make for a greater identity. No longer confined to Europe, nor to their own land, and not even to Africa or India, the Caribbean writer has a "country" of water and land thousands of miles square, full of history and important lives.

Today, at home or in exile the world over, Caribbean writers are creating works of sincerity and often of genuine talent. Influenced by the major currents, political and artistic, coming in from all continents, the Caribbean of English expression is particularly making over his heritage and beginning to take a deserved place in contemporary world literature.

Now the world "outside" ought to turn to these new writers who have conquered their inward space and found a humanity as complex and fascinating as any ever lived.

John Figueroa's poem "From the Caribbean, With Love" contains the lines:

We have sprung from the urge
To know the entrails
We are proud of such ancestral errors
As bred us here. . . .

Breadfruit from the South Seas
  Mangoes from the East
Salt fish from Canada
  Afu from Africa
Rice from Spain
  Curry from India
  Through searching, that gave us birth,
  Let us know our meaning
    and love it
  (It is the world's)

LIST OF WRITERS FROM THE WEST INDIES (By Country)

ANTIGUA

Clarke, Joy
Flax, Oliver
Franklyn, Michael
Hewlett, Agnes Cecilia
MacDonald, Hilda
Murdoch, Colin
Nanton, Gene
O'Marde, Andy
O'Marde, Dorbrene
Prince, Ralph
Richards, Novella Hamilton
Wescott, Lee

BAHAMAS

Culmer, Jack
Michael, Julia Warner
Missick, Rupert
Peek, Basil
Tree, Iris
Wallace, Susan T.

BARBADOS

Arthur, William S.
Barnes, W. Therold
Blackman, Peter
Braithwaite, J. Ashton (a.k.a. Odimumba Kwamdela)
Brathwaite, L. Edward (now: Edward Kamau Brathwaite)
Callender, Timothy
Chapman, Matthew James
Clarke, Austin Chesterfield (Tom)
Clarke, Elizabeth
Collymore, Frank A. (Colly)
Daniel, Eugene
Drayton, Geoffrey
Emtage, J.B.
Forde, A.N.
Foster, Denis
Foster, Michael
Gill, Margaret
Giuseppi, Undine
Hamilton, Aileen
Hamilton, Bruce (b. England)
Harney, Leonora
Hinkson, Anthony
Hutchinson, Lionel
Kellman, Tony
Kizerman, Rudolph
Lamming, George
Layne, Paul
Lewis, K.C.
Marshall, Harold
Marshall, Paule (b. U.S.)
Moore, H. Willoughby
Mottley, Elton
Payne, Millicent
Pragnell, Alfred
Sainsbury, Edward Bennett
St. John, Bruce Carlisle
Sealy, Karl
Skeet, Monica (née Martineau)
Spencer, Flora
Vaughan, Hilkton Augustus (b. Santo Domingo, D.R.)
Wickham, John

BELIZE

Barrow, Raymond
Cano, Luis E.
Sealy, Theodore

BERMUDA

Tucker, Nathaniel

BRITISH VIRGINS (TORTOLA)

Lettsome, Quincy V.F.
Penn, Verna Ernestine

CAYMAN ISLANDS

Fuller, Robert Sevier
Turen, Teppo

DOMINICA

Allfrey, Phyllis Shand
Bully, Alwin
Casimir, Joseph R.R.
Caudeiron, Daniel (b. Venezuela)
Ellis, Royston
Haweis, Stephen (a.k.a. Stephen Hawys) (b. England)
Honeychurch, Lennox
Jean-Baptiste, Emmanuel
Napier, Elma (b. Scotland)
Rhys, Jean
Scobie, Edward
Watt, Cynthia

GRENADA

de Coteau, Delana (pseudonym: Abdul Malik)
Lowhar, Syl
Marryshow, Theophilus Albert (pseudonym: Max T. Golden)
Redhead, Wilfred A.
Steele, Lorna

GUYANA

Agard, Clifford (pseudonym for Jamal Ali)
Agard, John
Apple, Arnold
Ali, Jamal (pseudonym: Clifford Agard)
Balgobin, Basil
Barrow, Charles
Bartrum, Eugene
Beke, X (pseudonym for G.H. Hawtayne)
Belgrave, F.A.
Benn, Denis Martin
Bourne, J.A.V.
Bourne, Tommy
Braithwaite, Edward R. (Ted)
Brathwaite, Percy A.
Cameron, Norman Eustace
Campbell, John
Carew, Jan Rynveld
Carter, Martin Wylde (Martin)
Cendrecourt, Esme
Chan, Brian
Charles, Bertram
Chase, Sam
Chattoram, Paul (pseudonym: Walter O. Smith)
Chinapen, Jacob Wellien
Craig, Dennis
Cruickshank, J. Graham
Dabydeen, Cyril
Daly, P.H.
Daly, Vere Trevelyan
Dalzell, Frank E.
Dathorne, Oscar Ronald
Davis, Leslie C.

De Weever, Jacqueline
D'Oliveira, Evadne
Dolphin, Celeste
Douglas, Syble G. (a.k.a. "Sylvia")
Ferreira, Albert S.
Farrier, Francis Quamina
Fraser, Winslow
Gilkes, Michael
Greene, Eustace (pseudonym for M.R. Monar)
Grange, Peter (a pseudonym of Christopher [Robin] Nicole)
Hamaludin, Mohamed
Harris, Wilson (pseudonym for poetry only: Kona Waruk)
Hawtayne, G.H. (pseudonym: X Beke)
Heath, Roy
Hopkinson, Slade
Kempadoo, Peter (pseudonym: Lauchmonen)
King, Sheila
Kona Waruk (pseudonym for Wilson Harris)
Lauchmonen (pseudonym for Peter Kempadoo)
Lawrence, Walter MacArthur
Leo (pseudonym for Egbert Martin)
Martin, Egbert (pseudonym: Leo)
McAndrew, Wordsworth
McLlelan, G. (pseudonym: Pugagee Puncuss)
McTurk, Michael (pseudonym: Quow)
Melville, Edwina
Mirglip, Knarf (pseudonym of Frank Pilgrim)
Mittelholzer, Edgar (pseudonym [used once]: H. Austin Woodsley)
Monar, Motilall R. (pseudonym: Eustace Greene)
Nicole, Christopher (Robin) (pseudonyms: Andrew York, Peter Grange)
Perry, Ernest
Pilgrim, Frank (pseudonym: Knarf Mirglip)
Puncuss, Pugagee (pseudonym for G.H.H. McLlelan)
Quow (pseudonym of Michael McTurk)
Ramcharitar-Lalla, C.E.J.
Rodway, James (b. England)
Rohler, Lloyd
Roth, Vincent (b. Tasmania)
Sadeek, Sheik M.
Sancho, Thomas Anson
Seymour, Arthur (A.J.)
Seymour, Elma
Singh, Rajkumari (Raj.)
Smith, Ricardo
Smith, Walter O. (pseudonym for Paul Chattoram)
Trotman, D.A.R.
Van Sertima, Ivan G.
Van Sertima, Sheila
Webber, A.R.F. (b. Tobago)
Westmaas, David
Williams, Denis
Williams, Milton
Woodsley, M. Austin (pseudonym for Edgar Mittelholzer)
Yardan, Shana
York, Andrew (pseudonym for Christopher Nicole)

JAMAICA

Aarons, Rudolph L.C.
Abrahams, Peter
Alves, H.E.B.

Anderson, Hopeton A.N.
Anon. (William Nicoll?)
Barrett, C. Lindsay (a.k.a. Eseoghene)
Barrett, Nathan Noble
Barsoe, Elsie (née Benjamin)
Baugh, Edward Alston Cecil
Baxter, Ivy
Beckwith, Martha Warren
Bell, Vera
Bennett, Alvin G.
Bennett, Henry Charles
Bennett, Louise Simone (Mrs. Eric Coverley; a.k.a. Miss Lou)
Berry, Francis
Bethune, Lebert
Black, Clinton (Vane de Brosse)
Bongo Jerry
Bowen, Calvin
Bunbury, Henry Shirley
Bunting, J.R.
Campbell, George
Campbell, William Alexander
Canoe, John (pseudonym for Oliver Austin Kirkpatrick)
Carberry, Hugh Doston
Cargill, Morris (pseudonym: John Morris, when collaborating with John Hearne)
Cassidy, Frederic G.
Chapman, Esther (married name Esther Marshall Hepher)
Clerk, Astley
Cooper, Eileen (née Ormsby)
Corbett, Len
Coulthard, Gabriel (George Robert)
Cundall, Frank (b. England)
Curtin, Marguerite
Da Costa, Jean Constantine
Dawes, Neville
De Lisser, Herbert George
Dodd, E.A. (see under pseudonym: E. Snod)
Du Quesnay, Frederick J. Le Mercier
Durie, Alice
Durie, Sally
Ellis, Hall Anthony
Endicott, Stephen (pseudonym for Walter Adolphe Roberts)
Eseoghene (see C. Lindsay Barrett)
Escoffery, Gloria
Fazakerley, F.R. (b. England)
Frazer, Fitzroy
Ferguson, Merrill
Ferland, Barbara
Figueroa, John (Joseph Maria)
Fowler, Greta (née Todd—formerly Greta Bourke)
Frazer, Fitzroy
Garrett, Clara Maud (pseudonym: C.M.G.)
Ghisays, Bobby
Gladwell, Joyce (née Nation)
Goodison, Lorna Gaye
Gradussov, Alex (b. Europe)
Hamilton, Norma
Hasell, Vivian
Hearne, John (b. Canada) (pseudonym: John Morris)
Hendricks, A.L. (Micky)
Hendricks, Vivette
Henry, Ainsley E.T. (A.E.T.)
Hill, Frank
Hillary, Samuel
Hinds, Donald
Hollar, Constance
Ho Lung, Richard

Hutton, Albinia C. (née McKay; name by previous marriage—Davis)

Ingram, Kenneth E.N.

Iremonger, Lucille (née Parks)

Jekyll, Walter (b. England)

Jones, Evan

Kent, Lena (pseudonym of Lettice A. King)

King, Audvil

King, Lettice A. (see under pseudonym: Lena Kent)

King, Washington

Kirkpatrick, Oliver Austin (pseudonym: John Canoe)

Lashley, Cliff

Lee, Easton Hugh

Lewin, Olive

Lindo, Archie

Lindo, Cedric George

Lockett, Mary F.

Lucie-Smith, (John) Edward (McKenzie)

Lyon-Tippling, Carmen

MacDermot, Thomas H. (better known as Tom Redcam)

MacKenzie, Rhoda Elizabeth (pseudonym: "Auntie Lizzie")

Mais, Roger

Manley, Carmen (b. Panama)

Manley, Edna (b. England)

Manley-Ennevor, Rachel (b. England)

Marr-Johnson, Nancy (N.J. Marr) (b. England)

Marshall, H.V. Ormsby

Marson, Una Maud

Matthews, Tony

McDowell, Rudolph

McFarlane, Basil Clare

McFarlane, John Ebenezer Clare

McFarlane, R.L.C.

McKay, Claude

McNeil, R. Anthony (Tony)

Merson, H.A. (pseudonym for Harold Watson)

Mills, Charles Wade (b. England)

Mockyen, Alma Hyacinth (née Hylton)

Morris, John (pseudonym [collective] for Morris Cargill and John Hearne, q.v.)

Morris, Mervyn

Morrison, Hugh Panton (b. Canal Zone, Panama)

Morrison, William

Moulton-Barrett, Arabel (b. England?)

Murray, Reginald Myrie

Murray, Tom (b. England)

Myrie, Daisy (née Baxter)

Nettleford, Rex Milton

Nicholas, Arthur E.

Nicholas, Eva

Norman, Alma (b. Canada)

Ogilvie, William George Graham (b. Panama)

Palmer, C. Everard

Patterson, Horace Orlando

Pereira, Joseph Raymond

Perkin, Lily

Quayle, Ada

Rae, Norman

Ramson, Joyce M.

Ras Dizzy

Record, Barry

Redcam, Tom (pseudonym for Thomas H. MacDermot)

Reid, V. S. (Vic) (Victor Stafford)

Rhone, Trevor D.
Roberts, Walter Adolphe
Robinson, Carey
Robinson, Rudolph Oscar Athelston (Ruddy)
Rogers, Joel Augustus
Roy, Namba
Salkey, Andrew (b. Panama)
Scott, Dennis C.
Scott, Michael (b. Scotland)
Sealy, Theodore (b. Belize [Br. Hond.])
Senior, Olive
Sherlock, Hilary
Sherlock, Sir Philip Manderson
Sibley, Inez K. (pseudonym: Pennibb)
Simmons, Ulric (b. Cuba)
Simpson, Louis (a.k.a. Louis Aston Marontz)
Smith, Basil (b. England)
Smith, M.G.
Smith, Pamela C.
Snod, E. (pseudonym for E.A. Dodd)
Taylor, Stanley Arthur Goodwin
Thompson, Claude Alphonso
Thompson, Ralph C.
Tomlinson, Frederick Charles
Townsend, Mitzie
Twiney, Harriette (Harrie) M.E. (née Ormsby)
Usherwood, Vivian
Tropica (pseudonym for Mary Adella Wolcott)
Vaz, Noel D.
Virtue, Vivian (Vivian Lancaster)
Waite-Smith, Cicely (Howland)
Wallace, George B.
Walrond, Eric
Watson, Harold (pseudonym: H.A. Merson)
Wiles, Alan Richard
Williams, Gershom
Williams, James
Wilmot, Cynthia (Mrs. Fred Wilmot)
Wilmot, Frederic (Fred) Alexander
Wilson, D.G. (Don)
Wilson, Jeanne
Wint, Pam
Wolcott, Mary Adella (see under pseudonym: Tropica)
Wynter, Sylvia (a.k.a. Wynter Carew)

MONTSERRAT

Markham, E.A.
Pond, Wilfred Oscar Morgan

ST. KITTS

Margeston, George Reginald
Redmill, Felix

ST. LUCIA

Aubertin, Mike
Dixon, McDonald
Francois, Hunter J.
King, Cameron G.O.
Lee, Robert
Raymond, Arthur
Reid, Stanley
St. Omer, Garth
Walcott, Derek
Walcott, Roderick

ST. VINCENT

Daisy, Al T.
Keane, Ellsworth McG.
Stephenson, Michael
Williams, Cecil
Williams, Daniel (b. U.S.A.)

TRINIDAD AND TOBAGO

Alladin, M.P.
Als, Michael
Anthony, Michael
Archibald, Douglas
Ashby, Osborne
Ashtine, Eaulin
Augustus, Earl
Barker, J.S.
Bastien, Elliot
Bhajan, Selwyn
Brown, Lennox
Brown, Wayne
Cambridge, Arnold
Capildeo, Devendranath
Carr, Ernest A.
Cartey, Wilfred
Charles Faustin
Clarke, Alfred McDonald
Clarke, Sebastian
Connor, Edric
Constantine, Learie
Cromwell, Liz
Davis, Wayne Edward
De Boissiere, Ralph A.C.
Donaldson, Robert N.
Elder, John D.
Espinet, Charles Albert
Frederick, Rawle
Galt, Roy
Garneth, Philbert J.
Giuseppi, Neville
Gomes, Albert
Gonzalez, Anson John
Gonzalez, Maria
Gonzalez, Sylvia
Gray, Cecil Roderick
Griffith, Reginald (Reggie)
Guy, Rosa
Hamilton, Doreen
Hannays, Kitty (see under pseudonym: Macaw)
Herbert, Cecil L.
Hercules, Frank
Hill, Errol
Hodge, Merle
Holder, Geoffrey
Hosein, Clyde
James, Cyril Lionel Robert (often called CLR)
James, Leroy Martin
Jarvis, Euton
John, Errol
John, Frank
Jones, Barbara Althea
Jones, Marion Patrick (Mrs. Marion Glean O'Callaghan)
Keens-Douglas, Paul
Kelshall, Jack
Khan, Ismith
King, Lloyd
Kissoon, Freddie
Ladoo, Harold S.
La Fortune, Knolly S.
Laird, Christopher
La Rose, John A. (pseudonym: Antony La Rose, for verse)

Leighton-Mills, Horace E.
Lewis, Enid Kirton
Lovelace, Earl W.
Lushington, Claude
Macaw (pseudonym for Kitty Hannays)
Mahabir, Dennis Jules
Maloney, A.H.
Mansoor, Ramon
Maraj, Jagdip
Maxwell, Marina (now known as Marina Omowale)
McBurnie, Beryl
McDonald, Ian
Mendes, Alfred H.
Miles, Judy
Mills, Therese
Naipaul, Seepersad
Naipaul, Shiva
Naipaul, Vidiadhar Surajprasad (V.S.)
Omowale, Marina (pseudonym for Marina Maxwell)
Ottley, Carlton Robert
Questel, Victor D.
Ramon-Fortuné, Barnabas J.
Ramon-Fortuné, Joseph Alex (José)
Raphael, Lennox
Roach, Eric M.
Rogers, De Wilton
Samaroo, Daniel Joseph
Sealy, Clifford
Selvon, Samuel (Sam)
Simmonds, Austin M.
Slinger, Francisco (The Mighty Sparrow)
Taylor, Daphne Pawan
Telemaque, Harold Milton
Thomas, G.C.H.
Thomasos, Clytus Arnold
Thompson, Clarence C.
Warner, Keith Q.
Williams, Eric
Wyke, Marguerite
Yetming, Cline

VIRGIN ISLANDS

U.S.

Cancryn, Addelita (née Parott)
Coombs, Tram
Creque, Cyril F.W.
Ellington, Richard
Gimenez, J.P.
Hatchette, Wilfred Irwin
Hill, Valdeman A.
Jarvis, José Antonio
Lee, Erica B.
Paiewonsky, Isidor
Rasmussen, Eric
Richards, Edward A.
Tiwoni, Habib
Todman, Gerwyn

LIST OF WRITERS BORN OUTSIDE OF THE WEST INDIES

CANADA

Carbury, Hugh Doston (assoc. with Jamaica)

Hearne, John (assoc. with Jamaica)

Norman, Alma (assoc. with Jamaica)

Wilmot, Cynthia (Mrs. Fred Wilmot–assoc. with Jamaica)

Wilmot, Frederick (assoc. with Jamaica)

CUBA

Simmons, Ulric (assoc. with Jamaica)

DOMINICAN REPUBLIC

Vaughan, H.A. (assoc. with Barbados)

ENGLAND

Anon. (William Nicoll?—assoc. with Jamaica)

Barker, J.S. (assoc. with Trinidad)

Bennett, Henry Charles (assoc. with Jamaica)

Bunting, J.R. (assoc. with Jamaica)

Chapman, Esther (assoc. with Jamaica)

Coulthard, Gabriel G.R. (assoc. with Jamaica)

Cundall, Frank (assoc. with Jamaica)

Ellis, Royston (assoc. with Dominica)

Hamilton, Bruce (assoc. with Barbados)

Haweis, Stephen (assoc. with Dominica)

Fazakerley, G.R. (of Jamaican parents)

Jekyll, Walter (assoc. with Jamaica)

Manley, Edna (assoc. with Jamaica)

Manley-Ennevor, Rachel (assoc. with Jamaica)

Marr-Johnson, Nancy (assoc. with Jamaica)

Mills, Charles W. (assoc. with Jamaica)

Moulton-Barrett, Arabel (assoc. with Jamaica)

Murray, Tom (assoc. with Jamaica)

Rodway, James (assoc. with Guyana)

EUROPE

Gradussov, Alex (assoc. with Jamaica)

IRELAND

Bunbury, Henry Shirley (assoc. with Jamaica)

NIGERIA

Dawes, Neville (assoc. with Jamaica)

PANAMA

Manley, Carmen (assoc. with Jamaica)

Morrison, Hugh Panton (assoc. with Jamaica)

Ogilvie, William (assoc. with Jamaica)

Salkey, Andrew (assoc. with Jamaica)

SCOTLAND

Napier, Elma (assoc. with Dominica)

Scott, Michael (assoc. with Jamaica)

SOUTH AFRICA

Abrahams, Peter (assoc. with Jamaica)

TASMANIA

Roth, Vincent (assoc. with Guyana)

U.S.A.

Marshall, Paula (assoc. with Barbados)

Williams, Daniel (assoc. with St. Vincent)

VENEZUELA

Caudeiron, Daniel (assoc. with Dominica)

WALES

Smith, Basil (assoc. with Jamaica)

Volume I Entries: A to Z

AARONS, Rudolph L.C.

b. April 5, 1905, Jamaica; d. 1977.
Shortstory writer.

Educated at Titchfield High School, Jamaica, Aarons entered the Jamaica Civil Service, in the Collector General's Department, and retired as Assistant Collector General, (1925-64). He served in several cultural groups and associations, including International P.E.N. (Jamaica Centre), the Jamaica Library Board, the Jamaica Library Association, and The National Council on Libraries, Archives and Documentation.

Writings: Short Stories: *The Cow that Laughed and Other Stories,* Kingston, Printers Ltd., 1944 [93 pp.]; *In Jamaican short stories . . .,* Kingston, Pioneer Press, 1950 [135 pp.].

Most stories were published in local papers and magazines, including the now defunct English magazine, *Life and Letters,* and some in *The Independence Anthology,* Kingston, 1962. Some stories were broadcast on BBC programs, *Caribbean Voices.*

ABRAHAMS, Peter

b. 1919, Vrededoro (outside of Johannesburg, South Africa; emigrated to Jamaica, 1957).
Novelist, storywriter, broadcaster, editor.

Abrahams first visited Jamaica in 1955 in order to write *Jamaica: An Island Mocaic.* He had become by that time a regular contributor to the international press including the *Observer* and the *Herald Tribune.* For a time he was the vigorous editor of the PNP's *Public Opinion;* and then later edited with Eddie Young, the *West Indian Economist* (1952-64).

Subsequently, he has become a well-known broadcaster, news analyst, commentator, and controller of *West Indian News* (Jamaica, 1955-64).

In *Contemporary Novelists,* Bernth Lindfors writes:

> *Peter Abrahams left South Africa in 1939 when he was only twenty years old but the racial and political problems of that twisted land have continued to dominate his imagination.*

But Abrahams has not been in any way twisted by his early experiences; his BBC broadcasts, printed in the *Listener,* of his reactions to being "free" in England are really enlightening insights into self analysis and into how easily habitual experiences can lead one to misinterpret the actions of others. He has always shown a deep understanding of what it means to toe party lines of one kind or another.

His books are all interesting and often enlightening about social and political problems, and, as one would have expected, about relations between the "races." His 1966 novel *This Island Now* is to some extent like his *Udoma* (which was set in Africa in early independence days), for there is the not unexpected and lethal struggle between those who were once close in the fight for "Independence," and who now find themselves in command of the "New Nation."

Abrahams is clearly one who cares about the full development of the country he has adopted—however that has changed since he made it his own.

Writings: Novels: *Song of the City,* London, Crisp, 1945; *The Path of Thunder,* New York, Harper, 1948, London, Faber, 1952; *Wild Conquest,* New York, Harper, 1950, London,

Faber, 1951; *A Wreath for Udomo,* New York, Knopf, London, Faber, 1956; *A Night of Their Own,* New York, Knopf, London, Faber, 1965; *This Island Now,* London, Faber, 1966, New York, Knopf, 1967.

Others: *Return to Goli* (rapportage), London, Faber, 1953; *Tell Freedom: Memories of Africa,* New York, Knopf, London, Faber, 1954; *Jamaica: An Island Mosaic,* London, Her Majesty's Stationery Office, 1957; *The Influence of Ideas,* 196?; *The World of Mankind,* with others, New York, Golden Press, 1962.

Short Stories: *Dark Testament,* London, Allen and Unwin, 1942.

Editor, with Nadine Gordimer, *South Africa Writing Today,* London, Penguin, 1967.

Biographical/Critical Sources: D. Herdeck, *African Authors, 1300-1973,* Washington, D.C., Black Orpheus Press, 1973, rev. ed., 1974; B. Lindfors' biography, *Contemporary Novelists.*

AGARD, Clifford

(pseudonym for **Jamal ALI**)

AGARD, John

b. ca. 1930, Guyana.
Poet, shortstory writer, journalist, actor.

Agard is a lively contributor, with his wife, to the art scene of Guyana. He has contributed poetry to *Expression* (edited by Janice Lowe); *Plexus* (ed. R.C. McAndrew) and the *Sunday Chronicle.*

His short stories have been broadcast.

Writings: Poetry: *Shoot Me with Flowers,* Georgetown, n.d.

Biographical/Critical Sources: Robert E. McDowell, *Bibliography of Literature from Guyana,* Arlington, Texas, 1975.

ALI, Jamal

(pseudonym of **Clifford AGARD**)

b. ca. 1942, Guyana.
Playwright, poet.

Ali has put two plays into performance and has contributed poetry to several journals, including *Savacou.* The poet in "To Find A Root" admits to the name "Angus Louis Martin Payne" which is even more Brittanic than Clifford Agard.

Writings: Plays: *Black by Night,* London, Performed Oval Theatre, 1972; *Black Feet in the Snow,* London, Performed Commonwealth Institute, 1973.

Poetry: In various journals: "De Bum (Calypso)" and "To Find a Root" appear in *Melanthika: An Anthology of Pan-Caribbean Writing* (1977).

ALLADIN, M.P.

b. January 11, 1919, Trinidad.
Poet, writer, educator, painter, designer.

Educated in Trinidad, England, U.S.A. (M.A.Columbia University, New York), and Europe, Alladin was an assistant teacher from 1938-1946 and later Director of Culture in the Ministry of Education. He has been very active in the arts world of Trinidad and has traveled broadly in India, Europe and North America.

Writings: Poetry: *And Where is Human Man? Forty Poems* (Dedicated to Truth), Port of Spain, Trinidad, n.d. (1968?); *The Monstrous Angel—Forty Poems,* details not known.

Folk Stories: *Folk stories and legends of Trinidad,* Port of Spain; *Folk Dances of Trinidad and Tobago,* n.d., but pub. 1970; *Folk chants and refrains of Trinidad and Tobago,* Port of Spain, 1969; *The Folk Arts in Trinidad and Tobago,* Port of Spain.

General: *Man is a creator,* Port of Spain; *A Village in Trinidad,* Port of Spain, n.d., but probably 1970.

Plays: *3 One-Act Plays* (Brainser, 1945; Hosay, 1946; *The PS,* 1955), Port of Spain, by author, n.d.

Biographical/Critical Sources: "Alladin—the poet laments dehumanisation of man," Michael Gibbes, *Trinidad Guardian* (June 16, 1968).

ALLFREY, Phyllis Shand

b. Oct. 24, 1915, Dominica.
Novelist, poet, journalist, politician.

Phyllis Allfrey is the daughter of Francis Shand, former Crown Attorney of Dominica. She was educated privately in Dominica, with emphasis on English Literature and French. She spent two years while a teenager in the United States. Later she lived and studied in England, Belgium, Germany and France.

She began writing from a very early age—poems and short stories. She married Robert Allfrey, an Englishman, while still very young. She lived between the United States and the U.K.; their two children were born in the U.S.A. However, she always maintained a great interest and sympathy for her homeland and its people. In London she met some of the world's great writers and politicians and became a socialist; she became involved in the Fabian Society, the British Labour Party, and the Parliamentary Committee for West Indian Affairs.

In 1953 she entered three poems for a contest run by the Society of Women Writers and Journalists, V. Sackville West being one of the judges; she was awarded second prize for her poem "While the young sleep." Encouraged by this success, and by a literary agent, Phyllis Allfrey completed her novel *The Orchid House* in four months, and sold it, in 24 hours, to Constable (1953). It was also published by Dutton (U.S.A.); and then by Librairie Stock (France) as *La Maison des Orchidées* (1955).

The Orchid House is her one published novel. The leading personality in the book is a Negro nurse "Lally" who analyses with fidelity and independence the children she cared for. This novel, then, is not, like much of West Indian literature, about the black oppressed or underprivileged, who are struggling up, but about a white family whose powers are waning.

Her verse is modernist; the following extract is almost Poundian:

The White Ladies walk between the trees,
choosing their steps with care, so as not to soil
their shoes, which are whiter than their faces:
for these are the untarnished ones, the wives of officials.
We are the trees, the silent spies,
we know their gowns are imported from Paris,
and therefore precious.
We know that they conceive their children in rooms
with the jalousie blinds drawn, the mosquito net tucked in.
We are not jealous of their love-making.

(From "The White Lady [Martinique]")

She has published four collections of poems.

In 1954 she returned to Dominica. She and her husband had, for a period, renounced the maelstrom and diversions of politics on leaving England; but soon she found herself caught up against her will in the political struggle of the relatively newly enfranchised in the British controlled islands who were soon to have a ministerial system and then a federal election.

Phyllis Allfrey founded a party, the Dominica Labour Party, was elected as one of the federal MPs for Dominica and then chosen as a Minister of the Federal Government. She became Minister of Social Services in the W.I. Federal Government (1958-62). She moved to Port of Spain, Trinidad, the Federal Capital.

During this period her literary work and output suffered. When the Federation was dissolved in 1962, she returned to Dominica, to restart life under difficult and hostile circumstances. She became a $1.00 a year Editor of a small opposition weekly paper—the *Dominica Herald;* then she was editor of the even smaller *Dominica Star,* owned and published by her husband. However the *Star* has outlived the *Herald* and one of its greatest contributions has been the cultivation and encouragement of young local writers.

Phyllis Allfrey continues her great socio-political concern for the Caribbean—she and her husband have adopted Indian children. They fight an uphill battle as "the opposition" in a small community; one hopes that she will write much more. Her autobiography would be particularly interesting. One of the main themes underlying her work is the "Palm and Oak" motif: the tropic and nordic strands in her character and cultural heritage being clearly revealed.

Writings: Novels: *The Orchid House,* London, Constable, 1953, and New York, Dutton, 1954, republished as *La Maison des Orchidées,* Paris, Librairie Stock, 1955.

Short Stories: *Governor Pod,* London, 1951; and numerous short stories published in many newspapers and magazines, the best known being "O Stay and Hear"; and "A Real Person" (Argosy); "A Talk on China" (The Windmill); "Breeze" (Pan-Africa); "The Eyrie" (Heinemann Collection); "The Untanglers" (Writers Guild Publication), 1950.

Poetry: (collections): *In Circles: Poems,* Harrow Weald, Middlesex, Raven Press, 1940; *Palm and Oak: Poems,* London, Privately printed, 1950; *Contrasts,* Barbados, Advocate Press, 1955; *Palm and Oak II,* published 1973, Star Printery; published 1974 in limited edition of 300 copies: contains poems from *In Circles, Palm and Oak (I)* and *Contrasts.*

Poems published variously and broadcast.

Biographical/Critical Sources: L.E. Brathwaite's review of *The Orchid House,* in *BIM,* No. 37; Barrie Davies, "Neglected West Indian Writers. No. I. Phyllis Allfrey. *The Orchid House,* in *World Literature Written in English,* II, 2 (Nov. 1972), pp. 81-83; Kenneth Ramchand, *The West Indian Novel and its Background,* London, Faber, 1970, Barnes and Noble, Inc., N.Y., 1970, references: pp. 223n, 224, 225-228.

ALS, Michael

b. 1946, Trinidad.
Poet.

Much concerned with workers' activities, Als was a founder of the Young Power Movement in Port of Spain, Trinidad and Tobago.

Writings: Poetry: *Speaking of My Country: A Collection of Political Poems,* published by Camalas Business Services, Trinidad, 1975; *Poems on Life and Soul,* San Fernando, Vanguard. He appears in *Breaklight* (A. Salkey, ed.), 1973.

ALVES, H.E.B.

b. ca. 1926, Jamaica.
Poet.

Alves' one known collection of poetry: *Verses wise and Otherwise,* Kingston, Dailey's Publishing Co., 1956, deals mainly with daily personal experiences.

ANDERSON, Hopeton A.N.

b. August, 1950, Jamaica.
Poet.

Anderson early lived in New York but later studied at Dawson College, Montreal,

Quebec. He has published in several poetry journals and has one collection of his work in print.

Writings: Poetry: *Out of the Woods,* Montreal (?), 1970. Individual poems (in *Drums to Drums*): "Watermelon Blues," "Crucifixion" (in *St. Catherine St. Good*); "Transition and Ghosts were the Generals."

ANON. (William Nicoll?)

b. ca. 1746, probably England.
Poet.

Author of possibly the earliest poem celebrating Jamaica, the unknown writer's work is extant in xerographic copy made by the Institute of Jamaica, West Indies Reference Library, in 1969.

Writings: Poetry: *Jamaica, a poem, in three parts. Written in that Island, in the year MDCCLXXVI. To which is annexed, a Poetical Epistle from the author in that Island to a Friend in England.* London, Printed for William Nicoll, 1777. [Copies at Institute of Jamaica and U.C.W.I., Mona, Jamaica.]

ANTHONY, Michael

b. February 10, 1932, Mayaro, Trinidad.
Novelist, journalist.

A relaxed and charming person, Anthony hides a great deal of power behind a quiet style. Educated in Trinidad, he has been living in San Fernando since 1970 as an official of the Ministry of Culture. Previously he had lived in London (1955 and 1968) and for two years worked in Brazil.

Gerald Moore, in *Contemporary Novelists,* 1972, states: "The appearance of Anthony's first novel, *The Games Were Coming,* added a distinctive voice to West Indian fiction." But Anthony himself tells us that it was as a poet that he first tried to make his mark. It was apparently Vidia Naipaul, then editor of the BBC's Caribbean Voices Programme, who persuaded Anthony to give up verse; his attempts at prose were immediately successful.

He has written a number of short stories, although his novels are better known. *The Year in San Fernando* recalls some of his own early experiences when he worked for a rural family during his 12th year. Perhaps Subramani's comment on Anthony's *Green Days by the River* can be applied, with slight differences of emphasis, to all his novels: "... an authentic imaginative work rendered in a precise and deceptively simple prose ... skillfully controlled, moves through apparently trivial incidents, towards a subtle climax."

Somewhat more tense than his other work is *The Games Were Coming* (1963), which is concerned, to put it baldly, with the tense and dedicated preparation of a champion for victory in the 15 mile bicycle race, a victory which takes its personal toll. Although Anthony lived in England for 14 years—he worked at Reuters, London from 1964-1968—he himself says that he

has never had any desire to write about England. What is more he did not even develop any of the unfortunate feelings of frustration and disturbance that sometimes bedevil "the writer in exile."

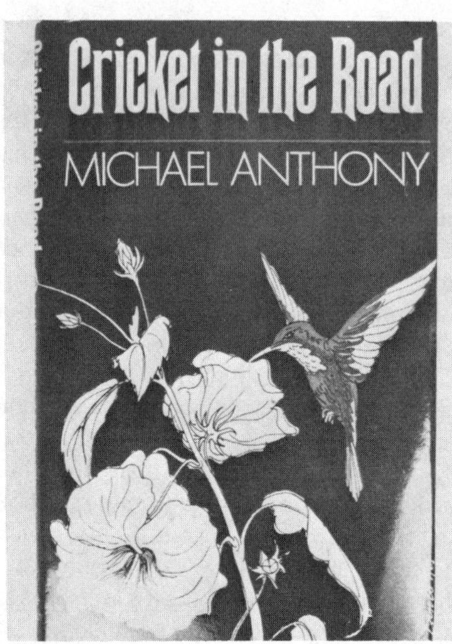

His most recent novel, *Streets of Conflict,* is set in Brazil.

Writings: Novels: *The Games Were Coming,* London, Deutsch, 1963, Boston, Houghton Mifflin, 1968, and in Heinemann Caribbean Writers Series, London, 1973; *The Year in San Fernando,* London, Deutsch, 1965, Caribbean Writers Series, No. 1, London, Heinemann, 1970, introduction by Paul Edwards and Kenneth Ramchand; *Green Days by the River,* London, Deutsch, 1967, Caribbean Writers Series, No. 9, London, Heinemann, 1973, introduction by Gareth Griffiths; *Streets of Conflict,* London, 1976.

Short Stories: *Sandra Street and other stories,* London, Heinemann Secondary Readers, 1973; *Cricket in the Road,* London, Deutsch, 1973; London (Caribbean Writers Series No. 16), Heinemann, 1973, introduction by the author; this selection of short stories made by the author includes the nine stories in the collection *Sandra Street.* He has contributed to many anthologies and journals including: *Caribbean Prose; Island Voices—Stories from the Caribbean; Response; The Sun's Eye; West Indian Narrative; BIM; The Bajan.* Of this collection the author says, in his introduction: "I would like to say that this collection represents my complete work in short stories, because although I have written many others these are the only ones that have 'survived'." Individual short stories in BIM (cf. An index to BIM, comp. Reinhard Sander, p. 27) from 1942-1972.

General: *Glimpses of Trinidad and Tobago: with a glance at the West Indies,* Port of Spain, Columbus Publishers, 1974.

Tales: *Folk Tales and Fantasies,* Port of Spain, Columbus Publishers, 1976.

Biographical/Critical Sources: Review by Subramani: "Anthony Michael. *Green Days by the River,"* in *World Literature Written in English,* 19 (April 1971), pp. 84-85; Louis James (ed.), in his introduction to *The Islands in Between,* London, 1968; Paul Edwards and Kenneth Ramchand in their introduction to *The Year in San Fernando,* 1970; in *London Magazine,* Vol. 7, No. I (April 1967), pp. 117-120; Harold Marshall, a review of *The Games Were Coming,* in BIM, No. 28 (January-June 1964), p. 145; Derek Walcott, a review of *The Games . . .* in *Sunday Guardian,* Trinidad (November 24, 1963), p. 10; also a review of *The Year in San Fernando,* in *The Sunday Guardian* (Trinidad, March 14, 1965), p. 5; Arthur Kevyn, review of *The Year . . .* in BIM, No. 41 (June-December 1965), pp. 70-71; Kenneth Ramchand, in his *The West Indian Novel and its Background,* Chapter XII, "The Novels of Childhood," pp. 205-222; Gareth Griffiths in his introduction to *Green Days by the River;* Michael Anthony's own introduction to *Cricket in the Road,* Heinemann, 1973. Also see Sylvia Wynter's review of *Green Days by the River* and *The Games Were Coming,* in *Caribbean Studies,* IX, pp. 111-118.

APPLE, Arnold

b. ca. 1932, Dalgin, Guyana.
Autobiographer.

Born into a large family of a dozen children of mixed Indian and African heritage, Apple was a pugnacious and active child. After lumbering, hunting, diamond-mining, he emigrated to England in March 1961 to work and to study. He took a diploma in Applied Science and other courses and settled down in Stratford, East London for a period.

His only published work to date is *Son of Guyana* (1973) which details his precarious childhood and his subsequent search for education and a way out of the poverty of his origins. His book ends with the story of his magical first trip by ship across the Atlantic to Genoa and the long train ride to Calais and the final arrival in England to begin his new life.

Apple is now back in Guyana and is farming up the Demerara River. He is married, with six children.

Writings: Autobiography: *Son of Guyana,* London, Oxford University Press, 1973 (both case and Three Crowns Press paper).

ARCHIBALD, Douglas

b. April 25, 1919, Port of Spain, Trinidad.
Playwright, novelist, historian, civil engineer.

A well known and interesting playwright, Archibald has written many performed and published plays, some of which also have appeared on BBC TV and British and Caribbean radio. Archibald is actively engaged in completing a four-volume history of Trinidad. He has taught creative writing at the U.W.I. in Trinidad.

Writings: Plays: *The Rose Slip* (4-acts, written 1960, first performed October 26-29, 1962, Port of Spain by The Company of Players and directed by Jean Herbert), winner of Theatre Guild award, New York, 1963; *Old Maid's Tale*—Caribbean Plays: One-Act Play XII (written 1962), Extra Mural Department, U.(C.)W. I. 1966, Trinidad and Tobago; *Junction Village—A play in two acts* (written 1952), Mona, Jamaica, Extra Mural Department, University College of West Indies, 1958 (Caribbean Plays No. 9); *Anne-Marie*—a full length play in 3 acts (written 1957), Port of Spain, Trinidad, Extra Mural Department, University (C) West Indies, 1967 (Caribbean Plays); *Island Tide* ("A Full Length Play in 3-Acts"), Trinidad, U.W.I. Extra Mural Studies, 1972.

In ms: *Defeat with Honour,* 1950; *Cito's Tavern,* 1951; *Once Upon a Time,* 1955; *The Bamboo Clump* (a full-length play in 2 acts), written 1961.

Novel: *Isadora and the Turtle,* 1964.

Historical Works: *The Spanish Galleon; Bande de l'Est: Don Damien de Churruca; Noel and Chacachacare; Fort San Andres; A Review of Archeological Investigation in Trinidad.*

ARTHUR, Kevin Alan

b. ca. 1932, Barbados.
Poet, playwright, storywriter, journalist.

Kevin has published in BIM and has worked as a journalist with Radio Guardian, the Advocate newspaper and Barbados rediffusion.

He has contributed fiction to BIM 41, "Memoirs of a Lesser Casanova," and "Episode" in BIM 34.

Writings: Play: *Violin on a Wet Horseback* (A play for radio), BIM 39 (July-December 1964).

ARTHUR, William S.

b. 1909, Barbados.
Poet, storywriter.

Arthur is a retired headmaster of Buxton Boys' School, Barbados. His verse appears in *BIM* and in the Anthology *Caribbean Voices* Vol. I (selected by J. Figueroa). His short story "Sequel to Murder" is in *BIM* 13 (pp. 49-54).

Writings: Poetry: *Whispers of the Dawn,* Coles Printery, Barbados, 1941; *Morning Glory; Poems,* Barbados, Advocate Press, 1947 (or 1944?); *No Idle Winds,* Bridgetown, Barbados, Advocate Printery, 1955.

Biographical/Critical Sources: Review of *No Idle Winds* by George Lamming in BIM 22 (June 1955), pp. 132-133.

ASHBY, Osborne

b. ca. 1936, Trinidad.
Playwright, labour officer.

Ashby has published two plays.

Writings: Plays: *Sailors Ashore.* Caribbean Plays: One Act Play VIII, Trinidad & Tobago Extra Mural Dept., U.C. of W.I., 1966. Adapted by Ashby: *The Doctor in Spite of Himself* (from Moliere's *Le medecin malgre lui*), Port of Spain, Extra Mural Dept., U.C. of W.I., 1966; Caribbean Plays: One-Act Play VII.

ASHTINE, Eaulin

b. ca. 1936, Trinidad.
Folklorist, librarian.

Ashtine has published two collections of traditional tales.

Writings: Tales: *Crick-crack! Trinidad and Tobago Folk Tales Retold ...,* illustrated by Wilhemina McDowell, St. Augustine, Trinidad, U. of W.I., Extra Mural Dept., 1966. (New World Life and Love Series: Special Vol. 1); *Nine Folk Tales* (retold), 1968.

AUBERTIN, Mike (Michael)

b. ca. 1948/1949, St. Lucia.
Poet, playwright.

Mike Aubertin is a graduate of St. Lucia's Teachers Training College. His poetry has been published in *Link* (a quarterly magazine of St. Lucia), and his play "The Invocation" was produced by the Creative and Performing Arts Society in 1970.

AUGUSTUS, Earl

b. October 27, 1934, Trinidad.
Folklorist, playwright, critic, storywriter.

Educated in Trinidad and at U.W.I., Mona, Jamaica, where he did the Diploma in Education, a teacher and one-time lecturer at Teachers' College, Trinidad, Augustus has been very active in efforts at "local consciousness' and the study of local culture and folklore.

His *Baka* (56 pages), written with Winston Moore, Winston Rennie and William Alexander (latter also the illustrator) with introductory "Over View" by Augustus, is a rather originally organized book. Augustus sets out the purpose of *Baka* in the introduction:

> *We have tried to communicate some "things" which we considered basic to our understanding of the problem of creating what is called a "national identity. . . . We must discriminate between a false consciousness and an authentic consciousness.*

Writings: Plays: *Gambage,* St. Augustine, Trinidad, U.C.W.I., 1966 (children's play).

Critical reviews and stories: in *Voices* (ed. C. Sealy).

BALGOBIN, Basil

b. ca. 1915, Guyana.
Storywriter, playwright.

Balgobin has contributed to local periodicals, including *Kyk-over-al,* and the *Chronicle Christmas Annual.*

Writing: Play: *Asra. A Political Play of India,* performed Guyana, 1945.

Biographical/Critical Sources: Robert E. McDowell, *Bibliography of Literature from Guyana,* Arlington, Texas, Sable Publishing Corporation, 1975.

BARKER, J.S.

b. 1910, Yorkshire (lived in Trinidad and traveled widely in West Indies).
Journalist, sports writer (cricket), critic and playwright.

Barker, a lively writer on manners and sports, mainly cricket, holds a senior post in the Thompson Newspaper enterprises. He and Espinet earned gibing references in the first production of Walcott's *Drums and Colours* at the inception of the ill-fated West Indian Federation. But Jack has always given as much and more than he has taken; a lively companion in the press box.

Writings: Plays: *Bond of Matrimony,* Caribbean Plays Edition, Kingston, U.C.W.I. 1955, and republished, Trinidad and Tobago, Extra Mural Department, U.C.W.I. 1966 (Caribbean Plays: One-Act Play XVII); *Vulnerable Doubled* (Caribbean Plays Edition, One-Act Play V), Trinidad and Tobago, U.C.W.I. 1966.

Sports: *Summer Spectacular: The West Indies v. England, 1963,* Collins, London, 1963.

Articles (about manners and mores): in a variety of West Indian, U.K. and U.S. papers and journals.

BARNES, W. Therold

(pseudonym: **BENDIX)**

b. ca. 1913, Barbados; d. February 11, 1965.
Poet, storywriter, editor, painter, composer.

Therold Barnes was co-editor of BIM (a literary magazine of Barbados) from 1943 to 1964, a man of great creative talent. He composed lyrics and music for revues, designed stage sets and costumes and drew cartoons for the newspaper *The Advocate.*

He contributed 28 short stories, 13 poems and numerous articles to BIM. One of his stories was entitled "The Book (Synopsis for a Novel)" in BIM No. I, pp. 15-17. One of his articles was about the well known Barbadian sculptor, Broodhagen (BIM 8, pp. 25-26).

He also wrote poetry under the pseudonym of Bendix.

Biographical/Critical Sources: Cf. "Notebook" BIM 41 (June-Dec. 1965) the obituary from *The Sunday News* of February 12, 1965, entitled "Cultural Benefactor" and written by E.L. (Jimmy) Cozier, one of the founding editors with Therold of BIM.

BARRETT, C. Lindsay

(a.k.a. **ESEOGHENE**)

b. September 15, 1941, Jamaica.
Novelist, storywriter, poet, playwright, journalist, teacher.

Educated in Jamaica, on leaving school Barrett worked for *The Daily Gleaner,* and served as news editor of Jamaica Broadcasting Corporation. In 1961 he went to England where he worked for the BBC and the Transcription Centre, but spent some time in Paris, and travelled in

Europe and North Africa as a journalist and feature writer. He attended the 1966 Dakar Arts Festival and went on to lecture at Fourah Bay College in Sierra Leone. He taught for a period in Ghana, then at the University of Ibadan (African and Afro-American Literature).

During the Biafra War Barrett was head of the Information Service for East Central State. He plans to remain in Nigeria, where he married a leading actress, Beti Okotie.

His poems are militant, crisp, often concerned with racial prejudice as in the poem "In My Eye and Heart" which concerns Bull O'Connor and his dogs in the bad Alabama days of the 1960's. He won the Conrad Kent Rivers award in 1970 (a. U.S. prize).

Writings: Poetry: *The State of Black Desire: 3 Poems . . . 3 Essays,* Alencon, Imp. Corbiere et Jugain, 1966 (illustrations by Larry Potter); *The Conflicting Eye,* London, Paul Bremen, 1973. His poetry has also appeared in various collections and reviews.

Novel: *Song for Mumu,* London, Longmans, 1967. Also: "Leap Skyward," in manuscript.

Plays: *Jump Kookoo Makka,* directed by Cosmo Pieterse and performed at Leicester University Commonwealth Arts Festival in 1967; *Sigh of a Slave Dream,* Mbari [Ibadan, Nigeria] group performance in London; *Home Again,* performed 1967 by Wole Soyinka's Company; *And After This We Heard of Fire,* performed Ibadan Arts Theatre; *Blackblast,* performed in London, 1973. His plays have been performed at the Mbari Theatre, University of Ibadan, and on the Nigerian National Radio.

Writings: Essays: "Revolution;" "Two Cities," "The New African;" "Magnet News;" "Daylight."

Biographical/Critical Sources: Review of *Song for Mumu,* by Edward Baugh in *Caribbean Quarterly,* Vol. 13, No. 4, pp. 53-54 and in *Trinidad Guardian* (September 14, 1968).

BARRETT, Nathan Noble

b. ca. 1933, Jamaica.
Novelist.

Barrett has published one novel to date. *Bars of Adamant: A Tropical Novel* (New York, Fleet Publishing Co., 1966 [287 pp.]).

BARROW, Charles

b. ca. 1940, Guyana.
Poet.

Barrow's poetry has appeared in *Plexus* (ed. R.C. McAndrew) and *Expression Six* (ed. Janice Lowe).

BARROW, Raymond

b. 1920, British Honduras (Belize).
Poet, government official.

Educated at St. John's College in Belize and at Catherine's College, Cambridge, Barrow was the son of a district judge. He is a civil servant in Belize.

He has contributed to "Poetry of the Negro" and the BBC "Caribbean Voices" program. He appears in the following anthologies: *Kyk-over-al: An Anthology of West Indian Poetry* (Special Issue Mid-Year 1952). No. 22, 1957 ed.); *Caribbean Voices,* Vol. 11, John Figueroa, ed.; *Caribbean Verse,* O.R. Dathorne, ed.; and *West Indian Poetry,* K. Ramchand and Cecil Gray (eds.).

Writings: Journal Articles: In BIM No. 11, "Poetry"; *Caribbean Quarterly,* Vol . 5, No. 3 (1958).

Comment: A note on verse in British Honduras, in *Caribbean Quarterly* Vol. 2, No. 2.

BARSOE, Elsie

(née **Benjamin**)

b. ca. 1915, Jamaica; d. 1974.
Editor, journalist, critic.

Active in the forties, particularly in theatre circles, Elsie Barsoe also has edited a number of journals. She also actively has encouraged many to act, dance and read poetry. She played a great part in "the development of a Jamaican drama and an indigenous theatre" with her theatre group, "People's Theatre." She edited, contributed to, and published *Pepperpot: Jamaican Potpourri,* an annual Jamaican Review, for 21 years. This magazine is now being published by Elsie Bowen.

Writing: Article: "Toward a Native Drama," *Theatre Arts* 29 (5) (May, 1945), pp. 313-314.

Biographical/Critical Sources: See "Obituary" by Elsie Bowen, in *Pepperpot* (December 1974) p. 53; Henry Fowler's article in *Jamaica Journal* Vol. 2, No. 1 (March 1968), on "A History of Jamaican Theatre."

BARTRUM, Eugene

b. ca. 1915, Guyana.
Storywriter, civil servant.

Educated at Berbice High School, Bartrum contributed stories to *Kyk-over-al, Chronicle Christmas Annual, Caribia,* and other periodicals. He is now a national pensioner.

BASTIEN, Elliot

b. 1941, Trinidad.
Playwright, poet, actor, petroleum engineer.

Bastien has had an active career as a chemical engineer and petroleum production expert after college work and graduate studies in operational research at the University of Toronto. He played the part of Jules in Derek Walcott's *The Sea at Dauphin* in the production of The New Company and the Whitehall Players, directed by Errol Hill. He takes an active interest in civil rights matters and has written a handbook on race relations for Cambridge University Press, published in the late 1960's.

Writings: Play: *Anancy Story,* produced by the Caribbean Theatre Workshop (Friday, July 24, and Sunday, July 26, 1971) at Central Technical Auditorium, Toronto, Ontario.

Poetry: in various journals, including *Voices* (Port of Spain), and in collections such as *Breaklight: The Poetry of the Caribbean,* New York, Anchor, 1973, edited by A. Salkey.

Essay: "The Weary Road to Whiteness and the Hasty Retreat into Nationalism," in *Disappointed Guests,* London, Oxford University Press, 1965.

Study on "Race Relations," in a handbook published by Cambridge University Press.

Biographical/Critical Sources: S.O. Asein, "Bastien's Anancy Story: A Critique," in *Black Images,* I, 2 (Summer 1972), pp. 25-27.

BAUGH, Edward Alston Cecil

b. January 10, 1936, Port Antonio, Jamaica.
Poet, critic, teacher, actor.

Baugh attended University College of the West Indies (1954-1958); Queens University, Ontario; the University of Manchester. He has been senior lecturer at U.W.I., Mona, since September 1969. Earlier he taught English at Victoria College, B.C. (1959-60), and in Jamaica at Kingston College (1960-62), and was assistant lecturer in the English Department, Cave Hill, Barbados (1964-65).

Baugh is an accomplished actor who made his mark with the Green Room group in Barbados—the company for which Frank Collymore and Alfred Pragnel so often "starred." His quiet manner sometimes hides him in a crowd or at a conference, but he must be one of the most sensitive and thorough (and graceful) of practicing West Indian critics.

His poetry appears mainly in BIM and *Seven Jamaican Poets.* For some years the "greatness" of being Chairman of the English Department, Mona, has been "thrust upon" him, and he is completing some studies on Derek Walcott's *Another Life.*

Writings: Poetry: His work is in *Seven Jamaican Poets,* ed. by Mervyn Morris, Bolivar Press,

Jamaica, 1971. Poems published in various West Indian, Canadian, English periodicals and various anthologies, including *Independence Anthology,* 1962 (eds. Hendicks and Lindo).

Reviews and Commentary: "Plainness and Metaphor in the Poetry of Derek Walcott," *Literary Half-Yearly,* XI (July 1970), 47-48; *West Indian Poetry* 1900-1970 [pamphlet], 1971; "Questions and Imperatives for a Young Literature;" *Humanities Association Review,* XIV (written 1973), pp. 13-21; "Frank Collymore: A Biographical Portrait"; in *Savacou* 7/8 (January-June 1973), pp. 139-148; many reviews (e.g. in BIM): of *This Island Now* by Peter Abrahams (BIM 44, pp. 298-299), London, Faber & Faber, 1975; L.E. Brathwaite's *Rights of Passage* and *Masks* (BIM 45 and BIM 47); Alejo Carpentier's *The Kingdom of this Earth,* tr. by Harriett de Onis, London, Gollancz, 1967, (BIM 46, pp. 136-137); *Nor Any Country,* by Garth St. Omer (BIM 50, p. 128).

Biographical/Critical Sources: Anson Gonzalez, " 'Possibility' in West Indies Creative Writing," *The New Voices,* No. 4, pp. 44-46.

BAXTER, Ivy

b. ca. 1940, Jamaica.
Dancer, choreographer, essayist.

One of the pioneers of local dancing in modern Jamaica, Baxter often uses literary sources as her inspiration. She was educated in Jamaica and Canada and has taught and worked with schools a great deal. Her major efforts have been in the collection of folkloric material.

Writing: The Arts of An Island, Scarecrow Press, Inc., New York, 1970.

Biographical/Critical Sources: Mentioned for her part in the development of the dance in Henry Fowler's article "A History of Theatre in Jamaica" in *Jamaica Journal,* Vol. 2, No. 1 (March 1968).

BECKWITH, Martha Warren

b. 1871, Jamaica.
Folklorist.

Beckwith's pioneering studies of Jamaican folklore are interesting in themselves and very useful for later writers and scholars.

Writings: Folklore: *Black roadways: a study of Jamaican folk life,* Chapel Hill, N.C., University of North Carolina Press, 1929.

Editor: *Jamaica Proverbs,* Poughkeepsie, New York, Vassar College, 1925; *Jamaican anansi stories . . .* with music recorded in the field by Helen Roberts, New York, American Folk Lore Society, 1924, xiii, 295 pp. (memoirs of the American Folklore Society, vol. xvii), *Jamaica Folk-lore,* New York, American Folklore Society (1930), 67, 95, 137, 47 page long articles (Memoirs of the American Folk-lore Society, v. 21). Also: *Folk games in Jamaica,* 1922 (with Helen Roberts); *Christmas Mummings in Jamaica,* 1923.

BEKE, X.

(pseudonym for **G. H. HAWTAYNE**)

BELGRAVE, F.A.

b. ca. 1834, Guyana; death date undetermined.
Poet.

Belgrave was one of the very earliest of published Guyana poets.

Writings: Poetry: *Poems,* 1864.

BELL, Vera

b. June 16, 1906, Jamaica.
Poet, storywriter, editor.

After high school in Jamaica at Wolmer's Girls' School, Bell edited the *Welfare Reporter,* was a clerical assistant, and a government of Jamaica executive officer of the Social Welfare Commission. After study at Columbia University's School of Library Service, New York City, and London University, (Dip. in Archaeology), she emigrated to England. She has published much poetry, a few stories, and has written one pantomime.

Writings: Poetry: *Ogog* (Epic Poem), 1971. Her poetry appears in various journals and anthologies, including: *Focus; The Independence Anthology of Jamaican Literature,* 1962; *New Ships; Life Lines—One Hundred Poems for Junior Schools,* 1972; *Caribbean Quarterly* (Vol. 5, No. 3), and *An Anthology of West Indian Poetry* (Federation Commemoration Issue, April 1958).

Stories: in *Jamaican short stories . . .,* Kingston, Pioneer Press, 1950.

BENN, Denis Martin

b. ca. 1933, Guyana.
Playwright.

Benn has one published work, *Pickpockets Anonymous* (British Guiana, 1963). In typescript are two plays: *Atta,* Cuffy, and *Accabre: An Historical play in Verse in Four Acts,* and *Toussaint L'Ouverture; A Struggle for Freedom: An Historical Drama in Verse.*

BENNETT, Alvin G.

b. March, 1918, Jamaica.
Journalist, novelist.

Bennett's novel *Because They Know Not* arises out of his involvement with West Indians in London, whither he had gone as correspondent of the Jamaica *Daily Gleaner* in 1954. His other novel, *God the Stonebreaker,* appears in Heinemann's Caribbean Writers' Series. It is an interesting treatment of Granny Brown (G.B.) which Louis James in part describes as G.B.'s "rake's progress from Swine Lane to a neat detached bungalow of the suburbia of Kingston." The book is structurally weak but contains much clear and honest observation, much of it quite funny. His introduction of God and religion in a serious mode isn't always successful. But he clearly knows the beliefs and mores of those about whom he writes.

> *Sixty-seven-year-old mother Crocks. . . . [p. 42, GS] alias Mother Young Gal, traditionally collected money to produce for the Harvest what she called 'God's Corncake,' but which her enemies nicknamed "Dog's Corncake." The money left over after purchasing the ingredients for this item were kept by Mother Crocks as payment for her labour. She insisted that God was not like a capitalist, wanting people to work for nothing."*

Writings: Novels: *God the Stonebreaker,* London, Heinemann, 1964; Caribbean Series, 1973; *Because They Know Not,* London, Phoenix Press, 1958, 1961.

Poetry: in various Jamaican journals.

Biographical/Critical Sources: Kenneth Ramchand, *The West Indian Novel and Its Background,* London, Faber, 1970.

BENNETT, Henry Charles

b. ca. 1905, England.
Poet.

An Englishman who resided in Jamaica over a long period of time, Bennett long has lived in the hills of St. Catherine above Kingston. He has published two collections of his poetry and appeared in several anthologies.

Writings: Poetry: *Sojourner and Other Poems,* published in London, c. 1910; *Thirteen Poems and Seven,* Edgar G. Dunsten, London, 1935.

Also verse in J.E.C. McFarlane's two Anthologies: *Voices from Summerland,* and *A Treasury of Jamaican Poetry.*

BENNETT, Louise Simone

(**Mrs. Eric Coverley;** a.k.a. **Miss Lou**)

b. September 7, 1919, Jamaica.
Poet, actress, folklorist, popular singer, entertainer, radio personality.

Despite Mervyn Morris' excellent essay, "On Reading Louise Bennett Seriously," Miss Lou's image as Miss Matty and as a vibrant actress and entertainer is such that her poetry has not had quite the serious reception and careful reading which it fully deserves. Like so many other Caribbean persons of talent hers has not been a highly specialized professional, or personal, existence, mining one vein for all it is worth. So she gets full scholarly praise from Fred Cassidy in his *Jamaica Talk,* is much in demand to do "commercials" (in "dialect") on the radio, and has dominated the annual Jamaican Christmas Pantomime to an extent that might not have been tolerated in any other artist. (It might be well to note that the Jamaican Pantomime is *sui generis,* and not to be confused with its namesake in London. That it has become a popular, and often critical success year after year is due in part to Louise—but many others have contributed, including politician Robert Lightbourne, academic/political critic Sylvia Wynter, Greta Fowler—to name at random a few persons. Some of these indeed had reservations about Miss Lou's use of the dialect in Jamaican radio advertising—feeling that unfortunate stereotypes both of people *and* language are encouraged by it.)

Jamaica
Dialect
Poems by LOUISE BENNETT
Jamaica Labrish
With Notes & Introduction by Rex Nettleford

Perhaps Edward Lucie-Smith strikes the best note about Louise's poetry. He wrote of her part in the Royal Court reading at

the Commonwealth Festival of Arts (1965): her performance of her own works ". . . went a long way towards proving that a large part of the job of poetry in a new nation is not to make or break images, but to tell the truth so that it sounds true," a profound remark that one did not fully appreciate at the time. The reading had been brilliantly organized and directed by George Lamming, and presented many other poets who seemed so much more "serious"—and *political*—than Louise. Good though they all were, and striving to be truthful in a complicated situation, none sounded, at least to the Jamaican ear, as authentic as Louise. This, of course, poses one of the major problems for writers in a multi-dialectical society; for not all need speak like Miss Lou's persona Miss Matty—though they all know her voice very well.

But her sounding *true*—it is very important to realize—is not only a matter of that particular ability which she has with the Jamaican language, especially with certain aspects of it. It is very much, as one would have expected, a matter of grasping the insides of a certain type of Jamaican experience, which is typically Jamaican, but not unknown to others.

Wat a joyful news, Miss Mattie,
I feel like me heart gwine burs'
Jamaica people colonizin
Englan in reverse. . . .

What a islan! What a people!
Man an woman, old an young
Jusa pack dem bag an baggage
An tun history upside dung! . . .

Wat a devilment a England!
Dem face war an brave de worse,
But I'm wonderin how dem gwine stan
Colonizin in reverse.

And of the Jamaican who wants, perhaps, to do his bit for the war effort, but finds it all a bit distant and impersonal: (he is accustomed to fighting only when really annoyed!):

Me dah-dead fe-go a war,
But me kean fight widout me bex!

Louise Bennett is a distinguished comic poet who for that reason gets very close to what could be considered the tragic and absurd elements of life, but the touch is light; and the sharper the irony the sweeter the relish. This is especially true when, in the true ballad tradition, she performs with a delivery, vitality and delight that are entirely her own. She has received many awards among which are the Musgrave Silver Medal, Institute of Jamaica, an M.B.E., and a Jamaica National Award, the Order of Jamaica.

Writings: Poetry: *Verses in Jamaican Dialect,* compiled and published by George Bowen, Kingston, The Herald Ltd., 1942; *Jamaican humour in dialect,* Kingston, published under the sponsorship of the Jamaican Press Association, 1943; *Jamaican dialect poems,* Kingston, Gleaner, 1948; *M's' Lulu sez: a collection of dialect poems,* Kingston, Gleaner Co., Ltd., 1949: *Lulu Says, Dialect Verses with Glossary,* 1952; *Laugh with Louise,* a pot-pourrie of Jamaican folk-lore, stories, songs and verses (with a foreword by Robert Verity), Kingston, City Printery, 1961; *Jamaican Labrish,* Jamaica, Sangster's Book Stores, 1966 (with notes and introduction by Rex Nettleford).

Stories: *Stories and dialect verse by L.B. and others,* Kingston, Jamaica Pioneer Press, 1951 (introduction by P.M. Sherlock); *Anancy stories and dialect verse,* Kingston, Pioneer Press, 1957.

Contributed to Anthologies: *Caribbean Voices* (Vol. 2); *Breaklight; Independence Anthology of Jamaica; Bite in;* Contributed to Journals/Newspapers: *The Sunday Gleaner.* Five Poems and notice of Award in *Jamaica Journal,* Vol. 6, No. 2 (June 1972), pp. 25-30. (With Noel Vaz) *Bluebear and Brer Nancy,* Kingston, Little Theatre, 1949.

Essay: in anthology *Jamaican Song and Story,* ed. W. Jekyll, New York, Dover Publications, 1966.

Biographical/Critical Sources: in Introduction (pp. 15-17) in *The Islands in Between,* Louis James, ed., London, A Three Crowns Book, 1968; Mervyn Morris, "On Reading Louise Bennett, Seriously," in *Jamaica Journal* I (1967), pp. 69-74; Dennis Scott, "Bennett on Bennett Interview," *Caribbean Quarterly,* Vol. XIV, Nos. 1 and 2, pp. 97-101, 1968; Edward Baugh, "West Indian Poetry 1900-1970," (Pamphlet), p. 15. Reviews of *Jamaica Labrish* in *Daily Gleaner,* Kingston (Jan. 15, 1967); in *Public Opinion,* Nov. 25, 1966; *Times Literary Supplement* (Dec. 15, 1966); *Books and Bookman* (May 1967), p. 28.

BERRY, Francis

b. ca. 1915, Jamaica.
Poet.

Berry's work centers around his experiences in and around Jamaica's Morant Bay and the famous rebellion along its margin.

Writings: Poetry: *Morant Bay and other poems,* London, Routledge and Keegan Paul, 1961; *Face of Jamaica—6 The Morant Bay Rebellion.*

BETHUNE, Lebert

b. 1937, Kingston, Jamaica.
Novelist, poet.

Bethune emigrated with his family to New York City where he attended New York University (B. Sc.) and then went to France. He has written articles, plays, a novel and Court-Metrage documentaries (films).

The first stanza of the title poem of his one collection: "A Juju of my own" reads:

For I was tired of strange ghosts
Whose cool bones
Lived on the green furnace of my blood.

Writings: Novel: *Skate's Dive,* details not known.

Poetry: *A Juju of my own,* Paris, 1965, seven poems appeared earlier in *Présence Africaine* magazine (Paris). Also, poems in *Twenty Poems by Jamaicans living in Paris.*

BHAJAN, Selwyn

b. ca. 1945, Trinidad.
Poet.

Bhajan has contributed to *The New Voices,* (ed.-publisher Anson Gonzalez), and published one modest collection of verse (58 pp.).

Writings: Poetry: *Season of Song,* Siparia, Trinidad, printed for author at Sookhai's Printery, 196? (no date in book).

BLACK, Clinton

(Vane de BROSSE)

b. August 26, 1918, Jamaica.
Storywriter, folklorist, collector, historian, government archivist.

Clinton Black is probably best known as an archivist and a person particularly interested in words, their use and history. He has accordingly played an important part in the building up of the literature, folklore and arts of Jamaica, as his list of publications will show. His *Tales of Old Jamaica,* first published in 1952, has been a great favorite. It was redone in 1966, and had four more printings through 1972.

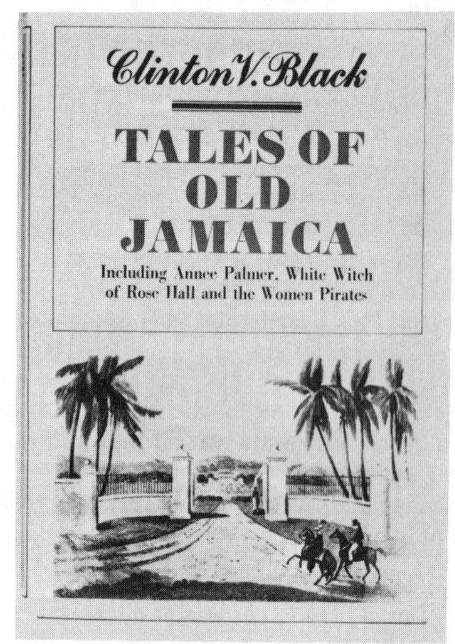

Writings: Stories: *Tales of Old Jamaica,* Kingston, Jamaica, Pioneer Press, 1952 (New enlarged edition, London, Collins, 1966); *Living Scenes in Jamaica's History,* Kingston, Welfare Ltd., 1948 (deals with six famous names in Jamaica's history—Moses Baker, Richard Hill, Mary Seacole, Rev. W.M. Webb, Andrew D. Mowatt, Ex-Sergeant William Gordon).

History: *Capitals of Jamaica,* 1952; *History of Spanish Town: Spanish Town, the Old Capital ... Jamaica,* Glasgow, Maclehose, 1960; *The Story of Jamaica from prehistory to the Present,* London, Collins, 1965; *History of Jamaica,* London, Glasgow, Collins, 1958, 2nd edition, revised, London, Collins, 1961, 3rd edition, London, Collins, 1965.

Archives: "A list of the records in the Jamaica Archives by main groups with an indication of extent and approximate covering dates, as well as a note of the contents of the neighboring Island Record Office and Registrar General's Department," August 1965. Also: Report on the "Archives of British Guiana," 1955; "The

Archives of Trinidad and Tobago" (1958—co-author); "Our Archives," 1962.

Tales and Stories: Contributor to various journals including *Caribbean Quarterly* and *Jamaica Journal;* also *Independence Anthology,* 1962.

BLACKMAN, Peter

b. ca. 1920, Barbados.
Poet.

Blackman emigrated to Britain in 1933 and visited Africa in 1937. He has one published collection of verse.

Writings: Poetry: *My Song is for All Men;* London, Lawrence and Wishart Ltd., 1952. Republished, Kraus Reprint, 1970 with works by other Caribbean authors. Set to music by Alan Bush.

BONGO JERRY

b. ca. 1934, Jamaica.
Poet.

One of the new poets, a "Rasta," writing in a newer, "freer" way but in a language some elements of which are not all that new! See, for instance, Claude McKay's early work or many parts of *Tom Cringle's Log* which records common songs and speech, which must have been in existence at least from the middle of the eighteenth century.

But, of course, Bongo Jerry's work is much more consciously oriented to changing our actual perception of the society in which Jamaicans live. He is concerned, among other things, but very powerfully, with BLACK POWA.

Only time will tell whether Bongo Jerry's way is the way of the future in the Caribbean, or a necessary way of jolting our complacencies. In the meantime it is interesting, and perhaps instructive, to compare McNeill's ending of "Ode to Brother Joe":

Meantime in the musty cell,
Joe invokes, almost from habit,
the magic words:
Hail Selassie I
Jah Rastafari,
But the door is real and remains shut.

with Jerry's ending of "Mabrak":

for the white world must come to blood bath
and blood bath is as far as the white world
can reach; so when MABRAK
start skywriting,
LET BABYLON BURN
JEZEBEL MOURN
LET WEAK HEART CHURN
BLACK HOUSE STAND FIRM: for
somewhere under ITYOPIA rainbow
AFRICA WAITING FOR I.

Bongo Jerry's work appears in *Savacou* and in *Caribbean Rhythms* (ed. James T. Livingstone), and is discussed by Gerald Moore in BIM, 57 (March 1974), pp. 71, 72, 73.

BOURNE, J.A.V.

b. ca. 1910, Guyana.
Storywriter, poet.

Bourne has contributed stories and poetry to *Kyk-over-al* and has one collection of stories: *Dreams, Devils, Vampires* (Georgetown, F.A. Persick, 1940).

BOURNE, Tommy

b. ca. 1923, Guyana.
Playwright.

Bourne was one of the earliest Guyanese playwrights to be published.

Writings: Plays: *Hassa Curry: A Caribbean One Act Play* (Br. Guiana, Labour Advocate, 1958); *MacKenzie Blues: A Play in One Act* (typescript).

BOWEN, Calvin

b. ca. 1924, Jamaica.
Poet, journalist.

Calvin Bowen showed great interest in writing from his early school days at St. George's College, Kingston. He became one of the better known journalists in Jamaica, having worked for a number of papers, including the *Gleaner*. He did a stint in London in the late forties and also worked for the Jamaica Tourist Board. He was also involved and concerned with the arts, folklore and cultural development of Jamaica.

Writings: Article: "Jamaica's John Canoe," in *Caribbean Commission Monthly Information Bulletin* 8 (I) (August 1954, Port of Spain), pp. 11-12. Other articles and poems appeared in *Gleaner* over a period of years.

BRAITHWAITE, Edward R. (Ted)

b. June 27, 1912, Georgetown, Guyana (then British Guiana).
Novelist, teacher, diplomat.

Braithwaite was educated in Guyana; New York (City College, B.S., 1940); Cambridge University; Gains College (M.Sc., Physics, 1949); and London University Institute of Education. He served in the R.A.F. in World War II (1941-45). He has served as Ambassador of Guyana to Venezuela (1968-69), having been previously Permanent Representative to the United Nations.

He lived in London for a long time, having been a school teacher there (1950-57), and a London County Council Welfare Officer (1958-60). He has also lived in Paris, where he was Human Rights Officer in the Veterans' Foundation (1960-63), and has been Lecturer and Education Officer, UNESCO (1963-66).

2755 NEW ENGLISH LIBRARY U.K...6/- (30p)
Paid Servant
The Brilliant
Sequel To
'To Sir, With Love'
E.R.Braithwaite

A quiet and charming man, Braithwaite's success in the literary field has surprised some, and generated a certain amount of controversy. His writings seem to many rather simple and, perhaps, too directly connected with a kind of autobiography, to be genuine works of the creative imagination. He has also been attacked on what might be called ideological grounds. Nonetheless, his still popular *To Sir With Love* (1959) won the Anisfield-Wolf Award in 1960, and was filmed (with Sidney Poitier as leading actor). Most

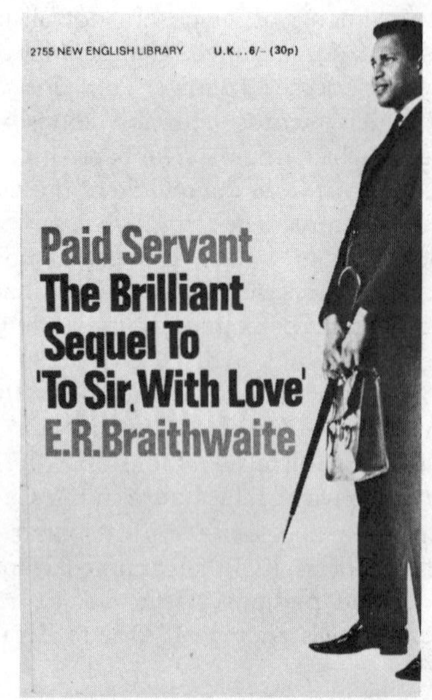

of his books have been published both in the United Kingdom and the United States.

He has been anthologized often in such journals as: *West Indian Narrative; West Indian Stories; The Sun's Eye;* and *Thieme's Anthology of West Indian Literature;* and had the signal honor of having his *To Sir With Love* banned from Jamaican schools by the then distinguished Minister of Education, Edward Allen, B.A.

Writings: Novels: *To Sir With Love,* London, Bodley Head, 1959; and London, Four Square, paperback, 1962, Toronto, Signet Books, 1968; Englewood Cliffs, Prentice-Hall, 1960 and 1962, New York, Pyramid, 1973 (made into a film by Columbia Pictures); *A Kind of Homecoming,* Englewood Cliffs, N.J., Prentice Hall, 1962; and London, Muller, 1963; *Paid Servant,* London, Bodley Head, 1962; and New York, McGraw Hill, 1968; Pyramid, 1972; London, Four Square Paper Books, 1965; London, New English Library, 1968, 1969 (new edition); *Reluctant Neighbours,* London, Bodley Head, 1972, and New York, McGraw Hill, 1972; *A Choice of Straws,* London, Bodley Head, 1965; New York, Pyramid, 1972, and soft cover, London, Pan Books, 1968, and Indianapolis, Bobbs-Merrill, 1967.

Essay: "The 'Coloured Immigrant' in Britain" as chapter to special issue "Color and Race" of *Daedalus* magazine (Spring 1967).

Travel (in South Africa): *Honorary White: A Visit to South Africa,* London, 1975.

Biographical/Critical Sources: Kenneth Ramchand, "The Myth of Sir, With Love," in *Voices,* Vol. I, No. 5 (December 1965), pp. 13-20; review of *A Choice of Straws,* by Arnold Kettle, in *Journal of Commonwealth Literature* (1966-67); F.M. Bisbalsingh "To John Bull, with Hate," in *Caribbean Quarterly;* Joseph and Johanna Jones, *Authors and Areas of the West Indies* (People and Places in World-English Literature No. 2), 1970, pp. 10-11.

BRAITHWAITE, J. Ashton

(a.k.a. **Odimumba KWAMDELA**)
b. ca. 1945, Barbados.
Poet, novelist.

Braithwaite has been editor and co-publisher of *Spear,* Canada's first black magazine, founded in 1971. As a young man, he emigrated to England and has traveled widely in the Middle East, Africa, and the United States and Canada.

Writings: Prose: *Black British Soldier; Souls in the Wilderness; Niggers ... This is Canada,* Toronto, 21st Century Book, 1971.

Poetry: *The Righteous Blackman,* Toronto, 21st Century Book, 1970, 1971, 1972.

BRATHWAITE, L. Edward

(now: **Edward Kamau BRATHWAITE**)
b. May 11, 1930, Barbados.
Poet, critic, storywriter, teacher, historian, editor.

Born in Barbados, Brathwaite attended Harrison College, won the Barbados Scholarship in 1949, and went to Cambridge to read History at Pembroke College. He obtained his B.A. in 1953, and his Certificate in Education in 1954. He was later, after working in Ghana and the West Indies, to return to England to do his Ph.D. at the University of Sussex, on

the development of creole society in Jamaica, 1770-1820. He has been an active Extra Mural Tutor of the Univ. of West Indies, in St. Lucia. He lived, studied and worked off and on in England and Ghana; more recently he has been on a number of lecture tours in the United States, and has been teaching, on a short stint, at Boston University.

Brathwaite is another West Indian who defies the usual metropolitan ideas on specialization. A knowledgeable jazz enthusiast and expert, a leading West Indian historian, a man with great interest in how language operates, he is also a poet of international fame.

He and Walcott were born in the same year, and have shared the experience of rave reviews abroad. Brathwaite lived for seven years in Ghana, where he worked as Education Officer, teaching and supervising over a wide area, and taking the opportunity to get to the bottom of those African forms and traditions—Masks?—which crossed by the narrow and anquished Middle Passage to the Caribbean. What exactly was the *kind* of sea change which accompanied the brutal transportation of African customs to the Caribbean?—that has been one of the constant controversies surrounding Brathwaite's work and activities as a publicist.

All his poetry has received outstanding reviews in the metropolitan centres.

Of *Rights of Passage* the *Critical Quarterly* said: "The particular vitality of *R. of P.* is nearer to the American than to the English tradition, but different from either." (The reviewer no doubt meant the *North* American; after all the Caribbean has been part of the Americas for a long time!). . . . "the poet is equally at home with experimental and traditional forms."

And the *Sunday Times* said of *Islands*, the third part of Brathwaite's trilogy,

> *This book together with its earlier sections is enough to place Mr. Brathwaite among the finest living poets in the Western hemisphere.*

He is a remarkable reader of his own poetry; and he controls his native Barbadian dialect brilliantly. His poems have been sometimes criticized because he does not seem to have indicated on the printed page, and through the usual traditions of verse writing, just exactly how their rhythm is to be vocalized. Perhaps his brilliance as a reader, enhancing though it is to his performances, is a hidden handicap to him as a writer for people who will never hear him.

His major work, in verse, so far, has been an attempt to *place* the main Caribbean cultural experience especially as it has been related to Africa. One of his great admirers, Anne Walmsley, who on the whole compares Walcott to him unfavorably says this:

> *Brathwaite is himself so articulate an expositor of his own verse that his own explanations of titles can be quoted.* Rights of Passage, *he tells us on the record sleeve, is "based on my own experience of that old triple journey: in my case, from the Caribbean to Europe, to West Africa and back home again . . . the journey of the 'passage' of the title, becomes, in other words, a ritual, a rite, which is also a right, a possession. It is a rite and the posession of the Negro peoples of the New World!"*

She also quotes him as telling the Caribbean Artists Movement:

> *I attempt to find a home which is the answer for the traveling. I postulate that Africa is the spiritual home for the West Indians.*

This "spiritual home" view, which seemed to have been a large part of what Brathwaite was saying at the famous ACLALS meeting in Jamaica early in 1973, appears, to the simple minded, to exclude from the right (or is it "rite") to be West Indians such persons as: Naipaul, Selvon, Jagan, Ian McDonald and Frank Collymore to name a few. One wonders whether Walmsley has reported the exact context in which the remark was made.

Brathwaite's carefully orchestrated long poems, which have been very popular, have been criticized on other than ethnic and ideological grounds. Edward Baugh is less enthusiastic than many, and C.L.R., the indefatigable, takes a self-revealing swipe at both Brathwaite and Walcott!

Baugh says of *Masks:*

> *I have to add that my final impression is that there is, on the whole, rather more pattern than pith. This impression only confirms what I had felt on reading* Rights of Passage. *Too much is claimed for* Masks. *This is the first time so far as we know, that a West Indian has come so intimately to terms with his African heritage. The statement seems to confuse intimate knowledge with the business of coming to terms.*

And the old Guru, C.L.R. James, has this to say:

> *As for Brathwaite, I don't make it very much with him, but that is a matter of taste. I believe he is working hard. There are parts of his poems that seem to me come straight from Aimé Césaire's* Cahier d'un retour au pays natal. *Well certain things that Césaire says, Brathwaite says. He has been making a reputation for himself. He and Walcott—I don't think they're of the quality of the old generation, and I much prefer those two young men, Earl Lovelace and Michael Anthony, who are natural writers. There is something artificial about Brathwaite . . .*
>
> *Kas-Kas,* (Occasional Pub. of the African and Afro-American Research Institute, The University of Texas at Austin), p.31.

At a later date Baugh was also to write something central to considering, in any serious sense, Brathwaite both as a practicing poet and a man of culture, and an educator, in the Caribbean:

> *He (Brathwaite) has set himself in his internationally acclaimed trilogy, to write the great poem of the Black Man, on the basis of the idea that it is in cultivating his black continuities that the West Indian will realize his full potential!*

Notice not that "Brathwaite will," but "that the West Indian will."

Brathwaite is also very much an organizer and the center of a movement; he is the vigorous editor of *Savacou,* and of its publications; he led the formation of the Caribbean Artist Movement in London. He has also been a leader in experimenting in verse forms, and in the use of non-standard English in West Indian Verse.

He is also a critic much interested in the relationship of jazz to Caribbean writing, and to the whole question of *Caribbean Studies* done, as it were, from the *inside.*

He gives the impression, rare among poets, of knowing exactly where he wishes to get to, and of sparing no efforts to arrive at that chosen destination. And his range is wider than one thinks—see BIM (No. 29), for instance.

Brathwaite has received many awards including: Poetry Book Society Recommend, (*Rights of Passage),* 1967; Hampstead Arts Festival Poetry Prize, U.K., 1967; Arts Council of Great Britain Poetry Bursary, 1967; Cholmondeley Award, 1970; Guggenheim Foundation Fellowship, 1971; Bussa Award, 1973; In 1971 he recorded the entire trilogy (*Rights of Passage; Masks; Islands)* for Argo Recording Company. He also reads on "West Indian Poets Reading Their Own Poetry," Caedmon (No. T.C. 1379), edited by John Figueroa.

A poet of international fame, and one with many admirers and followers in the Caribbean, he paid tribute to Frank Collymore in a generous and moving manner by putting together, at the cost of much time and effort, *Savacou 7/8.*

Writings: Poetry: *Rights of Passage,* London, Oxford University Press, 1967; *Masks,* London, Oxford University Press, 1968; *Islands,* London, Oxford University Press, 1969; *The Arrivants,* London, Oxford University Press,

1973; the Trilogy of the three publications above republished; *Other Exiles,* London, Oxford University Press, 1975; *Days and Nights,* Caldwell Press, Mona, Kingston, Jamaica, 1975; *Mother Poems,*London, Oxford University Press, 1977.

Plays: *Odale's Choice,* London, Evans Brothers, 1967, performed in Bishop's Auditorium, Port of Spain, Trinidad, May 25, 1973 by Derek Walcott's Theatre Workshop; *Four Plays for Primary Schools,* London, Longmans, 1964 (written while author was Education Officer in Ghana: two of the plays are nativity plays recast in West African setting and two are based on traditional West African folktales).

Other: *The People Who Came,* Bk. I, 1968 and Bk. II (Ed. and Co-author), 1969.

History: *The Folk Culture of Jamaican Slaves,* London, New Beacon Books, 1969; *Creole Society in Jamaica 1770-1820,* Oxford, Clarendon Press, 1971 (based on his doctoral thesis, University of Sussex, 1968).

Critical Essays and Articles (including): "Sir Galahad and the Islands. An Essay on the Theme of Migration in Br. West Indian Literature," in *Iouanola: Recent Writing from St. Lucia* (ed. E. Brathwaite), Castries, St. Lucia, Dept. fo Extra Mural Studies, U.W.I., 1963, pp. 50-59; "Caribbean Critics," in *Critical Quarterly,* XI, 3 (1969), pp. 268-276; "West Indian Prose Fiction in the Sixties," in *The Critical Survey* (Winter 1967), pp. 169-174; "Jazz in the West Indian Novel," in BIM 44, pp. 275-284, in BIM 46, pp. 115-126; several essays in *Contemporary Poets of the English Language,* London, 1970; "The Caribbean Artists' Movement," in *Caribbean Quarterly,* Vol. 14, Nos. I and II (March-June, 1968), pp. 57-59; "Movement to overcome isolation of West Indian novelists," in two parts, BIM, Vol. 8, No. 31 (July-Dec. 1960), pp. 199-210, and BIM, Vol. 8, No. 32 (Jan.-June 1961), pp. 271-280; "The controversial tree of time" (on works of Wilson Harris), in BIM, Vol. 8, No. 30 (Jan -June 1960), pp. 104-114; "Roots": a commentary on West Indian Writers," in BIM, Vol. 10, No. 37 (July-Dec. 1963), pp. 10-21; list of his reviews of others' works in *Commonwealth Caribbean Writer: A Bibliography,* Merriman and Christiani, comps., Georgetown, Guyana, 1970.

Co-editor and Contributor to BIM and *Savacou.* He has contributed verse to numerous journals, reviews, and anthologies including: *Poetry from Cambridge, 1947-50; Caribbean Voices* (ed. J. Figueroa) Vol. II; *Commonwealth Poems of Today* (ed. Howard Sergeant); *New Voices of the Commonwealth,* 1968 (H. Sergeant); *The Sun's Eye* (A. Walmsley); *Penguin Modern Poets* 15, 1969; *N.Y. Times Anthology of Poetry,* 1969; *Times Ed. Supplement; Contemporary Poets of the English Language.*

Recording: Gramophone Records: *The Making of a Drum from "Masks,"* 1968; *Rights of Passage,* 1969; *Masks,* 1973; *The Arrivants,* 1973. Recorded readings of his own poetry on Caedmon Record, No. T.C. 1379: *Poets of the West Indies* (ed. J. Figueroa).

Short stories: in various journals and collections including: BIM; *Stories from the Caribbean* (ed. A. Salkey); *Caribbean Prose* (ed. A. Salkey).

Biographical/Critical Sources: Jean DaCosta, "The poetry of Edward Brathwaite," *Jamaica Journal,* Vol. 2, No. 3 (Sept. 1968), pp. 24-28; Louis James in his Introduction to *The Islands in Between,* London, 1968; Damian Grant, "Emerging Image: The Poetry of Edward Brathwaite," in *Critical Quarterly,* XII, 2 (1970), pp. 186-192; K. Senann, "Brathwaite's Song of Dispossession in *Universitas,* I, I (1969), pp. 59-63; Anne Walmsley, "Dimensions of Song: A Comment on the Poetry of Derek Walcott and Edward Brathwaite" in BIM XIII, 51 (1970), pp. 152-167; Gordon Rohlehr, "The Historian as Poet" (on Brathwaite's *Islands*), in *The Literary Half-Yearly,* XI, 2 (July 1970), pp. 171-178, Nos. 3 and 4 (Sept-Dec. 1971), pp. 54-71; review of *Four Plays for Primary Schools,* Longmans by Harold Marshall in BIM 41, pp. 71-72; *Rights of Passage,* Oxford University Press, reviewed by Edward Baugh in BIM 45, pp. 66-68; review of *Masks*, Oxford Uiversity Press, by Edward Baugh, in BIM 47, pp. 209-211; review of *Islands*, Oxford University Press, by Gerald Moore, in BIM 51, pp. 186-189; review of *Other Exiles*, Oxford University Press, in the *Daily Gleaner*, (Feb.22,1976) Kingston, Jamaica; Edward Baugh, "A Brief Account of West Indian Poetry 1900-1970"—pamphlet, Savacou Publications Ltd, references: pp. 1,2, 13, 17-18; Anson Gonzalez, " 'Possibility' in W.I. Creative Writing," in *The New Voices,* No. 4 (June 1974), Trinidad and Tobago, pp. 3, 45, 46; *Authors and Areas of the West Indies* by Joseph and Johanna Jones in *People and*

Places in World-English Literature No. 2, Austin, Texas, p. 12; List of reviews of his work up to 1970 in *Commonwealth Caribbean Writers: A Bibliography*, Merriman and Christiani, eds. and comps., Georgetown, Guyana, 1970.

BRATHWAITE, Percy A.

b. ca. 1933, Guyana.
Folklorist, editor, musicologist.

Percy Brathwaite has published much needed studies of local songs and stories of Guyana.

Writings: Folklore: *Folksongs of Guyana: Queh-Queh, Chanties and Ragtime*, Georgetown, C.H. Welshman, 1964; *The Legend of Christmas: Stories and Verse*, Georgetown, Guyana, 1973.

Editor (with Serena Brathwaite): *Guyanese Proverbs and Stories*, Georgetown, 1966.

Musicology: *Musical Traditions*, Georgetown, Guyana, C.A. Welshman, 1962 (only Vol. I issued).

BRETT, William Henry (Rev.)

b. ca. 1831, Guyana.
Folklorist.

Brett is possibly the earliest Guyanese student of local legends, particularly those of Amerindian origin.

Writings: Folklore: *Legends and Myths of the Aboriginal Indians of British Guiana*, London, W. Gardner, 1860, 1861; *The Indian Tribes of Guiana: Their Condition and Habits*, London, Bell and Daldy, 1868.

Compiler of: *Guianese Legends:* London, Society for the Propagation of the Gospel in Foreign Parts, n.d. (49 p.), as *Guiana Legends*, 1931, with Leonard Lambert as editor.

BROWN, Lennox

b. 1935, Port of Spain, Trinidad.
Playwright, critic, poet, musician.

Born in a multi-racial slum, the East Dry River District, which was simply called by the residents "Behind the Bridge," Brown used his early years there in his play *A Ballet Behind the Bridge*. He worked for a period at Magistrate's Court in Port of Spain but moved on to gain a B.A. in Journalism (First Class honors) at the University of Western Ontario in 1961. He served as editor-reporter for the Canadian Broadcasting Corporation 1965-1968 in Toronto, and then earned an M.A. in journalism at the University of Toronto (1969), his thesis being on Samuel Selvon, the well-known Trinidad novelist.

At 18, Brown began his own personal educational program by doing extensive reading at a local library in Trinidad and began to write for the *Trinidad Guardian* and the *Evening News*, many of his stories covering the gang wars of the Port of Spain slums. Brought up as a Roman Catholic, he gave up the church at 16. Though his work quite naturally reflects the gross poverty, violence and widespread suffering of his home neighborhood, Brown also recalls the music, dance, the steel bands and the general vivid life, too. In 1968 he visited Trinidad after a considerable absence with the Trade Winds, a combo with which he was then singing and playing guitar. He took part in Carifesta, Guyana, 1972, and also visited Trinidad at that time.

Writings: Plays: *The Voyage Tonight*, runner up in Norma Epstein National (Bienniel) Creative Award, Univ. of Toronto; *The Captive*, first prize in Ottawa Little Theatre Playwriting Competition (in mimeograph copy only); *A Ballet Behind the Bridge*, written 1969, performed by Negro Ensemble Theatre in New York; *The Trinity of Four*, published in J.T. Livingston's *Caribbean Rhythms*, New York, Washington Square Press, 1974; *Saturday Druid of Man Against Himself*, one-half hour radio play recorded by CBC; *Prodigal in Black Stone*, premiered at Eugene O'Neill National Playwrights Conference, 1972; *Jour Ouvert* (or *Daybreak*), Ottawa, Ottawa Little Theatre, 1966 (?), in mimeograph version only; and *The Meeting*, also Ottawa and in mimeo, 1966; *Night Sun*, first prize in annual Ottawa Little Theatre Canadian Playwright Competition, and Birks Medal and Solange Karsh award of $250.

BROWN, Wayne

b. 1944, Trinidad.
Poet, critic.

Brown's university work (with Honors) was done first at U.W.I., Mona. He has been on the editorial staff of the *Trinidad Guardian,* has done research in England, and has published a book on Edna Manley. On this book and on Naipaul's *Guerrillas,* Brown gave his opinions in an interview in the *Trinidad Guardian* (Jan. 11, 1976).

Lively conversationalist, though quiet, Wayne Brown is clearly not only a young poet of whom much is expected, but one who makes great demands on himself. Of his collection (p. 48) Ted Hughes writes:

> *There are quite a few beautiful poems here and they seem to me to be pressing beyond even their present sophistications, moving towards something really unusual and fine.*

Some of his poems seem distant and rather too refined, but others cluster with moving imagery:

> *. . . the frail, smoking sea-pit of sky*
> *capsizes slowly, as in dreams,*
> *letting fall, in luxuries of vertigo,*
> *blue wildernesses, like clouds. . . .*
>
> (from "Fisherman's Son")

Writings: Poetry: *On The Coast,* London, Andre Deutsch, 1972, Poetry Book Society Recommendation. Individual poems appear in BIM, *The Voices, Savacou, Caribbean Quarterly* (Vol. 18, No. 4, December 1972), and other journals; also in *Breaklight; Poetry and Audience* (Leeds University: Vol. 21, No. 6); and *The Literary Half-Yearly* (Mysore, India), XI, 2 (July 1970).

M.A. Thesis: "The Use of Tragicomedy in the Development of a National Consciousness in West Indian Literature: a Study of Samuel Selvon's *The Housing Lark,* unpublished, University of Toronto, 1969.

Essays: "A Black Castle, The Cultural Crisis in Black Canada," *Black Images,* I, 1, 4; "A Crisis: Black Culture in Canada," *Black Images* (Jan., 1972), pp. 4-8.

Biographical/Critical Sources: Jo Jo Chintoh, "Profile of Lennox Brown, A Black Playwright," *Black Images,* I, 1, 28.

Critical Articles and Reviews: in *Trinidad Guardian* including: "West Indian Poetry of the 1940's," (September 13, 1970); "New West Indian Writers of the Past Years," (September 6, 1970); "West Indian Literature of the Past Year," (August 30, 1970); "The First Generation of West Indian Novelists," in *Sunday Guardian (*June 7, 1970); "The Little Magazine in the West Indies," *Trinidad Guardian* (August 16, 1970).

Biography: *Edna Manley,* London, Andre Deutsch, 1975.

Reviews: *The Expatriates* by Faustin Charles, "An exciting Trinidad Poet" in *Trinidad Guardian* (August 2, 1970); *The Humming Bird Tree,* Ian McDonald, in *Trinidad Guardian* (June 2, 1970); *Crick-Crack Monkey,* by Merle Hodge, in *T.G.* (June 28, 1970); of *Savacou,* in *T.G.* (August 16, 1970).

Biographical/Critical Sources: Review of *On The Coast,* in *Sunday Guardian* (February 25, 1973), p. 8, which was favorable, and in *Trinidad Guardian (*January 12, 1973), by E. Roach, which was unfavorable; *On The Coast,* Lee S.D. Johnson, in *Caribbean Quarterly,* Vol. 18, No. 4 (December 1972), pp. 84-86; Edward Baugh, "West Indian Poetry 1900-1970" (pamphlet), Savacou Publications Ltd., p. 18.

BULLY, Alwin

b. ca. 1935, Dominica.
Poet, storywriter, playwright, artist, dancer, producer.

Alwin Bully, a graduate of the University of the West Indies, is also a teacher. For the last three years he has been using and developing his rich creative talents in Roseau, Dominica.

A friend of Robert Lee of St. Lucia, he did the Cover Design and illustrations for Lee's poetry collection *Vocation* (St.

Lucia, 1975). Bully himself wrote an interesting piece on the Cover Design.

Along with Daniel Caudeiron, and Lennox Honeychurch of Dominica, he has edited *Wahseen*, and *Free Your Mind*, two Dominican literary magazines. He has adapted the novel *Ruler in Hiroona* by G.C.H. Thomas into a play.

Writings: Plays: *Good Morning Miss Millie; Streak; Ruler in Hiroona.*

BUNBURY, Henry Shirley

b. April 24, 1843, Watford, Ireland, but lived in Jamaica from 1911; d. 1920.
Poet.

Educated at Magdalen College School and King's College, London University, Bunbury retired from the English Civil Service in 1903 and settled in Jamaica in 1911. He was a prolific writer and contributed poems and letters to the *Daily Gleaner* and *Jamaican Times.* His poetry appears in *Voices from Summerland* (1929), and *A Treasury of Jamaican Poetry* (1950).

Biographical/Critical Sources: Mentioned in J.E. Clare McFarlane's *A Literature in the Making,* Pioneer Press, Jamaica, 1956 (main reference—Chapter 2, p. 18).

BUNTING, J.R.

b. 1929, England.
Poet, educator, civil servant.

Born in England, Bunting lived in Jamaica (with which he identified) for many years. Educated at Oxford, he taught at Munro College, Malvern, and was an energetic Headmaster of Wolmer's Boys's School, Kingston, and afterwards Education Officer, Nigeria, a country which he represented at the 1959 Education Conference, Oxford.

Later, a consultant to Evans Brothers, London, he dealt with many publications for the West Indies and the rest of the post-independence British-English speaking world. He was one of the group who published early in *Focus.*

Writings: Contributed to *Focus* and *Caribbean Voices,* Vol. 2. His poems also were broadcast in BBC's *Caribbean Voices.*

CALLENDER, Timothy

b. ca. 1936, Barbados.
Storywriter, painter, teacher.

Callender became well known for his short stories from the time he was a student at Combermere in Barbados. He did graduate and postgraduate studies at the University of the West Indies, at Mona, Jamaica. He taught for three years in St. Kitts, where he continued his research on "The Woman in the West Indian Novel." He is now back on Barbados, teaching English and Art at Combermere. He has also written and published poetry.

He has been a regular and prolific contributor of short stories to BIM (over 50). His stories have been broadcast over Radio Barbados and Rediffusion. His stories have been published in various West Indian newspapers and journals including *New World* and *Savacou.* He was one of the fifty contributors in *Savacou 7/8* which was brought out in honor of Frank Collymore. One of his contributions, "The Boyfriends," was listed under the Section (III) BIM CLASSICS in the company of such writers as George Lamming, Edgar Mittelholzer, Derek Walcott, Michael Anthony, Frank Collymore, Austin Clarke—to mention a few.

He has now published his first collection of short stories.

Writing: It So Happen, Belfast, (Dublin), Ireland Christian Journals Ltd., 1975.

CAMBRIDGE, Arnold

b. ca. 1937, Trinidad.
Playwright.

Cambridge's play, *Cockadoo*, was performed by the Rosary C.Y.O. players, on May 1964, at C.Y.O., Port of Spain, Trinidad. It won three prizes in the C.Y.O. competition: Best performed play, Best principal actor, Best actress. In 1965 it won second prize in the comedy section of the Trinidad and Tobago Arts Festival.

Writing: Play: *Cockadoo*, (Caribbean Plays: One Act Play XLV), Trinidad and Tobago, Extra Mural Dept., U.C.W.I., 1967.

CAMERON, Norman Eustace

b. January 26, 1903, New Amsterdam, British Guiana, now Guyana.
Editor, teacher, playwright, scholar.

Norman Cameron is one of those who has been long in the field of culture and the fine arts in the English speaking West Indies. He was awarded the M.B.E., and later the Golden Arrow of Achievement of Guyana. Educated in Guyana and the United Kingdom, and a Cambridge M.A., Cameron was founder of both a secondary school and the Association of Assistant Masters and Mistresses of Secondary Schools, British Guiana.

His *Guianese Poetry* collection (covering the hundred year period 1831-1931) provides interesting material for the historian of literature and its relations with society.

Writings: Plays: *Three Immortals* (a collection of three plays), Georgetown, Persick, 1953, (*Adoniya: A Play in Three Acts)*, British Guiana, F. A. Persick, 1953 and in *Three Immortals*, performed, Georgetown, Queen's College, 1943; *Ebedmelech: A Play in Three Acts*, British Guiana, F. A. Persick, 1953 and in *Three Immortals; Sabaco: A Play in Three Acts*, Persick, 1953; *Balthasar*, Georgetown, Argosy Co., 1931; *Jamaica Joe: A Play in Three Acts*, British Guiana, De Souza's Printery, 1962, (performed Georgetown, 1946); *The Trumpet: A Play in Three Acts*, Georgetown, *Daily Chronicle*, 1969; *The Price of Victory: A Play in Two Parts* (based on a Nigerian legend), British Guiana, Labour Advocate Job Printing Department, 1965; *Kayssa, or Hear the other side: Programme and text of play*, British Guiana, Adana Printing Service, 1959.

Poetry: *Interlude: Original Poems*, Georgetown, Argosy Co., 1944.

Editor of: *Guianese Poetry* (covering the hundred year period 1831-1931), British Guiana, Argosy Co., 1931, and Nendeln, Kraus, 1970 (Reprint).

His verse appears in anthologies: *Themes of Song; Sun is a Shapely Fire;* and local periodicals, including: *Kyk-over-al*, and *Kaie*.

Others: *The Evolution of the Negro*, 2 vols., Georgetown, Argosy Co., 1929, 1934, and Westport, Connecticut, U.S., Negro University Press, 1970; *Adventures in the Field of Culture*, Georgetown, *Guyana Daily Chronicle*, 1971; *Gilchrist Scholarships in the Caribbean*, Georgetown, Guyana Graphic, 1963; *Thoughts on Life and Literature*, British Guiana, F.A. Persick, 1950 (172 pp.); *Guyanese Library and its Impact*, Georgetown, 1971; *Poetry and Philosophy in Drama*, Georgetown, Labour Advocate Job Printing, 1973; *A History of the Queen's College of British Guiana*, Georgetown, 1951; *Worrying Features in our Politics*, Georgetown, Labour Advocate Job Printing, 1964; *Clearing the Political Air*, Georgetown, Labour Advocate Job Printing, 1963; *Communism and British Guiana*, Georgetown, Guyana, Labour Advocate Job Printing, 1963; *Thoughts on a co-operative state; An Introduction to our Social Philosophy*, Georgetown, Guyana, 1965; *Thoughts on the Making of a New Nation*.

Articles and Essays: in *Kyk-over-al* and *Kaie*.

Biographical/Critical Sources: Review, p. 26, n. 2, notes on *The Evolution of the Negro*, in *The West Indian Novel and its Background* by Kenneth Ramchand, New York, Barnes & Noble, 1970. Also see *Guide to the Published Work of a Guyanese Author and Playwright*, Guyana, Labour Advocate Job Printing, 1966 (Annotated Bibliography to Cameron's work).

CAMPBELL, George

b. 1918, Jamaica.
Poet, playwright.

Campbell has lived for many years in New York, where he and his wife (Odilla Orane of Jamaica) and three daughters make their home. He was in the '40's *the* bright star of Jamaican poetry, and he influenced the early Walcott who was introduced to his poetry by Harry Simmons. Walcott in *Another Life* quotes Campbell's well known lines:

Holy be the white head of a Negro . . .

The refrain "Holy be . . ." is in fact built with much subtlety into *Another Life*—a tribute, in a way, to one of the most promising of Caribbean poets who has produced but little recently.

One of Campbell's more recent poems "we tear our leaders down" appears in *Caribbean Voices II,* and embodies a feeling and a reality only too true to Caribbean experience:

We tear our leaders down
Like a man who hates nature
Turns from trees, live, offering,
And lays bare the day
For material gain.
. . . .
. . . .
. . .
And yet the nightingale
Sings best in the night
For the passing ear,
And the lion hunts best his own way.
wounded in the wing the song bird
Sings only suffering
And the wounded lion hates the day.

Writings: Poetry: *First Poems*, Kingston, Jamaica, City Printery, Ltd., 1945 (dedicated to E.M. and N.W.M. the People of Jamaica) and republished in volume entitled *Bamboula dance and other poems* (Jose Antonio Jarvis, ed.) Nendeln, Liechtenstein, Kraus Reprint, 1970); *A Play without Scenery: A Fantasy in Focus,* edited by Edna Manley, 1948, pp. 257-279 (produced Jamaica, 1946 and 1947). Individual poems in *Caribbean Voices,* Vols. I and II (1966, 1970): *Focus* (1943, 1948, 1956, 1960); *Caribbean Quarterly,* Vol. 5, No. 3) *An Anthology of West Indian Poetry* (April 1958), Federation Commemoration Issue), and *The Independence Anthology,* 1962.

Biographical/Critical Sources: Edward Baugh, *West Indian Poetry 1900-1970. A Study in Cultural Decolonisation* (pamphlet), Kingston, Savacou-Publications, pp. 8-9.

CAMPBELL, John

b. ca. 1936, Guyana.
Poet, playwright.

Campbell has contributed poetry to various periodicals and collections, including Monar's *Poems for Guyanese Children,* and has published four volumes of poetry and two plays.

Writings: Poetry: *Poems to Remember*, Georgetown, 1968; *Poems for All*, Georgetown, 1971; *Our Own Poems*, Georgetown, 1973; and *Trends 12*, Georgetown, 1973.

Plays: *Come Back to Melda*, performed Guyana, 1963; *Cuffy, The Brazen: One Act Play; Dhanwattie: A Play in One Scene*, performed, Georgetown, and in *Writers in Uniform* (see below), 1966; and in ms. *Don't Look Back: A Play in One Act* (composed 1963).

Editor of: *Writers in Uniform*, Guyana, Guyana Police Force Publication, 1972 (contains one play, two stories, 13 poems).

CAMPBELL, William Alexander

b. ca. 1877, Jamaica.
Storywriter.

Campbell authored but one known work, a pioneering story published in 1907.

Writing: Novelette: *Marguerite: A story of the Earthquake,* Kingston, The Times Printery, 1907.

CANCRYN, Addelita

(née **PAROTT**)
b. ca. 1945, St. Thomas, U.S. Virgin Islands.
Biographer, teacher, musician.

Cancryn has had a long and successful career as an educator. She did her professional studies, B.A., M.A. (Ed.), at Hampton Institute in Virginia, U.S.A. During her years of teaching at the Abraham Lincoln School in St. Thomas, now renamed for José Antonio Jarvis, she met Jarvis and worked closely with him. This association has resulted in her biography of Jarvis which is her first publication. She is Principal of the Wayne Aspinall Junior High School in St. Thomas, and very active in creative, musical and civic and church affairs. She has given an excellent record of Jarvis' contribution to the U.S.A. Virgin Islands as a journalist, poet, artist, playwright and historian.

Writing: Biography: *Man of Vision* (of José Antonio Jarvis), St. Thomas, Virgin Islands, Val-Hill Enterprises, 1975.

CANO, Luis E.

b. 1927, Belize (British Honduras).
Poet, artist.

Cano has published one collection of his verse.

Writing: Poetry: *The middle way*, 1972.

CANOE, John

(pseudonym for **Oliver Austin KIRKPATRICK**).

CAPILDEO, Devendranath

b. ca. 1934, Trinidad.
Poet.

Better known as a mathematician and as a politician, Capildeo has published two collections of simple poems.

Writings: Poetry: *10 Short Poems*, Port of Spain, Trinidad, Horsford Printerie, 1969; *"Maracas Bay" and other short poems*, Port of Spain, Trinidad, Superservice Printing, 1972. Verse published in BIM, *Caribbean Medlay* (Poems), a collection of W.I. Poetry in BIM 52 (January-June 1971).

CARBERRY, Hugh Doston

b. 1921, Montreal, Canada (of Jamaican parentage).
Poet, bibliophile, barrister.

A well known collector of Jamaican Literature and West Indian books, Carberry belonged to the early group of writers including George Campbell and Kenneth Ingram, but has not written much poetry recently. He is one of the few "modern" writers to be in *A Treasury of Jamaican Poetry*. He appears also in recent anthologies such as *Breaklight* and *Caribbean Voices*. He was educated at Jamaican College, Jamaica, St. Catherine's Oxford, and the Middle Temple, London.

One time president of the West Indian Student Union, London, at a critical time in its history and the history of the West Indies; Carberry has ever been an encourager of intellectuals and writers.

Writings: A West Indian in England (with Dudley Thomas), 1950. Contributor to anthologies: *Focus; The Sun's Eye; Caribbean Voices*, Vol. 1 (1966) and Combined Edition (1971, 1973); *Breaklight; The Poetry of the Negro; A Treasury of Jamaican Poetry; Caribbean Quarterly* Federation Commemoration Issue, Vol. 5, No. 3 (April 1958); *Independence Anthology*, 1962.

Biographical/Critical Sources: Edward Baugh, *West Indian Poetry 1900-1970* [pamphlet], Kingston, Savacou, p. 9.

CAREW, Jan Rynveld

(a.k.a. **Jan Alwyn CAREW**)

b. September 24, 1925, in Agricola, British Guiana, now Guyana.
Novelist, critic, teacher, playwright, poet, editor.

Educated at Berbice High School in Guyana, and at several universities in the United States and Europe, Jan Carew is at present Professor of African American

Studies and Chairman of that Department at Northwestern University (United States). He has also been Senior Lecturer in the Council of Humanities and Lecturer in the Department of Afro-American Studies, Princeton University.

From 1966-69 he resided in Toronto, Canada, where he edited *Cotopaxi*, a

review of Third World literature and current events. In 1969 he was recipient of a Canada Arts Council Fellowship. He has edited a number of journals including *De Kim*, Amsterdam, Holland; *The Kensington Post*, London, and *The African Review*, Ghana.

Carew is a very lively and concerned person and writer; full of energy, he is a formidable adversary, but not without a great deal of charm. Ivan Van Sertima feels that if Carew does have a fairly constant theme it is that "of flights from origins and quest for roots." But Carew does not seek an easy communal "identity," for, in *The Last Barbarian*, for instance, he portrays someone doing his best to find *himself*, to become an artist in his own right.

Despite Carew's heavy administrative and promotional duties, he continues to write fiction ("Waiting for the American"), and he is working on a collection of poems with Andrew Salkey, for Princeton University Press. He also has a play, "Boni Doro," in manuscript.

He has received many awards, and in 1975 Princeton University established the Jan Carew Annual Lectureship. He was awarded in 1974 and 1975 the Burton Annual Fellowship, Howard University, Graduate School of Education.

Carew's books range over a wide area—even as he has lived in many places, and done many things: write, edit, act and paint. He deals not only with the "green fires in the jaguar's eyes" but also with the complicated fires of racial discrimination and misunderstanding smouldering in the eyes of the socialist brothers. In *Moscow is Not My Mecca*, he deals with the impact of a new white society on a colored observer. He seems to be suggesting "a plague on both your houses," but, of course, he is writing a novel, and is not a man for simple slogans. As a matter of fact, as Ivan Van Sertima shows, Carew points, in *Moscow*

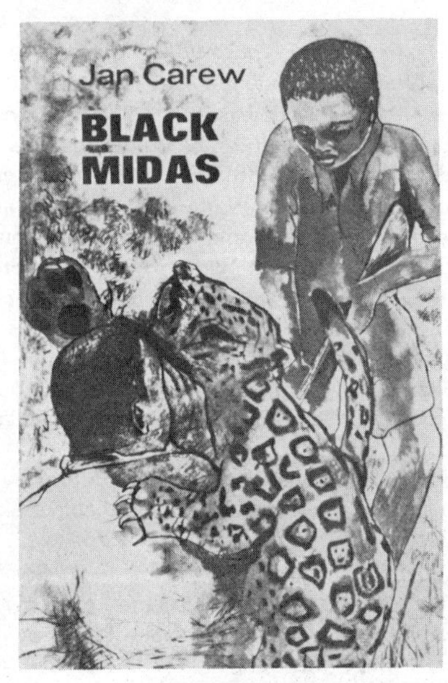

is Not My Mecca, "prophetically to the future alignment of the 'coloured' races in a Third World stance against the 'white' super-powers."

Black Midas, Carew's first novel, is colorful. His portraits of the porknockers and prostitutes are vigorous, and ring true. The folklore and forests of Guyana are very much present.

He has written many short stories and plays, and *Black Midas* was translated into the Georgian language. His review in the New York Times of George Lamming's *Natives of My Person,* was helpful, sensitive and interesting.

It is only fair to add that like all powerful writers Jan Carew has had his critics. Oliver Jackman, for instance, sounds what he himself calls a "sour note" in his review of *The Wild Coast:*

> "... *Few of the characters in this book come alive. Mr. Carew seems to know next to nothing about* people....

but he praises the ability of the writer in his

> *set pieces.... The wild-hog hunt is a fine piece of writing, spare, without frills and completely convincing.*

Writings: Novels: *Black Midas,* London, Secker and Warburg, 1958, and as *A Touch of Midas,* New York, Coward McCann, 1958, and Longman-Caribbean, 1969; *The Wild Coast,* Secker and Warburg, 1968; *The Last Barbarian,* London, Secker and Warburg, 1961; *Moscow is Not My Mecca,* London, Secker and Warburg, 1964, and as *Green Winter,* New York, Stein and Day, 1965, and as *Winter in Moscow* (Special edition for non-native speakers of English), New York, Avon Books, 1967); *The Wild Coast,* London, Secker and Warburg, 1963; *Cry, Black Power,* Toronto, McClelland and Stewart, 1970. *A Touch of Midas* appeared in Georgian translation as *Cernyj Midas* by N. Gudzabidze, Tbilisi, U.S.S.R., Sabcota Sakartvelo.

Juvenile Fiction: *The Third Gift,* Boston, Little Brown, 1972; *Sons of the Flying Wind,* Toronto, McClelland and Stewart, (Juvenile), 1970; *Rape the Sun,* New York, Third Press, 1973; *Children of the Sun,* Boston, Little Brown, 1976; *The Twins of Ilora,* Boston, Little Brown, 1977.

Stories: In various journals and collections, including: "The Coming of Amalivaca: A Guianese legend," in *West Indian Stories* (ed. A. Salkey); "Hunters and Hunted," in *Stories from the Caribbean: An Anthology;* extracts from his novels in *The Sun's Eye; Caribbean Narrative; West Indian Narrative; New World* (1966; Guyana Independence Issue); and *Caribbean Prose.* Also see short story: "Ti-Zek," published in *Fiction Midwest* and in *Caliban* (ed. by Roberto Marquez), Hampshire College, Mass. (received Illinois Arts Council Annual Award for fiction).

Poetry: in various journals and anthologies, including: *Kyk-over-al; New World (*Fortnightly); *Kaie; Caribbean Voices,* Vol. I; *My Lovely Native Land; Themes of Song; Breaklight.*

Plays: *Miracle in Lime Lane,* with Sylvia Wynter, adaptation of a play by Coventry Taylor (produced Spanish Town, Jamaica, 1962); *University of Hunger* (produced Georgetown, Guyana, 1966); *Gentlemen Be Seated* (produced Toronto, 1967 and CBC-TV), and Toronto Workshop Productions: December 31, 1967, presented at Brecht West Theatre, New Jersey, United States, 1969; *The University of Hunger,* a play in three acts, broadcast on the BBC radio, 1961, and on BBC radio, 1962, as *The Big Pride.*

Plays (Radio and TV): *Anancy and Tiger,* BBC early 1960's; *Atta,* BBC, early 1960's; *The Baron of South Boulevard,* a one-hour TV play, televised BBC, 1963; *The Day of the Fox,* BBC-TV, 1962; *The Conversion of Tiho,* BBC-TV, 1963; *The Smugglers,* BBC-TV, 1963; *Behind God's Back,* CBC-TV, November 1969; *Exile from the Sun,* written 1963, televised BBC; *Legend of the Nameless Mountain,* BBC radio, early 1960's; *The Riverman,* BBC radio Home Service, October 1968, and World Service, May 4, 7, 8, and 9, 1969; *A Roof of Stars,* written 1963 for TV.

A Stage Play: *Black Horse, White Rider,* performed at Venice Festival (Canada), 1969.

Critical Essays: (including) "British West Indian Poets and Their Culture." in *Phylon* (journal), 1958; read on Jamaica Radio, 1960; "An Artist in Exile—from the West Indies," in *New World,* Vol. I, Nos. 27 and 28 (November

12, 1965), pp. 23-30; "A West Indian Student at an American University," in *Kyk-over-al*, Vol. 2, No. 9 (December 1949), pp. 16-18; "The Coup in Ghana," in *New World*, Vol. I, No. 40 (May 13, 1966), pp. 9-18; "Black Studies Seek Universal Goals," Georgetown *Sunday Chronicle* (December 29, 1975), p. 7; "Literature and Language in Developing Countries," in *New World* (Fortnightly), Part I—22 (1965), p. 25 and Part II—23 (1965), p. 23; "The Origins of Racism in the Americas," (to be published) in *African Themes*, Northwestern University, United States.

Biographical/Critical Sources: Wilfred Cartey, "The rhythm of society and landscape: Mittelholzer, Carew, Williams, Dathorne," in *New World*, Guyana Independence Issue, 1966, pp. 96-104; Joyce L. Sparer, "Carew—an unfinished search for identity," in *Sunday Chronicle*, Guyana (April 30, 1967); Ivan Van Sertima, essay on Carew in *Caribbean Writers: Critical Essays*, by Sertima, London, New Beacon, 1968, pp. 30-32; Joyce L. Sparer, "Attitudes towards 'race' in Guyanese Literature," in *Caribbean Studies*, Vol. 8, No. 2 (July 1968), pp. 23-63; Reviews of *The Last Barbarian*, by Frank Collymore, BIM 34 (January-June 1962), pp. 149-150; of *Moscow is Not My Mecca*, by Alex Gradussov, BIM 43 (July-December 1966), pp. 224-225; *The Third Gift*, in *Black Orpheus*, No. 20 (August 1966), pp. 23-25; *The Wild Coast*, by Oliver Jackman, BIM 29 (June-December 1959), pp. 64-67; *Black Midas* by A.J. Seymour, in *Kyk-over-al, Vol. 8, No. 24 (December 1958), pp. 86-87; University of Hunger* by Monica Jardine, *New World*, Vol. 1, No. 48 (September 19, 1966), pp. 23-25; Colin Richard, "Carew returning home to live: Jan picks Rio Potaro to build dream house," article in *Guiana Graphic*, (May 4, 1966); Kenneth Ramchand, *The W.I. Novel and its Background* (1970), pp. 112, 119, 167n. Also see Robert McDowell, *Bibliography of Literature from Guyana*, Arlington, Texas, Sable Publishing Corporation, 1975, for detailed listing of books.

CAREW, Wynter
(see **Sylvia WYNTER**)

CARGILL, Morris
(pseudonym: **John MORRIS,** when collaborating with John Hearne)
b. June 10, 1914, St. Andrew, Jamaica.
Novelist, journalist and radio commentator, solicitor, company director, planter.

Educated in Jamaica and England, Cargill was a former Federal M. P. for St. Mary (elected 1958; resigned 1960) and served as Deputy Leader of Opposition in Gordon House, Kingston, Jamaica.

A very lively and well-known Jamaican columnist, Cargill has been the goad of the dull, the bumptious and the "progressive!"

Writings: Novels: under pseudonym (with John Hearne): *Fever Grass*, London, Collins, 1969, paperback, Fontana, 1970; *The Candywine Development*, London, Collins, 1970, Fontana paperback, London, 1971.

Editor: *Ian Fleming introduces Jamaica*, London, Andre Deutsch, 1965; *Jamaica and England*.

Article: "Jamaica and Britain," *History Today*, Vol. 6, No. 10 (October 1956), pp. 655-663.

CARR, Ernest A.

b. March 7, 1902, Trinidad; d. 1975(?).
Poet, shortstory writer, essayist, folklorist.

Carr was an early member of the literary group of the 1920's centered around Alfred Mendes and C.L.R. James and the cultural/political journals, *Trinidad* (1929-30) and *The Beacon.* He has contributed many stories and poems to BIM and was the "elder statesman" to George Lamming and others of the new writers in the islands at that time. He served as president in the 1960's of P.E.N. Club of Trinidad and Tobago. His poems and short stories have been broadcast on the BBC and in the U.S.A. He received in 1953 a travel grant to Northwestern University in the field of folklore. He served as president of the Trinidad Art Society.

Writings: Stories: (with A.M. Clarke) *Ma Mamba and other stories,* Port of Spain, Trinidad. [Frasers Printerie], n.d. (1939?), 199 pp.

Editor with others, and contributor to: *Caribbean Anthology of Short Stories,* Kingston, Pioneer Press, 1953. His stories have been published in various British, Canadian and U.S. journals.

Poetry: in various journals and collections, including: BIM; *Voices, Nouvelle Somme (New Sum of Poetry from the Negro World),* Paris, *Présence Africaine* Commemoration Issue); *World's Fair Anthology of Verse,* 1937; *Caribbean Literature,* 1966.

Articles: (Folklore) "A Rada Community in Trinidad Pierrot Grenade," in *Caribbean Quarterly,* Vol. 4, Nos. 2 and 3 (March and June 1956), "Calypso in Trinidad; The Cultural Personality of Trinidad and Tobago."

CARTER, Martin Wylde

b. 1927, Georgetown, Guyana.
Poet, politician, historian.

A gifted and complicated person, Carter has been a revolutionary, information officer for Bookers, Minister of Information Guyana, historian, and direct, moving poet, and excellent reciter of all kinds of poetry including his own.

He was detained for some months in 1953, the experience being reflected in these lines:

I have not eaten for four days.
My legs are paining, my blood runs slowly.
It is cold tonight, the rain is silent and sudden
And yet there is something warm inside of me.

("On the fourth night of hunger strike," from *Caribbean Voices,* Vol. 11, p. 126)

Carter has done much practical work for Guyana, representing her at the Guyana Constitutional Conference in London, 1965; and was a member of Guyana's delegation to the United Nations, 1966-67.

He has been an activist and a dreamer, as well as a respectable Minister of Government:

and so
if you see me
looking at your hands
listening when you speak
marching in your ranks
you must know
I do not sleep to dream, but dream to change the world.

(*Caribbean Voices,* Vol. I, p. 102)

Carter's 1977 collection *Poems of Succession* offers selections of most of his earlier volumes plus his newest work.

Writings: Poetry: *The Hill of Fire Glows Red* (Miniature Poet Series), British Guiana, Master Printer, 1951; *To a Dead Slave,* 1951; *The Hidden Man,* Georgetown, 1952; *The Kind Eagle,* 1952; *Returning,* 1953; *Poems of Resistance from British Guiana,* preface by Neville Daves, London, Lawrence and Wishart, 1954, and as simply *Poems of Resistance* (with one new poem, "A Banner for the Revolution"), Georgetown, Guyana, University of Guyana, 1964 (both 18 pp.); *Poems of Shape and Motion,* 1955; *Jail Me Quickly,* 1966; *Poems of Succession,* London, New Beacon Books, 1977.

He has contributed to *Caribbean Voices*, Vols. I-II; *West Indian Poetry; Talk of the Tamarinds; Caribbean Rhythms; Breaklight; My Lovely Native Land; New Writing in the Caribbean; Caribbean Verse,* and other West Indian anthologies. He has also contributed to several journals, including *Kyk-over-al, Kaie, New World,* Editor (Fortnightly) (with George Lamming) *New World: Guyana Independence Issue,* Georgetown, Guyana.

Biographical/Critical Sources: see Louis James' Introduction to *The Islands in Between,* London, Three Crown's Book, 1968, pp. 34-35; and A. J. Seymour's "The Arts of Guiana," *Kyk-over-al,* 27 (1960), p. 97 (correspondence); also "West Indian Poetry 1900-1970," by Edward Baugh (Savacou Publications, Ltd., a pamphlet), p. 13; review of *New World: Guyana Independence Issue,* New World Group, 1966 (ed. with George Lamming) by Anne Walmsley in BIM 44, pp. 297-298. Interview with Carter by A. J. Seymour appears in *Kaie,* No. 2 (1966), pp. 18-21. For detailed listings of his work see Robert E. McDowell, *Bibliography of Literature from Guyana,* Arlington, Texas, Sable Publishing Corporation, 1975.

CARTEY, Wilfred

b. 1931, Port of Spain, Trinidad.
Critic, editor, teacher, poet.

Cartey was educated at Queens Royal College, U.W.I. (Mona), and Columbia University, New York. Although growing increasingly blind during his university days, he achieved his doctorate, and continues to be productive. He has taught Spanish, English and Comparative Literature and has been visiting professor at a number of universities, including U.W.I. and the University of Ghana. In 1969 Cartey was director of Black and Puerto Rican Studies Programme at City College New York, and in 1971 was elected to membership in the Black Academy of Arts and Letters. He has been consultant to a number of organizations.

In 1955 he received a Fulbright travel grant ('55-'59) to study Afro-Antillan and Latin American Literatures. Although Cartey's base is now outside the Caribbean, he has kept in close contact with the culture and people of that area. He has also worked across some of the language barriers, having worked with Puerto Ricans and lectured at the University of Puerto Rico. He is also a member of the Hispanic Institute of the U.S.A.

Cartey, a concerned and widely informed person, was named, in 1972, the first Martin Luther King Jr. Distinguished Professor at Brooklyn College, City University of New York.

Writings: Poetry: *The House of Blue Lightning,* New York, Emerson Hall, 1973.

Criticism and Literary History: *Whispers from a Continent: The Literature of Contemporary Black Africa,* New York, Vintage-Random House, 1969; *The West Indies: Islands in the Sun.*

Articles: "The Rhythm of Society and Landscape" (Mittelholzer, Carew, Williams, Dathorne), in *New World,* Vol. II, No. 3 (Guyana Independence Issue), pp. 97-104; "The Knights Companion—Ganesh, Biswas and Stone," in *New World Quarterly,* Vol. II, No. 1 (Dead Season, 1968), pp. 93-98; "The Novels of John Hearne," in *The Journal of Commonwealth Literature,* Vol. VII (July 1969), pp. 45-58; "I've been reading of the realities of Four Negro Writers," in *Columbia University Forum,* Vol. 9, No. 3 (Summer 1966), pp. 34-42.

Biographical/Critical Sources: Eric Roach's review of *The House of Blue Lightning,* in *Trinidad Guardian* (September 16, 1973), p. 6; "This is Dr. Cartey," critique in *Express* (Trinidad, May 25, 1972), p. 4; "Our Society is growing not flowering," critique in the *Trinidad Guardian* (July 20, 1969).

CASIMIR, Joseph Raphael Ralph

b. September 26, 1898, St. Joseph, Dominica.
Poet, editor.

Casimir was educated in the Government Primary School; he served as a pupil teacher from January 1915 to November 1916 and then left St. Joseph to live in Roseau, the capital of Dominica, where he still resides. He was appointed assistant teacher at the Roseau Boys Government Primary School. Roseau, in 1922, resigning in 1923. He has worked in capacities other than that of teaching and for many years has been a Solicitor's Clerk.

In the thirties and forties Casimir was very interested in politics, during which time he was organizer and Assistant Secretary of the Dominica Taxpayers Reform Association, a political organization, (1931-32); Assistant Secretary of the West Indian Conference held in Dominica (Oct. 28-Nov. 4, 1932); and he has served two terms as an elected member of the Roseau Town Council.

He has always maintained a great interest in writing, especially verse, and has always devoted time to this great interest and to his reading. He is also a skillful bookbinder.

He has published booklets of his verse and four anthologies of Dominican verse. He has contributed articles and poems to American and West Indian magazines, and newspapers; he was correspondent of the *Pittsburg Courier* (New York Edition) from 1950-1952.

Writings: Poetry: *Pater Noster and Other Poems* (Religious), 1967; *Africa Arise and Other Poems,* 1967, by Author; *A Little Kiss and Other Poems,* 1968; *Farewell and Other Poems,* 1971; *Dominica and Other Poems,* 1968: all published in Roseau, Dominica, by Chronicle Press.

Editor: Anthologies: (Collected and edited): *Poesy, Book I,* Joseph Press, Dominica, 1943; *Poesy, Book II,* Chronicle Press, Dominica, 1944; *Poesy, Book III,* Chronicle Press, Dominica, 1946; *Poesy Book IV,* Advocate Press, Barbados, 1948.

Biographical Essay: *The Negro Speaks,* Chronicle Press, Dominica, 1969.

CASSIDY, Frederic G.

b. October 10, 1907, Jamaica.
Poet, linguist, teacher.

Cassidy was educated at Jamaica College, Jamaica; Oberlin College (B.A.,M.A.); and the University of Michigan (Ph.D., 1938). A quiet hard-working man who has kept up his connections with Jamaica and the West Indies, although he has lived abroad for so long, Cassidy at present is Professor of English, University of Wisconsin, Madison (since 1939). He was a Fulbright Research Fellow, University College of the West Indies (1951-52 and 1958-59) and has collaborated with R.B. LePage on the *Dictionary of Jamaican English* which is internationally known, as is his long-standing and pioneering work on the language situation in Jamaica. Since 1965 he has been Director of the *Dictionary of American Regional English.* He recently was elected to the American Academy of Sciences. He was awarded the Silver Musgrave medal, Institute of Jamaica, 1962 for the Study of Language and Folklore.

Writings: Linguistics: *Jamaica Talk,* MacMillan, London, 1961, reprinted (revised) 1971; *Dictionary of Jamaica English,* Cambridge University Press, 1967 (with R.B. Le Page).

Poetry: Poems published in *West Indian Review,* about 1930; in *West Indian Language and Literature; Writers on the Other Side of the Horizon,* NCTE, Champaign, Ill., 1964, pp. 35-43. Also: long unpublished poem on the White Witch of Rose Hall (A Jamaican Legend), first written in 1930, revised in 1974.

CAUDEIRON, Daniel

b. ca. 1940, Venezuela (long-time resident of Roseau, Dominica).
Poet.

Caudeiron along with Alwin Bully and Lennox Honeychurch, has edited *Wahseen* and *Free Your Mind,* two Dominican literary magazines.

Son of a Venezuelan father and a Dominican mother, he has published two volumes of verse.

Writings: Poetry: *Poems,* Roseau, Dominica, Printer: Hilton Services Ltd.; *Seconds,* Privately printed. (A collection of satirical poetry about life in Dominica), c. 1974.

CENDRECOURT, Esme

b. ca. 1903, Guyana.
Playwright.

Cendrecourt has written a number of plays which exist only in typescript, however.

Writings: Plays: *Captain's Party: A Play,* (published(?), New York, 19??; *A Night in the Caribbean,* New York, 19??; *Grandpapa's Pride: A Play in Three Acts* (Performed Georgetown, 1942) and in mimeo, British Guiana, 1933; *Romance of the Kaiteur: A Play in Three Acts,* British Guiana, 1931; *New Probationer: A Play in Three Acts* (British Guiana, 1939); *Unmasked: A Play in Three Acts* (British Guiana, 1944).

CHAN, Brian

b. ca. 1942, Guyana.
Poet.

Chan is a very promising poet. He went to Queen's College, worked with the British Council for a couple of years and then retired to devote himself to writing. His poetry has appeared in *Expression* and *Poet,* 13, I (1972). See R.E. McDowell's *Bibliography of Literature from Guyana,* 1975, for details.

CHAPMAN, Esther

(married name: **Esther Marshall Hepher**)
b. ca. 1897, Essex, England (lived in Jamaica many years).
Novelist, playwright, journalist, editor.

A very active, socially and politically conscious editor and writer, who was the mainstay for many years of *West Indian Review* which she founded, Chapman was also the publisher of *Jamaica 1954* and successive annuals for many years. She has also been managing director of The Arawak Press, Ltd.

Writings: Novels: *Punch and Judy: A comedy of living, in two acts and an interlude,* London, Constable, 1927 (Jamaican fiction); *Study in Bronze,* first published by Constable, London, 1928, and then London, Chantry Publications, 1952; *Pied Piper,* London, Duckworth, 1939; *Too much summer, a novel of Jamaica,* London, Chantry Publications, 1953.

Plays: *West Indian: a play in verse showing the historical development of the West Indies* (for 70 players and dancers; produced at the Ward Theatre, Kingston, Jamaica, 1936?/1938?); and the revue, *Travelling Light,* 1950.

Others: *Pleasure Island: the Book of Jamaica,* 5th ed., Kingston, Arawak Press, 1961, 7th ed., 1968; *Development in Jamaica: Year of Progress, 1954,* Kingston, Arawak Press.

Articles: "Matters of some importance: the West Indian," in *West Indian Review,* new ser., Vol. 2, No. 10 (October), pp. 13-15; "Political experiment in Jamaica: a promising start," in *Crown Colony,* Vol. 16, No. 170 (January 1946), pp. 15-16; "The truth about Jamaica," in *West Indian Review,* Vol. 4, No. 10 (June 1938), pp. 13-18.

Biographical/Critical Sources: Mentioned in "A History of Theatre in Jamaica" by Henry Fowler in *Jamaica Journal*, Vol. 2, No. 1 (March 1968).

CHAPMAN, Matthew James

b. 1796 (?), Barbados; d. 1865.
Poet, medical doctor.

Chapman's one known publication is *Barbados and other poems* (1835).

CHARLES, Bertram

b. ca. 1937, Guyana.
Playwright, shortstory writer.

Charles is primarily a playwright, having composed at least nine known works, but he has also published one collection of his stories (1972).

Writings: Plays: *The Pains of Abortion: Play in One Act*, Guyana, 1967; *A Virgin Child: Play in Two Acts*, 1967; *Another Man: Play in Two Acts*, Guyana, 1968; *The End of the Affair*, Georgetown, 1968; *Another Place, Somewhere: Play in Two Acts*, 1969; *It Tolls Not for Thee: Play in One Act*, 1970; *The Lost Husband: Play in One Act*, 1970; *The Alexin of Our Cure*, Georgetown, 1970; *Within Our Narrow Walls: Play in Five Acts*, performed Guyana, 1971. Also: *The Human Predicament*, broadcast Guyana Broadcasting Service, 1971; *The Pains of Abortion* (one-act), Guyana, 1967.

Short stories: *Our Dilemma* (published privately), Georgetown, 1972.

CHARLES, Faustin

b. 1944, Trinidad.
Poet.

After local schooling, Charles went to England in 1962 to study at London University (philosophy). He soon turned, however, to literature and the writing of fiction and poetry. In 1969 he published his first collection of verse, *The Expatriate*, and in 1973, his second, *Crab Track*.

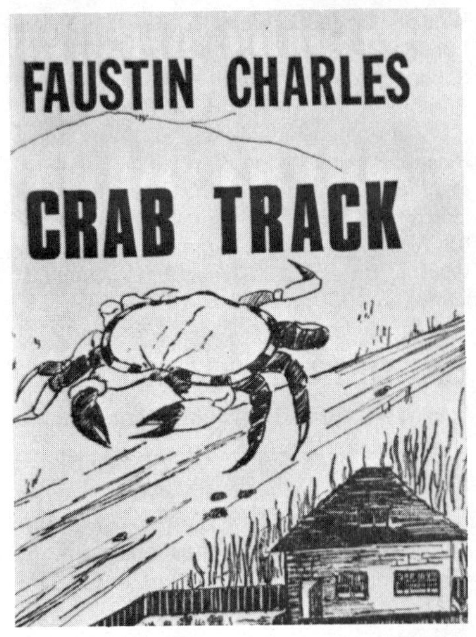

For many years Charles has been Visiting Lecturer at the Commonwealth Institute in London.

Writings: Poetry: *The Expatriate: Poems, 1963-1968*, London, Brookside Press, 1969; *Crab Track*, London, Brookside Press, 1973; and individual poems in many journals and collections, including *Breaklight* (A. Salkey, ed.), New York, Anchor, 1973. The poems "At Mittelholzer's Tomb" and "Days and Nights in the Magic Forest" are in the anthology *Melanthika*, 1977.

Biographical/Critical Sources: Review of *The Expatriate* by Wayne Brown: "An Exciting Trinidad Poet," in *Trinidad Guardian* (Aug. 2, 1970), p. 13. Review of *Crab Track*, by Andrew Salkey, in *Melanthika*, 1977, pp. 30-31.

CHASE, Sam

b. ca. 1910, Guyana; d. ca. 1965(?).
Playwright, comedian.

Sam Chase was a national figure performing in the theatre and writing at least six plays. Some of his performances were satirical, or comedy skits—a form of every day comment. His skit on the Public Hospital was notable.

His father was Aston Chase, a well-known Guyanese trade unionist and politician.

Writings: Plays: *The Collapsible Bridegroom; The Dreamer and the Jar; Gentlemen, the King; Guardroom Jitters; The Mare and the Bonds; The Ruler and the Boo-Boo Man.*

CHATTORAM, Paul

(pseudonym: **Walter O. SMITH**).
b. ca. 1940, Guyana.
Playwright, storywriter.

A play of Chattoram's was performed in Guyana in 1970 and his stories have been published in local periodicals such as *Kaie* and *Caribia,* but have never been collected.

Writing: Play: *The Fall of an Idol,* performed Guyana, 1970.

CHINAPEN, Jacob Wellien

b. 1931, Guyana; d. ca. 1965(?).
Poet, teacher.

Chinapen was a well-known headmaster who was very concerned and professionally involved with his work among young teachers. Besides his writing he also painted.

His poetry is in A. Seymour's *Themes of Song,* Elma Seymour's *Sun is a Shapely Fire,* as well as other local collections and individual poems are also in periodicals, including *Kyk-over-al, Kaie,* and *A New Guyana.* His one collection is *Albion Wilds,* British Guiana, B.G. Lithographic Co., 1961.

CLARKE, Alfred McDonald

b. August 13, 1912, Trinidad.
Poet, playwright, storywriter, novelist, biographer.

A graduate of Government Training College for Teachers, Clarke also has a B.A. from London University (Honors, medieval and modern History). He studied law in the Middle Temple, being called to the Bar in 1962. In 1967 Clarke studied International Relations at the University of the West Indies, St. Augustine, Trinidad.

After long residence in England, he returned to Trinidad to take up a private law practice and has been in local theatre and poetry circles. His verse play, *Green Magic,* is set in the Trinidad of the 1920's and much of his work, including an unpublished novel on civil strife in and around Port of Spain in early independence days of the 1960's, reflects his historical training and interests.

Clarke has contributed to *The New Voices, Caribbean Quarterly,* Vol. 5, No. 3 (April 1958) Federation Commemoration Issue, and various local journals.

Writings: Poetry: (with H.M. Telemaque): *Burnt Bush,* Port of Spain, Trinidad, Fraser's Printerie, 1947.

Compiler and Editor: *Best Poems of Trinidad* (Anthology), Port of Spain, Trinidad, Fraser's Printerie, 1943.

Short Stories: (with R.C. Brown): *Collected Short Stories,* Port of Spain, Trinidad, Fraser's Printerie, 1938; and (with E.A. Carr): *Ma Mamba and other stories,* Port of Spain, Trinidad, Fraser's Printerie, 1939.

Biography: "Learie Constantine," in ms.

Novel: in ms. (on riots in 1961-62 period in Trinidad).

Other: *Wheels within Wheels,* Trinidad and Tobago, 1975.

Verse—Drama: *House of Love,* produced Port of Spain Town Hall, 1967, mimeographed, (28 pp.); and *Green Magic: A Folk Tale in Verse,* in ms., never produced, written in 1952.

Play: *Road to Glory,* produced Queen's Hall, 1964 (written 1952).

Biographical/Critical Sources: Review of *Burnt Bush* (with H.M. Telemaque) by G.O. Bell in BIM No. 9, pp. 74-77.

CLARKE, Austin Chesterfield (Tom)

b. July 26, 1934, Barbados.
Novelist, storywriter, playwright, broadcaster, teacher, lecturer.

Austin Clarke, as he is known to most of the literary world, particularly in Canada and the U.S.A., is Tom to Barbadians, who have reestablished direct contact with him through his leadership of the Caribbean Broadcasting Corporation. For after a long absence from Bimshire, Tom has returned to both broadcasting and his home ground.

His early education in Barbados was both at Combermere and Harrison in Barbados. He has also done university work at Toronto University and at Indiana, Bloomington. He has lectured at a number of North American universities, including Duke, North Carolina and Texas. He has acted in a diplomatic capacity for the Government of Barbados, and was cultural officer in the embassy in Washington just before returning to Barbados in 1975.

Austin Clarke is a lively man and a lively writer. He has an excellent feeling for local speech patterns, and probes nicely the relations between the immigrant and his newly found environment.

He is particularly well-known in Canada both as a broadcaster and as a writer. He has received a number of literary and art awards in that country: President's medal, University of Western Ontario, 1966; Belmont Short Story Award, 1965; and Canada Council Senior Arts Fellowship, 1967, 1970.

Writings: Novels: Toronto Trilogy: *The Meeting Point,* Toronto, Macmillan, London, Heinemann, 1967, Boston, Little Brown, 1972; *Storm of Fortune,* Boston, Little Brown, 1972; *The Bigger Light,* Boston, Little Brown, 1975. Also: *Among Thistles and Thorns,* Toronto, McClelland and Stewart, London, Heinemann, 1965; *The Survivors of the Crossing,* London, Heinemann, 1964, Toronto, McClelland and Stewart, 1964; and *The Impuritans,* Atlantic Highlands, Dolman—Humanities, 1974.

Stories: *When He Was Free and Young and He used to Wear Silks,* Toronto, House of Anansi Press, 1971, Waltham, Mass., Little Brown, 1974; *The Land of the Living,* London, Faber, 1961; *The Eye of the Storm,* Boston, Little Brown, 1958; Also: Stories in *Canadian Writing Today* (Penguin); *Evergreen Review; Evidence; Tamarack Review; CBC Anthology;* BIM; *From the Green Antilles* (Barbara Howes, ed.)

Play: *Son of Learning: A Play in Three Acts,* Chester Srings, Pa., Dufour, 1974.

Poetry: *Poems,* New York, Oxford University Press, 1974 (Austin is one of several authors in the volume).

Biographical/Critical Sources: Keith Jeffers, "Clarke: Promise and Insight with Flaws" in *Black Images,* I, I (Jan. 1972); Anthony Boxill, "The Novels of Austin Clarke," in *The Fiddlehead 75* (Spring 1968); Kevyn Alan Arthur, review of *The Survivors of the Crossing* in BIM 40, pp. 291-292; Harold Marshall, review of *When He Was Free and Young and He Used to Wear Silks* in BIM 54, pp. 113-116; Clare MacCulloch, "Look Homeward Bajan (A Look at the Work of Austin Clarke, Barbadian Expatriate as Seen by an Outsider)," BIM 55, pp. 179-182; Lloyd H. Brown, "The West Indian Novel in North America: a study of Austin Clarke," in *Journal of Commonwealth Literature,* No. 9 (July 1970), pp. 89-103; Kenneth Ramchand, *The West Indian Novel and its Background* (Barnes and Noble, New York, 1970), references: *Amongst Thistles and Thorns,* pp. 110-111, 119, 206; *Survivors of the Crossing,* p. 193.

CLARKE, Elizabeth

b. ca. 1943, Barbados.
Poet.

One of the young promising Bajan writers mentioned by Edward Brathwaite in his notes on contributors to *Savacou 7/8* (Jan -June 1973), dedicated to the honor of Frank Collymore. Brathwaite links Elizabeth Clarke with Anthony Hinkson and Margaret Gill. She contributed to the *Savacou 7/8* issue, "Signs and Wonders." Brathwaite speaks of her "Mudda Africa" (see A.J. Seymour's *New Writing in the Caribbean*) as a classic.

CLARKE, Joy

b. ca. 1943, in Antigua.
Storywriter, teacher.

Joy Clarke was educated at the Antigua Girls' High School, and at Waterloo University, Canada. She teaches in Trinidad.

Her short story "De Trip" is included in the Anthology: *Backfire* (Macmillan, London, 1973), compiled by Neville and Undine Giuseppi for use in Secondary Schools.

CLARKE, Sebastian

b. 1948, Trinidad.
Poet.

After local schooling, Clarke went to England in 1964, staying for five years in London. He was very active in Caribbean and black groups in the U.K. and came to know many black American poets and their work.

Writings: Poetry: *Saint and Sinner Join in Merriment on the Battlefront,* New York, 1973 or 1974; poems in various reviews and collections including *Breaklight* (A. Salkey, ed.), New York, Anchor, 1973.

CLERK, Astley

b. 1868, Jamaica; d. 1944.
Poet, musician, folklorist, editor.

One of Clerk's main interests was the collecting and editing of Jamaican folk songs, many of which he has set to music. He edited *Musical Monthly* for many years. He is a medallist, Institute of Jamaica, 1937.

Writings: Musicology: *Music and Musical instruments of Jamaica: a lecture. . .,* Kingston, Cowen Music Rooms, 1913 (28pp. illus.; include sections on Arawak musical instruments and music, Afro-Jamaican music and the musical instrument of the Maroons [the abeng]).

Compiled and edited: *A Volume of Jamaican School Songs,* many written and set to music by the author.

Poetry: Verse in *A Treasury of Jamaican Poetry.*

COLLYMORE, Frank A. (Colly)

b. January 7, 1893, Barbados.
Poet, teacher, actor, editor, broadcaster.

Colly is without doubt the grand old man of W.I. literature. And so much has been written about him—there is so much that could be said—that we will limit ourselves in this entry to the bare essentials. Colly has been many things in his long life: teacher, cricketer, actor, painter, poet, shortstory writer and great reader on the radio. His rendition of short stories on Radio Barbados is much appreciated by people from all walks of life. And the personal stories he tells about teaching, or well-known characters or cricket, are much appreciated by friends or acquaintances lucky enough to hear them. But perhaps what one cherishes most about him is his remarkable ability to be a teacher, in the broadest sense, and to be a friend, in the most exact sense. At school he taught, just to name a very few, George Lamming, Frank Worrel, Austin (Tom) Clarke and Timothy Callender. But through BIM, and in many other ways, he was a teacher in a much wider sense—not least of all of a decent gentleness and open heartedness, not too frequently encountered in these days of *"Powa"* and "commitment." He has also taught that kind of dedication and attention to detail, and willingness to work without fuss, which has seen BIM off the press, in good days, and in bad, for 58 numbers, from

1942 to 1975, during which year Colly eventually, in his 82nd year, handed over completely to others the little magazine to which West Indian Literature owes so much.

Colly taught at Combermere School from 1910-1963; became an editor of BIM from Number 3 (it had been started in 1942 by the Young Men's Progressive Club of Barbados); Colly was awarded the O.B.E. in 1958; and an honorary degree from U.W.I., Mona, in 1968. He has acted in a variety of plays in the local theatre,

including Noah and the Barretts. He has published six collections of poems, and various editions of his well-known *Barbadian Dialect.* He has done a number of illustrated poems which have not been (but should be) published. Many of his notebooks are quite remarkable for their sketches and drawings.

His poems are of a great variety, varying from short humorous couplets (I think that I shall never see/A poem livelier than a flea) to serious, but witty, comments on such things as a secondary education in Barbados,

Yes, he won't have to use a hoe or lie out
in the open
Wondering about what things are or why
they go,
Physical Georgraphy, the Cadet
Company and the Tables
will have taught him all there really
is to know . . .
(from "Voici la plume de mon oncle," *Caribbean Voices* 11, pg. 91)

Colly's help to George Lamming has been described by the latter in *Kas-Kas:*

> *Writers lived somewhere else. They were dead, not people you lived with.* (Lamming had learnt from the attitude of the school he went to) . . . *But, I was very fascinated by Collymore. He used to write a great deal in private. I always remember the very first time I went to his house. He had these volumes of poems in a sort of exercise book. He was a great doodler and he painted. He would have poems written on one page, and this doodling on the next page . . . But I don't think any of the boys in the school knew that, except the people who had visited his house. He was very separate from the school scene. He had a tremendous library which I literally took over. . ."*

Lamming dedicated his first novel, *In the Castle of My Skin,* to his mother [and Frank Collymore, Sr.]. Colly spotted Derek Walcott's talent and achievement very early, and as has ever been his way, he unobtrusively and generously gave all the help that was necessary to get D.W. published in Barbados.

A constant letter writer, Colly has offered fellowship, support and advice to a variety of writers. His amateur work on the language of Barbados is a real contribution to the field of language study in the Caribbean; first published in 1955, it had by 1970 gone into its third edition, and is full of the "socio" implications of the Bajan language:

> ecky-becky. *Another name for the* redleg *or poor* backra. *The following bit of doggeral refers to their clannishness and*

refusal to mingle with the Negro population.

> *Ecky-becky is a nation, true botheration: As you touch dem, dem run at the station.*

Savacou 7/8 (Jan.-June 1973) was dedicated to Frank Collymore, and should be consulted for further details about him. Perhaps two quotations from that issue can best end this brief note on (and *ipso facto* tribute to) Colly:

> *1. The only printed book completely related to the West Indies I knew at first was (your) Bajan dialect; I had a copy at Elementary School. My father was proud to buy it—he bought it without questioning why I wanted it, as he usually did, because, he said, you had taught him at school. That, perhaps, was the best reason there could be* (p. 9: Tribute by Timothy Callendar).

> *2. I should like to introduce to you this evening the work of Derek Walcott of St. Lucia: a small volume recently published entitled* 25 Poems. *His name may be familiar to some of you, for I remember being shown a few years ago some MS poems of a schoolboy of that name, and being greatly impressed by their promise. That promise has now been fulfilled, and* 25 Poems, *although the product of one who has not yet attained his majority—he is just nineteen years of age, must be regarded as the work of an accomplished poet.*

> *I use the word "poet" advisedly. There are some of us who write poetry: to us the spirit comes and goes and we are deeply grateful if at some time in our lives it is our good fortune to be blessed with the divine gift. But there are others, a select band, who are poets from birth: to them poetry is all in all, the very breath of life; and I do not think I am mistaken when I make this claim for Derek Walcott.*

That last quotation, from *Savacou*, is reprinted from BIM 10, and reports the words spoken in *1949* by Frank Collymore, three years before *In A Green Night*, twenty-four years before *Another Life*—at a time before Derek Walcott had met Colly.

Colly's voice, reading some of his poems, may be heard on Caedmon Record No.TC 1379, *Poets of the West Indies* (ed. J. Figueroa).

Writings: Poetry: *Thirty Poems*, Bridgetown, Barbados, 1944; *Beneath the Casuarinas*, Bridgetown, Barbados, 1945; *Flotsam*, Advocate Co., Bridgetown, Barbados, 1948; *Collected Poems*, Advocate Co., Bridgetown, Barbados, 1959; (light verse) *Rhymed Ruminations on the Fauna of Barbados*, Advocate Co., Ltd., Bridgetown, Barbados, 1968; *Selected Poems*, Cole's Printery Ltd., Bridgetown, Barbados, 1971.

Other: *Barbadian Dialect:* (Notes for a Glossary of Words and Phrases of Barbadian Dialect), first published 1955; second impression 1956, 2nd edition, 1957; 3rd edition, 1965; 4th edition, 1970.

His poetry appears in various anthologies including: *Caribbean Voices* Vols. I and II (ed. J. Figueroa); *Commonwealth Poems of Today* (ed. Howard Sergeant); *The Sun's Eye* (ed. Anne Walmsley); *Talk of the Tamarinds* (ed. A.N. Forde); *Kyk-over-al, Special Issue Mid Year 1952* and No. 22 (1957) (ed. A.J. Seymour); *Caribbean Rhythms* (ed. James Livingston); *Caribbean Quarterly*, Vol. 5, No. 3 (April 1958) Federation Commemoration Issue; *Caribbean Verse* (ed. O.R. Dathorne); *From the Green Antilles* (ed. Barbara Howes); *New Voices of the Commonwealth* (ed. Howard Sergeant); the *Poetry of the Negro* (eds. Langston Hughes and Arna Bontemps).

He has been editor and a regular and prolific contributor to BIM; contributing poetry, short stories, plays, articles on literature and language, reviews on books, art and theatre, and miscellaneous articles. He uses the pseudonyms of Frank Appleton and Capricorn in his writings in BIM at times. His article "An Introduction to the poetry of Derek Walcott" appears under the section BIM CLASSICS in *Savacou 7/8* which was brought out on the occasion of his 80th birthday (ed. Edward Brathwaite, Savacou Publications Ltd., Kingston, Jamaica, June 1973.)

Biographical/Critical Sources: Savacou 7/8 (ed. E. Brathwaite); review of *Flotsam* by Henry

Swanzy, BIM 9, pp. 77-79; review of *Collected Poems* by M.H. Combe Martin, BIM 30, pp. 137-139; review of *Selected Poems* by Edward Baugh, BIM 53, pp. 58-60; "West Indian Poetry 1900-1970" pamphlet by Edward Baugh (Savacou Publications Ltd.) reference pp. 7-8; Introduction to *An Index to BIM* by Edward Baugh, main reference to Collymore, pp. 15-16; *Authors and Areas of the West Indies* by Joseph and Johanna Jones, discussed in some detail by George Lamming in his interview during his visit to the University of Texas at Austin in *World Literature Written in English* No. 19 (April 1971), reference p. 20; "Magazines," "Frank Collymore and the Miracle of BIM," Edward Baugh in *New World* (Barbados Independence Issue, 1966), pp. 29-133; "The Story of BIM," Jimmy Cozier in BIM Vol. 12, No. 48 (Jan.-June, 1969), pp. 245-248; *Kas-Kas:* Interviews with Three Caribbean Writers in Texas (ed. Ian Munro and Reinhard Sander), Austin, Texas, 1972; F.C. is mentioned by George Lamming in his interview.

CONNOR, Edric

b. ca. 1928, Trinidad.
Singer, actor, song-writer.

Edric Connor once was one of the real personalities in the West Indian community in London.

Writings: Songs: (Editor) *Songs from Trinidad* (arranged for voices, guitar, drum and bass by Gareth Walters), London, Oxford University Press, 1958.

CONSTANTINE, Learie

b. ca. 1900, Trinidad; d. 1971.
Essayist, autobiographer, sports-journalist, barrister.

Constantine was one of the greatest of all Empire cricketers, and son and nephew and brother of other great players. A dynamic person, he later turned to sports writing, broadcasting, and politics, and was knighted for his achievement on and off the playing field. He has written interesting books on Test Cricket and on his own career and experiences in that difficult and exciting game.

He was Trinidad High Commissioner in London. He ended his days in the House of Lords— a most unusual distinction for a West Indian.

Writings: Autobiographical: *Cricket and I,* (with C.L.R. James), London, P. Allan, 1933; *Cricket in the Sun,* London, St. Paul, 1948; *Cricketer's Carnival,* London, St. Paul, 1948.

Biographical/Critical Sources: Undine Giuseppi, *Learie Constantine,* London, Nelson, 1964; and unpublished biography of Constantine, by A. M. Clarke.

COOMBS, Tram

b. ca. 1926, St. Thomas, U.S. Virgin Islands.
Poet.

Coombs is an interesting and unusual poet who has published in, and showed a great interest in, BIM.

Writings: Poetry Collections: *Pilgrim's Terrace: Poems,* Editorial La Nueva Salamanca, San Juan, 1957 (86 pp.); *But Never Mind: Poems, 1946-1950,* Golden Mountain Press, San Francisco, 1961 (unpaged); *Saint Thomas: Poems,* Middletown, Conn., U.S.A., Wesleyan University Press, 1965 (83 pp.); *Briefs: Poems,* Franklin, Hillside Press, 1966 (80 pp.); *Ceremonies in Mind: Artists, Boys, Cats, Lovers, Judges, Priests,* St. Thomas, The Art Shop, 1959 (30 pp.).

COOPER, Eileen

(née **Ormsby**)
b. ca. 1926, Jamaica.
Poet.

Eileen Cooper is a niece of Barbara Stephanie Ormsby and Harrie Ormsby Twiney, to mention a few of the well known Ormsby family.

J.E. Clare McFarlane discusses her work in his book, *A Literature in the Making,* in the chapter he devotes to "The Ormsbys."

She is included in the anthology *Seed*

and Flower which represents the prose and poetry of the Ormsby Family, Kingston, Jamaica, 1956.

CORBETT, Len

b. ca. 1890, Jamaica.
Poet.

An unpretentious and at times witty versifier, Corbett often presented his work in the *Gleaner* during the Twenties. He wrote "Current Gossip," "Gleaner News Rhymelets." "Able Notes to Notables" (1924) is another one of his playful titles and contains the following bit of light wisdom which is still so applicable to visits by H.M. the Queen to the Mona Campus, U.W.I., and by various high African dignitaries to Jamaica:

In welcoming Sir Frederick Field
And Squadron, it appears
Miss Market Pier was made to wear
Her brightest coat in years.

When Frederick Junior, decades hence,
With modern vessels quaint
Drops anchor here, we'll give Miss Pier
Another coat of paint.

COULTHARD, Gabriel (George Robert)

b. August 6, 1921, Bradford, England; d. August 10, 1974, Merida, Mexico.
Linguist, translator, critic, teacher.

Educated in the Bradford Grammar School, then at Oxford and London Universities (Ph.D., 1952), Gabriel Coulthard was one of the very first to take on the task of interesting the Anglophone Caribbean in Latin American literature. He spoke Spanish and French beautifully, and was well versed in the literatures of both languages, although he concentrated on the Spanish of the Caribbean and of Latin America. He was one of the first of the modern anthologists with his *Anthology of Caribbean Literature* (1966). He was particularly interested in Cuba and in the African influences in Caribbean literature.

His criticism, although at times given to the general rather than the particular, was nonetheless seminal for the necessary realization of the Pan Caribbean aspects of culture in *La Cuenca del Caribe.* He did his best to interest teachers in the language and culture of Mexico, and it was there in Merida that he died, in 1974, while conducting a summer course in Spanish for teachers from Jamaica. He had joined U.C.W.I. staff in 1950 as a lecturer, and had been named Professor of Latin American Literature in 1971, having been professor in charge of the Spanish Department since 1967.

Coulthard published widely, and did translations from poetry, as well as critical articles which will be of interest and value for a long time.

Writings: Anthologies, Critical Books: *La Literatura de las Antillas Inglesas,* Santiago de Cuba, Universidad de Oriente, 1954; *Raza y color en la literatura antillana,* Seville, Collección "Mar Adentro," 1958; *Race and Culture in Caribbean Literature,* Oxford University Press, 1962; *La revaloración de la cultura indigena en la novela peruana,* Universidad de Yucatan, 1964; *Anthology of Caribbean Literature,* London, University of London Press, 1966; *The Spanish American Novel (1940-1965), Caribbean Quarterly,* Vol. 12, No. 4, December 1966; University of the West Indies, Extra-Mural Department (500 copies published as off-prints); *New Chronicle and Good Government: Guaman Poma de Ayala* (Translation, Notes and Introduction), Jamaica, University of the West Indies Library, 1968.

Articles: "The Emergence of Afro-Cuban Poetry," *Caribbean Quarterly,* Vol. II, No. 3 (1954); "The Theme of Africa in West Indian Writing," *Caribbean Quarterly,* Vol. 4, No. 1 (1955); "Rechazo de la civilización occidental y búsqueda del alma negra, Torre," *Revista de la Universidad de Puerto Rico* (April-June 1956), pp. 123-143; "La mujer de color en la poesia antillana," *Asomante* (Puerto Rico 8, 1958); "Literature of the British West Indies

(1900-1958)," *Panorama Das Literaturas Das Americas,* Vol. III (Nova, Lisboa, 1959); "Cuban Literary Prizes for 1963," *Caribbean Studies* (Puerto Rico), Vol. 4, No. 4; "The Position of the Writer in Revolutionary Cuba," *Journal of Caribbean Studies,* Rio Piedras, University of Puerto Rico, Institute of Caribbean Studies, 1967; "The Bolivarian Ideal," *Jamaica Journal,* Vol. I, 1967, Institute of Jamaica, Kingston; "La négritude en la literatura Hispano-americana," *Revista de la Universidad de Guayaquil,* No. 15 (December 1967); "El mito indigena en la literatura hispano-americana contemporánea," *Cuadernos Americanos,* No. 1 (January-February, 1968); "Arguedas: Un problema de estilo," *Mundo Nuevo,* Numero 19, Paris (January 1968); "Parallelisms and Divergencies between *négritude* and *indigenismo,*" *Journal of Caribbean Studies,* Vol. 8, No. 1 (1968), Institute of Caribbean Studies, University of Puerto Rico; "Commentary on and translation of Spanish and Portuguese inscriptions on Jewish gravestones in the Hunt's Bay Cemetery," *Jamaica Journal,* Institute of Jamaica, Kingston (March 1968); "A New Vision of the Indian in Mexican Literature of the post-revolutionary period," *Caribbean Studies,* Vol. 2, No. 4, University of Puerto Rico; "La enanjenación en las letras latinoamericanas, *Mundo Nuevo* (Paris, December 1, 1969); "Reality and Mystification in négritude," *Caribbean Quarterly,* University of the West Indies, Extra-Mural Centre (March 1970); "Paralelismo y divergencia entre indigenismo y negritud," *Anuario de Estudios Latinoamericanos,* II, pp. 65-73; "The search for identity in the Caribbean," *Planet,* IV; "¿Crisis o agotamiento de la negritud?" *Actas del Tercer Congreso Internacional de Hispanistas;* translation of a poem of Guillen as "My Name," in *Savacou,* 1971.

Biographical/Critical Sources: Anson Gonzalez, " 'Possibility' in W.I. Creative Writing," *The New Voices,* No. 4, pp. 6-7.

CRAIG, Dennis

b. 1929, Guyana.
Poet, teacher, storywriter, expert in linguistics.

Craig has now lived for many years in Jamaica. First educated in Guiana, he did an external London B.A. there. He subsequently went to Mona to do his Diploma in Education. He has done further post-graduate work in the United States and the United Kingdom and has completed his doctorate at London University. Although not primarily a literary person, Craig has made his mark through a number of poems published in a variety of journals, and through the light his research has thrown on many aspects of Jamaican English and the Creole continuum.

Writings: Poetry in: *Sunday Gleaner, Chronicle Christmas Annual,* BIM, *Caribbean Quarterly,* and *Savacou.* Also in: anthologies: *Caribbean Voices,* Vol. II; *New Ships; Bite In.*

Academic Articles on Linguistics: in *Creole Languages,* and *English Teaching.*

CREQUE, Cyril F.W.

b. ca. 1904, Charlotte Amalie, St. Thomas, Virgin Islands.
Poet, economist.

Creque was educated in St. Thomas, at Moorehouse University, Atlanta and at Harvard University. He has served as Commissioner of the Department of Housing and Community Renewal, Virgin Islands of U.S.A.

Writings: Poetry: *Trade Winds,* Newport, Franklin Printing House, 1934 (110 pp.); *Panorama,* St. Thomas, Virgin Islands; *Poems,* Wauwatosa, Kenyon Press Publishing Co., 1947 (81 pp.).

Other: *The U.S. Virgins and the Eastern Caribbean; Planning a Balanced Development Program for Small Business in the U.S. Virgin Islands.*

CROMWELL, Liz

b. ca. 1945, Trinidad.
Poet.

Cromwell was a well-known journalist in Trinidad and Tobago, working on major newspapers with articles appearing in many local publications. She currently lives in Canada.

Writings: Poetry: *Canadian jungle tea*. Toronto, Canada, 1975; her "Fairy Tale" is in *The New Voices*, No. 6.

CRUICKSHANK, J. Graham

b. ca. 1875, Guyana; d. ca. 1950(?).
Essayist, folklorist.

Cruickshank published two pioneering studies of Guyana speech and humor. A close friend of James Rodway, he published two articles, "James Rodway," in *The Daily Argosy* (Sunday, December 19, 1926), "Religion of a Naturalist; Mr. Rodway Not an Atheist." He also wrote the preface to Rodway's *Story of Georgetown*. Cruickshank also contributed articles to *Timehri*, the magazine of the Royal Agricultural and Commercial Society.

Writings: Negro Humour, Being Sketches in the Market, on the Road and at My Back Door, Georgetown, Argosy Co., 1905; *"Black Talk": Being Notes on Negro Dialect in British Guiana with (inevitably) a Chapter on the Vernacular of Barbados*, Demerara, Argosy Co., 1916.

CULMER, Jack

b. ca. 1918, Bahamas.
Editor, compiler.

Culmer's one known collection of verse is *A Book of Bahamian Verse*, (London, Bailey Bros., 1930; 2nd ed., London, Author, 1948).

CUNDALL, Frank

b. ca. 1858 (came to Jamaica at age of 33, in February 1891); d. 1937.
Folklorist, historian, bibliographist, compiler.

One of the fine early scholars of the culture of the "old days," much of Cundall's historical and bibliographical work is still essential to anyone working on nineteenth and early twentieth century Jamaican and West Indian materials. He was for many years the chief mover of the Institute of Jamaica in all its activities. A full bibliography of his work, which is very extensive, is to be found in the West Indian Reference Library, Kingston, Institute of Jamaica.

He was Secretary and Librarian of the Institute of Jamaica from 1891 to 1937. He had a great interest in art, and organized an Art Gallery at the Institute. Before he came to Jamaica he had already organized six Art Exhibitions.

Writings: Stories and Folklore: *Jamaica negro proverbs and sayings*, collected and classified according to subjects, Kingston, Institute of Jamaica, 1910, (with Izett Anderson), 2nd ed. rev. and encl., illus. by Lilly G. Perkins, London, published for the Institute of Jamaica by the West India Committee, 1927; *Three Fingered Jack, the terror of Jamaica*, London, West India Committee Circular, 1930 (illustrated); Extract from the W.I. Commission Circular January 9, January 23, February 6, 1930, which includes bibliography of 16 entries on the literary and dramatic history of "Obi" or "Three Fingered Jack"; *Historic Jamaica*, London, published by W.I. Commission for the Institute of Jamaica, 1915; (with J.L. Pietersz) *Jamaica under the Spaniards*, abstracted from the archives of Seville, Kingston, Inst. of Jamaica, 1919; *Bibliographia Jamaicensis*, Kingston, Inst. of Jamaica, 1902, and Supplement, 1908; *Bibliography of the West Indies* (excluding Jamaica), Kingston, Inst. of Jamaica, 1909; *The Press and Printers of Jamaica prior to 1820* . . . , Worcester, Mass., American Antiquarian Society, 1916; *Pine's painting of Rodney and his officers*, West India Commission, Vol. 39 (June 5, 1924); "Sculpture in Jamaica," *Art Journal* 69 (March 1907).

History of Painters: *The Landscape and Pastoral Painters of Holland;* and *Reminiscences of the Colonial and Indian Exhibition* (published pre-1891).

Edited: *Lady Nugent's journal: Jamaica One Hundred Years Ago*, London, (published for the Institute of Jamaica by the West Indian Committee, 1934).

Biographical/Critical Sources: "The Achievement of Frank Cundall" by H.P. Jacobs in *Jamaica Journal,* Vol. 2, No. 1 (March 1968).

CURTIN, Marguerite

b. 1934, Jamaica.
Poet.
One of the new writers included in *The New Voices,* edited by Anson Gonzalez, Trinidad and Tobago (No. 4, June, 1974), Curtin has one separate volume in print, the booklet poem "Nanny and Maroon," *New Voices,* No. 5, 1975.

DABYDEEN, Cyril

b. ca. 1942, Guyana.
Poet.

Dabydeen attended Queen's College in Georgetown, Guyana, and the University of the West Indies. His collection of poems has a foreword by A.J. Seymour in which A.J. comments: "One of the fine younger poets developing a personal idiom in Guyana and winner of a number of national poetry prizes in recent years." Dabydeen gained the Sandbach Parker Gold Medal in 1964 and the A.J. Seymour Prize in 1967. The poem that won the Seymour Prize—"Poem To Your Own"—is included in his collection.

He has been published in *New World; Kaie;* and *Voices* (Trokman, ed.).

Writings: Poetry: *Poems in Recession,* Georgetown, Sheik Sadeek, 1972 (foreword by A.J. Seymour, 24 pp.).

DA COSTA, Jean Constantine (née Creary)

b. January 13, 1937, Jamaica.
Storywriter, critic, teacher.
DaCosta was educated at St. Hilda's Diocesan High School and St. Hugh's High School, Jamaica; then at the U.C.W.I., Mona, Jamaica, and at Oxford and Indiana Universities. She is currently Senior Lecturer in the Department of English, U.W.I., and is married to the Jamaican journalist and broadcaster, David DaCosta.

Her children's books have caught the particular Jamaican atmosphere beautifully and use the Jamaican speech rhythms with great accuracy and insight. DaCosta has also written critical articles and literary essays.

She currently is working on the imagery in Jamaican novelist Roger Mais' fiction, and another children's novel to be entitled "Voice in the Wind." Her work in linguistics, especially on Jamaican Creole, is also well known.

Writings: Sprat Morrison (Ministry of Education), Jamaica, Collins-Sangster, 1972; *Escape to Last Man Peak* (Blue Mountain Series, illustrated by Imre Hofbauer) Kingston, Longman Caribbean Ltd., 1975.

Critical Studies: of *The Hills were Joyful Together* and *Brother Man.* In Longmans' *West Indian Authors,* (ed. by Mervyn Morris), London, 1976; and critical essay on Roger Mais in *The Islands in Between,* edited by Louis James, Oxford, Oxford University Press, 1968.

DAISY, Al T.

b. ca. 1939, St. Vincent.
Poet.

Daisy has published three known volumes of verse: *Bitter Harvest* (date not known); *The Naked I* (1969); *Dedications on Turning Thirty* (1971).

DALY, P.H.

b. ca. 1911, Guyana.
Poet, novelist, essayist, biographer, teacher.

Daly is now a retired Head Teacher whose last school was Diamond Government. He wrote an unpublished novel, extracts from which were published in *Kyk-over-al* 13 and 17 (1951 and 1953). His poetry was published in local periodicals.

Writings: Biography: *Story of the Heroes,* Georgetown, Daily Chronicle, Book I, 1940; Book II, 1941; Book III, 1943.

Essays: "Walter MacArthur Lawrence," in *Kyk-over-al* 2, (1946), p. 18; "West Indian Freedom and West Indian Literature," *Daily Chronicle,* Georgetown, Daily Chronicle, 1951.

Compiler and Biographer: *The Poet of Guiana, Walter MacA. Lawrence* (Selected with a Biography), Georgetown, Daily Chronicle, 1948.

History: *Revolution to Republic,* Georgetown, Daily Chronicle, 1970.

DALY, Vere Trevelyan

b. Guyana, November 29, 1909.
Shortstory writer, educator, historian, lecturer.

Daly wrote poetry and short stories which were published in local periodicals; he possessed a great interest in historical research and trade unionism.

His work is included in Cameron's anthology, *Guianese Poetry,* and verse and short stories are in various periodicals, including: *Christmas Tide, Kyk-over-al,* and *A New Guyana.*

Writings: General: *The Making of Guyana,* London, Macmillan, 1974.

DALZELL, Frank E.

b. ca. 1932, Guyana.
Poet, civil servant.

Dalzell has appeared in A. Seymour's anthologies: *My Lovely Native Land* (with Elma Seymour); *Fourteen Guianese Poems for Children; Themes of Song;* Elma Seymour's *Sun is a Shapely Fire* and is in many local periodicals, including *Kyk-over-al* and *Chronicle Christmas Annual.* He is a Guyanese Civil Servant.

Writings: Poetry: *Moments of Leisure,* British Guiana, 1952 (Miniature Poet Series).

DANIEL, Eugene

b. 1931, Barbados.
Poet, storywriter.

Daniel was educated St. Michael's Girls' School and at Queen's College Barbados. He published his stories in the *Barbados Advocate* and *The Children's Corner* and his poetry in BIM.

DATHORNE, Oscar Ronald

b. November 19, 1934, Georgetown, Guyana.
Novelist, storywriter, essayist, anthologist, teacher.

Educated in Guyana and England, Dathorne took his B.A., M.A. and Ph.D. at Sheffield University, and his Cert. Dip. Ed. from London University. He has taught at a number of universities in Africa and the United States, including Howard, the University of Wisconsin, and Ohio State. He was UNESCO Consultant to the Government of Sierra Leone (1967-68), and for a period was co-editor of *Black Orpheus* magazine, Ibadan.

Dathorne's *Caribbean Verse,* an anthology with some biographical and critical comment and one of the earliest of such collections, is quite widely used. The introduction to his *Caribbean Narrative* (1966) has worn well, for it is still cogent and perceptive.

Besides writing interesting, and sometimes provocative novels, he has contributed critical articles to a number of journals in Africa, the United Kingdom and the United States.

Dathorne is quoted in *Contemporary Novelists* as saying that often the new contact with reality which comes upon his antagonists cannot "be resolved on a rational level and this is why in plays and poetry I have moved towards an 'irrational' approach which expresses bewilderment." But besides this non-rational element there is invariably a real touch of the comic—and the odd—in his writings.

Writings: Novels: *Dumplings in the Soup,* London, Cassell, 1963; *The Scholar Man,* London, Cassell, 1964; *One Iota of Difference,* London, Cassell, 19??.

Anthologies: Editor: (with others): *Young Commonwealth Poets '65,* London, Heinemann, 1965; (with Willfried Feuser), *Africa in Prose,* London, Penguin, 1969; and Editor of: *Caribbean Narrative,* London, Heinemann, 1966; *Caribbean Verse,* London, Heinemann, 1967; *African Poetry for Schools and Colleges,* London, Macmillan, 1969.

Essays: "Africa in the Literature of the West Indies," *Journal of Commonwealth Literature,* I (1965), pp. 95-116; "The African Novel: Document to Experiment," *Bulletin of the Association for African Literature in English* 3 (1965), p. 18; "Africa in West Indian Literature," in *Black Orpheus* No. 16 (1964), pp. 42-56; "The Theme of Africa in West Indian Literature," *Phylon,* XXVI, 3 (1965), pp. 254-276; "The Writers of Guyana," *Times Literary Supplement* (May 26, 1966), p. 480.

Article: "Two Black Latin Poets: Juan Latino and Francis Williams," *Black Orpheus,* No. 21 (1967), pp. 53-56.

Uncollected Short Stories: "Hodge," in *Nierian Radio Times* (Ibadan), 1967; "The Nightwatchman and the Baby Nurse," in *Black Orpheus* (Ibadan, 1967); "The Wintering of Mr. Kolawole," in *Black Orpheus* (Ibadan, 1967); "Constable," in *Political Spider,* London, Heinemann, 1969. He is also represented in *Stories from the Caribbean* (ed. A. Salkey).

Poetry: in *Young Commonwealth Poets '65; Commonwealth Poems of Today; New Voices of the Commonwealth;* and in *Black Orpheus* (Ibadan); *Transition* (Kampala); *Outposts* (London); *Présence Africaine* (Paris).

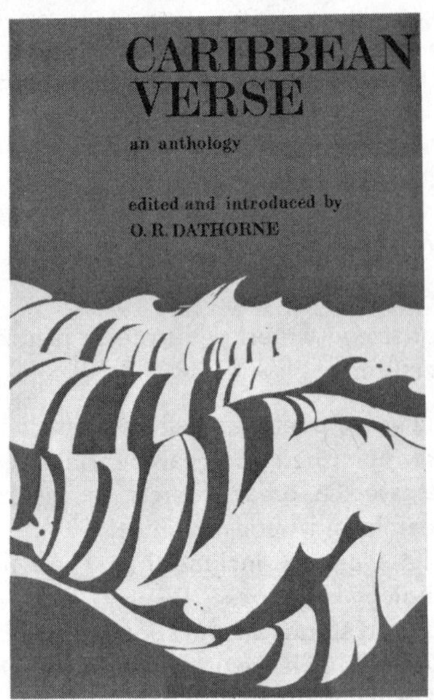

Literary Criticism: *The Black Mind. A History of African Literature,* Minneapolis, University of Minnesota, 1975.

Bibliography: in *Bibliography of Neo-African Literature from Africa, America and the Caribbean,* by Janheinz Jahn, London, Deutsch, 1965, and New York, Praeger, 1965.

Biographical/Critical Sources: Review *"The Scholar Man"* by L.E. Brathwaite in BIM 41 (June-December), pp. 68-69; Review *"Dumplings in the Soup,"* by Harold Marshall in BIM 39, pp. 226-227; In a review by Mervyn Morris of "West Indian Literature: Some Cheap Anthologies," *Caribbean Quarterly,* 13, 2 (June 1967), pp. 37-38; "Guyanese Writers," by Wilfred Cartey, in *New World,* Georgetown, Guyana, 1966; *The Chosen Tongue,* by Gerald Moore, London, Longman, 1969; Kenneth Ramchand, *The West Indian Novel and its Background,* London, 1970, pp. 159-160.

DAVIS, Leslie C.

b. ca. 1928, Guyana.
Poet.

Davis is head of a private secondary school and has published two collections.

Writings: Poetry: *Invocation to Sivananda*, British Guiana, Adana Printing Service, 1957; *Eternal Tribute*, British Guiana, 1958; and has contributed to *Kyk-over-al* and other journals.

DAVIS, Wayne Edward

b. ca. 1940, Trinidad.
Poet.

Davis, high school principal in San Fernando, has contributed verse to *The New Voices* and has one published collection.

Writings: Poetry: *Old Oracle/Timeless Dream*, Trinidad and Tobago, 1975.

DAWES, Neville

b. June 16, 1926, Warri, Nigeria (of Jamaican parents).
Novelist, poet, teacher.

Dawes grew up in Sturge Town, in the hills of St. Ann, Jamaica. He was educated in Jamaica, then at Oriel College, Oxford (M.A. in English). He has taught at Calabar High School, Jamaica, and Kumasi College of Technology, and at Achimoto, both Ghana. He has been visiting professor of English, University of Guyana. One-time editor of *Okyeame,* a Ghanaian literary journal, Dawes has returned to live in Jamaica to serve as the head of the Institute of Jamaica. He has always been a genial companion and champion of the arts.

Dawes has not kept the early promise of his verse which showed a strong feeling for the Jamaican countryside and for the rhythms of common Jamaican speech. His novel *The Last Enchantment* deals with an interesting group of Jamaicans, including some who look very much like famous pre-independence politicians. And his old school, Jamaica College, is not exactly absent from his characterization of the class/color context of the Jamaica in which he grew up. Because he has always shown a keen interest in the relations between Africa and the Caribbean, and in the writers of both areas, he was, for a time, closely connected to the Nkrumah regime in Ghana, and to the political developments in that country.

Dawes' poetry mainly has appeared in reviews and anthologies.

Writings: Novel: *The Last Enchantment*, London, Macgibbon and Kee, 1960.

Contributed to: BIM; *Focus; Schwarzer*, 1964; *Young Commonwealth Poets*, 1965; *Caribbean Voices*, 1966, 1970; *The Sun's Eye*, 1968; *Caribbean Narrative, Caribbean Prose; Sepia*, 1957; *Caribbean Quarterly, Federation Commemoration Issue* (April 1958); and *Independence Anthology*, 1962.

Biographical/Critical Sources: Review of *The Enchantment*, by E. Brathwaite, in BIM, Vol. 9, No. 33, (July-December 1961), pp. 74-75.

De BOISSIERE, Ralph A.C.

b. ca. 1899, Trinidad.
Novelist, storywriter.

De Boissiere comes from an old French-Creole family of means. He was an early member of the literary circle surrounding Alfred Mendes and C.L.R. James in the 1920's in Trinidad and a frequent contributor to the cultural journals *Trinidad* (1929-1930) and *The Beacon*. In 1940 he emigrated to Australia where he has resided ever since, publishing three novels.

Cliff Sealy writes of *Crown Jewel,* set in Trinidad during the heady revolts of 1937, that it "... is the story of Andre du Coudray's journey towards self-discovery. But man is a social animal; and Andre's growing self-consciousness is but a parable of the birth of a new society out of the womb of the old, a new society of which in a modified form we are the inheritors. *Crown Jewel* is thus our most important political novel; it is the fundamental work of fiction in our society."

Writings: Novels: *Crown Jewel*, Melbourne, Australasian Book Society, 1952 and Leipsig, Panther Books (Paul List Verlag Leipsig), 1956; *Rum and Coca-Cola*, London, Panther Books, 1956, 2nd ed., Melbourne, Australasian Book Society, 1956; *No Saddles for Kangaroos*, Melbourne, Australasian, 1964.

Stories: in various journals: "Miss Winter," "Booze and the Coberdaw" in Christmas issue of *Trinidad* (1929), and "Woman on the Pavement," in *Beacon* (1931).

Biographical/Critical Sources: Review of *Crown Jewel* and general comments on his life and writings in "A Note on Ralph de Boissiere" by Clifford Sealy in *Voices*, Vol. 2, No. 3 (Port of Spain, March 1973); "The Novels of Ralph De Boissiere," *Journal of Commonwealth Literature* 9 (1970), p. 104.

DE COTEAU, Delano

(pseudonym: **Abdul MALIK**)
b. 1940, Grenada (has lived primarily in Trinidad; d. 1974.
Poet.

Malik was taken as a child of two to Trinidad and thereafter for 20 years moved between it and Grenada, finally remaining in Trinidad after 1962. He attended Presentation College in Grenada and the Grenada Boys' Secondary School. From the notes he wrote for the front of his book of poems, *Revo* (1975), we learn that he was ". . . expelled from the former, dropped out of the latter at 17, continued the learning process in the streets and public libraries of Port of Spain and St. George's."

His first published collection of poems was *Black Up 1* (May 1972), and the second collection "takes up where *Black Up* left off." He also commented that he had been "experimenting with words in one form and another for the past twenty-one years."

At one time Malik was very active politically and was cited for desecration and sedition in Trinidad in 1970. He had become a Muslim in 1968, and was given the name of Abdul Malik at that time. He co-founded the Trinidad Black Panther Organisation, which later merged to form the N.J.A.C. He was tried and executed for murder in Trinidad in 1974. His story is the basis for V. S. Naipaul's novel *Guerrillas.*

Writings: Poetry: *Black Up*, Trinidad, Free Press, 1972; *Revo*, printed for the author by the Tapia House Printing Co., 1975.

Biographical/Critical Sources: Mentioned in Anson Gonzalez's article "Possibility in W.I. Creative Writing," in *The New Voices*, No. 4 (June 1974), p. 47, and also in F. Gordon Rohlehr's article "West Indian Poetry," in BIM 54 (Jan-June 1972), p. 81.

De LISSER, Herbert George

b. 1878, Falmouth, Jamaica; d. 1944.
Novelist, editor, journalist.

DeLisser was for years editor of the *Daily Gleaner* and as such held much power over public opinion *in* Jamaica, and about it, abroad. Once closely associated with Sir Sydney Oliver, the Fabian Socialist, to whom his remarkable and early novel *Jane's Career* is dedicated, he came later to symbolize a certain part of the local and imperial establishment. But he never lost the common touch, as witness his humorous columns in the *Gleaner*. DeLisser came of that particular Portuguese-Jewish heritage, which with or without an added African element, has played so great a part in the cultural development of the Caribbean.

Kenneth Ramchand showed in his introduction to the reissue of *Jane's Career* in the Colonial Novel Library, that DeLisser had a scorn for rising browns and

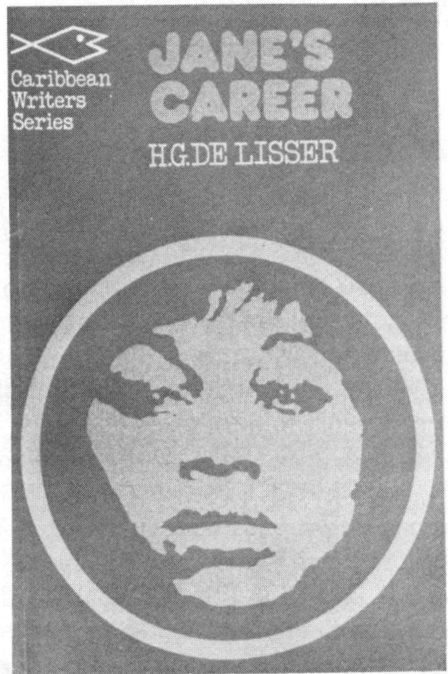

light browns of his own day, and that he is unfair to Gordon and to Bogle in his *Revenge* (1918). H.G.D., as he was known to many, also opposed adult suffrage in 1938—as did many others who now forget that they did. He apparently was much upset by what he considered to be the "mob rule" presaged by the 1938 disturbances and "riots." Yet as John Figueroa puts it ". . . it is he who first wrote about a black maid seriously and in depth; it is he who shows a close knowledge of the language of the people, and of their customs both in old Kingston and in the country."

DeLisser's writings are an undoubted must for those who wish to understand the complications of the pre-independence, over-facile rhetoric of colonialism/imperialism/neocolonialism which sometimes now too readily explains, and explains away, all the genuine and frightening problems which beset the Caribbean. A good study is needed of what first made men like DeLisser sympathetic and then afterwards rather "reactionary." Whether his fiction is read with this kind of enquiry in mind or not, it usually gives pleasure and a certain amount of insight. Perhaps some of his humorous writings in the *Gleaner* unfortunately made fun of what needed reformation rather than of those who should have been helping, but did not.

Writings: Novels: *Jane: A Story of Jamaica*, Kingston, Jamaica, Gleaner Co., 1913; *Jane's Career: A Story of Jamaica*, London, Methuen, 1914, and published in U.S.A., 1971, by African Publishing Corp., New York, with an introduction by Kenneth Ramchand, London, Rex Collings, Colonial Novel Library, 1971; and also appears in edition by Heinemann, Caribbean Writers Series, No. 5, London, 1972, introduction, K. Ramchand; *Susan Proudleigh*, London, Methuen, 1915; *Triumphant Squalitone: a tropical extravaganza*, Kingston, The Gleaner Co., Ltd. Printers, 1917; *Revenge—a tale of Old Jamaica*, Kingston, printed for the author by the Gleaner Co., Ltd., 1918; *The White Witch of Rosehall*, London, Ernest Benn, 1929 (with three editions and 13 printings by 1970); *Under the Sun: a Jamaica comedy*, London, Ernest Benn, 1937; *Psyche*, London, Ernest Benn, 1952; *Morgan's Daughter*, London, Ernest Benn, 1953 (paperback edition by Benn by 1961); *The Cup and the Lip, a romance*, London, Ernest Benn, 1956; *The Arawak Girl*, Kingston, Pioneer Press, 1958.

An extract from *Susan Proudleigh* is in the *Independence Anthology* (1962).

Biographical/Critical Sources: Jane's Career, review article, *World Literature Written in English*, pp. 97-105, 1973, by John Figueroa; Kenneth Ramchand, *The West Indian Novel and its Background*, New York, 1970, especially Chapter IV, part ii, pp. 55-62; and Ramchand's introduction to Africana edition of *Jane's Career*, New York, 1971. Also see W. Adolphe Roberts, "Herbert George de Lisser," in *Six Great Jamaicans*, Kingston, The Pioneer Press, 1952.

DE WEEVER, Jacqueline

b. ca. 1935, Guyana.
Poet, storywriter.

Educated at Charlestown Convent in New York, DeWeever attended New York

University and the University of Pennsylvania (Ph.D.). She is a specialist in English medieval literature. She writes poetry and fairy tales and her work has appeared in *Kyk-over-al.* Her story "The Rice Fairies" is in *My Lovely Native Land* (eds. A. and E. Seymour).

DIXON, McDonald

b. October 1, 1945, Marchand, Castries, St. Lucia.
Poet, playwright, painter.

Educated first at Anglican Infant and Primary schools in St. Lucia, Dixon won a C.T.B. scholarship to St. Mary's College in 1955. He began a banking career upon graduation in 1960, joining the staff of the Royal Bank of Canada, and later was appointed accountant at the Viėux-Fort Branch before transfer to Grenada in 1973.

Dixon joined the St. Lucia Arts Guild in 1964 and was thenceforth strongly influenced by Roderick Walcott and Derek Walcott. His poems have been published in such journals as *Link*, BIM and *Caribbean Quarterly*, but much of his work remains either unpublished or uncollected. *Pebbles* (1973) is his first volume of verse.

His poem "Poet's Corner. . . . Walcott" begins:

Perplexed by the bloods
That warm these veins,
Like you I cannot choose.
Home to me, is this brittle shore
A cluster of shacks at the teeth
of the wind.

Writings: Poetry: *Pebbles,* with foreword by Robert Lee, Castries, St. Lucia, printed at St. Lucia Government Printing Office, 1973.

Plays (all in ms.): *Toussaint: A history of the Haitian Revolution; The Glass Doll; The Stick Fighters; Kesnoe or Portrait of a man in black; Tales of Brer Rabbit; Diablotin;* and *A Hero Always.*

DODD, E. A.

(see under pseudonym: **E. SNOD**)

D'OLIVEIRA, Evadne

b. ca. 1942, Guyana.
Poet, playwright, storywriter, journalist.

Evadne D'Oliveira has been writing from a very early age; she has been a journalist in Guyana and in London. She writes and has written a number of stories and plays for children, often using local legends and folklore. She was one of the six women who contributed to and published *Guyana Drums.* She was also one of the six writers who produced "Stories from Guyana" for Canada Expo '67. She has won awards in local competitions for her poems and short stories. In the notes on her in *Guyana Drums* we are told that "she will be well remembered for her Guyanese fantasy, *The Scattered Jewels,* a play for children which she wrote and directed herself with great success." She is planning to publish a book of spiritual poems shortly. She was included in the P.E.N. collection for Human Rights Year, 1968.

Writings: Plays: (in typescript): *The Female of the Species: A Play for Radio; If Freedom Fails: A Play for Radio; The Shadow and the Substance; The Scattered Jewels* (performed 1969).

Poetry: in *Guyana Drums,* Georgetown, Guyana, 1972; *Voices* (collection by P.E.N., 1968); and *Voices of Guyana,* 1968 (ed. Trotman). Also is in various local periodicals.

Short Story: "Drama at Tukeit" was broadcast by the BBC, under the title "The Choice" in 1968.

DOLPHIN, Celeste

b. ca. 1913, Guyana.
Storywriter, editor, broadcaster (radio and television).

Educated in Guyana, Dolphin trained as a radio and TV broadcaster in London and the United States and has been the head of Government Broadcasters to Schools Service since 1954. She was the Editor of *Kaie,* publication of the National History and Arts Council from 1964. She did a series of broadcasts over Radio Demerara in 1953 which were later collected in one volume *Children of Guiana* (Georgetown, 1953). An extract from this is in *My Lovely Native Land*—"The Little Chinese Boy," (pp. 92-98). She made a great contribution to the organization of Carifesta, Guyana, 1972.

Her stories have appeared in various periodicals including *Chronicle Christmas Annual; My Lovely Native Land; An Anthology of Guyana* (Arthur and Elma Seymour, eds.), Trinidad, 1971.

DONALDSON, Robert N.

b. October 28, 1912, Trinidad.
Novelist, journalist, free-lance writer.

Donaldson is principal of a Commercial College and has been active in private education.

Writing: Novel: *Heart's Triumph* ("a moving story of love's conquest over race and color"), Trinidad, 1944, printed for author; reprinted, 1963, at Rahaman Printery Ltd. (rewritten by author).

DOUGLAS, Syble G.

(a.k.a. **"Sylvia"**)
b. ca. 1942, Guyana.
Poet, artist, teacher, journalist.

Douglas was Woman's Page editor of the now defunct *Daily Argosy.* She has written three plays, two having been staged locally. She has been editor and contributor to *Guyana Drums,* Georgetown, 1972. Her work is in *Sun is a Shapely Fire;* and *Voices of Guyana; P.E.N. Anthology "Voices,"* 1968; and *A New Guyana.*

Writings: Poetry: *Fulfillment: A collection of poems,* Georgetown, 1967.

DRAYTON, Geoffrey

b. 1924, Barbados.
Novelist, storywriter, poet, journalist, critic.

Geoffrey Drayton was educated in Barbados and the U.K. He attended Cambridge University, taking a degree in political science. He moved on to Canada, where he worked as a research economist with the Canadian Government; later he taught for a period.

During 1951-1953 he worked as a journalist in the U.K., Canada and Spain. In 1953 he became a staff member of the *Petroleum Times,* and later was to serve the paper in an editorial capacity. In the 1970's he was a member of the *Economist* Intelligence Unit and project director for the journal's Oil Department.

He was a frequent contributor to BIM, publishing both verse and short stories. His short story "Mr. Dombey the Zombie," which was broadcast on the BBC and appears in A. Salkey's *West Indian Stories* (1951), is probably one of his best.

An extract of his first novel *Christopher*, appeared in BIM, Vol. 7, No. 26 (Jan-June 1958). This novel recalls his childhood spent on a sugar plantation. Kenneth Ramchand in his *The West Indian Novel and its Background* makes two very pertinent points (among others) on Drayton's work: one in relation to the fact that it is a West Indian novel of childhood and the other in relation to the use of "obeah and cult practices" in Drayton's novel.

> *A third West Indian novel of childhood,* Christopher *(1959) by Geoffrey Drayton, invests like* The Year in San Fernando *(Michael Anthony, 1965), in the very particular consciousness of an isolated boy; and again like Anthony's novel it does not have an explicit social or political drive. But* Christopher *concentrates on a crucial period in the life of a boy. . . ."* (p. 207); and:

> *Obeah and cult practices occur in novels by West Indians of every racial origin; the degree of prominence given to them varies from novel to novel; and the author's attitudes to their raw material differ widely. J.B. Emtage introduces Negro terror of the fetish in a mocking and comic spirit (*Brown Sugar, *1966), but another White West Indian uses obeah differently in the novel of childhood* Christopher *(1959): the boy's increasing involvement with the Negro world around him, and his growing-up process, are subtly correlated with his development, away from an exotic view, to an understanding in psychological terms of how obeah operates.* (p. 123)

Writings: Novels: *Zohara*, London, Secker and Warburg, 1961; *Christopher*, London, Collins, 1959 and London, Heinemann, Caribbean Writers Series, 1972.

Poetry: *Three Meridians: Poems*, Toronto, Ryerson Press, 1951. Also: verse published variously including Anthologies: *Caribbean Voices* (ed. J. Figueroa), London, Evans Bros. Vol. I [1966]; *The Sun's Eye* (ed. A. Walmsley), Longmans, Green and Co., London, 1968. Verse also published in various journals and reviews including: BIM; *Contemporary Verse;* and *Canadian Forum*.

Critical Articles: Numerous articles published in West Indian, Canadian and British magazines.

Biographical/Critical Sources: Barrie Davies, review in *World Literature Written in English*, XII, I (April 1973), pp. 119-121; A.N. Forde, review of *Christopher* in BIM Vol. 8, No. 29, (June-Dec 1959), p. 64; Harold Marshall, review of *Zohara*, in BIM, Vol. 9, No. 34 (Jan-June 1962), p. 152; Frank Collymore, review of *Three Meridians* in BIM, Vol. 4, No. 14, (June 1957), pp. 144-145; R.B. LePage, review of *Three Meridians* in *Caribbean Quarterly*, Vol. 2, No. 1, p. 45; K. Ramchand, review of *Christopher* in "Terrified Consciousness," in *Journal of Commonwealth Literature* (July 1969), No. 7, pp. 8-19; and K. Ramchand in *The West Indian Novel and its Background*, London, Faber, 1970, Barnes and Noble, New York, 1970, review of *Christopher*, references: pp. 123, 207, 223, 224, 228-230.

Du QUESNAY, Frederick J. Le Mercier

b. 1923, Jamaica.
Novelist.

Du Quesnay's one known work, a romantic novel, is based on the life and times of Mary Carleton, a notorious lady in both London and Port Royal Society.

Writing: Novel: *A Princess for Port Royal*, Ilfracombe, N. Devonshire, Arthur H. Stockwell, 1960.

DURIE, Alice

b. ca. 1909, Jamaica.
Novelist.

Only one work is known by this all but forgotten writer.

Writing: Novel: *One Jamaica Gal*, Kingston, Jamaica Times, 1939.

DURIE, Sally

b. ca. 1940, Jamaica.
Poet, actress, playwright.

A talented actress and poet now living in England, Sally Durie will be remembered for her acting in Jamaica production of Derek Walcott's *In a Fine Castle.* She has published her verse in various journals, and has gained awards for her poetry in the National Jamaican Festival Competitions.

Writings: Poetry: "Anaktoria," "Country Store," (winner of Certificates of Merit 1970); "No Moe (winner of Certificates of Merit, 1970); "No More Myth," (Bronze Medal, Festival, 1971); "Seth" (Certificate of Merit, Festival, 1971).

ELDER, John D.

b. ca. 1932, Tobago.
Storywriter, folklorist, editor.

Elder is chairman of the Trinidad National Cultural Council and is a well known commentator on Trinidad Culture.

Writings: Folklore Publications: *National Cultural Council Art and Culture,* Port of Spain, 1972; *From Congo drum to steelband. A socio-historical account of the emergence and evolution of the Trinidad steel orchestra,* Trinidad, University of the West Indies, 1969, (21 pp.); "Folk song and folk life in Charlotteville. Aspects of village life as dynamics of acculturation in Tobago folk song tradition," Paper presented at the Twenty-first Conference of the International Music Council, Kingston, Jamaica, Aug. 27-Sept. 3, 1971, Port of Spain National Cultural Council of Trinidad and Tobago, 1972, (79 pp.).

Articles: "Evolution of the Traditional Calypso of Trinidad and Tobago: A Socio-Historical Analysis of Song-Change." *Univ. Microfilms,* Ann Arbor, Michigan, 1971; "The Male/Female Conflict in Calypso," *Caribbean Quarterly,* Vol. 14, No. 3 (Sept. 1968), pp. 23-41; "Kalinda—Song of the Battling Troubadours of Trinidad," *Journal of the Folklore Institute,* Vol. III, No. 2 (Aug. 1966), pp. 192-203; "Colour, Music and Conflict; A Study of Aggression in Trinidad with reference to the Role of Traditional Music," *Ethnomusicology,* Vol. 8, No. 2 (1964), pp. 128-136.

Editor: *Ma Rose Point* (An Anthology of rare and strange legends and myths from Trinidad and Tobago), Port of Spain, National Cultural Council of Trinidad and Tobago, 1972, (79 pp.).

Story: "Tank Halla," dramatized for Trinidad stage for Trinidad and Tobago Festival at Queen's Hall, 1968 as a folk opera, two acts, by the Mausica Teachers' College Alumni Choir.

Biographical/Critical Sources: "Eternal Triangle"—That's Tank Halla: A Novel Attempt at Complete Integration of Song and Dance," in *Trinidad Guardian* (April 29, 1968).

ELLINGTON, Richard

b. ca. 1908, St. John, U.S. Virgin Islands.
Novelist.

Ellington's five known published works are in the detective thriller vein.

Writings: Novels: *It's a Crime,* 1948; *Shoot the Works,* 1948; *Stone Cold Dead,* 1950; *Exit for A Dame,* 1951; *Just Killing Time,* 1953, all New York, William Morrow.

ELLIS, Hall Anthony

b. 1936, Jamaica.
Poet, actor.

Ellis' early schooling was in Jamaica. He then studied agriculture and science in Canada but later moved on for studies of the theater in the U.S. for three years before going to the United Kingdom for more drama training. He has played the Ghost in Hamlet and other minor parts.

Writings: Poetry: Living: *Poems and Sayings,* Lindsay, Ontario, Blewett, 196? (probably 1969).

ELLIS, Royston

b. February 10, 1941, England (?), (and lives in Dominica).
Novelist, poet, biographer, TV and radio commentator, administrator.

Royston Ellis is a man of many parts. From 1957-61 he was a radio and TV commentator, from 1961-63 he was Assistant Editor of the Jersey News and Feature Agency; from 1963-66 he was Associate Editor of the *Canary Islands Sun;* from 1966 to the present he has been administrator of the Emerald Hillside Estates, Dominica. He is a member of the Royal Commonwealth Society and Dominican Arts Council Writers Workshop. He is the author of five volumes of poetry, four novels and four biographies. He has also been a university lecturer. He has been awarded several Dominican National Day Poetry Prizes (1970, 1971, and 1973).

Writings: Novels: *The Flesh Merchants; The Rush at the End; Myself for Fame; Flesh Game.*

Poetry: *Jiving to Gyp,* 1959; *Rave,* 1960; *The Rainbow Walking Stick,* 1961; *A Seaman's Suitcase,* 1963; and *The Cherry Boy,* 1967.

Biographies: *Rebel; The Big Beat Scene; Drifting with Cliff Richard;* and *The Shadows by Themselves.*

Articles: in many journals and collections including: *Dominica Star, Phoenix, University Magazines, New Writing in the Caribbean.*

EMTAGE, J.B.

b. ca. 1914, Barbados.
Novelist.

Emtage left Barbados in 1934 and went to live and work in Britain, where he still resides.

Writing: Novel: *Brown Sugar, A Vestigial Tale,* London, Collins, 1966.

Biographical/Critical Sources: Review of *Brown Sugar*—in K. Ramchand's "Terrified Consciousness," *Journal of Commonwealth Literature* (July 1969), No. 7, pp. 8-19; K. Ramchand, *The West Indian Novel and its Background* (Barnes and Noble, Inc., N.Y., 1970), p. 123, 129, pp. 223-224.

ENDICOTT, Stephen

(pseudonym for **Walter Adolphe ROBERTS**)

ESEOGHENE

(see **C. Lindsay BARRETT**)

ESCOFFERY, Gloria

b. 1923, Jamaica.
Poet, painter, teacher.

Educated at St. Hilda's High School from which she won the Jamaica Scholarship, Gloria Escoffery was very active in Jamaica in literature and music circles from her late teens. She lived for a long time in England, having done her first degree in Montreal, but is now settled in Jamaica where she works as a painter and teacher. She taught one year in Barbados and became associated with BIM magazine and successfully encouraged other Jamaicans to send contributions to that review. She won poetry awards from the Jamaica Festival: 1970—Certificate of Merit, 1973—Bronze Medal.

Writings: Poetry: In BIM and in anthologies: *Breaklight,* 1973; *Caribbean Voices,* Vol. II, 1970, Vol. I, 1966, and the Combined Edition, London, 1971 and Washington, Robert Luce, 1973.

Short Stories: in *Focus;* BIM.

Miscellaneous articles on theatre and art and reviews: in BIM.

Biographical/Critical Sources: Interview with Alex Gradussov, editor of *Jamaica Journal* at that period, with representations of her paintings as "Gloria Escoffery talks to Alex Gradussov" in *Jamaica Journal,* Vol. 5, No. 1 (March 1971), pp. 34-40.

ESPINET, Charles Albert

b. June 14, 1907, Trinidad.
Folklorist, editor, journalist.

Member of the Trinidad Art Society and the Folklore Society, Espinet has always had a lively interest in culture and the arts.

Writings: Musicology: (with H. Pitts): *Land of Calypso: Origin and Development of Trinidad's Folksong,* Port of Spain, Trinidad, 1941.

FARRIER, Francis Quamina

b. 1938, Guyana.
Playwright, actor, producer.

Farrier has written and had broadcast many radio plays.

Writings: Plays: *The Plight of the Wright* (one act), Georgetown, Guyana, Autoprint, 1969; *The Slave and the Scroll* (one act), Georgetown, Guyana, Autoprint, 1969; *Gaylanda,* three act musical comedy, performed 1966; *Air Partner: A Play in the Vernacular in One Act* (performed 1963); *Manaka: A Play in One Act* (performed 1965); *Loafer's Lane;* and *Border Bridge: A Play in One Act* (performed 1963). For a complete list of his radio plays see R.E. McDowell's *Bibliography of Literature from Guyana,* 1975.

FAZAKERLEY, G.R.

b. ca. 1929, Liverpool (of Jamaican parents).
Novelist.

Fazakerley has never visted the West Indies. His one novel, *A Stranger Here,* is about a rather prissy educated West Indian's efforts to find work and an acceptable wife in prejudiced England. There is no direct experience of the West Indies as such.

Writing: Novel: *A Stranger Here,* London, Macdonald, 1959.

Biographical/Critical Sources: Barrie Davies, "The Sense of Abroad: Aspects of the West Indian Novel in England," in *World Literature Written in English,* Vol. II, No. 2 (November 1972), pp. 67-80.

FERGUSON, Merrill

b. ca. 1930, Jamaica.
Novelist, journalist and commentator.

Ferguson works as a journalist in England. He has contributed to *Alienation—A symposium,* 1960 and his short stories were published variously.

Writing: Novel: *Village of Love,* London, MacGibbon and Kee, 1960 (or 1961).

FERLAND, Barbara

b. 1919, Jamaica.
Poet.

Educated at Brampton and Wolmer's Girls' School, Jamaica, Ferland worked in Jamaica before leaving to live in England to work for the Music Department of the British Council. Although she has never had a collection of poems published, some of her work is outstanding, and she has been published in *Focus* and *Caribbean Voices.* She was a contributor to BBC's Caribbean Voices program. She also is an accomplished musician with interest in folklore. "Expect No Turbulence" is one of her better known poems. It ends:

For we, two lost, two hungry souls, will meet
At common board, with common need for bread.
You in the wood, will gather berries sweet;
I in the dark, taste the salt flesh of the dead.

Ferland is a distinguished writer whose output of verse is small but whose quality is remarkable.

Writings: Poetry: in BIM, and several journals and various Anthologies, including *Caribbean Voices,* Vol. I; Vol. II; *Focus; Caribbean Quarterly,* Vol. 5, No. 3; Federation Commemoration Issue (April 1958); *Independence Anthology* (1962).

FERREIRA, Albert S.

b. ca. 1916, Guyana.
Novelist, storywriter.

Ferreira has published short stories in local periodicals including *Chronicle Christmas Annual* and *Caribia.*

Writing: Novel: *A Sonata is Simple,* Georgetown, British Guiana Lithographic Co., 1946.

FIGUEROA, John (Joseph Maria)

b. August 4, 1920, Jamaica.
Poet, critic, storywriter, university teacher, editor, broadcaster, consultant in education.

Educated at St. George's College, Jamaica, and Holy Cross College, Worcester, Massachusetts, Figueroa did his postgraduate work at London University. He then taught in England for five years before

returning (1953) to Jamaica to be Senior Lecturer in Education at U.C.W.I., Mona. He was the first Jamaican to take up a chair in U.C.W.I. and the first Dean of the Faculty of Education. He also has taught at Indiana University, and lectured at Moscow Pedagogic Institute, University of Washington (Seattle), Makerere University and other schools. He left the U.W.I. in 1971, first on secondment to the University of Puerto Rico, and then finally in 1973, to join Centro Caribeño de Estudios Postgraduados. By that time the Department of Education under his leadership was offering the Ph.D., M.A., Cert. Ed., B.Ed., having started in 1953 with the Diploma in Education only.

Figueroa was the first General Editor of Heinemann's *Caribbean Writers Series,* and he has read papers at international conferences in the West Indies, Santo Domingo, Colombia, Chile, Peru, the U.S.A., the United Kingdom, Russia, France, and in many parts of Anglophone Africa. He has received awards from the British Council, Carnegie and Guggenheim Fellowships. He is a member of International P.E.N., and one-time President of the Jamaica Centre.

Figueroa, who likes to consider himself *un hombre del Caribe,* knows well the whole Caribbean basin. His writings include, besides poems and short stories, work in the fields of criticism, linguistics, education, and sport, having broadcast the Olympics and many cricket matches. This diversity has no doubt affected, adversely, his work in poetry and fiction; but he does write a clear, clean line.

Called by James T. Livingston "perhaps the most classical of West Indian poets . . ." he has also written poems which use the dialect; and poems of a religious as well as experimental nature.

Perhaps Figueroa will be best known for his book *Society, Schools and Progress in the West Indies,* and for his anthology *Caribbean Voices.* The former, although receiving good reviews in many parts of the English-speaking world (e.g.: "the twelfth and perhaps the best in . . . the series . . ."—*Education,* London) did not please the Ministry of Education, Jamaica. The anthology, though adversely criticized in certain of its aspects by Collier (*Commonwealth Newsletter,* June 6, 1974), gets a warm welcome from Cecil Gray (BIM 55, July-Dec 1972):

> *Summarily put, C V is THE comprehensive anthology of West Indian verse, and*

John Figueroa, who holds a chair in education, deserves un-qualified praise for producing it and for demonstrating, incidentally, the indistinguishable oneness of culture—of which poetry is perhaps the highest expression—and education.

Vol. I (completed in 1963, published in 1966), has gone to six impressions; Vol. II (completed in 1966, published in 1970), has gone to two editions. There is also a combined edition published in both the United Kingdom and the United States. The long delay between selection and publication dates has caused some confusion and queries about who should and should not have been included.

Figueroa reads poetry well; he was one of the main readers on the BBC's *Caribbean Voices* for a long time. He and George Lamming have arranged and given readings in many parts of the English-speaking world. Figueroa is the editor and producer of one of the few records of West Indian verse—Caedmon TC 1379, "West Indian Poets reading their own work." And he recorded a series of poems for the Moscow Pedagogic Institute for the Teaching of Languages. His most recent collection is *Ignoring Hurts* (1976).

One of Figueroa's aims is to stress the likeness-in-variety of culture in the Caribbean basin. For this reason he has always kept close contact with El Caribe Hispanico, and with the Spanish language from which he has "imitated" a number of poems including Garcia Lorca's *Despedida:*

If I die
Leave the shutters open
The stumbling child reaches out startling doves
Through open shutters I've seen him
The striding farmer presses plough to earth
Through open shutters I've seen him
If I die
Leave the shutters open

Writings: Poetry and Anthologies: *Blue Mountain Peak* (A collection of poetry and prose), Kingston, Jamaica, 1944; *Caribbean Voices*, Vol. I, London, Evans Brothers, 1966 (Sixth impression, 1974); *Love Leaps Here* (Poetry), London, Evans Brothers, 1962 (Reprinted in volume entitled *Bamboula Dance* [J.A. Jarvis, ed.], Kraus, 1970, Nendeln); *Caribbean Voices*, Vol. II, (*The Blue Horizons*), London, Evans Brothers, 1970 (Second Edition, 1973); *Caribbean Voices* (combined edition of Vol. I and II) London, Evans Bros., 1971; *Caribbean Voices* (combined edition), Washington, D.C., Luce, 1973; *Ignoring Hurts*, Poems, Washington, D.C., Three Continents Press, 1976. Verse in many anthologies, including: *Focus*, 1956, 1960; *The Independence Anthology of '1962; Verse and Voice*, 1965; *Caribbean Voices; Caribbean Verse; Commonwealth Poems of Today; Caribbean Rhythms.* His poem "From the Caribbean with Love" was commissioned for the Commonwealth Festival of 1965.

Pedagogy: *Society, Schools and Progress in the West Indies*, Oxford, New York, Pergamon, 1971.

Chapters in Books: "West Indian Novels" in *Commonwealth Literature*, Heinemann, London, 1965; "Needs and Problems," in *Language Teaching, Linguistics and the Teaching of English in a Multilingual Society*, U.W.I. Faculty of Education, 1965; "Creole Studies," in *Pidginization and Creolization of Languages*, (edited Dell Hymes, Cambridge, Cambridge University Press, 1971; "Poetry and the Teaching of Poetry," in *Literary Studies*, (edited by John H. Dorenkamp), Worchester, Holy Cross College, 1973.

Articles: "The Teacher as Artist: who or what is the efficient cause of Education?" *British Journal of Ed. Studies*, London, 1954; "The Use of Literature in the Teaching of Language?" in PILEI, *Actas*, Bogota, Colombia, 1966; "Language Teaching: Part of a General and Professional Problem," in *English Language Teaching*, London, 1962; "The Value of Philosophy," in *The Idea of a University*, U.C.W.I., Mona, 1961; Bibliographical Article on the theme of *Love* in philosophy, *Cross Currents*, New York, 1952; "V.S. Reid," in

Contemporary Novels, New York, St. Martin's Press, 1972; "John Hearne, West Indian Writer" in *Revista Inter Americana,* Vol. II, No. 1 (San Juan, Puerto Rico, Spring 1972), pp. 72-79; "A Note on Derek Walcott's Concern with Nothing," in *Revista Inter Americana,* Vol. IV, No. 3, pp. 422-428; Review: Walcott's *Another Life,* BIM, No. 58 (1975); Introduction to *A Morning at the Office,* London, Heinemann, pp. vii-xx, 1974; Review of *Jane's Career, World Literature Written in English* (1973), pp. 97-105; Review of V.S. Naipaul's *Overcrowded Barracoon* in *Caribbean Studies,* U.P.R., Puerto Rico (1975); "Tales of the Islands"—a long article on Derek Walcott's *Tales of the Islands* in *World Literature Written in English,* University of Texas (April, 1976).

Poems, reviews, short stories and critical articles have appeared in many magazines and journals, including: BIM; *Caribbean Quarterly; Jamaica Journal; London Magazine; America* (New York); *The Critic* (Chicago); and *BBC* (London).

Short Story: "Ars Long: Vita Brevis" in *West Indian Short Stories* (ed. A. Salkey).

In Progress: "The Poetry of Derek Walcott," for Three Continents Press, 1980 (about 260 pp.).

Biographical/Critical Sources: review of collection *Ignoring Hurts* by Stuart Hall in *Melanthika,* 1977, pp. 38-40; review of *Caribbean Voices,* Cecil Gray, BIM 55 (July-Dec 1972); review by Derek Walcott of *Love Leaps Here,* in *Trinidad Guardian* (1962).

FLAX, Oliver

b. ca. 1942, Antigua.

Shortstory writer, playwright.

Flax was educated in Antigua and at the University of the West Indies, Mona, Jamaica. He has written short stories and a play, "The Legend of Prince Klass"—Carifesta (Guyana), 1972. He is working on short stories for children.

His play "Tantie Gertrude" was performed by the Little Theatre Group of Antigua, and is included in the anthology *Backfire,* compiled and edited by Neville and Undine Guiseppi (London, Macmillan, 1973).

He is editor of the Company Magazine of the W.I. Oil Co., Antigua, where he is Administrative Assistant.

FORDE, A.N. (Freddie)

b. 1923, Barbados.

Poet, playwright, storywriter, editor.

Long connected with writing and cultural activities, Freddie Forde has been one of Barbados' best known civil servants. He has done much work on the literary magazine BIM, has had his work broadcast on the BBC, and has taught for many years.

He was educated at Harrison College, Barbados, did the London University External B.A., and then, some seven years after, took his postgraduate Certificate of Education at Southampton University (1954).

His combined concern for literature and education has found interesting expression in his anthology, *Talk of the Tamarinds,* which is intended for secondary schools in the Caribbean. He has travelled, worked and studied in many countries, including Canada, Scotland, Grenada and Tobago.

Writings: Stories: stories in various journals and anthologies, including: BIM; *From the Green Antilles,* (ed. Barbara Howes), London, Souvenir Press Ltd., 1967, London, Panther, 1971, New York, Macmillan, 1966; *Island Voices: Stories from the West Indies* (ed. A. Salkey), Liveright, 1970; *Response,* (ed. Cecil Grey), Nelson and Sons, London, 1969; *Stories from the Caribbean* (ed. A. Salkey), Dufour, Philadelphia, 1965.

Poetry: (booklet) *Canes by the Roadside* in Miniature Poets series, Guyana. His individual verse appears in various journals and anthologies, including: *Kyk-over-al, Caribbean Quarterly;* BIM; *Caribbean Voices,* Vols. I and II (ed.

J. Figueroa), London, Evans Brothers Ltd., 1970, combined edition, Evans Brothers, 1971 and Washington, Robert Luce Co., Inc., Washington, 1973; *Commonwealth Poetry* (ed. Peter Ludwig Brent), London, Heinemann, 1965.

Play: *The Passing Cloud: a one-act play,* Extra Mural Dept., U.W.I., Mona, Jamaica, n.d. mimeographed, 1966; then published Port of Spain, Trinidad, Extra Mural Dept., U.W.I., 1966 (a psychological drama on civil servants' jealousies).

Editor: Anthology—*Talk of the Tamarinds: an Anthology for Secondary Schools,* London, Edward Arnold and Trinidad, Columbus Publishers, 1971.

Critical reviews in BIM: *Artists-Boys-Cats-Lovers-Judges-Priests,* (Tram Combs), St. Thomas, Virgin Islands, BIM 32, pp. 290-291; *Christopher,* (C. Geoffrey Drayton), BIM 29, p. 64; *Love Leaps Here* (John Figueroa), BIM 37, pp. 63-65; *Muet,* A.L. Hendriks (Micky), BIM 55, pp. 186-188; *These Green Islands* (A.L. Hendriks), BIM 55, pp. 185-188; *Seven Jamaican Poets* (ed. Mervyn Morris), BIM 54, pp. 116-117; *The Shadow which the Soul Must Pass* (Jacqueline Pointer), Regency Press, BIM 51, pp. 194-195; *Turn Again Tiger* (Samuel Selvon), BIM 29, pp. 60-61; *Themes of Song: An Anthology of Guianese Poetry* (ed. A.J. Seymour), BIM 35, pp. 224-225; *In a Green Night* (Derek Walcott), BIM 36, pp. 288-290. *Biographical/Critical Sources:* Review of *Talk of the Tamarinds* (anthology) by John Wickham, in BIM 54, pp. 109-113; Edward Baugh, "West Indian Poetry 1900-1970"; pamphlet—(Savacou Publications Ltd.), pp. 10-11; Andrew Salkey, review of *Talk of the Tamarinds,* in *Caribbean Quarterly,* Vol. 18, No. 3 (Sept. 1972), pp. 80-81.

FOSTER, Denis

b. ca. 1940, Barbados.
Storywriter, poet.

Foster published along with Robert Lee and Paul Layne *Posthumous Papers* (Aug. 1970) and *Banjo Notebook* (Nov. 1970)—the title of the publication was taken from his story "Banjo" which was published in BIM 53 (July-Dec 1971). On the occasion of Paul Layne's death in 1971, Lee and Denis Foster brought out *Music Men* (July 1972) in the name of the trio Foster/Layne/Lee. Denis also helped to publish his brother's work posthumously— (Michael Foster— publication: *Things*).

His verse is in *Caribbean Medlay (Poems),* (BIM 52, Jan-June 1971) and *Caribbean Collage* (BIM 55, July-Dec. 1972).

FOSTER, Michael

b. 1945, Barbados; d. January 8, 1965.
Poet.

Michael Foster was a young Barbadian poet of great promise who met an untimely end at the age of twenty, leaving a number of unpublished poems. A selection of these was prepared and published posthumously under the title of *Things.* Later on his brother Denis Foster, also a writer, together with Robert Lee of St. Lucia and Paul Layne of Barbados, brought out (privately printed) a collection called *Posthumous Papers* (August 1970). Unfortunately, in 1971, Paul Layne was also to die tragically.

Foster had had verse published in BIM (Barbados) before he died; after his death he was published in two mini-collections of poems of West Indian writers in BIM: *Caribbean Mosaic: Poems,* BIM 41 (June-Dec. 1965) and *Caribbean Mosaic II (Poems)* in BIM 43 (July-Dec. 1966). He was also published in *Savacou 7/8* (Jan-June 1973), edited by Edward Brathwaite in the form of a tribute to Frank Collymore.

The poem, "She Was Just Standin There," by Foster was selected and placed in the section BIM CLASSICS.

His poem appears also in the anthology:

Caribbean Voices Vol. II, edited by John Figueroa (London, Evans, 1970).

Writings: Poetry: *Things*, Barbados, Cole's Printery, 1965.

Biographical/Critical Sources: Review of *Things* by E.B.B. Massiah, BIM, Vol. II, No. 42 (Jan-June 1966), pp. 141-143; an appraisal of his work is in BIM 42.

FOWLER, Greta

(née **Todd**—formerly **Greta Bourke**)
b. ca. 1932, Trelawny, Jamaica.
Playwright, theatre producer, teacher.

Educated in Jamaica, Toronto, Canada, and Nova Scotia, Fowler has been very involved with Theatre in Jamaica. Organizer and Founder with a committee of prominent theatrical personnel of the "Little Theatre Movement" in 1941, she has served as president of the L.T.M. Committee which built the Little Theatre. Fowler has directed and produced pantomimes over many years.

Writings: Play: *Out of many, one people, a pageant in ten episodes*, Kingston, Government Printery, 1962.

Biographical/Critical Sources: The importance of the "growth of the Little Theatre Movement over the last 27 years . . . and the opening in 1961 of the Little Theatre" are stressed by Henry Fowler in his "A History of Jamaican Theatre" in *Jamaica Journal*, Vol. 2, No. 1 (March 1968), pp. 52-59.

FRANCOIS, Hunter J.

b. ca. 1918, St. Lucia.
Poet.

Hunter Francois, one-time Minister of Education and Social Services, St. Lucia, is a widely read man. "Hunter," as he is popularly known, can quote enormous passages of prose and poetry from memory—much of Macauly, all of Omar.

Writings: Poetry: *First and Last Poems*, Bridgetown, Barbados, Advocate Company, n.d.
Critical Essays: articles on poetry of the West Indies in various journals.

Biographical/Critical Sources: Review of *First and Last Poems* by J.W.B. Chenery, in BIM, Vol. 3, No. 12, pp. 353-354.

FRANKLYN, Michael

b. ca. 1928, Guyana.
Playwright.

Franklyn is one of the poets published in *Harambee Speaks* (Antigua).

FRASER, Winslow

b. ca. 1928, Guyana.

Fraser has been one of Guyana's most prolific writers of drama, many of them performed but not yet published.

Writings: Plays: *Andel: A Play in One Act* (typescript); *Auntie Annette: A Play in One Act; Bacra Dead ah Backdam: A Play in One Act; Inside the Forum: A Sketch*, performed Guyana, 1958; *Death Cell 13: A Play in One Act* (typescript); *No. 55 Wildroot Alley: A Play in One Act; Death was the Bridegroom: A Play in One Act* (typescript); *Strange Secret*, performed Guyana, 1965 (typescript); *Professor John: A Play in One Act*, performed Guyana, 1963; *Village Delinquent: A Play in Two Acts*, performed Guyana, 1968; *Valley of Tears: A Play in Four Acts*, performed 1969; *Backward Turn Backwards: A Play in Two Acts* (typescript); *Murder in the Playhouse: A Play in Three Acts*, 1970, (typescript); *Life is but an Empty Dream: A Play in Two Acts*, performed Guyana, 1970; *Trouble at Arvida: A Play*, 1971; *Winds of Change: A Play*, performed Guyana, 1971; and *Death Dream of Cassell Barry*, performed Guyana, 1971.

FRAZER, Fitzroy

b. 1936, Jamaica.
Poet, novelist.

Frazer is one of the younger enthusiasts of literature in Jamaica. He has worked as a schoolmaster and written radio scripts and poems. He now lives in Germany.

Writings: Poetry: *The Coming of the Harvest,* Kingston, Mutual Publishing Co., n.d.; *Monologue: Poems,* Kingston, Mutual Publishing Co., 1960; poems in *Focus,* 1960.

Novel: *Wounds in the Flesh,* London, Hutchinson (New Authors), 1962.

FREDERICK, Rawle

b. ca. 1945, Trinidad.
Poet, teacher.

After completing his secondary schooling in Trinidad, Frederick worked for the Inland Revenue Department, Port of Spain, and for the Federation Chemicals Ltd., in Savonetta for several years before going to Canada. Frederick took his B.A. at Presentation College, Canada (1967) and his M.A. in English literature at McGill University, Montreal, where he then began his teaching career. In the years 1973-74 he taught in Tanzania with a grant received from the Canadian Government.

Writings: Poetry: *Transatlantic Cargo,* introduction by Fred Anderson, Montreal, Quebec, Work-Study-Institute's Black Writers' Workshop, 1973.

FULLER, Robert Sevier

b. ca. 1937, Cayman Islands.
Storywriter.

Fuller's one known published work is *Duppies is* (Grand Cayman, Cayman Authors Ltd., 1967).

GALT, Roy

b. June 14, 1922, Trinidad.
Poet.

Galt manages his own book shop in Port of Spain.

Writings: Poetry: *First Try, a book of verse 1943-55,* Trinidad, Guardian Commercial Printery (195?). He has contributed verse to *Voices,* Independence Anniversary Issue, 1964.

GARNETH, Philbert J.

b. ca. 1907, Trinidad.
Novelist.

Garneth began writing his first novel at age 22, in 1929, but was unable to devote sufficient time to complete it as he pursued his career in the construction industry. The work was eventually published in 1974.

Writings: Novel: *The Unfortunate Hero,* San Fernando, Trinidad, by the author, 1974.

GARRETT, Clara Maud

(pseudonym: **C.M.G.**)
b. ca. 1880, Jamaica.
Writer, poet.

Clara Garrett has long lived in the United States but she has kept a concern for her homeland. According to J.E.C. McFarlane, she belonged to that well-known early group of Jamaican women writers, namely, Constance Hollar, Albinia Hutton, Lena Kent, Arabel Moulton-Barrett and "Tropica" (Mary Adela Wolcott). He considers her a "gifted and versatile writer." She is included in his anthology, *A Treasury of Jamaican Poetry.*

Biographical/Critical Sources: Mentioned in J.E. Clare McFarlane's *A Literature in the Making,* Pioneer Press, Jamaica, 1956 (main reference: Chapter 10, pp. 70-75).

GHISAYS, Bobby

b. November, 1935, Kingston, Jamaica.
Playwright, actor, director, teacher, journalist.

Son of a Colombian father and Lebanese mother, Ghisays caught his stage fever from his mercantile family. After schooling at Campion Hall, at Gaynstead High and St. George's College, he tried his hand at the hotel and grocery business without much success. His bent was always theatrical, and as early as his 14th year he had been a member of the chorus in *Busha Blue Beard* in Kingston. In 1935 he played the Prince of Aragon in *The Merchant of Venice* and shortly thereafter he directed his first revue *Travelling Light* with Esther Chapman and Orford St. John in the lead roles.

While taking his B.A. in the U.S., Ghisays also did much college and amateur drama work and then went on to London where he studied at the Royal Academy of Dramatic Arts. After minor roles as a reporter or policeman in such films as *The Reclining Figure* and *Make a Million,* he determined to return to Jamaica. By now married to the Welsh actress Sylvia Aberyswyth, Ghisays began to write plays. The next years however saw the couple back in England, twice in Italy, acting, teaching, and translating. He caught on as a reporter with Reuters covering the Italian film scene particularly in the late 1960s.

He directed *Picnic in Town* and *To Dorothy a Son* and did some plays for BBC in London, and in 1970, once again home in Jamaica, he worked at the Jamaica Broadcasting Company in Public Affairs. In 1971 he acted in *Rockstone Annancy* and *Two for the Sea-saw,* the latter also being directed by him. There followed his own play *Is Everybody Happy* during which his wife died in an automobile crash.

In 1974 Ghisays converted the Way Out Discotheque at the Pegasus Hotel, Kingston, into an intimate review theatre format and in August put on his very successful *8 o'clock Jamaica Time Strikes Again,* the first of several productions, including one in Toronto that fall which was billed along with Louise Bennett and Jerry Craig in a Jamaica promotional show.

Other works of his performed were *Two's a Crowd, The Man in the Moon is a Ms,* both revues, and *Come Home to Jamaica,* which also found an enthusiastic audience in a New York run.

Plays he has directed besides those cited were *Dat; Annie Get Your Gun;* and *Peter Pan.*

Biographical/Critical Sources: "The Busiest Director in Town," by Verena Reckord, interview with Ghisays, in *The Jamaica Daily News* (Sunday May 29, 1977), pp. 6-7.

GILKES, Michael

b. 1933, Guyana.
Literary critic, essayist, dramatist, and university teacher.

Gilkes is a distinguished critic who combines teaching, research and creative writing. He has recently become tenured lecturer in English at U.W.I., Cave Hill, Barbados.

Writings: Plays: *Couvade,* London, Longman Caribbean, 1975; and *In Transit,* performed, Georgetown, 1969.

Essays: "The Art of Extremity—Wilson Harris' Ascent to Omai," *Caribbean Quarterly* 17, 3 and 4 (1971), p. 33; "Racial Identity and Individual Consciousness in the Caribbean Novel," (text of 1974 Edgar Mittelholzer Memorial lectures); "The Role of Drama in the University," *New World Quarterly* 2, 2 (1964). p. 3; "The Spirit in the Bottle: A Reading of Mittelholzer's *A Morning at the Office,*" in *World Literature Written in English* 14, I (1975), p. 237.

Literary Criticism: *Wilson Harris and the Caribbean Novel,* London, Longman Caribbean, 1975.

GILL, Margaret

b. ca. 1947, Barbados.
Poet, teacher.

Edward Brathwaite links Margaret Gill, Elizabeth Clarke and Anthony Hinkson as three of the "Young Bajans" who are most talented and promising writers. They belong to a literary group which operates out of the Erdiston Teachers College and produced *Unchained* for Carifesta in Guyana (1972). Brathwaite in his notes on these writers in *Savacou 7/8,* a tribute to Frank Collymore, remarks that Margaret Gill's poem "Canecutter" has already become a classic: it appears in *Savacou 7/8,* (Jan-June 1973), Savacou Publications Ltd., Kingston, Jamaica.

GIMENEZ, J.P.

b. ca. 1923, U.S. Virgin Islands.
Poet, folklorist.

Gimenez is one of the earliest published poets from the Virgin Islands.

Writings: Caribbean Echoes, New York, Galleon Press, 1934 (62 pp.); *Deep Waters,* St. Thomas, The Art Shop, 1939 (72 pp.); *Voice of the Virgin Island's Mystic Poet,* Philadelphia, Dorrance and Co., 1952 (50 pp.); *Virgin Islands Folklore and other Poems,* New York, Harding, 1953 (contains folklore and other poems with strong overtones of American patriotism).

GIUSEPPI, Neville

b. December 26, 1909, Trinidad.
Essayist, poet, editor, free-lance writer.

Giuseppi has edited and selected with Undine Giuseppi (his wife) the collection of short stories for use in secondary schools; *Backfire* (London, Macmillan, 1973). His work appears in various anthologies including the Federation Commemoration Issue of *Caribbean Quarterly* Vol. 5, No. 3 (April 1958) and his work has been broadcast over the BBC. He has been a retired civil servant since 1969.

Writings: Poetry: *Verse and Prose,* 1940; *The Light of Thought: a Book of Poems,* Port of Spain, Trinidad, Guardian Commercial Printery, 1943; also by the same printery, *From Grave to Gay,* 1959; *Selected Poems,* 1972/3?, Trinidad.

Essays: *A Modern Pilgrim's Script (being a collection of original aphorisms and reflections with some brief miscellanies),* London, Stockwell, 1938.

GIUSEPPI, Undine

b. ca. 1914, Barbados (lives and works in Trinidad).
Biographer, poet, storywriter, teacher, compiler, editor.

Undine Giuseppi, formerly Vice Principal of St. Augustine's Girls' High School, Trinidad and now Principal of the University School, is the wife of Trinidadian novelist and poet, Neville Giuseppi. With Neville she compiled *Backfire;* they also published in 1976 an anthology of verse for secondary schools, *Out for Stars* (Book 2, Macmillan, London).

She started writing from a very early age. At the age of eight she won a school writing competition; and she had stories published in an English children's magazine at age 11 and again at age 12. She has written biographies on two of the greatest West Indian cricketers, Learie Constantine and Frank Worrell. She published a collection of short stories and poems in 1944, has produced a series of school readers, edited text books and produced a television series on creative writing. She edits a periodical, *Small World,* for children which includes stories, poems, and regular features. It is published by Key Caribbean Publications.

Writings: Stories and Poems: *These Things are Life* (a collection of short stories and poems), 1944.

Biographies: *Sir Frank Worrell,* London, Nelson, 1969; *Learie Constantine,* London, Nelson, 1974.

Compiled: *Writing is Fun,* a collection of short stories and light verse published during International Book Year, Trinidad, 1972.

Edited and selected with Neville Giuseppi: *Backfire,* a collection of various pieces for Secondary Schools, London, Macmillan, 1973.

Biographical/Critical Sources: Review of *Sir Frank Worrell* by Zac Perez in *Trinidad Guardian,* (March 5, 1969): "The Start of Worrell's Immortality," and Review of *Sir Frank Worrell,* by John Wickham in BIM 49, pp. 59-64.

GLADWELL, Joyce

(née **NATION**)
b. ca. 1939, Jamaica.
Autobiographer, teacher.

Gladwell was educated in Jamaica and at London University. She did research for two years in the old Department of Education, Mona, U.W.I., Jamaica. Her one work deals with the major social issues and personal problems of our time—race, color, human relationships, mixed marriage, and the search for God.

Writings: Autobiography: *Brown Face, Big Master,* London, Inter-Varsity Press, May 1969.

GOMES, Albert

b. March 25, 1911, Trinidad; d. January 13, 1978, London.
Poet, novelist, storywriter, editor, politician.

Bertie Gomes, as he was known to all and sundry in the Caribbean, loomed large, in more senses than one, in politics for some thirty years until about 1962, the year of the dissolution of the ill-fated West Indian Federation. He lost, by a large margin, his seat in the Trinidad House, and for a number of reasons, interestingly set out in his Autobiography, *Through a Maze of Colour,* left the West Indies to live in London, which he had so often visited as a V.I.P. on Government business.

But, although known as a politician, he had not only written poetry, but was a stalwart upholder of folk arts and folk ways; had written critical articles, and of course, was part of that cultural reawakening which clustered around *The Beacon.* As he puts it:

> *I had been away in the United States during 1928-1930 . . . someone sent me . . . a collection . . . that Alfred M. Mendes, another Trinidadian of Portuguese ancestry, had compiled . . . I was very excited. . . .*
>
> *Back in Trinidad, I discovered that Mendes had gathered around him a small circle of young men who shared his interest in literature and music, argued way into the night, and read excerpts from each other's writings. . . . from it arose the movement of the Thirties that played such an important part in the literary development of the island. . . . It was around my magazine 'The Beacon' that this movement grew, the movement giving "The Beacon" the initial push forward. (p. 16)*

Gomes's poetry is of the rather spontaneous, loose variety. He appears in BIM and *Caribbean Voices.* A collection is soon to come out in New York. He was one of the people who spotted the genius of Derek Walcott early. Of a pugnacious nature, the "enfant terrible" of early local independence politics, his writing is often humorous and polysyllabic. He returned his CMG to the English Government when they perpetrated the Immigration Act. His introduction to his autobiography ends with the following paragraph:

> *I was born into this polychromatic maze and, although considered "white," was elected to the highest offices available to natives at the time. Indeed, for the better part of some two decades, there was hardly an area of public activity where my influence was not felt. It is of this that I have written and, in a final chapter, of yet another which promises to be quite as unique and as exciting: for I am now a citizen of the United Kingdom where, because of my swarthiness—a throwback, doubtless, to some remote Moorish ancestor—I am for all practical purposes "coloured."*

Gomes was one of the earliest enthusiasts and supporters for the steel bands gradually developing pan music and calypso in the back ways of Trinidad.

Writings: Autobiography: *Through a Maze of Colour,* Port of Spain, Trinidad, Key Caribbean Publications Ltd., 1974.

Editor: *From Trinidad: Poems and short stories,* Port of Spain, Trinidad, 1937; a new collection bearing that title, edited by Reinhard Sander was published by Houghton-Stoddard, 1978.

Published with A.H. Mendes, Ernest Carr, C.L.R. James and others: *The Beacon,* 1931-1933.

Novel: *All Papa's Children,* East Molesey (Surrey, England), Cairi Publishing House, 1978.

Biographical/Critical Sources: Anson Gonzalez in *Self-Discovery Through Literature (Creative Writing in Trinidad and Tobago),* (Trinidad, 1966), has this to say of Albert (Bertie) Gomes: "One of the giants, unacknowledged that is, of our literary world, who was making an effort to create a literary tradition not only for Trinidad and Tobago but for the entire West Indies as well, . . . *The Beacon* was his baby and brainchild. . . ."

GONZALEZ, Anson John

b. ca. 1934, Trinidad.

Poet, essayist, teacher, critic, free-lance journalist, dramatist, photographer.

Anson Gonzalez has a clear interest in the literature and culture of Trinidad and Tobago. He is a part-time tutor for the Extra Mural Dept., U.W.I., and has taught English at Mausica Teachers College for many years. He is a Fellow of the International Poetry Society. The poem "Cadence" from his book *Score* exploits the rhythms of the steel band and the imagery of carnival in a saddened atmosphere of loss as the once hearty life of the spontaneous islanders becomes the raw material for tourist shows and mock-gay "Panorama" night. The "pan" beat of the steel oil drums becomes "pan-ic" in this poem:

> *The sound of silence*
> *is the sound of fear*
> *is the empty sound*
> *of the steel pan-ic*
> *orchestration,*
> *Oh listen to that cadence*
> *of suspense of suspicion*
> *and pause suspended*
> *while the maestro massa*
> *with arms upraised*
> *freezes the status quo.*

Gonzalez' *Trinidad and Tobago Literature on Air* (1974) has informative discussions on C.L.R. James and Alfred H. Mendes, DeWilton Rogers, H.M. Telemaque, Sam Selvon, V.S. Naipaul, Earl Lovelace, and many others.

Writings: Poetry: *The Love Song of Boysie B and other poems.* (60 poems), Port of Spain, privately printed, 1974; *Score* (written with Victor D. Questel), Trinidad and Tobago, 1972; and verse in various journals; verse in *Voices* (C. Sealy, ed.).

Essays: *Self-Discovery Through Literature: Creative Writing in Trinidad and Tobago,* St. Augustine, privately printed, 1972 (54 pp.); "25 Years of Reading/51 Years of Writing," work paper for a seminar on Caribbean literature in English (Nov. 30-Dec. 1, 1973—Port of Spain), on file in Central Library of Trinidad and Tobago, Port of Spain; *Trinidad and Tobago Literature on Air,* Port of Spain, Trinidad, National Council of Trinidad and Tobago, 1974.

Editor/Publisher: *"The New Voices" Trinidad-Tobago;* first published in Feb. 1973, "A forum for regional writers."

GONZALEZ, Maria

b. 1964, Trinidad.
Poet.

The daughter of Anson and Sylvia Gonzalez, both writers, Maria Gonzalez published her first volume of poems at ten years of age, *Step by Step.* It was highly commended by the Commonwealth Poetry Adjudicators. She has been featured on local radio and TV, and has been selected for *New Voices* writer of the year, 1974.

Writings: Poetry: *Step by Step,* Trinidad and Tobago, 1974. In 1974 her work was published in *Poems* (Ministry of Education and Culture); *Express; Caribbean Contact;* the *St. James R.C. Church Newsletter,* and *The New Voices.*

GONZALEZ, Sylvia

b. ca. 1940, Trinidad.
Poet, essayist, folklorist.

Sylvia Gonzalez' work, verse and prose, has appeared in various publications, including *The New Voices.* She is an educationalist interested in folklore. One of her articles: "Steel Band 15 years ago" is an important source of information on this Trinidad phenomenon.

GOODISON, Lorna Gaye

b. August 1, 1947, Kingston, Jamaica.
Poet, art teacher, advertising copywriter.

Goodison was educated at St. Hugh's High School, and the Art Students League, New York. Her poems have been published in the local newspapers and the *Jamaica Journal*—Institute of Jamaica, and her work has been used by the actors Mathews and Ken Corsbie of Guyana.

Illustrations done by her will be in Mervyn Morris' forthcoming collection of poems dealing with Holy Week.

A young writer of efficiency, insight and charm, she is currently working on a book of poems to be published by Sangster's Books Ltd.

GRADUSSOV, Alex

b. ca. 1930 (now resident in Jamaica).
Playwright, scholar, folklorist, teacher, editor, writer.

Gradussov has contributed much to advance Jamaican and West Indian knowledge of local culture and history by his elegant editing of *Jamaica Journal.* He has not himself written much fiction, but he did co-author with Sylvia Wynter the Jamaica Pantomime, *Rockstone Anancy,* which broke new ground. He has published many reviews and interviews.

Writings: Editor: *Anancy in Love* (Tales collected by Lily Perkins), Kingston, Jamaica Publishing House, 1971; and (with Sylvia Wynter): *Rockstone Anancy, a magical morality* (Jamaican Pantomime), produced in Jamaica, 1970.

GRANGE, Peter

(pseudonym for **Christopher [Robin] Nicole**)

GRAY, Cecil Roderick

b. February 11, 1923, Trinidad.
Shortstory writer, editor, poet, critic, university teacher, actor.

Educated in the "good old days" of "payment by results," Gray worked his way up to Teachers Training College by doing excellently in examinations. He then read externally for his London B.Sc. degree. He was awarded a scholarship to do the Post Graduate Diploma Education, U.C.W.I., Mona. He was taken on to the staff of U.W.I.'s Dept. of Education and has worked there ever since. He is now Director, In-Service Diploma in Education Programme, U.W.I., Mona.

Although his short stories have not been collected, there can be no doubt that he is a master of that genre—as a look at some of the older BIMs will show. He has also published verse. More recently he has been concentrating on books which promote and help the teaching of English in the schools of the West Indies. He has also done much to promote drama and the teaching of drama among teachers in training at the university. An outstanding actor, his performance in the Nigerian playwright Wole Soyinka's *The Road* will not soon be forgotten.

His poems and reviews have appeared in BIM and *Savacou.* Another one of those gifted West Indians who have not been able to—(who could not *humanly* choose to?)—concentrate on writing poems and short stories.

Writings: School Texts: *Response* (anthology of W.I. stories), Thomas Nelson, 1969 (Reprinted five times); *Language For Living: Stage I,* (School text for language teaching), Longmans, 1969 (Reprinted several times); *Stage 2,* 1970 (Rerinted several times); *Stage 3,* 1971 (Reprinted several times); *Stage 4,* 1973; *Stage 5,* 1973.

Poetry: *West Indian Poetry* (anthology with K. Ramchand), London, Longmans, 1971; *Bite In One* (anthology of poems for secondary education), London, Thomas Nelson, 1972; *Bite In-Two,* London, 1972; *Bite In-Three,* London, 1972 (all three books reprinted three times).

His poems are in *Images* (anthology of W.I. stories), London, Thomas Nelson, 1973, and *Teachers' Herald,* Trinidad; BIM; *Savacou; Caribbean Rhythms; Torch* (Min. of Education, Jamaica).

Stories: in BIM and on *Caribbean Voices,* BBC program.

Play: *Family Name: a play in one act,* Kingston, Extra Mural Dept., U.C.W.I., (n.d.), 14 pp., mimeo.

Professional articles: in *Caribbean Quarterly; Teacher Education* (O.U.P.); *Teacher Education for New Countries* (O.U.P.); *Teaching* (O.U.P.); *Jamaica Journal; Torch* (Min. of Ed. Jamaica).

Biographical/Critical Sources: John Wickham, review of *Response* in BIM, Vol. 13, No. 49, (July-Dec. 1969), p. 59.

GREENE, Eustace

(pseudonym for **M. R. MONAR**)

GRIFFITH, Reginald (Reggie)

b. April 4, 1937, Trinidad.
Playwright, writer, actor, guitarist.

Educated in Trinidad and at Wisconsin University, U.S.A., Griffith is an agricultural research worker in Redring disease in coconuts. He has contributed to *Art* and *Man Magazine,* 1968, and has recorded the song "Scrunting Man."

Writings: Cas Brain and Other Stories, (a collection), 1968.

Plays: *Home on the Hills, a one-act play,* Barataria, Trinidad, Tri Color Printery, 1967; *Justina,* performed by Cumuto Village Council, 1975; placed second in the Best Village Competition and won numerous awards; *Perils of San Jose.*

GUY, Rosa

b. ca. 1925, Trinidad.
Novelist.

A long-time resident of Harlem, Rosa Guy was taken to the United States as a child. Involved in the American Theatre Movement and a student of drama during World War II, she later attended New York University to study writing under Viola Brothers Shaw. She helped to found the Harlem Writers' Guild.

Writings: Novel: *Bird at My Window,* New York, Lippincott, 1965, London, Souvenir Press, 1966; *Friends,* 1973.

HAMALUDIN, Mohamed

b. ca. 1938, Guyana.
Poet, playwright, shortstory writer.

Hamaludin's poetry is in *Kyk-over-al*, Cameron's *Guianese Poetry*, and appeared in local newspapers. His short stories have appeared in *Chronicle Christmas Annual*. With R.C.G. Potter he is the composer of the Guyana National Anthem.

Writings: Plays: (in typescript): *Gentlemen-at-Alms—A Play in One Act; Whom the Gods Love: A Tragedy in Three Acts;* and *Much Married Mary*, performed Guyana, 1968.

HAMILTON, Aileen

b. ca. 1934, Barbados.
Poet, storywriter, painter.

She has done frontispieces for BIM, especially one of Frank Collymore in BIM 38 (Jan-June 1964), and her verse and short stories have appeared in BIM.

HAMILTON, Bruce

b. 1900, England (lived for many years in Barbados); d. 1975 or 1976.
Novelist, poet, playwright.

Bruce Hamilton is an Englishman who lived a long time in Barbados and became a great friend of Frank Collymore and of BIM. He now lives in Hove, Brighton, England. He is the brother of Patrick Hamilton (author of *Gaslight*), whose biography he has written. He was an Assistant Master at Harrison College, Barbados, from 1927-1929 and 1938-1950. He was the first Principal of the Barbados Evening Institute. He left Barbados c. 1960.

He published poetry, drama, and miscellaneous articles in BIM.

He also contributed a tribute to Frank Collymore in *Savacou 7/8* dedicated to Collymore (Edward Brathwaite, ed.), (Jan-June 1973), Savacou Publications Ltd.

Writings: Novel: *Too Much of Water*, London, Cresser Press, 1958 (illustrated).

Plays: *Smartly Outsmarted: A Perversion of Shakespeare (In One Act)*, in BIM 11, pp. 203-208; *Gettysburg Night (A Play in One Act)*, in BIM 21, pp. 35-43.

Theatre Reviews: *Gaslight* (Patrick Hamilton), A Bridgetown Players Production, BIM 10, pp. 172-175; *The Shop at Sly Corner*, Bridgetown Players, BIM 15, pp. 222-223; *The Circle* (Somerset Maughan), The Bridgetown Players, BIM 16, pp. 292-293.

Other Works: *Cricket in Barbados*, 1947; *Barbados and the Confederation Question*, 1956; *The Light Went Out*.

Biographical/Critical Sources: Review of *Too Much of Water* by M. Combe Martin in BIM 29, pp. 61-62.

HAMILTON, Doreen

b. ca. 1935, Trinidad.
Storywriter, medical social worker.

Hamilton's story "Obituary for Doolarie" in *Voices* (1964) is thoughtful, compassionate, and a touch dramatic. She is the wife of Clifford Sealy, writer and editor and owner of the well-known The Book Shop, Port of Spain.

Hamilton's stories and articles have been published in Trinidad and have been broadcast on the BBC.

HAMILTON, Norma

b. ca. 1944, Jamaica.
Storywriter, poet, playwright.

One of the "new" writers, Hamilton's short stories, plays and poetry have gained awards in the Jamaica National Festivals.

Writings: Short Stories: "Run, Billy, Run" (Honour Award, 1964); "Death of Howard," (Bronze Medal, 1970), (with Trevor Burrowes); "Birthday Drive," (Silver Medal, 1972).

Play: (Three-Act) *These People Never Learn* (Bronze Medal, 1970).

Poetry: "Do Offica Do" (Bronze Medal), 1971; "Black Yout Pleas Middle-Class Social Conscious Jamaica," (Certificate of Merit, 1973).

Biographical/Critical Sources: Gerald Moore's article "Use Men Language," in BIM 57 (March 1974), pp. 69, 70.

HANNAYS, Kitty

(see under pseudonym: **MACAW**)

HARNEY, Leonora

b. ca. 1933, Barbados.
Storywriter.

Harney is a member of the Writers' Guild of Barbados; her work appeared in BIM, Nos. 37 and 40.

HARRIS, [Theodore] Wilson

(pseudonym for poetry only: **KONA WORUK**)
b. March 24, 1921, New Amsterdam, British Guiana (Guyana).
Novelist, critic, poet.

Wilson Harris was educated at Queen's College, Georgetown. He was a Government surveyor, becoming Senior Surveyor, 1955-1958. He travelled extensively through Guyana; now makes his home in the U.K. But he has travelled widely lecturing and holding posts of writer-in-residence—in Australia, New York, Texas, Toronto, Cuba. He has also lectured at the University of the West Indies.

Wilson Harris has added new dimensions to Caribbean fiction—he almost calls into question the category of Caribbean as he brings into play a continental landscape, rather than one of islands and the sea. This is particularly important to note in Harris, for as Hena Maes-Jelinek puts it, "The landscape always acts as a prime mover to consciousness in Wilson Harris's novels, stirring man's imagination and helping him to define himself." (*Contemporary Novelists,* St. James Press Ltd., 1972, p. 564).

Harris has been much acclaimed by many critics including C.L.R. James. Anthony Boxhill speaks of his "tremendous success in evoking the timelessness and mystery of the forests, rivers, and waterfalls of his setting, and in suggesting their effects upon the personalities of the Caribs . . ." Ramchand also is clearly impressed by his work.

Harris is at the far end of the scale from the social realism which was instituted by Mendes, and which has continued to be one of the main modes of West Indian fiction. But, of course, Harris, in being innovative, runs great risks, and he ignores the usual formalities of the novel to such an extent that it is not always easy for the reader to follow whither he is being led. According to Ramchand, Harris is "trying to create a sense of man's original condition of terror and freedom prior to the accretions of history and civilization." But was there ever a time really of this kind?

There can be no doubt that, whatever might be the difficulties, Harris is engaged in a central deviation from the usual descriptive, realist, ostensive type of Caribbean fiction towards the *using* of the landscape to make puzzles of human existence carry a meaning that radiates outward with further meanings. Oddly enough in this respect he is nearest to one who differs from him in many ways—George Lamming (cf. *In The Castle,* and of *Natives of My Person*).

Harris has a further ingredient in his experience which he exploits excellently—he is one of the few West Indian writers who has lived and worked with Amerindians. And this, in an odd way, links him closely with the islands where the Caribs and the Arawaks have strong mythological influence but are mostly notable by their actual absence.

Harris is a conscious artist, and is not unaware of some of the difficulties of his particular approach. He says of his imagery which "has as an exotic device but as a subjective alteration of form in order to relate new content or new existences to a revised canvas of community." (Introduction to the paper-covered edition of the *Whole Armour,* Faber, 1973)

Louis James tackles this problem of Harris's difficulty, and attempts to take seriously some of what appears to be weaknesses in his work in an interesting article in the *New World Guyana Independence Issue.* He suggests that Harris's poetry and prose/ cum poetry have to be taken together. He feels that many of Harris's preoccupations in the novels are clarified in the verse, and the more difficult parts of the poem become easier to understand after studying the prose. But he does not entirely reassure the reader by stating "For Harris, time and space are exploded, and as in atomic physics, matter is transformed into energy and vice versa, a person may turn into a place, a place into an aspiration." In fact, Harris takes *seriously* the central place of *fiction* in man's struggle with his inner and outer environments, with his trying to put together the present and the past, the moment with movement, eternity and season, the everflowing river and the everlasting sea. He attempts in novels what older writers attempted in long poems. In order to come to grips with his experience of the world, not least of all the primal Guiana forests, he does what Penelope did for a different reason: in the daytime he weaves the mighty web, and at night he unravels the same.

It is not Harris's fault that many a reader who will accept in films the bizarre, and also a completely unrealistic, mosaic line of development, will nonetheless ask of his novelist some form of social realism and many aspects of the documentary! But it is Harris's weakness that at times his medium, that of words, does not seem to have embodied his deep fictional insights. In some ways he is most like the Cuban Carpentier. But Carpentier, even when most probing and complicated, has a limpidity of statement which is closer to Martin Carter's way of statement—even in his deepest poetry, than Harris's.

There can be little doubt that Harris has introduced a genuine new and interesting element to West Indian fiction: he has a unique vision, a unique imaginational approach to man's place in his environment, and especially to the human existence of those who struggle with the forest and the river and the sea. It is just that at times we long for the sun to burst forth:

> *Clouds experience youth and age when they glance so quickly across the earth, and fall to the deep world around in tiny raindrops and mist. Skies clear and vision finds the torrent sparkling in the sun.*
>
> ("Spirit of the Fall" in *Eternity to Season,* p. 42).

Wilson Harris has received many awards, including the Arts Council Grant, 1968. He was Visiting Lecturer, State Univ. of New York, Buffalo, 1970; Writer in Residence, Scarborough College, University of Toronto, 1970; Visiting Lecturer

University of the West Indies, Mona, Jamaica; Commonwealth Fellow in Caribbean Literature, Leeds University, Yorkshire, U.K., 1971; Delegate to the National Identity Conference, Brisbane, 1968; Delegate to U.N.E.S.C.O. Symposium on Caribbean Literature, Cuba, 1968; Visiting Professor of Ethnic Studies and English at University of Texas at Austin, Spring 1972.

Most recently, Harris has added two new novelettes to his long list of titles in the combined volume *Da Silva, Da Silva's Cultivated Wilderness,* and *Genesis of the Clowns* (1977). The first deals with a Brazilian-born painter, English educated, who with his spirited wife, lives in a vividly alive London. *Genesis* in contrast returns to Harris' favorite character, a surveyor, busy in charting the still mysterious rivers of upper Guyana.

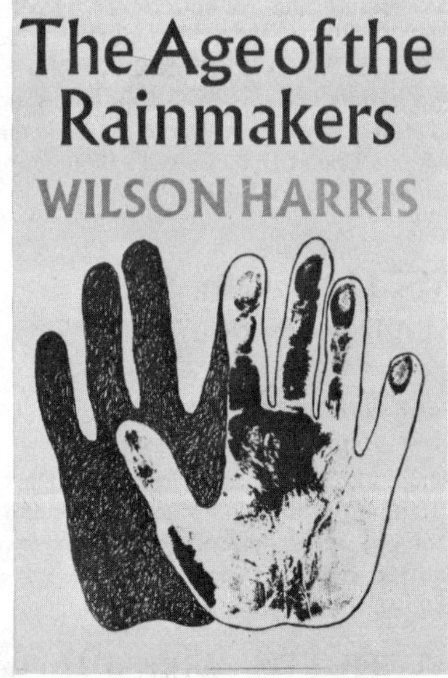

Writings: Novels: *Palace of the Peacock,* London, Faber, 1960; in paperback by Faber, London, 1968, (preface by Kenneth Ramchand); *The Far Journey of Oudin,* London, Faber, 1961; *The Whole Armour,* London, Faber, 1962; in combined volume with *The Secret Ladder* (Faber, 1963); *The Secret Ladder,* London, Faber, 1963; in combined volume with *The Whole Armour* (Faber, 1962); *Heartland,* London, Faber, 1964; *The Eye of the Scarecrow,* London, Faber, 1965; *The Waiting Room,* London, Faber, 1967; *Tumatumari,* London, Faber, 1968; *Ascent to Omai,* London, Faber, 1970; *Black Marsden,* London, Faber, 1972; *Companions of the Day and Night,* London, Faber, 1975; *Genesis of the Clowns,* London, Faber, 1975, and republished with *Da Silva, Da Silva's Cultivated Wilderness,* London, Faber & Faber, 1977.

Short Stories: *The Sleepers of Roraima: A Carib Trilogy,* London, Faber, 1970; *The Age of the Rainmakers,* London, Faber, 1971. His short stories and extracts from novels appear in various journals and collections including: *Kyk-over-al; Ariel; Black Orpheus; West Indian Stories; My Lovely Native Land; West Indian Narrative; Caribbean Rhythms;* Thieme's *Anthology of West Indian Literature.*

Verse: (pseudonym Kona Waruk for first two titles): *Fetish,* British Guiana, 1951 (Miniature Poet Series); *Eternity to Season,* British Guiana, Magnet Printery, 1952, and *Eternity to Season* (Poems of separation and reunion), British Guiana, privately printed, 1954, and reprint, Kraus, Nendeln, 1970; *The Well and the Land* (Studies in Time), British Guiana, 1952. His verse appears in journals and collections including: *Kyk-over-al; Kaie; New World* (1966); *Guyana Independence Issue; Caribbean Voices; The Sun's Eye; Poet 13, I* (1972); *Themes of Song; Fourteen Guianese Poems for Children; West Indian Poetry; My Lovely Native Land; Caribbean Verse.*

Others: *History, Fable and Myth in the Caribbean and Guianas,* Text of 1970 Edgar Mittelholzer Memorial Lectures, Georgetown, National History and Arts Council, 1970; *Tradition and the West Indian Novel,* London, West Indian Students Union, 1965; introduction by C.L.R. James (A Lecture delivered to the London West Indian Students Union, May 15, 1964); and London and Port of Spain, Trinidad, New Beacon Books, 1965; Also: *Tradition, the Writer and Society: Critical Essays,* London, and Port of Spain, Trinidad, New Beacon Books, 1967; and New York, Panther House, 1971.

Critical Essays: "The Phenomenal Legacy," in *The Literary Half-Yearly* (Mysore, India, XI, 2, July 1970), pp. 1-6; "The Enigma of Values," in

New Letters, 40, No. I (Oct. 1973) which is the author's analysis of the leading contrapuntal themes in his *Tumatumari* and *The Palace of the Peacock;* and "The Manuscript of Ascent to Omai" discusses the acquisition of the ms. of that work by the Humanities Research Center of the University of Texas at Austin in 1970; "Interior of the Novel: Amerindian/European/ African Relations," National Identity Papers delivered at the Commonwealth Conference University of Queensland, Brisbane, August 9-15, 1968 (K.L. Goodwin, ed.), London, Heinemann, 1970, (p. 138); "Impressions After Seven Years," *New World* (Fortnightly) 44 (1966), p. 17; "The Guiana Book by A.J. Seymour," *Kyk-over-al,* 7 (1948), p. 37; "The Question of Form and Realism in the West Indian Artist," *Kyk-over-al* 15 (1952), p. 23 (in Harris' *Tradition, the Writer and Society*).

Biographical/Critical Sources: Joyce Sparer, "Wilson Harris and the Twentieth Century Man," *New Letters,* 40, I (1973), p. 49; and "The Art of Wilson Harris," *New Beacon Reviews* I (1968), p. 22 (John LaRose, ed.); also "Tumatumari and the Imagination of Wilson Harris," *Journal of Commonwealth Literature,* 7 (1967); introduction by C.L.R. James to *Tradition and the West Indian Novel,* 1965. Also *Kas-Kas, Interviews with three Caribbean Writers in Texas,* Austin, The University of Texas at Austin (Occasional Publication of the African and Afro-American Research Institute, 1972); "The Writer as Alchemist, The Unifying Role of Imagination in Wilson Harris' Novels," by Hena Maes-Jelinek, in *Language and Literature* (Copenhagen) Autumn 1971; and *Ascent to Omai,* review in *Literary Half-Yearly* (Mysore) Jan. 1972; C.L.R. James, "Wilson Harris—A Philosophical Approach," from a lecture given April 1965, at St. Augustine, U.W.I., Trinidad; Kenneth Ramchand, *The West Indian Novel and Its Background,* New York, Barnes and Noble, 1970, references: Oeuvre outlined, 8-12, pp. 41, 72, 153; Gerald Moore, *Chosen Tongue,* London, Longman, 1969; *The Naked Design:* a reading of *Palace of the Peacock* by Hena Maes-Jelinek, Dangaroo Press, (Dept. of Commonwealth Literature at Aarhaus University, Denmark, Sept. 1975); *Enigma of Values: an introduction* (Ann Rutherford and Kirsten Holst Peterson, eds.), Dangaroo Press, Denmark, May 1975; "The introductory chapter describes the critical approach to literature of the West Indian Critic and novelist W.H.; the remaining six chapters (including one by W.H.) apply this critical approach to several novels by W.H. plus other well-known works . . ." (quote from the press release by Anna Rutherford); Wilson Harris, in *Contemporary Novelists* by Hena-Maes Jelinek (St. Martin's Press, New York, 1972); Review of *Eternity to Season* by A.J. Seymour in BIM 22, pp. 133-135; Review of *Palace of the Peacock* by F.A. Collymore, in BIM 33, p. 76; Review of *The Far Journey of Oudin* by Karl Sealy in BIM 35, pp. 223-224; *Tumatumari,* review by Gerald Moore in BIM 51, pp. 193-194: *The Waiting Room,* review by Joyce Sparer in *Caribbean Quarterly,* Vol. 14, Nos. I and II, pp. 148-151; Dennis Scott, "Novels of Wilson Harris reveal Guyana History," in *Sunday Gleaner,* Jamaica, (Feb. 22, 1970), pp. 4-10; W.J. Howard, "Wilson Harris and the Alchemical Imagination," in the Literary Half-Yearly, XI, 2 (July 1970); Michael Gilkes, *Wilson Harris and the Caribbean Novel,* (London, Longman Caribbean, 1975); John Hearne, "The Fugitive in the Forest: A Study of Four Novels by Wilson Harris," *The Journal of Commonwealth Literature,* IV (Dec. 1967), pp. 99-112; also his essay in *The Islands in Between,* (Louis James, ed.), London, O.U.P., 1968. For a more detailed listing, see Robert E. McDowell's *Bibliography of Literature from Guyana,* 1975.

HASELL, Vivian

b. ca. 1926, Jamaica.
Poet.

Hasell's poetry has appeared in two modest volumes in the 1960's.

Writings: Poetry: *Poems,* Ilfracombe, Devon, U.K., Arthur Stockwell, 1956; *First fruits of me,* Ilfracombe, Devon, U.K., Arthur H. Stockwell Ltd., 1965 (63 pp.).

HATCHETTE, Wilfred Irwin

b. ca. 1918, U.S. Virgin Islands.
Poet.

Hatchette's one collection of verse, one of the earliest ever from the Virgins, was *Youth's Flight,* St. Thomas, Art Shop Press, 1938.

HAWEIS, Stephen

(a.k.a. **Stephen HAWYS**)
b. July 23, 1878, London, England (long associated with Dominica); d. ca. 1968.
Autobiographer, poet, painter, amateur biologist, botany writer.

Stephen Haweis was the son of the Rev. Hugh Reginald Haweis of St. James' Church, Marylebone and Mary Eliza Joy, whose father taught drawing to Prince Albert and did royal portraits of Victoria's children and their pets at Windsor Castle. Eliza Joy herself painted professionally and illustrated a *Chaucer for Children* and helped her improvident, if brilliant, husband send Stephen to Westminster School and then to Peterhouse College, Cambridge. When she died in 1898, Stephen left the university without a degree, preferring to study painting in Paris. After a show in London of his French work he drifted to the South Seas, then to East Africa, finally coming to Dominica in 1929.

Settling down in his island home, he soon felt himself almost a "native" of the place. His *Mount Joy* tells his story of setting up a household and a garden of his highland farm. Though he at times seems obtuse about the descendants of Africans living and working all about him, he is genuinely outraged by racism and colonial arrogance. His weekly column of Dominican news published in the Barbados *Advocate* was summarily stopped in the early 1960's for "ill-timed" remarks. His interest in plants and agriculture in general also made him a testy critic of colonial policies in the island. He was fined by the Government for an attack on the colonial program during the Second World War and he was once led handcuffed to jail when he refused to pay the fine, on the grounds that freedom of speech was one of the reasons for fighting the war against Hitler.

Haweis published a little poetry—his "Madonna of the Fisherman" is given in full in E.C. Baker's article in *Caribbean Quarterly,* but much was left in manuscript. His oil painting THE BLACK MADONNA hangs in the Bishop's Residence, Montserrat, and another work of his hangs in the Barbados Museum's Art Gallery. He also did the background painting for the Insect House of the National Zoo, Washington, D.C.

In 1966 Haweis went to England to arrange for the publication of his memoirs and in 1967 changed his name to "Hawys." He died in England a few years later at the age of 90.

Writings: Autobiography: *Mount Joy,* London, Duckworth, 1967; *Dominican Lyrics,* Rosen, 1963.

Poetry: in various journals; seven poems are in BIM Vol. No. 8/17; 8/51; 11/240; 19/145; 25/66; 26/79.

General Guide: *Anything about Dominica,* Roseau, Dominica, n.d. (illustrated and written by Haweis.

Marine Biology: *The Book About the Sea Gardens of Nassau, Bahamas,* New York, Collier, 1917.

Biographical/Critical Sources: "Stephen Haweis of Dominica," by E.C. Baker, in *Caribbean Quarterly,* Vol. 16, No. 3 (Sept. 1970), pp. 64-70; Bea Howe's *Arbiter of Excellence,* London, Harvill, 1967; Alec Waugh's *Where the Clock Chimes Twice,* London, Cassell, 1952; *Pearl Diver* by V. Berge and H.W. Lanier, New York, Doubleday Doran, 1930 [where Hawys has 30 line-drawings of fish, sailing vessels, and other subjects].

HAWTAYNE, G.H.

(under pseudonym **X. Beke**)
b. ca. 1854, Guyana (?).
Folklorist.

Hawtayne's *West Indian Yarns* (Georgetown, 1884, 1890) are among the earliest collections of oral literature from the area.

HAWYS, Stephen

(see **Stephen HAWEIS**)

HEARNE, John

(pseudonym: **John Morris** [when collaborating with Morris Cargill])
b. February 4, 1926, Montreal, Canada (of Jamaican parents).
Novelist, historian, teacher, commentator, journalist.

Hearne was educated at Jamaica College, Jamaica; Edinburgh University (1947-49); London University (1949-50) (T.D.). He served in the Royal Air Force as an Air Gunner (1943-46). He then taught in London and Jamaica (1950-59 and 1962) and was an Information Officer for the Government of Jamaica, a Resident Tutor, Department of Extra Mural Studies, U.W.I. (1962-67) and from 1968-74 was Head of the Creative Arts Center, Mona, U.W.I. He has been an Assistant to the Prime Minister of Jamaica. He has been a

visiting fellow in Commonwealth Literature, University of Leeds (1967), and O'Connor Professor in Literature, Colgate University, Hamilton, New York (1969-70). He has been the Recipient of the Rhys Memorial Prize (1956); and the Institute of Jamaica's Silver Musgrave Medal (1964).

Hearne's books have been well received —particularly in England, and a number of them have been translated. He is a fascinating story teller, and has a remarkable ability to describe physical events— the opening of *Stranger at the Gate* is a case in point. Those who have, perhaps too easily, characterized W.I. fiction as being "peasant," have problems with John Hearne. Louis James makes the rather paradoxical statement that "J.H. is essentially a West Indian novelist; at the same time he lies outside the main stream of the Caribbean novel." Perhaps the Caribbean is a little more complicated than our critical concepts, developed for more homogeneous societies, allow. The uneasiness one experiences with Hearne at times is possibly not so much related to ideology as to one of his strengths—his ability to evoke the physical aspects of the Caribbean, and of love-making, with such impact. For sometimes the *significance* of the details escapes us. Paradoxically Hearne understandably believes that only in *fiction* could something be said "about the way we live," yet often it is in the matter of overtones, so important to fiction, that he seems to be disappointing.

His first novel, *Voices Under the Window,* is beautifully structured; and although many feel that *Land of the Living* is his best novel, John Figueroa argues for *Autumn Equinox* (in *Revista Interamericana,* Vol. II, No. 1: John Hearne; "Too sharp distinctions," or "Caught in between,"). J.H. has evoked quite strong reaction from George Lamming, Sylvia Wynter and Frank Birbalsingh, yet beyond a doubt, as Mervyn Morris has pointed out, his writings are "the carefully worked creations of a very conscious artist."; and not least of all his short stories.

A close friend of many other writers,

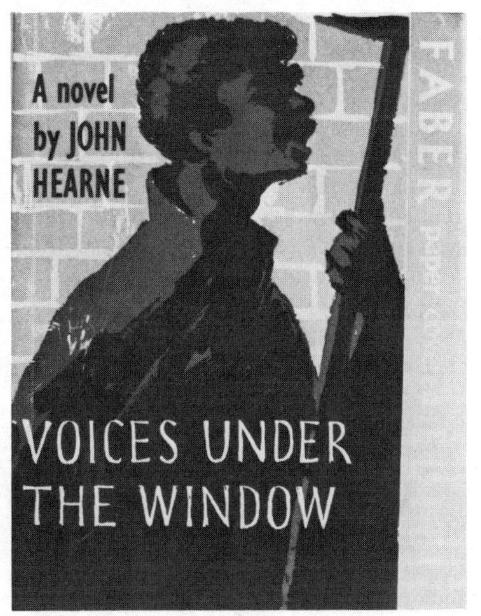

Hearne early spotted the real genius of Derek Walcott. He has taught, and encouraged the teaching of Creative Writing at a number of universities, and helped to bring back West Indian writers to the U.W.I. for short spells from time to time. He was a very close friend of Roger Mais, and together with him and Zacky Matalon, lived and worked through hard times in London and the South of France before achieving his "style and technique," and being published and accepted with *réclame.*

Writings: Novels: *Voices Under the Window,* London, Faber, 1955 and paper edition 1973; *The Faces of Love,* London, Faber, 1957; Boston, Little Brown, 1958, but entitled *The Eye of the Storm; A Stranger at the Gate,* London, Faber, 1956; Jamaica, Collins and Sangster, 1970; *Autumn Equinox,* London, Faber, 1959; New York, Vanguard Press, 1961; *The Land of the Living,* 1961, London, Faber, New York, Harper, 1962.

Written with Morris Cargill under the pseudonym of John Morris, two 007-type thrillers: *Fever Grass,* London, Wm. Collins, 1969, and Fontana Books, 1970; and *The Candywine Development,* London, Wm. Collins, 1970, and in Fontana (paper) Books, 1971.

His work has been translated into Swedish, German, Portuguese and Russian.

Uncollected Short Stories: "At the Stelling," in *West Indian Stories,* London, 1960, and in *Atlantic* (Boston), 1960; "The Lost Country," in *Stories from the Caribbean,* London, 1965, and in *Atlantic* (Boston, September 1961); "A Village Tragedy" in *From the Green Antilles,* London, 1966 and in *Atlantic* (Boston) November 1958. Also: "The Wind in this Corner" in *From the Green Antilles* in *West Indian Stories,* and also in *Atlantic* (Boston) May 1960. Extract from the *Autumn Equinox* in the *Independence Anthology,* 1962.

Plays: *Freedom Man* (based on the life of John Sharpe), in mimeo, 11 pages, one act, produced in Jamaica in 1957); *The Golden Savage* (produced London, 1968); both plays produced on television in England.

Articles and Reviews (partial listing): "The Fugitive in the Forest"—a study of four novels by Wilson Harris, in *Journal of Commonwealth Literature,* No. 4 (December 1967), pp. 99-112); "Landscape with Faces," in *Ian Fleming Introduces Jamaica* (Morris Cargill, ed.), London, Andre Deutsch, 1965, pp. 41-70; "Who Killed the King?" in *Focus* (Edna Manley, ed.), Jamaica, 1960; "European heritage and Asian influence in Jamaica," in *Our Heritage,* Kingston, Department of Extra Mural Studies, U.W.I., 1963, pp. 7-37, (Public Affairs in Jamaica, No. I (5)).

Biographical/Critical Sources: Barrie Davies, "The Seekers": the novels of John Hearne, in *Islands in Between* (Louis James, ed.), London, 1968; Wilfred Cartey, "The Novels of John Hearne," in *Journal of Commonwealth Literature,* No. 7 (July 1969), pp. 45-58; Sylvia Wynter: *Jamaica Journal,* Vol. 3 No. I (March 1969); George Lamming, *The Pleasures of Exile,* Michael Joseph, London, 1960; Frank Birbalasingh, "Escapism in the novels of John Hearne," *Caribbean Quarterly,* Vol. 16, No. I (1970), pp. 28-38; Mervyn Morris, "Pattern and Meaning in *Voices Under the Window,*" *Jamaica Journal,* Vol. 5, No. I (March 1971), pp. 53-56; John Figueroa, John Hearne: "Too sharp distinctions" or "Caught in between?" *Revista Americana,* Vol. 2, No. I (Spring 1972), pp. 72-79. Many reviews in leading newspapers and journals, including the *Observer* and the *London Times.*

HEATH, Roy

b. ca. 1942, Guyana.
Novelist, storywriter, essayist, playwright.

After completing his secondary education at Central High School in Georgetown, Heath worked for a period and then went to England at the age of 24 to read Modern Languages at London University. He taught for some time, was called to the Bar in 1964, London, and to the Guyana Bar in 1973. One comment on his one novel says: "*A Man Come Home* has a vigour and freshness, a humour and unpatronising sympathy quite of its own. No one has written like this before of the Guyana 'yard'. . . ."

Writings: Novel: *A Man Come Home,* London, Longman Caribbean, 1974.

Short Stories: in *Savacou 9/10* (1974), and Seymour's *New Writing in the Caribbean.*

Poetry: in *Kyk-over-al* (1953), p. 5 and p. 116 (1954).

Play: *Inez Combray,* performed, Georgetown, 1972.

Essay: "The Function of Myth," in *Kaie* 8 (1971), p. 19.

HENDRIKS, A.L. (Micky)

b. April 17, 1922, Kingston, Jamaica.
Poet, journalist, broadcaster, executive.

Hendriks was educated at Jamaica College, Jamaica; Ottershaw College, United Kingdom.

One of the many gifted West Indians who now lives abroad permanently, Hendriks as a young man showed great interest in the arts, and was himself a good actor. He appears to be a poet by nature, to find his lines easily, but that is probably a deceptive appearance, for his work is so consistent. As Mervyn Morris says (in BIM 43) of his *On This Mountain:* "Judged by itself; nearly every poem in this book is well-wrought and interesting; some of the poems are very attractive, and some go deeper than that."

His style, his tone, is usually that of understatement, of suavity—"the well-springs of silence are inviolably still"—but there is more than a suggestion of power and movement beneath the smooth surface. His concern is not only for various moments of quiet personal insight; it is also for the whole of the Caribbean; and for the whole of the "space-ship earth":

So when the perennial falsehood
mutters and
hints of hatred among islands or,
between planets, wars,
I may send out from the shore of a
small island
love to you in St Lucia, and to you in
Mars.

This is not today quite as popular a vision of human existence as is the national, racial, anti-imperial view. But today is a short moment, and Hendriks' wider concern for the human condition across the globe—of his "Solemn Light"—might yet return to popularity when, perhaps, it begins to appear that some old scores have been settled, and we are brave enough to listen to the human voice whereever it weeps or sings. As he puts it in his poem "For A Young Writer":

Make a little music in the warm, still air,
strum six wires of words,
pluck cittern notes for a newheard
phrase
and let these taut notes ring. You
cannot walk beside blue flowers
and forget wizened roots of thin
Jewish girls
thirsting to dry death in barren lands;
and in quiet gardens you remember
broken stalks
or sepia children
listless in the dust of lightless places:

for them you will make music
and for them grieve at starbreak. . . .

Writings: Poetry: *On This Mountain and Other Poems,* London, Andre Deutsch, 1965; *These Green Islands and Other Poems,* Jamaica, Bolivar Press, 1971; *Muet,* London, Walton-on-

Thames, Surrey, England; Outposts Publications, 1971; *Madonna of the Unknown Nation,* London, Workshop Press, 1974 (Introduction by Norman Hidden).

Edited (with Cedric Lindo): *The Independence Anthology of Jamaican Literature,* with an introduction by Peter Abrahams. A Publication of The Arts Celebration Committee of The Ministry of Development and Welfare, Jamaica, 1962. Contributed two poems to the Anthology: "Across Cold Skies" and "Road to Lacovia." Has contributed to many journals including BIM, *Anglo-Welsh Review, Caret, Here Now, Outposts, Phoenix, Poet, Savacou, The Christian Science Monitor, Focus* and *The London Magazine;* also to many anthologies, among which are: *Caribbean Voices,* Vol. II, *New Voices of the Commonwealth, Commonwealth Poems of Today,* and *Seven Jamaican Poets.*

Biographical/Critical Sources: The Islands in Between, (edited by Louis James), London, 1968, pp. 31 f.; Mervyn Morris, a review of *On This Mountain,* in BIM, Vol. II, No. 43 (July-December 1966), pp. 225-228; A.N. Forde, a review of *Muet,* in BIM 55, pp. 186-188; A.N. Forde, a review of *These Green Islands,* in BIM 55, pp. 186-188; Stewart Brown (ed.), a review of *Muet* in *NOW* (first issue), pp. 25-27; and Edward Baugh, "West Indian Poetry 1900-1970," (Pamphlet), p. 12.

HENDRIKS, Vivette

b. ca. 1925, Jamaica.
Poet.

Vivette Hendriks grew up and lived her early life in Jamaica but she now lives in Ireland.

A writer of power who, unlike her brother, Micky, has produced in print only a handful of poems. Her work has appeared in *Caribbean Voices,* Vols. I and II, *Focus,* 1960, and the *Independence Anthology* of 1962. She has been a regular contributor to the BBC *Caribbean Voices* program in the 1940's. The following lines which end her "Leda and the Swan" are well known:

Through her cries,
She knows at last
The power of his head,
The sensuous weight of breast and
throat and bill,
And in the cold, unmoving eyes,
The triumph of a hunter at the kill.

HENRY, Ainsley E.T. (A.E.T.)

b. 1911, Jamaica.
Journalist, humorist, storywriter, columnist.

AET's columns in *The Gleaner* and *The Star* used to be a "must" for many Jamaicans. He lived for a longish spell in London, working regularly for the BBC, and doing free-lance journalism. Almost Dickensian in style, AET is adept at catching a certain kind of Jamaican spirit and attitude to life.

Writings: Articles and Columns (collected): *Sheets in the Wind,* Kingston, Jamaica, Printed by the Gleaner Co., 1942; *Bats in the Belfry,* Jamaica, City Printery, 1945; *Pickapeppa,* Jamaica, The Gleaner Co., 1948.

Humorous Short Story: "Mein Kampf"—Extract, in the *Independence Anthology* (1962). Over the years regular columns appeared in the Gleaner and the Star.

HERBERT, Cecil L.

b. 1926, Trinidad.
Poet, teacher, land surveyor.

Educated in Trinidad, Herbert was an early contributor to BIM, and a close friend of George Lamming, half of whose boat-fare to England he paid for the future famous novelist's first trip out of the Caribbean. Herbert was a gifted poet who has published little recently, but much of his early work stands up remarkably well.

Writings: His work appears in various reviews and collections, including: *Kyk-over-al;* BIM; *Tamarack Review; Caribbean Voices,* Vols. I and II; *Caribbean Verse: Young Common-*

wealth Poets, 1965; *Caribbean Quarterly* (Vol. 5, No. 3, 1958), Federation Commemoration Issue. His work also has been broadcast on the BBC.

Biographical/Critical Sources: Anson Gonzalez, " 'Possibility' in W.I. Creative Writing," in *The New Voices,* No. 4 (June 1974), p. 49.

HERCULES, Frank

b. ca. 1920, Trinidad.
Novelist.

After schooling in Trinidad, Hercules then read law at Middle Temple, London. He emigrated to New York City during the Second World War and engaged in business. He became an American citizen in 1959. He was awarded the Fletcher Pratt Memorial Fellowship in prose.

Writings: Novels: *Where the Humming Bird Flies,* New York, Harcourt Brace, 1961; *I Want a Black Doll,* London, Collins, 1967.

Biographical/Critical Sources: review of *I Want a Black Doll* by Colin Richards, in *Books and Bookmen,* Vol. 12, No. 9 (June 1967), p. 23.

HEWLETT, Agnes Cecilia

b. December, 1948, St. John's, Antigua.
Poet.

Hewlett is at present living in New York, working at Barclay's Bank, New York. She has published one collection of her verse: *'Allo et Au'voir,* Elms Court, Ilfracombe, Devon, Arthur H. Stockwell Ltd., 1972.

HILL, Errol

b. August 5, 1921, Trinidad.
Playwright, poet, editor, actor, teacher.

Educated in Trinidad, Hill later attended London University (R.A.D.A.) and the Yale School of Drama (M.F.A., B.F.A.).

Hill has been a most active Professor of Drama at Dartmouth College, New Hampshire, U.S.A., since 1968; earlier (1968-69) he was a teacher in Nigeria (University of Ibadan) and the City University of New York, (1967-68); before that he had been for years a leader in the Extra Mural Department of U.C.W.I. and in drama circles in Jamaica and all over the West Indies (1953-65). He was also active in Carnival productions in Trinidad, and has produced an impressive book on Carnival. He is full of intellectual energy; it is most unfortunate that his splended abilities and deep interest have had to function outside of the Caribbean, whither he has returned from time to time, but only briefly.

Hill has been the recipient of the following awards: British Council Scholarship, 1949-1951; Rockefeller Foundation Fellowship, 1958-1960; Theatre Guild Play Writing Fellowship, 1961-1962; Humming Bird Gold Medal, 1973; Humanities Fellowship, 1973. He is working on a "History of the Caribbean Theatre."

Writings: The Trinidad Carnival: Mandate for a National Theatre, Austin, University of Austin Press, 1972; (Joint author): *Why Pretend?,* 1973.

Dramatic Verse: *Man Better Man,* performed during the Commonwealth Festival of Arts in Britain, 1965; also performed on a West End stage; published in *Three Plays from the Yale School of Drama,* New York, Dutton, 1964 (John Gassner, ed.).

Plays: *The Ping Pong: a backyard comedy in one act,* Mona, Jamaica, Extra Mural Department, U.C.W.I., 1955, mimeo, with introduction by Eric Williams; printed version, U.W.I., 1966. *Wey - Wey: a play in one act,* Mona, mimeo, 1958, published in book form, 1966, Mona, U.W.I.; *Broken Melody: a family drama in one act,* Kingston, Jamaica, U.C.W.I., 1966; (Caribbean Plays: One-Act Play XIX); *Dance Bongo, a one act play in verse,* produced by Studio Players, Trinidad, later performed by Ghana Dance Studio, University of Ghana, Lagon, November 28, 1970, and later, directed by Sandy Arkhurst; first published as *Dance Bongo: a fantasy in one act,* in *Caribbean Plays,* Vol. 2, Extra Mural Department, U.C.W.I., 1966, pp. 9-32, and republished in separate volume as *Dance Bongo: A Fantasy in*

One Act, Port of Spain, Extra Mural Department, U.W.I., 1972; included in *Caribbean Literature* (G.R. Coulthard, ed.), 1966; *Oily Portraits; a satirical comedy in one act,* Mona, U.C.W.I., 1966; *Square Peg; a drama in one act,* Mona, in mimeo, n.d., and later printed, Port of Spain, 1966, Extra Mural Department, U.C.W.I.; One act play XXVI Caribbean Plays: *Square Peg* (One-Act Play No. 26) in U.C.W.I., Trinidad, 1966; *Strictly Matrimony; a comedy in one act,* Kingston, U.C.W.I., 1966; *Dilemma,* Port of Spain, Extra Mural Department, U.C.W.I., 1966 (Caribbean Plays XXVIII); *What Price a Slave,* in *The Literary Half-Yearly* (Mysore, India), xi, 2 (July 1970), pp. 69-99.

Poetry: in various reviews, including some five poems in BIM, and also in *Caribbean Voices,* Vol. I, and the *Caribbean Quarterly,* Federation Issue, April 1958.

Editor of: *Caribbean Plays,* Vol. I, Kingston, Jamaica, Extra Mural Department, U.C.W.I., 1958, and Vols. 1 and 2, Trinidad, U.C.W.I., 1966 (done with A.M. Sampson).

Editor and contributor: *The Artist in West Indian Society,* 1963, and Editor: *Bulletin of Black Theatre,* 1972.

Bibliography: "Plays of the English Speaking Caribbean," in *Bulletin of Black Theatre* (6 issues so far). First issue, Vol. 1, No. 2, Winter 1972.

Biographical/Critical Sources: Review of *Man Better Man,* by Barrie Davies, in BIM, Vol. 10, No. 40 (January-June 1965), pp. 293-294, and review of same work by Louis James in *Caribbean Quarterly,* XIII, 2, pp. 53-55. See also the unfortunate and sometimes bitter exchanges between Hill and Walcott in the *Trinidad Guardian* in the 1964 period.

HILL, Frank

b. November 25, 1910, Jamaica.
Playwright, journalist, broadcaster, commentator.

Hill was much involved in the P.N.P. (Peoples National Party) of early days. More recently he has been doing historical research and working on and chairing various Government Boards. He is an incisive commentator.

Writings: Plays: *Betrayal,* a play in one act, published in *Focus* (Jamaica, 1943); *Upheaval,* a play in three acts, produced Jamaica, 1939.

Biographical/Critical Sources: Mentioned in Henry Fowler's "A History of Jamaican Theatre," *Jamaica Journal,* Vol. 2, No. 1 (March 1968), pp. 53-59.

HILL, Valdeman A.

b. ca. 1905, St. Thomas, U.S. Virgin Islands.
Poet.

Hill published his one and only collection of verse, the 33-page volume: *Ripples* (St. Thomas, The Art Shop, 1935).

HILLARY, Samuel

b. ca. 1936, Jamaica.
Playwright.

Hillary has written at least four plays, some of them prize-winners in various island competitions.

Writings: Plays: *Chippy:* A play in one act, Kingston, Extra Mural Department, University College of West Indies, 1966, Caribbean Plays Edition, U.W.I.; Port of Spain, 1966; *Departure in the Dark:* A play in two acts, three scenes, Kingston, U.C.W.I. (61 pp., mimeo), n.d., stencilled; *A Broken Wing:* A full length play—Award of high commendation, National Festival, 1965; *Favours of Lovers:* Bronze Medal Festival Award, 1966.

Biographical/Critical Sources: Mentioned in Henry Fowler's "A History of Jamaican Theatre"' in *Jamaica Journal,* Vol. 2, No. 1 (March 1968), pp. 52-59.

HINDS, Donald

b. 1934, Jamaica.
Storywriter.

Hinds was educated in Jamaica but went to England in 1955, and has remained there. His long experiences were distilled into his study of West Indians in the United Kingdom: *Journey to an Illusion.*

Writings: Stories: *Island Voices:* "Busman's Blues" and "Any Lawful Impediment": also represented in *Stories from the Caribbean.*

Study of W.I. Emigration: *Journey to an Illusion: The West Indian in Britain,* London, Heinemann, 1967 (Dedicated to Claude Jones, Trinidadian Editor of the *West Indian Gazette*).

Biographical/Critical Sources: Colin Richards, a review of *Journey to an Illusion,* in his collection, *Caribbean Bookshelf,* Port-of-Spain, Trinidad Guardian (April 20, 1967).

HINKSON, Anthony

b. ca. 1943, Barbados.
Poet, playwright, storywriter.

Hinkson is the leading writer in the Writers' Workshop, Barbados. In 1974, he won a Writers' Workshop Scholarship from the University of Toronto. He was at Paul Engle's International Writing Program, University of Iowa, Ames.

His plays, and some stories, adapted, have been read or played on TV and radio, Barbados. His plays have been produced in Jamaica, Guyana and Barbados.

He contributed "Tradition," written in dialect, to *Savacou 7/8* (Jan-June 1973), edited by Edward Brathwaite as a tribute to Frank Collymore on the occasion of his eightieth birthday. Brathwaite links Hinkson, Margaret Gill and Elizabeth Clarke as three of the young "Bajan" outstanding writers among others in their writers' group. Brathwaite notes Hinkson's poem about the riots of '37 as a classic.

HODGE, Merle

b. 1944, Trinidad.
Novelist, translator, teacher.

Growing up in Curepe, Trinidad, Merle Hodge was an excellent student and won the Trinidad and Tobago Girls' Island Scholarship in 1962, enabling her to study French at University College, London (B.A. 1965 and M. Phil. 1967). She has traveled widely in England, France, Den-

mark, Spain, and elsewhere in eastern and western Europe. She has worked as a governess, typist, and has translated a collection of Leon Damas' poetry (unpublished). In the 1970's she became lecturer in French at the University of the West Indies.

Her first novel, *Crick Crack Monkey,* (1970) shows a young girl, Tee, amidst a chaotic family of relatives, especially of Tantie and her "uncles" passing through town. Aunt Beatrice is very important, for she slowly cleaned Tee up and transmogrified her into "Cynthia" so she could begin to cope with the caste system of Trinidad where shades of darkness and light are apparently still terribly important.

Writings: Novel: *Crick Crack Monkey,* London, Deutsch, 1970.

Translations: The poems of Léon Gontran Damas, in ms.

Biographical/Critical Sources: Review of *Crick*

Crack Monkey, by Elizabeth Harvey in *World Literature Written in English*, No. 19 (April 1971), p. 87; and review of novel by Wayne Brown, "Growing Up in Colonial T'dad" in *Trinidad Guardian* (June 28, 1970), p. 6.

HOLDER, Geoffrey

b. August 1, 1930, Trinidad.
Storywriter, dancer, painter, choreographer, actor.

Geoffrey Holder is best remembered in Trinidad as a painter and a dancer. He has lived for many years in New York where he has made a name for himself as a many-talented man of the arts. He is dynamic and shows, in a very creative way, that West Indian many-sidedness which, when properly disciplined, flies in the face of the specialization of "more developed" societies: he is a dancer who paints, and a painter who writes and a writer who acts.

He collaborated with Tom Harshman on a book of stories and has published an island recipe cookbook.

Writings: Stories: (with Tom Harshman) *Black Gods, Green Islands*, New York, Dolphin Books, 1959.

Criticism: Review of two of Samuel Selvon novels: *An Island is a World* in BIM, Vol. 6, No. 23 (December 1955), p. 202; and *A Brighter Sun*, in BIM 16, pp. 295-296.

HOLLAR, Constance

b. 1880, Jamaica; d. 1945.
Poet.

Constance Hollar was a favorite among the older folk in the late thirties and early forties, but her manner, and that of her circle has gone out of style. It is perhaps more than fashion that is in question. Although clearly dedicated to poetry and to fashioning it, she seems, except on rare occasions, much more concerned with the Fancy than with the Imagination. There is an interesting preoccupation with night in some of her work, and its seems a pity that she did not quarry that vein a bit more deeply.

Yet why weep for fallen stars—
Fruit of Infinity—

Who planned the orchard there,
Planned their hereafter. . . .

Gold are the fruit of night,
Golden for laughter.

Those who remember her recall a charming and a lively person, member of a famous group of sisters, one of whom was Miss Anna Hollar who taught Latin to many generations of young Jamaican men and women, and who was one of the first women students to attend London University.

Writings: Poetry: *Flaming June*, Kingston, New Dawn Press, 1941; contributor to *Caribbean Voices*, Vol. 1 (1966); *A Treasury of Jamaican Poetry*, 1949; *The Poetry of the Negro*, 1949; *Voices from Summerland, An Anthology of Jamaican Poetry*, 1929; *Independence Anthology*, 1962.

Editor of the Anthology: *Songs of Empire*, with a foreword by Sir William Morrison, Kingston, Jamaica (printed by the Gleaner Co.), 1932.

Biographical/Critical Sources: Edward Baugh, *West Indian Poetry 1900-1970* [Pamphlet], p. 6; mentioned in J.E. Clare McFarlane's *A Literature in the Making*, Kingston, Jamaica, Pioneer Press, 1956 (Chapter 6, pp. 40-47 is main reference).

HO LUNG, Richard

b. September 17, 1939, Highgate, St. Mary, Jamaica.
Poet, teacher, Jesuit priest.

Ho Lung was educated at Boston College and Syracuse University. His poems have been published in various journals, including BIM, *Jamaica Journal, Envoy*, and *Savacou*, and general newspapers.

He has been an innovator in the use of the Jamaican dialect and often employs local rhythms in his hymns and in his liturgical writings. He is an active promotor of poetry readings and concerts and is a professor at U.W.I., Mona. He is presently working on a collection of his verse scheduled for publication by Sangster's, Kingston.

Recordings of his work: "Caribbean Bread and Wine;" "Marianna;" "Jasmine and Jeremiah;" "Letter: Job to John;" and "Missa Vitae: A Caribbean Mass."

Biographical/Critical Sources: Gerald Moore's article, "Use Men Language," in BIM 57 (March 1974), p. 72.

HONEYCHURCH, Lennox

b. December, 1952, Portsmouth, Dominica.
Storywriter, poet, actor, broadcaster, journalist, artist.

Honeychurch was educated at St. Mary's Academy, Dominica and the Lodge School, Barbados. He is an established personality of Dominica and in April 1975 became a nominated member of the Dominican House of Assembly.

Together with Alwin Bully and Daniel Caudeiron he has edited and published *Wahseen* and *Free Your Mind,* two Dominican literary magazines.

His book *The Dominica Story, A History of the Island,* was first presented by him as a dramatized radio series, "tracing the origin and development of this beautiful and often mysterious island from its formation up to the attainment of Associated Statehood with Britain in 1967." The book is dedicated to his grandmother, Elma Napier, herself a well-known writer. The maps and line drawings are by Lennox Honeychurch. The whole effort shows enterprise and insight, and is beautifully put together. (Photographs by Curtis Henry and Peter Green). On the "fly-leaf" below his dedication, Honeychurch cites a verse written by Phyllis Shand Allfrey, another Dominican writer, personality and politician of Dominica:

Love for an island is the sternest passion pulsing beyond the blood through roots and loam it overflows the boundary of bedrooms and courses passed the fragile wall of home.

Writings: History: *The Dominica Story—A History of the Island,* Barbados, Letchworth Press Ltd., 1975.

HOPKINSON, Slade

b. November 3, 1934, Guyana.
Poet, actor, playwright, teacher.

Slade Hopkinson is best known as an actor of remarkable ability and range. Educated in his home country and Barbados (Harrison College) and at U.C.W.I., Mona, he took an active part in student life, being (at university) a member of the Walcott, Llanos, Slade group of high livers, actors, and playwrights. He played Papa Bois/Planter/Devil in the original version of Walcott's *Ti Jean.* He also did a remarkable Lear. In later days he played Lastrade in *Dream.*

His work as man of the theatre, and encourager of the arts, was carried on over a wide area of the Caribbean and has certainly made its mark. He founded the Theatre Guild Company in Trinidad in 1970.

He was editor of *Public Opinion* (Jamaica Weekly Journal) and Information Officer in the Public Relations Office of Jamaica Government from 1959-61. He also served as drama critic for *The Nation* from 1961-63.

Writings: Plays: *The Onliest Fisherman,* Port of Spain, Trinidad, U.C.W.I., Extra Mural Department, 1967 (Caribbean Plays Edition); *The Blood of a Family: A Play in One Act,* performed Jamaica, 1957; *Fall of a Chief: A Play in Nine Scenes,* performed, Georgetown, Theatre Guild, 1965; *Spawning of Eels,* performed Georgetown, 1968 (rewritten as "Sala" and presented at the Little Carib Theatre by the Caribbean Theatre Guild, Trinidad, October 1975).

Poetry: *The Four and Other Poems,* Barbados, Advocate Publishing Co., 1954 (20 pp.); *Rain over St. Augustine*, Guyana, Freedom Year, 19??; His verse appears in various journals and anthologies, including: BIM; *Savacou; New World (Monthly); Caribbean Voices of the Commonwealth; Breaklight; The Literary Half-Yearly* (Mysore, India) XI, 2 (July 1970); *Caribbean Quarterly* 5, 3 (April 1958) (Federation Commemoration Issue).

Biographical/Critical Sources: Review of *Rain over St. Augustine* in *The Literary Half-Yearly* Vol. 11, No. 2 (1970), pp. 149-150; Review of *"Sala"* by Mauby in *Trinidad Guardian* (Thursday, October 16, 1975), p. 4; "Dilemma of an educated country boy."

HOSEIN, Clyde

b. ca. 1940, Trinidad.
Critic, poet, script-writer.

Hosein is a producer and script-writer for Radio Trinidad. He has travelled in Europe and has been associated with British publishing houses and newspapers. He has written a novel and three television plays.

Among his critical articles are: a critique of K. Ramchand's *The West Indian Novel and its Background* in "Focus on the Arts:" *Trinidad Guardian* (August 26, 1970), Criticism of *Themes*, in *Trinidad Guardian* (May 27, 1970); "Agony of Expression—West Indian Fact": *Trinidad Guardian* (July 22, 1970); "Bridging Many Gaps," Criticism of Ramon Mansoor's *Lirio Enamorado*, in *Trinidad Guardian* (July 29, 1970); review of *Themes 2*, in *Trinidad Guardian* (January 27, 1971); "James Baldwin and Commitment," in *Voices*, Vol. I, No. 3 (March 1965).

Writings: Poetry: in *Voices*.

HUTCHINSON, Lionel

b. ca. 1921, Barbados.
Novelist, commentator, free-lance journalist.

Hutchinson joined the RAF at the age of 19, during World War II. After the war he turned to journalism. He has been a contributor to press, radio and TV. He is an informed commentator on the history of Barbados. In 1948 he was appointed Librarian to the House of Assembly and in 1953 he was awarded a British Council Scholarship.

Writings: Novels: *Man From the People*, London, Collins, 1969 (256 pp.); *One Touch of Nature*, London, Collins, 1971 (317 pp.).

Other: *Behind the mace* (a history of the Barbadian House of Assembly), 1951.

Biographical/Critical Sources: Review of *Man from the People* by John Wickham in BIM 51, pp. 189-193.

HUTTON, Albinia C.

(née **McKay;** name by previous marriage: **Davis**)
b. 1894 in Kingston, Jamaica (of Scottish parentage).
Poet.

Hutton was one of the earliest published Jamaican poets.

Writings: Poetry: *Poems*, 1912; *Hill Songs and Wayside Verses*, Kingston, Gleaner Co., 1932; *Sonnets of Sorrow* (for private circulation, 1939); included in *A Treasury of Jamaican Poetry* (Anthology).

Prose: *Life in Jamaica*, A prose work, 1930.

Biographical/Critical Sources: Mentioned in J.E. Clare McFarlane's *A Literature for the Making*, Jamaica, Pioneer Press, 1956 (Chapter 4, pp. 27-33 is main reference).

INGRAM, Kenneth E.N.

b. 1921, St. Ann's Bay, Jamaica.
Poet, bibliographer.

Ingram attended Jamaica College, Kingston; he did his B.A. at the University of Nottingham, Library Science in London, and an M. Phil. at UC London. He worked at the Institute of Jamaica and then since

1950, at the University of West Indies Libary, Mona, where he is now University Librarian. His wife (née Renée) is a well-known secondary school teacher.

Ingram belonged to that "renaissance" of lyric poetry which was evident throughout the Caribbean in the late thirties and early forties. He produced at that time some fine and sensitive lyrics, but has not written much poetry recently. A sensitive and religious man, he has been ever helpful to scholars and poets alike.

Although he has not published a book, his work, poetic and scholarly, has appeared over a wide area, and he has been the recipient of a number of fellowships and awards.

Writings: Poetry: Verse published in various anthologies such as *Focus* (1943, 1948, 1956, 1960); *Life and Letters* (Apr -Nov. 1948); *Kyk-over-al; Anthology of West Indian Poetry,* edited by A.J. Seymour (1952); *The Poetry of the Negro 1746-1949,* edited by Langston Hughes and Arna Bontemps (1949); *Poetry for Children* (1950); *Caribbean Quarterly Federation Commemorative Issue* (April 1958); *The Independence Anthology of Jamaican Literature,* edited by A.L. Hendricks and Cedric Lindo (1962); *Caribbean Voices,* edited by John Figueroa, 2 vols. (1966-1970); *The Sun's Eye,* edited by Anne Walmsley (1968); *New Ships, an Anthology of West Indian Poems,* edited by D.G. Wilson (1971, 1975); *West Indian Poetry, an anthology for schools,* edited by Kenneth Ramchand and Cecil Gray (1972).

Essays and Scholarships: "W. Osburn, Naturalist—His Journal and His Letters," *Jamaican Historical Review,* Vol. 2, No. 1 (December 1949), pp. 33-37; "The West Indian Trade of an English Furniture Firm in the Eighteenth Century," *Jamaican Historical Review,* Vol. 3 (March 1962), pp. 22-37; "Bibliographical Control of Commonwealth Caribbean Government Publications," in *Research Library Co-operation in the Caribbean,* edited by Alma Jordan (American Library Association, 1973), pp. 87-100; "Review of Bradford F. Swan," *The Spread of Printing: the Caribbean Area,* in *The Library* (Birmingham, March 1973), Vol. 28, No. 1, pp. 72-74; Review of Edward Scobie, *Black Britannia: a History of Blacks in Britain,* in *Caribbean Studies* (Puerto Rico, October 1973), Vol. 13, No. 3, pp. 146-148; *Manuscripts Relating to Commonwealth Caribbean Countries in United States and Canadian Repositories* (London, Caribbean Universities Press in association with Bowker, 1975); *Libraries and the Challenge of Change,* papers of the International Library Conference held in Kingston, Jamaica, April 24-29, 1972, edited by K.E. Ingram and Albertina A. Jefferson (London, Mansell, 1975).

IREMONGER, Lucille

(née **Parks**)
b. ca. 1921, Jamaica.
Novelist, collector of folktales.

Iremonger attended Wolmer's Girls' School, Kingston, where she won the Jamaica Scholarship. She went on to England for her university education.

Writings: Novels: *Creole,* London, Hutchinson, 1951; *The Cannibals, a novel,* London, Hammond, 1952; *The Ghosts of Versailles,* London, Faber, 1957; *Love and the Princess,* London, Faber, 1958; *And His Charming Lady,* London, Secker and Warburg, 1961; *Yes, My Darling Daughter,* London, Secker and Warburg, 1964. An extract from the novel *Creole* is in the *Independence Anthology,* 1962.

Folklore: *West Indian Folktales: Anansi Stories, Tales from West Indian Folklore retold for English Children,* London, Harrap, 1956.

Juveniles: *The Young Traveller in the South Seas,* London, Phoenix, 1952; *The Young Traveller in the West Indies,* London, Phoenix, 1955.

JAMES, Cyril Lionel Robert

(often called **CLR**)
b. January 4, 1901, Trinidad.
Novelist, critic, political theorist, historian, sports writer, teacher.

CLR is a lively talker and a most engaging writer. His main work has not been in literature, but in historical and political thought. He has influenced greatly many younger Caribbean writers in many fields, including George Lamming who is in many ways one of his most ardent disciples. James combines a strong ideology with great independence of mind. He is not one for the bandwaggon—"My objection to Cruse's book is that he doesn't like West Indians, he doesn't like Jews, he doesn't like too many people. There is too much subjective response to events in the book" (CLR). Compare this with Lamming's "The finest book I have yet read on this whole matter, by the way, is *The Crisis of the Negro Intellectual* by Harold Cruse." (Both quotations are from *Kas-Kas,* Ian Munro, Reinhard Sander, University of Texas at Austin.)

James was schooled in Trinidad—". . . we were well educated in the liberal tradition of the British." He taught for a while at his old school, Queen's Royal College, and was in the group around Alfred Mendes, and *The Beacon,* and *Trinidad.*

James, like so many others, decided that he had to go abroad: "You could join the government, or you could go abroad. But to start the fight there at that time couldn't be done. The man who really led the fight in Trinidad was a white man—Captain Cipriani." James became one of the leaders in the Pan-African Movement. He was also active in the U.S.A., often under an assumed name. The dates of his movements are not very easily ascertained, but the pattern was, roughly, 1932 to England, where he lived until 1938, writing for the press, mostly on cricket. He went to the States in 1938; in 1953 he returned to England, which became his base. He spent 1958-60 in the West Indies. More recently he has been teaching in the U.S.A. as Professor of Humanities at Federal City College, Washington, D.C., since 1972.

James' main book of fiction is *Minty Alley,* which was certainly a pioneer book, but has undoubtedly been overpraised. Louis James comments: ". . . (CLR) . . . hoped that a second novel would be his major work but this never appeared. *Minty Alley,* however, assures him a place in Caribbean fiction."

The James book that has probably been his most influential is *The Black Jacobins* (1938). It was better known to African leaders in the 40's and 50's than to those of the Caribbean, but in recent years it has been well known "at home" as well. (It was republished in paperback in New York in 1963, as a Vintage book.)

James is a highly civilized man and a polished writer. His *Beyond a Boundary* is a classic of the genre, and displays that great West Indian passion for cricket as an art form. His political books, which were many and influential, are not here being commented on. Clearly his work would be even better known as *his,* had he not published under assumed names, when as a Trotsky socialist (since 1934) he felt it wise not to be too visible.

James does not seem to think that a great deal has changed in the West Indies—not in certain fields, at least: ". . . independence has meant . . . a national flag, and a national anthem and a visit by the Queen (or members of the Royal Family). But the old economic and financial domination of the European civilization still exists." The fault lies with the new "black middle class" which defends the status quo "because it is profitable." (*Washington Post* interview, Aug. 25, 1973).

Despite his long absence, James has always been in touch with the West Indies, and was, in 1972, awarded an honorary doctorate by The University of the West Indies.

Writings: Novel: *Minty Alley,* London, Secker and Warburg, 1936; reprint in paper by New Beacon Books, London, 1971.

Sport: *Cricket and I,* with L.N. Constantine, London, Allan, 1933.

Political/Social Studies: *The Life of Captain Cipriani.* Privately printed, 1933; abridged as *The Case for West Indian Self-Government,* London, Hogarth Press, 1933. New York, University Place Bookshop, 1967; *World Revolution* 1917-1936: *The Rise and Fall of the Communist International,* London, Secker, and New York, Pioneer Publications, 1937; *A History of Negro Revolt,* London, Fact, 1938, and New York, Haskell, 1967, 1969 and issued as paperback with title: *A History of Pan African Revolt,* Washington, D.C., Drum and Spear Press, 1969; *Mariners, Renegades and Castaways, Melville and the World We Live In,* privately printed, 1953; *Party Politics in the West Indies,* San Juan, Trinidad, Vedic Enterprizes, 1961; *Beyond a Boundary,* London, Hutchinson, 1963; *Notes on Dialectics: Hegel and Marxism,* Detroit 1971; *The Black Jacobins: Toussaint L'ouverture and the Santo Domingo Revolution,* New York, Dial Press, 1938, and London, Secker and Warburg, 1938—in paperback, New York, Vintage, 1963; *Modern Politics,* Port of Spain, P.N.M. Publishing Co., 1960; *Marxism and the Intellectuals,* Detroit, Facing Reality Publishing Comittee, 1962; *Lenin, Trotsky and the Vanguard Party: A Contemporary View,* Detroit, Facing Reality Publishing Committee, 1964; "Peasants and Workers," "George Jackson," and "The Way Out: World Revolution," all in *Radical America,* Nos. 5 and 6 (1971), pp. 5-60; *State Capitalism and World Revolution,* 1950.

Literary Criticism: "Introduction to Tradition and the West Indian Novel," as end-word to Wilson Harris' *Tradition, The Writer and Society,* London, 1967; *Wilson Harris—A Philosophical Approach,* Port of Spain, Trinidad, U.C.W.I., 1965; "The Artist in the Caribbean, Kingston, U.C.W.I., 196?; "Discovering Literature in Trinidad: The Nineteen Thirties," *Savacou,* No. 2 (1970), pp. 54-60, and also in *Journal Commonwealth Literature,* No. 7 (1969), pp. 73-80; introduction to *Froudacity: West Indian Fables Explained,* London, New Beacon Books, 1969 (original edition, 1889); *The Future in the Present, Selected Writings.*

Plays: *The Black Jacobins* (in mimeo): completed London, 1967, 2 parts (autographed copy at St. Augustine, Trinidad campus of U.W.I.), London, Allison and Busby, 1977; *Nkrumah and the Ghana Revolution,* London, Allison and Busby, 1977 (but earlier partly published in 1962, 1964, and 1969 as occasional essays or speeches); *Toussaint L'Ouverture,* also in ms. only.

Stories: "Triumph," James' first story, written 1928 or 1929 and is probably the first story to picture "yard life" or slum life in Port of Spain, published in *Island Voices,* New York, Liveright, 1930; "La Divina Pastora" in *Saturday Review of Literature* (Oct. 15, 1927) and also in E.J. O'Brien's *The Best British Short Stories of 1928,* New York, Dodd, Mead, 1928; also in *Caribbean Prose; Stories from the Caribbean;* and *West Indian Narrative: An Introductory Anthology.*

Biographical/Critical Sources: K. Ramchand in *The West Indian Novel and Its Background,* London, 1970; Eric Roach's review of new printing of *Minty Alley:* "Minty Alley Revisited," *Trinidad Guardian* (April 29, 1973), p. 6; review of *A History of Pan-African Revolt,* by Angele Blackwell, *Black Scholar,* Vol. 2, No. 7 (March 1971), pp. 54-57; Martin Glaberman, "CLR James—The Man and His Works," in *Flambeau,* No. 6 (Nov. 1966), pp. 22-23; *Kas-Kas, Interviews with Three Caribbean Writers in Texas,* Austin, The University of Texas at Austin (Occasional Publication of the African and Afro-American Research Institute), 1972; *The Island in Between,* Louis James, ed., London, 1968, pp. 24-25; Interview of Alfred Mendes by Reinhard W. Sander of October 6, 1972, in Port of Spain, "The Turbulent Thirties in Trinidad," in *World Literature Written in*

English, XII, 1 (April 1973), pp. 66-79; Tony Martin, "C.L.R. James and the race/class question," in *Race,* Vol. 14, No. 2 (Oct. 1972), pp. 183-193; Ivar Oxaal, *Black Intellectuals Come to Power: The Rise of Creole Nationalism in Trinidad and Tobago,* Cambridge, Mass., Schenkman Publishing Co., 1968.

JAMES, Leroy Martin

b. ca. 1945, Trinidad.
Novelist, poet.

James has published one biographical novel and two collections of poems.

Writings: Novel: *A short peaceful walk,* Trinidad, Crest Publications, 1975.

Poetry: *Rhythm of Coger Street,* San Fernando, Trinidad, Rahaman Printery, n.d. [21 pages]; *A quiet resort* (Part 1), Trinidad, Crest Publications, 1975.

JARVIS, Euton

b. ca. 1941, Black Rock, Tobago.
Storywriter, novelist.

Educated at Gloster Lodge Moravian School, and at Belmont and Osmond High Schools, Jarvis quickly found a cub-reporter job with the *Chronicle* (now defunct), and then became clerk for the Water Department in Tobago. He took a noon lunch hour to write a prize-winning story, "A Budget for Christmas" on December 14, 1967, for which the deadline was the next day. Jarvis was a lightweight boxer in his early days.

His short story "King Belshazzar" appearing in the March, 1965 volume of *Voices opened with these lines:*

. . . And for two days like puppets under his spell, we would jig, shuffle and jump-up while the sun penetrated our tireless bodies: bodies fired by draughts of rum: rum running down the sides of our mouths as we sang:

Cannaval is ah bacchana!
We doh care!
We drink we rum an' we tumble dong!
We doh care!

Writings: Stories: in various journals; and "A Budget for Christmas" in *Sunday Guardian* (Jan. 8, 1967), with review by Carl Jacobs, republished in *Voices,* edited by Cliff Sealy.

Novel: in manuscript.

JARVIS, José Antonio

b. November 22, 1902, St. Thomas, U.S. Virgin Islands; d. July 23, 1963.
Poet, playwright, artist, historian, journalist, editor, critic, commentator.

Mrs. Addelita Cancryn in her biography of José Antonio Jarvis, *Man of Vision,* notes that Jarvis' "place as journalist, playwright, poet, artist, and historian will have to await the judgment of time. . . ." but that he "contributed significantly to almost every phase in the development of the United States Virgin Islands."

As a poet he wrote simply, directly, expressing concern for all things in Nature, Life and Religion that touched him deeply. He published some of his verse but he left behind many unpublished works, which show the wide interests and concerns he had. In "Virgin Island Market" he portrays a vivid and real Caribbean scene:

Black women, ample breasted, stand
by trays
High heaped with red gold carrots
banked on green
And luscious spinach damp with crisp
curled leaves
They fling rich happy laughter over
limes
That nudge tomatoes into beds of peas,
And prod virginal cabbages in ranks
To rival fat bananas gathered close.

He wrote the scripts for many pageants performed at Carnival time, and many short plays, but he left only two serious works of drama—*Bluebeard's Last Wife* (1957) and *The King's Mandate.* The first work was based on a Virgin Island folk tale, which was first written down in a literary form by Charles Edwin Taylor in 1880. Jarvis' version was more of an epic poem, written in the classic Greek tradition. The second work, *The King's Mandate,* was a longer effort, but written in the same form—blank verse—as *Bluebeard's Last Wife.* The title "The King's Mandate" referred to the proclamation given out by the then Governor of the Virgin Islands, in accord with a mandate from the Danish King, Christian VIII, that all who were "unfree" in the Danish Virgin Islands were now "free," and dealt with the liberation of the Negro slaves of the Virgin Islands.

Jarvis was one of the main founders of the *Daily News* and served as its first editor. He felt very strongly that his role and that of the paper was to keep the people fully informed on all relevant topics affecting the society, especially in political and business matters, as well as to express opinions and comments that would be "an inspiration" to the people.

Jarvis wrote a *Brief History of the Virgin Islands* and another work in which he accounts for the *Virgin Islands and Their People.* The works are not to be considered as being historical in the usual sense, but they are valuable accounts for the special insights and intimate knowledge he had of the islands and his fellow men.

In January 1952, he was commissioned by the then Governor of the Islands to do research abroad and in the islands in the preparation of a textbook on the history of the Virgin Islands. Jarvis, then principal of a Government School, was relieved of his duties in the school in the summer of 1962 so as to take up this commission. He travelled to the United States, England and Denmark in pursuit of the research he needed for the commissioned work. Unfortunately his health began to deteriorate and in the early months of 1963, he was forced to resign from his educational post on May 31, 1963. His health continued to deteriorate; he died soon thereafter.

Many tributes were paid him throughout the island, but he was praised especially for "his constant and accurate recording of the history and his vivid interpretations of the culture of these Virgin Islands." His was the first effort of a native Virgin Islander to present a comprehensive account of the Islands to the world.

Writings: Poetry: *Fruits in Passing* (Book of poems), St. Thomas, Virgin Islands, Art Shop Press, 1932; *The Bamboula Dance and other poems,* St. Thomas, V.I., Art Shop Press, 1936;

Plays: *Bluebeard's Last Wife,* Charlotte Amalie, St. Thomas, V.I., Jarvis Art Gallery, 1951 (dramatic poem); *The King's Mandate,* Charlotte Amalie, St. Thomas' Academy, Limited Editions, 1960 (three acts, written in 1948).

Other: *Brief History of the Virgin Islands,* St. Thomas, V.I., The Art Shop, 1938; *The Virgin Islands and Their People,* Philadelphia, Dorrance and Co., 1944; and with Martin, Rufus: *Virgin Islands Picture Book,* St. Thomas, The Art Shop Press, 1949; Also: *The Three Islands,* n.d. (a description of the Islands).

Articles: in various newspapers and magazines, including *The Record* (weekly magazine) and editorials and a commentary entitled "Observation Tower."

Biographical/Critical Sources: Addelita Cancryn, *Man of Vision: A Biography of José Antonio Jarvis,* St. Thomas, Virgin Islands, Val-Hill Enterprises, 1975.

JEAN-BAPTISTE, Emmanuel

b. 1939, Dominica.

Poet, novelist, shortstory writer, critic, playwright, teacher.

After local schooling Jean-Baptiste went to England in 1966 to study at Oxford with a scholarship where he did his major work in English literature. He then went on to the Sorbonne for philosophy and then became a teacher in a private school in Switzerland as a Latin instructor. He is currently a teacher of English language and literature at a Swiss State Gymnasium.

Writings: Poetry: in *Breaklight,* New York, Anchor, 1973.

JEKYLL, Walter

b. ca. 1877, England (long resident in Jamaica).
Folklorist, compiler, editor.

Jekyll was the first major influence on Claude McKay, strongly recommending that he should write in Jamaican English. His tolerance and social ideas obviously influenced McKay whom he entertained at his home while earning the rancour of the English Governor General—whom, with upper class sang froid, he considered an "upstart"—by declining to offer "His Excellency" similar hospitality. It was, perhaps, Jekyll's early respect for McKay's promise which inclined the latter to be wary of taking up racist stands on any issue, and to realize that even the most vexing problems demand consideration from many angles, and that human help comes from many directions.

Writings: Folklore: *Jamaica Song and Story: Anancy Stories, digging songs, ring tunes and dancing tunes,* London, published for the Folk-Lore Society by D. Nutt, 1907, xxxviii, 288 pp.; *Folk Songs of Jamaica; The Greedy Goat* (A West Indian Folk Tale); *Jamaican Song and Story . . .* with new introductory essays by Philip Sherlock, Louise Bennett and Rex Nettleford, New York, Dove Publications, 1966.

JOHN, Errol

b. ca. 1918, Trinidad.
Playwright, actor, writer (radio, television, cinema and stage).

Errol John is the founder member of the Whitehall Players. He won a Guggenheim Fellowship in 1958, after the success of his play *Moon on a Rainbow Shawl* which won first prize in the London Observer's Play competition of 1957. This work was also performed in new productions in Hungary, Holland, Iceland, Australia, Argentina and the United States. A revised version was presented January 15. 1962 at the East 11th Street Theatre, New York City by Kermit Bloomgarden and Harry Joe Brown, Jr., and directed by George Roy Hill. John spent some time in Hollywood as a film actor and script writer. Three of his film scripts have been published in one volume. He had roles in: *Heart of the Matter; Odongo; The Nun's Story;* and *Sins of Rachel Cade.* He has lived for a time in Mexico.

Writings: Plays: *The Gateway*—rewritten and produced as *How Then To-morrow,* 1948; *Moon on a Rainbow Shawl,* a play in three acts, London, Faber, 1958; and New York, Grove Press, 1962; *The Tout,* Trinidad, Tobago, Extra Mural Dept., U.C.W.I., 1966 (Caribbean Plays: one act play XI); *Three Screen Plays: Force Majeure; The Dispossessed; Hasta Luego, London, Faber, 1967; Horseman Pass By,* written for BBC TV.

Biographical/Critical Sources: J. A. Ramsaran, a review of *Moon on a Rainbow Shawl,* in *Black Orpheus,* No. 5 (May 1959), pp. 54-55; Bridget Jones, review of *Screen Plays: Force Majeure; The Dispossessed; Hasta Luego,* in *Caribbean Quarterly,* Vol. 13, No. 3, (Sept. 1967), pp. 57-59.

JOHN, Frank

b. November 14, 1941, Trinidad.
Poet, playwright.

Locally educated, John travelled to England in 1967. He soon began promoting the work of his contemporaries and his own poems, well received, were collected in *Black Songs.*

Writings: Play: *Orange Lady,* London, by author, 196?.
Poetry: *Black Songs,* London, Longman, 1970; *Light a Fire,* London, Paul Bremen Ltd.,

Heritage Series, 1972; *Black Waves,* London, 1973; poems in various collections, including *Breaklight* (A. Salkey, ed.).

JONES, Barbara Althea

b. ca. 1937, Trinidad; d. 1972.
Poet.

Barbara Jones worked as a research scientist in agriculture in Trinidad in the 1960's, and was making a name for herself as a scientist and poet when she left Trinidad to live in Canada.

Her poem "Escapist's Dream" (published in Cliff Sealy's magazine *Voices*) was from her manuscript of verse being prepared for publication at the time of her untimely death in Montreal, Canada in 1972. Her collection *Among the Potatoes* is divided into four parts: The Real and the Unreal; Love and Nothing; Tropic Phase; Campus and Nature. The book is illustrated by lino-cuts done by her. Anson Gonzalez in his series "Literature On the Air," says: "She looks at and writes on the ambivalences in life and uses both traditional and modern approaches in addition to strong sexual imagery."

Writings: Poetry: *Among the Potatoes: a collection of modern verse,* Ilfracombe, Stockwell, 1967. Her verse work also has appeared in newspapers and in *Voices.*

Biographical/Critical Sources: Anson Gonzalez, *Trinidad and Tobago Literature "On the Air,"* (N.C.C., T.T.).

JONES, Evan

b. 1927, Hector's River, Eastern Portland, Jamaica.
Playwright, poet, biographer, TV and radio script writer.

Son of a major banana planter in Jamaica, Evan Jones attended local schools including Munro College. He attended Wesleyan University in the United States, and worked one year in Israel with the American Friends Service Committee, doing relief work among the Arab refugees in 1949. He now lives mainly in London, writing mostly TV and cinema scripts. He did some teaching in the U.S.

One of his most popular and most widely anthologized poems is "Song of the Banana man" which begins:

"Tourist", white man, wipin' his face,
Met me in Golden Grove market place.
He looked at m'ol'clothes brown wid stain,
An'soaked right through wid de Portland rain,
He cas' his eye, turn'up his nose,
He says, "you're a beggar man, I suppose?"
He says, "Boy, get some occupation."
Be of some value to your nation."

But even more moving is his "Lament of the Banana man," which ends:

. . . Gal, I'm tellin'you, I'm tired for'true,
Tired of Englan', tired o'you,
I can'go back to Jamaica now—
But I'd want to die there, anyhow.

One of the distinguished West Indian writers who, while not cutting himself off from the local scene, works, lives and produces entirely abroad. He has done a TV series on slavery.

Writings: Plays: *The Damned,* film-script, completed 1962; *Eve,* film-script, completed 1963; *Funeral in Berlin,* film-script adapted from Len Leighton's novel, 1966; *Go Tell it on Table Mountain,* one act, produced Jamaica, 1970; *In a Backward Country,* a play in two acts, produced by BBC TV, London, 1959, and in Guyana, 1964; *The Madhouse in Castle Street,* TV play, completed 1964; *Modesty Blaise,* film-script, 1966; *Return to Look Behind,* TV play, 1963; *The Spectators,* produced in England, 1962; *Two Gentlemen Sharing,* film-script, 1969; *The Widows of Jaffa,* TV play, 1957.

Poetry: in various journals and collections, including *Caribbean Voices,* Vol. I; *Commonwealth Poems of Today; New Voices of the Commonwealth; The Sun's Eye; Young Commonwealth Poetry; Breaklight; Cannot Shot and Glass Beads: Modern Black Writing; Independence Anthology of 1962.*

Biography: *Protector of the Indians* (a biography of Bartolomé de Las Casas), London, Nelson, 1958.

Other: *Trappers and Mountain Men,* 1961.

JONES, Marion Patrick

(**Mrs. Marion Glean O'CALLAGHAN**)
b. ca. 1943, Trinidad.
Novelist, librarian.

A graduate of St. Joseph's Convent, Port of Spain, Jones won the Girls' Open Island Scholarship of 1950 and was one of the first two girl students admitted to the Imperial College of Agriculture. She left Trinidad for the U.S. in the mid-fifties and lived in Brooklyn working in a ceramics factory for one year. She returned to Trinidad and worked at the Carnegie Free Library where she qualified as a Chartered Librarian. In 1959 she entered London University (B.Sc.); did postgraduate work in Social Anthropology submitting a thesis on "The Chinese Community in Trinidad." She is one of the founders of C.A.R.D. (Campaign Against Racial Discrimination) in London. She now lives in Paris working in the field of Race Relations and Human Rights.

Her first novel, *Pan Beat,* covers the period in the mid-1960's in Trinidad, and catches the growing crisis of racial and national identity of its people, and particularly of the "failure" of the middle-class of the 1940's, in the crisis of underdevelopment. Andrew Salkey commented on the work: "An important feature is the crucial symbolism of the steel band and the pan and fete culture endemic in the historical formation and thrust of Trinidad and Tobago."

Jones' second novel, *J'Ouvert Morning* (1976), is a warm study of the passionate, often defeated people spanning three generations in a place much like Trinidad.

Writings: Novel: *Pan Beat,* Port of Spain, Columbus Publishers Ltd., 1973; *J'Ouvert Morning,* Port of Spain, Columbus Publishers, 1976.

Biographical/Critical Sources: A. Salkey's introductory comments to *Pan Beat,* 1973; Elma Reyes, *Trinidad Express* (Jan. 21, 1973), p. 29.

KEANE, Ellsworth McG.

(a.k.a. **Shake**)
b. May 30, 1927, St. Vincent.
Poet, musician, teacher.

Popularly known as Shake (for the immortal bard?), Keane is a lively mind and man, who has played jazz on the flügelhorn.

Keane, educated at St. Vincent's Grammar School, taught there from 1947-1952. He went to England to London University to take a degree but preferred work on perfecting his trumpet techniques. He played with the West Indies saxophonist Joe Harris in the Indo-Jazz fusion style of the late 1950's in England. He has lived in Cologne, Germany, where he was a member of the popular Kurt Edelhagen band. He studied there as well.

He has contributed poems to BIM and

other journals and has published two volumes of poetry. He was a friend and ally of Owen Campbell and Daniel Williams, the "trio" of St. Vincent writing.

His work was read on BBC programs during his days in England. He has now returned to St. Vincent as Government Cultural Officer, where he has been organizing and stimulating local cultural activities.

Writings: Poetry (Collections): Volume I: *L'Oubli,* Bridgetown, Barbados, Advocate Co., 1950; Volume II: *Ixion,* Georgetown, Guyana (Miniature Poet Series), 1952; *Nanacitori,* a long narrative poem (for Dannie [Daniel] Williams) with drums, presented at the Lyric Theatre, Cologne, August 11, 1972. His poetry appears in BIM (Literary magazine, Barbados); *Caribbean Verse* (O.R. Dathorne, ed.), London, Heinemann, 1967; *Caribbean Voices* Vol. II, selected and edited by John Figueroa, Evans, London, 1970, Combined Edition, Robert Luce Co., Inc., Washington, N.Y., 1971; *Kyk-over-al, An Anthology of West Indian Poetry,* 1952, 1957 (A.J. Seymour, ed.); *Savacou* (A Journal of the Caribbean Artists' Movement), Savacou Publications Ltd., Kingston, Jamaica.

Articles: "The Contribution of the West Indian to Literature" in BIM 14, pp. 102-106; "Some Religious Attitudes in West Indian Poetry" (I) in BIM 15, pp. 169-174; "Some Religious Attitudes in West Indian Poetry" (II), in BIM 16, pp. 266-271.

Biographical/Critical Sources: Review of *L'Oubli* in BIM 13, pp. 69-71, by Daniel Williams; he is mentioned in *West Indian Poetry 1900-1970* by Edward Baugh (Pamphlet No. I, Savacou Publications Ltd.), p. 13 and p. 16; and also in "West Indian Poetry: Part II" by F. Gordon Rohlehr in BIM 55, (July-Dec. 1972), p. 143.

KEENS-DOUGLAS, Paul

b. September, 1942, Trinidad.
Poet, actor, broadcaster.

Keens-Douglas spent most of his early life in Grenada. He attended Sir George Williams University, U.S.A., and did post-graduate work at U.W.I., Mona, Jamaica, in Sociology. Active for the last twelve years in drama, he has acted in the U.S.A., Canada, Jamaica and Trinidad. He has also been an announcer/researcher for special programs at Radio Trinidad. He writes in dialect as well as standard English.

Writings: Poetry: *When Moon Shine,* St. Augustine, Trinidad, 1975 (Introduction by Victor D. Questel: Printed by Scope Publishing Caribbean).

Biographical/Critical Sources: Introduction by Victor Questel to *When Moon Shine.*

KELLMAN, Tony

b. ca. 1945, Barbados.
Poet.

Kellman has one known collection of verse, *The Black Madonna and other poems,* Bridgetown, Barbados, the Author, 1975.

KELSHALL, Jack

b. ca. 1942, Trinidad.
Poet.

While detained during the 1971 Trinidad State of Emergency, Kelshall, a lawyer and labor organizer, produced a collection of poems: *Song from a prison courtyard (and other poems),* Curepe, Trinidad, Moko Enterprises Ltd., 1972. He has otherwise not published.

KEMPADOO, Peter

(see under pseudonym: **LAUCHMONEN**)

KENT, Lena

(pseudonym of **Lettice A. KING**)
b. ca. 1888, Jamaica.
Poet, prose writer.

Medallist of the Institute of Jamaica, 1931, Kent's poems appeared regularly in the *Daily Gleaner.*

Writings: Poetry: *Spiritual Counsels for Young Christians,* 1918; *The Hills of St. Andrew,* 1931, two other collections, mainly of a religious nature, include *Dews on the Branch,* 1933; work represented in the *Treasury of Jamaican Poetry.*

Biographical/Critical Sources: Mentioned in J.E. Clare McFarlane's *A Literature in the Making,* Kingston, Jamaica, Pioneer Press, 1956, see especially Chapter 5, pp. 34-37.

KHAN, Ismith

b. 1925, Port of Spain, Trinidad.
Novelist, storywriter, journalist, librarian, teacher.

From the "East Indian" tradition, Khan was educated at Queens Royal College, Trinidad, then attended Michigan State University and the New School for Social Research in New York City. He was a reporter for the *Trinidad Guardian,* later assistant to Elliott Coleman's creative Writing Seminar at Johns Hopkins University (Baltimore, Md.), and was recently

named director of Third World Studies at the University of California at San Diego.

Khan's first novel, ***The Jumbie Bird*** (1961), is a semi-autobiographical novel in which a youth struggles to understand the East Indian world of his grandfather in Asia and the new confused cultural world of Trinidad. His second novel, *The Obeah Man,* is set in carnival season in Port of Spain when violence and release from the year-long tensions of crowding and poverty excuse most excesses. There is, in this work, also a sympathetic treatment of genuine African elements in the community.

Khan has been recently working on a survey of the use made in Caribbean schools of local literature and culture.

Writings: Novels: *The Jumbie Bird,* London, MacGibbon and Kee, 1961, and New York, Obolensky, 1963; *The Obeah Man,* London, Hutchinson, 1964. In ms., "The Crucifixion."

Play: *The Obeah Man,* London: The BBC, 1970.

Stories: in various journals and collections, including "The Red Ball," in *New Writing in the Caribbean* (A.S. Seymour, ed.), and in J.T. Livingston's *Caribbean Rhythms,* New York, Four Square Press, 1974; *From The Green Antilles* (Barbara Howes, ed.), N.Y., Macmillan, 1966.

Biographical/Critical Sources: R.M. Lacovia, "Ismith Kahn and the Theory of Rasa," in *Black Images,* Vol. I, No. 3 and 4, pp. 23-27; K. Ramchand has a discussion of Ismith in *The West Indian Novel and Its Background,* New York, Barnes and Noble, 1970, and London, Faber, 1970; review of *The Obeah Man,* by M.S. Blundell, in *Caribbean Quarterly,* Vol. II, Nos. 1 and 2, pp. 95-97.

KING, Audvil

b. 1943, Jamaica.
Poet, journalist, editor, publisher.

King was educated at Buxton High School and the West Indies School of Public Health, which he completed in 1967. He works on environmental matters for the city of Kingston.

King has been a contributor to and publisher, editor and writer for the revolutionary newspapers and magazines, *Harambee, Bongo-Man, Blackman Speaks,* and *Abeng.*

Writings: Poetry: *Revolutionary Poems,* Vols. 1, 2, 3 and 4.
Sociology-Journalism: *A Look at the Black Struggle in Jamaica.*
Selected and Edited: *One Love,* London, 1971, Bogle L'Ouverture Publications (Introduction by Andrew Salkey). Included in *One Love.*

Biographical/Critical Sources: Review article of *One Love* in *Caribbean Studies,* Vol. 12, No. 3 (October, 1972), by Sylvia Wynter—"One Love —Rhetoric or Reality—Aspects of Afro-Jamaicanism." Article "Use Men Language" in BIM 57 (March 1974) by Gerald Moore, pp. 69, 70, 72.

KING, Cameron G.O.

b. ca. 1935, St. Lucia.
Critic, teacher.

King won the Walter Allen Prize for his study of Derek Walcott while at the University of the West Indies. He writes with Louis James on "The Poetry of Derek Walcott" in the chapter "In Solitude for Company" in *The Islands in Between.* (Louis James, ed.), London, A Three Crowns Book, 1968. In *Caribbean Quarterly,* Vol. 10, No. 3, (Sept. 1964), pp. 3-30, he writes on "The Poems of Derek Walcott."

He contributed a chapter, "Jamaican Literature" in *Ian Fleming Introduces Jamaica* (Morris Cargill, ed., London, Andre Deutsch, 1965).

He is presently head of the English Dept., St. Vincent Grammar School, and was External Affairs Secretary in the Government.

Writings: Poetry: *Volume of Poems,* 1970.

KING, Lettice A.

(see under pseudonym: **Lena KENT**)

KING, Lloyd

b. ca. 1935, Trinidad.
Poet, shortstory writer.

An active member of the Modern Languages staff of the U.W.I., King has published at various levels. A regular contributor to *The New Voices* (Anson Gonzalez, ed.-pub.), King published one short story in *Kairi,* and has done translations as well as original poems.

King, like the late Gabriel Coulthard, has had a great socio-cultural interest in Caribbean and Latin American literature.

KING, Sheila

b. ca. 1942; Guyana.
Poet, playwright, storywriter, artist.

At present, King is organizing secretary for the Council on Affairs and Status of Women in Guyana. She was one of the contributors to *Stories from Guyana,* produced for Expo '67. She won the prize winning essay for "The Curelist Test" in the Human Rights Year Essay Competition (1968). She has a poem in the P.E.N. anthology *"Voices."* She has also won prizes for three plays entered in local History and Arts Council and Theatre Guild Competitions; one was staged—*Bourdabounty* (Three Acts), and one was produced for radio—*Fo' Bettin' or Worse: A Two Act Play in the Vernacular,* performed Georgetown, Theatre Guild, 1966 and also still in typescript is *Hands Across the River* (One Act) and *A Matter of Policy* (One Act).

She has four poems in *Guyana Drums,* Georgetown, Guyana, 1972; and is represented in Trotman's *Voices of Guyana.*

KING, Washington

b. ca. 1936, Jamaica.
Poet.

King attended the Alpha Boys' School in Jamaica. He started his own school for children when he was just 16. He served as Secretary of the Tobolski Coffee Group for five years and has worked for the Peoples' Co-operative Bank for two years. He was Headmaster of Windsor Infant School Parish of Clarendon. He was news correspondent for *Daily Gleaner* and *The Star.* He went to the United Kingdom to live in the 1960's.

Writings: Poetry: "In Our Opinion," *New Modern Poems,* Bristol, published by author, 1966.

KIRKPATRICK, Oliver Austin

(pseudonym: **John CANOE**)
b. June 12, 1921, Jamaica.
Storywriter, poet, librarian.

Kirkpatrick was educated at Wolmer's Boys' School, Kingston, Jamaica, and New York University (B.Sc.); Columbia University—M.S., Library Science. He broadcasted regularly over station ZQI, Jamaica, during the war, in penetrating and witty Jamaican speech. He now lives in Brooklyn.

From 1953-1964 Kirkpatrick worked at the New York Public Library. In 1964 he joined the Brooklyn Public Library as Senior Librarian and at present is the Supervising Librarian, Adult Services. He is working on *Pukka Sahib,* a novel of Jamaica, and on "Percy Bysshe's Bike" and "The Shark Papers," both children's books.

Writings: Stories: *Country Cousin,* A selection of dialect talks (broadcast from ZQI, first radio station in Jamaica), printed by the Gleaner Co., Kingston, Jamaica, 1941; *Naja the Snake and Mangus the Mongoose,* New York, Doubleday, 1960.

Poetry: Verse published at various times in *Bitteroot Magazine.*

KISSOON, Freddie

b. ca. 1928, Trinidad.
Playwright, director, actor.

After local schooling through the Government Training College, Kissoon began amateur and then professional acting and playwriting. He founded the Strolling Players who did 263 performances through 1973 in Trinidad, Tobago, and Grenada. He taught acting classes and directing in summer school sessions at the University of the West Indies in 1966, 1967, and 1971. He was commissioned by Radio Trinidad to do a radio serial, *Calabash Alley*—and 78 episodes were done from November 2, 1970 through February 17, 1971. The series has been re-run in its entirety on Sundays, August 22 to December 19, 1971.

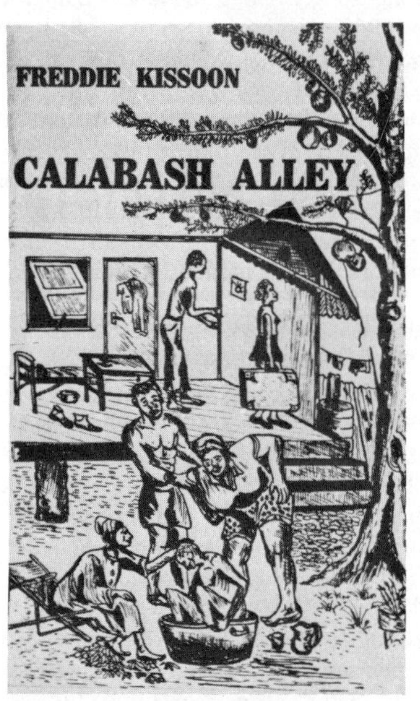

Kissoon has played the role of Ti-Jean in the play of that name by Derek Walcott (1958) and Ram, the West Indian coolie who became a general of the Maroon revolutionary army, in Walcott's *Drums and Colours.* Kissoon lives in Diego Martin, Trinidad.

He wrote the first full-length film script ever composed by a Trinidadian, *The Right and the Wrong,* directed by Harbance Kumer.

Writings: Plays: *Calabash Alley: a full-length play,* Port of Spain, Hi-Grade Printery, 1973;

Do Your home-lesons, Daddy: a one-act play, first performed in 1968, in mimeo version, 1969; *Doo-doo, one act,* first performed 1966, in mimeo, 1969: awarded first prize in Arts Festival in 1965; *God and Uriah Butler,* performed Town Hall, five-day run [covers prophet Butler's life from 1929-1950 from first vision to his disappointment in 1950 elections], done in a three-hour long performance without intermission and performed 11 separate occasions; *Zingay,* Kissoon's first play, performed 112 times on stage in islands and in Ibadan, Nigeria: it was first local play to be performed on Trinidad TV, May 1966; *We Crucify Him,* performed 27 times; *Papa, Look De Priest Passing; King Cobo, a full-length play in three acts,* 1969, which won $1000 as first prize in People's National Movement Competition; *Like hog love mud, one act,* 1969 but first performed in 1965, in mimeo version, 1963; *Mamaguy; a West Indian play in one act,* Champ Fleurs, Trinidad, 1961, and Port of Spain, Extra Mural Department, 1966, with 140 performances in the islands and in London and New York by West Indian students; *Pahyol, one act,* 1969, but first performed in 1966, in mimeo version; *A Promise for Christmas,* one act, three scenes, 1969, and first performed in 1969; *Fugitive from the Royal Jail, one act,* 1969, first performed 1968; other plays: *Girls Wanted; The Cleaner and the Boss* (done with strolling players); *Suicide on the Rails* (done with strolling players); *Christmas Ham* (performed by St. James Secondary School); *Common Entrance* (performed by St. James), and *Obeah Man* (performed with Youth Training Centre and California Government School); *He died for us: a passion play,* P.O.S., 196?.

Film Script: *The Right and the Wrong,* produced by Delinke Film International.

Biographical/Critical Sources: Review of *God and Uriah Butler,* by Jeremy Taylor, *Express* (June 18, 1973), p. 10; Review of same play by Elma Reyes, "Two Views of Freddie Kissoon's *God and Uriah Express, Express,* (June 18, 1973), p. 6; Eric Roach review of same play, in *Trinidad Guardian* (April 12, 1973).

KIZERMAN, Rudolph (Rudi)

b. 1934, Barbados.
Poet, playwright, novelist, actor.

After local schooling, Kizerman went to England in 1952 to study medicine, but he has instead become an actor and playwright after graduating from the Rose Spaulding Drama School. He lived in London for 18 years, then went to Montreal, and has travelled to South Africa, India and Kenya. His novel, *Stand Up in the World* (1968), was his first separately published work.

Kizerman's collection of poems, *I'm Here,* in the words of Andrew Salkey from his introduction, reflects ". . . the borrowed soul from the Black American revolutionary process," but "he has renewed and deepened its original definition and made it appropriately his own." Kizerman had originally completed the collection in 1971 but had to wait for the currents of interest in Black poetry to rise before he could find a publisher.

On August 2, 1975, Kizerman, while walking with his girl friend, was arrested for the possession of "a dangerous weapon," a freshly washed milk bottle he was returning to a nearby milk crate. After many court appearances he was acquitted on April 8, 1976. His bitter poem "The System" (from *I'm Here*) has these lines:

> *I wasn't bombing trains,*
> *looting, burning, tossing bricks*
> . . .

and ends:

> *not even evolution will conceal it!*
> *The victim of the System*
> *WILL NOT FORGIVE.*

Writings: Novels: *Stand Up in the World,* London, Blackbird Books, 1968; "A Tear for the Strangers," in ms.

Poetry: *I'm Here,* London, Blackbird Books, 1975, individual poems in various collections and journals.

Plays: *Yes please, No Please Officer* (or "The Last Bully") is soon to be published. Other plays also in ms.

KONA WARUK

(pseudonym for **Wilson HARRIS**)

LADOO, Harold S.

b. ca. 1942, Trinidad; d. 1973.
Novelist.

Ladoo has lived in Toronto since completing his secondary education in Trinidad.

Of Ladoo's first novel, *No Pain Like this Body,* Victor Questel has this to say: Ladoo "blazed a furious path across the Caribbean literary scene in what is probably the most violent work of Caribbean fiction." His second novel, *Yesterdays,* was published after his death. Christopher Laird says in his review of that work that the "mood and narrative technique is different from *No Pain. . . .*"

Writings: Novels: *No Pain Like This Body,* Toronto, Anansi Press, 1972; *Yesterdays,* Toronto, Anansi Press, 1974 (published posthumously).

Biographical/Critical Sources: Emile Espinet, "Ladoo, Harold S.—*No Pain Like this Body,*" review in *Black Images,* II, I (Spring 1973), pp. 60-62; Victor Questel, review of *No Pain Like this Body* in *Kairi* I, 1974; Christopher Laird, review of *Yesterdays* as "The Novel of Tomorrow Today," *Kairi,* 1974.

LA FORTUNE, Knolly S.

b. 1920, Trinidad.
Poet, folklorist, teacher.

After schooling in Trinidad, La Fortune went to England where he has resided most of his adult life. He is a Grammar School teacher in London. His poem "Breaklight" begins:

Breaklight,
glow!
The old, dark night
was our vision.
We stared the sun
into blindness
and counted ourselves wise.

and the poem ends:

Breaklight!
We understand might.
We know the power of hate.
We've closed the gaps in our story
for our own good.

Writings: Folklore: *Legend of T-Marie, A Tale of Trinidad Folklore,* London, (privately printed), 1968.

Poetry: *Moments of Inspiration,* Port of Spain, Guardian Commercial Printery (privately printed), 1946; his work is in many collections, including *Breaklight,* edited by Andrew Salkey (New York, 1973), which takes its name from La Fortune's poem of that name and which is found of course in the volume. His work is also in *Caribbean Voices,* I (J. Figueroa, ed., London & Washington); *Caribbean Quarterly,* Federation Issue, (April 1958); and poems in *Trinidad Guardian; Port of Spain Gazette* and *Catholic News.*

LAIRD, Christopher

b. ca. 1945, Trinidad.
Poet, writer, editor.

Laird's poetry has been published in *The New Voices* and *Kairi.* He is also the editor of *Kairi,* the aim of which is to "publish creative work from and about Trinidad and Tobago and the Caribbean."

Writings: Editor of Collection (with Basil Smith): *Rising Poems* (listed in *Caribana,* Sangster's Bookstores, Kingston, Jamaica).

LAMMING, George

b. 1927, Barbados.
Novelist, poet, critic, broadcaster, teacher.

George Lamming was born in Barbados, son of a Barbadian woman of strong character. He has many distinctions, not least of which is giving to a Caribbean reality the important verbalization "it was my mother who fathered me." He attended elementary school and then won a scholarship for Combermere High School where he read much and played cricket on the same team as the young Frank Worrell—later to be Sir Frank Worrell, and an international hero of that graceful sport.

He left Barbados at the age of 18 to teach in Trinidad, at a Venezuelan college for boys. The post had been arranged partly through the good offices of Jimmy Cozier and Frank Collymore of BIM.

It was for Lamming the end of one life and the beginning of another: as the end of *In The Castle of My Skin* has it:

> *... Words and voices falling like a full shower and the old man returning with the pebble under the grape leaf on the sand....*
>
> *The earth where I walked was a marvel of blackness and I knew in a sense more deep than simple departure I had said farewell, farewell to the land.*

Lamming was first a poet— as old copies of BIM will show, and even after going to London, on leaving Trinidad, he produced the impressive poem, "The Swan."

Lamming's school days (as one learns from *Kas-Kas,* [African and Afro-American Research Institute, The Univ. of Texas at Austin, Texas, 1972], and from his novels) were none too rewarding or happy. He survived at Combermere secondary school (Barbados) mainly because of Frank Collymore who not only taught him at school but also put at his disposal an extensive library, and provided him with a refuge—on Saturday mornings at least!

In the Castle of My Skin, Lamming's first novel, which was such a widely heralded success in England and the States, and to some extent in France, is dedicated to

> *My Mother*
> *and*
> *Frank Collymore*
> *whose love and help*
> *deserved a better book.*

The praises of *In the Castle of My Skin* were impressive; even in the literary pubs, the book, while still in manuscript, created ripples all over. One remembers how impressed people like John Grenfell Williams, Head of BBC Overseas, was.

Lamming had brought one chapter to London; he finished it there, giving up his original idea of doing an arts degree, and "settled down" to writing, broadcasting, and the literary life.

At first George Lamming did not agree with what Simone Weil called "The Need for Roots," but he later became very "committed" and particularly concerned about the politics of Africa with all the arguments about "colonization," "imperialism," "independence" and the rest. He took over and developed the imagery and myths connected with the latter day, hindsight reading of the *Tempest,* some of which had been put forward quite early by O. Manoni.

In later life, Lamming became a friend of C.L.R. James, who impressed him with his Marxist interpretations of history, but in turn Lamming has no doubt made James reexamine his earlier readings of Melville's *Moby Dick.*

George Lamming's remarkable talent, as shown in *In the Castle of My Skin,* perhaps always suffered by being apparently not infused enough with structural and disciplined form. Some critics also found a tendency to overwrite. He seemed to be too detailed where he did not really need it—as in *Water With Berries* (1971)—and not detailed enough when we did need it—as in *The Emigrants* (1955).

Though some critics felt that Lamming's works following *Castle* were a falling-off, the appearance of *Natives of My Person* and the earlier *Season of Adventure* were major efforts. Certainly *Season of Adventure* had been well ahead of its time by exploring, in fictional and moving terms, not the preliminary maneuvers of "independence," but the much more important and lasting question of what happens when the very people who have struggled for independence begin to rule and govern and really be in control. He makes his narrator say, through the rather awkward mechanism of an author's note:

> *. . . Exactly two months and four days after the episode which brings this book to a close, enough evidence was found to prove beyond doubt who murdered Vice-President Raymond. It was Powell. . . .*
>
> *. . . Believe it or not: Powell was my brother: my half brother by a different mother.*
>
> *Until the age of ten Powell and I had lived together, equal in the affection of two mothers. Powell had made my dreams; and I had lived his passions. Identical in years, and stage by stage, Powell and I were taught in the same primary school.*
>
> *And then the division came. I got a public scholarship which started my migration into another world, a world whose roots were the same, but whose style of living was entirely different from what my childhood knew. . . .*
>
> *. . . I believe deep in my bones that the mad impulse which drove Powell to his criminal defeat was largely my doing. I will not have this explained away by talk about environment; nor can I allow my own moral infirmity to be transferred to a foreign conscience, labelled imperialist. I shall be beyond my grave in the knowledge that I am responsible for what happened to my brother.*
>
> *Powell still resides somewhere in my heart, with a dubious love, some strange, nameless shadow of regret: and yet with the deepest, deepest nostalgia. For I have never felt myself to be an honest part of anything since the world of his childhood deserted me.* (pp. 331-332)

This central idea of accepting responsibility for one's own complicities—and overt acts— is evidence of the fictional depth of Lamming, and certainly was a new and "revolutionary" note when he produced it. At the same time the self-accusation "I have never felt myself to be an honest part of anything since the world

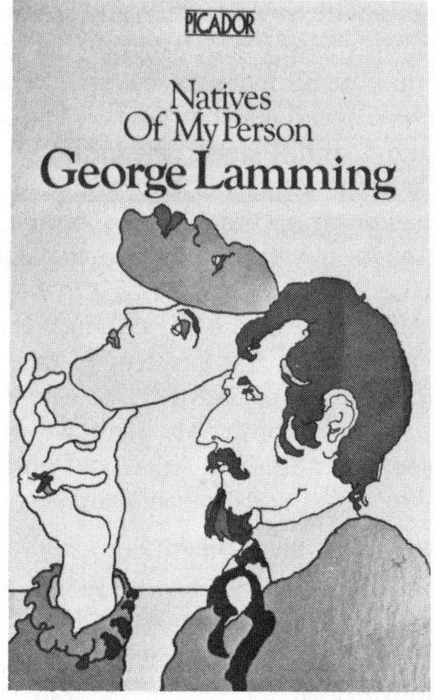

of his childhood deserted me" points up, perhaps, some of the difficulties of over-self consciousness, of an almost compulsive, repetitiveness which we meet often in Lamming's fiction. There is also some unexplained tension between the sentence just quoted and the earlier declaration "I will not have this explained away by talk about *environment*" . . . (emphasis added).

Lamming's fiction is rewarding and rich;

it struggles with the complexities of the culture of the Caribbean Basin—cultures and peoples and regimes and languages in contact and conflict; his imagination is also deep and moving even if at times bizarre and violent. His control of langauge, at a variety of levels and registers and dialects, is powerful and impressive. Perhaps because of the complexities of the data, but also one feels, because of an overestimation of the importance of detail, and of a tendency to overwrite—Lamming does not often enough achieve that clear light of epiphany which one longs for as one reads his rightly demanding and penetrating books.

Lamming was once an excellent broadcaster—both as performer and maker of programs. His Frank Worrell memorial program was a masterpiece; and some of his BBC readings (at times with John Figueroa and Pauline Henriques) were really outstanding. It is to be regretted that he has given up broadcasting, but he has started in recent years to teach and lecture at a variety of universities. He started at the University of the West Indies, Mona, Jamaica, under the auspices of the Creative Arts Centre and the Department of Education. He has continued this work in places as far apart as Arhaaus, Denmark; Austin, Texas; and Tanzania and Australia.

Lamming has long had his center of operation in London, and this perhaps has added to the feeling of alienation in some of his work, but from the beginning his fiction has been concerned with "the other's interference." When, in *In the Castle of My Skin,* "G" is perturbed by the disappearance of the pebble on the beach, he says:

> *I had no overwhelming sense of the supernatural, but I was getting a strange feeling that something had interfered. I didn't know how to relate the situation because I didn't know how I should describe this sense of the other's interference.*

Perhaps one of the most unresolved underlying main ideas in Lamming's rich and interesting work is precisely whether "the other" is enemy or "neighbor." He has also been much concerned with the role of women in the socio-political development of "San Cristobal" and its surrounding sea of islands, and in the world as a whole—see his impressive *Natives of My Person.* It is through a woman that we meet one of his most moving moments, Penelope, an English woman, visiting in a foursome, San Cristobal, has discovered, in an embarrassing way, that she is homosexual. We read in her diary:

> *My imagination had played no part in this deception, nor was it the feeling which was the first sign of my difficulty with Marcia. These were inactive during my sleep. It was one other part of me which substituted Marcia for Bill. For the first time I felt ashamed. Not only my hands, but my entire body had deceived me . . . I shall become Penelope in spite of being Penelope . . . They will never use the accident of my experience against me, but I shall always feel the mark, "in spite of," branded on my presence. . . . It would be better to lose one's status completely and be seen wholly as a new thing; much better than to have have one's status granted with a certain reservation . . . The Negro, the homosexual, the Jew, the worker . . . he is a man, that is never denied, but he is not quite ready for definition until these reservations are stated, and it is the reservation which separates him from himself. He is a man in spite of . . . I shall be Penelope in spite of . . . .*

More recently (1974), Lamming was invited by the General Secretary of the Barbados Workers' Union to organize the opening of their first Labour College. That Institution is now a reality. In 1976 he received the Writers Award from the Association of Commonwealth Literature and later made an extensive lecture tour of India and Australia. In 1977 he served as visiting professor at the University of Texas (Austin) and then accepted a professorship at the University of Pennsylvania which had been vacated by Ezekiel Mphahlele.

In 1966 he served on the jury in Havana of the National Union of Artists and Writers, which for the first time made an award to Caribbean writers working in English. (Winners were Noel Williams, James Carnegie [both in prose], and Edward Brathwaite [poetry]).

Writings: Novels: *In the Castle of My Skin,* London, Joseph, and New York, McGraw Hill, 1953; *The Emigrants,* London, Joseph, 1954; New York, McGraw Hill, 1955; *Of Age and Innocence,* London, Joseph, 1958; *Season of Adventure,* London, Joseph, 1960; *Water with Berries,* London, Longman, 1971; *Natives of My Person,* New York, Canada, Holt, Rinehart and Winston, 1972.

Other: *The Pleasures of Exile,* London, Joseph, 1960.

Anthology (Editor): *Cannon Shot and Glass Beads,* London, Pan Books, 1974.

Short Fiction: in various anthologies including: *Caribbean Narrative* (O.R. Dathorne, ed., Heinemann Ltd., London, 1966); *Caribbean Prose* (A. Salkey, ed., Evans, London, 1967); *From the Green Antilles* (Barbara Howes, ed., Macmillan, New York, 1966); *Island Voices* (A. Salkey, ed., Liveright, New York, 1970); *Stories from the Caribbean* (A. Salkey, ed., Dufour, Philadelphia, 1965); *West Indian Stories* (A. Salkey, ed., Faber, London, 1960); *Caribbean Rhythms* (James T. Livingston, ed., Pocket Books, New York, 1974).

Poetry: in various anthologies, including: *Young Commonwealth Poets '65* (Peter Brent, ed., Heinemann, London, 1965); *Caribbean Voices,* Vols. I and II (ed. and selected by John Figueroa, Evans, London, 1966, 1966, 1970, and Combined edition, Robert Luce Co., Inc., Washington, New York); *Caribbean Verse* (O.R. Dathorne, ed., Heinemann, London, 1968); *Caribbean Quarterly,* Vol. 5 No. 3 (April 1958), Federation Commemoration Issue; *Kyk-over-al,* No. 22 (1957); *Kyk-over-al, Special Issue* (Midyear, 1952), Vol. 1, No. 14. He has also been published in various journals including BIM (Barbados); *Savacou; New World; Casa de las Americas* (Cuba).

Biographical/Critical Sources: Reviews of: *In the Castle of My Skin,* by Gloria Escoffery in BIM 18, pp. 153-155; *The Emigrants,* by Bruce St. John, in BIM 22, pp. 130-132; *Of Age of Innocence,* by M. Combe Martin, in BIM 29, pp. 62-64; *The Pleasures of Exile,* by Harold Marshall, in BIM 32, pp. 289-290; *Season of Adventure,* by John Wickham, in BIM 33, pp. 69-72; *New World: Guyana Independence Issue* (Ed. with Martin Carter) by Anne Walmsley in BIM 44, pp. 297-298; *New World: Barbados Independence Issue,* (ed.) by Elizabeth Wardrop, in BIM 44, pp. 299-300; *Water with Berries,* by Chalmer St. Hill, in BIM 55, pp. 189-191; *Natives of My Person,* by Jan Carew in the *New York Times Book Review;* and Thomas Lask, *New York Times;* Stuart M. Hall, "Lamming, Selvon and some trends in the West Indian Novel," in BIM Vol. 6, No. 23 (Dec. 1955), pp. 172-178; Joseph and Johanna Jones, *Authors and Areas of the West Indies* (People and Places in World-English Literature, No. 2, Austin, Texas, 1970), p. 32; *Kas-Kas: Interviews with Three Caribbean Writers* (Occasional Publication of 1972), pp. 5-20; Kenneth Ramchand, *The West Indian Novel and its Background,* (Barnes and Noble Inc., New York, 1970), references: George Lamming, pp. 6, 52, 73, 135; *In the Castle of My Skin,* pp. 73, 207; *Seasons of Adventure,* pp. 29, 52, 108, 109, 131, 135-149, 239, 267, 272; *The Emigrants,* pp. 107, 108; "The Negro Writer and his World," p. 6 [refers to article in *Caribbean Quarterly,* Vol. 5, No. 2 (Feb 1958)]; *The Pleasures of Exile,* pp. 4, 25-26, 72, 138 n.i., 142; Also see: Edward Baugh, "West Indian Poetry 1900-1970," (Pamphlet No. I, Savacou Publications Ltd., Jamaica), pp. 11-12, 14-15; Gordon Rohlehr, "West Indian Poetry: Part II," BIM 55, p. 143, Anson Gonzales "'Possibility' in W.I. Creative Writing," *The New Voices,* (No. 4, June 1974, Trinidad and Tobago), references: pp. 3, 6, 8, 9, 10; "The Historical Imagination,' *The Literary Half-Yearly* XI, 2 (Mysore, July 1970), pp. 35-46; J.A. Ramsaran, *New Approaches to African Literature,* Ibadan, Ibadan University Press, 1964, 1970; Anthony Boxhill "George Lamming's Two Latest Novels," (*Water with Berries* and *Natives of My Person*), in *World Literature Written in English,* XII, I (April 1973), pp. 111-116; Ian Munro: "The Theme of Exile in George Lamming's *In the Castle of My Skin," World Literature Written in English,* No. 20, University of Texas at Arlington, Texas (Nov. 1971); Interview of October 15, 1970, entitled "Writing and Publishing in the West Indies, in *World Literature Written in English,* No. 19 (April 1971); Barrie Davies, "The Sense of Abroad: Aspects of the West Indian Novel in England," in *World Literature Written in English,* II, 2 (Nov. 1972), pp. 67-80; John Figueroa, in the chapter entitled "Some Provisional Comments on West Indian Novels," in *Commonwealth Literature* (John Press, ed.), London, Heinemann, 1965; R.M. Lacovia, "The Reach of Language and Music: and exploration of the works of George Lamming," in *Black Images,* II, 4; Gerald Moore, *The Chosen Tongue,* London, Longmans, 1969; Wilfred Cartey, "Lamming and the search for freedom," in *New World Quarterly,* Barbados Independence Issue, Vol. III, Nos. 1 and 2, (Dead Season, 1966 and Croptime, 1967), pp. 121-128; Mervyn Morris, "The poet as novelist: the novels of George Lamming," chapter in *Islands in Between* (Louis James, ed.), London, 1968, pp. 73-85; Stella Merriman, *Commonwealth Caribbean Writers: A Bibliography,* Georgetown, Guyana, 1970, pp. 52-63; C.L.R. James, review of *Natives of My Person* in *Cross Currents,* Vol. XXII, No. 3 (Summer-Fall 1972).

LA ROSE, John A.

(pseudonym: **Anthony LA ROSE,** for verse)
b. December, 1917, Trinidad.
Poet, critic, publisher, teacher.

John La Rose became prominent through his work in politics during the late pre-independence period in the British West Indies and Guiana (Guyana). He has taught in High School, been an insurance salesman, journalist (which included editing *Freedom,* an organ of the West Indian Independence Party), and also a manual worker in the building trades.

Moving to England in the 1950's, La Rose runs a book shop in London specializing in Third World books. He has served as secretary of the Caribbean Artists' Movement in London, and organized the Island publishing house of New Beacon Books Ltd. He has also issued his own two volumes of poetry and the work of others, including Adolph Edwards (*Marcus Garvey, 1887-1940*); Wilson Harris (*Tradition, The Writer and Society*); and *Ivan Van Sertima* (Caribbean Writers).

He has served as Chairman of the Race Relations Institute of London. In 1956 he was an unsuccessful candidate in the Trinidad general elections.

La Rose's first volume of poetry, *Foundations,* was published in 1966; the second in 1971. The last two verses of his poem "The Uprooted" from *Foundations* are typical of his style and motifs:

When you chant our circumstance,
The night owl screeches,
Dredging haunted huts
For unwilling coffins.

We jump like fish
Fleeing into the dust;
Roots that but touch
The earth do wither.

Writings: Poetry: *Foundations,* London and Port of Spain, New Beacon Publications, 1966, (first work published by N.B.P.); *Islets of Truth Within Me,* Port of Spain, New Beacon, 1971; Verse in various journals including BIM; *New World Fortnightly; Vanguard; Voices; New World Quarterly.*

Editor of: *New Beacon Reviews; Collection One,* Port of Spain, New Beacon Books, 1968; co-author with Raymond Quevedo of *Kaiso—A Review.*

Biographical/Critical Sources: Interview by Sebastian Clarke in *Journal of Black Poetry,* Special West Indian Issue, Vol. I, No. 17 (Summer 1973), pp. 25-28; review of *Foundations* by Peter Figueroa in BIM, Vol. 12, No. 48 (Jan-June 1969), pp. 270-271; review of *Foundations* by Derek Walcott in *Sunday Guardian* (Trinidad), Jan. 15, 1967, p. 8; review of *Foundations* by Colin Richards in *Books and Bookmen,* Vol. 12, No. 8 (May 1967), p. 28; review of *Foundations* by R.H. Foakes, in *Journal of Commonwealth Literature,* No. 6 (Jan. 1969), p. 149; review of *New Beacon Reviews: Collection One* (Ed.) by Mervyn Morris in BIM, No. 50, pp. 131-132.

LASHLEY, Cliff

b. September 21, 1935, Jamaica.
Poet, librarian, teacher.

Educated at University of West Indies, University of Western Ontario and School of Librarianship, Northwestern Polytechnic, London, Lashley has taught at Seneca College, Toronto, Livingston College, and Rutgers University.

Lashley now works in the New York office of A.P.I., Jamaica. He is a regular contributor to *Black Images* magazine, established in 1972, and four of his poems appeared there in a group entitled "Poems of Exile."

According to Drayton in his *Black Orpheus* essay of 1969, Lashley explores "West Indian Self-Hood" in the "face of cultural schizophrenia."

Writings: Poetry: *Letter from home* in *Jamaica Journal,* Institute of Jamaica, Vol. I, No. 1 (December 1967), p. 78; Five poems in *Black Orpheus,* No. 22 (August 1967), pp. 48-53.

Journals: *Black Orpheus,* BIM, *Folio, Jamaica Journal;* and anthology: *New Voices of the Commonwealth,* 1968.

Biographical/Critical Sources: Arthur D. Drayton: "The Poetry of Cultural Precariousness: Introducing Cliff Lashley: a new Caribbean Voice," in *Black Orpheus,* No. 22 (August 1967), pp. 49-63.

LAUCHMONEN

(pseudonym for **Peter KEMPADOO**)

b. 1926, Guyana.
Novelist, broadcaster, teacher, publisher, lecturer.

Lauchmonen grew up on a sugar estate in British Guiana. After leaving school he worked for a time in the sugar factory; then he became a teacher and later a reporter in Georgetown. He has traveled widely in the Caribbean and spent some time in Barbados with his family working as a publisher. He has returned to Guyana. But his home and base for a number of years was England where he has written and published. He has been a consultant in Rural Development and has been a publisher of school texts.

His novels reflect the life of sugar farmers on the large estates of cane and rice in Guyana, with which he was familiar from his growing up years. His novel *Guiana Boy* is really a series of episodes in the life of Lilboy on the sugar estate. From the notes on the cover of this book we read "What is most impressive about this novel is the author's very real sense of humor; his ability to drape that humor around a whole set of raffish earthy characters that stay in the mind." The cover design and illustrations for the book were done by his wife Rosemary Kempadoo.

Writings: Novel: *Guiana Boy,* Crawley, Sussex, New Literature, 1960; *Old Thom's Harvest,* London, Eyre and Spottiswoode, 1965. Extracts from his novel *Guiana Boy* appear in the anthologies: *The Sun's Eye* ("Rice Money"); and in *My Lovely Native Land* ("The Rice Cutting Season").

Biographical/Critical Sources: Kenneth Ramchand in *The West Indian Novel and its Background* (Barnes and Noble, 1970) makes a reference to *Guiana Boy* (p. 208) in the chapter on "Novels of Childhood."

LAWRENCE, Walter MacArthur

b. 1896, Guyana; d. 1942.
Poet.

Lawrence was educated at St. Thomas Scots School and Queen's College. He began submitting his early poems to a Georgetown newspaper in 1920. He has been called the "poet of Guyana." One of his best known poems, "Kaiteur," contains the following lines:

Who, who can behold thee, O glorious
Kaituer, let down as it were from the
fathomless blue,

A shimmering veil on the face of the
mountain obscuring its flaws from
inquisitive view,
Retouched with the soft, rosy glow of
the morning and freaking the flow of
desultory light,
Or bathed in the brilliant translucence
of noontide a mystical mirror
resplendently bright.

Writings: Poetry: *Meditation. Thoughts in the Silence,* Georgetown, 1933. He appears in *Caribbean Verse* (Dathorne, ed.); *Themes of Song; Sun is a Shapely Fire; Fourteen Guianese Poems for Children;* and *Guianese Poetry* (Cameron, ed.). He was also published in local periodicals including *Kyk-over-al.*

Biographical/Critical Sources: The Poet of Guyana, Walter MacA. Lawrence, selected with a biography by P.H. Daly, Georgetown, Daily Chronicle, 1948; Edward Baugh, *West Indian Poetry 1900-1970* (Savacou Publications, Pamphlet No. 1), p. 5. Also see "Introduction to the Poetry of Walter MacA. Lawrence," in *Kyk-over-al,* 6 (1943), p. 35.

LAYNE, Paul

b. ca. 1945, Barbados; d. 1971.
Poet, shortstory writer.

Paul Layne was a highly talented and creative person. John Wickham, writing of him on the occasion of his tragic death in Notebook, BIM 53 (July-Dec. 1971), said: "We are not so surfeited with the kind of industry and talent which Paul had that we can easily afford these losses."

Layne, along with Denis Foster and Robert Lee, produced *Posthumous Papers* (Aug. 1970) and *Banjo's Notebook* (Nov. 1970). The latter publication took its name from a short story by Denis Foster (published in BIM 53, 1971). It carried Layne's "Captain Cudjoe of the Maroons and Independence in the West Indies" which won posthumously for him the first prize of US$200 offered by the American based Association for the Achievement of Education in the Caribbean.

After his death the third publication of the trio Foster/Layne/Lee, *Music Men,* was brought out (July 1972).

His verse. and fiction appeared in BIM and *Caribbean Medlay (Poems),* BIM 52 (Jan-June 1971—posthumously).

Writings: Mixed Prose and Poetry: *Sunday blues: poems/stories,* Wildey, Barbados: Coles Printery, 1975 (63 pp., illus.; a posthumous publication).

LEE, Easton Hugh

b. February 19, 1931, Jamaica.
Playwright. actor, shortstory writer.

Easton Lee has long been involved in theatre and drama circles, radio and TV. He wrote and directed Jamaica's first TV play. He was the winner of the Best Actor Award, Jamaica, 1958; the Seprod Journalism Award, 1965. He is the Art Director of the Jamaica Folk Singers led by Olive Lewin. He has written several plays and short stories.

LEE, Erica B.

b. ca. 1909, St. Thomas, U.S. Virgin Islands.
Poet.

Lee's one known published volume (50 pages) is *Reflections: A Collection of Poems* (San Juan, Padilla Printing Works, 1939).

LEE, Robert

b. May 6, 1948, Castries, St. Lucia.
Poet, storywriter, critic, director, actor.

Robert Lee went to St. Mary's College in Castries. After High School he worked for two years with the Royal Bank of Canada (1967-69), then left St. Lucia for U.W.I., Cave Hill, Barbados, where he studied mainly English and French literature.

At the Royal Bank he formed a close friendship with MacDonald Dixon, who encouraged him to write poetry and to develop a latent interest in the theatre.

This encouragement flowered in Barbados, where he made a name for himself as a writer (poetry, stories, and critical reviews) and as a theatre person (actor and director). He returned to St. Lucia in 1974 to take a teaching post at his old school, St. Mary's College. He is director of a theatre group, the New Day Theatre Workshop, which he founded. He is at present training a small group of actors in the Theatre Workshop, and working on plans for future programs which include community theatre, work in the media, and dramatization of West Indian literature.

In February 1975, his first collection of poetry, *Vocation and other poems,* was published by the local Extra Mural Dept. of U.W.I. (Iounaloa Series No. 3, General Editor, Patricia Charles, Resident Tutor). His poems and articles have been published in various periodicals and newspapers of the Caribbean, and in reviews in Canada.

He writes regularly for the local newspapers and has a regular critical column "Soul-to-Soul." He is at present planning to launch a St. Lucian Literary magazine called *Jou'ouvert.* Also pending is a collection of essays. He did a long critical study of the novels of Garth St. Omer, the St. Lucian novelist, part of which was published in *Tapia* (Trinidad) in 1974, and the *Crusader* (St. Lucia).

He says of himself: "I admire intensely the poetry and essays of Derek Walcott. I share with a kind of fanaticism his vision and his passion. James Baldwin, in many of his essays and novels, has provided me with guidelines to my own lifestyle. I admire Naipaul's intense honesty. Césaire and Fanon brought me to a kind of 'political' consciousness; Eliot and Larkin provided guidelines to a new kind of poetry; Lawrence, Camus and Gibran provided a romantic kind of philosophy that has its roots in the hard reality of what seems to be an 'absurd' existence.

"I read much more poetry than prose. "I am an individualist, hate and abhor bandwaggons, choose my company carefully, hate noise and violence, hate to be tied down (hence have avoided marriage). If I was not a writer, I would have liked to be a musician."

Lee, along with Paul Layne and Dennis Foster, privately printed *Posthumous Papers* by Michael Foster (the young Barbadian poet and brother of Dennis Foster) who died tragically in an auto accident at the age of 20, in January 1965.

Writings: Poetry (collections): *Vocation and other poems* (published by the Extra Mural Dept., The Morne, St. Lucia, Feb. 1975), with cover design and illustrations by Alwin Bully; With Foster and Layne: *Posthumous Papers,* August, 1970; *Banjo's Notebook,* November, 1970; *Music Men,* July, 1972 (all three publications privately printed in Barbados [Layne died in 1971]). Lee's verse has been published in the following periodicals: *Link* (St. Lucia); BIM (Barbados); *Savacou* (Jamaica); *Free your mind* (Dominica); *Wahseen* (Dominica); *New Voices* (Trinidad); *Caribbean Medley; Caribbean Collage; Kairi* (Trinidad); *Manna* (Canada); *The Greenfield Review* (Greenfield Center, N.Y. State), and in the following newspapers: *Pan-Africanist; The Cavite; Voices from the Cave* (U.W.I. Barbados); *Barbados Advocate News* (Barbados); *The Voices* (St. Lucia); and *Tapia* (Trinidad).

LEIGHTON-MILLS, Horace E.

b. ca. 1936, Tobago.
Playwright, poet, storywriter.

One-time principal of Independence College, Roxborough, Tobago, Leighton-Mills has published one play and a variety of stories and verse.

Anson Gonzalez in *Self-Discovery Through Literature (Creative Writing in Trinidad and Tobago),* comments: "Horace E. Leighton-Mills has written two volumes, which contain about 90 poems. . . . A sort of unofficial poet laureate, he often celebrates in verse the anniversaries of our independence. . . ." (p. 14).

Writings: Mixed prose and poetry: *Anthology of poems and a 3-act play, Flora,* Port of Spain, Busby's Printerie, 1966; *Second Anthology of poems and short stories,* Port of Spain, Busby's Printerie, 1968.

LEO

(pseudonym for **Egbert MARTIN**)

LETTSOME, Quincy F.V.

b. ca. 1913, Tortola, British Virgin Islands.
Poet.

Lettsome's one known collection is *Virgin Verses* (Road Town, Tortola, B.V.I., 1969); a second edition (Tortola, Caribbean Printing Co.) appeared in 1976.

LEWIN, Olive

b. ca. 1937, Jamaica.
Folklorist, musician, singer, musicologist.

Lewin is a collector of folklore and songs, and the leader of well-known and widely recognized group which interprets Jamaican folk music. She was awarded the Musgrave Silver Medal for her contribution in the field of folk music, 1970.

Writings: Musicology and Folklore: *Some Jamaican Folk Songs, Vol. I; Arawak Love Song (Words and Music),* recorded by author, Guyana, 1967, sung by E. Pieters, and published in *Jamaica Journal,* Institute of Jamaica, Vol. 1 No. 1 (Dec. 1967), p. 88; "Bungo Mulatto" (Folk Song), collected by Olive Lewin in *Jamaica Journal,* Vol. 2, No. 1 (March 1968), p. 77; "Folk Music of Jamaica—An outline for classification," in *Jamaica Journal,* Vol. 4, No. 2 (June 1970), pp. 68-72.

LEWIS, Enid Kirton

b. ca. 1940, Trinidad.
Storywriter, critic.

The stories in Lewis' one collection, *Voices of Earth* (1972) are good, strong, warm, showing a good ear for Trinidadian speech.

Writings: Stories: *Voices of Earth: Ten Short Stories of raw life in Trinidad in the Forties,* Gasparillo, Rillsprint, 1972 [96 pp.]; "The Locho," in *The New Voices* (No. 3, 1974).

Novelette: *The Beedoe* [A fiction based on life in "The Coffee."].

Critical Essays: "The World of Samuel Selvon: An Appraisal of the Works of the Versatile Caribbean Writer," in ms.; "The Syrian-Lebanese Community of Trinidad," in ms., a winner of a prize in the competition of 1970 for essays submitted to the U.W.I., St. Augustine, Trinidad.

LEWIS, K.C.

b. ca. 1903, Barbados.
Poet, civil servant.

Lewis' two volumes of poetry are *Floraspe* (1933), and *Weymouth poems* (1969).

LINDO, Archie

b. ca. 1919, Jamaica.
Poet, storywriter, novelist, playwright.

Archie Lindo has been better known in recent years as a broadcaster and firm supporter of the arts, but he has been a writer for a long time with many stories, plays, and poems in print. He edited the *Year Book Poetry League of Jamaica* in 1939 and 1945.

Writings: Plays: *Under the Skin*, published in *Bronze* (see below: *Tar Brush; Forbidden Fruit,* produced in 1942; *The White Witch of Rose Hall,* adapted from H.G. DeLisser's novel of that name, produced Jamaica, 1945; *The Maroon,* adapted from Captain Mayne Reid's novel of the same name, produced January 1947.

Short Stories (and other genres): *Bronze: Short stories, articles, a poem and a play,* Mandeville, Jamaica, printed by the College Press, 1944 or 1945; *My Heart Was Singing: poems and short stories*, Mandeville, Jamaica, printed by the College Press, 1945.

LINDO, Cedric George

b. January 23, 1913, Jamaica.
Newspaper columnist, reviewer.

Lindo was the BBC representative in the West Indies, 1942-1946, and 1956-63. In the early days he worked closely with Henry Swanzy in the collection of material for BBC's *Caribbean Voices*. More recently he organized for some time the literary page of the *Sunday Gleaner,* and he has been an active member of the Jamaica P.E.N.

Writings: Editor, with A.L. Hendricks: *The Independence Anthology of Jamaican Literature,* Kingston, The Arts Celebration Committee of the Ministry of Development, Welfare.

LOCKETT, Mary F.

b. ca. 1872, Jamaica.
Poet, novelist.

Lockett is one of the earliest Jamaican novelists.

Writings: Novel: *Christopher* (A Novel), New York, The Abbey Press, 1902.

Poetry: in *A Treasury of Jamaican Poetry.*

LOVELACE, Earl W.

b. 1935, Trinidad.
Novelist, storywriter, poet, civil servant.

Educated in Trinidad, Lovelace's first job after leaving school was as proofreader with the *Trinidad Guardian.* Later, he joined the Civil Service after which he has been a journalist and a literary critic. After the publication of his first novel (1965) he spent some time studying at Howard University U.S.A. In the 1950's he was professor at Federal City College, Washington, D.C.

The work which became his fist published novel, *While Gods Are Falling,* was first entered in a literary competition sponsored by British Petroleum (1964) and gained for him a $5,000 Trinidad prize. Anson Gonzalez in his *Literature of Trinidad and Tobago "On Air"* comments:

> *The book* While Gods Are Falling *deals mainly with Trinidad society in the fifties and early sixties, the heyday of gang warfare, an era of social change and for some, a time of political disillusionment."*

Writings: Novels: *While Gods Are Falling,* London, Collins, 1965; Henry Regnery, Chicago, 1966; *The School Master,* London, Collins, 1968; Henry Regnery, Chicago, 1968; and extract from his third novel, "Every Step Is A Station" (which according to editorial notes in *Voices* was to be published in 1970) is in *Voices,* Vol. 2, No. 1 (Sept-Dec 1969) under the title of "The Wine of Astonishment."

Poetry: in *Voices,* edited by Clifford Sealy.

Article: "Let's forget the image of the happy native," in *Express* (Port of Spain, Dec. 31, 1967), p. 8: this is Lovelace's defense of *While Gods Are Falling.*

Biographical/Critical Sources: Helen Pyne-Timothy, "Earl Lovelace: his view of Trinidad Society," in *New World,* IV, 4 (1968), pp. 60-65; Edward Brathwaite, "Priest and Peasant," in *Journal of Commonwealth Literature,* No. 7 (July 1969), pp. 117-122; a review of *The School Master;* another review of the same novel by Brathwaite is in BIM, Vol. 12, No. 48 (Jan-June 1969), pp. 273-277; Eric Roach, review of *The School Master,* in *Sunday Guardian* (Trinidad, Jan. 28, 1968), p. 16; interview with Lovelace and review by G.R. John of *While Gods Are Falling,* in *Sunday Mirror* (Trinidad, May 16, 1965), p. 19; Bertram Clasp, review of *While Gods Are Falling,* in *The National Annual,* 1965 and Clasp's "A Review of the Novels of Earl Lovelace," in *Express* (Trinidad, Jan. 19, 1969); George Panton, a review of *The School Master,* in the *Gleaner* (Kingston, Jamaica, April 14, 1968).

LOWHAR, Syl

b. 1935, Grenada.
Poet.

Lowhar studied at the University of West Indies, St. Augustine, Trinidad, and has since identified himself with Trinidad. He has been employed by the Trinidad and Tobago High Commissioner's Office, Georgetown, Guyana. His poetry is represented in Salkey's anthology: *Breaklight* (New York, Anchor, 1973), and in other journals and collections, including *New World Quarterly.*

LUCIE-SMITH, (John) Edward (McKenzie)

b. February 27, 1933, Jamaica.
Poet, autobiographer, art critic, journalist, broadcaster, freelance writer.

Lucie-Smith spent the first twelve years of his life in Jamaica, and then went in 1946 to Canterbury, England for a high school education. He subsequently won a History scholarship to Oxford. He has been writing since his 14th year and has published one book on art and has edited an anthology of Elizabethan verse. He is well known in literary circles as critic, poet, editor, and broadcaster. A sensitive poet and critic who has commented with insight on various West Indian writers, he is a Fellow of the Royal Society of Literature. He has been the recipient of many honors, including the John Llewellyn Rhys Memorial Prize (1961) and the Arts Council Award (also 1961).

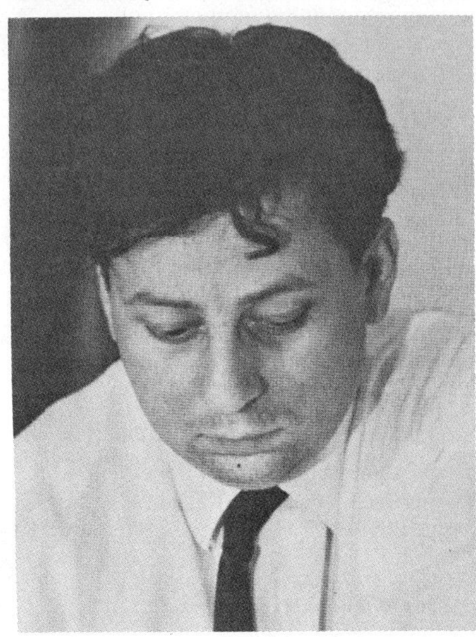

His recent collection of verse, *Well-Wishers* (1974), is more personal, intensely erotic, than his "literary" earlier ones. Particulary of interest is their melodic quality. The volume however has several translations from Latin or Greek or allusions to classical verse.

Writings: Poetry: *Seven Colours,* a very rare edition, (75 copies, signed and numbered, with prints by Michael Rothenstein), was published by Rampant Lion Press (London, n.d.). The seven poems have been republished in *Melanthika* (1977), pp. 63-67; *Fantasy Pamphlet No. 25,* 1954; *A Tropical Childhood and Other Poems,* New York, Oxford University Press, 1961; *Confessions and Histories,* New York, O.U.P., 1964; co-author of *Penguin Modern Poets,* No. 6, Harmondsworth, U.K., Penguin Books, 1964; *Jazz for the NUF,* London, Turret Books, 1965; *Borrowed Emblems,* London, Turret Books, 1967; *Toward Silence,* New York, O.U.P., 1968 (paper); *Snow Poem,* London, Turret Books, 1968; *More Beasts for Guillaume Apollinaire,* portfolio, 1968; *Egyptian Ode,* London, Daedalus Press, 1969; *The Well-Wishers,* London, Oxford University Press, 1974; in numerous journals including: *Audi-*

ence; Beloit Poetry Journal; Critical Quarterly; Encounter; Flame; Isis; Listener; London Magazine; Tribune; New Yorker. (c.f. full listing in International *Who's Who in Poetry 1974-75*.)

Autobiography: *The Burnt Child,* London, Gollancz, 1976.

Contributor to: *A Group Anthology,* 1963; *The Liverpool Scene,* 1967; *The Penguin Book of Elizabethan Verse,* 1965.

Editor of: *The Penguin Book of Satirical Verse,* 1967; *Holding Your Eight Hands: A Book of SF Verse,* 1969, 1970; *Penguin Book of Elizabethan Verse,* 1967; *The Liverpool Scene,* 1967; *British Poetry Since 1945,* 1970; *A Primer of Experimental Verse 1870-1922,* 1971.

Translations: *Jonah,* by Jean-Paul de Dadelsen, 1967; *Five Great Odes* by Paul Claudel, 1967.

Reviews: many, including: *The Islands in Between* (edited by Louis James), in *London Magazine,* Vol. 8, No. 4 (July 1968), pp. 96-108; review on "West Indian Poetry Reading," London, *Sunday Times,* 1965. His work appears in many anthologies, including: *Caribbean Voices* Vol. I; *The Sun's Eye; Commonwealth Poems of Today; Young Commonwealth Poetry.*

LUSHINGTON, Claude

b. 1925, Trinidad.
Poet, filmscript writer, essayist, painter, lawyer.

After local schooling in Trinidad and Tobago, Lushington served as a Flight Engineer in the RAF during the latter part of World War II, and after his return to civilian life he was a Housing Manager of the Office of Public Housing for the Trinidad Government. In 1955 he returned to England (where he had had wartime service) to read law at the Inner Temple. Although admitted to the bar, he practiced only for a short period, becoming increasingly engaged in writing scripts for films, in painting and other artistic pursuits. He has a novel and a collection of literary essays in manuscript.

Writings: Poetry: *The Mystic Rose,* Edited by Léonie Scott-Matthews, London, Magpie Press, 1969 (28 pp.); seven poems in *Breaklight* (A. Salkey, ed.), New York, 1973, and verse in other reviews and anthologies.

LYON-TIPPLING, Carmen

b. ca. 1938, Jamaica.
Playwright.

Lyon-Tippling has gained awards for her plays entered in the National Festival Competitions.

Writings: Plays: *See How They Run* (Silver Medal, Jamaica Festival, 1968); *The Comfortable Arrangement* (Certificate of Merit, 1969); *Decision, Decision* (Certificate of Merit, Jamaica Festival); *The Rope's End* (Honorablé Mention, Jamaica Festival, 1972); *The Stowaway* (Bronze Medal, Jamaica Festival, 1972).

MACAW

(pseudonym for **Kitty HANNAYS**)
b. ca. 1930, Trinidad.
Storywriter, journalist.

A talented and lively writer, Macaw has been a journalist and regular columnist for the *Trinidad Guardian* and the *Express,* both Port of Spain, Trinidad. Her popular pieces have been issued in one collection (1960).

V. S. Naipaul in his *Middle Passage* (1963) discusses dialect writing and Macaw's work in particular: " . . . the insecure wish to be heroically portrayed. Irony and satire, which might help more, are not acceptable; and no writer wishes to let down his group. For this reason the lively and inventive Trinidadian dialect, which has won West Indian writing many friends and as many enemies abroad, is disliked by some West Indians. They do not object to its use locally; the most popular column in Trinidad is a dialect column in the *Evening News* by the talented and witty person known as Macaw."

Writings: Stories: *Notebook by Macaw,* Port of Spain, Trinidad Publishing Co., 1960 (96 p.).

MacDERMOT, Thomas H.

(better known as **Tom REDCAM**)
b. 1870, Jamaica; d. 1933, in England.
Journalist, poet, novelist, playwright, critic.

According to Vic Reid as quoted by Peter Abrahams, Jamaican literature "began with Redcam." Son of an Anglican clergyman who died young, MacDermot grew

up in straightened circumstances. He was a school teacher, a journalist, and eventually editor of the *Jamaica Times.* He published his own poetry and assisted others with their publications. His verse is rather heavy and unenterprising. He was original for Jamaica (in his day) in being a fulltime writer and professional poet.

After a long illness he died in England away from the Jamaica which he really loved and whose literature he had so much influenced. The Poetry League declared him, posthumously, Jamaica's first poet laureate.

Because Redcam's poetry and novels are disappointing we might be wrongly tempted to underrate his path-finding contribution, for, as Ramchand argues, Redcam's attitudes as shown in *One Brown Girl And . . .* are quite modern, and not unlike the "sentiments of later Negritude writers from the Caribbean."

One is indebted to Ramchand for the following passage written by Redcam in *1909* (rather long but *still* relevant to this day in the Caribbean area):

> *I desire to get from this novel a reasonable return in money . . . Now I would make it very clear that I ask no one, on the sentimental grounds of patronising a local writer or supporting local literature to pay a shilling for what he or she does not want but this I ask as the minimum of fair-play to this or to any local independent publication, whether by myself or by another, that those who want to read the book and those who read it and like it, buy it . . . all the fine talk in the world, and all the nice expressions of enthusiasm and regard will avail little if the enthusiasts do not buy the local publications that they declare so well deserve support.*

Writings: Stories: *Becka's Backra Baby,* Kingston, Jamaica Time's Printery, 1907; *One Brown Gal and -, a Jamaican story,* Kingston, Jamaica Time's Printery, 1909; *Martha Brae: a story of Spanish Jamaica,* 1918.

Poetry: *Brown's Town Ballads and other poems,* Mona, Jamaica, Jamaica Library Service Pamphlet No. 3, 1958; *Orange Valley and Other Poems,* Kingston, Jamaica Pioneer Press, 1951, with an introduction by J.E. Clare McFarlane. His poetry appears in *A Treasury of Jamaican Poetry; Caribbean Voices,* Vol. II; *Voices from Summerland; The Poetry of the Negro, 1746-1949.*

Play: *San Gloria: A Drama of Christopher Columbus,* Kingston, Pioneer Press, 1920.

Biographical/Critical Sources: Mentioned in J.E. Clare McFarlane's *A Literature in the Making,* Kingston, Jamaica, The Pioneer Press, 1956 (Chapter I, pp. 1-11, is the main reference); also see Kenneth Ramchand's *The West Indian Novel and Its Background;* and Edward Baugh, *West Indian Poetry 1900-1970* (pamphlet), pp. 5-6.

MacDONALD, Hilda

b. ca. 1917, Antigua.
Poet.

MacDonald's one collection of verse is *Snowflakes and Stardust,* (Antigua, 1957). It was reviewed by Frank Collymore in BIM 25 (July-Dec. 1957), pp. 62-63.

MacKENZIE, Rhoda Elizabeth

(pseudonym: **"Auntie Lizzie"**)
b. ca. 1939, Jamaica.
Poet.

Rhoda MacKenzie has lived in the United Kingdom for many years, and is a social worker. Besides the works of poetry listed below, she has written two unpublished novels. A few poems are in Jamaican English but most are cast in somewhat outmoded diction and forced rhymes.

Writings: Poetry: *Jamaican Pocomania and Other Poems,* Glasgow, William MacLellan, 1969; *Jamaica Lucina, Second Poems,* foreword by S.B. Williams, Glasgow, William MacLellan, 1971.

MAHIBIR, Dennis Jules

b. April 24, 1920, Trinidad.
Novelist, editor, publisher, news commentator, lecturer.

Mahabir edited a magazine at age 21 and has been associated with many Trinidadian publications and various West Indian journals.

He studied law in London and Trinidad after completing his high school at Queens Royal College, Port of Spain. Active in public affairs, Mahabir has been mayor of Port of Spain and has served as city councillor. He was a founder member of the Caribbean Institute of Race Relations.

Mahabir, whose grandparents came from India, has employed his mixed cultural heritage in his first novel, *The Cutlas is Not for Killing.*

Writing: Novel: *The Cutlas is Not for Killing,* New York, Vantage Press, 1971.

MAIS, Roger

b. August 11, 1905, Kingston, Jamaica; d. 1955, in Jamaica.
Novelist, journalist, poet, painter, playwright.

Mais spent his early boyhood in Kingston; at the age of seven he moved with his family to the Blue Mountains in the parish of St. Thomas. His early formal education, in that rural, farm setting, was at home with his mother who was a teacher; he went to Calabar High School at fourteen; there he gained his Senior School Certificate. He joined the civil service, but was at heart a Bohemian, left the civil service within a year, and worked at many other jobs.

He was a journalist for the *Daily Gleaner* and later *Public Opinion.* A socialist, he was involved with the upheaval and nationalist movement of the thirties. Always outspoken and a champion of the underdog, he was imprisoned for six months in 1944 for writing the

notorious article "NOW WE KNOW," in the PNP weekly journal *Public Opinion* (July 14, 1944). His experience of prison and of the life of the poor plays a central part in his books.

He was surprised and appalled by the poverty of Spain—which he experienced around Barcelona—comparing it adversely with that of Jamaica, having lived and travelled in Europe—part of the time with John Hearne and Zacky Matalon—1952-54. He returned to Jamaica in 1954 and died the following year from cancer ("that fascist disease," as he called it). He was buried from Coke Church, at West Parade —the same church that figures in De Lisser's *Jane's Career.* The restless, generous, cussing and sometimes cussed, spirit had been worn out by many a battle and many a bout of argument and "good cheer." One of the most helpful commentaries (short) is Edward Brathwaite's introduction to the Caribbean Writers Series edition of *Brother Man* although one wonders whether Brother Man "unlike the ideal of the Rastas ... is not fully enough grounded in reality." (p. xii).

Mais was in a good position to have become a really major West Indian novelist; he knew both the rural and the urban people and ethos. He himself was from the middle class (his brother Reggie was to become a distinguished Permanent Secretary in the very Department which Roger could not take), and he empathized with everyone, including the dear old lady who helped him to get on the right "double-decker" in London after a rather too respectable West Indian party from which Roger had been "expelled" for using too frequently the then "forty shilling" expletive. (Roger loved to tell the tale, and that is why anyone who has heard one from his lips wants to repeat it but not in all *his* lurid detail!)

Further, he was a master of the Jamaican language; but he never really "came big." Perhaps there was too much for a sensitive man to struggle with in those days; perhaps he tried to do too many things. Perhaps it was just too hard to earn a living except in the traditional "trades." One of his loveliest bits of writing is his small poem, "Children coming from school":

I can hear the gospel
Of little feet
Go choiring down
The dusty asphalt street.

Beneath the vast
Cathedral of sky
With the sun for steeple
Evangling with laughter
Go the shining ones
The little people.

(Caribbean Voices, Vol. I)

Mais was much influenced by the Bible—and not only by the "rhythms of the King James' Version"—as his character Brother Man so clearly shows.

N.W. Manley wrote of Mais: "Here was a man by nature a genuine original, widely read, profoundly curious about experience and with a vast capacity for anger and passion. For years he had been shaping and sharpening his own tools and his weapons of war. He experimented with plays, with poetry, with short stories—he wrote a great amount that was never seen except by his closest friends." (from the foreword to a collection of novels entitled *The Three Novels of Roger Mais*, Cape, 1966, and in *Manley and The New Jamaica*, edited by Rex Nettleford, Longman Caribbean, 1971).

A collection of his unpublished work is at the University of West Indies Library, Mona, Jamaica.

Writings: Novels: *The Hills Were Joyful Together*, London, Cape, 1953; *Brother Man*, London, Cape, 1954 (with drawings by the author) and in Heinemann Caribbean Writers Series, introduced by E. Brathwaite, London, 1974; *Black Lightening*, London, Cape, 1955; *The Three Novels of Roger Mais*, with an introduction by Norman W. Manley, London, Cape, 1966 (the three novels first published 1953, 1954, 1955); still in manuscript: "Another Ghost in Arcady," written 1942; "The Seed in the Ground," 1943; "Blood on the Moon," 1950; "Storm Warning," 1950; "In the Sight of the Sun," 1952-53.

Short stories and verse (mixed): *And Most of All Man*, Kingston Printery, 1939; *Face and Other Stories*, Kingston, Universal Printery, 1942. Also, a one-volume collection (in xerox) of 23 stories appearing in *Public Opinion* (1942-45), called *Short Stories*, one copy at Institute of Jamaica (Kingston).

Poetry: in *Caribbean Voices; Caribbean Quarterly, Federation Commemoration Issue*, April 1958.

Essay: "Why I Love and Leave Jamaica," 1950, reprinted in *Public Opinion*, Kingston, (June 10, 1962).

Plays: published: *The Potter's Field* in *Public Opinion* (Jamaica, Dec. 23, 1950); *The First Sacrifice* in *Focus* (1956), edited by Edna Manley, Kingston, U.W.I., Extra Mural Dept. In manuscript are: *Masks and Paper Hats*, produced Jamaica, 1943; *Moon over Ajalon*, written in the period 1943-50?; *The Morning of Man*, radio-play, written 1943-50; *The Naked Truth*, radio-play, 194?-50; *The Old Mill Pool*, radio-play, written 1943-50; *Ordinary People*, 1953; *Rosalind and Roland*, 1947-50; and as *Rosamund and (sic) Rolando*, three acts, 1943-50; *Samson*, 1943; *Sons for the Night*, one act, 1943-50; *The Time of Our Lives*, 1943-50; *The White Oxen*, 1947-50, radio-play; *Afternoon of the Gods*, radio-play, 1943-50; *Apollo in Delos*, six scenes, 1943-50; *Atlanta in Calydon*, five scenes, 1943-50, (performed in 1950); *The Cuckoo Clock*, 1943-50; *Before Philippi* 1943-50; *Black Lightening*, five acts, 1943-50; *The Cloak*, 1943-50; *Dragon's Teeth in the Ground*, 1943-50; *General Joshua*, three acts, 1943-50; *George William Gordon*, 14 scenes, no date information; *The Golden Eagle*, radio-play, 1943-50?; *Hurricane*, produced Jamaica in 1943; *The Jest of Hassim*, five scenes, 1943-50; *Jorinda and Joringle*, one act, 1947-50; *The Little Green Man*, 1947-50, and as a radio play, 1943-50; *Love Came in Also*, 1943-50; and *Man about a Squirrel*, 1943-50.

Biographical/Critical Sources: W.I. Carr: "Roger Mais—Design from a Legend," in *Caribbean Quarterly*, Vol. 13, No. 1 (March 1967), pp. 3-28; R.M. Lacovia; "Roger Mais: An Approach to Suffering and Freedom," in *Black Images*, 1, 2 (Summer 1972); Karina Williamson, "Roger Mais: West Indian Novelist," in *Journal of Commonwealth Literature*, No. 2 (Dec. 1966), pp. 138-147; Jean Creary (Da Costa): "A Prophet Armed: The Novels of Roger Mais," in *The Islands in Between*, edited by Louis James, London, A Three Crowns Book (Oxford), 1968; K. Ramchand, *The West Indian Novel and Its Background*, New York, Barnes and Noble, 1970; K. Ramchand: "Literature and Society: The Case of Roger Mais," in *Caribbean Quarterly*, Vol. 15, No. 4 (Dec. 1969), pp. 23-30; J.E. Clare McFarlane: *A Literature in the Making*, Pioneer Press, Jamaica, 1956.

MALIK, Abdul

(pseudonym for **Delano de COTEAU**)

MALONEY, A. H.

b. ca. 1916, Trinidad.
Autobiographer.

Maloney early moved from Trinidad to the United States where he published one of the earliest autobiographies of an islander, *Amber Gold*, in 1946.

Writings: Autobiography: *Amber Gold,* Boston, Meader Publishing Co., 1946.

MANLEY, Carmen

b. ca. 1931, Panama (of Jamaican parents); d. 1975.
Storywriter, actress, broadcaster (TV and radio).

One of the most lively of spirits who died comparatively young, Carmen Manley was a well-known broadcaster and actor and writer of radio and television scripts. She lived for a while in England.

Writings: Tales/Stories: *Jamaican Stories for Children from the Land of Hill and Sully,* Kingston, Carmen Manley Publishing Co., Ltd., illustrated by Winnie Risden, designed and selected by Norman Rae; *The Land of Wood and Water,* Kingston, Jamaica, 1961, author, drawings by Edna Manley, 1961; *Folk Tales,* with sketches in black and white by Edna Manley.

Awards Jamaica Festival Competitions: Plays (Television): *Chi Chi Bad's Love* (Certificate of Merit, 1967); (Radio and Television): *My Brother's Keeper; No Fool Like an Old Fool; Coffee Party* (all winners of Certificates of Merit, 1967).

Short Stories: *The Isle of Springs* (Silver Medal, 1968); and story in the *Independence Anthology,* 1962: "When Fly Bodder Mauger Mule."

MANLEY, Edna

b. ca. 1913; Hampshire, England (long resident of Jamaica).
Editor, critic, sculptor.

Edna Manley is an artist in her own right, and, for as many years as most can remember, has been encouraging the arts and Jamaican artists. She is also, of course, widow of the late Norman Manley, distinguished barrister, King's Counsel, Rhodes Scholar, outstanding Jamaican Politician and West Indian Statesman, who was himself a great promoter of the arts—not least of all music. She is also mother of Michael Manley, the present Prime Minister of Jamaica.

Edna Manley was particularly influential as the editor of *Focus,* and as the center of a group of poets and theatre people, most of whom were involved in the Peoples National Party. She also encouraged painters and sculptors. Unfortunately, *Focus* published but few issues and those irregularly: it first appeared in 1943, then in 1948, 1956 and 1960. As Mrs. Manley says in the Foreword to the 1948 edition: "Five years ago when the first *Focus* was published, we had hoped to make it a yearly event. But the war and the difficulty of getting paper, coupled with the fact that so many of our writers had gone away, made it impossible . . . In any event the expense of publishing a book is great and the limitation and uncertainty of our market make it such a risk. . . ." Unfortunately, it was eight years before the second volume appeared, and none has appeared since 1960. (Nonetheless one could note that by comparison, for instance, BIM [58 issues]) has appeared in Barbados since 1942 with regularity, although not without serious problems of course.)

Fortunately for Jamaican and West Indian letters Mrs. Manley's influence, support and leadership in the arts have not depended only or mainly on *Focus.* Her own dedication to her particular art, and her insistence on the highest of standards from herself have been a great inspiration and example to writers as well as painters and sculptors.

In 1972 she accompanied a selection of Jamaican painting to CARIFESTA (Guyana), and more recently took a show of her own carvings to China.

Many writers have felt her influence and encouragement. A number of authors, including Sherlock, Campbell and Figueroa, have dedicated works to her.

In the 1960 *Focus,* in her Editor's Foreword, she reasserts her central work of keeping the society unPhilistine by her expression of concern for those writers who have not chosen "a greater freedom than the confines of the Caribbean can confer on the artist at present." "It is essential," she continues, "to the development of our literature especially, that regular channels of expression be open to our 'artists at home '."

Writings: Editor: *Focus,* 1943, 1948, published in Crossroads, Jamaica, City Printery; *Focus,* 1956, published by the Extra Mural Dept., U.C.W.I.; *Focus,* 1960—dedicated to Roger Mais, Kingston, City Printery; *An Anthology of Contemporary Writing,* with art plates (Edna Manley's own work was represented by a plate of her sculpture "Growth" which is owned by the Institute of Jamaica).

Biographical/Critical Sources: Crichlow Matthews, *Focus,* 1948 (E.M., ed.), *A Jamaican Anthology,* Jamaica, in BIM 10, pp. 175-176; Frank A. Collymore, *Focus,* 1960 (E.M., ed.), Jamaica in BIM 33, p. 76.

MANLEY-ENNEVOR, Rachel

b. July 3, 1947, England (resident of Jamaica).
Novelist, poet.

Manley-Ennevor was educated through high school in Jamaica and England but took her university degree at the University of the West Indies (Mona.). Her main occupation and interest has been writing and her first novel is in progress. Her poetry has appeared in the *Daily Gleaner* (Kingston) and one collection: *Prisms,* Hyde Held, England, by Blackburn, date unknown.

Biographical/Critical Sources: review of *Prisms* in *Now* (first issue, edited by Stewart Brown), pp. 38-40.

MANSOOR, Ramon

b. ca. 1939, Trinidad.
Poet, editor, teacher.

Educated at Fatima College, then at the University of Ottawa with a major in French, Mansoor took a second degree in Spanish at Carlton College, also in Ottawa. Of Syrian-Lebanese extraction, Mansoor was the editor and founder of *Reflexion,* a bi-lingual Hispanic-English magazine issued in Ottawa from 1968-1970, the first Spanish language journal ever to appear in Canada. He is a professor of Spanish at Carlton University, Ottawa.

Writings: Poetry: *Lirio Enamorado,* Spain, 1969; also appears in summer issue of *Reflexion,* 1970.

Biographical/Critical Sources: Clyde Hosein's review of *Lirio Enamorado,* in *Trinidad Guardian* (July 29, 1970); Eric Roach review in *Trinidad Guardian* (July 7, 1970).

MARAJ, Jagdip

b. 1942, Trinidad.
Poet.

Grandson of Indian parents who emigrated to Trinidad in the 19th century, Maraj's poems often reflect Hindu culture and religion. After local schooling he went to McGill University in Montreal, Canada, to study English and philosophy. He has won two Canadian poetry awards. His poem "The Flaming Circle" ends:

Let me soar
beyond the flaming circle,
to listen for the sound of petal on petal
and to feel the warmth of hands within
my reach.

Writings: Poetry: *The Flaming Circle,* Montreal, McGill University Press, 1966; McGill Poetry Series No. 10 (Louis Dudek, ed.). His verse is in several collections, including *Breaklight* (A. Salkey, ed.), New York, 1973 (which has "The Flaming Circle").

Biographical/Critical Sources: review of *The Flaming Circle* by Derek Walcott, in *Sunday Guardian* (June 19, 1966), p. 5.

MARGESTON, George Reginald

b. ca. 1876, St. Kitts.
Poet, commentator.

Margeston is possibly the earliest published poet from the Leeward Islands.

Writings: Poetry: *Songs of Life,* Boston, Sherman, French and Co., 1910; *The Fledgling Bard and the Poetry Society,* Boston, R.G. Badger, 1916.

Others: *England in the West Indies; A Neglected and Degenerating Empire,* Cambridge, Mass., privately published, 1906; and *Ethiopia's Flight: The Negro Question, or the White Man's Fear,* Cambridge, Mass., privately published, 1907.

MARKHAM, E.A.

b. 1941, Montserrat.
Poet, playwright.

Markham founded the Caribbean Theatre Workshop in England. After long residence in the U.K. (since his teens), he returned to his native island for a period to help produce his play *Dropping Out in Violence* which was performed in Montserrat in 1971. After teaching for a period in France he returned to England. His poetry has appeared in various journals. The poem "Patience" is in *Caribbean Quarterly,* Vol. 17, Nos. 3 and 4 (Sept.-Dec. 1971), p. 91.

Writings: Poetry: *Cross-Fire,* published by Outposts; *Mad* (Aquila); and *A Black Eye* (Bettiscombe): other details unknown.

Prose: "Goodbye," an autobiographical account of his early days in London, in *Melanthika,* 1977, pp. 68-74.

MARR-JOHNSON, Nancy

(N.J. MARR)
b. ca. 1921, England (long resident of Jamaica).
Prose writer, journalist.

Educated in England, Paris, The Royal Academy of Dramatic Art, and London University, Marr has lived in Jamaica since 1948. For a period she was regular contributor (of opinion on the arts) to the *Daily Gleaner.*

Writings: Home is where I Find it, London, Museum Press, 1950; *The Dark Divide: A Romance,* Museum Press, London, 1951; *Adam,* Museum Press, London, 1952; *Nigger Brown,* London, Museum Press, 1953.

MARRYSHOW, Theophilus Albert

(occasional pseudonym: **Max T. GOLDEN**)
b. November 7, 1887, Grenada; d. 1958.
Poet, commentator, editor, legislator.

Marryshow was educated at Wesley Hall Methodist School, St. George's Grenada, to 4th standard. Originally apprenticed to a carpenter, he soon joined the *Grenada Federalist* as an office boy; in 1909 he became Editor of the *Grenada Chronicle* and in 1915, with C.F.P. Renwick, launched the *West Indian,* of which he was Managing Editor. He wrote poetry under his own name and that of Max T. Golden; his poetry was published mainly in the *West Indian.* His other writings consist mainly of political and social comment; one series of articles, *Cycles of Civilization,* was published separately and was republished in 1973 by the Afroamerican Institute with a foreword and biographical sketch by Richard B. Moore.

In 1925 he became one of the first elected members of the Legislative Council, in which he served until 1958, when he resigned to become a member of the West Indies Senate.

He lived all his life in Grenada but travelled throughout the Caribbean and to the U.K., Europe and U.S.A.

MARSHALL, H.V. Ormsby

b. ca. 1926, Jamaica; deceased (date unknown).

Poet, compiler and editor, shortstory writer.

Very involved with the arts and International P.E.N., Jamaica branch. Her family, after one of whom Ormsby Memorial is named, all wrote. She, Violet, compiled *Seed and Flower, An Anthology of Prose and Poetry* by the Ormsby family, as a memorial to her brother. This collection has an introduction by the then very well known Bishop Percival Gibson, founder of Kingston College, who refers to the work of Joyce Ramson, herself closely connected to the Anglican communion, through her father, a Venerable Archdeacon, and through her writing of hymns.

Violet Ormsby Marshall did everything possible to keep P.E.N. going in the thinner years, when her charm and enthusiasm proved invaluable.

Writings: Stories and Verse: respresented in *Seed and Flower: An Anthology of Prose and Poetry by the Ormsby Family of Jamaica,* Kingston, Jamaica, The Gleaner Co., 1956; a short story, "V-for Victory" and three poems, in *Seed and Flower.* Short story in the *Independence Anthology of 1962,* "Poinsettia for Christmas," first published in the *Daily Gleaner.*

MARSHALL, Harold

b. ca. 1943, Barbados.
Poet, journalist.

Marshall was assistant editor of BIM for a period before emigrating to Canada. His one collection is *Full Fathom Five* [dedicated to Frank Collymore], 1973. Three poems from this collection appear in *Savacou 7/8,* Kingston, (Jan -June 1973), edited by Edward Brathwaite and dedicated to Frank Collymore as a tribute.

MARSHALL, Paule

b. April 9, 1929, Brooklyn, New York (of Barbados parentage).
Novelist, storywriter, librarian, journalist.

Paule Marshall grew up in Brooklyn and went to New York City Schools; she still lives in New York. Her first novel, *Brown Girl, Brownstones,* reflects a consciousness of the problem of the transplanted "Islander" to a big city and the problem in reverse for the one grown up in the city to adapt to an island community: the heroine Selina Boyce who was born and raised in the United States returns to the Caribbean island home of her parents.

Her second and major novel, *The Chosen Place, The Timeless People,* is also set in the Caribbean; an American research and development group works with the natives of a small Caribbean island "Bournehills." John M. Reilly, in *Contemporary Novelists,* tells us that "out of sympathy for the human predicament she portrays both aliens and natives in terms of the motives of guilt and frustration by which they comprehend their personal lives." Merle Kinbona stands out, as the novel develops, as the predominent character who, according to Reilly, "translates personal drama into general social meaning."

For her collection of the four excellent pieces in *Soul Clap Hands and Sing* she won an award of the American Academy of Arts and Letters. John Reilly sums up his commentary on her in *C.N.* thus: "Paule Marshall's art is remarkable. She manages the often summoned but rarely arriving synthesis of the particular and universal, for in revealing the rich texture of West Indian life within her fiction she also constructs a microcosm of the contemporary struggle to be free."

She has been the recipient of a Guggenheim Fellowship (1961); Rosenthal Award (1962); Ford Theatre Award (1964); and a National Endowment for Arts Grant (1966).

Writings: Novels: *Brown Girl, Brownstones,* New York, Random House, 1959; London, W.H. Allen, 1960; and New York, Avon Books, 1970 (paperback); *The Chosen Place, The*

Timeless People, New York, Harcourt, Brace, 1969; and London, Longmans, 1970.

Short Stories: *Soul Clap Hands and Sing,* New York, Atheneum, 1961; and London, W.H. Allen, 1962. Story: "Reena."

Article: "Shaping the World of My Art," in *New Letters* 40, No. 1 (Oct. 1973).

Biographical/Critical Sources: Peter Nazareth: "Paule Marshall's Timeless People," in *New Letters,* 40, No. 1 (Oct. 1973); *Brown Girl, Brownstones,* review by Gordon Bell in BIM 30, pp. 134-136; *Soul Clap Hands and Sing,* review by Karl Seal in BIM 35, pp. 225-228; John M. Reilly's commentary in *Contemporary Novelists* (ed. James Vinson), St. Martin's Press, New York, 1972.

MARSON, Una Maud

b. 1905, Jamaica; d. 1965.
Poet, playwright, broadcaster.

After attending Hampton School, Malvern, Jamaica, Marson went to England in 1932 and there took up duties as secretary to the League of Coloured Peoples; she later was private secretary for a period to the Emperor Haile Selassie during his exile in England in the mid-1930's.

She founded and edited *The Cosmopolitan* (1929-32). Returning to Jamaica in 1936, she helped establish several literary journals and produced several of her plays. After a second period in England to work for the BBC (1938-1947), Marson returned home, this time for good except for brief visits to the United States. In 1942, she had the distinction of starting the BBC's *Caribbean Voices* program. In Jamaica she was active as a publisher, journalist and social worker, especially for the Save the Children Fund. She was rewarded with the Musgrave Medal of the Institute of Jamaica (1930), for her poetry.

Writings: Poetry: *Tropic Reveries,* Kingston, Jamaica, The Gleaner Co., privately published, 1930; *Heights and Depths: poems,* Kingston, Jamaica, The Gleaner Co., 1931; *The Moth and the Star,* introduction by Philip Sherlock, privately published, 1937; *Towards the Stars: poems,* Brickley, Kent, University of London Press, 1945.

Plays: *At What a Price,* (written with Horace Vaz), produced in Jamaica, 1932; *London Calling,* 3 acts, produced in Jamaica, 1937; *Pocomania,* 3 acts, produced in Jamaica, 1938.

Editor: *Poetry for Children by Poets of Jamaica* (rev. ed. by W. Adolphe Roberts), Kingston, Pioneer Press, 1958.

Biographical/Critical Sources: In J.E. Clare McFarlane's *A Literature in the Making,* Jamaica, 1956; mentioned in H. Fowler's "A History of Jamaican Theatre," in *Jamaica Journal,* Vol. 2, No. 1 (March 1968), pp. 53-59.

MARTIN, Egbert

(pseudonym: **LEO**)
b. 1859, Guyana, d. 1887.
Poet.

Son of a tailor in Georgetown, Egbert Martin was one of the earliest West Indian poets writing in English to be published.

Writings: Poetry: *Poetical Works,* London, W.H.L. Collingridge Printers, 1883; *Leo's Local Lyrics,* Georgetown, 1886. He is in many anthologies, including: *Themes of Song; Fourteen Guianese Poems for Children; Sun is a Shapely Fire; Caribbean Verse; Guianese Poetry* (Cameron, ed.), and contributed to *Kyk-over-al.*

Biographical/Critical Sources: Arthur Seymour, "The Poetry of Egbert Martin (Leo)," *Kyk-over-al* 3 (1946), p. 19. Also Seymour's "Looking at Poetry," *Kaie,* 9 (1973), p. 7. (A series of broadcasts for schools given between January-March 1972: Seymour in his analysis uses poems from Guyanese writers including Egbert Martin.)

MATTHEWS, Tony

b. 1941, Jamaica.
Poet, documentary filmmaker, essayist, playwright.

After local schooling, Matthews moved to England in 1960 to study photography at Nottingham College of Art. He has done documentary films in London. His writing is at present mostly unpublished but he is preparing a collection of poetry for the press. Much of his verse is concerned with third-world efforts at achieving true independence—economic as well as political.

He has written many essays, plays and political articles (all in manuscript), and is preparing a book of poems for publication.

Writings: Poetry: In various collection, including four poems in *Breaklight* (A. Salkey, ed.), New York, Anchor, 1973.

MAXWELL, Marina

(now known as **Marina OMOWALE**)
b. 1934, Trinidad.
Singer, producer, poet.

Marina Omowale is a vibrant person, much concerned with the question of "identity," and much given to supporting real efforts at knowing and presenting West Indian culture. She has a splendid voice and did not always sing only that part of her musical heritage which is represented by "Canne Broulé"!

She lived for some years in Jamaica, having done her university work at Mona. In Jamaica she founded the Yard Theater, which aimed at popular audiences, and was experimental and radical. She has published articles, essays and poems in England and the Caribbean. She has recently returned to live in Trinidad.

Writings: Poetry: in various journals and collections, including *Breaklight* (A. Salkey, ed.), New York, 1973.

McANDREW, Wordsworth

b. ca. 1928, Guyana.
Poet, playwright, storywriter, folklorist, journalist, broadcaster.

McAndrew specialized in Guianese folklore and published five modest collections of his verse.

Writings: Poetry: *Blue Gauling*, British Guiana, 1958 (Miniature Poet Series); *Poems to St. Agnes*, British Guiana, 1962; *Meditations on a Theme*, Georgetown, 1963; *Selected Poems*, Georgetown, Erbar Press, 1966; and *More Poems*, Georgetown, 1970. He is in such anthologies as *My Lovely Native Land; Magnet; Sun is a Shapely Fire;* and *Breaklight; Poems for Guianese Children* (Monar, ed.), and journals, including: *Kyk-over-al; Chronicle Christmas Annual; New World.*

Pamphlets: *Ol'Higue*, British Guyana Lithograph, 1958; *Three P's*, Georgetown, 1961.

Play: *Freedom Street Blues*, performed, Guyana, 1971.

McBURNIE, Beryl

b. ca. 1930, Trinidad.
Folklorist, dancer.

Celebrated dancer and teacher of the dance, McBurnie was one of the most dynamic people for a number of years in Trinidadian Theatre, Dance and Arts. Her troupe performed in Jamaica and outside the Caribbean, always carrying with it verve, color and authenticity. Beryl herself has performed in many of the big metropolitan centers.

Writings: Outlines of the dances of Trinidad.

McDONALD, Ian

b. April 18, 1933, St. Augustine, Trinidad.
Novelist, poet, international tennis champion.

Completing his education at Cambridge University after local schooling in Trinidad, McDonald read history.

McDonald has been living in Guyana for a number of years. From a very European type of family in Trinidad, he is very much part of Caribbean writing and culture as, for instance, his remarkable poem "Jaffo, the Calypsonian" shows. He did not fall into the philistine habit of life and perception so often common among many West Indian sportsmen.

His novel, *The Humming Bird Tree,*

about growing up in Trinidad (autobiographical?), was awarded a prize by the Royal Society of Literature, London, 1969, and is a delight to read. It is sometimes lyrical in intensity: it raises some of the problems of growing up in a multiracial society in a poignant fashion, even if it does not manage to "solve" these! This novel has been reissued as one of Heinemann's Caribbean Writers Series, with an introduction by Dr. Gordon Rohlehr, which while being thorough and serious, appears to make a number of unanalyzed assumptions about the necessary relation between a writer's background and what in the end he must produce. It is, perhaps, just possible that those whose group have suffered, and feel that they have suffered, at the hands of gentlemen farmers and other powerful castes, will not be better at analyzing the real situation than are the sons of the "power oligarchy."

McDonald's university education was at Cambridge ("black mark"/"white mark"?) —and he was captain of the university tennis team, and later of Guyana and the West Indies.

His poems have appeared widely in journals: a number of them appear in a cyclostyled form simply called *Poems* (Georgetown, n.d.); and a dozen appear in *Poetry. Introduction 3,* Faber, London, 1975.

His "Yusman Ali, Charcoal Seller," which appears in *Savacou 7/8,* has in its last stanza the following lines:

He is useful still. I shake with pain to see him pass.
He has not lost his hating yet, there's that sweet thing to say
He farts at the beauty of the rain-dipped moon.
The smooth men in their livery of success
He curses in his killing heart
And yearns for thorns to tear their ease. . . .

Writings: Novel: *The Humming-Bird Tree,* London, Heinemann, 1969; (reprinted 1969); Caribbean Writers Series, No. 13, Heinemann, 1974, introduction by Gordon Rohlehr (Winifred Holtby Prize winner for best regional novel, Royal Society of Literature).

Short Story: "Pot O'Rice Horowitz's House of Solace," *International Playmen,* 1968.

Play: *The Tramping Man,* performed Georgetown: Theatre Guild, 1969; also broadcast Guyana Broadcasting Service, 1972; done with Bill Pilgrim, Frank Pilgrim, Ron Robinson, Pauline Thomas, Diane Ng Yen), script for *Advance to the Brink,* performed Georgetown: Theatre Guild, 1969.

Poetry: (collection) *Poems,* Georgetown, n.d. (cyclostyled); 12 poems in *Poetry. Introduction 3,* London, Faber, 1975. McDonald has contributed to various anthologies and journals, including: *Caribbean Voices; New Voices of the Commonwealth; Breaklight; Sun is a Shapely Fire; Commonwealth Poems of Today; Caribbean Verse; Thieme's Anthology of West Indian Literature; West Indian Poetry* (Ramchand and Gray, eds.); *Compass* (New York, Scott, Foreman, 1971); *New World* (Fortnightly); *Kyk-over-al;* BIM; *Kaie; Savacou; Jamaica Journal; Pembroke Magazine.*

Articles: (with Richard Allsopp and A.J. Seymour)—"The Literary Tradition in Guyana," Georgetown, The National History and Arts

Council, 1970; "The Unsteady Flame—A Short Account of Guyanese Poetry," *New World* (Fortnightly) Vol. 17 (1965), p. 10 for Part I; Vol. 18 (1965), p. 24 for Part II; Vol. 19 (1965), p. 19 for Part III.

Biographical/Critical Sources: Review of *The Humming-Bird Tree,* by John Wickham in BIM 49, pp. 59-64; Review of *Tramping Man,* by Ken Corsbie, in *New World,* Vol. 5, No. 4 (Special Issue, 1971), pp. 46-48.

McDOWELL, Rudolph

b. July 10, 1903, Jamaica.
Storywriter, journalist, newspaper and Hansard Reporter.

McDowell, a retired Government Social Welfare worker, was formerly private secretary to the late Rt. Rev. Thomas A. Emmet, S.J., Vicar Apostolic of Jamaica. At various times he was assistant editor of the journals *Catholic Opinion; West Indian Review; Jamaica Times;* and *The Voice.* At the present he is sub-editor of *The Daily Gleaner.* His stories have appeared in *The Gleaner* and other papers.

Writings: Collection of Stories: *Jamaican Christmas Chimes,* Kingston, Jamaica, (n.d.); published by author.

McFARLANE, Basil Clare

b. April 23, 1922, St. Andrew, Jamaica.
Poet, journalist, film and art critic, broadcaster.

McFarlane was educated in Jamaica. After high school he attended Jamaica School of Arts and Crafts. He has been a civil servant and served in the RAF in Britain during World War II. During the 1930's he was a journalist (1934-42) and has been since 1955 an editor of the Kingston *Daily Gleaner* and a radio journalist for Radio Jamaica. He is the son of the poet J.E. Clare McFarlane, founder of the Jamaica Poetry League, and brother of R.L.C. McFarlane. His poem "For a Poet in Death" dedicated to Ernest Hemingway, is very effective as one might see from a few lines even from the middle of the work:

... in Paris, it
seemed possible to make terms
with the terror of the world.
But art
was not enough. There were uneasy
corners of a man's desire not to be
choked with words: ...

He was one of the early poets to be included in *Focus.*

Writings: Poetry: *Jacob and the Angel and Other Poems,* Georgetown, British Guiana, privately published, 1952; republished by Kraus Reprint in 1970 with other Caribbean works in combined volume entitled *Bamboula dance and other poems* (J.A. Jarvis, ed.). And contributor to various anthologies and journals: (1962) *Independent Anthology; Seven Jamaican Poets; Focus; Caribbean Voices,* Vol. I; BIM; *Caribbean Quarterly; Kyk-over-al; Jamaica Journal; The London Magazine; Life and Letters; Phylon; Schwarzer Orpheus; West Indian Review; Magazine of Atlanta University; Public Opinion; Now.*

Biographical/Critical Sources: Edward Baugh, *West Indian Poetry 1900-1970* [Pamphlet], p. 8.

McFARLANE, J.E. (John Ebenezer) Clare

b. 1894, Jamaica; d. 1962, Jamaica.
Poet, essayist, anthologist, critic.

McFarlane was the founder of the Poetry League of Jamaica which in 1923 became a branch of the Empire Poetry League. McFarlane had a respect for, and did his best to keep alive an interest in, literature and the literary life. His *Voices from Summerland* (1929) was the first anthology of Jamaican poetry. In 1935 he was awarded the Musgrave Silver Medal for the encouragement of poetry, and in 1958 the Gold for poetry. It is from no want of respect for McFarlane, or poetry, that one feels that the awards might have been justly reversed.

As J. Jones puts it, "Readers of older poetry will be quick to detect the ring of the nineteenth century romantics, most especially Wordsworth, in McFarlane's lines . . . he belongs to a group no longer in fashion." But part of the reason for the fading away of that group is not mainly that they are derivative—which artist is not in some sense so?—but that their lines are so lacking in memorability.

Further, the school teachers of those days seemed to think that only the Romantics had ever written, and really only Wordsworth, Keats and Shelley—the latter two always pronounced almost as one word, as, in other fields, are Fichter and Schelling, or Worrell and Weeks. Byron was more or less taboo—and not quite serious enough! It is really a lack of humor and wit that affected McFarlane and his very worthy group adversely. Consider for instance all the choice ambiguities, clearly entirely unintentional, underneath the poem (AND its title) WHEN NATURE CALLS which McFarlane includes in his *Treasury of Jamaican Poetry* (and it is *not* the only one of its kind):

WHEN NATURE CALLS
(A Rondeau of the Early Morning)

When Nature calls, at dawn of some bright day,
And gives the invitation—"Come and play!"
With sweet imperious cadence, felt and heard.
In cool blue skies, wet grass, and fresh-voiced bird,
We leave all else her summons to obey!

. . . .

By some vague longing is the spirit stirred;
The room grows close, the book's dull page is blurred;
All out-door beckons, and we cannot stay—
When Nature Calls.

A veritable summons from the 'out-back'!

It should be noted that according to anthologist McFarlane the *Treasury* "is chiefly intended to bring examples of Jamaican poetry within the reach of every child of school age."

McFarlane, the critic and great lover of literature, had a strong feeling for his country, Jamaica, and for its position within an older concept of Empire; he ends his well-known poem, addressed to Jamaica, My Country, in this way:

And that strange peace
Be mine, that broods above thy mist-filled vales
At twilight, and upon thy purple hills;
Not silence, but a hushed expectancy,
A brimming joy that greets night unafraid,
When life stands tiptoe on the brink of time
And waits with fluttering pulses for the last
Sweet benediction, and the touch of hands;
And hope expires towards the Evening Star.

Writings: Poems: *Beatrice,* Kingston, Time's Printery, 1918; poems in Anthologies: Dathorne, Hendriks-Lindo, McFarlane, Seymour; *Daphne: A Tale of the Hills of St. Andrew, Jamaica,* (a narrative and philosophical poem), London, F. Wright, 1931; *Poems,* Kingston, Gleaner Co., 1924.

Editor of Anthologies: *Voices from Summerland* (1929), an early anthology of Jamaican Poetry; *A Treasury of Jamaican Poetry,* London, University Press, 1949; *Selected shorter poems, especially edited and arranged for use of Schools,* Kingston, Pioneer Press, 1954.

Miscellaneous: *The Challenge of our Time,* Jamaica, the New Dawn Press, 1945 (essays and addresses); *A Literature in the Making,* Kingston, Pioneer Press, 1956; *The Magdalen; a story of supreme love,* Kingston, The New Dawn Press, 1960; *Sex and Christianity* (a sociological work), Kingston, 1932, and London, 1934; *Jamaica's Crisis* (an economic and social survey), Kingston, 1937; *The Freedom of the Individual,* Jamaica, New Dawn Press, 1940 (from the 1933 Wilberforce address).

Article: "The Prospect of West Indian Poetry" in *Kyk-over-al,* Vol. 16 (1953), pp. 125-127.

Biographical/Critical Sources: Edward Baugh, *West Indian Poetry 1900-1970* [Pamphlet], p. 5.

McFARLANE, R.L.C.

b. July 20, 1925, Jamaica.
Poet, teacher.

McFarlane was educated in Jamaica, London University and in the United States, at Howard University (M.A.). He has been a civil servant and since 1971 head of the English Department at Wolmer's Boys' School. One of his quietly impressive lyrics appears in *Seven Jamaican Poets:*

The caterpillar sheers the leaf,
Barns the sweetness which he reaps,
In the long brown house. . . .

Writings: Poetry: *Selected Poems, 1943-1952,* Kingston, City Printery, 1953, republished by Kraus Reprint in 1970; combined volume: *Hunting the Bright Stream (Poems 1954-1960),* Kingston, City Printery, 1960; poems in various collections, including *Seven Jamaican Poets;* and *Focus* (1960).

McKAY, Claude

b. 1889, Jamaica; d. 1948; buried in Queens, New York.
Poet, novelist, critic.

A complicated, and in many ways, ambivalent figure, McKay is considered by many to be an Afro-American. But Mervyn Morris says: "Physically he never came home (i.e. to Jamaica which he left in 1912). But, psychologically, he was always basically ours." (paper, Department of English, U.W.I., February 20, 1975).

McKay was, like all sensitive human beings, involved in value conflicts almost from the beginning. During the Great Revival his father and mother were part and parcel of it, but he and his brother, well known in Jamaica as "U Theo"—as he signed his letters to the local press—were "free thinkers." By the time Claude went to the States—against the advice of many who knew the kind of trauma he would suffer there—he was agnostic. But he became, at the end of his life, a Catholic:

Of course I am not very political, especially since I became a Catholic, but

I try to see things from the stand point of right and wrong and when Soviet Russia is wrong I will say so. When the U.S. and Great Britain are wrong I will say so too, and the two latter in my mind are more often wrong than the Soviet nation. I am certainly never going to carry the torch for British Colonialism or American imperialism abroad.

(Letter to Max Eastman, dated August 28, 1946; quoted in *The Passion of Claude McKay,* Wayne Cooper, pp. 310/311, Schocken Books, New York, 1973).

This kind of refusal to say "my side, right or wrong" is never, of course, really appreciated, and black writers, including Marcus Garvey and Ted Poston accused McKay, on different occasions, of distorting Harlem and black life in America.

While being anti-imperialist he did not accept what the apologists for communism and the Soviet Union were wont to say in explanation of "leftist" behavior. His *Harlem: Negro Metropolis,* deals harshly with various aspects of what he considers to be communist duplicity and oversensitivity to criticism.

Perhaps in the end, McKay's letters will prove as interesting as any of his more formal literary work. Those to Max Eastman, as quoted, for instance, by Wayne Cooper, are really fascinating, and show him always unwilling to swallow hook, line and sinker any particular line.

Known as a lyricist of intensity, and a protest poet of fire—

If we must die, let it be not like hogs . . .

(which *Time* magazine with not unwonted ignorance, and very characteristic assurance, attributed September 27, 1971 to the rebellious prisoners at Attica State Prison!)—his verse from fairly early included a religious element—

Bow lowly down before
the sacred sight
Of man's Divinity alive in stone

(St. Isaac's Church, Petrograd; published 1925; see *Selected Poems,* p. 84; also in *A Treasury of Jamaican Poetry,* 1949).

Yet perhaps his best formal work is to be found in his novel *Banana Bottom,* 1933, and in his collection of essays and impressions *Harlem: Negro Metropolis,* 1940.

One of the puzzles of McKay, the man, which might not be irrelevant to McKay, the artist, is that for all the nostalgia about Jamaica in his poems, and the insight into Jamaican and (West Indian) country folk in his novels, he never did revisit the island which he left in 1912; nor did he return to any form of dialect verse, the writing of which, at the suggestion of his English friend and mentor, Walter Jekyll, first brought him fame.

His fight for racial justice was never simple-minded; he did not expect to find, nor write as if he did find, all justice and truth and enlightenment in any of the camps, racial and political, which he knew so well!

Sometimes over-sentimental in his poetry, and sometimes self indulgent in his other writings, he is often a real artist of language. His ambivalence, his refusal to see things only in black and white terms,

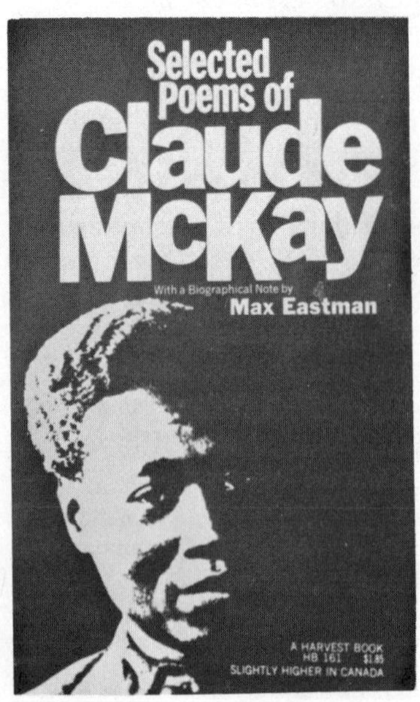

perhaps spring as much from his early experiences of Jamaican society as from his travels and his realization that many aspects of our world are inevitably linked, and interacting, and have consequences far deeper than we realize. His poem "Like a strong tree" (*Caribbean Voices*, Vol. I, p. 38) is a good image of how a poet (and poetry) grows and works.

Writings: Novels: *Home to Harlem,* New York and London, Harper, 1928, and New York, Avon (paperback), 1951; also New York, Pocket Books, Simon and Schuster, 1965; *Banjo, a story without a plot,* New York, Harper, 1929; Harvest Paperback, Harcourt Brace Jovanovich, 1970; *Banana Bottom,* New York, Harper, 1933 and New Jersey, Chatham Book Seller, 1970, in paper by Harcourt, Brace Jovanovich (A Harvest Book), New York.

Short Stories: *Sudom Lincha* [Under Lynch Law], Moscow, 1925; *Gingertown,* New York, arper, 1932, Freeport, New York: Books for Libraries, 1972.

Poetry: *Constab Ballads,* London, Watts and Co., 1912, Freeport, New York, Books for Libraries, 1972; *Songs from Jamaica,* London, Augener, 1912 (six songs set to music by Walter Jeckyll); *Spring in New Hampshire and other poems,* London, Grant Richards, 1920; *Harlem Shadows,* New York, Harcourt, 1922; *Songs of Jamaica,* Kingston, Aston W. Gardner, 1912, later edition: with an introduction by Walter Jekyll, Miami, Florida, Mnemosyne, 1969; *Selected Poems of Claude McKay,* New York, Harvest paperback, 1969, as *Negry i Amerike* (Russian trans.), Petrograd, 1923; Verse is included in many anthologies including: *Caribbean Voices; Poetry of the Negro; A Treasury of Jamaican Poetry; West Indian Narrative.*

Others: *Harlem, Negro Metropolis,* New York, Dutton, 1940, Harvest Paperback, 1972, *Selected Poems;* New York, Bookman Associates, 1953, Introduction by John Dewey (with biographical note by Max Eastman), New York, Bookman Associates, Inc.

Autobiography: *A Long Way From Home,* New York, L. Furnam, Inc., 1937 in paper-covered edition: New York, Harcourt, Brace and World, 1970.

Biographical/Critical Sources: "McKay's Human Pity," Arthur Drayton in *An Introduction to African Literature* (edited by Ulli Beier, Longmans, 1967), pp. 76-88; "A note on McKay's protest poetry showing that there is human pity evident in his earliest work which saves his protest from the cramp of strident hate," "Claude McKay in England, 1920," by Wayne Cooper and Robert C. Reindeers in *New Beacon Reviews* No. I; Jacqueline Kaye, "Claude McKay's *Banjo, Présence Africaine,* No. 73 (1970), pp. 165-169; "An account of McKay's activities and writings in the socialist and anti-racist causes in England," in J.E. Clare McFarlane's *A Literature in the Making,* Kingston Pioneer Press, 1956; *The Passion of Claude McKay (Selected Prose and Poetry, 1912-1948),* edited by Wayne Cooper with an Introduction and Notes, New York, Schocken Books, 1973; Edward Baugh, "West Indian Poetry 1900-1970," (pamphlet), p. 7. For a more detailed recent bibliography, see *The Passion of Claude McKay,* op. cit., pp. 350-358. Also see detailed introduction to McKay's *A Long Way from Home* (1970 edition) by St. Clair Drake.

McLLELAN, George H.H.

(pseudonym: **Pugagee PUNCUSS**)
b. ca. 1907, Guyana.
Folklorist, journalist.

McLlelan's tales were collected in *Old Time Story, some old Guianese yarns re-spun by "Pugagee Puncuss,"* Georgetown, British Guiana, *Daily Chronicle,* 1943. The Guiana Edition (No. 7) was edited by Vincent Roth from files of the *Daily Chronicle,* 1937-38, where they had appeared at irregular intervals.

McNEIL, R. Anthony (Tony)

b. December 17, 1941, Jamaica.
Poet, journalist, editor.

McNeil attended Excelsior School and St. George's College, Jamaica; Nassau Community College, United States; and earned his Ph.D. from the University of Massachusetts after his M.A. at Johns Hopkins (1971). He lives in Massachusetts. Tony McNeil has been a civil servant and worked as a journalist. Though born into a distinguished family of Jamaican politicians he was much attracted in his youth to the popular Rasta cult—see his poem "Ode to Brother Joe," which he reads beautifully on Caedmon's West Indian Poets (T.C. 1379).

A quiet but outstanding reader of his own work he came to the notice of Elliott Coleman, then in charge of the Hopkins creative writing seminar, at a reading held in Mona, at which Coleman, Brathwaite, Morris, McNeil and others read. (See Baugh's interesting comment on this particular event which had been organized by Morris and Figueroa, and which according to Baugh marked the coming of age of West Indian Poetry (cf. Baugh pamphlet, *West Indian Poetry 1900-1970*).

McNeil is undoubtedly one of the most accomplished and promising of the younger group of West Indian poets. His range is wider than at first appears:

Eg.:

(1) *Mind's ultimate trick*
is simply to strut
on one leg/ minus looking stupid . . .

(2) *Meantime in the musty cell,*
Joe invokes, almost from habit,
the magic words:
Hail Selassie I
Jah Rastafari,
But the door is real and remains shut.

And:

(3): *This morning I chose to stay home,*
To watch the cats and think of
Columbus. And the grass is precious
merely because it belongs to us.

These three quotations are from "Flamingo," "Ode to Brother Joe," and "Residue," all poems which appear in his *Reel from "The Life Movie."*

Judging from the quotations from his letters to Dennis Scott—in the latter's introduction to *Reel*—McNeil is interested in the theory of poetry and of writing. His concerns are the gut concerns that come out of a real knowledge and experience of a wide variety of Jamaican life; but his poems are not simply immediate reactions to these or any other experiences: he is clearly a conscious artist. Serious but not dull: ". . . the eight syllable line relates to my Lowellian concern with developing 'great power under great restrictive pressure'. Besides, it's fun."

There is a story probably not apocryphal that McNeil caused a change in the rules for the Jamaica Poetry Festival competition—apparently he submitted so many good poems at one time that it would have been difficult for others to receive prizes.

From then on the number of poems submitted by any one author was clearly restricted. He won the gold medal in 1966, and has been the recipient of many other prizes and awards.

His voice is distinctive; his concerns catholic.

Writings: Poetry: *Hello Ungod,* Baltimore, Peacewell Press; *Reel from "The Life Movie,"* Savacou Publications Ltd., 1972, with an introduction by Dennis Scott, in *Savacou 6;* reprinted in separate volume in *Poets Series-3* by Savacou Publications Ltd., 1975.

Poems: in various newspapers and journals, including *The Sunday Gleaner, Contraband Lynx, Public Opinion, Jamaica Journal,* BIM (Barbados) and the anthologies: *Breaklight; West Indian Poetry; Seven Jamaican Poets,* among others.

Record: L.P., "Poets of the West Indies," Caedmon T.C. 1379, edited by J. Figueroa, with two poems, read by author: "Ode to Brother Joe," and "Black Space."

Biographical/Critical Sources: See D. Scott's Introduction to McNeil's *Reel from "The Life Movie;"* and Review of *Reel from "The Life Movie"* in *NOW* (First issue), edited by Stewart Brown, pp. 13-18; Edward Baugh, *West Indian Poetry 1900-1970* (Pamphlet), p. 18.

McTURK, Michael

(pseudonym: **QUOW**)
b. ca. 1858, Guyana.
Folklorist.

McTurk published three of the earliest collections of stories and fables in Jamaica in the last decades of the 19th century.

Writings: Folklore and Essays: *Essays and Fables in verse, written in the Vernacular of Creoles of British Guiana,* Georgetown, Argosy Office, 1881 (and rhymed narratives, written in "Creolese"); *Essays and Fables—Written in the Vernacular of British Guiana,* A.W.B. Long, 1899; *Essays and Fables in the Vernacular,* Georgetown, Daily Chronicle, 1949; (Guiana Edition, Vincent Roth, ed.).

MELVILLE, Edwina

b. ca. 1926, Guyana.
Poet, storywriter, journalist.

Educated at Bishop's High School, Melville was a journalist for a time in British Guiana. She contributed "The Wapishana Indians" to A.J. and Elma Seymour's *My Lovely Native Land* and her poetry is in *Kyk-over-al* and *New World.*

Writings: Stories: *This is the Rupununi: A Simple Story Book of the Savannah Lands of the Rupununi,* British Guiana, Government Information Service, 1956.

MENDES, Alfred H.

b. 1897, Trinidad.
Novelist, poet, storywriter, critic, editor, legislator.

A Trinidadian of Portuguese ancestry, and son of a well-to-do father, Mendes, like many other West Indians of his intellectual and social background, including Norman Manley, fought in World War I—Mendes in the King's Royal Rifles. His experiences connected with the war affected him, politically and culturally, as did his knowledge of the Revolution in Russia. From those days, apparently, dates his political and intellectual awakening "... the motivating forces that drove us, willy-nilly, like a sort of one of the furies, into writing at all, stemmed from two world-shattering events of that early period of our lives.... the first world war where a large number of us had been abroad, and indeed even those of us who had not been abroad were influenced considerably by what was happening in the world, and the second event was the Russian Revolution." (Interview with Cliff Sealy, *Voices,* Vol. I, No. 5, December 1965).

Mendes feels that *The Beacon* was the "harbinger of events that so drastically changed the whole attitude of the people in Trinidad to what they considered to be their own life and manners" (op. cit., p. 7). It was around Gomes' *Beacon* that the Mendes group "kept stirring the pot." And some group it was: C.L.R. (Nello) James, R.A.C. De Boissiere, Ernest Carr, Alarnon Wharton et al. Gomes seems to feel that the group became too withdrawn and aesthetic and romantic: "... only two of them, C.L.R. James and De Boissiere, rose from this comfortable armchair aestheticism to the affirmation of political views ..." (Gomes, *Through a Maze of Colour,* p. 16). But this is probably a somewhat exaggerated view.

Mendes became a great reader and admirer of T.S. Eliot, and collected a 6000 volume personal library, which was open to young literati. But he himself learned not only from books, moving at one time from his comfortable surroundings to the slums of Park Street, so as to experience the language and life of the barrack yard, which he later used in his writings.

At Christmas 1929, and Easter 1930, Mendes and C.L.R. James published two issues of a Journal called *Trinidad.* It had a wide circle of contributors, and stirred up much opposition and controversy, mostly over its non-respectable approach, and its forthright use of language, including taboo words. Letters of protest flooded the *Guardian.* One is quoted, in part, by Ramchand: "Its [Christmas 1929 Number] disagreeable implications cast unwarrantable aspersions on the fair name of our beautiful Island . . ." Apparently the second issue of the journal was entirely the work of Mendes.

Mendes, like so many others, in time decided to migrate, going to New York, whereas James and so many others departed for London.

Mendes' short stories and novels were consequently published abroad. He is, undoubtedly, one of the real pioneers, although he generously gives much credit to Claude McKay ("In my private view, *Banana Bottom,* his latest book, is the finest novel that has come out of the West Indies." (Interview cited above.)

Mendes was not one of those encouragers of the arts and of criticism who make a great contribution from the outside as it were, without himself producing real works of worth: his own writing did much to establish social realism as the main mode of West Indian fiction.

In 1972, he was awarded an Honorary Doctorate in Literature from the University of the West Indies.

Writings: Novels: *Pitch Lake,* London, Duckworth, 1934; *Black Fauns,* London, Duckworth, 1935.

Poetry: *The Wages of Sin and other poems,* P.O.S., Trinidad, Yuille's Printerie, 1925.

Stories: In various journals and collections: "Afternoon in Trinidad" is in *Penguin New Writing,* No. 6, London, Penguin; and in J.T. Livingston's *Caribbean Rhythms,* New York, Washington Square Press, 1974; early work is in *Manchester Guardian, Stories* (H.E. Bates, ed.); *London Mercury; New Writing; Story Magazine;* and *The Magazine.* His "Lulu Gets Married" appeared in the O'Brien *Best Short Stories of 1936.*

Biographical/Critical Sources: Cliff Sealy's interview in *Voices,* Vol I, No. 5 (Dec. 1965), pp. 3-7; Kenneth Ramchand in *The West Indian Novel and its Background,* London, 1970; and an interview of October 6, 1972, Port of Spain, with Reinhard W. Sander, as "The Turbulent Thirties in Trinidad," in *World Literature Written in English,* XII, 1 (April 1973), pp. 66-79. Also see Anson Gonzalez' " 'Possibility' in W.I. Writing," in *The New Voices,* No. 4 (June 1974); R. W. Sander, *From Trinidad,* London, Hodder & Stoughton, 1977, an anthology which discusses Mendes in detail along with other writers of this period.

MICHAEL, Julia Warner

b. ca. 1879, Bahamas; death year undetermined.
Poet.

Michael's 12-page collection, *Native Nassau: A Memory of New Providence Island* (New York, H. Marchbank's Print Shop, 1909), is one of the earliest verse published by a native of the Bahamas. She contributed to *A Book of Bahamian Verse,* selected and edited by Jack Culmer (London, Bailey Bros., Ltd., 1930).

MILES, Judy

b. 1944, Trinidad.
Poet.

After local schooling, including the University of the West Indies, Mona (honors in English), Judy Miles went on to the University of British Columbia, Vancouver. She has contributed to various journals in Canada and the Caribbean, including *Breaklight* (A. Salkey, ed., New York, 1973), and *Voices,* Port of Spain, BIM (Bridgetown, Barbados).

Biographical/Critical Sources: in Introduction to *The Islands in Between* (Louis James, ed., London, A Three Crowns Book-Oxford, 1968), pp. 34-36.

MILLS, Charles Wade

b. January 3, 1951, England (of Jamaican parentage).
Storywriter, teacher.

Educated at Jamaica College, University of the West Indies, Mona, Jamaica, and Toronto University, Mills has taught at

College of Arts, Science and Technology (CAST), Jamaica. He was awarded the Jamaica Scholarship (1968) and the Commonwealth Scholarship to Canada (1973). (1973).

Besides being a gifted scholar, both in the Arts and Sciences (with a special interest in Philosophy), Mills is a shortstory writer of great merit. His first two stories won silver medals and the third won a gold medal in the Jamaica Festivals.

Writings: Short Stories: in *Jamaica Journal* by the Institute of Jamaica: "A Journey to The Exterior," Vol. 5, Nos. 2-3 (June-Sept. 1971), pp. 66-70; "Moonrise," Vol. 6, No. 3 (Sept. 1972), pp. 33-37; "The Man With The Red Shoes," Vol. 7, No. 3 (Sept. 1973), pp. 50-59.

MILLS, Therese

b. ca. 1932, Trinidad.
Storywriter (juvenile), journalist.

Mills has published eight works written for children. She works with the *Trinidad Guardian.*

Writings: Stories: *Caribbean Christmas,* Trinidad, December 1972; *The Shell Book of Trinidad Stories* (Printed in Trinidad by the College Press, 1973); *Christmas Stories,* Trinidad, December 1973; *Great West Indians,* Trinidad, Longman Caribbean, 1973; *A Kite for Christmas,* Trinidad, 1974; *Std 3 Christmas Concert,* Trinidad, 1975; *Ramesh of El Socorro* and *Peggy in Santa Cruz,* (both commissioned by the Ministry of Education, Trinidad and Tobago).

MIRGLIP, Knarf

(pseudonym for **Frank PILGRIM**)

MISSICK, Rupert

b. ca. 1940, Bahamas.
Poet.

Missick's only collection to date is *Naked Moon* (New York, 1970).

MITTELHOLZER, Edgar

(pseudonym [once used]: **H. Austin WOODSLEY**)

b. 1909, New Amsterdam, Guyana; d. May 6, 1965, England.
Novelist, playwright, poet.

Edgar Mittelholzer is one of the modern giants of Caribbean writing. From very early he decided to be a writer, and he pursued that aim relentlessly. His early experience was all of rejection slips, and of a philistine lack of understanding that one could be a full time writer, wholly dedicated to that art. His first novel, *Corentyne Thunder,* had an unbelievable series of mishaps, and was not really available until Heinemann brought it out in their *Caribbean Writers Series.* It is a pioneer work for Guyana dealing with the Great House and the peasantry, not least of all with East Indian women and their relations to their fathers and their men. His *Morning at the Office,* considered by some to be his best, came out in 1950, and deals with another society, Trinidad, and with a different section of society, with its color, class, ethnic, occupational tensions, and with the

relationship of all this to metropolitan/ colonial tensions.

Edgar Mittelholzer was a relentless, almost compulsive writer. When he first went to England, and was a filing clerk at a British Council office, he set himself the task to write a certain number of words per day—so many on the tube going to work, so many during tea break, so many during lunch, and so many on the way home. He stuck to this sort of schedule and his output became an "impressively long list" of novels. Unfortunately his compulsive relationship to his work means that some themes were overdone, not least of all that of the sins of the father being visited upon the sons—or daughters! Likewise he seemed rather heavily taken up with certain kinds of sexual relationships. On one occasion at least the daughter has to be seduced in the same fashion as had been the mother thus combining two of his great preoccupations. This was the more remarkable because in the ongoing affairs of life Mittelholzer gave the impression of being puritanical to the point of prissiness.

But in another sense he had a wide range. *My Bones And My Flute* is a delightful "entertainment" of the genus thriller. His *Kaywana trilogy* is painted on a very large canvas indeed. In portraying a Dutch family, and its Guianization, it stretches from 1611 until 1953, and gives the author ample opportunity to show some of his theories of inheritance, and of the innate superiority of some races, or groups of people. It is noteworthy that this book is called *Kaywana BLOOD* (emphasis added), and that the abridged version is called *The Old BLOOD* (emphasis added). Yet he does not seem to place Sylvia's predicament (In *The Life and Death of Sylvia*) within the context of her "mixed blood." She seems rather to be related to the tensions and disturbances of her time—the 1930's in the West Indies!

Both Louis James and Wilfred Cartey make the point that what appears to be Mittelholzer's dreams (or nightmares) are intimately connected with Guyana and with its history: "It is a holy land purified by

the blood of many peoples—Indian, Portuguese, Dutch and Negro and East Indian and Chinese . . ." (Cartey, *New World*, Guyana Independence Issue). But there is always something very much Mittelholzer in his prolific output, not least of all in his weaker work.

It is as well to remember that he produced not only novels, although they abound, but also radio and TV plays, short stories, comment, and an autobiography *Swarthy Boy*. It is fascinating and sad that some of Edgar's theory about the strong, and about the force of the early generations upon the later, caught up with him in a truly tragic way. For as Cartey puts it:

> *There existed an ambivalent relationship between Mittelholzer and his father, who resented the boy because of his dark complexion, but who at the same time seemed to have a measure of love for him . . .*
>
> *Mittelholzer seems to have admired his grandfather, whose eccentric and nonconformist pattern of living ap-*

pealed to him. His grandfather came and went like a vagabond and died under peculiar circumstances.

Later on Mittelholzer too, a vagabond artist, died under peculiar circumstances.

We could have done with more of him—and his quizzical smile. We must remember that it was his Miss Bisnauth who said:

I agree with what Arthur said once. . . . a novelist ought to laugh at his characters—and even at himself—but his laughter should be in respectful undertones.

Writings: Novels: *Corentyne Thunder,* London, Eyre and Spottiswoode, 1941; and London, Heinemann, Caribbean Writers Series, 1970; and London, Hutchinson paperback, 1970; and New York, Humanities, 1970; *A Morning at the Office,* London, Hogarth Press, 1950; and London, Heinemann, Caribbean Writers Series, 1974; and New York, Doubleday, 1950, under the title *Morning in Trinidad,* and in paper in Heinemann's Caribbean Writers Series, London, 1974; *Shadows Move Among Them,* London, 1951, and Philadelphia, Lippincott, 1951; and New York, Ace Books, 1961; and London, Four-Square, 1963; *Children of Kaywana,* London, Peter Nevill, 1952; and New York, John Day, 1952; London, Secker and Warburg, 1956, 1960; and London, Ace Books, 1959; and London, Four Square, 1962; *The Weather in Middenshot,* London, Secker and Warburg, 1952; and New York, John Day, 1953; *The Life and Death of Sylvia,* London, Secker and Warburg, 1953; and New York, John Day, 1954; and London, Ace Books, 1960; and London, Four Square, 1963 (under the title of *Sylvia*); also under the title *Sylvia:* London, New English Library, 1968. Also: *The Adding Machine: A Fable for Capitalists and Commercialists,* Kingston, Jamaica, Pioneer Press, 1954; *The Harrowing of Hubertus,* London, Secker and Warburg, 1954; and New York, John Day, 1955, under the title *Hubertus;* also London, Secker and Warburg, republished as *Kaywana Stock,* 1959; and London, Four Square, 1962; *My Bones and My Flute: A Ghost Story in the Old-Fashioned Manner,* London, Secker and Warburg, 1955; and London, Corgi Books, 1958; and London, New English Library, 1974; *Of Trees and the Sea,* London, Secker and Warburg, 1956; *A Tale of Three Places,* London, Secker and Warburg, 1957; *Kaywana Blood,* London, Secker and Warburg, 1958; and London, Four Square, 1962; abridged as *The Old Blood,* New York, Doubleday, 1958 and later New York, Crest, Fawcett, World, 1971; *The Weather Family,* London, Secker and Warburg, 1958; *A Tinkling in the Twilight,* London, Secker and Warburg, 1959; *Mad Mac Mullochs,* London, P. Owen, 1959, 1961 (first edition was published under pseud. H. Austin Woodsley); London, World Distributors, 1961; *Latticed Echoes: A Novel in the Leitmotiv Manner,* London, Secker and Warburg, 1960; *Eltonsbrody,* London, Secker and Warburg, 1960; *The Piling of Clouds,* London, Putnam, 1961; and London, Four Square, 1963; *Thunder Returning: A Novel in the Leitmotiv Manner,* London, Secker and Warburg, 1961; *The Wounded and the Worried,* London, Putnam, 1962; and London, Pan Books, 1965; *Uncle Paul,* London, MacDonald, 1963; and New York, Dell, 1965; *The Aloneness of Mrs. Chatham,* London, Library 33, 1965; *The Jilkington Drama,* London, Abelard-Schuman, 1965; and London, Corgi, 1966; *Savage Destiny,* New York, Dell Books, 1965.

The novel *Children of Kaywana* has been translated into Dutch by Hans de Vries, Danish by Sonja Rindom, German by Georg Goyert and Egon Strohm, French by Clément Leclerc and Italian by Egidio Modena. The novel *The Life and Death of Sylvia* has been translated into French by Jacques and Jean Tournier, and into Italian by Giuseppe Gogioso. *A Morning at the Office* has been translated into French by Ludmila Savitsky, and into Italian by Bruno Tasso. *Shadows Among Them* has been translated into German by E. Strohm, into French by Claude Vincent, into Dutch by Max Schuchart and Italian by A. Giorgi. *The Weather Family* was translated into German, and *The Weather in Middenshot* into French and Italian. Extracts from his novels have been published in various journals and collections including: The Tamarack *Review* 14 (1960); *Caribbean Narrative; West Indian Narrative.*

Autobiography: *A Swarthy Boy,* London, Putnam, 1963.

Dramatization: of *Shadows Move Among Them* (novel): as *The Climate of Eden* by Moss Hart, New York, Random House, 1953; of the novel *The Weather in Middenshot:* as *The Weather in Middenshot: A Serio-Comedy.*

Radio and TV Plays: *The Sub-Committee: sketch,* in BIM, IV, 15 (Dec. 1951), pp. 1

162; *Before the Curtain Rose,* one act, in BIM, VII, 28, (Jan-June 1959). In typescript or mimeograph: *The Aloneness of Mrs. Chatham: a sophisticated comedy,* 3 Acts (mimeo); *Fears and Mirages* (typescript); *The Savannah Years* (typescript); Other dramas: *Entirely Traditional,* 1954; *Ghosts at their Shoulders; No Guileless People.*

Short Stories: in BIM; *Caribia; Christmas Tide; Savacou;* and the anthologies: *Caribbean Rhythms; Carr's Anthology of Short Stories; West Indian Stories; Stories from the Caribbean.*

Poetry: in BIM, *Kyk-over-al,* in Figueroa's anthology, *Caribbean Voices.* He published *Colonial Artist in Wartime: A Poem* (British Guiana, 1941).

Essays: "Literary Criticism and the Creative Writer," in *Kyk-over-al,* V, 15, (1952), pp. 19-22; "Colour, Class and Letters," in *The Nation,* Vol. 188, No. 3(Jan. 17, 1959), pp. 54-57; "Of Casuarinas and Cliffs (an Essay)," in BIM, 5 (1945), pp. 6-7, 53-55; "Romantic Promenade: A Divertisment in Minor Chords," in BIM 8, pp. 12-13; "Van Batenburg of Berbice," in BIM, 19, pp. 172-174.

Others: *Creole Chips,* British Guiana, Lutheran Press, 1937; *With A Carib Eye,* London, Secker and Warburg, 1958.

Arthur and Elma Seymour selected from Mittelholzer's writings for inclusion in their anthology *My Lovely Native Land:* "The Canje" and "New Amsterdam."

Biographical/Critical Sources: Mittelholzer, Edgar Austin, (A Bibliography of M.'s works and works on him, with tributes by Martin Carter, William Dow, Daisy Hahnfeld, Edward V. Luckhoo, Lucille Mittelholzer, A.J. Seymour), published by the Public Free Library, Georgetown, 1968—a pamphlet produced for Guyana Week, 1968; Introduction to *The Islands in Between,* Louis James (ed.), London, Three Crown, 1968, pp. 37-42; Kenneth Ramchand, *The West Indian Novel and its Background,* New York, Barnes and Noble, 1970, references: p. 73; *A Morning at the Office,* p. 73; *Children of Kaywana,* p. 164 n.3; *Corentyne Thunder,* pp. 103-105; *Sylvia,* p. 44; A.J. Seymour, *Edgar Mittelholzer: The Man and His Work* as "The 1967 Edgar Mittelholzer Lectures," Georgetown, Guyana, Ministry of Education, 1968; F.M. Birbalsingh, "Edgar Mittelholzer: moralist or pornographer," *Journal of Commonwealth Literature* 7 (1969), pp. 88-103; Wilfred Cartey, "The Rhythm of Society and Landscape," *New World* (Guyana Independence Issue, 1966), p. 96; Obituary in *Daily Mirror* (Port of Spain, Trinidad), Friday, May 7, 1965; Patrick Anthony Guckian, "Failure in Exile: A critical study of the works of Edgar Mittelholzer," unpublished thesis, U.W.I., Cave Hill, Barbados, Dept. of English, 1970; Geoffrey Wagner, "Edgar Mittelholzer: Symptoms and Shadows" in BIM 33, pp. 29-34; Frank Collymore, "Edgar Mittelholzer: A Biographical Sketch," in BIM 41 (June-Dec. 1965), pp. 23-26; William J. Howard, "Edgar Mittelholzer's Tragic Vision," *Caribbean Quarterly,* XVI (Dec. 1970), pp. 19-28; Reviews in BIM of Mittelholzer's novels by Frank Collymore, John Harrison, Gloria Escoffery, Chalmer St. Hill, A.F. Crichlow Matthews, W.T. Barnes, Harold Marshall, Karl Sealy and A.J. Seymour, cf. *An Index to BIM* (compiled by Reinhard W. Sander), 1942-1972, pp. 81-82; novels reviewed: *Morning at the Office, Shadows Among Them, Children of Kaywana, The Weather in Middenshot, The Life and Death of Sylvia, The Harrowing of Hubertus, My Bones and My Flute, Of Trees and the Sea, A Tale of Three Places, Kaywana Blood, The Weather Family, A Tinkling in the Twilight, Latticed Echoes, Thunder Returning, The Piling of Clouds, The Wounded and the Worried, A Swarthy Boy, Eltonsbrody;* also reviewed: *With a Carib Eye:* Joseph and Johanna Jones, "Edgar Mittelholzer" in *Authors and Areas of the West Indies,* Steck-Vaughn Co., Austin, Texas, 1970, pp. 46-47; Colin Rickards, "A Tribute to Edgar Mittelholzer," in BIM 42, pp. 98-105. Also see "The Spirit in the Bottle—A Reading of Mittelholzer's *A Morning at the Office,*" by Michael Gilkes, in *World Literature Written in English,* Vol. 14, No. 1 (April 1975), pp. 237-252, and John Figueroa's extensive introduction to the Heinemann paper edition of *A Morning at the Office* (1974), pp. vii-xx. See R.E. McDowell's *Bibliography of Literature from Guyana,* 1975, for the most detailed general bibliography of Mittelholzer.

MOCKYEN, Alma Hyacinth

(née **HYLTON**)

b. November 15, 1928, Jamaica.

Radio broadcaster, TV/radio producer, editor, poet, dancer.

Educated at Wolmer's Girls' School, Jamaica, University of West Indies, Diploma Mass Communications, Mockyen has been a supervisor of Broadcasting at JAMAL and an assistant to Staff Tutor in Radio Education (Extra Mural Department, University of West Indies, Mona). She is working on a collection of verse (*Take 3*), and has published poems and short stories in the *Gleaner* (daily newspaper), and various small magazines and the anthology *Focus* (1960).

She did the "book" for the Jamaican musical, *Once Upon a Seaweed* (1961). Member and chairman of the Jamaica Festival Awards Commission, she has been the recipient of many awards: For contribution to the Jamaican Theatre (1961); Government of Jamaica award; Silver medal—poetry (Jamaica Festival Commission, 1967); Bronze Medal for poetry (Jamaica Festival Commission, 1972); Bronze Musgrave Medal for Choreography (1970); and numerous awards for dance, including an award of Honour 1965 (Jamaica Festival, Gold Medal, 1966).

MONAR, Motilall Rooplalln

(pseudonym: **Eustace GREENE**)
b. ca. 1944, Guyana.
Poet, editor.

Monar has contributed to anthologies including: *Voices of Guyana; Sun is a Shapely Fire; New Writing in the Caribbean;* and the journals *New World, Kaie,* and *Chronicle Christmas Annual,* among others.

Writings: Poetry: *Meanings,* Georgetown, 1972; *Patterns,* Georgetown, 1974.

Compiler-Editor: of *Poems for Guyanese Children,* Georgetown, Annandale Writers Group, 1974.

Story: *The Canefield Fire,* London, Macmillan, 1977.

MOORE, H. Willoughby

b. ca. 1910, Barbados.
Poet.

Moore was sometime Headmaster of Combermere School. His one collection of verse was *Barbados (Miscellaneous poems)*, published in Barbados in 1940.

MORRIS, John

(pseudonym [collective] for **Morris CARGILL** and **John HEARNE,** q.v.)

MORRIS, Mervyn

b. February 21, 1937, Kingston, Jamaica.
Poet, critic, teacher.

Morris was educated at Munro College, Jamaica; U.C.W.I., Mona; and St. Edmund Hall, Oxford. He has been a lecturer in the English Department, U.W.I.; a former school teacher; Assistant Registrar; and Warden, Taylor Hall, U.W.I. In 1975 he was named Secretary of the Creative Arts Center, Mona. He was a Rhodes Scholar and in his day an international class tennis player.

Morris is one of the "coolest" and best read of W.I. contemporary authors and critics. While in no way disassociating himself from the Caribbean culture of which he is so clearly a part, his style is rather more understated and formal than many of his contemporaries. His "Valley Prince" is evidence of his feeling for the contemporary, "non-standard" aspects of Jamaican culture:

and plenty people
want me blow straight.
But straight is not the way; my world
don't go so; that is lie . . .

And his well known "Literary Evening, Jamaica" shows that his knowledge of the metropolitan scene enables him to say something about the Caribbean that others might not manage half so well.

His criticism is thorough and perceptive.

He broke new ground with his piece "On Reading Louise Bennett Seriously," for which he was awarded the first prize in the 1964 Jamaica Festival Competition. He has taken other prizes.

His main collection of poems to date is *The Pond* (1973). The title poem shows a searching into the self, and a realization of meanings "beneath the surface," which is also characteristic of his religious type poetry.

His poetry and criticism are very much his own. Although obviously concerned, he is clearly not one for band-wagons. A strong individual, he is none the less close to other poets, with whom he often gives readings, and who value his criticism. He has always sought to encourage other poets—old and young, formally and informally.

Writings: Books: Editor of: *Seven Jamaican Poets, An anthology of recent poetry,* Kingston, Bolivar Press, 1971; *The Pond, a book of poems,* London, New Beacon, and Port of Spain, 1973.

Work in Progress: A new book of poems, probaby to be called *Asylum* (book ready, no publisher definite); An annotated edition of about 50 Louise Bennett poems, mainly for use in schools (to be published by Sangster's Bookstores); A critical account of Jamaican fiction and poetry since 1903 (for the Institute of Jamaica).

Short Story: "A Death," in *Caribbean Prose,* edited by Andrew Salkey, London, Evans Brothers, 1967, pp. 105-112; reprinted in *That Once Was Me,* London, Penguin English Project Stage 2, 1973, pp. 56-61.

Poetry: *The Pond,* London and Port of Spain, New Beacon Books, 1973; *On Holy Week,* Kingston, Jamaica, Sangster's, 1975; poems published in newspapers and journals including *The Sunday Gleaner; The Daily Gleaner; Public Opinion; The Daily News; Jamaica Journal; Caribbean Quarterly; Savacou* (Jamaica); BIM (Barbados); *Moko; Tapia* (Trinidad); *English; Outposts; The Times Literary Supplement* (England); *Pembroke Magazine* (U.S.A.); *The Literary Half-Yearly* (India); one poem translated into Spanish: "Velada literaria en Jamaica," (translation by Luis Suardiaz) in *Casa de las Americas,* número 90 (Juiy-August 1975), pp. 180-181. Poems published in many anthologies, including *The Independence Anthology of Jamaican Literature,* edited by A.L. Hendriks and Cedric Lindo (A Publication of the Arts Celebrations Committee of The Ministry of Development and Welfare, Jamaica, 1962); *Young Commonwealth Poets '65,* edited by P.L. Brent (Heinemann, London, in association with Cardiff Commonwealth Arts Festival, 1965) *Caribbean Literature,* edited by G.R. Coulthard (University of London Press, 1966); *Modern Poems for the Commonwealth,* edited by Maurice Wollman and John Spencer (Harrap, London, 1966); *Commonwealth Poems of Today,* edited by Howard Sergeant (John Murray, London, for The English Association, 1967); *New Voices of the Commonwealth,* edited by Howard Sergeant (Evans Brothers, London, 1968); *Caribbean Voices,* Volume 2, edited by John Figueroa (Evans Brothers, London, 1970); reprinted in *Caribbean Voices* Combined edition, 1971; *Seven Jamaican Poets,* edited by Mervyn Morris (Bolivar Press, Jamaica, 1971).

Poems on recordings: *Poets of the West Indies* reading their own works (edited by John Figueroa), Caedmon Records, New York, 1971: TC 1379.

Articles: "A West Indian Student in England (A Personal Reaction)," *Caribbean Quarterly,* Vol. 8, No. 4 (Dec. 1962), pp. 17-29; "On Reading Louise Bennett, Seriously," first published in *The Sunday Gleaner* (Jamaica, June 7, 14, 21 and 28, 1964), then in *Jamaica Journal* Vol. 1, No. 1 (Dec. 1967), pp. 69-74; "Feeling, Affection, Respect," in *Disappointed Guests,* essays by African, Asian, and West Indian students, edited by Henri Tajfel and John I. Dawson (Oxford University Press, 1965), pp. 5-26; "Some West Indian Problems of Audience," *English,* Vol. XVI, No. 94 (Spring 1967), pp. 126-131; "The Novels of George Lamming," in *The Islands in Between,* edited by Louis James (Oxford University Press, 1968), pp. 73-85; "Walcott and the Audience for Poetry," *Caribbean Quarterly,* Vol. 14, Nos. 1 and 2 (March-June 1968), pp. 7-24; "Black Power and Us," *Jamaica Journal,* Vol. 2, No. 4 (Dec. 1968), pp. 2-5; "This Broken Ground," Edward Brathwaite's trilogy of poems, *New World Quarterly,* Vol. 5, No. 3, pp. 14-26; "Pattern and Meaning in *Voices Under the Window,*" *Jamaica Journal,* Vol. 5, No. 1 (March 1971), pp. 53-56;

"The All Jamaica Library," *Jamaica Journal*, Vol. 6, No. 1 (March 1972), pp. 47-49; Introduction to V.S. Reid's *New Day* (London, Heinemann Educational Books, 1973); Introduction to Dennis Scott's *Uncle Time* (Pittsburgh, University of Pittsburgh Press, 1973), pp. xvii-xxiii; "Interdepartmental Links II: A West Indian in East Kent," *Overseas Universities*, No. 20 (Nov. 1973), pp. 25-26; "The Arts: a varied scene," on the arts in Jamaica, *The Financial Times* (Nov. 21, 1973), p. 28; "West Indian Literature: A Bibliographic Introduction to Critical Contexts," *Journal of English Teachers*, No. 5 (Feb. 1975), pp. 42-44; "The Arts in Jamaica," *Commonwealth* (April/May 1975), pp. 9-11; accepted for publication: "Contending values: The Prose Fiction of Claude McKay," *Jamaica Journal* (for next issue, Spring 1976).

Biographical/Critical Sources: Edward Baugh, *West Indian Poetry 1900-1970* (Pamphlet), p. 18; and information on him in Hugh Morrison's article in *Caribbean Quarterly*, Vol. 18, No. 4 (Dec. 1972), pp. 82-83.

MORRISON, Hugh Panton

b. February 21, 1921, Canal Zone, Panama (of Jamaican parents).
Poet, essayist, shortstory writer, reviewer, teacher, radio producer.

Morrison was educated at Calabar High School, Jamaica, the School of General Studies and Teachers College, Columbia University, New York, and at Indiana University, Bloomington, Indiana.

He taught at Calabar High School and Excelsior School, Kingston, Jamaica, and was Resident Tutor and Staff Tutor in Radio Education, University of West Indies, Mona. He prepares radio education programs on West Indian (Caribbean) subjects and has published short stories and poems in Caribbean anthologies, including *Focus* (1956 and 1960), and other magazines and newapapers. He also has a joint weekly book review column in the *Sunday Gleaner* (Jamaica). He received I.C.A., U.S.-AID, and Federal Republic of Germany Fellowships.

Writings: Critical Essays: in various journals, including review of *Seven Jamaica Poets* in *Caribbean Quarterly*, Vol. 18, No. 4 (Dec. 1972), pp. 82-83.

MORRISON, William

b. 1838, Jamaica; d. 1902.
Poet, teacher.

Morrison was a schoolmaster and headmaster. He was the father of Sir William Morrison, philanthropist, who wrote the Introduction to Constance Hollar's pioneering anthology, *Songs of Empire* (1929).

Writings: Poetry: *Poems*, Jamaica, 1906.

MOTTLEY, Elton

b. ca. 1932, Barbados.
Poet, teacher.

Elton Mottley is deeply committed to the arts, and serves as the Director of Yoruba House—"a cooperative project designed to develop artistic and critical talent among Barbadian youth." He is socially and politically committed to the full development of the Caribbean. His poem "Afrika—My Brother" was published in BIM 54 (Jan-June 1972).

In BIM 57 (March 1974) he has a long intense poem: "From Cherry Tree Hill" with a quotation from Faust—"I must act because I live."

I stand up here, alone,
helpless against the sky
when I see me staked out
like kite, to die
beneath mill and rotted hut.
. . . .

MOULTON-BARRETT, Arabel

b. ca. 1890, England(?), lived in Jamaica for much of her life; d. 1953.
Poet.

Moulton-Barrett was a contemporary with Constance Hollar and Lena Kent. J.E. Clare McFarlane devotes a chapter to her in his *A Literature in the Making* (1956). A member of the famous Barrett family, she wrote a great deal but only a small part of her work has been published. She is included in McFarlane's two anthologies: *A Treasury of Jamaican Poetry* and *Voices from Summerland.*

Biographical/Critical Sources: J.E. Clare McFarlane, *A Literature in the Making,* Kingston, The Pioneer Press, 1956 (Chapter 7, pp. 48-56 is the main reference).

MURDOCH, Colin

b. August 23, 1955, Antigua.
Poet.

Colin Murdoch attended the University of the West Indies, Cave Hill, Barbados. His verse has been published in *Outlet; Herambee Speaks* (Antigua); and the *Cavite* (Cave Hill, Barbados).

MURRAY, Reginald Myrie

b. ca. 1900, Jamaica.
Poet, mathematician, headmaster.

Beloved and much talked about head of both Wolmer's Boys' School, and Jamaica College, Murray was a great hiker in the Blue Mountains as his poems reflect. Some of the poems give the impression of being exercises or "imitations":

In a cleft remote
Where white mists float
Around Blue Mountain's Peak,
I rise unseen
Beneath the screen
Of fog-clouds dank and bleak;

But it must have been unusual, in those days, to have a Head Master not only interested in poetry, but in poetry concerned with the Jamaica scene.

Writings: Poetry: *Ramblings, (Poems, and),* Kingston, 193?, 33 pp. His work also is in *The Treasury,* Kingston, Jamaica Times, Press Ltd., and *Caribbean Voices.*

MURRAY, Tom

b. ca. 1900, England.
Editor, musician, teacher.

Murray originally came to work with the British Council in Jamaica, then stayed on to teach music at Mona (U.W.I.). He has remained a great supporter of the arts and music in Jamaica.

Writings: Songs and Folklore: *Folk Songs of Jamaica,* Oxford University Press, 1951 and New York, O.U.P., 1952; *32 Songs with Words and Music* (Words and Music for Unison Voices and Piano); *Three Jamaican Folk Songs* (with John Cavell); *Twelve Folk Songs from Jamaica,* London, O.U.P., 1960 (selected from larger collection of words and music, including voice parts and guitar).

MYRIE, Daisy

(née **BAXTER**)
b. March 25, 1908, Jamaica.
Poet.

Educated at Wolmer's Girls' School, Kingston, Jamaica, and the School of Radiography, Royal Northern Hospital, London, Daisy Baxter married Bertram Myrie. She worked for many years as a radiographer in the Government Service of Jamaica and is a strong promoter of literature and a dedicated member of the International P.E.N. (Jamaican Centre), with which she held the position of treasurer for many years.

Her poetry has appeared in various magazines and periodicals and she has contributed to several anthologies, including *Working with English,* (W.W. Dilworth, ed.), Collins and Sangster (Ja.) Ltd., 1969; *Caribbean Voices,* Vol. 1; *New Ships;* and *Focus* (1948). Her poems have been broadcast over local radio stations, CBC (1961), and Radio Eire (in Gaelic).

Her poem "A Christmas Carol" has been translated into Gaelic and French, and her poem "My Island Home" was translated into German by Mrs. Margit Vincenz.

She also set to music "A Christmas Carol" (c. 1950), later sung in Gaelic on an Irish National broadcast by Irish school children.

NAIPAUL, Seepersad

b. ca. 1906, Trinidad.
Storywriter, journalist.

Father of the well-known V.S. Naipaul and his brother Shiva Naipaul, Seepersad was one of the first Indians in Trinidad to attempt to sketch life in the new island home. His *Gurudeva and the other Indian Tales* appeared in 1946 and hesitantly faced many of the themes his son "V.S." has handled so subtly since.

Seepersad was a working journalist for a long period at the *Trinidad Guardian* and later worked as a social welfare officer in Dora Ibberson's short-lived Social Welfare Department.

His son, Vidia, is editing a collection of S. Naipaul's stories. Cliff Sealy (of *Voices*) has lectured on Seepersad Naipaul as a pioneer of Trinidadian-Indian writing.

Writings: Stories: *Gurudeva, and other Indian Tales,* Port of Spain, Guardian Commercial Printery for Trinidad Publications, 1946 [72 pp.].

NAIPAUL, Shiva

b. 1945, Trinidad.
Novelist, storywriter.

Naipaul attended Queens Royal College and St. Mary's College, both in Port of Spain, Trinidad, and then attended Oxford where his major study was Chinese language and literature.

Both of his novels are concerned with rural Indian laborers in Trinidad. John G. Moss, one critic, finds Naipaul's work to be less than convincing, but as brother of V.S. Naipaul and son of the early writer, Seepersad, Shiva is accomplishing the difficult task of making his own mark as a writer.

Writings: Novels: *Fireflies,* London, Andre Deutsch, and Penguin Books, 1970, New York, Knopf, 1971; *The Chip-Chip Gatherers,* London, Deutsch, 1973, New York, Alfred Knopf, 1973.

Stories: in various journals and reviews, including "The Tenant," in *Winters Tale,* 17 (London, Macmillan, 1971), pp. 145-172; and in *Penguin Modern Stories,* 4 (London, Penguin, 1970).

Biographical/Critical Sources: Review in *World Literatures Written in English* by John G. Moss, XII, 1 (April 1973), pp. 117-119; review of *The Chip-Chip Gatherers,* by Julian Symons, in *Trinidad Guardian* (April 22, 1973); interview by Jeff Hackett in *Express* (Port of Spain, March 1, 1970), p. 2.

NAIPAUL, Vidiadhar Surajprasad (V.S.)

b. August 17, 1932, Chaguanas, Trinidad.
Novelist, essayist, storywriter, journalist.

As a Banaras trained Brahman, Naipaul's grandfather came to Trinidad to teach and to work the cane fields. He prospered, and his son Seepersad, a reporter for the *Trinidad Guardian,* passed on to Naipaul his interest in writing and journalism. Naipaul developed the literary aspect of his heritage, but professed intolerance for ancestral Hinduism and for the colonial society into which he was born. While in the fourth form at Queens Royal College, Port of Spain, he inscribed in his Latin primer the vow to leave Trinidad within five years.

It took six years, but he emigrated just before his eighteenth birthday to England, where he read English at University College, Oxford. Following Oxford, he did some broadcasting, edited a weekly literary program for the BBC, and from 1958 to 1961 he was a prolific book reviewer, primarily for *The New States-*

man. His preference for working independently on his own books and for international travel, however, precluded extended regular employment. On numerous occasions he has journeyed back and forth from London to Africa, the Caribbean, India, South America, and the United States. Each of these places in time has found its way into his writing.

London remains Naipaul's metropolitan, commercial center, however he has confessed to feeling peripheral, detached from the local scene, even though he has lived there for many years. The cause is not far to seek: Naipaul guards his privacy on the one hand, and the tenor of his satirical point of view is inevitably that of the distanced observer. He carries within him the same sense of rootlessness and of unfulfilled expectation that pervades his books and articles from first to last. It is the stance of the traditional satirist, but Naipaul reworks conventional molds to assimilate characters, problems and themes from a post-colonial world of increasingly fragmented societies.

It was not until he was twenty-three that he began writing seriously as a career,

though by then he had already completed at least one book. His early efforts were obstructed by certain romantic notions about authorship and the relationship between fact and fiction. The worlds of Dickens, Conrad and Eliot were adapted in his mind to the reality of Trinidad. When he was confronted by the actual London, his distorted fantasy was exploded; and he admits being embarrassed at the prospects of setting down his own island experience in literary form. To his thinking there was something hallowed about the printed word and the sense of permanency associated with long-established cultures such as those which up until that time had been the only societies to produce great literature.

Fortunately Naipaul overcame, as he calls it, this "regional barrier." As is the case for a majority of Third World authors, he had to write for a foreign audience in a language and a literary tradition that were imposed on him from outside. He studied languages—Spanish, French, English; he read foreign literature; but he saw his own background as shapeless, unfounded, and absurd. He considered himself to be excluded from generations of writers who, because they built successively on each other, seemed to have removed any possibility of his participation in their collective creation—that is until he came upon stories that were being written about his own familiar surroundings. Then, recognizing his own reality in print, he concluded that all literature was regional, all language private.

In 1958, Naipaul complained that he could never get a serious reading abroad because his works were considered exotic comedies. By 1965, he realized that limitations he had considered unique to his situation were endemic to all creative artists. He learned as he earned his reputation; neither process came easily. He received £300 in five years for his first three books, but some critical acceptance began to build until he accumulated most of the major British literary prizes. His awards include the John Llewellyn Rhys Memorial Prize [for *The Mystic Masseur*], the Somerset Maugham Award [*Miguel Street*], the Hawthornden Prize [*Mr Stone and the Knights Companion*], the W.H. Smith Award [*The Mimic Men*], the Booker Prize [*In a Free State*], and the Phoenix Trust Award [general achievement].

Another kind of acceptance (one Naipaul seems disinclined to seek) continues to be withheld. Primarily because of his harsh treatment of colonial people and situations, he has enjoyed only limited popularity among Third World compatriots and writers. Naipaul disparages the propagandistic efforts of nationalistic writers, arguing that the artist best serves his country by perfecting his art. He mercilessly dissects the weaknesses of emerging societies, in fiction and in magazine articles, insisting that improvement begins with the admission of inequalities. In keeping with his commitment to esthetic values, Naipaul's primary complaint about much of the early criticism that came his way is that it was not legitimate literary criticism. It concerned itself with his attitude and the manner in which he depicted West Indian characters.

The Mystic Masseur (1957), *The Suffrage of Elvira* (1958), and *Miguel Street* (1959), Naipaul's first three novels, are light, satirical comedies. The first two center on politics and correspond respectively with elections in Trinidad in 1946 and 1950. In spite of the narrator's frequent comments, the novels tell their own stories. Ironically, a succession of failures leads the masseur Ganesh Ramsumair to international eminence where he ultimately sinks into resigned disillusionment. Accidents, eccentricities, chicanery, and bribery pave the road to an equally unsavory victory in *The Suffrage of Elvira*. In this second novel, the candidate is merely a pawn of chance. The picture is of a rootless society, imitative and aimless in its values. Lacking self-respect, the people are only concerned with getting ahead.

For the most part Naipaul's third novel, while less satirical in nature, is a rogues' gallery of Port of Spain's street people. More like a string of colorful vignettes than a plotted novel, *Miguel Street* dramatizes the frustrating meaninglessness of urban poverty. It seems that the only hope is escape; indeed the narrator, buying patronage, flies to the metropolis on the wings of "scholastic success." The most positive aspect of this depressed world is the indomitable spirit which continues to buoy up one character after another. The result is a poignant blend of bitterness and pathos.

Naipaul's fourth book, easily one of the finest to be written by a West Indian author and considered by many to be among the best novels in English literature, is *A House for Mr Biswas* (1961). The story of Mohun Biswas captures authentic West Indian life, but beyond that it transcends provincial boundaries and evokes concepts that are universal in their human implications. The novel has been called an epic and its protagonist an Everyman. Biswas' desperate fight to gain his own house is symbolic of man's need to develop an authentic identity.

A House for Mr Biswas culminates the early phase of Naipaul's artistic development. Combined with his use of vivid color and action is an increased depth of character exposition which anticipates the dark seriousness of his most recent work. The ambivalence of Biswas' desire for self-reliance echoes existential absurdity. Stifled by communal pressures, yet afraid of the chaos outside structured society, Biswas is in constant suspension. His marriage into the Tulsi household provides greater security than he has known before, but in return the family demands conformity and anonymity. More than the characters in the previous novels, he strikes out with desperation and foolishness, utilizing his imagination to impose his own sense of personal order on a meaningless, often malevolent, surrounding reality. On one level Biswas shows a courageous, individual struggle; on another his story is allegorical, dramatizing the legacy of colonial paternalism in a post-colonial world.

It is significant that immediately preceding publication of *A House for Mr Biswas*, Naipaul spent many months in the Caribbean preparing to write *The Middle Passage* (1962). In this exposé-travel book he judges the West Indies to be "a derelict land." Tourism, a new kind of slavery, continues to degrade the populace, keeping it a materialist, immigrant society without substance. Naipaul's nonfictional picture complements the fictional one and neither is favorable. One legitimate criticism of Naipaul's view is that it is narrow, that it is restricted to the isolated East Indian segment of society and that it excludes the recent progressive efforts made on behalf of *negritude* or Black Power. Naipaul's answer to this charge is that the society he saw was not cohesive; communities there are juxtaposed and mutually exclusive: "I can speak only out of my own experience."

Following *The Middle Passage*, Naipaul finally acted upon a decision he had reached in 1958, concerning what he called the "regional barrier." He had concluded that if he were ever to become a best-selling author he must cease writing about Trinidad. Three obvious avenues appeared to lie open, but he had to reject each one: to exploit sex would be embarrassing; to create a popular American or English hero would be bad art; to play on racial tensions would seem spurious. The method he chose required time and cultural adjustment, but by 1963, he had accustomed himself to the London scene well enough that he could write *Mr Stone and the Knights Companion*—and this in spite of his expressed doubt that he could ever absorb enough to be able to write about England.

Naipaul's fifth novel appears to be a complete break with the West Indies. In many respects it is, but he retains the familiar themes of individual isolation and of man's need to find himself. Mr. Stone's inspired effort to stave off retirement is lonely and almost futile. His plan for the Knights Companion is stolen from him and commercialized beyond recognition. What salvages the attempt is Mr. Stone's ultimate recognition of the value of survival. By limiting the scope to a few individuals, Naipaul brings off a convincing portrayal.

Though *Mr Stone and the Knights Companion* was good enough to win the prestigious Hawthornden Prize, it stands as a plateau in Naipaul's development. Sharing this plateau and broadening the staging area for Naipaul's future writing is his second travel book, *An Area of Darkness* (1964). Herein he records his personal impressions of India, the land of his ancestors. His initial reaction was one of withdrawal. He recognized how dependent he had become on the sense of being different, a sense that had supported him both in the islands and in London. Lost among the chaotic millions of India, he searched for and failed to find ancestral roots. Before he escaped back to London, he realized within himself and in India a philosophy of detached acceptance which he found to be humiliating. It explained his conviction that every man is an island, and his urgent need to shield himself from the corruption of causes. His concluding chapter is entitled "Flight," and in it he confesses that the self-discovery occasioned by the trip broke his life in two. With unbearable intensity he encountered a depth of despair and empty illusion which defies formulation.

Fortunately, this experience was not a dead end. Three years later, in 1967, Naipaul published both *The Mimic Men* and *A Flag on the Island*. The latter is a collection of short stories and the title novella. The novella is tightly knit, fast moving, and sophisticated—an American tourist trying to recapture the past, ending in a danse macabre as a hurricane fails to purge the island of life and corruption—but it is not equal to the accomplishment of *The Mimic Men*.

The Mimic Men returns to the subject of West Indian politics and, as its title suggests, the story undertakes the theme of colonial mimicry, the charade of purpose and meaning. The structure of the novel is complex, with the narrator-protagonist "Ralph" Kripal Singh breaking up chronology to piece together his autobiography. He spends his childhood on the island of Isabella, goes abroad to school in England, marries an English girl, returns to his newly independent homeland to make money and ride the swell of nationalistic fervor to political power. His eventual exile from Isabella is even more final than the spiritual downfall of Ganesh Ramsumair. He retires to lick his wounds, perhaps to begin again, but in his fate Ralph detects an all too familiar pattern: "I find I have indeed been describing .... a leader of some sort.... I have established his isolation, his complex hurt and particular frenzy. And I believe I have also established ... the deep feeling of irrelevance and intrusion, his unsuitability for the role into which he was drawn, and his inevitable failure. From playacting to disorder: it is the pattern."

For his next extended work, Naipaul turned to another form of writing, to history. *The Loss of El Dorado* (1969) manages to bring to life four centuries of West Indian history by focusing on two revealing but obscure episodes. The first centers on the last adventurers who sought the mythical El Dorado; the second is the senseless torture of an insignificant mulatto teenager named Luisa Calderon. Each event created a sensation when it occurred, then slipped into oblivion. As Naipaul concludes, it is the typical result of colonialism. Even while Luisa Calderon was being abused, the course of empire was shifting to the east; the slave islands of the West Indies were already becoming neglected outposts. *The Loss of El Dorado* is an advancement over Naipaul's two travel books. It is as sharply etched and vigorous as the earlier books, but the author has distanced himself effectively. His guidance through masses of information is a valuable asset, but he has learned to permit the ironies of cause and effect to convey their own impact.

In a single volume in 1971, Naipaul collected two journal entries, a novella, and two long short stories. All of these underscore in one way or another the significance of the title *In a Free State*. The journal serves as prologue and epilogue, and depicts Naipaul's personal involvement in and compassion for the world he describes. In the end, detachment gives way to an outburst of compassion as he intervenes between a man with a camelwhip and a group of Egyptian urchins who are scrambling for tourist handouts. The short story "One Out of Many" outlines the painful transition an East Indian must make as he tries to fit into American life. Incapable of adequate adjustment, he finally discovers that he is a stranger, separated by glass walls from the life around him. Freedom from his past teaches him only that he must feed and clothe his body for a limited number of years until life ends.

The title novella is set in a recently established African state, during a period of civil unrest. The English protagonist's general isolation and impotence are underscored by the fact that he is homosexual. Bobby is rejected at first in a sexual advance. He then fails to communicate with a female companion who rides with him to the shelter of a government compound. And in the end he is totally defeated by the knowing laughter of his black servant. When his façade shatters, his initial impulse is to escape; but when he cannot run he relinquishes his greatly prized liberal ideals and becomes the colonial master—he can dismiss the objectionable subordinate. Ultimately the free state does not refer to a political entity, but to a state of being. For Bobby, as for Mohun Biswas, freedom is as illusive as the lost El Dorado.

Throughout Naipaul's work there is a remarkable consistency between fictional and nonfictional presentations of basic themes. His concern over the demoralizing influence of colonialism, for example, is not merely a convenient assumption. One effect of the colonial outlook is a kind of insidious security, an assurance that the individual is not responsible for himself, that major decisions will be handled by someone else. In a 1971 interview, he describes England's attachment to the United States in these terms. Problems in London seem less important because they lack American chic and glamor. Naipaul prefers insecurity, a feeling constant with direct involvement. If he is to be taken at his word, the spiritual enervation reflected in most of his recent work is matched by his personal disenchantment with writing as a career. In another interview the same year, he confessed that the idea of writing fiction for the rest of his life was nightmarish. He thought commitment to a more active profession—journalism, politics, or business—might be more rewarding.

Perhaps because of this feeling, most of what Naipaul has produced since 1971 has been in the journalistic vein, including his book *The Overcrowded Barracoon* (1973). The previously published material assembled in this volume spans the years from 1958 through 1972. Most of Naipaul' interests are represented: the vagaries of politics from Africa to New York, the status of emerging nations, the relationship between the writer and society—himself, Norman Mailer, John Steinbeck. Such a collection was due; it focuses the discursive view of an acute mind.

Particularly interesting is his mention of Chaucer as an author meeting a language situation not unlike that of the modern West Indian in his multi-lingual, multi-dialectical situation. Of course, it could never have been only an accident of talent that enabled Naipaul to handle so many levels and registers of West Indian English with such mastery. One recalls, for instance, his comment on the West Indian attitude to "dialect" which he had met while traveling for the *Middle Passage* (1963):

> *The insecure wish to be heroically portrayed. Irony and satire, which might help more, are not acceptable; and no writer wishes to let down his group. For this reason the lively and inventive Trinidad dialect, which has won West Indian writing many friends and as many enemies abroad, is disliked by some West Indians. They do not object to its use locally; the most popular column in Trinidad is a dialect column in the* Evening News *by the talented and witty person known as Macaw. But they object to its use in books which are read abroad. "They must be does talk so by you," one woman said to me. "They don't talk so by me." The Trinidadian expects his novels, like his advertisements, to have a detergent purpose, and it is largely for this reason that there are complaints about the scarcity of writing about what is called the middle class.*

But *The Overcrowded Barracoon* points up one of the main problems raised by the existence and performance of a writer—a considerable writer—of Naipaul's particular style: are all man's foibles, or greatnesses, best probed by the scalpel, best seen by the blinding light of noon? Or do we not hear, and see, some things better in that particular evening light of the Caribbean, when hills no longer seem monolithic, when unexpected depths and fissures, and shadows, are revealed?

Naipaul's achievement, not least of all in catching the rhythms of the Caribbean speech at a variety of levels, remains and is remarkable. There also remain the controversies (esthetic and political) that surround him, and which apparently are not to be in any way lessened by the publication of his latest *Guerrillas* (1975). This study of postcolonial ennui and disillusionment is set in a fictional West Indian nation; but the fictional setting grows most immediately out of the real life experiences of "Michael X" (Abdul Malik) de Freitas, who was tried and executed for murder in Trinidad. To a large extent, what Naipaul reports about de Freitas in two lengthy articles for the *Sunday Times Magazine* in May 1974 becomes the fictional world of *Guerrillas.*

In 1977 Naipaul collected his thoughts and reworked his articles on his 1975-76 trip into *India, A Wounded Civilization,* which is a warm collection of essays on novelists, politicians, and simple villagers in the India of the last days of Mme Gandhi's Emergency.

V.S. Naipaul is the enemy of deceit, especially of self deceit. He encourages us to see *through* the evasions of our societies—evasions that have in no way diminished, though they may have changed, with the coming of Independence. But is it unfair to ask, as C.S. Lewis did a long time ago, *see through* to what? Perhaps not, but nevertheless—that gives us no right to ask the satirist to be what he is not.

Writings: Novels: *The Mystic Masseur,* London, Andre Deutsch, 1957; New York, Vanguard, 1959; *The Suffrage of Elvira,* London, Andre Deutsch, 1958; *Miguel Street,* London, Andre Deutsch, 1959, and New York, Vanguard, 1959; *A House for Mr Biswas,* London, Andre Deutsch, 1961; *Mr Stone and the Knights Companion,* London, Andre Deutsch, 1963; *The Mimic Men,* London, Andre Deutsch, 1967; New York, Macmillan, 1967. (All of these novels are in Penguin paperback.) *Guerrillas,* London, Andre Deutsch, 1975.

Essays: *The Overcrowded Barracoon,* London, Andre Deutsch, 1972; New York, Alfred Knopf, 1973.

Short Stories (collected): *A Flag on the Island,* London, Andre Deutsch, 1967; New York, Macmillan, 1967; *In a Free State,* London, Andre Deutsch, 1971; New York, Alfred Knopf, 1971; (both in Penguin paperback), second printing, 1971, and third printing, 1972.

Others: *The Middle Passage,* London, Andre Deutsch, 1962; *An Area of Darkness,* an experience of India, London, Andre Deutsch, 1964; New York, Macmillan, 1965 (both in Penguin paperback); and *India: A Wounded Civilization,* New York, Knopf, 1977.

Biographical/Critical Sources: Robert D. Hamner, ed., *Critical Perspectives on V.S. Naipaul,* Washington, D.C., Three Continents Press, 1977 (which has a definitive bibliography); Hamner: *V.S. Naipaul,* New York, Twayne Publishers, 1973; Hamner, "V.S. Naipaul: A Selected Bibliography," *Journal of Commonwealth Literature* (August 1975); Paul Theroux, *V.S. Naipaul: An Introduction to His Work,* New York, Africana Corp., 1972; William Walsh, *V.S. Naipaul,* Edinburgh, Oliver and Boyd, 1973; New York, Barnes and Noble, 1973; Robert Morris, *Paradoxes of Order: Some Perspectives on the Fiction of V.S. Naipaul,* Columbus, University of Missouri Press, 1975; Landeg White, *V.S. Naipaul: A Critical Introduction,* London, Macmillan, 1975; New York, Barnes and Noble, 1975; John Figueroa, review of *The Overcrowded Barracoon,* in *Caribbean Studies* (1976); J.A. Carnegie, review of *The Loss of El Dorado* in *Savacou,* No. 5 (1971); V.S. Naipaul, "What's Wrong with Being a Snob?" *Saturday Evening Post,* 240 (June 3, 1967); Israel Shenker, "V.S. Naipaul, Man Without a Society," *New York Times Book Review* (Oct. 17, 1971), and *Words and Their Masters,* Garden City, Doubleday, 1974; Ian Hamilton, "Without a Place," *Times Literary Supplement* (July 30, 1971), and *Savacou,* 9-10 (1974); R.H. Lee, "The Novels of V.S. Naipaul," *Theoria,* 27, (Oct. 1966); David Omerod, "In a Derelict Land: The Novels of V.S. Naipaul," *Contemporary Literature,* 9 (Winter, 1968); Gordon Rohlehr, "The Ironic Approach: The Novels of V.S. Naipaul," in *The Islands in Between,* Louis James, ed., London, Oxford University Press, 1968; Victor Ramraj, "The All-Embracing Christlike Vision: Tone and Attitude in *The Mimic Men* in *Commonwealth,* Anna Rutherford, ed., Aarhaus, Akademisk Boghandel, 1971; Barry Argyle, "A West Indian Epic," *Caribbean Quarterly,* 16, No. 4, (Dec. 1970); Peter Nazareth, "*The Mimic*

Men as a Study of Corruption," *East Africa Journal*, 7, No. 7 (July 1970), and *An African View of Literature*, Evanstown, Northwestern University Press, 1974; M. Bryn Daires, "Criticism from India," *Journal of Commonwealth Literature* No. 3 (July 1967); George Lamming, *The Pleasures of Exile*, London, Michael Joseph, 1960; Kenneth Ramchand, *The West Indian Novel and its Background*, London, Faber and Faber, 1970; John Thieme, "V.S. Naipaul's Third World: A Not So Free State," *Journal of Commonwealth Literature* (Aug. 1975); Anthony Boxill, "V.S. Naipaul's Starting Point," *Journal of Commonwealth Literature* (Aug. 1975); Keith Gurebian, "V.S. Naipaul's Negative Sense of Place," *Journal of Commonwealth Literature* (Aug. 1975); Review of *The Guerrillas* by Consuelo López de Villegas in *Revista/Review Interamericana*, Vol. V, No. 1; A review of Naipaul's *India: A Wounded Civilization* is Paul Scott's "India's Collective Amnesia," in the *Washington Post's* Book Review Section (Sunday, June 19, 1977), pp. K1 and K4.

NANTON, Gene

b. December 23, 1952, Antigua.
Poet.

Gene Nanton is greatly interested in Caribbean culture and literature. His verse has been published in various newspapers and the journal *Outlet*. Together with Elleton Jeffers, another Antiguan poet, he has been connected with the Afro/Caribbean Liberation Movement.

NAPIER, Elma

b. March 23, 1893, Scotland; d. at Calibishie, Dominica, November 12, 1973.
Storywriter, travel writer.

Elma Napier emigrated to Australia in 1915 and then to Dominica in 1932. She first married Maurice Gibbs in 1912; that marriage was dissolved and she married Lennox Napier in 1923. Her grandson, Lennox Honeychurch, dedicated his *The Dominica Story* to her.

She was elected to the Dominica Legislature in 1940, the first woman in Dominica and the West Indies to hold such a post. She served as elected and later, as nominated member, until 1954.

She travelled widely in Southeast Asia, the Pacific, Turkey, Syria and Europe.

Writings: Nothing So Blue, Jonathon Cape, London, 1928; *Duet in Discord*, Jonathon Cape, London, 1935; *A Flying Fish Whispered*, Jonathon Cape, London, 1938; *Youth is a Blunder*, Jonathon Cape, London, 1944; *Winter is in July*, Jonathon Cape, London, 1948; *Commonwealth Conference Nairobi 1954, Impressions*, Advocate Printery, 1955.

The bulk of her work consisted of travel articles and short stories in the *Manchester Guardian* (1930-41); *Blackwoods Magazine* (1948-59); BIM (Literary magazine, Barbados); *The West Indian Review* (Jamaica); and *The Strand* (London).

NETTLEFORD, Rex Milton

b. February 1933, Jamaica.
Essayist, editor, dancer, choreographer, educator.

Nettleford was educated in Jamaica through the U.W.I. and then at Oxford as an Issa Scholar (1956) and Rhodes Scholar (1957). He is the Special Adviser on Art and Culture to the Government of Jamaica.

Rex Nettleford is not basically a writer of fiction, either in poetry or prose, but he is a brilliant dancer, and outstanding organizer of the Jamaica Dance Company, which has left its mark on the cultural life of the Caribbean. Only Walcott's Trinidad Theatre Workshop rivals Nettleford's group for imaginative and disciplined team work.

Nettleford has used in his dancing, choreography and design his extensive knowledge of African culture and Jamaican folklore. A political scientist as well as an artist, his editing of N.W. *Manley and the New Jamaica: Selected Speeches and Writings 1938-1968* is a valuable background book for any one wishing to know something about the human culture out of which Jamaican creative writing has grown.

Nettleford has a wide international reputation, and has been honored at home and abroad. His *Mirror Mirror* gives a very special insight into growing up and coming into full consciousness in Jamaica of the sixties. The book has for its subtitle: "Identity: race and protest in Jamaica." It ends with a comment on one of the key decisions which will have to be made by the whole West Indian society:

> *... the Jamaican society ... will have to decide whether it wants ... institutions of learning which are serious in intent—institutions, which even at the risk of some disruptions ... can help to produce the innovators and creators and forge a quality of mind so widespread among its citizenry that there can come a quick end to that threatening mediocrity which is the bane of much that is Jamaican existence ...*

Writings: General Cultural Study: *Mirror Mirror Identity: Race and protest in Jamaica,* London, Collins; and Kingston, Sangster (Jamaica) Ltd., both 1970; Third impression, 1974.

Editor of: *Manley and the New Jamaica: Selected speeches and writings 1938-1968,* (edited with notes and introduction), London, Longman Caribbean, 1971.

Articles: "The African connexion—the significance for Jamaica," in *Our Heritage,* Kingston, Department of Extra Mural Studies, U.W.I., 1963, pp. 39-55. (Public Affairs in Jamaica, No. 1) (5, 11); "National Identity and attitudes to race in Jamaica," *Race* 7 (1) (1965) pp. 59-72; co-author with M.G. Smith and Augier, Roy, *The Ras Tafari movement in Kingston, Jamaica,* Kingston, University of the West Indies, 1960; *Political education in the developing Caribbean,* 1962; "New goals in education," in George Cumper, editor, *Reporter of the Conference on Social Development in Jamaica,* Kingston, Standing Committee on Social Services, pp. 94-97.

Biographical/Critical Sources: Nettleford is mentioned in H. Fowler's article, "A History of Jamaican Theatre" in *Jamaica Journal,* Vol. 2, No. 1 (March 1968), pp. 53-59; and in Errol Hill's paper to ACLALS, Jamaica (Jan. 1971). Also see Sylvia Wynter's "One Love—Rhetoric or Reality?" in *Caribbean Studies,* Vol. 12, No. 3, pp. 14.

NICHOLAS, Arthur E.

b. 1875, Jamaica; d. 1934.
Poet.

Nicholas was one of the earliest of published Jamaican poets. J.S.C. McFarlane said he was "One of the sweetest singers of Jamaica. . . ." and that he "enjoys a deserved reputation among poetry lovers."

Writings: Poetry: *Arcadia: Poems,* London, Books for Today, Ltd., 1949 (108 pp.). Also represented in *A Treasury of Jamaican Poetry.*

Biographical/Critical Sources: He is mentioned in J.E. Clare McFarlane's *A Literature in the Making,* Kingston, Pioneer Press, 1956.

NICHOLAS, Eva

b. ca. 1877, Jamaica.
Poet.

Sister of Arthur Nicholas, J.E. Clare McFarlane tells us Eva Nicholas "formed a literary association whose fruitfulness is reminiscent of the Wordsworths and the Rossettis." Her poetry appears in McFarlane's anthology, *A Treasury of Jamaican Poetry.*

Biographical/Critical Sources: Her work is discussed briefly in McFarlane's *A Literature in the Making,* Kingston, Pioneer Press, 1956 (Chapter 3: "Nicholas and his Sister" is the main reference, pp. 19-26).

NICOLE, Christopher (Robin)

(pseudonyms: **Andrew YORK; Peter GRANGE**)
b. December 7, 1930, Guyana.
Novelist.

Nicole was educated at Harrison College,

Barbados; and Queen's College, Guyana. He worked as a bank clerk in Guyana and the Bahamas (1947-50); went to England in 1956; settled in Guernsey, Channel Islands in 1957.

Nicole is a prolific writer who has produced serious novels, historical romances under the pseudonym of Peter Grange and a series of thrillers under the name of Andrew York. He has also written a history of West Indian Cricket and a history of the West Indies. He himself tells us that his first eight novels were concerned with the West Indies but that after living away from the West Indian scene for a long time he felt that he had said all he could.

Anthony Boxill in his commentary on Nicole in *Contemporary Novelists* (St. Martin's Press, N.Y., 1972) says that "if Nicole is to be taken as a serious writer, it is his books set in the West Indies which will qualify him for this title. He has written other works set in parts of the world where he has travelled, Poland for example, but these lack the intimacy of insight that he demonstrates when he is writing about the West Indies and Guyana, where he grew up."

Nicole, like Mittelholzer, produced a trilogy with his *Amyot's Cay, Blood Amyot,* and *The Amyot Crime.* Kenneth Ramchand classes his "coloured" heroine Yvonne Huntly in *Off White* with the heroines of Mittelholzer's *Sylvia* and Tom Redcam's *One Brown Girl And*—Ramchand says that these "authors do not push their characters in the direction of the stereotype" of the Coloured woman, but they all "are portrayed as having in common a sensuous beauty which, in real life, is the basis of a continuing popular image of the Coloured woman. . ."

Ramchand in his chapter on Aborigines "where he discusses how the contemporary Indians are portrayed in West Indian fiction specially refers to Nicole's *Shadows in the Jungle* (*The West Indian Novel and its Background,* Chapter VIII, p. 164 n.2.). And Boxill feels that Nicole is at his best in this novel where "he suggests the character of the jungle and develops the relationship between it and its inhabitants."

Writings: Novels: *Off White,* London, Jarrolds, 1959; *Shadows in the Jungle,* London, Jarrolds, 1961; *Ratoon,* London, Jarrolds, and New York, St. Martin's Press, 1962, and Bantam, 1973; *Dark Noon,* London, Jarrolds, 1963; *Amyot's Cay,* London, Jarrolds, 1964; *Blood Amyot,* London, Jarrolds, 1964; *The Amyot Crime,* London, Jarrolds, 1965; *White Boy,* London, Hutchinson, 1966; *The Eliminator* (as Andrew York), London, Hutchinson, 1966, and Philadelphia, Lippincott, 1967; *King Creole* (as Peter Grange), London, Jarrolds, 1966; *The Co-Ordinator* (as Andrew York), London, Hutchinson, 1967, and Philadelphia, Lippincott, 1967; *The Predator* (as Andrew York), London, Hutchinson, 1968, and Philadelphia, Lippincott, 1968; *The Self-Lovers,* London, Hutchinson, 1968; *The Devil's Emissary* (as Peter Grange), London, Jarrolds, 1968; *The Deviator* (as Andrew York), London, Hutchinson, 1969, and Philadelphia, Lippincott, 1969; *The Doom Fisherman* (as Andrew York), London, Hutchinson, 1969; as *Operation Destruct,* New York, Holt Rinehart, 1969, and New York, Dell, 1974; *The Thunder and the Shouting,* London, Hutchinson, 1969, and New York, Doubleday, 1969; *The Dominator* (as Andrew York), London, Hutchinson, 1969, and New York, Lancer, 1971; *Manhunt for a General* (as Andrew York), London, Hutchinson, 1970; as *Operation Manhunt,* New York, Holt Rinehart, 1970; *The Tumult at the Gate* (as Peter Grange), London, Jarrolds, 1970; *The Longest Pleasure,* London, Hutchinson, 1970; *The Infiltrator* (as Andrew York), London, Hutchinson, 1971, and New York, Doubleday, 1971; *Where the Cavern Ends* (as Andrew York), London, Hutchinson, 1971, and New York, Holt Rinehart, 1971; *The Face of Evil,* London, Hutchinson, 1971; *The Expurgator* (as Andrew York), London, Hutchinson, 1972; *Appointment in Kiltone* (as Andrew York), London, Hutchinson, 1972; as *Operation Neptune,* New York, Holt Rinehart, 1972, and New York, Dell, 1973.

Others: *West Indian Cricket,* London, Phoenix House, 1957; and *The West Indies: Their*

People and History, London, Hutchinson, 1965.

Biographical/Critical Sources: Anthony Boxill in *Contemporary Novelists,* (New York, St. Martin's Press, 1972), p. 946; Kenneth Ramchand, *The West Indian Novel and its Background* (New York, Barnes and Noble, 1970), pp. 44, 45 (*Off White*), p. 164, n. 2 (*Shadows in the Jungle*).

NORMAN, Alma

b. 1930, Canada (of Jamaican parents).
Poet, teacher.

Norman has demonstrated a great interest in helping young Jamaicans become aware of poetry, and of their historical heritage. His own work is accordingly mostly folkloric.

Writings: Ballads of Jamaica, Kingston, 1964, new edition with drawings by Dennis Rallston, Green and Co., London, Longmans, 1967; "Revolt of Chief Tacky" (from *Ballads*) is in *West Indian Poetry* (K. Ramchand and C. Grey, eds., London, Longman Caribbean, 1972).

OGILVIE, William George Graham

b. ca. 1923, Canal Zone, Panama (of Jamaican parents).
Novelist, playwright, poet, storywriter, teacher.

Ogilvie was educated in Jamaica at St. John's and St. George's School, Happy Grove and Mico. He has taught in country schools and several Kingston high schools. His work has appeared in United States and British reviews as well as Jamaican magazines. His novel, *The Ghost Bank,* won the Jamaican novelist's prize in 1953, the year of its issue. He is presently Principal of Wentworth High School.

Writings: Plays: *Etheldred Marlow; Hi, Mis Cleo; His English Wife,* written 1965; *Jezebel,* 3 acts, produced in Jamaica, 1966, and winner of first prize in Jamaica Festival competition in 1965; *The Legacy; Me tief,* 3 acts; *One dollar for Dog,* produced in Jamaica, 1964 and winner of bronze medal, Jamaica Festival, 1968; *One Sojer Man,* comedy in 3 acts, Jamaica, 1945; *The Sudden Guest,* produced in Jamaica as *Star Boarder,* 1962.

Novels: *Cactus Village;* and *The Ghost Bank,* both Kingston, Pioneer Press, 1953.

Poetry: in *Focus,* 1960.

Short Story: in *Jamaican short stories,* Kingston, Pioneer Press, 1950.

Biographical/Critical Sources: Kenneth Ramchand, in *The West Indian Novel and Its Background,* New York, Barnes and Noble, 1970. He is also mentioned in H. Fowler's article, "A History of Jamaican Theatre" in *Jamaica Journal,* Vol. 2, No. 1 (March 1968), pp. 53-59.

O'MARDE, Andy

b. April 21, 1954, Antigua.
Playwright.

O'Marde attended the Grammar School in Antigua and the University of the West Indies, St. Augustine, Trinidad. He is the brother of Dorbrene O'Marde, the playwright who has written and produced plays in Antigua and Barbados. His (unpublished) plays are *Tell it like it is* and *Oh Lord, Why Lord?*.

O'MARDE, Dorbrene

b. March, 1950, Antigua.
Poet, playwright.

Dorbrene O'Marde was educated in Antigua; he is a 1971 graduate of the University of the West Indies, Cave Hill, Barbados (B.Sc. Chem.). He did a post-graduate Diploma in Hospital Administration in Toronto, Canada, and is now in charge of the Hospital in Antigua. Before specializing in the field of Hospital Administration he was a teacher.

O'Marde has done readings of his poetry and has been published in the Antiguan journal *Herambee Speaks,* and his plays have been produced in Antigua and Barbados. O'Marde is a very lively and concerned person, very much involved with the arts.

Writings: Plays (unpublished): *Bad Play;* and *Homecoming.*

OMOWALE, Marina

(pseudonym for **Marina MAXWELL**)

OTTLEY, Carlton Robert

b. 1915, Tobago.
Writer, folklorist.

Ottley was educated at Bishops High School in Tobago and St. Mary's College in Trinidad and at Liverpool University. He was former Director of Community Development for Trinidad and Tobago. Retired in 1968, he at present delves into old historical documents, and is the author of several books on Trinidad and Tobago. He published *Creole Talk: Trinibagianese: How to Old Talk in Trinidad,* four more volumes between 1965-67 in *Words, Phrases and Sayings peculiar to the country,* and in 1971 produced one further volume.

Writings: Collection: *Creole Talk* (Trinibagianese), printed by Victory Printers for the author, Trinidad, 1971; *Tobago Legends and West Indian Lore,* Georgetown, Daily Chronicle, 1950 (137 pp.); *Legends: True Stories and Old Sayings from Trinidad and Tobago,* Port of Spain, College Press (71 pp.).

PAIEWONSKY, Isidor

b. ca. 1903, St. Thomas, U.S. Virgin Islands.
Poet.

Paiewonsky's one known work is *Croucher by the Fire* (New York, Galleon Press, 1933).

PALMER, C. Everard

b. ca. 1930, Kendal, Jamaica.
Novelist, teacher.

Palmer was educated in Jamaica and he now teaches in Canada. His novels are especially written for children. He was awarded a certificate of merit by the Jamaica Reading Association for his contribution to Jamaican Children's Literature.

Writings: Novels (Juvenile Fiction): *A Broken Vessel,* Kingston, Jamaica, Pioneer Press, 1960; *The Adventures of Jimmy Maxwell,* Jamaica Publications Branch, Ministry of Education, 1962 (illustrated by Barrington Watson); *A Taste of Danger,* Kingston, Publications Branch, 1963 (illustrated by Laszlo Acs); *The Cloud with the Silver Lining,* Pantheon Books, New York, 1967; and London, Andre Deutsch, 1966; *Big Doc Bitteroot,* 1968; *The Sun Salutes You,* 1970; *Humming Bird People,* 1971; *The Wooing of Beppoo Tate,* 1972); *A Cow Called Boy,* 1973 (and Indianapolis, 1962); *My Father, Sun-Sun Johnson,* 1974 (these last six by Andre Deutsch, London); *Babu and Mr. Big,* Indianapolis, Indiana, 1972.

PATTERSON, Horace Orlando

b. June 5, 1940, Jamaica.
Novelist, teacher, sociologist.

Educated at Kingston College, U.C.W.I., and London School of Economics (Ph.D., Sociology, 1965), Patterson is a scholar whose work is widely known. After having been a lecturer at U.W.I. he went to Harvard University where he is now a full professor and Allston Burr Senior Tutor.

His fiction has evoked differing responses. His *The Children of Sisyphus* won first prize at the Dakar Festival of Negro Arts, but others have been critical, feeling that his fiction is, perhaps, too documentary. He seems to write as one with a social philosophy which has not quite become the kind of vision which serious literature needs. As a writer of fiction he suffers by comparison with Mais in *The Hills were Joyful Together,* and with Lamming in *Season of Adventure,* and there is no way he can escape the comparison. But he has attempted to deal with an aspect of Jamaican life which needs a fictional treatment but which at the same time represents great problems even to the most gifted of creative spirits.

He has published essays on history and literature in various periodicals. He was a member of the Editorial Board of the *New Left Review*, London (1965-66).

Writings: Novels: *The Children of Sisyphus*, London, New Authors, 1964, and Boston, Houghton Mifflin, 1965; and Jamaica, Bolivar Press, 1968, 1971, and as *Dinah*, New York, Pyramid Books, 1968; *An Absence of Ruins*, London, Hutchinson, 1967; *Die the Long Day*, New York, Morrow, 1972.

Scholarship: *The Sociology of Slavery*, London, MacGibbon and Kee, 1967; *An Analysis of the Origins, Development and Structure of Negro Slave Society in Jamaica*, Rutherford, New Jersey, Fairleigh Dickinson University Press, 1968.

Biographical/Critical Sources: see introduction of Louis James in his *The Islands in Between* (anthology), London, A Three Crowns Book, Oxford, 1968, pp. 46-49, and Kenneth Ramchand, *The West Indian Novel and Its Background*, London, Faber, 1970.

PAYNE, Millicent

b. ca. 1911, Barbados; d. 1967.
Storywriter.

Payne published one collection, *Short Stories: Check and Mate: the Barbados Gift Book* (1941), and several short stories in BIM.

PEEK, Basil

b. ca. 1919, Bahamas.
Folklorist, editor.

Peek's one published volume is *Bahamian Proverbs* (arranged and illustrated by Basil Peek, published in London, J. Culmer, 1949).

PENN, Verna Ernestine

b. ca. 1946, Tortola, British Virgin Islands.
Poet, librarian, teacher, playwright.

Verna Penn, librarian at the main library in Road Town, has composed and broadcast plays on local radio.

Writings: Poetry: *The Essence of Life*, Tortola, Caribbean Printing Co., 1976.

Official: Program and Background of Tortola, "Visit of Her Majesty Queen Elizabeth II . . . to the British Virgin Islands . . . 26th October, 1977, Road Town, Tortola, Caribbean Printing Co., 1977.

PEREIRA, Joseph Raymond

b. September 23, 1945, Montego Bay, Jamaica.
Poet, university lecturer, critic.

Educated Cornwall College, U.W.I. (B.A. Sp. Hons.—1966), and winner of the Dip.Ed. (1967) Queens University, Canada (M.A. 1968), Pereira is at present lecturer in the Department of Spanish (U.W.I., Mona, Jamaica), and president of the West Indies University Graduates Teachers' Union.

Writings: Poetry: *Retamar: Revolutionary Poems*, Kingston, Savacou (Poets Series, No. 2), 1974.

Critical Essays and Articles: "Towards a Theory of Literature in Revolutionary Cuba," *Jamaica Journal*, Vol. 9, No. 1, pp. 28-38, and work in *Caribbean Quarterly*, Vol. 20, Nos. 1-2, pp. 62-73.

PERKIN, Lily

b. ca. 1941, Jamaica.
Folklorist, actress.

Perkins has collected folk tales which were edited by Alex Gradussov.

Writings: Collection: *Anancy in Love*, Jamaica, Jamaica Publishing House, 1971.

PERRY, Ernest

b. ca. 1940, Guyana.
Poet.

Perry's popular work has appeared in Monar's *Poems for Guianese Children*. Most of his collected verse was first published in local newspapers and periodicals, including *A New Guyana*.

Writings: Poetry: *A New Morn*, Georgetown, 1970; *Black Mahogany and Other Poems*, Georgetown, Bovell's Printery, 1971; *Guyana's Child*, Georgetown, 1973.

PILGRIM, Frank

(pseudonym: **Knarf MIRGLIP**)
b. December 5, 1926, Georgetown, Guyana.
Journalist, playwright, broadcaster, public relations officer.

A well-known worker in the field of culture in the Caribbean and Africa, Pilgrim has travelled extensively, and worked abroad a great deal: e.g., for the *London Observer* (1962-66), and for the BBC. He organized and ran CARIFESTA, Guyana 1972.

He has contributed stories and articles to various newspapers and periodicals. His plays have been performed in Georgetown, Guyana, and have been broadcast.

Writings: Plays: *Miriamy: a West Indian play in three acts*, (written 1955), published La Penite Rice, B.G., Lithographic Co., 1963 (67 pp.); *Skeleton at the Party: A Play in one Act*, London, Dean and Sons, 1954.

Radio Plays: *Singing Rum*, broadcast 1963, and staged Georgetown, 1964; *The Homecoming*, broadcast 1964 and 1971; *Christmas Reunion: A Thirty Minute Play for Radio in One Act*, 1964; *Rain Stop Play*, 1973.

Plays: (with Peter Anderson): *So This is the Brink*, performed in Georgetown by the Theatre Guild, 1967. (Pilgrim used the pseudonym Knarf Mirglip and Anderson the pseudonym Retep Neresand.); (with Michael Norsworthy): *On the Brink*, performed in Georgetown by the Theatre Guild, 1964; co-authored with Bill Pilgrim, Ian McDonald and others: the musical drama *Advance to the Brink*, performed 1969, by the Theatre Guild in Georgetown, Guyana.

POND, Wilfred Oscar Morgan

b. June 15, 1912, Plymouth, Montserrat.
Poet, teacher.

Wilfred Pond attended the Roman Catholic Primary School, and the Anglican Primary School, where he was appointed a pupil teacher in 1928. In 1932, he won a Leeward Islands Student scholarship, which took him to the Rawle Teachers' Training College, Barbados; he graduated in 1934 and was posted to Dominica where he has remained ever since.

Pond served in various capacities in the teaching field up to his retirement in 1969. He was an Acting Education Officer at the time of his retirement, having been Adult Education Officer, Acting Inspector of Schools, and Head Teacher in various schools.

He started writing verse at the age of 15, and has contributed to various magazines and newspapers. He wrote the words of

the Dominican National Song. A religious man and staunch supporter of the Anglican Church, Pond was ordained a Deacon (perpetual Diaconate) in August, 1974. He has written a number of harvest hymns with a West Indian flavor, which are used in various churches on the island.

PRAGNELL, Alfred

b. ca. 1925, Barbados.
Poet, broadcaster, actor.

Alfred Pragnell is a well-known broadcaster in Barbados, and an excellent actor. His verse has been published in BIM (Barbados); and in the anthology, *Caribbean Voices*, Vols. I and II, selected and edited by John Figueroa.

Pragnell is very good at imitations, taking off some "Bajan" characters to a "T." He brought the house down at Madison Square Gardens, and has two or three recordings of skits in which he plays a variety of persons; one, *Tea for 2*, has been a great success, as was "Laughin' Sport." The script of *Tea for 2* is by the well-known Jeanette Layne-Clarke. Pragnell is well described as "a perfectionist"; he is also a very human and *simpatico* person, unassuming but committed to the best values he knows and works for. He has been awarded the M.B.E.

Among his various writings is a review of *Voices under the Window* by John Hearne (Faber and Faber, Ltd., London, 1955) in BIM 23, p. 206.

PRINCE, Ralph

b. ca. 1938, Antigua.
Storywriter, free-lance journalist.

Ralph Prince was educated in Antigua and in Nevis, St. Kitts. He spent some time as a free-lance reporter elsewhere in the Caribbean, notably in St. Thomas of the Virgin Islands, before settling in Mackenzie, Guyana with his family. His short stories have been published variously in West Indian newspapers and literary journals. He is identified with Guyana.

His short stories appeared in BIM regularly. He was one of the fifty contributors to *Savacou 7/8* (Jan.-June 1973), edited by Edward Brathwaite, and published by The Caribbean Artists Movement and Savacou Publications Ltd., Kingston, Jamaica, the issue dedicated to Frank Collymore (editor of BIM) on the occasion of his 80th birthday. Prince's contribution "Ol Higue" is based on the folk lore of Guyana.

His stories have also been broadcast on the BBC. His work also appears in the Anthology *The Sun's Eye* (Anne Walmsley, ed.), London, Longman Caribbean, 1968, 1970, 1971.

PUNCUSS, Pugagee

(pseudonym for **G.H.H. McLLELAN**)

QUAYLE, Ada

b. ca. 1927, Jamaica.
Novelist.

Quayle served in Egypt and East Africa with the Women's Royal Air Force. After work with the BBC, she removed to Kenya where she now lives.

Writings: Novel: *The Mistress*, London, MacGibbon and Kee, 1957, and London, Four Square Books, 1961.

Biographical/Critical Sources: Frank Collymore, "*The Mistress,*" a review in BIM, Vol. 7, No. 27 (July-Dec. 1958), pp. 185-186.

QUESTEL, Victor D.

b. 1948, Trinidad.
Poet, critic.

One of the new active poets and literary personalities in Trinidad, Questel has won first prize for poetry in the National Cultural Council Literary Contest, 1973, and has published in a wide range of journals. He recently earned his doctorate at the University of the West Indies, St. Augustine (Trinidad).

Writings: Poetry: *Score; Poems* (by Victor D. Questel and Anson Gonzalez), published by the authors, Trinidad, 1972 (20 poems by V.D. Questel), entitled "Prelude" forms the first part of the book). His poetry has appeared in *Caribbean Rhythms; Voices,* (Vol. 2, No. 3, 1973); *Savacou,* (Pelican, 1969); *The New Voices; Black Images* (Canada); *Now;* BIM (57). He wrote the introduction to *When Moon Shine*—a collection of poems by Paul Keens-Douglas and he reviewed Anson Gonzalez's *Love Song of Boysie B and Other Poems* under the title "The Price of Self-hood" in *The New Voices,* No. 4 (June 1974).

Biographical/Critical Sources: Anson Gonzalez, " 'Possibility' in W.I. Creative Writing" in *The New Voices,* No. 4 (June 1974), p. 47.

QUOW

(pseudonym of **Michael McTURK**)

RAE, Norman

b. December 5, 1931, Jamaica.
Critic, producer, broadcaster.

Rae was educated in Jamaica, and at Oxford and London (M.A.).

For many years Norman Rae was a regular theatre, film and art critic, besides being a producer. His criticisms were sometimes thought to be too severe, and not considerate enough of local conditions and difficulties. However, his reviews were often witty and said what needed to be said on such occasions as the famous presentation of the obligatory basket of flowers to a distinguished ballerina by a charming young lady who rushed onto the stage just as the ballerina was reaching the climax of her performance.

On his TV program Rae did his best to encourage the arts and the intelligent discussion of the cultural side of life in Jamaica and elsewhere. Perhaps his most memorable production was that of the *Royal Hunt of the Sun.* He has collaborated with Carmen Manley in the production of her books and TV and radio scripts.

RAMCHARITAR-LALLA, C.E.J.

b. ca. 1904, Guyana.
Poet, compiler, teacher.

Ramcharitar was a graduate of the Government Training College for Teachers. He edited the *Anthology of Local Indian Verse* (Georgetown, Argosy, 1934).

His poetry appears in *Themes of Song; My Lovely Native Land,* in two of Seymour's anthologies, and in G. Singh's *Heritage.*

RAMON-FORTUNE, Barnabas J.

b. ca. 1905, Trinidad.
Poet, novelist, shortstory writer.

Retired October 1971, from the Civil Service of the Government of Trinidad, Ramon-Fortuné has published verse and stories in such journals as BIM; *Caribbean*

Quarterly, Vol. 5, No. 3 (April 1958), Federation Commemoration Issue; *Caribbean Voices; Response; Backfire;* and *West Indian Stories.* His poetry gained second prize in the National Cultural Council Contest of 1973.

Writings: Novel: "The Undertones of Victory," first prize winner of 1973 of the National Cultural Council's Literary Competition.

Story: *Parian Currents*, (Trinidad, Port of Spain, Gazette Ltd., 1949).

RAMON-FORTUNÉ, Joseph Alex (José)

b. 1917, Trinidad.
Poet.

Ramon-Fortuné has done many local children's TV programs.

Writings: Poetry: *Eh bien oui! An Anthology of 20 poems in English and Creolese*, Trinidad and Tobago, 19??; *Up With Your Hearts: A Collection of Poems and Metrical Translations*, Ilfracombe, Devon, England, Stockwell, 1971; poems in several collections, including *Caribbean Voices*, Vol. I, London, Evans, 1967, 1973; and metrical translation of New Testament.

RAMSON, Joyce M.

b. Jamaica; d. 1941.
Poet, hymn writer.

Ramson's *Poems and Hymns* were published posthumously by her father as a memorial to her very short life.

Writings: Poetry: *Poems and Hymns*, 1941; "Harvest Hymn" (celebrating the Jamaican scene) appears in H.V. Ormsby Marshall's *Seed and Flower.*

RAPHAEL, Lennox

b. 1938, Trinidad.
Playwright, journalist.

Educated in Trinidad, Raphael was a feature writer with the *Sunday Guardian* in the early 1960's. He moved to Jamaica to work on the *Gleaner's Newday* magazine for a few months, but soon went to Mexico, and then to the University of Brazil to study Latin American history. He has contributed to such U.S. journals as *Harper's, Esquire,* and *Better Living.*

Raphael's play, *Che,* which ran eleven months in New York, off-Broadway, was charged as an obscene work by New York authorities, but the American Civil Liberties Union fought his appeal and had 53 of the 54 charges dropped. In an interview in *Express* (Port of Spain, Trinidad), Raphael insisted "that he didn't like to talk very much about the past or the future . . . What I will say [is] that I refuse to get involved in anything that demeans the human spirit or anything that involves hate." He was working on musical and movie scenarios in the 1970's.

Writings: Plays: *Che,* performed 1960's in New York City; *Blue Soap,* performed in late 1960's in off-Broadway theatre.

Biographical/Critical Sources: Interview by Jeff Hackett in *Express* (Port of Spain, March 19, 1972), p. 16; Interview in *Express* (Jan. 19, 1976, Port of Spain, Trinidad).

RAS DIZZY

b. ca. 1925, Jamaica.
Poet, prose writer, painter.

Ras Dizzy, mentioned with respect by J.V. Owens in *Savacou 11/12,* came to the arts and to writing in an interesting and instructive way. He used to sell to members of the old Department of Education, U.W.I., a number of objects, including plants and roughly framed airways calendars. It was suggested to him that he himself could probably paint something more interesting than the calendars. He was skeptical at first, but on being supplied with materials, set to work, and after a while produced scenes on which were written tales cautionary and otherwise.

Extant is a painting by Ras of Wolmer's School at the North of the old Race Course. On this as on most of his paintings is a legend.

On the back of his painting of a drummer he has, for instance, the following, which is copied without change:

18-4-17- Jamaica
A Rastafarian Cult in Jamaica— He is Beating
a Drum call the Repeiter—it is 3 Drums
been used in Their Faith—The Doctrine is
Religious and They all Regard The King of Ethiopia
as the Messiah Devine Return on Earth—Rastas
uses even the Flag of Ethiopia and called and
Govt. Heads for Repatriation to Africa as Black
people—Their true Flag is the Rainbow like
in Ethiopia—Please See colors on the Drum to
Their Flag—
Read Revelation 19 - and Psalms 87

Owens says: "Ras Dizzy's prose is considerably more successful than his poetry. The latter tends to be rather disconnected and has little discernible rhythm," which is a very polite assessment of the situation. His prose work is described as being "interesting and entertaining." Yet in many ways his paintings, with or without the commentaries, seem to be his most expressive work.

Writings: The Human Guide Line, Kingston, 1969 (a 53-page pamphlet); *Rastafarians Society Watchman,* Kingston, 1971 (?) (c. 25 pp.); and numerous essays, many of which comment on the Jamaican political scene.

Biographical/Critical Sources: J.V. Owens' Article "Literature on the Rastafari: 1955-1974," in *Savacou-Caribbean Studies,* No. 11/12 (Sept. 1975), pp. 86-105; and see Gerald Moore's article in BIM 57 (March 1974), "Use Men Language," p. 72.

RASMUSSEN, Eric

b. ca. 1917, U.S. Virgin Islands.
Novelist.

Rasmussen has lived off and on in New York City for a long time. His one novel is *The First Night* (New York, Wendell Malliet Co., 1947).

RAYMOND, Arthur

b. 1947, St. Lucia.
Poet.

After local schooling, Raymond moved to England in 1966 to study law. He began to write poetry seriously in his London years and became in his own words, according to Andrew Salkey, a "former optimist." He is preparing a collection of poems for publications. His verse has appeared in various reviews; two poems are in *Breaklight* (A. Salkey, ed., New York, Anchor, 1973).

RECORD, Barry

b. ca. 1930, Jamaica.
Playwright, play producer, teacher.

Record was educated at Kingston College, Jamaica, and at university in England. A controversial, vibrant actor and producer and playwright, he worked very hard (with Errol Hill and others) to change the "image" of the Jamaican Theatre in the 50's. His brother, the distinguished producer, Lloyd Record, often produces his plays and has acted in many of them.

Perhaps Record's best play, paradoxically enough, was the *Skyvers,* especially in its Royal Court production. For whatever reason—distancing of the experience (?)—he had his great energy under real control in that plan, about English school children and was in "real form"; whereas the plays *Don't Gas the Blacks,* whether in London, or *A Liberated Woman,* placed in Jamaica, disappointed, and seem almost opportunistic—as both titles might suggest.

Jamaica Theatre, nevertheless would just not be the same without "Barry" who is once again back "at home," stirring things up.

Writings: Plays: *Skyvers,* in New English Dramatists 9, London, Penguin Books, 1966; and produced in London, 1963; *Adella: a radio script,* produced BBC, London, 1954; *Della,* in mimeo, produced Jamaica 1954, and in London as *Flesh to a Tiger,* 1958; *In the Beautiful Caribbean,* BBC TV, London, 1972; *Don't Gas the Blacks,* performed in London, 1969; and produced also in London as *A Liberated Woman,* 1970, and performed at the West Indian Conference on Commonwealth Literature, Kingston, Jamaica, January 1971; *Miss Unusual, 8 scenes,* produced Jamaica, 1956; *You in Your Small Corner,* produced in London, 1960, and in Jamaica, 1962; *The White Witch of Rose Hall*—comedy, 1975; produced in Jamaica.

REDCAM, Tom

(pseudonym for **Thomas H. MacDERMOT**)

REDHEAD, Wilfred A.

b. November 10, 1909, Grenada.
Playwright, essayist, administrator.

Wilfred Redhead was educated in Grenada. He is manager of the Grenada Sugar Factory Ltd. At one time a civil servant, he served as an Assistant Social Welfare Officer, and as Superintendent of Prisons. He retired in 1967. His main literary interest has been in amateur dramatics.

Writings: Plays: *Three Comic Sketches; Hoist Your Flag; Goose and Garden; Canaree and Pot* (all published by the Extra Mural Dept., U.C.W.I., Trinidad and Tobago, 1966). Also: *Just in Time; Thief from Thief; Now for Now* (no details).

Essay: "Truth, Fact and Fiction in Carriacou," a discussion of M.G. Smith's "Kinship and Community in Carriacou," (Yale University Press, New Haven, Conn., 1962), published in *Caribbean Quarterly,* Vol. 16, No. 3 (Sept. 1970), pp. 61-63; Smith's *Dark Puritan* (Mona, Jamaica, U.W.I., 1963) was also criticized in Redhead's essay; M.G. Smith's rejoinder "A Note on Truth, Fact and Tradition in Carriacou," in *Caribbean Quarterly,* Vol. 17, Nos. 3 and 4 (Sept-Dec. 1971), pp. 128-138.

REDMILL, Felix

b. ca. 1941, St. Kitts.
Poet.

Redmill's one collection to date is *The Fisherman and other poems,* published by Outposts Publications (Walton-on-Thames, Surrey, England, 1973). His verse has also appeared in various journals and collections, including BIM.

REID, Stanley

b. ca. 1921, St. Lucia (long resident in Jamaica).
Poet, editor, playwright, actor.

Reid has been General Editor of the *Link Magazine,* a quarterly publication of Castries, St. Lucia, which he founded.

His work has frequently appeared in *The Bajan* (Barbados); *The Augustinian* (of Trinidad); and *Link.* Two of his poems have been published in *Poets of the Seventies* (London, Regency Press). He produced along with Paul Kink, *The Shape of Things to Come* (Kingston, Jamaica, 1971).

In *Link,* Vol. 2, No. 1, he has a series of poems "In Memoria" for a number of his friends who had died young and tragic deaths. One, written for Sir Frank Worrell, the great Barbadian cricketer, begins:

Five o'clock evening time
you said "I'm tired Stan,
Very tired" and then how
Stupid I was not to
Recognise that you were
Mortal, that in the image

Larger than life, the
Artistry of bat and ball
Hid blood and brain,
Watching with blackbird's eye
My turn to hurl the ball again
Down at your stumps
Even then in your last
Innings it was a boundary.

Writings: Co-Editor of: *The Shape of Things to Come* (an anthology of West Indian poetry), Jamaica, 1972.

REID, V.S. (Victor Stafford)

(also known as **"VIC"**)
b. May 1, 1913, Kingston, Jamaica.
Novelist, storywriter, playwright, reporter, editor, businessman.

One time editor of *Public Opinion,* which was not only a political but also a cultural journal to which many Jamaican writers contributed, Reid started his journalism career with the *Daily Gleaner* which has for so many years dominated the news field in Jamaica, and of which H.G. DeLisser was for a number of years editor and prime mover. Vic Reid later in life was very much the man behind *Spotlight,* a successful news magazine, somewhat of the *Time* mode and mould.

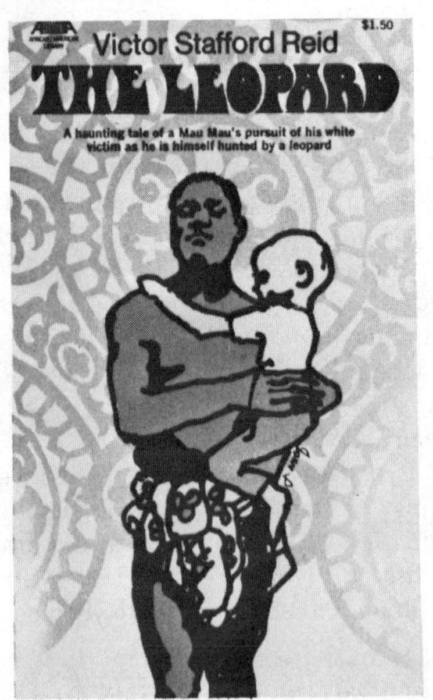

A quiet and retiring man, Reid has led a busy life; he has not perhaps had the real opportunity to produce as much as all readers of West Indian literature would have liked, but what he has done has been significant and carefully worked. He broke new ground with *New Day,* not only in the broadest political sense, but also in his use of the Jamaican cadences, and in his sympathetic treatment of all concerned—not least of all the children, who as always are dragged into battle devised by older and "wiser" heads. The flashback technique in *New Day* gives Reid a few moments of uncertainty, but he has succeeded—whatever ideologues and historians may say—in his avowed aim ". . . What I have attempted is to transfer to paper some of the beauty, kindness and humour of my people . . ."

In some ways his other full length novel *The Leopard* is even more noteworthy, especially in structure and symbolism. With marked economy he builds up suspense—meaningfully: an image of sick hunted and hunting man for the "upright man," as Walcott has it, "Seeks his divinity with inflicting pain."

John Figueroa says of Reid in *Contemporary Novelists:*

> *[he] is a flexible and varied writer, with, at times, a fist of mail beneath that gauntlet of silk. An innovator on the West Indian literary scene, he has written, besides the novels mentioned, a variety of short stories and books for young people.*

Reid has won many honors and awards, including the Musgrave Silver Medal for Literature (1950); and has been the recipient of a Guggenheim Fellowship (1959); a Canada Council Fellowship; and a Mexican Writers Fellowship.

Writings: Novels: *New Day,* Knopf, 1949, and London, Heinemann, 1950, and Kingston,

Jamaica, Sangster, 1970; this work also appears in Heinemann's Caribbean Writers Series, 1973; *The Leopard*, New York, Viking Press, and London, Heinemann, 1958, also New York, Collier, 1971 (in paper).

Novelettes for Children: *Sixty Five*, London, Longmans, 1960; *The Young Warriors*, London, Longmans, 1967; *Peter of Mount Ephraim*, Kingston, Jamaica Publishing House, 1971 (in association with the Ministry of Education, Jamaica), and illustrated by Dennis Ranston); extract from *New Day* is in the *Independence Anthology*, 1962.

Stories: *Fourteen Jamaican Short Stories*, by Vic Reid and others, Kingston, Jamaica, Pioneer Press, 1950; and in various collections, including *Focus; The Sun's Eye*, 1968; and *From the Green Antilles*, 1966.

Play: *Waterfront Bar*, one act, produced Jamaica, 1959.

Biographical/Critical Sources: Two Novels by V.S. Reid by Louis James in his chapter *Of Redcoat and Leopards*, in *The Islands in Between*, London, Three Crowns Book, 1968, pp. 64-72; Barrie Davies' review of *The Leopard*, in *World Literature Written in English*, II, 2 (Nov. 1972), pp. 83-85; Gregory Rigsby, introduction to *The Leopard*, New York, Collier, 1971; K. Ramchand, *The West Indian Novel and its Background*, London, Faber, 1970; Gerald Moore, in *The Chosen Tongue*, London, Longman, 1969, pp. 3-6; review of *New Day* by Charles H. Archibald, BIM, Vol. 3, No. 12 (1949); review of *New Day*, by P.M. Sherlock, in *Caribbean Quarterly*, Vol. 1, No. 1 (Apr.-May-June 1949), pp. 31-32; entry by John Figueroa in *Contemporary Novelists*, New York, St. Martin's Press (James Vinson, ed.), 1972, pp. 1054-1056.

RHONE, Trevor D.

b. March 24, 1940, Kingston, Jamaica. Playwright, film director, screen writer.

Rhone has a diploma in Drama and Speech from Rose Bruford College. He has taught in Kingston, Jamaica, and acted and broadcast in the United Kingdom. On returning to Jamaica he continued to broadcast and write plays.

He is a pioneer in Jamaica in the local making of films in the Caribbean. He has produced the feature film *The Harder They Come* which received the Cork Film International Award, and which has been widely acclaimed. He is now working on a musical, a screen play, and another play. His full-length feature film *Smile Orange* received the Diploma of Distinction from the French Institute, the Cork Film Festival International Award, and a gold plaque in the Virgin Islands Film Festival (Nov. 1975). It also won the special jury award in the category: "Films of Unusual Merit."

Smile Orange started as a very successfull play in the Barn Theatre in Kingston, which is Rhone's home base, and where his current success *Schools Out* has been playing to enthusiastic audiences. His plays, while *topical*, have wide appeal. They put before us, in fascinating and telling moments of drama, the social and ethnic culture and ambivalencies of the Jamaican scene. It is interesting to note that one of his favorite authors is Vidia Naipaul who in his books has also placed before us the realities of life in the Caribbean—though not as "sweetly" as Trevor Rhone does!

Writings: Plays: *Smile Orange, a play*; produced Jamaica, 1972; *Schools Out*, a play, produced Jamaica, 1975; *The Blue Socks Blues*, awarded Bronze medal, Jamaica Festival, 1970; *The Gadget*, produced Jamaica, 1969 (Silver medal award, Jamaica Festival, 1969); *I'm all right, Jack; I'm Human . . . Right? a revue*, produced Jamaica, 1968; *Music Boy, a Jamaican Pantomime*, produced Jamaica, 1971; *Yes, Mama (one act)*, produced Jamaica, 1968; *The Adventure of Ring* (awarded Bronze medal, 1967).

Films: *The Harder They Come* and *Smile Orange*.

Biographical/Critical Sources: Fred Wilmot, writing on "Entertainment" in *Pepperpot* (December, 1974), p. 43, mentions the Barn Theatre and its influence on the Theatre World in Jamaica.

RHYS, Jean

b. 1894, Dominica.
Novelist, storywriter.

Jean Rhys left Dominica for England in 1910; since then she has lived in England and on the continent. She belonged in the twenties to the "Left Bank" group, which included James Joyce, Hemingway and Ford Madox Ford, who encouraged her with her writing. She now lives permanently in Devon, England.

There can be no doubt of the outstanding quality of Jean Rhys' work, even though for years she seemed to be silent and ignored. But she poses, for the West Indian writer, reader and critic, the common problem—or is it a pseudo-problem—of trying to define exactly who is a West Indian writer.

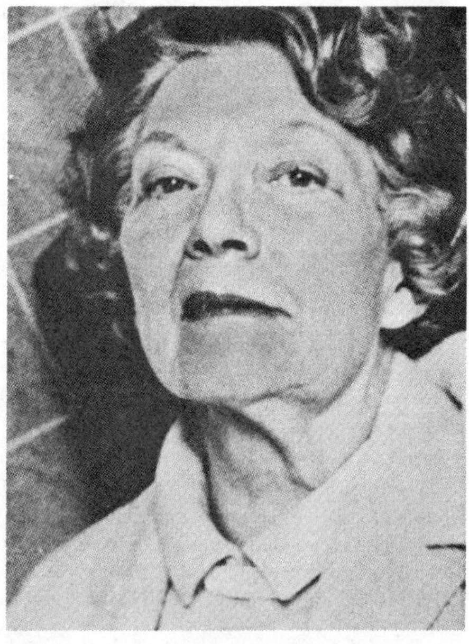

Without in any way trying to take over a person and a reputation one can say that it is impossible to imagine anyone but a West Indian writing that opening chapter of *Wide Sargasso Sea:*

> *They say when trouble comes close ranks, and so the white people did. But we were not in their ranks. The Jamaican ladies had never approved of my mother, "because she pretty like pretty self" Christophine said.*
>
> *She was my father's second wife. far too young for him they thought. and. worse still, a Martinique girl. . . .*

Of course, Christophine is the black maid—"blue black with a thin face and straight features"—and she teaches the narrator most of what she knows including the patois song from Martinique:

> *The little ones grow old, the children leave us, will they come back.*

Apparently *Wide Sargasso Sea* was started some *forty years* after Jean Rhys had left the Caribbean! This makes the whole accomplishment more remarkable, and the questions which it raises of origins even more difficult and profound. In the novel the young heroine is taunted by the "black" children:

> *. . . . 'Go away white . . .*
>
> *"Go away white cockroach, go away, go away." I walked fast, but she walked faster.*
>
> *"White cockroach, go away, go away. Nobody want you. Go away." . . .*
>
> *Old time white people nothing but white nigger now, and black nigger better than white nigger*

Her novel *Wide Sargasso Sea* won the W.H. Smith Award for 1967 and that same year the Heinemann award. The novel's heroine is Antoinette Cosway (the West Indian first wife of Jane Eyre's "Mr. Rochester" in Charlotte Bronte's famous gothic novel) and is the madwoman in the attic. Rhys shows us the happier earlier days of Antoinette's childhood in the Windward Islands and her honeymoon there with Rochester.

In October, 1976, Harper and Row brought out her new collection of stories, *Sleep It Off Lady*, which contains her latest pared-to-the-bone stories, most of which are set in the Caribbean and all dealing with death or old age or both.

All of her pre-War work has been re-issued in similar format by Andre Deutsch.

If, as *Penguin Books* states, *Wide Sargasso Sea* has a "largely autobiographical content, it is no wonder that embitterment is a recurring theme in Jean Rhys—whether because of "the shade of a person's skin, lack of money, or the mere fact of being a woman. All her heroines are born victims"—as Neville Braybrooke has it, in a very helpful entry in *Contemporary Novelists,* (St. James Press Ltd., 1972, U.S.A.).

Perhaps Jean Rhys' work symbolizes something about what the world likes to think of as being "in between." The old creole family at the time of Emancipation was neither new European rich, nor old African now released from bondage; and the women in the demi-monde are neither wife, nor established mistress, nor common-law companion.

Is the world's insistence on "pure categories" just a form of whistling in the dark; just a kind of "closed shop" mentality trying to protect itself from hard reality? Will the Caribbean always be the cross-roads of the world, always be the seed bed of constant cross fertilizations, somewhat disordered and, we hope, creative, or must we aim for, and achieve that state, so frighteningly put in the mouth of the woman, by Jean Rhys, at the end of Part Three of *Voyage in the Dark:*

> *Everything was always so exactly alike—that was what I could never get used to. And the cold; and the houses all exactly alike, and the streets going north, south, east, west, all exactly alike.*

Jean Rhys has been the recipient of the arts Council Bursary, 1967; W.H. Smith Literary Award, 1967; William Heinemann Award, 1967; Royal Society of Literature Prize.

Writings: Novels: *Postures,* London, Chatto and Windus, 1928; and as *Quartet,* New York, Simon and Schuster, 1929; *After Leaving Mr. McKenzie,* London, Cape and New York, Knopf, both 1931; *Voyage in the Dark,* London, Constable, 1934; and New York, Morrow, 1935; *Good Morning, Midnight,* London, Constable, 1939; and New York, Harper and Row, n.d.; *Wide Sargasso Sea,* London, Deutsch and New York, Norton, 1966.

Short Stories: *The Left Bank and other Stories,* London, Cape and New York, Harper, 1927; *Tigers are Better Looking,* eight stories (with a selection, including the preface, from *The Left Bank*), London, Deutsch, 1968; *Sleep It Off Lady,* New York, Harper and Row, 1976. Her work is included in *Penguin Modern Stories I,* (Judith Burnley, ed.), London, Penguin, 1969, and in various "Little Magazines" in Britain.

Memoir: *My Day,* New York, Frank Hallman, 975 (first published by *Vogue* magazine; piece "Close Season for the Old?" first published by *Times* (London) in somewhat different form.

Biographical/Critical Sources: Critical Study: Introduction by Francis Wyndham to *Wide Sargasso Sea;* Neville Braybrooke on Jean Rhys in *Contemporary Novelists* (James Vinson, ed.), St. Martin's Press, New York, 1972; Kenneth Ramchand, *The West Indian Novel and its Background,* Barnes and Noble, New York, 1970, reference to *Wide Sargasso Sea,* pp. 224 and 230-236; "Jean Rhys—Novelist" in *Authors and Areas of the West Indies* by Joseph and Johanna Jones and in "People and

Places" in *World-English Literature*, No. 2 (Austin, Texas, 1970); Review of *Wide Sargasso Sea* by Wally Look Lai, "The Road to Thornfield," in *New Beacon Reviews, Collection One*, (J. LaRose, ed., London, New Beacon Books, 1968), No. 1, pp. 38-52.

RICHARDS, Edward A.

b. ca. 1903, St. Thomas, U.S. Virgin Islands.
Poet.

Richards' published collections are *Shadows* and *The Reflector* (St. Thomas, 1933). His verse also appears in *Ebony Rhythm: An Anthology of Contemporary Negro Verse* (Beatrice M. Murphy, ed., New York, The Exposition Press, 1948), and *Books for Libraries* (New York, 1968).

RICHARDS, Novella Hamilton

b. 1917, Antigua.
Poet, novelist.

Novella Richards attended a local grammar school in Antigua and then went to England where he pursued studies in journalism at the London Polytechnic Institute. He became interested in politics and gave up a career in accountancy to edit Antigua's leading newspaper.

Elected to the West Indies Parliament during the time of the West Indian Federation, he in time became a Minister in the Council of the State. When the Federation was dissolved, he became president of the Antigua Senate. At present he is in diplomatic service, presently serving as Commissioner for the West Indies Associated States in Canada.

He has published a collection of verse and one novel.

Writings: Poetry: *Tropic Gems*, New York, Vantage Press, 1971.

Novel: *The Twilight Hour*, New York, Vantage Press, 1971 (217 pp.).

ROACH, Eric M.

b. 1915, Tobago; d. May, 1974, Port of Spain, Trinidad.
Poet, playwright, critic, journalist.

Educated in Tobago and Trinidad, Eric Roach has been also a soldier, teacher and civil servant.

Eric Roach's living voice was stilled in 1974 but his intense lyric poetry is still vivid:

Only the foreground's green;
Waves break the middle distance,
And to horizon the Atlantic's spread
Bright, blue and empty as the sky;
My eyot jails the heart,
And every dream is drowned in the shore water.

That claustrophobic feeling of being "penned up" in the islands, one feels, overcame him at the end. To some his feeling of what Livingston calls "the West Indian's tragic sense of displacement" was exaggerated, and sometimes ambivalent and ambiguous as appeared in the controversy he stirred up in criticizing some of the new, and admittedly, rather loosely organized poems in *Savacou 3/4*. He even went so far as to express the opinion, on occasion, that he was sorry that he had ever written in *English!*

But we who read him—whether his plays, or his criticism or his poems—can only be grateful to him that he did, and so excellently!

The poem, the first stanza of which is quoted above, ends in a very different way, on a note dear to the hearts of all West Indians of a certain age. From it was taken the title of Figueroa's comprehensive Vol. II of *Caribbean Voices:* (which it in fact ends):

The drunken hawk's blood of
The poet streams through climates of the mind
Seeking a word's integrity

A human truth. So, from my private
hillock
In Atlantic I join cry:
Come, seine the archipelago;
Disdain the sea; gather the islands' hills
Into the blue horizons of our love.

Writings: Poetry: Roach never made a collection of his poems but his work appears in many journals and collections, including BIM; *Breaklight*, 1973; *Caribbean Voices*, 1966; *Caribbean Literature*, 1966; *New Voices of the Commonwealth*, 1968; *Caribbean Quarterly* (Vol. 5, No. 3); *An Anthology of West Indian Poetry, Federation Commemoration Issue*, (April 1958); *Verse and Voice*, 1965; *Caribbean Verse*, 1967; *The Sun's Eye*, 1968. His poetry has been broadcast over the BBC.

Critical Articles and Reviews: in the *Evening News* and *Trinidad Guardian*—to mention two of the newspapers—and in many journals: some of these are: Review of *While Gods are Falling* by Earl Lovelace, in *The Evening News* (May 17, 1965), p. 6; *The Schoolmaster* by Earl Lovelace in *Sunday Guardian* (Jan. 28, 1968), p. 16; *The Mimic Men* by V.S. Naipaul, "As Naipaul sees us" (Part I), in *Trinidad Guardian* (May 17, 1967), p. 9; *On the Coast*, by Wayne Brown, in *Trinidad Guardian* (Jan. 12, 1973); *Ti-Jean and His Brothers*, by Derek Walcott in *Trinidad Guardian* (July 14, 1970).

Plays: *Belle Fanto*, performed in The Basement Theatre, Barbados, 1966, by the Derek Walcott Company and The Trinidad Theatre Workship; *Letter from Leonora* (Caribbean Plays, No. 33, one-act), Port of Spain, Trinidad, Extra Mural Department, U.W.I., 1966; *Calabash of Blood* (full-length, three acts), St. Augustine, Trinidad, Extra Mural Department, U.W.I., 1971.

Biographical/Critical Sources: Mentioned in Lee S.B. Johnson's review of *On the Coast*, Wayne Brown, in *Caribbean Quarterly*, Vol. 18, No. 4 (Dec. 1972), p. 84; Edward Baugh, *West Indian Poetry 1900-1970* (Pamphlet), Savacou Publications Ltd., p. 12; Anson Gonzalez, "'Possibility' in W.I. Creative Writing," in *The New Voices*, No. 4 (June 1974), p. 49.

ROBERTS, Walter Adolphe

b. 1886, Jamaica; d. 1962.
Novelist, poet, historian, editor, journalist.

Roberts was educated privately and in 1901 worked as a reporter for the *Daily Gleaner*. Although he always kept in touch with things Jamaican, he did live abroad for a long time, mainly in Paris and in the United States. When he returned to Jamaica he took a keen interest in the new writing besides carrying on his own historical research. He was one of the early nationalists.

Whereas his fiction has definite realistic elements, his poetry is rather distant and cool, but its versification is always accomplished as in "The Dancer" from which come these lines:

On beauty's scroll no record is more
fleet
Than the sweet patterns of lost dancing
feet. . . .

In 1936 Roberts founded the Jamaica Progressive League of New York. He was founder and editor of the *American Parade* (1925) and was awarded the National Order of Merit Carlos Manuel de Cespedes; the Musgrave Silver Medal for

Literature (1941) and the Musgrave Gold Medal (1954).

Writings: Novels: *The Top Floor Killer*, London, Nicholson and Watson, 1935; *The Pomegranate*, Bobbs-Merrill, 1941; *Royal Street, a Novel of Old New Orleans*, Indianapolis, Bobbs-Merrill, 1944; *Brave Mardi Gras, a New Orleans Novel of the '60s*, Indianapolis, New York, Bobbs-Merrill, 1946; *Creole Dusk, a New Orleans Novel of the '80s*, Indianapolis, Bobbs-Merrill, 1948; *The Single Star, a Novel of Cuba in the '90s*, Indianapolis, Bobbs-Merrill, 1949, Kingston, Jamaica, Pioneer Press, 1956; Also, a mystery: *The Mind Reader*, New York, Macaulay Co., 1929; and a detective story: *The Haunting Hand*, Macaulay Co., 1926, London, Hutchinson, 1929.

Poetry: *Pierrot Wounded and Other Poems*, New York, Britton Publishing Co., 1919; *Pan and Peacocks (Poems)*, Boston, Four Seas Co., 1928; *Medallions*, Kingston, Arawak Society, 1950. Work also has appeared in many anthologies, including *Caribbean Verse; The Poetry of the Negro;* and *A Treasury of Jamaican Poetry*.

Autobiography: Extract from "These Many Years," an autobiography in progress, is in *The Independence Anthology of 1962* (title of extract: "How war came in 1914").

History and Biography: *Semmes of the Alabama*, New York, 1938; *Lake Pontchartrain*, New York, 1946; *Havana: The Portrait of a City*, New York, 1953.

History and Biography: *Sir Henry Morgan; buccaneer and governor*, Covici, Friede, 1933, West Indian Edition, Kingston, The Pioneer Press, 1952; *Six Great Jamaicans; biographical sketches*, Kingston, the Pioneer Press, 1952, (covers Edward Jordan, George W. Gordon, Enos Nuttall, Robert Love, T.H. McDermott, H.G. DeLisser); *Lands of the Inner Sea. The West Indies and Bermuda*, New York, Coward McCann, 1948; *The Caribbean: Sea of Destiny*, Indianapolis, Bobbs-Merrill, 1940; *The Capitals of Jamaica, 1955—portrait of an Island*, New York, Kingston, Pioneer Press, 1955; *The French in the West Indies (1942)*: trans. into French *Self-Government for Jamaica*, New York, Jamaican Progressive League of New York, 1936; *Onward Jamaica*, New York, Jamaican Progressive League of New York, 1937; *We Advocate a Social and Economic program for Jamaica*, 1938 (with others) Jamaica, Progressive League, 1938.

Political Reviews and Articles: in *Jamaican History Review;* Current History Nation Survey Graphic; "The Future of Colonialism in the Caribbean: the B.W.I.," in E.F. Frazier and E. Williams, (eds.), *The Economic Future of the Caribbean*, Washington, D.C., Howard University Press, pp. 37-39.

Biographical/Critical Sources: Walter Adolphe Roberts bibliography: a preliminary check list prepared by the West Indian Reference Library; typescript, arranged alphabetically by title; in Jamaican Historical Society Bulletin: "Walter Adolphe Roberts 1886-1962," Memorial Number, Vol. 3, No. 8 (Dec. 1962), pp. 120-126 (arranged chronologically). Also see J.E. Clare McFarlane's *A Literature in the Making*, Jamaica, Pioneer Press, 1956 (main reference—Chapter 11, pp. 76-83); and Edward Baugh, *West Indian Poetry 1900-1970* (Pamphlet), pp. 5-6.

ROBINSON, Carey

b. November 26, 1924, Jamaica.
Playwright, radio information officer.

Educated at Calabar High School, Jamaica, and at Howard University (Washington, D.C.), Robinson worked on the editorial staff of the *Daily Gleaner* and *Spotlight News* magazine, and in 1952 became a reporter on Radio Jamaica. He was the recipient of the Musgrave Silver Medal for broadcasting (1970).

Writings: History: *The Fighting Maroons of Jamaica*.

Plays: *Mountain Lion*, produced in Jamaica, 1963 (and prize winner, Jamaica Festival of 1963); *The Runaway*, two acts, produced Jamaica 1960; Kingston, Jamaica, Extra Mural Department, U.C.W.I., n.d., Caribbean Plays, stencilled; *Time of Fury*, produced Jamaica for centenary celebrations of the Morant Bay Rebellion.

Biographical/Critical Sources: Mentioned in H. Fowler's article "A History of Jamaican Theatre," in *Jamaica Journal*, Vol. II, No. 1 (March 1968), pp. 53-59.

ROBINSON, Rudolph Oscar Athelston (Ruddy)

b. February 2, 1930, in Jamaica; d. ca. 1968/69.
Storywriter, teacher.

Educated at Calabar, Jamaica, and Trinity College, Cambridge, England, Robinson taught as a university professor in Toronto, Canada, at U.W.I. St. Augustine, Trinidad, and at the University of Ife, Nigeria. (Professor 1964-1968). Many of his stories have been broadcast on the BBC, African and Caribbean programs. Robinson died when still quite young; he, perhaps, never did have the opportunity to concentrate on writing, for he was an active mathematician and teacher.

Writings: Stories in various journals; no collected volume. His work appears in *Focus* (1956); *Island Voices: Stories from the West Indies*, 1970; and *Stories from the Caribbean*, 1965.

RODWAY, James A.

b. February 27, 1848, in Troubridge, England; lived in Guyana from 1870 to his death in 1927.
Novelist, commentator, historian, naturalist, chemist.

James Rodway was the son of a weaver and after leaving school he began his training to be a chemist as an apothecary's assistant. On reading an advertisement that such an assistant was wanted in Demerara, British Guiana, he applied, was accepted and sailed from Southampton, England on September 2, 1870, landing in Georgetown on September 26. He pursued his original profession but he set himself the task of learning about the history and botany of Guiana. He became Librarian and Assistant Secretary to the Royal Agricultural and Commercial Society in Georgetown in 1888, and maintained this position until his death. He contributed considerably to Guyana's history. He was elected Fellow of the Linnean Society (Botany).

The selections "Guiana" and "Kyk-over-al" from his writings are in the anthology *My Lovely Native Land* (A. and E. Seymour, eds.). He also wrote stories and poetry which appeared in local journals. He had many publications in scientific magazines on the flora and fauna of Guyana.

James Rodway's grandson, of the same name, but known to many as "Sonny," has been a distinguished teacher, education officer and principal in St. Lucia and Guyana. He was very helpful to Derek Walcott in his early days; and Walcott's remarkable *Epitaph For The Young* (1949), was dedicated to him with the Latin inscription: *namque tu solebas meas esse aliquid putare nugas.*

Writings: Novel: *In Guiana Wilds: A Study of Two Women*, London, Fisher Unwin, 1899, and Boston, 1899.

Histories: *History of British Guiana from the Year 1668 to the Present Time*, Georgetown, J. Thomson, 1891-1894; *The Story of Georgetown*, Georgetown, Argosy Co., 1920; *Guiana, British, Dutch and French*, London, Fisher Unwin, 1912.

Botany: *In the Guiana Forest; The Story of Forest and Stream*, Second Edition, London, Hodder and Stoughton, 1913.

Biographical/Critical Sources: "James Rodway" by Fred Undschans Deutz, translated from *De West Indische* for June 1927 by Walter E. Rith; J. Graham Cruickshank, articles in *The Daily Argosy* (Sunday, Dec. 19, 1926) on "James Rodway."

ROGERS, De Wilton

b. November 5, 1906, Trinidad.
Novelist, teacher, politician.

Rogers was educated in Trinidad and at Fisk (B.A., Sociology). He then taught at elementary and secondary levels in Trinidad. He was subsequently elected to many posts in Teacher's Unions and Associations, and was a founder of the People's

Education Movement. He was a member of the National Committee of Education, and Governor of the Gandhi Tagore College.

Rogers' style is unsophisticated, almost banal, but he produces sympathy for his ordinary characters, and he aims at awakening a social and political consciousness in his reader. In his introduction to his little novel, *Chalk Dust* (1943), he states: "We are on the dawn of another reformation and this time it is not coming from Germany." And the book itself predicts the needed changes in the Catholic Church, and by extension, in most of the colonial and European inheritance of the Caribbean people.

Writings: Novels: *Chalk Dust*, Gasparillo, Trinidad, 1945; Second printing, Gasparillo, 1973, for author by Rilloprint; *Lalaja, a tale of retribution*, Port of Spain, Trinidad, Fraser's Printerie, 1944; "Queen Daisy," details unknown, believed only to be in ms.

Stories: "Eight Short Stories," in ms., as of 1974.

Plays: "Blue Blood and Black;" "Silk-Cotton Grove;" "Trickidad."

Poetry: "Tagore" and "Kisagotami."

Songs: "Gasparee" and "My Island Home."

Other: *Education and Work Attitudes*, publish, details not known; "Sociology for Everyday Life," in ms.; "Life of John Donaldson" in ms.; "Autobiography of a Victorian Teacher"; "The Benwoods," both in ms.: *The Poetry of Tagore in comparison with a few poets of the West; together with Kisagotami*, Port of Spain, 1968.

Biographical/Critical Sources: Rogers is mentioned in *Black Intellectuals Come to Power*, Cambridge, Mass., 1968, by Ivar Oxaal, and in Anson Gonzalez's *Literature of Trinidad and Tobago "On Air,"* pp. 11-17.

ROGERS, Joel Augustus

b. 1880, Jamaica; d. 1966.
Novelist, scholar, journalist.

Rogers emigrated to the United States and took American citizenship in 1917. He had been a war correspondent and was a member of the Academy of Political Sciences of the U.S. Most of his work is polemical and concerned with race. One critic said Rogers' *From Superman to Man* was "the thinnest imaginable fictional excuse for a tract on the negro race."

Writings: Novel: *She Walks in Beauty*, Los Angeles, Western Publishers, 1963.

Tracts: *From Superman to Man*, Chicago, Donohue and Co. (printers), 1917; New York, Lennox Publishing Co., 1924; J.A. Rogers Publications, 1941; *World's Greatest Men of African Descent*, 1931; *Africa's Gift to America: The Afro-American in the Making and Saving of the United States*, Second Edition revised, 1961.

Article: "Jazz at Home," in *The Black Aesthetic*, Addison Gayle Jr. (editor), New York, Doubleday, 1971, and New York, Anchor, 1972.

ROHLER, Lloyd

b. September 21, 1928, Guyana.
Poet, playwright (radio), shortstory writer, TV personality, journalist.

Rohler, educated in Guyana, was a staff journalist on Guyana's leading newspapers from 1947-1952. In 1953 he became official reporter for the British Guiana legislature; in 1960, senior reporter for the Federal West Indian Government. In 1962, Rohler went on a study tour to London to do TV programming for BBC. He is now with Trinidad and Tobago Television. He was awarded a gold medal by the Theatre Guild of Guyana in its National Playwright's Competition. He is a member of the P.E.N. International—Guyana and Trinidad centers.

Rohler has written poems, short stories and radio plays, and is known in Trinidad as a TV personality. (cf. Notes on Contributors—*Voices*, Independence Issue, 1964, Port of Spain, Trinidad; editor: Clifford Sealy). "The Arts of Guyana," *Kyk-over-al*, 27 (1960), p. 97; has correspondence between Arthur Seymour and other writers, including Lloyd Rohler).

Writings: Play: *Thousands Cheer: A Historical Drama written for Radio,* British Guiana, 1960 (Broadcast 1962, in mimeograph).

Poetry: in *New World* (Fortnightly); *Voices* (C. Sealy, ed.)

Stories: in various journals and collections, including the *Chronicle Christmas Annual* (1957).

Other: *The First Nine Years* (Story of the B.G. Press Association), 1953.

ROTH, Vincent

b. ca. 1892, in Tasmania, lived from 1907 on in Guiana (Guyana).
Folklorist, autobiographer, editor, storywriter, legislator, naturalist.

Roth was Honorable Secretary of the Royal Agriculture and Commercial Society for many years. He edited the *Folklorist,* written by Michael McTurk (pseudonym: Quow); works by George McLlellan (pseudonym: Pugagee Puncuss); Henry Bolingbroke's travel book, *A Voyage to the Demerary;* and a "Series of Notes on the West Indies" under the title *Letters from Guiana* (1942); along with other books on Guyana. He was editor of the R.A. and C.S. Journal *Timehri,* and of the *British Guiana Edition,* published by the Daily Chronicle.

He was also Curator of the British Guiana Museum and published studies on the fish and animal life of Guiana.

Roth's folklore stories have been published in local periodicals.

His account "A Trip on the Baridi" (taken from his *Pepper Pot*) appears in Seymour's *My Lovely Native Land.*

Writings: Autobiography: *Pathfinding on the Mazaruni 1922-24,* Georgetown, Daily Chronicle, 1949; *Tales of the Trail,* Georgetown, Daily Chronicle, 1960.

ROY, Namba

b. 1910, Jamaica; d. 1961, in London.
Novelist, sculptor.

Namba Roy came from the Maroon country of the "Cockpit" mountain areas of Jamaica. His father had been a woodcarver in the old African tradition, for the Maroons had preserved some of the old culture. Roy himself worked in ivory and wood, but also in modern plastic. His one novel, *Black Albino* (1961), tells the story of the run-away slaves of the Spanish period who resisted all attempts to recapture them and whose descendants, "the Maroons," even now are treated specially by the independent government of Jamaica. He brings the albino son of the Maroon chief into conflict with the white-hating Maroons to show reverse racism, but the didactic purposes mar the insights, and blur the special experience of the author.

Writings: Novel: *Black Albino,* London, New Literature, 1961; an extract is in *The Sun's Eye* (Anne Walmsley, comp.), London, Longman Caribbean, 1968, 1970, 1971 and in *West Indian Narrative: An Introductory Anthology.*

Biographical/Critical Sources: Kenneth Ramchand, *The West Indian Novel and Its Background,* London, Faber, 1970.

SADEEK, Sheik M.

b. 1921, Guyana.
Novelist, shortstory writer, playwright, editor, publisher.

Sadeek started writing in the late '30's and since then has published two novels, two collections of poems, a number of dramas and dozens of short stories. His short stories have won many prizes in literary competitions.

His first novel *Bundarie Boy* was written from a manuscript version which won the National Gold Medal Award in a competition in 1961. In his interview with Robert McDowell of the University of Texas in *World Literature Written in English* (Vol. 14, No. 2, Nov. 1975), he says that he rewrote the original manuscript four times and expanded it from "250 to about 300 or 400 pages." He also comments that his second novel, *Song of the Sugar Canes,* deals with the period 1917 to 1953, from the time that the last immigrant ship bringing East Indians arrived in Guyana up to the year the British suspended the Constitution; he regards this as the end of an era.

He is a creative writer who has been involved in every aspect of the field of writing: with publishing, editing and bookselling besides the actual writing. He has published not only his own work but that of many other authors, and he has pointed out that a number of the privately run magazines that originally were responsible for publishing Guyanese writings—in which his work also appears—are now defunct; namely *Kyk-over-al; Chronicle Christmas Annual; Christmas Tide* and *Caribia. Kaie,* another journal in which he is published, is a Government-sponsored publications of the Guyana National History and Arts Council.

He has a great interest in the Guyanese Creole speech and has used the patterns of the Creoles in his writings. He has worked for the National History and Arts Council for a number of years and is at present engaged in gathering local material: Guyanese writings, folklore and stories as a special research project for use in literary forms such as plays.

Writings: Poetry: *Dreams and Reflections,* Georgetown, Sheik Sadeek, 1969; *Reflections and Dreams and More Poems,* Georgetown, Sheik Sadeek, 1974 (enlarged mimeo version of the 1969 book), *Dreams and Reflections; Song of the Sugar Canes,* 1975.

Stories: *Across the Green Fields and Five Other Stories,* Georgetown, Sheik Sadeek, 1974; *No Greater Day and Four More Adult Stories,* Georgetown, Sheik Sadeek, 1974; *The Porkknockers and Four Other Stories,* Georgetown, Sheik Sadeek, 1974; *Windswept and Other Stories,* Georgetown, Kitty, 1969. Stories are in local periodicals, including *Kaie; Chronicle Christmas Annual; Caribia,* and in Seymour's *New Writing in the Caribbean.*

Plays: *Black Bush: A One-Shot Radio Play,* prize winning entry in a Georgetown Demba Play Competition, 1966; *Fish Koker,* Georgetown, Sheik Sadeek, 1962 (winner of the Jagan Gold Medal, 1961); *Namasté,* Georgetown, Sheik Sadeek, 1965 (first prize Theatre Guild Playwrighting Competition, 1960, Georgetown); *He. A Guyanese Play* (one-act, one-scene), Guyana, 1967; *Bound Coolie,* 1958; *Goodbye Corentyne,* 1974; *No Greater Day,* 1965; *Pork Knockers,* 1974; *Savannah's Edge,* 1968.

Novel: *Bundarie Boy,* Georgetown, Sheik Sadeek, 1969 (adapted from original prize-winning ms.).

Biographical/Critical Sources: "Interview With Sheik Sadeek—A Guyanese Popular Writer" (in Georgetown, April 11, 1975), in *World Literature Written in English* (pp. 525-535) by Robert E. McDowell (Vol. 14, No. 2, Nov. 1975).

SAINSBURY, Edward Bennett

b. ca. 1923, Barbados.
Poet.

Sainsbury's one collection of verse is *The Light of the World* (New York, Zephyrs, 1953).

ST. JOHN, Bruce Carlisle

b. December 24, 1923, Barbados.
Poet, educator.

Bruce St. John is a Lecturer in Spanish at the University of the West Indies, Cave Hill, Barbados, and Vice-Dean of the Faculty of Arts and General Studies. He studied at London University and in Toronto, Canada.

He specializes in dialect Barbadian poetry and has published several collections of his dialect verse. He specializes in reading his poetry and has given readings in the U.S.A., Puerto Rico, and Canada, and has recorded his poetry. He does a great deal to encourage young writers, especially through the Writers' Workshop in Barbados. He received a Bussa Award in 1973.

St. John's verse has appeared in many journals, including: BIM; *Savacou; Contact; Tapia; New Writing; Greenfield Review; Manna; Revista de Letras; Kairi,* and others.

ST. OMER, Garth

b. ca. 1938, Castries, St. Lucia.
Novelist, storywriter.

Garth St. Omer was educated in St. Lucia and at the University of the West Indies, Mona, Kingston, Jamaica; his B.A. degree was in French. He then went to France to continue his studies. After spending many years working in Africa, he returned for a short while to St. Lucia, but settled in London for some time. Most recently he has been living in the United States. He is another of the West Indian artists who have lived abroad and travelled much but never can forget the Caribbean.

A careful and skilled artist, spare in his style, and almost bleak in his sensitivity, St. Omer has great powers of evoking, through the most economic means, scenes that ring true, and which are almost overpowering in the way they can hit off human confusion and miscommunication.

His novella *Syrop* made a deep impression when it was first read on the BBC Caribbean Voices program. His first novel, *A Room on the Hill* (1968), evoked tremendous praise from Andrew Salkey on the BBC World Service: "Garth St. Omer is a writer of rare distinction. There is no other West Indian writer with his relaxed narrative tone, or with his control and implicit assurance . . . a compelling first from the leader of the new wave of West Indian novelists." His fictional hero John Lestrade is caught up in the dilemma of dealing with rapidly changing conditions and opportunities in the islands. *Shades of Grey* was also published by Faber in 1968. This book, made up of two short novels, again centers on the frustrations and conflicts of Caribbean Society. Wallace Hldick in *The Listener* speaks of *Shades of Grey* as "one of the most genuinely daring and accomplished works of fiction." He added: "More than any other living writer, Mr. St. Omer reminds me of Lawrence. He does so not simply in the vivid, subtly rhythmic intensity of many of his passages, but also in his themes . . ."

St. Omer's third book, *Nor Any Country* (1969), was once more received with high praise. The hero, Peter, a West Indian, returns to his West Indian home from England. He finds his wife and mother and the whole country changed, more demanding and less hopeful. St. Omer portrays the concerns vividly and with a skilful tact that gives the reader an awareness of a particular encounter with a significant social and spiritual climate.

Gerald Moore in his assessment of St. Omer's work in *Contemporary Novelists* describes aptly the language and style used by St. Omer in his writings. "St. Omer is particularly good at rendering the speech of those who, though educated elsewhere, are still very close to the islands . . ." Again, "St. Omer's dialogue is full of sharp, perfectly registered dialogue . . . His narrative and descriptive passages are rendered throughout in short, rather spikey paragraphs and staccato sentences, which carry the same burden of unease as the lives they describe." (p. 1085).

Writings: Novels: *A Room on the Hill,* London, Faber, 1968; *Shades of Grey,* London, Faber, 1968, contains: *The Lights on the Hill; Another Place Another Time; Nor Any Country,* London, Faber, 1969; *J. Black Bam and the Masqueraders,* London, Faber, 1972.

Novella: "Syrop" in *Introduction II,* London, Faber, 1968.

Stories: in various journals, including BIM.

Biographical/Critical Sources: Gordon Rohlehr, "Small Island Blues," in *Voices* II, 1 (Trinidad, 1969), pp. 22-28; review of first three of St.

Omer's novels, in *Trinidad Guardian* (Nov. 30, 1969); Leonie Star, review of *Nor Any Country*, in *World Literature Written in English*, 19 (April 1971), p. 92; Bernard Graham, review of *A Room on the Hill*, BIM 47, pp. 208-209; John Wickham, review of *Shades of Grey*, BIM 49, pp. 59-64; Edward Baugh, review of *Nor Any Country*, BIM 50, pp. 128-130; Gerald Moore, *Contemporary Novelists* (James Vinson, ed., New York, St. Martin's Press, 1972), pp. 1084-1086).

SALKEY, Andrew

b. January 30, 1928, Colon, Panama.
Novelist, poet, editor, broadcaster, critic.

Educated in Jamaica and the University of London, (B.A. English), Salkey is one of the best interviewers in the radio business and does regular work for the BBC. He is a

novelist, a poet, and an editor of great energy and scope. He has also taught English and Latin in London schools. His output has been remarkable, and his editing vigorous. His first novel, *A Quality of Violence*, received a number of enthusiastic reviews. It is, as the *Listener* put it, "A vigorous, imaginative and quite unusual novel," but it might be that, *Escape to an Autumn Pavement*, his second novel, has even more to recommend it. Self-revelation and self-choice are so clearly insisted upon:

> *I was heading nowhere in particular. . . .*
>
> *I had a choice of lives before me. A choice of loves . . .*

and earlier:

> *I didn't want to run away from a bloody thing. I didn't love Fiona. I didn't love Dick. I didn't even love myself. I simply wanted money. Loads and loads of it!"*
>
> *. . . and only that was worth waiting for: the truth about myself, and the courage and the ability to recognise it when it came.*

That is the second to the last sentence in the novel; the last being:

> *It was a cold morning. Not a trace of rain, anywhere.*

One of the paradoxes about Salkey's writing is that, as Sylvia Wynter has pointed out, his handling of the Jamaican dialect of which he is so fond, and of which he makes such an issue, is so weak. Perhaps she overstates her case, but she does have a point: "The use of the Jamaican dialect as a medium of language, as indeed the use of all language, calls for a process of selectivity. . . . This is Mr. Salkey's bugbear. The moment he touches the dialect his artistic skill lapses, and the use of dialect which he employs in order to justify the use of dialect, is highly fraudulent."

His long poem *Jamaica* does suffer from this lack of touch with the "dialect."

> *All o' we losin out,*
> *'cause we won't own up to weself,*
> *grab we soul,*
> *grab weself like we know weself,*
> *an' tradition-up we tradition,*

Salkey worked on *Jamaica* from 1951 until 1971, and it is, as the publisher tells us, "the very first poem of its kind published by a Jamaican writer."

Mr. Salkey's work as an editor has been of great service not only to authors whose work he has collected but also to all people interested in West Indian writing. He has made available much that otherwise would be so difficult to come upon. It is a real pity that through no fault of his own he has had to work for so long away from the mountains and hills and people of whom he is so fond, and to whose literature and political development he is so committed.

He has been the recipient of many awards, e.g.: Thomas Helmore Prize, University of London, 1955; Guggenheim Fellowship, 1960; Deutscher Kinderbuchpreis, 1967 (for the German edition of *Hurricane*).

Writings: Novels: *A Quality of Violence*, London, New Authors, 1959, and London, Four Square, 1962; *Escape to an Autumn Pavement*, London, Hutchinson, 1960, and London, Four Square, 1966; *The Late Emancipation of Jerry Stover*, London, Hutchinson, 1968; *The Adventures of Catallus Kelly*, London, Hutchinson, 1969; *Come Home, Malcolm Heartland*, London, Hutchinson, 1972.

Juvenile Novelettes: *Hurricane*, London, 1964; *Earthquake*, London, 1965; *Drought*, London, 1966; *Riot*, London, 1967 (these four novels are illustrated by William Papas and published by the Oxford University Press); *Jonah Simpson*, London, 1969, and Roy Publishers, New York, 1970; *Joey Tyson*, London, Bogle L'Ouverture Publications, 1974; *The Shark Hunters*, London, Nelson, 1966 (illustrated by Peter Kesteven).

Other: (Travel and Reportage): *Havana Journal*, London, Penguin, 1971; *Georgetown Journal—A Caribbean Writer's Journey from London via Port of Spain to Georgetown, Guyana, 1970*, London, New Beacon Books, 1972.

Poetry: *Jamaica*, a long historical poem, Hutchinson and Co., 1973.

Radio Play: *Where to Gabriel?* (unpublished).

Short Stories: *Anancy's Score*, London, Bogle L'Ouverture, 1973.

Editor of: *West Indian Stories*, London, Faber, 1960; *Stories from the Caribbean*, London, Elek, 1965, and as *Island Voices*, New York, Liveright, 1970; Caribbean Section of *Young Commonwealth Poets '65*, London, Heinemann, 1965; *Caribbean Prose*, London, Evans, 1967; *Breaklight: Caribbean Poetry*, London, Hamish Hamilton, 1971; *Caribbean Essays*, London, Evans, 1972; *The Poetry of the Caribbean*, New York, Anchor, 1973; *Writing in Cuba since the Revolution*, London, New Beacon Books, 1972.

Editor with others of: *Savacou, A Journal of the Caribbean Artists Movement Quarterly* (the fourth issue each year is devoted to the publication of creative work and artistic creation).

His work is in *Caribbean Narrative; The Sun's Eye; West Indian Narrative: An Introductory Anthology; Caribbean Voices*, Vol. II; *The Independence Anthology of 1962*, and others.

Biographical/Critical Sources: W. Carr's discussion of "The Novels of Andrew Salkey," as chapter entitled "A Complex Fate" in *The Islands in Between*, (Louis James, ed.), London, 1968; David Arnason, review of *The Late Emancipation of Jerry Stover* and *The Adventures of Catallus Kelly* in *World Literature Written in English*, 19 (April 1971), pp. 91-92; Barrie Davies, "The Sense of Abroad: Aspects of the West Indian Novel in England," in *World Literature Written in English*, 1, 2 (Nov. 1972), pp. 67-80; Victor Questel, review of *Anancy's Score* in *Kairi* 2 (1974); E. Brathwaite, review of *A Quality of Violence* in BIM 31; Harold Marshall, review of *West Indian Stories* in BIM 33; Gerald Moore, review of *The Late Emancipation of Jerry Stover* in BIM 48; Arthur Drayton, "Awkward Questions for Jamaicans," review of *Jerry Stover* in *Journal of Commonwealth Literature,* No. 7 (July 1969); Sylvia Wynter, in review article on *One Love,* in *Caribbean Studies,* Vol. 12, No. 3 (Oct. 1972); John Figueroa, in *Tribune,* London (Summer 1960) with review of *Escape to an Autumn Pavement.*

SAMAROO, Daniel Joseph

b. August 27, 1927, Trinidad.
Storywriter, social worker, businessman.

Of East Indian descent, locally educated through high school, Samaroo attended University in London. He has served as a Justice of Peace in Trinidad, but more recently has been a sole director for Kirpalani's Ltd., an island-wide chain of department stores. His stories are ordinarily cast into the form of inward musings, or internal monologues. Most of his stories originally appeared in BIM.

Writings: Story: "Big Brains" in J.T. Livingston's *Caribbean Rhythms,* New York, Washington Square Press (paper edition) 1974, originally in BIM, Vol. 13, No. 53, 1971, and represented in *From the Green Antilles* (Barbara Howes, ed.), 1966.

SANCHO, Thomas Anson

b. ca. 1932, Guyana.
Poet, teacher, essayist, historian.

Sancho served for a period as a member of the Legislative Council of Guyana and has been an active trade unionist. He has published two modest volumes of poetry, five works on history and labor, and has written one play.

Writings: Poetry: *Lines and Rhymes: A Collection of Verse,* British Guiana, Labour Advocate Printing Department, 1962; *Ballad of 1763: The Story of Cuffy's Rebellion Narrated in Verse,* Georgetown, 1970.

Critical Study: *C.L.R. The Man and His Work,* A Carifesta Publication, Guyana, 1972 (foreword by A.J. Seymour).

Histories: *Supermen of History,* Georgetown, Part I, 1956, Part II, 1957; *Highlights of Guyanese History; To England and Back,* Georgetown, Daily Chronicle, 1967; *Octave.*

Labor Study: *Anatomy of Labour.*

Play: *Spectacles for Drama* (typescript), 1967, contains *A Woman's Vengeance* and *The Happy Hypocrite.*

Articles: "The Importance of Our Literature in Caribbean Secondary Education," *Kaie* 11 (1973), p. 78; "West Indianism," in *New Writing in the Caribbean,* (A.J. Seymour, ed.), p. 250.

SCOBIE, Edward

b. May 23, 1918, Roseau, Dominica.
Poet, storywriter, journalist, teacher.

Edward Scobie was educated at the Roseau's Government School; and Dominica Grammar School where he passed the Cambridge (Overseas) Junior and Senior Examinations (1932 and 1934). In 1941 he volunteered for Air Crew Duties in the Royal Air Force and flew as a Navigator in Bomber Command (World War II); he was demobilized in 1946. He then studied journalism, gaining his Diploma in London, in 1949.

Scobie remained in England for 23 years. During that time he became a correspondent for the *Chicago Defender* and *Ebony* and *Jet* magazines of Chicago, Ill., U.S.A. He contributed to many London newspapers and magazines and the wire services. He became a frequent BBC broadcaster and scriptwriter for radio and television. He wrote several major historical radio features dealing with the black experience, particularly during the centuries of the African slave trade and slavery in North America and the Caribbean.

He edited the following monthly magazines published in London and directed to a reading public in Africa and the Caribbean mainly: *Checkers* (1948); *Bronze* (1954-1955); *Tropic* (1960-1967) and *Flamingo* (1961-1963). He also wrote verse and won many prizes for his work in Dominica.

His poems and short stories have been broadcast on the BBC Caribbean network. His verse appears in *Poesy*, Book II, an anthology published by J.R. Ralph Casimir of Dominica.

Scobie was very active in sports in Dominica, and has been swimming and table tennis champion of the island. He was also interested in politics and was vice-president of the Dominica Freedom Party, the official Opposition Party. He was twice Mayor of Roseau, the capital of Dominica. From 1968-1972 he was owner-publisher and editor of the *Dominica Herald*, a weekly newspaper.

From 1972-73 he was assistant professor in the Afro-American and Political Science Department at Livingston College, Rutgers University. He is now Associate Professor in the Black Studies Department at the City College of the City University of New York, where he teaches Caribbean and Afro-American History and Political Science.

In 1972, Scobie published *Black Britannia*, which deals with blacks in Britain. A second book, *Black Othello*, a biography of Ira Frederick Aldridge, the nineteenth century black Shakespearean actor, is in the press; and a third work dealing with the historical and socio-political development of the Caribbean has been commissioned by his publishers and his Department at City College, N.Y.

Writings: Poetry: in anthology *Poesy II* (Ralph Casimir, ed.), Joseph Press, Dominica, 1944.

History: *Black Britannia*, Chicago, Johnson Publishing Co., 1972.

Biography: *Black Othello*, in press.

Biographical/Critical Sources: Kenneth Ingram, review of *Black Britannia: A History of Blacks in Britain* in *Caribbean Studies* (Puerto Rico, Oct. 1973), Vol. 13, No. 3, pp. 146-148.

SCOTT, Dennis C.

b. December 16, 1939, Jamaica.

Playwright, poet, actor, producer, dancer, teacher, editor.

Scott was educated at Jamaica College, U.W.I., Mona; B.A.; and took a diploma in Drama Education, New Castle upon Tyne. He won a Schubert Playwriting Fellowship (University of Georgia). He is a member of the Jamaica National Dance Theatre and at one time was executive editor of the *Caribbean Quarterly*. One of the most all-around and talented of young West Indians working in the arts, he has a striking presence and reads his poetry in a controlled but brilliant manner—as can be heard on the Caedmon Record No. TC 1379, *Poets of the West Indies*. A friend of poets and artists, and a great encourager of workers in the field, he is also an actor and producer of note and is an editor of *Caribbean Quarterly*.

Scott has a remarkable facility with

verse, and an ability to use a very wide range of the kinds of English endemic to Jamaica. He is in fact the kind of person and artist who brings home the paradox that in the Caribbean to be authentic does not mean to be "nativist," or as Sylvia Wynter might put it, to practice "black-ism." "You in your winter grief and I in mine" comes as truly from his lips as:

Grampa, how come you t'in so?
an' him tell me, is so I stay
me chile, is so I stay
laughin, an' fine. . . .

I cry now. Wash him. Lay him out.

He knows his poets, West Indian and others; the last single line quoted above is in the tradition of the now well-known line of Derek Walcott's:

You in the castle of your skin
I the swineherd

(later used by George Lamming for the title of his *In the Castle of My Skin*).

Further, many of his poems are in the Browning/Pound tradition of catching the dramatic moment, not only in tone and diction but also in the particular point of entry into the structure of the "fiction" which he chooses for his readers (each line numbered below is [are] opening line[s]):

(1) *I came on you at sunrise, putting out the flesh . . .*
(2) *Here, if I stayed too*
long, the skin would tear, scrawling
(3) *something glitters. She is waiting.*
(4) *So, good-bye to dark:*

Mervyn Morris is so right to underline in his introduction to Scott's *Uncle Time* the grand achievement of "No sufferer," the final poem in that collection. It not only is a tribute to Scott's honesty in refusing to claim that in any simple sense he, too, is a sufferer (others would have been tempted to say that literary people are really also WORKERS, and that in any case we are all *black*—even those who reap all the benefits of at least *apparently* not being so). The poem is really a result of his being serious and hard working enough not merely to see and record the rich tensions and confusions about him, but much more to MAKE something of them; to build them into a significant song, rather than to jump on the bandwagon, waving the bright banners that, alas, fade so soon.

Mrs. Manley in *her* introduction—for the book apparently needed at least three mid-wives to slap it into existence—speaks of Scott's sharing "with the poets of our country . . . a special kind of tolerance." One knows the quality to which she refers, but wonders if it is not something richer than tolerance. Something not unconnected with the true actor's art: that ability to get under the skin, of whatever color, and class, of other humans. It is doubtful that Scott has really been born in "A more integrated period" than Campbell—or in many significant senses, a "freer" period, but he does, as Mrs. Manley puts it, have a happier mind—a mind perhaps braver, more able and willing to use all that is at hand: a religious background, the realities of the sufferers, Anancy, birds, learning, varieties of language.

In the end his poetry promises great things for the human spirit, not least of all in the Caribbean, because he shares with Walcott the true poet's hard won gift, that of MAKING, of fashioning, of *using* language and experience, rather than of simply recording, repeating, reproducing —holding a mirror up.

"Bird of Passage," the title to the first poem in *Uncle Time,* has an ironic twist to it, as does the poem. We hope that what with the other major activities which Scott engages in, he will not become a mere bird of passage as far as the written word of poetry goes:

That is because the bird is not really
dead. Yet.
Clap a little.

One can wish and hope that the bird (favorite image with this author) will clap its wings for a long while. But *time* also flies:

Me Uncle Time smile black as sorrow. . . .

Watch how 'im spin web roun' yu house,
an' creep
inside; an' when 'im touch yu, weep. . . .

Scott was the recipient of the bronze and silver medals as awards for his poetry in the Festival Commission Competitions (1968-1972).

Writings: Poetry: *Journey and Ceremonies, Poems: 1960-1969,* Jamaica, privately printed, 1969; *Uncle Time* (collection of poems), Pittsburgh, University of Pittsburgh Press, 1973 (this work was an International Poetry Forum Selection and also a Jamaican Selection—with introduction by Mervyn Morris, preface by Edna Manley; and works in many collections and journals, including *Seven Jamaican Poets* (edited by Mervyn Morris), Jamaica, Bolivar Press, 1971; *Breaklight,* 1971; *Caribbean Voices,* Vol. 11, 1970; *Anthology of W.I. Poems,* 1971; Journals: *Jamaica Journal, London Magazine* (U.K.); *East Indian Review; Focus* (1960).

Plays: *Terminus,* a play in one act, Kingston, Jamaica Extra Mural Department, U.C.W.I., Caribbean Plays; (n.d.), in manuscript; *Breakfast with a Witch: a grim fairy tale,* produced Jamaica, 1964. in Secondary School Drama Festival; *The Caged,* produced Jamaica, 1961; *Chariots of Wrath,* full-length play (winner of Gold Medal in Jamaica Festival Literary Competition of 1966); *Cold Equation* (adapted from a story by Tom Godwin), produced Jamaica, 1959; *The Crime of Anabel Campbell,* one act, produced Jamaica, 1970; *The Passionate Cabbage* (Bronze Medal, Jamaica Festival Award, 1969).

Short Story: "Dragon on a Green Field," (Bronze Medal, Jamaica Festival Award, 1969).

Novel: in manuscript.

Biographical/Critical Sources: Edward Baugh, *West Indian Poetry 1900-1970,* (Pamphlet), p. 18.

SCOTT, Michael

b. 1789, Glasgow, Scotland; d. 1835.
Prose narrator, poet.

At age 16 Scott arrived in Jamaica where he passed most of his life except for several trips throughout the Caribbean. After a brief trip back to Scotland in 1831 to marry, he returned to Jamaica with his wife, staying for his last four years. As a young man Scott was a sea-going yarn spinner on ships which sailed to the Caribbean, and his books depicting his sea-

faring experiences were first published as serials in *Blackwood's Magazine* under a pseudonym and were, from the beginning, well-received critically. He shows an extraordinary acquaintance with Jamaican speech, as well as with what he calls the hot tempered Jamaican creole. His *Tom Cringle's Log* shows how clearly even across national borders the culture of "La Cuenca del Caribe" achieves a certain unity.

Writings: One of his few extant poems appeared in *Caribbean Voices*, Vol. II; *Tom Cringle's Log*, London, Macmillan, 1895, first published 1832, Edinburgh, in *Blackwood's Magazine*, later issued in Dent's Everyman's Series, London, 1915, and New York, Dutton, 1915 (both reprints); and *The Cruise of the Midge*, Paris, 1936.

SEALY, Clifford

b. November 27, 1927, Trinidad.

Poet, shortstory writer, playwright, editor, businessman.

After local schooling, Sealy moved to England where he stayed for many years. He returned in 1968 to Port of Spain, Trinidad where he edited until recently, *Voices*, a quarterly. He manages The Bookshop in Port of Spain, which he founded, specializing in Caribbean books and literary readings. His work appears in British and Canadian journals. He is president of P.E.N. of Trinidad and Tobago.

Sealy was an early contributor to BIM and was closely associated with such Caribbean writers in London as George Lamming. His play, *The Professor, A Comedy in One Act*, spoofs the pretensions of a social-climbing amateur artist whose husband, daughter and maid are down-to-earth Trinidad types not to be impressed by the "artistic" jargon of a great painter who turns out to be the maid's long-lost husband. A touring Trinidad play-group in 1967 performed the work with great applause in San Francisco. His *Smell of Damp* is also a diverting satire on island middle-class ways.

Sealy has been at the center of much of the literary stir in Trinidad; very helpful to other writers and to those wishing to know about the writing and culture of the West Indies.

Left to Right: Clifford Sealy, Donald Herdeck, George Lamming.

Writings: Poetry: in various journals such as BIM, and in collections such as *Breaklight* (A. Salkey, ed.), New York, 1973. Included in *Caribbean Medlay (Poems)* a collection of W.I. poetry in BIM 52 (Jan.-June 1971).

Plays: *The Professor,* Saint Augustine, Trinidad, Extra Mural Department, U.C.W.I., 1967; first published in *Caribbean Plays,* Vol. 2, Extra Mural Department, U.C.W.I., 1965, pp. 119-148; *Smell of Damp,* in mimeograph.

Stories: in various journals, including BIM; "The Interview" is in *British Broadcasting Service* and a winner of the BBC World Service short story competition of 1967, and represented in *Response* (Cecil Gray, ed.).

Reviews: "Crown Jewel: A note on Ralph de Boissiere," *Voices,* Vol. 2, No. 3 (March 1973).

Editor, Publisher and Contributor to: *Voices* —Port of Spain, Trinidad, several volumes were brought out in collaboration with the P.E.N. Club of Trinidad and Tobago and Independence Anniversary issue of *Voices* 1964, and complete set in reprint by Kraus Reprint, Liechtenstein.

SEALEY, Karl

b. ca. 1932, Barbados.
Storywriter, poet, critic.

Sealey's work has appeared in several journals, including BIM and various anthologies including *From the Green Antilles; New Voices of the Commonwealth;* and *West Indian Stories.* He wrote with R. Atherly the short story "The Song of the Fiddler," published in BIM 18, pp. 90-92.

Writings: Book Reviews: *The Far Journey of Oudin,* by Wilson Harris in BIM 35, pp. 223-224; *Soul Clap Hands and Sing,* by Paule Marshall in BIM 35, pp. 225-228; *The Wounded and the Worried,* by Edgar Mittelholzer, in BIM 36, p. 293; *The Hills of Hebron,* by Sylvia Wynter, in BIM 36, p. 292.

SEALY, Theodore

b. November 6, 1909, British Honduras (Belize).
Prose narrator, storywriter, journalist.

Sealy was educated in Jamaica and early joined *The Gleaner's* editorial staff, November, 1928.

Sealy has lived most of his life in Jamaica and his account of his early days there is fascinating. One can only hope that he is working on an in-depth autobiography. He has done little creative writing of the usual fictional kind, but his special pieces on a variety of subjects, including travel and boxing, have been part of the Jamaican cultural scene for a long time. And he has of course influenced a variety of matters, artistic and political, by his editing of the *Gleaner* newspaper over a number of years, and by the hard work he has done on a number of important cultural and community committees.

Sealy has been the recipient of many awards: C.B.E. (1956); the Jamaica Independence Medal (1962); Musgrave Gold Medal (1966) for services to the Arts; Officer National Order of Merit Carlos Manuel de Cespedes, a Cuban award, among others.

Writings: Autobiographical Short Story: in *Focus* (1960), "Sentimental Journey," pp. 81-84.

SELVON, Samuel (Sam)

b. May 20, 1923, Trinidad.
Novelist, journalist, playwright (radio & TV).

Of the Trinidad East Indian community, Sam Selvon, after local schooling entered the Royal Naval Volunteer Reserve, and served as a wireless operator on a minesweeper, 1940 to 1945. He published his early stories in the *Trinidad Guardian,* and lived for a period in Tacarigua, between Paradise and El Dorado! He was a journalist with the *Guardian* from 1946 to 1950, when he emigrated to England.

There he wrote his first novel, *A Brighter Sun* (1952). His work, which he reads remarkably well, is full of humor, often of the quiet, peasant kind by which the apparently naive shows that he is quite capable of coping with the big city—even if he does do it by wearing heavy clothes in the Summer, and going about in shirt sleeves in the Winter. Or even by catching sea gulls from the roof to provide curry or soup or any other kind of meal during "hard times," in good old London. It has been often felt that Sam's particular kind of writing, and his very Trinidadian voice, should be more anchored in an actual presence in Trinidad. But Sam continues to make London his home, and he seems to continue to write well.

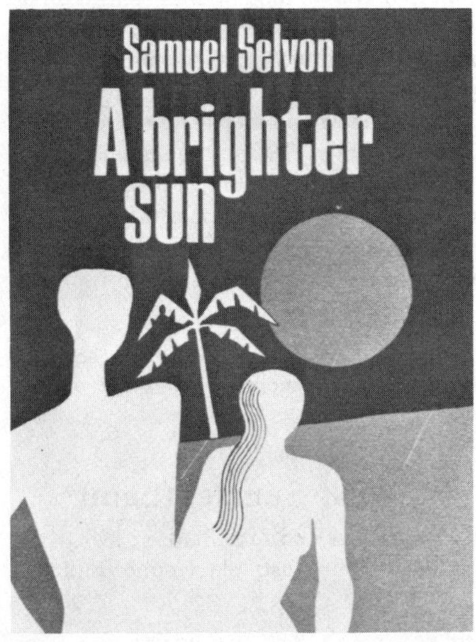

He has visited Trinidad and other parts of the Caribbean, once on a Trinidad Government grant, once with the support of the Caroni Sugar interests. He, like George Lamming, was also invited, through the combined efforts of the English, Creative Arts, and Education Departments (Mona), to visit U.W.I., and to give readings and lectures. Sam Selvon has been the recipient of many awards, including the Guggenheim (twice), and the Humming Bird (Trinidad).

Sam has dealt, in a humane and humorous way, with the new and old immigrants to England. He portrays their valiant efforts, not always orthodox, to cope—with the locals, with fellow immigrants, with rent and girl friend problems.

More recently he has returned, in his *The Plains of Caroni*, to the Trinidadian scene. And he has been doing some lecturing at one of the English universities and in Canada in the late 1970s.

His artistic control of Trinidad speech rhythms is superb; his use of the Caribbean version of English is a joy to experience.

His renditions of sections of *The Lonely Londoners*, and of *The Housing Lark*, have pleased and "instructed" audiences in many parts of the English speaking world—for, in many ways, he is a writer who draws heavily on the oral tradition, laughing mostly *with* rather than *at* his characters.

The Lonely Londoners has been made into a film. Selvon also did a musical about West Indians in London, which the *Sunday Times* critic Kenneth Pearson—*King of Spades*, staged in the West End of London.

Selvon's most recent novel, *Moses Ascending* (1975), returns to the hero of *The Lonely Londoners* who now is a landlord of a terrible property in *Shepherd's Bush* with a new set of friends and problems.

Writings: Novels: *A Brighter Sun*, London, Wingate, 1952, New York, Viking Press, 1953; reprint in (London) Longman Caribbean, 1972; *An Island is a World*, London, Wingate, 1955; *The Lonely Londoners*, London, Wingate, 1956; New York, St. Martin's Press, 1957; and (London) Longman Caribbean, 1972, and London, Mayflower Books, 1967, and *The Lonely Londoners* (paperbound), reissued under the title *The Lonely Ones*, London, Brown, Watson, 1959; *Turn Again, Tiger*, London, MacGibbon and Kee, 1958, New York, St. Martin's Press, 1959; and London, Four Square, 1962; *I Hear Thunder*, London, MacGibbon and Kee, 1963, New York, St.

Martin's Press, 1963; *The Housing Lark*, London, MacGibbon and Kee, 1965; *The Plains of Caroni*, London, MacGibbon and Kee, 1970; *Those Who Eat the Cascadura*, London, Davis-Poynter, 1972; *Moses Ascending*, London, Davis-Poynter, 1975.

Children's Novels: *A Drink of Water*, London, Nelson, 1968, illustrated by Aubrey Williams; *Carnival in Trinidad*, New Zealand, Department of Education, 1964.

Short Stories: *Ways of Sunlight*, London, MacGibbon and Kee, 1957, St. Martin's Press, New York, 1957. Individual short stories have appeared in various magazines and collections, including: BIM; *Caribbean Literature; Caribbean Narrative; From the Green Antilles; Island Voices—Stories from the Caribbean; The Sun's Eye; West Indian Stories.* His poetry is in *Caribbean Voices*, Vol. II; poem "Variation" in *Breaklight*. He also writes plays for radio and television.

Biographical/Critical Sources: Review of *The Plains of Caroni* in *World Literature Written in English*, 19 (April 1971), pp. 92-93, by Andrew P. Scott; review of *Lonely Londoners* by Eric Roach, as "Time Has Not Tarnished This Novel: Selvon Revisited," in *Trinidad Guardian* (Aug. 28, 1973); Review by Roach of *Those Who Eat the Cascadura*, in *Trinidad Guardian* (March 6, 1972); interview with Rosemary Stone in the *Express* (Trinidad, March 2, 1972), p. 13; review, *A Brighter Sun*, G.A. Holder, in BIM 16, pp. 295-296; review, *An Island is a World*, G.A. Holder, BIM 23, p. 202; review, *The Lonely Londoners*, Bruce Hamilton, BIM 25, pp. 61-62; review, *The Ways of Sunlight*, Frank Collymore, BIM 27, pp. 185-186; *Turn Again Tiger*, A.N. Forde, BIM 29, pp. 60-61; *The Plains of Caroni*, John Wickham, BIM 51, pp. 189-193; *Those Who Eat the Cascadura*, BIM 55, p. 189, reviewed by Chalmer St. Hill.

SENIOR, Olive

b. ca. 1938, Jamaica.
Poet, playwright, editor.

Senior has been an editor of the journal *Social and Economic Studies* (of the Institute of Social and Economic Research, Mona, Jamaica), and has published some poetry and one play.

Writings: Poetry: in various journals. "To my Arawak Grandmother" won the Bronze Medal (1972); "Hill Country" the Bronze (1968).

Plays: *Down the Road Again* (Bronze Medal, 1968); *Stranger in Our House*, full length work, published in *Savacou*, 11/12 (Sep. 1975), and winner of the Certificate of Merit.

SEYMOUR, Arthur James (A.J.)

b. 1914, Guyana.
Essayist, poet, critic, storywriter, editor.

One of the established and acknowledged "God-Fathers" of West Indian literature, Seymour is himself a poet, and a man of strong Christian principles and action. He has ever been a help to other writers, and a collector and publisher of the work of others.

His contribution that is best known is his editing of the literary journal of *Kyk-over-al* (also written *Kykoveral*) from 1945-1961. But he has been active in many other ways, including a stint in Puerto Rico as Development Officer (Information and Culture) in the Central Secretariat of the

Caribbean Organization (1962-1964). He has also had a senior post with Demerara Bauxite Company.

He was one of the main organizers of the Carifesta held in Guyana in 1972, and was in charge of the literary side of that occasion. His poems have a strong feeling for Guyana; a number of them have been translated into Russian, German and Hindi. His work is serious—perhaps even to a fault; yet in contrast, on reading his *My Lovely Native Land* (an elegant anthology edited with his wife, Elma), one would hardly remember the real and serious human problems which face him and all his fellow citizens in that lovely but divided country.

Arthur Seymour is, in a sense, a romantic writer, who kept the torch of interest in culture and literature and history alight in a society in which it might easily have smouldered out. And for this no West Indian writer can be but grateful even if he should agree with the rather strict opinion of Edward Baugh in his *West Indian Poetry 1900-1970* (Pamphlet No. 1, Savacou Publications Ltd.):

> *He (Seymour) belongs in large measure to the old ornamental tradition of routinely noble sentiments and "local" poetry which is really a grafting of local names on to borrowed stock. At the same time he vigorously encouraged the idea of a new cultural awakening which would produce a truly West Indian literature. . . . In his own poetry we find him purposefully digging about in Guyanese history and legend, asserting continuities, going back to the Amerindians in the search for a Guyanese spirit. But with him history is really not much more than romance. . . .*

Seymour himself makes an interesting point in writing about West Indian novelists (BIM 43, July-Dec. 1966):

> *. . . in the English tradition, perhaps the time has passed for us to talk about race and political indepedence. The time has come to close national and regional ranks on the need for a better life for all, and it is a good thing for the West Indian novelist to be conscious of the social forces he is serving. . . .*

That his statement will seem to some too old fashioned and to others eminently sensible is the strength and misfortune of Arthur Seymour, and marks him as the kind of transitional figure, who, understandably, is likely to be criticized by those very people who owe their ability and willingness to criticize, precisely to such characters as Arthur Seymour.

He is Deputy Chairman of the Guyana National History and Arts Council. In 1970 he was awarded the Golden Arrow of Achievement, for his work in Literature, by the Republic of Guyana, a clearly and fully deserved honor.

Writings: Poetry: Collections: *Verse,* Georgetown, British Guiana, Daily Chronicle, 1937; *More Poems,* Georgetown, Daily Chronicle, 1940; *Over Guiana Clouds,* Georgetown, Demerara Standard, 1944; *Sun's in My Blood,* Georgetown, Demerara Standard, 1945; *Poetry in these Sunny Lands,* "Caribia," 1945, British Guiana; *Six Songs,* Georgetown, author, 1946; *We Do Not Presume to Come . . . Seven Poems,* Georgetown, Author, 1948; *Leaves from the Tree,* British Guiana, Master Printery, 1951 (Miniature Poet Series); *Ten Poems,* Georgetown, Argosy, 1953, reprint of *Kyk-over-al* 16 (1953); *Three Voluntaries,* Georgetown, Master Printery, 1953; *Selected Poems,* British Guiana, Lithographic Co., 1965; *Monologue. Nine Poems,* Georgtown, author, 1968; *Patterns,* Georgetown, author, 1970; *Passport,* Georgetown, Labour Advocate Job Printing Dept., 1972; *Song to Man,* Georgetown, Labour Advocate, 1973; *Love Song,* Georgetown, author, 1975; *Italic,* Georgetown, author, 1974; *I, Anancy,* Georgetown, author, 1971; *Guiana Book,* British Guiana, Argosy Co., 1948; *Black Son,* Labour Advocate, 1971; *A. Bethlehem Alleluia,* Georgetown, 1974; *Tomorrow Belongs to the People. El Mañana Pertenece al Pueblo.* (Bilingual text: translated by Norma Psaila), Georgetown, 1975.

He also edited the "Miniature Poets" Series in Georgetown, putting out the verse of Martin Carter, Philip Sherlock, Basil McFarlane,

Harold Telemaque and others including himself.

Editor of Anthologies: *Kykoveral No. 22's* Anthology of West Indian Poetry, 1957; *Kyk-over-al, Special Issue Mid Year 1952,* Vol. 4, No. 14; with Celeste Dolphin he compiled *The Genius of the Place: Personal Anthology of Poetry from the British Commonwealth; Kyk-over-al* 16 (1953), p. 170 (a British Council Broadcast); *Themes of Song: An Anthology of Guianese Poetry,* Georgetown, B.G. Lithographic, 1961; *Magnet,* Georgetown, 1962; *New Writing in the Caribbean,* Georgetown, Guyana Lithographic Co., 1972; with Elma Seymour he compiled *My Lovely Native Land: An Anthology of Guyana,* London, Longman Caribbean, 1971; *Twelve West-Indian Poems for Children,* Georgetown, 1952; *Fourteen Guianese Poems for Children,* B.G. Master Printery, 1953.

Short Stories: in local periodicals, including *The Chronicle Christmas Annual.*

Essays: (including): "Nature Poetry in the West Indies," *Kyk-over-al* 11, (1950), pp. 39-47; *Caribbean Literature,* British Guiana, F.A. Persick, 1951, (ten 15-minute radio talks for the Extra Mural Dept., U.C.W.I. (1950); "Culture in Commonwealth Caribbean Development," in *With Eyes Wide Open* (by David Mitchell), Barbados, CADEC, 1973; *Edgar Mittelholzer, The Man and His Work,* (National History and Arts Council, 1968) which is text of E.M.'s Memorial Lectures given in 1967; "Main Currents in Caribbean Literature," *Commonwealth Journal of the Royal Commonwealth Society,* 14, 6 (1970), p. 245; "The Novel in the British Caribbean," BIM 42 (1966), p. 83—Part I; BIM 43 (1966), p. 176—Part II; BIM 44 (1967), p. 238—Part III; BIM 45 (1968), p. 75—Part IV; "The Novels of Wilson Harris," BIM 38 (1964), p. 139; "The Poetry of Egbert Martin (Leo), *Kyk-over-al* 3 (1946), p. 19; "Introduction to the Poetry of Walter MacA. Lawrence," *Kyk-over-al* 6 (1948), p. 35; *Window on the Caribbean,* Georgetown, Persick, 1952.

His criticism and general essays appear in various journals including: *Kyk-over-al;* J. Jahn's *Schwarzer Orpheus; Sunday Chronicle; Chronicle Christmas Annual;* BIM; *Kaie;* and in various anthologies including: *Caribbean Voices; Sun is a Shapely Fire; Bite In, Stage I; Bite In Stage III; Commonwealth Poems of Today; West Indian Poetry: The Sun's Eye;* Thieme's Anthology of West Indian Literature; Caribbean Verse; Caribbean Rhythms; Caribbean Quarterly, 5, 3, (1958) Federation Commemoration Issue; *Savacou 7/8; Talk of the Tamarinds.*

Literary Comment: With Ian McDonald and Richard Allsopp: *The Literary Tradition in Guyana,* Georgetown, The National History and Arts Council, 1970; "The Literary Adventure of the West Indies," *Kyk-over-al* 10 (1950), (a special issue dealing with Jamaica, Belize, Antigua, St. Lucia, Barbados, Trinidad and Guyana); "The Arts of Guyana," *Kyk-over-al* 27 (1960), p. 97, which is correspondence with Allan Young, Mary Woods, Martin Carter, Lloyd Rohler, Ken Taharally.

Biographical/Critical Sources: "*Kyk-over-al* and the Radicals: an assessment of *Kyk-over-al* and the work of Seymour (Carter and Harris)," E. Brathwaite in *New World,* Guyana Independence Issue, 1966; Introduction to the *Islands in Between,* (Louis James, ed.), London, 1968, pp. 27-28; Celeste Dolphin, "The Poetry of A.J. Seymour," in *New World* (Fortnightly), I, 13, (1965), pp. 31-39; E. Brathwaite in *Contemporary Poets of the English Language* (1970); E. Baugh, "A Brief Account of West Indian Poetry 1900-1970" (Savacou Publications, Pamphlet No. 1), pp. 4, 7-8, and 15-16; Mentioned in "'Possibility' in W.I. Creative Writing," by Anson Gonzalez in *The New Voices* 4 (June 1974); Reviews of: *The Guiana Book,* by Gordon Bell, in BIM 10, pp. 176-178; *The Kyk-over-al* (ed.) *Anthology of West Indian Poetry,* by A.F. Crichlow Matthews in BIM 16, pp. 298-299; *Themes of Song* (ed.) by A.N. Forde in BIM 35, pp. 224-225; *Selected Poems,* by Frank Collymore in BIM 42, pp. 143-147; Kenneth Ramchand, *The West Indian Novel and its Background* (1970), p. 72. The most complete list of his works is in R.E. McDowell's *Bibliography of Literature from Guyana,* 1975.

SEYMOUR, Elma

b. ca. 1920, Guyana.
Anthologist, editor, teacher.

Elma Seymour has devoted much of her attention to education, including interest in child development and welfare. She is co-editor with her husband, A.J. Seymour, of *My Lovely Native Land, An Anthology of Guyana* (1971).

Writings: Editor: *Sun is a Shapely Fire,* Georgetown, Labour Advocate, 1973 (anthology).

SHERLOCK, Hilary

b. ca. 1934, Jamaica.
Storywriter, teacher.

Sherlock was educated at St. Andrew High School; St. Joseph's, Trinidad; Oberlin College, United States (B.A.); and earned an M.A. (Elementary Education, Bank Street College, New York, specializing in early development of children). For the last four years she has been living and working in London, England, at the Hornsey Centre for handicapped children. She returned to Jamaica in 1975, and is now working with the Experimental School for Handicapped Children, Mona. She is a promising shortstory writer.

Writings: (jointly with [Sir] Philip Sherlock, her father): *Ears and Tails and Common Sense; A Collection of Animal Stories,* New York, Thomas T. Cromwell Co., 1974.

SHERLOCK, Sir Philip Manderson

b. 1902, Portland, Jamaica.
Poet, storywriter, historian, educator.

Sir Philip's interest in, and contribution to, the whole Caribbean are so great and cover so many fields that only the literary side will be covered in this entry in any detail. He was knighted in 1967 for his distinguished contribution in education.

Sir Philip has always shown a lively interest in the creative arts—as the Creative Arts Centre at Mona witnesses. He has always been an encourager of writers, and has himself produced interesting and concerned poetry—that he has not produced more is no doubt due to the many administrative tasks which he has taken on for the West Indies and the wider Caribbean, and because his chosen field has been history and civics.

His poems have been widely published in anthologies and journals, and he reads and quotes verse with relish and feeling. He brought out in the spring of 1976 a dramatic sequence of poems in tribute to Samuel Sharpe—"Shout Freedom." One of the remarkable things about Sherlock is the constancy of his commitment not only to "La Cuenca del Caribe," but to writing and the arts. In 1940, in what now looks like another era, he wrote his poem "Dinner Party 1940," which begins:

Do you mind the news while we eat?

and ends, twenty lines later after the news has been recited, amidst the drinks, the distant deaths:

Cold mutton is delicious with guava-jelly
And does not seriously incommode
Like cold lead in the belly.

Even at that dress parade in Jamaica, to Sherlock the news of war and struggle could not be distanced from the full belly of the safe civilian.

Some thirty-three years after that he writes about his experience of being at a special mass in Santo Domingo, in the lovely city built by Spaniards looking for another and more delightful Spain than the one they knew "at home." He is in Santiago de los Caballeros; now Secretary General of the Association of the Universities and Research Institutes of the Caribbean (in Spanish, U N I C A), a post he assumed on retiring from that of Vice Chancellor of the University of the West Indies. He attends a Mass of celebration—he, the lay preacher, and son of a Methodist parson! Once again his heart, concerned for the West Indies, is not there confined. His knowledge of history is not merely bookish, nor his feeling for people, and their societies, monodimensional: this recent long poem begins:

Singing the new mass
young lips moulding the language of
Spain

and it ends:

Madre y Maestra's student-choir
brown-skinned mestizos mingling their praise
of Mary the blessed, Mary the Mother,
mingling of lands and mingling of peoples
Niger and Tagus, Congo and Ebro
Kumasi, Cadiz, Angola and Andalusia
skin-tinge and contours of face
sing a fusion of peoples
nor see
presences thronging the fields.
the viga the vale of Cibao
Fusion of races with whip-lash and spear-thrust
passion at sword-point
hateful begetting.

Blessed Mother who seest all
give not, oh give not to these
the eyes of yesterday.

Sir Philip, historian though he is, cannot limit his vision of the Caribbean Basin to "the eyes of yesterday"; in fact, especially in the fields of culture and the arts, he has often been in the vanguard of those who know that "development is difficult," and that it is not by bread alone that humans live, build and hope.

He is at work on "Manley and Jamaica's Independence"—a life of Norman Manley up to 1954, with special reference to Manley's contribution to the constitutional development of his country, which will be published by Macmillan. He also is engaged on a long essay under the title "Development through a Tribal Eye," for the International Development Research Centre of Canada.

Writings: Tales: *Jamaica Way,* London, Longmans, 1962; *The Iguana's Tail,* Crick Crack Stories from the Caribbean, New York, Crowell, 1969; essay in *Jamaican Song and Story,* W. Jekyll, editor, New York, Dover, 1966, originally published in 1907; *Three Finger Jack's Treasure,* London, Macmillan, 1961, New York, St. Martin's Press, 1961; *Anansi, the Spider Man,* London, Macmillan, 1956, New York, Crowell, 1954; *The Man in the Web and other folk tales,* London, Longmans, 1959; *West Indian Folk Tales,* London, Oxford University Press, 1966; *West Indian Story,* London, Longmans, 1960, second Edition, 1964, third edition, 1971, second impression, 1973; *Anancy Stories* (with Arthur J. Newman), 1936, London, Gunn Co.; *Ears and Tails and Common Sense* (with Hilary Sherlock), New York, Thomas Y. Cromwell Co., 1974, a collection of Caribbean animal stories.

Histories and Readers: *The Aborigines of Jamaica,* Kingston, Institute of Jamaica, 1939; *Jamaica Today,* Kingston, Tourist Board, 1940; *History for Use in Secondary Schools,* London, Macmillan, 1956; *A Short History of the West Indies* (with John Parry), London, Macmillan, 1956; *Caribbean Citizen,* first edition, London, Longmans, 1957, second edition, London, Longmans, 1963; *Jamaica: a Junior History,* London, Collins, 1966; *West Indies,* London, Thames and Hudson, 1966, New York, Walker and Hudson, 1966; *The Land the People of the West Indies,* Philadelphia, Lippincott, 1967; *This is Jamaica,* London, Hodder and Stoughton, 1968; *Belize: a Junior History,* London, Collins, 1969.

Poetry: *Ten Poems,* British Guiana, Master Printery, 1953 (The Miniature Poets, 12); *Shout for Freedom*—a dramatic sequence of poems in tribute to Samuel Sharpe (published by Macmillan, London, Spring 1976). His poetry has appeared in many anthologies, including: *Focus* (1956, 1960); *Caribbean Voices; Caribbean Verse; A Treasury of Jamaican Poetry; The Independence Anthology of 1962; Caribbean Quarterly,* Vol. 5, No. 3, (Federation Commemmoration Issue, April 1968).

Editor of: the *New Age Poetry Books,* Longmans Green & Co.; Joint Editor, *Caribbean Readers,* Ginn and Co.

Reviews, Essays and Articles: in many journals.

Biographical/Critical Sources: Good listing in Commemoration Issue, April 1968). *A Bibliography* (edited by S.E. Merriman), Georgetown, Guyana, 1970; Pen—Portrait—"Philip Sherlock" in *Kyk-over-al,* Vol. 3, No. 12 (mid-year 1951), pp. 94-96; Edward Baugh, *West Indian Poetry 1900-1970,* (Pamphlet), p. 9; Anson Gonzalez, " 'Possibility' in W.I. Creative Writing," in *The New Voices,* No. 4, p. 5.

SIBLEY, Inez K.

(pseudonym: **PENNIBB**)
b. ca. 1908, Jamaica.
Storywriter.

Sibley's work is folkloric and employs local English. Her one book, *Quashie's Reflections in Jamaican Creole,* has "more" than "power of phrase and an appreciation of

Jamaica Talk; more than shrewd observation and a sense of humour," in Philip Sherlock's words. Writing in the brief introduction to the second edition of the book, he continued: "here we find that knowledge and understanding which is a sort of 'being', which is not so much deliberate as intuitive, which sees and knows the modes of our way of expressing ourselves without having to ponder over them."

Her story "What's in a Name?" begins:

> *Dis lang time me did waan fe go travel tou-out fe we Islan as one touris tel me it ah crying shame me lib yah so lang, an no noa any furda dan me doah mout.*

Writings: Stories: *West Indian Folk-Tales,* London, Oxford University Press, 1966; *Quashie's Reflections in Jamaican Creole,* Jamaica, Bolivar Press, 1968 (introduction and glossary by Joan McLaughlin, illustrated by Carl Abrahams), revision of original *Quashie's Reflections (in native dialect),* by Pennibb, Kingston, The Herald Ltd. Printers, 1939.

SIMMONDS, Austin M.

b. ca. 1929, Trinidad.
Folklorist.

Ivy Lawrence, in her foreword to *PAN!* a study of the Steelband written by Simmonds, says that " 'Will' Simmonds has lived among Panmen, has been the friend and adviser to 'the boys' in the hills of Laventille."

Simmonds was asked to write this study by the Department of Extra Mural Studies, (Trinidad and Tobago), U.C.W.I., to accompany the Exhibit on "Pan" in cement sculpture by Raphael 'Boy Blue' Samuel. *PAN* is a useful book for all interested not only in "steele" music but also in the multicultural and innovative nature of Trinidadian and Caribbean culture.

Writings: PAN and PANMEN (A Study of the Steelband), produced by Shell (Trinidad Ltd., Trinidad, January 1959).

SIMMONS, Ulric

b. November 24, 1920, Guantanamo, Cuba (of Jamaican parents).
Storywriter, journalist, political commentator.

Although Ulric has been best known as an interesting political commentator for the *Gleaner*—where he seemed to glory in a "Jamaica First" stance, he is also a writer of fiction. For many years he influenced political attitudes in Jamaica through his regular *Gleaner* column.

Writings: Stories: published in *Jamaican short stories . . . ,* Pioneer Press, Kingston, Jamaica, 1950. His short story "Grannie Bell" is included in the *Independence Anthology of 1962,* pp. 21-27.

SIMPSON, Louis

(a.k.a. **Louis Aston MARONTZ**)
b. March 27, 1923, Jamaica.
Poet, editor, teacher.

The son of a famous Jamaican lawyer, Louis Simpson is, of course, well known as one of the outstanding United States poets. But his autobiographical *North of Jamaica* makes his connection with the West Indian scene quite clear, and its first chapters certainly contain important insights into what Jamaican society was like not so long ago. Jamaica possibly lost a lawyer when young Simpson packed and left; but the United States undoubtedly gained an excellent poet who has received many awards, including the Prix de Rome (1957), the Pulitzer (1964) and the S.C. Poets Award (by S.C. Review, 1972).

He has earned numerous awards: Hudson Review Fellow in Poetry, 1957; Prix de Rome, 1957; Distinguished Service Award School of General Studies, Columbia University, 1960; Edna St. Vincent Millay Award, 1960; Pulitzer Prize for Poetry, 1964; Columbia University Award for Excellence, 1965, and several fellowships: American Academy in Rome; and the John Simon Guggenheim Memorial Foundation.

Among his many moving poems, the sadness and the reality of "My father in the night commanding No" hits one very hard who has grown up in a certain section of Jamaican society. Simpson's father was a hard working lawyer; his mother a Russian lady of the stage ("And then my mother winds the gramophone") somewhat lost in Jamaican society; and the poet, like so many other Jamaicans of his class and talents, will journey all about:

And I have been in Thule! It has come true—
The journey and the danger of the world, . . .

But the stark question remains:

Father, why did you work? Why did you weep,
Mother? Was the story so important?
"Listen!" the wind

Said to the children, and they fell asleep.

Writings: Poetry: *The Arrivistes, Poems, 1940-49,* New York, Fine Edition Press, 1952; *Good News of Death and Other Poems*—in *Poets of Today* 11, New York, Charles Scribner's Sons, 1955; *A Dream of Governors,* Wesleyan University Press, Middletown, Connecticut, 1959; *At the End of the Open Road,* Middletown, Wesleyan University,. 1963; *Selected Poems,* New York, Harcourt, Brace and World, 1965; *Adventures of the Letter I,* London, Oxford University Press, 1971; *Three on the Tower,* New York, William Morrow, 1975. He has contributed to various journals, magazines, anthologies, including *Hudson Review, Paris Review, Harper's Magazine, The New Yorker, New Statesman, Times Literary Supplement, Critical Quarterly;* and anthologies: *Caribbean Voices,* Vol. 11; *Commonwealth Poems of Today; New Voices of the Commonwealth; The Poetry of the Negro, 1746-1949.*

Novel: *Riverside Drive,* New York, Atheneum, 1962.

Autobiography: *North of Jamaica,* United States, 1972, published in England as *Air with Armed Men.*.

Non-Fiction: *James Hogg: A Critical Study,* New York, St. Martin's Press, 1962, and in Edinburgh by Oliver and Boyd; *An Introduction to Poetry. Edited with Donald Hall and Robert Pack: New Poets of England and America,* New York, Meridian Books, 1957.

Biographical/Critical Sources: *Three on the Tower,* reviewed by Richard D. Lingerman, in *New York Times* (July 15, 1975).

SINGH, Rajkumari (Raj.)

b. ca. 1936, Guyana.
Poet, storywriter.

Raj is a leading figure (recently its president) in the Guyana Writers Group, and is otherwise very involved in literary activities despite her crippling affliction. She has written four plays and a wide variety of stories and verse.

She has contributed to G. Singh's *Heritage,* Trotman's *Voices of Guyana;*

My Lovely Native Land; Kaie, among other collections.

Writings: Poetry: *Collection of Poems,* Georgetown, 1971.

Stories: *A Garland of Stories,* Devon, Arthur Stockwell.

Editor: *Days of the Sahib,* Georgetown, 1971.

Plays: *Roraima: A Radio Play,* winner of 1966 Demba Radio Play contest; *Hoofbeats at Midnight: A Play in One Act* (typescript): *Sound of the Bells,* 1971; *A White Camellia and a Blue Star* (typescript).

SKEETE, Monica

(née **MARTINEAU**)
b. ca. 1920, Barbados.
Storywriter, poet, teacher.

Monica Skeete started publishing in BIM from 1946, when her poem "Two pigs going to the slaughter" appeared under her maiden name Monica Martineau. Her short stories for which she is better known, date from BIM 31 (1960).

In *Savacou 7/8* (Jan-June 1973), edited by Edward Brathwaite, she has a long poem in dialect dedicated to Frank Collymore on the occasion of his eightieth birthday. (This issue of *Savacou* was specially brought out as a tribute to Collymore.)

SLINGER, Francisco

(The Mighty Sparrow)
b. ca. 1933, Trinidad.
Calypsonian singer-poet.

Of wide fame is Slinger's total somatic presentation of the calypso, an ongoing embodiment of the oral tradition which is so important to Caribbean writing, Sparrow is here mentioned for another reason —that being the verve and originality of the verse forms of many of his calypsoes, and for the social comment and cleverness of many—such as "Dan is the man in the van"! There are problems, however, over the expressed desire to promote him as one of the "greatest poets" of the West Indies: first, it is not clear how many of his lyrics are written entirely by him, for internal (and external) evidence seem to suggest that "many hands" are involved in what we usually think is *his* poetry.

Nonetheless the results are often worth examining even separate from his splendid musical presentation of them, which in itself would be worth a long article. Despite the notoriety of his more risque lyrics he does sing quite a variety of material—"I never eat a white meat yet," "Dan is the man in the van," "Krushchev and Kennedy," "Leave the damn doctor alone," etc., etc.

Slinger has, of course, made numerous recordings.

Writings: One hundred and twenty calypsoes to remember, by the Mighty Sparrow, Port of Spain, Trinidad, Caribbean Printers, 1963? (92 pp.).

Biographical/Critical Sources: "Sparrow and the language of the calypso," St. Augustine 1968; Gordon Rohlehr: "The Calypso" in *Caribbean Background,* Trinidad, Centre for Multi-Racial Studies, 1969; *"Political Calypsos," St. Augustine, 1970.*

SMITH, Basil

b. 1946, Monmouthshire, Wales (brought to Jamaica at age of one).
Poet, journalist.

Smith was educated in Jamaica and then went to England in 1966 to study journalism at the London College of Journalism. In 1968, he took a Diploma Course in the technique of film directing, returning to Jamaica in 1970. He has experimented with multi-voice readings of his work.

Writings: Poetry: *Rising Poems,* with C. Laird: poems published in various journals and collections, including *Breaklight* (A. Salkey, ed.), New York, Anchor, 1973.

SMITH, M.G.

b. 1921, Kingston, Jamaica.
Poet, anthropologist, teacher.

M.G. Smith has gained many awards for his anthropological work and he has published a number of distinguished pieces of research. He has been a university teacher in the West Indies, the United States and the United Kingdom. He was first recognized in Jamaica as one of the outstanding poets in the *Focus* group who gathered around Mrs. Edna Manley.

His early style is very lyrical and nationalistic, rather "free" in its rhythms:

This is the land that knows no level
Water rushes through this land
So river
Silver river
Flow
Forever
Under time.

For a poet who has published comparatively little, Smith is well known and much admired in a variety of circles. *Savacou 11/12* is dedicated to Philip Sherlock, Henry Swanzy and "M.G." himself. Brathwaite says in his preface to that edition of *Savacou:* "m.g. smith is central. do his poems become a *framework* for caribbean studies?" There is no doubt that his work as a scholar and advisor to governments and Prime Ministers is powerful and central but one doubts that his poetry, as so far published, could be the framework for anything so varied and rich as Caribbean Studies would have to be in order to do justice to the entire Caribbean reality, past and present.

Some of his poems deal with his experience of London, where he did his postgraduate work. *Focus 1956* contains three of his longer and more remarkable poems, including "Testament," which starts:

A day ends and a way ends and a world ends here. . . .

This exultant poem has a deep religious feeling:

There is a morning in all human night
And life and birth and beauty beyond death. . . .

The poem ends:

O great to praise
O glory glory be
O Source and Way and Stillness
Home of peace. . . .
And first and last for this committed light
Of presence in these hands to love and know
The harmony that moves in touch, O glory be
Unto the Lord, and glory, glory be
Unto the coming of the Lord in light.

It is not clear whether M.G. Smith has written any verse recently. Now that he is again working, at least part of the time, in Jamaica, perhaps his great creative powers will once again express themselves in poetry.

Writings: Poetry: in *Focus; Caribbean Literature,* 1966; *Caribbean Verse,* 1967; *A Treasury of Jamaican Poetry,* 1940; *Independence Anthology,* 1962; Caribbean Voices, Vol. 1; *Caribbean Quarterly; Anthology of West Indian Poetry* (Federation Commemoration Issue, April 1958).

Play: *The Leader,* in *Focus,* Vol. 1 (Edna Manley, ed., Kingston City Printery, 1943).

Among his main publications (on the Caribbean): *The Plural Society of the British West Indies,* Berkeley and Los Angeles, University of California Press, 1965, XVII (359 pp.); *Stratification in Grenada,* Berkeley and Los Angeles, University of California Press, 1965, XIII (271 pp.); *West Indian Family Structure,* Seattle, University of Washington Press, 1962; *Dark Puritan,* Kingston, Department of Extra Mural Studies, U.W.I. (139 pp.); *The Ras Tafari Movement in Kingston, Jamaica,* U.W.I., 1960 (with Augier and Nettleford); *Report on Labour Supply in Rural Jamaica,* Kingston, Government Printery, 1956; *A Framework for Caribbean Studies,* Extra Mural Dept., U.C.W.I., 1955; (with G.J. Kruijer) *A Sociological Manual for Extension Workers in the Caribbean,* Extra Mural Dept., U.C.W.I., 1957; "Family Patterns in Rural Jamaica," *Welfare Reporter,* Vol. 16, No. 3 (Kingston, 1957), pp. 24-25; "Ethnic and Cultural Pluralism in the British Caribbean," Document 11, INGIDI Conference, Lisbon,

1957; "Community Organization in Rural Jamaica," S. & E.S., Vol. 5, No. 3, pp. 295-312; "The African heritage in the Caribbean," in Vera Rubin editor, *Caribbean Studies: A Symposium*, second edition, Seattle, University of Washington Press, pp. 34-53; "Short Range Prospects in the British Caribbean," 1962, in A. Singham, L.E. Brathwaite (editors), Special Number of *Social Economic Studies on the Conference of Political Sociology in the British Caribbean* (Dec. 1961), *Social Economic Studies* 11 (4) (Dec.), pp. 392-408; "Some Aspects of Social Structure in the British Caribbean about 1820," S. & E.S., Vol. 1, No. 4, pp. 55-80; "Slavery and Emancipation in Two Societies," S. & E.S., Vol. 3, Nos. 3 and 4, pp. 239-290; "Education and Occupational Choice in Rural Jamaica," 1956; and *Kinship and Community in Carriacou*, New Haven, Yale University Press (341 pp.).

Biographical/Critical Sources: Joseph J. Doherty, "The Life of Contemplation in M.G. Smith's *Testament*, BIM 25, pp. 36-42; Edward Baugh, *West Indian Poetry 1900-1970* (Pamphlet), p. 8.

SMITH, Pamela C.

b. ca. 1869, Jamaica.
Folklorist.

One of the earliest students of Jamaican tales, Smith is known to have published two collections of her work.

Writings: Folklore: *Anancy Stories*, New York, R.H. Russell, 1899; *Chim-Chim: folk stories from Jamaica*, London, "The Green Sheaf," 1905.

SMITH, Ricardo

b. ca. 1936, Guyana.
Playwright.

Smith was long a civil servant; he also worked in various capacities in a commercial firm and then went over to the *Graphic* newspaper where he served as manager for a short period. He eventually migrated to Canada.

Writings: Miss Phoebe; or Guyana Legend: A Play with Music in Three Acts (performed, Georgetown, for Independence Celebrations, 1966: adapted from an earlier play version: *Miss Phoebe: One Act Musical and Historical Play on Early Demerara*, 1963).

SNOD, E.

(pseudonym for **E.A. DODD**)
b. ca. 1875, Jamaica.
Storywriter.

Snod's studies of the Maroon mountain people (1905) are among the early creative works in Jamaican literature, though, according to Ramchand, they are comic sketches of the inferior sort.

Writings: Stories: *Maroon Medicine* (and three other stories), Kingston, Times' Printery, 1905.

Biographical/Critical Sources: K. Ramchand, *The West Indian Novel and its Background*, London, Faber, 1970.

SPENCER, Flora

b. ca. 1936, Barbados.
Storywriter, radio script writer, painter.

Flora Spencer is noted for her television series "Barbados, Past and Present." She was the script writer for "Bimshire," an annual performance first produced for Barbados Independence in 1966. She also writes short stories and scripts for radio. Some of her work has appeared in West Indian textbooks.

Spencer is a member of the Executive Committees of the Barbados Arts Council and the Commonwealth Caribbean Resource Centre.

STEELE, Lorna

b. ca. 1936, Guyana.
Playwright.

Lorna Steele, a poet in her own right, happens also to be the mother-in-law of Denis Foster, the Barbadian poet. Her one collection is *Reflections* (published c. 1974).

STEPHENSON, Michael

b. 1952, St. Vincent.
Poet, dancer.

After emigrating to the United States, Stephenson joined the U.S. Army and while on tour in Germany began writing poetry in 1972. His work has appeared in various little magazines and in the collection *The New Voices of American Poetry 1976*.

While undergoing basic training in Alabama, Stephenson began to develop his own idiom of dance, a freely organized working out of his ideas of modern dance and with a Caribbean quality. In Alabama he appeared on a television show of poetry and dance, and began his professional career. In Washington, D.C., in the mid-70s, he has established his own company, the Caribbean Ensemble.

Writings: Poetry: *Another Shade of Black: The Caribbean Experience—Here and There*, Washington, D.C., IVth Dynasty Press, 1977.

TAYLOR, Daphne Pawan

b. ca. 1917, Trinidad.
Writer, folklorist.

Taylor has a great interest in folklore and made one collection of island tales. She worked at I.D.C., Trinidad Promotions Department in 1972 and produced the I.D.C. *Directories of Industry in Trinidad and Tobago*. She is now working on a book on Trinidad "parrans."

Writings: Stories: *The Pompous parrot and other West Indian Tales*, Macmillan, Canada, 1947.

TAYLOR, Stanley Arthur Goodwin

b. 1894, Jamaica.
Novelist.

Taylor's work has been to capture the more dashing aspects of Jamaica's turbulent past in three historical fictions.

Writings: Novels: *The Capture of Jamaica: A historical novel*, Kingston, Jamaica, Pioneer Press, (c. 1951) xv, 164 pp. illus. fold. map; *Buccaneer Bay*, Kingston, Jamaica, Pioneer Press, 1952 (243 pp.); *Pages from our past*, Kingston, Jamaica, Pioneer Press, 1954 (183 pp.).

TELEMAQUE, Harold Milton

b. August 20, 1909, Plymouth, Tobago.
Poet, teacher.

Educated in Trinidad and the United Kingdom where he did special work in Educational Administration, Telemaque possess a remarkably fine reading voice. He has not written as much verse as one would have hoped, but he has appeared in journals in Germany, Russia and Sweden, reflecting his wide travels in Europe, the U.S.A. and the Caribbean.

He has contributed poetry to various anthologies and West Indian periodicals including: *Caribbean Voices; Caribbean Verse; Trinidad Anthology; Caribbean Federal Supplement; American Anthology; Bite In; Kyk-over-al; Beacon;* BIM; *Voices; NOW;* as well as in various European anthlogies (Sweden, Germany, Russia, Czechoslovakia), and his poetry has been broadcast over the BBC. He has been the recipient of many awards, including: a prize for the best contribution to poetry by the American Literary Society (1949); the National Golden Award for distinguished services to education, the Community and Teachers Union by the Union of Trinidad and Tobago Teachers Union.

His home is filled with his own ceramics and paintings and he plays jazz and listens to classical music in his free time. He serves as Church Warden and lay reader, and is a member of the Diocesan council of the Anglican Church. He has been a high school principal and published *A Caribbean Geography* and study guides.

His first collection, *Burnt Bush*, was sold from door to door by Clarke and Telemaque to pay the printer. When enough copies were sold, they went back to order new copies, until they had exhausted their informal market.

Telemaque's poetry is not easily available—although he is in Seymour's (1957) *Kyk Anthology*, in Figueroa's *Caribbean Voices*, and has very much more recently appeared in *NOW*, edited by Stewart Brown (St. Ann's Bay, Jamaica). *Kyk* and *C.V.* both published his well known "Our Land," the first stanza of which is:

In our land,
Poppies do not spring
From atoms of young blood,
So gaudily where men have died:
In our land
Stiletto cane blades
Sink into our hearts,
And drink our blood.

NOW published his "Homecoming," the last of which is:

I am home and give indeed
No place to Gonerils.
For love of my beginnings:
Deep and dark and high.
No hate
Will walk with me
Day nor night;
No frills and frompings
To my pinnacle.
And far beneath in vast embrace
Shall lie
The long white line of my exalted shore.

Writings: Poetry: (with A.M. Clarke) *Burnt Bush*. Fraser's Printerie, Trinidad, 1947; *Scarlet*, Georgetown, British Guiana (Guyana), Master Printery, 1953 (listed in Addenda of Literature of the English- and French-speaking West Indies in the University of Florida Library, bibliography comp. by Karl S. Watson.

Biographical/Critical Sources: G.O. Bell's review of *Burnt Bush* in BIM 9, pp. 74-77; and see Anson Gonzalez's *Literature of Trinidad and Tobago on Air.*

THOMAS, G.C.H.

b. ca. 1932, Trinidad.
Novelist.

Thomas begins his first novel, *Ruler in Hiroona*, in the autobiographical vein and goes on to say: ". . . I shall be writing about the nineteen-fifties and sixties, and the West Indian islands were incredible places during those times. They still are in some respects." The work deals with the thoughts and experiences of Jerry Mole who, former teacher and cop, organizes a labor union with his friend Joe Pittance, an intelligent dock worker. Mole in time becomes the Prime Minister of Hiroona, corrupt and arrogant. His subsequent fall cannot be regretted but it offers him an opportunity to put down on paper the rapid trajectory from colonial squalor to the glitter of power of independence.

Andrew Salkey has written "*Ruler in Hiroona* is an important contribution to Caribbean writing. . . . It is also one of the very few Caribbean political novels written with integrity and wise maturity."

Writings: Novel: *Ruler in Hiroona*, Port of Spain, Columbus Publishers Ltd., 1972; dramatic version by Alwin Bully with same title has been performed in West Indies.

THOMASOS, Clytus Arnold

b. 1907, Trinidad.
Poet, shortstory writer.

Thomasos was educated in Arima Boys' R.C. School in Trinidad. He was a member of the Legislative Council from 1956 to 1961 and then Deputy Speaker; in 1961 he became M.P. for Arima, and Speaker of the House of Representatives.

Writings: Poetry: *Poems*, Port of Spain, Fraser's Printerie, 1939. His work has appeared in *The Beacon* and various West Indian anthologies. During the 1940's his poems were broadcast on "Calling the West Indies" Programme.

THOMPSON, Clarence C.

b. ca. 1944, Trinidad.
Poet.

Thompson reads and dramatizes his poetry, and has published one collection.

Writings: Poetry: *Portrait of a People; a collection of 29 poems,* published by Free University for Black Studies, London, 1974.

THOMPSON, Claude Alphonso

b. 1907, Jamaica.
Poet, storywriter, broadcaster.

Thompson was educated at Wolmer's Boys' School, Jamaica and later was a civil servant and a newspaperman. He now lives in London. An occasional writer of short stories, he also does broadcasts.

J.E. Clare McFarlane wrote, "Mr. Thompson's "Afoot in Jamaica" affords a vivid description of some of Jamaica's most delightful mountain scenery."

His short stories have been published in: *Focus; Stories from the Caribbean;* and the *Independence Anthology of 1962,* and some verse in *A Treasury of Jamaican Poetry.*

Writings: These My People, Kingston, Jamaica, The Herald Ltd. Printers, 1943; "Afoot in Jamaica" (poetry), in manuscript.

THOMPSON, Ralph C.

b. 1928, Jamaica.
Storywriter, broadcaster, company executive.

Thompson was educated at St. George's College, Jamaica; Fordham University, New York (Doctor of Laws degree, 1951).

His short stories have appeared in the *West Indian Review* and his poems in the *Daily Gleaner.* He was a winner of the Bronze medal for Poetry in the Festival Competition of 1975 for "Planes." He has also won two Certificates of Merit for "Leda" and "Rain."

Thompson also paints interestingly—figures and scenes from around Port Antonio, Jamaica, and is a great promoter of the Arts. He first brought the musical version of Walcott's *Ti Jean* to Jamaica, and has since then, along with his wife and his Company, brought other Walcott plays to Jamaica.

Writings: Article: "The Role of Capitalism in Jamaica's Development," in *Caribbean Quarterly* (June 1966).

TIWONI, Habib

b. 1939, St. Thomas, U.S. Virgin Islands.
Poet.

Habib Tiwoni is currently a student at Pace University in New York. He is working on his third book of poetry, "What Time is the Sun," a verse account of his travels in Mexico.

In the notes on the back cover of his *Islands of My Mind* it is stated that "his works have appeared in publications in China, Africa, Europe, Caribbean America, South America and the United States. In March 1974 his poems were translated into Dutch and read over Radio KRO in Holland."

Writings: Poetry: *Attacking the Moncada of the Mind,* New York, El Pueblo Publications, 1970; and represented in *Islands of My Mind,* New York, Casha Publications, 1975.

TODMAN, Gerwyn

b. ca. 1891, St. Thomas, U.S. Virgin Islands.
Poet.

Todman's one collection of verse was *St. Thomas: A Retrospection* published by George A. Audain, Printer (St. Thomas, 1921, 58 pp.).

TOMLINSON, Frederick Charles

(pseudonym: **Frederick CHARLES**)
b. 1867, Jamaica.
Novelist.

Tomlinson's one work, *The Helions,* is one of the earliest Jamaican novels.

Writings: Novel: *The Helions; or the deeds of Rio: a political comedy* (by Frederick Charles), London, Simpkin, Marshall (etc.), 1903.

TOWNSEND, Mitzie

b. ca. 1935, Jamaica; d. 1974, Jamaica.
Playwright, poet, actress, scriptwriter.

Active in Jamaica and Guyanese Theatre, Mitzie Townsend was a dynamic personality and friend to many writers. She died prematurely in Guyana. She received many awards in the Jamaica National Festival Competitions for her plays and poetry.

Townsend worked as a director and script writer in the Guyana Information Service and was one of the six women who contributed to and published *Guyana Drums* (Georgetown, Guyana, 1972). She was also known throughout the Caribbean for her special artistic and creative talents. For two consecutive years in the Jamaica Drama Festival she won the "Best Actress" award.

Writings: Plays: *Apartment to Let* (First Class Award, 1965); *Heavens Above* (full length play, Award of High Commendation and an Alcan Award, 1966); and a one-act play, *The Job* (Silver Medal and an Alcan Award, 1966).

Poetry: published in various newspapers and journals; and included in Douglas' *Guyana Drums* (name spelled in collection as "Townshend").

TREE, Iris

b. 1889, Bahamas.
Poet.

Tree's very early collections were *Poems* (New York, John Lane, 1919, 144 pp.), and *The Traveller and Other Poems* (New York, Boni and Liveright, 1927, 89 pp.).

TROPICA

(pseudonym for **Mary Adella WOLCOTT**)
b. ca. 1874, Jamaica, (her parents were American Missionaries).
Poet.

Tropica's work is mentioned in J.E. Clare McFarlane's *A Literature in the Making,* Jamaica, Pioneer Press, 1956, the main reference is Chapter 9, pp. 64-69.

Writings: Poetry: *The Island of Sunshine,* New York, Knickerbocker Press, c. 1904, and poems in *A Treasury of Jamaican Poetry.*

TROTMAN, D.A.R.

b. ca. 1935, Guyana.
Poet, anthropologist.

Trotman's work appears in journals and collections, including: *Kyk-over-al; Kaie; Magnet; Themes of Song; Sun is a Shapely Fire; Voices of Guyana* (contributor, editor), and he has one collection of his verse in print: *Poems for My People* (British Guiana, 1965).

Writings: Editor: *Voices of Guyana,* Georgetown, Sheik Sadeek, 1968.

TUCKER, Nathaniel

b. ca. 1750, Bermuda; d. 1807.
Poet.

Nathaniel Tucker grew up in Bermuda then in 1771 moved to South Carolina U.S.A. In 1775 he revisited Bermud before setting out for London to begin hi studies in medicine and where he pub lished his two known works.

Joseph and Johanna Jones include him in their *Authors and Areas of the Wes Indies* and in their commentary on hir explain their reason for his inclusion. H "worked hard at trying to establish th permanent poetic reputation whic eluded him" but "John Adams thought *The Bermudian's* description of the enchanting island, and everything else" offered "proofs of a rich vein of poetry no less than of moral and social feeling without which human life would not be tolerable." (p. 68)—and that "he represents with peculiar force the efforts of colonial island communities to make themselves heard."

Writings: Poetry: *The Anchoret: a Poem,* London, Murray, 1776; and *The Bermudian,* London, Author, 1774.

TUREN, Teppo

b. ca. 1936, Cayman Islands.
Writer.

Turen's *The invulnerable rulers of banner reef* (Grand Cayman, Caribbean Colony Ltd., 1966), of unknown genre, is one of the few works published by a native of the Cayman Islands.

TWINEY, Harriette (Harrie) M.E.

(née **ORMSBY**)
b. December 1867, Jamaica; d. December 1953.
Poet.

One of the many poetic Ormsbys, Harriette Twiney published two volumes of her work.

Writings: Poetry: *Ideal Jamaica and Other Poems,* London, Arthur Stockwell, n.d., Short poems about Jamaica, and her verse is in *Seed and Flower: An Anthology of Prose and Poetry* (by the Ormsby Family of Jamaica), Kingston, Jamaica, 1956.

USHERWOOD, Vivian

b. ca. 1960, Jamaica.
Poet.

Vivian Usherwood published the collection, *Poems,* when only 12 years old, while attending school in Hackney, London.

Writings: Poetry: *Poems,* London, Centerprise 1972.

VAN SERTIMA, Ivan Gladstone

b. January 26, 1935, Guyana.
Poet, critic, storywriter, teacher, scholar, broadcaster.

After schooling in Guyana, Van Sertima took a degree in African languages and culture at London University. For a period (1957-1959) he served as Press and Broadcasting Officer of the Government Information Services, British Guiana, but then moved to London for his studies and work with BBC. During the next ten years he published poetry in various small journals and did much critical writing, some of it aired on the radio. His first volume of verse, *River and the Wall,* appeared in 1958 in Guyana but the bulk of his creative work was done in England.

In 1970 on his first trip to the United States, Van Sertima came upon the three-volume work of Leo Weiner's entitled *Africa and the Discovery of America* (published in the 1920's) and it and the archeological discoveries of giant Olmec period heads with negroid features dating to 814 B.C. by Alexander von Wuthenau, led to his writing *They Came Before Columbus* (1977). This work argues the compelling evidence for believing Africans had early arrived in the Americas and made their mark. Citing a wide range of factual, anthropological, and documentary sources, Van Sertima's work became the object of a vitriolic attack by the Cambridge University scholar Glyn Daniel who termed the thesis "ignorant rubbish" and its author one more of the "deluded." Van Sertima mildly responded that Daniel was ". . . . a man impervious to original thought." Stimulated by the vast attention gained by the book and film *Roots* by Alex Haley, Random House brought out a second printing of *They Came Before*

Columbus in 1977 and the Book of the Month Club made the work its special May selection. Van Sertima has said, "Many people feel a certain kind of happiness when they read my book. A certain kind of shadow lifts. The psyche of blacks is raised. No man who believes his history began with slavery can be a healthy man. If you lift that shadow, you help repair that damage." Later in his interview with a *Washington Post* reporter, he added, "... Columbus is not just a man. He is a symbol. It was with the coming of Columbus that the twilight of the red and black races began. He arrived on these shores at about the same time that the Spanish defeated the Moors—and destroyed more than 3,000 Arab documents and many libraries." He concluded: "How many of us know the African influence on ancient Greece and Rome? There is also a vast body of knowledge to be uncovered about Africa and America. When you push one door, other doors begin to open."

Writings: Poetry: *River and the Wall*, British Guiana, Master Printery, 1958 (Miniature Poet Series). He has contributed to such anthologies as *Schwarzer Orpheus* (1964); *Nouvelle Somme de poésie du monde noir* (1966); *Breaklight; Sun is a Shapely Fire; Themes of Song;* and has appeared in many journals.

Stories: *Caribbean Writers, Critical Essays*, London, New Beacon, 1968, and New York, Panther, 1971.

Stories: in *Kyk-over-al* 26 (1956); the story "Black Prince" is in *New Writing in the Caribbean.*

Criticism: *Caribbean Writers, Critical Essays*, Londo, New Beacon, 1968, and New York, Panther, 1971.

Compiler: *Dictionary of Swahili Legal Terms*, Dar es Salaam, University of Dar es Salaam, 1973.

Cultural History: *They Came Before Columbus*, New York, Random House, 1977, second printing also 1977, Book of the Month Club, 1977.

Biographical/Critical Sources: Glyn Daniel, review of *They Came Before Columbus*, in *New York Times Book Review* (March 13, 1977); Hollie I. West, " 'Before Columbus,': Roots of a Dispute," *Washington Post*, Section B, pp. 1, 3, (May 9, 1977).

VAN SERTIMA, Sheila

b. ca. 1935, Guyana.
Playwright, storywriter.

Van Sertima has had short stories published in various periodicals, including *Christmas Chronicle Annual* and has written two plays.

Writings: Plays: *It's Brickdam! a play in One Act*, in *Kyk-over-al* 25 (June 1959), pp. 139-147; *Admit Joe*, broadcast during "History and Culture Week," 1964.

VAUGHAN, Hilkton Augustus

b. 1901, Santo Domingo (of Barbadian parents, long resident in Barbados).
Poet, historian, diplomat, editor, judge.

"H A," as he is known to all in Barbados, is a man of the establishment who has written poetry of remarkably advanced sentiments. But his poetry is lyrical and in no way pedestrian or propagandistic.

H A has been a judge, a Member of the Barbadian House of Assembly, and his country's Ambassador to the U.S.A., and to the United Nations. His special interest is the history of Barbados. He has been working on a biography of Sir Conrad Reeves, and has been a moving force among historians in his country. He has served as editor of the *Barbados Recorder.*

Like so many other distinguished Barbadians, he is an alumnus of Harrison College—and a Barrister at Law, having taken silk in 1964. He has had not only a literary career, but has served in many posts in the State: judge, minister without portfolio, Attorney General, Minister of State.

Although his poems are "old fashioned"

in form, they were well ahead of their times in their concerns. The much quoted "Revelation" is proof of this. But so too is his "The old Convict" which begins:

Look at me, I am Ishmael,
Ham's heir, the spit and spawn of Cain
The outcast with the twisted brain.
Lord of Cats Castle, fit for Hell....

and ends, four stanzas later,

Reform, you say? Reform indeed!
Let's all reform. They must not quit
The Golden Rule, and I from it
Will not stray once. That is our need.

H.A. Vaughan has an unusual, and slightly old world, reading style. He comes through interestingly on the Caedmon record, *Poets of the West Indies*, number TC 1379, edited by John Figueroa.

Writings: Poetry: *Sandy Lane and Other Poems*, Barbados, 1945. He has contributed to anthologies including: *Caribbean Voices* (John Figueroa, ed.), Evans Bros., Vol. I (1966), Vol. II (1970); Robert Luce Co., Inc., New York, Washington, (1971); *The Poetry of the Negro* (Langston Hughes and Arna Bontemps, eds., Doubleday, New York, 1949); *Kyk-over-al* (A. Seymour, ed.); *Anthology of West Indian Poetry*, 1957; *Caribbean Quarterly: Federation Commemoration Issue* (April 1958), Vol. 5, No. 3. He has also published poetry in various journals, including BIM.

Articles: on Barbadian history and folk music in various journals.

Editor of: the *Barbados Recorder.*

VAZ, Noel D.

b. ca. 1920, Jamaica.
Essayist, poet, actor, producer, teacher.

Noel Vaz has written little but has had a marked effect on the modern theatre of Jamaica. Educated at Calabar High School, Vaz always had a great interest in the theatre, and was awarded, in 1946, a British Council scholarship to study in England. He had before that produced a well-remembered version of "Twelfth Night" which featured spectacle, including the dancing of the pupils of the Hazel Johnson School. (It is interesting to note that the production was a kind of turning point and was supported by many who have since been clearly connected with the theatre and the arts in Jamaica: e.g. Mike Campbell [deceased], Ralph Thompson, Dorothy Alexander, John Figueroa and Greta Fowler.)

But Vaz's most outstanding work has been as Extra Mural Tutor, U.C.W.I. He toured many islands encouraging drama as part of education, and working on local material—to the extent that he had the distinction of having one of his productions banned in Antigua—because parts of the script were written in "dialect," Antiguan dialect none the less!!

A producer of the highest standards and a rather quiet, uncommunicative man, he has sometimes run afoul of the younger groups in the theatre who consider him rather conservative and "Euro-centric," without perhaps knowing that Vaz in his day too found the cultural climate suffocating and did something about it.

His somewhat controversial "Creative Potential at Home" (*Focus*, 1960) is still worth reading:

> *A most pertinent question we should ask our writers abroad ... is why don't they come home? ... an artist being ahead of his time is essentially an exile from his society and has a hard time anywhere whether he is writing in the hills of St. Andrew, painting in Basseterre, carving in Bridgetown or pontificating in Putney or Soho.*

He collaborated with Louise Bennett on *Bluebear and Brer Nancy*, Little Theatre, 1949.

Biographical/Critical Sources: Mentioned in Henry Fowler's article, "A History of Jamaican Theatre," *Jamaica Journal*, Vol. 2, No. 1 (March 1968).

VIRTUE, Vivian

(a.k.a. **LANCASTER**)
b. November 13, 1911, Jamaica.
Poet, translator, broadcaster.

Educated Kingston College, Jamaica. Vivian Virtue's name has long been associated with the poetry of Jamaica. He was an active member (and for a while Librarian) of the Poetry League. His work appears in *Focus* and *The Treasury of Jamaican Poetry;* he was awarded the Musgrave Medal for Poetry by the Institute of Jamaica (1960) and also the Constance

Hollar Memorial prize for Poetry, Poetry League of Jamaica (1950).

Virtue has done a number of translations from the French and Spanish. He is fond of the sonnet form, and his translations seem to have more vital push than his own original poems which sometimes remind one of Roy Campbell's famous questions to the poet whose work was so well polished. . . .

One of his "Villanelles" has for its first stanza:

Take me again the burning desert way,
After the shading palms, the living
springs.
O pain to-day! for joy was yesterday.

His sonnet translation from Lopez Goldaras of Cuba ends:

While love and lust, inseparable twain,
Dance measures of fantastic imagery
To the rhythm that your lyric hips
contain.

He was a frequent broadcaster in the former Caribbean Voices program, BBC. In 1961 he retired as a civil servant and he now lives and writes in London.

He is a Fellow of the Royal Society of Arts and in Jamaica was a co-founder of the New Dawn Press; was on the Advisory Board of the Pioneer Press, Kingston; was a Foundation member and former Vice-President of the Jamaican Center of International P.E.N. Club. He represented the Center at the P.E.N. Congress in Lausanne (1951), London (1956), Brussels (1962), and Oslo (1964). He participated in the Commonwealth Arts Festival (London, 1965) as a commissioned Poet; c.f. *Verse and Voice a festival of Commonwealth Poetry.*

Among his translations number a completed translation of eighty sonnets from the French of José Maria de Heredia's *Les Trophées.* He has other translations from French and Spanish Caribbean poets.

Writings: Poetry: *Wings of the Morning,* Kingston, Jamaica, New Dawn Press, 1938. He contributed to various anthologies, including *Caribbean Voices,* Vols. I and II, 1966, 1970; *New Poems,* 1966; *New Voices of the Commonwealth,* 1968; *West Indian Poetry,* 1971; *Focus; Independence Anthology of Jamaican Literature,* 1962; *A Treasury of Jamaican Poetry,* 1949; *Jamaica, Portrait of an Island,* 1955; *Verse and Voice,* 1965; *Caribbean Quarterly, Federation Commemoration Issue* (April 1958), Vol. 5, No. 3 and also to several newspapers and journals: "Salute to a National Hero: Marcus Garvey, 1887-1940."

Biographical/Critical Sources: In J.E. Clare McFarlane's *A Literature in the Making,* Jamaica, Pioneer Press, 1956 (main reference, Chapter 15, pp. 104-109); Edward Baugh, *West Indian Poetry 1900-1970* (Pamphlet), p. 6.

WAITE-SMITH, Cicely (Howland)

b. ca. 1913, Jamaica.
Storywriter, playwright.

Very active for a number of years in Jamaica Theatre, especially at the time when the appropriate meaning and style of the theatre was being actively discussed, Waite-Smith is one of the most published playwrights of the Caribbean.

Writings: Stories: *Rain for the plains and other stories,* Kingston, Jamaica, The Gleaner Co., 1943.

Plays: *African Slingshot,* one act, Kingston, U.W.I., Extra Mural Department, 1958, also published in Errol Hill's *Caribbean Plays,* Vol. I, Kingston, U.W.I., 1958, and new edition: by University of W.I., Trinidad and Tobago, 1966; *The Creatures,* one act, Port of Spain, Trinidad, U.W.I., 1954, in mimeo, produced in Trinidad, 1954, also published in Edna Manley's *Focus Jamaica,* 1956, Kingston and published Port of Spain, U.W.I.; *Grandfather is Dying,* in *Focus,* Jamaica, 1943, The City Printery; *The Impossible Situation,* Port of Spain, U.W.I., 1966, produced Jamaica, 1957; *The Peoples' Champion,* 2 acts, typescript only, completed 1957; *The Ravishers,* produced Jamaica, 1958; *Return to Paradise,* one act, Port of Spain, U.W.I., 1966; *Storm Signal,* a radio play, *Focus,* Jamaica, 1948, The City Printery; and produced by CBC, Canada; *Uncle Robert of Family Poem,* 3 acts, Kingston, U.W.I., 1957, and produced Jamaica in 1957, new edition, Trinidad, U.W.I., 1967 (expanded to 77 pp. from original 56); *The Wild Horses,* one act and five scenes, acting and mime, in *Public Opinion Chrismas Annual,* 1955, Kingston, Jamaica 1955; Waite-Smith also wrote introduction to *Sleepy Valley; a Jamaican morality,* created by Knox Summer School (Jamaica), 1952, published Port of Spain, U.C.W.I., 1955. (The play was based on a story written by Waite-Smith but its subjects and situations were discussed and analyzed by group of 12 persons led by Errol Hill and then written and rewritten. The group effort was performed October 1966 and twice earlier as the group sought to improve their work.) Also: *The Long Run,* London, Gollance, 1961.

Biographical/Critical Sources: Mentioned in Henry Fowler's article "A History of Jamaican Theatre" in *Jamaica Journal,* Vol. 2, No. 1 (March 1968), pp. 53-59.

WALCOTT, Derek

b. January 23, 1930, St. Lucia.
Poet, playwright, producer, teacher, journalist, painter.

Walcott was educated at St. Mary's College, Castries, St. Lucia, and at U.C.W.I., Mona, Jamaica. By the time he was nineteen he had produced *25 Poems.* Harry Simmonds at that time replied to Collymore's request for biographical material on Walcott in this way:

> *Derek was nineteen years old on the 23rd of January of this year (1949). He won an exhibition scholarship to St. Mary's College where he is now an assistant master teaching English to the Higher Certificate Class, and French. He is a prolific writer, and this volume represents his own selections. He is also a painter in water colours and oils. His father, Warwick Walcott, was a Barbadian. His mother is a prominent social worker, one of our most successful head teachers, and a producer of amateur dramatics.*

His father was, in fact, English; a watercolorist with a great interest in the theatre and opera. He died while Derek, his twin Roderick, and their sister Pam, were quite young. *25 Poems* bears the inscription: . . . "for A.W." (his mother) "and the memory of my father."

Walcott's aubobiographical poem, *Another Life,* speaks of himself as "The Divided Child . . . of the wrong colour." His heritage was indeed a mixed one because not only were his parents of different countries and different ethnic groups, but his family was staunchly Methodist in the midst of the French, almost prerevolutionary Roman Catholicism of St. Lucia. Further, he would have had a very early experience of a variety of language backgrounds, because French Patois is one of the living languages of St. Lucia, together with a number of varieties of English, as well as standard French. Of course these languages and religious differences also indicated great cultural and stylistic differences. It is one of Walcott's remarkable achievements to have drawn, strongly and creatively, on all these different traditions. In many ways he has been the leader in a tendency, much needed in the Caribbean arts, of acknowledging and using creatively, the mixed and sometimes conflicting cultures which have come together in the Caribbean Basin.

Walcott has now been for some time a full-time writer and producer of plays, having instituted the Trinidad Theatre Workshop which he long directed but recently left. But he has also made his living as a teacher—of Latin, as well as French and English, and as a journalist. After university he taught successfully in Jamaica, and was afterwards a lively commentator, mainly on the arts, in the *Trinidad Guardian.* In fact, many of his pieces in that paper would be quite worth collecting and publishing.

Whatever might be the controversies which have arisen about Walcott's poetry or ideology, or about his producing his own plays, or about the difficult balance he tries to hold about the Caribbean heritage, and about those who would profit by every new bandwagon which trumpets along, there can be little doubt that he is a literary genius. In an early essay (written at the U.W.I.), he himself quotes as applicable to himself, Pope's "I lisped in numbers," and his touch was recognized very early by such persons as Harry Simmonds, Frank Collymore, and James (Sonny) Rodway, to whom *Epitaph For The Young* (1949) is dedicated.

Collymore called *25 Poems* "the work of an accomplished poet"...."there are (those) ... who are poets from birth: to them poetry is all in all, the very breath of life; and I do not think I am mistaken when I make this high claim for Derek Walcott." Collymore, well read as he was, and having at that time completed the ninth issue of BIM, went on to say about Walcott: "These two qualities ... imagery and sincerity ... combine in a poetic fervour sufficient to assure me that Derek Walcott is a poet of whom any community might be proud." That was in 1949.

As many will know, *In a Green Night,* published thirteen years after, elicited the following from Robert Graves: "Walcott handles English with a closer understanding of its inner magic than most (if not any) of his English-born contemporaries." And of his *Another Life* (1973), George Lamming has this to say: "... how truly to name what the society sees is the intricate task and the burden of Walcott's turbulent meditation on the dilemma of his time. The result is a formidable achievement."

So that in the case of Walcott we are not dealing with a powerful flash in the pan, but with a talent which has worked hard and produced consistently for some twenty-five years. Further, as has been often noted, Walcott has done most of this while using the Caribbean as his home

and working base—although he has travelled, and although the structure and style of his plays have been clearly influenced by "outside" traditions. He has not found it necessary—so far anyway—to live and work outside the Caribbean. In fact even those plays which have achieved considerable acclaim abroad have had their premieres in the Caribbean, and have often travelled around the islands before being taken abroad. This is particularly important because Walcott believes that without the experience of art, people find it very difficult really to see what is right in front of them. From this point of view the theatre is clearly central to a people's perception of *the* world, and their world.

It is no accident that one like Walcott, to whom Collymore early attributed the quality of *sincerity,* has taken so strongly to the theatre and has brought into existence, and enabled to develop, such a splended artistic entity as the creative and disciplined Trinidad Theatre Workshop, for he is essentially a "sooth-sayer" in the old sense of a "truth-teller." But he realizes that truth is complicated, and many layered, (and like beauty, difficult!). He knows the truth is just as easily (or as difficultly) grasped through the imagination, structured and well disciplined, as through the easy slogans of the politicians —academic, cultural, power-conscious or wedded to what *they* consider history.

Of course, a "truth-teller" can often be wrong, but, it must be realized, that the nearer he is to being right, the less will he be liked. Walcott's "What the Twilight Says: An Overture," the introductory essay to his *Dream on Monkey Mountain, and Other Plays,* is a masterpiece of grappling with the truth and letting the chips and the spittle and the counterfeit haloes (and crowns of thorn) fall where they may: "But Carnival was meaningless as the art of the actor confined to mimicry. And now the intellectuals, courting and fearing the mass, found values in it that they had formerly despised. They apotheosized the folk form, insisting that calypsos were poems . . . they wanted politically to educate the peasant yet leave him intellectually unsoiled; they baffled him with schisms and the complexities of Power while insisting that he needed neither language nor logic . . ."

> *Once we have lost our wish to be white we develop a longing to become black, and those two may be different, but are still careers. . . ."*
>
> *And their poems (i.e. those of our writers) remained laments, their novels propaganda tracts, as if one general apology on behalf of the past would supplant imagination, would spare them the necessity of great art* . . . (p. 10).

For Walcott, without great art nothing is possible. And his latest efforts in the Theatre have brought, through music and dance, as well as through his thick magic words, that art closer and closer to more Caribbean people, in St. Croix, Barbados, Castries, Trinidad and Jamaica. His latest collaborator in this work was Galt MacDermot—not only of Hair fame, but of Anglo-Jamaican ancestry. (MacDermot is a collateral descendant of Jamaica's Tom Redcam, q.v.)

But he has not abandoned poetry outside of the theatre. In fact, his output has been remarkable in bulk as well as quality: *Another Life* alone, a "formidable achievement" in anybody's book, is four thousand lines long. And there has been another collection since then.

Although Walcott displays in his play, at times, a really humorous touch, he tends to give, especially in his early work, an impression of melancholy, controlled anger and deep dissatisfaction with *life,* and with the way in which, for instance,

Devouring Time, which blunts the Lion's claws,
Kept Cosimo, count of curios fairly chaste,
For Mama's sake, for hair oil, and for whist;
Peering from balconies for his tragic twist.

(from *Tales of the Islands,* Chapter II—"Qu'un sang impur")

He himself, especially in his younger drinking days, could be morose and melancholy beyond belief. But there appears to be a movement in his verse, from rather thick, clotted evocations to insightful and clear epiphanies, from, as John Figueroa argues, exorcism to benediction. He certainly sets himself, as Lamming points out, the task of naming what he and our society *see,* but he goes beyond naming. He seems to have experienced the depth of Nothing and to have understood, or achieved, its relationship with All. The Nada, apparent in the early poems—not least of all in "Tales of the Islands" (and in *Poems,* published in Jamaica while he was at university) achieves a very positive meaning in *Another Life.*

Anna, I wanted to grow white-haired
as the wave, with a wrinkled
brown rock's face, salted,
seamed, an old poet,
facing the wind
and nothing, which is,
the loud world in his mind.

(p. 148)

And oddly enough that old-fashioned word "sincerity" is perhaps more adequate than one thought at first, that ability to struggle with the truth, not as a philo-

sophic abstraction, nor away from philosophy, but as a part of life's struggle, which for any but the maimed, includes the battle of the imagination not only to sympathize with the other but to know itself:

. . . . Not
to enter the knowledge of God
but to know that His name
had lain too familiar on my tongue,
as this one would day "bread,"
or "sun," or "wine." I staggered,
shaken at my remorse, as one
would say "bride," or "bread,"
or "sun," or "wine," to believe—
and that you would rise again,
when I am not here, to catch
the air afire, that you need not
look for me, or need this prayer.
(from *Another Life,* pp. 146-147)

Walcott has received many honors and awards. In 1957 he was awarded a Fellowship by the Rockefeller Foundation to study the American Theatre; (on his return to Trinidad he founded the Trinidad Theatre Workshop). In 1961, the year before his first volume of poetry *In a Green Night* was published, he received the Guiness Award for Poetry. His second collection *The Castaway* gained for him a Royal Society of Literature Award; and in 1969 he received the Cholmondeley Award for his collection *The Gulf.* In July 1969 he took part in the Poetry International Festival in London. For his autobiographical *Another Life* (1973) he received the award of the 1974 Jock Campbell/New Statesman Prize.

He received the Eugene O'Neill Foundation-Wesleyan Fellowship for Playwrights. In 1969 he produced with great success *Dream on Monkey Mountain* at the Eugene O'Neill Memorial Theatre at Waterford. For *Dream* also, he won an OBIE award for the most distinguished foreign off-Broadway production in 1971. His plays have been performed throughout the English-speaking Caribbean, in Canada and America; in 1960 two of his one-act plays were performed at the Royal Court Theatre. His musical *Joker of Seville* (with Galt MacDermot) was commissioned by the Royal Shakespeare Company of Great Britain in 1974.

He has been the recipient of an Honorary Doctorate of Letters from the University of the West Indies (1972); and has been decorated by St. Lucia.

His very recent play, *O Babylon,* a musical with Galt MacDermot, maintains the high standard of the previous work; it probes, in a witty manner, some of the problems of the Rastas (a Jamaican religious sect), and of the wholly inadequate posturings of many of the politicians who struggle with the relationships, in a place like Jamaica; between not only the "haves" and the "have nots," but also between the "developed" and "developing" world.

While "Playwright in Residence" in St. Croix, Walcott wrote *Remembrance* which premiered in St. Croix and Road Town (Tortola) in December, 1977. The serio-humorous three-act play is set in Port of Spain in the early 1970's.

Writings: Poetry: *25 Poems,* Port of Spain, Trinidad, Guardian Commercial Printery, 1948; *Epitaph for the Young—a poem in XII Cantos,* Bridgetown, Barbados, Advocate, 1949; *Poems,* Kingston, Jamaica, City Printery, 1953; *In a Green Night: Poems 1948-1960,* London, Cape, 1962; *Selected Poems,* New York, Farrar Straus, 1964; *The Castaway and Other Poems,* London, Cape, 1965, Reissued in 1969; *The Gulf and Other Poems,* London, Cape, 1969, and as *The Gulf,* New York, Farrar Straus, 1970; *Another Life,* London, Cape and New York, Farrar Straus, 1973. His poetry has also been published in various magazines and journals, including: *The New Statesman; The London Magazine; Encounter; Evergreen Review; The Caribbean Quarterly; Tamarack Review;* and BIM.

His work appears in numerous anthologies, including: *Caribbean Literature* (G.R. Coulthard, ed.); *Caribbean Verse* (O.R. Dathorne, ed.); *Caribbean Voices* (J. Figueroa, ed.) Vols. I and II; *Commonwealth Poems of Today* (H. Sergeant, ed.); *From the Green Antilles* (Barbara Howes, ed.); *New Voices of the Commonwealth* (H. Sergeant, ed.); *The Sun's Eye* (A. Walmsley, ed.);

Young Commonwealth Poetry, (Peter Ludwig Brent, ed.).

He records a reading of his poetry on Caedmon Record TC 1379, *Poets of the West Indies,* (J. Figueroa, ed.).

Plays: *Henri Christophe* (A Chronicle in seven scenes), Bridgetown, Barbados, Advocate Co., 1950, (produced St. Lucia, 1950, and London, 1951), published Kingston, Jamaica, Extra Mural Department, U.C.W.I., in mimeographed form; *Henri Dernier* (A Play for Radio Production), Bridgetown, Barbados, 1951; *Wine of the Country,* U.C.W.I., Mona, Jamaica, 1953(?), 1954(?); *The Sea at Dauphin,* a play in one act, Mona, Jamaica, Extra Mural Dept., U.C.W.I., 1954 (Caribbean Plays 4); second edition, 1958, and produced, Trinidad 1954; London, 1960; Included in *The Dream on Monkey Mountain and Other Plays* (New York, Farrar Straus and Giroux, 1970); *Ione—a play with music,* Mona, Jamaica, Extra Mural Dept., U.C.W.I., 1957 (Caribbean Plays 8), produced, Trinidad 1957; *Drums and Colours* (an epic drama commissioned for the opening of the First Federal Parliament of the West Indies), April 23, 1958, and published in *Caribbean Quarterly,* Special Issue, Vol. 7, Nos. 1 and 2, Kingston, Jamaica, (March-June 1961); *In a Fine Castle,* produced in Jamaica, 1970; in Trinidad, 1971; in Los Angeles, California, 1972; *The Dream on Monkey Mountain,* produced Toronto, 1967; Waterford, Connecticut, 1968; New York, 1971. Included in *The Dream on Monkey Mountain and Other Plays,* New York, Farrar, Straus and Giroux, 1970. (This latter also contains, besides *The Dream on Monkey Mountain: Ti-Jean and His Brothers; Malcauchon; Sea at Dauphin;* and the essay, "What the Twilight Says.") Also: *Malcauchon, or Six in the Rain,* Caribbean Plays Edition, Port of Spain, Trinidad, University of the West Indies, 1966; *Jourmard,* Caribbean Plays Edition, Port of Spain, Trinidad, U.W.I., 1967; *The Charlatan,* Caribbean Plays Editions, Port of Spain, Trinidad, U.W.I., 1967; *Ti Jean,* Caribbean Plays Edition, Kingston, Jamaica, U.W.I., n.d.; *Dream on Monkey Mountain and other Plays,* New York, Farrar, Straus and Giroux, 1970.

Musical: *The Joker of Seville* (with Galt MacDermot), recorded under the heading "trinidad theatre workshop, original cast album," 1975; *Joker of Seville* and *O Babylon,* New York, Farrar, Straus and Giroux, 1978.

Critical Articles and Reviews: A review of V.S. Naipaul's *Mr. Stone and the Knights Companion,* in *Sunday Guardian,* Trinidad (July 7, 1963), p. 15; review of V.S. Naipaul's *Middle Passage,* in *Sunday Guardian,* Trinidad (Sept. 30, 1962), p. 9; review of Samuel Selvon's *The Housing Lark,* in *Sunday Guardian,* Trinidad (June 27, 1965), p. 7; a review of Selvon's *I Hear Thunder,* in *Sunday Guardian,* Trinidad (May 5, 1963), p. 4; a review of A.J. La Rose's *Foundations,* in *Sunday Guardian Magazine* (Jan. 15, 1967), p. 8; introduction to *Dream on Monkey Mountain and other Plays,* "What the Twilight Says: An Overture" (Farrar, Straus and Giroux, New York, 1970).

Biographical/Critical Sources: Keith Alleyne, a review of *Epitaph for the Young: a poem in XII cantos* in BIM, Vol. 3, No. 11, pp. 267-272; Aubrey Douglas-Smith, a review of *Henri Christophe,* in BIM, Vol. 3, No. 12, pp. 349-353; John Figueroa, a review of *In a Green Night* in *Caribbean Quarterly,* Vol. 8, No. 4 (Dec. 1962), pp. 67-69; A.N. Forde, review of *In a Green Night* in BIM Vol. 9, No. 36 (Jan.-June 1963), pp. 288-290; K.L. McShine, review of *Selected Poems* in *Sunday Guardian,* Trinidad (June 7, 1964), p. 4; L. Edward Brathwaite, review of *The Castaway* in BIM, Vol. 11, No. 42 (Jan.-June 1966), pp. 139-141; Kevin Ireland, a review of *The Castaway* in *Journal of Commonwealth Literature,* No. 2 (Dec. 1966), pp. 157-158; Alan Rose, review of *The Castaway* in *London Magazine,* Vol. 5, No. 10 (Jan. 1966), pp. 88-91; John Melser, review of *The Dream on Monkey Mountain,* in *Trinidad Guardian* (Jan. 29, 1968), p. 11 (author's name wrongly spelt as John Mercer); Roy Fuller, review of *The Gulf* in *London Magazine,* Vol. 9, No. 8 (Nov. 1969), pp. 89-90; Gordon Rohlehr "Withering into truth: a review of Derek Walcott's *The Gulf . . . poems,*" in *Trinidad Guardian* (Dec. 10, 1969), p. 18; and "Power in desolation," review of *The Gulf* in *Trinidad Guardian* (Dec. 11, 1969), p. 17; and "Making love look more like despair," in *Trinidad Guardian* (Dec. 13, 1969), p. 8, concluding Dr. Gordon Rohlehr's review of *The Gulf;* Bill Carr, "The significance of Derek Walcott," in *Public Opinion* (Jamaica, Feb. 28, 1964), pp. 8, 9, 14; Frank Collymore, a review of Walcott's poems in BIM Vol. 4, No. 15 (Dec. 1957), pp. 224-227; Winston Hackett, "Identity in the poetry of Walcott," in *Moko,* No. 8 (Feb. 14, 1969), p. 2; C.G.O. King, "The poems of Derek

Walcott," in *Caribbean Quarterly,* Vol. 10, No. 3 (Sept. 1964), pp. 3-30; Cameron King and Louis James, "In solitude for company; the poetry of Derek Walcott," in the *Islands in Between* (Louis James, ed.), London, O.U.P., 1968, pp. 85-99; Mervyn Morris, "Walcott and the audience for poetry," in *Caribbean Quarterly,* Vol. 14, Nos. I and II (March-June 1968), pp. 7-24; three reviews by John Figueroa: "Tales of the Islands by Derek Walcott," in *World Literature Written in English,* Vol. 15, No. 1 (April 1976); article on *Another Life,* in BIM 58, (June 1975), pp. 160-170; "A Note on Derek Walcott's Concern with Nothing," in *Revista Inter Americana,* Vol. IV, No. 3, (San Juan, P.R.), pp. 422-428; John Figueroa's review of *Another Life* in *Melanthika* (1977), pp. 117-125.

Also see Edward Baugh, *West Indian Poetry 1900-1970* (Pamphlet), (Savacou Publications Ltd.), pp. 1, 13, 14, 16-18; Anson Gonzalez, " 'Possibility' in W.I. Creative Writing," in *The New Voices,* No. 4 (June 1974), pp. 1, 6, 43, 45, 46, 48; *Authors and Areas of the West Indies,* by Joseph and Johanna Jones, in *People and Places in World-English Literature,* No. 2, Austin, Texas, p. 72; Bruce McM. Wright, "No Longer Blinded by Our Eyes. The Poetry of Derek Walcott: The Return of the Exile as Exile," in *Shango* I (I) (1973); *The Poetry of Derek Walcott,* a full-length treatment by John Figueroa, is being prepared for publication by Three Continents Press (Washington, D.C.).

WALCOTT, Roderick

b. January 23, 1930, St. Lucia.
Playwright, producer.

Roddy, as he is known throughout Caribbean Theatre, has done many interesting things, but none, perhaps, as remarkable as his two musical plays based on the tradition of "the Battle of the Roses" in St. Lucia. "La Rose" was produced with much success at Carifesta, Guyana, 1972; and "La Marguerite" was specially done for the Commonwealth Heads of Governments meeting in St. Lucia in 1974.

Roddy has spent many years studying the Theatre—he has just finished his graduate work in this field in Toronto. But like his twin, Derek Walcott, he has also done a great deal with theatre workshops.

He works closely with his cast and musicians in the creation and preparation of his productions; he sometimes plays in the orchestra himself.

He has a powerful control of the Creole of St. Lucia and uses it to remarkable effect in his work. He has not published a great deal, but his work has had its affect in St. Lucia and elsewhere. His return home after graduate study in Canada will no doubt be very important to St. Lucia, and to the continuance of the remarkable work already done in that country in the theatre. Roddy has a gentle humor, and often shows a quiet and peaceful delight in his work.

He manages to use St. Lucian traditions and folklore without affectation, and with great relevance to the question of good and evil that beset people everywhere, but which, of course, have their special forms in St. Lucia. His character, the Banjo Man (from his recent play of that name) is a character and a symbol at the same time, and his sweet smile and surface levity reverberate to deeper meaning long after the play is over. It is hard to understand the kind of problems which Roddy Walcott's work used to have with the upholders of *public* morality in St. Lucia. But it is also a tribute to that very same complex, small, and interesting society that he was recalled from his studies to create a suitable "entertainment" for the Commonwealth Caribbean heads of Governments meeting in St. Lucia in 1974. And like the true Walcott he is, the entertainment was *not* the usual fare one gets at such conferences. It was long, funny, full of life and music, and underneath it all, of serious intent. One felt that it was something that had *grown* under his green finger, and as a result of his work with people like composer Charles Cadet, pianist "Bam" Charles, and the local chorus and orchestra. It might have needed pruning, but in typical fashion, it never lacked life.

He directed Derek Walcott's *Malcauchon, or Six in the Rain,* 1959, with the St. Lucia Arts Guild.

Writings: Plays: *The Harrowing of Benjy,* Caribbean Plays Edition, Kingston, Jamaica, University of the West Indies, 1958; *Shrove Tuesday March: A Play of the Steel Band,* Caribbean Plays Edition, Port of Spain, Trinidad, U.W.I., 1966; *A Flight of Sparrows,* Caribbean Plays Edition, Port of Spain, Trinidad, U.W.I., 1966; *Albino Joe,* Caribbean Plays Edition, Port of Spain, Trinidad, U.W.I., 1966; *Malfinis or the Heart of a Child,* Caribbean Plays Edition, Port of Spain, Trinidad, U.W.I., 1967; *The New Jamaica,* Kingston, Jamaica Welfare Ltd., Walkerwood Pioneer Club, 1945; *Banjo Man,* performed Carifesta, Guyana (Aug. 25-Sept. 15, 1972), for Caribbean Festival of the Creative Arts; *Chanson Marianne,* commissioned for the Conference of Prime Ministers of the West Indies, St. Lucia, 1974.

WALLACE, George B.

b. ca. 1920, Jamaica.
Poet, storywriter.

Wallace was a popular and prolific writer, often appearing in the *Daily Gleaner* and the *Sunday Gleaner.*

Writings: Poetry and Stories: *"You and I," a collection of verses* (with an introduction by Sir Philip M. Sherlock), Kingston, Gleaner Co., 1950; *"Scattered petals:" a collection of verses and short stories* (with an introduction by Kenneth B. Crooks), Kingston, Gleaner Co., 1951; *Ineffable moments: a collection of verses,* 1954; *"High Lights," a collection of verses old and new, in commemoration of "Jamaica 300,"* with an introduction by J.J. Mills, Kingston, Gleaner Co., 1955; *Flights of Fancy: a collection of verses and a short, short story,* Jamaica Times (Press) Ltd., 1961; *Reach for the Higher,* Kingston, United Printers, 1963; *Nestling blossoms; a collection of verse,* Kingston, Lithographic Printers, 1965 (Foreword by A.J. Newman).

WALLACE, Susan J.

b. ca. 1935, West End, Grand Bahama.
Poet, teacher.

After early schooling in West End and at St. John's College, Nassau, Wallace studied at the Nassau Teacher-Training College, the University of Exeter Institute of Education, and the University of Miami. After teaching elementary and high school classes, she taught at the Nassau Teacher-Training College and from 1968-69 was an official at the Bahamas Ministry of Education.

Married to an officer of the Department of Civil Aviation she writes poetry in her free time while teaching and raising her five children. Most of her poems are written in an easy sing-songy local English. "Shoppin' Trips" begins:

Sophisticated Nassau gals
Ar fin'in' erry day
Dat shoppin' in dey local shops,
Mos' certainly don' pay.

Writings: Poetry: *Bahamian Scene,* Philadelphia, Dorrance & Co., 1970, five printings by September, 1972.

WALROND, Eric

b. ca. 1896, Jamaica; d. 1966.
Storywriter, journalist.

Eric Walrond was a friend of the American

poet-critics Arna Bontemps, Langston Hughes and other members of the Harlem Renaissance group of the 1920's. His stories are realistic and generally sad. His view of life is grim but not quite completely pessimistic. His short stories are often set in a frustrating *ambience*—from a lonely shack in Guyana, to Barbados, and the West Indian slums of Panama.

Writings: Short Stories: *Tropic Death,* New York, Boni and Liveright, 1926; republished New York, Macmillan (Collier paperback), 1972.

Editor of: *Black and Unknown Bards,* Aldinton, Kent, Hand and Flaver, 1958.

WARNER, Keith Quinley

b. March 7, 1943, Port of Spain, Trinidad.
Poet, storywriter, critic, teacher.

After Warner completed his schooling at Queen's Royal College in Trinidad and at the University of West Indies, St. Augustine, he was awarded a French Governmental scholarship and completed his studies in French literature at Caen University in Normandy (licence ès lettres, 1967, doctorat de l'université, 1969).

For three years he taught francophone African literature and French literature at Howard University, Washington, D. C. In the Spring of 1971 he returned to Trinidad to teach the same subjects at the U.W.I. campus at St. Augustine.

Writings: Poetry and Fiction: in various journals and critical essays including *Black Images,* and *Voices;* collection: "Thoughts Can be Poems" (ms).

Editor and Collector of: *Voix Françaises du Monde Noir: Anthologie d'auteurs noirs francophones,* New York, Holt Rinehart and Winston, 1971.

In Progress: *Critical Perspectives on Léon Gontran Damas,* and *Black Shack Alley,* trans. of Joseph Zobel's *La Rue Case Négre,* both for Three Continents Press (Washington, D. C.).

Articles: "Eboué," in *Présence Africaine,* No. 82 (1972), "Negritude Revisited: an interview with Léon Damas," *Manna,* No. 3 (March 1973), and many others.

WATSON, Harold

(pseudonym: **H.A. MERSON**)
b. ca. 1912, Jamaica.
Poet, essayist, chemist.

Watson was sub-editor of *Catholic Opinion* from 1942 on for many years. Watson was, with Crab Nethersole and others, one of the group of middle-class intellectuals who at Sabina Park (Kingston Cricket Club) and elsewhere discussed endlessly, and with gusto, Socialism and Christianity, Independence and all that in the heady days of the arguments about Universal Adult Suffrage. He unfortunately did not really continue to write verse although he does have in manuscript a few good religious poems. He is one of that too large band of Jamaicans who after a promising start appear simply to give up writing poetry. He is the author of "Easy Essays," unpublished. McFarlane commented: "under the pen-name of H.A.

Merson, Mr. Watson, then a young man of twenty-eight, contributed four sonnets to *From Overseas* (Wright S. Fowler, ed., London, Marin Press, 1924), which raised great hopes in literary circles."

He contributed poems to the *Gleaner* and other newspapers and journals, and his verse is in *Caribbean Voices,* Vol. I (1966).

Two sonnets of his appeared in *A Treasury of Jamaican Poetry.*

WATT, Cynthia

b. November 27, 1923, Portsmouth, Dominca.
Storywriter, poet, newspaper columnist.

Cynthia Watt began writing at the age of ten, but had to wait many years to get some of her poems published in the mid-forties in the U.S.A. At present Watt is a newspaper columnist for the *Star,* a Dominican weekly, in which she has popularized "Ma Titine," a homely Dominican housewife who exposes all the foibles of current affairs in their real light. One of the "Ma Titine" series was broadcast over Radio Antilles (Montserrat). She is at present working on a novel.

Writings: Poetry: in *Talent: Song writers and Poets of Tomorrow,* New York, Haven Press, 194(?), and some poems in *Poesy IV,* J.R. Casimir (ed.), published by Advocate Press Barbados, 1948.

WEBBER, A.R.F.

b. ca. 1887, Tobago; lived in Guyana from youth; and died in Guyana (date not known).
Novelist, poet, journalist, editor.

Webber became the editor of a leading daily newspaper and also served as a legislator and politician. His novel *Those That Be in Bondage* first appeared in serial form, one of the first works of fiction to deal with East Indian immigration into the Caribbean.

Writings: Novel: *Those That Be in Bondage,* Georgetown, Daily Chronicle, 1917.
Poetry: in Cameron's *Guianese Poetry;* He also was published in local papers. His one separate volume is *Glints from an Anvil,* Georgetown, Daily Chronicle, 1918.
Commentary: *A Centenary History and Handbook of British Guiana,* Georgetown, Argosy, 1931.

WESCOTT, Lee

b. ca. 1920, Antigua.
Poet.

Wescott is one of the writers who has been writing for a long time in Antigua. He has published poetry variously. He has produced one volume and is working on another.

Writings: Poetry: *The Garden of Life, a Collection of Poems,* Barbados, Letchworth Press Ltd., n.d. (86 pp.).

WESTMAAS, David H.

b. ca. 1918, Guyana.
Storywriter, playwright.

Westmaas has had stories published in local periodicals. He is interested in Creole speech and published an essay in *Kyk-over-al* (1948): "On Writing Creolese."

Writings: Plays: *The Harvesters: A Play in the Vernacular in Three Scenes;* and *Old Suit, New Cloth: A Comedy.*

WICKHAM, John

(a.k.a. **Clemensford WILSDEN**)
b. 1923, Barbados.
Storywriter, critic, editor.

John Wickham, very much a son of the soil, has nonetheless lived and worked in many places outside of his beloved *Bimshire:* in Trinidad, England, France and Switzerland. He worked for the World Meteorological Organization in Geneva. His father was a well-known journalist in

Barbados, being editor of the *Herald,* a weekly, in the late twenties and early thirties.

Wickham has always been one of the mainstays of BIM, and he has now taken over the editing of that magazine from Frank Collymore. He has been facing the problems of rising costs in the midst of a depression, but already he is leaving his stamp on that most hardy of literary journals. He has held many important public service posts, being very much a community man: Secretary of the Writers' Guild, Port of Spain, Trinidad; President, Barbados Arts Council; Chairman Caribbean Resource Centre, Barbados. He has been a close friend to writers, including Collymore and Lamming, and one of his favorite writers is V.S. Naipaul.

Wickham is a quiet observer with a slow smile that lights up beautifully, as he faces an editor's problems or recalls an old Barbadian story—about his father perhaps. *Today* says of his collection of stories, *Casuarino Row,* that "West Indian culture [is] at its best showing how crucial personal identity is to any man but at the same time there is that shrewd thread of knowing how to live and share life in a society that draws its heartbeat from various cultures."

In 1975 he was awarded a Research Associateship by the International Development Research Centre of Canada. He is working on a novel: *Patriarchs and Prodigals,* and has been doing a certain amount of travelling in connection with it. Wickham is one of those persons in the Caribbean who over a number of years has been quietly writing, and making sure that the Philistines do not completely take over—but he has not been a full-time writer, having earned his living in other professional fields. One looks forward with great interest to his forthcoming novel, and with hopes that his powerful efforts will keep BIM alive and kicking for many more years.

Writings: Collection of Short Stories: *Casuarina Row,* Belfast, Ireland, Christian Journals Ltd., 1974. His short stories have appeared in many journals and anthologies, including: BIM; *Black I,* Ottawa, 1973; *Caribbean Rhythms* (James T. Livingston, ed.), Washington Square Press, New York, 1974; *34 x Schwarze Liebe* (German Anthology); *New Writing in the Caribbean,* Georgetown, Guyana, 1972; *BBC Short Stories,* London, BBC, 1967.

Essay: "West Indian Writing," BIM 50, pp. 168-180.

Autobiographical-Travel: "A Fragment of an Autobiography," BIM 54, pp. 72-77; "Notes from New York," BIM 34, pp. 135-140; "Dutch Excursion," BIM 25, pp. 17-24; "A Look at Ourselves," BIM 22, pp. 128-130; "Letter from Geneva," BIM 39, pp. 192-200; "Letter from Ferney," BIM 43, pp. 147-150; La Baie Revisited," BIM 52, pp. 248-252.

Reviews by Wickham: (in BIM): *Dream on Monkey Mountain* (Derek Walcott), in BIM 48, pp. 267-268; *A Wreath for Udomo* (Peter Abrahams), BIM 25, pp. 59-61; *Talk of the Tamarinds: An Anthology of Poetry for Secondary Schools* (A.N. Forde, ed.), BIM 54, pp. 109-113; *Sir Frank Worrell* (Undine Giuseppe), BIM 49, pp. 59-64; *Response* (Cecil Grey, ed.), BIM 49, pp. 59-64; *Man from the People* (Lionel Hutchinson), BIM 51, pp. 189-193; *Season of Adventure* (George Lamming), BIM 33, pp. 69-72; *Weymouth Poems* (K.C. Lewis), BIM 49, pp. 59-64; *The Hummingbird Tree* (Ian McDonald), BIM 49, pp. 59-64; *The Chosen Tongue: English Writing in the Tropical World* (Gerald Moore), BIM 51, pp. 189-193; *The West Indian Novel and its Background* (Kenneth Ramchand), BIM 52, pp. 255-256; *Shades of Grey* (Garth St. Omer), BIM 49, pp. 59-64; *The Plains of Caroni* (Samuel Selvon), BIM 51, pp. 189-193; *Froudacity: West Indian Fables Explained,* with an introduction by C.L.R. James (J.J. Thomas), BIM 51, pp. 189-193; *The Sun's Eye* (A. Walmsley, ed.), BIM 49, pp. 59-64.

WILES, Alan Richard

b. May 29, 1920, Kingston, Jamaica. Poet.

Wiles is a descendent of James Wiles, a famous botanist who brought breadfruit to

Jamaica with Captain Bligh. His poems appeared regularly in the *Daily Gleaner,* Kingston, and were collected in 1949 under the title of *Reveries,* with an introduction by J.E.C. McFarlane, the last paragraph of which must rate highly in the art of writing Forewords.

> *There is in Wiles' work no lack of the essential stuff of poetry; but I should expect that as his taste ripens and his skill increases with practice, much of his early work will be discarded or revised. This will be in keeping with the established principles of growth. For the present he is a fledgling bird singing to other fledglings of the beauty and mystery of the vast pageantry of Life of which he is himself a part.*

Writings: Poetry: *Reveries,* Kingston, printed by The Gleaner Co., Ltd., 1949.

WILLIAMS, Cecil ("Blazer")

b. ca. 1936, St. Vincent.
Poet, playwright.

Williams' two known verse collections are *The Crowd, a selection of poems* (Printed at The Model Printery, Kingstown, St. Vincent), and *Chains* (details not known).

WILLIAMS, Daniel (Danny)

b. 1927, New York City (of St. Vincent parentage); d. February, 1972, in St. Vincent.
Poet, lawyer.

Danny Williams, another of the many West Indian "all rounders" who played many roles in their society, was an affable person and generous. He was always socially involved in his community. At the same time he was well known beyond that community—even though his output as poet was not great. But in many ways it was remarkable, as John Figueroa put it in his memorial poem "For Danny Williams," written and read at Carifesta, 1972:

> *Your poems gentle in your way*
> *Seeped through our foo-foo stuffed bodies*
> *Enlightening them. They will lift*
> *Our youth quietly to see our skies.*
> (from *Ignoring Hurts*)

Williams was a close friend of two other significant St. Vincent writers, Shake Keane and Owen Campbell. While in no way inactive over social issues, there is about his work a certain calm strength, combined with a strong feeling for nature. In this latter feeling he combines his experience of temperate climates with his intimate knowledge of that arrangement of clouds and sea which is special to St. Vincent:

> *For here we have loved*
> *The wet mud clinging the hoemen's feet.*
> *Here in the soil our blood is green and*
> *In our wine the vine is parched with the*
> *Heat of our hope....*
> ("Over here," from *Caribbean Voices,* Vol. II, p. 81, J. Figueroa, ed.)

Danny died tragically in an automobile accident in St. Vincent at Carnival time.

Writings: Poetry: in various reviews and collections, including: *Caribbean Verse; Caribbean Voices; Caribbean Quarterly; Kyk-over-al* (No. 22 of 1957).

Critical reviews: in various journals. His review of E. McG. Keane's *L'Oubli,* published by the Advocate Co. of Barbados, is in BIM 13, pp. 69-71.

WILLIAMS, Denis

b. 1923, Georgetown, Guyana.
Novelist, painter, teacher.

A lively and active worker, Denis Williams started out as a painter and teacher of art. In the Sudan, where he became very attached to the desert, he started working on his novel *Other Leopards.* He often used to comment that the desert was the true begetter of great religions. As the hero of that book puts it: "Between Europe and

Africa there is this desert.... Between black and white, this mulatto divide. You cannot cross, whoever you are, and remain the same.... I have given this desert my soul ..."

Denis Williams was educated in Guyana and at the Camberwell School of Art in England (1950-1957). He has taught and lectured widely in England, Khartoum, Ife and Lagos. He has held exhibitions in London and Paris.

In Khartoum a new kind of perception and sensibility, almost one might say a new kind of thinking, was forced upon him by the mode of art and drawing and patterning he found there. He was Lecturer in Fine Arts at the Khartoum Technical Institute of African Studies, and then at the University of Ife in Nigeria.

His *The Third Temptation* employs a sharply focussed series of "Viewpoints" of very different people in a few hours at an English seaside resort.

Denis Williams has now settled in Guyana and is working with a new day of seeing his surroundings. He had always been interested in the theoretical side of art—as well as in its craft—this theoretical interest comes out clearly in his Mittelholzer Memorial Lectures, "Image and Idea in the Arts of Guyana."

Writings: Novels: *Other Leopards,* London, Hutchinson, 1963; *The Third Temptation: A Novel,* London, Calder and Boyars, 1968.

Commentary: "An Exchange of Letters," in *Kyk-over-al* 24 (1958), p. 96 (D.W. and A.J. Seymour).

Essays: *Image and Idea in the Arts of Guyana,* Georgetown, National History and Arts Council, 1969 (text of Edgar Mittelholzer Memorial Lectures); "Guiana Today," *Kyk-over-al* 9 (1949), p. 9; "Art and Society," *Kaie* 11 (1973), p. 100 (paper given at Carifesta, 1972).

Stories: in various anthologies, including: *Stories from the Caribbean; Caribbean Narrative* (with extract from novel); *New Writing in the Caribbean* (extract from novel).

Biography: *Giglioli in Guyana 1922-1972,* Georgetown, National History and Arts Council, 1973.

Biographical/Critical Sources: review of *The Third Temptation* by K.L. Goodwin, in *World Literature Written in English,* No. 19 (April 1971), p. 93; Kenneth Ramchand, *The West Indian Novel and its Background* (London, Faber and Faber, 1970), pp. 159, 161-163 (discussion of *Other Leopards*).

WILLIAMS, Eric

b. September 25, 1911, Trinidad.
Essayist, historian, statesman.

This distinguished West Indian historian, and Prime Minister of Trinidad and Tobago, is not, of course, a literary man in the usual sense of that term. But his writings have had a wide-spread influence on the thinking and writing of the Caribbean. Dr. Williams graduated from Oxford in 1935; and received his doctorate from that university in 1938. He was Professor of Political and Social Science at Howard University, and served with the Caribbean Commission. In 1962 he became the first Prime Minister of Trinidad and Tobago, having been previously first Chief Minister.

He has been the Political Leader of the P.N.M. since its inception in 1956.

Writings: Critical Essay: "Four poets of the Greater Antilles," *Caribbean Quarterly,* II, 4, (1952).

History: *The Negro in the Caribbean,* Bronze Booklet, No. 8 (Associate in Negro Folk Education) 1942; New York, Haskell, 1970; *The Economic Future of the Caribbean* (joint author with E. Franklin Frazier), Washington, D.C., Howard University Press, 1944; *Capitalism and Slavery,* Chapel Hill, University of North Carolina Press, 1944; London, Deutsch, 1964, 1944; *History of the People of Trindad and Tobago,* London, Deutsch, 1964; *British Historians and the West Indies,* Port of Spain, P.N.M. Publishing Co., 1964; New York, Africana, 1972; *Documents on British West Indian History—1807-1833,* Port of Spain, Historical Society of Trinidad and Tobago, 1952; *Inward Hunger: The Education of a Prime Minister,* introduction by Sir Denis Brogan, Chicago, University of Chicago Press, 1971; *From Columbus to Castro. The History of the Caribbean,* London, Deutsch, 1970; and New York, Harper and Row, 1971; *Some historical reflections on the church and the Caribbean,* Trinidad, Public Relations Division, Office of the prime Minister, 1973.

Numerous pamphlets and articles in historical journals and work on selective documents relating to West Indian history.

WILLIAMS, Gershom

b. 1936, Jamaica.
Novelist.

Williams emigrated to Canada in 1965 and has held many jobs, including that of hospital orderly while trying to support his writing. On his own account he risked $1,500 to publish 1,000 copies of his first novel, *The Native Strength.*

Writings: Novel: *The Native Strength,* Toronto, published by author, 1968.

Biographical/Critical Sources: review by Darryl Dean, "A Jamaican Native Shows His Strength," in *Express* (Port of Spain, Dec. 25, 1968), p. 16.

WILLIAMS, James

b. ca. 1804, Jamaica; death year undetermined.
Autobiographer.

An apprenticed laborer in Jamaica, Williams' *A Narrative of Events,* published in the first third of the 19th century is one of the early bits of writing in English connected with Jamaica.

Writings: Autobiography: *A Narrative of Events since the first of August, 1834,* third edition, London, W. Ball, 1837 (30 pp.).

WILLIAMS, Milton

b. 1936, Guyana.
Poet.

After schooling and miscellaneous jobs at home, Williams emigrated to England in 1959, and presently lives in New Castle-upon-Tyne.

Williams' poetry appears in *Breaklight; My Lovely Native Land; Poet 13,* I, and other local collections; also it is in journals, including *Kyk-over-al* (to which he was a regular contributor); *Kaie; Nouvelle somme de poésie du monde noir* (Paris, Présence Africaine, No. 57, 1966).

Writings: Poetry: *Pray for Rain,* Georgetown, Argosy Co., 1958 (Miniature Poets Series). Three of his poems, "For Martin Carter," "Sister Alno," and "Black Boy" appear in *Melanthika, An Anthology of Pan-Caribbean Writings* (1977).

WILMOT, Cynthia

(Mrs. Fred WILMOT)

b. ca. 1920, Canada (has lived in Jamaica for many years).
Playwright (radio and TV), storywriter, journalist.

Wilmot has been very involved in radio, TV, press and art circles in Jamaica and currently is producer/director in the films section of API (formerly Jamaica Information Service). She has won many awards in the Jamaica National Festival Competitions for her plays.

Wilmot has published stories and articles in numerous magazines and newspapers. With her husband she has for the past 35 years written radio drama and documentaries for the Canadian Broadcasting Corporation as well as for Jamaican radio and television.

Writings: Plays: Radio: *Mistress of the Revelles* (Certificate of Merit, and an Alcan Award—Festival, 1967); *The Phantom Riders* (Bronze Medal—Festival, 1968).

Television: *Monster Among Us* (Bronze Medal—Festival, 1968); *Morning Encounter* (Bronze Medal—Festival, 1968); *Visitors to Tea* (Bronze Medal—Festival, 1970).

WILMOT, Frederic (Fred) Alexander

b. October 10, 1918, Toronto, Canada (of Jamaican parents).
Journalist, radio script writer, broadcaster, public relations expert.

Wilmot was a radio writer (1944-45), Associate Editor of *The Advocate* (Vancouver, 1945-46), and author of many radio plays and series for CBC over the past 35 years. He has lived in Jamaica since the early 1950s. He was also editor of *Public Opinion* (Jamaica, 1951-54), Assistant Editor of *Spotlight* News Magazine (1954-56), and a script writer, producer, and free-lance broadcaster in Jamaica on radio, and JBC, radio and television. He was at one time associated with the Jamaica Tourist Board and now runs his own public relations office.

Wilmot has published stories and articles in various magazines and newspapers.

WILSON, D.G. (Don)

b. ca. 1921, Jamaica.
Poet, teacher, editor.

Educated at St. George's College, and at universities in both the United States and the West Indies, Don Wilson has done further work at London University. Always interested in the teaching of English, he encouraged, and worked with a group of teachers, starting when many of them were in their Dip. Ed. year in the old U.W.I. Department of Education. In the end he and they produced *New Ships,* which was first published in *Savacou,* and more recently by Oxford University Press.

He has also done interesting work on the English spoken by children in their schools, in Jamaica; and on the teaching of reading.

Writings: Editor of Anthology: *New Ships,* Kingston, Savacou Publications, 1971, and London, Oxford University Press, 1975.

WILSON, Jeanne

b. ca. 1932, Jamaica.
Playwright, novelist.

Jeanne Wilson has gained many awards for her plays in the Jamaica National Festival Competitions and has been active in literary circles; she became professor of the P.E.N. International Jamaica branch in 1975 on the retirement of Daisy Myrie. Her historical novel is to be published by Macmillan, London and in the United States by M. Evans Inc. of New York. The second novel—a sequel—is in the hands of Macmillan, London.

Writings: Plays: *The Heiress,* one act, produced in Jamaica, 1962, at Secondary Schools Drama Festival; *A Legacy for Isabel,* one act, London, Evans Bros., 1967; *A Question of Loyalty,* one act, produced Jamaica, 1966, Secondary Schools Drama Festival; *No Justice in October,* one act, London, Evans Bros., 1967; produced Jamaica, 1961, Secondary Schools Drama Festival; *No Medicine for Murder,* one act, High Commendation, Festival 1965; *Reality is Relative,* one act, High Commendation, Festival 1965; *No Truth at All,* one act, Certificate of Merit, Festival 1966.

WINT, Pam

b. 1953, Jamaica.
Writer, librarian, dance group director.

Pam Wint was educated at the Convent of Mercy Academy, Jamaica. She has been Assistant Librarian of the Jamaica Library Service, and a part-time teacher of Dance and Drama. She directs "The Heroes," a children's dance group.

She contributed to the anthology, *One Love,* edited by Audvil King, London, The Bogle-L'Overture Publications, 1971.

WOLCOTT, Mary Adella

(see under pseudonym: **TROPICA**)

WOODSLEY, H. Austin

(pseudonym for **Edgar MITTELHOLZER**)

WYKE, Marguerite

b. ca. 1928, Trinidad.
Poet, potter, politician.

Wyke has served as a Senator in the former West Indian Parliament. She works with several art forms—clay, mosaics and glass. Her verse has been published in *Voices; Canadian Forum;* BIM; and included in the *Caribbean Quarterly, Federation Commemoration Issue—Anthology of West Indian Poetry* (Vol. 5, No. 3, April 1958). She is very active in the culture and fine arts of Trinidad and Tobago.

WYNTER, Sylvia

(a.k.a. **Wynter CAREW**)
b. ca. 1932, Cuba (of Jamaican parents).
Critic, playwright, novelist, dancer, actress, teacher.

After her high school education in Jamaica, she went on to university studies in London and Madrid. She worked for some time at U.W.I, Mona, and is now teaching in the United States.

Sylvia Wynter is another example of the fact that life is not as specialized in the West Indies as it is elsewhere. A vibrant person, she has many talents, but more recently she seems to have been concentrating on criticism, working out perhaps in greater detail the ideas she put forward at ACLALS meeting in Jamaica in February 1971 on the relation of "plantation and plot" to the whole cultural complex of places like Jamaica. Perhaps the best place to date to see her criticism at work is in her "One Love: Rhetoric or Reality?—Aspects of Afro-Jamaicanism," a rather long and powerful article in *Caribbean Studies* (Oct. 1972). She challenges such well known personalities as Louise Bennett, Rex Nettleford and Andrew Salkey. She also says much that is positive and enlightening on the use of language (including the so-called "dialect"), and on what might rather vulgarly be characterized as "bandwagonism" in the whole cultural Afro field.

Her *Rockstone Anancy* (with Alex Gradussov) attempted to use the very popular Jamaica Pantomime to put across a "new" view of Brer Anancy—for Sylvia Wynter is not above having a moral to her tales. "Rockstone" was somewhat too wordy, but was a very interesting experiment in using an "entertainment" to "instruct"; the title, incidentally, has nothing to do with Rock—hard or soft, but is the usual Jamaican word for *stone,* and is usually pronounced *rak-toun.*

Sylvia Wynter (who wrote under the name of Wynter Carew while married to Jan Carew) has now joined the long list of talented West Indians, who, for one reason or another, have found it necessary or expedient to leave the U.W.I. and/or the West Indies to work and make their contribution elsewhere. One looks forward to any further work she might do in the field of criticism in the Caribbean—a field which needs much development by those who can, and will, take the local cultural realities truly into account.

She has translated and adapted several classical Spanish prose works for the BBC.

Writings: Novel: *The Hills of Hebron: a Jamaican novel,* New York, Simon and Schuster, 1962, and Jonathan Cape, London, 1962; adaptation (for children) of Jan Carew's novel *Black Midas,* London, Longmans, 1970.

Plays: (with Jan Carew) *The University of Hunger,* performed Georgetown Theatre Guild, 1966; also broadcast BBC, 1961 (televised BBC 1962 as *The Big Pride*); (with Jan Carew) *Miracle in Lime Lane,* Spanish Town, Jamaica, Folk Theatre, 1962; *1865 Ballad for a Rebellion, epic story of Morant Bay Rebellion,* produced Jamaica, 1965; *Brother Man* (adaptation of Roger Mais' novel of the same name), produced Jamaica, 1965; *Rate of Exchange* typescript; *Ssh ... it's a Wedding,* musical, Jamaica, 1961?; *Under the Sun* (adaptation of her novel [in manuscript] of that name, three acts, in mimeo version only; *Rockstone Anancy, a magical morality* (Jamaican Pantomime) with Alex Gradussov, produced in Jamaica, 1970; *Breakout,* three acts, in ms. (with Jan Carew).

Critical Essays: in various journals: "We must learn to sit down together and talk about a little culture, reflections on West Indian Writing and Criticism," in *Jamaica Journal,* Vol. 2, No. 4 (1968), pp. 23-32, and Vol. 3, No. 1 (1969), pp. 27-42; *Lady Nugent's Journal,* review article in *Jamaica Journal,* Vol. I, No. 1 (Dec. 1967), pp. 23-34; "One Love: Aspects of Afro-Jamaicanism," in *Caribbean Studies,* Vol. 12, No. 3 (Oct. 1972), pp. 64-99; "Bernardo de Balbuena: epic poet and Abbot of Jamaica 1562-1627," in two parts, *Jamaica Journal,* Vol. 3, No.3 (Sep. 1969), pp. 3-12 and Vol. 3, No. 4 (Dec. 1969); "An Introductory essay to an adaptation of Garcia Lorca's *The House of Bernardo Alba,"* and an extract from the adapted play, entitled *The House and Land of Mrs. Alba,* in *Jamaica Journal,* Vol. 2, No. 3 (Sep. 1968), pp. 48-56; "Jonkonnu in Jamaica," in *Jamaica Journal,* Vol. 4, No. 2 (June 1970), pp. 34-48; article: "Towards the interpretation of Folk Dance as a Cultural Process."

Poetry: in various journals, including *New World Quarterly* (Dead Season), Vol. 2, No. 1 (1965), p. 12.

Biographical/Critical Sources: Kenneth Ramchand, *The West Indian Novel and its Background,* London, Faber, 1970; Karl Sealy, review of *The Hills of Hebron* in BIM, Vol. 9, No. 36 (Jan-June 1963); George Pantin, "Bedward in new guise": a review of *The Hills of Hebron,* in *Sunday Gleaner* (Kingston, Jamaica, July 22, 1962); "Loss of a prophet": a review of *The Hills of Hebron* in *Times Literary Supplement,* No. 3161 (Sep. 28, 1962), p. 75.

YARDAN, Shana

b. ca. 1942, Guyana.
Poet.

Shana Yardan is comparatively a new writer on the Guyanese scene. She is one of the six women who contributed poetry and published *Guyana Drums* (Georgetown, Guyana, 1972). Before *Guyana Drums* she won second prize and two honorable mention awards for her poetry entries in the National History and Arts Open Competition, 1972.

Yardan's work is included in Arthur Seymour's *New Writing in the Caribbean,* and she has also been published in *Kaie.*

YETMING, Cline

b. ca. 1936, Trinidad.
Playwright, poet.

Yetming studied creative writing at the University of British Columbia under Earle Birney.

Writings: Play: *An Echo of Drums; a play in two acts,* performed March 1966 at Town Hall, Port of Spain, in mimeo at U.W.I., St. Augustine, Trinidad.

Poetry: in various collections, including Sealy's *Voices.*

YORK, Andrew

(pseudonym for **Christopher NICOLE**)

Supplementary List of Writers from Belize

FULLER, Hugh F.

b. 1918, Belize.
Poet, administrator, broadcaster, vaudeville entertainer, elocutionist.

Fuller has held a myriad of administrative posts in the recently conceived and constructed neo-Mayan city of Belmopan, Belize's new capital. He is presently with the Office of Reconstruction and Development.

His poetry as well as his prose has been called both virile and patriotic. In "Mayan Reverie" he celebrates the natural beauties of the country and the sanctity of domestic life.

This is the land I love. The murmuring of
pines and palm trees,
And bearded baboons filling nights with
eerie chatter.
Clear from the river dark, hard backed,
the alligators bark,
And yellow lights gleam from the
thatched-roof villaged
Like fireflies signalling in the night.

Writings: Poetry: in *Belizean Poets,* Belmopan, Belize, Government Printing Information Service, n.d.

HYDE, Evan X.

b. 1947, Belize City, Belize.
Poet, playwright, storywriter, politician.
After local schooling, Hyde won a United States sponsored scholarship offered through the State Department. He attended Dartmouth College in New Hampshire and graduated magna cum laude with his B.A. in English. Joining the active black movement in the U.S., he began to think about issues at home in new ways and on his return turned to politics. He also launched the literary group "Amandaal" which had political intentions as well toward pushing for complete independence.

His first collection of poems, *North Amerikkkan Blues* (1971) speaks of American society which "spin the web of whiteness around me." In his preface "Before I do" he characterizes his writing as a special brand . . .

This story is written and it is a kind of English and you cannot interrupt me when you are not sure of what I am saying . . .

It would be better if I could talk this story to you in raw creole and you could top me when you are not sure of what I am saying."

His poem "About poems" says it this way:

We didn't know
no better
we was small
we was slaves

and the poet complains he was told:

Poems is like this
Trees by Joyce Kilmer
God can make a tree
poems by a fool like me
poems is like this-
they have to rhyme
in every line
and every time
poems must be nice

in his poems, he insists:

They is violence
they is not nice
neither proper
nor correct
most uncourteous.

His play *Haad Times* won the 1971 Wesley College festival in Belize City. Written in "raw creole" it was found "unintelligible" by Robert A. Johnston, an American critic, who published *Theatre of Belize* (1973).

The play deals with the triumph of love over the usual deep privation and isolation of the Caribbean poor.

In his story "A Guilty Man" the protagonist is a victim of his wife's flight to New York and of the last shreds of a colonial administration. The same note is struck in "So you're leaving" where the abandoned husband cries after his wife:

You're not going to no Cayo
It's L.A. on your mind.

The governing party in Belize, the P.U.P. of George Price, was believed by Hyme to be inimical to his politico-literary efforts, but in 1975 his collection *Feelings,* an anthology of stories, poems, and one play, was published under the patronage of C.L.B. Rogers, the Deputy Premier.

Writings: Poetry: in miscellaneous journals and in two collections: *Belize. The Voices of Your Children,* Belize City, n.d., and *Feelings,* Belize City, 1975.

Play: *North Amerikkkan Blues,* Belize City, 1971.

Political: *The Crowd call UBAD: The Story of a People's Movement,* Belize City, 1970.

MARTINEZ, James S.

b. ca. 1900, Belize; d. ca. 1945.
Poet.

Possibly the first published collection of poetry by a Belizean was Martinez' *Caribbean Jingles* (1920). Though heavily encrusted with outmoded 19th century language and diction, he could occasionally break free into an earthy, simple creole. With no formal education and growing up in the mahogany forest-cutting camps, his work naturally is full of the concerns and joys of the lumberman's life.

Compare the sentimental valentine of "Life's Success":

What is the success of life I pray
Is it the wealth that we possess?
Of treasures hoarded day-by-day?
Is that the success of life you say?

with these lines from "Fus Lag Day":

Talk about a time at Benk w'en Cutter's
feelin' gay,
Jus' go an' see dem at de time
w'en it is Fus Lag Day!

De fo'man o' de work would den put up a
nice big treat,
wid quite a lot of rum to drink an'
lat's o' t'ings to eat.

Writings: Poetry: *Caribbean Jingles,* London, 1920; two poems cited above appear in *Belizean Poets,* Vol. II, Belmopan, Belize, Government Printing Information Service, n.d.

PRICE, George Cadle

b. 1919, Belize City, Belize.
Poet, statesman, historian.

Price attended a Catholic seminary in Mississippi (U.S.A.) from 1934 to 1936 when he returned home to enter politics.

After founding the People's United Party in 1950 in the former British Honduras, Price remained at the head of the independence movement, becoming Prime Minister of Belize in 1964, a position he still holds.

The bulk of Price's poetry is patriotic. He writes in Spanish and English and often employs the local English creole as in his "Limestone Pillars of Belikin" which glorifies the new capital up-country from old Belize City:

Belikin awoke united and saw mol-cab
dawn of nationhood.
From northern sky by silver bird brings
new zac stranger.
But at his coming limestone pillars and
temples rise again
At tunben-cah safe site of tropic beauty,
and
Maya splendour returns to Belikin.

Writings: Poetry: "Limestone pillars of Belikin" and "Beliceños unánomos para construir nuestra nación," in local journals and collected with other verse in the volume, *Belizean Poets,* Vol. II, Belmopan, Belize, Government Information Service, n.d.

Frank Collymore

Louise Bennett

Derek Walcott

WEST INDIAN LITERATURE AND CULTURE: BIBLIOGRAPHIES

A Select List of Works on the British Caribbean. Prepared by the University of the West Indies Library, 13th February, 1964.

An Index to BIM (Reinhard Sander, comp. and ed.). University of the West Indies, Extra Mural Studies Unit, Trinidad and Tobago, St. Augustine, 1973.

Boxill, Anthony. "Bibliography of W.I. Fiction," in *World Literature Written in English Newsletter,* 1970, pp. 24-44.

Caribbean Studies (each issue has a selected bibliography [current] of the Caribbean [general], edited by Neida Pagan).

Comitas, Lambos. *Caribbeana: A Topical Bibliography 1900-1965,* published for Research Institute for the Study of Man, Univ. of Washington Press, Seattle, and London, 1968.

________. *The Complete Caribbeana 1900-1975. A Bibliographic Guide to Scholarly Literature.* 3 vols. Millwood, N. Y., Kto Press (Kraus-Thomson), 1977.

Carifesta '72 (Catalogue). Book Exhibition: August 25-September 15, at Public Free Library, Georgetown, Guyana.

Christiani, Joan (comp.). *A.J. Seymour. A Bibliography.* Georgetown: Georgetown National Free Library, Georgetown, Guyana.

Commonwealth Caribbean Writers (A Bibliography). Stella Merriman and Joan Christiani (comps.). Georgetown: Public Free Library, 1970 (on Brathwaite, Carew, Harris, Hearne, Lamming, Sherlock, Wynter).

Contemporary West Indian Literature: An Annotated Book List prepared by the Kingston and St. Parish Library to accompany an "Exhibition of Contemporary West Indian Literature" to celebrate Jamaica's Independence, August 6, 1962.

Creative Writers in Trinidad and Tobago; a bibliography, by Maritza Pantin and Diane Hunte. St. Augustine, Trinidad, University of the West Indies Library, 1970; prepared on the occasion of the opening of the John F. Kennedy Library, U.W.I., St. Augustine.

Cundall, Frank. *Bibliographia jamaicensis.* Kingston: Institute of Jamaica, 1902; Supplement, 1908.

________. *Bibliography of the West Indies* (excluding Jamaica). Kingston: Institute of Jamaica, 1909.

Current Caribbean Bibliography. Vol. 7. San Juan, Puerto Rico: Caribbean Commission, 1957 (Special feature: A Bibliography of West Indian Literature).

Georgetown Public Library—Guyanese Plays and their Location; a bibliography. Georgetown, Guyana: Public Library, 1970.

Harris, L.J. and Ormerod, D.A. *A preliminary check-list of West Indian Fiction in English 1949-1964.* London, 1966; extract from *20th Century Literature,* Vol. 2 (1965-1966).

Ingram, K.E. "Bibliographical Control of Commonwealth Caribbean Government Publications," in *Research Library Cooperation in the Caribbean,* edited by Alma Jordan (American Library Association, 1973), pp. 87-100.

Kingston Institute of Jamaica. *A Guide to Jamaican Reference Material in the West Indian Reference Library,* by Rae Delattre, 1965.

Kingston Institute of Jamaica, West Indian Reference Library. *Jamaican Accessions,* 1964, 1965, 1966, 1967.

Literature of the English and French-Speaking West Indies in the University of Florida Libraries. Bibliography compiled by Karl Watson, Center for Latin American Studies, Gainesville, Florida, 1971.

McDowell, Robert E. *Bibliography of Literature from Guyana.* Arlington, Texas, Sable Publishing Corporation, 1975.

Manuscripts Relating to Commonwealth Caribbean Countries in United States and Canadian Repositories, Caribbean Universities Press in association with Bowker Publishing Co., 1975.

New York Public Library. *List of Works in the New York Public Library relating to the West Indies.* New York, 1912.

"Plays of the English Speaking Caribbean" (Bibliography), in *Bulletin of Black Theatre* (6 issues so far), by Errol Hill (first issue, Winter, 1972).

Public Library Barbados. *Our Common Heritage* (A bibliography of Barbadian writers), 1971.

"Representative West Indian Authors," p.v., Contents, in *Savacou* Journal of the Caribbean Artists Movement, annual listing of West Indian work.

Ramchand, Kenneth. *The West Indian Novel and its Background.* New York, Barnes and Noble, 1970 (Author bibliography: pp. 274-281; Year by Year bibliography: 1903-1967: pp. 282-286; Secondary bibliographies: pp. 287-289.

Roth, Vincent. *Bibliography of British Guiana,* compiled under the aegis of the British Guiana Bibliography Committee by its chairman, Hon. Vincent Roth, M.L.C., by direction of the Governor, 1943.

Short Bibliography of Recent Literature on Jamaica: Relative Comparative Literature on British West Indies; prepared list in Library, University of the West Indies, Mona, Kingston, Jamaica (general).

University of the West Indies. Cave Hill Campus, Barbados. *Main Library Check List of Items in the West Indian Collection at 29th June, 1971.*

Trinidad and Tobago Central Library. A Selection of West Indian Novels. Port of Spain, Trinidad: Adult Education Centre, 1964.

West Indian Drama in English: A Select Bibliography by Lloyd W. Brown, University of Southern California, *Studies in Black Literature—6* (1975).

West Indian Literature: A Select Bibliography. Compiled by the University of the West Indies Library, Mona, Kingston, Jamaica, 1964. Supplement 1964-1967.

West Indies University Department of Extra Mural Studies, St. Augustine, U.W.I. *Publications: Caribbean Plays; Folklore; West Indian Literature,* etc., St. Augustine, Trinidad, U.W.I., Extra Mural Department, 1967.

Wright, Philip. *List of Jamaican and other West Indian Newspapers in the West Indies Reference Library of the Institute of Jamaica.* On cards up to 1959. Contents: Alphabetical List of titles, List of holdings, List of titles year by year.

Walkley, Jane (comp.). "A Decade of Caribbean Literary Criticism: A Select Annotated Bibliography," in *The Literary Half Quarterly* (Mysore, India) XI, 2 (July 1970), pp. 187-195.

THE WEST INDIES: CRITICAL STUDIES

Abrahams, Peter. *Jamaica: An Island Mosaic.* London: H.M. Stationery Office, 1957.

Abrams, Ovid S. *Guyana Metagee (Folk Songs Queh Queh).* Georgetown: Labour Advocate Job Printing, Bustar Republic Issue, 1970.

Allsopp, Stanley R.R. "Folklore in Guyana: Building a Guyanese Tradition," *Kaie,* No. 4 (1967), 37-41.

Aykroyd, W.R. *Sweet Malefactor: Sugar, Slavery and Human Society.* London: Heinemann, 1967.

Baker, S.J. "The Literature of Pidgin English," in *American Speech,* Vol. 19 (1944), 271-275.

Baugh, Edward. 'Frank Collymore and the Miracle of BIM," *New World,* Barbados Independence Issue, 1966, 129-133.

___________. "West Indian Poetry, 1900; a study in cultural decolonisation," in *Savacou* (1971), 19-20.

___________. "Toward a West Indian Criticism," in *Caribbean Quarterly,* XIV, Nos. 1-2 (1968), 140-144.

___________. *West Indian Poetry: A Study in Cultural Decolonisation.* Pamphlet No. 1, Savacou Publications, 1972.

Blackman, Margot. "Barbadian Proverbs," BIM 11, No. 43 (1966), 158-163.

Boxill, H.F. "The Novel in the West Indies, 1900-1962." Unpublished Ph.D. dissertation, University of Brunswick, 1968.

Braithwaite, Edward. "Jazz in the West Indian Novel," BIM, Vol. 11, No. 44 (1967), 275-284; Vol. 11, No. 45 (July-December 1967), 39-51; Vol. 12, No. 46 (January-June 1968), 115-126.

___________. "The New West Indian Novelists," BIM, Vol. 8, No. 31 (July-December 1960), 199-210; BIM, Vol. 8, No. 32 (January-June 1961), 271-280.

___________. "West Indian Prose Fiction in the Sixties, a Survey," BIM, Vol. 12, No. 47 (July-December 1968), 157-165.

___________. "West Indian Prose in the Sixties: a Survey," *The Critical Survey* (Winter 1967), 169-174.

Braithwaite, P.A. and Serena. *Folk Songs of Guyana in Words and Music (Queh-Queh, Chants and Plantation Themes).* Kingston: Institute of Jamaica, West Indies Reference Library, 1966.

___________. *Folk Songs of Guyana.* Georgetown, 1970.

Brett, William H. (comp.) and Leonard Lambert (ed.). *Guiana Legends.* London: S.P.C.K., 1931.

Brown, Lloyd W. "The Calypso Tradition in West Indies Literature," in S.O. Mezu's *Modern Black Literature.* Buffalo: Black Academy Press, 1971.

Bryden, Ronald. "West Indian Writing," in *The New Statesman,* Vol. 219, No. 1771 (February 19, 1965), 278 ff.

"Caribbean Voices," in *The Times Literary Supplement* (August 5, 1955), XVI XVII, in Special Autumn Issue: "Writing Abroad."

Carr, W.I. "Reflections on the Novels of the British Caribbean," *Queen's Quarterly*, Vol. 71, 585-597.

Cartey, Wilfred. "The Rhythm of Society and Landscape." *New World.* Vol. II No. 3, Guyana Independence Issue (1966), 97-104.

Cassidy, Frederick G. *Jamaica Talk: 300 Years of the English Language in Jamaica.* New York: Macmillan, 1961.

Clasp, Bertram. "The extent to which West Indian Writers are hindered by conventional British Literature," in *Education Magazine* (Trinidad and Tobago League of Literary and Cultural Clubs).

Collymore, F.A. "Writing in the West Indies: A Survey," in *Tamarack Review*, No 14 (Winter 1960), 111-124.

Coulthard, George R. (ed.). *Race and Colour in Caribbean Literature.* London: Oxford University Press, 1962.

__________. "Caribbean literature reviewed," in *Times Literary Supplement*, No. 3 (March 24, 1966), 245.

__________. "The literature of the West Indies," in *The Commonwealth Pen.* Ithaca, New York: Cornell University Press, 1965, 185-202.

__________. "Literature of Latin America and the Caribbean," in *Caribbean Quarterly*, Vol. 10, No. 4 (December 1964), 46-54.

__________. "Rejection of European culture as a theme in Caribbean literature," in *Caribbean Quarterly*, Vol. 5, No. 4 (June 1959), 231-244.

Daly, P.H. *West Indian Freedom and West Indian Literature.* Georgetown, Guyana: Daily Chronicle Press, 1951.

Dathorne, O.R. "Africa in the Literature of the West Indies," in *Journal of Commonwealth Literature*, Vol. I (September 1965), 95-116.

__________. "Africa in West Indian Literature," in *Black Orpheus*, No. 16, 42-54.

Dewar, Lilian. "Jamaica in the Novel," in *Kyk-over-al*, Vol. III, No. 12 (Mid-Year 1951), 108-113.

Derrick, Anthony. "An Introduction to Caribbean Literature," in *Caribbean Quarterly*, Vol. 15, Nos. 2 and 3 (June-September 1969), 65-78.

Drayton, Arthur D. "The European Factor in West Indian Literature," in *The Literary Half Yearly*, XI, 1 (1970), 71-95.

__________. "West Indian Consciousness in West Indian Verse: an Historical Perspective," in *Journal of Commonwealth Literature*, No. 9 (July 1970), 66-88.

__________. "West Indian Fiction and West Indian Society," in *Kenyon Review*, Vol. XXV, No. 7 (Winter 1963), 127-141.

Figueroa, John. "Some Provisional Comments on West Indian Novels," in *Commonwealth Literature* (John Press, ed.). London: Heinemann, 1965.

Freeth, Zohra. *Run Softly, Demarara.* London, Allen and Unwin, 1966.

Gershator, David. "Poetry of the Virgin Islands: Past and Present," in *Revista Interamericana,* Vol. II, No. 3.

Gonzalez, Anson. *Self-Discovery through Literature: Creative Writing in Trinidad and Tobago.* St. Augustine, privately printed, 1972.

__________. *Trinidad and Tobago Literature: On Air.* Port of Spain, Trinidad: National Cultural Council of Trinidad and Tobago, 1973 (copyright), published 1974.

Gray, Cecil. "Folk Themes in West Indian Drama: an analysis," in *Caribbean Quarterly,* Vol. 14, Nos. 1-2 (1968), 102-109.

Green, James W. "Culture and Colonialism in the West Indies," in *Journal of Interamerican Studies and World Affairs,* Vol. 14, No. 4 (November 1972), 489-495.

Hall, Stuart M. "Lamming, Selvon and some trends in the West Indies Novel," BIM, Vol. 6, No. 23 (December 1955), 172-178.

Harris, Wilson. *Tradition, The Writer and Society.* London: Port of Spain, Trinidad, New Beacon Press, 1967.

Henriques, Fernando. "A Survey of West Indian Literature for 1965," in *Journal of Commonwealth Literature,* No. 2 (1966-1967), Leeds: School of English, Leeds University.

Hill, Errol. *Plays of the English Caribbean, Part II: Guyana; a Bibliography of the Black Theatre* in *Black Images,* No. 3 (Winter 1973).

Iremonger, Lucille. *The Young Traveller in the West Indies.* London: Phoenix, 1955.

Irish, James. "Magical Realism: A Search for Caribbean and Latin American Roots," *The Literary Half-Yearly,* XI, 2 (July 1970), 127-139.

James, C.L.R. *The Artist in the Caribbean.* Trinidad: Open Lecture Series, U.C.W.I., 1965.

__________. *Black Jacobins.* New York: Dial Press, 1938; New York: Random House, 1963.

__________. "Discovery Literature in Trinidad: 1. The 1930's," in *Journal of Commonwealth Literature,* No. 7 (July 1969), 73-80.

James, Louis. "Islands of Man: Reflections on the Emergence of a West Indian Literature," *Southern Review.* Adelaide, Australia, 150-163.

Jekyl, W. *Jamaica Song and Story: Anancy Stories, Digging Sings, Ring Tunes, and Dancing Tunes.* Introduction by A. Werner. New Jersey, U.S.A.: Dorker, 466.

Jones, Joseph. *Terranglia.* New York: Twayne Publishers, 1965.

__________, and Johanna Jones. *Authors and Areas of the West Indies.* Austin, Texas: Steck-Vaughn, 1970.

King, Audvil, with Althea Helps, Pam Wint and Frank Hastal. *One Love.* Kingston: Bogle-L'Overture Publications, 1971.

King, Bruce. *Literatures of the World in English* [includes West Indies, Nigeria, Kenya, S. Africa]. Boston: Routledge and Kegan Paul, 1975.

Klass, Merton. *East Indians in Trinidad: A Study of Cultural Persistance.* Philadelphia: Lippincott, 1961.

Lacovia, R.M. "Caribbean Aesthetics: A Prologomena," in *Black Images* (Monograph No. 1) Vol. 2, No. 2.

__________. "Caribbean Literature in English, 1949-1970," in *Modern Black Literature.* S.O. Mezu (ed.). Buffalo: Black Academy Press, 1971.

Lamming, George. "Caribbean Literature: the black rock of Africa," in *Africa Forum,* Vol. 1, No. 4, 32-52.

LaRose, John. *New Beacon Reviews, Collection One.* Port of Spain, New Beacon Books, 1968.

Le Page, R.B. "Dialect in West Indian Literature," *Journal of Commonwealth Literature,* No. 7 (July 1969), 1-7.

Livingston, James T. *Caribbean Rhythms: The Emerging English Literature of the West Indies.* New York: Washington Square Press, 1974.

Lucie-Smith, Edward. "West Indian Writing," *London Magazine,* Vol. 8, No. 4 new series (1968), 96-102.

MacDonald, Bruce. "The Growth of Social Consciousness in Trinidadian Fiction," unpublished Ph.D. dissertation, University of New Brunswick, 19??

McFarlane, J.E. Clare. *A Literature in the Making.* Kingston, Jamaica: Pioneer Press, 1956.

McLeod, A.L. (ed.). *The Commonwealth Pen.* Ithaca, New York: Cornell University Press, 1961.

McTurk, Michael ("Quow"). *Essays and Fables in Prose and Verse Written in the Vernacular of the Creoles of British Guiana.* Demerara: Argosy Office, Georgetown, 1891; reprinted Georgetown: The Daily Chronicle, 1949.

Mills, Therese. *Great West Indians: Life Stories for Young Readers.* London: Longman Caribbean, 1973.

Mittelholzer, Edgar. *Creole Chips.* Borbice, Lutheran Press N.A., 1937.

Moore, Gerald. *The Chosen Tongue: English Writing in the Tropical World.* London: Longmans, 1969.

__________. "The Negro Poet and His Landscape," in *Black Orpheus,* No. 22 (1967), 33-44.

Naipaul, V.S. *The Middle Passage.* London: Deutsch, 1962.

Oxaal, Ivan. *Black Intellectuals Come to Power in Trinidad.* Cambridge, Massachusetts: Schenkman Publishing Co., 1968.

Patterson, H. Orlando. *The Sociology of Slavery.* London: MacGibbon and Kee, 1967.

Pearce, Andrew. "West Indian Themes," *Caribbean Quarterly,* Vol. 2, No. 2, 12-23.

Pearcy, G. Etzel. *The West Indian Scene.* New York: Van Nostrant, 1965.

Pope-Hennessy, James. *West Indian Summer: A Retrospect.* London: Batsford, 1943.

Press, John (ed.). *Commonwealth Literature.* London: Heinemann, 1965.

Ramchand, Kenneth. "Decolonization in West Indian Literature," *Transition,* No. 22, 48-49.

__________. "Dialect in West Indian Fiction," *Caribbean Quarterly,* Vol. 14, Nos. 1 and 2 (March-June 1968), 27-42.

__________. "The Negro and the English Language in the West Indies," *Savacou,* I, 1 (1970), 33-44.

__________. "Obeah and the Supernatural in West Indian Literature," *Jamaica Journal,* II, 2 (June 1969), 52-54.

__________. "Some West Indian Novelists," in *Ibadan,* Vol. 4 (October 1958), 19-22.

__________ (ed.). *The West Indian Novel and Its Background.* London: Faber, 1970; and New York: Barnes and Noble, 1970.

__________. "Some West Indian Novelists," in *Ibadan,* Vol. 4 (October 1958), 19-22.

Ramsaran, J.A. "West Indian and French Caribbean Literature," in *New Approaches to African Literature: a guide to Negro-African Writing.* Ibadan: Ibadan University Press, 1965 [Chapter III, pp. 94-134].

Roberts, W. Adolphe. *Biographical Sketches of Six Great Jamaicans.* Kingston, Jamaica: The Pioneer Press, 1951 [of Jordan, Nuttall, Robert Love, Gordon and writers Redcam and DeLisser].

Rohlehr, F.G. *West Indian Poetry: Some Problems of Assessment* (mimeo copy in University of Trinidad, St. Augustine, dated 30 July 1971) and published with changes as "A Look at New Expressions in the Arts of the Contemporary Caribbean," in *Caribbean Quarterly,* Vol. 17, Nos. 3 and 4 (September-December 1971), 92-113.

Sander, Reinhard W. (comp.). *An Index to BIM,* foreword by E.M. Ramesar, introduction by Edward Baugh, and with an interview with Frank Collymore, Port of Spain, Trinidad: University of the West Indies, 1973.

Sertima, Ivan van. *Caribbean Writers: Critical Essays.* London: New Beacon, 1968; and Port of Spain: New Beacon Books, 1968.

Seymour, A.J. "The Novel in the British Caribbean," in BIM, Vol. 11, No. 42 (January-June 1966), 83-85, Vol. 11, No. 43 (July-December 1966), 176-180; Vol. 11, No. 44 (January-July 1967), 238-242, No. 46 (January-June, 1968), 75-80.

__________. "From Raleigh to Carew: the books of Guiana," in *Kyk-over-al,* Vol. 9, No. 27 (December 1960), 74-82.

__________. "Guianese Poetry," in *Kyk-over-al,* Vol. 1, No. 2 (June 1946), 13-16.

__________. "The Themes of West Indian Novels," in *Kyk-over-al,* Vol. 8, No. 24 (December 1958), 60-103.

Shaw, Bradley (comp. & ed.). *Latin American Literature in Translation: An Annotated Bibliography.* New York: Center for Inter-American Relations, 1976.

Shepherd, Phyllis. *Guyanese Plays and Their Location.* Georgetown: Guyana Public Library, 1967.

Sherlock, Philip M. *The West Indies.* London: Thames and Hudson, 1966; and New York: Walker and Hudson, 1966.

Smith, Rowland (ed.). *Exile and Tradition: Studies in African and Caribbean Literature.* New York/Halifax, Africana/Dalhousie University Press, 1976.

Sparer, Joyce. "Attitudes toward Race in Guyanese Literature," in *Caribbean Studies,* VIII, 2, 23-63.

Todd, Loreto. *Pidgins and Creoles.* Boston: Routledge and Kegan Paul, 1975.

Twiggs, Robert D. *Pan-African Language in the Western Hemisphere.* North Quincy, Massachusetts: Christopher, 1973.

Walcott, Derek. "The figure of Crusoe; on the theme of isolation in West Indian Writing, with a reading of his [own] poems," (mimeographed), 13 pp., at Library of University of the West Indies, St. Augustine, Trinidad.

Walkley, Jane (comp.). "A Decade of Caribbean Literary Criticism: A Select Annotated Bibliography," in *The Literary Half Quarterly* (Mysore, India) XI, 2 (July 1970), 187-195.

Walsh, William. *Commonwealth Literature.* Oxford/London: Oxford University Press, 1973.

__________. *A Manifold Voice: Studies in Commonwealth Literature.* London: Chatto and Windus, 1970.

Waters, Harold A. [See same item in French critical section.]

Wickham, John. "West Indian Writing from a lecture given at the Multi-Racial Centre," University of the West Indies, Cave Hill, BIM, Vol. 13, No. 50 (January-June 1970), 68-80.

Williams, Denis. *Image and Idea in the Arts of Guyana; being the text of the 1969 Edgar Mittelholzer memorial lectures.* Georgetown: National History and Arts Council, Ministry of Information, 1969.

Williams, Eric. *History of the People of Trinidad and Tobago.* London: Deutsch, 1964.

Williams, Aubrey. "The Predicament of the Artist in the Caribbean," in *Caribbean Quarterly,* Vol. 14, Nos. 1 and 2 (March-June 1968), 60-62.

Wyndham, Francis. "The New West Indian Writers," BIM, Vol. 7, No. 28 (January-June 1959), 188-190.

Wynter, Sylvia. "Reflections on West Indian Writing and Criticism," in *Jamaica Journal,* Vol. 2, No. 4 (December 1969), 23-32, and Vol. 3, No. 1 (March 1969), 27-42.

WEST INDIAN LITERATURE: GENERAL ANTHOLOGIES AND COLLECTIONS

Anderson, Izett and Frank Cundall (comps.). *Jamaican Negro Proverbs and Sayings, Collected and Classified According to Subjects.* Kingston, Jamaica: 1910; London, 1927.

Ashtine, Eauline. *Crick-Crack.* New World Life and Lore Series: Special Volume I. Port of Spain, Extra Mural Dept., University of the West Indies, 1966.

BBC Short Stories from the BBC. British Broadcasting Corporation, London, 1967.

Barteaux, Marion C. *Grandmother's Stories.* Barbados, 1st. ed., January, 1964; 2nd. ed., May, 1964.

———. *More Grandmother Stories.* Barbados, January 1965.

Beckwith, Martha W. *Jamaica Anansi Stories: With Music Recorded in the Field by Helen Roberts.* New York: American Folklore Society, 1924. Vol. 17 of Memoirs of the American Folklore Society.

Belizean Poets. Belize City: Government Information Service, n.d. (41 pp.).

Bennett, L. *Anancy Stories and Dialect Verse.* Kingston, Jamaica: Pioneer Press, 1957.

———. *Jamaica Labrish.* Kingston: Sangster's Bookstores, 1966.

Binney, E.M. *English in the Caribbean.* London: University of London Press [1961] & v. contains excerpts from West Indian literary works for the study and teaching of English language.

Brathwaite, P.A. *Folk Songs of Guyana; Queh-queh, Chanties and Rag Time.* Georgetown: CA Welshman, 1964.

Brathwaite, Edward (ed.). *Iounaloa; recent writing from St. Lucia.* Castries, St. Lucia: Government Printing Office (Dept. of Extra Mural Studies, U.W.I.), 1963.

Bremen, Paul (comp. and annot.). *You better believe it; black verse in English from Africa, the West Indies, and the United States.* Harmondsworth, England; and Baltimore: Penguin, 1973.

Brent, Peter Ludwig (ed.). *Young Commonwealth Poets '65.* London: Heinemann, 1965 (pages on West Indies: 189-209).

Brown, John. *Poems and Stories of St. Christopher, Nevis and Antigua.* Basse Terre, Leeward Islands: Extra Mural Dept., 1959.

Cameron, Norman Eustace (ed.). *Guianese Poetry (covering the hundred years' period 1831-1931).* Nendeln, Liechtenstein: Kraus Reprint, 1970; 1st ed.: Georgetown, Guiana, 1931, by the Argosy Company.

Caribbean Quarterly: an anthology of West Indian Poetry. Caribbean Quarterly: Federation Commemoration Issue. Vol. 15, No. 3 (Mona, Jamaica, University College of the West Indies, 1958, 121-226).

Carr, Ernest A. et al. *Caribbean Anthology of Short Stories.* Kingston: Pioneer Press, 1953.

Carter, Martin and George Lamming. *New World Independence Issue.* Place unknown: New World Associates, 1967.

Casimir, Joseph R.R. (ed.). *Poesy. An Anthology of Dominica Verse,* 4 Vols. Roseau, Dominica. (Vol. I: 1943; Vol. II: 1944; Vol. III: 1946; Vol. IV: 1948), 1953.

Clarke, A.M. *Best Poems of Trinidad.* Trinidad: Fraser's Printerie, 1943.

Collins, Marie. *Black Poets in French.* New York: Scribners, 1972.

Collymore, Frank. (ed.) Various Journal Anthologies in BIM—Literary Journal. St. Michael, Barbados.

Coombs, Orde (ed.). *Is Massa Day Dead? Black Moods in the Caribbean.* New York: Doubleday, 1974. (This Doubleday anthology is of historical and cultural developments).

Connor, Edric. *Songs From Trinidad.* (Arranged for voices, guitar, drum and bass by Gareth Walters). London: Oxford University Press, 1958.

Coulthard, G.R. (ed.). *Caribbean Literature, An Anthology.* London: University of London Press, 1966.

__________. *Caribbean Narrative.* London: Oxford University Press, 1966.

__________. *Caribbean Poetry.* London: Oxford University Press, 1967.

Culmer, Jack (comp.). *A Book of Bahamian Verse.* 2nd ed. London: J. Culmer, 1948; London: Bailey Bros., Ltd., 1930.

Dathorne, O. Ronald (ed.). *Caribbean Verse.* London: Heinemann, 1967.

__________. *Caribbean Narrative.* London: Heinemann, 1966.

Douglas, Syble G. (ed.). *Guyana Drums.* Georgetown, Guyana, 1972.

Duperly, Denis. *Calypso, Calypso: Menschliches, allsumenschliches aus Jamaica.* Berlin, 1967.

Figueroa, John J. (coll. and ed.). *Caribbean Voices: An Anthology of West Indies Poetry.* London: Evans, Vol. I, 1966; *Dreams and Visions.* Vol. II: *The Blue Horizons,* 1970; Combined Edition, Evans, 1971; Washington and New York: Robert Luce, 1973.

Fitts, Dudley. *Anthology of Contemporary Latin-American Poetry.* Norfolk, Connecticut: New Directions, 1942.

Forde, Alfred N. (ed.). *Talk of the Tamarinds: an anthology of poetry for secondary schools.* London: E. Arnold, 1971. (World poetry but some Caribbean authors are included).

Francisco, S. (pseudonym: "Mighty Sparrow"). *120 Calypsos to Remember.* Port of Spain, Trinidad: Caribbean Music Co., 1959.

Galperina, Eugenie. *Freedomways (periodical):* "The People of the Caribbean Area"; Complete issue, Vol. 4, No. 3, Summer 1964. (Includes poems, essays, short stories).

__________ (ed.). *The Time of Flambouy Trees. An Anthology of West Indian Poetry.* Moscow, 1961.

Gambage's New World Life and Lore Series: Vol. I by E. Augustus and others. Port of Spain: Extra Mural Dept., University of the West Indies, 1966. (Anancy Folk Stories).

Gershator, David. "Poetry of the Virgin Islands: Past and Present," in Revista *Interamericana Review,* Vol. II, No. 3, 408-414.

Gomes, Albert M. (comp.). *From Trinidad, a selection from the fiction and verse of the Island of Trinidad, British West Indies.* Port of Spain: Frasers, 1937.

Gray, Cecil (with K. Ramchand). *West Indian Poetry.* Longmans, 1971.

Gray, Cecil. *Images.* (Anthology of West Indian Stories). London: Thomas Nelson, 1973.

__________. *Bite In.* (three books) Anthology of poems for Secondary Schools. London: Thomas Nelson, 1972.

__________. *Response: A course in narrative comprehension and composition for Caribbean secondary schools.* London, 1970. (Contains 22 stories by West Indians).

Griffin, Ella Washington (ed.). *Stories and Verses to Read and Share.* Illus. by Georges Remponeau, Kingston, Jamaica: Pioneers Press, 1953.

Guiseppi, Neville and Undine (comps.). *Backfire.* London: Macmillan, 1973. (short stories for use in secondary schools).

__________. *Out of the Stars* I and II (In Print II). Anthology of Poetry for use in Secondary Schools. London: Macmillan.

Guyana Independence Number. Georgetown, Guyana: New World, 1966.

Harris, Rodney E. et al. *Contes et poèmes d l'Afrique noire et des Antilles.* Glenview, Illinois: Scott, Foresman and Co., 1973.

Heaven, Violet. *Jamaica Proverbs and John Canoe Alphabet.* Kingston and Montego Bay, 1896.

Hendricks, A.L. and Cedric Lindo (eds.). *The Independence Anthology of Jamaican Literature.* Kingston: Ministry of Development, 1962.

Herring, Robert (ed.). *Life and Letters.* (Journal Anthology) continuing the London Mercury. London: Brendin Pub. Co. An Anthology of Jamaican poetry, short stories, articles and reviews. Vol. 57, No. 128 (April 1948); Vol. 59, No. 135 (November 1948); West Indies and London: Brendin, 1948.

Hill, Errol. *Caribbean Plays.* Mona, Jamaica: Extra Mural Dept., University of the West Indies, 1958.

Hollar, Constance. *Songs of Empire.* Collected and arranged by C.H.; Foreword by Sir William Morrison, Kingston, Jamaica: Printed Gleaner Co., 1932.

Howes, Barbara (ed.). *From the Green Antilles: Caribbean Writing.* London: Souvenir Press, 1967; New York: Macmillan, 1966.

Hughes, Langston (ed.). *Best Short Stories by Negro Writers.* New York: Harcourt Brace, 1922.

Hughes, Langston and Arna Bontemps. *The Poetry of the Negro 1746-1949.* New York: Doubleday and Co., Inc., 1949; and with Introduction by Garth St. Omer—St. Lucia, and stories by other writers, London: Faber and Faber, 1964.

Jahn, Janheinz. *Schwarzer Orpheus.* Munchen: C. Hanser, 1955.

__________, (ed.). *Afrika Lacht: anthology of African and West Indian Short Stories.* (includes Timothy Calender [Barbados]).

Jamaican Proverbs. New York: Negro Universities Press, 1970.

Jamaican Short Stories. Kingston: Pioneer Press, 1970.

James, Louis. *The Islands in Between.* London: Oxford University Press, 1968.

Jekyll, Walter (ed.). *Jamaican Song and Story.* New York: Dover, 1966; 1st. ed., London, 1907.

__________. *Jamaican Song and Story: Anancy Stories, Digging Songs, Ring Tunes, and Dancing Tunes.* New York: Dover Publishing Co., 1966.

Jones, Edward A. *Voices of Negritude; the expression of black experience in the Poetry of Senghor, Cesaire and Damas.* Valley Forge, Pa., 1971.

Khan, Yusuf S. *Anthology of Political Poems.* Guyana (details unknown).

King, Audvil, and others. Introduction by A. Salkey. *One Love.* London: Bogle L'Ouverture Publications, 1971. (Prose and verse with revolutionary and Rastafarian contents).

Kyk-over-al Anthology of Guianese poetry (A.J. Seymour, ed.). Vol. 6, No. 19, British Guiana: Argosy Co., 1962; revised, *Kyk-over-al,* No. 22, British Guiana: Daily Chronicle, 1957.

Lamming, George (ed.). *Cannon Shot and Glass Beads: Modern Black Writing.* London: Picador, 1974.

Landeck, Beatrice. *Echoes of Africa in Folksongs of the Americas.* New York, 1961.

La Rose, John (ed.). *New Beacon Reviews: Collection One.* London: New Beacon Press, 1968.

Le Page, R.B. *Jamaican Creole . . . and Four Jamaican Creole Texts.* London.

Lindo, Archie (comp.). *The Year Book of the Poetry League of Jamaica. 1941-45.* Kingston, Jamaica: The New Dawn Press, 1945.

Livingston, James T. (ed.). *Caribbean Rhythms.* New York: Washington Square Press, 1974.

McAndrew, R.C. (ed.). *Plexus: A New Magazine of Young Writings.* Georgetown, Guyana, 19??.

McDowell, Robert E. and Edward Lavitt. *Third World Voices for Children.* New York: Third Press, 1971, 1972.

McFarlane, J.E. Clare (ed.). *Selected Shorter Poems specially edited and arranged for use of schools.* Kingston, Jamaica: Pioneer Press, 1954.

__________ (ed.). *A Treasury of Jamaican Poetry.* London: University of London Press, 1950. Selected short poems specially edited and arranged for use of schools.

__________. *Voices from Summerland.* Anthology of Jamaican Poetry. London: Fowler Wright, 1929.

Manley, Edna (ed.). *Focus: An Anthology of Contemporary Jamaican Writing.* Kingston, Jamaica: City Printery, 1943, 1948, 1956, 1960.

Marshall, H.V. Ormsby (comp. and ed.). *Seeds and Flower: an anthology of prose and poetry by the Ormsby family of Jamaica.* Kingston, Jamaica: The Gleaner Co., 1956.

Mills, Therese. *Caribbean Christmas: A Book for Children.* Port of Spain: The College Press, 1973.

____________. *Christmas Stories.* Port of Spain: The College Press, 1972.

____________. *The Shell Book of Trinidad Stories.* Port of Spain: The College Press, 1973.

Monar, Motilall R. (comp.). *Poems for Guyanese Children.* Georgetown: Annandale Writers Group, 1974.

Morris, Mervyn (ed.). *Seven Jamaican Poets.* Kingston, Bolivar Press, 1971.

Murphy, Beatrice M. *Ebony Rhythm: An Anthology of Contemporary Negro Verse.* New York: The Exposition Press, 1948.

Murray, T. (ed.). *Folk Songs of Jamaica.* London: Oxford University Press, 1951.

____________. *Twelve Folk Songs from Jamaica* (ed. and arranged by T. Murphy and John Gavall). London: Oxford University Press, 1960.

New World Quarterly (Journal) Vol. 1, No. 1 (March 1963). Georgetown, Guyana: Printed by Guiana Graphic Ltd. for the publisher Clive Y. Thomas, 1963.

New World—Guyana Independence Issue. George Lamming and Martin Carter, (eds.). Pub. by New World Group Assoc., Georgetown.

New World—Barbados Independence Issue (May 1966-67), George Lamming, (ed.).

Norman, Alma. *Ballads of Jamaica.* London: Longmans, 1967.

O'Brien, Edward (ed.). *The Best British Stories of 1928.* New York: Dodd, Mead, 1928.

Ottley, C.R. *Legends, true stories and old sayings from Trinidad and Tobago.* Port of Spain: The College Press, 1962.

Papa bois—Trinidad, Port of Spain Gazette Ltd. (Collection of a group of writers—Prose and poetry under the aegis of "Papa bois" rural deity of the forest of Trinidad).

Parsons, Elsie Clews. *Folklore of the Antilles, French and English.* New York: American Folklore Society, Memoir 26, Part I, 1933, 1936.

____________. *Folk-Tales of Andros Island, Bahamas.* New York: Memoirs of the American Folklore Society, XIII, 1918.

Poetry for Children by Poets of Jamaica. Kingston: Pioneer Press, 1950.

Poets of Jamaica (Poetry for Children). Jamaica: Pioneer Press, 1958.

Pouchet, E. (comp.). *Life Lines: One Hundred Poems for Junior Secondary Schools.* Port of Spain, 1972.

Powan-Taylor, Daphne. *The Pompous parrot and others. West Indian Tales for Children.* Canada, 1947; Port of Spain: I.D.C., 19??.

Ramchand, Kenneth (ed.). *West Indian Narrative.* London: Nelson, 1966.

__________ and Cecil Gray. *West Indian Poetry; an anthology for schools.* Port of Spain: Longman Caribbean, 1971.

Ramcharitar-Lalla, C.E.J. (ed.). *Anthology of Local Indian Verse.* Georgetown, Guyana: Argosy, 1934.

Ramón-Fortune, José. *Eh bien oui! An Anthology of Twenty Poems in English and Creolese.* Port of Spain, Trinidad: Guardian Commercial Printery, 1954.

Reid, Victor Stafford. *14 Jamaican Stories by Vic Reid (and others).* Kingston: Pioneer Press, 1950.

Revista/Review Interamericana, Vol. IV, No. 3, 1974, Special Caribbean Literature Issue. Published by the Inter American University of Puerto Rico, Hato Rey, Puerto Rico. (John Zebrowski—Director Editor).

Rutherford, Anna (ed. along with Donald Hannah). *Commonwealth short stories* (an anthology for Secondary School level). London: E. Arnold, 1971.

Salkey, Andrew (ed.). *Caribbean Prose.* London: Evans, 1967.

__________. *Breaklight: The Poetry of the Caribbean.* New York: Anchor, 1973; and London: Hamish Hamilton Children's Books Ltd., 1971.

__________. *Stories from the Caribbean.* London: Elek, 1965, 2nd ed., 1972.

__________. *West Indian Stories.* London: Faber, 1960, reprinted 1971-1973.

Savacou Literary Journal, Special Issue 3/4 and 7/8 as a tribute to Frank Collymore. (Eds. Edward Brathwaite, Kenneth Ramchand, Andrew Salkey), Kingston, Jamaica: Caribbean Artist Movement and Savacou Publications Ltd.

Sealy, Clifford (ed.). *Voices,* Independence Anniversary Issue (in collaboration with the P.E.N. Club of Trinidad and Tobago). Port of Spain, Trinidad, 1964.

Seawar, Lloyd (ed.). *Cooperative Republic.* (Study of aspects of Our Way of Life.) Georgetown: Government of Guyana, 1970 (essays and poems).

Sergeant, Howard (ed.). *Commonwealth Poems of Today.* London: Murray, 1967. (Pages on West Indies: 257-271)

__________. *New Voices from the Commonwealth.* London: Evans, 1968.

Seymour, A.J. and Elma Seymour (comps.). *My Lovely Native Land: an anthology of Guyana.* Port of Spain: Longman Caribbean, 1971.

Seymour, A.J. (ed.). *Anthology of West Indian Poetry,* Georgetown, Guyana: by *Kyk-over-al,* journal, in No. 14 (1952), and in No. 22 (Autumn 1957).

__________. *New Writing in the Caribbean.* Georgetown, Guyana: Guyanese Lithographic Co., 1972.

__________. *Themes of Song: an Anthology of Guyanese Poetry.* La Penitence, Guyana, 1961.

__________. *Over Guiana Clouds.* British Guiana: Demerara Standard Estb., 1944.

__________. *Fourteen Guianese poems for children.* 1953. (An Anthology of Guianese poems).

__________. *Kyk-over-al,* (Journal) No. 22, Anthology of West Indian Poetry, 1957. *Kyk-over-al,* Special Issue Year—end 1954. *Kyk-over-al,* Special Issue Mid Year, 1952, Vol. 4, No. 14. (with Celeste Dolphin) compiled *The Genius of the Place: Personal Anthology of Poetry from the British Commonwealth.*

__________. *Magnet.* Georgetown: Guyana Lithographic Co., 1972.

__________. *Twelve West Indian Poems for Children.* Georgetown, 1952.

Seymour, Elma (ed.). *Sun is a Shapely Fire.* Georgetown, Guyana: Labour Advocate, 1973.

Sherlock, Sir Philip M. (ed.). *Anansi the Spider Man.* London: Macmillan, 1956.

__________. *The Iguano's Tail.* New York: Crowell, 1969.

__________, with Hilary Sherlock. *Ears and Tails and Common Sense: A Collection of Animal Stories.* New York: T. Cromwell, 1974.

__________. *West Indian Folk-Tales.* London: Oxford University Press, 1966.

Singh, Gora (ed.). *Heritage.* Georgetown: author, 1973 (Collection of poems).

__________ (ed.). *Heritage.* Georgetown: author, 1973. (Program Commemorating 135th anniversary of Indian migration to Guyana: May 5, 1838).

Sterling, Philippe (ed.). *3 Contes.* Port-au-Prince, 1953. (Stories by Jamaican authors)

Tamarack Review. West Indian Number (Winter 1961). Toronto, Canada: Toronto University Press.

Thieme, John, Annette Warren and George Cave (eds.). *Anthology of West Indian Literature.* Georgetown, University of Guyana.

Trotman, Donald (ed.). *An Anthology: Voices of Guyana.* Georgetown, Guyana, 1968. (Poetry only)

Van Sertima, Ivan. *Caribbean Writers: Critical Essays.* London, 1968; Port of Spain, Trinidad: New Beacon Books, 1968.

Verse and Voice: A Festival of Poetry. Poems and Ballads of the Commonwealth at the Royal Court Theatre. September 20-25. London: Poetry Book Society, 1965.

Walmsley, Anne (comp.). *The Sun's Eye: West Indian Writing for Young Readers.* London: Longmans, 1968, 1970, 1971.

Walrond, Eric (ed.). *Black and Unknown Bards.* Aldington, Kent: Hand & Flaver, 1958 .

Weaver, Robert (ed.). "The First Five Years," in *Tamarack Review,* Toronto.

Wilson, D.G. (ed.). *New Ships, an anthology of West Indian Poems.* Kingston: Savacou Publications, 1972. (Junior High School Level).

Wright, S. Fowler. *From Overseas: An Anthology of poems from the old British Empire.* London: Marin Press, 1924.

LITERATURE
PRE-1900
BACKGROUND BOOKS (SELECTED)

Breen, Henry H. *Warrawarra, the Carib Chief. A Tale of 1770.* 2 Vols. London, 1876.

Brooke-Knight, Captain. *The Captain's Story; or Jamaica sixty years ago.* London, (n.d., but 1860).

Crookall, L. *Br. Giuani, or work and wanderings among the Creoles and Coolies, the Africans and the Indians of the wild country.* London, 1898. (Cultural-Travel-Comment)

Cumberland, Richard. *The West Indian; a comedy.* London, 1771. Reprinted in Dent's Everyman's Series. J. Hampden, (ed.). Eighteenth century plays.

Ireland, W. Alleyne (pseudonym: Langton). *Demerariana*—Essays Historical, Critical and Descriptive. Demerara, Br. Guiana, 1897.

Grainger, James. *The sugar-cane: a poem in four parts.* London, 1764.

Hillhouse, William. *Indian Notices: or Sketches of the Habits, Characters, Languages . . . of the several Nations* (of Br. Guiana). Georgetown, 1820.

The Koromantyn slaves; or West Indian sketches. London, 1828.

Lewis, Matthew Gregory (Monk Lewis). *The Monk—a gothic novel.* London, 1795.

__________. *Journal of a West Indian Proprietor.* London: Murray, 1834.

Marly; or, A planter's life in Jamaica . . . Glasgow, Scotland, 1828.

Nugent, Maria. *Lady. A journal of a voyage to and residence in the island of Jamaica from 1801 to 1805.* London, 1839. (Edited later by Frank Cundall, pub. Institute of Jamaica. Third Edition, pub. 1939. Philip Wright edited *Lady Nugent's Jamaica Journal,* 1966).

Orderson, J.W. *Creolana; or social and domestic scenes and incidents in Barbados in days of yore.* London, 1842.

Radcliffe, John. *Lectures on Jamaica Proverbs* . . . . Kingston, Jamaica: G. Henderson, Savage and Co., 1859.

__________. *Lectures on negro proverbs, with a preliminary paper on negro literature.* . . . Kingston, Jamaica: M. DeCordova, McDougall and Co., 1869.

Scott, Michael. *The cruise of the Midge.* Paris, 1836.

__________. *Tom Cringle's Log.* Edinburgh: Blackwood, 1833. Issued in Dent's Everyman's Series.

Senior, Henry. *Charles Vernon: a trans-Atlantic tale.* 2 Vols., London, 1849.

Van Sertima, J. *Scenes and Sketches.* Georgetown, 1899. (Reprints in book form of pieces published in the *Argosy,* Georgetown, Guiana.)

Veecock, Walter J. *Notes on Legends of Br. Guiana. West Indian Quarterly,* Vol. 3 (July 1887), p. 306.

HISTORICAL WRITINGS
PRE-1900
BACKGROUND BOOKS (SELECTED)

General:

Caribbeana, containing letters and dissertations, together with poetical essays on various subjects and occasions, chiefly written by several hands in the West Indies. . . . London, 1741. (2 Vols.).

Thomas, J.J. *Froudacity; West Indian fables by James Anthony Froude* . . . London, 1889.

Underhill, Edward B. *The West Indies: their social and religious conditions.* London, 1862.

Antigua:

Flannigan (Mrs.). *Antigua and the Antiguans.* London, 1844 (2 Vols.).

Barbados:

Ligon, Richard. *A true and exact history of the Island of Barbados.* 2nd ed. London, 1673.

Ligon, Richard. *Memoirs of the first settlement of the island of Barbados and the other Caribee Islands* . . . Barbados, 1741.

British Guiana:

Rodway, James. *A History of Br. Guiana.* Georgetown, 1891-94. (3 Vols.).

Dominica:

Atwood, Thomas. *The history of Dominica.* London, 1791.

Jamaica:

Gardner, William J. *A history of Jamaica.* London, 1909. First published 1873.

Feurtado, W.A. *Official and other personages of Jamaica, from 1655 to 1790, to which is added a chapter on the peerage, etc. in Jamaica, compiled from various sources.* Kingston, Jamaica, 1896.

St. Lucia:

Breen, Henry H. *St. Lucia: historical, statistical and descriptive.* London, 1844.

St. Vincent:

Shephard, Charles. *An historical account of the island of St. Vincent.* London, 1831.

Trinidad and Tobago:

Fraser, Lionel M. *History of Trinidad.* Port of Spain, Trinidad (n.d.)

Joseph, Edward. *History of Trinidad.* Port of Spain, Trinidad, 1838. (2 Vols.).

Woodcock, Henry. *A History of Tobago.* Eyr, 1867.

Virgin Islands (British)

Lewisohn, Florence. *Tales of Tortola and the British Virgin Islands: Recounting nearly Five Centuries of Lore, Legend and History* . . . Printed for author by International Graphics, Inc., Hollywood, Fla., 1966, rev. ed., 1973.

Description—Pre-1900:

Beckford, William. A descriptive account of the island of Jamaica. London, 1790 (2 Vols.).

Kingsley, Charles. *At last; a Christmas in the West Indies.* London, 1872.

Madden, Richard R. *A twelve month's residence in the West Indies during the transition from slavery to apprenticeship.* Philadelphia, 1836 (2 Vols.).

Roth, Vincent (ed.). *A soldier's sojourn in British Guiana, 1806-1808.* Georgetown, Br. Guiana, 1947. Being selections from the author's work published in 1834.

Wentworth, Trelawny. *The West Indian Sketch Book.* London, 1834 (2 Vols.).

GENERAL BACKGROUND STUDIES ON VARIOUS ISLANDS POST-1900

Abraham, Peter. *Jamaica: An Island Mosaic.* London: H.M. Stationery Office, 1957.

Aykroyd, W.R. *Sweet Malefactor: Sugar, Slavery and Human Society.* London: Heinemann, 1967.

Augier, F.R., et al. *The Making of the West Indies.* London: Longmans, 1961.

Bell, Wendell, with M.G. Smith and R. Nettleford. *Jamaican Leaders: Political Attitudes to a New Nation.* Berkeley, Cal.: University of California Press, 1961.

Black, Clinton. *History of Jamaica.* (2nd. rev.). London: Collins, 1961.

Brathwaite, L.E. *Creole Society in Jamaica. 1770-1820.* Oxford: Clarendon Press, 1971.

Burnham, Forbes. *A Destiny to Mould.* New York: Africana Publishing Corp., 1970.

Comitas, Lambros. *Work and Family Life: West Indian perspectives.* New York: Doubleday, 1973.

Carley, Mary Manning. *Jamaica, the old and the new.* London: Allen and Unwin, 1963.

Carmichael, Gertrude. *History of the West Indian Islands of Trinidad and Tobago 1948-1900.* London: Redman, 1961.

Clarke, Edith. *My Mother who Fathered me.* London: Allen and Unwin, 1957.

Clementi (Sir), Cecil. *The Chinese in British Guiana.* Georgetown: Argosy Co., 1915.

Cumper, George (ed.). *The Economy of the West Indies.* Kingston, Jamaica: Institute of Social and Economic Research, U.C.W.I., 1960.

Daly, P.H. *Revolution to Republic.* Georgetown: Daily Chronicle, 1970.

Daly, Vere T. *The Making of Guiana.* London: Macmillan, 1974.

Easter, B.H. *St. Lucia and the French Revolution.* Castries, St. Lucia: The St. Lucia Archaeological and Historical Society, 1969.

Fermor, Patrick Leigh. *The Traveller's Tree; a Journey through the Caribbean Islands.* London: Murray, 1950.

Figueroa, John J. *Society, Schools and Progress in the West Indies.* Oxford and New York: Pergamon, 1971.

Gordon, Shirley (comp.). *A Century of West Indian Education. A Source Book.* London: Longmans, 1963.

Goveia, Elsa. *The Slave Society in the British Leeward Islands at the End of the 18th Century.* New Haven: Yale University Press, 1965; paperback edition, Rio Piedras: Institute of Caribbean Studies, University of Puerto Rico, 1969.

Hall, Douglas. *Free Jamaica, 1838-1865. An Economic History.* New Haven: Yale University Press, 1959.

__________. "Independent Jamaica. Ten Years after 1962." *Jamaica Journal,* Vol. 6, No. 7 (December 1972), 2-3.

Hoyos, F.A. *The rise of West Indian democracy: the life and times of Sir Grantley Adams.* 1963.

Henriques, Fernando. *Family and Colour in Jamaica.* London: Eyre and Spottiswoode, 1953.

Horowitz, M.M. *Peoples and Cultures of the Caribbean.* Garden City, New York: Natural History Press, 1971.

Jacobs, H.P. "The New Economic Pattern." *Pepperpot.* Vol. 4 (Jamaica 1954), 25-32.

Jagan, Cheddi. *The West on Trial: My Struggle for Freedom.* London: A. Deutsch, 1966.

James, C.L.R. *Party Politics in the West Indies.* Trinidad: Vedic Enterprises, 1962.

Jesse, C. (Rev.). *Outlines of St Lucia's History.* Castries, St. Lucia: The St. Lucia Archaeological and Historical Society, 1970.

Kerr, Madeline. *Personality Conflicts in Jamaica.* Liverpool: University Press, 1952.

Lamming, George. *The Pleasures of Exile.* London: M. Joseph, 1960.

LePage, R.B. "The Language Problem in the British Caribbean." *Caribbean Quarterly,* Vol. 4, No. 1 (1955), 40-49.

Lewis, Arthur. *Industrial Development in the Caribbean.* Trinidad: Caribbean Commission, 1950.

Lewis, Gordon. *The Growth of the Modern West Indies.* New York: Monthly Review Press, 1968 (paperback).

Lowenthal, David. *West Indian Societies.* London: Oxford University Press, 1972.

Manley, D.R. and Clarence Senior. *Report on Jamaica Migration to Great Britain.* Kingston, Jamaica: Government Printer, 1956.

Mintz, Sidney W. "The Caribbean as a Socio-Cultural Area." *Journal of World History,* Vol. IX, No. 4 (Neufchâtel, Switzerland, 1966).

Mitchell, (Sir) Harold. *Caribbean Patterns.* Berkeley, Calif.: University of California Press, 1968.

Mordecai, (Sir) John. *The Federal Negotiations.* Cambridge, Mass.: Schenkman Publishing Co., 1968.

Naipaul, V.S. *The Loss of El Dorado. A History.* London: A. Deutsch, 1969; and Harmondsworth, England: Penguin Books Ltd., 1973.

__________. *The Middle Passage. The Caribbean Revisited.* New York: Macmillan, 1963.

Nettleford, Rex. *Mirror Mirror. Identity: Race and Protest in Jamaica.* Kingston: Collins, Sangster (Jamaica) Ltd., 1970; 3rd printing, 1974.

__________, (ed.). *Manley and the New Jamaica: Selected speeches and writings 1938-1968;* with notes and introduction by editor. Kingston: Longman Caribbean, 1971.

__________. (co-author with M.G. Smith and R. Augier). *The Ras Tafari Movement in Kingston, Jamaica.* Kingston: University of the West Indies, 1960.

Parry, H. and P.M. Sherlock. *A Short History of the West Indies.* London: Macmillan, 1956.

Patterson, H. Orlando. *The Sociology of Slavery.* London: MacGibbon and Gee, 1967.

Sherlock, P.M. *The West Indies.* London: Thames and Hudson, 1966.

__________. *Caribbean Citizen.* London: Longmans, 1957.

Smith, M.G. *A Framework for Caribbean Studies.* Kingston, Jamaica: Extra Mural Department, U.C.W.I., 1955.

__________. *The Plural Society in the British West Indies.* Berkeley, Calif.: University of California Press, 1965.

__________. *West Indian Family Structure.* Seattle: University of Washington Press, 1962.

Ethnic and Cultural Pluralism in the British Caribbean. Document 11, INCIDI Conference, Lisbon, 1957.

Smith, Raymond. *British Guiana.* London: Oxford University Press, 1962.

__________. *The Negro Family in British Guiana.* London: Routledge, 1956.

Williams, Eric. *The Caribbean: From Columbus to Castro.* London: Deutsch, 1970.

__________. *Capitalism and Slavery.* Chapel Hill, N.C.: University of North Carolina Press, 1944; London: Deutsch, 1944, 1964.

__________. *History of the People of Trinidad and Tobago.* Port of Spain, 1962.

Wright, Philip (ed.). *Lady Nugent's Jamaica Journal,* 1966.

WEST INDIAN LITERATURE: SELECTED JOURNALS

Artana 2-5, Guyana Centre of the Arts, 294 Murray St. Georgetown, Guyana. (Quarterly).

The Bajan, Carib Publicity Co. Ltd., Bridgetown, Barbados. A news magazine with occasional literary articles; includes book reviews.

The Beacon, Port of Spain, Trinidad, issued 1931-1933.

BIM, The Editors, Ferney, Atlantic Shores, Christchurch, Barbados, West Indies (Semi-Annual)

Black Images, Black Images Inc., Toronto, Canada. (Quarterly)

CACLALS (Canadian Association for Commonwealth Language and Literary Studies) Journal, c/o R.T. Robertson, Chairman, CACLALS, Dept. of English, Univesity of Saskatchewan, Saskatoon, Sask. S7N 0W0, Canada.

Caribbean Quarterly, Dept. of Extra Mural Studies, Univ. of the West Indies, Mona, Kingston, Jamaica, West Indies. (Quarterly)

Caribbean Studies, Institute of Caribbean Studies, University of Puerto Rico, Rio Piedras, Puerto Rico. (Quarterly).

Cavite, Univ. of the West Indies, Cave Hill Campus, Barbados, West Indies.

Expression, A magazine of Creative Writing from the Caribbean (Editor, Janice Lowe). Expression was founded by Noel Williams and Brian Cotton. Distribution and Correspondence: c/o J. Shinebourne, c/o U.G. Library, Turkeyen, East Coast, Demerara, Guyana.

Focus, Kingston, Jamaica. Issues were 1943, 1948, 1956, 1960.

Jamaica Journal, Journal of the Institute of Jamaica, 12-15 East St., Kingston, Jamaica, West Indies. (Quarterly)

Journal of Commonwealth Literature, Univ. of Leeds, Leeds, LS2 9JT, England.

Journal of Commonwealth Literature, Univ. of Aarhaus, Denmark.

Free Your Mind, Literary magazine of Dominica, West Indies.

Herambee Speaks, Literary magazine of Antigua, West Indies.

Kaie, Official Organ of the National History and Art Council of Guyana. The Council, 49A Main St., Georgetown, Guyana.

Kairi (editor, Christopher Laird), Port of Spain, Trinidad, West Indies.

Kyk-over-al, A. J. Seymour, early editor, Georgetown, Guyana. Issued 1945-1961.

Melanthika: An Anthology of Pan-Caribbean Writing. Edited by Nick Toczek, Philip Nanton, and Yann Lovelock. L.W.M. Publications, Birmingham, England, 1977.

Link, Castries, St. Lucia, P. O. Box 216. (Quarterly)

New Beacon Reviews, J. LaRose, editor, New Beacon Publications, 2 Albert Road., London, N.4, England.

New World Fortnightly, published by New World Associates, 215 King St., Georgetown, Guyana.

New World (Quarterly), (Dead Season; Crop Time; High Season; Crop Over). Published by New World Group Ltd., P.O. Box 221, U.W.I., Mona, Kingston 7, Jamaica, West Indies. (A Quarterly Journal of Caribbean Affairs). Special Issues: Independence of Guyana; Independence of Barbados.

Pepperpot, (Editor, Elsie Bowen), Box 147, Kingston 8, Jamaica, West Indies. Annual Jamaica Review.

Revista Inter Americana, (Inter American University Press) G.P.O. Box 3255, San Juan, Puerto Rico 00936.

Savacou, Journal of the Caribbean Artists' Movement. P.O. Box 170, Mona, Kingston 7, Jamaica, West Indies. (Editors: Edward Brathwaite, Kenneth Ramchand, Andrew Salkey). Quarterly: March, June, September, and December; the fourth issue each year is devoted to the publication of creative work and artistic criticism. A comprehensive listing of current publications by the West Indies is included annually.

The New Voices, (Editor, Anson Gonzalez), Port of Spain, Trinidad, West Indies.

Tapia, Tapia House, 82-84, St. Vincent, St. Tunapuna, Trinidad, West Indies.

Voices, (Editor, Clifford Sealy), The Book Shop, Frederick St., Port of Spain, Trinidad, West Indies.

World Literature Written in English, "WLWE", Univ. of Texas at Arlington, Arlington, Texas, U.S.A.

Late Addition:

Melanthika: An Anthology of Pan-Caribbean Writing. Nick Toczek, Philip Nanton, Yann Lovelock, editors, Birmingham, England, L.W.M. Publications, 1977.

Volume II

Francophone Literature from the Caribbean

Hommage à Marie-Ange Jolicoeur

Marie-Ange Jolicoeur from her earliest youth was devoted to art, with poetry and music her passion. She composed several musical pieces which were not published, but she was successful in offering the public three collections of her poems.

Her songs, natural, poignant, and fresh, remain eloquent contributions to Haitian poetry.

Marie-Ange was denied the opportunity of maturing her art, perishing in her mid-twenties—but we wish, here, to pay our tribute to her and to all other young artists who left careers too early to make their full impression on Caribbean literature.

Maurice A. Lubin
February 10, 1979

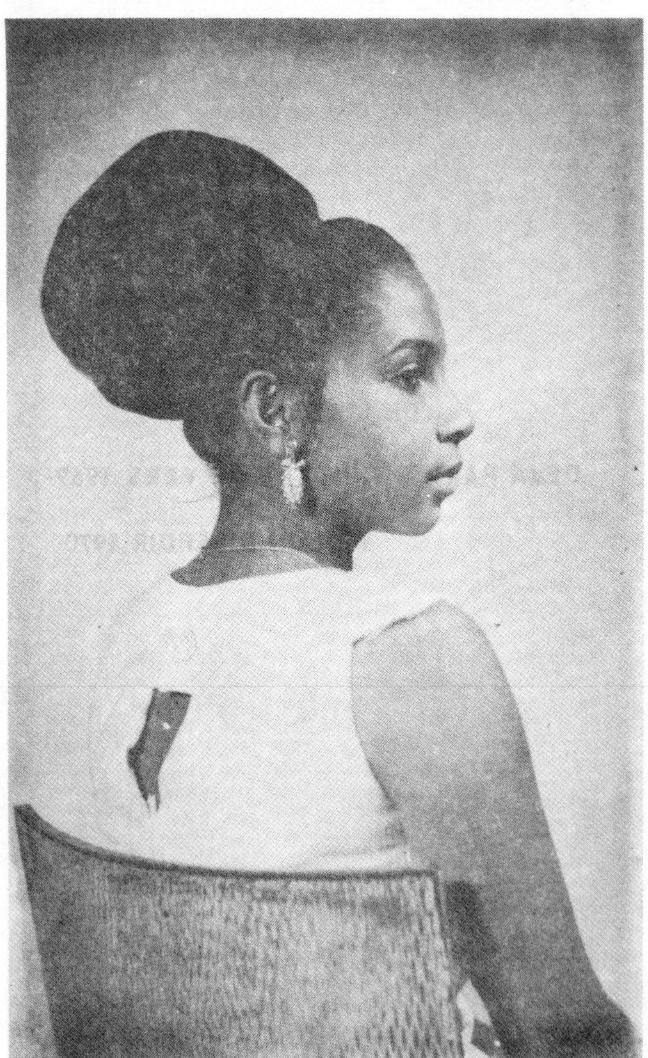

ESSAY ON THE LITERATURE OF HAITI

Haiti, the western third of the large island of Hispaniola, has since its independence in 1804 experienced a tumultuous history. Ceded by Spain to the French in 1697 by the Treaty of Ryswick, the territory became in time the "Pearl of the Antilles" and producer of great fortunes in France. Sweated by the owners of plantation and mill were the Africans who neither shared in the prosperity nor enjoyed even the rudiments of education. Liberated by their own efforts and led by Toussaint Louverture, Jean Jacques Dessalines, Alexandre Pétion and Henri Christophe after a decade of ferocious fighting, the Haitian people awoke to freedom as the first black nation in the New World and a pariah as far as the United States and other slave-holding states were concerned.

As the French had all departed, by exile or death, the continuing internal battles between the almost white, the rather white, and the ethnically pure African stock would provide the fuel for much of the island's repression, and eventual counter-revolt in a cycle of violence not yet completed. Permitted to suffer alone in a splendid isolation of increasing poverty, the Haitian people had to create in a collapsed society (African in origin and intensity but European in language and orientation) a state strong enough to maintain independence and stable enough to allow a better life.

From the very beginning there would be counter-pulls. One tug, a relatively intellectual one, would come from France and many Haitians for the next century or more would seek in Paris an escape from the ennuies or threats of Port-au-Prince in exchange for the pleasures of European art and society. For these, the French language was the tongue they chose to perfect, and to create in, were they artists. The contrary tug would be that of the heart which could best speak in the rich créole (evolved over five generations or more) of the perfumes and colors of the tropics—of the pride of freedom and the glory of victory.

A brief sketch of the Haitian literary periods, might be given this way:

The Pre-Colonial Period and the first few years of independence (1700-1804)

II: The Early Independence Period (1804-1836)
III: The Romantic Period (1836-1890)
IV: The Symbolist and Realistic Period (1890-1928)
V: The Indigenist Period (1928-1946)
VI: The Contemporary Period (1946-Present)

• • • • •

Boisrond Tonnerre (1776-1806) and Juste Chanlatte (1766-1828) may be cited as two of Haiti's rare pre-independence writers. The French who resided in the island were not of the literary sort and there was no other group yet which could express the feelings or experiences of the people.

With the formal coming of independence in 1804, journals, patriotic poems, and the first stirrings of historical interest, would produce the first works of a free nation. Coriolan Ardouin (1812-1835) and Ignace Nau (1812-1845) are two of the better writers. Others were Jules-Solime Milscent (1778-1842) and Céligny Ardouin (1806-1849) and his brother Alexis Ardouin (1796-1865).

The Romantic Period obviously reflected the major movement of the European 19th century. Most Haitians of means lived for at least a period in France, there producing a literature hardly, if at all, different from the lesser productions of native Frenchmen. At home or abroad, they celebrated women's beauty, the glories of a sunset, the world of fashion or spiritual hunger—all in excellent French. Leading prose writers were Alibée Fery (1819-1869), Tertulien Guilbaud (1856-1934), Amédée Brun (1867-1896), and some of the more interesting poets were Paul Lochard (1835-1919), Oswald Durand (1840-1906), and A. de Pommayrac (1844-1908).

Emile Nau in *L'Union* (November 6, 1836) had written: "La source de l'inspiration est en nous et chez nous . . . Célébrer Haiti, ses fastes et ses gloires militaires, évoquer ses nuits intenses et son ciel profond, ses supersititions et ses légendes, le charme ardent de ses femmes et la ruse finaude de ses paysans, le tout en un français le plus possible pittoresque et coloré . . ." This local color or "créolisme" produced *Contes créole* by Ignace Nau and the poetry of Oswald Durand. Called "Haitianisme" long afterwards, it is still a useful term, for it marked the first genuine efforts to seize the Haitian experience and to cast it into patterns more complex than had the earlier nationalistic writings.

The La Ronde Period, beginning in 1898 and ending with the American occupation (1915) was marked by such writers as Solon Ménos (1859-1918), Louis Borno (1865-1942), Etzer Vilaire (1872-1951), Justin Lhérisson (1873-1907), Dantès Bellegarde (1877-1966), and Georges Sylvain (1866-1925) which group also supported *La Jeune Haiti.*

The escapism of the last wave of European romanticism and the newly popular symbolism persisted for two decades, but the cold water of the American occupation of 1916 encouraged a sterner sort of literature. A growing racial self-consciousness and concomitant pride quickly developed in reaction to the continuing stay in Haiti of American troops, the great majority of them drawn from the former confederate states of the old south.

Burr-Reynaud would write in his "Anathèmes" of 1916:

Et puisque nul affront et puisque nul danger
N'atteignit l'étranger,
De quel droit les Yankees, au nom de quelle règle
Font-ils planer sur nous les ailes de leur aigle?

The journal of the resistance, *La Nouvelle Ronde,* ironically chosen, and the review *La Trouée,* carried the voices of the short-lived *Revue de la Ligue de la Jeunesse Haitienne* (founded February 1916 by George N. Leger, Fernand Hibbert, Léon Laleau, L. Henry Durand, and others) to all parts of the country.

Aware as never before that they were Caribbeans and Afro-Caribbeans, too long cut off from mother Africa, the French "connection" seemed less important. Georges Sylvain with his modest effort to reinterpret Fontaine's *Fables* in creole in *Cric-Crac* as early as 1901, and the more original efforts of T. Guilbaud, M. Coicou, D. Vieux and Vaval created the ground for the next wave of artists and intellectuals.

The Indigenist Period (1928-1946) brought the work of Jean Price-Mars and Jacques Roumain. Their journal *La Revue Indigène* would urge the cosmopolite Port-au-Princiens to rediscover their African heritage and, more important, to accept the culture of the rural masses, including the vestigal Dahomeen religion termed Voudou, as the genuine culture of the nation.

A balancing of African feeling with what was useful in European culture (now including Anglo-Saxon) was the call and need. Price-Mars' *Ainsi parla l'oncle* (1928) was the first great book of this movement, with its essays examining many subjects from folk-ways and religion to music and literature.

Roumain, poet and novelist, anthropologist, diplomat, and political radical, was no less important—and his posthumously published (1945) romance *Gouverneurs de la rosées* (*Masters of the Dew* in its English translation by Mercer Cook and Langston Hughes) show Manuel, a strong peasant worker just back from the cane-fields of Cuba, trying to combine the warmth and integrity of the country people with the international spirit of reform and progressivism in a Marxist parable. The relative innocence of this Afro-Haitian or "back-to-the-people" period might be considered over by the time of the short-lived revolution of 1946 in which an entire new generation came forward.

Toward the end of this period one might claim to find a surrealist school with such poets as Magloire St. Aude, Hamilton Garoute, Davertige and Serge Legagneur whose work obviously was influenced by the French poets Eluard, Aragon, Desnos, Tzara and André Breton who himself paid a visit to Haiti in 1945, and by other poets of the 1920's. Working in both of the later periods of this century are Jean Joseph Vilaire (1881-1967) and the cited Bellegarde and Laleau.

The Contemporary Period (1946-Present) would see the review *Les Griots* even more assertively proclaiming the African connection, a negritude amplified by the work of Césaire, Damas, and Senghor being done in Paris, elsewhere in the

Caribbean, and, eventually, in mother Africa itself. After the failure of the 1946 efforts at reform, many of the best were in exile or prison. Some got to Cuba, others to New York or Montreal, or Africa. Often Marxist, revolutionary, they despise their country's dictatorships and write or wrote accordingly.

Jacques Stéphen Alexis (1922-1961), a strong supporter of Roumain, argued for what he called "réalisme merveilleux" and produced *Compère Général Soleil* (1955) whose main character Roumal is a lightly veiled evocation of Roumain, and *Les Arbres musiciens* (1957), the latter dealing with events in 1941-42 when the Catholic Church made strenuous efforts to weaken Voudou.

Important journals of the recent period were *La Ruche* involving the major figure, René Dépestre (b. 1926), *Semences* with René Philoctète (b. 1928), Roland Morisseau (b. 1933), Anthony Phelps (b. 1928), and for the present time *Le Petit Samedi Soir.* The latter was noted for its courageous staff, one of whom, Gasner Raymond, was brutally murdered.

Lacking a reasonably large and educated audience at home, and often themselves far from home, Haitian writers must perforce battle against private despairs and the evils of exile. No longer seeing Haiti as the lone black state in the Caribbean, or as a uniquely troubled one, will help in time, for the artist will find his universality in his condition. Accepting the themes of home or exile, and wielding a supple new French (call it créole if you wish), Haitian authors will inevitably mold their thoughts in words and artistic structures which will embody the inner and outer realities of being Haitian.

Laleau in his "Musique nègre" had posed the need—and the challenge:

Ce coeur obsédant, qui ne correspond
Pas avec mon langage et mes coutumes,
Et sur lequel mordent, comme un crampon,
Des sentiments d'emprunt et des coutumes
D'Europe, sentez-vous cette souffrance
Et ce désespoir à nul autre égal
D'apprivoiser, avec des mots de France,
Ce coeur qui m'est venu de Sénégal?

The poet will probably first sing most fully the sound of a united and healthy Haiti.

One could characterize the course of Haitian writing as being documentary and nationalistic at the beginning, escapist (in subject and manner) in the long middle years when Haitian life was all too uncomfortable for the sensitive artist, and increasingly activist, realistic, and finally revolutionary in the past two generations. With some exceptions, most good Haitian writing has been accomplished in exile.

Jean Brierre (b. 1909), creator of scores of works in a wide range of genres, is possibly Haiti's most gifted modern writer. The past and present are his subjects, his goal—the liberation of the poor and downcast everywhere. He is today living in Dakar, entrusted with important duties in the Senegalese Ministry of Culture; for him, at least, the great circle of being is complete.

ESSAY ON THE LITERATURE OF THE FRENCH ANTILLES

The writers of The French Antilles, along with those from Puerto Rico, have had to develop a literature completely immured in the colonial situation. For them none of the glories and crises of independence and "where-do-we-go-from-here" difficulties after a period of national liberation. Puerto Rico, though it has had to deal with two major colonial tutelages, has a strong national consciousness, but the French islands, so isolated in a sea of Spanish- and English-speaking peoples, and so closely held to France's overly protective bosom, could only dream of producing a "national" literature. Only in the last decade or so have writers begun to break away from Paris as they woke up to developments elsewhere in the Caribbean and/or Africa.

Typical of writers in the early period were Poirié de Saint-Aurèle (1795-1855) who, living in France, could lament his lost island paradise:

> *J'aime, oh! j'aime avant tout la sensible créole*
> *A la paupière noire, à la taille espagnole*
> . . .

Another early writer was Eyma, born in Saint Pierre, the ancient capital of Martinique. For a period he edited the French section of a New Orleans journal *L'Abeille,* and quitting his early verse efforts decided to become the "Balzac des Tropiques." His five historical novels, all published in the 1860's, his collection of poems and stories, *Emmanuel* (1841), and many other works make him one of the historically important early writers of the Antilles.

During the 18th and 19th centuries writers of French origin produced the first local work, mostly derivative as might be expected. Even today, island writers and intellectuals are strongly oriented toward Europe and Saint-John Perse (1887-1975), the only Nobel prize winner born in the Caribbean, stands outside most literary histories of the French Antilles. (He is not so much as referred to, for instance, in Jacques Nantet's *Panorama de la litterature noire d'expression française.* Perse was of course of pure French extraction but his family has been for centuries resident in the Antilles.)

It should not be surprising therefore to note that the créole of the Antilles has not diverged as much from standard "school" French as did Haitian popular French and the small populations have been unable to generate the "critical mass" for a genuine indigenous literature against pressures of the French orientation of the educational system. However, the Haitian example of Jean Price-Mars and Jacques Roumain of the 1920's and thereafter was of some utility. Paul Niger (b. 1917 in Guadeloupe) was touched to some degree by it, and even more was Guy Tirolien (also b. 1917 in Guadeloupe) who commonly employed negritude or Africanist themes. Tirolien's turn to Guinea (from whence came most of the island's population) was, however, more exotic and in the light of the more authentic developments elsewhere his verse seems somewhat naively insistent on the beauties of the nostalgically re-evoked mother Africa:

Tes seins de satin noir rebondis et luisants
tes bras souples et longs dont le lissé ondulé
ce blanc sourire
des yeux
dans l'ombre du visage
éveillent en moi ce soir
les rythmes sourds.

Gilbert Gratiant (b. 1901 in Martinique) would primarily use the island créole and folklore, and Etienne Léro (1909-1939) also from Martinique, would try in such works as *Lucioles* to evoke Africa in poems touched as much by Freud and Marx as by African culture. Along with René Ménil and Jules Monnerot, Léro helped found the first short-lived, but historically very significant journal *Légitime défense* in 1934 in Paris.

Obviously with the pressures of French control, even the inventor of the term *négritude,* Aimé Césaire (b. 1913 in Martinique) has had to be content with evoking the thoughts of Haiti's Henri Christophe or Zaire's Patrice Lumumba in his plays. Even his poetry which treats of the cruelties of the past, recent or near, is less than revolutionary or secessionist in tone. Harsher, terser, more obviously struggling in the toils of the Gallic mother python, is Léon Gontran Damas (b. 1912 in Guyane) who is willing to employ créolisms and popular speech. His sarcasm is also refreshing:

Mes amis j'ai valsé
valsé comme jamais mes ancêtres
les Gaulois
au point que j'ai le sang
qui tourne encore
à la viennoise

Senghor, born 1906 in Senegal, Damas, and Césaire would issue their own journal *L'Etudiant Noir* (one issue published, five or six more printed but never distributed) in 1934 in which *négritude* was more fully enunciated than in Léro's *Légitime défense.* This journal might properly be called the first cultural bugle-call to a genuine independence and acceptance of Africa in the Antilles.

Even earlier of course, René Maran (b. 1887 in Martinique of Guyanese parents) had published *Batouala,* winner of the Prix Goncourt in 1921. Considered by most to be the founding father of modern Antillean literature, Maran had served in the French colonial empire in Africa for a decade, though he finished his life in Paris and lived there almost thirty years after being forced out of the service because of the uproar ensuing the publication of *Batouala.* Set in Africa, the novel reflects a sad and rapidly decaying African society in the Ubangi Shari (today's Central African Empire). Though conceived in sympathy with the Africans, the work is essentially written by an outsider, no matter how pure his African lineage. The preface was more provocative than the text, for Maran could write there:

> *Ah! M. Bruel, in a scholarly study you were able to declare that the population of Ubangi-Shari was climbing to 1,350,000 inhabitants. But why didn't you say instead that in a certain small village of Uahm, in 1918, there were no more than 1,080 individuals of the 10,000 who had been counted seven years before? You spoke of the richness of that immense country. Why didn't you say that famine was mistress there?*

But with all his vehemence, Maran never even hinted at France pulling out of either Africa or the Antilles. At least for rhetoric's sake he posed as one Frenchman appealing an injustice of other Frenchmen. Nevertheless, he had thrown down the gauntlet and the newer writers would claim him as the great stimulus, and his apartment in Paris would become the rendez-vous for two generations of black writers from America, the Caribbean, and Africa.

More directly and recently a major influence has been Césaire's *Cahier d'un retour au pays natal* (1939 and later editions) which showed how the surrealism of a Breton or Aragon, allied to a subterranean energy of bitterness and growing Marxist orientation, could utter unspeakable truths in a French as clear as it had to be and as murky as strong emotion and need for concealment would make it. Here are the famous opening lines from *Cahier:*

> *Partir. Mon coeur bruissait de générosités emphatiques.*
>
> *Partir . . . j'arriverais lisse et jeune dans ce pays mien et je dirais à ce pays dont le limon entre dans la composition de ma chair: "J'ai longtemps erré et je reviens vers la hideur désertée de vos plaies."*

Daniel Boukman (b. 1936 in Martinique), deserter from the French Army in Algeria in 1961 and there long resident, has composed dramatic poems, midway between chants and cabinet drama. Much of his work is clearly concerned with recapturing the ancestral past:

Partons! partons!
Fuyons au beau pays d'Afrique

Là-bas
les hommes les dieux
face à face se contemplent
sans baisser les yeux
Viens.
Que te réservent ces îles pitieuses?

And Boukman's *Orphée nègre* (dedicated to Martinique's famous Frantz Fanon) refers particularly to the Guadeloupe uprising of 1967:

La liberté
n'est pas la pièce au creux d'une main, Jetée
ni le salaire d'un long temps de sourire et de génuflexions
La liberté vraie
c'est une perle étincelante tombée au fond de l'océan

More vigorous yet is *Eia! Man-maille-la* (1968), a play by Macouba (pseudonym of August Armeth, b. 1939) which uses the events of a communist-inspired riot in Fort-de-France, Martinique, in 1959.

Several of the more interesting writers from the past several decades would be the Martiniquan Edouard Glissant (b. 1928), poet and critic who works in the Césairean mode but is more mistily concerned with the feel of place than the contemporary scene; and Eugène Emile Dervain (b. 1928), poet, playwright, and storywriter who has married an African and settled in the Ivory Coast. His plays *Saranou la reine scélerate* and *La Langue et le Scorpion* (both 1968) retell in dramatic form two of the great tales handed down by the griots of the Bambara world of King Da Monson, ruler of 18th century Segou. Joseph Zobel (b. 1915) is an important novelist with his *Diab'la* (1946), *La Rue Cases-Nègres* (1950), *Les Jours Immobiles* (1946), *La Fêté à Paris* (1953) and *Le Journal de Samba Boy* (195?), and other works.

The Guadeloupians are Jean-Louis Victor (called Baghio'o, born ca. 1915) who fought the Nazis in the French underground and continued his personal struggle against oppression in his three novels and one collection of poetry; Paul Niger (Albert Béville, 1915-1962), poet, and Henri Corbin (b. 1932).

One author long associated with Martinique, though born in the West Indian neighboring island of Dominica, was Daniel Thaly (1879-1950) whose family orientation was French (as is the case with many Dominicans even after 200 years of British control). Thaly dreamed of Africa:

Depuis, la nostalgie habite dans son âme;
Rien ne l'a consolé de sa lointaine Afrique
Où sont les fleuves bleus chers à l'hippopotame?

In Guyane, several important poets besides the famous Damas deserve mention: Serge Patient (b. 1934) and Elie Stephenson (1944). Born in France (1945) but resident in Guyane and associating himself with Guyane also is the poet, novelist, and painter, Patrick Langlois.

The major novelist from Guyane, and one of the best from the Caribbean, is Bertène Juminer (b. 1927), author of the novels *Les Bâtards* (1961), *Au seuil d'un nouveau cri* (1963) and *La Revanche de Bozambo* (1968), now translated (1976) into English as *Bozambo's Revenge: or Colonialism Inside Out,* one of the few translated francophone Caribbean works. The latter work provides the mirror image to European colonialism by positing a long Baoulian (the major people of the Ivory Coast) occupation of the lands of the "primitive" peoples living along the Sekuana River (read Seine) and their slow movement toward recapturing their own culture and political freedom.

René Jadford (1901-1947) also wrote three novels: *Deux hommes et l'aventure* (1945), *Nuits de Cachiri* (1946), and the unpublished "Cipango ou les trésors du lendemain." Hardly remembered today, but a very early novelist, was Jean Galmot (1879-1928), who, though born in France, long was resident in Guyane and even joined in efforts to achieve independence. His two works were *Quelle étrange histoire* (1918) and *Un mort vivait parmi nous* (1922).

Moving beyond the nostalgia of *négritude* was Raphael Tardon of Martinique who yet wrote *Starkenfirst* (1947) which deals with the slave trade and *La Caldeira* (1948), centered on the disastrous eruption of Mt. Pelée in 1902 and the equally vicious racial prejudices of whites and blacks in Martinique. His *Christ au poing* (1950), set in French Tahiti, provided him an esthetic (geographical?) distance in which to lament the loss of innocence and the grossness and disease coming fast with occidental civilization.

Until recently, there have not been many women writers from the Caribbean, but Marie-Magdalene Carbet (b. 1906) is an accomplished poet as these few lines might indicate:

Trois roses, Passion
Orgueil, flammes, rayon.
Spectres chers au regard.
Larmes, prismes fluides

and after a voyage to Africa she would recall the ancient city of Gao on the Upper Niger in such poems as "Hautes Eaux" and "Beau piroguier" in the collection *Rose de ta grâce.* She also has published five novels, including the recent one, *Au péril de ta joie* (1972) and many volumes of verse.

Other women writers are: Marie Berte, Thèrèse Betzon, Mayotte Capecia, Marie-Thérése Julien-Lung-Fou, Kiki Marie-Sainte, and Irmine Romanette, all from Martinique. Some of the Guadeloupian writers are Simone Schwarz-Bart, novelist and co-author with her husband, André, of *La Mulâtresse Solitude* (1972); Maryse Condé, critic; Michèle Lacrosil; Jacqueline Manicom, and Florette Morand-Capasso.

Not a creative writer in our sense, but possibly the most important writer from the Antilles, was Frantz Fanon (b. 1925, Fort de France; d. 1961) but who so identified himself with the Algerian struggle against colonialism that he could shout: "Je suis algérien, . . . Nous, patriotes algériens," and who later served as Algeria's first ambassador to Ghana and would become a friend of Nkrumah and Patrice Lumumba. Among his works, by now world famous, were *Peau noire, masques blancs* (1952), translated as *Black Skin, White Masks* (1967); *Les Damnés de la terre* (preface by Sartre, 1961), and translated as *The Wretched of the Earth* (1965); and *Pour la révolution africaine* (1964) and in translation, *Toward the African Revolution* (1966).

The problem for all the Antillean writers, whatever their "language of expression," is that of dealing with, or expressing, two or more cultures. Césaire in his introduction to Juminer's *Les Bâtards,* wrote:

> *Telle est la situation de l'Antillais, le bâtard de l'Europe et de l'Afrique, partagé entre ce père qui le renie et cette mère qu'il a reniée . . . C'est le problème d'hommes privés de leur propre culture et acculturés à une autre civilisation, mais au prix de quelles mutilations!*

That is also the situation posed in Mme. Schwarz-Bart's novel cited above. Solitude, born of violence on board a slave-ship, must live out her life despised by her mother, and half-petted, half-hated by her white "owners." Only as she identifies herself with rebellion and Africa can she find a peace of sorts. Her madness and the cryptic prose-verse of a Césaire is testimony to terrible strain in the Antilles. *That is still the problem . . .*

LIST OF WRITERS FROM HAITI

Abderrahman (pseudonym for Dr. François Duvalier)
Abélard, Charles Alexandre
Adry-Carène (pseudonym for Adrien Carrénard)
Albert, Pasteur Auguste
Alexandre, Antoine C.
Alexandre, MacDonald
Alexis, Jacques Stéphen
Alexis, Stéphen
Alphonse, Emile J.
Ambroise, Fernand (pseudonym: Félix de Saint-Laurent)
Ambroise, Ludovic
Ambroise, Lys (pseudonym: Jean Libose)
André, Constant
André, Démétrius
Anselin, Charles
Antoine, Yves
Ardouin, Alexis Beaubrun
Ardouin, Charles Nicolas Céligny
Ardouin, Gustave Léonard Coriolan
Audain, Julio Jean-Pierre
Audain, Dr. Léon
Audain (père), Dr. Louis
Auguste, Jules
Auguste, Nemours
Auguste, Nemours (b. 1883: see under Alfred Nemours)
Backer, Desaix (see under pseudonym: Aimard Le Sage)
Baguidy, Joseph D.
Baguidy-Gilbert, Serge
Battier, Alcibiade Fleury (also: Fleury-Battier)
Bauduy, Robert
Beaubrun, Théodore (pseudonym: Languichatte)
Beaugé, Jacqueline
Beaulieu, Raymond
Bec, Marie (pseudonym for Marie-Thérèse Colimon)
Bélance, René
Bellegarde, Jean-Louis Windsor
Bellegarde, Louis Dantès
Benoît, Clément
Benoît, François Pierre Joseph (pseudonym for Dr. Rosalvo Bobo)
Bergeaud, Eméric
Bernard, Regnor Charles
Bervin, Antoine
Besse, Martial
Bissainthe, Max
Blanchet, Jules Antoine
Blot, Probus Louis
Bobo, Dr. Rosalvo (pseudonym: François Pierre Joseph Benoît)
Boisrond-Tonnerre, Louis
Bonhomme, Arthur (pseudonym: Claude Fabry)
Bonhomme, Colbert
Bonnet, Guy-Joseph
Borno, Louis Eustache Antoine François Joseph
Bourand, Anne-Marie (née Lerebours; see under pseudonym: Annie Desroy)
Bourand, Etienne
Bréville, Pierre (pseudonym for Dominique Hippolyte)
Brierre, Jean Fernand (also Jean François)
Brouard, Carl
Brun, Adolphe Pascal
Brun, Amédée
Brun, Lélio
Bruno, Camille
Brutus, Edner

Brutus, Timoléon César
Burr-Reynaud, Frédéric
Calixte, Démosthène Pétrus
Calvin, Jean Max
Camille, Roussan (pseudonym: Nassour El Limac)
Campfort, Gérard
Carrénard, Adrien (pseudonym: Adry-Carène)
Carrié, Pierre
Casias, Rose-Marie Perrier (also: Rose-Marie Perrier)
Casséus, Maurice A.
Castera, Georges
Catalogne, Gérard de
Cédras, Dantès
Célestin, Clément
Célestin, Julio B.
Célestin-Mégie, Emile
Chanlatte, Juste (also: Comte de Rosiers)
Charles, Carmin
Charles, Christophe
Charles, Jean-Claude
Charles, Joseph D.
Charles-Pierre, Derville
Charlier, Aymon (see under Marie Vieux)
Charlier, Etienne Danton
Charlier, Jacques Roumain
Charmant, Antoine Alcius
Charmant, Dr. Rodolphe
Chassagne, Roland
Chauvet, Henri
Chauvet, Marie-Vieux (see under Marie Vieux)
Chenet, Gérard
Chevalier, André Fontanges
Chevry, Arsène
Chrisphonte, Propser
Cinéas, Jean-Baptiste
Coicou, Clément A.
Coicou, Massilon
Colas, Justin L.
Colibri (pseudonym for Marie Vieux)
Colimon, Marie-Thérèse (pseudonym: Marie Bec)
Colombel, A. Noël
Corvington, Hermann
Courtois, Félix
Courtois, Mme Joseph (née Julienne Bussière Laforest)
Cyprien, Anatole (pseudonym for Claude Dambreville)
Damne, Konrad (pseudonym for Eddy Arnold Jean)
Danache, Berthoumieux
Darfour, Félix
Darlouze, René (pseudonym for Charles Moravia)
Daumec, Gérard
Dauphin, Marcel
Davertige (pseudonym for Villard Denis)
David, Placide
Delorme, Démesvar
Denis, Lorimer (pseudonym: Aristide de Sabe)
Denis, Villard (pseudonym: Davertige)
Dennery, Germaine
Dépestre, Edouard
Dépestre, René
Deschamps, Marguerite (pseudonym for Michaëlle Lafontant-Medard)
Deslandes, Emile
Deslandes, Célie-Diaquoi (see under: Célie Diaquoi-Deslandes)
Desroussels, Félix (pseudonym for Jean-Baptiste Dorismond)
Desroy, Annie (pseudonym for Mme Etienne Bourand, née Lerebours)

Destouches, Dantès
Dévieux-Dehoux, Liliane
Diaquoi-Deslandes, Célie (also: Célie-Diaquoi Deslandes)
Dodard, Antoine
Domingue, Jules
Dorcély, Roland
Doret, Frédéric
Dorismond, Jacques
Dorismond, Jean-Baptiste (pseudonym: Félix Desroussels)
Dorsainvil, Justin Chrysostome (also: J.C.)
Dorsinville, Hénec
Dorsinville, Jean-Baptiste
Dorsinville, Luc
Dorsinville, Max
Dorsinville, Roger
Dorval, Gérard
Dougé, Gérard
Douyon, Ernest
Drice, Mirabeau (or: Mirabbo)
Duc, Gérard
Ducasse, Vendenesse
Dumervé, Constantin Eugène
Dumesle, Hérard
Duplessis, Jean-François Fénelon
Duplessis-Louverture, Louis (also: Louis Duplessis Louverture)
Dupoux, Antoine
Dupré, Antoine
Durand, Charles Alexis Oswald
Durand, Louis-Henry
Duval, Amilcar
Duvalier, François (pseudonym: Abderrahman)
Edouard, Emmanuel
El Limac, Nassour (pseudonym for Roussan Camille)
Elie, Abel (pseudonym: Franck)
Elie, Louis Emile
Emile, George Léon
Ethéart, Liautaud
Etienne, Gérard Vergniaud
Eugène, Grégoire
Fabry, Claude (pseudonym for Arthur Bonhomme)
Fardin, Dieudonné (pseudonym: Louis Marie Benoît Pierre)
Faubert, Ida
Faubert, Pierre
Féquiere, Fleury
Féry, Alibée
Féthiere, Sténio
Figaro, Georges Jacques
Figaro, Morille P. (or Maurille)
Fignolé, Jean-Claude
Firmin, Anténor Joseph
Fleury-Battier (pseudonym for Alcibiade Fleury Battier)
Fligneau, Pierre
Fouché, Franck
Fouchard, Jean
Franck (pseudonym for Abel Elie)
Fraeniel (pseudonym for Madeleine Dominique Paillère)
Franketienne (see under Frank Etienne)
Fureteur, Jean Le (pseudonym for Auguste Magloire)
Gaillard, Roger
Garoute, Hamilton
Garoute, Louis
Gédéon, Max
Georges, Guy D.
Gérard, Marie (pseudonym for Luc Grimard)
Giordani, Roland
Godefroy, Justin
Gouraige, Ghislain
Grimard, Luc (pseudonyms: Marie Gérard and Lin Dège)

Guérin, Mona Rouzier
Guéry, Fortuna Augustin
Guilbaud, Tertulien Marcelin
Hall, Louis Duvivier
Héraux, Edmond
Heurtelou, Daniel
Hibbert, Pierre Fernand
Hippolyte, Alice
Hippolyte, Dominique (pseudonym: Pierre Bréville)
Hyppolite, Ducas
Hyppolite, Michelson Paul
Inginac, Joseph Balthazar
Innocent, Antoine
Jacob, Kléber Georges
Jacques, Maurice (see supplement)
Janvier, Louis-Joseph
Jastram, Gervais
Jean, Eddy Arnold (pseudonym: Konrad Damné)
Jean-Baptiste, Ernst
Jean-Louis, Dulciné
Jérémie, Cadet (also: Joseph)
Jolicoeur, Renée Marie-Ange

Labonté, Louis Roger
Labossière, Abel
Labuchin, Rassoul (pseudonym for Yves Medard)
Lafontant, Jean Délorme
Lafontant-Médard, Michaëlle (pseudonym: Marguerite Deschamps)
Laforest, Antoine
Laforest, Edmond
Laforest, Georges Florvil
Laforest, Jean-Richard
Lahens, Léon
Laleau, Léon
Lamarre, Joseph P.V.
Languichatte (pseudonym for Théodore Beaubrun)
Lanier, Dr Clément (pseudonym: Jean Robion)
Lapierre, Alix
Laraque, Paul (pseudonym: Jacques Lenoir)
Large, Camille
Large, Josaphat Robert
Laroche, Louis Arnold
Laroche, Maximilien
Lassègue, Franck
Lataillade, Robert
Latortue, Paul Emile
Laurent, Gérard Mentor
Lavelanet, François (see supplement)
Leconte, Vergniaud
Lefèvre, Louis
Legagneur, Serge
Léger, Georges Nicolas
Légitime, Denis
Lemaire, Emmeline Carriès
Lemoine, Lucien (see supplement)
Lenoir, Jacques (pseudonym for Paul Laraque)
Léon, Rulx
Lerebours, Anne-Marie (see under pseudonym: Annie Desroy)
Lerebours, Michel Philippe
Lérémond, Jean Jacques
Leroy, Félix Moriseau (or Morisseau-Leroy)
Leroy, Frantz
Le Sage, Aimard (pseudonym for Desaix Backer)
Lescot, Léocardie Elie
Lescouflair, Arthur
Lescouflair, Georges
Lespès, Anthony
Lespès, Pascher
Lestage, Willy
Lhérisson, Camille

Lhérisson, François Romain
Lhérisson, Justin
Libose, Jean (pseudonym for Lys Ambroise)
Lin Dège (pseudonym for Luc Grimard)
Lochard, Paul
Louhis, Léon
Louis, Mme Jeanine Tavernier (see under Jeanine Tavernier)
Louis, Michel Salmador
Louverture, Isaac
Louverture, Pierre François Dominique Toussaint
Lubin, Maurice Alcibiade (pseudonym: Malu)
Madiou, Alexandre
Madiou, Thomas
Magloire, Auguste (pseudonym: Jean Le Fureteur)
Magloire, Francis L. (see under: Francis L. Séjour-Magloire)
Magloire, Clément fils (see under Magloire Saint-Aude)
Maglóire, Nadine
Malu (pseudonym for Maurice A. Lubin)
Mangones, Victor Michel Raphaël
Manigat, Leslie François
Manigat, Thalès
Marc, Jules André
Marcelin, Emile
Marcelin, Frédéric
Marcelin, Pierre
Mariamour, Jean Hubert (pseudonym for Hubert Papailler)
Mars, Dr Jean Price (see under Dr Jean Price-Mars)
Martineau, Fernand
Mathon, Alix
Mathon, Etienne
Mayard, Constantin
Mayard, Pierre
Medard, Yves (see under pseudonym: Rassoul Labuchin)
Mégie, Emile Celestin (see under Emile Celestin-Megie)
Ménos, Solon
Mentor, Etienne Victor
Mercier, Louis
Metellus, Jean (see supplement)
Milscent, Jules Solime
Moïse, Rodolphe
Moravia, Adeline
Moravia, Charles (pseudonym: René Darlouze)
Moreau de Saint Méry, Médéric Louis
Morisseau, Roland
Morisseau-Leroy, Félix (see under Félix Morisseau Leroy)
Morpeau, Louis
Najac, Paul E.
Nau, Auguste Théodore Eugène
Nau, Auguste Emile
Nau, Ignace
Nemours, Alfred (also: Nemours Auguste or Géneral Nemours)
Neptune, Louis
Niger, Emilius (pseudonym for Emile Roumer)
Numa, Edgar Nérée
Paillère, Madeleine Dominique (pseudonym: Fraeniel)
Papailler, Hubert (pseudonym: Jean Hubert Mariamour)
Papillon, Pierre
Paret, Timothée L. J.
Pereira, Roger
Perez, Jeanne
Perrier, Rose-Marie (also: Rose-Marie Perrier Casias)
Pétion, Alexandre Sabès

Phelps, Anthony
Philoctète, Raymond
Philoctète, René
Pierre, Claude C.
Pierre, Louis Marie Benoît (see under pseudonym: Dieudonné Fardin)
Pierre-Louis, Ulysse
Piquion, René
Pommayrac, Alcibiade
Pompilus, Pradel
Posy, Bonnard
Pouilh, Duraciné
Pradel, Seymour
Pressoir, Charles Fernand
Price, Philippe Hannibal
Price-Mars, Dr Jean (also: Jean Price Mars)
Raymond, Julien
Renaud, Alix Joseph
Rey, Dantès
Rey-Charlier, Ghislaine
Ricot, Justinien
Ricourt, Volvick
Rigaud, André
Rigaud, Milo (also: Emile)
Robion, Jean (pseudonym for Clément Lanier)
Rochemont, Serge (see supplement)
Romain, Dr Jean-Baptiste
Romane, Jean-Baptiste
Rosarion, Ulrick
Rose, Samuel Luzincourt
Rosemond, Jules
Rosiers, Comte de (see under Juste Chanlatte)
Roumain, Jacques (Jean-Baptiste)
Roumer, Emile (pseudonym: Emilius Niger)
Rouzier, Maximilien (also: Sémexant or Saint-Mexant)
Roy, Francis Joachim
Roy, Hérard, L.C.
Sabe, Aristide de (pseudonym for Lorimer Denis)
Saint-Amand, Edriss
Saint-Aude, Magloire (born Clément Magloire fils)
St-Cyr, Frantz Colbert
Saint-Jean, Serge
Saint-Louis, Carlos
Saint-Rémy, Joseph
Saint-Robert (pseudonym for Félix Viard)
Salès, Pierre Marc
Salgado, Antoine
Sampeur, Marie Angelique Virginie
Sannon, Horace Pauléus
Sansaricq, Walter
Savain, Pétion
Séjour-Magloire, Francis L. (also: Francis L. Magloire)
Simonise, Alfred
Staco, Louis
Sylvain, Georges
Sylvain, Louis François Normil (a.k.a. Normil-George)
Sylvain-Bouchereau, Madeleine G.
Sylvain-Comhaire, Suzanne
Tavernier, Jeanine (also: Jeanine Tavernier Louis)
Théard, Gaston
Thébaud, Fritz Vély
Thévenot, René Larivière
Thoby, Armand
Thoby-Marcelin, Philippe
Toulanmanche, Karl
Trouillot, Ernst
Trouillot, Hénock
Valcin, Mme Virgile (also: Cléanthe Desgraves Valcin)
Vastey, Baron (originally Pompée Valentin de Vastey)

Vallès, Max
Vaval, Duraciné
Vaval, Jean-Baptiste F.
Verne, Marc
Viard, Félix (pseudonym: Saint-Robert)
Victor, René
Vieux, Antonio (also: Antoine)
Vieux, Damoclès
Vieux, Isnardin
Vieux, Marie (also published under married names: Aymon Charlier, Marie Vieux Chauvet and pen-name: Colibri)
Vilaire, Etzer
Vilaire, Jean-Joseph
Villevaleix, Charles Séguy
Vincent, Sténio
Vixamar, Claude
Voltaire fils, Jean-Auguste
Werleigh, Christian
Wiener, Jacqueline
Wiener, Wanda Ducoste
Williams, Charles D.
Wolff, Carl (or Karl)
Zéphyr, Jacques J.

LIST OF WRITERS FROM DOMINICA, GUADELOUPE, GUYANE AND MARTINIQUE

Dominica

Thaly, Daniel Désiré Alain

Guadeloupe

Agricole, Eugène
Alante-Lima, Willy
d'Anglemont, Alexandre Privat
Baghio'o, Jean-Louis (pseudonym for Victor Jean-Louis)
Baudot, Paul
Bazile, Corneille
Beauvallon, Jean Baptiste Rosemond de
Bellaire, Ancelot
Beville, Albert (pseudonym: Paul Niger)
Bonhomme, Jacques
Campenon, François Nicolas Vincent
Chambertrand, Gilbert Suandeau de
Clermont, Raymond
Condé, Maryse
Corbin, Henri
Coussin, J.H. Joseph
Delisle, Gérard
Elot, Maryse
Estoup, Valentine Eugènie (b. France)
Giraud, Octave
Hennique, Léon
Jean, Antoine
Jean-Louis, Victor (pseudonym: Jean-Louis Baghio'o)
Jeffry, Antonio
Kermadec, Jeanne de
Lacrosil, Michèle
Lara, Oruno
Lara, Sully-Moïse
Léger-Léger, Alexis (pseudonym: Saint-John Perse)
Léonard, Nicolas Germain
Manicom, Jacqueline
Marsolle, Edouard
Morand-Capasso, Florette
Niger, Paul (pseudonym for Albert Béville)
Perse, Saint-John (see Alexis Léger-Léger)
Poirié, Jean-Aurèle Pierre (see under pseudonym: Poirié de Saint-Aurèle)
Porto, Louis (pseudonym for Camille Rousseau)
Rousseau, Camille (pseudonym: Louis Porto)
Rupaire, Sonny
Saint Aurèle, Poirié (pseudonym for Jean-Aurèle Pierre Poirié)
Saint-John Perse (pseudonym for Alexis Saint Léger-Léger)
Schwartz-Bart, Simone
Talbom, Léon
Thomarel, André
Tirolien, Guy

Guyane

Bonneton, André
Cabassou, Lionel George André (pseudonym for Léon G. Damas)
Chatenay, Libert
Cupidon, Antoine
Damas, Léon Gontran (pseudonym: Lionel George André Cabassou)
Eboué, Adolphe Félix Sylvestre
Galmot, Jean (b. France)
Jadfard, René
Juminer, Bertène
Llero, Auguste (pseudonym for Christian Rolle)
Langlois, Patrick

Lohier, Michel
Métro, Henri
Monnerville, Gaston Charles François
Nago, Jules
Othily, Georges
Patient, Serge
Rolle, Christian (pseudonym: Auguste Llero)
Stephenson, Elie

Martinique

Achard, Marcel (pseudonym: Jean Foyal)
Adréa, Albert
André, Marcel
Armeth, Auguste (pseudonym: Auguste Macouba)
Attuly, Lionel
d'Avrigny, l'Oeillard
Berte, Marie (pseudonym: Emmbe)
Betzon, Thérèse (Mme Thérèse Blanc; also Melle DeSolms)
Blanc, Mme Thérèse (see under Thérèse de Betzon)
Bonneville, Renẽ
Boukman, Daniel
Capécia, Mayotte
Carbet, Claude
Carbet, Marie-Magdalene (a.k.a. "Magdeleine")
Césaire, Aimé
Chalonec, Frantz
Clarac, René
Cléry, Pierre
Coquille, Jean
Dervain, Eugène
Desportes, Auguste
Desportes, Georges
Du Prey, Pierre de la Ruffinière
Duquesnay, Victor
Ega, Françoise
Emmbe (pseudonym for Marie Berte)
Etchart, Salvat (b. Netherlands)
Eyma, Louis Xavier
Fanon, Frantz
Florentiny, Edouard
Gentille, Antoine de
Glissant, Edouard
Grandmaison, Daniel
Grassely, Abbé Paul
Gratiant, Gilbert (pseudonym: Jean Nous-Terre)
Helm, Danyl
Herpin, Thérèse
Houel, Drasta (née Hurard; pseudonym: Huel or Houël)
Joyau, Auguste
Joyau-Dormoy, Alice
Julien-Lung-Fou, Marie-Thérèse
Lavigne, Mark (pseudonym: Emmanuel-Flavia Léopold)
Léméry, Hélène
Léopold, Emmanuel-Flavia (pseudonym: Mark Lavigne)
Léro, Etienne
Levilloux, A.
Linval, Paule Cassius de (Jean Marx)
Macouba, Auguste (pseudonym for Auguste Armeth)
Maran, René
Marbot, François Achille
Marie-Sainte, Kiki
Marraud de Sigalony, Joseph
Marraud de Sigalony, Louise
Marx, Jean (pseudonym for Paule Cassius de Linval)
Mauvois, Georges
Melon-Degras, Alfred
Ménil, René

Miramant, Yves (see under Irmine Romanette)
Monnerot, Jules Marcel
Monplaisir, Emma
Nous-Terre, Jean (pseudonym for Gilbert Gratiant)
Orville, Xavier
Osénat, Pierre
Padoly, Yves
Placoly, Vincent
Plinval, Robert
Polius, Joseph
Pulvar, César
Relouzat, Claude
Richer, Clément
Romanette, Irmine (pseudonym: Yve Miramant)
Rouil, Marie-Thérèse
Saint-Maurice, Rémy
Saint-Prix, Rone Eleuthère
Sainville, Léonard
Salavina (pseudonym for Virgile Savane)
Savana, Virgile (see under pseudonym: Salavina)
DeSolms, Melle (pseudonym for Thérèse de Betzon)
Tardon, Raphaël
Thaly, Fernand
Zizine, Albert Pierre
Zobel, Joseph

Volume II Entries: A to Z

ABELARD, Charles Alexandre

b. February 10, 1932, Léogane, Haiti. Playwright.

Abélard attended the school of the Christian Brothers for his primary classes in Léogane, and went to Port-au-Prince for his secondary studies, attending the College of Saint-Vincent de Paul and the Lycée Pétion.

He was a student at the Conservatoire National d'Art Dramatique where he was graduated. He founded a company of actors, La Société des Messagers de l'Art, and he staged the classical works of Corneille, Racine, Molière, the *Ecole des Maris* by Franck Fouché, *L'Oiseau de ces Dames* by Mona Rouzier Guérin, an adaptation of *Masters of the Dew* by Jacque Roumain, and Albert Camus' *Caligula* for which he was awarded a prize.

He became the manager of the Conservatoire National d'Art Dramatique and director of Radio Port-au-Prince.

In October of 1969 Abélard was named Cultural Attaché at the Haitian Embassy in Paris and he later served as Minister Councellor until June, 1972.

Writings: Plays: *David, tragedy in 5 acts, Port-au-Prince, Les Presses Libres, 1961; La leçon du bicolore* (historical play, unpublished); *Mariage ou Duel à mort* (unpublished).

Poetry: *Croche et double croche,* followed by *Déclaration paysanne,* Port-au-Prince, Fardin, 1974.

ACHARD, Marcel

(pseudonym: **Jean FOYAL**)

b. 1892, Fort-de-France, Martinique; d. December, 1950, Lyon, France. Poet, lawyer.

Achard attended the Lycée Schoelcher in Fort-de-France, Martinique, then the law school in Toulouse, France, and won his doctorate. He became deputy attorney at Pointe-à-Pitre. His career took him finally to Indo-China where he served as a judge. He served in Haiphong, Phnom-Penh, Tonkin, and in Cambodia.

Achard's poetry was influenced by Daniel Thaly's work but discloses a greater feeling of loss of his island roots than Thaly's nostalgic poetry often written in exile in France.

In this poem dedicated to Daniel Thaly, Achard expressed his sadness and his nostalgic feeling for his island:

Comme toi, dans une île où l'azur environne
La noble pourpre et l'or d'un somptueux jardin
Je naquis dans l'ardeur d'un soir incarnadin
Dans une ile de feu qu'un noir volcan couronne.

Mais, moins heureux, hélas, mon humeur pérégrine,
M'éloigne trop longtemps du tendre sol natal,
Et par delà les mers du monde oriental.

Je donne libre essor à mon âme chagrine,
Et je revois, en songe, aux plaintes des ramiers,
Glisser la lune pâle aux faîtes des palmiers.

Writings: Poetry: *La Muse pérégrine* (sonnets), Toulouse, Ed. Guitard, 1924; *La Cendre empourprée,* 1927.

ADREA, Albert

b. April 8, 1901, Saint Esprit, Martinique.
Poet, playwright, essayist.

Adréa attended schools in Fort-de-France but he was forced to interrupt his studies. A self-made man, he worked as a photographer, but was active in many cultural activities.

He has written many poems and delivered several lectures.

He received many rewards for his works, among them the Lauréat des jeux de l'Olympe and the Médaille d'Or à l'Exposition du Tricentenaire.

Writings: Poetry: *Bluets d'Avril,* poèsies, Fort-de-France, Impr. La Presse, 1944; *Dans l'oasis du coeur,* Fort-de-France, 1947; *Brises de jeunesse,* 1951; *Fleurs du soir (vers et prose),* Fort-de-France, Ed. des Horizons Caraibes, 1957;*Sommets (poèmes philosophiques),* Fort-de France, Ed. Berger, 1960; *Roses d'automne,* Fort-de-France, Impr. Antillaise Saint-Paul, 1967; *Le chant des sources,* Fort-de-France, Impr. Antillaise Saint-Paul, 1967; *Beautés, grandeurs, tristesses,* 1970.

Essay: *Société de l'Humanité solidaire,* Fort-de-France, Impr. Officielle, 1948.

Play: *Trois Bonnes Fortunes.*

ADRY-CARENE

(pseudonym for **Adrien CARRENARD**)

AGRICOLE, Eugène

b. June 8, 1835, Basse-Terre, Guadeloupe; d. April 30, 1901, in Sainte Marie, Martinique.
Poet, public servant.

Agricole was educated in Basse-Terre where he came to settle with his family in Martinique. He was elected Mayor of Sainte-Marie and later Town councillor. He became president of the general council.

As poet, Agricole contributed to the anthology *Fleurs des Antilles* published the World's Fair of 1900 (Paris, A. Challamel, ed., 1900).

Many of his poems and articles appeared in newspapers of Guadeloupe and Martinique.

Writings: Poetry: *Les Soupirs et les rêves* (posthumous), Nantes, Impr. Méchinaud et Giraudet, 1936.

ALANTE-LIMA, Willy

b. ca. 1942, Grand-Bourg, Ile de Marie-Galante (Guadeloupe).
Poet, critic, storywriter.

Alante-Lima's first collection was published in German as *Mancinelen Blauten* (Mancenils Flowers), but his first verses had already appeared in *La Revue Guadeloupéene.* He has published many

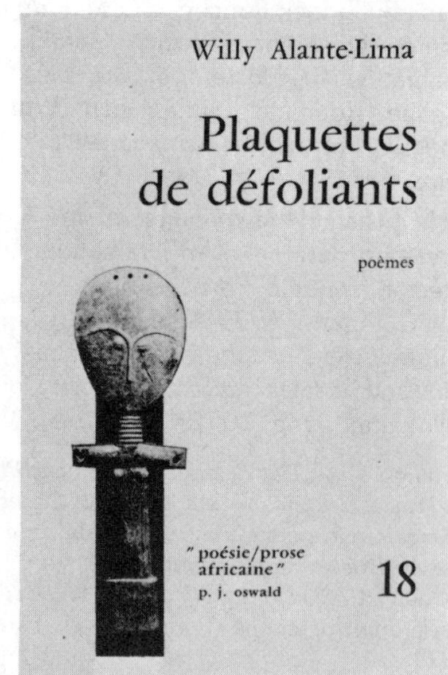

reviews and critical essays, commencing with an article in *Le Nouvelliste de la Guadeloupe;* Recherche de l'antillianité" appeared in *Présence Africaine* and "Le Critique noir et son peuple comme producteur de civilisation" was read at the Yaoundé Conference of the Société Africaine de Culture. His critical work continues to appear frequently in *Présence Africaine.*

Writings: Poetry: *Plaquettes de défoliants,* Paris, Pierre Jean Oswald, 1976. (Details are unavailable on the German-language version of his early poetry.)

Phonograph Recording: *Clindindins des îles* (on the subject of the fauna and flora of the Antilles).

Stories: various, several broadcast by Radio-Guadeloupe in 1972-1973.

ALBERT, Pasteur Auguste

b. September 7, 1860, Cap-Haitien, Haiti;
d. April 17, 1926, Cap-Haitien.
Journalist, teacher, preacher.

Albert was educated at the Institution Saint-Nicolas, directed by Nelson Desroches, and later at the Collège Capois with Saint-Surin Manigat as Director. After schooling, he started as a sales agent and became a teacher and the principal of the school for boys, in Cap-Haitien. He was also a notary.

As a journalist, he protested with other Haitian leaders the American military forces who occupied Haiti by founding the patriotic papers *Le Maringouin, l'Argus* and *L'Opinion Nationale.* He left many articles and sermons unpublished.

Writings: Essay: *Comment fêter le centenaire?,* Cap-Haitien, Impr. du Progrès, 1903.

ALEXANDRE, Antoine C.

b. March 23, 1917, Léogâne, Haiti.
Poet, teacher.

Alexandre attended the school of the Christian Brothers in Léogane, then went to Port-au-Prince to be educated at the Lycée Pétion.

He was a teacher in several schools, became Professor at the Lycée Pétion and finally was Inspector and head of the secondary education division at the Department of National Education.

Writings: Poetry: *Chansons nègres; poèmes,* Port-au-Prince, Impr. V. Valcin; *Rythmes indigènes, poèmes,* Port-au-Prince, Impr. V. Valcin, 1946.

ALEXANDRE, MacDonald

b. August 25, 1862, Cayes, Haiti;
d. June 30, 1931, Port-au-Prince.
Teacher, poet.

Alexandre was educated at the Petit Séminaire Collège St-Martial and at the Lycée Philippe Guerrier of Cayes. He was graduated from the law school of Cayes. He was a teacher from 1881-1902, and served as Mayor (Magistrat Communal) of Cayes and later was National Deputy (1900-1914).

Alexandre favored the progress of music in Cayes and he founded the magazine *La Petite Revue* in 1891, which lasted until 1900.

Most of Alexandre's work was directed at juveniles or was prepared for school texts of literature.

Duraciné Vaval, who knew him, expressed this about his work: "Mac Donald Alexandre n'exprime que des sentiments qu'il a réellement éprouvés. Il excelle à découvrir le côté poètique des choses les plus vulgaires. Il sait donner à tout ce qu'il touche une forme brève et originale."

Writings: Poetry: *Les Chants intimes* (unpublished).

Anthology: *La poèsie haitienne à l'école et dans la famille* (with Arsène Chevry, unpublished).

ALEXIS, Jacques Stéphen

b. April 22, 1922, Gonaives, Haiti;
d. ca. 1961.
Novelist, playwright, essayist, storywriter, physician.

Alexis started his education at the College Stanislas in Paris and completed his studies at the Institution Saint-Louis de Gonzague of Port-au-Prince. He studied medicine at the Faculty of Medicine of Port-au-Prince and in Paris. He contributed to the 1946 political movement that overthrew the government of his time after which he went to France and traveled extensively, visiting many countries, including those in the Middle East and Russia and China. He was very much interested in Africa and has been virulently anti-Western in his work. At the Congress of Black Artists and Writers, Paris, 1956, he spoke out for "le réalisme merveilleux."

Alexis slipped back into Haiti clandestinely in 1961, having fled for political reasons after an earlier sojourn, and is believed to have perished after his secret arrest.

His life was short but his novels were of good quality and received wide praise.

Writings: Novels: *Compère Général* Soleil, 1955; *Les Arbres musiciens,* 1957; *L'espace d'un cillement,* 1959, all Paris, by Gallimard.

Essays and Critical Works: "Modern Haitian Thought," in *Books Abroad,* Vol. 30 (1965), pp. 261-265; "Conditions d'un roman national chez les peuples noirs," in *Présence Africaine,* No. 13 (April-May 1957); "Du réalisme merveilleux chez les Haitiens," (speech at the first Congress of Black Writers, Paris, 1956) in *Présence Africaine,* Nos. 8-10 (June-Nov. 1956), pp. 245-273; "Contribution à la Table Ronde sur le Folklore et le Nationalisme," in *Optique* (Jan. 1956), No. 23, pp. 25-34; "Les Littératures noires et la France," *Optique* (Dec. 1956), No. 34 (April 1957), pp. 31-42; "La Belle Amour Humaine," in *Europe* (Jan. 1971), pp. 20-27; preface to *Oeuvres Choisies de Jacques Roumain,* Moscow, 1967.

Stories: "La rouille des ans," (extract), *Présence Africaine,* No. 16 (Oct-Nov 1957), pp. 89-93; *Dits du Vieux Vent Caraibe,* Paris, Gallimard, 1958; "Dieu-Premier" (part of an unfinished novel entitled "L'Eglantine"), this fragment published in *La Nouvelle Revue Française,* (1972), pp. 49-67.

Translation of Fiction: *Les arbres musiciens:* in Russian as *Derev'ja Muzy Kanty,* Moscow, Hudoz, 1964; *Compère Général Soleil:* in Albanian as *Gjenerali i mire diell,* Tirana, Naim Frasheri, 1966; in Hungarian as *Nap Tabornok,* Budapest, Kossuth, Kiado, 1966; in Japanese as *Taiyo Shogun, Mezameru Haiti,* Tokyo, Shin Vishon Shuppanoha, 1965, in Czech as *General Slvoko,* Bratislava, V.P.L., 1963; in Spanish as *El Compadre General Sol* (preface by René Dépestre), Havana, Casa de las Américas, 1974; trans. of collection of stories: *Dits du Vieux Vent Caraibe,* into German as *Der Tanz der Goldenen Blü,* Berlin, Volk, U. Welt, 1965, and earlier as *Die Singendem Baume,* Berlin, Vorlag Volk und West, 1961.

Biographical/Critical Sources: René Dépestre, "Un grand roman haitien, *Compère Général Soleil,* par Jacques S. Alexis," *Présence Africaine,* 16 (Oct.-Nov. 1957), pp .91-92; "Les Arbres musiciens by Jacques S. Alexis, *Présence Africaine,* No. 16 (Oct.-Nov.), 1957, pp. 188-189; "Pour la Révolution, Pour la Poésie," in *Parler de Jacques Stéphen Alexis,* Quebec, Léméac, 1974, pp. 172-204 (all above by René Depestre); *Revue Europe,* No. 501 (Jan. 1971), carried several studies on Jacques Alexis and Haitian literature; Beverley Ormerod, "French Caribbean Literature: The Contemporary Situation," in *The Literary Half-Yearly* (West Indian Number), Vol. XI, 2 (July 1970), pp. 113-126 (discussion of *L'espace*

d'un cillement); Jacques Nantet, *Panorama de la littérature noire d'expression française,* Paris, Fayard, 1972; pp. 211-212; Ghislain Gouraige, *Histoire de la littérature haitienne,* Port-au-Prince, Impr. N.A. Théodore, 1960, pp. 356-360; Pradel Pompilus & les Frères de l'Instruction Chrétienne, *Manuel illustré d'histoire de la littérature haitienne,* Port-au-Prince, H. Deschamps, ed., 1961, pp. 483-495; Robert Cornevin, *Le théâtre haitien, des origines à nos jours,* Québec, Léméac, ed., 1973, pp. 149; Eddy A. Jean & Justin O. Fièvre, *Pour une littérature haitienne nationale et militante,* Lille, Editions Jacques Soleil, 1975, pp. 138-159; Mudimbe-Boyi Mbulamwanza, *L'oeuvre romanesque de Jacques-Stéphen Alexis, écrivain haitien,* Kinshasa, Editions du Mont Noir, 1975; Michael Dash, "Jacques Stéphen Alexis," in *Black Images* (Toronto, 1975); Jorge Ruffinelli, "Jacques Stéphen Alexis: Maravilla y terror en Haiti," trans. into Spanish by Ida Vilarina in *Hispameric,* Vol. 2, pp. 41-49; Barbara S. Lynch, "The Collision of Cultures in the Novels of Miguel Angel Asturias, Jacques Stephen Alexis and Chinua Achebe," noted in *Dissertations, Abstracts International,* No. 34; Maximilien Laroche, *Jacques Stéphen Alexis,* Paris, Fernand Nathan, 1977.

ALEXIS, Stéphen

b. November 29, 1889, Gonaives, Haiti; d. August 15, 1962, Caracas, Venezuela.
Novelist, biographer, historian, playwright, diplomat, journalist.

Alexis was educated at the Lycée of Gonaives. He practiced journalism and was a founder and manager-editor of *L'Artibonite.* He used to write articles under the pseudonym of "Stephalex," but when writing his daily chronicles for *La Presse,* he used the name "Agathon II." After teaching at the Lycée of Gonaives, he was named Chargé d'Affaires in Brussels in 1926. He published a novel, *Le nègre masqué,* in 1933, and wrote one play. He was Jacques Alexis' father.

He became the second director of the National Museum of Port-au-Prince and served as Haitian Ambassador to London and later as Representative of Haiti to the United Nations.

After the political events of the 1960's in Haiti, he went into exile in Venezuela where he died.

Writings: Novel: *Le nègre masqué; tranche de vie haitienne,* Port-au-Prince, Impr. de l'Etat, 1933.

Play: *Le Faisceau,* on the second prize at the dramatic contest held in 1933 by the Department of Public Instruction.

Histories: Toussaint Louverture, libérateur d'Haiti, translated into English by William Sterling as *Black Liberator: the Life of Toussaint Louverture,* New York, Macmillan, 1949; *Abrégé d'histoire d'Haiti: 1492-1946,* Port-au-Prince, Ed. H. Deschamps, 1946; Editor of: *Catalogue du Musée National, Fondation Sténio Vincent,* Port-au-Prince, Impr. de l'Etat, 1941.

ALPHONSE, Emile J.

b. ca. 1941, Port-au-Prince, Haiti.
Poet, essayist.

Alphonse received his education in Port-au-Prince. His verse has appeared in various journals and he has collected his works in three volumes.

Writings: Poetry: *Jets de lumière,* Art Graphique Presse, 1961; *Les yeux et la lumière,* 1962; *Rose-sur-le-Sable,* Impr. M. Rodriguez, 1964 (all in Port-au-Prince).

AMBROISE, Fernand

(pseudonym: **Félix de SAINT-LAURENT**)

b. December 9, 1881, Jacmel, Haiti; d. April 7, 1938, Jacmel.
Poet, teacher.

Ambroise was educated at the Petit Séminaire Collège Saint-Martial. Later he was appointed professor of physical sciences at the Lycée Pinchinat of Jacmel. He became an official of the local government of Jacmel and finally an administrator of finances.

He was fond of poetry and published his verses under the pen-name of Félix de

Saint-Laurent in *L'Essor-Revue, Le Temps-Revue* and *Le Nouvelliste.*

Writings: Poetry: A collection of poems still unpublished in book form.

Essay: *Recherche sur les causes naturelles de notre malaise social,* Port-au-Prince, Impr. St-Jacques, 1910.

History: *Le Général Magloire Ambroise a-t-il été tué ou s'est-il suicidé?* Port-au-Prince, Impr. N. Telhomme, 1937.

AMBROISE, Ludovic

b. August 12, 1879, Jacmel, Haiti;
d. September 7, 1940, Port-au-Prince.
Poet, lawyer, accountant.

Ambroise came to Port-au-Prince for his education at the Petit Séminaire Collège Saint-Martial. He studied law and accountancy. He long worked for the government and was eventually named General Postmaster.

Writings: Poetry: *Epanchements (poèmes),* Port-au-Prince, Impr. N. Telhomme, 1939.

AMBROISE, Lys

(pseudonym: **Jean LIBOSE**)
b. August 15, 1911, Cap-Haitien, Haiti.
Poet, military and consular officer.

Ambroise was educated in Cap-Haitien at the Lycée Phillipe Guerrier, thereafter studying at a local military academy and then serving several years in the Haitian army. He served more than ten years as the Haitian consul at Le Havre in France.

Writings: Poetry: *Bouquet à la naiade,* 1941; *Une palme et des roses,* 1941; *La Corbeille* with Edgard N. Numa, Dominique Hippolyte, Luc Grimard), 1943—all three works: Port-au-Prince, Impr. du College Vertières; *Grappes de souvenirs,* 1947; *L'Ile songeuse,* 1947; both Port-au-Prince, Société d'Editions et de Librairie; *Les Cendres du passé,* 1948; *C'est la voix de L'Afrique,* 1951: both Port-au-Prince, Impr. du Séminaire Adventiste; *Confidences,* 1951 and *Valparaiso,* 1951: both Port-au-Prince, Collection Capoise, 1951; *L'Ile Paradisiaque (La Tortue)* with *Cinq Sonnets à Ma Mère,* Port-au-Prince, Impr. du Seminaire Adventiste, 1955.

ANDRE, Constant

b. May 11, 1904, Cap-Haitien, Haiti.
Ethnographer, physician.

Dr. André attended primary and secondary schools in Cap-Haitien and went to Port-au-Prince where he completed his education at the Lycée Pétion. He won a diploma at the Central School of Agriculture and became a school teacher of machine drawing at the vocational school of Cap-Haitien. He then gave up this position and returned to Port-au-Prince to study medicine and graduated from the Faculty of Medicine.

At home, he practices medicine, but he also has been a director of the local asylum Sténio Vincent (Cap-Haitien), and physician and later head of the Justinien Hospital. He supported the cultural Griot movement with Dr. François Duvalier and has published many articles on folklore and medicine in the journals *La Montée, Le Septentrion, Le Nouvelliste* and *Les Griots.*

Writings: Ethnography: *Nos vendeuses de rues et l'avenir de ce trafic en Haiti* (Collection Capoise), Les Presses Nationales d'Haiti, 1966.

History: *L'Hôpital Justinien du Cap-Haitien, de sa fondation en 1890 à l'année 1966* (Collection Capoise), Port-au-Prince, Les Presses Nationales, 1967.

ANDRE, Démétrius

b. September 13, 1866, Cap-Haitien, Haiti; d. July 27, 1915, Port-au-Prince.
Biographer, lawyer, politician.

André was educated in Cap-Haitien at the College Grégoire and he studied law. He was a teacher of history at the Lycée Philippe Guerrier of Cap-Haitien. He founded with Pasteur Auguste Albert the paper *L'Argus.* He died in the prison of Port-au-Prince with 167 political prisoners, prior to the day the American Marines landed in Haiti.

Writings: Biography: *L'anniversaire ou éloge de Joseph Anténor Firmin: 19 Septembre 1912,* Port-au-Prince, Impr. J. Verrollot, 1912.

ANDRE, Marcel

b. ca. 1932, Martinique.
Novelist, playwright, storywriter.

André has written many stories and published three novels and three plays.

Writings: Novels: *Passeport pour l'enfer; Tragiques amours; Andromaque 67* (details not known).
Stories: *Antinéa, mon amour, conte philosophique.*
Plays: *Jésus de Nazareth; La Fille du Sénateur,* Ducoa, Martinique, Impr. M. André; *La Révolution,* Ducoa, Martinique, Impr. M. André, 1962.

d'ANGLEMONT, Alexandre Privat

b. August 21, 1815, Sainte-Rose, Guadeloupe; d. July 18, 1859, Paris.
Traveloguist, essayist, artist.

After local schooling, Privat d'Anglemont went to Paris to study at the famous Lycée Henry IV. He returned home after he completed his classes, but remained only a short time and returned to Paris. He lived the bohemian life, was a good friend of Murger, and served as a model for many characters in Murger's *Scènes de la vie de Bohème.* He died in fitting poverty.

He did picturesque sketches of artisans in and around Paris, but all his works appeared only after his death, edited by Alfred Delvau and Victor Cochinat.

Writings: Travels: *Paris Anecdote, avec une préface et des notes par Ch. Monselet, and 50 sketches by J. Belon,* Paris, 1885; *Paris inconnu, avec une étude sur la vie de l'auteur par A. Delvau* (with 63 sketches by Goindre), Paris, 1886.

ANSELIN, Charles

b. 1841, Haiti; d. June, 1932, Paris.
Poet.

Anselin was one of Haiti's more scholarly poets.

Writings: Poetry: *Album poètique ou la nature de l'homme,* Paris, 1890.
Scholarship: *L'art d'être facile à la riposte, de faire le trait d'esprit, d'avoir le mot pour rire; suivi de notices utiles sur les arts et les lettres,* Paris, 1885; and *L'art de bien vivre; pensées morales et sociales pour la conduite pratique de la vie,* Paris, 1887.

ANTOINE, Yves

b. December 12, 1941, Port-au-Prince, Haiti.
Poet, essayist, storywriter.

Yves Antoine studied at the Lycée Pétion of Port-au-Prince and took a degree from the Faculty of Medicine in the capital. He has also earned other degrees from Montreal and Ottawa universities. He has lived in Canada since 1969.

Writings: Poetry: *La Veillée,* preface by Dr. Pradel Pompilus, Port-au-Prince, Impr. Serge L. Gaston, 1963; *Au gré des heures,* 1970; *Les sabots de la nuit,* Canada, Impr. Gasparo, 1974; *Alliage,* Quebec, Impr. Gasparo, 1978.
Stories: *Fleurs d'Ebène,* Port-au-Prince, Impr. Serge L. Gaston, 1965.

ARDOUIN, Alexis Beaubrun

b. April 30, 1796, Petit Trou des Baradères, Haiti; d. August 30, 1865, Port-au-Prince.
Essayist, playwright, translator, historian, journalist, diplomat, statesman.

Ardouin lived through the violence of independence and was self-taught, mostly from the great French encyclopedia. Early, he had come to Port-au-Prince from the country with his family to become a typographer-trainee at the printing office of the government. In 1821 he was named assistant-judge at the Supreme Court of Port-au-Prince. He became Commissaire du Gouvernement near the Civil Court of Port-au-Prince and was elected Senator in 1832. Reelected many times, he came to serve as President of the Senate during the administrations of Presidents Boyer and Riché. He became Minister of Justice, Public Instruction and Religion under President Philippe Guerrier. He was named Haitian Minister and Plenipotentiary to Paris (1846-1849). His brother Céligny Ardouin was executed by Soulouque in 1849 and Beaubrun was forced to quit his post but remained in France until 1860, dying five years later shortly after returning to Haiti.

His history of Haiti began as a study of his great friend, General Borgella, but, with the enforced leisure of his exile, he was enabled to exploit French archives for a larger work, expanding and correcting the earlier history of Madiou. Ardouin's work carries the Haitian story to the time of President Boyer in the 1840's.

Writings: History: *Etudes sur l'histoire d'Haiti,* followed by *La vie du Général J.M. Borgella,* Paris, Typ. de Prévot et Drouard, Tomes I and II, 1853; Tomes III to XI, Dezobry & E. Magdeleine, Lib. Ed., 1853, 1854, 1856, 1858, 1860; a second edition, Paris, Impr. Donnaud, 1860; and an abortive third edition, only 3 vols., published 1926-1927, Port-au-Prince, M. Chéraquit (Dr. François Dalencour edited one single big vol., Impr. Condé-sur Noireau, 1958).

Geography: *Géographie de l'ile d'Haiti, précédée d'un précis et de la date des évènements les plus remarquables de son histoire (1492-1830),* Port-au-Prince, Impr. de la "Feuille du Commerce," 1832; a second edition, Port-au-Prince, Impr. Telismon Bouchereau, 1856.

Law: *Instructions sur le jury,* Port-au-Prince, Impr. du Gouvernement, 1829.

Politics: *Réponse du Sénateur Ardouin à un écrit intitulé: "Apologie des destitutions pour opinions politiques, ou dogme de l'obéissance passive prêché aux fonctionnaires publics par un Sénateur et réfuté par un citoyen privé,* Port-au-Prince, Impr. de Pinard, 1840; *Réponse du Sénateur . . . à une lettre de M. Isambert,* Port-au-Prince, Impr. de Pinard, 1842.

Biographical/Critical Sources: Hénock Trouillot, *Beaubrun Ardouin,* Mexico, D. F. Instituto Panamericano de Geografia e Historia, 1950; Biographical note on A. B. Ardouin by Dr. François Dalencour in new edition of *Etudes sur l'histoire d'Haiti,* 1958; Auguste Viatte, *Histoire littéraire de l'Amérique française,* Quebec, 1953, pp. 368-371; Pradel Pompilus & Frères de l'Instruction Chrétienne, *Manuel illustré d'histoire de la littérature haitienne,* Port-au-Prince, Ed. H. Deschamps, 1961, pp. 63-73.

ARDOUIN, Charles Nicolas Céligny

b. 1806, Petit Trou de Nippes, Haiti; d. August 7, 1849, Croix des Bouquets, Haiti.
Essayist, historian, politician.

Céligny Ardouin was the half-brother of Beaubrun and Coriolan Ardouin. He was active in politics and was a deputy and afterwards Senator. He became Minister of Interior to Emperor Faustin I.

Writings: Histories: *Essais sur l'histoire d'Haiti publiés par Beaubrun Ardouin,* Port-au-Prince, Chez T. Bouchereau, Impr. 1865; *Siège de Jacmel,* Port-au-Prince, Impr. de T. Bouchereau, E. Nau et Cie., n.d., *Précis des évenément de la Révolution à Saint Domingue, et principalement dans la province de l'Ouest,* (no publishing date).

ARDOUIN, Gustave Léonard Coriolan

b. December 11, 1812, Port-au-Prince, Haiti; d. July 12, 1835, Port-au-Prince.
Poet.

Younger brother of Beaubrun Ardouin and Céligny, important political figures in their days, Coriolan was educated, as was Ignace Nau, at Jonathas Granville Institution. He suffered severely throughout his life from various illnesses. The day of his birth, one of his brothers died; as he put it:

Car un papillon noir, le jour de ma naissance
posa sur mon berceau.

Coriolan Ardouin, certainly one of the tragic and short-lived romantic poets which his period produced, lost in just one year, 1824, his mother, father, nephew, and his oldest sister. His wife had died five months after their marriage. He could well write:

En ce monde il n'est rien qui t'énivre
ou t'enflamme;
Ni l'étoile du ciel, ni l'amour de la
femme,
La brise, ni les fleurs:

. . . .

Pauvre jeune homme âgé de vingt-et-un
ans à peine,
Je suis déjà trop vieux. Oui l'existence
humaine
est bien nue à mes yeux.
Pas une île de fleurs dans cette mer
immense!
Pas une étoile d'or qui, la nuit, se
balance,
Au dôme de mes cieux!

He himself slipped away into death at age 22. For Coriolan, life is only sadness:

Oh! si mon coeur est plein de larmes,
d'amertume,
Comme une onde de sable, ou comme
un ciel de brume,
C'est que je n'ai connu que peines
et douleurs,
C'est qu'enfant je n'ai bu qu'un lait
mêlé de pleurs,
C'est que le jour fatal où m'a souri
ma mère,
Dans la chambre voisine, on couvrait
d'un suaire

Le cercueil de mon frère! J'ai bien vu
depuis!
J'ai passé, l'oeil ouvert et mouillé, bien
des nuits!
Depuis, j'ai vu mourir à quinze ans
père et mère!
Tout le miel a tari! reste l'absinthe
amère!

Though ever lyric effusions of sorrow, Coriolan's poems were full of the natural wonders of Haiti and of nature in general. His poems were published in France by *La Revue des Colonies, La Revue Contemporaine,* and *La Revue des Deux Mondes,* and, in Haiti, in *L'Union.* Emile Nau collected Coriolan Ardouin's poems and published them in 1835 under the title *Poèsies; reliques d'un poète haitien.*

Writings: Poetry: *Poèsies;, reliques d'un poète haitien,* Impr. Bouchereau, 1837(?); *Poèsies de Coriolan Ardouin,* Impr. Ritt Ethéart, 1881; *Poèsies complètes; supplément de la Revue de la Ligue de la Jeunesse Haitienne,* Impr. de l'Abeille, 1916: all Port-au-Prince.

Biographical/Critical Sources: Beaubrun Ardouin (brother of Coriolan) describes his brother and discusses his work in "Notice biographique," in *Poèsie de Coriolan Ardouin,* Port-au-Prince, 1881; Etzer Vilaire has a long poem dedicated to Coriolan Ardouin in *La Ronde;* Franck Fouché, "Coriolan Ardouin est de tous les poètes haitiens, le plus romantique. La vie et l'oeuvre du poète justifient-elles ce jugement?" in *Guide pour l'étude de la littérature haitienne,* pp. 46-52, Eds. Panorama, 1964; Noémi M. Garret, *The Renaissance of Haitian Poetry,* Paris, Présence Africaine, 1963; Pradel Pompilus & Frères de l'Instruction Chrétienne, *Manuel illustré d'histoire de la littérature haitienne,* Ed. H. Deschamps, 1961, pp. 41-51; Hérard Jadotte & Dieudonné Fardin, *Cours d'histoire de la littérature haitienne,* Tome I (1804-1860), Mimeographed, 1965, pp. 33-37; Hénock Trouillot, *Les origines sociales de la littérature haitienne,* Impr. N.A. Théodore, 1962, pp. 132-139: all Port-au-Prince unless otherwise noted.

ARMETH, Auguste

(see under **Auguste MACOUBA**)

ATTULY, Lionel

b. 1900, Fort-de-France, Martinique.
Poet.

Attuly was a brilliant student at the Lycée Schoelcher in Fort-de-France. Urged to enlist by his brother, Attuly served in the French army during the first world war and he was awarded several medals for valor.

After Attuly dropped his courses at the School of Public Works, he went to Africa to enter business. Eventually, he found a position in the civil services of a West Africa State.

Attuly's poetry was always more African than Antillean and expressed his constant feelings for his African heritage.

Writings: Poetry: "Par-dessus la frontière," (unpublished collection); some of his work appears in the L.G. Damas-edited: *Poètes d'expression française,* Paris, Seuil, 1947, pp. 120-133.

AUDAIN, Julio Jean Pierre

b. 1903, Port-au-Prince, Haiti.
Essayist, diplomat, journalist.

Audain was educated at the Institution Saint-Louis de Gonzague of Port-au-Prince for his classical studies. He went to France to study engineering at Normal Institute of Electronics in Paris.

When he returned to Haiti, he became a teacher of mathematics at the Tippenhauer Institute from 1928 to 1930. He was editor-in-chief of *La Presse,* the leading nationalist newspaper against the American occupation. Later, Audain founded his own paper *La Réaction,* then *L'Action Haitienne* and at last *L'Action Nationale.* For his articles, he was put in jail.

Audain served as chief of the private Cabinet of President Sténio Vincent and many diplomatic posts. He was Chargé d'Affaires in Mexico, Plenipotentiary Minister in Lima and Ambassador in Mexico. He ran as presidential candidate for the 1957 elections in Haiti. After some years as Ambassador in Mexico, he resigned and is still residing there.

Writings: Essays: *Haiti, su Historia y su porvenir,* Lima, 1948; *Le Chaos haitien,* Mexico, 1957; *Les ombres d'une politique néfaste,* Mexico, Impr. Arana, 1976.

AUDAIN, Dr. Léon

b. December 17, 1863, Port-au-Prince, Haiti; d. September , 1930, Paris.
Essayist, physician, medical scholar.

Son of Dr. Louis Audain who was Director of the School of Medicine, deputy and senator, Léon Audain was educated in France. He was graduated from the Faculty of Medicine of Paris and became assistant to the famed French surgeon, Dr. Péan.

He returned to Port-au-Prince in 1891 to practice medicine and where he applied the newest medical methods. In 1898, Audain founded the Polyclinic Péan.

He became Director of the Faculty of Medicine of Port-au-Prince in 1902, and was named Minister Plenipotentiary of Haiti to Paris and Berlin and later served as Minister of Public Instruction, 1916.

Writings: Essays: *Choses d'Haiti; explications et conseils,* Port-au-Prince, Impr. de l'Abcille, 1916; *Le Mal d'Haiti, ses causes et son traitement,* Port-au-Prince, Impr. J. Verrollot, 1908.

Medicine: *De l'hémostase préventive dans les opérations chirurgicales; étude théorique et pratique du pincement préventif des vaisseaux combiné au morcellement, suivant la méthode de Mr. Péan,* Paris, G. Steinhel, 1891; *De l'hérédité et de la prédisposition héréditaire devant la doctrine microbienne,* Port-au-Prince, 1900; *Des formes cliniques de la* filariose génitale chez l'homme, de leur pathologie, de leur traitement, Port-au-Prince, Impr. Vve. J. Chenet, 1894; *Des hémomicroblastocytes,* Port-au-Prince, 1906; *L'organisme dans les infections* (ouvrage couronné par l'Académie de Médecine de Paris, Prix Desportes) Paris, Maleine Ed., 1912; *Les bases rationnelles de la médication leucogène dans les infections médicales et chirurgicales,* Paris, A. Maleine et fils Ed., 1916; *Pathologie intertropicale,* Port-au-Prince, Impr. J. Verrollot, n.d.; *Varicocèle lymphatique et filariose testiculaire,* Port-au-Prince, Impr. Vve. J. Chenet, 1898; *Fièvres intertropicales; diagnostic hématologique et clinique* (with Drs. Charles Mathon, Brun Ricot, Gaston Dalencour, V. Lissade and Paul Salomon), Port-au-Prince, Impr. J. Verrollot, 1909.

Biographical/Critical Sources: Dantès Bellegarde: *Ecrivains haitiens,* Ed. Henri Deschamps, 1950, *Léon Audain,* pp. 177-183; *Hommage au Dr. Léon Audain* (Port-au-Prince, le 18 Janvier 1918), Impr. Aug. A. Héraux, 1918.

AUDAIN (père), Dr. Louis

b. August 25, 1828, Port-au-Prince, Haiti; d. 1896, Port-au-Prince.
Essayist, letter-writer, physician, public official.

Audain was educated in Port-au-Prince and France. After earning his medical degree, he practiced and in time was named professor at the School of Medicine and later became the Director. He was a national deputy, and finally a senator.

Dr. Audain contributed his essays to several newspapers such as *Le Bien Public* and *L'Opinion Nationale.*

Writings: Speeches: *Discours à trois jeunes haitiens récemment couronnés au grand concours de la Sorbonne; discours lu le 12 Aout 1858, dans un banquet offert à ces trois jeunes lauréats,* Paris, Impr. de Moquet, 1858; *Entretien offert au public, au Musée du Petit Séminaire Collège sur la nécessité de l'assistance publique en Haiti,* Port-au-Prince, Impr. H. Amblard, 1894.

Essays: *Du changement de nationalité parmi les haitiens,* Port-au-Prince, Impr. de Mme F. Smith, 1903; *Quelques fragments inédits de notre histoire contemporaine et des aperçus sur l'éducation du peuple d'Haiti,* Port-au-Prince, Impr. de Mme F. Smith, 1903.

Letters: *Lettre ouverte à M. le Général Paul Tirésias Augustin Simon Sam, Président de la République d'Haiti,* Port-au-Prince, Impr. H. Amblard, 1896; *Quelques lignes de reconnaissance à M. Victor Hugo pour son article "Un mot sur John Brown" par trois haitiens interprètes des sentiments de leurs compatriotes,* Paris, Impr. de Moquet, 1869: (co-authors: Prosper Elie et Edmond Paul).

AUGUSTE, Jules

b. 1855, Cap-Haitien, Haiti; d. September 17, 1902, Limbé, Haiti.
Poet, politician.

After his primary classes in Cap-Haitien, Auguste was sent to Europe for his higher education. He remained in Europe for many years and on his return to Haiti, he was involved in politics and died in a riot at Limbé.

Writings: Poetry: *La mort de Gambetta (poem),* Paris, Auguste Ghio, 1888; *Parfums créoles; gerbes d'amitié, enthousiasmes et révoltes* (preface by Paul Théodore Vibert), Paris, Berger-Levrault, 1905.

Politics: *Quelques vérités à propos des récents évènements de la République d'Haiti; exploitation et injustice,* Paris, Libr. Nouvelle de droit et de jurisprudence, 1891.

AUGUSTE, Nemours

b. June 10, 1849, Cap-Haitien, Haiti; d. ca. 1914.
Essayist, journalist, physician, public servant.

Auguste was educated in Cap-Haitien and completed his studies in Paris where he studied medicine and earned his degree. He came back to Haiti, practiced medicine as a "sacerdoce" and was elected a deputy and later a senator.

Auguste contributed to *Messager du Nord* and *Le Rèveil,* publishing many articles regarding the welfare of the people.

With the United States occupation of Haiti, the former educational system was questioned and two groups squared off face to face; one praising the French educational system and criticizing the Anglo-Saxon model or vice versa. Dantès Bellegarde expressed the educational confusion this way: "Sur la question du choix d'une éducation qui opposait les anglo-saxonnistes (Auguste Magloire, Fleury Féquière) aux partisans de la culture latine (Georges Sylvàin, Nemours Auguste) . . ." he urged the adoption of a position of "un éclectisme éducationnel." Auguste wrote: "Inspirons-nous de l'exemple de tous les peuples, et en particulier du grand peuple anglais que Fleury Féquière et Auguste Magloire ont bien raison de proposer avec tant de conviction, à l'admiration des Haitiens. Mais gardons jalousement le contact avec la France."

Writings: Essay: *Sur le choix d'une discipline: l'anglo-saxonne ou la française,* Cap-Haitien, Impr. La Conscience, 1909.

Politics: *Le dernier outrage: Mr. Thoby et Boyer Bazelais,* Port-au-Prince, n.d.; *Lettre ouverte à Mr. L. Nau, juge d'instruction, à propos de la loi du 25 avril 1900 sur les consolidés 12% et 6%,* Cap-Haitien, Impr. La Conscience, 1904.

Medicine: *De l'hygiène de la flanelle,* Paris, Typog. Parent, 1876 (his thesis of medicine, University of Paris).

AUGUSTE, Nemours (b. 1883)

(see under **Alfred NEMOURS**)

d'AVRIGNY, l'Oeillard

b. ca. 1760, Saint Pierre, Martinique; d. ca. 1819.

Poet.

D'Avrigny's poetry derives from Lebrun and his heroic odes are influenced by Abbé Delille, as in his poem "Mexique conquis."

Writings: Poetry: *Poèsies nationales* (odes); *Le départ de La Pèrouse ou les navigateurs modernes,* Paris, 1807; *Mexique conquis* (poème hèroique).

BACKER, Desaix

(see under pseudonym: **Aimard LE SAGE**)

BAGHIO'O, Jean-Louis

(pseudonym for **Victor JEAN-LOUIS**)

b. ca. 1915, Saint-Anne, Guadeloupe.

Novelist, poet.

Trained as an engineer, Baghio'o earl[y] went to France where he soon took a[n] active role in the French resistance move[-]ment during the Nazi occupation, deal[t] with in his novel *Fugue mineure.* In 194[5] he became Technical Director of th[e] broadcasting services of the French over[-]seas radio.

Author of three novels and one volum[e] of poetry, Baghio'o is always concerne[d] with the still living colonial legacy in th[e] Caribbean, most of it bad. His secon[d] work, *Les jeux du soleil: Poèmes* (1960) claimed to be about the author's ancest[or] who arrived in Guadeloupe aboard a[n] ancient slaver, a far come-down for th[e] once "Sultan" of Timbouctou. In h[is] recent *Le flamboyant à fleurs bleu[es]* (1973), he studies the slave revolts of th[e] revolutionary period and the violen[t] events of the early decades of the 19th century in the French Antilles while the great flame tree of *blue* flowers watches over all. Everything here leads to the new, this time, Marxist-inspired, explosions of 1848.

Writings: Novels: *Issandre le mulâtre,* introduction by Catherine Dunham, Paris, Fasquelle, 1949; *Fugue mineure,* details not known; *Le flamboyant à fleurs bleues,* Paris, Calmann-Lévy, 1973.

Poetry: *Les jeux du soleil, Poèmes,* Paris, Soulanges, 1960.

Essays: "La prise de son," and "Rèves de neige" (about the creation of poetry).

BAGUIDY, Joseph D.

b. September 18, 1915, Jérémie, Haiti.
Poet, essayist, journalist, diplomat.

Baguidy studied first at the Lycée Nord Alexis of Jérémie and went to Port-au-Prince where he completed his education, graduating from the Faculty of Law.

He was Sous-Inspecteur of the Jérémie schools, and later Chef de Bureau au Cabinet particulier du Président d'Haiti and Sous-chef de Protocole. He was named first secretary at the Haitian Embassy of Paris, and Chargé d'Affaires at Anvers. Later, Baguidy became Minister of Foreign Affairs and Ambassador to Spain, and then to Switzerland.

He practiced journalism and founded with Paul Blanchet the magazine *Panorama.*

Writings: Poetry: *Sous les futaies,* preface by Arsène Pompée, Port-au-Prince, Impr. du Collège Vertières, 1938.

Essays: *Aperçus sur la pensée haitienne,* Impr. de l'Etat, 1941; *Considérations sur la conscience nationale,* Impr. H. Deschamps, 1945; *Esquisse de sociologie haitienne,* Impr. de l'Etat, 1946; *Incidences; essais de témoignages,* 1955: all in Port-au-Prince. Also see: *Dynamique d'une révolution: 1946 à Haiti,* Berne Coloroffret, n.d. (1976?).

BAGUIDY-GILBERT, Serge

b. July 19, 1943, Haiti.
Poet.

Baguidy-Albert was educated in Port-au-Prince. He is now living in Canada.

Writings: Poetry: *Poèmes dits dans un miroir,* Port-au-Prince, Coll. Hounguenicon, Impr. Rodriguez, 1966.

BATTIER, Alcibiade Fleury

(also: **Alcibiade FLEURY-BATTIER**)
b. July 8, 1841, Petite Rivière de Nippes, Haiti; d. February 23, 1883, Port-au-Prince.
Poet, teacher.

Battier was educated in Port-au-Prince and was a professor at the Lycée Pétion for several years. He was Chef de Division at the Ministry of Public Instruction. He died from smallpox.

Battier was best known for his patriotic verse celebrating the heroes of Haiti's earliest days. The following verse from an unknown poem is characteristic of his nationalistic fervor:

Salut, ô Dessalines, ô Pétion, ô Guerrier!
Salut, brave Magny, modèle du guerrier!
Et toi, vaillant Lamarre, à la bravoure antique!
Et vous tous, fondateurs de cette République!

He made some effort to celebrate Haiti's African origins in such mildly sentimental verses as this from the "Le Vrai Ouanga":

Mais quoi de plus doux que le miel?
Qui peut, en nous versant l'ivresse,
Nous faire oublier terre et ciel?
—C'est le baiser d'une négresse!

Writings: Poetry: *Luména ou le génie de la liberté; poèsie,* Impr. Télismon Bouchereau, 1869; *Le génie de la patrie,* Impr. J.J. Audain, 1877; second edition, Impr. Chéraquit, 1930; *Par mornes et par savanes; rimes glanées,* no date; *Sous les bambous: poèsie,* Paris, Kugelmann, 1881. The print-shop of Bouchereau also published Battier's *La journée d'adieux ou le Jeudi Saint au mont Sinai,* Télismon Bouchereau, 1869, reprinted in *Chaîne d'Union* of Paris (Dec. 1874 and Feb. 1875): all Port-au-Prince, except *Sous les bambous.*

Biographical/Critical Sources: Ghislain Gouraige, *Histoire de la littérature haitienne,* Port-au-Prince, Impr. N.A. Théodore, 1960, pp. 45-49; Pradel Pompilus & Frères de l'Instruction Chrétienne, Ed. H. Deschamps, 1961, pp. 103-105; Hénock Trouillot, *Les Origines sociales de la littérature haitienne,* Impr. N. A. Théodore, 1962, pp. 201-208: both in Port-au-Prince.

BAUDOT, Paul

b. June 29, 1801, Pointe-à-Pitre, Guadeloupe; d. March 6, 1870.
Poet, fabulist, playwright, storywriter, theatre critic (much work in créole).

His family was from France, Nièvre, but Baudot was educated in Guadeloupe. He was employed by a public notary and became a notary on November 28, 1827. He was a city councellor of Pointe-à-Pitre.

Writings: Opera (in one act): *Fondoc et Thérèse,* performed in Basse-Terre, 1856.

Parodies, Sermons and Political Speeches: unpublished.

Collected works: *Oeuvres créoles: Poèsies, fables, théatre, contes,* Basse-Terre, Impr. Officielle, 1923, new edition 1935.

BAUDUY, Robert

b. December 21, 1940, Jacmel, Haiti.
Poet, playwright, folkloric group director.

Bauduy was educated at the primary school of the Christian Brothers and the Lycée Pinchinat of Jacmel. He graduated from the Conservatoire National of Dramatic Art (C.N.A.D.) in Port-au-Prince under the guidance of Gabriel Imbert, and he later was a student at the Faculty of Ethnology. He is now serving at the Cultural Division of the Ministry of Foreign Affairs.

Bauduy has long devoted himself to the theater and he is the manager of various folkloric groups such as "The Comedians of Haiti," "Lambi Club," and "Les Caracos Bleus" (Blue Jackets).

Writings: Poetry: *Oracle du Mal d'Aurore,* Port-au-Prince, Ed. Henri Deschamps, 1973.

Drama Essay: "Un second souffle pour le théâtre haitien," in *Conjonction,* No. 124 (Fall 1974), pp. 55-71.

BAZILE, Corneille

b. ca. 1895, Guadeloupe.
Novelist.

Corneille Bazile was a school teacher who published two novels. Bazile said in the introduction: "Ce titre (la Terreur Noire) dissimule les vices, les grands maux qui corrompent le monde guadeloupéen. En écrivant ce livre, je dévoile des vérités profondes, sans me soucier de leur naïveté un peu crue."

Writings: Novels: *La Terreur noire à la Guadeloupe,* Pointe-à-Pitre, Impr. L'Information, 1925; *Le Meilleur mariage, Pointe-à*-Pitre.

BEAUBRUN, Théodore

(pseudonym: **LANGUICHATTE**)
b. 1923, Port-au-Prince, Haiti.
Playwright, actor.

Théodore was educated in Haiti's capital and from his youth delighted in comedy. Since 1935 he has performed in his own dramatic productions, acting in some 35 works and becoming one of the most popular entertainers ever in Haiti.

Robert Bauduy, dramatist, said of Languichatte: "Il y a chez Languichatte une peinture permanente de la psychologie des classes moyennes lorsqu'elles renoncent à assumer leur propre condition pour adopter cette vie de façade, du devoir être, en dépit de la dégradation des conditions d'existence. Languichatte instaure un théâtre de boulevard, attaché aux structures traditionnelles de la farce et de la comédie de moeurs."

Writings: Plays: *Anna* (comedy in two acts), Eds. Panorama, 1962; *La Haine au Service de l'Amour* (comedy in two acts), Impr. de l'Etat, 1963: both Port-au-Prince.

BEAUGE, Jacqueline

b. February 7, 1932, Jérémie, Haiti.
Poet, teacher.

Beaugé was educated mostly in Jérémie and afterwards in Port-au-Prince. She has published two collections of her verse.

Writings: Poetry: *Climats en marche,* Impr. des Antilles, 1962; *A vol d'ombre,* preface by Phito Gracia, Impr. Serge L. Gaston, 1966: both Port-au-Prince.

BEAULIEU, Raymond

b. August 5, 1931, Jacmel, Haiti.
Poet.

Beaulieu first attended the school of the Christian Brothers in Jacmel but he completed his education in Port-au-Prince. He spent some years in Venezuela. He was named an official of the Department of Foreign Affairs, but he went into exile and is now living in New York.

Writings: Poetry: *Soleil* (preface by Joseph Thévenin), Port-au-Prince, Impr. Pierre-Noel, 1950.

BEAUVALLON, Jean Baptiste Rosemond de

b. April 1, 1819, Basse-terre, Guadeloupe; d. July 21, 1903.
Novelist, travel writer, journalist, historian, lawyer.

After his primary schooling in Guadeloupe, Beauvallon went to Paris to complete his education. There he studied law and practiced journalism, founding in his 19th year the magazine *La Revue Coloniale* with the slogan: "Ce sont aussi des Français."

Always a frank personality, Beauvallon's articles in *Le Globe* and elsewhere were controversial, one leading to a long debate in the press and finally a duel. Killing his opponent, Beauvallon spent eight years in prison. Finally released, he embarked on wide travels, writing a book on Cuba and becoming a member of the Royal Academy of Madrid.

Writings: Travel: *L'Ile de Cuba,* Paris, 1844, later translated into Spanish, details not known but for which he received the award of Isabella La Catolica.

Novels: *Hier! aujourd'hui! demain!,* published in Coulommiers, France, Impr. de Brodart and Gallois, 1885; *La Charmeuse,* Coulommiers, 1885.

History: *Les Corsaires de la Guadeloupe sous Victor Hughes*, Paris, Paul Dupont, 1901.

Biographical/Critical Sources: Auguste Viatte, *Histoire littéraire de l'Amérique française, 1954, pp. 490-491.*

BEC, Marie

(pseudonym for **Marie-Thérèse COLIMON**)

BELANCE, René

b. September 28, 1915, Corail, Haiti. Poet, teacher.

Bélance received his education in Port-au-Prince and then graduated from the Normal School [Teachers'] when Damoclès Vieux was the director. He spent some time teaching and then became a government employee at the Department of Justice and at the new Department of Commerce. He then became engaged in creole language teaching for adults. He spent several years in Puerto Rico and he is now living in the United States as a teacher at Brown University, Providence, Rhode Island.

His first collection of verse, *Rythmes de mon coeur,* recalls the past and the voodoo drums and dances, as can be seen in this extract from "Coin de tonnelle":

Gronde, gronde encore,
tambour enroué
de l'Afrique opprimée,
dis toujours ton rêve
ton grand rêve avorté
en la cale des négriers.

"Ma Vocation" reveals the nature of Bélance's verse. He says of himself:

Je suis l'artiste muet qui soupire en sourdine de sentir qu'en mon âme
il passe des accords que je voudrais chanter;
or, mes doigts inhabiles n'ont pas osé saisir
la note qui a'allonge, s'écoule
en la musique . . .

His poetry often is close to surrealism in its complex associational and personal cryptic qualities. Senghor commented in the preface to his famous *Anthologie de la nouvelle poèsie nègre et malgache de langue française:*

> *Bélance est le plus doué des jeunes poètes haitiens. Esprit aigu, explorateur d'au-delà le royaume de la nuit, il avance par lianes-serpents et marais putrides . . .*
>
> *En images de voyance, voilà comment explose, chez lui, le tourment du nègre nouveau. Sans éloquence, dans un style où l'angoisse vrille les ténèbres, mais non sans le rythme négre du sang qui donne au vers sa chaleur émotionnelle.* (page 129)

Writings: Poetry: *Rythmes de mon coeur* (preface by Léon Lahens), Port-au-Prince, Impr. Modèle, 1940; *Luminaire (poèmes),* Impr. Morisset, 1941; *Pour célébrer l'absence (poèmes),* Impr. Chrysostome Beaubrun, 1943; and second edition, Québec, 1947; *Survivances (poèmes),* Impr. de l'Etat, 1944; *Epaule d'ombre* (poèmes), Impr. de l'Etat, 1945: all Port-au-Prince, except as noted; *Nul ailleurs,* Montréal, Nouvelle optique, 1978.

Recording: Bélance reads his own poetry for J.S. Library of Congress, and poetic and inter-iew material on file at Library of Congress, Vashington, D.C.

3iographical/Critical Sources: Naomi M. Gar-et, *The Renaissance of Haitian Poetry*, Pré-ence Africaine, 1963, pp. 175-184.

3ELLAIRE, Ancelot

. ca. 1922, Guadeloupe.
'oet, journalist.

3ellaire was educated at the Lycée Carnot nd completed his education in France.

He was a practicing journalist and ontributed his work to many newspapers uch as *Bulletin d'Information de la Guadeloupe; Liberté; Dimanche Sportif t Culturel; Revue Guadeloupéenne;* and ne journal *Le Miroir de la Guadeloupe*.

Bellaire won many prizes awarded by uropean societies.

Vritings: Poetry: *Sacerdoce; De mon florilège*, aris, Editions L'Amité par la plume, n.d.; *astels Guadeloupéens; Pour toi*, 1952; *Sans me ni raison; La fête*, Guadeloupe, in *Revue Guadeloupéenne*, No. 46, p. 40.

3ELLEGARDE, Jean-Louis Windsor

. January 26, 1872, Port-au-Prince, Haiti; d. February 16, 1930, Port-au-Prince.
ssayist, historian, teacher, journalist.

ellegarde was educated at the Lycée étion in Port-au-Prince. After he com-leted his education with his later well-nown schoolmates, Justin Lhérisson, lirabeau Drice and Seymour Pradel, he ounded the successful literary review, *La eune Haiti*.

Bellegarde taught at the Ecole Lancas-rienne and at the National Pensionnat of Girls whose principal was his aunt, Mme. rgentine-Bellegarde Foureau.

He went to France on a grant with Mirabeau Drice where both became students at l'Ecole Normale Supérieure de Paris.

On his return Bellegarde was appointed professor of philosophy at the Lycée Pétion. Later, he was elected Deputy for Arcahaie in 1905 and eventually he was named Director General of Secondary Education at the Ministry of Public Education.

He campaigned for the expansion of education in Haiti and wrote:

> *L'ignorance de la masse constitue en Haiti plus qu'ailleurs un danger social que, dans un double but de solidarité nationale et de préservation personnelle, nous devons combattre avec énergie. L'ensemble d'idées contenues dans l'expression* extension universitaire *répond parfaitement à la nécessité d'organiser, non seulement l'oeuvre post-scolaire pour ceux de nos compatriotes qui ont quitté l'école avec un bagage insuffisant, mais aussi des "Cours d'adulte" en faveur de ceux qui n'ont pas eu le bonheur de passer par l'école et à qui ne s'est révélé que sur le tard le besoin de savoir.*

Seymour Pradel expressed these sentiments about Bellegarde:

> *W. Bellegarde est un esprit pondéré toujours préoccupé des questions sociales , morales et historiques. Son style est sobre, clair, limpide, nourri de faits et d'idées, une observation toujours en éveil et une curiosité toujours aux aguets. Il méditait longuement et écrivait lentement. Il avait le goût des recherches.*

Works: School Texts: *Manuel d'instruction civique et morale*, Impr. de l'Abeille, 1905; *Manuel d'instruction civique et morale à l'usage des écoles de la République; exposé méthodique, questionnaires, sujets de rédaction; ouvrage rédigé conformément au programme officiel pour l'enseignement de l'instruction civique et morale*, Impr. Chéraquit, 1926; later edition, Impr. Chĕraquit, 1931. Also: *Petite histoire d'Haiti: 1492-1915, à l'usage des écoles primaires de la République,* Impr. du journal "Les Nouvelles," 1922; other editions, Impr. L'Abeille, 1921, and Impr. Chéraquit, 1925; *Manuel d'histoire à l'usage des écoles de la République* (with Justin Lhérisson), 1907; other editions, under his own authorship, Impr. Saint-Jaques, 1914; Impr. Bernard, 1923: all Port-au-Prince.

Report: *Rapport général (Congrès des professeurs de l'enseignement secondaire, Janvier 1904),* Port-au-Prince, Impr. de l'Abeille, 1904.

Study: *Etude sommaire pour un projet d'établissement agricole,* (with Charles Dubé), Paris, Ateliers Haitiens, n.d.

BELLEGARDE, Louis Dantès

b. May 18, 1877, Port-au-Prince, Haiti; d. June 13, 1966, Port-au-Prince.

Critic, autobiographer, scholar, lawyer, statesman.

Bellegarde attended the Lycée Pétion in the capital and began teaching there in 1894 after his graduation. There followed university work and a professorate of philosophy, then service as Chief of Division at the Ministry of Public Instruction. He became Minister in 1918 for three years of that Ministry. He was named Haiti's Minister to Paris, then to the Vatican, and two or three times he served as Minister or Ambassador to Washington, D.C. He presided in 1949 at Haiti's Constitutional Congress. Bellegarde became a sitting judge on the World Court at the Hague and was a member of the Commission on Slavery and Forced Labor of the League of Nations and after the second World War he was Haiti's Permanent Delegate to the United Nations. The French Legion d'Honneur also made him an officer and the University of Montréal awarded him a doctorate, *honoris causa.*

His prose style is natural and fresh, and his strongly-held feelings are always close to the surface. Nonetheless, his work is generally philosophical in spirit, even meditative, though never resigned or passive.

Writings: Literary Criticism: *Ecrivains haitiens; notices biographiques et pages choisies,* first series, Société d'Editions et de Librairie, 1947; second edition, H. Deschamps, 1950; *Un Haitien parle,* Impr. Chéraquit, 1934; *Pour une Haiti heureuse,* 2 vols., Impr. Chéraquit, 1927, 1929: all works in Port-au-Prince.

History: *La Résistance haitienne (l'occupation américaine d'Haiti), récit d'histoire contemporaine,* Montreal, Ed. Beauchemin, 1937; *Dessalines a parlé,* Port-au-Prince, Société d'Edition et de Librairie, 1948; *Haiti et son peuple,* Paris, Nouvelles Editions Latines, 1953; *Histoire du peuple haitien,* Port-au-Prince, 1953; *La nation haitienne,* Paris, J. de Gigord, 1938; *Pages d'histoire,* Port-au-Prince, Impr. Chéraquit, 1925.

Autobiography: *Au service d'Haiti; Appréciations sur un haitien et son oeuvre,* Port-au-Prince, Impr. N.A. Théodore, 1962.

Speeches: *Haiti, centre de culture française en Amérique* (Communication présentée à la conférence américaine des commissions nationales de coopération intellectuelle, November 15, 1941), Port-au-Prince, Impr. de la Phalange, 1942; *La République d'Haiti et les Etats-Unis devant la justice internationale,* Paris, Lib. de Paris-Livres, 1924.

Essays: *Haiti et ses problèmes,* Montreal, Ed. B. Valiquette, 1943; *Haiti and her problems,* Rio Piedras, Puerto Rico, U. of P.R. University Press, 1936.

Education: *L'instruction publique en Haiti,* Port-au-Prince, Impr. Nationale, 1908.

Textbooks: *L'écolier haitien* (the school reader) with Sténio Vincent; *Lectures haitiennes* (cours élémentaire), Port-au-Prince, Ed. H. Deschamps, 1950; *The Haitian American Anthology* (Haitian readings from American Authors), with Mercer Cook, Port-au-Prince, Impr. de l'Etat, 1944.

Editor: *Morceaux choisis d'auteurs haitiens, prose et vers,* 2 vols. (with Solon Ménos, Amilcar Duval, and Georges Sylvain), Port-au-Prince, Impr. de Mme. F. Smith, 1904. (The two books were awarded a prize by l'Académie Française.)

Biographical/Critical Sources: Jules Blanchet: *Peint par lui-même ou la résistance de Mr. Bellegarde,* Port-au-Prince, Impr. V. Valcin, 1935; Hénock Trouillot: *Dantès Bellegarde, Un écrivain d'autrefois,* Port-au-Prince, Impr. des Antilles, 1957; Dr. Ghislain Gouraige, *Histoire de la littérature haitienne,* Port-au-Prince, Impr. N.A. Théodore, 1960, pp. 469-471; Pradel Pompilus & Frères de l'Instruction Chrétienne, *Manuel illustré d'histoire de la littérature haitienne,* 1961; Léon Laleau: "Dantès Bellegarde," Port-au-Prince, *Conjonction,* No. 116, 1972; Patrice Bellegarde-Smith: *Expression of a Culture in Crisis: Dantès Bellegarde in Haitian Social Thought,* (Ph.D. thesis).

BENOIT, Clément

b. September 1, 1904, Port-au-Prince, Haiti.
Poet, teacher.

After his classical studies, Benoit studied at the school of the technical service of Agriculture "Damien." He was a school teacher, and was graduated from the Faculty of Law.

A pioneer in the folkloric field, he broadcast his program "L'heure de l'Art Haitien" with a regular supporting cast. He was named Consul of Haiti to the Bahamas in 1958 but is now living in exile in New York.

Benoit's poetry sought Haiti's African roots and vivid pictures of the ancestral life dance through most of his verses.

Writings: Poetry: *Chants sauvages,* Port-au-Prince, Impr. Collège Vertières, 1940; *Rythmes nègres,* Port-au-Prince, Impr. H. Deschamps, 1945.

BENOIT, François Pierre Joseph

(pseudonym for **Rosalvo BOBO**)

BERGEAUD, Eméric

b. 1818, Cayes, Haiti; d. February 23, 1858, Saint-Thomas Island.
Novelist.

Bergeaud received a good education in France and served as secretary to his uncle, General Borgella.

After the bloodshed on April 16, 1848, in Port-au-Prince, and the riot against Faustin Soulouque in Cayes, he sought exile in Saint Thomas. There, in 1850, he wrote *Stella,* the very first novel by a Haitian. He employed the Roman founding twins as the polar combattants of his symbolic work: Romulus as the man of pure African descent, and Remus as the Creole mulatto's rival. Very ill, he went to Paris to restore his health. The novel in manuscript, left to Beaubrun Ardouin as executor, was published in 1859 after the author's death. The 330-page work has not been republished since 1887.

Writings: Novel: *Stella,* Paris, Dentu, 1859, and 1887.

BERNARD, Regnor Charles

b. October 18, 1915, Jérémie, Haiti.
Poet, essayist, teacher, journalist.

After his primary schooling, Bernard went to Port-au-Prince where he studied at the Lycée Pétion and at the Normal School. Taking his degree, he became a teacher and in time served as a president of UNIH (Association des Instituteurs Haitiens). In this capacity, he attended many international educational meetings, Jamaica (1947), Canada (1950), and Malta (1951).

He practiced journalism and was a frequent contributor to *La Nation,* the biweekly of the P.S.P. (Parti Socialiste Populaire).

Bernard was a member of the revolutionary generation of 1946 and he often attacked the Catholic Church for aiding, he believed, in the continued exploitation of the Haitian black masses. His poem "Fête" has:

Il y a fête au dehors
on dit que c'est Noël et qu'un enfant
est venu
qui doit sauver les hommes!
Quels hommes?

and he ends the poem with another question:

Y a-t-il un enfant capable de sauver
les hommes
à peau noire?

Writings: Poetry: *Le souvenir demeure (poèmes),* Port-au-Prince, Impr. Séjour, 1940; *Pêche d'étoiles; poèmes,* Port-au-Prince, Impr. La Nation, 1943; *Nègre!!!* Port-au-Prince, Impr. N. Telhomme, 1945; His poem "C'était à l'Arcahaie" received first prize at the poetic contest for the Flag commemoration, and was printed with Jean F. Brierre's play *Au milieu des flammes* with work by Clovis Bonhomme: Collection du Cent-cinquantenaire, Port-au-Prince, Impr. de l'Etat, 1953.

Essay: *Sur les routes qui montent,* Port-au-Prince, Les Presses Libres, 1945 (contains a study of Robert Lataillade).

BERTE, Marie

(pseudonym: **EMMBE**)

b. May 4, 1893, Saint-Pierre, Martinique. Novelist, storywriter.

Born in Saint-Pierre where her father was a comptroller of Customs, and from a family which emigrated to Martinique from Europe, Berté received her education at the Couvent des Soeurs de Saint Joseph de Cluny, in Fort-de-France.

She contributed to newspapers and published one of her novels in the journal *La Paix,* Fort-de-France.

Writings: Novels: *Un roman gai* [by Emmbé], Fort-de-France, Impr. L'Aurore, 1935; *Miss Canne à Sucre,* Paris, Les Livres Nouveaux; *Sous les filaos,* Fort-de-France, Impr. Officielle, 1941; *Le baiser imprévu,* 1946.

Stories: *Nouveaux Ombrages,* Fort-de-France, Impr. du Gouvernement, 1941; *Thérèse de Castelroc,* published in *La Paix de Fort-de-France.*

BERVIN, Antoine

b. June 11, 1901, Port-au-Prince, Haiti. Biographer, essayist, storywriter, diplomat.

Antoine Bervin received his education in Port-au-Prince. He served as a librarian at the Service National de la Production Agricole directed by the American officials of Damien. He later went to Washington, D.C., where he worked as a translator at the Office of Panamerican Union.

Bervin became Minister Plenipotentiary of Haiti in Havana and served as Assistant Commissaire General of the World Fair of Port-au-Prince for its bicentennial in 1949.

Writings: Biography: *Louis-Edouard Pouget, Homme d'état, diplomate, tribun,* Port-au-Prince, Impr. de l'Etat, 1945; *Benito Sylvain, apôtre du relèvement social des Noirs,* Port-au-Prince, Impr. La Phalange, 1969.

Essay: *Pantal à Paris,* Port-au-Prince, Impr. de l'Etat, 1953.

Report: *Mission à la Havane,* printed in Switzerland, 1954.

Story: *La vie étourdissante de Jean Lucksa, e roi des veinards,* Port-au-Prince, Presses Nationales d'Haiti, 1975; *Reflets d'Haiti,* Port-au-Prince, Impr. des Antilles, 1977.

BESSE, Martial

b. September 15, 1759, Terrier-Rouge, (near Trou), Haiti; d. 1816, Cap-Haitien. Memoirist, soldier.

Besse was educated in France as was his brother, Engineer Henri Besse, who contributed in building Christophe's La Ferrière, the eighth wonder of the world, according to Charles Lindberg. He was still in France when the French Revolution began. He was enlisted as a common soldier and was sent with the expedition to Saint Domingue, when all natives of Saint Domingue who were residents in France, were arrested. Martial Besse was put in the same Fort-de-Joux where Toussaint Louverture was incarcerated. He later served as a secretary of the former Governor and made a fair copy of *Les Mémoires de Toussaint Louverture.*

Besse returned to Haiti when he was freed, living in Cap-Haitien under King Henri I and was ennobled as the Comte de Sainte Suzanne and was made Commanding Officer of the First Arrondissement of the first military division in the North.

Writings: "Memoires" (unpublished); *Martial Besse, Général de Brigade: Appel à l'opinion publique, Paris le 15 messidor, an 6, (1797),* Paris, Impr. de J. Baillio, 1797; and *Deuxième appel à l'opinion publique,* Paris, de l'Impr. de J. Baillio, an 6, (1797).

BETZON, Thérèse de

(also: **Melle DE SOLMS, Mme Thérèse BLANC**)

b. ca. 1850, Martinique; d. ca. 1912. Novelist.

Betzon's one novel *Yvette* is one of the island's first "studies" of a creole woman.

Writings: Novel: *Yvette, histoire d'une jeune créole* (Les colonies, feuilleton, 1888), Paris, J. Hetzel, 1880 (other editions: 1882-1890).

BEVILLE, Albert

(see under pseudonym: **Paul NIGER**)

BISSAINTHE, Max

b. November 11, 1911, Port-au-Prince, Haiti; d. April 15, 1978, New York. Essayist, bibliographer, biographer, translator, journalist.

Bissainthe was educated in Port-au-Prince, and was on the staff of the Ministry of Interior. He went to the United States to study library science. He spent many years

as Director of the Public Library of Port-au-Prince and as Inspector of all public libraries in the country.

Bissainthe was also a practicing journalist and served as chief editor of *Zinglins,* and was a frequent contributor to *Maintenant: Reflets d'Haiti; Le Nouvelliste* and to *Conjonction.*

Until his death recently, he was living in New York working as a Reference Librarian for the New York University Libraries.

Writings: Bibliography: *Dictionnaire de bibliographie haitienne,* Washington, D.C., Scarecrow Press, 1951; *Dictionnaire de Bibliographie haitienne: Premier Supplément,* Metuchen, N.J., The Scarecrow Press, 1973.

Translation: *Toussaint Louverture* (by Wendell Phillips), Port-au-Prince, Impr. de l'Etat, 1950.

BLANC, Mme Thérèse

(pseudonym for **Thérèse de BETZON**)

BLANCHET, Jules Antoine

b. January 24, 1913, Port-au-Prince, Haiti.
Essayist, journalist, government official, sociologist.

Blanchet was educated in Port-au-Prince. He studied law and after taking his degree, he served many years in the President's private office, becoming Director of the Tobacco Excise Office. He is presently Prime Counsellor of the Audit Office.

He began early writing for several newspapers: *L'Action Nationale, L'Assaut, Haiti-Journal, Le Matin,* and *Le Nouvelliste,* and he is now the main contributor to *Panorama.* He was the chief editor of the noted magazine, *La Relève.*

Writings: Essays: *Politique étrangère et représentation extérieure,* Impr. V. Valcin, 1936; *Peint par lui-même ou la résistance de M. Bellegarde,* Impr. V. Valcin, 1936; *La Mission de l'Institution Communale,* Port-au-Prince, N. Telhomme, 1938; second edition, Impr. du Collège Vertières, 1938; *Essai sur la culture* (with Dr. René Piquion); preface by Dumayric Charlier, Impr. V. Valcin, 1940: all Port-au-Prince.

Literary essays: *Le destin de la jeune littérature,* Port-au-Prince, Impr. de l'Etat, 1939

Economy: *Aspects of Haitian economy* (from the *Social Sciences in Mexico and South and Central America,* Vol. 1, No. 4 (Mexico D.F.) pp. 39-46.

Dissertation: *Idéologies et transformations sociales,* Port-au-Prince, Eds. Panorama, Impr de l'Etat, 1955. (ext. from *Bulletin International des Sciences Sociales, Revue trimestrielle,* Vol. V, No. 1 (1953).

BLOT, Probus Louis

b. May 15, 1876, Cap-Haitien, Haiti;
d. February 6, 1937, Port-au-Prince.
Poet, public official.

Descended from the Baron de Saint-Cap, Blot studied in Cap-Haitien before going on to the capital of Haiti for advanced schooling. He went to Paris where he attended university and there he became a marked boulevardier and elegant habitué of the cafés. He contributed to the popular illustrated journals of the French capital, mostly publishing the Parnassian poetry then in vogue.

On return to Haiti he was named chief of the Division of Public Instruction, and later served in the same capacity at the Ministry of Agriculture. He later became director of secondary education. He was elected a Deputy in 1902.

Beginning as a Parnassian poet, Blot turned to symbolism, and was always extremely refined and "précieux." A member of the important *La Ronde* group, he contributed much to the poetry of his times, and published some criticism in various journals, including *Haiti Littéraire et Scientifique.* Much of his work recalls the symbolism of French poet Henri de Régnier.

Writings: Poetry: no single collection. "Les

efforts et le triomphe" is the title of one of his unpublished verse manuscript collections.

Biographical/Critical Sources: Auguste Viatte, *Histoire littéraire de l'Amérique française,* Quebec, 1953, p. 409.

BOBO, Dr. Rosalvo

(pseudonym: **François Pierre Joseph BENOIT**)
b. January 29, 1873, Cap-Haitien, Haiti; d. November 29, 1929, Paris.
Poet, essayist, physician, lawyer, politician.

Bobo was educated in Haiti and France. He studied medicine and law and graduated from both the Faculty of Medicine and the Faculty of Law of the University of Paris.

He was an active politician and was a strong opponent of the American occupation and the "officials of the treaty" as Haitians used to call the American administrators. He refused accordingly to seek the presidency of Haiti with American support, though urged to do so. Tired of political harassment, he went to France where he died at 56 years. He composed the hymn, "L'Artibonitienne" (music and words).

Writings: Medicine: *De la rupture spontanée de l'aorte et de ses anévrismes dans le péricarde; étude clinique, anatomologique et expérimentale,* Paris, Henri-Jouvé, 1898.

Politics: *A propos du centenaire; proposition faite à Mr. Ls. Edouard Pouget,* Cap-Haitien, Impr. "La Conscience," 1903; *Pour l'histoire de la révolution haitienne par le parti progressiste,* Saint-Thomas, Lightbourn's Press, 1908; *Lettre ouverte au Général A. T. Simon, président de la République,* Cap-Haitien, 1909; *Lettre ouverte au Président de la République adressée à la classe cultivée de mes concitoyens,* Cap-Haitien, Impr. du Progrès, *1909; Aux Progressistes Haitiens,* Saint-Thomas, Impr. Fort-de-France, 1908; *Voies de réforme,* Cap-Haitien, Impr. La Conscience, 1910; *Adresse à ceux de mes concitoyens qui partagèrent mes vues nationales et à mes collaborateurs politiques de l'an 1915,* Paris, 1915; *Exploits de yankees; remerciements à mes concitoyens,* Port-au-Prince, 1916; *Lettre ouverte à M. Le Président et aux Membres du Sénat Américain* (Washington), Port-au-Prince, Impr. Saint-Jacques, 1922.

Herbal Medicine: *Flore des Antilles,* rev. edition of work by Descourtilz, but never published.

BOISROND-TONNERRE, Louis

b. 1776, Torbeck, Haiti; d. October 18, 1806, Port-au-Prince.
Prose writer, poet, autobiographer.

Louis "earned" the name *Tonnerre* on the day of his birth when lightning struck his cradle but left him unharmed. His uncle, Louis Boisrond, deputy of Saint Domingue to the Council of Cinq Cents, brought him to Paris where he studied at the Colonial Institute.

He came back to the country very bitter against both the colonial system with all its injustices and French racial prejudices. He was named General Geffrard's secretary and at Camp Gérard he was introduced to the Commander-in-Chief, Jean-Jacques Dessalines, who selected him as his own secretary. He became a trusted aide to Emperor Dessalines who liked him for his impetuous character.

Boisrond Tonnerre wrote *L'Acte de l'Indépendance,* the most important political document in Haitian history. Written in an incandescent style it led the way to the period's feverish production of nationalist poetry and patriotic essays, most of which is extant:

> *Ce n'est pas assez d'avoir expulsé de notre pays les barbares qui l'ont ensanglanté depuis deux siècles; ce n'est pas assez d'avoir mis un frein aux factions toujours renaissantes qui se jouaient tour à tour du fantôme de liberté que la France exposait à nos yeux; il faut par un dernier acte d'autorité nationale, assurer à jamais l'empire*

de la liberté dans le pays qui nous a vus naitre; il faut ravir au gouvernement inhumain qui tient depuis longtemps nos esprits dans la torpeur la plus humiliante, tout espoir de nous réasservir; il faut enfin vivre indépendant ou mourir.

Jurons à l'univers entier, à la postérité, à nous-mêmes, de renoncer à jamais à la France, et de mourir plutôt que de vivre sous sa domination.

De combattre jusqu'au dernier soupir pour l'indépendance de notre pays!

When Emperor Dessalines was assassinated at Pont-Rouge on October 17, 1806, Boisrond Tonnerre was imprisoned and later executed. Boisrond Tonnerre scratched with a nail this quatrain on the walls of his cell:

Humide et froid séjour, fait par et pour le crime,
Où le crime en riant immole sa victime.
Que peuvent inspirer tes fers et tes barreaux,
Quand un coeur pur y goûte un innocent repos?

Writings: Political: *L'Acte de l'Indépendance,* January 1, 1804; *Proclamation du Général en chef au Peuple d'Haiti,* January 1, 1804; *Acte des Généraux de l'armée qui nomment le général en chef, Dessalines, gouverneur général à vie,* January 1, 1804.

Poetry: "Chant National" (sur l'air de "la Marseillaise") in Lélia J. Lhérisson's *Manuel de littérature haitienne,* Port-au-Prince, Impr. Collège Vertières, 1945, pp. 312-313.

Autobiography: *Mémoires, pour servir à l'histoire d'Haiti, précédés de différents actes politiques et d'une étude historique et critique,* Paris, Libraire, 1851.

Biographical/Critical Sources: H. Pauléus Sannon's biography: *Boisrond-Tonnerre et son temps,* Port-au-Prince, Impr. Auguste A. Héraux, 1904; Pradel Pompilus & frères de l'Instruction Chrétienne, *Manuel illustré d'histoire de la littérature haitienne,* 1961, pp. 25-29; Auguste Viatte, *Histoire littéraire de l'Amérique française,* 1953, pp. 335-336.

BONHOMME, Arthur

(see under pseudonym: **Claude FABRY**)

BONHOMME, Colbert

b. 1904, Petit-Goâve, Haiti; d. May 27, 1977, Paris.
Essayist, lawyer, teacher.

Bonhomme studied in Port-au-Prince and graduated from the National Law School of Port-au-Prince. He started his career as a teacher in various schools and founded his own college with Justin Marcelin.

He practiced law before the courts and served as Judge at the Civil Court of Port-au-Prince. He later became Minister of Justice and President of the Supreme Court of Haiti. He was sent as Ambassador to the Vatican and later served at the Court of St. James in Great Britain.

Writings: Political Essays: *Les origines et les leçons d'une révolution profonde et pacifique,* preface by Samuel Dévieux, Port-au-Prince, Impr. de l'Etat, 1946; *Révolution et Contre-Révolution en Haiti de 1946 à 1957,* Port-au-Prince, Impr. de l'Etat, 1957.

Law: *La non-rééligibilité du chef de l'Etat et la portée politique de la procédure de révision constitutionnelle dans les constitutions haitiennes depuis 1946,* Paris, Memoir of Political Sciences, 1966.

BONHOMME, Jacques

b. ca. 1931, Guadeloupe.
Novelist.

Bonhomme's one novel concerns Antoine Dalbéra, first mate of the banana boat *Font-Fleur-de-l'Epée.* Dalbéra's love affair with Rose-Aimée moves from innocence to complications and Rose-Aimée's horrible illness. The work analyzes character and love, and is also descriptive of the island, both in its touristic-scenic reality and the inner sense of the daily routine of its inhabitants.

Writings: Novel: *Adieu Foulards, Adieu Madras,* Paris, Soulanges, 1961.

BONNET, Guy-Joseph

b. June 10, 1773, Léogâne, Haiti; d. January 9, 1843, Saint Marc, Haiti.
Military man, government official.

Bonnet had the opportunity to receive some education. As a soldier, he was an aide-de-camp to General André Rigaud, Commander-in-Chief for the southern part of Saint Domingue. He participated in the wars of independence and was among the signers of the Independence Act of Haiti (January 1, 1804), in Gonaives. He was among the first senators and became Secretary of State. Later, he was appointed Commandant of the Arrondissement of Saint Marc where he died.

Writings: Memoirs: *Souvenirs historiques de Guy-Joseph Bonnet, Général de Division des Armées de la République d'Haiti, ancien aide-de-camp de Rigaud; documents officiels relatifs à toutes les phases de la révolution de Saint-Domingue, recueillis et mis en ordre par Edmond Bonnet* (son fils), Paris, Lib. Auguste Durand, 1864.

Politics: *Au Directoire Exécutif et au Corps Législatif,* Paris, Impr. de J.F. Sobry, 1798; *Exposé de la conduite du Général Rigaud dans le commandement du Département du Sud de Saint Domingue, adressé au Directoire Exécutif,* Paris, Impr. de J.F. Sobry, 1796.

BONNETON, André

b. January 3, 1925, Cayenne, Guyane.
Poet, playwright, shortstory writer, musician, physician.

Dr. André Bonneton completed his secondary education at the Lyceé de Cayenne and then went to the University of Montpellier (France), where he took his P.C.B. He then attended, simultaneously, the Medical School and the "Faculté des Lettres" of the University of Montpellier, subsequently serving his internship at a psychiatric hospital and writing a well-known thesis entitled "Manifestations Neuro-Psychiâtriques et Anachlorhydrie gastriques ou Syndrome Neuro-Anachlorhydrique." Dr. Bonneton presently resides in Paris where he practices medicine and is known for his plan, "l'amaigrissement sans aucun régime" which he calls "psychosomatic weight loss."

He has written works in the field of medicine, biographies, novellas, plays, a novel and literary criticism, but poetry is the dominant genre of his literary output. He describes his style in a word of his own coinage, "irréalisant" which means that he transposes the living experience into images which are frequently violent and unexpected and makes allusions of such a nature that the uninitiated would consider his work allegorical.

There is a degree of pessimism running throughout the works of Dr. Bonneton which is an expression of his view of life as a "merdier" to which, he believes, we accommodate ourselves too easily and by so doing often show ourselves indifferent to certain values and essential problems.

Writings: Poetry: *Etoiles amères,* Paris, Dehan, 1951; *Aquilon,* Paris, Eds. de la Licorne, 1953; *Echo,* Paris, Subervie, 1965; *Takari* (preface by F.-J. Temple), Paris, Subervie, 1968; *Mage,* Paris, Jean Grassin, 1973.

Unpublished Works: *Salammbô* (play); *Le Bourreau* (play); *Iole (La Trachinienne),* (three-act tragedy); *Les Trois Pendus, Un rat-à-l'huile* and *Le crâne* (three novelettes); and *Jean Galmot: le mort qui vit en Guyane Française* (monograph); and the 1,135 page ms., *Gaston Monnerville: tracer droit le sillon* (biography), deposited in the Bibliothèque Nationale, Paris.

Medicine: article in *L'Encyclopédie Médicale et Familiale,* Paris, Eds. du Club Familial, 1964. Also: *Médecine Psychosomatique: regards sur les énigmes de la médecine,* Paris, Maloine, 1964.

BONNEVILLE, René

b. ca. 1870, Saint-Pierre, Martinique; d. May 8, 1902, Saint-Pierre.
Novelist, journalist.

Bonneville received his education in France, but he came back to live in Martinique where he died on May 8, 1902, a victim of the Mont-Pélé explosion, which destroyed Saint-Pierre in one great eruption. (Mont-Pélé killed 30,000 people in Saint-Pierre in a few seconds, snuffing out all life except one prisoner in an underground cell in the then capital of the island.)

His writing is strongly oriented towards the subjects of social conflict and race prejudice and his novels *Le Fruit défendu* and, especially, *Soeurs ennemies,* deal directly with the problem of the Martiniquian over-consciousness of gradations of skin coloring. His interests were violently attacked by white journalists and Bonneville often *literally* had to fight them.

Writings: Anthology: *Fleurs des Antilles* (poèsies de Eug. Agricole, Victor Duquesnay, M. Rosal, R. Bonneville, Salavina, A. Sédécias, E. St-Prix René, Daniel Thaly, Eug. Deslandes, J. Rivières, Pièces de Clavius Marius, P. Heyne, Paul de Beuze, Th. Célestin, Th. Baude, T. Titi), Paris, Challamel, 1900.

Novels: *Le Fruit défendu, roman de moeurs créoles; La Vierge endormie; Le Triomphe d'Eglantine,* Paris, Alcan Lévy, 1899; *Les Soeurs ennemies,* Paris, A. Challamel, 1901; *Les voluptueuses; L'Idéale maîtresse; Névrose; Tamai-Ha (pastorale créole); Moeurs créoles; Mal d'amour,* Paris, Challamel, 1902.

BORNO, Louis Eustache Antoine François Joseph

b. September 20, 1865, Port-au-Prince, Haiti; d. July 29, 1942, Pétionville.
Poet, lawyer, statesman (President of Haiti).

Borno studied at the Collège Polymathique and the Petit Séminaire Collège Saint-Martial. He went to Paris where he took a degree in law from the University of Paris.

When he returned to Haiti, he had a busy career in law and public affairs. He was a professor in the Faculty of Law, and Minister Plenipotentiary to the Dominican Republic. He was a Cabinet Minister for Foreign Affairs, Finance and Commerce, and became a judge at the Tribunal de Cassation. He was elected President of Haiti, April 14, 1922, was reelected in 1926, and left power on April 12, 1930.

Writings: Poetry: *Offrande mariale,* Port-au-Prince, 1921; several of his poems appeared in *La Ronde, Haiti Littéraire et Scientifique.*

Speech: *La Crise Morale, conférence faite au Musée du Petit Séminaire, Collège Saint-Martial, le 10 Mai, 1895,* Port-au-Prince, Impr. H. Amblard, 1895.

Law: *Code Civil d'Haiti annoté,* Paris, Lib. Giard et Brière, 1892; *Code de Commerce Haitien,* Port-au-Prince, Impr. de l'Abeille, 1910.

Diplomatic: *Rapport à Monsieur le Président de la République d'Haiti,* Tome 1, Port-au-Prince, Impr. Nationale, 1918.

BOUKMAN, Daniel

b. 1936, Martinique.
Poet, playwright, teacher.

After local schooling Boukman went to Paris for university study. Enlisted in the military, he deserted the French army in 1961 and fled to Algeria where he is now a professor.

Boukman's political drama, *Chants pour hâter la mort du temps des Orphée,* is in three dramatic-verse sections: "Les voix des Sirènes," written in 1959 and published in various journals; "Orphée nègre," which is dedicated to the famous Martiniquian psychologist and writer Franz Fanon; and "Des voix dans une prison," which treats of civil disorders in Guadeloupe in 1967.

His play *Les négriers* (1971) attacks the conservative leaders of Martinique who cannot even conceive of independence or a culture less than absolutely French. Boukman's 1976 drama, *Et jusqu'à la dernière pulsation,* deals with Palestine and the massacre in September, 1970, of Palestinians.

Writings: Verse-Play: *Chants pour hâter la mort du temps des Orphée ou Madédina île esclave,* Honfleur, P.-J. Oswald, 1967, 1971.

Prose Plays: *Les nègriers,* Honfleur, P.-J. Oswald, 1971; *Ventres pleins, ventres creux,* Honfleur, P.-J. Oswald, 1971; *Et jusqu'à la dernière pulsation de nos veines* (5 acts), Paris, Eds. l'Harmattan, 1976.

Biographical/Critical Sources: Juliette Eloi-Blézes' review of Boukman's two plays in *Acoma,* No. 3 (Feb. 1972), pp. 135-137.

BOURAND, Anne-Marie

(née **LEREBOURS**)
(see under pseudonym: **Annie DESROYS**)

BOURAND, Etienne

b. June 10, 1892, Gonaives, Haiti; d. 1958, Port-au-Prince.
Poet, playwright, teacher, lawyer.

Bourand was educated in Port-au-Prince and graduated from the Law School of the capital. He was named secretary at the Haitian Legation in London. On his return, he was appointed Commissaire du Gouvernement to the Civil Court of Port-au-Prince. He spent several years as professor of the Faculty of Law. His wife, Annie Desroys (pseudonym), was also a writer.

Writings: Poetry: *L'éternel adolescent,* Port-au-Prince, Impr. Modèle, 1928.

Plays: *Ménage de poète,* performed in 1915; *Le coeur décide,* performed in 1915; *L'imprévu* (adapted from Georges Rivolet's short story), performed in 1918; *En retenue,* performed in 1920; *Le goût du fard,* performed in 1921; *Feu de paille,* performed in 1921.

Biographical/Critical Sources: Ghislain Gouraige, *Histoire de la littérature haitienne,* 1960, pp. 333-336; Robert Cornevin, *Le théâtre haitien, des origines à nos jours,* 1973, pp. 137-138.

BREVILLE, Pierre

(pseudonym for **Dominique HIPPOLYTE**)

BRIERRE, Jean Fernand

(or **Jean François**)

b. September 28, 1909, Jérémie, Haiti.
Poet, playwright, novelist, biographer, teacher.

Brierre, one of the most prolific writers and one of the best poets of Haiti, attended the school of the Christian Brothers of Jérémie and the Lycée Nord Alexis of this city. He continued his education at the Service Technique d'Agriculture and he became teacher and later principal of the rural school of Châtard, located in the northern part of the country. He began his writing career when he was proclaimed laureate in a poetry contest organized by Charles Moravia.

Brierre took part in the student strike of 1929 in Haiti, and then was named Secretary of the Haitian Legation at Paris, where he remained twelve months. Returning to Haiti, he studied law and practiced journalism. He founded the opposition newspaper *La Bataille* and was put in prison on frequent occasions for political activities. He was Inspector des Ecoles of Jérémie in 1941 and came to the United States to study at Columbia University for a year, 1942-1943. Since then, he has held a number of posts: head of the Cultural Division of the Ministry of Foreign Affairs, Director of the Tourist Bureau, and later Under-Secretary of State of the Ministry of Tourism. Brierre was also member of the Government Council and was named Ambassador from Haiti to Buenos-Aires. Since 1965, Brierre has been living in Dakar where he is an important member of the Senegalese Ministry of Cultural Affairs. He was an active participant in the World Festival of Negro Arts at Dakar in 1966.

Brierre's first important poem was "Le Drame de Marchaterre" (1930), called forth by outrage at the shooting by U.S. marines of the occupying forces of unarmed peasants in late 1929 who were protesting new high taxes on tobacco and alcohol. Widely popular, the poem itself was in the old French alexandrine form, for he had not yet moved to more contemporary forms. That same year he wrote a dramatic poem "Au coeur de la Citadelle" in which he imagined King Christophe meeting other heroes and martyrs of Haiti's past to swear fidelity to the nation, its flag, and its people. After these early patriotic effusions he went off to Paris as political secretary and profitted by the wider experiences offered there, producing the work going into his first collection, *Chansons secrètes* (1933).

Through his various new experiences, imprisonments and exiles, he gained maturity, and having met Langston Hughes, the great American poet at Columbia, Brierre more than ever wanted to concern himself with the folkloric and Afro-Caribbean aspects of his country's culture. By 1944 he had moved stylistically to a freer verse in the wake of Jacques Roumain and Hughes. In 1945 he published 21 poems in *Nous garderons le dieu . . .* dedicated to the memory of Roumain, who had just died. These poems, written between August 25-September 7, 1945, celebrates Roumain, the poor and downcast black people of the world everywhere. Two of the poems are addressed to Marian Anderson and one each written "for" Paul Robeson and Toussaint Louverture ("L'adieu à la marseillaise"). Many of the poem titles later were used for his plays.

Brierre's historic sketch in one act, the drama *Les aieules* (1946), celebrates the heroic women who fought for Haitian independence. Another sketch of the same sort was "Vers le même ciel," seeking to dramatize the neglected orphans of Haitian society.

His work is in a wide range of forms and

reflective of much personal suffering and exile. Possibly he is Haiti's most gifted poet, certainly he is one of its most active artists and playwrights.

Writings: Lecture: *Le petit soldat* (causerie prononcée à l'Association des étudiants en Droit), Port-au-Prince, Impr. Haitienne, 1932.

Poetry: *Chansons secrètes (poèmes)*, Port-au-Prince, Impr. Haitienne, 1933; *Gerbes pour deux amis* (with Roussan Camille and F. Morisseau-Leroy), Port-au-Prince, Impr. H Deschamps, 1945; *Nous garderons le dieu: en hommage au grand leader haitien de gauche: Jacques Roumain*, Port-au-Prince, Impr. H. Deschamps, 1945; *Poems* in *Edition Spéciale de Noël des Poèmes de Jean F. Brierre, Haiti-Journal*, 1945; *Vers le même ciel* (sketch en vers), Numero spécial de *Haiti-Journal* (Noel, 1946), Port-au-Prince, 1946; *Black-soul; poème*, Havana, Ed. Lex, 1947; *Dessalines nous parle* (Collection du Sesquicentenaire de l'Indépendance d'Haiti), Port-au-Prince, Impr. H. Deschamps, 1953; *La Source: poème*, Buenos-Aires, 1956 (Collection du Jubilé du Docteur Jean Price-Mars); *La Nuit; poème*, Lauzanne, Impr. Held, 1957, but written May-Oct 1955; *Images d'or, poèmes pour 7 enfants avec 6 dessins originaux sur lino*, Port-au-Prince, 1959; *Aux champs pour Occide, sur un clavier bleu et rouge. Hommage au Maitre Occilius Jeanty* (Collection Librairie Indigène), Port-au-Prince, 1960; *Cantique à trois voix pour une poupée d'ébène; poème* (Collection Librairie Indigène), Port-au-Prince, 1960; *Découvertes*, Paris, Présence Africaine, 1966; *Or, Uranium, cuivre, radium*, Port-au-Prince, 1961; *Formes et couleurs* appeared in 1954. In manuscript, several poems, one concerns the great political figure from Guyana, and is so entitled: "Gouverneur Général Eboué."

Plays: *Le drapeau de demain, poème dramatique en deux actes*, Port-au-Prince, Impr. Haitienne, 1931; *Les Aieules*, Port-au-Prince, Ed. H. Deschamps (performed in the Lycée des Jeunes Filles, June 26, 1945); *Belle*, Impr. de l'Etat, 1948 (performed at the Club Hotel de Belladères, Oct 30, 1948); *Au milieu des flammes, pièce patriotique en deux actes et quatre tableaux* (with Clovis Bonhomme), in Collection du Cent cinquantenaire, Port-au-Prince, Impr. de l'Etat, 1953; *Pétion y Bolivar* with *L'Adieu à la Marseillaise*, French and Spanish language texts, Buenos Aires, Ed. Troquel; *La Première Marie* and *La cîme du calvaire*, both in Spanish, dates unknown; *Gorée "Son et lumière,"* Paris, Impr. André Rousseau, 1966.

Novel: *Les horizons sans ciel. Province*, Port-au-Prince, Ed. H. Deschamps, 1953.

Biography: *Marian Anderson* (with René Piquion), in Collection du Bi-Centenaire de Port-au-Prince, Port-au-Prince, Ed. H. Deschamps, 1950.

Mixed form: *Volonté*, a meringue [dance] by Jules Héraux, words by Jean F. Brierre, Port-au-Prince, 1949.

Recording: His reading of his own work made in 1953 at the Music Division, U.S. Library of Congress, Washington, D.C.

Literary Criticism: "A Oswald Durand," in *Haiti Journal*, Edition spéciale (1945); "Etzer Vilaire," in *Conjonction* (Aug. 1951), where Brierre calls Etzer Vilaire the "plus grand poète haitien de tous les temps"; preface to Gérard Chenet's *El Hadj Omar; Chroniques de la guerre sainte*, Honfleur, P.J. Oswald, 1968.

Biographical/Critical Sources: Richard Constant's "Paroles d'aîné: Jean Brierre," in *La Relève* (Aug. 1933), pp. 9-14; Naomi M. Garret's *The Renaissance of Haitian Poetry*, Présence Africaine, 1963; Maurice A. Lubin, "Jean F. Brierre and his work," translated from the French by Martha K. Cobb, in *Black World*, (Jan. 1973), pp. 36-49; Maurice A. Lubin, "Jean Brierre, Haitian poet," same article adapted for *Américas*, Vol. 26, No. 10 (Oct. 1974): the article is also available in Spanish and Portuguese; Ghislain Gouraige, *Histoire de la littérature haitienne*, 1960, pp. 385-390 and 431-433; Pradel Pompilus & Frères de l'Instruction Chrétienne, *Manuel Illustré d'histoire de la littérature haitienne*, 1961, pp. 390-400 and 448-454; Robert Cornevin, *Le théâtre haitien, des origines à nos jours*, 1973, pp. 146-147.

BROUARD, Carl

b. July 5, 1902, Port-au-Prince, Haiti; d. November 29, 1965, Port-au-Prince. Poet, essayist, journalist.

Born into a wealthy family, Brouard started his studies at Erima Guignard school, with Dr. Catts Pressoir as a teacher. He completed his education in France. Carl Brouard early gave up the luxury of his home in the Bois Verna of Haiti's capital for the tumultuous, bohemian life of artist-poet in the workers' section of Bourg Salomon. Loving, drinking and taking refuge in simple pleasures, employing in his verse an unadorned language, he set himself to depict the often harsh sorrows and passions of the masses of poor.

A member of the nativist "indigenism" or "negrism" group in Paris in 1926 with Jacques Roumain, Philippe Thoby-Marcelin and others, Brouard returned to Hajti in 1927. He was a contributor to *La Trouée* and *Le Petit Impartial,* helped to found *La Revue Indigène* which lasted only until 1928. His pioneering collection, *Le tam-tam angoissé* was put together in 1927 also, but was never published in its original form.

In 1938 he became the director of *Les Griots* magazine, a very important organ for the negritudist movement in Haiti and he was successful in keeping it going until 1940. For students of Haitian literature, Brouard is the Caribbean "François Villon," though he is without Villon's depth and emotional range.

Writings: Poetry: *Ecrit sur du ruban rose (poèmes),* Impr. Modèle, s.d. (1938); special commemorative volume, 1962, second edition, Panorama, 1965; *Pages retrouvées,* Panorama, 1963. Many poems are in periodicals and magazines; 12 poems in *Panorama de la poèsie haitienne,* edited by Carlos Saint-Louis and Maurice A. Lubin, H. Deschamps, 1950: all in Port-au-Prince.

Critical Essays: "Promenade à travers la littérature," in *La Bataille* (March 5, 1932), which states his admiration for Price-Mars; "La nouvelles école et l'idée d'une éthique haitienne," in *Les Griots* (Oct.-Dec. 1938), pp. 172-173; "L'art au service du peuple," also in *Les Griots* (Oct.-Dec. 1938).

Biographical/Critical Sources: Edner Brutus' "Carl Brouard vu de dos," in *La Relève* (Aug. 1932), pp. 2-8; "Carl Brouard: Fol de coeur," *La Relève* 3 (Ed. spéciale), pp. 7-32 (Sep. 1937); Franck Fouché's "Y a-t-il un cas Brouard dans la littérature haitienne," in *Guide pour l'étude de la littérature haitienne,* Port-au Prince, Panorama, 1964; Roger Gaillard's *La Destinée de Carl Brouard,* Port-au-Prince, H. Deschamps, 1968 (documents and photographs are also provided in this volume along with some extracts of his work); J. Jahn, *Neo-African Literature,* New York, Grove, 1968; Naomi M. Garret, *The Renaissance of Haitian Poetry,* Présence Africaine, 1963; Max Dorsinville, "Carl Brouard," in *La Relève,* pp. 4-6; Auguste Viatte, *Histoire littéraire de l'Amérique française,* Quebec, 1954, pp. 463-465; Ghislain Gouraige, *Histoire de la littérature haitienne,* 1960, pp. 234-238; Dr. Pradel Pompilus and les Frères de l'Instruction Chrétienne, *Manuel illustré d'histoire de la litterature haitienne,* 1961, pp. 374-381. Also see: Maurice A. Lubin, "Carl Brouard," in *Présence Francophone,* No. 12 (Spring 1976), pp. 141-149; Eddy A. Jean and Justin O. Fièvre, "Carl Brouard," in *Pour une littérature haitienne et militante,* pp. 9-40 (Lille, Eds. Jacques Soleil, 1975); and Frère Raphael Berrou and Pradel Pompilus, *Deux poètes indigéniste: Carl Brouard et Emile Roumer,* Port-au-Prince, Eds. Caraibes, 1973.

BRUN, Adolphe Pascal

b. September 26, 1889, Jacmel, Haiti; d. February, 1965, Jacmel.

Poet, scholar, teacher, merchant, journalist.

Brun was educated in Jacmel by his father who acted as his tutor and later at the Lycée Pinchinat of Jacmel, where he was to become a professor.

He was very fond of the sciences and especially of mathematics. He was chief editor of the Jacmelian paper *L'Abeille,* founded by his father. He contributed to many magazines and papers of Haiti and abroad.

Writings: Essays: *Qu'est-ce au juste que le Patrimoine Social de la Nation Haitienne,* (Premier prix du concours de la "Ligue de la Jeunesse Haitienne"), Jacmel, Impr. Typog.,

"L'Abeille," n.d. (1917?); *Observations relatives à notre present état économique et de la nécessité d'établir le budget de la République sur des recettes probables de moins de six millions de dollars,* Jacmel, Impr. Typog., "L'Abeille," 1931.

Poetry: *Rêves et pleurs,* Jacmel, Impr. de L'Abeille, n.d.

Mathematics: *Solution par l'algèbre élémentaire du fameux problème de la droite segmentée de Fermat, suivie de considérations sur le génie prodigieux d'Archimède, l'emploi de la méthode intuitive dans les mathématiques et la nature de certains rayons caloriques qui peuvent avoir été découverts, permettant de propager l'incendie et de mettre le feu aux soutes à poudre, dépôts de munitions, etc., malgré les obstacles, à n'importe quelle distance,* Jacmel, Impr. de l'Abeille, 1931; *Réflexions à propos de la synthèse des ondes et des corpuscules de M. Karl K. Darrow,* Jacmel, Impr. de l'Abeille, 1933 (mimeo); *Solution générale de la fameuse proposition de Fermat "Xn plus Yz égale Zn ne peut être résolue en nombres entiers que pour n égale 2," suivie d'une autre proposition qui la complète et de considérations diverses et variées,* Jacmel, Impr. de l'Abeille, 1935. Also: *Simple lettre à Mr. Jacques Fonteneau, philosophe qui a sollicité mes impressions au sujet de son ouvrage, Faisons le point: bons sens et verité,* Jacmel, Impr. de l'Abeille, 1938; *Suite obligée de ma lettre en date du 22 Mars 1938 à Monsieur Jacques Fonteneau,* Jacmel, Impr. de l'Abeille, 1938; *Le point, son essence, sa transcendance, fantaisie mathématique; doctrine complète (1 figure), discussion* etc., *en 18 pages d'un texte simple à la portée de quiconque sait seulement lire,* Jacmel, Ed. L'Abeille, n.d.; *Dans les champs de la transcendance. Démonstration rigoureuse de l'énigme diophantienne dite théorème de Fermat,* Port-au-Prince, Impr. H. Deschamps, 1954.

Metaphysics: *Un miracle constant et probablement éternel qui prouve l'existence en dehors des êtres et des choses d'une intelligence supérieure,* Port-au-Prince, "La Presse," 1931; *Une nouvelle hypothèse pour expliquer les phénomènes mystérieux et inexplicables découverts par MM Nouillard et Dupré,* Jacmel, Impr. de l'Abeille, n.d.

BRUN, Amédée

b. April 5, 1868, Jacmel, Haiti; d. September 1, 1896, Port-au-Prince.
Poet, storywriter, novelist, lawyer.

Born into a French family in Jacmel, Brun studied at the Petit Séminaire Collège, Saint-Martial, then went to Paris for university studies in 1888. Returning to Haiti in 1892 at the age of 26, with a law degree, Brun began a public and legal career.

He contributed to many of the literary journals of the day and he sought to express the nation's political moods in his poetry particularly. His style was smooth and conservative, often highly pictorial or descriptive. Though he wrote much, he published little, leaving in manuscript a novel, sheaves of verse, and several stories. His prose is considered mediocre stylistically and influenced by Poe, but he did employ folkloric elements from Haiti in a touch of early realism. His poetry, richly parnassian, is considered much better. Brun's verse style may be seen in this fragment from "Sakountala":

Oh! tuer la pensée assassine, à son tour,
Dans l'endormement noir du haschich étoilé,
Et fuir, l'âme dissoute en un élan d'amour
D'un grand vol de houris fraîchement constellé!

Writings: Stories: *Deux amours (contes des tropiques),* Port-au-Prince, Impr. Vve. J. Chenet, 1895; *Pages retrouvées,* Paris, Albert Savine, 1895; "Sans pardon," followed by "Faute vénielle," "Peine d'amour," "Isabella," Port-au-Prince, Impr. de l'Abeille, 1909.

Poetry: *Poèsies,* in the latter part of the volume *Sans Pardon,* Port-au-Prince, Impr. de l'Abeille, 1909.

Biographical/Critical Sources: Auguste Viatte, *Histoire littéraire de l'Amérique française,* 1954, pp. 387-388; Ghislain Gouraige, *Histoire de la littérature haitienne,* 1960, pp. 144-147; Dr. Pradel Pompilus & Frères de l'Instruction Chrétienne, *Manuel illustré d'histoire de la littérature haitienne,* 1961, pp. 258-262.

BRUN, Lélio

b. August 28, 1931, Jacmel, Haiti.
Poet, geologist.

Brun studied at the Brothers of Christian Education's school in Jacmel and at the Lycée Pinchinat. He graduated from the Ecole Normale Supérieure of Port-au-Prince. With a scholarship granted by the French government, he went to Paris where he studied geology. He is presently working in Algeria.

Writings: Poetry: *Bouquets de violettes* (with Bonnard Posy), mimeographed; *Blanc et noir,* preface by Paul E. Najac, Port-au-Prince, Impr. Les Presses Libres, 1952.

BRUNO, Camille

b. September 8, 1838, Port-au-Prince, Haiti; d. after 1902.
Economist, politician, teacher, orator.

Bruno was educated in France. When he returned to Haiti he was appointed professor at the Lycée Pétion and was eventually promoted to Director. He was later named President of the Audit Office. When he was driven into exile during Salomon's presidency, he founded a college in Kingston, Jamaica, during the 1884-1888 period.

Returning home, he was again appointed director of the Lycée Pétion and auditor of the Bank of Haiti.

Writings: Speeches: *Discours prononcé au cimetière de la Capitale le 8 Février 1897 à l'occasion de l'inauguration du monument funéraire érigé à la mémoire d'Edmond Paul,* Port-au-Prince, Impr. J. Verrollot, 1897. Biographic speech: *A la mémoire de Victorin Plésance; paroles et discours* (with various speakers), Por-au-Prince, Cérant Arnoux, Impr., 1902.

Administration: *L'Agriculture et le Budget; projet de budget du Département de l'Agriculture, précédé d'une lettre ouverte aux membres des pouvoirs exécutif et législatif,* Port-au-Prince, Impr. de l'Abeille, 1909.

Essay: *Eloge d'Edmond Paul,* Port-au-Prince, Impr. J. Verrollot, 1897.

BRUTUS, Edner

b. April 20, 1911, Jérémie, Haiti.
Historian, essayist, critic, lawyer, diplomat.

Brutus started his studies in Jérémie and came to Port-au-Prince where he completed them at the Christian Brothers' school. He graduated from the Faculty of Law.

Brutus contributed to many newspapers and magazines such as *Haiti-Journal, Le Nouvelliste,* and *La Relève.*

He was secretary at the President's office and went as Haitian Chargé d'Affaires to Rome; he later became Minister Plenipotentiary to Brazil and Holland.

Brutus was named Minister of Public Education and from 1971-78 he served as Minister of Foreign Affairs.

Writings: Biographical and Literary Critical Essays: in *La Relève.*

Education: *Instruction Publique et Haiti: 1492-1945,* Port-au-Prince, Impr. de l'Etat, 1948.

History: *Révolution dans Saint Domingue,* Paris, Eds. du Panthéon, 2 vols., 1970.

BRUTUS, Timoléon César

b. March 26, 1886, Port-au-Prince, Haiti; d. September, 1971, Port-au-Prince.
Biographer, lawyer, historian.

Brutus was educated in Port-au-Prince and studied pharmacy, but he settled in Jérémie to become a teacher at the Lycée Nord Alexis. Later he was mayor of the city.

Named Prefect of Jérémie, Brutus then became the chief of the private office of the President of the Republic, and soon Secretary of State of Public Works and Commerce.

In 1947, Brutus chaired the private committee in charge of collecting funds to pay the International debt to the United States, after which he was named Minister of Foreign Affairs.

As historian, Brutus argued Haitians should cease looking overseas for their culture and ideologies; instead, he urged, they should build on their own climate, social, and historical experiences.

Writings: Political: *Mémoire à la chambre des Représentants du Peuple,* Port-au-Prince, Impr. Aug. A. Héraux, 1917.

Biographies: *Rançon du génie ou la leçon de Toussaint Louverture,* 2 vols., Port-au-Prince, Impr. N.A. Théodore, 1945; *L'homme d'airain; étude monographique sur Jean-Jacques Dessalines, fondateur de la Nation Haitienne; histoire de la vie d'un esclave devenu empereur jusqu'à sa mort, le 17 Octobre 1806,* 2 vols., 1er. vol.; *L'éveil d'une nation,* Port-au-Prince, Impr. N.A. Théodore, 1946; second vol. is *Du sang sur le trône,* Port-au-Prince, Impr. de l'Etat, 1947.

Study of Medicinal Herbs: *Les plantes et les légumes d'Haiti qui guérissent: Mille et une recettes pratiques,* Tome 2 (in collaboration with Arsène Vaugelas Pierre Noel), Port-au-Prince, Impr. de l'Etat, 1960.

BURR-REYNAUD, Frédéric

b. July 9, 1884, Port-au-Prince, Haiti; d. February 3, 1946, Port-au-Prince. Poet, playwright, lawyer.

Burr-Reynaud studied at the Lycée Pétion. He was active in public affairs and served as deputy of Léogane in the Chamber of Deputies in 1930. He contributed to such journals as *La Phalange* and was the founder and the director of *La Forge.* He was a member of the Haitian Society of Arts and Letters.

Much of his work deals with the Indian period of Haiti's history. His *Poèmes quisqueyens* (the latter word an old Indian name for Hispaniola) is a sonnet collection providing a detailed, if poetic, evocation of the lost Indian culture. The poem "1804" is one of his patriotic works having been inspired by his attendance at a concert by the gifted Haitian artist, Occide Jeanty.

Writings: Poetry: *Ascensions, poèmes,* Paris, Ed. de la Revue Mondiale, (Impr. Floch), 1924; *Poèmes quisqueyens, époque indienne,* Paris, Ed. de la Revue Mondiale (Impr. Floch), 1926; *Au fil de l'heure tendre, dizains,* Impr. La Presse, 1929; *Anathèmes,* Impr. La Presse, 1930; *C'est la guerre, poèmes,* Impr. du Collège Vertières, s.d.; *La Corbeille* (Poems of F. Burr-Reynaud, Dominique Hippolyte, Jean Libose, Edgard N. Numa, and Luc Grimard), Impr. du Collège Vertières, 1943: all Port-au-Prince, except first two.

Plays: *Anacaona* (dramatic poem in 3 acts and verse written with Dominique Hippolyte), performed at Ciné-Variétés (Feb. 19, 1927), Port-au-Prince, Impr. N. Telhomme, 1941; *Le soupçon,* with Luc Grimard, details not known.

Botany: *Visages d'arbres et de fruits haitiens,* Port-au-Prince, Impr. du Collège Vertières, 1940.

Biographical/Critical Sources: Naomi M. Garret: *The Renaissance of Haitian Poetry,* Paris, Présence Africaine, 1963; Auguste Viatte, *Histoire littéraire de l'Amérique française,* 1954, pp. 455-456; Ghislain Gouraige, *Histoire de la littérature haitienne,* 1960, pp. 208-214; Dr. Pradel Pompilus et les Frères de *toire de la littérature haitienne,* Port-au-Prince, Impr. H. Deschamps, 1961; pp. 332-337 and 441-448; Robert Cornevin, *Le théâtre haitien des origines à nos jours,* Montréal, Léméac, 1973, p. 135.

CABASSOU, Lionel George André

(pseudonym for **Léon Gontran DAMAS**)

CALIXTE, Démosthène Pétrus

b. August 6, 1896, Fort-Liberté, Haiti; d. December 7, 1970, Port-au-Prince. Autobiographer, military officer.

Calixte attended the school of Fort-Liberté. When the American Forces of occupation came to Haiti, they abolished the Haiian Army and organized the Gendarmerie d'Haiti. He was among the first soldiers of this military organization, in time rising to the rank of colonel and then Chief of the Garde d'Haiti, after its "haitianization."

He was later dismissed by the Haitian government, but was soon named Inspector of Embassies and Consulates of Haiti in Europe, and as a final appointment, Haitian ambassador to Spain.

Writings: Politics: *Haiti, the cavalry of a soldier,* New York, W. Malliet, 1939 (the English edition was translatd into French as *Le calvaire d'un soldat (Haiti),* New York, W. Malliet, 1939).

CALVIN, Jean Max

b. June 1, 1945, Port-au-Prince, Haiti. Poet.

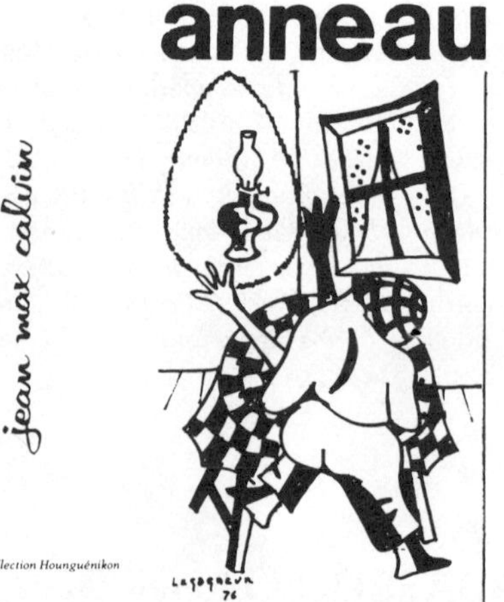

Collection Hounguénikon

Calvin attended schools in Port-au-Prince.

Writings: Poetry: *Le légende de l'ombre,* Port-au-Prince, Les Presses Nationales d'Haiti, 1966; *Anneau,* New York, Atelier Haiti, 1976.

CAMILLE, Roussan
(pseudonym: **Nassour EL LIMAC**)

b. August 27, 1912, Jacmel, Haiti; d. December 7, 1961, Port-au-Prince. Poet, journalist.

Roussan Camille, one of the best poets of Haiti, began his education at the Christian Brothers' school and the Lycée Pinchinat of Jacmel. He later studied in Port-au-Prince at the Tippenhauer College.

Under Charles Moravia's directorship, he entered the field of journalism, published articles, poems and the column "Bel aujourd'hui" under his pen-name Nassour El Limac for the new Haitian lottery in *Haiti-Journal, Temps-Revue* and *L'Action Nationale.* He became director of *Haiti-Journal* after Moravia's death.

Roussan Camille was named Secretary of the Haitian Legation to Paris and traveled extensively throughout Europe.

Returning to Haiti, he was Chef-de-Division of the Department of Public Instruction in the 1940's and was head also of the Mouvement de Coopération Intellectuelle Haitiano-Cubaine.

He was Co-director with René Piquion and Séjour Laurent of the paper, *Le National,* during 1955-1956.

He was appointed Haitian Vice-Consul in New York, returned to Haiti to become Secretary General at the Ministry of Public Health, and finally at the Ministry of Tourism.

He was awarded the Dumarsais Estimé poetry prize for his collection of poems, *Multiple présence.*

As a young man he visited New York City where he fell under the influence of Langston Hughes; and the great Cuban poet, Nicolás Guillen also turned him toward developing a more personal and black-conscious verse. While a diplomat in Paris, he traveled widely as noted, and was influenced by European artists he read and visited, and began to consider his own country's anguished history. Most of his work is expressive of Hughes' idea that black poets should use their verse for protest and social purposes.

In Paris he became a close friend of the Latin American poets Jorge Royo fils, Eduardo Aviles Ramirez, and Guillermo Benavides. Camille's *Assaut à la nuit,* though published much later, in 1940, contains much of his work from this period. The poem "Poison dans le coeur" from that collection (it first appeared in *La Relève*), expresses an anti-U.S. feeling occasioned by the American occupation of Haiti:

Moi-même!
Immensité fantastique,
faite de mille millions de douleurs
lointaines et proches
que d'autres subirent . . .

In "Christ" he expresses the blessings bestowed upon humanity and black man's desire for the fulfillment of that promise:

Le monde va renaitre
aux accents de ta voix
répercutés par les siècles
et tout au long des foules.
Nous voulons des Pâques,
et des cènes
et des noces,
où le mouton,
le poisson
et le vin
feront librement tout le tour de la table.

The poem Mercer Cook considers the "most moving in recent Haitian literature" is Camille's "Nedjé" which takes a hard look at the cabaret girl he had briefly seen in a dance in Casablanca:

Un soir sanglant
qui n'était qu'une minute
de l'éternel soir sanglant de l'Afrique
. . . .
les faubourgs noirs de Londres
les bordels de Tripoli,
Montmartre
Harlem
tous les faux paradis
où les nègres dansent et chantent
pour les autres.

Writings: Poetry: *Assaut à la nuit,* Port-au-Prince, Impr. de l'Etat, 1940; *Gerbe pour deux amis* (written with contributions also by Jean Fernand Brierre and Félix Morisseau-Leroy) in honor of Dr. and Mrs. Mercer Cook, Port-au-Prince, Ed. H. Deschamps, 1945; *Multiple présence,* (awarded the Dumarsais Estimé poetry prize), Quebec, Eds. Naaman, 1978; unpublished is "Douze poèmes pours enfants," preface by René Bélance.

Biographical/Critical Sources: Mercer Cook, "Trends in Recent Haitian literature," in *The Journal of Negro History* (April 1947); Franck Fouché, *Symphonie en noir majeur,* Port-au-Prince, Art Graphic Press, 1961; Bonnard Posy, *Roussan Camille, le poète d'assaut à la nuit,* Port-au-Prince, Impr. des Antilles, 1962; Naomi M. Garret, *The Renaissance of Haitian Poetry,* Présence Africaine, 1963, pp. 167-175; Ghislain Gouraige, *Histoire de la littérature haitienne,* 1960, pp. 167-175; Pradel Pompilus & Freres de l'Instruction Chrétienne, *Manuel illustré d'histoire de la littérature haitienne,* 1961, pp. 400-406.

CAMPENON, François Nicolas Vincent

b. March 29, 1772, Sainte-Rose, Guadeloupe; d. November 24, 1843, Villecresnes, Seine-et-Oise, France.
Poet, travel writer, memoirist.

As a young man, Campenon went to France to attend schools at Sens and afterwards in Paris. He was a royalist and composed a romance for Marie-Antoinette, but, when the work failed to please, the author fled France and took shelter in Switzerland, where he wrote this first book, *Voyage de Grenoble à Chambéry.* Later, back in France during the Consulate, Campenon was named head of the Department of Theatre at the Ministry of Interior. Managing to avoid political difficulties, Campenon even became Secretary of the King's Chamber at the time of the Restoration (Louis XVIII).

Campenon was elected member of the famed Académie Française in 1813 to Delille's seat. During his academic campaign for the election, an epigram was circulated against him:

> *Au fauteuil de Delille aspire Campenon,*
> *Son talent suffit-il pour qu'il s'y campe?*
> *Non.*

Ever faithful to classicism, Campenon vigorously opposed the new movement of romanticism. He died at 71 and was succeeded at the Academy by Saint-Marc de Girardin. When Victor Hugo, on January 16, 1845, answered Saint-Marc de Girardin's reception address, he praised Campenon with these words:

> *Chacune de ses oeuvres est comme une production nécessaire dont on retrouve la racine dans quelque coin de son coeur. Son amour pour la famille engendre ce doux et touchant poème de "L'Enfant prodigue"; son goût pour la campagne fait naitre "La Maison des Champs" cette gracieuse idylle; son culte pour les esprits éminents détermine les* Etudes sur Ducis, *livre curieux et intéressant au plus haut degré par tout ce qu'il fait voir et par tout ce qu'il fait entrevoir; portrait fidèle et soigneux d'une figure isolée, peinture involontaire de toute une époque.*

Writings: Travel: *Voyage de Grenoble à Chambéry,* 1791.

Poetry: *La Maison des champs,* Paris, 1809; *L'Enfant prodigue,* Paris, 1811; *Epitre aux femmes; Stances à Mr. Desarps; Poèsies et opuscules,* 2 vols. (verse and prose), Paris, L'advocat, 1823.

Memoirs: *Mémoires,* 1824.

Translation: *Histoire d'Ecosse* (by Robertson); *Histoire d'Angleterre* (from English); *Odes et Satires d'Horace* (from Latin).

CAMPFORT, Gérard

b. January 11, 1942, Port-au-Prince, Haiti.
Poet, essayist, literary critic.

After his classical studies, Campfort attended the Ecole Normale Supérieure and the Faculty of Ethnology in Port-au-Prince. After teaching in the capital in various colleges, he emigrated to New York.

Writings: Poetry: *Eaux, poèmes 1964-1966,* Collection Hounguenikon, Port-au-Prince, Impr. M. Rodriguez, 1966; *Clés,* Collection Hounguenikon, Port-au-Prince, Impr. M. Rodriguez, 1970.

CAPECIA, Mayotte

b. ca. 1928, Carbet, Martinique; d. 1953.
Novelist.

Capécia was educated in Fort-de-France, but she spent most of her later years in France.

Capécia was famed for her two novels. The first had a commercial as well as a critical success and concerns Ce Carbet, the "fille de couleur," who grows up in a small village of Martinique. Capécia's works have frequently been criticized for reflecting the old self-shame of many Creoles in their portion of African heritage and her too obvious belief that everything white is or was wonderful and superior. However, Dr. Mercer Cook, the sagacious American literary critic, also considered her novel, *Je suis Martiniquaise,* a revealing study of race relations in the French West Indies."

Fanon used her novels as examples of Caribbean alienation in his study *Les Damnés de la terre,* and his disdainful treatment of her work probably gave her the attention she otherwise would have seriously lacked. In her second novel, the images of Afro-Caribbean characters are more subtle, but the same alienation dominates throughout.

Writings: Novels: *Je suis Martiniquaise,* Paris, Eds. Correa, 1948 (Grand Prix des Antilles, 1948); *La Négresse blanche,* Paris, Eds. Correa, 1950.

Biographical/Critical Sources: Mercer Cook, book review, in *Journal of Negro History* 34 (July 1949), p. 370; Elizabeth Brooks, "Three Martinican Novelists," unpublished Ph.D. dissertation, Howard University, 1953; Beatrice Smith Clark, "The Works of Mayotte Capécia," in *CLA Journal,* XVI (June 1973), pp. 415-425; Clarisse Zimra, "Patterns of Liberation in Contemporary Women Writers," in *L'Esprit Createur,* XVII, No. 2 (Summer 1977), pp. 103-114.

CARBET, Claude

(a.k.a. **CLAUDE**)
b. October 24, 1893, Fort-de-France, Martinique.
Teacher, novelist, musician.

Carbet was educated in Martinique and in France. After schooling, she was appointed professor of literature and English in Martinique. She wrote two collections of melodies and songs for Suzy Solidor.

Carbet joined her talent to another teacher, Anna-Maria Magdeleine, to write and publish books on Martinique. They both adopted in this work of collaboration the pseudonyms of "Claude" and "Magdeleine" Carbet. They published for some years a useful collection, the "Ceux d'Outre-Mer" series printed in Paris (1939).

Her stories are based on close personal observance of the customs of the Martinican peasants and petty bourgeoisies.

Carbet was a major supporter for many years of the publishing house in Fort-de-France, "Les Presses de la Cité," and actively participated in the publication of the *Revue Dialogue.* She travelled widely in Europe and met political leaders in France. In her last years, Carbet lived in her villa "Balata" in Fort-de-France with her children and grandchildren.

Writings: Novels (published in collaboration by Claude and Magdeleine Carbet): *Féfé et Doudou, Martiniquaises,* Paris, Ed. J. Cres, 1936; *Braves gens de la Martinique,* Fort-de-France, La Cité du Livre, 1957; *Piment Rouge,* Paris, Les Cahiers d'Art et d'Amitié, 1938; *Cà et là dans la Caraibe,* Paris, Ceux d'Outre-Mer, 1939.

Poetry: *Chansonnette, l'Ile aux Oiseaux!* Fort-de-France, Cité du Livre, 195(?); *La Voix des Isles,* Paris, Ed. Orphée, 195(?).

History: *Questions sur l'histoire de la Martinique* (both in collaboration with Gilbert de Chambertrand), Fort-de-France, Impr. Antillaise, Saint-Paul, n.d.; and Carbet (alone) published *Musique noire,* Fort-de-France, Ed. de la Revue Dialogue, 1958; and *Et Lazare sortit du tombeau,* 1967.

CARBET, Marie-Magdalene

(a.k.a. **MAGDELEINE**)
b. ca. 1906, Martinique.
Novelist, teacher, poet.

Marie-Magdalene studied in France and long taught in Troyes, Martinique, but she has recently retired. She collaborated on several works with Claude Carbet. She has been active in the movement against racism in Martinique.

Marie-Magdalene Carbet was ever happy to celebrate her small island. Her verse-style can be seen in this example from the title poem for the volume *Viens voir ma ville:*

Trois roses, Passion
Orgueil, flammes, rayon.
Spectres chers au regard.
Larmes, prismes fluides.

Buisson d'espoirs à vif
Chanson rouge de sang.
Témoignage obstiné
Du quotidien miracle.
Voix de l'éternité.

She was glad to discover Africa, as she sought a return to the mother continent. Her poem "Hautes Eaux" from *Rose de ta grâce* recalls her visit to the upper Niger at Gao, and "Beau Piroguier" was written on the banks of the Niger. "Des bords du Niger . . ." and other poems from this collection are shown to have been written in Bamako, Mali, or in Abidjan, Ivory Coast.

Writings: Novels (published alone): *Au péril de ta joie,* Quebec, Ed. Léméac, 1972; *D'Une rive à l'autre* (preface by Robert Cornevin), Montreal, Ed. Léméac, 1975; Written with Claude Carbet: *Féfé et Doudou, Martiniquaises,* Paris, J. Crés, 1936; *Piment rouge,* Paris, Les Cahiers d'Art et d'Amitie, 1938; *Ça et là dans la Caraibe,* Paris, Ceux d'Outre-Mer 1939; *Braves gens de la Martinique,* Fort-de-France, La Cité du Livre, 1957;. . . *Et merveille de vivre,* 1973.

Poetry: *Chansonnelle, l'ile aux oiseaux,* Fort-de-France, La Cité du Livre, 195(?); *Point d'Orgue,* Paris, La Reproductrice, 1958; *Ecoute, soleil-dieu, poèmes,* Paris, Le Choix, 1961; *Viens voir ma ville,* Paris, Impr. La Reproductrice, 1963; *Suppliques et chansons, poèmes,* Paris, Ed. du Cerf-Volant, n.d.; *Rose de ta Grâce,* winner of the Prix des Caraibes awarded by the Association des Ecrivains de Langue Française, Paris, 1971.

Essay: *Questions sur l'histoire de la Martinique* (written with Claude Carbet and Gilbert de Chambertrand), Fort-de-France, Impr. Antillaise Saint-Paul, 1965.

Genre Unknown: *Comptines et chansons antillaises,* Montreal, 1975.

Stories: *Au village en temps longtemps,* Montréal, Ed. Léméac, 1977.

CARRENARD, Adrien

(pseudonym: **ADRY-CARENE**)
b. January 29, 1880, Bainet, Haiti;
d. November 3, 1971, Jacmel.
Poet, lawyer.

Carrénard received his education in Port-au-Prince, but spent all his life in Jacmel. He served as Commissioner of Government at the Civil Court of Jacmel, and later became Judge.

Carrénard contributed to *Le Nouvelliste, Le Matin* and especially *L'Abeille,* whose editor-manager was his close friend, Pascal Brun.

Writings: Poetry: *Les Pervenches, poèsies,* Port-au-Prince, Impr. H. Chauver, 1917; "Les Roses naines," unpublished.

CARRIE, Pierre

b. May 27, 1919, Gonaives, Haiti.
Poet, novelist, playwright, teacher.

Carrié started his schooling in Gonaives and completed his studies in Port-au-Prince at the Petit Séminaire Collège Saint Martial, where he became a teacher. Later, he was named as Secretary at the Haitian Embassy in Rio de Janeiro and some years later in the same capacity at the Organization of American States.

He is living now in New York.

Writings: Poetry: *Heures intimes, poèmes,* preface by Stéphen Alexis, Port-au-Prince, Impr. H. Deschamps, 1945.

Play: *La légende de l'eau.*

Novels: *Crépuscule, roman* (présentation de Léon Laleau, de l'Académie Ronsard), Port-au-Prince, Impr. de l'Etat, 1948; *Bonjour New York,* Canada, n.d. (but 1972?).

CASIAS, Rose-Marie Perrier

(also: **Rose-Marie PERRIER**)
b. ca. 1944, Jérémie, Haiti.
Poet, storywriter.

Perrier received her education partly in Jérémie and partly in Port-au-Prince.

Writings: Poetry: *La Nuit de mon exil,* Port-au-Prince, 1963; *Cantilène à Zouki,* preface by Ulysse Pierre-Louis, Port-au-Prince, Impr. M. Rodriguez, 1965.

CASSEUS, Maurice A.

b. April 18, 1909, Port-au-Prince, Haiti; d. January 16, 1963, London.
Poet, novelist, teacher, diplomat.

Casséus was educated in Port-au-Prince at the Petit Séminaire Collège Saint Martial and the Lycée Pétion. He spent some years as assistant professor at this same Lycée. He lived for many years in New York before serving as secretary in the Private Office of the President and thereafter as Secretary of the Haitian Embassy in London where he died.

Writings: Poetry: *Entre les lignes,* Port-au-Prince, Ed. "La Presse," n.d.

Novels: *Viejo* (preface by Dr. Price Mars), Port-au-Prince, Impr. "La Presse," 1935; *Mambo, roman,* Port-au-Prince, Impr. du Séminaire Adventiste, 1949.

CASTERA, Georges

b. December 27, 1936, Port-au-Prince, Haiti.
Poet, essayist, painter.

Castera attended school in Port-au-Prince at the Institution Saint-Louis de Gonzague. After many years in Spain he now lives in New York.

Writings: Poetry: *Le retour à l'arbre* (illustrations by Wai), New York, Calfou, New Orientation, 1974; *Koubèlan* (poems in creole), mimeo., 1972; *Jak Roumin* (poem in creole dedicated to the poet for his 70th anniversary), Ed. "A contre-courant," May 1977.

Biographical/Critical Sources: Louis Lamothe "Georges Castera" in *Los Mayores poetas latino-americanos de 1850-1950,* Mexico, B. Costa Amic Editor, 1959.

CATALOGNE, Gérard de

b. June 19, 1905, Cap-Haitien, Haiti; d. November 24, 1974, Nice, France.
Critic, literary historian, journalist, politician.

Gérard de Catalogne was entirely educated in France. He attended the Pensionnat de Passy, the Lycée Louis Le Grand and the Institut Catholique de Paris, where he won his licence ès-lettres. In Paris, he had close contact with the "L'Action française" group and with writers such as Charles Maurras, Léon Daudet, and increasingly became interested in writing criticism.

When he came back to Haiti, around 1931, he spent many years in Cap-Haitien. He managed Les Hostelleries du Roi Christophe. He moved on to Port-au-Prince as chief editor of *La Phalange* and founded *Le Soir,* when he left the catholic newspaper. Years later he founded *Le Nouveau Monde.* De Catalogne later became Director General of the Bureau of Tourism.

Writings: Literary History-Criticism: *Henri Bataille ou le romantisme de l'instinct* (fragments), Paris, Ed. de la Pensée Latine, 1925; *Le message de Thomas Hardy; préface de François Mauriac,* Paris, Lib. de France, 1926; *Dialogue entre deux mondes; enquête,* Paris, Lib. de la Revue Française (Alexis Ridier Ed.), 1931.

Politics: *Haiti devant son destin* (preface by Louis Zéphirin), Port-au-Prince, Impr. de l'Etat, 1939; *Les compagnons du spirituel,* Montreal, Valiquette, 1946; *Les nostalgies de San Francisco,* Port-au-Prince, Impr. H. Deschamps, 1945; *Notre révolution,* 3 vols., Montreal, Bernard Valiquette, 1943, 1944, et 1945 (Vol. 1: *Tragédie dans le monde;* Vol. 2: *Hommes et doctrines du vingtième siècle;* Vol. 3: *Entretiens dans la tourmente*); *Haiti à l'Heure du Tiers-Monde. Précédé d'une "Lettre ouverte" au Général De Gaulle,"* Port-au-Prince, Ed. du

Nouveau Monde, 1964; *Discours sous le soleil,* Port-au-Prince, Office national du Tourisme et de la Propagande, 1965.

Essay: *Une génération,* Paris, Ed. "Le Rouge et le Noir," 1930.

Tourism: *A Guide to Cap-Haitien* and *The Citadel of King Christophe,* Cap-Haitien, 1956.

CEDRAS, Dantès

b. April 4, 1915, Jérémie, Haiti.
Poet, teacher, public servant.

Cédras attended the School of Christian Brothers of Jérémie and the Lycée Nord Alexis of this city. He came to Port-au-Prince and took his law degree. He was a teacher in Jérémie and later supervisor of the schools.

He is presently assistant to the secretary-general at the Department of Coordination.

Writings: Poetry: *Morsures (poèmes),* Haiti (Jérémie?), 1938.

CELESTIN, Clément

b. March 5, 1887, Port-au-Prince, Haiti; d. February 3, 1973, Port-au-Prince.
Essayist, historian, public servant.

Célestin received his education in Port-au-Prince. He was engaged in commercial activities and became General Inspector at the Department of Commerce.

Writings: Annuaire Général d'Haiti (with Berthoumieux Danache), Port-au-Prince, Impr. Modèle, 1926; *Bulletin de renseignements, d'adresses et de réclames,* Port-au-Prince, Cie. Lithog., 1923.

Essays: *Idées et opinions; la réforme de l'Etat, réorganisation de l'armée, plan politique, administratif et social, plan financier, économique et terrien,* Port-au-Prince, Impr. M. Gachette, 1940; La crise *économique haitienne,* Port-au-Prince, Impr. du Commerce, 1947.

History: *Compilations pour l'histoire,* 4 Vols., Impr. N.A. Théodore, Tome I, 1958, Tome II, 1959, Tome III, 1959, and Tome IV, 1960.

CELESTIN, Julio B.

b. March 20, 1950, Port-au-Prince, Haiti.
Folklorist, novelist, teacher.

After studying at the School of Christian Brothers in Haiti, Celestin briefly studied in Paris before taking his B. A. from Brooklyn College in New York and his M. A. at New York University's School of Education. At present he is a director of an educational center in New York City.

His first major published work is *Sous les Manguiers,* a collection of seven folkstories which are, however, written in French rather than the island créole in which they had been told over the centuries. Publishing in exile no doubt made such a move obviously appropriate. Nevertheless, Célestin has employed many créole terms (furnishing a glossary) and attempted to preserve as authentic a local (and linguistic) flavor as possible.

Writings: Folklore: *Sous les manguiers,* Québec, Naaman, 1976.

CELESTIN-MEGIE, Emile

b. October 17, 1922, Marigot, Haiti.
Poet, novelist (in créole), biographer.

After his classes, Emile Célestin-Mégie was a teacher at the primary school at Marigot and later became a public notary there. Some years later he moved to Port-au-Prince where he became a member of the staff of ONEC (Office National d'Analphabétisation et d'action communautaire).

Célestin-Mégie has been a strong supporter of creole as a language of the country to replace standard French, which is spoken by only a very small minority. He has consequently published a great number of collections of poems in creole. Following Frankétienne, who has just published the first novel in creole, *Dezafi,* Mégie became the second to compose and publish a novel in creole with his *Lanmou pa gin baryè.*

Writings: Poetry in French: *Feuilles d'Ortie,* Port-au-Prince, Togiram Press, 1958; *Coeur de Silex,* Port-au-Prince, 1963; *Faisceau Multicolore,* mimeo., Atelier ONEC, 1967; *Vers la Nouvelle Saison,* Port-au-Prince, Atelier ONEC, 1968; *Bouquets de Glanures I,* Port-au-Prince, Ateliers Fardin, 1974; *Bouquets de Glanures II,* Port-au-Prince, Atelier-Fardin, 1976.

Poetry in Creole: *Dizhuitt Mé (18 Mai),* Port-au-Prince, Togiram, 1955; *Trayizon (Trahisons),* Port-au-Prince, Togiram, 1955; *Tenifiantsana (Paròl chanté),* Port-au-Prince, Togiram, 1965; *Kité-m Palé,* Port-au-Prince, Atelier, ONEC, 1967; *Vouayaj,* Port-au-Prince, Atelier-Fardin, 1968; *Byin Viv,* Port-au-Prince, Atelier-Fardin, 1973; *Sinsérité Nan Lanmou,* Port-au-Prince, Atelier-Fardin, 1974.

Novel in Creole: *Lanmou Pa Gin Baryè,* Port-au-Prince, Eds. Fardin, 1975.

Biography: *Ulrick Henry, poète,* Port-au-Prince, Pierre-Noel, 1953.

CESAIRE, Aimé

b. June 26, 1913, Basse-Pointe, Martinique.

Poet, teacher, playwright, political leader.

Aimé Césaire was born in 1913 into a family of seven children in Basse-Pointe, a town on Martinique's northeastern Atlantic coast which lies in the afternoon shadow of the volcano Mont Pelée. Son of a father who worked as an accountant for the colonial internal revenue service, and a mother who was a seamstress (references to both appear in *Cahier d'un retour au pays natal*), Césaire was an outstanding student at the local elementary school, and earned a scholarship in 1924 to attend the Lycée Schoelcher in Fort-de-France, the island's main city. There he met Léon Damas, a Guianan classmate who would contribute to the birth of *négritude* ten years later; Octave Mannoni, an instructor whose subsequent theories about the psychology of colonization Césaire was to attack in *Discours sur le colonialisme;* and Gilbert Gratiant, E. Rivert, and Louis Achille, later writers all.

Success at Schoelcher, where he was the top student in 1931, winning prizes in English, French, Latin, and History, earned Césaire a scholarship for further study in Paris at the prestigious Lycée Louis-le-Grand. Arriving in France, Césaire encountered Ousmane Socé Diop and Léopold Sédar Senghor, the first of a small group of Africans who would introduce him to the cultures of his ancestors.

Soon after his arrival in September, 1931, the Nardal sisters, Paulette and Jane, two Martinican women, and Dr. Leo Sajous, a Haitian, launched *La Revue du Monde Noir,* a bilingual French-English journal devoted to news from all parts of the Black world. Césaire read the short-lived review (Nov. 1931-April 1932), although he did not join Senghor in attending the weekly salon of the Nardal sisters and their group, whom he considered as a little too middle-class and "salonnard." Nevertheless, *La Revue du Monde Noir* contributed, along with many other sources (e.g. the French Communist review *Le Nouvel Age,* which published Afro-American poetry; Afro-American journals and novels; ethnographic studies of African cultures), notably *Légitime Défense,* to the new currents of interest in Black culture which Césaire absorbed during the early 1930's. Considerably more militant in tone than *La Revue du Monde Noir, Légitime Défense* was produced June 1, 1932, and impressed both Césaire and Senghor, although both felt that the single issue of the review lacked a concrete program to deal with the problems of assimilation which its young Afro-Caribbean editors so vehemently attacked.

During this period, Césaire was an extremely intense student who read deeply in Marx, Freud, and the precursors of surrealism, Lautréamont and Rimbaud. Although he preferred reading to socializing, he was active enough to be elected president of the French West Indian student association at the beginning of the 1934-35 school year. With Senghor, who was head of the African students, and Damas, he produced *L'Etudiant Noir,* a four-page, single-sheet student newspaper which appeared five or six times over the next two years before lack of funds, poor sales, and the intervention of French authorities forced them to cease publication. While Senghor stressed the importance of their African cultural heritage, Césaire protested in his articles West Indian tendencies toward total assimilation of French cultural values. According to Damas, it was in a *L'Etudiant Noir* editorial that Césaire first used the term *négritude* to symbolize the new awareness and activity for Black culture.

At about this time Césaire stopped writing poetry in the French mold. Deciding that he would never be a poet, he began to write in prose, and kept a notebook of his ideas and observations. He continued to prepare for the competitive entry exams for France's highest institution of learning in the liberal arts, L'Ecole Normale Supérieure, nearly burning himself out, physically and emotionally, in the process. After successfully passing the exam in July, 1935, he went off to Yugoslavia with a classmate, Petar Guberina, to recuperate. At the Guberina home on the Adriatic, Césaire remembers the sight of an island called Martinska, or St. Martin's Island, which reminded him of home and no doubt contributed to the notes which were to become, by 1938, *Cahier d'un retour au pays natal.*

Between 1935 and 1938, Césaire earned a *licence* and then a *Diplôme d'études supérieures* with an essay on "Le Thème du sud dans la poésie nègre américaine." At the same time, he continued to work on *Cahier d'un retour au pays natal,* and his homework began to reflect this growing preoccupation with poetry. In 1938, after a rejection by a French publisher, and at the encouragement of one of his teachers, Prof. Petitbon, he submitted the manuscript to Georges Pellorson, director of the Parisian review *Volontés,* who published it in August, 1939, just as Césaire was returning to Martinique to take up a position as a teacher of classical and modern literature at the Lycée Schoelcher.

Césaire's return to Martinique in 1939 was not, however, his first return to his native land, for in 1936 he had gone home during the summer. He experienced at that time the cultural re-entry shock which provided a series of powerful images of physical decay, poverty, hunger, and resignation in the first part of *Cahier d'un retour au pays natal.* It is this reaction which launches the narrator into a cultural dialectic involving real and imagined returns to Martinique and Africa. The complex structure of the poem, plus striking imagery, often unorthodox syntax, hammering rhythms, and an extremely wide vocabulary, including several neologisms, serve to transform the narrator from observer to messiah. The narrator's passionate expression of his *négritude* in the poem is the only documented use of the neologism which has survived the 1930's.

Unnoticed in Paris, *Cahier d'un retour au pays natal* was discovered by the leader of the surrealist movement, André Breton, when he was forced to stop in Martinique while fleeing from Paris to New York in 1941. Breton's essay on Césaire, "Un grand poète noir," appeared in 1943 in a New York-based French-English review, *Hémisphères,* and served as the preface to the first edition, an expanded version of the original text which appeared simultaneously in 1947 in Paris and, as *Memorandum on My Martinique,* in New York.

In the poem, Césaire showed the first flashes of surrealist technique which he was to develop in his subsequent wartime poetry. It was, in fact, the first poem published after *Cahier d'un retour au pays natal* ("Les pur-sang" in *Tropiques,* April, 1941), which caught Breton's eye and led to the meeting of the two writers. But if Breton appreciated a kindred spirit in what he described as the Martinican's ability to sing in his poetry, the refugee from Paris merely confirmed, rather than initiated, Césaire's tendencies to experiment with a Western technique aimed, for him, at several rather specific goals: to communicate in code language with other Martinicans during the Vichy occupation of the island; to probe the collective subconscious in order to rediscover what had been lost in transit between Africa and the New World; and to sound the depths of his own subconscious.

Césaire was a remarkably effective teacher at the Lycée Schoelcher during the war, as evidenced not only by his popularity, but also by the theretofore unheard of success of his students on standardized exams. Meanwhile, he, his wife Suzanne, René Ménil, Aristide Maugée,and other Martinican intellectuals sought to extend the process of cultural revival to the assimilated élite of Martinique via a quarterly cultural journal, *Tropiques. Tropiques* was launched not only to combat cultural assimilation, but also to respond to the new threat which had quite literally appeared on the horizon in the form of Admiral Robert's isolated Vichy fleet. Robert took over the island, fired many of the Black mayors, and soon began to pressure Césaire to stop publication of *Tropiques.* By Spring 1943, after an unsuccessful attempt to oust Césaire from his post at the Lycée Schoelcher, the Robert government finally closed down the review, labeling it "revolutionary, racial, and sectarian." But after the Allied blockade and the riots of July and August 1943, provoked by discrimination in the distribution of the island's dwindling supplies, the Robert régime toppled and *Tropiques* appeared again until September, 1945. That the efforts of the *Tropiques* group were successful is evident in Fanon's 1955 essay, "Antillais et Africains," where he points out that before 1939, no West Indian could safely take pride in being Black. By 1945, notes Fanon, one no longer had to feel ashamed of one's color.

At the request of Pierre Mabille and the President of Haiti, Elie Lescot, the Provisional French Government, which took over Martinique in 1943, sent Césaire to Haiti as a cultural ambassador. From May to December 1944, he lectured on French poetry, discussed new developments in Black culture, and demonstrated new teaching methods. At the same time, he absorbed some of what would eventually result in two works celebrating Haiti's past: *Toussaint Louverture: la Révolution française et le problème colonial* (1960), a historical study which stresses the indigenous origins of the Haitian revolution, and his first play written expressly for the stage, *La Tragédie du roi Christophe* (1963).

Invited by friends to speak about Haiti

upon his return home, Césaire turned out to be an extremely gifted orator who drew standing-room-only audiences. He was subsequently asked to stand for the municipal elections on the Communist ticket in May, 1945. Although the Martinican section of the *Parti communiste* garnered only a few hundred votes in prewar elections, it became overnight a major political force, with Césaire leading the ticket, to control of Fort-de-France. As Mayor, he discovered first-hand the low priority of the city in France's system of dealing with immediate postwar shortages. Elected to the Assemblée Nationale Constituante in October, Césaire left for Paris to help form a new republic which, he hoped, would provide Martinicans with the same benefits accorded their metropolitan counterparts. But if he was successful in pushing through the departmentalization law which gave his constituents full citizenship, Césaire was obliged, because of a special provision, to wage separate legislative battles for the normally automatic privileges of French natives: minimum wages, social security, medical care, etc.

Between frequent trips back and forth across the Atlantic and speeches on the floor of the Assemblée Nationale, Césaire began to publish some of his wartime poetry, much of which was incomprehensible to his metropolitan comrades in the Communist Party. To one leader writing in the party newspaper, *L'Humanité*, Césaire's first collection, *Les Armes miraculeuses* (1946), represented the decadent influence of André Breton on their most effective, if impressionable, young orator. But the poet was nevertheless encouraged during this early postwar period by the publication of *Cahier d'un retour au pays natal* (1947), and Sartre's high praise of his poetry in *Orphée noir,* a preface to Senghor's 1948 *Anthologie de la nouvelle poésie nègre et malgache de langue française.*

Césaire's fighting self-confidence during this period was reflected in his speeches at a series of international peace conferences, the Assemblée Nationale, and, in particular, the 1948 centennial celebration of the abolition of slavery in France. Invited with Senghor to participate in the official government ceremony marking the event at the Sorbonne, Césaire destroyed the atmosphere of self-congratulation with a stinging attack on the French bourgeoisie, and in particular, its efforts to block the plans of the abolitionist Victor Schoelcher.

His poetry of the period echoes this new feeling. In *Soleil cou coupé* (1948), Césaire began to develop a less hermetic style which is especially apparent in "Tornade," where he refers to the condition of Afro-Americans, and "Depuis Akkad, depuis Elam, depuis Sumer," an evocation of the long history of enslavement which his race has known.

By 1950, however, Césaire reached something of a literary and political turning point in his career, signaled in part by *Corps perdu,* a collection of less optimistic poetry, and, to a more noticeable degree, by the pamphlet *Discours sur le colonialisme.* In *Corps perdu* (1950), he appeared to withdraw into the racial and geographic fortress of his island, and seemed to question the validity of his symbolic search for Africa. The title poem offers one of his favorite images, that of the volcano which explodes with unexpected fury. Comparing himself with Mont Pelée's Indonesian counterpart, Krakatoa, the poet declares that he will have to work against the forces of nature—human nature—to achieve the liberation of the islands which have seemed for so long to live as appendages to the metropole. "Je commanderai aux îles d'exister!" he shouts in defiance to the world. In spite of occasional optimism in some of the island imagery, the poet reaches a low point in the last poem, "Dit d'Errance," where he wonders out loud about his poetic creation of a personal cosmogony. The magical African world he had created, and toward which he had strained, as a tree strains toward the sun, seemed to disappear as the poet began to cut down what he called "les arbres du paradis."

By 1950, the left wing had lost much of its strength in the Assemblée Nationale, and a conservative government had become embroiled in bloody rebellions throughout the French empire. For Césaire, the French Union was a disaster, and the departmentalization law he had worked for merely another form of colonization. His criticisms of government policy at the Assemblée Nationale were rejected from the floor by cries of "who taught you how to read?" and "insulter of the fatherland!" Césaire finally exploded with a carefully-wrought polemic, *Discours sur le colonialisme* (1950) in which he exposed racist tendencies in 19th and 20th century French thought, and warned the West to change its colonial policies.

In the 1950's, Césaire became increasingly dissatisfied with the French Communist Party's paternalistic attitude toward the overseas sections (and especially its unwillingness to allow the establishment of a Martinican Communist party), failure to condemn Stalin's crimes after they had been exposed by Kruschev, and efforts to discourage Black members from involvement in international black cultural meetings (notably the Premier Congrès des Ecrivains et Artistes Noirs at the Sorbonne in September 1956). On the eve of the Hungarian rebellion in October, 1956, Césaire left the Party, outlining in his *Lettre à Maurice Thorez,* Party chief, the reasons for his action. To implement his desire for a political organization free to deal directly with local problems, Césaire founded his own party in 1958, the *Parti progressiste martiniquais.* During this same period, he became increasingly active in the new series of international congresses devoted to Black culture, speaking both in Paris and Rome on the interdependence of political and cultural freedom in the Third World.

Césaire's last collection of poetry, *Ferrements* (1960), reflected both the shock of the break with the French Communist Party and a new sense of leadership on the part of the poet. One poem in particular, "Séisme," echoes feelings generated by the rupture. References to events in the U.S. ("Sur l'état de l'Union"), Africa ("Pour saluer le Tiers Monde" and "Salut à la Guinée"), and Caribbean history ("Mémorial de Louis Delgrès") reveal a new appreciation of the broader, more historical, and less personal perspective necessary for communication with a larger public.

To achieve what he termed a "multiplication de la force poétique," Césaire turned to the theater with the 1956 stage version of his wartime dramatic poem "Et les chiens se taisaient," which the first published fragments of the work in *Tropiques* had revealed. With the subsequent plays, *La Tragédie du roi Christophe* (1963), *Une saison au Congo* (1966), and *Une tempête* (1969), Césaire became the leading black dramatist of French expression in the world.

La Tragédie du roi Christophe, Shakespearean in tone and style, is considered by many to be Césaire's best play. With remarkable use of historical material from the reign of Henry Christophe, one of Haiti's earliest leaders, Césaire sought to illustrate for the benefit of newly-installed African statesmen the pitfalls of independence. Christophe's soaring vision, manifested in his towering mountaintop fortress, La Citadelle La Ferrière, and his growing insensitivity to the immediate needs of his people, provided an example of both tremendous accomplishment and tragic failure. Under the direction of the late Jean-Marie Serreau, the play was successfully staged at the Premier Festival Mondial des Arts Nègres in Dakar (1966), Expo 67 in Montreal, and throughout Europe. Césaire, Serreau, and their troupe of African and Afro-Caribbean actors modified the script frequently by the addition of new material, especially references to Africa, which was developed spontaneously in successive productions of the play.

In an effort to keep the Serreau company going, Césaire wrote *Une saison au Congo* (1966), a less successful play which highlights in Brechtian style the rise of Congolese premier Patrice Lumumba and the outside forces which destroyed him soon after independence. The play was modified in 1967 to reflect changes in the Congo and its leadership, and was modified again in 1973 to show further developments in the Mobutu/Mokutu character.

Césaire's last play, *Une tempête,* has drawn the most negative commentary, mainly from Western critics who view it as Shakespeare incomprehensibly adapted. However, by modifying the Shakespearean version of the good master/humble servant theme, Césaire attempts to destroy a myth which has permeated Western civilization (e.g. as analyzed in O. Mannoni's *Caliban and Prospero: The Psychology of Colonisation*), rather than merely "translate" a Western classic for the edification of Third World peoples. In this sense, *Une tempête* represents in literary terms the culmination of a life-long war against the mythology which Césaire and his people encounter in their daily lives. The dramatist focuses not only on the political and social aspects of the conflict between Prospero and Caliban, but, above all, stresses the fundamental cultural gulf between master and servant. Where Shakespeare had given Caliban no recognizable cultural characteristics, Césaire's Caliban is the inheritor of a rich heritage spanning time and the oceans to include bits of an African language, African gods, and African, Afro-American, and Afro-Caribbean chants, songs, and expressions. The success of *Une tempête* outside of Paris, not only in the provinces and in many parts of Europe, but also in the Middle East, Africa, and, most recently (1972), in Martinique, underscores the significance of Césaire's reinterpretation of Shakespeare for Third World audiences. (One should not forget, however, the Robert Browning poem "Caliban Upon Setebos," first elaborated a rebellious Caliban who used his master's language to curse his servitude.)

Césaire's considerable role in politics and literature over the years has not been free from criticism both at home and in France. The Gaullist Right condemns him as a revolutionary bent on independence for Martinique while the Extreme Left criticizes him as a reformer whose actions do not match his rhetoric. In this crossfire, he attempts to achieve what he considers the possible as an opposition *députémaire* whose powers are highly circumscribed by the centralized French system of government: schools, housing, sanitation, and a greater sense of political awareness on the part of his constituents. As he has done for thirty years, he continues to commute between Paris and Fort-de-France to attend the sessions of the Assemblée Nationale and deal with problems in Martinique.

Four decades after he and his comrades began to discuss their sense of *négritude,* Césaire admits to a feeling of frustration as he sees the term debated, condemned, and popularized in ways he had never imagined. In an important 1971 interview with Lilyan Kesteloot (*Aimé Césaire, l'homme et l'oeuvre,* pp. pp. 227-243), he reiterated his view of négritude:

> *I still hold to a kind of negritude (. . .) which consists in saying quite simply that I am a Black and that I know it, I am a Black and I consider that I come from a tradition, and that I must devote myself to the enrichment of this heritage . . .My conception of negritude is not biological, it is cultural and historical . . . Negritude raised the Black question, it awakened the Black man to his situation, and it gave all Blacks a sense of Black world solidarity.*

André Breton, an admirer of Aimé Césaire, expressed the following comment on his works:

> *... cette faculté d'alerter sans cesse de fond en comble, le monde émotionnel jusqu'à le mettre sens dessus dessous, ce mouvement, cette exubérance qui caractérisent la poèsie authentique par opposition à la fausse poèsie ... cette poèsie qui vaut au plus haut point par le pouvoir de transmutation qu'elle met en oeuvre, et qui consiste à partir des matériaux les plus déconsidérés parmi lesquels il faut compter les laideurs et la servitude même à produire, on sait bien que ce n'est plus l'or ou la pierre philosophale, mais bien la liberté.*

Moreover, in his free-verse comment on Césaire's poetry, André Breton paid homage to the man himself:

> *Aimé Césaire est un Noir*
> *qui est non seulement un Noir*
> *mais tout l'homme*
> *qui en exprime toutes les interrogations,*
> *toutes les angoisses,*
> *tous les espoirs et toutes les extases,*
> *et qui s'imposera de plus en plus à moi*
> *comme le prototype de la dignité.*

Léopold Sédar Senghor, his long-standing friend, characterized Césaire's works by stating:

> *Césaire se sert de sa plume comme Louis Armstrong de sa trompette. Ou plus justement peut-être, comme le fidèle du Vaudou, de son tam-tam. Il a besoin de se perdre dans la danse verbale, au rythme du tam-tam, pour se retrouver dans le Cosmos.*

The many books, dissertations, special issues of journals, articles, symposia and colloquia devoted to Césaire in recent years have helped to document his role in the history of *littérature négro-africaine.* The great extent to which his works are studied in schools and universities, and the impact of his ideas on young blacks has been documented in several surveys. But most importantly, the frequency with which subsequent generations of Black writers from Africa, South America and Afro-America refer to his writings in dedications and citations suggests that Césaire is probably the most significant and widely read black author of French expression in the world today.

Writings: Césaire's collections of poetry, his drama, some of his historical and political writings, and a few of his speeches are available in the three-volume *Oeuvres complètes* (Vol. I, Poésie, Vol. II, Théâtre, Vol. III, Oeuvre Historique et politique), Fort-de-France, Editions Désormeaux, 1976. The following bibliography of his writings is selected from a listing of nearly 500 texts. For more information, see *Les Ecrits de Césaire: bibliographie commentée* (Thomas A. Hale, Montréal, *Etudes Françaises/* Presses de l'Université de Montréal, 1978), a chronological bibliography from 1935 to 1978 which contains excerpts and commentary on 494 texts. For critical sources through 1973, see Frederick Ivor Case's *Aimé Césaire: bibliographie,* Toronto, Manna Publishing Co., 1973.

Poetry: *Cahier d'un retour au pays natal,* original version in *Volontés* (Paris), No. 20 (August, 1939). Subsequent rev. eds., Paris, Bordas, 1947; New York, Brentano's, 1947; Paris, Présence Africaine, 1956. Both 1947 editions and the current 1971 Présence Africaine edition have prefaces by André Breton. *Les Armes miraculeuses,* Paris, Gallimard, 1946; 2nd rev. ed., 1970; *Soleil cou coupé,* Paris, Eds. K, 1948; reprinted with many changes in *Cadastre,* Paris, Le Seuil, 1961; original reprinted in *Poems from Martinique,* Nendeln, Kraus Reprint, 1970; *Corps perdu,* Paris, Fragrance, 1950, with drawings by Picasso; rev. eds. *Cadastre,* Paris, Le Seuil, 1961; *Ferrements,* Paris, Le Seuil, 1960 (Prix René Laporte, 1960); *Noria,* in Vol. I of *Oeuvres complètes,* Fort-de-France, Désormeaux, 1976.

Theatre: *Et les chiens se taisaient,* dramatic poem in *Les Armes miraculeuses,* Paris, Gallimard, 1946; modified for stage and reprinted, Paris, Présence Africaine, 1956; 2nd ed. of original version modified and reprinted, 1970; performed in German version in Basel, 1960, and in Hanover, 1963; *Tragédie du roi Christophe,* Paris, Présence Africaine, 1963; rev. ed.,1970; premiere at the Salzburg Festival in 1964 under the direction of Jean-Marie Serreau; subsequent performances in Venice, Berlin, Brussels; Paris premiere at the Odeon theatre in 1965; Festival des Arts Nègres, Dakar, 1966; Exposition 1967, Montréal; Fort-de-France, Cultural Festival, Martinique, 1978; *Une saison au Congo,* Paris, Le Seuil, 1966; rev. eds., 1967 and 1973; premiere in Brussels in 1966 under direction of Rudi Barnet; subsequent versions under the direction of Jean-Marie Serreau in Venice, 1967; Paris premiere at the Théâtre de l'Est Parisien, 1967; *Une tempête, Présence Africaine,* No. 67, 1968, rev. ed., Paris, Le Seuil, 1969; premiere at the Hammamet Festival in Tunisia, 1969; subsequent performances in Venice; Paris premiere at the Théâtre de l'Ouest Parisien; other performances at the Baalbeck Festival, 1970, and at the Fort-de-France Cultural Festival, 1972.

Selected Non-Fiction Texts: "Nègreries. Jeunesse noire et Assimilation," *L'Etudiant Noir* (Paris), March, 1935; "Introduction à la poésie nègre," *Tropiques* (Fort-de-France), No. 2, July, 1941, pp. 37-42; "Introduction au folklore martiniquais," *Tropiques,* No. 4 (January 1942), pp. 7-11; "Vues sur Mallarmé," *Tropiques,* No. 5 (April 1942), pp. 53-61; "Isidore Ducasse, Comte de Lautréamont. La Poésie de Lautréamont belle comme un décret d'expropriation," *Tropiques,* No. 6-7 (February 1943), pp. 10-15: " Lettre ouverte à Monseigneur Varin de la Brunelière, Evêque de Saint-Pierre et de Fort-de-France," *Tropiques,* No. 11 (May 1944), pp. 104-106; "Poésie et Connaissance," *Tropiques,* No. 12 (January 1945), pp. 157-170; also in *Aimé Césaire, l'homme et l'oeuvre,* Lilyan Kesteloot & Barthélemy Kotchy, Paris, Présence Africaine, 1973; (see also the reprinted version of *Tropiques* for more information on Césaire's other texts in the journal he directed from 1941 to 1945, Paris, Editions Jean-Michel Place, 1978); Speeches at the Assemblée Nationale on changing Martinique to an overseas department, *Journal Officiel de la République Française, Annales de l'Assemblée Nationale,* March 5, 12, 14, 1946; "Commémoration du centenaire de l'abolition de l'esclavage," text of speech given at the Sorbonne, April 27, 1948, in *Commémoration du Centenaire de l'abolition de l'esclavage,* Paris, Presses Universitaires de France, 1948, pp. 20-33; *Discours sur le colonialisme,* Paris, Editions Réclame, 1950; Paris, Présence Africaine, 1955; "Sur la poésie nationale," *Présence Africaine,* New Series, No. 4 (Oct.-Nov. 1955), pp. 39-41; *Lettre à Maurice Thorez,* Présence Africaine, 1956; "Culture et Colonisation," speech presented at the Premier Congrès International des Ecrivains et Artistes Noirs, the Sorbonne, Paris, September 19-22, 1956, in *Présence Africaine,* New Series, Nos. 8-10 (June-Nov. 1956), pp. 190-205; "L'Homme de culture et ses responsabilités," speech presented at the Deuxième Congrès des Ecrivains Noirs, Rome, March 26-April 1, 1959, in *Présence Africaine,* New Series, No. 24-25 (February-May 1959), pp. 116-122; *Toussaint Louverture: la Révolution française et le problème colonial,* Paris, Club française du livre, 1960, Présence Africaine, 1962; "Discours sur l'art africain," text of speech given at the Premier Festival Mondial Club français du livre, 1960, Présence Afri-*Etudes Littéraires,* Vol. 6, No. 1 (April 1973), pp. 99-109.

Prefaces and Introductions to Works of Others: "Wilfredo Lam," introduction to reproductions of works by Cuban artist Wilfredo Lam in *Cahiers d'Art,* No. 20-21, 1945-46, p. 357; "Victor Schoelcher et l'abolition de l'esclavage," introduction to *Esclavage et Colonisation,* collection of writings by Victor Schoelcher, selected and annotated by Emile Tersen, foreword by Charles-André Julien, Paris, Presses Universitaires de France, 1948; preface to *Végétations de Clarté* by René Depestre, Paris, Seghers, 1951; introduction to *Les Antilles décolonisées* by Daniel Guérin, Paris, Présence Africaine, 1956, reprinted in *Présence Africaine,* New Series, No. 7 (April-May 1956), pp. 7-12, and also in *Aimé Césaire,* by Lilyan Kesteloot, Paris, Seghers, 1962; preface to *Expérience guinéenne et unité africaine* by Sekou Touré, Paris, Présence Africaine, 1959, 1961; reprinted in *Présence Africaine,* No. 29 (December 1959-January 1960), pp. 65-73; preface to *Les Bâtards* by Bertène Juminer, Paris, Présence Africaine, 1961, reprinted in *Présence Africaine,* No. 36, 1961, pp. 160-61; introduction to *Lamba* by Jacques Rabemananjara, Paris, Présence Africaine, 1961, reprinted in *J. Rabemananajara,* Paris, Fernand Nathan, 1970, p. 26; "Liminaire," introductory note to *Nouvelle somme de poésie du monde noir,* special issue of *Présence Africaine,* No. 57, 1966, p. 3; preface to *L'Abolition de l'esclavage* by Guy Fau, Paris, Le Burin & Martinsart, 1973.

Selected interviews: "Entretien avec Aimé Césaire," Jacqueline Sieger, *Afrique,* No. 5 (October 1961), p. 64-67; "Pour un théâtre l'inspiration africaine: Aimé Césaire," Claude Stevens, *La Vie Africaine,* No. 59 (June 1965), pp. 40-41; "Une saison au Congo: fresque de la négritude dans le monde moderne. Une interview avec Aimé Césaire," Claude Stevens, *L'Afrique Actuelle,* No. 23, 1967, pp. 49-52; "An Interview with an Architect of Négritude: Aimé Césaire," Ellen Conroy Kennedy, *Negro Digest,* (May 1968), pp. 53-61; "Entrevistas con Aimé Césaire," Sonia Aratán and René Depestre, *Casa de las Américas,* No. 49 (July-August 1968), pp. 130-142 (two separate interviews, that by Depestre also in English in *Discourse on Colonialism,* New York, Monthly Review Press, 1972, *Savacou,* No. 5 (June 1971), and *Radical America,* Vol. 5, No. 3 May-June 1971; "Un poète politique: Aimé Césaire," François Beloux, *Magazine Littéraire,* No. 34 (November 1969), pp. 27-32; "Aimé Césaire: 'Nous sommes à la veille de 1789'," Pierre Benichou and Jean-Pierre Joulin, *Le Nouvel Observateur,* No. 329, (March 1, 1971), pp. 33-35; "Entretien avec Césaire," Lilyan Kesteloot, in *Aimé Césaire, l'homme et l'oeuvre,* by Kesteloot and Barthélemy Kotchy, Paris, Présence Africaine, 1973, pp. 227-243; "Entretien avec Aimé Césaire," Michel Benamou, *Cahiers Césairiens,* No. 1 (Spring 1974), pp. 4-8; "Ce que j'aurais dit à Giscard," Guy Sitbon, *Le Nouvel Observateur,* No. 528 (December 22-28, 1974, pp. 18-19; "Interview avec Aimé Césaire à *Fort-de-France, le 12 janvier 1977,"* Gérard Georges Pigeon, *Cahiers Césairiens,* No. 3 (Spring 1977), pp. 1-6; "Entretien avec Aimé Césaire par Jacqueline Leiner," introduction to *Tropiques* reprint, Paris, Editions Jean-Michel Place, 1978, Vol. 1, v-xxiv.

Press Conference: "Conférence de presse à Québec," in *Aimé Césaire, l'homme et l'oeuvre,* by Lilyan Kesteloot & Barthélemy Kotchy, Paris, Présence Africaine, 1973, pp. 212-224.

Translations (Poetry): *Memorandum on My Martinique,* Lionel Abel & Ivan Goll, New York, Brentano's, 1947; *Return to My Native Land,* Emile Snyder (based on Abel & Goll version), Paris, Présence Africaine, 1968; *Return to My Native Land,* John Berger and Anna Bostock, Harmondsworth, Penguin, 1969; *Zurück ins Land der Geburt,* Janheinz Jahn, Frankfurt, Insel-Verlag, 1962, Suhrkamp, 1967; *Ritorno al paese natale,* trans. anon., Reggio Emilia, Poligrafici, 1967; *Le Armi miracolose,* Anna Vizioli and Franco De Poli, Parma, Guanda, 1962; *Cadastre,* Emile Snyder and Sanford Upson, New York, Third Press, 1973; there are also several translations which draw from many of Césaire's collections: *State of the Union,* Clayton Eshleman and Denis Kelly, Bloomington, Caterpillar, 1966; *Sonnendolche,* Janheinz Jahn, Heidelberg, Wolfgang Rothe, 1956; *An Afrika,* Janheinz Jahn and Friedhelm Kemp, München, Hanser, 1968; *Poezija,* Bozo Kukolja, Zagreb, Mladost, 1967 (Serbo-Croatian); *Trpky Cas,* Bohumila Grögerová and Ladislava Novák, Prague, Odeon, 1968 (Czech); *Poésias,* trans. anon., Havana, Casa de las Américas, 1969.

Translations (Theatre): *Und die Hunde Schweigen,* Janheinz Jahn, Emsdetten, Verlag Lechte, 1956; *La Tragedia del Re Christophe,* Luigi Bonino Savarino, Turin, Einaudi, 1968; *Die Tragödie von König Christoph,* Janheinz Jahn, Cologne, Kiepenheuer & Witsch, 1964; *The Tragedy of King Christophe,* Ralph Manheim, New York, Grove Press, 1970; *La Tragedia del Rey Christophe,* Carmen Kurtz, Barcelona, Barral, 1972 (includes trans. of *Une tempête*); *Im Kongo,* Monika Kind, Berlin, Wagenbach, 1966; *A Season in the Congo,* Ralph Manheim, New York, Grove Press, 1969; *En tid i Kongo,* Ingemar & Mikaela Leckius, Stockholm, FIBs Lyrikklubb, 1969; *Ein Sturm,* Monika Kind, Berlin, Wagenbach, 1970; *Una Tempestad,* Carmen Kurtz, Barcelona, Barral, 1972.

Translations (Non-Fiction): *Uber den Kolonialismus,* Monika Kind, Berlin, Wagenbach, 1968; *Discourse on Colonialism,* Joan Pinkham, New York, Monthly Review Press, 1972; *Toussaint Louverture: La Revolución francesa y el problema colonial,* trans. anon., Havana, Instituto del Libro, 1967.

Biographical/Critical Sources: Books: Hubert Juin, *Aimé Césaire, poète noir,* Paris, Présence Africaine, 1956; Lilyan Kesteloot, *Aimé Césaire,* Paris, Seghers, 1962; Lilyan Kesteloot, *Les Ecrivains noirs d'expression française: naissance d'une littérature,* Bruxelles, Université Libre de Bruxelles, 1963; in English, *Black Writers in French,* Ellen Conroy Kennedy, trans., Philadelphia, Temple University Press, 1975; René Piquion, *Les "Trois Grands" de la Négritude,* Port-au-Prince, Editions Henri Deschamps, 1964; Simon and Monique Battestini, *Aimé Césaire,* Paris, Editions Fernand Nathan, 1967; Hénock Trouillot, *L'Itinéraire* d'Aimé Césaire, Port-au-Prince, Impr. des Antilles, 1968; Marie-Françoise Bourgin, *Etude sur Cahier d'un retour au pays natal d'Aimé Césaire,* Fort-de-France, Les Documents du Centre d'Etudes Antilles-Guyane, 1973; Susan Frutkin, *Aimé Césaire, Black Between Worlds,* Washington, D.C., Center for Advanced International Studies, University of Miami, 1973; Rodney E. Harris, *L'Humanisme dans le théâtre d'Aimé Césaire,* Sherbrooke, Editions Naaman, 1973; Lilyan Kesteloot and Barthélemy Kotchy, *Aimé Césaire, l'homme et l'oeuvre,* Paris, Présence Africaine, 1973; Graziano Benelli, *Aimé Césaire,* Florence, *Il Castoro,* (October 1975); M. a M. Ngal, *Aimé Césaire: un homme à la recherche d'un pays,* Dakar, Nouvelles Editions Africaines, 1975; Bernadette Cailler, *Proposition poètique: une lecture de l'oeuvre d'Aimé Césaire,* Sherbrooke, Editions Naaman, 1976.

Articles: Aristide Maugée, "Aimé Césaire, poète," *Tropiques,* No. 5 (April 1942), pp. 13-20; André Breton, "Un grand poète noir," *Hémispheres* (New York), No. 2-3 (Fall-Winter 1943-44), pp. 5-11; reprinted as preface to both 1947 editions of *Cahier d'un retour au pays natal* and the current edition; René Etiemble, "Aimé Césaire et *Tropiques,*" *L'Arche* (Algiers), (June-July 1944), pp. 137-42; Maurice Nadeau, "Aimé Césaire, surréaliste," *Revue Internationale,* No. 10, 1946, pp. 289-294; Jean-Paul Sartre, *Orphée noir,* preface to *Anthologie de la nouvelle poèsie nègre et malgache de langue française,* Léopold Sédar Senghor, ed., Paris, Presses Universitaires de France, 1948; Aimé Patri, "Deux poètes noirs de langue française," *Présence Africaine,* No. 3, 1948, pp. 378-387; Léopold Sédar Senghor, *Postface* to *Ethiopiques,* Paris, Le Seuil, 1956; Edouard Glissant, "Aimé Césaire et la découverte du monde," *Les Lettres Nouvelles,* No. 34 (January 1956), pp. 44-54, reprinted in *L'Intention poètique,* Paris, Le Seuil, 1969, pp. 143-150; Pierre Marteau, "La Mort de l'impossible et mot du printemps," *Présence Africaine,* No. 30 (February-March 1960), pp. 82-95; Lilyan Kesteloot (listed as Lilyan Lagneau), "En marge de *Ferrements* d'Aimé Césaire," *Synthèses* (Brussels), No. 168 (April-July 1960), pp. 248-255; Pierre Marteau, "A propos de *Cadastre* d'Aimé Césaire," *Présence Africaine,* No. 37, 1961, pp. 125-135; Lilyan Kesteloot (listed as Lyliane Lagneau-Kesteloot), "*La Tragédie du roi Christophe,* ou les indépendences africaines au miroir d'Haiti," *Présence Africaine,* No. 51, 1964, pp. 131-145; René Ménil, "Le Romanesque et le réalisme dans *La Tragédie du roi Christophe,*" *Action* (Fort-de-France), No. 6 (December 1964-January 1965), pp. 51-56; Michel Leiris, "Qui est Aimé Césaire?" *Critique,* Vol. 21, No. 216 (May 1965), pp. 395-402, also: in *Brisées,* by the same author, Paris, Mercure de France, 1966, pp. 269-278; as an introduction to *Aimé Césaire, l'homme et l'oeuvre* by Kesteloot and Kotchy, Paris, Présence Africaine, 1973, and to the *Oeuvres complètes,* Fort-de-France, Editions Désormeaux, 1976, Vol. 1, pp. 15-25; Hélina Bobrowska-Skrodzka, "Aimé Césaire, chantre de la grandeur de l'Afrique," *Présence Africaine,* No. 59, 1966, pp. 33-56; Abiola Irele, "Aimé Césaire: An Approach to His Poetry," in *Introduction to African Literature,* ed. Ulli Beier, Evanston, Northwestern University Press, 1967, p. 59-69; Jean Decock, "Faut-il jouer Césaire?" *African Arts/Arts d'Afrique,* Vol. 1, No. 1, 1967, pp. 36-39, 72-73, 75; Frédérique Dutoit, "Quand le Congo ne sera plus qu'une saison que le sang assaisonne," *Présence Africaine,* No. 64, 1967, pp. 138-145; Jacqueline Ormond, "Héros de l'impossible et de l'absolu," *Les Temps Modernes,* No. 259 (December 1967), pp. 1049-1073; Eric Sellin, "Aimé Césaire and the Legacy of Surréalism," *Kentucky Foreign Language Quarterly,* Vol. 13, Supplement, 1967, pp. 71-79; Abiola Irele, "Post Colonial Negritude: The Political Plays of Aimé Césaire," *West Africa,* (January 27, 1968), pp. 100-101; Juris Silenieks, "Deux Pièces antillaises: du témoignage local vers une tragédie moderne," *Kentucky Romance Quarterly,* Vol. 15, No. 3, 1968, pp. 245-254; Marcien Towa, "Les Pur-Sang (négritude césairienne et surréalisme)," *Abbia* (Yaoundé), No. 23, 1969, pp. 71-82; Seth Wolitz, "The Hero of Negritude in the Theatre of Aimé Césaire," *Kentucky Romance Quarterly,* Vol. 16, No. 3, pp. 195-208; Mineke Schipper de Leeuw, "Noirs et Blancs dans l'oeuvre d'Aimé Césaire," *Présence Africaine,* No. 72, 1969, pp. 124-147; Gérard Durozoi, "De Shakespeare à Aimé Césaire: notes sur une adaptation," *L'Afrique Littéraire et Artistique,* No. 10 (April 1970), pp. 9-15; Frederick Ivor Case, "Aimé Césaire et l'occident chrétien," *L'Esprit Créateur* (Kansas), Vol. 10, No. 3 (Fall 1970), pp. 242-256; Emile Snyder, "A Reading of Aimé Césaire's *Return to My Native Land,*" *L'Esprit Créateur,* Vol. 10,

No. 3 (Fall 1970), pp. 197-212; Georges Ngal, "De Shakespeare au drame des Nègres," *Cahiers de Littérature et de Linguistique Appliquée,* No. 2 (December 1970), pp. 171-179; reprinted in *Tendances actuelles de la littérature africaine d'expression française,* by the same author, but listed as Ngal Mbawil a Mpaang, Lubumbashi, Editions du Mont Noir, pp. 49-61; Georges Ngal, "Le Théâtre d'Aimé Césaire: une dramaturgie de la décolonisation, *Revue des Sciences Humaines* (Lille), Vol. 35, Fascicule 140 (October-December 1970), pp. 613-636; Sandra Williams, "La Renaissance de la tragédie dans l'oeuvre dramatique d'Aimé Césaire," *Présence Africaine,* No. 76, 1970, pp. 63-81; Pierre Laville, "Aimé Césaire et Jean-Marie Serreau: un acte politique et poètique. *La Tragédie du roi Christophe* et *Une saison au Congo,"* in *Les Voies de la création théâtrale,* ed. Jean Jaquot, Paris, Centre National de la Recherche Scientifique, Vol. 2, 1970, pp. 237-296; August Armet, "Césaire et le Parti Progressiste Martiniquais: le nationalisme progressiste," *Nouvelle Optique* (Montréal), Vol. 1, No. 2 (May 1971), pp. 57-84; Robert P. Smith, Jr., "Aimé Césaire Playwright Portrays Patrice Lumumba Man of Africa," *College Language Association Journal,* Vol. 14, No. 4 (June 1971), pp. 371-379; Georges Ngal, "Chronologie de la vie d'Aimé Césaire: principaux événements," *Présence Francophone,* No. 3 (Autumn 1971), pp. 163-167; René Richard, "Césaire et Shakespeare," in *Actes du colloque sur le théâtre négro-africain, Abidjan, 15-29 avril 1970,* Paris, Présence Africaine, 1971, pp. 122-134; Ruby Cohn, "Black Power on Stage: *Emperor Jones* and *King Christophe,"* *Yale French Studies,* No. 46, 1971, pp. 41-47; Prescott Nichols, "Césaire's Native Land and the Third World," *Twentieth Century Literature,* Vol. 18, No. 3 (July 1972), pp. 157-166; Robert P. Smith, "The Misunderstood and Rejected Black Hero in the Theatre of Aimé Césaire," *College Language Association Journal,* Vol. 16, No. 1 (September 1972), pp. 7-15; Vere Knight, "The West Indian Attitude to Tragedy—The Example of Aimé Césaire," *Bulletin of the African Studies Association of the West Indies,* No. 5 (December 1972); the following appeared in *Etudes Littéraires,* Vol. 6, No. 1 (April 1973): August Armet, "Aimé Césaire, homme politique," pp. 81-96; Thomas A. Hale, "Sur *Une tempête* d'Aimé Césaire," pp. 21-34; Lilyan Kesteloot, "Première lecture d'un poème de Césaire, 'Batouque'," pp. 49-72, reprinted in her volume *Aimé Césaire, l'homme et l'oeuvre,* Paris, Présence Africaine, 1973; Bruno Jobin, "*Cadastre,* lecture transcendante," pp. 73-80; Maximilien Laroche, "*La Tragédie du roi Christophe* du point de vue de l'histoire d'Haiti," pp. 35-47; Hervé Fuyet, Guy Levilain, *et al.,* "Décolonisation et classes sociales dans *La Tragédie du roi Christophe* d'Aimé Césaire, *French Review,* Vol. 46, No. 6 (May 1973), pp. 1101-1116; E. A. Hurley, "A Theatre of Frustration: the Theatre of Aimé Césaire," *Black Images,* Vol. 2, No. 1 (Spring 1973), pp. 13-15, 43; Frederick Ivor Case, "L'Intention poètique d'Aimé Césaire," *Présence Francophone,* No. 6 (Spring 1973), pp. 41-57; Henry Cohen, "History, Invention and Césaire's Roi Christophe," *Black Images,* Vol. 2, No. 3-4 (Autumn-Winter 1973); Renée Riese Hubert, "Aimé Césaire, French Poet," *Dada/Surréalisme,* No. 3, 1973, pp. 53-60; Graziano Benelli, "Il teatro di Aimé Césaire," *Letture* (Milan), No. 4 (April 1972), pp. 277-296; Thomas A. Hale, "Aimé Césaire: A Bio-Bibliography," *Africana Journal,* Vol. 5, No. 1, 1974, pp. 3-29; the following appeared in *Cahiers Césairiens,* No. 1 (Spring 1974): Graziano Benelli, "L'Oeuvre de Césaire en Italie," pp. 9-19; Judith G. Miller, "Césaire and Serreau: 'une sorte de symbiose'," pp. 20-25; Auguste Armet, "A propos des élections législatives 1973 à la Martinique: Césaire, le Parti Progressiste Martinquais, et les électeurs du centre," pp. 26-31; Rodney E. Harris, "The English Translations of Césaire's Theatre," pp. 32-34; Thomas A. Hale, "Aimé Césaire et *Tropiques,"* pp. 35-38; Michel Benamou, "Demiurgic Imagery in Césaire's Theatre," *Présence Africaine,* No. 93, 1975, pp. 31-43; Lilian Pestre de Almeida, "Rire haitien, rire africain (le comique dans *La Tragédie du roi Christophe* de Césaire," *Présence Francophone,* No. 10 (Spring 1975), pp. 59-71; the following appeared in *Cahiers Césairiens,* No. 2 (Autumn 1975): Michel Benamou, "Sémiotique du *Cahier d'un retour au pays natal,"* pp. 3-8; Frederick Ivor Case, "Sango Oba ka so: les vodoun dans *La Tragédie du roi Christophe,"* pp. 9-24; Rodney E. Harris, "The Scrupulous Aimé Césaire," pp. 25-28. Michael J. Dash, "The Example of Césaire," in *A Celebration of Black and African Writing,* Bruce King and Kolawole Ogungbesan, eds., Zaria and Ibadan, Ahmadu Bello University Press and Oxford University Press Nigeria, 1975, pp. 74-86; Thomas

A. Hale, "Structural Dynamics in a Third World Classic: Aimé Césaire's *Cahier d'un retour au pays natal,*" *Yale French Studies,* No. 53, 1976, pp. 163-174; Hilary Okam, "Aspects of Imagery and Symbolism in the Poetry of Aimé Césaire," *Yale French Studies,* No. 53, 1976, pp. 175-196; Lilian Pestre de Almeida, "Christophe, cuisinier entre nature et culture," *Conjonction* (Port-au-Prince), No. 130 (September 1976), pp. 33-61, reprinted in *Présence Africaine,* No. 105-106, 1978, pp. 230-249; Aliko Songolo, "Césaire's Surrealism and the Quest for Africa," *Ba Shiru* (Wisconsin), Vol. 7, No. 2, 1976, pp. 32-40; Emile Snyder, "Aimé Césaire, the Reclaiming of the Land," in *Exile and Tradition: Studies in African and Caribbean Literature,* Rowland Smith, ed., New York, Africana Publishing Co., 1976, pp. 31-43; the following appeared in *Cahiers Césairiens,* No. 3 (Spring 1977): Gérard Georges Pigeon, "Le Rôle des termes médicaux, du bestiaire et de la flore dans l'imagerie césairienne," pp. 7-24; Jonathan Ngaté, " 'Mauvais Sang' de Rimbaud et *Cahier d'un retour au pays natal* de Césaire: la poésie au service de la révolution," pp. 25-32; A. James Arnold, "*Cahier d'un retour au pays natal;* Reflections on the Translations into English," pp. 33-41; Jacqueline Leiner, "Césaire et les problèmes du langage chez un écrivain francophone," *L'Esprit Créateur,* Vol. 17, No. 2 (Summer 1977), pp. 133-142; Aliko Songolo, "*Cadastre* et *Ferrements* de Césaire: une nouvelle poétique pour une nouvelle politique," *L'Esprit Créateur,* Vol. 17, No. 2 (Summer 1977), pp. 143-158; Maurice Lecuyer, "Rythme, Révolte, et Rhétorique, ou aimer Césaire," *Rice University Studies,* Vol. 63, No. 1 (Winter 1977), pp. 85-111; Gregson Davis, "Towards a 'Non-Vicious Circle': The Lyric of Aimé Césaire in English," *Stanford French Review,* Vol. 1, No. 1 (Spring 1977), pp. 135-146.

CHALONEC, Frantz

b. April 10, 1929, Lorrain, Martinique; d. 1967.
Poet.

Chalonec attended school at Fort-de-France, completing his studies at the Lycée Schoelcher, after which he entered private business. He has published many poems in various journals, winning in 1960 the title "Lauréat des Jeux Floraux," given in Martinique to locally published poets.

Writings: Poetry: Poems in various journals, including: *Caraibes 56* (pub. in Toulouse); *Le Progressiste; La Vigie;* and *Le Musée Vivant,* edited by Madeleine Rousseau. The poem "Un homme face au soleil" is in *Littérature Antillaise (Poèsie),* E.G. Desormeaux (ed.), Fort-de-France, 1971, p. 290.

CHAMBERTRAND, Gilbert Suandeau de

b. February 13, 1890, Pointe-à-Pitre, Guadeloupe; d. 1973(?).
Poet, novelist, playwright, storywriter (in French and creole), journalist, artist.

Chambertrand received his education at the Lycée Carnot in Pointe-à-Pitre, Guadeloupe, and he then went to France where he spent many years in Toulon.

He returned home to become professor of drawing at the Lycée Carnot and afterwards served as librarian in Pointe-à-Pitre. He later became attaché at the Musée de la France d'Outre-Mer in Paris.

Adolphe Lara, who wrote many sketches on the leading personalities of Guadeloupe, offered this comment about Chambertrand: "Grand remueur d'idées, travailleur infatigable, d'une étonnante activité, Gilbert Chambertrand, avec une vie intense, des dons brillants, fait penser à Alexandre Dumas."

An hyperactive journalist, he contributed to *Le Nouvelliste de la Guadeloupe; Le Bulletin de la Société des Artistes Antillais; En Avant; A.B.C. Magazine; Monde Colonial Illustré; La Vie; Vu; Le Commerce; Beaux Arts; Gazette du Foyer; Sie Und Er; Revue des Monats;* and *Das Deutche Lichtbild.*

His poetry is filled with regional flavor but shows Parnassian influences. One typical example may be cited, the poem "Femme créole," from the collection

Images Guadeloupéennes:

Elle est extrêmement sensible aux madrigaux.
Son madras rutilant a deux bouts inégaux
Ainsi que le prescrit la mode des Antilles.

Dans sa démarche lente, et molle par moment,
Elle a de la souplesse et du balancement,
Et sa chair est pareille aux chairs de sapotille.

Chambertrand won a poetry prize in 1938 given by le Groupement "Ceux d'outre-mer" for his collection *Images Guadeloupéennes.*

In his plays, the characters very often employed creole in their dialogue rather than standard French.

Writings: Plays: *L'honneur des Montvoisin* (comédie en un acte), Pointe-à-Pitre, 1917; *Les méfaits d'Athénaise,* Pointe-à-Pitre, 1918; *Le prix du sacrifice,* Pointe-à-Pitre, 1918.

Poetry: *Les sept péchés capitaux, poèmes,* Pointe-à-Pitre, 1919; *Images guadeloupéennes, poèmes,* Paris, Ceux d'Outre-mer, 1929 (Prix de Poèsie "Ceux d'Outre-Mer"); *D'azur et de sable, poèmes,* Paris, l'auteur, Maisons-Alfort, 1961; *Reflets sur l'eau d'un puits,* 1965; *L'Album de famille,* 1969; and poetry in various journals, including: "Terre-de-Hauts-des-Saintes" in *Caribbean Voices,* John Figueroa (ed.), 1967, 1973.

Legends: *Choses et Gens de mon patelin,* Pointe-à-Pitre, 1924, with drawings, Paris, Souanges, 1961; *Mi io* (drawings and legends), Pointe-à-Pitre, 1926; and *Mi io! Les voici! Here they are! Aqui estan!;* Basse-Terre, Impr. Officielle, 1963.

Stories: *Titine Grosbonda, récits guadeloupéens,* Paris, Ed. Fasquelle, 1947.

Novel: *Coeurs créoles,* Point-à-Pitre, Impr. La Reproductrice, 1958.

Scholarship: "Proverbes et dictons," in *Nos Antilles* (Paris, 1935), pp. 291-304.

Travel: *La Guadeloupe,* Pointe-à-Pitre, 1957.

Astrology: *La lune et ses influences,* Paris; *La Maison Rustique,* 1947; *Les causes cosmiques de la guerre de 1939,* Paris, Adyar, 1946; *Pour comprendre et pratiquer l'astrologie moderne,* Paris, Adyar, 1947 (with R.P.G. de Cursac); *Les dates exactes de la vie du Christ,* Paris, Adyar, 1947.

History: *Questions sur l'histoire de la Martinique* (in collaboration with Claude and Magdeleine Carbet), Fort-de-France, Impr. Antillaise Saint-Paul, 1965.

Biographical/Critical Sources: Bettina Lara and Roger Fortuné, *Un héraut du régionalisme antillais: Gilbert de Chambertrand,* Basse-Terre, 1948; Auguste Viatte, *Histoire littéraire de l'Amérique française,* 1954.

CHANLATTE, Juste or Comte de Rosiers

b. 1766, Arcahaie, Haiti; d. October 13, 1828, Port-au-Prince.
Poet, playwright, essayist.

Educated in France, Chanlatte on his return to Saint Domingue sided with the British during the independence struggles in Haiti and was forced to flee to the United States. He subsequently became a leading spokesman for Dessalines. He wrote several official documents.

Chanlatte was named the Comte de Rosiers in the imperial period of Haitian history and was a court writer of poetry for King Christophe, but like many courtiers, turned against his benefactor when the latter fell. His last verse is, however, honestly critical of the excesses of Christophe, and the Martiniquian poet Aimé Césaire makes use of some of Chanlatte's lines in his own *La Tragédie du Roi Christophe,* written in Shakespeaian mode. Since the court was at Christophe's fantasmagoric chateau "Sans-Souci" in the mountains, the setting for the poetry and of Césaire's later tragedy is appropriately grandiose.

Chanlatte's *Cri de la nature,* a powerful plea for racial equality, was one of the earliest of its sort anywhere. His play *Nehri* celebrates Christophe's victories over the French.

Writings: Poetry: *Recueil de chants et de*

couplets à la gloire de leurs majestés et de la famille royale d'Hayti . . . à l'usage de la cour et des Haytiens, Sans-Souci, Haiti, Impr. Royale, 18??; *Ode à l'Indépendance; La Ville du Cap-Henry; La Triple palme ou Ode à Boyer.*

Plays: *L'entrée du Roi en sa capitale; opéra-vaudeville,* Sans-Souci, de l'Impr. Royale, 1818; *Nehri* (Henry Christophe's anagram).

Essays: *Le cri de la nature,* Cap-Henry, 1810; second edition, Paris, Ed. de la Revue Encyclopédique, 1819; *Haiti reconnaissante en réponse à un écrit intitulé "L'Europe châtiée et l'Afrique vengée,"* Sans-Souci, De l'Impr. Royale, 1819.

CHARLES, Carmin

b. October 28, 1916, Jérémie, Haiti.
Poet, storywriter, teacher.

Charles schooled at the Christian Brothers' School in Jérémie and afterwards at the Lycée Pétion. He graduated from the Faculty of Law in Port-au-Prince.

He was a teacher at the Lycée Nord Alexis of Jérémie and later at different colleges of Port-au-Prince. He got a scholarship to study in Bogota and he studied philology at the Caro Y Cuervo Institute and at the same time he taught French at the Panamerican Center of Literature and Languages of Bogota.

Writings: Law: *Le Droit dans la vie moderne,* Port-au-Prince, Impr. Les Presses Universitaires, 1950.

Stories: *Contes des tropiques,* Port-au-Prince, Ed. Panorama, 1962.

CHARLES, Christophe

b. April 29, 1951, Port-au-Prince.
Poet, literary critic.

After Charles graduated from the Faculté des Lettres and Pedagogie, Port-au-Prince, he taught in several lycées and colleges in the capital. He contributed to such newspapers and magazines as *Le Nouvelliste, Oedipe, Le Nouveau Monde, Le Petit Samedi Soir,* and *Conjonction.*

Charles has commented on his own works by saying, "Je suis aussi le poète de l'insolite, le poète des sensations fugitives et des émotions fugaces."

Writings: Poetry: *Neuf hai-kai pour Magloire St-Aude,* Port-au-Prince, 1971; *L'aventure humaine,* 1971; *Le cycle de la parole,* 1973; *Hurler,* 1974; *L'Aventure Humaine,* Tome Ie, *L'ardent sanglot,* 1974, Tome II, *Désastre,* 1975: all his works, Port-au-Prince, Atelier Fardin.

Literary Criticism: *Dix nouveaux poètes et écrivains haitiens,* Port-au-Prince, Collection UNHTI, 1974.

CHARLES, Jean-Claude

b. 1949, Port-au-Prince, Haiti.
Poet, novelist.

After schooling in Port-au-Prince, Charles studied at Haiti's School of Ethnology, and in Strasbourg, France where he attended courses in journalism. Subsequently he travelled in Mexico, the United States, and now lives in Paris.

Writings: Poetry: *Négotiations,* Paris, J.P. Oswald, 1972.

Novel: *La sainte dérive des cochons,* Paris, 1977.

CHARLES, Joseph D.

b. November 15, 1907, Limbé, Haiti
d. November 16, 1966, Cap-Haitien.
Essayist, orator, lawyer, professor, diplomat.

Charles was educated at the College of Notre Dame du Perpétuel Secours. He attended the law school of Cap-Haitien where he took his degree.

He then taught at the College Notre Dame and became deputy commissioner of the Civil Court and later a judge.

He was named Minister of Public Instruction and later elected as Deputy of

Limbé. In 1946, Charles was appointed Ambassador to Washington, D.C., and to the Organization of American States. For several years he taught International Law at the law school of Cap-Haitien.

Writings: Essay: *Graines au vent,* Port-au-Prince, Impr. du Collège Vertières, 1938.

Orations: published in various journals.

CHARLES-PIERRE, Derville

b. December 24, 1863, Fort-Liberté, Haiti; d. ca. 1910(?).
Essayist, teacher, lawyer, merchant.

Charles-Pierre studied in Cap-Haitien through law school. He was a teacher, having abandoned the practice of law, and also turned to commercial activities in Fort Liberté. He contributed many essays to newspapers printed in Cap-Haitien or in Port-au-Prince.

Writings: Law: *La profession d'avocat,* Cap-Haitien, Impr. "La Conscience," 1909.

CHARLIER, Aymon

(see under **Marie VIEUX**)

CHARLIER, Etienne Danton

b. June 12, 1904, Aquin, Haiti; d. December 26, 1960, Port-au-Prince.
Essayist, historian, lawyer, scholar.

Charlier came to Port-au-Prince where he received his education. He then studied law in France and won his degree at the University of Paris. He returned to Haiti to practice law and to serve as a professor at the Faculty of Law of Port-au-Prince.

Charlier contributed to such newspapers as *Le Matin, Le Nouvelliste, L'Action,* and *La Nation.*

Dr. Ghislain Gouraige commented on Charlier's works:

> *L'histoire socialiste de l'indépendance d'Haiti est écrite par Etienne Charlier sur le modèle de Louis Blanc, de Jaurès et surtout de James. Dans son* Aperçu sur la formation historique de la nation haitienne, *Charlier reprend l'affirmation de Gabriel Debien selon laquelle les blancs à Saint Domingue étaient d'extraction bourgeoise. Ce qui rend aisé sa thèse de la lutte des classes dans la colonie ... L'aisance avec laquelle il soutient sa thèse est peut-être la seule originalité de son oeuvre ingénieuse.*

Writings: Essays: *Fascisme, nazisme ou socialisme scientifique,* Port-au-Prince, Impr. Aug. A. Héraux, 1934; "Haiti," from *Pensamiento economico latino-americano,* Mexico, Fondo de Cultura Economica, 1945, pp. 223-237.
Law: *De l'aménagement du principe de la liberté individuelle de travail en droit français* (thèse de doctorat en droit), Paris, 1932.
History: *Aperçu sur la formation historique de la nation haitienne,* Port-au-Prince, Les Presses Libres, 1954; *En marge de Notre "Aperçu sur la formation historique de la nation haitienne,"* (réponse to Mr. Emmanuel C. Paul), Port-au-Prince, Les Presses Libres, 1955.

Biographical/Critical Sources: Ghislain Gouraige, *Histoire de la littérature haitienne,* 1960, pp. 474.

CHARLIER, Jacques Roumain

b. May 4, 1945, Port-au-Prince, Haiti.
Poet, novelist.

Jacques Charlier was educated in Port-au-Prince, and since 1965 has lived in New York.

Writings: Poetry: *Le Scapulaire des Armuriers,* New York, Impr. French Printing, 1976; *La Part des pluies,* New York, 1977.

CHARMANT, Antoine Alcius

b. June 26, 1856, Jacmel, Haiti; d. March 28, 1936, Jacmel.
Journalist, lawyer, politician, polemist.

Charmant was educated in Jacmel. He started working in the field of law as a legal clerk before becoming a very successful lawyer.

Before the American occupation, Charmant had enjoyed a fine local career in politics and had been a deputy of Jacmel. His numerous adventures with local authorities made him a legend in his own time. His son, Dr. Rodolphe Charmant, published a narrative of his father's life in his book *La vie incroyable d'Alcius.*

He was a strong opponent of the U.S. occupation of Haiti and pushed his views as chief editor of *L'Intransigeant.*

Writings: Politics: *Notre appréciation sur le traité d'Arbitrage,* Port-au-Prince, Impr. Aug. A. Héraux, 1890; *Une réplique aux "Quatre mois de Ministère,* Jacmel, Brun, 1891; (*Quatre mois de Ministère* was by Dr. Roche Grellier); *Pétition aux membres du Corps Législatif,* Port-au-Prince, Impr. V. Valcin, 1932.

Political Sociology: *Haiti vivra-t-elle; (*étude sur le préjugé *des races; race noire, race jaune, race blanche; et sur la doctrine de Monroe),* Tome I, second edition, Le Havre, Impr. et Lithog. F. Le Roy, 1905.

Polemics: *Une réfutation; Monsieur P.N. Lhérisson et son contrat devant le Sénat de la République,* Port-au-Prince, Impr. de La Jeunesse, 1893; *La mort de Chicoye,* Le Havre, Impr. et Lithog. Duval et Davoult, 1907; *Le spectre de Chicoye,* Le Havre, Impr. et Lithog. Duval et Davoult, 1907; *Un assassinat maçonnique,* Port-au-Prince, Impr. H. Chauvet, n.d.

CHARMANT, Dr. Rodolphe

b. November 4, 1884, Jacmel, Haiti; d. ca. 1969, Port-au-Prince.
Essayist, biographer, physician, teacher.

Charmant attended the school of the Christian Brothers of Jacmel and completed his education at the Petit Séminaire Collège Saint Martial in Port-au-Prince. He later graduated from the School of Medicine. He was President of the Red Cross for many years and General Inspector in all Schools of Port-au-Prince for health education. His biography of his father, Antoine Alcius, appeared under the title *La vie incroyable d'Alcius.*

Writings: Essay: *La République d'Haiti, sa faillite et sa rédemption,* Port-au-Prince, Impr. de l'Abeille, 1917.

Biography: *La vie incroyable d'Alcius,* Port-au-Prince, Société d'Ed. et de Lib., 1946.

Hygiene: *Aide-mémoire d'hygiène et de puériculture,* Port-au-Prince, Impr. V. Valcin, 1944; *Manuel d'hygiène appliquée,* Port-au-Prince, Impr. de l'Etat, n.d.

Education: *Vers les sommets; par l'éducation et la santé,* Port-au-Prince, Impr. de l'Etat, 1953.

CHASSAGNE, Raymond

b. 1929, Jérémie, Haiti.
Poet, essayist.

Chassagne was educated partly in his natal city and partly in Haiti's capital. He served for a period as an officer in the Haitian Army but resigned in 1957, emigrating to Montreal to study for a B.A., an M.A. and thereafter, his doctorate in French and Canadian literature.

He has contributed to various Haitian

magazines such as *Optique* and *Conjonction.* He is preparing for the press a study of the three novels of Edouard Glissant and a second study of the work of Aimé Césaire.

Writings: Poetry: *Mots de Passe,* Canada, Eds. Naaman, 1976.
Recording: *Mots de Passe, Raymond Chassagne,* recited by Anthony Phelps.

CHASSAGNE, Roland

b. August 13, 1912, Jérémie, Haiti;
d. date unknown.
Poet, novelist.

Chassagne was educated in Jérémie and Port-au-Prince. He was a boyhood friend and schoolmate of future poets Jean F. Brierre and Robert Lataillade, also of Jérémie. He, like Lataillade, who died young, was preternaturally concerned with the fleeting moment and death. He once seriously considered the priesthood as a career and studied at a seminary but came to feel the pull of the flesh and other worldly pleasures. He entered the military school of Port-au-Prince and served as commissioned officer for several years in the Haitian army.

His verse is free, hardly ever cast in the classical French modes, but is otherwise little touched by the concerns of the Haitian patriot-nationalists such as Roumain and Price-Mars. Instead, his work is ironic, distant, influenced by the French poet Jules Laforgue, who so strongly influenced the early work of T.S. Eliot. Chassagne's "Prière" seems clearly reflective of his reading of Laforgue's "Noël sceptique."

A brief example of his earlier work are these lines from "Murmure":

Valse, la vie n'est que toi, et la souplesse
Que moule une prison mouvante de dentelles.

Writings: Poetry: *Le tambourin voilé,* preface by Stéphen Alexis, Port-au-Prince, Impr. Haitienne, 1933.
Novels: two manuscripts unpublished.

Biographical/Critical Sources: Naomi M. Garret, *The Renaissance in Haitian poetry,* 1973, pp. 163-167; Edner Brutus essay, "Roland Chassagne," in *La Relève* (March 1935), pp. 20-32; and Grimard's article in *Temps-Revue* (April 8, 1933), pp. 24-25; Ghislain Gouraige, *Histoire de la littérature haitienne,* 1960, pp. 319-323; Pradel Pompilus & Frères de l'Instruction Chrétienne, *Manuel illustré de la littérature haitienne,* 1961, pp. 356-359.

CHATENAY, Libert

b. July 7, 1905, Cayenne, Guyane.
Poet, novelist, journalist.

Chatenay attended a college in Cayenne and the Lycée of Toulouse in France. He later studied medicine at the University of Toulouse. He published in such papers as *L'Express du Midi, Bulletin des Républiques Pyrénéennes,* and *Mercure de France.* He founded his own review *Restauration* in which he published his poems, his one play, *Gisèle,* and articles of literary and philosophical criticism.

Chatenay participated in the second World War and was a prisoner for a period. He later published in the journal *Chanteclair* in the post-war period.

Writings: Poetry: *Naufrages* (unpublished collection), various poems in *Restauration* and other journals.
Politics: *Décret d'Insurrection,* 1935.
Play: *Gisèle,* published in *Restauration,* 19??.

CHAUVET, Henri

b. July 23, 1863, Port-au-Prince, Haiti;
d. December 19, 1928, Port-au-Prince.
Poet, playwright (in French and creole), journalist, geographer.

After his primary education at the Petit Seminaire Collège Saint-Martial, Chauvet went to France to complete his education and received a degree in letters at the University of Paris. Returning to Haiti, he became a professor at the Collège Saint-Martial, and later at the Lycée Pétion. He was President Florvil Hyppolite's reporter during his trips all over the country. He later became a deputy, representing Port-au-Prince (1899-1903). He founded the humorous paper, *Le Zinglin,* and years later, *Le Matin,* with Guillaume Chéraquit. He left the new periodical to become director of *Le Nouvelliste,* now the leading Haitian newspaper. He served as Haitian Consul in Amsterdam. Chauvet was an officer of the Academy of Arts and Sciences.

He has published in *Le Nouvelliste* his own work as well as that of many others.

Writings: Poetry: *La fleur d'or, poème patriotique haitien,* Port-au-Prince, Impr. Vve J. Chenet, 1892; second edition, Impr. H. Chauvet, 1899; *Fleurs et pleurs,* Port-au-Prince, Impr. H. Chauvet, n.d.

Prose Plays: *Toréador par amour; comédie bouffe en un acte,* Impr. Nationale, Port-au-Prince, 1892; *Le bon à marier; comédie bouffe en un acte* (with Georges Sioen), Port-au-Prince, Impr. Nationale, n.d.; *Une nuit de noces* (with Fleury Féquière), Port-au-Prince, Impr. H. Chauvet and Cie, 1901; and the creole language play: *Macaque ac chien* (a satire in two acts), dates unknown of production and publication, if any. Also, one verse play: *La fille du Kacik* (5 acts), Paris, Vve Victor Goupy, 1894.

Travel: *A travers la République d'Haiti; Par mornes et par savanes,* Paris, Vve Victor Goupy, 1894.

Georgraphy: *Grande géographie de l'Ile d'Haiti* (with Robert Gentil), Paris, Impr. de Goupy, 1896.

CHAUVET, Marie Vieux

(see under **Marie VIEUX**)

CHENET, Gérard

b. April 14, 1929, Port-au-Prince, Haiti. Playwright, poet.

After Chenet completed his education in Port-au-Prince, he studied law. He contributed to the launching in 1946 of the important newspaper *La Ruche,* with René Dépestre and Jacques S. Alexis, and helped oust from his office the President of Haiti, Elie Lescot. He subsequently went to Europe for further studies. He lived many years in East Germany and Hungary. He then was a professor of History in Conakry, Republic of Guinea. He is now living in Dakar, Senegal, where he is a secretary of the National Commission of UNESCO and at the same time "Secrétaire de la Conférence des Ministres de l'Education des Etats Africains et Malgaches d'expression française."

Chenet is a militant writer who has sought to understand the African heritage of Haiti. His first drama, *Les Fiançailles tragiques,* appeared in 1968. It is an adaptation of a study of Omar, the Islamic reformer of the Toucouleur people of eastern Senegal, written by Djibril Tamsir Niane. Omar gradually swayed the Toucouleur and their king Yimba Sanko to a renewed effort of Islamic and national spirit. Although Omar was defeated in time by the French general Faidherbe, the message "to fight on" is very clear for Africains everywhere.

Writings: Plays: *Les Fiançailles tragiques* (performed in 1968); *El Hadj Omar: Chronique de la guerre sainte,* preface by Jean F. Brierre, Honfleur, P. J. Oswald, 1968; *Zombis nègres,* a new play, details unknown.

Poetry: *Poèmes du village de Toubab Dyalaw,* Dakar, Nouvelles Editions Africaines, 1974.

Biographical/Critical Sources: J. Nantet, *Panorama de la littérature noire d'expression française,* 1971; and Robert Cornevin, *Le Théâtre Haitien des origines à nos jours,* pp. 230-285.

CHENET, Jean-Baptiste

b. 1788, Cap-Haitien, Haiti; d. 1851, Gonaives, Haiti.
Poet, businessman, surveyor.

Born in Cap-Haitien, Chenet spent his entire life in Gonaives as a surveyor and businessman. He reflected the French preacher-poet Boileau in his one 558-page book of verse, but his poetry was naturally romantic, repudiating Greek gods and other classical devices, he wrote that Haiti needed something different:

Sous un beau ciel, sous un riant tropique,
La fiction d'un climat tempéré
Est refusée aux enfants de l'Afrique.
Point de guérets, Vertumne est ignoré.

Chenet praises strong feeling as a source of poetry:

Malheur au froid auteur
Sans âme en ses écrits, qui brigue sa faveur.

Writings: Poetry: *Etudes poètiques ou chants du barde glanés chez les muses,* Paris, Impr. Administrative de Paul Dupont, 1846.

Letter: "Réponse à Monsieur Saint-Rémy fils," in *Le Manifeste* (Jan. 27, 1848).

Biographical/Critical Sources: Auguste Viatte, *Histoire littéraire de l'Amérique française,* 1953, pp. 354-356; Hénock Trouillot, *Les origines sociales de la littérature haitienne,* 1962, pp. 151-155.

CHEVALIER, André Fontanges

b. 1877, Cayes, Haiti; d.April, 1953, Port-au-Prince.
Novelist, playwright, politician.

Chevalier was educated in Port-au-Prince and very early entered politics. He served as General Post Master and later was named Minister Plenipotentiary to the Dominican Republic. He was Deputy Commissioner for the World Fair in 1949 held for the bicentennial of Port-au-Prince.

Chevalier promoted theatre and sports, particularly soccer, tennis, and swimming, and became Commissioner of Sports in Haiti. He contributed to many newspapers and founded the magazine *Aya Bombé* (a term meaning, in an old Indian language of Haiti, "Live free or die"). He published two novels, *Aya Bombé* and *Bakoulou.*

Writings: Folkloric Narrative: *Aya bombé; évocation quisqueyenne,* Port-au-Prince, Ed. Academia, 1945; *Bakoulou; audience folklorique* (in collaboration with Luc Grimard), Port-au-Prince, Soc. d'Ed. et de Libr., 1950.

Plays: *La marquise de Périgny; comédie locale en un acte,* performed at Ciné Variétés in 1918, published Port-au-Prince, Impr. Moderne, 1918; *Dambala Ouèdo; comédie locale en 2 actes,* Port-au-Prince, Impr. Moderne, 1919; *Les mosquerettes,* Port-au-Prince, Impr. Moderne, n.d.; *L'amiral Killick,* in collaboration with Charles Moravia (drame historique en 3 tableaux), Port-au-Prince, Impr. Collège Vertiéres, 1943.

Tourism: *Mon petit kodack; clichés d'hier,* preface by Henri Chauvet, Port-au-Prince, Impr. Edm. Chenet, 1916, and new edition, Port-au-Prince, Impr. La Presse, 1930; *Remembrance,* Port-au-Prince, Impr. de l'Etat, 1936.

Sports: *Règlements et participation haitienne aux jeux olympiques,* Port-au-Prince, Impr. de l'Etat, 1938.

CHEVRY, Arsène

b. July 14, 1867, Port-au-Prince, Haiti;
d. February 16, 1915, Port-au-Prince.
Poet, journalist, essayist.

Chevry completed his studies at the Collège Saint Martial in Port-au-Prince. He was a teacher at the Lycée Pétion. He became director and founder of the journal, *Le Devoir* (1902), and contributed to many literary reviews. The critic Clément Magloire wrote of Chevry the day after his death: "On ne verra plus passer ce frêle et doux poète, mince, court, comme effacé, qui portait cependant une âme d'acier qui ne plia jamais."

Magloire considered his own verse "délicats et travaillés" and the product of the purest inspiration. Much of his verse dealt with Amerindian themes.

Writings: Poetry: *Les areytos: poèsies indiennes,* Port-au-Prince, Impr. de la Jeunesse, 1892; *Voix perdues, poèsies,* Port-au-Prince, Impr. H. Chauvet, 189?; *Les voix du centenaire, poemes héroiques,* Port-au-Prince, Impr. de l'Abeille, 1904; *Voix de l'exil; fatale expiation,* Saint-Thomas, Leroy Nolte printer, 1908.

Critical-Literary Essays: *Causerie sur la littérature haitienne: saynètes créoles; La poèsie haitienne à l'école et dans la famille,* details unknown.

CHRISPHONTE, Prosper

b. January 14, 1903, Port-au-Prince, Haiti.
Poet, teacher, biographer, essayist.

Chrisphonte was a teacher of English at the Lycée Pétion in Port-au-Prince.

Writings: Poetry: *Rèves et chants (poèmes),* Paris, Impr. Jouve, 1929.

Biography: *Le poète de la Dessalinienne* (portrait, essai, critique), Port-au-Prince, Imrp. N. Telhomme, 1941; *Noces d'or de Monsieur L.C. Lhérisson* (portrait, essay critique), Port-au-Prince, Impr. N. Telhomme, 1939.

Various: *L'après-guerre; pour une licence ès-lettres,* Port-au-Prince, Impr. N. Telhomme, 1946; *Deuxième thèse de doctorat,* Port-au-Prince, Impr. Beaubrun, 1950; *Seconde partie d'un écrivain par les textes; deuxième travail de licence ès-lettres et 4ème tome sur Massillon Coicou,* Port-au-Prince, Impr. du Séminaire Adventiste, 1954; *Comment on fait un cinquième tome sur une même figure nàtionale,* Port-au-Prince, 1958; *Traits-d'union entre deux tomes et 3ème thèse,* Port-au-Prince, Impr. du Séminaire Adventiste, 1964.

CINEAS, Jean-Baptiste

b. June 5, 1895, Cap-Haitien, Haiti;
d. July 5, 1959, Port-au-Prince.
Novelist, lawyer, judge.

Cineas received a good education at l'Ecole Notre-Dame du Perpétuel Secours of Cap-Haitien and graduated from the Free Law School of that city. He was a teacher at the Collège Notre-Dame. He was elected as the Députy from Limbé in 1930, and spent many years as a judge on the Supreme Court in Port-au-Prince.

Cinéas was an active writer in the "indigenist" tradition and built his novels around the conditions of the African peasants of Haiti.

Writings: Novels: *Le drame de la terre; roman paysan,* Cap-Haitien, Impr. du Séminaire Adventiste, 1933; *La vengeance de la terre; roman paysan,* Impr. du Collège Vertieres, 1933; *L'héritage sacré; roman paysan,* Impr. Deschamps, 1945; *Le choc en retour,* Impr. Deschamps, 1948: the last three in Port-au-Prince.

Informal Essay: *Le collège de jadis; causerie . . . ,* Port-au-Prince, Impr. de l'Etat, 1954.

CLARAC, René

b. October 10, 1912, in the Southwest of France (but of Martinican parents).
Novelist, lawyer.

Clarac completed his education in France and graduated from the School of Law, Paris University.

He came to Martinique to practice law and was an attorney at the Court of Appeals. At the same time, he was named professor at the School of Law, Fort-de-France, and lecturer.

Clarac later went to Africa where he served as an attorney at the Court of Appeals, Abidjan, Ivory Coast.

Writings: Novels: *Bagamba, nègre marron,* Paris, Les Ed. de la Nouvelle France, year unknown; *L'espagnole de la Vera-Cruz,* Paris, Seuil, 1947; and *Le vert,* Paris, Les Grandes Editions Françaises, 1947.

CLERMONT, Raymond

b. ca. 1929, Guadeloupe.
Poet, dental surgeon, photographer.

After locally schooling in Guadeloupe, Clermont went to France where he graduated from a dental school.

He has contributed to several journals in which he published many rondels, his favorite genre.

Writings: Poetry: *D'un cahier retrouvé,* (Les Editions Françaises), Paris, Ed. Bellemand, 1959.

CLERY, Pierre

b. April 18, 1930, Rivière-Pilote, Martinique.
Poet, painter and musician, playwright.

Cléry attended the Lycée Schoelcher of Fort-de-France. His poems have been published in the review *Horizons Caraibes* and anthologies and magazines.

Writings: Play: *Ti timbale en argent. Missié* Isido-a (3 acts), details unknown.

COICOU, Clément A.

b. November 22, 1895, Miragoâne, Haiti; d. July 1, 1952, Port-au-Prince.
Poet, lawyer.

After primary schooling at home, Coicou completed his education in Port-au-Prince where he attended the Faculty of Law. He was for many years Professor of Law, and general counsel to the Labor Department.

Writings: Poetry: *Reflets,* Port-au-Prince, Impr. C. Beaubrun, 1947; *Les labours,* Port-au-Prince, Impr. C. Beaubrun, 1948; *Aux souffles des tropiques,* Port-au-Prince, Impr. V. Valcin, 1948; *Dans la cité de l'Exposition du Bi-Centenaire,* Port-au-Prince, Impr. V. Valcin, 1949, (these poems were dedicated to President Dumarsais Estimé who was the prime mover of this Exposition in commemoration of 200 years of Port-au-Prince).

COICOU, Massillon

b. October 7, 1867, Port-au-Prince, Haiti; d. March 15, 1908, Port-au-Prince.
Poet, playwright, novelist.

Coicou was a student at the School of the Brothers of Christian Education, and completed his studies at the Lycée Pétion, where he graduated in 1885 with great distinction.

He was named teacher at the Lycée Pétion and later headed the office of the President of Haiti, Tirésias Simon Sam. He was named Secretary of the Haitian Legation in Paris under Anténor Firmin as Minister.

He remained many years in Paris where he was appreciated by French writers, and where he contributed to many magazines and papers and published several volumes of his work.

When he returned to Port-au-Prince, he taught at the Lycée Pétion, devoting much energy to dramatic performances.

In 1905, Coicou served as the director of the unofficial Haitian National Theatre. (Forty-five years later President Dumarsais Estimé [February 7, 1950] gave the name "Massillon Coicou" to the government's open-air theatre in Port-au-Prince.)

Coicou was executed without trial at the orders of President Nord Alexis, during one of the many purges of the enemies or critics of the corrupt rulers of Haiti at the turn of the 19th and beginning of the 20th centuries. His poetry was considered by the government as too inflamatory in its call for patriotic sacrifices, honesty, and working for the common good.

Though published only in 1903 in book form, Coicou's earliest poetry, "Passions," dates to his twelfth year (1879). Although he loved France and its culture, he protested the plight of black men, too, crying out in a mixed mood of self-doubt in his *Complainte d'esclave:* "Pourquoi donc suis-je nègre? Oh! pourquoi suis-je noir?"

He authored several novels but only *La noire* saw print (1905), a work studying the colonial roots of racism and conflict in Haiti.

Writings: Poetry: *Poèsies nationales,* Paris, Impr. Victor Goupy et Jourdan, 1892; *Passions; primes vers d'amour et variations sur de vieux thèmes,* Paris, Librairie des Mathurins, 1903; *Impressions: rêve des jours de trêve,* Paris, Librarie des Mathurins (Dujarric et Cie, Ed.), 1903; *L'oracle; poème dramatique haitien,*

Plays: *Liberté* (drama in 4 acts and in verse), produced 1894 (Haiti) and 1904 (Paris.); *Les fils de Toussaint,* produced 1895 in Haiti; *L'Empereur Dessalines,* Port-au-Prince, Impr. Chenet, 1906; *Féfé candidat,* comedy produced in Théatre-Haitien, Oct. 7, 1906; *Féfé ministre,* comedy produced at Port-au-Prince Théatre National, in 1906; *L'Art triomphe,* 1895; *Faute d'actrice,* 1895; *L'Ecole mutuelle,* 1896; *L'école des proverbs; L'alphabet,* 1905; *Saint Vincent de Paul,* 1907.

Essay-Discourse: *Le génie français et l'âme haitienne* (lecture, July 23, 1904), Paris, Lib. de la Renaissance Latine, 1904.

Novel: *La noire,* published only as a pamphlet, Paris, 1905.

Biographical/Critical Sources: Pradel Pompilus, "Massillon Coicou, poète," in *Conjonction,* No. 105, pp. 60-68 (Oct. 1967); Frère Raphael, "Impressions of Massillon Coicou ou un poète de l'inquiétude religieuse," *Conjonction,* No. 105, pp. 69-73 (Oct. 1967); Duraciné Vaval discusses the Féfé plays in his *Histoire de la littérature haitienne,* Port-au-Prince, 1933; Ghislain Gouraige, *Histoire de la littérature haitienne,* Port-au-Prince, Impr. N.A. Théodore, 1960, pp. 94-98; Pradel Pompilus & Frères de l'Instruction Chrétienne, *Manuel illustré d'histoire de la littérature haitienne,* 1961, pp. 152-162; Hénock Trouillot, *Les origines sociales de la littérature haitienne,* 1962, pp. 215-222; Robert Cornevin, *Le théâtre haitien, des origines à nos jours,* 1973, pp. 108-109.

COLAS, Justin L.

b. 1918, Cap-Haitien, Haiti.
Poet, novelist, physician.

Colas was educated in his native city and later went to Port-au-Prince to study medicine. After some years practicing medicine, he travelled to Montreal, Munich, Cologne, and Paris for advanced training.

Writings: Poetry: *Mosaiques,* Chicoutimi, Canada, 1969.

Novel: *Port ensablé,* Canada, Ed. du Phare Desbiens, 1970.

COLIBRI

(pseudonym for **Marie-Vieux CHAUVET**)

COLIMON, Marie-Thérèse

(pseudonym: **Marie BEC**)
b. April 11, 1918, Port-au-Prince, Haiti.
Poet, novelist, essayist, playwright, educator.

Marie-Thérèse Colimon received her education in Port-au-Prince. After graduation from the Normal School for girls, she has taught in various schools and colleges.

Colimon has also contributed to many cultural or social activities and she was for many years the president of the Women's League of Social Action. She was a managing editor of *La Revue de la Femme Haitienne,* and has published a great number of articles on education, the Haitian school system, and women's world and problems.

Writings: Plays: *La fille de l'esclave* (under pen-name of Marie Bec), (3 acts, for girls), Port-au-Prince, Impr. Daudin Brothers, 1949; *Vision d'Anacaona* (in collaboration with Elodie de Wend); *Marie-Claire Heureuse,* 1955; *Bernadette Soubirous,* 1955; *Le chant du musicien,* 1960; *Le message des aieules,* 1974.

Novel: *Fils de Misère* (1973 Prize: France-Antilles), Port-au-Prince, Eds. Caraibes, 1974.

Poetry: *Mon cahier d'écritures,* No. 1, Port-au-Prince, Atelier Fardin, 1973.

Stories: *Une autre histoire de Bouqui* (first prize in contest sponsored by Haitian-American Institute); *La Source* (tales for children), 1973; *Les rois l'avaient dit . . . ; L'irrésistible appel;* Le chant des sirènes (to be published soon).

Essays: *Femmes Haitiennes* (in collaboration with various members of Ligue Féminine d'Action Sociale), Port-au-Prince, Impr. de l'Etat, 1950; *L'émancipation de la jeune fille (êtes-vous pour ou contre?),* Port-au-Prince, 1954; "Femmes écrivains d'Haiti," in magazine *Pot-Pourri,* Port-au-Prince, 1977.

COLOMBEL, A. Noël

b. December 25, 1786, Saint-Michel-du-Fond-des-Nègres, Haiti; d. in shipwreck, 1823.
Biographer, journalist.

Colombel was educated in France. Returning to Haiti, he was a teacher and served in the national administration as President Boyer's secretary. It is believed he was the author of the letter by which Haiti recognized the independence of Greece.

He contributed to the first literary magazine *L'Abeille Haytienne.* The manuscript of his study of Alexandre Pétion was lost.

Writings: Compte de l'examen public du lycée National, rendu par N.A. Colombel, membre de la Commission d'Instruction Publique et Sécrétaire particulier de S. Ex. le Président d'Haiti, Port-au-Prince, Impr. du Gouvernement, 1820; *Examen d'un pamphlet ayant pour titre "Essai sur les causes de la révolution et des guerres civiles d'Haiti,* etc., Port-au-Prince, 1819.

CONDE, Maryse

b. ca. 1936, Pointe-à-Pitre, Guadeloupe.

Playwright, critic, journalist, reviewer, teacher.

Condé started her studies in Guadeloupe, but travelled to Paris to complete her education at the University of Paris and in London. She has taught in many countries of Africa but mostly in Ghana. She has been a speaker and journalist for BBC, and has contributed to several French and English newspapers.

Condé is now living in Paris and is a professor at the University of Paris VII (Jussieu). She is a contributor to *Présence Africaine* as a reviewer.

Writings: Editor of: *Anthologie de la littérature africaine d'expression française,* Accra, Ghana Institute of Languages, 1966.

Novel: *Hérémakhonon,* Paris, Union Générale d'Editions, 1976.

Plays: *Le Morne de Massabielle,* performed in 1970 at Théâtre-des-Hauts de Seine de Puteaux (unpublished); *Dieu nous l'a donné,* Paris, Pierre-Jean Oswald, 1972; *Mort d'Oluwemi d'Ajumako,* Paris, Ed. Pierre-Jean Oswald, 1973.

Studies: "Autour d'une littérature antillaise, in *Présence Africaine,* No. 81, 1972, pp. 170-186; "Three female writers in modern Africa: Flora Nwapa, Ama Ata Aidoo and Grace Ogot," in *Présence Africaine,* No. 82 (2nd quarter 1972), pp. 132-144; "Pourquoi la négritude? Négritude ou révolution," in *Les Littératures d'expression francaise: Négritude africaine-Négritude caraibe,* Paris, Eds. de la Francité, 1973; "Negritude ou révolution," Colloquy at the University of Paris, Eds. de la Francité (1973); "Négritude césairienne, Négritude senghorienne," in *Revue de Littérature comparée,* Nos. 3-4 (July-Dec. 1974), pp. 409-420.

Literary Criticism: *Le roman antillais* (2 vols.), Paris, Fernand Nathan, 1977; *La poèsie antillaise,* Paris, Fernand Nathan, 1977.

COQUILLE, Jean

b. ca. 1780(?), Martinique; d. 1811, Haiti.
Poet.

Coquille, of African race, was a teacher at the Ecole aux Cayes and his verse is cited in Sannon's *Histoire de Toussaint Louverture.*

Biographical/Critical Sources: Pauléus Sannon, *Histoire de Toussaint Louverture,* 2 vols., Port-au-Prince, 1932 (see Vol. 2, p. 147).

CORBIN, Henri

b. ca. 1932, Guadeloupe.
Poet, playwright.

Corbin's play *Baron-Samedi* is a highly imaginative treatment of voodoo and a voodoo god's intervention in human affairs.

Writings: Poetry: in *Nouvelle somme de poèsie du monde noir,* Paris, Présence Africaine, No. 57, 1966: Poems are "Humidité lente," "Cavalier du vent," "Voleur de nuage," and "Et dans l'anneau;" and many others are published in *Les Temps Modernes,* No. 52 (Feb. 1950); and in *Acoma* (his four-page poem "Province Ténébreuse"), No. 3, (Feb. 6, 1972).

Play: *Baron-Samedi,* Special Issue of *Présence Africaine,* New Series, No. 43, 1962; and in Special Issue entitled *Antilles-Guyane;* "L'ombre de la falaise" is in *Acoma,* No. 1 (Jan-March 1971).

CORVINGTON, Hermann

b. ca. 1891, Port-au-Prince, Haiti; d. November 2, 1964, Port-au-Prince.
Essayist, historian, lawyer, teacher.

Corvington received his education in Port-au-Prince where he also took his law degree. He was appointed as professor at the Faculty of Law, and his main field was international law and the problems of nationality. He served for many years as adviser to the Department of Foreign Affairs. His work in history was concentrated on the pre-colombian period.

Writings: Essays: *Histoire humaine des aborigènes d'Haiti: origine et provenance des aborigènes,* Port-au-Prince, Impr. S. Dévieux, n.d.

Biographies: *Caonabo, Seigneur de la Maguana,* Port-au-Prince, Impr. S. Dévieux, 1944; *Deux caciques du Xaragua, Bohéchio et Anacaona,* 1944; *Guacanagaric,* Port-au-Prince, Impr. S. Dévieux, n.d.; *Guayacuya (Le cacique Henri),* Port-au-Prince, Impr. S. Dévieux, n.d.

Law: *Etude sur la condition juridique de l'étranger en Haiti, envisagée sous l'aspect des droits réels immobiliers de 1804 à 1934,* Port-au-Prince, Impr. N. Telhomme, 1934; *Examens des diverses doctrines relatives au conflit des lois; contribution officielle des Gouvernements en Europe* . . . (livre ler, fascicule No. 1), Port-au-Prince, Impr. Gachette, 1935; *Projet de convention internationale sur l'extradition,* Port-au-Prince, Impr. S. Dévieux, 1944.

COURTOIS, Félix

b. February 4, 1892, Port-au-Prince, Haiti.
Novelist, storywriter, journalist.

After completing his studies at the Lycée Pétion in Haiti's capital, Courtois studied law and entered into an active governmental career. He became chief of the Division of Foreign Affairs and later served as Secretary of the Legation to Paris. His most recent post has been as Assistant Commissioner of the Government at Haiti's Supreme Court.

He has published articles and stories in various Haitian journals. In 1920 he published his first novel, *Deux pauvres petites filles,* and 56 years later, his second, *Scènes de la vie port-au-princienne.*

Though writing much later, Courtois is of the school of Flaubert and de Maupassant in his evocation of the memories of youth, though his own nostalgic scenes of Haiti are of course very much his own. Adding to his strengths are his pictures of politicians and other ephemeral phenomena who flicker in the depths of the unchangeable people whose character remain much the same through generations. His style is rich and opaque to avoid any difficulties with the powers that be, though there is all the clarity needed when he wants to use more chiseled phrases.

Writings: Novels: *Deux pauvres petites filles,* Port-au-Prince, Impr. Héraux, 1920; *Scènes de la vie port-au-princienne,* Port-au-Prince, Impr. des Antilles, 1975; *Durin Belmour,* Port-au-Prince, Impr. des Antilles, 1977.

Story: in various journals; "Marie-Eve ou le petit bar," in *Nouvelliste,* 114, 4(1970), pp. 57-69.

COURTOIS, Joseph Madame

(née **Julienne Bussière Laforest**)
b. 1789, Cap-Haitien, Haiti; d. December 24, 1853, Port-au-Prince.
Journalist, essayist, biographer, editor.

Julienne Bussière went to France in 1795 with her father Etienne Bussière Laforest who had just been elected Deputy of Saint Domingue to the French National Assembly. Etienne also served during this period as a member of the French Council of Five Hundred.

After Julienne completed her education she married Joseph Courtois who had also gone to France to study. On returning to Haiti, she founded a private school for students of both sexes in 1818. With her husband she also founded in 1829 the newspaper *La Feuille du Commerce* in the capital, working as the managing editor until her death in her 66th year.

COUSSIN, J.H. Joseph

b. 1773, Basse-Terre, Guadeloupe; d. 1836.
Novelist.

Coussin was clerk at the Royal Court in Guadeloupe. Influenced by Chateaubriand's romances, *René* and *Atala,* Coussin celebrated the unfortunate Carib Indians of the islands.

He stated in the introduction to his novel, *Eugène de Cerceil:*

> Souvent dans ma jeunesse, en parcourant les montagnes aspères (sic) *de ma terre natale, et en m'égarant sous les dômes des forêts vierges qui la couvrent encore en grande partie, je m'affligeais que les tableaux sublimes dont j'étais enveloppé, n'eussent point encore rencontré ni de peintres qui eussent essayé de les rendre ... Lorsque je lus la description du désert dans* Atala, *je reconnus avec transport des scènes pareilles à celles que, depuis longtemps, j'admirais dans ma patrie, et que j'y admirais à peu près tout seul.*

Coussin was not only a Chateaubriand disciple, but he was a follower of Rousseau with his "bon sauvage" doctrine, for René, Chateaubriand's hero, had declared:

> *J'ai quitté l'Europe pour fuir des moeurs et des préjugés qui répugnaient à mon coeur . . . Allons ensemble vivre avec les sauvages. Nous ne leur apprendrons de la civilisation que les choses qui sont véritablement bonnes et utiles: la religion seule les comprend toutes.* (Vol. II, p. 16)

Writings: Novel: *Eugène de Cerceil,* 3 vols. Paris, 1824.

CUPIDON, Antoine

b. ca. 1908, Guyane.
Poet.

After his primary studies, Cupidon went to France for university work. Taking his law degree he received several appointments from the French government so that he remained in France for a period. In time he returned to Guyane to serve as supervisor of the Registry Office.

Most of his work has appeared in Guyanese papers and journals. He asserts the dignity and value of his homeland in much of his verse:

> *Car ma Guyane est belle, riche de tous les présents,*
> *Car plus que ses trésors son mystère ensorcèle*
> *Le poète qui rêve et le pauvre artisan*
> *Et le marin errant à l'errante nacelle.*

Writings: Poetry: miscellaneous work in journals and manuscript, including two unpublished collections: "Les Fruits amers," and "Le chant des Palmistes."

CYPRIEN, Anatole

(pseudonym for **Claude DAMBREVILLE**)

b. ca. 1932, Port-au-Prince, Haiti.
Novelist, chronicler.

Dambreville was educated in Port-au-Prince. He has been a practicing journalist from his earliest adult years and his chronicles in *Le Nouvelliste* on travellers and tourists going and coming in Haiti are useful sources for the period.

Writings: Novel: *Coup de tonnerre,* Port-au-Prince, Eds. Panorama, 1966.

DALENCOUR, Dr. François Stanislas Ramir

b. 1880, Port-au-Prince, Haiti; d. 1959, Paris.
Historian, biographer, essayist, physician.

Dalencour was educated in Port-au-Prince and later graduated from the Faculty of Medicine. He practiced medicine in Haiti and for many years in Venezuela. He died in Paris after almost a lifetime of exile.

Writings: History: *Alexandre Pétion devant l'humanité; Alexandre Pétion et Simon Bolivar; Haiti et l'Amérique Latine ... et "Expédition de Bolivar" par le Sénateur Marion ainé,* n.d.; *Histoire de la nation haitienne,* chez l'auteur, 1930; *La fondation de la République d'Haiti par Alexandre Pétion,* chez l'auteur, 1944; *Le drapeau national haitien,* chez l'auteur, 1939; *Précis méthodique d'histoire d'Haiti; cinq siècles d'histoire (1492-1930),* chez l'auteur, 1935; *Simon Bolivar, champion de la liberté, défenseur de la démocratie, (conférence)*, 1934; *Francisco de Miranda et Alexandre Pétion. L'expédition de Miranda. Le premier effort de libération Hispano-Américaine. Le premier vagissement du Panaméricanisme*, chez l'auteur et Paris, Librairie Berger-Levrault, 1955; Editor of: *Ardouin Alexis Beaubrun: Etudes sur l'histoire d'Haiti; suivies de la vie du Général J.M. Borgella, 2ème édition conforme au texte original, annotée et précédée d'une note biographique sur B. Ardouin, par le Dr. François Dalencour*, chez l'éditeur, 1958, all Port-au-Prince.

Biography: *Marcelin Berthelot, (conférence)*, 1928; *Pasteur, conférence*, 1923; *Biographie du Général François Capoix, le héros de la Bataille de Vertières (18 Novembre 1803), laquelle détermina la capitulation et l'évacuation des troupes françaises de Saint Domingue*, chez l'auteur et Paris, Lib. Cart., 1956: all Port-au-Prince.

Essays: *Essai d'une synthèse de sociologie économique*, Paris, Lib. des Sciences Politiques et Sociales, 1937; *La force de l'idée*, Port-au-Prince, 1905; *La vie de jeune homme, (conférence)*, Port-au-Prince, 1908; *La philosophie de la liberté; comme introduction à la synthèse humaine*, Port-au-Prince, chez l'auteur, 1947.

Medicine: *L'hérédité de la tuberculose*, Port-au-Prince, 1947; *La lésion anatomique et le trouble fonctionnel; une page de philosophie médicale*, Port-au-Prince, Impr. H. Amblard, 1903; *La philosophie des fièvres des pays chauds; essai d'une synthése de pyrétologie tropicale*, Port-au-Prince, Impr. H. Amblard, 1907; *Le lait de chaux dans le traitement de la fièvre typhoide*, Port-au-Prince, 1907; *Questions d'hématologie (à propos des microcytes du sang)*, Paris, A. Maloine, 1908; *Un cas de plaie pénétrante de la poitrine avec paraplégie inférieure*, Port-au-Prince, Impr. H. Amblard, 1904.

Politics: *Appel à la Jeunesse Haitienne: 1-Patriotisme et travail*, Impr. Centrale, 1919; *La croisée des chemins; adresse au Peuple haitien*, Impr. Modèle, 1926; *Le sauvetage national par le retour à la terre* (in several pamphlets), Impr. Aug. A. Héraux, 1922, 1923, 1925, 1935, all Port-au-Prince.

DAMAS, Léon Gontran

(pseudonym: **Lionel George André CABASSOU**)

b. March 28, 1912, Cayenne, Guyane;
d. January 22, 1978, Washington, D. C.

Damas received his primary education in Cayenne and went to Fort-de-France to attend the Lycée Schoelcher where he met Aimé Césaire for the first time. He completed his education in Paris. He studied law and oriental languages, but dropped them to devote his efforts to creating a new black culture-oriented literature.

Damas was introduced to Léopold Sédar Senghor from Africa by Césaire and the trio launched *L'Etudiant Noir* (1934), and with it the cultural movement internationally known as NEGRITUDE.

Among the three poets of Negritude, Damas was the first who published poems, these early works appearing in the review *Esprit* in 1934. In 1937 appeared Damas' *Pigments*, this collection of verses receiving the most appreciative welcome in France and French Africa. The poems were soon "found" to be dangerous to French security in the colonies, however, and the volume was banned in 1939. However, it was translated into at lease one African language.

Damas always believed that Negritude was not limited to one country, for he collected poets and poems from different French-speaking countries and published *Poètes d'expression française, 1900-1945*. This anthology includes poets from most francophone African countries and Guadeloupe, Martinique, Guyane, Indochina, Madagascar, and Réunion, covering some 35 poets and offering 172 poems.

Analyzing the situation of these French-speaking countries at that time, Damas stated:

> *La pauvreté, l'analphabétisme, l'exploitation de l'homme par l'homme, le racisme social et politique dont souffre l'homme de couleur noire ou jaune, le travail forcé, les inégalités, les mensonges, la résignation, les escroqueries, les préjugés, les complaisances, les lâchetés, les démissions, les crimes commis au nom de la liberté, de l'égalité, de la fraternité, voilà le thème de cette poèsie indigène d'expression française.*

Damas went to his homeland on a mission for the Musée de l'Homme in Paris, and on his return he published *Retour de Guyane*.

During the early 1960's, Damas served as editor of the Overseas Department of *Editions Fasquelles,* and in the mid-1960's he travelled widely in the Caribbean and Brazil, doing research on African culture, supported by grants from UNESCO and various foundations. Since 1966 he has been the representative of the Société Africaine de Culture (SAC) at UNESCO, where he is also consultant on African and South African cultural matters. Among his awards and honors are: Officer of the National Order, *Honneur et Mérite,* of the Republic of Haiti; membership in the Société des Africanistes; the Executive Council of SAC; of the Syndicat National des Ecrivains de France; of the Société des Gens de Lettres; and of PEN Club International.

Damas served for a brief period in the French National Assembly in the 1950's, representing Guyana. A life-long socialist, Damas is a militant anti-colonialist and has struggled for Guyanese independence. Though he maintained the family's house in Cayenne until its recent destruction by fire in 1971, he lived most of his life after the thirties in Paris. In the summer of 1970 he came to Georgetown University in Washington, D.C., to lecture on Caribbean and African literature and then received an appointment as professor of literature at Federal City College in Washington. For seven years he was a Visiting Lecturer on African literature and negritude at Howard University's Institute of African Studies and served as Acting Director of Howard's African Studies Department.

Of the negritude group, Damas is considered to be the most original in his use of African motifs from both the Antilles and Africa itself. His verse employs the repetitive, circular pattern of much African dance and song; it often is staccato and acerbic, and is neither nostalgic nor free-associational and surrealistic as is Senghor's on the one hand or Césaire's on the other. In *Pigments* (1937), and *Graffiti* (1952), he uses duplications and repetitions of sound which are not aimed at developing a concept, but, rather, at advancing a feeling of motion and emotion. (The closest thing to his verse technique for readers of English would be the writings of Gertrude Stein.) Damas' early interest in African music bore fruit in his *Poèmes nègres sur des airs africains* (Negro Poems Written to African Airs), published in 1947.

Damas, in his *Black-Label* (1956), an 84-page poem in four parts, sought for more complex expression. Employing his basic technique of staccato lines and overlapping, repetitive phrases and lines, he produced a complex intellectual structure through the device of "leitmotives" and recurring images which "key" his poetic ideas or themes from one part of the poem to the other. The harmonic interrelationships are evocative of the polyphonic textures of traditional African works played on the talking drum and accompanied by dance and chorus and, of course, a music also widely prevalent in the West Indies.

Neuralgies (Neuralgies), issued in 1966, reflects Damas' growing pessimism and deepening mood of hurt and sorrow. He is planning a new volume of poems, many of them written in America, tentatively entitled "Mine de riens" (Mine of Nothing).

Stories collected and adapted for French appear in *Veillées noires* (Black Vigils), published in 1944. An autobiographical work is *Retour de Guyane* (Return from Guyana), published before the war in 1938.

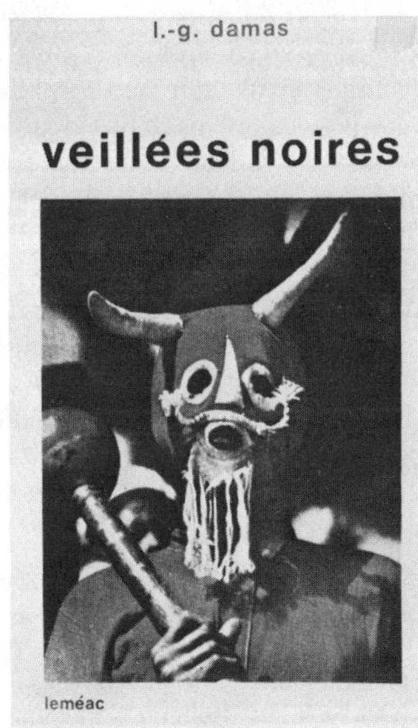

During the past several years in the United States, Damas has also lectured and spoken at many schools and conferences. He attended the Conference on Negritude in Dakar in 1971. Personal friend of Langston Hughes and other great contemporaries in Afro-American poetry, Damas has been active in helping young poets and has "sat for his portrait" to many graduate students in America for their studies of negritude and of black writing. He is represented in many anthologies and has edited several important ones in both French and English.

Writings: Poetry: *Pigments, poèmes,* preface by Robert Desnos, woodcuts, by Frans Maserel, Paris, G.L.M., 1937; A definitive edition introduced by Robert Goffin, Paris, Présence Africaine, 1962 (illustration by Max Pinchinat); *Poèmes nègres sur des airs africains,* Paris, Ed. Guy Levis-Mano, 1948; *Graffiti, poèmes,* Paris, Seghers, 1952; *Black Label,* Paris, Gallimard, 1956; *Névralgies, poèmes* (incl. *Graffiti*), Paris, Présence Africaine, 1964; *Pigments, Névralgies,* Paris, Présence Africaine, 1972.

Essay: *Retour de Guyane,* Paris, Ed. José Corti, 1938.

Stories: *Veillées noires, contes guyanais,* Paris, Stock, 1944; second edition, Montreal, Editions Léméac, 1972.

Editor of Anthologies: *Poètes d'expression française, 1900-1945,* Collection Latitudes Françaises, Paris, Ed. du Seuil, 1947; and *Nouvelle somme de poèsie du monde noir,* (in collaboration with others), Paris, Présence Africaine, 1966 [Cahier spécial No. 57].

Article: "Price-Mars, the father of Haitianism," in *Présence Africaine,* 32-33.

Biographical/Critical Sources: René Piquion: *Léon Gontran Damas, un poète de la négritude,* Port-au-Prince, (mimeo.), 1964; Malu (Maurice A. Lubin): *Etapes d'une visite culturelle,* Port-au-Prince, Impr. de l'Etat, 1964; René Piquion: *Les trois grands de la négritude (Damas, Senghor, Césaire),* Port-au-Prince, Ed. Henri Deschamps, 1964; Ellen C. Kennedy: "Léon Damas: Pigments and the colonized personality. Poems from *Pigments,*" translated into English, *Black World* (Chicago Issue, Jan. 1972), pp. 4-28; Keith Warner, "New Perspectives on Léon Damas" in *Black Images,* II, 1, (Spring, 1973), pp. 3-6; also: "On the Poetry of Negritude" in *The World of Translation* (Papers delivered at the Conference on Literary Translation, held in New York City in May 1970 under the auspices of P.E.N. American Center), New York, P.E.N., North American Center, 1971; Edward A. Jones (ed.), *Voices of Negritude: The Expression of Black Experience in the Poetry of Senghor, Césaire and Damas,* Valley Forge, Pa., Judson, 1971; Mercer Cook, "The Poetry of Léon Damas" in *African Forum,* No. 4 (Spring 1967), pp. 129-132; J.U. Ita, "A propos" (on Léon Damas' *Black Label*), in *African Arts/Arts d'Afrique*, 3, No. 2 (1970), pp. 84-87; Miriam Koshland & Ulli Beier, *African songs of Love, War, Grief and Abuse* (translation of *Poèmes Nègres sur des airs africains*, Ibadan, Nigeria, Mbari Press, 1961.

DAMBREVILLE, Claude

(see under pseudonym: **Anatole CYPRIEN**)

DAMNE, Konrad

(pseudonym for **Eddy Arnold JEAN**)

DANACHE, Berthoumieux

b. November 9, 1878, Saint Marc, Haiti; d. June 6, 1949, Port-au-Prince.
Memoirist, essayist, teacher, lawyer.

After Danache was educated in Saint Marc and Port-au-Prince where he studied law, he spent many years working for the the government. Serving as a chief of the cabinet of President Sudre Dartiguenave, he sadly witnessed the problems and humiliations the Haitian president faced with the American Forces of Occupation and his several books are detailed reports of this period.

Writings: Album: *Annuaire Général d'Haiti* (with Clément Célestin), Port-au-Prince, Impr. Modèle, 1926.

Memoirs: *Choses vues; récits et souvenirs*, 1902, Port-au-Prince, Impr. Chéraquit, 1939; *Le Président Dartiguenave et les Américains*, Port-au-Prince, Impr. de l'Etat, 1950.

DARFOUR, Félix

b. ca. 1790, Darfour, Sudan, East Africa; d. September 2, 1822, Port-au-Prince, Haiti.
Journalist, surveyor, lawyer.

Darfour's name came from his birthplace, Darfour, a region of East Sudan, whence the future Haitian had been taken up by a French general on a mission to Egypt with Bonaparte's army and brought to France. Darfour lived there and received some European education and came to marry a French wife.

After Haiti proclaimed its independence and invited all blacks to become citizens of the new black country, Darfour emigrated to Haiti with an uncle of Beaubrun Ardouin who was returning after forty years of absence. Darfour settled down as a newspaper editor and supported his fellow Afro-Haitians, always seeing Haiti as a potential paradise for Africans.

He founded and managed first *L'Eclaireur ou le Parfait Patriote,* the initial issue being August 5, 1818, and later *L'Avertisseur.* His ideas were esteemed too liberal for the strong-willed President Boyer and Darfour was accused of fomenting social divisions based on color prejudice: light-skinned citizens (mulâtres) looking down on black-skinned people (noirs). He was also charged with being a spy for France. He dared protest to the national parliament, but was indicted and finally sentenced September 2, 1822, and executed. Later considered a martyr, Darfour became a symbol for Haitian writers seeking free expression.

Biographical/Critical Sources: J.B. Francisque, "Hommage aux mânes de Darfour," in *Le Patriote* (July 13, 1848); Pauléus Sannon, "Une victime du journalisme sous Boyer," in *La Ronde* (Oct. 1889); Robert Cornevin: *Le théâtre haitien, des origines à nos jours,* Quebec, 1973, pp. 48-49.

DARLOUZE, René

(pseudonym for **Charles MORAVIA**)

DAUMEC, Gérard

b. 1928, Port-au-Prince, Haiti; d. November 18, 1976, Port-au-Prince.

Poet, politician.

Gérard Daumec received his education in Port-au-Prince. Involved in politics, he became a close confidant to the President, Dr. François Duvalier.

Camille commented on Daumec's négritude and these few lines offer some testimony:

Ils allaient noirs comme une nuit sans étoiles
Les fils d'Afrique aux muscles de metal
Ils allaient berçant leurs craintes et leurs angoisses
Au tangage douloureux du négrier fatal.

Writings: Poetry: *Reflets d'ombre,* preface by Roussan Camille, Port-au-Prince, Impr. de l'Etat, 1952.

Politics: *Réponse à Jacques St-Lôt,* Port-au-Prince, Impr. de l'Etat, 1957; *La Trahison des Maréchaux,* Port-au-Prince, Presses Nationales d'Haiti, 1966; *Rencontre de Deux Grands Leaders de Tiers-Monde* (treating of Emperor Haili Selassie's visit to Dr. François Duvalier), 1966.

DAUPHIN, Marcel

b. July 23, 1910, Port-au-Prince, Haiti.
Poet, playwright, teacher.

Dauphin studied at the Petit Séminaire, Collège Saint-Martial, and graduated from the Faculty of Law of Port-au-Prince. He was a teacher at the Petit Séminaire for many years and later founded his own college named after Jean Jacques Dessalines.

A militant in his poetry, Dauphin's *La Sérénade des opprimés* protests the arrest of peasants who, shoeless and in rags, were caught by police in the streets of the capital. He is now a contributor to the newspaper, *Le Nouvelliste,* with his column "La Rue."

Writings: Poetry: *Cantilènes tropicales,* preface by Léon Lahens, Impr. N. Telhomme, 1940; *Le culte du drapeau,* Impr. du Collège Vertières, 1943; *La sérénade des opprimés,* Impr. du Collège Vertières, 1946; *Reflet des heures,* Compagnie Lithog. d'Haiti, 1961; *Haiti, mon pays* (Edition Mercédès Westen), Impr. Dorsinville, 1963; *Hommage au drapeau, Dix-huit Mai 1803,* 1953; *Le chant de l'esclave,* Ed. Mercédès Westen, 1950; *Flammèches,* Eds. Fardin, 1976: all published in Port-au-Prince.

Plays: *Boisrond Tonnerre* (3 acts), Port-au-Prince, Impr. Dorsinville, 1954; *Neila,* 1955; *Pierre Sully,* Port-au-Prince, Impr. de l'Etat, 1960.

DAVERTIGE

(pseudonym for **Villard DENIS**)
b. September 2, 1940, Port-au-Prince, Haiti.
Poet, painter.

Davertige studied at Colbert Bonhomme's College, and at Toussaint Louverture Lycée. He published his collection of poems, *Idem,* which at first failed of any attention. However, after a favorable review by the French critic, Alain Bosquet, who proclaimed his talent, Seghers published in Paris a revised edition of *Idem* with Alain Bosquet's preface.

Writings: Poetry: *Idem . . . avec un poème autographe illustré par l'auteur: Poèsies 1960-1961,* Collection Haiti Littéraire, Port-au-Prince, Impr. N.A. Théodore, 1962; *Idem et autres poèmes,* Paris, Seghers, 1964; *Idem,* followed by *Le passage et les voyageurs,* Montréal, Nouvelle Optique, 1978.

DAVID, Placide

b. September 9, 1885, Gonaives, Haiti; d. October 5, 1967, Pétionville, Haiti.
Playwright, lawyer, historian, journalist.

David received his education in Port-au-Prince, including a degree from the law school in the capital. Entering politics very early, aided by his father, David in time became Counsellor of State and later head of the President's Office. He later became Director of the National Museum.

He was chief editor of the famed journal,

La Presse, that led the opposition against the American occupation and the Haitian government of Louis Borno, President of Haiti.

David was named Haitian Ambassador in Paris and later went in the same capacity to Madrid under the Duvalier administration.

Writings: Anthology: *Discours parlementaires* (in collaboration with Daniel Apollon and Edouard Dépestre), Port-au-Prince, Impr. de l'Abeille, n.d. (but 1911).

History: *Sur les rives du passé; choses de Saint-Domingue,* Paris, Ed. "La Caravelle," 1947 (this book won the Grand Prix de Littérature des Antilles, Paris, 1947); a second edition appeared in Canada, Léméac, 1972, but it carried one addition, a study of Pierre Pinchinat; *L'héritage colonial en Haiti,* Madrid, Langa & Cia, 1959.

Play: *Le torrent* (3 acts, written in collaboration with Dominique Hippolyte). This play was awarded the first prize at the dramatic contest sponsored by the President of Haiti, Sténio Vincent (1938).

DELISLE, Gérard

b. 1929, Basse-Terre, Guadeloupe.
Poet.

Delisle completed his classical studies in the Lycée Carnot in Pointe-à-Pitre and then went on in 1947 to Paris to study law. Belatedly attracted to poetry, especially Rimbaud, Verlaine and Plekanov, he dropped his legal studies to seek out a career as a full-time writer.

Writings: Poetry: *Rhapsodie Caraibe,* Paris, Gallimard, 1960; the title poem is found in *La Poésie Antillaise,* Maryse Condé, ed., Paris, Fernand Nathan, 1977.

DELORME, Démesvar

b. February 10, 1831, Cap-Haitien; d. December 25, 1901, Paris.
Novelist, storywriter, essayist, memoirist, educator, diplomat.

Delorme attended the primary school of Cap-Haitien and the Lycée Philipe Guerrier. He taught in a grade school for boys, then at the College Adelina, before entering government service in the Ministry of Public Instruction. He was elected Deputy of Cap-Haitien in 1862. He was Minister of the Interior, Agriculture and Navy under President Salnave, before being named Minister Plenipotentiary at Berlin and at the Holy See from 1890 to 1895.

Delorme practiced journalism. He started the periodical *L'Avenir* and contributed to *Le Progrès, L'Opinion Nationale, Le Ralliement* and for some time was the Director of *Le Moniteur.*

Delorme, one of Haiti's earliest professional men of letters, studied in Europe from 1853-1859, and was more European than Haitian in his interests. He was instrumental in a heavy purchase of books looking to the establishment of a National Library and organized many literary conferences to revive Haitian culture after the oppressive 12-year regime of Emperor Soulouque.

When Delorme died, a French journal paid homage to him:

> *La nation haitienne perd en lui un de ses plus glorieux enfants, la littérature française se voit privée d'un remarquable représentant; le monde entier est dans le regret de la disparition d'une belle intelligence, d'une rare force morale dont l'humanité avait le droit d'être fière. Il ne m'appartient pas d'apprécier la personnalité politique de Démesvar Delorme, nombre d'haitiens sont autrement désignés pour satisfaire à cette tâche avec une compétence plus sûre. Mais, comme écrivain de langue française, il est intimement lié, et par la valeur de sa production et par la nature de ses rapports avec les plus célèbres esprits de son temps, à l'histoire littéraire de notre propre pays.*

Though most of his published work was in the area of his career experiences, he wrote many stories and published two novels in the 1870's. Inspired by Goethe's *Sorrows of Werther* and by Hugo and Dumas, he made the hero of his *Francesca, les jeux du sort* an oriental prince, and the hero of his *Le damné* a Germanic figure, Ulrick von Krussnacht. Considered by his contemporaries "le doyen des lettres haitiennes," he suffered from a reaction against the over-gallization of Haitian culture in the 1890's and though now considered a literary and intellectual figure of some importance, he is no longer seen as in the mainstream of Haitian cultural development.

Writings: Novels: *Francesca, les jeux du sort,* Paris, Ed. Dentu, 1873; *Le damné,* 2 vols., Paris, Challamer, 1877.

Story: *L'Albanaise.*

Essays: *Les Petits; la Hollande,* Brusells, Soc. Anonyme C. Schepens, 1898; *Les théoriciens au pouvoir; causeries historiques,* Paris, 1870; *Réflexions diverses sur Haiti,* Paris, E. Dentu, 1873; "Le sang latin en Amérique," in *Revista Latino-Americana* (1874).

Politics: *Les paisibles,* Paris, Impr. Alcan-Lévy, 1874; *La reconnaissance du général Salnave,* Paris, Impr. Centrale des Chemins de Fer (A. Chaix et Cie.), 1868; *La démocratie et le préjugé de couleur aux Etats-Unis,* Paris, n.d. (but 1862); *Les nationalités américaines et le système Monroe,* 1862.

Memoirs: *1842 au Cap; tremblement de terre* (published and prefaced by his nephew, Jean M. Lambert), Cap-Haitien, Impr. du Progrès (E. Almonacy), 1942 (a fragment of his otherwise unpublished memoirs).

Biographical/Critical Sources: Ernst Trouillot, *Démesvar Délorme,* Impr. N.A. Théodore, 1958; Hénock Trouillot, *Le cas Démesvar Délorme ou Introduction à une sociologie de la littérature haitienne,* Impr. des Antilles, 1968; Georges Sylvain, article on Délorme in *La Ronde* (Oct. 5, 1898); Auguste Viatte, *Histoire littéraire de l'Amérique française,* Quebec, 1953, pp. 383-386; Ghislain Gouraige, *Histoire de la littérature haitienne,* 1960, pp. 30-34; Pradel Pompilus & Frères de l'Instruction Chrétienne, *Manuel illustré d'histoire de la littérature haitienne,* 1961, pp. 165-176: all Port-au-Prince except as noted.

DENIS, Lorimer

(pseudonym: **Aristide DE SABE**)

b. October 20, 1904, Cap-Haitien; d. August 17, 1957, Port-au-Prince.
Critic, scholar, teacher.

Denis' schooling started in Cap-Haitien and was completed in Port-au-Prince at the Lycée Pétion and the Faculty of Law. He was a teacher in many secondary schools of Port-au-Prince, became Director of the Bureau of Ethnology created by Jacques Roumain. He was a special Representative of Haiti at the Centennial of the Republic of Liberia in 1947.

On or about 1932, Louis Diaquoi is credited with having popularized the word GRIOT as the term for the story teller of Africa, by his articles in *Le Nouvelliste or l'Action Nationale* on the past glories of Africa. Lorimer Denis, with Dr. François Duvalier, Carl Brouard, Kléber Georges Jacob and Clément Magloire St-Aude, founded a cultural movement which stressed Africanism and "Haitianism." Their magazine which expressed their ideas and carried their studies of Haitian culture was naturally entitled *Les Griots.* It lasted some five issues (1938-1940), not too bad considering the histories of little reviews.

Writings: Criticism: *Les tendances d'une génération* (with Dr. François Duvalier and Arthur Bonhomme), Impr. du Collège Vertières, 1934.

Sociology: *Le problème des classes à travers l'histoire d'Haiti* (with Dr. François Duvalier), Impr. de l'Etat, 1948, second printing, 1965; *Evolution stadiale du vodou* (with Dr. François Duvalier), Impr. de l'Etat, 1944; *Chants et jeux des enfants haitiens,* Impr. de l'Etat, 1949; *Essai d'organographie haitienne* (with Emmanuel C. Paul), Publication du Bureau d'Ethnologie de la République d'Haiti, Impr. V. Valcin, 1948: all in Port-au-Prince, *Le musée du Bureau d'Ethnologie d'Haiti,* Impr. de l'Etat, 1953.

Polemics: *L'avenir du pays et l'action néfaste de Mr Foisset* (with Dr. François Duvalier, Michel Aubourg, and Léonce Viaud).

DENIS, Villard

(see under pseudonym: **DAVERTIGE**)

DENNERY, Germaine

b. ca. 1909, Cayes, Haiti.
Poet, storywriter, journalist.

Germaine Dennery studied in Port-au-Prince and has contributed to various literary journals. She is a member of the Société des Lettres et des Arts. Her one published volume is the product of a trip made to Europe.

Writings: Tourism: *Chants du souvenir,* preface by Gaston Picard, Port-au-Prince, Cie. Lithographique, 1939.

DEPESTRE, Edouard

b. August 18, 1880, Jacmel, Haiti;
d. August 15, 1939, Saint Marc, Haiti.
Storywriter, folklorist, physician.

Depestre started his studies in Jacmel and completed them in Port-au-Prince. He was a teacher at the Lycée Pétion and went to work at the Haitian parliament. He studied medicine and became a physician at the Military Hospital of Saint Marc.

His 1958 re-publication of Father Marco Dépestre's stories, originally appearing in *La Presse, Le Temps,* and *Haiti-Journal,* was preceded by Edouard Dépestre's study of Haitian folkloric themes.

Writings: Anthology: *Discours parlementaires* (in collaboration with Daniel Apollon et Placide David), Port-au-Prince, Impr. de l'Abeille, n.d.

Politics: *La faillite d'une démocratie; politique et administration haitienne (1908-1915),* Port-au-Prince, Impr. de l'Abeille, 1916.

Stories: *Contes du docteur, Thèmes du folklore haitien,* Petit-Goâve, La Presse du Sauveur, 1958.

DEPESTRE, René

b. August 29, 1926, Jacmel, Haiti.
Poet, storywriter, essayist, journalist, novelist.

Depestre started his primary classes at the Frère Clément School of Jacmel, his secondary studies at the Lycée Pinchinat and the Lycée Pétion of Port-au-Prince. He has been editor-in-chief of *La Ruche* (Organe de la Jeunesse Révolutionnaire) in the capital which was banned by the government in 1945, and he took part in the revolution of January, 1946, which overthrew and then exiled President Elie Lescot.

He went to France and attended the Institut d'Etudes Politiques of the University of Paris, taking the *Licence ès-lettres* at the Sorbonne and a diploma in history and art at Paris' Musée de l'Homme. He traveled to eastern Europe in the late forties and reportedly joined the Communist Party in France in 1946.

His revolutionary volume of verse, *Etincelles,* written when he was only 19, went through two editions in 1945 and quickly established Depestre as the leading spokesman for the radical young generation.

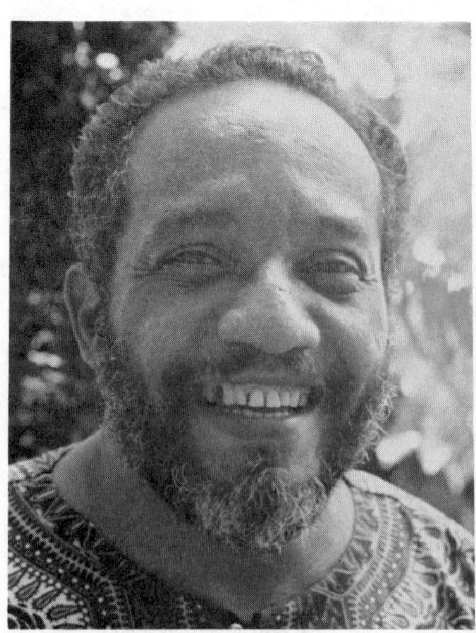

Despite his efforts at establishing a new regime, his own uncompromising communist orientation and sympathy for the masses led to his being forced into exile in France. In Paris he continued to write his polemical Marxist poetry, all of which is still banned in Haiti.

After 11 years abroad, Depestre returned home in 1958, but dissatisfied with Duvalier's government, he left Haiti and settled down in Cuba. His many poems and essays make him possibly the most well-known speaker for the radical poets in the Pan-African world. Aimé Césaire, his colleague, gives such a definition of René Dépestre: "Il est la poète de la fraîcheur, de la sève qui monte, de la vie qui s'épanouit, du fleuve de l'espoir qui irrigue le terreau du présent et le travail des hommes."

Paulène Aspel, commenting on *Poète à Cuba* (1976), says Depestre ". . . seeks to demonstrate that poetry and revolution do fertilize and grow from a common soil. And later she writes, "The poet's idiom is relaxed yet firm, with numerous pleasant metaphors. Free from traditional French rhythms, the prosaic journey of René Dépestre is liberated by a multiple re-entry permit into poetry."

Writings: Poetry: *Etincelles,* Port-au-Prince, Impr. de l'Etat, 1945, in two separate editions; *Gerbe de sang,* Port-au-Prince, Impr. de l'Etat, 1946; *Végétation de clartés,* preface by Aimé Césaire, Paris, Seghers, 1951; *Traduit du grand large, poème de ma patrie enchainée,* Paris, Seghers, 1952; *Minerai noir,* Paris, Présence Africaine, 1957, in Spanish: *Mineral negro,* Havana, Revolución, 1962; *Journal d'un animal marin,* Paris, Seghers, 1964; *Un arc-en-ciel pour l'occident chrétien, poème mystère vaudou,* Paris, Présence Africaine, 1966, in Spanish as *Un arcoiris para el Ocidente cristiano,* Havana, Casa de las Américas, 1967; prose and poetry in *Por la revolución,* Havana, 1969, and his verse is in many reviews and collections, including *Negritude: Black Poetry from Africa and the Caribbean,* New York, October House, 1970, edited by N. R. Shapiro. Also: *Cantata de octubre,* Havana, Instituto del Libro, Arte y Literatura, 1968 (160 pp.); and in original French text as *Cantate d'Octobre: à la Mort du Commandant. Ernesto Che Guevara,* Algiers, Société Nationale d'Edition et de Diffusion, 1969; and *Poète à Cuba,* Paris, Oswald, 1976.

Novel: *El Palo Ensebado,* Havana, Instituto del libro, 1975; Santo Domingo, Ediciones de Tailler, 1977.

Essays: "Une rose de vents noirs (chronique par David Diop, Bernard Dadié et J. Rabemananjara," in *Présence Africaine,* No. 11 (Dec. 1956 and Jan. 1957), pp. 110-115; "Les sept piliers de l'innocence: Makandal, Toussaint Louverture, Dessalines, Antonio Maceo, Charlemagne Peralte, Patrice Lumumba, Malcolm X," in *Présence Africaine,* No. 57 (1966), pp. 205-213; "Les métamorphoses de la négritude en Amérique," in *Présence Africaine,* No. 75 (1970), pp. 19-33; "Jean Price-Mars et el mito del Orfeo Negro," in Depestre's *Por la revolucion,* op. cit.; "Introduction à un art poètique haitien," in *Optique,* No. 24 (Feb. 1956); *La responsabilité des intellectuels devant leur peuple,* Port-au-Prince, Eds. Coumbite, 1958 (the text of a speech delivered in Haiti, March, 1958, before the Société Nationale d'Art Dramatique); "Langston Hughes, ou la main sur la charrue de la poèsie," in *Présence Africaine,* No. 58 (1966), pp. 189-193; "Problemas de la identidad del hombre negro en las literaturas antillanas," in *Casa de las Américas,* No. 53 (1969); and see his preface to Auguste Macouba's play: *Eia! Man-maille-la,* Honfleur, P.J. Oswald, 1968 (Macouba is the pen-name of Martinican writer Auguste Armet). Also see: *Pour la révolution, pour la poèsie,* Havana, Institut du Livre, 1968; second edition, Quebec, Léméac, 1974; *Cantate d'Octobre* (ed. bilingue), Havana, Institut du Livre, 1968; "Problems of identity for the Black Man," in *Caribbean Literature* (Sep. 1973), pp. 51-61; and preface to Jacques S. Alexis' *El Compadre General Sol* (Havana, 1974).

Stories: *Alléluia pour une femme-jardin,* Quebec, Léméac, 1973, folkstories of fantasy, sensuality, and pure delight in the flesh; anti-puritan and hardly Marxist.

Translation of Depestre's work: *Arc-en-ciel . . . ,* rendered in Spanish by Herberto Padillo as *Un arcoiris para el occidente christiano: Poema, misterio, vodu,* Havana, Casa de las Américas, 1967.

Translations by Depestre into French: *Le grand Zoo* of N. Guillén, Paris, Seghers, 1966;

Poèsie cubaine, an anthology, Havana, Institut du Livre, 1959, 1966, 1967; *Avec les mêmes mains* of Roberto Fernández Retamar, Paris, P.J. Oswald, 1968.

Biographical/Critical Sources: Dépestre, Poeta a Cuba, Studio e Antologia (in Italian), by Ugo Salati, Milano, Edizioni Academia, 1973, and review by Paulène Aspel of *Poète à Cuba,* Paris, Oswald, 1976 (201 pp.), in *World Literature Today* (Spring 1977); Valentin Y. Mudimbe, "Un goût de la parole, *Le journal d'un animal marin* [de René Dépestre]," in *Présence Africaine,* No. 79 (1971), pp. 85-95; Naomi M. Garret, *The Renaissance of Haitian Poetry,* Paris, Présence Africaine, 1963; Jacques Nantet, *Panorama de la littérature noire d'expression française,* Paris, 1972; Keith K. Warner, "René Depestre, the not so terrible 'enfant terrible'," in *Black Images,* No. 3 (Toronto), pp. 46-54; Hal Wylie, "Creative Exile: Dennis Brutus and René Dépestre," paper for African Literature Association, April 8, 1978.

DERVAIN, Eugène Emile

b. February 4, 1928, Saint-Esprit, Martinique.

Poet, playwright, storywriter, painter, lawyer, judge.

Born into a family of teachers on both sides, Dervain started his studies at the primary school of Saint-Esprit. He was a student at the Lycée Victor Schoelcher where he had Aimé Césaire as his teacher. With his schoolmates, Georges Desportes, Félix Jouanelle, Edouard Glissant, and Fourneuf, Dervain founded a weekly magazine, *La Jeune Tribune;* and through the works of Leo Frobénius and Jules Monnerot they discovered Africa and became familiar with the surealism of André Breton and Desnos.

In 1947, Dervain went to Paris and met many African students at the Foyer des Etudiants de la France d'Outre-Mer. After earning a law degree in France in 1959, he emigrated to Guinea in West Africa where he was named a judge in the early days of independence. Later, he and his wife removed to the Ivory Coast, his wife's home, where he is now serving as judge and where he is now an Ivorien citizen.

Dervain's first works are based on African themes. The two plays he has published exploit the griot stories of the great Bambara epics based on the life of King Da Monson, ruler of 18th-century Segou. Dervain has of course introduced into his work a certain modern psychology and feeling for the need of unity for a still divided Africa. (Da Monzon who extended the Bambara empire to the Kingdom of Kong [today's Ivory Coast] then to Timbucto in the north, and finally to Gao to the east.)

A painter and designer, Dervain has also illustrated the books *Kiroa,* by Moune de Rivel, and *Bakary, enfant du Mali,* by André Clair.

Writings: Poetry: "Chant pour un chef," followed by "Poème à Koffi," in Lilyan Kesteloot's *Anthologie négro-africaine,* Verviers, Belgium, Gérard & Cie., 1967; "Grand Bassam," in *Fraternité Matin,* No. 1220 (Dec. 17, 1968).

Plays: *Saran ou la reine scélérate,* followed by *La Langue et le scorpion* (4 acts, both in one volume, introduction by Lilyan Kesteloot), Yaoundé, CLE, 1968; *Termites*, Paris, 1976; and also unpublished plays: *La Reine Pokou; Chaka; Antigone; Macouba Congo; La dixième part.*

Biographical/Critical Sources: Review by Kamissoko Gaoussou: "Triomphe de Termites, Samedi," in *Fraternité Matin*, No. 1625 (April 21, 1970), p. 2; Richard Bonneau, review of *Saran ou la reine scélérate* and *La Langue et le Scorpion*, Eburnéa (Abidjan), No. 54 (Dec. 1971), pp. 38-39.

DESCHAMPS, Marguerite

(pseudonym for **Michaëlle LAFONTANT-MEDARD**)

DESLANDES, Célie-Diaquoi

(see under **Célie DIAQUOI-DESLANDES**)

DESLANDES, Emile

b. December, 1863, Port-au-Prince, Haiti; d. 1920's(?), Port-au-Prince.
Playwright, lawyer.

Deslandes attended the schools of Port-au-Prince and completed his studies at the Lycée Pétion of Port-au-Prince. He became a lawyer.

He was head of office at the Department of Justice. He served as government commissioner for the Court of Port-au-Prince, and later was named Minister of Interior.

Writings: Plays: *Nigra*, and *Les cinq puissances*, both performed in 1882, but unpublished.

DESPORTES, Auguste

b. ca. 1925, Fort-de-France, Martinique; d. ca. 1962.
Poet.

Desportes completed his schooling through the Lycée Schoelcher in Fort-de-France. Despite his untimely death at an early age, he was considered one of the most promising poets of his generation.

Auguste was the younger brother of Georges Desportes, the disciple of Aimé Césaire, and a founder of the *Revue Caravelle*.

Writings: Poetry: in Auguste Joyau's *Anthologie des poètes martiniquais*, Fort-de-France, Eds. des Horizons Caraibes, 1961; in N.R. Shapiro's *Negritude Black Poetry from Africa and the Caribbean*, New York, October House, 1970 (the poem is "Ecoeurement et Départ"); and in several journals.

DESPORTES, Georges

b. 1921, Ducos, Martinique.
Poet, journalist, storywriter.

Desportes received his education at the Lycée Victor Schoelcher, where Aimé Césaire was his teacher and strongly influenced his development. He completed his education in France.

Considered by some critics to be the most brilliant disciple of Césaire, Georges Desportes was born into a well-to-do middle class mulatto family. Often ill and unable to participate in strenuous physical activity, Desportes turned to writing, and in the period of great literary activity which followed the fall of the Vichy regime in Martinique in 1943, he participated in a series of short-lived newspapers and reviews: *Le cri des jeunes, France-Jeu*, and *Horizons Caraibes*. Desportes founded the student journal *Caravelle* in 1947 to spread pan-African and negritudist ideas.

Desportes has worked in publicity, journalism, and the local office of the French government broadcasting system, the ORTF. His poetry has appeared in two collections, *Les Marches souveraines* (1956), and *Sous l'oeil fixe du soleil* (1961). Both collections testify to his concern for his people and the future of the island.

In *Kaleidoscope,* he writes:

Mais il y a une île dans la mer des Antilles,
Une ile de bambous, de cases, de manguiers;
C'est le pays où les nègres vont pieds nus!
Les femmes capresses et les coupeurs de cannes!
C'est ce pays que chante le poète nègre.

and also in these verses extracted from *Autodafé*:

Nous avons délaissé les hordes, les défroques,
Nous nous sommes dépouillés de nos vêtements d'Europe
En brutes magnifiques et barbares que nous sommes;

Et nous crions notre joie d'être libres
Nous chantons notre délivrance et notre affranchissement
Sous le ciel lumineux des tropiques caraibes;
Et le tam-tam résonne notre allégresse . . .
Sur nos faces épanouies, larges et détendues;
. . .
Et nous lançons au monde notre défi primitif
Notre défi prognathe!

His recent book, *Cette ile qui est la nôtre,* is a provocative prose-poem with certain sections written in dialogue. The poet searches for a new truth and finds French colonialism and racial prejudice everywhere in his beloved isle.

Writings: Poetry: *Les marches souveraines,* Paris, Ed. P. Seghers, 1956; *Sous l'oeil fixe du soleil; poèmes masquès,* Paris, Debresse, 1961; *Soliloques pour mauvais rêves,* Fort-de-France, Sonaubry, 1958; also verse in *Nouvelle somme de poèsie du monde noir,* Paris, Présence Africaine, 1966. His most recent volume is: *Cette île qui est la nôtre,* Ottawa, Ed. Léméac, 1973.

DESROUSSELS, Félix

(pseudonym for **Jean-Baptiste DORISMOND**)

DESROY, Annie

(née **Anne-Marie Lerebours; Mme Etienne Bourand**)

b. May 4, 1893, Port-au-Prince, Haiti; d. October 2, 1948, Port-au-Prince.
Novelist, playwright, teacher.

Mme. Etienne Bourand, born Anne Marie Lerebours, was educated in Port-au-Prince. She started her career as a teacher and became a Director of Centre d'Etudes Universitaires where Haitian girls first received their baccalaureate first and second parts.

When the Ligue Féminine d'Action Sociale was organized by women claiming their rights and demanding an amendment of the law regarding women, Mrs. Bourand became a militant member.

Writings: Novel: *Le Joug,* Port-au-Prince, Impr. Modèle, 1934.

Plays: *Et l'amour vient* (comedy), performed in 1921; *La cendre du passé* (also a comedy, performed in 1931).

Biographical/Critical Sources: Ghislain Gouraige, *Histoire de la littérature haitienne,* 1960, pp. 362-363; Robert Cornevin, *Le théâtre haitien, des origines à nos jours,* 1973, p. 138; also see article by Yvette Tardieu Feldman, "Une Romancière haitienne méconnue: Annie Desroy (1893-1948)," in *Conjonction,* No. 124, (Port-au-Prince, Aug. 1974), pp. 35-52.

DESTOUCHES, Dantès

b. February 6, 1862, Port-au-Prince, Haiti; d. January 22, 1912, Port-au-Prince.
Travel-writer, physician.

Educated in Haiti and France, Destouches had a long public career in Port-au-Prince and was professor of medicine in the capital's medical school (1883-1902).

He contributed personal essays, mostly on his travels, to local journals and published works on Haitian plants.

A statue of him has been erected in Port-au-Prince and an important street bears his name.

Writings: In manuscript: *Etudes sur la flore haitienne; Carnet de voyage.*

Biographical/Critical Sources: Le Docteur Destouches, by many contributors, including Seymour Pradel, Port-au-Prince, Impr. de l'Abeille, 1912; Dantès Bellegarde, *Ecrivains haitiens,* article on Dantès Destouches, Port-au-Prince, Ed. Henri Deschamps, 1950, pp. 166-171.

DEVIEUX-DEHOUX, Liliane

b. December 29, 1942, Port-au-Prince, Haiti.
Poet, novelist, storywriter.

Liliane Dévieux received her education in Port-au-Prince. She went to Paris to further her studies. In Montreal she won her Licence-ès-lettres and later graduated from the Ecole Normale Supérieure. She lives in Montreal with her family.

Dehoux has published several poems in *Poèsie Québec* and *Prométhée* and many articles in *Digest Eclair.*

Writings: Novel: *L'Amour, oui. La Mort, Non,* Sherbrooke, Eds. Naaman, 1976; *Le Vent de l'amandier* (to be published).

Short Stories: "Complainte pour un voleur" and "Métempsychose" in *L'Atelier des Inédits* (Radio, Canada); "Un Immigrant," in *Actualité,* and "Le dahlia."

DIAQUOI-DESLANDES, Célie

(also: **Célie-Diaquoi DESLANDES**)
b. September 11, 1907, Gonaives, Haiti.
Poet, civil servant.

Célie Diaquoi was educated in Port-au-Prince and has been involved in many social programs as an employee of the government.

Writings: Poetry: *Chants du coeur,* Port-au-Prince, Impr, Serge Bissainthe, 1963; *Arpent d'amour; chansons feutrées,* Port-au-Prince, Eds. Henri Deschamps, 1967; *Crépuscule aux cils d'or,* Port-au-Prince, La Phalange, 1969.

DODARD, Antoine

b. August, 1923, Gonaives, Haiti.
Poet.

Dodard began his studies in Gonaives at the Christian Brothers' school and the Lycée of Gonaives, completing them in Port-au-Prince at the Petit Séminaire Collège Saint Martial. He was an employee at the Bank of the Republic of Haiti in Gonaives for a period during which time he contributed to *Artibonite-Journal,* edited by Hébert Magloire.

Dodard eventually emigrated to the United States to live in New York City.

Writings: Poetry: *Tambour (poèmes),* published with *Face à face* by Louis Duplessis-Louverture in same volume, Gonaives, Les Editions des Presses Artibonitiennes, 1954.

DOMINGUE, Jules

b. 1862, Port-au-Prince, Haiti; d. March 7, 1940, Port-au-Prince.
Novelist, essayist.

Domingue completed his education in Paris after studying in Port-au-Prince. When returned to Haiti, he settled in Pétionville, where he was a practicing agriculturist. Later, he served in the national administration under President Florvil Hyppolite.

Writings: Essay: *La Tortue et la Gonave,* Port-au-Prince, Goldmann et Cie., 1887.

Novel: *Les deux amours d'Adrien ou l'hérédité psychologique; moeurs haitiennes,* Corbeil Impr. Typ. Ed. Crété, 1902; *Melanie* (unpublished).

DORCELY, Roland

b. 1931, Port-au-Prince, Haiti.
Poet, painter.

Unlike most Haitian poets, Dorcely was born in a very modest household, his father being a butcher. From 1952-53, after local schooling in Haiti, with help from the Institut Français d'Haiti, he studied painting in Paris. Again, because of his having sprung from simple stock, his work, both art and poetry, is natural, full of sympathy for the everyday sights or experiences of the ordinary people, with little of the strain and intellectual effort evident in even the most "engagé" of the bourgeois poets and artists of his country.

Writings: Poetry: no separate volume, but his work appears in *HAITI, poètes noirs,* Paris, Présence Africaine, 1951, Special Issue No. 12; in *Conjonction,* (Feb., June and Oct. 1949 and Feb. and April 1951); and in *Les Temps Modernes,* Paris (Feb. 1950).

Biographical/Critical Sources: Philippe North, "Au Centre d'art, L'Exposition Dorcély-Lazarre," in *Conjonction* (June 1949), a publication of the Institut Français d'Haiti; see also Michel Leiris' "Martinique, Guadeloupe, Haiti," in *Temps modernes* (Feb. 1950), pp. 1345-1385; and Naomi M. Garret, *The Renaissance in Haitian Poetry,* Paris, Présence Africaine, 1963.

DORET, Frédéric

b. January 12, 1866, Miragoâne, Haiti; d. January 17, 1935, Paris.
Creole-writing scholar, storywriter, translator, engineer.

Doret studied at the Collège Saint-Martial and the Ecole Nationale Supérieure des Mines in France, in preparation for his life's work as an engineer. In 1902, he founded the Ecole des Sciences Appliquées in Port-au-Prince (with engineers Jacques and Chavineau Durocher, Horace Ethéart, Louis Roy and the lawyer Auguste Bonamy), the nation's first school of engineering, of which he became the first director.

Doret always had a strong interest in literature, however, and his creole adaptation of the *Fables* of La Fontaine was one of the earliest efforts to employ the local patois as a language of instruction and entertainment. Publishing many articles in local journals, he also edited the French magazine, *La Petite Revue,* for many years during his long sojourn in Paris, where he died in his 69th year.

Writings: Abécédaire à l'usage de la jeunesse haitienne et précis historique, chronologique et géographique sur l'ile d'Haiti jusqu'en 1900, Paris, Ateliers Haitiens (L.W.N. Doret), 1900; *Petit syllabaire haitien basé sur la langue populaire d'Haiti; adopté par le Département de l'Instruction Publique pour les écoles primaires,* Port-au-Prince, chez l'auteur, 1905; *Les premiers pas dans la grammaire,* Paris, 1924; *Pour amuser nos tout petits,* Paris, Impr. des Orphelins-apprentis, 1924.

Politics: *Comment je conçois une constitution d'Haiti,* Port-au-Prince, Impr. de l'Abeille, 1916.

Education: *Lettre au Congrès Haitien de l'Education Nationale,* Paris, Impr. des Orphelins-apprentis d'Auteuil, 1922.

Essay: *Quelques suggestions au sujet de l'Ecole des Sciences Appliquées,* Port-au-Prince, 1917.

Biographical/Critical Sources: Dantès Bellegarde: *Ecrivains Haitiens,* lère partie, Port-au-Prince, Ed. Henri Deschamps, 1950, essay, "Frédéric Doret," pp. 183-190.

DORISMOND, Jacques

b. October 8, 1924, Port-au-Prince, Haiti.
Poet, journalist, public servant.

Dorismond received his education in Port-au-Prince. He practiced journalism and he published poems and articles in *Chantiers, Flambeau, Le Soir* and *Le Nouvelliste.*

He is a long-time employee of Haiti's Department of Finance.

Writings: Poetry: *La Terre qui s'ouvre* (Collection Haitiana), Port-au-Prince, Impr. de l'Etat, 1950.

DORISMOND, Jean-Baptiste

(pseudonym: **Félix DESROUSSELS**)

b. October 27, 1891, Port-au-Prince, Haiti; d. late 1950's(?).

Poet, journalist.

Dorismond was educated in Port-au-Prince. He spent all of his life as an employee of the General Printing Office of the government.

Writings: Poetry: *Vers le jour, la lumière; poèmes,* Port-au-Prince, Impr. de l'Etat, 1941; *Sur les traces de Caonabo et de Toussaint Louverture; poèmes caraibes,* Port-au-Prince, Impr. de l'Etat, 1953; *L'Ile d'Amour (à la recherche des lumières du monde), poèmes caraibes,* Port-au-Prince, Impr. de l'Etat, 1954. (All of his collections appeared under his pseudonym, Félix Desroussels, with prefaces by Jean-Baptiste Dorismond.)

DORSAINVIL, Jean-Baptiste

b. June 17, 1865, Port-au-Prince, Haiti; d. 1928, Paris.

Essayist, historian, teacher, diplomat.

Dorsainvil was educated at the Lycée Pétion of Port-au-Prince where he was later professor and then the Director in 1896. He was elected Deputy of Port-au-Prince in 1901. He served as Minister of Haiti in London.

Writings: Essays: *Essai historique sur l'esclavage,* Port-au-Prince, 1886; *Histoire des flibustiers et boucaniers de Saint Domingue,* Port-au-Prince, Impr. H. Amblard, 1886; *Essai sur l'histoire de l'établissement des institutions et des moeurs de Saint Domingue jusqu'en 1789,* 1ère partie, Port-au-Prince, Typ. L'Haitienne, 1892; 2ème partie, Ed. Impr. H. Amblard, 1893.

History: *Cours complet d'histoire d'Haiti à l'usage des écoles,* Paris, Impr. Dubois et Bauer, 1912; *Cours d'histoire d'Haiti à l'usage de l'enseignement primaire supérieur (1492-1804),* Paris; *Cours d'histoire d'Haiti à l'usage de l'enseignement secondaire (1630-1789),* Port-au-Prince, Impr. Ed. Chenet, n.d.; *Cours d'histoire d'Haiti à l'usage de l'enseignement secondaire (1804-1889),* Paris, Impr. Dubois et Bauer, 1912.

Economics: *Etudes économiques sur Haiti: du travail,* Port-au-Prince, Impr. B. Chapotin, 1883; *La monnaie, la circulation fiduciaire et les échanges internationaux,* Paris, M. Giard & E. Brière, Lib. Ed., 1913; *Les sociétés coopératives de crédit,* Port-au-Prince, Impr. H. Amblard, 1899.

Law: *De la démocratie représentative; histoire et principes,* Port-au-Prince, Impr. J. Verrollot, 1900; *Eléments de droit constitutionnel; étude juridique et critique sur la constitution de la République d'Haiti,* Paris, M. Giard & E. Brière, Lib. Ed.,1912.

DORSAINVIL, Justin Chrysostome

(usually called **J.C.**)

b. December 20, 1880, Port-au-Prince, Haiti; d. September 8, 1942, Port-au-Prince.

Essayist, teacher, scholar, physician.

Dorsainvil, considered one of the major Haitian scholars, completed his schooling at the Lycée Pétion of Port-au-Prince. He entered the Faculty of Medicine where he graduated in 1905. He taught at the L'Ecole Lancastérienne and the Lycée Pétion. He long served as Head of the Education Division at the Department of Public Education.

Writings: Essays: *Militarisme et hygiène sociale,* Port-au-Prince, Impr. C. Magloire, 1909; *L'échec d'hier et l'effort pour l'avenir,* Port-au-Prince, Impr. H. Amblard, 1915.

Education: *Le problème de l'enseignement primaire en Haiti,* Port-au-Prince, Impr. Centrale, 1922.

History: *Lectures historiques,* Port-au-Prince, Impr. Aug. A. Héraux, 1922, and new edition, Port-au-Prince, Cie Lithogr., 1927, and last edition, Port-au-Prince, Impr. La Presse, 1930; *Manuel d'Histoire d'Haiti* (with the collaboration of Brothers of Christian Education), preface by Brother Archange, Procure des Frères, 1924.

Politics: *Organisons nos partis politiques,* Port-au-Prince, Impr. Chéraquit, 1925; *Quelques vues politiques et morales (questions haitiennes),* Port-au-Prince, Impr. Modèle, 1934.

Religion: *Une explication philologique du vodou,* Port-au-Prince, Impr. V. Pierre-Noel, 1924; *Vodou et névrose,* second edition, Port-au-Prince, La Presse, 1931; *Vodou et magie,* Port-au-Prince, Impr. N. Telhomme, 1937.

Scholarship: *Essais de vulgarisation scientifique et questions haitiennes,* Port-au-Prince, Impr. Théodore, 1952 (introduction by Mesmin Gabriel who also published the work).

DORSINVILLE, Hénec

b. July 26, 1882, Port-au-Prince, Haiti; d. 1927, Port-au-Prince.

Essayist, journalist, lawyer.

Dorsinville was educated at the Petit Séminaire Collège Saint Martial. He later graduated from the law school.

He served as employee in various government offices and became Councellor of State and finally Minister of Public Instruction.

He contributed to many newspapers and served as the chief-editor of *L'Essor,* first a magazine and afterwards a daily paper. He published many literary essays in the journals of the day.

Writings: Politics: *Lettre à mes pairs,* Port-au-Prince, Impr. de l'Essor, 1917.

DORSINVILLE, Luc

b. 1885, Port-au-Prince, Haiti; d. ca. 1961, Port-au-Prince.

Biographer, teacher, politician.

Dorsinville received his education in Port-au-Prince. Very early, he became interested in business and especially the coastal trade. He also farmed on the small island of La Gonave. He served for a period in the President's private office.

Dorsinville spent many years as a professor at the Lycée Pétion and he founded the college Guy Joseph Bonnet.

Writings: Biography: *Toussaint Louverture, soldat de la liberté, précurseur de l'Indépendance d'Haiti,* Port-au-Prince, (mimeo.).

History: *Toussaint Louverture, général haitien,* Port-au-Prince, Impr. de l'Etat, 1953.

Politics: *Aperçu sur l'histoire politique de la Chambre de 1914,* Port-au-Prince, Impr. de l'Abeille, 1916; *La Chambre des Députés représentait-elle la Nation?* Port-au-Prince, Impr. Aug. A. Héraux, 1930; *Tout pour Haiti dans l'union qui fait la force,* Port-au-Prince, Impr. N. A. Théodore, 1957.

Bibliography: *Catalogue du Musée National d'après le dernier inventaire,* Port-au-Prince, Impr. N. A. Théodore, 1953.

DORSINVILLE, Max

b. 1938, Port-au-Prince, Haiti.

Essayist, literary critic, teacher.

Max Dorsinville was born in Port-au-Prince but his education has been achieved abroad because his family has spent a great number of years in many countries while his father served in the diplomatic service of Haiti or as a high officer in various United Nations missions. He did his higher education in Canada and the United States. Now he is teaching at McGill University in Canada.

Writings: Essays: *Caliban Without Prospero: Essay on Quebec and Black Literature,* Erin, Ontario, Press Porcepic, 1974; "Senghor or the Song of Exile," in *Exile and Tradition: Studies in African and Caribbean Literature,* Rowland Smith, (ed.), New York, Africana Publishing Company, 1976.

DORSINVILLE, Roger

b. March 11, 1911, Port-au-Prince, Haiti.
Poet, novelist, playwright, historian, diplomat.

Dorsinville's education was completed in Port-au-Prince, after which he entered the military school and was commissioned adjutant. Later, he was in charge of adult education in the Creole language. He became Chef de Cabinet of the President of Haiti, then Haitien Consul in New York. He also served as Minister of Public Health, and later Ambassador to Brazil, Costa Rica, Venezuela, Senegal, and Liberia. He is now living in Dakar, Senegal.

One critic, writing in *Présence Africaine* about his novel *Kimby* said: "Roger Dorsinville aime à penser que d'être devenu

depuis quatorze ans, Africain, n'a fait que mieux situer, éclairer et approfondir une haitianité inséparable de ses sources africaines."

Dorsinville is now Vice-President of the publishing house, Nouvelles Editions Africaines, of Dakar.

Writings: Poetry: *Pour célébrer la terre,* Port-au-Prince, Les Presses Libres, 1955; *Le grand devoir, poème,* Madrid, Taller Grafico, 1962, this work also appeared in *Présence Africaine,* No. 44 (1962), pp. 166-172.

Novels: *Kimby ou la loi de Niang,* Paris, Présence Africaine, 1973; *L'Afrique des rois,* Paris, Union générale d'éditions, 1975; *Un homme en trois morceaux,* Paris, Union générale d'éditions, 1975; *Sainte Esther,* Montréal, Nouvelle Optique, 1978.

Plays: *Barrières,* Port-au-Prince, Ed. Henri Deschamps, 1946; *La Fresque,* (history of Black people from remote times until now) performed January 12-30, 1977, for the Second Festival of Black Art (FESTAG) in Lagos, Nigeria.

Political Essays: *Lettre aux hommes clairs,* Port-au-Prince, Impr. de l'Etat, 1946; *Lettre à mon ami Serge Corvington,* Port-au-Prince, Impr. de l'Etat, 1947; *Lettre à Daniel Fignolé,* Port-au-Prince, Impr. H. Deschamps, 1947.

History: *Toussaint Louverture ou la vocation de la liberté,* Paris, René Julliard, Coll. Les Temps Modernes, 1965.

Ethnological Studies: *Mythologie de l'hinterland libérien,* Alger, S.N.E.D., 1970; *The Bassa Mask: A Stranger in the House* (with Mario Meneghini), Zurich, Faculté d'Ethnologie, University of Zurich, 1973.

DORVAL, Gérard

b. ca. 1947, Haiti.
Storywriter, novelist, teacher.

Dorval completed his education at the Faculty of Ethnology and the Normal School, Port-au-Prince. He is presently teaching in many colleges of the capital.

Writings: Novels: *Les Chemins de l'action, Dans la melée,* Vol. I (1972) and *Les Pouilleux,* Vol. II (1974), both Port-au-Prince, Eds. Fardin; *Ma terre en bleu,* Port-au-Prince, Eds. Fardin, 1975.

Criticism: *Etudes et peintures, Premier Cahier,* Port-au-Prince, Fardin, 1975.

DOUGE, Gérard

b. June 8, 1923, Port-au-Prince, Haiti.
Poet, novelist, essayist.

After Dougé was educated in Port-au-Prince, he went to the Ecole Polytechnique, from which he graduated. He has worked primarily, however, as a writer. His research in literature leads Dougé to launch what he coined the term *Pluréalisme* as "a method of research put at the disposal of the artist."

Writings: Poetry: *Femme noire,* 1969; *La lune l'Amérique,* 1969; *Souvenir,* 1969; *Pollen,* Port-au-Prince, Impr. Centrale, 1971, all others Les Presses Port-au-Princiennes in Port-au-Prince.

Novel: *Transfert* (3rd Prize of Concours des Editions de l'An 2000), unpublished.

Essays: "Littératures traditionnelles et nouvelles esthétiques," in *Le Nouvelliste,* 4 and 5, 6, 7 Septembre 1972; "Manifeste du mouvement pluréaliste" in *Le Petit Samedi Soir,* No. 16 "Pluréalisme et culture haitienne," in *Le Nouvelliste* (Feb. 23, 1973); "Le créole: arme de défense culturelle ou instrument de travail?" in *Le Nouvelliste* (Nov. 22, 1973); "Révolution créole et culture bilingue," in *Le Nouvelliste* (Dec. 10, 1973); "Dynamique des relations inter-culturelles" (Lecture), unpublished.

DOUYON, Ernest

b. December 8, 1885, Port-au-Prince, Haiti; d. January 10, 1950, Port-au-Prince.

Poet, storywriter, critic, lawyer, teacher.

Douyon started his studies in Port-au-Prince and completed his education in Martinique in 1903 with a Bachelier-ès-lettres. Returning to Haiti, he was a professor of literature at the Lycée des Cayes (1905-1914) and a professor at the School of Law, also in Cayes (1912-1915), and otherwise active in educational and juridical circles. He was named Minister of Finance with the government of President Eugène Roy and later served as President of the Tribunal de Cassation (1932-1946).

Douyon's work saw print in the journals of *Le Matin, Le Nouvelliste, La Phalange,* and *Le Temps-Revue.*

Writings: Criticism-Eulogy: *L'année d'Oswald,* Port-au-Prince, Impr. de l'Abeille, 1906.

Essay: *La Guadeloupe,* Port-au-Prince, Impr. H. Amblard, 1905.

Poetry: in miscellaneous journals.

DRICE, Mirabeau

(or **MIRABBO**)

b. 1875, Port-au-Prince, Haiti; d. 1919, Port-au-Prince.

Storywriter, critic.

An excellent student, Drice won a French governmental grant to complete his education in Paris, becoming a fine classicist and ardent student of Plato at the Ecole Supérieure in the French capital. Returning to Haiti, he taught Greek and Latin at the Lycée National of Port-au-Prince. He lived only a few years after returning to Haiti and published no separate volume of his delicate "fantasies" which appeared in *La Jeune Haiti* and *La Ronde.* With Justin Lhérisson and Seymour Pradel he had helped establish *La Jeune Haiti,* one of the earliest important literary magazines of the island.

Pradel wrote of his perished friend: "Sa phrase est d'une souplesse merveilleuse, vivante et chantante . . . Il a une sensibilité très digne, une âme grondante et tourmentée."

DUC, Gérard

b. October 20, 1925, Saint-Marc, Haiti.

Novelist, storywriter, essayist.

Duc was educated partly in Saint-Marc and Port-au-Prince. He spent many years as a teacher and is now living in exile.

Duc has published many articles in *Le Matin, Le Nouvelliste,* and *Le National,* all in Port-au-Prince.

Writings: Poetry: *Agoué ou le dieu des Caraibes,* Port-au-Prince, 1959.

Novels: *Les Trésors du Roi Christophe,* preface by Antonio Vieux, Port-au-Prince, Les Presses Libres, 1954; *Terre en Gésine,* Port-au-Prince, Impr. de l'Etat, 1935; *L'île damnée,*

Paris, Eds. d'Hablouin, 1970.
Essay: *La lutte pour l'existence dans le processus d'évolution des collectivités humaines,* Port-au-Prince, 1962.

DUCASSE, Vendenesse

b. March 27, 1872, Port-au-Prince, Haiti; d. March 27, 1902, Port-au-Prince.
Playwright, lawyer, teacher.

Ducasse attended the Lycée Pétion and later graduated from the Law School, and then practiced law.

From his schooldays, he has been fond of theatre. Possessed of a fertile imagination, he produced as many serious dramas as comedies. He pointed out Toussaint Louverture's fortitude in front of Napoléon Bonaparte, when he had Toussaint delivering these lines:

En voulant m'abaisser, il s'abaisse lui-même,
Car l'on dira demain que le fameux vainqueur
N'est qu'un homme mesquin et de plate rancoeur.

When Mars Plaisir, his servant and companion of misfortune, bemoaned his fate, Toussaint exclaimed:

Ah! tu me fais rougir de tant de défaillances:
Sache que le martyre ennoblit l'innocence
Et les derniers instants des grands coeurs mutilés,
Que l'outrage grandit les fronts immaculés . . .

Writings: Plays: *Fort de Joux ou les derniers moments de Toussaint Louverture; drame historique en un acte* (performed in 1896), published Port-au-Prince, Ed. Vétéran, 1957 (with a list of actors of the original 1896 production). Other plays (unpublished): *1804 (drama in 4 acts and verse); Place vacante* (comedy); *L'amour et l'argent* (3 acts and verse); *Factionnaire; 13 Novembre; Philistins; Noirs et Jaunes; En ménage* (sketch); *Les Elections* (sketch); *Les duels de mon pays; Haitiens et Syriens.*

Biographical/Critical Sources: Duraciné Vaval: *Histoire de la littérature haitienne, ou l'âme noire,* Port-au-Prince, Impr. Aug. A. Héraux, 1933; Robert Cornevin, *Le Théâtre haitien, des origines à nos jours,* Quebec, Ed. Léméac, 1973, pp. 115-117.

DUMERVE, Constantin Eugène

b. October 20, 1883, Môle Saint Nicolas, Haiti; d. January, 1969, Port-au-Prince.
Journalist, musical composer.

Dumervé started his first studies in Môle Saint Nicolas and went to Port-au-Prince, where he completed his education at the Petit Séminaire Collège Saint Martial. There Father Albert Saint Clair taught him music.

Dumervé studied law and became a member of the Attorneys' Bar in Port-au-Prince. In 1930, he was the delegate to the Congress which elected Eugène Roy as a provisional president of Haiti to restore the Haitian Parliament, abolished since the American occupation of Haiti in 1917.

He contributed essays to many magazines and newspapers on music and Haitian musicians. He also composed some pieces of music, including "La Baie du Môle Saint-Nicolas," a waltz, and "Hymne de la Libération Financière."

Writings: Recueil de chants patriotiques à l'usage des écoles de la République, Port-au-Prince, 1952; *Histoire de la musique en Haiti* (preface by Maurice A. Lubin), Port-au-Prince, Impr. des Antilles, 1968.

DUMESLE, Hérard

b. June 16, 1784, Cayes, Haiti; d. June 22, 1858, Kingston, Jamaica.
Poet, journalist, biographer, politician.

Hérard Dumesle received a good education in his native city. Very early, he practiced journalism and he founded in 1819 the political-cultural journal, *L'Observateur,* in which he published light poetry and some verse satires.

He was elected Deputy of Cayes in 1822 and was reelected many times, for he was a powerful antagonist of Boyer's dictatorship. When President Boyer was ousted by the 1843 Revolution and Hérard's cousin, Rivière Hérard, became President of Haiti, Dumesle was named Secretary of State for War and Foreign Affairs. He became a powerful official and acted as vice-president. He was eventually banished by the government of President Guerrier and spent the last years in Kingston, where he died after 15 years of exile.

His *Voyage dans le Nord d'Haiti* celebrates Haiti's natural grandeurs and attacks materialists in pleasant verse stanzas mixed with polemical prose.

Writings: Poetry: *Dithyrambe élégiaque sur la mort de Jonathas Granville; imprimé par souscription des citoyens des Cayes,* Port-au-Prince, 1839; *Voyage dans le Nord d'Haiti ou révélation des lieux et des monuments historiques,* Les Cayes, Impr. du Gouvernement, 1824.

Politics: *Réflexions politiques sur la mission des Commissaires du Roi de France près la République d'Haiti,* Les Cayes, Impr. du Gouvernement, 1816.

Biography: *Eloge du général de division I.D. Marion,* Port-au-Prince, Impr. de J. Courtois, 1841.

Biographical/Critical Sources: Pradel Pompilus et les Frères de l'Instruction Chrétienne: *Manuel illustré d'histoire de la littérature haitienne,* Port-au-Prince, Ed. Henri Deschamps, 1961, pp. 18-20.

DUPLESSIS, Jean François Fénelon

b. May 16, 1826, Port-au-Prince, Haiti; d. June 6, 1904, Port-au-Prince.
Poet.

Fénelon Duplessis was educated in Port-au-Prince, and was named secretary of the Haitian Legation in London. He later became Administrator of Finances of Port-au-Prince.

Writings: Poetry: *Chants et pleurs, poèsies: 1849-1880,* Port-au-Prince, Impr. de l'Abeille, 1908 (published after his death by his niece Luce Archin-Lay).

Biographical/Critical Sources: Georges Sylvain's comments in *Revue de la Société de Législation* (Jan. 1909), p. 153.

DUPLESSIS-LOUVERTURE, Louis

b. 1887, Saint-Michel de l'Attalaye, Haiti; d. 1961, Saint Michel de l'Attalaye.
Poet, lawyer, notary.

Duplessis-Louverture was educated in Haiti and France. He graduated from the law school in Port-au-Prince, and served as Deputy of Saint-Michel de l'Attalaye.

Duplessis-Louverture generally employed free verse in his work and expressed his Negritude in these typical stanzas:

Oh! ne plus savoir ce que c'est
D'avoir la peau d'un nègre, un cerveau de français
Et le coeur de l'Afrique au fond de la poitrine!

Car tout le mal est là, tout le mal.
Il est trop de contraires par notre sang charrié,
Tout le mal,
Tout le mal est d'être trop proche de la brousse
Tout le mal est d'être un être d'élection.
De s'émouvoir du cuir heurté d'un tambour
En même temps que des Chopin et des Corot,
De goûter l'onomatopée et les palabres
Et de mourir aussi des sanglots d'un Verlaine.

or:

Ancêtre, il n'est pas loin le jour où ta poussière
Dansera parmi l'or des matins de bonheur,
Que tu riras avec nos lèvres et nos yeux.
Car nous aurons repris notre place au soleil.

Writings: Poetry: *Avec et sans rimes (poèmes),* Port-au-Prince, Impr. du Collège Vertières, 1944; *Face à Face,* published in combined volume with Antoine Dodard's *Tambour,* Gonaives, Haiti, Presses Artibonitiennes, 1953; Some poems ("Scènes vaudouesques") appeared in *Les Griots* magazine, Vols. 2-3, Nos. 2-3 (Oct. 1939-March 1940), p. 638.

Play: in the last part of the first verse-book is found *Marivaudage,* a fairy-scene in one act and verse.

Biographical/Critical Sources: Pradel Pompilus & Les Frères de l'Instruction Chrétienne, *Manuel Illustré d'Histoire de la littérature haitienne,* Port-au-Prince, Ed. H. Deschamps, 1961, pp. 353-357.

DUPOUX, Antoine

b. May 17, 1910, Jérémie, Haiti.
Poet.

Dupoux started his schooling at the Lycée Nord Alexis of Jérémie and completed it in Port-au-Prince. He graduated from the Faculty of Law and became an accountant. He spent several years as a teacher.

Dupoux is a social activist and his verses attacked the continued poverty and degradation of the vast majority of the Haitian people.

Writings: Poetry: *Face à la vie,* Port-au-Prince, Impr. Le Réveil, 1949; *Fleurs des bouges, poèmes,* preface by Regnor C. Bernard, Port-au-Prince, Impr. N. Telhomme, 1940.

Manifesto: (written with Carlos Saint-Louis) *Manifeste de l'école réaliste Haitienne,* Port-au-Prince, Ed. H. Deschamps, 1948.

DUPRE, Antoine

b. ca. 1782, Saint-Marc, Haiti; killed in a duel, January 13, 1816.
Poet, playwright, politician.

Dupré was one of Haiti's earliest published poets and possibly its first performed playwright, producing his own plays and those of others in a theatre he founded in Port-au-Prince. Little is specifically known about him except that his "Hymne à la liberté," written and sung in 1812, won for him the title of national bard given him by his contemporaries. Patterned after the famous French anthem, his hymn begins:

Haiti, libre et guerrière
A reconquis sa liberté
Et montre aux tyrans de la terre,
L'homme libre, l'homme indompté.

or, "le dernier soupir d'un haitien":

Haiti, mère chérie,
Reçois mes derniers adieux,
Que l'amour de la patrie
Enflamme tous nos neveux.

Si quelque jour, sur tes rives
Osent venir des tyrans
Que leurs hordes fugitives
Servent d'engrais à nos champs!

According to Saint-Rémy, "Antoine Dupré célèbre tour à tour la gloire, la liberté et l'amour."

Writings: Poetry: *Hymne à la liberté,* Port-au-Prince, Impr. du Gouvernement, n.d.

Play: *La mort du général Lamarre, (drama),* Port-au-Prince, Impr. J. Courtois, 1844. (It dramatized an historical event of 1810. The play was hissed during its premiere performance [1813] in England, but was well accepted in its 1815 Port-au-Prince production.); *Odéide ou la honte d'une mère,* this title according to Beaubrun Ardouin, but *La jeune fille* according to Joseph Saint-Rémy des Cayes (performed in Dupré's theatre in Port-au-Prince, in 1813).

Biographical/Critical Sources: Naomi M. Garret's *The Renaissance in Haitian Poetry,* Paris, Présence Africaine, 1963; Auguste Viatte, *Histoire littéraire de l'Amérique Française,* Quebec, Presses Universitaires Laval, 1953.

DU PREY de la RUFFINIERE, Pierre

(pseudonym: **TEXTU**)
b. August 30, 1911, Fort-de-France, Martinique.
Novelist, journalist, storywriter.

Duprey attended the primary school of Fort-de-France and completed his education at the Lycée Henri IV in France. After winning his baccalaureate, he worked in several hotels in Paris for his living, and during a two-year period (1931-1932), he completed his military service in Morocco.

He travelled extensively, spending some time in Spain and Italy, and went on to the Ivory Coast. He settled in the region of Grand-Lahou-Divo, where he had the opportunity to study the customs and usages of the people, and wrote his book, *Histoire des Ivoiriens,* based on these experiences.

Duprey worked in the Ivory Coast as a forester, living far into the interior. Later he was named to the staff of the Ministry of the Interior, and then became technical advisor for the Tourism Department. He is now head of the cabinet of the Ministry of Tourism.

He founded a newspaper, *La Concorde,* and early was an organizer of the journals *La Côte d'Ivoire libre* and *L'Essor.*

He is a member of the Société des Gens de Lettres de France.

Writings: Novels: *Le Coupeur de bois,* Paris, Nouvelles Editions Latines, 1946; *Bli, homme pensant,* Paris, Nouvelles Editions Latines, 1949.

Stories: "Elisa the Hustler," in *From the Green Antilles,* London, Souvenir Press Ltd., 1967, reprinted London, Panther, 1971.

History: *Histoire des Ivoiriens,* preface by the Minister of Education, Abidjan, Impr. Nationale, 1962.

Tourism: *La Côte d'Ivoire de A à Z,* Abidjan, Ed. TEXTU, 1970.

Biographical/Critical Sources: G.K. "Le tour de la Côte d'Ivoire en 384 étapes: une interview de Pierre Duprey," *Fraternité Matin,* No. 1590 (March 10, 1970); N'Guessan Gbohourou (Bertin), "La Côte d'Ivoire de A a Z: un répertoire de nos vertus in *Fraternité Matin,* No. 1613 (April 7, 1970), p. 8.

DUQUESNAY, Victor

b. 1872, Marin, Martinique; d. 1920, Martinique.
Poet.

Locally educated, Duquesnay served in government offices in and around Marin most of his life, where he served in the field of internal revenue administration.

Duquesnay's works show fancy and a certain originality, both in metrics and in their treatment of subject. He often employed free verse. An example of his work from the poem "Madinina," written in 1895, shows his characteristic style:

J'aime, ô mon beau pays, tes belles
indolentes,
Ces filles à peau d'ambre, aux caresses
brûlantes . . .
. . . J'aime, autour du tam-tam, la
câpresse attifée . . .
J'aime ton doux parler, harmonieux et
tendre,
Ce créole naif . . .

And of course the poetic, somewhat cliché handling of the beautiful, langorous creole, is typical of the island poetry of the day.

Writings: Poetry: *Madinina,* 1895, in *Fleurs des Antilles,* edited by René Bonneville; *Les Martiniquaises,* Paris, Librairie Fischbacher, 1903; *La chanson des iles* (posthumous), Toulon, Impr. du Sud-Est, 1926.

DURAND, Charles Alexis Oswald

b. September 17, 1840, Cap-Haitien, Haiti; d. April 22, 1906, Port-au-Prince.
Poet (in French and creole), journalist, statesman.

Durand's parents died in the cataclysmic

earthquake of 1842 which destroyed Cap-Haitien, and he was reared by his grandmother in Ouanaminte, where he was educated. He began to write verses while working as a tinsmith and was encouraged by Démesvar Délorme, the well-known writer, to consider publishing his work.

Forced into exile in 1883 for a short period, he gained a certain amount of sophistication and returned in a short while to win a seat in the national assembly in 1885. Reelected six times, he served one session as chairman of the Chambre des Représentants. In 1888 he travelled to France and was introduced to the Société des Gens de Lettres by François Coppée, who read Durand's then famous poem, "Idalina," for the occasion. In Haiti, Durand directed the official journal, *Le Moniteur.*

He has been called the "Mistral of the Tropics," the Whitman, and the Verlaine of the Tropics. Predominantly a love poet, he did concern himself, however, in some of his work, with race prejudice and the concern over Haiti's future as it went from one tumultuous year to the next.

His first collection of verses, *Rires et pleurs* (1896), was very popular in Paris where it was published, and his poem "Idalina," celebrating "la brune fille des grèves," was even more so, being given a second printing in the French journal in which it had originally appeared. Even more liked was his poem "Choucoune," written in creole and which appeared in many journals. Ghislain Gouraige considered Durand to have been the first Haitian poet to offer "the realities of Haiti in simple words and tender images." "Choucoune" is a ballad to a Cuban-African girl, there called a "marabou," and this and other creole works by Durand helped establish the local Haitian dialect of French as an acceptable vehicle for a serious poet.

Though influenced later by Hugo, Sainte Beuve, Musset, and Gauthier, Durand was always his own man and more "Haitian" than most poets of his generation.

Durand also wrote vernacular verse farces, which appear not to have seen publication, and he directed in 1876 the satirical review *Les Bigailles*,, and again in 1901.

Once condemned to execution, Durand rose to be president of the National Assembly and proclaimed as the nation's laureate. Today his work is still held in good esteem by younger poets.

Georges Sylvain in his *Confidences et Mélancolies* said of Oswald Durand:

> *Pour mon goût, le véritable Oswald Durand n'est pas, l'avouerai-je, cet artiste au travail menu . . . même pas ce poète au verbe sonore, aux courtes mais superbes envolées . . . C'est le chantre de Choucoune, la Marabout, c'est avant tout le poète local, le poète créole. Oswald Durand est nôtre, sans mélange d'exotisme. . . .*

On August 25, 1905, Frédéric Marcelin, then Minister of Finance, successfully urged the Haitian Parliament to create a retirement pension for Oswald Durand as "un chef d'Etat de l'Esprit, de l'Imagination, de la Poèsie et de la Pensée."

Writings: Poetry: *Rires et pleurs, (1869-1896),* 2 vols., Paris, Impr. Ed. Crété, 1896; *Quatre nouveaux poèmes,* Cap-Haitien, Impr. Lib. La Conscience, 1900; *Oswald Durand: Poèsies choisies, avec une étude bibliographique,* Pradel Pompilus, (ed.), Port-au-Prince, Impr. des Antilles, 1964; In Manuscript: "Dates et nouveaux poèmes," "Primes fleurs et ballades," and "Les mosaiques."

Biographical/Critical Sources: Ernest Douyon, *L'année d'Oswald Durand,* Port-au-Prince, Impr. de l'Abeille, 1905; Félix Viard, *La dernière étape; Oswald Durand et ses admirateurs,* Montpellier (France), Ed. des Nouvelles Annales, 1906; Jean F. Brierre, "A Oswald Durand," in *Haiti-Journal,* Edition spéciale, 1945; Franck Fouché's "Peut-on parler de primitivisme à propos d'Oswald Durand?" in *Guide pour l'étude de la littérature haitienne,* Port-au-Prince, Panorama, 1964, pp. 66-67; Gouraige Ghislain's *Histoire de la littérature haitienne,* Port-au-Prince, 1961; Pradel Pompilus, *Les classiques de la littérature haitienne: Oswald Durand,* Port-au-Prince, Impr. des Antilles, 1964; Auguste Viatte, *Histoire littéraire de l'Amérique française,* Quebec, 1953, pp. 391-393; Jean-Claude Fignolé's essay devoted to Durand: *Les grands écrivains de la littérature haitienne,* Port-au-Prince, 1968.

DURAND, Louis-Henry

b. June 21, 1887, Cap-Haitien, Haiti; d. June 23, 1943, Port-au-Prince.
Poet, playwright.

After early schooling in Haiti, Durand completed his education in France at the Lycée Janson de Sailly and the Collège Chapsal. When he returned to Haiti, he took part in the work of the review *L'Essor* and the group led by Héneck Dorsinville. Durand was a founder of a new group and its journal *Printania* in Cap-Haitien. His play *Cléopatre,* adapted to music by Justin Elie, was his greatest success.

He worked as a translator at the Custom House of Port-au-Prince and also served in this capacity at the Department of the Interior. He also had minor business interests.

In 1916 he helped found the anti-U.S. journal, *La Revue de la Ligue de la Jeunesse Haitienne,* to counter the impact of the American occupation. His colleagues were Georges Léger, Fernand Hibbert, Frédéric Duvignaud, Paul Barjon and Léon Laleau.

Writings: Poetry: *Les pétales s'effeuillent (poèmes),* Ed. de la Ligue de la Jeunesse Haitienne, Port-au-Prince, Impr. de l'Abeille, 1916; *Roses rouges; poèmes,* Paris, Jouve et Cie, 1930; *Trois poèmes* (Après le sacrilège, l'Aube; Ave Juventus), Port-au-Prince, La Presse, 1930.

Play: *Cléopâtre; pièce en quatre tableaux et en vers, avec musique de Justin Elie,* Port-au-Prince, Impr. Bernard & Cie, 1919; *Crépuscule* (unpublished) in one act.

Biographical/Critical Sources: Robert Cornevin: *Le théâtre haitien, des origines à nos jours,* Quebec, Ed. Léméac, 1973, pp. 131-132; Pradel Pompilus & Les Frères de l'Instruction Chrétienne, *Manuel illustré d'histoire de la littérature haitienne,* Port-au-Prince, Ed. H. Deschamps, 1961, pp. 343-346; Ghislain Gouraige, *Histoire de la littérature haitienne,* Impr. N. A. Thédore, pp. 188-191.

DUVAL, Amilcar

b. October 17, 1875, Port-au-Prince, Haiti; d. March 6, 1949, Port-au-Prince.
Playwright, poet, storywriter, journalist.

Duval studied at the Lycée Pétion and took his law degree in 1902. He was a professor at the Lycée Pétion and later division chief at the Department of Foreign Affairs. His career in the diplomatic service saw him as secretary of legation at Washington, D.C., at Paris as secretary, Chargé d'affaires and Consul General at Rome, then Chief of Protocol in the Foreign Affairs Ministry. He was a judge in 1930 and later minister of Interior and Justice in the 1940's.

His literary interests made him a director of the review *Le Bronze* (1897), and brought him into the La Ronde group, in whose journal he published many of his stories. His work is based on closely observed details of daily life and local customs, but at times there is a bizarre, even fantastic imagination remolding the quotidian subject matter into exotic psychologies and experiences.

Duraciné Vaval said of him:

> *Amilcar Duval a du goût pour le théâtre. Son dialogue est alerte, spirituel, naturel. On y sent le chroniqueur attitré de* La Ronde *où il se révéla comme un fin observateur des mille petits riens de notre milieu qui ont pourtant leur importance à les envisager sous un certain angle.*

Writings: Plays: *Un cas de conscience; Etapes* (3-act comedy); *Pour elle* (comedy of manners).

Stories: *Le miroir trop fidèle,* collected 1933,

typeset by Edition de La Revue Mondiale, but never placed on sale.

DUVALIER, François

(pseudonym: **ABDERRAHMAN**)
b. April 14, 1907, Port-au-Prince, Haiti; d. April 21, 1971, Port-au-Prince.
Physician, poet, politician, head of state.

Duvalier studied at the Lycée Pétion of Port-au-Prince and entered the Faculty of Medicine, where he graduated in 1934. He practiced medicine in rural areas and specialized in the treatment of a tropical disease, the yaws. Doctor Duvalier, as a physician, published many articles relating his experiences as a medical practitioner.

He was Director General of the Public Health Service in 1946, became Under-Secretary of Labor in 1948-1949, and Secretary of State of the same department in 1949-1950.

He was elected President of Haiti September 22, 1957, reelected for a second term on April 30, 1961, and elected for life in 1964.

He participated in literary activities and used to co-author all his literary and ethnological writings with Lorimer Denis. It was an unusual partnership and it was said that "Duvalier and Denis were intellectual twins." With Lorimer Denis, Carl Brouard, Magloire St-Aude and Kléber Georges-Jacob, he helped found a cultural movement which stressed the importance of the African heritage in Haitian culture. Until that time, the Haitian elite found its sole pride in its cultural ties with France. This Griot movement, as it is called, instead put in evidence the aspects by which Haiti is attached to Africa. Africanism and Haitianism are the two poles of griot concept. The declarations of principles and the doctrine were exposed in the magazine, *Les Griots.* After the disappearance of the original magazine, there were subsequent journals published under the same title. Jean Price-Mars and Jacques Roumain deepened and widened the Griot initiatives.

Duvalier's *Les tendances d'une génération,* written with others, called for an end to colonial tendencies still evident in Haitian writing and a revival of national pride as American Occupation forces were being withdrawn after 18 years in the island state.

Writings: Criticism-Sociology: with Lorimer Denis and Arthur Bonhomme: *Les tendances d'une génération,* Port-au-Prince, Impr. du Collège Vertières, 1934.

Sociology: *Le problème des classes à travers l'histoire d'Haiti,* with Lorimer Denis, Port-au-Prince, Impr. de l'Etat, 1948.

Politics: *L'avenir du pays et l'action néfaste de Mr Foisset* (with Lorimer Denis), Port-au-Prince, Impr. de l'Etat, 1949; *Pour affronter les temps durs,* Ed. SID, Port-au-Prince, Impr. de l'Etat, 1960; *Face au peuple et à l'histoire,* Port-au-Prince, Impr. de l'Etat, 1961; *Oeuvres essentielles,* 4 vols., Port-au-Prince, Impr. de l'Etat, 1958; *Bréviaire d'une révolution,* Port-au-Prince, Impr. de l'Etat, 1967; *Mémoire d'un leader du Tiers-Monde. Mes négociations avec le Saint-Siège ou une tranche d'histoire,* Paris, Hachette, 1969; *Hommage au martyr de la non-violence, le Révérend Dr Martin Luther King, Jr,* édition spéciale, Port-au-Prince, Les Presses Nationales, 1968; *A Tribute to the Martyred Leader of Non-violence, Reverend Dr Martin Luther King, Jr* (trans. from French by John E. Pickering), Port-au-Prince, Les Presses Nationales, 1968; *Politique étrangère; histoire diplomatique. Politique frontérale, géographie politique,* Port-au-Prince, Les Presses Nationales, 1968; *Hommage au Marron Inconnu,* Port-au-Prince, Les Presses Nationales, 1969.

Medicine: *Contribution à l'étude du pian en Haiti, l'aspect médico-social et l'oeuvre de la Mission Sanitaire Américaine,* Canada, 1945; *La valeur de la pénicilline dans le traitement du pian en Haiti,* Canada, 1948; *Sur un cas de sulfamido-pénicillino-résistance traité par la terramycine,* Canada, 1951; *A propos d'un cas de pneumonie primitive atypique,* Canada, 1952; *Contribution à l'étude des Acxémies par piqûre vénimeuse, Deux études extraites des Oeuvres scientifiques: Le Traitement du Pian pqr la Terramycine pure; De la valeur relative du cyto et du séro-diagnostic dans la Tréponé-*

matose sous les tropiques, Port-au-Prince, Impr. de l'Etat, 1962.

Various: *Considérations sur cent cinquante ans d'évolution du régime alimentaire dans le prolétariat urbain et rural en Haiti, (1804-1954),* Extrait du Bulletin de l'Association des Médecins de Langue Française du Canada, Canada, 1953.

Memoirs: *Souvenirs d'autrefois (bric-à-brac), 1926-1948,* Port-au-Prince, Les Presses Nationales d'Haiti, 1968 (published under pseudonym of Abderrahman).

EBOUE, Adolphe Félix Sylvestre

(usually **Félix,** and nicknamed **Fé-Fé**)
b. December 26, 1884, Cayenne, Guyane;
d. May 17, 1944, Cairo, Egypt.
Statesman, government official, amateur historian and folklorist.

Eboué attended a Roman Catholic primary school and the college in Cayenne, and went to France to complete his secondary school education at the Lycée Montaigne of Bordeaux, where he won his baccalaureate. He entered the Colonial School in Paris and in 1908 was assigned as student-administrator in Oubangui-Chari (now Central African Empire). After many years, Eboué was named Administrator of Colonies, becoming Secretary General in Martinique at the government office, and then acting governor, and moved in the same capacity to the Soudan (now Mali) in 1934.

He was promoted to Governor (of colony), and was the first true black to reach this position, being named Governor in Guadeloupe in 1936 and Chad in 1938. By August 1940, during the Second World War, he rallied French Equatorial Africa behind the Free French forces of General Charles de Gaulle.

Eboué was promoted to Governor General of French Equatorial Africa in 1942. Unfortunately, he became ill after the Brazzaville conference and he died in Cairo, where he was seeking rest and medical treatment.

General Charles de Gaulle, Commander-in-Chief, could not travel to the funeral, but issued in these sad circumstances the following statement:

> *Le pays, la nation et l'Empire sont en deuil par la mort du Gouverneur Général Félix Eboué de l'Afrique Equatoriale Française, compagnon de la Libération. Tout français se rappelle qu'en maintenant le Tchad en guerre à la plus triste période de notre histoire, Félix Eboué a mis un point à l'esprit de capitulation dans ce territoire placé en bordure du Sahara. Félix Eboué, un grand français, est mort en servant la France.*

René Pleven, de Gaulle's delegate, attended the funeral, and made the eulogy to Eboué:

> *Eboué a apporté une importante contribution à l'empire et pouvait continuer à influencer la politique coloniale d'après-guerre. Je déclare avec tristesse que la perte soufferte aujourd'hui par la France dans sa personne affaiblit le pays pour le moment et l'appauvrit pour l'avenir. . . . Vous restez pour tout l'empire où vous êtes né, la preuve que la France ne connaît d'autres distinctions que celles que donne le mérite.*

Writings: Folklore/Scholarship: *Grammar: African customs: La clef musicale des langages tambourinés et sifflés,* extract in Archives Nationales de France, Section d'Outre-Mer, Br. 4093; *Langues sango, banda, baya, mandjia: notes grammaticales, mots groupés d'après le sens, phrases usuelles, vocabulaire,* Paris, Larose, 1918; "La musique et le langage des Banda," in *La Revue du Monde Noir,* Paris, Vol. II, No. 6 (April 1932), pp. 32-34; *Les Peuples de l'Oubangui-Chari: essai d'ethnographie, de linguistique et d'économie sociale,* Paris, Comité de l'Afrique Française, 1933; Also printed as articles in *Bulletin de la Société des Recharches Recherches Congolaises,* No. 17, 1932, pp. 31-*Congolaises,* No. 17, 1932, pp. 31-51; No. 18, 1933, pp. 57-86; Also, in *Renseignements coloniaux de l'Afrique Française,* No. 11, 1932, pp. 401-414, No. 12, 1932, pp. 452-462; No. 1, 1933, pp. 14-24; *Les sociétés d'initiés en pays banda; Bulletin de la Société des Recherches Congolaises,* No. 13, 1931, pp. 3-15; *Les Bayas de l'Ouham Pendé: organisation familiale-fiançailles et mariage; Bulletin de la Société des Recherches Congolaises,* No. 9, 1928, pp. 32-38 (with N. Simonin).

Administration: *Le Coton en Oubangui-Chari: Le Monde Colonial Illustré* (Oct. 1926), pp. 225-227; *Politique indigène de l'Afrique Equatoriale Française,* Brazzaville, Afrique Française Libre, 1942.

Sport: "Le Sport en Afrique Equatoriale," in *Le Monde Colonial Illustré,* No. 103 (March 1932), pp. 6-61.

Biographical/Critical Sources: Jean De La Roche, *Le Gouverneur Général Félix Eboué, 1884-1944,* Paris, Hachette, 1957; René Maran: *Félix Eboué: grand commis et loyal serviteur, 1885-1944,* Paris, Les Editions Parisiennes, 1957; Albert Maurice, *Félix Eboué: sa vie et son oeuvre,* Brussels, Institut Royal Colonial Belge; Ulrick Sophie, *Le Gouverneur Général Félix Eboué,* preface by M.G. Monnerville, Président du Conseil de la République, second edition, Paris, Larose, 1950; Brian Weinstein, *Eboué,* New York, Oxford University Press, 1972; Félix Eboué, 1884-1944, *Album imprimé à l'occasion de l'inauguration officielle du monument Eboué, le 21 Janvier 1957,* Guadeloupe, n.d.; Brian Weinstein, *Félix Eboué and the Chiefs: Perceptions of Power in Early Oubangui-Chari,* in *Journal of African History,* Vol. XI, No. 1 (1970), pp. 114-115; Général P. Marchand "Le Gouverneur Général Eboué" in *Tropiques,* Fort-de-France, July 1949, pp. 3-9; *Félix Eboué, Compagnon de la libération,* L'hommage du Gouvernement de la France Libre, Basse-Terre, Impr. Officielle, 1945; Eugène Graëve, *Georges Mandel et le Gouverneur Félix Eboué,* Union Française et Parlement, No. 36 (March 1953), p. 14; Egon Kaskeline, "Félix Eboué and the Fighting French," in *Survey Graphic;* "Color, Unfinished Business of Democracy," Special Vol. XXXI, No. 11 (Nov. 1942), pp. 522-523, 548-50; Camille Lhuerre, *10e anniversaire de la mort du Gouverneur Général Félix Eboué, Souvenirs; Parallèle* 5, Cayenne, No. 7 (June 1, 1954), p. 5; Albert Maurice, "René Maran et Félix Eboué, une amitie," in *Hommage à René Maran,* Paris, Présence Africaine, 1965, pp. 209-220; Monnerville, Président, Paul Coste-Floret et M. Roussel, *Hommage à Victor Schoelcher et Félix Eboué à l'occasion du transfert de leurs cendres au Panthéon le 20 Mai 1949,* Cayenne, 1949; Ginette Eboué, "18 Juin 1940, au coeur de l'Afrique Noire avec Félix Eboué; Voix et Visages," in *Bulletin Mensuel de l'Association Nationale des Anciens Déportés et Internés de la Résistance,* No. 2 (May-June 1958), pp. 1, 2, 4; *Les Fêtes funèbres organisées par les loges maçonniques de Fort-de-France, les dimanches 18 Juin 1944 et 17 Juin 1945, à la mémoire du regretté et éminent Félix Eboué,* Fort-de-France, Impr. officielle, 1945; René Maran, "Autour d'une nomination de Gouverneur," in *Je suis partout* (Jan. 19, 1937).

EDOUARD, Emmanuel

b. September 27, 1858, Anse-à-Veau, Haiti; d. August 13, 1891, Port-au-Prince.
Poet, memoirist.

After Edouard's schooling in Haiti, he studied law in France. He led the delegation of homage, including Justin Dévot (Haitian vice-president), Georges Sylvain, Anténor Firmin, and others to Victor Hugo's funeral in 1885.

After returning to Haiti, he published much prose and verse, but died very young at the age of 33 years.

Writings: Poetry: *Rimes haitiennes, poèsies, 1874-1881,* Paris, Dentu, 1882.

Poetry and Essays: *Le Panthéon haitien . . .* (précédée d'une lettre à L.L. MM. l'Empereur du Brésil et le Roi d'Espagne), Paris, Auguste Ghio, 1885.

Memoir: *La République d'Haiti à l'apothéose de Victor Hugo, documents commémoratifs,* Paris, Derenne, 1885.

Politics: *Essai sur la politique intérieure d'Haiti; proposition d'une politique nouvelle,* Paris, A. Challamé, 1890.

EGA, Françoise

b. November 27, 1924, Case-Pilote, Martinique; d. March, 1976, Marseille.
Novelist, storywriter.

Françoise Ega received her education in the Perrinon School of Fort-de-France after which she went to France in 1946. After marriage to Saint-François Xavier, she entered the French Air Force and served in Indochina, Djibouti and Madagascar. Her last years were spent in Marseilles. She has published one autobiographial narrative, *Le Temps des madras* (1967), and has in manuscript two other works: the novel "Cité des Aulx" and "Lettres à Carolina."

EL LIMAC, Nassour

(pseudonym for **Roussan Camille**)

ELIE, Abel

(pseudonym: **FRANCK**)
b. January 15, 1841, Port-au-Prince, Haiti; d. November, 1876, Port-de-Paix, Haiti.
Poet.

Elie left Haiti as a child with his family who lived in exile in France where the poet spent many years and where he was educated. He published many poems under the pseudonym of Franck in *L'Opinion* and *Le Bien Public.* He died at the age of 33 and failed to published any collection of his verse.

Frédéric Marcelin, one of his friends, favorably commented on the works of Elie: "Il avait l'âme tendre, l'imagination ardente, la confiance loyale qui caractérise ces êtres privilégiés."

Writings: Poetry: "Premiers accords," unpublished collection; miscellaneous verse in journals and anthologies.

ELIE, Louis Emile

b. February 28, 1884, Port-au-Prince, Haiti; d. ca. 1955.
Biographer, historian.

Elie was educated in Port-au-Prince, and later served as Haitian Consul in Cuba. When he returned to Port-au-Prince, he was employed as an agronomist at the Technical Service of Agriculture. His writings focussed on slavery, Haitian politics, and the biographies of Boyer, Dessalines and Christophe.

Writings: Biographies: "Alexandre Pétion et l'opposition du Sénat," in *Le Temps* (Jan. 31 and Feb. 1, 2, 4, 5, and 6, 1929), *Le Président Boyer et l'Empereur de Russie Alexandre Ier (une mission diplomatique à Saint Pétersbourg, 1821),* Port-au-Prince, Impr. du Collège Vertières, 1942; "Le Libérateur Dessalines et son temps" (unpublished); "La vie tragique d'Henri Christophe" (unpublished); (The two unpublished manuscripts cited above are in the archives of the Brothers of Christian Education, Port-au-Prince.); *Fabre Geffrard et son temps: 1806-1878* (manuscript).

History: "Esclaves, Affranchis et Colons. La vie coloniale à Saint-Domingue" (feuilleton historique), in *Haiti-Journal* (April 2-May 9, 1930); "Les causes véritables des guerres de l'indépendance," in *Le Temps* (Sep. 10, 11, and 12, 1928); "Auguste Magloire, ses idées et ses opinions," in *Le Temps,* 8è année, 1939; *Histoire d'Haiti,* 3 vols., Port-au-Prince, 1944, 1945; Vols. 4 and 5 in manuscripts, uncompleted.

ELOT, Maryse

b. 1914, Bretagne, France (of Guadeloupian father).
Poet, novelist.

Elot was born in Bretagne but her father was a Guadeloupean. She received her education in France. Happy to return to her father's land, she accepted appointment as professor of literature at the Lycée of Basse-Terre.

Elot has contributed articles to several newspapers and to many cultural activities. She is presently living in New York.

Writings: Poetry: *Le carnaval des Muses, poèmes,* 1933; *L'encens des crépuscules,* 1933; *La symphonie d'amours,* 1935; *A fleur de soir,* 1938; *Symphonie des Antilles,* Malines, Belgium Cahiers de la Tour de Babel, 1953, and Paris, Ed. du C.E.L.F., n.d.; *Sérénité d'après-midi,* published in *Revue Guadeloupéenne,* No. 20 (March-April, 1949).

Novel: *Mosquito,* 1943.

EMILE, Georges Léon

b. July 21, 1915, Port-au-Prince, Haiti.
Poet, teacher.

Emile was educated in Port-au-Prince, attending the Petit Séminaire Collège Saint Martial and the Lycée Pétion. He published one collection of verse.

Writings: Poetry: *Les Préludes,* Port-au-Prince (?), 1941.

EMMBE

(pseudonym for **Marie BERTE**)

ESTOUP, Valentine Eugénie

b. October 8, 1891, Toulouse, France; d. October 16, 1961, Guadeloupe.
Poet.

Estoup was born at Toulouse and was educated there. She married Henri Corbin, then a student at the Faculty of Medicine, and has spent all her life in Guadeloupe.

Writings: Poetry: *Les Heures changeantes,* Toulouse, Eds. du Bon Plaisir, 1928; *La danse des images,* 1929.

ETCHART, Salvat

b. ca. 1932, Netherlands (associated with Martinique).
Novelist.

Etchart came to settle in Martinique and was named Director of Martinique Radio, but as he was too fervent in his attacks on colonialism, he was dismissed from his post.

His works face social issues directly and some more sensitive critics (those whose own predilections or prejudices are affronted) have found him too harsh. Also, he is called "Le Céline des tropiques," and his book, *Le Monde tel qu'il est,* was awarded the Prix Renaudot in 1967.

Writings: Novels: *Une bonne à six,* Paris, Ed. Julliard, 1962; *Les Nègres servent d'exemple,* Paris, Ed. Julliard, 1964; *Le Monde tel qu'il est,* Paris, Mercure de France, 1967; *L'Homme empêché,* Paris, Mercure de France, 1977.

ETHEART, Liautaud

b. March 9, 1826, Port-au-Prince, Haiti; d. November 21, 1888, Port-au-Prince.
Playwright, poet, storywriter, statesman, scholar.

Ethéart studied in Port-au-Prince and was the founder of the Collège Wilberforce, which he headed from 1853-1858. Active in public affairs, he was named Chef de Division au Département de l'Instruction Publique. He became minister of Finances and of Commerce (1872-1875), and finally of Foreign Affairs (1878-1879). He was also at one time the director of the journal *Le Moniteur.*

He was a fertile dramatist and writer of farces and monologues. His best play is considered *La fille de l'Empereur,* set in the time of Dessalines.

Most of his work was published in three volumes (Paris, 1857-1860).

Writings: Plays: *Génie d'enfer* (drama in one act); *Guelfes et Gibelins* (historical drama in 3 acts, 6 scenes); *La fille de l'Empereur* (drama); *Un duel sous Blanchelande* (historical drama in 4 acts and 6 scenes); *Un espoir déçu* (drama); *Le monde de chez nous* (comédy in 5 acts); *Le parc aux cerfs.*

Vaudevilles: *Deux étudiants* (2 acts); *Binettes de classiques* (2 acts).

Monologue: *Faute d'un habit* (one act in verse).

Essays and Articles: *Miscellanées,* Port-au-Prince, Impr. J. Courtois, 1885.

Economics and History: *Discussions économiques et documents d'histoire,* Port-au-Prince, Impr. Ritt Ethéart, 1882; *Le Gouvernement du Général Boisrond-Canal, la France et l'emprunt de 1875,* Port-au-Prince, Impr. Ritt Ethéart, 1882; *La vérité à Mr Vouillon,* Port-au-Prince, Impr. Ritt Ethéart, 1884.

ETIENNE, Franck
(or **FRANKETIENNE**)
b. April 12, 1936, Saint-Marc, Haiti.
Poet, novelist in creole, playwright, teacher.

Franck Etienne received his education partly at the Petit Séminaire Collège Saint-Martial and partly at the Lycée Pétion in Port-au-Prince. He is a teacher and the head of his own college.

Frankétienne has published many collections of poems, but he is particularly credited with being the author of the first novel written in creole, *Dezafi.* Thanks to him and many supporters, Haiti is in possession of a remarkable collection of literary works in creole.

Writings: Poetry: *Au fil du temps,* Impr. des Antilles, 1964; *La Marche,* Eds. Panorama, 1964; *Mon Côté Gauche,* Impr. Serge L. Gaston, 1965; *Vigie de Verre,* Impr. Serge L. Gaston, 1965; *Chevaux de l'Avant-Jour,* Impr. Serge L. Gaston: all in Port-au-Prince.

Novels (in French): *Mur à crever,* Port-au-Prince, 1968; *Ultravocal,* Port-au-Prince.

Novel (in creole): *Dézafi,* Port-au-Prince, Eds. Fardin, 1975.

Play: *Trou-Forban,* tragedy performed at Rex Theatre, December, 1977; *Pèlin-Tèt,* performed in 1978.

ETIENNE, Gérard Vergniaud
b. May 28, 1936, Cap-Haitien.
Poet, novelist, essayist, teacher.

Etienne's schooling began in Cap-Haitien and was completed in Port-au-Prince. He then taught in Haiti and was a journalist, writing critical essays primarily. Presently, Etienne lives in Canada, where he is a university professor.

Writings: Poetry: *Au milieu des larmes,* Port-au-Prince, Togiram-Presse, 1960; *Plus large qu'un rêve,* Port-au-Prince, Impr. Dorsinville, 1960; *La raison et mon amour,* Port-au-Prince, Les Presses Port-au-Princiennes, 1961; *Gladys,* Port-au-Prince, Eds. Panorama, 1963; *Dialogue avec mon ombre,* Eds. Francophones, Canada, 1972.

Essays: *Essai sur la négritude,* Port-au-Prince, Ed. Panorama, 1962; *Le nationalisme dans la littérature haitienne,* Port-au-Prince, Ed. du Lycée Pétion, 1964; *Lettre à Montréal,* Canada, Ed. Estérel, 1966.

Novel: *Le nègre crucifié,* Canada, Eds. Francophones, 1974.

EUGENE, Grégoire
b. March 12, 1925, Grande-Rivière-du-Nord, Haiti.
Playwright, teacher, lawyer.

Eugène attended the school of Christian Brothers in Grande-Rivière-du-Nord for his primary classes and went to the Collège de Notre Dame, in Cap-Haitien and the Petit Séminaire Collège Saint-

Martial for his secondary studies. He graduated from the Faculty of Law.

Eugène was a professor at the Lycée Pétion and later became Under-secretary of State at the Department of Justice. He is now professor at the Faculty of Law, Port-au-Prince, and the principal of his own private college.

Writings: Play: *Une ombre au tableau ou les droits du coeur,* performed April 26, 1969 and 1972 (unpublished); *Le Séducteur* (tragedy in 5 acts, unpublished).

EYMA, Louis Xavier

b. 1816, Saint-Pierre, Martinique; d. 1876.

Poet, novelist, storywriter.

Eyma studied in Paris, but moved with his father to Louisiana. Eyma went to New Orleans and was editor of the French section of the journal *l'Abeille.*

His career began as a poet, but he dropped poetry to write novels. His wish was to become the "Balzac des Tropiques."

Writings: Novel: *Emmanuel,* Fort-de-France, 1841 (novel and poems).

Stories: *Les Peaux noires; scènes de la vie des esclaves,* Paris, M. Lévy, 1857; *Excentricités américaines,* 1860; *Légendes, fantômes et récits du Nouveau Monde,* Paris, A. Lacroix, 2 vols., 1862; *Scènes de moeurs et de voyage dans le Nouveau Monde,* Paris, Poulet-Malassis, 1862.

Historical Novels: *Le Roi des tropiques,* Paris, Michel Lévy, 1860; *Aventuriers et Corsaires,* 1861; *Le trône d'argent,* Paris, M. Lévy, 1861; *Les poches de mon parrain,* 1863; *La chasse à l'esclave,* Paris, Brunet, 1866.

Essay: *Introduction à une politique générale.*

Politics: *Les deux Amériques,* 1853; *Les Femmes du Nouveau Monde,* 1860; *La République américaine,* 1861; *Les 34 étoiles de l'Union Américaine,* 1862.

Biographical/Critical Sources: Auguste Viatte, *Histoire Littéraire de l'Amérique française,* Laval, Quebec, Presses Universitaires, 1954, pp. 274-275 and 491-492.

FABRY, Claude

(pseudonym for **Arthur BONHOMME**)

b. June 19, 1910, Port-au-Prince, Haiti.

Poet, diplomat.

Born into a Baptist family, Fabry received his first education from his father and later studied at the Lycée Pétion where his father was a professor. After earning his baccalaureate, he entered the Military School where he graduated as an officer. One of a group of young officers who had conspired to overthrow the government, Fabry was sentenced by a general court-martial to be shot, but the death penalty was changed to life in prison. Eventually released, Fabry worked with the Nobel Prize-winner Franck Lauback and promoted the education of the Haitian masses in creole rather than in French.

He was elected Senator in 1957 and became Minister of Public Works in the government of Dr. François Duvalier. He served as Ambassador of Haiti in Washington, D.C., and represented Haiti at the Conference of American Heads of State at Punta del Este in Uruguay, in 1969.

Writings: Poetry: *L'âme du lambi,* Port-au-Prince, Impr. Telhomme, 1937.

Criticism (with Lorimer Denis and François Duvalier), *Les tendances d'une génération,* Port-au-Prince, Impr. du Collège Vertières, 1934. (Fabry's contribution was the essay, "La nouvelle génération littéraire," first prepared for a literary lecture, July 24, 1932.)

FANON, Frantz

b. July 20, 1925, Fort-de-France, Martinique; d. December 6, 1961, Washington, D. C.

Physician, social scientist, scholar.

Fanon attended the primary school and the Lycée Schoelcher in Fort-de-France where one of his teachers had been Aimé Césaire, who had a great influence on him. He went to France to complete his education. During the Second World War, he had joined the French army and fought under General De Lattre de Tassigny's command.

After the war, Fanon studied medicine at the Faculty of Lyon, and his specialization was psychiatry.

The year after his graduation, Fanon published his famous book *Peau noire, masques blancs.* By 1953, he was named director of psychiatric service at Blida-Joinville Hospital, in Algeria. Fanon was an activist. While a student in Lyon, he edited a magazine, *Tom-Tom,* and contributed to *Le Progrès de Lyon* and to *Esprit,* and in Algeria he published articles in the local press. In Tunis, he was a member of the Press Services of F.L.N., and was a contributor to *El Moudjahid.*

When he analyzed the situation of the Antillean people and especially the Caribbean writer, he said:

> *Jusqu'en 1939, l'Antillais vivait, pensait, rêvait, composait des poèmes, écrivait des romans exactement comme l'aurait fait un blanc. On comprend maintenant pourquoi il ne lui était pas possible de chanter comme les poètes africains la nuit noire, "La femme noire aux talons roses." Avant Césaire, la littérature antillaise est une littérature d'Européens. L'Antillais s'identifiait au blanc, adoptait une attitude de blanc, "était un blanc."*

Fanon did not hesitate to express his thoughts harshly when he felt the need, and he did so without reservation. One day, he met a friend, a schoolmate, and told him:

> *Alors, vous faites encore de la* politique *aux Antilles et en Guyane? Un de ces jours, c'est à coups de pied au cul que la France vous obligera à prendre votre indépendance. C'est à l'Algérie que vous le devez, notre Algérie qui aura été la putain de l'Empire colonial français.*

His second book was *Les damnés de la terre.* As a specialist of psycho-pathology, accustomed to human traumas, Fanon perceived the aberrations of racism and colonialism as well as the limitations of Negritude and Arabism. Although born in Martinique—an historical accident—he felt Algerian, and as he became a supporter of the Algerian cause, a fighter among the Algerian "guerilleros" he shouted, "Je suis Algérien ... Nous, patriotes algériens."

Fanon was Ambassador of Algeria in Ghana, where he became a close friend of Kwame Nkrumah and became an advisor to Patrice Lumumba.

His last work, the as yet unpublished "El Moujahid," envisioned a better humanity and he voiced this message:

> *La condition humaine, les projets de l'homme, la collaboration entre les hommes pour des tâches qui augmentent la totalité de l'homme sont des problèmes neufs qui exigent de véritables inventions.*
>
> *Décidons de ne pas imiter l'Europe et bandons nos muscles et nos cerveaux dans une direction nouvelle. Tâchons d'inventer l'homme total que l'Europe a été incapable de faire triompher.*
>
> *Pour l'Europe, pour nous-mêmes et pour l'humanité, il faut faire peau neuve, développer une pensée neuve, tenter de mettre sur pied un homme neuf.*

As Karl Marx and Lenin were the inventors of the doctrines of a non-capitalist system, Frantz Fanon has become not only a spokesman of the oppressed people whatever their place or race, but remains the leading intellectual influence of the Third World.

Fanon, suffering from leukemia, was brought to Bethesda Hospital near Washington, D. C. in December, 1961, and died there.

An eulogy published by Présence Africaine said:

> *Frantz Fanon savait que tous les opprimés, tous les colonisés, tous les bannis de la dignité humaine sont solidaires, à travers le monde, dans le combat qu'ils poursuivent ensemble pour la libre jouissance de leur émancipation, pour la récupération de leurs droits et que ce combat est le même sur tous les fronts de l'oppression.*

Writings: Political Works: *Peau noire, masques blancs,* preface by Francis Jeanson, Paris, Eds. du Seuil, 1952; *Black Skin, White Masks,* trans. by Charles Lam Markmann, New York, Grove Press, 1967; *Les Damnés de la terre,* preface by J.P. Sartre, Paris, F. Maspéro, 1961; trans. as *The Wretched of the Earth* by Constance Farrington, New York, Grove Press, 1965; *The damned,* Paris, Présence Africaine, 1963; German: *Die Verdammten dieser Erde,* Frankfurt, Surkamp, 1966; Danish: *Fordomte her pà Jorden,* Kobenhavn, Rhodos, 1966; Spanish: *Los Condenados de la tierra,* Mexico, F. de C.E. 1964; Portuguese: *Os Condenados da tierra,* Lisboa, Ulisseia, n.d.; Turkish: *Dunyanin Panetleri,* Istambul, Ciner Matbaasi, 1965; Yugoslavian: *Upor prekletik,* Ljubljana, Cankayeva Zalozba, 1963; *L'An V de la révolution algérienne,* Paris, F. Maspéro, 1959, trans. as *Studies in a Dying Colonialism* by Haakon Chevalier, New York, Monthly Review Press, 1965, and as *A Dying Colonialism,* New York, Grove Press, 1967; *Pour la révolution africaine,* Paris, F. Maspéro, 1964, trans. as *Toward the African Revolution* by Haakon Chevalier, New York, Grove Press, 1966; and "El Moudjahid" (unpublished).

Essay: "Antillais et Africains" in *Esprit,* Paris, (Feb. 1955), p. 263-268; "La plainte du Noir," by F. Fanon, L. T. Achille, J. F. Povers, *Esprit,* Paris, Mai 1951.

Biographical/Critical Sources: David Caute, *Frantz Fanon,* trans. by Guy Durand, Paris, Seghers, 1970; Renate Zahar, *L'Oeuvre de Frantz Fanon,* Paris, Eds. Maspéro, 1970; Philippe Lucas, *Sociologie de Frantz Fanon,* Paris, S.N.E.D. Etudes et Documents, 1971; Pierre Bouvier, *Fanon,* Paris, Eds. Universitaires, 1971; *Hommages à Frantz Fanon,* Paris, Présence Africaine, New Series, XL (First Quarter, 1962), pp. 118-142; M. Pablo, *Les Damnés de la terre. Quatrième Internationale,* 1962; J.M. Domenach, "Les Damnés de la terre," in *Esprit* (April 1962); G.K. Grohs, "Frantz Fanon et les problèmes de l'indépendance," in *La Pensée* (Feb. 1963); I.L. Gendzier, "Frantz Fanon: In Search of Justice," in *Middle East Journal* (1966); F.M. Gottheil, "Fanon and the Economics of Colonialism," in *Review of Economics and Business,* Vol. 7, No. 3 (Autumn 1967); F. Stambouli, "Frantz Fanon face aux problèmes de la décolonisation et de la construction nationale," *Revue de l'Institut de Sociologie,* Nos. 2-3 (1967); A. Zolberg, "Frantz Fanon: A Gospel for the Damned," *Encounter* (Nov. 1966); A. & R. Zolberg, "The Americanization of Frantz Fanon," in *The Interest,* No. 9 (1967); R. Barnard, "Frantz Fanon," *New Society* (Jan. 4, 1968); P. Geismar and P. Worsley, "Frantz Fanon: Evolution of a Revolutionary," *Monthly Review* (May 1969); M. Staniland, "Frantz Fanon and the African Political Class," in *African Affairs* (Jan 1969); R. M. Lacovia, "Frantz Fanon: A rehabilitating of our living-dead," in *Black Images,* Vol. 1, No. 3-4 (Autumn-Winter 1972), pp. 49-62; Fanon's name is invoked and his presence felt in Taban Lo Liyong's *Frantz Fanon's Uneven Ribs, with poems more and more,* London, Heinemann, 1971.

FARDIN, Dieudonné

(pseudonym for **Louis Marie PIERRE BENOIT**)

b. November 18, 1936, Saint Louis du Nord, Haiti.

Poet, novelist, storywriter, anthologist, editor.

Pierre Benoit was educated at the Lycée Tertulien Guilbaud of Port-de-Paix. He started his career as a teacher.

Benoit founded his mimeographed paper, *Le Petit Samedi Soir,* to create a literary life in the North-West Department. After many years, he moved to Port-au-Prince where his journal is playing a very important role in the current Haitian literary scene. He even voices criticism of public practices and measures notwithstanding the censorship imposed on the Haitian press. As editor, Dieudonné Fardin is doing fine work in reprinting many Haitian books long out of print.

Writings: Poetry: *Isabelle (Sur les Rives de l'Histoire* (poèsies et pensées), Port-de-Paix, Impr. La Petite Bourse, 1958; *Mélancolie des Heures Vécues, poésies et pensées,* Port-de-Paix, Impr. La Petite Bourse, 1958; *K. . . .K. . Chate* (poems in creole), Port-de-Paix, Atelier Capois La-Mort, 1960; *Déblosailles* (poems in creole), Port-de-Paix, Atelier Capois-La-Mort, 1961; *Lyre Déclassée,* Port-de-Paix, Atelier Capois-La-Mort, 1962; *Sept Fleurs Soleil,* Port-de-Paix, Atelier Capois-La-Mort, 1963; *Collier la Rosée, poèmes créoles,* Port-de-Paix, Atelier Capois-La-Mort, 1964; *Port-de-Paix Multicolore,* Port-de-Paix, Atelier Capois-La-Mort, 1965; *Létilia* (poems in creole), Port-de-Paix, Atelier Capois-La-Mort, 1966; *Mon poème de chair,* Port-au-Prince, Impr. of ONAAC, 1967; *Les grandes orgues followed by Aux Saisons de moi-même,* Port-au-Prince, Atelier Fardin, 1973.

Anthology: *Anthologie des Poètes et Ecrivains du Nord-Ouest, Tome I, Les Poètes,* Port-de-Paix, Atelier Capois-La-Mort, 1962; *Cours de Littérature haitienne,* 4 vols., mimeo., 1968-1969.

FAUBERT, Ida

(née **SALOMON**)

b. 1883, Port-au-Prince, Haiti; d. 1968, Paris.

Poet, storywriter.

Daughter of Haitian president Lysius Félicité Salomon, Ida went to Paris for her education and later married André Faubert. She spent all her life in Paris.

Her orientation to verse was accordingly contemporary, refined, and not at all touched by nativist sentiments. Her poetry recalls that of Marceline Desbordes-Valmore and is melancholic and subjective. Her most popular poems were "Pour Jacqueline," first published in 1912, but only collected in her 1939 volume, *Coeur des Iles,* and "Pierre Loti," for which she won a prize.

Writings: Poetry: *Coeur des Iles,* Paris, Impr. Spéciale des Editeurs Débrosse, 1939.

Stories: *Sous le ciel caraibe; histoire d'Haiti et d'ailleurs,* introduction by Pierre Dominique, Paris, Office Librairie Bord, 1959, and Paris, O.L.B., 1960.

Biographical/Critical Sources: Léon Laleau, "Ida Faubert," in *Femmes Haitiennes, Ligue Féminine d'Action Sociale,* (Collection du Tricinquantenaire de l'Indépendance d'Haiti), Port-au-Prince, Impr. Henri Deschamps, 1954, pp. 247-254.

FAUBERT, Pierre

b. March 1, 1806, Cayes, Haiti; d. July 13, 1868, Paris.

Poet, playwright.

Faubert received his education in France. When he returned to Haiti, he was for a period aide-de-camp and secretary to President Jean-Pierre Boyer. He became Director of the Lycée Pétion.

When Boyer was overthrown by the 1843 revolution, Faubert went to France where he spent much of his life. He was disgusted with the strife between mulatto and African stock Haitians, both in Paris and at home, and warned in his poem "Aux Haitiens" that the United States, supported by slave labor, was dreaming of the flowery field of conquest of new plantation lands in Haiti, and thus unity was a necessity:

Union, mot bien vieux, frères, mais mot sublime!
Ah! qu'il pénètre chaque coeur!
Dieu même nous le dit; Dieu qui, dans l'homme estime
L'âme seule, et non la couleur.

His poetry followed the pattern and music of the French poet Lamartine, then the most esteemed poet of the mid-century.

He exalted the beauty of the black girl:

Je suis fier de le dire, ô négresse, je t'aime!
Et ta noire couleur me plait. Sais-tu pourquoi? . . .
C'est que, nobles vertus, chaste coeur, beauté même
Tout ce qui charme enfin, le ciel l'a mis en toi.

Some of his poems celebrated the love of a white man for a Haitian creole girl, but one of his last poems ends with his love of a French girl:

O vous d'un ciel brumeux étoile éblouissante,
Qu'un seul de vos regards charmants
Sur moi vienne briller; et, sans regret, j'oublie
Le beau ciel bleu de ma patrie,

Ses palmiers toujours verts, ses alizés si doux,
Pour vivre à jamais près de vous!

His one play, *Ogé ou le préjugé de couleur,* was performed in 1841 by his students at the school where he was the principal.

In 1860 he helped to negotiate a Haitian Concordat with the Vatican, but he finished his life in exile. He was made a Roman Count by the Vatican State.

Writings: Play with Poetry: *Ogé ou le préjugé de couleur,* (historical drama), followed by *Poèsies fugitives et de notes,* Paris, Impr. de Moquet, 1856.

Speech: *Discours funèbre à la mémoire de Claire-Amélie-Alexandrine Célie Pétion* (the daughter of the then Haitian president, Alexandre Pétion), Port-au-Prince, Impr. du Gouvernement, 1827, delivered Port-au-Prince (Sep. 28, 1827).

FEQUIERE, Fleury

b. August 19, 1860, Petit-Trou-de-Nippes, Haiti; d. March 9, 1941, Port-au-Prince.
Playwright, scholar, statesman.

Most of Féquière's schooling was in Port-au-Prince. He was a frequent contributor to local journals and had an active public career, serving as chef de division at the Department of Navy in 1887, and later as Membre de la Chambre des Comptes in 1895-1899. He was elected Deputy in 1899.

Also active in education, Fequiere helped found the Ecole Elie Dubois and the Ecole Libre des Sciences Appliquées. His *L'éducation haitienne* stimulated improvement in the Haitian school system.

Writings: Play (with Henri Chauvet): *Une nuit de noces* (one act), Port-au-Prince, Chauvet, 1901.

Education-Sociology: *L'éducation haitienne,* Port-au-Prince, Impr. de l'Abeille, 1906; *Le jeu en Haiti; La Morale et le Code; L'Alcoolisme et ses ravages,* details unknown.

Report: *Promenade à l'Exposition du 22 décembre 1901 (Orphelinat de la Madeleine),* Port-au-Prince, Impr. de l'Abeille, 1902.

FERY, Alibée

b. May 28, 1819, Jérémie, Haiti; d. January 28, 1896, Port-au-Prince.
Poet, essayist, playwright.

Fery studied in Port-au-Prince, and then lived as a literary man, although he was inordinately fond of his title of general.

A classicist, Féry was an imitator of the best Greek and Latin models. He was only 20 years old when he wrote his two comedies, *Les Rimeurs* and *Le barbon amoureux.* His youthful poetry, *Les Bluettes,* was modeled on French poets of this time, particularly Beranger, and he published historical notes with *Les Esquisses.*

Writings: Essays: *Essais littéraires,* 4 vols., Port-au-Prince, Impr. Robin, 1876. (The volumes are: I—*Les rimeurs, Le barbon amoureux;* II—*Les bluettes, Les échantillons;* III—*Les esquisses* [folklore]; and IV—*Les mélanges);* the play *Le trésor supposé,* written in 1843, is lost.

Biographical/Critical Sources: Edmond Laforest, *Alibée Féry, sa vie et son oeuvre,* Port-au-Prince, date unknown.

FETHIERE, Sténio

b. July 1, 1908, Cayes, Haiti.
Poet, agronomist.

After Fethière completed his secondary education, he studied at the Technical School of Agriculture where he graduated. He then served as an agricultural agent in many localities in Haiti. He also studied law.

He became head of an agricultural district and then Director General of the Agriculture Department, and, finally, the Undersecretary of Agriculture.

Influenced by such nativist poets as Oswald Durand, Féthière would write in

"Archipels":

Non, ce n'est pas Vénus, car Vénus
n'est pas noire,
Mais elle en a les seins, l'épaule et
les hanches,
Cette femme aux grands yeux que le
buisson contemple. . . .

Writings: Poetry: *Archipels,* Port-au-Prince, Impr. de l'Etat, 1945.

FIGARO, Georges Jacques

b. August 8, 1918, Port-au-Prince, Haiti.
Poet.

Figaro was educated in Port-au-Prince. He taught in several schools and practiced journalism. He became Director of the Office of Government Publicity, and later served the government of Dr. François Duvalier as Minister of Coordination and Information. He was also a Mayor of Port-au-Prince, and he is now Préfet de Port-au-Prince.

Writings: Poetry: *L'écrin de mes rêves,* Port-au-Prince, Impr. du Collège Vertières, 1941; *Les ailes au vent,* Port-au-Prince, Impr. V. Valcin, n.d.; *Fusées, poèmes,* Port-au-Prince, Impr. Beaubrun, 1945; *L'Angoisse (poèmes),* Port-au-Prince, Impr. V. Valcin, 1942 (?); *Dialogue avec une ombre (poème),* Port-au-Prince, Impr. de l'Etat, 1946; *Stèle à Jean Rémy,* Port-au-Prince, Ed. Le Soir, 1948; *Le coffret de Cèdre,* preface by Léon Laleau, Port-au-Prince, Les Presses Nationales d'Haiti, 1972.

Story: *Le Papillon noir* (nouvelle), Port-au-Prince, Impr. de l'Etat, 1953.

FIGARO, Morille P.
(or **Maurille**)

b. October 21, 1922, Quartier-Morin, Haiti.
Poet, novelist.

Figaro spent all his life in Port-au-Prince, where he was educated. He was a teacher in several schools and a contributor to many journals.

He served as Minister of the Interior and National Defense in the Government of Dr. François Duvalier. He is now a member of the Grand Conseil Technique.

Writings: Essays: *Feuilles à la brise,* Port-au-Prince, Impr. de l'Abeille, 1937; *Le Duc de Tabara révolutionnaire (Histoire d'Haiti en roman),* Port-au-Prince, Impr. Barthélemy, 1948; *Voyage en pays nègre; thèse pour ma licence-ès-sciences ethnologiques,* Port-au-Prince, Impr. Barthélemy.

Poetry: poems published in various journals, including: *Panorama de la Poèsie Haitienne,* Port-au-Prince, Ed. H. Deschamps, 1950, edited by Maurice A. Lubin and Carlos Saint-Louis.

Novel: *Cadidja, la noire négresse,* Port-au-Prince, Impr. Le Soir, 1947; *La fleur qui s'ouvre,* Vol. 1, Port-au-Prince, Impr. de l'Etat, 1958; *Du Soleil sur les sables,* Port-au-Prince, Impr. de l'Etat, 1959.

FIGNOLE, Jean-Claude

b. May 24, 1942, Jérémie, Haiti.
Poet, essayist, teacher.

After completing his classical studies, Fignolé studied agronomy, law and economics. He is now teaching literature in Port-au-Prince.

Writings: Poetry: two collections: "Prose pour un homme seul," and "Fantasme" (both unpublished); individual poems in various journals.

Essay: *Oswald Durand,* Haiti, 1968; *Etzer Vilaire, ce méconnu,* Port-au-Prince, Eds. Fardin, 1970; *Pour une poésie de l'authentique et du solidaire,* Port-au-Prince, n.d.

FIRMIN, Anténor Joseph

b. October 20, 1851, Cap-Haitien, Haiti; d. September 19, 1911, St. Thomas, V.I., U.S.A.
Biographer, letter writer, statesman, scientist, historian.

Firmin was educated in Cap-Haitien and was thereafter employed by a business enterprise where he studied German and became familiar with financial problems. He was appointed a school teacher in the primary school for boys and afterwards was assistant supervisor for all the schools of Cap-Haitien.

In 1878, he founded the newspaper *Le Messager du Nord.* He went to France in 1884 and was received as a member of the Société d'Anthropologie. The next year he published *De l'Egalité des races humaines.*

He returned to Haiti after President Félicité Salomon was overthrown, and contributed to the work on the new Constitution of 1889. He was named by President François D. Légitime the Minister of Finance and Foreign Affairs.

Firmin served as Minister Plenipotentiary of Haiti to France, but in his effort to reach the highest office, he was defeated for the presidency in 1902 by Nord Alexis. Exiled, he moved to St. Thomas where he wrote a polemical biography of President Theodore Roosevelt of the United States, and a study of Haiti.

While most of his writing was not in the literary area, his style was crisp and his thinking always clear, as were his public addresses.

Writings: Ethnography: *De l'égalité des races humaines, anthropologie positive,* Paris, Cotillon, 1885.

Law: *Lettre ouverte aux membres de la Société de Législation de Port-au-Prince,* Basse-Terre, Guadeloupe, Impr. Ouvrière, 1904; *Deuxième lettre ouverte aux membres de la Société de Législation de Port-au-Prince, 10 Juillet 1905,* Basse-Terre, Guadeloupe, Impr. Ouvrière, 1905.

Letters: *Lettres de Saint-Thomas; études sociologiques, historiques et littéraires,* Paris, V. Giard et E. Brière, 1910; *Diplomates et diplomatie; lettre ouverte à Mr Solon Ménos,* Cap-Haitien, Impr. du Progrès, 1899.

History: *Monsieur Roosevelt, Président des Etats-Unis et la République d'Haiti,* New York, Hamilton Bank Note Engraving and Printing Co., and Paris, F. Pichon et Durand Auzias, 1905.

Essays: *Haiti au point de vue politique, administratif et économique, conférence faite au Grand Cercle de Paris, le 8 Décembre 1891,* Paris, F. Pichon, 1891; *L'Effort dans le mal,* Port-au-Prince, Impr. H. Chauvet et Cie, 1911, and San Juan, Puerto Rico, Tip Real Hermanos, 1911; *La République d'Haiti et ses relations économiques avec la France,* Paris, Soc. des Etudes Coloniales et Maritimes, 1892; *Une défense: Mr Stewart et les finances haitiennes,* Paris, F. Pichon, 1892.

Biographical/Critical Sources: Démétrius André, *L'Anniversaire ou éloge de Joseph Anténor Firmin,* September 19, 1912, Port-au-Prince, Impr. J Verrollot, 1912; Léonce Viaud, *La personnalité d'Anténor Firmin, étude psychologique,* Port-au-Prince, Impr. V. Valcin, 1948; Georges Benjamin, *La diplomatie d'Anténor Firmin, ses péripéties ses aspects,* Paris, A. Pedone, 1960; Claude Moise, "Memoire de sortie su Anténor Firmin," in *Conjonction,* (December 1971); Dr. Jean Price-Mars, *Anténor Firmin, le mal aimé,* Port-au-Prince, Impr. Séminaire Adventiste, 1978.

FLEURY-BATTIER

(pseudonym for **Alcibiade FLEURY-BATTIER**)

FLIGNEAU, Pierre

b. ca. 1774, Cayes, Haiti; d. in 19th century.
Playwright.

Fligneau was a member of the free-colored group who were afforded some opportunity to receive education. He was fond of the theatre and wrote the play *L'haitien expatrié,* performed in Cayes on November 12, 1804, and dedicated to General Geffrard, major-general in the Department of the South. Until recently, *L'haitien expatrié* was considered the first work written in Haiti after independence. According to Jean Fouchard's information, the play was printed in 1840 by the author's nephew, Alfred Gicquel. The sole existing copy known is in the Bibliothèque Nationale de Paris.

Writings: Play: *L'haitien expatrié; comédie en trois actes, en prose,* performed Les Cayes, 1804; published Paris (?), 1840.

FLORENTINY, Edouard

b. ca. 1934, Sainte-Marie, Martinique.
Poet.

Édouard FLORENTINY
LES ANTILLES TOUTES NUES
ÉDITIONS LOUIS SOULANGES
20, Rue de l'Odéon – PARIS (VIe)

After a happy childhood in his natal village near the sea, it was only natural for Florentiny to join the merchant marine. Three times he has sailed around the world and visited many lands. Returning, he wrote a "memoir" of his childhood and a philosophical introspective examination of Martinique (Les Antilles). His third novel (some 158 pages) is a soft-focus study of the relationship between French and Martiniquais and shows a young doctor from the island "envying" his old professor from France stricken while on a visit to Martinique.

Writings: "La vie et les déboires d'un enfant noir," in *Gazette de la Martinique* (April 1964), Paris, Eds. Soulanges, 1964; *Les Antilles: toutes nues,* Paris, Eds. Soulanges, 1966.

Essays and Pensées: *Le Plus Petit sera le plus grand,* Paris, Eds. Soulanges, 1969.

FOUCHE, Franck

b. November 27, 1915, Saint-Marc, Haiti; d. January 3, 1978, Montréal, Canada.
Poet (in French and creole), critic, literary historian, playwright.

Fouché was educated in Port-au-Prince and graduated from the Faculty of Law of Port-au-Prince. He was professor at the Lycée Sténio Vincent of Saint-Marc for many years and later at several colleges of Port-au-Prince. He contributed to magazines and newspapers, including *La Relève, Horizons,* and *Optique,* and became the editor-in-chief of the unofficial gazette, *Le National.* He also served as First Secretary of the Haitian Embassy in Mexico. He was a teacher in Montréal at the time of his death in 1978.

Writings: Poetry: *Message,* Port-au-Prince, Impr. Nemours Telhomme, 1946; *Symphonie en noir majeur, poème,* Port-au-Prince, Art Graphic Press, 1961 (dedicated to Roussan Camille); *Les Lambis de la Sierra* (in Russian in

Le temps des flamboyants, Moscow, U.S.S.R., 1960), trans. into Spanish by Nicolás Guillén.

Essays: *Guide pour l'étude de la littérature haitienne*, Port-au-Prince, Ed. Panorama, 1964; *Vodou et Théâtre. Pour un Nouveau Théâtre Populaire*, Montreal, Eds. Nouvelle Optique, 1976.

Plays: *Yerma*, adapt. in creole from *Yerma* of Federico Garcia Lorca, in magazine *Optique*, Haiti (1965); *Un fauteuil dans un crâne*, in

Optique (Haiti, 1957); *Oedipe-Roi* (in creole), Port-au-Prince, 1958; *Trou de Dieu* (1st version) in *Théâtre vivant*, Holt, Rinehart & Winston, Montreal, 1968; *Bouqui au Paradis* in *Les Cahiers de Sainte Marie*, Montreal, 1968; *Général Baron-La-Croix ou le silence masqué, (tragédie moderne en 2 calvaires, 28 stations et une messe en noir et rouge)*, Montreal, Léméac, 1974; unpublished manuscripts: "Les Cymbales du Vent de l'EST"; "Un Toit de soleil pour Charlemagne Péralte"; "Adjipopo"; "Bouki pa Bouki"; "tézin"; "La dernière porte";

FOUCHARD, Jean

b. March 2, 1912, Port-au-Prince, Haiti. Journalist, historian, diplomat, essayist.

Fouchard was educated at the Petit Séminaire Collège Saint-Martial and graduated from the Faculty of Law. He early entered journalism and contributed much to *Petit Impartial* and *Haiti-Journal*, of which he became the Director. He was later Managing Editor of the noted magazine *La Relève*, founded by Jacques C. Antoine. He was Chef du Cabinet of President Sténio Vincent, and served as Minister of Haiti to Cuba. He spent several years in Africa, where he was manager of commercial enterprises.

For the Fair of the Bicentennial of Port-au-Prince, Fouchard was the Commissaire Général. He is an elected officer of the Order of the Arts and Letters of France.

Writings: History: *Les Marrons du syllabaire*, Port-au-Prince, Ed. H. Deschamps, 1953; *Plaisirs de Saint-Domingue*, Port-au-Prince, Impr. de l'Etat, 1955; *Le théâtre à Saint-Domingue*, Port-au-Prince, Impr. de l'Etat, 1955; *Artistes et répertoire des scènes de Saint-Domingue*, Port-au-Prince, Impr. de l'Etat, 1955; *Les marrons de la liberté*, Paris, Eds. de l'Ecole.

Speeches: *Trois discours*, Port-au-Prince, Impr. de l'Etat, 1962.

Literary Essays: *Cahiers de Guinée (Liens de sang et de culture entre Haiti et la Guinée. Options culturelles du Parti démocratique de Guinée. Révolution démocratique africaine)*, Conakry, 1966; *Langue et littérature des aborigènes d'Ayti*, Paris, Eds. de l'Ecole, 1972; Also: *La méringue*, Quebec, Ed. Léméac, 1973.

Various: *La gerbe des quatre dits*, (private printing), Port-au-Prince, 1962.

Biographical/Critical Sources: Maryse Condé, "Jean Fouchard: Les Marrons de la liberté," Présence Africaine, No. 85, (First Quarter 1973), pp. 236-239.

FRAENIEL

(pseudonym for **Madeleine Dominique PAILLERE**)

FRANCK

(pseudonym for **Abel ELIE**)

FRANKETIENNE

(see under **Franck ETIENNE**)

FURETEUR, Jean Le

(pseudonym for **Auguste MAGLOIRE**)

GAILLARD, Roger

b. April 10, 1923, Port-au-Prince, Haiti.
Critic, essayist, teacher.

Gaillard received his education at Saint Louis de Gonzague Institution. He started very early as a newspaperman at *Le Soir* in Port-au-Prince (1941), and became editor-in-chief in 1946. He went to France with a scholarship granted by the French government. He studied at the Sorbonne (1946-1949) and won a degree in philosophy with four certificates. He was appointed teacher in Bulgaria and taught French and philosophy.

Gaillard returned to Haiti in 1958. He was a contributor to *Le Matin* and is now working for *Le Nouveau Monde*.

He has been a professor in several lycées and colleges.

Writings: Literary Criticism: *L'Univers romanesque de Jacques Roumain,* Port-au-Prince, Ed. H. Deschamps, 1965; *La destinée de Carl Brouard,* Port-au-Prince, Ed. H. Deschamps, 1966; *Etzer Vilaire, témoin de nos malheurs, Etude critique sur l'auteur des "Dix hommes noirs"* with integral text, notes and commentary, Port-au-Prince, Les Presses Nationales, 1972.

Stories: *Charades haitiennes,* Port-au-Prince, Eds. de l'An 2000, 1972.

Tourism: *Cette Amérique où nous vivons* (Mexico, Ecuador, Guatemala), Port-au-Prince, Impr. Oedipe, 1967.

History: *Les Cent-Jours de Rosalvo Bobo ou une mise à mort politique,* Port-au-Prince, Presses Nationales, 1973.

School texts: *Manuel de français* (classe de troisième), 1955; (classe de seconde), 1965, both Sofia, Eds. Pédagogiques.

Biographical/Critical Sources: Marguerite Deschamps, *Clé pour Charades Haitiennes,* Port-au-Prince, 1974.

GALMOT, Jean

b. June 1, 1879, Monpazier, Dordogne, France; d. August 5, 1928, Guyane.
Novelist.

Born in France, Galmot came to settle in Guyana and became so fond of this country that he became a citizen. Additionally, he decided to join the struggle to obtain economic and political independence.

He faced a great number of difficulties and he swore in these terms:

> *Je jure de lutter jusqu'à mon dernier souffle . . . Je demande à Dieu de mourir en combattant pour le salut de ma patrie, la Guyane immortelle.*

Writings: Quelle étrange histoire!, Paris, Ed. Bellenand, 1918; *Un mort vivait parmi nous,* Paris, A la Sirène, 1922.

GAROUTE, Hamilton

b. January 12, 1920, Jérémie, Haiti; d. date unknown.
Poet, soldier.

Hamilton Garoute started his primary studies in Jérémie and completed his education in Port-au-Prince at Saint Louis de Gonzague. He entered the Military Academy to be commissioned sub-lieutenant. He eventually became a colonel and a member of the general staff of the Haitian Army.

Although Garoute's poems were surrealistic and influenced by André Breton, these verses express his own personal style:

> *Nous sommes les enfants de l'heure grave*
> *où lutter est la loi.*

and:

> *Encore les bras tendus vierges de renoncements*
> *Encore les yeux lavés vers les mêmes sommets*
> *qu'importe, qu'importe,*
> *si le poème est beau!!!*

Jacques Stéphen Alexis made these comments on Garoute's one book of verse: "Hamilton Garoute, fils du XXè siècle, et poète véritable, paie le tribut et un beau tribut avec ses *Jets lucides.*"

Writings: Poetry: *Jets lucides,* Port-au-Prince, Ed. H. Deschamps, 1946.

Biographical/Critical Sources: "La lyre et l'épée; Témoignage sur des *Jets Lucides,*" par Jacques S. Alexis, in *Cahiers d'Haiti,* Vol. III, No. 3 (Oct. 1945), pp. 24-27.

GAROUTE, Louis

b. October 25, 1904, Jérémie, Haiti.
Biographer, lawyer, public servant.

Born in Jérémie, Garoute moved to Port-au-Prince for his education in order to attend the Petit Séminaire Collège Saint-Martial and the law school. He served as an employee in several offices of the Ministry of Commerce and Finances and became an official in the head office of the Department of Agriculture and Interior.

Writings: Biographies: *Instantanés; portraits,* Port-au-Prince, Impr. N. Telhomme, 1942.

GEDEON, Max

b. February 3, 1908, Léogâne, Haiti.
Novelist, lawyer.

Gedeon was educated in Port-au-Prince and later graduated from the Faculty of Law, Port-au-Prince.

He served in the Lycée Pétion administration office and later became a judge on the Civil Court of Port-au-Prince. He also served as examining magistrate of the Criminal Court. He wrote two works of fiction.

Writings: Novels: *Diagnostics différentiels,* Port-au-Prince, Impr. V. Valcin, 1934; *Le portefeuille,* Port-au-Prince, Impr. La Presse, 1934.

GENTILLE, Antoine de

b. 1900, Saint-Pierre, Martinique; d. April 7, 1964.
Poet, journalist.

Gentille has published his poems and articles in many newspapers, with most of his poetry in *Lucioles,* edited by Auguste Joyau, Ernest Thermes, Gilbert Gratiant, and Daniel Grandmaison.

Writings: Poetry: *Les Guirlandes; Silhouettes et fantômes,* followed by *Poèmes inachevés et pages de jeunesse,* Paris, Jouve, 1922.

GEORGES, Guy D.

b. January 6, 1941, Cayes, Haiti.
Poet, storywriter.

Georges received his education in the schools of Port-au-Prince; he has published three collections of verse.

Writings: Poetry: *L'Immense Profondeur,* Port-au-Prince, Serge L. Gaston, 1965; *La cité du Soleil,* Port-au-Prince, 1964; *Poèmes d'amour pour un amour inconnu,* Port-au-Prince, Impr. Serge L. Gaston, 1967.

GERARD, Marie

(pseudonym for **Luc GRIMARD**)

GIORDANI, Roland

b. ca. 1914, Cap-Haitien, Haiti; d. ca. 1965, Port-au-Prince.
Poet.

Giordani received his education in Cap-Haitien and studied law in Port-au-Prince. He has served as civil servant in the Bureau of Internal Revenue.

Writings: Poetry: *La chanson de l'espoir,* Port-au-Prince, Impr. H. Deschamps, 1954; *Les fuites du coeur,* Port-au-Prince, Impr. H. Deschamps, 1957.

GIRAUD, Octave

b. ca. 1827, Guadeloupe; d. ca. 1889.
Poet.

Giraud went to France at an early age and was educated there. He sojourned in Guadeloupe around 1860 and there he wrote most of the poems of his collection, "Fleurs des Antilles."

Giraud exalted his feeling for the tropical climate, the coconut trees, the humming birds, the lazy Creoles and especially for the island's famous black beauty, in words which today seem terribly unnecessary:

Venez voir, venez voir, trop
orgueilleuses blanches,
Les négresses n'ont pas moins de grâces
que vous . . .

Writings: Essay: *Les Devoirs du poète,* 1857.
Poetry: *Rêves d'avenir,* 1859; *Fleurs des Antilles,* Paris, Poulet-Malassis, 1862.
History: *L'Abolition de l'esclavage. . . .,* 1861.

GLISSANT, Edouard

b. September 21, 1928, Sainte-Marie, Martinique.
Poet, novelist, playwright, educator.

Edouard Glissant was born in Sainte-Marie, a town of 20,000 on the east coast of Martinique. His father was a plantation manager and his mother, a household servant. He attended the Lycée Schoelcher in Fort-de-France during Aimé Césaire's tenure from 1939-1945, and participated with Frantz Fanon in Césaire's election campaign of 1945.

He went to the Sorbonne to earn a licence in philosophy and, at the same time, he studied ethnology at the Musée de l'Homme. After taking his doctorate in philosophy, Glissant worked for a period at the Centre National de la Recherche Scientifique in Paris.

During the 1950's, he was active in the Société Africaine de Culture and various left wing West Indian political groups in Paris.

Glissant encountered difficulties with the French government during the Algerian war. With Paul Niger of Guadeloupe, he was one of the directors of the "Front antillo-guyanais pour l'independance." Because of his activities, he was forbidden to return to Martinique from 1959 to 1965, and even prevented from leaving France to go to Algeria.

Since his return to Martinique in 1965 he has participated in the development of a variety of cultural activities centered around the Institut Martiniquais d'Etudes (IME), a private secondary school he founded. One of the projects was the review *Acoma,* which appeared four times from 1970 to 1973.

Glissant has published a number of collections of poetry: *Un champ d'Iles* (Dragon, 1953), *La Terre inquiète* (Dragon, 1954); *Les Indes* (Falaize, 1956); *Le Sel noir* (Le Seuil, 1960), *Le Sang rivé* (*Présence Africaine,* 1961), the first three of which were collected and reprinted in *Poèmes* (Le Seuil, 1965).

In addition to his poetry, he has published two volumes of essays, *Le Soleil de la conscience* (1956) and *L'Intention poétique* (1969), plus a play, *Monsieur*

Toussaint (1961). But he is perhaps best known for his novels, *La Lézarde* (1958, Prix Renaudot), *Le Quatrième Siècle* (1970), and, most recently, *Malemort* (1975).

In the first two novels, Glissant attempts to cultivate a sense of Caribbean culture based on a careful analysis of the past. The novels are related, and are best understood if read in reverse order of publication.

In *Le Quatrième Siècle,* the author uses the device of a young archivist and an aging *quimboiseur* to reconstruct the history of the island in the form of two families: the first, descending from maroons, or escaped slaves, the second from house slaves. The two different families, traced from the day of arrival on the slaveship which carried them from Africa, represent the struggles, hopes, defeats, contradictions, repressions and inhibitions which have characterized the two different social classes on the island through the centuries.

In *La Lézarde,* Glissant brings together these two strains, the one from the high country, the other from the plains, in the characters of students after the liberation of the island during World War II. Thaël descends from the maroon tradition far from the main town of Lambrianne. He voyages to the south, where he meets his compatriots who are planning the assassination of an agent sent to put down the movement of the younger generation. The river Lézarde serves as a temporal and spatial symbol of the link between the past and the present. The fatal journey by Garin with his intended executioner Thaël down the river complements that made in time by Mathieu through the archives of the town and in the company of Longoué, the *quimboiseur.*

Malemort, Glissant's last novel, deals with life among the lower classes of the island, and is centered around a murder committed by a hired killer at election time.

Dr. Jean Price-Mars of Haiti said about Edouard Glissant:

> *Poète fasciné par l'attraction des symboles, son roman est imprégné de symbolisme. Il dénonce sans en avoir l'air l'inquiétude et exprime les aspirations confuses de la jeunesse antillaise qui est travaillée par un besoin d'évasion sans que nul parmi ces jeunes n'arrive à expliciter vers quoi tendent le désir et l'espérance de ses camarades.*

Auguste Viatte commented on Glissant's style:

> *Glissant écrit dans un style original et contourné, qui rappelle tantôt les procédés du Nouveau Roman, tantôt ceux du romancier haitien Jacques Stéphen Alexis.*

Writings: Poetry: *Un champ d'iles,* Paris, Ed. Instance, 1953; *La Terre inquiète,* Paris, Eds. du Dragon, 1955; *Les Indes; Poèmes de l'une et l'autre terre,* Paris, Falaize, 1956; *Le Sel noir,* Paris, Eds. du Seuil, 1960; *Le Sang rivé,* Paris, Présence Africaine, 1961. (Glissant's poetry was republished in five parts in *Poèmes,* Paris, Ed. du Seuil, 1965.)

Novels: *La Lézarde,* Prix Renaudot, published Paris, Seuil, 1955; *La Lézarde* was translated into English by Frances Frenaye under the title *The Ripening,* New York, G. Braziller, 1959; *Le Quatrième Siècle,* Prix Charles Veillon, Paris, Eds. Seuil, 1964; *Malemort,* Paris, Ed. du Seuil, 1975.

Essays: *Soleil de la conscience,* Paris, Eds. Falaize, 1956 (contains the poem "Novembre" and extracts from "Elements," earlier published in *Le Sang rivé*); *L'intention poètique,* Paris, Ed. Seuil, (consists of essays mostly composed between 1953-1961, many of them published first in *Les Lettres Nouvelles.* The essay on Alejo Carpentier of Cuba (pp. 136-142) appeared originally in the review *Critique. Le Soleil* was reprinted in *L'Intention poetique.*) Also see: "Culture et colonisation: l'équilibre antillais," in *Esprit* (Paris, 1962), No. 305, pp. 588-595; "Introduction à une étude des fondements socio-historiques du déséquilibre mental," in *Acoma* (Fort-de-France), No. 2 (April 1971), pp. 78-93; "Structure de groupes et tensions de groupes en Martinique," in *Acoma,* No. 1 (1971), pp. 31-43; *Poètique et inconscient martiniquais* (lecture given at Indiana

University, U.S.A., Conference on Cultural Identity), March 28-30, 1974.

Play: Monsieur Toussaint, Paris, Ed. du Seuil, 1961.

Biographical/Critical Sources: Guy Ducornet, "Edouard Glissant and the Problem of Time: prolegomena to a study of his poetry," in *Black Images,* II, 3 (1973), trans. by Z. Ellis, same issue, pp. 13-17; Marcel Oddon, "Les tragédies de la décolonisation: Aimé Césaire et Edouard Glissant," in *Le théâtre moderne II: depuis la deuxième guerre mondiale,* Jean Jacquot, ed., Paris, Eds. du Centre National de la Recherche Scientifique, 1967; Jacques Nantet, *Panorama d'expression française,* Paris, Fayard, 1972. Also see discussion of *La Lézarde* in Beverly Ormerod's essay, "French Caribbean Literature: The Contemporary Situation," in *The Literary Half-Yearly,* Vol. XI, 2 (July 1970), pp. 113-126; F.I. Case, "The Novels of Edouard Glissant," in *Black Images,* II, 3 and 4 (Autumn-Winter), pp. 3-12; and "Théâtre, conscience du peuple," in *Acoma* magazine, No. 2 (July 1971).

Also See: Frederick Ivor Case, "The Novels of Edouard Glissant," in *Black Images,* Vol. 2, Nos. 3 & 4 (1973), pp. 3-13; Vere W. Knight, "Edouard Glissant. The Novel as History Rewritten," in *Black Images,* No. 3, pp. 19-23; Beverley N. Ormerod, "Beyond Negritude: Some Aspects of the Work of Edouard Glissant," in *Contemporary Literature,* No. 5, pp. 360-369.

GODEFROY, Justin

b. June 19, 1875, Port-au-Prince, Haiti; d. July 4, 1907, Port-au-Prince.
Storywriter, essayist, poet, teacher.

Schooled in his natal Port-au-Prince through the Lycée Pétion, Godefroy was a member of the group which established the journal *La Ronde* as an important literary review at the turn of the century. He was a remarkable teacher at the Lycée Pétion. He wrote some poetry but is best remembered as a writer of stories.

Writings: Stories: "A ma fantaisie"; "Dans le vague"; Nocturne"; "Esquisse"; "La Mulâtresse"; "Renouveau"; Pessimisme de Jeunes."

Biographical/Critical Sources: Dantès Bellegarde, "Justin Godefroy" (article), in *Ecrivains haitiens,* Port-au-Prince, Ed. H. Deschamps, 1950, pp. 269-275.

GOURAIGE, Ghislain

b. ca. 1925, Port-au-Prince, Haiti; d. June 10, 1978, New York City.
Essayist, literary critic, playwright, teacher, scholar.

After he completed his secondary education in Port-au-Prince, Ghislain Gouraige went to Canada where he won his licence-ès-lettres from the University Laval, Quebec. Later, in Paris, he obtained his doctorate at the Sorbonne. During the same period, he attended some courses at l'Ecole des Hautes Etudes Politiques.

When he returned to Haiti, Gouraige taught at the Lycée Pétion, at l'Ecole Normale Supérieure and at the Institute of International Studies. He left Haiti in 1966 and was until his death teaching Haitian and African literatures at the State University of Albany in New York (U.S.A.).

Writings: History: *L'Indépendance d'Haiti devant la France,* Port-au-Prince, 1955.

Literary Criticism: *Histoire de la littérature haitienne,* Port-au-Prince, Impr. N.A. Théodore, 1960; another edition, *Histoire de la littérature haitienne de l'indépendance à nos jours,* Port-au-Prince, Impr. des Antilles, 1963.

Play: *Mon exil et toi,* performed in New York City, March, 1977.

Anthology: *Les meilleurs poètes et romanciers haitiens* (pages choisies), Port-au-Prince, Impr. La Phalange, 1963.

Essays: *La Diaspora d'Haiti et l'Afrique* (winner of the Prix des Caraibes, 1975), Sherbrooke, Ed. Naaman, 1975; *Amour: Révolution de la femme. La femme et l'amour, de l'antiquité à nos jours,* Sherbrooke, Canada, Eds. Naaman, 1976; *Continuité Noire,* Dakar-Abidjan, Les Nouvelles Editions Africaines, 1977.

GRANDMAISON, Daniel de

b. September 12, 1901, Saint-Pierre, Martinique.
Poet, journalist.

Grandmaison received his education in France. Upon returning to Martinique, he worked as a journalist and served as editor-in-chief of *Le Courrier des Antilles*. He also served as secretary of the magazine *Lucioles* with Auguste Joyau and E. Thermes beginning in 1925.

Writings: Poetry: *Amour et Nostalgie, poèmes*, Paris, Eds. de la Jeune Académie, 1930.
Novel: *Rendez-vous au Macouba*, Paris, Ed. Littré, 1948.

Biographical/Critical Sources: Review of *Rendez-vous au Macoùba* by John Harrison, in BIM, No. 16, pp. 252-261.

GRASELY, Abbé Paul

b. ca. 1922, Martinique.
Poet, storywriter.

Grasely's work generally is descriptive of the island and of small emotional range in "pastels" and "miniatures."

Writings: Poetry: *Mosaiques*, Paris, Eds. de la Revue Moderne, 1952; *Poèmes et propos d'un imagier*, Paris, Eds. de la Revue Moderne, 1959.
Stories: *Eaux fortes et pastels (Paysages, scènes et types martiniquais)*, Paris, Eds. de la Revue Moderne, 1953; *Sanguines et Fusains*, Paris, Eds. de la Revue Moderne, 1955; *Fresques et Miniatures*, Paris, Eds. de la Revue Moderne, 195(?); *Silhouettes et Paysages de la Martinique*, Paris, Eds. Debresse, 1963.

GRATIANT, Gilbert

(pseudonym: **Jean NOUS-TERRE** or **NOUS-TOUS**)
b. 1895, Saint-Pierre, Martinique.
Poet (in French and creole), teacher, novelist, critic, scholar.

Son of Gabriel-Labadie, a teacher of English, Gratiant grew up in a cultured home. He studied at the Lycée Schoelcher IV in Paris. After several years of study in Paris, he returned to Guadeloupe with the agregation in English, and became an English teacher at the Lycée Schoelcher.

In 1926, with August Joyau and Octave Mannoni, Gratiant helped found the short-lived (two years) review *Lucioles* as the organ of the first Pan-franco literary movement in the Caribbean.

In 1928, he returned to France where he taught at the Lycées Molière and Claude Bernard in Paris throughout the war years. During the occupation he used the pseudonym "Jean Nous-Tous" to publish a 300-verse poem "Métal non ferreux" attacking the Nazis for seizing and melting down French bronze sculptures, many of them by the greatest French artists.

Gratiant, a mulatto, was one of the earliest Martiniquans to take pride in his African heritage when, in some of his *Poèmes en vers faux* (1930), he refers to the political and racial situation on the island. In his *Credo du Sang-mêlé* (ca. 1948) he argued for a cultural synthesis of both European and African racial strains which could remain attached to what he termed the essential France of 1789.

Gratiant later turned to communism and produced a committed and pacifist poetry which some critics have found somewhat prosaic, as perhaps seen in his *Sel et Sargasses*.

Gratiant is perhaps best known for his efforts to encourage a literature written in creole. Senghor published several of his poems in a bilingual French-creole format in *Anthologie de la nouvelle poèsie nègre et malgache de langue française* (1948). In 1958, Gratiant published a collection of this poetry, *Fab' Compè Zicaque* (Horizons Caraibe).

In his preface to the second edition of *Credo*, Gratiant goes over events in Africa and elsewhere in the thirteen years since the first edition (1948), and he ends by hoping the best aspects of France will come to the fore in a Martinique independent of colonial domination. In singing "La France" he will sing only that kind of France. Though a confirmed Marxist and conscious of his dual racial origins, he still wants some of the better French qualities of culture and literature discussed in his "essai d'une poèsie martiniquaise dite nationale" in 1956. He is (despite the early attacks on his depth of commitment to his African ancestral culture by Etienne Lero), one of Martinique's most outspoken Negritudists and movers for a greater recognized African presence in island culture.

Auguste Viatte considered Gratiant's early verse successful in its Baudelairean tendencies as in the following from *Poèmes en vers faux* (1931):

Le vénéneux Ennui s'agrippe à mon coeur blême,
Radiante racine enlaçant l'âme même,
Parasite grimpant rongeant l'arbre qu'il aime.

Gratiant's *affirme multiple* (his multiple inheritances) produces instead of an imbalance—riches and harmony, as in these lines from *Credo des sang-mêlé:*

Terre de l'antilope et du lion
Terre africaine,
Tu es ma terre,
Colline tourangelle dans le fini inscrite
Des horizons de la mesure,
Tu es ma terre,
Et terre de l'Indien, jardin de l'Amérique,
Mon ile inégalée où les volcans fleuris
Rêvent au bord des mers,
Tu es ma terre,
Mais voici mon climat:
La présence française.

Gratiant often published in creole and his "La Farine Sèche" (air connu) is well known. The first stanza reads:

Manman moin fai du riz doux
Du riz dou-ou, du riz dou-ou
Manman moin fai du riz dou
I ba doudou-a i pa ba moin ai en:
Touit l'année man la farine sèche
To ka di man ka vini gros
Touit l'année man la farine sèche
Yo ka di man ka vini gras."
Béké-à fai gro lagen
Gro l'agen-en gro lagen-en.

Auguste Viatte expressed his comments on Gilbert Gratiant:

> *Gilbert Gratiant nous apporte un "au-delà du racisme," une synthèse, dégageant sa personnalité des servilismes comme des violences et assignant à son métissage une fonction conjointe à l'oeuvre unificatrice de l'esprit français: si ce n'est le dernier mot, c'est du moins une réponse neuve et sincère aux controverses sur le nationalisme littéraire. Mais il n'aurait pas ainsi réfléchi sur lui-même s'il n'avait d'abord été pris vivement à partie par les tenants de l'africanisme. Ils le réléguaient, ainsi qu'Emmanuel-Flavia Léopold, parmi "ces poètes de caricature . . ."*

An additional manifestation of Gratiant's "nationalist" efforts is his production of several poetic works in francophone creole. His *Fab' compè Zicaque* and his *Cinq poèmes martiniquaises* are major contributors to the growing body of Caribbean literature moving away from the cultural hegemony of France.

Writings: Poetry: *Poèmes en vers faux,* Paris, "La Caravelle," 1931; "Metal non ferreux," privately printed, Paris, 1943; *An moué,* Fort-de-France, Impr. Populaire, 1950; *Credo des sang-mêlé our Je veux chanter la France,* Fort-de-France, Impr. Courrier des Antilles, 1948, 1950 and Paris, Soulanges, 1961; *Fab' compè Zicaque (poèmes en créole),* dedicated to his mother, Rosena Hermani Gratiant-Labadie, Fort-de-France, Horizons Caraibes, 1958; trans. as *Fab' compè Zicaque (poèmes traduits du créole),* Paris, Maspéro, 19??; *Cinq poèmes martiniquais en créole,* Hauteville, Ain, 1935; *Sel et Sargasses; poèsies de France et des Antilles,* Paris, Soulanges, 1963.

Poetry and Essays: *Une fille majeure. Credo des sang-mêlé; Poème Martinique à vol d'abeille,* Paris, Soulanges, 1961; *Credo des sang-mêlé ou Je veux chanter la France (poème en français* and *Fab' compè Zicaque* (in creole), Fort-de-France, Impr. Courrier des Antilles

1950, and Paris, Soulange, 1961; Poems in L.S. Senghor's *Anthologie de la nouvelle poèsie nègre et malgache de langue française*, Paris, Presses Universitaires de France, 1948, third edition 1972, and in N.R. Shapiro's *Negritude: Black Poetry from Africa and the Caribbean*, New York, October House, 1972.

Creole Poetry in manuscript: "Dghiab la ka mandé an ti manmaille (poème chorégraphique inédit," and "Bel palé pou bel moune;" Manuscript in English: "Along My Neighbor's Path."

History: *Ile fédérée française de la Martinique*, Paris, Soulanges, 1961.

Essays: "D'une poèsie martiniquaise dite nationale," in *Présence Africaine*, New Series, No. 5 (1955-1956); "La Place du créole dans l'expression antillaise," in *Présence Africaine*, New Series, Nos. 14-15, pp. 252-255; "Martinique Conditionnel Eden," in *Les quatre Samedis des Antilles* and poems in French translation from creole: *Poèmes Martiniquais* 1) "Ti Manmzelle-la," 2) "Debout! Joseph," 3) "Pou si couri vini," and 4) "La Part du nègre,": in *Les quatre Samedis*, pp. 94-105.

Prose in manuscript: *Minimis malheuresse*.

Novels: *Vacances créoles* (in ms.); *Gérard mangé par le loup* (in ms.).

Translation: of J.B.S. Haldane's *Science advances* as *La Science en marche*, Paris, Presses Universitaires, 1952.

Essay in manuscript: "Cris d'un jeune."

Editor of: *La Lanterne antillaise* (a collection of 500 poems by various authors).

Biographical/Critical Sources: Auguste Viatte, *Histoire littéraire de l'Amérique française*, Laval, Quebec, Presses Universitaires, 1954, pp. 496-502; Keith Q. Warner, "Gilbert Gratiant and the Predicament of the Double Mulatto," in *French Caribbean Literature*, Black Images, Canada, 1975, pp. 64-70.

GRIMARD, Luc

(pseudonyms: **Lin DEGE** and **Marie GERARD**)

b. January 30, 1866, Cap-Haitien, Haiti; d. October 24, 1954, New York.

Poet, journalist, educator.

After local schooling, Grimard became a teacher at the Lycée Philippe Guerrier of Cap-Haitien. Through his stimulus and that of Louis Mercier and Christian Werleigh, the Lycée became a fortress of nationalism during the American Marines' occupation of Haiti.

Grimard was named Haitian Consul at Le Havre in France. On his return, he became, on Charles Moravia's retirement, director of the review *Le Temps*, and held the position of Inspector of the Ecole Normale des Instituteurs. He later was named director of the daily paper *La Phalange*, a Roman Catholic organ. He was also conservator of the Musée Sténio Vincent, president of the Société Haitienne des Lettres et des Arts and corresponding member of the Cuban Academy of Arts and Letters.

He was the first Rector of the University of Haiti, and died in this capacity in New York.

His style was precise, very sharply etched, but never severe or mannered. His debt to Mallarmé can be seen in his "Vespérale":

Le soir, sur Léogâne, est d'une ample beauté . . .
Les palmiers ont senti descendre le mystère

Sur leur feuillage triste. Un silence
enchanté . . .
La fleur du Songe éclôt dans le coeur
solitaire.

Writings: Poetry: *Ritournelles, poèmes,* Paris, Eds. de la N.R.F., 1927; *Sur ma flûte de bambou, poèmes,* Paris, Ed. de la N.R.F., 1927; *L'offrande du laurier,* Port-au-Prince, La Phalange, 1950; *La corbeille* (with Frédéric Burr-Reynaud, André Fontainas, Dominique Hippolyte, Edgard Numa, Jean Libose), Port-au-Prince, Impr. du Collège Vertières, 1943; *Quelques poèmes . . . quelques poètes,* Port-au-Prince, n.d.

Recording: Grimard's reading of his poetry, recorded in 1953, is in Music Division archives of the Library of Congress, Washington, D.C.

Stories: *Du sable entre les doigts,* Port-au-Prince, Impr. du Collège Vertières, 1941; *Bakoulou* (written with André F. Chevallier), Port-au-Prince, Ed. H. Deschamps, 1950; "Colombes de Paplagonie," in *Optique,* June 1954, No. 4, pp. 46-53.

Play: *Jours de gloire* (written with Dominique Hippolyte).

Literary Essay: "Existence historique du théâtre haitien," in *World Theatre,* Brussels, UNESCO (Sep.-Dec. 1967), pp. 534-535.

Biographical/Critical Sources: Ernst Trouillot, *Hommage à Luc Grimard,* Port-au-Prince, Impr. de l'Etat, 1955 (composed of speeches on Grimard by Luc Dorsinville, Edmond Sylvain, George Marc, Franck St-Victor, Ernst Trouillot, and others).

GUERIN, Mona Rouzier

b. October 9, 1934, Port-au-Prince, Haiti.
Poet, playwright, essayist, teacher.

Mona Rouzier Guérin attended the school of Sisters of Saint Joseph of Cluny where she completed her classical secondary studies. In 1959, recipient of a scholarship from the Conseil des Arts du Canada, she studied contemporary literature at Ottawa University.

She contributed to the newspapers *Le Matin, Conjonction,* and especially to *Le Nouvelliste,* where she published a weekly chronicle, "Le Coin de Cécile."

Writings: Poetry: *Sur les vieux thèmes . . .,* Port-au-Prince, Impr. N.A. Théodore, 1958.

Essay: "Les trois coups et mille problèmes," in *Conjonction,* Vol. XXIV, No. 69, pp. 19-23.

Plays: *L'oiseau de ces dames,* performed at Rex Theater, August 24, 1966, published Port-au-Prince, Impr. H. Deschamps, 1973, pp. 89-157; *Les cinq chéris,* performed at Institut Français, (Sep. 4, 1969); *La Pieuvre,* performed at Centre Culturel, (Sep. 2, 1971), published Port-au-Prince, Impr. H. Deschamps, 1973, pp. 1-86; *La Pension Vacher* (2-act comedy), Port-au-Prince, Eds. du Soleil, 1978 (performed January 14, 15, 1977).

GUERY, Fortuna Augustin

b. ca. 1894, Port-au-Prince, Haiti; d. 1975, Port-au-Prince.
Memorialist, storywriter.

After her classes in Port-au-Prince, Guery attended the newly established Normal School for girls directed by Mrs. Lerebours. She was a teacher for a period and became Director of Primary Schools and then Supervisor of Primary Education at the Ministry of Public Instruction.

Writings: Memoirs: *Témoignages,* Port-au-Prince, Ed. H. Deschamps, 1950.

GUILBAUD, Tertulien Marcelin

b. May 22, 1856, Port-de-Paix, Haiti; d. September 19, 1939, Port-au-Prince. Poet, playwright, journalist, storywriter.

Guilbaud started his primary classes in Port-de-Paix, studied for his humanities at the Lycée Philippe Guerrier of Cap-Haitien and the Lycée Pétion of Port-au-Prince. He attended law school at the University of Paris. He returned to the practice of law in his natal city, and was named a teacher at Philippe Guerrier. He then founded the Première Ecole Libre de Droit du Cap-Haitien. He was a member of the Constituent Congress which drew up the 1889 Constitution in Gonaives. During his public career he was elected Senator, served as Minister of Public Instruction, and as Minister Plenipotentiary of Haiti at Paris from 1916. For several years he was his country's representative at the Versailles Treaty Conference in 1919. He refused the Haitian presidency in 1917.

A patriotic poet par excellence, Guilbaud's verse ever exhorted his fellow Haitians to cease fighting each other and to work instead for the peace and prosperity of all citizens and classes of Haiti. Other countries have had their problems, he stated in "Hymne de foi" in the collection *Patrie* (1885), his most famous work, and Haiti would one day be past its own worst tribulations. After all, he wrote, " . . . le pin de la forêt met cent ans à grandir," and Haitians must have patience. By and large, he was a follower of Victor Hugo in his style and social goals.

Guilbaud's two plays poke gentle fun at the ways of island politicians, where his novelette *Higuenamota* is a rare study of Indian customs.

Writings: Poetry: *Patrie, espérances et souvenirs,* Paris and Versailles, Impr. Léopold Cerf, 1885; *Feuilles au vent, poèmes,* Paris, Léopold Cerf, 1888.

Novelette: *Higuenamota,* Port-au-Prince, 1876.

Plays: *Moeurs électorales,* Paris, details not known.

Biographical/Critical Sources: Naomi M. Garret's *The Renaissance of Haitian Poetry,* Paris, Présence Africaine, 1963; Auguste Viatte, *Histoire littéraire de l'Amérique française,* Quebec, 1954, pp. 296-398; Robert Cornevin, *Le théâtre haitien, des origines à nos jours,* Montreal, Léméac, 1973, p. 102.

HALL, Louis Duvivier

b. March 7, 1905, Cayes, Haiti. Poet, teacher.

Hall was first educated by his father, Duvivier Hall, who was a very good teacher, and the son then went to Port-au-Prince, where he completed his schooling. He was a teacher at the Lycée Philippe Guerrier of Cayes and then came to Port-au-Prince to teach humanities at the Lycée Pétion.

Hall spent some time at Columbia University to study education and he became head of the division of secondary schools in Haiti. Later, he founded a college under his own name. He then went into exile and lived for years in Puerto Rico.

Hall was one of the earliest poets to employ African motifs in his work and to show voodoo traditions and dances in a sympathetic light.

Writings: Poetry: *A l'ombre du mapou,* Les Cayes, Impr. Bonnefil, 1931.

HELM, Danyl

b. 1902, Saint-Pierre, Martinique. Poet, musician.

Helm was born the same year her parents died in the 1902 eruption of Mont Pelé, which killed 30,000 inhabitants of Saint-Pierre, then the capital of Martinique. As a girl, Helm went to France where she was educated and where she remained.

She was a talented musician, but poetry was her love. She said in the introduction to her collection of poems:

> *Musicienne et poète, j'ai choisi la poèsie des mots comme expression. . . . Mais je n'ai pu m'empêcher de garder le sens, le goût, et quelque peu de la technique, et d'en retrouver le concours dans l'orchestre de ma pensée où le caprice de l'image se marie aux jeux de la mélodie.*

Anatole France, who prefaced her collection of poems, stated: "Elle a trouvé une musique intime dans le ton de son rêve et au timbre de son âme."

Writings: Poetry: *Nocturne inconnu; Préludes,* preface by Anatole France, Paris, Bernard Grasset, 1918.

HENNIQUE, Léon

b. November 4, 1850, Basse-Terre, Guadeloupe; d. December 25, 1935, Paris.
Novelist, playwright, storywriter, naturalist, journalist.

Hennique spend his childhood in Guadeloupe and went very early to France where he received his education. He was a follower of the naturalist school and he contributed several works to this literary movement. His short story, "L'Affaire du Grand Sept," appeared in *Soirées de Médan* in collaboration with Emile Zola, Guy de Maupassant, Henri Céard, J. K. Huysmans, Alexis, Octave Mirbeau.

Hennique was a close friend of Zola and the brothers Goncourt, and he was chosen one of the first members of the famed Académie Goncourt. He had also joined others in the tentative creation of a Free Theatre in Paris.

Hennique was elected President of the Goncourt Academy and he remained at this post until 1912. He kept vivid his memories of his native island and his novels *Poeuf* and *Les Anolis* are full of Guadeloupean images long stored up in his mind.

He practiced journalism and contributed to the papers, *Voltaire, La Vérité,* and *La Revue de Paris.* His "noces d'or littéraires" were celebrated in November, 1928.

Hennique was made a Chevalier de la Légion d'Honneur in 1895, and an Officer of the National Order.

Writings: Novels: *La Dévouée,* 1879; *Elizabeth Couronneau; Benjamin Rozès,* 1881; *Les Hauts faits de Mr de Ponthau,* 1880; *L'accident de Mr Hébert,* 1884; *Poeuf,* 1887; *Un caractère,* 1889; and *Minnie Brandon,* Paris, Ed. Fasquelle, 1889.

Stories: *Deux Nouvelles,* 1881; *Les Soirées de Médan,* new ed., Paris, Charpentier, 1893.

Plays: *Pierrot sceptique; L'Empereur Dassoucy* (comedy); *Jacques Damour; Esther Brandis; La mort du duc d'Enghien; La menteuse; Deux patries; Amour; L'argent d'autrui, comédie en 5 actes,* Paris, Tresse et Stock, 1894; *La petite paroisse; Reines des Rois.*

Biographical/Critical Sources: Léon Louis Deffoux, *Le Groupe de Médan: Emile Zola, Guy de Maupassant, J.K. Huysmann, Henri Céard, Léon Hennique,* followed by two essays on "naturalisme," Paris, Payot, 1920.

HERAUX, Edmond

b. May 8, 1858, Cap-Haitien, Haiti; d. February 17, 1920, Port-au-Prince.
Poet, lawyer, physician.

Héraux attended primary schools in Cap-Haitien and came to Port-au-Prince where he completed his education at the Petit Séminaire Collège Saint-Martial. He studied medicine and later law, but he practiced law only.

He was Deputy Commissioner of Government of the Tribunal de Cassation, then became a deputy inspector of schools in Port-au-Prince. He was elected Député, and became a judge of the Supreme Court of Port-au-Prince. He later was named Minister of Finance and Minister of Public Education.

He contributed to several newspapers

and magazines and served as chief editor of the paper *Le Devoir.*

Writings: Poetry: *Les préludes, poèsies,* Paris-Versailles, Léopold Cerf & Cie, 1883; *Fleurs des mornes, poèsies,* Grasset, 1883.

Essays: *Mélanges politiques et littéraires,* Corbeil, Impr. Crété, n.d.

Law: *Principes de droit,* Port-au-Prince, (mimeograph).

Politics: *Considérations politiques sur Haiti,* Port-au-Prince, Impr. Aug. A. Héraux, 1886; second edition, Port-au-Prince, Impr. Aug. A. Héraux, 1891.

Prosecution Speech: *Réquisitoires prononcés avec le texte des arrêts,* Corbeil, Impr. Typ., Ed. Crété, 1896.

HERPIN, Thérèse

b. ca. 1899, Martinique.
Novelist.

Herpin's one work had a fairly large success but August Joyau dismissed it as "... assez superficiel d'ailleurs et dont le succès ne fut que passager."

Writings: Novel: *Cristalline Bois-Noir ou les dangers du Bal Doudou,* Paris, Ed. Plon, 1929.

HEURTELOU, Daniel

b. December 19, 1906, Port-au-Prince, Haiti.
Playwright, journalist, businessman.

Heurtelou studied at the Petit Séminaire Collège Saint-Martial in Port-au-Prince, and graduated from the Faculty of Law. He was first a schoolteacher, and then worked some time at the Health Department. Later, Heurtelou became Private Secretary to President Lescot, and was named Minister of Commerce in 1953.

Heurtelou contributed to many newspapers and magazines, including: *Nouvelle Ronde; Revue Indigène; L'Aurore; Le Matin; Le Nouvelliste; La Relève,* and *Cahiers d'Haiti.* He founded, with engineers Félix Bayard and André Liautaud, the humorous journal *Pangloss.*

Writings: Poetry: in many journals, including: *La Revue Indigène,* No. 4, and *La Trouée.*

Plays: *Alcius* (satirical comedy in one act), preface by André Liautaud, Port-au-Prince, Impr. de l'Etat, 1939; *La montée; pièce en trois actes,* Port-au-Prince, Impr. de l'Etat, n.d. (1944?), édition hors commerce.

Biographical/Critical Sources: Robert Cornevin, *Le théâtre haitien, des origines à nos jours,* Quebec, Ed. Léméac, 1973, p. 140.

HIBBERT, Pierre Fernand

b. October 8, 1873, Miragoâne, Haiti; d. December 19, 1928, Port-au-Prince.
Novelist, storywriter, playwright, teacher, historian.

After local education in Port-au-Prince at the Petit Séminaire Collège Saint-Martial, Hibbert studied in France in preparation for a career. When he returned to Haiti, he was named teacher of history and French literature at the Lycée Pétion; he became head of a division at the Ministry of Foreign Affairs, and was Haitian Minister

to Cuba (1915-1921) during the first troubled years of the U.S. occupation of Haiti. In 1921, Hibbert came home to be Minister of Public Instruction, keeping that post for just one year.

He contributed to and supported the work of the patriotic anti-U.S. group and its organ, *La Revue de la Ligue de la Jeunesse Haitienne,* and was closely associated with nationalists L.H. Durand, Léon Laleau, and Georges Léger. His many novels deal with the corrupt politicians and frivolous women, and are full of the local color of the capital.

Writings: Novels: *Séna,* Port-au-Prince, Impr. de l'Abeille, 1905; trans. into Spanish by Juan Paredes, Buenos-Aires, Imp. W.M. Jackson, 1957; *Les Thazar,* Port-au-Prince, Impr. de l'Abeille, 1907; *Romulus,* Port-au-Prince, Impr. de l'Abeille, 1908; *Les Simulacres,* Port-au-Prince, Impr. Chéraquit, 1923; *L'aventure de M. Hellénus Caton,* Port-au-Prince, Impr. Chéraquit, 1923; *Le manuscrit de mon ami,* Port-au-Prince, Impr. Chéraquit, 1923.

Stories: *Masques et visages,* Port-au-Prince, Impr. du Matin, 1919.

Novelettes: *Une mulâtresse, fille de Louis XIV; Un nègre à la cour de Louis XIV; Le Prince Zaga; Le Néronisme de Rochambeau—La Bacchante.*

Plays: *La réclamation Hopton, comédie en deux actes,* Port-au-Prince, Impr. de l'Abeille, 1916; *Une affaire d'honneur, un acte.*

Biographical/Critical Sources: H. Pauléus Sannon, "Autour d'une vie: Fernand Hibbert," in *Le Temps,* April 16-22, 1929;Ghislain Gouraige, *Histoire de la littérature haitienne,* 1960, pp. 129-140; Pradel Pompilus & Frères de l'Instruction Chrétienne, *Manuel illustré d'histoire de la littérature haitienne,* 1961, pp. 285-297; Robert Cornevin, *Le théâtre haitien des origines à nos jours,* 1973, p. 137; Hénock Trouillot, *Les origines sociales de la littérature haitienne,* 1962, pp. 313-336; and see special issue of *Conjonction* (Port-au-Prince), Nos. 122-123, pp. 23-74.

HIPPOLYTE, Alice

b. ca. 1936, Port-au-Prince, Haiti.
Novelist.

Educated in Port-au-Prince, Alice Hippolyte published in local journals before bringing out her first novel (dedicated to Renée Ménos Lafontant, her mother, and Dominique Hippolyte, her father-in-law). Awarded the "Prix Littéraire Henri Deschamps" the first year of its existence (1976), the novel is a domestic feminine drama with some guarded allusions to contemporary affairs in Haiti.

Writings: Novel: *Ninon, ma soeur,* Port-au-Prince, Ed. H. Deschamps, 1976.

HIPPOLYTE, Dominique

(pseudonym: **Pierre BREVILLE**)

b. August 4, 1889, Port-au-Prince, Haiti; d. April 8, 1967, Port-au-Prince.
Poet, playwright, storywriter, lawyer, government official.

Hippolyte completed his secondary schooling at the Lycée Pétion in Haiti's capital. He graduated from the Faculty of Law, and was for a period a teacher at the Lycée Pétion. He was appointed Commissaire du Gouvernment near the Civil Court of Port-au-Prince, and later elected Bâtonnier of all attorneys of Port-au-Prince.

He was the President of the Haitian Commission of Intellectual Cooperation, and also President of the Alliance Française of Port-au-Prince. He was honored by the award of Doctor "Honoris Causa," by Laval University of Canada.

Hippolyte was early interested in the theatre and he paid his literary debt to Massillon Coicou in these words:

> *Massillon Coicou est l'écrivain haitien qui a exercé la plus efficace influence sur ma formation intellectuelle. Il m'a donné le goût de la poèsie. J'ai toujours rapporté à sa mémoire mes humbles succès au théâtre.* (From Prosper Chrisphonte's statement in his *Supplément à trait d'union entre deux tomes,* Port-au-Prince, Impr. du Séminaire Adventiste, 1965.)

At a time when Price-Mars and Jacques Roumain were discovering and dignifying with serious scholarship the African religious and other traditions of the peasantry of Haiti, Dominique Hippolyte was responsible in *La Revue Indigène* (Oct. 1927, pp. 133) for the publication of early work by the young American black poet Countee Cullen.

Though busy with his law career, Hippolyte also wrote several plays and published poetry and stories in many journals. He published his stories under the pseudonym of Pierre Bréville, but his other work was under his own name.

Auguste Viatte states his belief that Hippolyte's prose drama, *Le forçat,* is the best Haitian play ever written.

Writings: Poetry: *La route ensoleillée, vers,* Paris, Ed. de la Pensée Latine, 1927; Two collections of his poems remain in manuscript. Many of his poems appeared in *La Revue Indigène, La Relève, Le Temps-Revue, Les Griots,* and others. He read his poems in 1953 for the Library of Congress, Washington, D.C., where the recordings are stored by the Music Division.

Plays: *Quand elle aime* (in one act), performed in 1917, Port-au-Prince, Impr. Nationale, 1918; *Le baiser de l'aieul* (play in 3 acts and in prose), Paris, Ed. de la Revue Mondiale, 1924; *Le forçat* (dramatic comedy in 4 acts), Paris, Jouve, 1933; *Tocaye,* performed in 1940; *Le Torrent* (in 3 acts), won the Prize of the President of Haiti, 1939 (written with Placide David), Impr. de l'Etat, 1965; *Anacaona* (dramatic poem in 3 acts and one scene, written with Frédéric Burr-Reynaud), Port-au-Prince, Impr. Telhomme, 1941; *Jour de gloire* (with Luc Grimard).

Law Scholarship: *Eléments de droit usuel haitien,* Port-au-Prince, Telhomme, 1947.

HOUEL, Drasta

(or **HUEL,** pseudonym of **Mrs. HURARD**)

b. ca. 1886, Martinique; d. ca. 1949.

Poet, novelist, storywriter, historian.

Houel attended schools in Martinique but went to France as a young woman and spent most of her life there.

She wrote a very nuanced prose and verse. Her later prose poems, *Cruauté et tendresse,* are considered better than the verse in her *Les vies légères,* written in 1916.

André Fontainas said of Drasta Houel:

> *Evoquant les Antilles, Mme Drasta Houel drape les vies légères des créoles. Ce "morceau de nu," Baigneuses, est, d'un rythme et d'une musicalité qui n'appartient qu'à elle. Le volume modeste s'emplit de lumière mobile d'une beauté frêle et fraîche. Et ces transcriptions fidèles de naives "chansons nègres," c'est un vrai ravissement!*

Writings: Poetry: *Les vies légères; évocations antillaises* (poems in prose), Paris, Les Oeuvres Nouvelles, 1916.

Novel: *Cruauté et tendresse,* Paris, Ed. Payot, 1925.

HYPPOLITE, Ducas

b. 1844, Port-au-Prince, Haiti; d. November 27, 1868, Port-au-Prince.

Poet, journalist, songwriter, lecturer.

Hyppolite was educated in Port-au-Prince and was a teacher. In the field of poetry, he was very romantic, writing in one letter:

> *Ma poèsie à moi, c'est la poèsie des pleurs, parce que je suis malheureux; c'est la poèsie des souvenirs parce que je fus heureux un temps; c'est la poèsie de l'amour parce que j'ai vingt ans.*

He died at the age of 26 with no collected works in print.

Biographical/Critical Sources: Frédéric Marcelin: *Ducas-Hippolyte; son époque, ses oeuvres,* Le Hâvre, Impr. A. Lemale ainé, 1878; Enélus Robin, *Recueil de paroles funèbres prononcées aux funérailles de M. Ducas Hippolyte précédé d'une notice nécrologique,* Port-au-Price, Impr. du Réveil, 1868.

HYPPOLITE, Michelson Paul

b. ca. 1921, Haiti.
Storywriter, folklorist, essayist.

Hyppolite received his education in Port-au-Prince and studied ethnology at the Faculty directed at that time by Dr. Jean Price-Mars. He was a teacher for a period and later joined the Bureau of Ethnology. He is now living in the United States, teaching a program of creole language and literature at Indiana University.

Writings: Essays: *Littérature populaire haitienne,* Port-au-Prince, Impr. de l'Etat, 1950; *Une étude sur le folklore haitien,* Port-au-Prince, Impr. de l'Etat, 1954; *La mentalité haitienne et le domaine du rêve (Essai d'oniromancie locale) Psychanalyse de quatre rêves prémonitoires ou prophétiques,* Port-au-Prince, Impr. de l'Etat, 1965.

Stories: *Contes dramatiques,* 2 vols., Port-au-Prince, Impr. de l'Etat, 1956.

INGINAC, Joseph Balthazar

b. 1777, Léogane, Haiti; d. May 9, 1847, Port-au-Prince.
Memoirist, essayist, merchant, government official.

Inginac was educated by his father and had a good intellectual background. He spent some early years in Kingston, Jamaica, returning to Saint-Domingue during the Independence wars. He helped negotiate an agreement between the French colonial generals and Haitian General-in-Chief Jean Jacques Dessalines.

Inginac was named director of the Land Registration Office, and served as secretary to Dessalines, to Pétion and Boyer, and was later Secretary of State.

Dr. Rulx Léon commented on Inginac:

> *Le Général Joseph Balthazar Inginac est certainement l'une des figures les plus curieuses et les plus sympathiques de notre histoire nationale . . . L'étendue de ses connaissances et le sérieux de son caractère contrastaient avec la superficialité et le manque de préparation de nombre de ses contemporains, sa constance avec leur humeur changeante, son désintéressement avec leur ambition.* (From *Propos d'histoire d'Haiti, Port-au-Prince, Impr. de l'Etat, 1945, p. 1.)*

When President Boyer was ousted in 1843, Inginac went into exile in Jamaica. By President Guerrier's decree, Inginac was permitted to return to Haiti in 1845.

Writings: Essays: *Etrennes à mes concitoyens, nécessité de l'éducation morale et religieuse en Haiti,* Port-au-Prince, 1841.

Agriculture: *Culture du tabac,* Port-au-Prince, 1839; *Industrie agricole; Culture du caféier et préparation de sa fève pour être livrée au commerce,* Port-au-Prince, 1840.

Politics: *A ses compatriotes et principalement à ceux qui ont dirigé les affaires populaires de la République depuis la fin de Janvier dernier* (March 15, 1843), Port-au-Prince, 1843; *Adresse du Général Inginac aux haitiens, ses compatriotes,* Kingston, Jamaica, A.D.Y. Henriquez, 1844.

Memoirs: *Mémoires de J.B. Inginac, Ex-Sécrétaire Général près son Excellence l'ex-Président d'Haiti, depuis 1797 jusqu'à 1843,* Kingston, Jamaica, Impr. J.R. de Cordova, 1843.

INNOCENT, Antoine

b. April 21, 1874, Port-au-Prince, Haiti; d. April 12, 1960, Port-au-Prince.
Novelist, storywriter, theatre director, actor.

Antoine Innocent completed his secondary studies at the Lycée Pétion in Port-au-Prince and in time was a professor at the Collège Louverture and l'Ecole Polymathique.

He was very early active in the theatre as an actor, playwright, and director, and is remembered for his vivid performance in the works of Liautaud Ethéart, Vandenesse Ducasse, Massillon Coicou and Charles Moravia. In 1909 he was selected as director of the Théâtre Haitien.

An associate of the *La Ronde* group, he published much of his work in that review, but he is considered by most critics as being primarily a novelist. Strongly influenced by the experimental novels of Emile Zola, Innocent's naturalistic novel *Mimola* treats African beliefs positively, and characters in the work who scoff at African religion and other ideas are severely punished. Though the novel was originally attacked as being outrageously "primitive," and in fact as "pro-voodou," the work is now seen to have been the pioneering effort the author intended it to be.

In his "Notice to the Readers," he said:

> *J'ai voulu montrer les analogies, les affinités qui existent entre le Vaudou et les religions de l'antiquité. J'ai essayé de faire voir que l'origine des divinités africaines est la même que celle des divinités romaines, grecques et hindoues. Leur source se trouve dans ce besoin qu'a l'homme de croire, à chaque âge de l'humanité, à l'existence d'êtres supérieurs et invisibles, qu'ils nomment lares, mânes, dieux, ancêtres ou saints . . . La vérité et la fidélité des faits sous une robe locale: telle a été ma seule préoccupation dans la reproduction de ces scènes burlesques dont j'ai été maintes fois témoin.*

Writings: Novel: *Mimola ou l'histoire d'une cassette; petit tableau de moeurs locales,* Port-au-Prince, Impr. E. Malval, 1906, and second edition, Port-au-Prince, Impr. V. Valcin, 1935.
Other Works: *Neiges d'Antan; Impression; Journée grise; Souvenirs du jour de l'an.*

Biographical/Critical Sources: Dantès Bellegarde, "Antoine Innocent," in *Ecrivains haitiens,* 1950, pp. 260-268; Pradel Pompilus & Les Frères de l'Instruction Chrétienne, *Manuel illustré d'histoire de la littérature haitienne,* 1961, pp. 302-306; Ghislain Gouraige, *Histoire de la littérature haitienne,* 1960, pp. 140-144; Duraciné Vaval, *Histoire de la littérature haitienne . . . ,* 1933; See also: Special Issue of *Conjonction,* Nos. 122-123, (Port-au-Prince), pp. 87-100, 141-144.

JACOB, Kléber Georges

b. 1905, Port-au-Prince, Haiti; d. July 26, 1956, Port-au-Prince.
Essayist, scholar, journalist.

Jacob received his education at the Lycée Pétion and became a teacher. He soon dropped this activity to engage in journalism, contributing to such papers as *Le Nouvelliste* and *Le Matin.* He later became editor of *Le Nouvelliste.*

Jacob served some years at the Department of Public Education. He strongly supported the Griot group with Dr. Francois Duvalier, Lorimer Denis, Carl Brouard, and Clément Magloire Saint-Aude, which fought for the recognition of the important contribution of African culture to the Haitian personality and culture. Much of his work appeared in *Les Griots* (1938 and 1939).

Writings: Sociology: *L'ethnie haitienne,* Port-au-Prince, Impr. de l'Etat, 1941; *Contribution à l'étude de l'homme haitien,* Port-au-Prince, Impr. de l'Etat, 1946; miscellaneous articles in *Les Griots* and other journals.

JADFARD, René

b. 1901, Guyane; d. 1947.
Poet, novelist.

Jadfard was born in Cayenne where he attended college. He went to France where he completed his education at the Lycée of Toulouse. He served in the French colonial service for a long period, much of it in Africa.

He was elected a deputy of Guyane to the French National Parliament. He died in 1947 in an accident.

Writings: Novels: *Deux hommes et l'aventure* (written with Georges Madal), Toulouse, Ed. S.T.A.E.L., 1945; *Nuits de Cachiri,* Paris, Fasquelle, 1946; *Cipango ou les trésors du lendemain* (unpublished). An extract of *Nuits de Cachiri,* with analysis by Léonard Sainville is in *Romanciers et conteurs négro-africains,* Paris, Présence Africaine, Vol. II (1968), pp. 215-219.

JANVIER, Louis-Joseph

b. May 7, 1855, Port-au-Prince, Haiti; d. March 24, 1911, Paris.

Novelist, biographer, critic, essayist, physician, lawyer, diplomat.

Janvier was educated in Port-au-Prince at the Lycée Pétion, and was a recipient of a scholarship to France. He studied medicine and graduated in 1881, and also received diplomas in law, political science, economics and finance. He was named Secretary of the Haitian Legation in London from 1889 to 1892, then Chargé d'Affaires, and later Minister, from 1892 to 1904. He was also chancellor at the Haitian Legation in Paris. He returned to Haiti after 30 years of residence abroad in 1904.

He was a vigorous defender of Salomon and the National Party against the Liberals. He ran without success for mayor of Port-au-Prince, his successful opponent being Sténio Vincent.

His works covered the span of novels, travel, criticism, politics and government, but he also published medical studies and some books concerned with Haiti and the race question. His single novel was influenced by Balzac and shows no sign of the then new experimental naturalism of Emile Zola.

Writings: Novel: *Une chercheuse,* Paris, G. Marpon and E. Flammarion, 1889.

Criticism: *L'évolution littéraire en Haiti,* Paris, 1894.

Travel: *Promenade au Quartier Latin,* Paris, 1883.

Tourism: *La République d'Haiti et ses visiteurs (1840-1882), réponse à Victor Cochinat,* Paris, Marpon et Flammarion, Lib. Ed., 1883.

Polemics: *L'égalité des races,* Paris, G. Roucier et Cie, 1884; *Les affaires d'Haiti (1883-1884),* Paris, Marpon et Flammarion, 1885; *Haiti aux Haitiens,* Paris, Impr. A. Parent, 1884; *Les détracteurs de la race noire et de la République d'Haiti,* 1882.

Essays: *Les haitianides (idyles et épisodes).*

Biographies: *Quatre grandes figures haitiennes: le Cacique Henri, Toussaint, Dessalines, Boisrond-Tonnerre.*

Sociology: *Le vieux piquet, scènes de la vie haitienne,* Paris, Impr. A. Parent, 1884; second edition, Port-au-Prince, Panorama, 1965.

Government: *Les Constitutions d'Haiti (1881-1885),* Paris, Marpon et Flammarion, 1886; *Du gouvernement civil en Haiti,* Lille, Le Bigot Frères, 1905.

Education: *La caisse d'épargne et l'école en Haiti, Conférence faite à l'église Wesleyenne, le 10 Avril 1906,* Port-au-Prince, Impr. de l'Abeille, 1906.

Medicine: *De la phtisie pulmonaire,* 1881.

Biographical/Critical Sources: Marie Edouard Lenoir, *Biographie du Dr Louis-Joseph Janvier;* Le Biographe-VII, 5ème livraison, 1884, pp. 67-71.

JASTRAM, Gervais

b. August 12, 1899, Jacmel, Haiti; d. October 26, 1963, Port-au-Prince.

Poet.

Jastram studied in Jacmel then removed to Port-au-Prince where he served as an official in the administration of the Haitian Armed Forces.

Writings: Poetry: *Juvenilia, poèmes,* Paris, Jouve et Cie, 1928; *Dans la solitude,* Impr. de l'Etat, Port-au-Prince, 1956.

JEAN, Antoine

b. December 17, 1923, La Retraite (Commune de Baie Mahault), Guadeloupe. Novelist, critic, painter, singer, composer.

Antoine is primarily a painter and musician. He won a prize of merit in the Fourth World Festival of Students and Youths (Bucharest, August 1953). His paintings have been exhibited at the Chambre de Commerce of Pointe-à-Pitre (1959-1964), in Galeries (Art and Folklore) (1960) and Realités Guadeloupéennes (1965), both in Pointe-à-Pitre, and at the Galerie Soulanges, Paris, 1965.

Writings: Novel: *Le secret de vivre (sous le ciel des Antilles, roman vécu),* Paris, Soulanges, 1964.

Poetry: *Des côtes d'Afrique aux rives d'Amérique (recueil); Echos et visions (recueil); Les ruines qui parlent (recueil).*

Criticism: Conférences et articles: Le vrai visage de la Poèsie;" "La Glorieuse."

JEAN, Eddy Arnold

(pseudonym: **Konrad DAMNE**)

b. November 5, 1952, Saint-Marc, Haiti. Poet, literary critic.

After his primary studies, Eddy Jean came to Port-au-Prince where he completed his education at the Institution Saint-Louis de Gonzague.

He taught Haitian literature in Haiti and afterwards travelled in many countries, including Jamaica, Costa Rica, Canada, and the United States. He is now studying medicine in Lille, France.

Writings: Poetry: *Bohio au Soleil* (composed with his brother Raynold Arnold Jean), Port-au-Prince, Impr. Les Presses Citadelle, 1968, second edition 1969; *Symphonie du Nouveau Monde* (translated into English and Spanish), preface by Francis Blanc, Port-au-Prince, Impr. Serge L. Gaston, 1970; *Orcus* (under pseudonym of Konrad Damné), Paris, Eds. Jacques Soleil, 1976.

Biography: *Carl Brouard, cet immortel,* Port-au-Prince, 1976.

Essays: *L'immense cri des damnés de la terre* (with Justin O. Fièvre), Brooklyn, New York, Presses Haitiennes, 1975.

Literary Criticism (with Justin O. Fièvre): *Cahiers de Littérature Haitienne,* 7 vols., mimeo.; *Pour une littérature haitienne nationale et militante,* Lille, France, Eds. Soleil, 1975.

JEAN-BAPTISTE, Ernst

b. March 28, 1949, Port-au-Prince, Haiti. Poet, literary critic, storywriter.

Jean-Baptiste studied at the Lycée Pétion of Port-au-Prince and later attended the faculty of Law. He is presently a member of the staff of the National Bank of Haiti.

Jean-Baptiste has published various articles and literary studies in *Le Nouvelliste.*

Writings: Poetry: *Les heures hallucinées,* Port-au-Prince, Impr. Centrale, 1972; "Les miroirs animés" (unpublished).

Novel: *Remous et monologues* (to be published).

JEAN-LOUIS, Dulciné

b. December 23, 1837, Jacmel, Haiti; d. May 27, 1906, Port-au-Prince, Haiti. Folklorist, botanist, essayist, public official.

After local schooling, including study under Mr. Debray aîné, an exiled Frenchman in Jacmel, Jean-Louis was appointed an employee in the administration of Finance of Jacmel. He also was a teacher at the Lycée Pinchinat of Jacmel and became Inspector of Schools. Later, he was elected senator. His work with herbs and the local plants was an important pioneering task and he sought to bring into repute the local customs of the peasantry.

Writings: Manuels de culture appropriés au climat et au terroir d'Haiti; I-Café, Jacmel, Impr. de l'Indépendance d'Haiti, 1877; *Manuels de culture appropriés au climat et au terroir d'Haiti;* II-*Canne à sucre,* Jacmel, Impr. de l'Indépendance d'Haiti, 1877; 2ème édition, 1880; *Manuels de culture appropriés au climat et au terroir d'Haiti;* I-*Café; 2ème édition suivie de questionnaires, de commentaires sur le manuel et d'un rapport sur la culture du cacao,* Port-au-Prince, Impr. Vve J. Chenet, 1891; 3ème édition, Bruxelles, Impr. Lithog. Populaire, 1893; *Documents pour la flore indigène d'Haiti,* ler fascicule, Port-au-Prince, Impr. H. Amblard, 1899.

Tourism: *Haiti; choses de la campagne; excursions de Port-au-Prince à Jacmel,* première livraison, Port-au-Prince, Impr. du Bulletin Officiel de l'Agriculture, 1901; *Haiti; choses de la campagne ....* 2ème livraison, Port-au-Prince, Impr. E. Malval, 1906.

Herbal Medicine: *Dictionnaire de médecine créole, d'après le Père Labat,* Fort-de-France (Martinique), Lib. Populaire, 1910.

Geography: *Géographie de l'île d'Haiti contenant des notices historiques, statistiques, géognostiques, etc. et suivie des premiers éléments de la cosmographie à l'usage des écoles primaires et des écoles rurales: premíer cahier* (with M. Jacques Thébaud jeune) Jacmel, Impr. L.N. Rameau et Cie, 1886.

Biographical/Critical Sources: Dantès Bellegarde: *Ecrivains haitiens:* Dulciné Jean-Louis, pp. 91-98, Port-au-Prince, Eds. Henri Deschamps, 1950.

JEAN-LOUIS, Victor

(see **Jean-Louis BAGHIO'O**)

JEFFRY, Antonio

b. 1940, L'île de Saint Martin (Guadeloupe).
Novelist.

After completing his work at the Lycée Gerville-Réache in the early 1960's, he enrolled at the Ecole Supérieure for journalism, in Paris.

His first work, *Soleil nègre,* is 43 pages long, really a "Journal" of meditation about being "nègre" and being French, of speaking créole, of discovering himself.

Writings: Novels: *Soleil nègre,* Paris, Soulanges, 1963; *Débauches; Soleils des Antilles; Pensées de Nègres.*

JEREMIE, Cadet or Joseph

b. March 21, 1858, Port-au-Prince, Haiti; d. March 2, 1958, Port-au-Prince.
Memoirist, scholar, statesman, government official.

Jérémie was among the first students of the Petit Séminaire Collège Saint-Martial where he was educated. He studied law later with attorney Jacques Thébaud.

He was a teacher and government official, becoming chief of division at the Department of the Navy. He was elected Député (1887-1888). Jérémie was appointed Judge at the Tribunal de Cassation (1894-1902) and was named Secretary of State of Justice, Public Education and finally Minister of Foreign Affairs. He was a hundred years old less nineteen days when he died.

Writings: Biographies: *Dessables (Nègre affranchi d'Haiti, fondateur de Chicago),* Port-au-Prince, Impr. de l'Etat, 1948; *Un apôtre de la civilisation* (a biography of Msgr. Guilloux), Port-au-Prince, Impr. N. Telhomme, 1945.

Essays: *De l'éducation populaire,* Paris, Impr. Victor Goupy et Jourdan, 1891; *Deux conférences sur le christianisme,* Paris, Impr. Victor Goupy et Jourdan, 1892; *Inauguration de l'Association du centenaire de l'Indépendance nationale et de l'école du soir,* Paris, Impr. Victor Goupy et Jourdan, 1892; *L'effort,* Port-au-Prince, Impr. de l'Abeille, 1905; *Haiti indépendante,* Port-au-Prince, Chéraquit, Impr. et Ed., 1929; *La culture intellectuelle et la charité,* Port-au-Prince, Impr. de l'Abeille, 1908; *Instruction et travail,* Paris, Impr. Goupy, 1894; *Mission de l'homme dans la vie,* Port-au-Prince, Impr. de l'Abeille, 1916; *Requête d'un prévenu,* Port-au-Prince, Impr. de l'Abeille, 1912; *Le Balliléisme,* Port-au-Prince, Impr. de l'Etat, 1946; *Pour bien vivre, Méditations,* Port-au-Prince, Impr. de l'Etat, 1952.

Memoirs: *Lourdes; impressions et souvenirs,* Lourdes, Impr. de la Grotte, 1927; *Lourdes; impressions et souvenirs d'un pèlerin haitien*

Lourdes, Impr. de la Grotte, 1933; *Action catholique à Lourdes,* Port-au-Prince, Impr. N. Telhomme, n.d.; *Souvenirs d'une enfance heureuse et d'une jeunesse déjà lointaine,* Port-au-Prince, Impr. N. Telhomme, 1940; *Mémoires, Tome I—Anniversaires,* Port-au-Prince, Impr. de l'Etat, 1950.

History: *La paroisse de Sainte-Anne; Le Morne à Tuf,* Port-au-Prince, Impr. de l'Abeille, 1922; and second edition, Impr. La Presse, 1931; *Une colonisation par le café,* Port-au-Prince, Impr. Henri Deschamps, 1946; *Haiti et Chicago,* Port-au-Prince, Impr. H. Deschamps, 1950; *Le Concordat,* Port-au-Prince, Impr. de l'Etat, 1951.

Biographical/Critical Sources: Dantès Bellegarde, "Monsieur Jérémie," in *Ecrivains haitiens,* Port-au-Prince, Ed. Henri Deschamps, 1950, and second edition, 1958; "Le Jubilé de Mr. Jérémie," Port-au-Prince, Chéraquit, 1941.

JOLICOEUR, Renée Marie-Ange *

b. July 20, 1947, Jacmel, Haiti; d. July 23, 1976, Lille, France.

Poet, musician.

Jolicoeur studied in Port-au-Prince at the Lycée de Jeunes Filles and studied medicine in Lille, France.

Léon Laleau, the dean of Haitian poets, expressed this comment about Marie-Ange Jolicoeur:

> Elle préfère *l'évocation à la confidence, la suggestion à l'aveu... L'avenir s'ouvre à deux battants devant elle. C'est d'un pas apparemment léger, cependant assuré, qu'elle y pénètre. Et la chanson originale et personnelle qui rythme cette ascension, enchante l'esprit, car la poètesse est aujourd'hui, plus maîtresse encore de ses moyens, et séduit le coeur—car elle a gardé intactes, et sa fraîcheur et sa grâce et sa personnalité et sa sensibilité . . .*

* See p. 262 for special "Hommage"

Writings: Poetry: *Guitare de vers,* preface by Laurore St-Juste, Port-au-Prince, Impr. Serge Gaston, 1969; *Violon d'espoir,* preface by Maurice A. Lubin, Port-au-Prince, Impr. Serge Gaston, 1970; *Oiseaux de mémoire,* preface by Léon Laleau, Port-au-Prince, Impr. du Séminaire Adventiste, 1972; "Mon Ile," an English translation of his work, "My Island," appeared in *New Writing in the Caribbean,* Georgetown, Guyana, 1972; the poem being from the collection *Oiseaux de mémoire.*

Biographical/Critical Sources: "A la mémoire de la poètesse Renée Marie-Ange Jolicoeur, *Le Petit Samedi Soir,* No. 155, July-Aug., 1976.

JOYAU, Auguste

b. September 3, 1903, Fort-de-France, Martinique.

Poet, storywriter, essayist, biographer, scholar.

Joyau was locally educated in the primary school and later at the Lycée Schoelcher, Fort-de-France, after which he worked for the colonial government in Martinique.

In 1926, he founded with Ernest Thomas the literary review *Lucioles* which lasted into 1928 and centered particularly around Gilbert Gratiant who proclaimed in the first issue:

> *En nos pays, pays du soleil qui se couche, écrivait-il notamment, l'ombre est tôt venue. L'ombre est faite de lumière en allée et de pensée défunte. Que voulons-nous? Reculer un peu le couchant en attirant sur notre commencement de nuits les rayons les plus féconds qu'un soleil les avait laissés derrière lui dans la vieille Europe.*

and then:

> *Malgré l'effort rouge de la lumière, l'Occident en demeure le tombeau.*

Joyau established a second review *Horizons Caraïbes* which lasted from 1953 to 1955 and therein published many writers' works.

Writings: Poetry: *Les conquêtes de Cristal,* Paris, Eds. de la Jeune Académie, 1929; *L'Empire des roses, poémes,* Fort-de-France, Eds. du Courrier des Antilles, 1939.

Stories: *Les Dames des Isles du temps jadis, récits historiques,* Paris, Nouvelles Eds. Latines, 1948; *Héroines et aventurières de la mer caraibe,* Fort-de-France, Eds. des Horizons Caraibes, 1959, new edition Paris, Grassin, 1960.

Biographies: *Belain d'Esnambuc et la conquête des Isles du Vent,* Paris, Ed. Bellenaud, 1950; *Théodore Baude, sa vie et son oeuvre* (with F. Soubie, G. Debien, et al.), Fort-de-France, Impr. Bezaudin, 1953.

Editor of: *Anthologie des poètes martiniquais,* Fort-de-France, Eds. des Horizons Caraibes, 1961.

Essay: *La Martinique: Carrefour du Monde caraibe,* Fort-de-France, Eds. des Horizons Caraibes, 1968, Prix Broquette-Gonin de l'Académie Française.

Anthology: *Panorama de la littérature à la Martinique,* T.1, *XVIII and XIXth* Centuries, Martinique, Eds. des Caraibes, 1974.

JOYAU-DORMOY, Alice

b. ca. 1921, Diamant, Martinique.
Poet, novelist.

Joyau was educated in Fort-de-France, and later studied in France. She married, but lost her husband very early on. She became a business manager and later worked in children's education.

Writings: Genre unknown: *France à bientôt,* 1943.

Poetry: *Chant des îles,* Paris, Ed. Bellenand, 1953; *La Saison éternelle; Nouveaux chants des Iles,* Fort-de-France, Ed. des Horizons Caraïbes, 1957; *Echo des océans; cantique des îles,* Fort-de-France, Ed. des Horizons-Caraïbes, 1971; *La Moisson du passé,* Ed. des Horizons-Caraïbes, 1971.

Novel: *Guiablesse Martinique,* Paris, Jean Grassin, 1958 (written in collaboration with Auguste Joyau); *Mayouta au pays des flamboyants,* Martinique, Eds. des Horizons Caraibes, 1977.

JULIEN-LUNG FOU, Marie-Thérèse

b. May 11, 1909, Rivière Salée, Martinique.
Playwright in French and créole, sculptor

Julien-Lung Fou was educated at the Pensionnat Colonial of Fort-de-France She went to France to study sculpture at L'Ecole Nationale Supérieure des Beaux Arts de Paris.

She won the first prize in a contest of sculpture at the Ministry of Commerce and Industry in 1933, and also a bronze meda at the Grand Salon des Artistes Français

After she married, she spent about ten years in Indochina and came back to Martinique in 1947. She created a bust of Schoelcher and other statues which are in public buildings and collections. She founded in 1956 the magazine *Dialogue* with Edgard Rodap.

Writings: Fables: *Fables créoles, transposées et illustrées,* Fort-de-France, Eds. Dialogue, 1958 *Nouvelles Fables créoles,* n.d.

Plays: *Trois Comédies: Sin-le-Noble* (near Paris), Impr. Wigerolle, 1969; *Le crucifix* (one act; winner of first prize in 1969 in island play competition); *Le Saint Joseph* (one act; about superstitions of peasants); *Pauvres pisseuses* (one act; a comedy about a couple and their 13 daughters).

Stories: *Les Piments doux,* Fort-de-France Impr. Antillaise Saint-Paul, 1976.

JUMINER, Bertène

b. August 6, 1927, Cayenne, Guyane.
Novelist, playwright, shortstory writer and physician.

Dr. Bertène Juminer completed his secondary schooling at the Lycée Carnot in Pointe-à-Pitre, Guadeloupe, and then went to the University of Montpellier (France) where he took a medical degree in 1953. After medical school, Dr. Juminer's first two positions were at a hospital in Saint-Laurent, Moroni, Guyane (1956-

1958) and then at the Institut Pasteur in Tunis (1958-1960). He has since served on the faculties of the Medical Schools at Mesched, Iran (1966-1967), and the University of Dakar (1967-1973). He is presently a Professor on the faculty of the Medical School of the University of Picardie (Amiens, France).

In addition to more than one hundred scientific articles, Dr. Juminer has written three novels: *Les Bâtards,* 1958; *Au seuil d'un nouveau cri,* 1963; and *La Revanche de Bozambo,* 1968. The latter novel has been translated into English under the title *Bozambo's Revenge: Colonialism Inside Out.* Dr. Juminer has also written a play, "L'Archiduc sort de l'ombre," adapted from *La Revanche de Bozambo,* which won first prize from the French National Radio-Television Organization (ORTF) in 1970. Finally, Dr. Juminer has written two short stories, "Le Résistant" and "La Pimentade."

Like the poems of his compatriots, Léon-Gontran Damas, Serge Patient and Elie Stéphenson, the novels of Dr. Juminer are principally concerned with the problem of cultural identity. *Les Bâtards,* for example, explores the anguish of the educated, black élite (cultural bastards) who have, to a great degree, been assimilated into French culture, but who are, nevertheless, aware of and responsive to their black cultural heritage. His second novel, *Au seuil d'un nouveau cri,* is didactic in that its first part, "Le Cri," uses an epic myth as an example (to the modern-day Blacks of the novel's second section, "L'Echo") of the struggle incumbent upon those who wish to be free men. Dr. Juminer's latest novel, *La Revanche de Bozambo,* is a satirical work in which the author ridicules the rhetoric and actions of those who advocate the superiority of one culture or race over another.

Juminer's third novel is a sparkling spoof on colonization—everything is reversed—the whites fight against black colonial rule and the African colonial officials leave wives home in Africa and take up with native white girls in Europe and America. Africains set up new independent white quasi-puppet states and send back by jet from Duke Ellington Airport long imprisoned white rebels to set up new governments under African tutelage who are expected to follow the ways of the superior African governmental forms.

Juminer's style is deft, ironic, imaginative. Aimé Césaire in his introduction to *Les Bâtards* writes:

> *Ici le Père-celui qui détient le pouvoir, celui qui a la force, celui qui régente, celui qui administre, c'est la France. La mère, une mère lointaine, reniée, mais dont la voix se fait soudain étrangement proche et tendre dans les moments de désespoir, c'est l'Afrique.*
>
> *Telle est la situation de* l'Antillais, *le "bâtard" de l'Europe et de l'Afrique, partagé entre ce père qui le renie, et cette mère qu'il a reniée.*

Further elaborating on this theme Chambord (the protagonist) agonizes:

> *Il continuait à faire partie de cette race d'hommes blancs d'esprit, noirs de corps; il ne pouvait plus choisir, trop*

marqué qu'il était dans sa constitution même par trois cents ans d'exil et de domination. Là était son destin; être condamné pour toujours à errer en quête d'une terre promise au-delà d'une Guyane attardée, en deçà d'une Europe en marche; végéter sans option réelle entre ceux qui s'oublient pour avoir trop subi, et d'autres qui vous oublient parce qu'ils sont trop préoccupés de faire subir.

Writings: Novels: *Les Bâtards,* preface by Aimé Césaire, Présence Africaine, 1961; *Au seuil d'un nouveau cri,* Paris, Présence Africaine, 1963; *La Revanche de Bozambo,* Paris, Présence Africaine, 1968, and translated as *Bozambo's Revenge* by Alexandra Bonfante Warren, Washington, D.C., Three Continents Press, 1976. Novel in progress: "La Sentence du Réel" (tentative title).

Plays: *De Dunkerque à Maripassoula?* in *Présence Africaine,* 1962, supplement to No. 42, pp. 260-273; and *L'Archiduc sort de l'ombre* (based on *La Revanche de Bozambo*), performed Paris, ORTF (French radio-television network), in 1970.

Stories: "Le Résistant" in *Awa,* 1972 (number unknown); and "La Pimentade," unpublished.

Essay: "Hommage à Franz Fanon," *Présence Africaine,* No. 40 (Paris, 1962), pp. 125-129.

Biographical/Critical Sources: Randolph Hezekian, "Bertène Juminer and the Colonial Problem," *Black Images,* Vol. 3, No. 1 (Spring, 1974); Gary Warner, "Bertène Juminer: The Ethics of Revolt," *Black Images,* Vol. 3, No. 3 (Autumn, 1974). Also see Paul L. Thompson, "Three Novels by Dr. Bertène Juminer and the Themes of Assimilation, Alienation and Revolt," unpublished Ph.D. diss., Pennsylvania State University, 1974.

KERMADEC, Jeanne de

b. February 8, 1873, Petit-Canal, Guadeloupe; d. August 5, 1964.
Poet, teacher.

Kermadec was educated at the Externat des Soeurs de Saint Joseph in Pointe-à-Pitre.

She was appointed a teacher at Jabrun and afterwards at Morne-à-l'Eau.

Writings: Poetry: *Feux du soir,* Paris, Collection Alternance, 1966; *Refuge poètique,* Paris, Collection Alternance, 1966; *Sanglots,* Paris, Collection Alternance, 1966; *Karukéra.*

LABONTE, Louis Roger

b. ca. 1928, Port-au-Prince, Haiti.
Playwright, poet, essayist, teacher, priest.

Labonté completed his Haitian education at the Petit Séminaire College Saint-Martial. After teaching and working in cooperatives at home he emigrated to Canada where he studied to be a priest, taking orders subsequently and remaining there as a religious.

Writings: Poetry: *Miroir d'Haiti,* Quebec, Eds. du Renouveau, 1971; *Lumière dans ma nuit,* Port-au-Prince, Impr. L'Action Sociale, 1952.

Play: *Une efficace coopération* (three acts), Port-au-Prince, La Phalange, 1962.

Songs: *Chansons coopératives* (preface by Edouard A. Tardieu), Port-au-Prince, 1954, n.d.

Essay: *Notre caisse populaire: coopérative d'épargne et de prêts* (preface by Father Jean Parisot), Port-au-Prince, La Phalange, 1959.

LABOSSIERE, Abel

b. October 27, 1902, Cayes, Haiti.
Novelist, teacher, lawyer.

Labossière attended the school of Christian Brothers and the Lycée Philippe Guerrier of Cayes. He was graduated from the Free Law School in this southern city.

He was appointed as professor at the Lycée Philippe Guerrier and he became deputy commissioner at the civil court of Cayes. At present he is serving as judge on the same court.

Writings: Novels: *Dette d'honneur; roman haitien,* Les Cayes, Impr. Bonnefil Frères, 1923; *La princesse adoptive; roman haitien,* Les Cayes, Impr. Bonnefil Frères, 1927.

LABUCHIN, Rassoul

(pseudonym of **Yves MEDARD**)
b. March 30, 1939, Port-au-Prince, Haiti.
Poet in creole, storywriter, playwright.

Yves Médard started his primary classes at the School Jean-Marie Guilloux of the Christian Brothers and completed his studies at the Lycée Pétion, Port-au-Prince.

Médard has been active in many cultural activities and contributed to the founding of the *Jeunesse Progressiste Haitienne* and *Mouvement Théâtral Ouvrier* with Rony Lescouflair. He is a strong supporter of creole as a language of learning and literature.

Médard is now teaching at several colleges of Port-au-Prince.

Writings: Poetry in creole: *Trois Colliers Maldioc* (Collection Haiti Littéraire), Port-au-Prince, Impr. des Antilles, 1962; *Compère* (poems in creole), preface by Maurice A. Lubin (in French), Port-au-Prince, Impr. des Antilles, 1966; *Compère followed by Dégui,* Port-au-Prince, Impr. des Antilles, 1968; *Le Ficus (with Michaelle Lafontant Médard),* Port-au-Prince, Impr. N.A. Thédore, 1970.

Play: *Le Roi Moko,* performed at Institut Français, January 10 and April 11, 1975.

Biographical/Critical Sources: Marguerite Deschamps: *A la découverte de Rassoul Labuchin, poète du réalisme merveilleux,* Port-au-Prince, 1974; Maximilien Laroche: "La figure du sujet dans le Roi Moko de Rassou Labuchin" in *Conjonction,* No. 127-128, (Dec. 1975), pp. 57-74.

LACROSIL, Michèle

b. 1915, Basse-Terre, Guadeloupe.
Novelist, teacher.

Lacrosil attended schools in Guadeloupe, and completed her education in France.

She married professor Henri Galliard, member of the Academy of Medicine. She is living in Paris and is a professor of litterature in a college in the Seine district of France.

She has published novels that have won modest, but critical success.

In *Sapotille,* the central character, troubled by the subtle but carefully nourished distinctions of skin-coloring throughout the Antilles, eventually seeks release in a hoped for less race-conscious Paris.

Cajou, the creole heroine of the novel *Cajou,* loves Germain, a French boy. Only after tender and often painful expressions of love do the two come to accept each other, but Cajou's fear of ruining Germain and her obsessive belief in her "ugliness" leads on to madness.

Demain Jab-Herma pits the people of Pâline, an old settlement of Guadeloupe, one against the other in a rivalry of love and power—of race and former loyalties, where, under a calm surface, violence is ready to explode. Jab-Herma, chauffeur and sorcerer, watches all and plans for his own special moments. The year is 1952 (and the work is dedicated to Sartre and Beauvoir).

Writings: Novels: *Sapotille et le Serin d'argile,* Paris, Gallimard, 1960; *Cajou,* Paris, Gallimard, 1961; *Demain Jab-Herma,* Paris, Gallimard, 1967.

Biographical/Critical Sources: Discussion of *Demain Jab-Herma* by Beverly Ormerod in "French Caribbean Literature: The Contemporary Situation" in *The Literary Half-Yearly,* Vol. XI, 2 (July 1970), pp. 113-126; Robert P. Smith, Jr., "Michèle Lacrosil: Novelist with a Color Complex," in *French Review,* XLVII (March 1974), pp. 783-790; Léonard Sainville, *Anthologie de la littérature négro-africaine* (Paris, Présence Africaine, 1963), pp. 407-410; Clarisse Zimra, "Patterns of Liberation in Contemporary Women Writers," in *L'Esprit Createur,* XVII, No. 2 (Summer 1977), pp. 103-114.

LAFONTANT, Jean Delorme

b. ca. 1894, Côtes-de-Fer, Haiti; d. ca. 1952, Port-au-Prince.
Novelist, storywriter.

Lafontant received his education in Port-au-Prince and was a businessman most of his life. He published two novels in his early maturity but did little in literature since.

Writings: Novels: *Célie,* Port-au-Prince, Impr. N. Telhomme, 1939; *Le Soir ou Fleurs haitiennes de sensibilité,* Port-au-Prince, Impr. du Collège Vertières, 1942.

LAFONTANT-MEDARD, Michaëlle

(pseudonym: **Marguerite DESCHAMPS**)
b. May 29, 1949, Port-au-Prince, Haiti.
Poet, essayist.

Lafontant was educated at the Institution of Sacré-Coeur de Turgeau, and later graduated from the Ecole Normale Supérieure. She is now working in the field of library science and teaching French and social sciences in several colleges of Port-au-Prince.

She married Yves Médard with whom she has collaborated on many projects.

Writings: Poetry: *Brumes de Printemps,* Port-au-Prince, Impr. M. Rodriguez, 1964; *Pour que renaisse ma Quisqueya,* Port-au-Prince, Impr. Serge L. Gaston, 1967; *Le Ficus* (with Rassoul Labuchin), Port-au-Prince, Impr. N.A. Théodore, 1970.

Essays: *A la découverte de Rassoul Labuchin, poète du réalisme merveilleux,* Port-au-Prince, 1974; *Clefs pour Charades Haitiennes de Roger Gaillard,* Port-au-Prince, 1975.

LAFOREST, Antoine

b. August, 1871, Jérémie, Haiti; d. April 5, 1919, Port-au-Prince.
Storywriter, essayist, printer, newspaper editor.

Laforest was educated in Jérémie. While still a very young man, he engaged in the coasting trade of visiting many cities of the country. He then became a printer.

He was named consul of Haiti in Jamaica. He returned to Port-au-Prince, and helped Frédéric Marcelin to edit *Haiti Littéraire et Politique.* He was later editor of *Haiti Littéraire et Sociale.*

He was elected Deputy of Corail and finally Director of Customs of Jérémie.

Writings: Fiction: *Croquis haitiens,* Port-au-Prince, Impr. de l'Abeille, 1906.

Souvenirs: *Impressions et souvenirs de la Jamaique,* Port-au-Prince, Impr. de l'Abeille, 1904.

Tourism: *38 jours de voyage; le général Antoine Simon, Président de la République, dans le Département du Sud,* Port-au-Prince, Impr. de l'Abeille, 1910 (written with Rocher Osson).

Statistics: *Bulletin des statistiques de la République d'Haiti* (Oct. 1912-Sep. 1913), Port-au-Prince, Impr. de l'Abeille, 1913.

Essay: *Etude industrielle; l'intérieur d'une famille d'ouvriers* (this paper won the prize in Saint Lucien Hector's contest), Port-au-Prince, Impr. Athanase Laforest, 1893.

LAFOREST, Edmond

b. June 20, 1876, Jérémie, Haiti; d. October 17, 1915, Port-au-Prince.
Poet, critic, biographer, teacher.

Laforest was educated by his father in Jérémie. He was long a teacher in Jérémie and other secondary schools, and for a good period at the new Lycée Nord Alexis. He was an head of a division at the finance administration. In 1911, he was named division chief at the Ministry of Interior, and later became Inspector General of Public Instruction. The U.S. Marine occupation of Haiti in 1915 was a blow for Laforest and he wrote a strong article against the Haitian American Convention, feeling so strongly that he committed suicide on the anniversary of Dessalines' death, October 17.

His "Baiser du jour" from *Cendres et flammes* has this valerian passage:

Le rayon promenant des antennes légères—
Songe de femme nue, étreintes mensongères!—
Se vautre, boit du miel, bourdonne, abeille d'or,
Sous le nombril fleuri de la vierge qui dort.

Nephew of Etzer Vilaire, one of Haiti's finest poets, Edmond Laforest was a melancholic artist, his work often saturated with thoughts of death. Influenced by Baudelaire and the later French symbolists, he published many volumes of his verse and founded with Frédéric Marcelin the journal *Haiti Littéraire et Sociale.*

Edmond's grandson, Jean Richard Laforest (b. 1940), also has published some promising verse.

Writings: Poetry: *L'évolution; poème,* Port-au-Prince, Impr. Mme. F. Smith, 1901; *Poèmes mélancoliques (1894-1900),* Port-au-Prince, Impr. H. Amblard, 1901; *La dernière fée; fantaisie en vers,* Port-au-Prince, Impr. de l'Abeille, 1909; *Sonnets-médaillons du dix-neuvième siècle,* Paris, Lib. Fischbacher, 1909; *Cendres et flammes; poèsies,* Paris, A. Messein, 1912; *Sonnets haitiens et Thrène pour Haiti* (patriotic work set against U.S. occupation), in ms., unpublished.

Critical-Biographical Essays: *L'oeuvre poétique de M. Etzer Vilaire,* Jérémie, Impr. du Centenaire, 1907; *Alibée Féry, sa vie, son oeuvre,* Port-au-Prince; *L'oeuvre des poètes* (lecture), Port-au-Prince, Impr. de l'Abeille, 1908; *A propos de culture allemande (question d'actualité),* Port-au-Prince, Impr. de l'Abeille, n.d.

Biographical/Critical Sources: Ghislain Gouraige, *Histoire de la littèrature haitiene,* Port-au-Prince, Impr. N.A. Théodore, 1960, pp. 182-188; Normil Sylvain, "Le souvenir d'Edmond Laforest," in *La Revue Indigène,* No. 4 (Oct. 1927), pp. 172-175; Pradel Pompilus & Frères de l'Instruction Chrétienne, *Manuel illustré d'histoire de la littérature haitienne,* Port-au-Prince, Ed. H. Deschamps, 1961, pp. 252-258.

LAFOREST, Georges Florvil

b. October 9, 1911, Port-au-Prince, Haiti.
Poet, journalist.

Laforest was educated at the Lycée Pétion of Port-au-Prince and other colleges of the capital. He served as an employee at the Department of Public Health in many cities such as Saint-Marc, Port-de-Paix, Gonaïves and Port-au-Prince.

He contributed poetry to many newspapers and published four collections of his verse.

Writings: Poetry: *Complaintes,* Port-au-Prince, Impr. de l'Etat, 1963; *Joies et Pleurs,* Port-au-Prince, Eds. Panorama, 1963; *Chagrins,* 1974; *Cris d'un coeur,* 1975.

LAFOREST, Jean-Richard

b. 1940, Jérémie, Haiti.
Poet, playwright.

Soon after his birth in the poetic city of Jérémie, Laforest moved to Port-au-Prince with his parents and there completed his education at the Centre d'Etudes Secondaires.

In 1960 his first book of verse appeared with some twenty-three poems: *Insoupçonné.*

He is the grandson of the fine Haitian poet Edmond Laforest.

Writings: Poetry: *Insoupçonné,* Port-au-Prince, Librairie Indigène, 1960.

Plays: (recording) *Les Puits Errants* (with Anthony Phelps); *Pierrot Le Noir* (with Emile Olivier); *Le divan des alternances,* Montreal, Nouvelle Optique, 1978.

Biographical/Critical Sources: Maurice Lubin's "Five Haitian Poets" in *Young Poetry of the Americas,* Washington, D.C., Pan American Union, 1968.

LAHENS, Léon

b. March 22, 1889, Port-au-Prince, Haiti;
d. April 4, 1965, Port-au-Prince.
Essayist, lawyer, teacher.

Lahens was educated at the Petit Séminaire Collège Saint-Martial, and graduated from the capital's law school.

He was a teacher and became chef de bureau at the Department of Foreign Affairs. He was appointed judge on the civil court of Port-au-Prince and later judge on the Court of Appeals of Gonaïves. He spent many years as professor at the Lycée Pétion.

Writings: Essays: *Ce que disent des lettres,* Port-au-Prince, n.d.; *L'élite intellectuelle,* Port-au-Prince, Impr. de l'Abeille, 1916.

Law: *De la possession d'état en matière de filiation naturelle,* Port-au-Prince, Impr. de l'Abeille, 1912.

LALEAU, Léon

b. August 3, 1892, Port-au-Prince, Haiti. Poet, playwright, storywriter, novelist, journalist, diplomat.

After lower schooling in the classes of "Les dames de Roux" and the Collège Louverture, Laleau went on to the Lycée Pétion in Port-au-Prince. He graduated from the law school and he also had many government positions, including sub-inspector of schools, chief of protocol, and four times was Minister of Foreign Affairs, of Public Works, and, recently, of National Education and Agriculture. He served in many diplomatic posts such as Chargé d'Affaires in Rome, Minister in Lima, in Santiago de Chili, and in London.

While in France he contributed to the *Mercure de France, Le Divan, Paris-Revue, Comoedia, Figaro* and other leading periodicals.

Laleau represents the transition between the *La Ronde* group of 1898 gathered around Georges Sylvain and Damoclès Vieux and the new movement grouped about the journal *La Revue Indigène* of Jacques Roumain and his associates. Although he by and large sought to ignore the American occupation beginning in 1915, he did join the circle of Georges Léger, Fernand Hibbert, Louis H. Durand and *La Revue de la Ligue de la Jeunesse Haitienne,* established February 1916 to protest the U.S. Marine invasion of Haiti. His favorite subjects were the natural beauties of Haiti and his experience in France and Italy in his younger days. However, by the 1930's, his verse, though still elegant, was nationalistic and conscious of African themes important to Haiti. Also by 1932, the year his novel *Le Choc* appeared, he was able to take stock of the impact of the U.S. power over his country and the implications and events of the early reactions to a non-Latin and highly race-conscious occupying force.

Laleau became editor-in-chief of the Haitian newspaper *Le Matin,* and manager-editor of *Haiti-Journal* and *Le Nouvelliste,* two other important periodicals of their day. In 1934, he was named Commander of the Legion of Honor and in 1962 he was awarded the Prix Edgar Poe, offered by the Maison de Poèsie in Paris to distinguish poets writing in French who are not French nationals. He was elected a member of the Académie Ronsard in Paris in 1965.

Laleau's poetry was increasingly brief as can be seen in these lines from *Abréviations:*

L'azur, d'un bleu fidèle, illumine Paris.
Les marronniers du bois sont en vert . . .
Tu souris.

or some sketches from "Paris bohême":

Les longs mollets bronzés de Joséphine
Baker, conquièrent les Parisiens
Eberlués . . . Garçon, une fine
Et qui sente bon les jours anciens.

In his "Trahison," Laleau expresses the consciousness of his African-Haitian heritage:

Ce coeur obsédant, qui ne correspond
Pas avec mon langage et mes costumes,
Et sur lequel mordent, comme un
crampon,

Des sentiments d'emprunt et des coutumes

D'Europe, sentez-vous cette souffrance
Et ce désespoir à nul autre égal
D'apprivoiser, avec des mots de France,
Ce coeur qui m'est venu du Sénégal?

Writings: Poetry: *A voix basse,* Port-au-Prince, Impr. Moderne, 1919; *La flèche au coeur, poèmes,* preface by Maurice Rostand, Paris, Eds. Parville, 1926; *Le rayon des jupes ou treize poèmes pour Tristan Derème,* first edition, Saint Calais, Sarthe, France, Impr. par Emile Lefleuvre, 1926, second edition, Paris, Collection des Amis de Tristan Derème, 1928; *Abréviations,* poèmes, Paris, Librairie de France, 1929; *Musique nègre, poèmes,* Port-au-Prince, Impr. de l'Etat, 1933; *Ondes courtes, poèmes,* Port-au-Prince, Impr. de l'Etat, 1933; *Orchestre,* Paris, Ed. Divan, 1937; poems in many anthologies including N.R. Shapiro's *Negritude: Black Poetry from Africa and the Caribbean,* New York, October House, 1970; Senghor's pioneering *Anthologie de la nouvelle poèsie nègre...,* Paris, Presses Universitaires de France, 1948, 1972.

Biographies: *Maurice Rostand intime,* Paris, Les Eds. du Monde Moderne, 1926; *Apothéoses,* (Etudes sur Dessalines, Christophe, Ludovic Lamothe, Ernest Douyon, Caïus Lhérisson, Constantin Henriquez, Frédéric Marcelin, et al.), Port-au-Prince, Ed. Henri Deschamps. 1952.

Novels: *La danse des vagues (roman haitien),* Port-au-Prince, Impr. Aug. A. Héraux, 1919; *Le choc, chronique haitienne des années 1915 à 1918,* Port-au-Prince, Impr. La Presse, 1932.

Story: *Jusqu'au bord, (nouvelle),* Port-au-Prince, Impr. de l'Abeille, 1916.

Plays: *Amitiés impossibles (lever de rideau en un acte),* written with Georges Léger, Port-au-Prince, Impr. de l'Abeille, 1916; *Une cause sans effet, comédie en deux actes,* (written with Georges Léger), Port-au-Prince, Impr. de l'Abeille, 1916; *L'étau, comédie,* 1917; *La pluie et le beau temps,* 1919; *Le tremplin,* 1921; *L'attelage—Les petites marionnettes;* "De Bronze et d'ivoire," (unpub.); "Pensées en vers," (unpub.).

Biographical/Critical Sources: Review by Jean Fouchard, "Léon Laleau: *Les ondes courtes,*" in *La Relève,* (April 1933), pp. 12-20; also various essays on Laleau in "Hommage à Léon Laleau" by Jean Fouchard, Pradel Pompilus, Maurice Rat in *Conjonction,* Edition spéciale, Nos. 87-88 (1963) with bibliography of Laleau's works; Frère Rapheal's "Léon Laleau, poète indigéniste," in *Le Nouvelliste* (April 1970); and Raphael's "*Le choc* (1932) ou un roman de l'occupation américaine en Haiti," in *World Theatre,* No. 114 (1970), pp. 44-52; Maurice Rat's "Lèon Laleau, Haitien et poète français," in *La Muse Française* (June 15, 1937), pp. 263-264; Naomi M. Garret's *The Renaissance of Haitian Poetry,* Paris, Présence Africaine, 1963; Franck Fouché's *Guide pour l'étude de la littérature haitienne,* Port-au-Prince, Eds. Panorama, 1964; Ghislain Gouraige, *Histoire de la littérature haitienne,* Port-au-Prince, Impr. N.A. Théodore, 1960, pp. 310-316, 351-354, 371-372; Pradel Pompilus et les Frères de l'Instruction Chrétienne, *Manuel illustré de la littérature haitienne,* Port-au-Prince, Ed. H. Deschamps, 1961, pp. 346-353; Robert Cornevin, *Le Théâtre haitien, des origines à nos jours,* Quebec, Ed. Léméac, 1973, pp. 139-140; and see Special Issue devoted to Laleau in *Conjonction,* Nos. 87-88 (Port-au-Prince, 1963), with bibliography; and Special Issue of *Le Petit Samedi Soir* (for Laleau's 80th anniversary), (Port-au-Prince, August 3, 1972).

LAMARRE, Joseph P.V.

b. May 8, 1918, Port-au-Prince, Haiti.
d. ca. 1957, Port-au-Prince.
Poet, government official.

Lamarre was educated in Port-au-Prince and studied bookkeeping. He served many years in the Haitian Internal Revenue Service.

Writings: Poetry: *L'aube rouge, (Poèmes),* "Collection Le Glaive," Port-au-Prince, Impr. V. Valcin, 1946.

LANGLOIS, Patrick

b. September 29, 1945, Melun, France.
(assoc. with French Guyane).
Novelist, playwright, poet, essayist, artist, teacher.

Although not French Guyanese by birth, Patrick Langlois adopted the country as his home and is contributing to its artistic output.

At a very early age Langlois was enrolled at the "école-mixte Barbizon-Fontainebleau" where he followed in the footsteps of his well-known artist father by taking up painting and drawing. At seven, his parents enrolled him in the "Institut pour le développement harmonique" which Georges Ivanovitch Gurdjieff established at Avon.

He has engaged in multiple and often parallel activities such as drawing and copper engraving, the study of the clarinet at the Conservatoire National, drawing and painting at the "Académie Kolwalsky," advanced studies in drafting at "l'école supérieure technique de dessin appliqué," and has participated in a number of painting exhibitions in the vicinity of Fontainbleau. He has also had some notable experience as a jazz musician.

During his military service he was sent to Guadeloupe, Martinique and French Guyane. After his release, he travelled in Brazil, but returned to French Guyane where he settled and continued to paint, sculpt, write and participate in the theater, particularly with the "Troupe Angéla Davis." His association with this troup has given him the opportunity to meet and work with the leading writers of French Guyane.

Langlois believes that literature should be addressed to the people and not be a special preserve of the elite. To the end that all men benefit from literature, Langlois feels that simplicity of expression should be stressed. His most consistent theme is the victory of man over himself, for he believes that an aware man is neither possessed nor possessive, but free.

Patrick Langlois currently resides in Montjoly, French Guyane, where he teaches drawing and, with his French Guyanese wife, pursues the arts.

Writings: Novel: *Une merveilleuse science,* Paris, La Pensée Universelle, 1974.

Unpublished Novels: *L'Accord Parfait* (novel in four volumes); *Il;Ne lisez pas ce livre c'est de la merde; Nya'lo; Vous n'y comprenez rien* (anti-novel).

Poetry: *Tue-toi si tu veux vivre.*

Short story: *La mirée girette.*

Essay: *Mixologie d'une opinion.*

Plays: *Les coulisses du théâtre* (surrealist play); *Pluralité* (avant-garde play).

LANGUICHATTE

(pseudonym for **Théodore BEAUBRUN**)

LANIER, Dr Clément

(pseudonym: **Jean ROBION**)
b. November 23, 1879, Saint-Marc, Haiti; d. 1967, Port-au-Prince.
Biographer, historian, physician, teacher, journalist.

Clément Lanier studied in local institutions and at the end of his studies for his humanities degree at the Lycée Pétion of Port-au-Prince he earned the "Prix d'honneur" in Philosophy in 1900. He was licensed to practice medicine in 1905 and took advanced scientific studies at the Institute Pasteur in Paris in 1922.

Active in education, Lanier founded in 1904 the Collège Lanier in Saint-Marc and served as an Inspector of Schools in Saint-Marc, from 1910-1915. He was Deputy of Saint-Marc, became the first Director of the Lycée Sténio Vincent when it was founded by President Sténio Vincent. He was a member of the Constitutional Congress of 1950.

Lanier published many historical and scientific articles in such local papers as *Horizons, Le National, Le Temps-Revue, La Presse, La Phalange, La Revue de la Société d'Histoire et de Géographie d'Haiti* and some foreign journals and was a member of many scientific and scholarly societies at home and abroad.

In the competition of 1903 to establish the text, music and title of Haiti's national anthem, Lanier's suggested title, "La Dessalinienne," was accepted. The words were by Justin Lhérisson and the music by Nicolas Geffrard.

Writings: History: *La lumière aux îles alizées; Des rives du passé; Les beaux visages de l'amitié; La campagne en Géorgie en 1779; La campagne en Floride en 1781; La Pologne: Dessalines et les Polonais; Miranda et Haiti; La flotille du Congrès du 18 mai 1803.*

Biography: *Demesvar Delorme and Antoinette Dessalines.*

Science: *Le coup de chaleur; Tuberculose humaine—Climat insulaire.*

LAPIERRE, Alix

b. April 11, 1931, Jacmel, Haiti.
Novelist, poet.

Alix Lapierre received his education at the primary school "Frère Clément" of the Christian Brothers of Jacmel and at the Lycée Pinchinat, also in Jacmel. Some years later he left Jacmel to live in Port-au-Prince.

He has published various poems in the literary magazine *Optique* and a great number of political articles in *Le Nouvelliste* and *Le Nouveau Monde.*

Writings: Novel: *Les Oubliés de Dieu,* Port-au-Prince, Impr. des Antilles, 1976.

LARA, Oruno

b. January 20, 1879, Pointe-à-Pitre, Guadeloupe; d. ca. 1942.
Poet, essayist, storywriter, novelist, literary critic/historian, editor.

Lara attended school at Pointe-à-Pitre. He began life as an apprentice typographer and was a self-made man.

After working at *La Vérité,* and the *Courrier de la Guadeloupe,* Lara became editor of *La République* and later editor-in-chief of *Indépendant,* edited in Pointe-à-Pitre.

Writings: Poetry: *L'année fleurie,* 1901; *L'idylle rose,* 1907; *L'art des vers,* 1911; *Les emblèmes,* 1909.

Essays: *Guadeloupe et Martinique,* 1909.

Editor of Anthology: *Fleurs tropicales.*

History of Literature: *Sous le ciel bleu de la Guadeloupe (essai sur la littérature créole),* Paris, Librairie Fischbacher, 1912; *La littérature antillaise; aux pays bleus: notes de littérature et d'art; études critiques; la littérature antillaise et le régionalisme,* preface by André Blancan, Paris, Libr. Le progrès vulgarisateur (Impr. du Progrès à Sartrouville), 1913.

History: *Histoire de la Guadeloupe,* 1923.

Novel: *Question de couleur (Blanches et Noires) roman de moeurs,* Paris, Nouvelle Librairie Universelle, 1923.

LARA, Sully-Moïse

b. August 14, 1867, Pointe-à-Pitre, Guadeloupe; d. December 8, 1950.
Playwright, novelist, teacher.

Lara received his education in Guadeloupe; he first was named a teacher at Goyave, afterwards at Pointe-à-Pitre.

Writings: Plays: *La chambre consignée,* (one act); *Rodolphe se venge* ("Comédie-vaudeville en 2 actes").

Novels: *La fiancée du Maître d'école* (roman en feuilleton); *Sous l'esclavage,* Pointe-à-Pitre, Impr. Officielle de la Guadeloupe, 1935; second edition, Paris, Eds. Ophryx, 1936; *Courtisane* (moeurs créoles), Basse-Terre, Guadeloupe, 1968.

Agriculture: *Traité élémentaire d'Agriculture tropicale,* Ophryx, 1935.

LARAQUE, Paul

(pseudonym: **Jacques LENOIR**)
b. September 21, 1920, Jérémie, Haiti.
Poet (in French and creole), essayist.

Laraque was educated in Port-au-Prince. He entered the military school of Port-au-

Prince and was commissioned adjutant. He followed a military career and became a deputy to the head of the Haitian Army. He is presently living in New York.

Writings: Poetry: *Ce qui demeure* (poèmes), Montreal, Ed. Optique, 1973; *Fistibal* (poems in creole), Montreal, Ed. Nouvelles Optiques, 1974.

Political Essay: *Pour une alternative de gauche,* (mimeo.), 1975.

LARGE, Camille

b. October 24, 1898, Jacmel, Haiti.
Novelist, storywriter, teacher.

Camille Large began his studies in Jacmel and went to Port-au-Prince to complete his education and graduated from the Faculty of Law. He spent many years teaching French at the Lycée Pétion of Port-au-Prince. Later, he became Director of the Lycée Nord Alexis and afterwards Inspector of the Department of Labor in Jérémie. He was called to Port-au-Prince as Supervisor of Secondary Education at the Ministry of National Education. He was teaching in different colleges and in 1972 his colleagues and former students celebrated his 50th year in the field of education. He has published many articles on education in *Education Sans Pleurs, Le Nouvelliste, Le Matin, La Revue de la Société d'Histoire et de Géographie,* and *Conjonction.*

Writings: Novel: *Carrefour sans visage* (with Alfred Icart), New York, Société Haitienne de Publication, 1969.

LARGE, Josaphat Robert

b. November 15, 1942, Jérémie, Haiti.
Poet.

Large started his education in Jérémie and came to Port-au-Prince to complete it. He is now living in New York and is the director of the experimental theatre "Kouidor."

He has published many texts in English in the collection *Hyn Anthology,* published in New York (year unknown).

Writings: Poetry: *Nerfs du Vent,* preface by Gérard Campfort, Paris, P.J. Oswald, 1975.

LAROCHE, Louis Arnold

b. 1869, Cap-Haitien, Haiti; d. 1890, Paris.
Poet, musician.

A brilliant student at the Lycée du Cap-Haitien, Laroche continued his studies in Paris, but committed suicide in his 21st year in the French capital.

Laroche's first volume of verses was published when he was but 17 and his last book in his 20th year.

Writings: Poetry: *Les bluettes (1882-1885),* Paris, Impr. G. St-Aubin, 1887; *Miragoâne; mémoire d'un assiégé* (poetic narrative in which the author pointed out his sympathy for the military adventures of Boyer Bazelais, in Miragoâne, in 1883), Paris, Arthur Rousseau, Impr. G. St-Aubin, 1889.

LAROCHE, Maximilien

b. 1937, Cap-Haitien, Haiti.
Essayist, literary critic, teacher.

Laroche attended the schools of his native city but emigrated to Canada where he took his university work. He is presently a professor at Laval University, Montreal.

Writings: Essays: *Portrait de l'Haitien,* Montréal, Eds. de Ste-Marie, 1968.

Literary Criticism: *Haiti et sa littérature,* Cahiers No. 5, Quebec, Ageum, 1963; *Le miracle et la métamorphose. Essai sur les littératures de Quebec et d'Haiti,* Canada, Eds. du Jour, 1970; "Image du nègre et rhétorique dans la littérature haitienne," in *Etudes littéraires* (Canada, 1974); "A propos de la négritude," in *Canadian Journal of African Studies,* No. 8 (1974), pp. 62-66; "L'Américanité ou l'ambiguité du 'Je' " in *Etudes Littéraires,* No. 8 (Canada), pp. 103-128; "Magloire St-Aude, l'exilé de l'intérieur," in *Présence Francophone,* No. 10 (Sherbrooke, Canada), pp. 49-57; "Mythe africain et mythe antillais: le personnage du Zombi," in *Canadian Journal of African Studies,* No. 9 (1975), pp. 479-491. Also see recent *L'Image comme écho,* Montréal, Eds. Nouvelle Optique, 1978; and *Jacques Stéphen Alexis* in Fernand Nathan, Series Classiques du Monde, Paris, 1978.

LASSEGUE, Franck

b. October, 1892, Jérémie, Haiti;
d. December 6, 1940, Paris.
Poet, musical composer, dentist.

Franck Lassègue attended the Lycée Nord Alexis of Jérémie and completed his education in Port-au-Prince. He graduated from the School of Dentistry of Port-au-Prince. For professional purposes, he visited many cities such as Miragoâne, Jacmel, Saint-Marc, Gonaïves, Port-de-Paix, and Cap-Haitien.

In 1923, Lassègue went to Paris where he spent many years before he died. He was a talented composer; some of his works are: "Chansons du Rivage," "Antillaises," "Marchand de pâtés," "Pages d'Album," and "Bacchanales."

Luc Grimard said of him:

> *Lassègue, musicien, a su rendre la quintessence parfumée de l'âme populaire haitienne, la poser pour l'opposer avec sa tristesse invincible, son filet de source mélodique, sa passion frémissante, ses possibilités latentes, son curieux et savoureux mélange afro-français, son inexprimable mélancolie séculaire.*

Writings: Etudes sur la musique haitienne; lère série, Port-au-Prince, Impr. du Sacré-Coeur, 1919; *Ciselures; la musique à travers Haiti; pages haitiennes; figurines,* Albert (France), Lib. A. Crossel, 1929.

Music: *Pages d'Album,* Paris, Librairie Musicale R. Legoux.

LATAILLADE, Robert

b. November 28, 1910, Jérémie, Haiti;
d. June 28, 1931, Jérémie.
Poet, teacher.

Lataillade was the nephew of the poet Edmond Laforest and the son of Nerva Lataillade, an amateur poet. He was educated in Jérémie and had Roland Chassagne and Jean F. Brierre as his schoolmates. All of the three went on to distinguished careers in writing and swelled the role of important Haitian authors from Jérémie.

When the final classes were suppressed in all provincial lycées, Robert Lataillade went to Port-au-Prince and spent two years at the Agricultural College established by the Americans at Damiens, close to Port-au-Prince. He was named director of a "ferme-école" (rural farm-school) near Jérémie. He died in his 21st year, in 1931.

Lataillade's verse was personal, indwelling. This was in interesting contrast to his training in the agricultural college where it was hoped by Haiti's U.S. controlled government that the youth of the island would learn "practical" things. No match for his often more husky and brawling comrades at Damiens, Lataillade was increasingly ill. Knowing he had little time he feverishly collected his experience of love and death into one modest volume, *L'urne close,* which was published two years after his death.

Writings: Poetry: *L'urne close,* Port-au-Prince, Impr. La Press, 1933, posthumous collection edited by Jean F. Brierre.

Biographical/Critical Sources: Naomi Garret, *The Renaissance of Haitian Poetry,* Paris, Présence Africaine, 1963; Edner Brutus "Robert Lataillade intime," in *La Relève* (July 1933), pp. 27-37; and Brutus, "Robert Lataillade" in *La Relève* (July 1939), pp. 21-27.

LATORTUE, Paul Emile

b. May 14, 1850, Gonaïves, Haiti;
d. October 5, 1921, Gonaïves.

Poet, journalist.

He was educated at the Petit Séminaire Collège Saint-Martial of Port-au-Prince. He was a teacher for many years.

He was elected deputy of Gonaïves and became Vice-President of the Constituent Assembly of Gonaïves in 1888. He also was a Senator.

Writings: Poetry: *Poèmes patriotiques,* Port-au-Prince, n.d. (vers français et créoles); *Le Palmier de l'Indépendance,* Port-au-Prince, n.d. (large sheet; music and verse); *Un épisode de l'Indépendance d'Haiti; récit familier des esclaves; Saint Domingue, 1803 (en vers),* Port-au-Prince, Impr. H. Chauvet et Cie, 1896; *Le palmier d'Haiti; chant de la reine des Antilles;* "Hymne du Centenaire" (musique de St-Jean Jeune des Gonaïves), Paris, A. Bourlant Ladam, 1903.

LAURENT, Gérard Mentor

b. December 14, 1921, Port-au-Prince, Haiti.
Biographer, historian, accountant.

Laurent attended the Institution of Christian Brothers and then studied accounting. He has taught history at many colleges.

He was secretary general at the Lottery of the Haitian State and was an administrator of the orthopedic hospital of the Institute of Social Insurance. He is now the curator of the National Museum of Haiti.

Writings: Biographies/History: *J.J. Dessalines, guerrier intrépide, génie organisateur,* Port-au-Prince, Impr. de l'Etat, 1947; *Coup d'oeil sur la politique de Toussaint Louverture,* Port-au-Prince, Ed. Henri Deschamps, 1949; *Six études sur J.J. Dessalines,* Port-au-Prince, Les Presses Libres, 1951; *Toussaint Louverture à travers sa correspondance,* Madrid, Industrias Graficas, 1953; *Documentation historique pour nos étudiants,* Port-au-Prince, Impr. La Phalange, 1958; *Pages d'histoire d'Haiti,* Port-au-Prince, Impr. La Phalange, 1960; *Le Commissaire Sonthonax à Saint-Domingue, Tomes I et II,* Port-au-Prince, Impr. La Phalange, 1965; *Tomes 3 et 4,* Port-au-Prince, Impr. Adventiste, 1974; *A Brief History of the Republic of Haiti for Foreigners,* Port-au-Prince, Impr. La Phalange, 1970; *Pèlerinage Historique à Sainte Anne,* Port-au-Prince, Impr. La Phalange, 1970; *Haiti et l'Indépendance américaine,* Port-au-Prince, Impr. Séminaire Adventiste, 1976; *800 Black Volunteers from Santo Domingo (Haiti) in Savannah,* trans. by Chevallier-Daguilh, n.d., 1977.

Tourism: *Haiti: Much To Know, Much To See, Much To Do,* Port-au-Prince, Impr. La Phalange, 1970.

LAVIGNE, Mark or Marc

(pseudonym for **Emmanuel-Flavia LEOPOLD**)

LECONTE, Vergniaud

b. 1866, Cap-Haitien, Haiti; d. October 17, 1932, Cap-Haitien.
Playwright, historian.

Leconte received his education in Cap-Haitien. He wrote three plays, all published in 1926. On Leconte's theatre, Dr. Ghislain Gouraige gave this comment:

> *Il n'y a nul souci de vérité psychologique. Son théâtre est un théâtre d'intrigues où la seule qualité appréciable est le style. L'auteur supplée par la composition à l'absence dans ses pièces de vie, et pour être plus précis de véritable intérêt humain.*

Writings: Plays: *Le Roi Christophe,* performed in 1901; *Coulou,* performed in 1916; *Une princesse aborigène,* Paris, Société d'Impr. et du journal d'Issoudun, 1926. (All of these were collected in a single volume.)

History: *Henri Christophe dans l'histoire d'Haiti,* Paris, Berger-Levrault, 1931; *L'Eglise du Cap de 1860 à 1942,* Port-au-Prince, Impr. de l'Etat, 1942.

Biographical/Critical Sources: Dr. Ghislain Gouraige: *Histoire de la littérature haitienne,* Port-au-Prince, Impr. N.A. Théodore, 1960, pp. 369-372; Robert Cornevin, *Le théâtre haitien, des origines à nos jours,* Quebec, Ed. Léméac, 1973, pp. 135-136.

LEFEVRE, Louis

b. August 17, 1855, Jacmel, Haiti;
d. November 14, 1896, Jacmel.
Poet, teacher.

Lefèvre was educated in Jacmel and was a teacher of primary education. He later became an inspector of schools in Jacmel. He published many articles on history and literature.

Writings: Poetry: *Un cri patriotique,* Jacmel, B.H. Lachataignerie, 1880.
Politics: *Le clergé,* Paris, Rennes, Typ. Oberthur, 1891.

Biographical/Critical Sources: A.V. Catulle Voyard: *Le clergé et Monsieur Louis Lefèvre,* Jacmel, Impr. L.A. Brun, 1891.

LEGAGNEUR, Serge

b. January 10, 1937, Jérémie, Haiti.
Poet, surrealist, storywriter, teacher.

Legagneur started his primary classes in Jérémie and completed his studies in Port-au-Prince. He was very close to the group of poets Philoctète, Phelps, Morisseau and Davertige (who formed the *Haiti-Littéraire* circle). He has written prefaces to many of the volumes of poetry published by members of the group and was a contributor to their later magazine, *Semences.* For the past ten years, Legagneur has been living in Canada where he is a teacher.

Writings: Poetry: *Textes Interdits,* Montreal, Ed. Esterel, 1966; *Textes en croix,* Montréal, Nouvelle Optique, 1978.

LEGER, Georges Nicolas

b. January 29, 1890, Port-au-Prince, Haiti; d. ca. 1950, Port-au-Prince.
Playwright, lawyer, diplomat.

Léger received his education in France where he attended the Lycée Michelet. He graduated from the Faculty of Law in Paris.

He practiced law in Haiti in his father's law office and served as secretary to the Haitian Legation in Paris, but returned to be elected Deputy in 1917. A member of the anti-U.S. group of writers of the *Revue de la Ligue de la Jeunesse Haitienne* established in 1916, Léger was in the forefront of the intellectual opposition to the American occupation of the island. He worked closely with such writers as Fernand Hibbert, Léon Laleau, and Louis Henry Durand to make the reassessments necessary to cope with the frontal assault on Franco-African values so long unchallenged.

He was named Minister of Foreign Affairs and Finances in the newly independent government of President Sténio Vincent during the 1936-38 period.

Always an amateur of the theatre, Léger wrote two plays, one of them with his old friend Léon Laleau.

Writings: Plays: *Amitiés impossibles* (with Laleau) in one act, Port-au-Prince, Impr. de l'Abeille, 1916; *Une cause sans effet* (comedy in two acts), Port-au-Prince, Impr. de l'Abeille, 1916.

LEGER-LEGER, Alexis

(see under pseudonym: **Saint-John PERSE**)

LEGITIME, Francois Denys

(or **DEUS**)
b. November 2, 1841, Jérémie, Haiti;
d. 1935, Port-au-Prince.
Writer, statesman.

Légitime attended the primary school in Jérémie, but he was a self-made man, saying he believed in books because they are the tools of human achievement.

He was enlisted as a youngster in the Haitian army as a soldier and was rapidly promoted. He became director of the custom house of Port-au-Prince, later

Minister of Agriculture and later Senator and Minister of the Interior. Finally, he was made President of Haiti in 1888-1889.

Under the government of President Louis Borno, he was named President du Conseil d'Etat.

Writings: Politics: *Ils ont osé,* Paris, Typ. Lahure, 1876; *Programme de gouvernement,* Port-au-Prince, Impr. Mme. Eyron Chapotin, 1888; *Principes politiques du Général Légitime; documents publiés en Haiti en Aout et Septembre 1888,* Paris, Ernest Leroux, 1891; *Onze années de luttes (précédé de "A la population de Jérémie,"* Port-au-Prince, n.d.; *Une année au Ministère de l'Agriculture et de l'Intérieur,* Paris, Challamel aîné, 1883; *Histoire du Gouvernement du Général Légitime, Président de la République d'Haiti,* Paris, E. Lerroux, 1891; *La voix de la patrie, réplique aux "voix de l'exil," Port-au-Prince, n.d.; A notre tour maintenant,* Port-au-Prince, Impr. de l'Abeille, 1903.

Speech: *Discours du Vice-Président du Comité Central de SOUSCRIPTION-LOUVERTURE, à l'occasion de la première réunion des Membres de ce Comité,* Port-au-Prince, 1877.

Essays: *Haiti; nation maritime, ou le cabotage en Haiti,* Port-au-Prince, 1885; *L'armée haitienne; sa nécessité, son rôle,* Paris, E. Dufossé, 1879; *Question financière,* Port-au-Prince, Impr. Bouchereau et Cie, 1880; *Industrie sucrière et une solution économique,* Port-au-Prince, Impr. Ritt Ethéart, 1884; *Haiti, son commerce et ses industries,* Port-au-Prince, Impr. Mme. D. Chapotin, 1888; *La nation ou la race haitienne,* Port-au-Prince, Impr. Athanase Laforest, 1888; *La propriété foncière en Haiti,* Port-au-Prince, 1866; *La République d'Haiti; ou réfutation de la brochure intitulée "Mémoire pour être communiqué aux gouvernements des puissances étrangères sur l'état de cette République,"* Port-au-Prince, 1889; *L'Indépendance nationale d'Haiti,* Port-au-Prince, Impr. de l'Abeille, n.d.; *Le Môle Saint-Nicolas,* Port-au-Prince, Impr. Ritt Ethéart, n.d.; *La question des chemins de fer (contrat Faubert),* Port-au-Prince, n.d.; *Questions économiques et sociales; le papier-monnaie,* Port-au-Prince, Impr. H. Chauvet et Cie, 1897; *Questions économiques et sociales; le papier-monnaie (deuxième partie; les finances haitiennes . . .),* Port-au-Prince, Impr. H. Amblard, 1897; *Some general considerations on the people and the government of Haiti* (in Universal Races Congress), London, 1911, papers on interracial problems, London, 1911, pp. 178-184; *La force publique,* Port-au-Prince, Impr. Nationale, 1918.

Sociology: *La vérité sur le vaudoux,* Port-au-Prince, n.d.; *La république d'Haiti et les races africaines en général; premier congrès universel des races tenu à Londres du 26 au 29 juillet 1911,* Port-au-Prince, Impr. de l'Abeille, 1911.

Scholarship: *La voie, la vérité, la vie,* Port-au-Prince, n.d.; *Le monde, l'homme et les sciences,* Port-au-Prince, Impr. J. Verrolot, 1907.

Biography: *Vie du Général Denys Légitime père,* Paris, 1881; *Les souvenirs historiques sur Salnave.*

LEMAIRE, Emmeline Carriès

b. June 20, 1899, Jacmel, Haiti.
Poet, essayist.

Lemaire was educated in Jacmel for her primary schooling and then went to Port-au-Prince to attend the school of Sainte Rose de Lima. She is an avid traveller, and has spent many years in Venezuela. She is presently living in the United States.

Writings: Poetry: *Mon âme vous parle (poèmes),* Port-au-Prince, Impr. du Collège Vertières, 1941; *Chant pour toi,* Havana, Editorial Lex, 1944; *Poèmes à Bolivar,* Port-au-Prince, 1948; *Coeur de héros, coeur d'amant,* Port-au-Prince, Impr. Le Matin, 1950; *Hommage à Simon Bolivar el Libertador* (à l'occasion du dévoilement de la statue de Bolivar, don du Gouvernement Vénézuélien au gouvernement Haitien), Poèmes en Espagnol, en français et en Anglais.

Essay: *Hispaniola; estudio histórico, geografico y politico de la isla de Haiti* (in Spanish and French), Havana, Talleres Tipog. de Editorial Lex, 1944.

LEMERY, Hélène

b. 1902, Paris (of Martiniquain parents); d. 1936, Paris.
Poet, novelist.

Daughter of Henry Léméry, formerly a Senator in the French national parliament, Hélène lost all her family during the Mont Pélé eruption in 1902. Though "abroad" all her life, she remained at heart a Martiniquain.

Léméry was educated in France and married there. Her first marriage brought her sadness, however, and she became melancholic. A visit to several cities in Italy gave her some comfort. She confessed to a friend:

> *L'Italie, autour de mon désarroi moral suscita l'ambiance souhaitée de détente, de réconfort. Peu à peu, le rythme des mots me préoccupa, puis me subjugua, ce rythme qui m'émouvait lorsque j'étais enfant au point de faire répéter à moi-même, longuement, à cause de sa seule sonorité, telle phrase d'un texte latin qui me restait totalement incompréhensible.*

Back to Paris, feeling renewed, she started writing. She burned a manuscript of a novel that she had come to think of little value. But her later work, strongly influenced by Claudel (who prefaced her first collection, *Enchantements*) was of literary value.

Writings: Poetry: *Enchantements,* Paris, Ed. du Monde Nouveau, 1924; *La Voie passionnée,* Paris, Ed. du Monde Moderne, 1925; *Fenêtre d'Ostie,* Paris, Editeurs Associés, 1928.

Novel: *Bérangère ou la symphonie amoureuse et la fenêtre d'Ostie,* Paris, Albin Michel, 1927.

LENOIR, Jacques

(pseudonym for **Paul LARAQUE**)

LEON, Rulx

b. December 2, 1890, Cayes, Haiti.

Essayist, biographer, physician, historian.

Rulx Léon started his classes in Cayes, and went to Port-au-Prince where he completed his education in the Petit Séminaire Collège Saint-Martial and then studied medicine. He served as physician in the government Health Service and became after many years the Director General of Public Health Service and eventually Under-Secretary of State for Public Health. During the Second World War, Dr. Léon was appointed Haitian Consul General in New York.

Dr. Léon published a great number of articles dedicated mostly to Haitian and French physicians of the past in such journals as *Le Matin, Le Nouvelliste, Aya-Bombé, Oedipe* and *Conjonction.*

Writings: Biography: "Jean Paul, Mayor of Port-au-Prince," in the series of *Oedipe* (1943-1944); *Notes bio-bibliographiques; médécins et naturalistes de l'armée coloniale française de Saint-Domingue,* Port-au-Prince, mimeo., 1937.

History: *Propos d'Histoire d'Haiti,* preface by Sténio Vincent, Port-au-Prince, Impr. de l'Etat, 1945, Tome I, and Tome II, Port-au-Prince, Ed. Panorama, 1976.

Medicine: *La législation de l'hygiène, de l'Assistance Publique, de l'Enseignement et de l'exercice de la Médecine,* Port-au-Prince, mimeo., 5 vols. 1933-1937; *La pratique médicale à Saint-Domingue,* Paris, Les Presses Modernes, 1928; *Les Maladies en Haiti* (collection of Tri-Cinquantenaire), Port-au-Prince, Impr. de l'Etat, 1953; *Phytothérapie Haitienne (nos simples),* Port-au-Prince, Impr. de l'Etat, 1959.

LEONARD, Nicolas Germain

b. March 16, 1744, Basse-Terre, Guadeloupe; d. January 26, 1793, Nantes, France.

Poet, letter-writer, novelist, autobiographical verse, diplomat.

Born in Guadeloupe, Leonard went in his early years to France where he received a classical and artistic education. Thanks to the protection of the Marquis Chauvelin, then French Minister for Foreign Affairs, he was appointed as secretary of the French legation in Liège (1773), and was later promoted to Chargé d'Affaires. Resigning this post he returned to Paris and then went to Guadeloupe where he was appointed on August, 1782, the Lieutenant de Juge to the Court of this colony. Leaving his native land once again he returned to France where he finished his years.

Leonard was appreciated for his poems, many of which were translated into English and Italian. Ste Beuve made extensive comments about him in *Journal des Débats* (issue of April 21, 1847), and Michaud in his important *Biographie Universelle* dedicated an article to Léonard, writing:

> *L'oeuvre de Léonard est remarquable par la douceur des sentiments, la grâce des images et l'harmonieuse élégance de la versification.*

Writings: Poetry: *Les Saisons,* 3 vols., *Le Temple de Gnide* (1772); *Idylles morales* (1776, 1771, 1775).

Novel: *Lettres des deux amants de Lyon,* Paris, 1792.

Memoirs: *Mémoires historiques sur l'Etat de Liège,* Paris, Esprit des Journaux, 1779.

Stories: *Voyages aux Antilles,* 1787; and *Oeuvres complètes,* 3 vols., Paris, 1798.

Biographical/Critical Sources: Sainte Beuve: "Léonard," *Journal des Débats* (April 21, 1847); Vaucheist: *La Guadeloupe, ses enfants célèbres,* Paris, Challamel, Impr. Coloniale, 1894; Raphael Barquissau: *Les poètes créoles du XVIII-ième siècle,* Paris, J. Vigneau, 1949; François Tulou: *Petits poèmes érotiques du XVIII-ième siècle,* Paris, Garnier Brothers, 1880.

LEOPOLD, Emmanuel-Flavia

(pseudonym: **Mark LAVIGNE**)
b. May 9, 1896, Fort-de-France, Martinique; d. June 22, 1962.
Poet, teacher, essayist.

Son of a small businessman in Fort-de-France, Leopold studied at the Lycée Schoelcher and the University of Toulouse, where he earned *licences* in history and geography. He also earned an *agregation* in English and taught English for a period at the Lycée of Montauban. He spent 24 years as a teacher at the Lycée Carnot in Pointe-à-Pitre, Guadeloupe, and, after the death of his Toulousan wife in 1955, he taught in Albi and Montauban.

In 1925 he translated poetry by Langston Hughes, Claude McKay, Jean Toomer, and Countee Cullen. He published many collections of poetry about the beauty of Martinique, among them *La Clarté des jours* (1924), *Suite pour un visage* (1926), *Le ciel dans mon âme* (1927), *Le Vagabond* (1932), *Adieu Foulards, adieu madras* (1948), *Poèmes* (1949), *Soleils Caraïbes* (1953), *Passage saccarère* (1956), *Paroles pour une nativité* (1957), and *Le Château du Tanzia* (1963) posthumously.

Leopold's poetry is noted for an exotic lyricism which was attacked early in his career by the editor of *Légitime Défense.*

He published his own first verses under the pen-name of Marc Lavigne.

Writings: Poetry: *La clarté des jours,* Paris, Eugène Figuière, 1924; *Poèmes,* Paris, Ed. Seghers, 1949; *Soleils caraïbes,* Paris, Seghers, 1953; *Passage Saccarère,* 1956; *Paroles pour une Nativité,* 1957; *Le chateau de Tanzia,* 1963.

Leaflets (Prose pieces): *Suite pour un visage,* 1926; *Le ciel dans mon âme,* 1927; *La vagabonde,* 1932; *Adieu foulards, adieu madras* (1948); *Chants pour la terre créole,* Paris, Eds. Littré, 1958.

LEREBOURS, Anne-Marie

(see under pseudonym: **Annie DESROY**)

LEREBOURS, Michel Philippe

b. ca. 1929, Port-au-Prince, Haiti.
Playwright, art critic.

Lerebours was educated in Port-au-Prince at the Institution Saint-Louis de Gonzague. After schooling he devoted much of his energy to the local theatre and served as secretary general of the magazine *Coumbite* (1953), published by la SNAD (Société Nationale d'art Dramatique).

For a period he was a teacher for UNESCO in the then Belgian Congo and thereafter moved to New York City where he has remained.

Lerebours' play *Le Roi* was performed in New York (November 15, 1970). He has in progress an extensive study of Haitian painting.

Writings: *Le Roi,* with *Temps Mort,* New York, Eds. Connaissance d'Haiti, 1972.

LEREMOND, Jean Jacques

b. 1825, Coteaux, Haiti; d. October, 1844.
Poet.

Lérémond came very early to Port-au-Prince for his education. He was shipwrecked on his way back home to Coteaux and perished. Lérémond was considered the finest lycéen poet of his day. Close follower of the French poet Lamartine, Lérémond's only known published work was "Stances," given in its entirety in Auguste Viatte's *Histoire Littéraire de l'Amérique Française.*

Biographical/Critical Sources: *Nécrologie:* "Manifeste" (Oct. 20, 1844); "Stance" in Edgard La Selve's *Histoire Littéraire de l'Amérique française,* Quebec, Presses Universitaires Laval, 1953, pp. 361-363.

LERO, Etienne

b. August 3, 1910, Lamentin, Martinique; d. October 28, 1939, Paris.
Poet, scholar, storywriter.

Léro was educated at Lycée Schoelcher in Fort-de-France. He went to Paris where he studied at La Sorbonne, won a *licence* in English, and the *agregation* in philosophy.

He published his first verses in *Lucioles,* edited by Gilbert Gratiant, but he later regretted them as "péchés de jeunesse."

Léro was very busy in intellectual and Antillean circles in Paris in the 1930's and was the founder, with Jules Monnerot and René Ménil, of the first "black" journal in France, *Légitime Défense* (1932). It drew on Marxist and Freudian ideas and the aesthetics of such surrealists as André Breton, and decried the corrupt colonial regimes in the Caribbean and Africa. Suppressed almost immediately by the French authorities, the 20-page work still stirred up comment and became the historical first concerted effort to reestablish black dignity and the value of black cultural values. With his friends Jules Monnerot and René Menil, he is considered the father or grandfather of what was to become known as the Negritude movement.

Léro's poetry, published in various journals, is now seen as academic and derivative, but it does manifest some of the new efforts to develop an original African voice in French verse.

Grateful to surrealism, Léro said:

> *C'est l'honneur et la force du surréalisme d'avoir intégré toujours plus à fond la fonction poèsie, d'avoir mis à poil la poèsie . . .*

Beyond the question of Léro's personal

poetic talents is the general one of facing the inhibition to any artist who works inside a restrictive racial and political order. Léro himself put it this way in his essay in *Légitime Défense:*

> *Le caractère exceptionnel de médiocrité de la poèsie antillaise est nettement lié à l'ordre social existant. . . .*

and he added:

> *L'antillais, bourré à craquer de morale blanche, de culture blanche, d'éducation blanche, de préjugés blancs, étale dans ses plaquettes l'image boursoufflée de lui-même. D'être un bon décalque d'homme pâle lui tient lieu de raison sociale aussi bien que de raison poètique.*

Writings: Short Stories: "L'évasion;" "Dix huitième année," 1929; "Evelyne," 1930.
Essay: "Misère d'une poèsie," in *Légitime Défense,* Paris, 1932.

LERO, Yva

b. ca. 1910, Martinique.
Poet, storywriter, painter.

Mme. Léro published one collection of original stories and one collection of her poetry. Yva was the wife of Etienne Léro, one of the earliest Antillean writers in the Paris movement preceding Negritude. (In 1932, with Jules Monnerot and others, Etienne published the now famous *Légitime Défense* which criticized harshly all earlier writing in the Antilles and called for the use of surrealism and more originality in subject matter and techniques. The journal had only one issue.)

Writings: Stories: *Doucherie* (for children), Fort-de-France, Eds. Horizons Caraïbes, 1958.
Poetry: *Peau d'ébène,* poèmes, Fort-de-France, Eds. des Horizons Caraïbes, 1960 (put to music by Moune de Rivel).

LEROY, Félix Morisseau
(or **Félix MORISSEAU-LEROY**)

b. March 13, 1912, Grand-Gosier, Haiti.
Novelist, teacher, playwright, poet (in French and creole).

Morisseau-Leroy spent his childhood in Jacmel where he studied at Condorcet Leroy's school and afterwards at the Lycée Pinchinat in Jacmel. He completed his education in Port-au-Prince and graduated from the Faculty of Law. He was teacher at the Lycée Pinchinat, then was named *chef de division* at the Ministry of Public Instruction in 1941. After a long period studying education at Columbia University in New York, he became Director General of Education in Haiti.

Morisseau-Leroy from the first practiced journalism and was a chief editor of *Sud-Ouest,* a local paper of Jacmel, and a contributor to many other papers as well as serving as editor of *Le Matin.*

He has sought to write for the 95 per cent of his people who generally were ignored by Haiti's more classically inclined writers. He used two things: creole language, and plays, to get in touch with the great masses. Rustic scenes, colloquial languages and humble situations are constants in his work. His close study of the Haitian dialect of French (creole) convinced him it should be dignified as a national language.

The ideas and efforts of Price-Mars and Jacques Roumain with regard to reclaiming the peoples' African roots were also important to Morisseau-Leroy. In his novel *Récolte* he pictures student life in Port-au-Prince in the turbulent 1930's when the young artists felt a strong fellowship with the youth of Asia and Africa as well as Latin America.

Morisseau Leroy spent five or six years in Ghana for a UNESCO mission, and he is living now in Dakar working for the Ministry of Culture in the field of theatre.

COLLECTION WOÏ
Kasamansa
poèmes de
Félix
Morisseau-Leroy
Les
Nouvelles
Editions
Africaines

Writings: Novel: *Récolte,* Port-au-Prince, Ed. Haitienne, 1946; "Les Djons" (to be published; another version exists in dramatic form.)

Poetry (in French): *Plénitude,* Port-au-Prince, Impr. N. Telhomme, 1940; *Gerbe pour deux amis* (written with Roussan Camille and Jean F. Brierre), Port-au-Prince, Impr. H. Deschamps, 1945.

Poetry (in English): *Ten Selected Poems,* Kingston, Jamaica, *Jadin Kréyòl,* 1978 (printed in Tarrytown, New York).

Poetry (in creole): *Diacoute 1,* Port-au-Prince, Ed. H. Deschamps, 1953; *Diacoute 2,* Montreal, Ed. Nouvelle Optique, 1972.

Verse Story: *Natif-Natal,* Port-au-Prince, Ed. Haitienne, 1948; *Kasamansa,* Dakar, Les Nouvelles Editions Africains, 1977.

Plays in French: *La maison hantée, drame* (performed at Rex-Théâtre Populaire in France, also London, Greece, Dahomey, and New York); *Doguicimi, tragédie,* adapted from Paul Hazoumé's Dahomean novel, *Doguicimi,* mimeo., Accra, Ghana, 1961, performed by the Drama Studio, Accra, Feb. 1962; *Akosombo, épopée ghanéenne,* details not known.

Plays in Creole: *Antigone en créole,* first performed, Port-au-Prince in 1953, later played at Théâtre des Nations in Paris, 1959; published in French version by Edris St Amand, Morne Hercule, Pétionville, Culture, 1953; Creole version, in mimeo., by "Culture," 1956; *Anatole, drame Rara,* and *Ti Sonson* (co-authored by Mme Dilliah Vieux).

Essay: *Le destin des Caraïbes,* Port-au-Prince, Impr. N. Telhomme, 1951; "La littérature haitienne d'expression créole, son avenir" in *Présence Africaine,* Vol. 17, pp. 46-59 (Dec. 1956-Jan. 1957); "Le Théâtre dans la révolution africaine," in *Présence Africaine,* No. 52 (1964), pp. 60-67; "African National Theatre," in *Okyeame,* Vol. 4, No. 1, (December 1968), pp. 91-94.

Essay in Creole: *Jadin kréyol,* Dakar, Les Nouvelles Editions Africaines, 1977.

Prefaces: several of particular interest in his prefaces to Jules Blanchet's *Le destin de la jeune littérature,* Port-au-Prince, Impr. de l'Etat, 1939.

Recording: Morisseau Leroy reading his poetry, on Library of Congress discs made in Port-au-Prince, 1953, available in Library of Congress, Music Division.

Biographical/Critical Sources: Emmanuel C. Paul, "Le message de *Diacoute*" in *Optique,* No. 27 (May 1956); Ghislain Gouraige, *Histoire de la littérature haitienne,* Port-au-Prince, Impr. N.A. Théodore, 1960, pp. 394-397; Robert Cornevin, *Le théâtre haitien, des origines à nos jours,* Quebec, Ed. Léméac, 1973, pp. 200-212.

LEROY, Frantz

b. ca. 1932, Port-au-Prince, Haiti.
Poet, storywriter.

Frantz Leroy completed his education in Port-au-Prince. After some trips to the United States, he decided upon a career in business. Tried for political reasons by the Haitian Courts, he has experienced the sadness of jail and has taken such opportunity to express his deep feelings about personal freedom through his poetry.

Writings: Poetry: *Du bec et des ongles,* Port-au-Prince, 1962; *Poèmes en prison,* Port-au-Prince, Les Presses Port-au-Princiennes, 1977.
Short Stories: *La Cravate,* Port-au-Prince, 1967.

LE SAGE, Aimard

(pseudonym of **Desaix BACKER**)
b. September 8, 1890, Cap-Haitien, Haiti; d. ca. 1967, Port-au-Prince.
Novelist, storywriter, playwright.

Backer completed his education in Port-au-Prince and then entered the Congregation of Saint-Esprit as a Brother, taking the name "Brother Alippe." After teaching at the Petit Séminaire Collège Saint-Martial he was sent to Africa where he spent many years during the colonial era. He described his observations and experiences in two narratives but he had some troubles with his home Congregation because his work was deemed immoral and he was forced to resign. When he returned to Haiti, he taught at the Lycée Pétion and later founded and led as director his own college.

Writings: Novels: *Les Amazones d'Haiti,* Port-au-Prince; *L'Amant idéal,* Port-au-Prince, 1926.
Stories: *Dans les brousses africaines,* Port-au-Prince, Impr. Chéraquit, 1935.
Play: "Docteur Muflard ou double amour," (unpub.)

LESCOT, Léocadie Elie

b. December 9, 1883, Saint-Louis du Nord, Haiti; d. November, 1974, Port-au-Prince.
Memoirist, teacher, diplomat, politician, President of the Republic.

Lescot was educated in Cap-Haitien where his family originated. He attended the Lycée Philippe Guerrier. He served as interpreter at the Customs House of Cap-Haitien, then was named Haitian Consul in Antilla, Cuba. He was elected a Member of the Legislative Assembly, became Commissioner of the Civil Court of Port-au-Prince, and later Examining Magistrate on the same Court. Commissioner at the Court of Cassation, he left this position to become Secretary of State of Public Instruction and Agriculture during the administration of President Borno. He was named Minister of the Interior, after that, Minister Plenipotentiary to the Dominican Republic and, later, in this same capacity, to Washington, D.C. He was elected Senator in 1940 and became President of the Republic in 1941. He was overthrown January 6, 1946, by a revolution.

Writings: Speeches: *Paroles de liberté et de foi en l'honneur de Toussaint Louverture, à l'occasion du Jour Panaméricain, 14 Avril 1942,* Port-au-Prince, Impr. de l'Etat, 1942; *Toussaint, Précurseur de l'amitié américano-haitienne,* Port-au-Prince, Impr. de l'Etat, n.d.
Memoirs: *Avant l'oubli,* Port-au-Prince, Ed. Henri Deschamps, 1974.
Miscellaneous Papers: *Témoignage d'admiration et d'affection à deux nations ehères: Etats-Unis d'Amérique et France ... à l'occasion du débarquement des forces expéditionnaires américaines sur les côtes françaises de l'Afrique du Nord le 8 novembre 1942,* Port-au-Prince, Impr. de l'Etat, 1942; *Message à l'occasion du départ de la* délégation haitienne pour San Francisco, le 18 avril 1945, Port-au-Prince, Impr. de l'Etat, 1945.

LESCOUFLAIR, Arthur

b. November 24, 1885, Jérémie, Haiti; d. 1967, Port-au-Prince.

Poet, biographer, teacher, storywriter, physician.

Arthur Lescouflair was educated in Port-au-Prince, at the Petit Séminaire Collège Saint-Martial. He entered the Faculty of Medicine and on graduation, he became professor on this faculty.

He published several short stories in the newspapers and magazines, *L'Essor* and *Le Temps-Revue,* but he never collected them.

Writings: Biography: *Thomas Madiou, homme d'état et historien haitien,* Mexico, Instituto Panamericano de Historia e Geografia, 1950.

Essay: *Pasteur à travers son oeuvre,* Port-au-Prince, Impr. Edm. Chenet, 1923.

LESCOUFLAIR, Georges

b. December 11, 1882, Jérémie, Haiti; d. 1959, Port-au-Prince.

Poet, essayist, diarist, lawyer.

Georges Lescouflair was educated in Port-au-Prince and took a law degree in the capital.

He spent several years as a teacher at the Lycée Pétion of Port-au-Prince and was later named a judge and examining magistrate.

Writings: Poetry: *Simple album; poèmes,* preface by J.L.L. d'Artrey, Paris, Ed. de la France Universelle, 1927; *Visages familiers,* Paris, Les Eds. d'Artrey, n.d. (1954).

Notebook and Travel: *Mon vieux carnet; voyages, pensées, considérations, journal, 1927,* Montreal, Beauchemin, 1958.

Biographical/Critical Sources: Ghislain Gouraige, *Histoire de la littérature haitienne,* Port-au-Prince, Impr. N.A. Théodore, 1960, pp. 219-221; Pradel Pompilus & Frères de l'Instruction Chrétienne, *Manuel illustré d'histoire de la littérature haitienne,* Port-au-Prince, Ed. H. Deschamps, 1961, pp. 328-332.

LESPES, Anthony

b. February 7, 1907, Cayes, Haiti; d. December 26, 1978.

Poet, agronomist, journalist, political scientist.

Lespès attended schools at the Institution of Saint Louis de Gonzague and then was a student at the School of Agriculture in Damien, graduating there. He served many years as Agricole Agent and later as an agronomist, as head of agricultural districts and adviser at the Department of Agriculture. Lespès is a specialist in soil conservation.

He entered politics and was a member and secretary general of the former socialist party of Haiti or the P.S.P. and he was chief editor of the journal *La Nation.*

Lespès was in 1938 the manager of a "colonie agricole" in Biliguy and his one novel depicts the living conditions of the settlers. Influenced by the work of Jacques Roumain and Dr. Price-Mars, Lespès' work is full of the daily lives of the rural Haitians.

He said in one of his poems:

Un mot de plus, un mot de moins, ça ne fait rien
à l'affaire. Les jours passent, notre victoire s'annonce,
on fait bien ce qu'on peut, au mieux de sa conscience.

Writings: Poetry: *Quelques poèmes . . . quelques poètes* (Léon Laleau, Abel Lacroix, Anthony Lespès, Damoclès Vieux, Luc Grimard), Port-au-Prince, n.d.; *Les clefs de la lumière* (avec illustration d'Elzire), Port-au-Prince, Cie Lithog., 1955; In m.s.: "Contre-chant."

Novel: *Les semences de la colère,* Port-au-Prince, Ed. Henri Deschamps, 1949.

Essays: *Débats sur la culture, FRAGMENTS sur une philosophie de l'art; Etudes sociologiques,* all unpublished; "La voie tracée par Jacques Roumain" in collaboration with Georges Castera, for the 70th anniversary of Jacques Roumain, collection of En Avant, published in Montreal, 1974.

Biographical/Critical Sources: Pradel Pompilus & Les Frères de l'Instruction Chrétienne, *Manuel illustré d'histoire de la littérature haitienne,* Port-au-Prince, Ed. Henri Deschamps, 1961, pp. 479-483; Ghislain Gouraige, *Histoire de la littérature haitienne, Port-au-Prince, Imp. N.A.* Théodore, 1960, pp. 436-440 and 400-403.

LESPES, Pascher

b. June, 1845, Port-au-Prince, Haiti.
Poet, lawyer, journalist.

Pascher Lespès received his education at the Ecole Polymathique whose director was Charles Séguy Villevaleix. He later studied law. After many years of practice he became Commissioner of the Government and he was the prosecutor general for the Consolidation trial in 1907.

He contributed to the newspapers *Le Réveil; Le Civilisateur; L'Eclaireur; L'Union,* and he published his verses in *La Jeune Haiti* and *La Ronde.* His poetry remains uncollected.

Writings: Haiti devant la France . . . réponse à Monsieur Paul de Cassagnac, second edition, Port-au-Prince, Typog. "L'Haitienne," 1891.

LESTAGE, Willy

b. November 28, 1916, Jérémie, Haiti.
Poet, bank official.

Lestage attended schools in Jérémie, the Christian Brothers' School, and the Lycée Nord Alexis.

He is presently serving on the staff of the Bank of the Republic of Haiti.

Writings: Poetry: *Voix du coeur,* Port-au-Prince, Impr. de l'Etat, 1942.

LEVILLOUX, A.

b. ca. 1805, Martinique; d. ca. 1872.
Novelist.

Born in Martinique, Levilloux was educated in France, and he spent more than 17 years in Europe.

His novel *Les Créoles ou la vie aux Antilles* is full of the spirit of the revolution in the late 18th century and its protagonist is a mulatto friend of the historic leaders of the rebellious slaves, Ogé and Chavannes. This pioneering work attacks the entrenched and racist French plantation owners and came to be a harbinger of such works produced throughout the Caribbean world.

Writings: Novel: *Les Créoles ou la vie aux Antilles,* 2 vols., Paris, Souverain, 1835.

LHERISSON, Camille

b. April 10, 1901, Port-au-Prince, Haiti;
d. 1971, in New York.
Essayist, physician, scholar.

Lhérisson attended the Collège Louverture founded by his father, Caius Lhérisson, and was a student at the Petit Séminaire Collège Saint-Martial and the Lycée Pétion of Port-au-Prince. He studied medicine at the Faculty of Medecine in Port-au-Prince and received special training in Canada at McGill University and in the United States at Harvard.

Dr. Lhérisson taught biology and parasitology at the Faculty of Medicine in Port-au-Prince. He was named Secretary of State of National Education and Public Health in 1951.

As a fine scholar, Dr. Lhérisson contributed to several domestic and foreign magazines his many studies and papers on biology and medicine. He was a member of many scientific organizations of Europe and America and served as president of the Haitian Association of scientific studies. He organized in this capacity and chaired the International Congress of Philosophy held in Port-au-Prince in September, 1944.

Professor Jacques Maritain, who was the Honorary President, delivered at the opening session the following remarks:

> *Le Congrès de philosophie de Port-au-Prince a une importance exception-*

nelle, non seulement par le haut témoignage qu'il rend en pleine guerre aux vertus de la pensée, et par la qualité des nombreux travaux qui y seront présentés, mais aussi parce qu'il est la première grande manifestation internationale dans laquelle, sur le plan des oeuvres de l'esprit, des représentants des peuples libres aient pu, depuis que le monde est en feu, se rencontrer pour travailler ensemble au grand ouvrage jamais interrompu de la connaissance et de la culture. Je salue avec joie cette initiative de la Nation Haitienne.

Dr. Lhérisson left Haiti after the unpleasant 1957 events and established a new home in New York where he died.

Writings: Speeches: *L'Université de Harvard et la civilisation américaine* (contribution à "Harvard's tricentenary" par un médecin haitien), Port-au-Prince, 1936; *La leçon de l'histoire; le drapeau, idée nationale* (discours prononcé le 18 mai 1953), Publication du Comité Exécutif du Cent-cinquantenaire de l'indépendance nationale), Port-au-Prince, Impr. de l'Etat, 1953.

Philosophy: *Travaux du Congrès International de Philosophie consacré aux problèmes de la connaissance, organisé par la Société d'Etudes scientifiques et tenu à Port-au-Prince du 24 au 30 Septembre 1944, sous les auspices du gouvernement haitien,* Port-au-Prince, Impr. de l'Etat (Papers submitted by prominent personalities who attended this Congress).

Essays: *De la responsabilité des élites dans la société moderne,* Port-au-Prince, Impr. de l'Etat, 1947.

Medicine: "Studies on the Specificity of Intradermal Tests in the Diagnosis of Filariasis," *The American Journal of Hygiene,* Vol. 43, No. 1 (Jan. 1946); *Lecture on First Aid,* mimeo. (April 2, 1941); *La Réaction de Hinton; Une nouvelle réaction de floculation pour le sérodiagnostic de la syphilis,* Paris, Masson et Cie, 1936 (written with Miss O. Stuart); "De la valeur relative des coefficients thermiques en biologie," *Protoplasma,* Tome XXXI, No. 4 (Berlin, 1938), pp. 535-539.

Bio-psychology: *Essai de Biopsychology. De la personnalité de l'être à la connaissance,* preface by Dr. J.C. Dorsainvil, Port-au-Prince, Impr. de l'Etat, 1951.

LHERISON, François-Romain

(his son and later descendants called themselves **LHERISSON**)

b. March 26, 1798, Aquin, Haiti; d. May 8, 1859.

Poet, songwriter.

Born six years before Independence, Lhérison received a good intellectual training and was a teacher. His grand nephew was Justin Lhérisson.

Lhérison's *Chansons créoles* may well be the earliest Haitian collection to employ the local creole speech but copies are no longer extant. His songs were popular even in French. "On chantait du Béranger, du Désaugiers et du Lhérisson." They helped to overthrow President Boyer in 1843. A one-time supporter of Emperor Faustin Soulouque, he made the mistake of joking at the proud leader and was sentenced to prison. His natural death in May 15, 1859, just before he was to be led away, cheated the punishment.

In his "Epître â Milscent," he questioned his talent to write in many literary genres.

Les Muses, tu le vois; sont sourdes à ma voix . . .
Pourrai-je enfin me taire? Hélas? peut-être non.

Writings: Poetry: "Epître à Milscent," in *L'Abeille Haytienne,* (April 1-August 1, 1819); "Satire sur un chymiste," *L'Abeille Haytienne,* (Jan. 1, 1818); "La bergère somnambule," (May 1, 1818), also in *L'Abeille Haytienne.*

Songs: *Chansons créoles,* Aux Cayes, 1819, but no copies extant.

Biographical/Critical Sources: Séméxant Rouzier has an article on Lhérison in *Haiti Littéraire et Sociale* (Sep. 5, 1907); Auguste Viatte, *Histoire littéraire de l'Amérique française,* Quebec, 1953, pp. 349-350.

LHERISSON, Justin

b. February 10, 1873, Port-au-Prince, Haiti; d. November 15, 1907, Port-au-Prince.

Novelist, poet, storywriter, biographer, editor, teacher.

Lhérisson studied at the Lycée Pétion of Port-au-Prince, and then became a teacher of Haitian history and geography at that lycée. He later graduated from the Law School. He founded a literary review, *La Jeune Haiti,* and contributed poetry to the new review, *La Ronde,* which was seeking to offer a new voice in Haitian writing. Having begun to write poetry in his fourteenth year, he never ceased though he may best be remembered as a fiction writer for his novels *Zoune chez sa nainaine* (1906), and *La famille des Petite-Caille* (1919).

An active journalist, Lhérisson was the director of *Le Soir* and a historian and literary critic. His poem "La Dessalinienne" won the first prize in a poetry contest and was adopted as the national hymn in 1903.

His first verse collection was *Passe-Temps,* 1895, parnassian poems, and in 1898 he published *Chants de l'aurore,* more parnassian verse, with some sonnets on the ancient period of Haiti.

Writings: Novels: *La famille des Petite-Caille,* Port-au-Prince, Impr. Aug. A. Héraux, 1905; a second edition in 1906; a third edition of *La famille des Petite-Caille* appeared in Paris, Typ. Firmin Didot & Cie, 1919; *Zoune chez sa nainnaine,* Port-au-Prince, Impr. Aug. A. Héraux, 1906; a second edition appeared the same year; *Fan'm gain sept sauts pou li passé,* Port-au-Prince, Dorsinville, 1953.

Poetry: *La Dessalinienne; chant national* (with Nicolas Geffrard who wrote the music), Port-au-Prince, Impr. D. Bernard, 1903; *Myrtha; poème érotique,* Port-au-Prince, Impr. Haitienne, 1892; *Les chants de l'aurore; primes rimes,* Port-au-Prince, Impr. de la jeunesse, 1893; *Passe-temps; poèsies,* Tour, Impr. Deslis Frères, 1893.

Biographical Sketches: *Portraitins,* 1ère série, Port-au-Prince, Impr. H. Amblard, 1894.

History: *Les enseignements de l'histoire,* speech delivered in 1897, Port-au-Prince, Impr. H. Amblard, 1897; *Le marronnage et le caudoux,* Port-au-Prince, n.d.; *Manuel d'histoire à l'usage des écoles de la République,* (with Windsor Bellegarde), Port-au-Prince, 1907.

Almanac: *Almanach du bon haïtien,* Port-au-Prince, Impr. Edm. Chenet, 1907.

Biographical/Critical Sources: Prosper Chrisphonte, *Le Poète de la Dessalinienne (Portrait, essai critique),* Port-au-Prince, Impr. N. Telhomme, 1941; Hénoch Trouillot, *Les origines sociales de la littérature haitienne,* 1962, pp. 336-343; Ghislain Gouraige, *Histoire de la littérature haitienne,* 1960, pp. 121-129; Pradel Pompilus et les Frères de l'Instruction Chrétienne, *Manuel illustré d'histoire de la littérature haitienne,* 1961, pp. 297-302; and see Special Issue of *Conjonction* (Port-au-Prince), Nos. 122-123, pp. 75-86; Michel Amer: "Justin Lhérisson, spécifique et subversif," Lakansiel, No. 1, (March 1975), pp. 19-25.

LIBOSE, Jean

(pseudonym: **Lys AMBROISE**)

LIN DEGE

(pseudonym for **Luc GRIMARD**)

LINVAL, Paule Cassius de

(pseudonym: **Jean MARX**)

b. October 23, 1890, Saint-Joseph, Martinique; d. August 16, 1970.

Novelist.

Linval attended the Convent School of Saint-Joseph de Cluny in Fort-de-France, then went to France to complete her education.

She published one novel about the great explosion of Mont-Pélé in 1902. This work is considered the best book dealing with the catastrophe which wiped out in a few seconds 30,000 people and Martinique's capital city, Saint-Pierre. The author herself lived in the doomed city almost to the last and employs many documents and other sources to gain authenticity. From today's vantage point her silence on color or race prejudice is unfortunate, however, for a certain dimension of unreality comes in with this ever, and still, important aspect of life being denied. It is instructive to compare her work to Raphael Tardon's *Starkenfirst* (1947) which deals with race prejudice in the same doomed Saint-Pierre.

Writings: Novels: *Coeurs Martiniquais,* Paris, Figuière, 1912; *Réminiscences,* Paris, Ed. de la Revue Moderne, 1959.

Folklore: *Mon pays à travers les légendes,* Paris, Eds. Revue Moderne, 1960.

LLERO, Auguste

(pseudonym for **Christian ROLLE**)

LOCHARD, Paul

b. June 15, 1835, Petit-Goâve, Haiti; d. July 15, 1919, Port-au-Prince.

Poet, journalist, teacher, protestant minister.

Lochard was educated in Port-au-Prince. He began his adult career as a high school teacher. He served for a period as director of Customs in Port-au-Prince (1889-1896). He was also director of the official Haitian governmental journal *Le Moniteur* for a short while.

Unlike many poets of his generation, Lochard was, in the words of Anténor Firmin, who introduced one of his collections of verses:

> *Mr Lochard est un Haitien et plus noir que blanc. Il n'a jamais quitté le sol de la république d'Haiti et sa mentalité est absolument nationale. Ces faits ne sont pas contestables. Eh bien! qu'on lise ces poèsies où le chantre des Antilles a mis toutes les notes de sa lyre, pourra-t-on jamais s'apercevoir de la forte dose de sang africain qui coule dans ses veines? Non, sans nul doute; car, soit dans la structure de sa phrase, soit dans son tour d'esprit, il n'y a rien, mais rien, qui le distingue d'un poète français issu du plus pur sang gaulois. Et qu'on ne croie point que cette complète appropriation de la langue de Racine, de Lamartine et de Victor Hugo soit un simple jeu d'imitation. Tout en se servant de cette belle langue française avec une aisance, une délicatesse et une élégance qui en font un vrai charme, le chantre haitien reste pourtant lui-même, gardant toujours le cachet de sa personnalité poètique.*

Lochard was a minister of a protestant group and he wrote poetry which was sternly Christian. These lines show the grim faith:

> *Pour moi, Seigneur, dont la pensée*
> *Parcourt les champs de l'infini,*
> *Dont la voix au ciel élancée,*
> *Dès mon aurore t'a béni,*
> *Du fond du désert de mon être,*
> *Je te sacrifie, ô mon maître,*
> *Mon existence, chaque jour!*
> *Je veux t'aimer, t'aimer encore!*
> *Je veux sur ma lyre sonore*
> *Sans cesse exalter ton amour!*

Writings: Poetry: *Les chants du soir; poèsies,* Paris, Impr. Typog. Kugelmann, 1878; *Les feuilles de chêne,* preface by M. Anténor Firmin, Paris, Ateliers Haitiens, 1901.

Biographical/Critical Sources: Hénock Trouillot, *Les origines sociales de la littérature haitienne,* Port-au-Prince, Impr. N.A. Théodore, 1962, pp. 235-245; Pradel Pompilus & Frères de l'Instruction Chrétienne, *Manuel illustré d'histoire de la littérature haitienne,* Port-au-Prince, Ed. H. Deschamps, 1961, p. 149; Ghislain Gouraige, *Histoire de la littérature haitienne,* Port-au-Prince, Impr. N.A Théodore, 1960, pp. 49-53.

LOHIER, Michel

(pseudonym: **Irac OUBO**)

b. January 24, 1891, Iracoubo, Guyane; d. November 1, 1973, Paris.

Essayist, biographer, storywriter, entomologist.

Lohier was educated in his native Iracoubo and Cayenne. He served as an employee in the Custom Administration before becoming a teacher in Iracoubo, Mana and then Cayenne. Appointed curator of the Cayenne National Museum, he also was a director of the main library.

During the ten year period from 1950 to 1960, Lohier was the managing editor of *Parallèle 5* and did research tracing the biographies of the outstanding personalities of the country. He also published many legends in creole collected in Guyane.

Writings: Stories: *Légendes et contes folkloriques guyanais en patois avec traduction française par l'auteur,* Cayenne, P. Laport, 1960.

Biography: *Mana et la Mère Javouhey,* 1962.
History: *Histoire de la Guyane,* 1970.
Memoir: *Les Mémoires de Michel,* 1972.

LOUHIS, Léon

b. December 4, 1867, Lascahobas, Haiti; d. January 17, 1935, Port-au-Prince.
Poet, playwright, professor, lawyer.

Louhis came to Port-au-Prince and attended the Lycée Pétion where he received the honor prize for his achievements as a student. He then served as professor at the Lycée Pétion and became Inspector of Schools in Gonaïves.

Louhis was appointed Director of Customs at Aquin and finally was elected Deputy of Mirebalais.

He published his poems and two short stories in *Haiti Littéraire et Sociale,* edited by Frédéric Marcelin.

Writings: Poetry: "Fleurs des tropiques," unpublished collection.

Play: *Rivalité* (pièce locale en 5 actes et vers), unpublished.

Stories: in various journals: The story "Voix de femme" appeared in *Haiti Littéraire et Sociale.*

LOUIS, Jeanine Tavernier

see under **Jeanine TAVERNIER**)

LOUIS, Michel Salmador

b. February 5, 1939, Limbé, Haiti.
Poet, journalist, teacher.

Salmador Louis was educated at the School of the Christian Brothers in Cap-Haitien and the College of Holy Cross Priests. He came to Port-au-Prince to study law. He also won a diploma at the Faculty of Ethnology.

He practiced journalism in Port-au-Prince and later in Quebec. He is presently teaching in Montreal.

Writings: Poetry: *Rhapsodie champêtre, poèmes,* preface by Hugo W. Pierre, 1963; *Les Variations (poèmes et études),* Port-au-Prince, Impr. Serge Gaston, 1966; *Pluie d'étoiles (poèmes),* Port-au-Prince, Impr. La Phalange, 1970.

LOUVERTURE, Isaac

b. November, 1782, Ennery, Haiti; d. September 16, 1856, Bordeaux, France.
Poet, memoirist.

Son of Toussaint Louverture, Isaac was sent very early to France where he was educated at the military school of Liancourt and at the Collège de la Marche.

On Napoleon Bonaparte's order, he came back to Saint-Domingue with his brother Placide Louverture and their tutor l'Abbé Coisnon to persuade his father from any military action against France. When the Governor General Toussaint Louverture became a prisoner, Isaac was taken to France with all members of his father's family.

Isaac Louverture established a home in Bordeaux where he died.

Writings: Poetry: various poems published in different magazines.

Prose: *Mémoires et Notes,* for which see: Antoine Marie-Thérèse Metral, *Histoire de l'expédition militaire des français à Saint-Domingue sous le consulat de Napoléon Bonaparte, suivie des mémoires et notes d'Isaac Louverture sur la même expédition et sur la vie de son père,* Paris, 1841.

LOUVERTURE, Pierre François Dominique Toussaint

b. May 20, 1743, Cap-Français, Saint-Domingue (now Haiti); d. April 7, 1803, France.

Statesman, memoirist.

Through his godfather, Pierre Baptiste, a lettered servant-nurse at the hospital of the Fathers of Charity, Pierre learned to read and write.He received a religious education from the Superior, Father Luxembourg. His master, Bayon de Libertad, employed him as a herdsman and later as his personal coachman, and then steward of Bréda. In 1777, Toussaint was liberated at 34 years of age, and married Suzanne Simon Baptiste who bore his two sons, Isaac and Saint Jean.

The political events in France raised even in faraway Saint-Domingue the question of civil and political rights for freed men (or "affranchis") and then for slaves who rebelled in the night of August 22, 1791, burning plantations and killing the French owners. Meanwhile, the personality of Toussaint Louverture emerged. He fought Spanish and British troops who invaded Saint-Domingue and expelled them. He became a Lieutenant in the government of the colony and the then Governor Etienne Laveaux declared to the colonial assembly:

> *Here you behold the saviour of the officially constituted authorities, the Negro Spartacus who, as the Abbé Raynald foretold, has come to avenge the wrongs done to his race. From this day forth I shall do nothing without him, and my labors will be his.*

Step by step, Toussaint Louverture was promoted to Governor General and became the official representative of France. His achievements, such as unification of the whole island and the promulgation of the self-government constitution, annoyed Napoléon Bonaparte. A 23,000-man French army was dispatched to wipe out in Saint-Domingue all the measures originally adopted by the French Revolution for the benefit of the Africains. Toussaint's armies proved their bravery in several circumstances, especially at the battles of Crête à Pierrot and Ravine-à-Ccouleuvre. The black governor became a prisoner through some treachery. On the ship *Le Créole,* Toussaint Louverture was transferred to *Le Héros.* In response to an unpleasant remark made by a French officer, he responded:

> *By overthrowing me you have merely succeeded in cutting the trunk of Saint-Domingue's Tree of Liberty; but it will grow again, for the roots are deep and many.*

After he reached France, he was jailed in the citadel of Fort-de-Joux where he died on April 7, 1803.

Dr. Jean Price-Mars made this statement about Toussaint Louverture:

> *Quand un homme a su, par la puissance de sa volonté, la pénétration, la finesse de son jugement, l'acuité de son coup d'oeil, la perspicacité, la justesse et la promptitude de ses décisions, déjouer la trame des contingences historiques, briser les obstacles, dompter les éléments pour se hisser comme César ou Napoléon au rôle de conducteur d'hommes et se montrér chaque fois supérieur aux moyens dont il use, qu'importe que cet homme-là sache l'orthographe de la langue qu'il emploie. Les mots, les idées, les hommes sont les outils dont il se sert pour produire de l'action.*
>
> *Sur le théâtre où se déployait son activité, il fut plus grand que tous les hommes—nègres, blancs, mulâtres—qu'il côtoyait et dont il se servit pour réaliser sa volonté de puissance. Il fut plus grand que les évènements qu'il maîtrisa et dont il sut captiver la marche pour les amener au terme fatidique de concrétiser sa pensée de domination et de grandeur. Il fut plus grand que le Destin lui-même qui, l'ayant abattu à l'apogée d'une carrière éblouissante, ne put qu'étayer sur les dépouilles de son rêve, l'idée dont il était la magnifique*

incarnation. Il ne fut ni un affranchi, ni un sang mêlé. Sorti du troupeau d'esclaves, cet homme se servit des esclaves comme le potier pétrit la glaise pour en faire jaillir la nouvelle matière humaine d'où naîtra la nationalité haitienne. En vérité, Wendel Philips a raison de trouver que ce nègre prodigieux n'a point de pairs dans l'histoire humaine et c'est par une intuition de visionnaire que Lamartine dira de lui, "Cet homme fut une nation."

Writings: Extrait du "Rapport adressé au Directoire Exécutif par le citoyen Toussaint Louverture, général en chef des forces de la République Française à Saint-Domingue; première conférence entre le commissaire Sonthonax et le général en chef, relative au dessein du premier de déclarer la colonie de Saint-Domingue indépendante de la France et d'égorger tous les européens, Cap-Français, chez Pierre Roux, Impr. 1797; *Récit des évènements qui se sont passés dans la partie du Nord de Saint-Domingue depuis le 29 Vendémiaire jusqu'au 13 Brumaire, an dixième de la république Française, une et indivisible, 4 novembre, 1801,* Au Cap-Français, chez Pierre Roux, Impr. du Gouvernement, 1801; *Réfutation de quelques assertions d'un discours prononcé au Corps Législatif le 10 Prairial, an Cinq, par Vienot Vaublanc, Toussaint Louverture, Général en chef de l'armée de Saint-Domingue au Directoir Exécutif,* Cap-Français, Pierre Roux, Impr. de la Commission, 1797; *Rapport fait par Toussaint Louverture, Général en chef de l'Armée de Saint-Domingue au Directoire Exécutif,* Cap-Français, Pierre Roux, Impr. 1798; *A tous les bons français, aux vrais et sincères amis de la liberté, à tous ses défenseurs,* Cap-Français, Pierre Roux, Impr. 1799; *Réponse du Citoyen Toussaint Louverture, Général en chef de l'Armée de Saint-Domingue, aux calomnies et aux écrits mensongers du Général de Brigade André Rigaud, Commandant de Département de sud,* Cap-Français, Pierre Roux, Impr. 1799; *Mémoires du Général Toussaint Louverture écrits par lui-même; précédés d'une étude historique et critique; avec un appendice contenant les opinions de l'Empereur Napoléon Ier sur les évènements de Saint Domingue,* Paris, Impr. de Moquet, 1853 (published by Joseph Saint-Rémy); *Lettre inédite qu'on pourrait appeler testament politique de Toussaint Louverture (24 Germinal, an VII);* extracts in *Annales d'Afrique;* publiée par M. Hippolyte de Saint Anthoine, Paris, Bureau des Annales d'Afrique, 1855; *Documents; letters of Toussaint Louverture and Edward Stevens,* 1798-1800, New York, 1910, Extracts from *American Historical Review,* Vol. XVI, No. 1(Oct. 1910), pp. 64-101.

Biographical/Critical Sources: M. Dubroca, *The life of Toussaint Louverture, chief of the French rebels in St-Domingo, to which are added interesting notes respecting several persons who have distinguished parts in St-Domingo,* (trans. from French), London, H.D. Simonds, 1802; *La vie de Toussaint Louverture, chef des Noirs insurgés de Saint-Domingue, contenant son origine, les particularités de sa jeunesse, sa réunion aux fameux Biassou, Bouckman et Jean François, les atrocités de la guerre, les actes de son indépendance . . . suivie de notes précieuses sur Saint-Domingue, sur plusieurs personnes qui ont joué un rôle dans la révolution de cette île,* Paris, Dubroca, 1802; Cousin d'Avalon: *Histoire de Toussaint Louverture, chef des Noirs insurgés de Saint Domingue, précédée d'un coup d'oeil politique sur cette colonie, et suivie d'anecdotes et faits particuliers concernant ce chef des Noirs, et les agens directoriaux envoyés dans cette partie du Nouveau Monde, pendant le cours de la révolution,* Paris, Pillot Fr., an 11, 1802. Also: James Stephen: *Buonaparte in the West Indies, or the History of Toussaint Louverture, the African Hero,* London, printed for J. Hatchard by J. Brettell, 1803; S. M. Y.: *Histoire du Consulat de Bonaparte, contenant tous les évènements politiques et militaires de l'an VIII jusqu'en l'an XI . . . l'histoire des troubles de Saint-Domingue et notamment de la guerre avec Toussaint-Louverture,* Paris, Testu, An II, 1803, 3 vols.; Also: Joseph St-Rémy: *Vie de Toussaint Louverture,* Paris, Moquet, 1850; Rev. John R. Beard, *The Life of Toussaint L'Ouverture, the Negro Patriot of Hayti,* London, Ingram. Cooke and Co., 1853; Alphonse de Lamartine: *Toussaint-Louverture, poème dramatique,* Nouvelle éd., Paris, Michel Lévy Fr., 1854; Gragnon-Lacoste: *Toussaint Louverture, général en chef de l'armée de Saint-Domingue, surnommé le Premier des Noirs. Ouvrage écrit d'après des documents inédits et les papiers historiques et secrets de la famille*

Louverture, orné du portait authentique du célèbre général et du facsimilé de sa signature, Paris, Durand et Pedone-Lauriel, 1877; Wendell Phillips: *Discours sur Toussaint Louverture, traduction et préface de Bétancès,* Paris, Impr. Hispano-américaine et Poissy, 1879; *Toussaint Louverture,* Extrait de Modern Eloquence, Vol. VI, pp. 846-867, Philadelphia, John D. Morris & Co., 1901; *Toussaint Louverture, discurso traducido del ingles por un Puerto-Riqueño,* New York, Levy & Voytis, 1869; *Toussaint Louverture,* Port-au-Prince, Impr. de l'Etat, 1950; Victor Schoelcher: *Conférence sur Toussaint-Louverture, général en chef de l'armée de Saint-Domingue. Compte rendu par Raoul de Loménie,* Paris, Libr. centrale des publications populaires, 1879; *Vie de Toussaint Louverture,* Paris, Paul Ollendorf (ed.), 1889; Also: Georges Le Gorgeu: *Etude sur Jean-Baptiste Coisnon. Toussaint Louverture,* Viré (Calvados), A. Guérin, 1881; M. Pierre Laffitte: *Toussaint Louverture. Extrait du Cours sur les Grand Types de l'Humanité, 1881-1882,* P. Dubuisson (ed.), Paris, au bureau de la Revue Occidentale, 1882; Rev. C.W. Mossell: *Toussaint Louverture, the Hero of Saint Domingue, Soldier, Statesman, Martyr, or Hayti's Struggle, Triumph, Independence, and Achievements,* Lockport, New York, Ward & Cobb, 1896; Baille, commandant du Fort-de-Joux: *Documents pour l'histoire. Correspondance du commandant Baille, commandant du Fort-de-Joux et geôlier de Toussaint Louverture, avec l'amiral Decrès, ministre de la Marine et des Colonies, au sujet de la captivité de ce prisonnier d'Etat jusqu'à sa mort,* Port-au-Prince, Impr. H. Chauvet, 1904; H. Pauléus Sannon, *Histoire de Toussaint-Louverture,* Port-au-Prince, Impr. Aug. A. Héraux, 3 vols., 1920, 1932, 1933; Also: Duraciné Vaval: *Conférences historiques: Dessalines devant l'histoire,* (conférence faite aux Cayes, le 10 Oct. 1903); *Toussaint-Louverture à travers la littérature nationale* (conférence faite au théâtre Haitien le 7 Septembre 1905), Port-au-Prince, Impr. de l'Abeille, 1906; Moravia Morpeau: *Documents inédits pour l'histoire. Correspondance concernant l'emprisonnement de Toussaint-Louverture. Procès-verbal de l'autopsie de son cadavre au Fort-de-Joux et rapport des médecin et chirurgien. Mémoire du Commissaire Julien Raymond sur la colonie de Saint-Domingue au Premier Consul Bonaparte,* Port-au-Prince, Impr. du Sacré Coeur, 1920; *Conférence sur Toussaint-Louverture, prononcée en 1921 au Théâtre cinématographique aux Gonaives et à Parisiana à Port-au-Prince,* Port-au-Prince, Impr. V. Pierre-Noel, 1922; Général Nemours: *Histoire militaire de la guerre d'Indépendance de St-Domingue,* 2 vols., Paris, Ed. Berger-Levrault, 1925, 1928; *Histoire de la captivité et de la mort de Toussaint-Louverture. Notre pèlerinage au Fort-de-Joux,* Paris, Ed. Berger-Levrault, 1929; *Quelques jugements sur Toussaint-Louverture,* Port-au-Prince, Impr. V. Valcin, 1938; *Histoire de la famille et de la descendance de Toussaint-Louverture avec des documents inédits et les portraits des descendants de Toussaint-Louverture jusqu'à nos jours,* Port-au-Prince, Impr. de l'Etat, 1941; *Histoire des relations internationales de Toussaint-Louverture, avec des documents inédits,* Port-au-Prince, Impr. du Collège Vertières, 1945; Also: Percy Waxman: *The Black Napoleon. The story of Toussaint-Louverture,* New York, Harcourt, Brace & Co., 1931; Michel Vaucaire: *L'étrange destin de Toussaint-Louverture,* Paris, Les Eds. de France, 1933; *Toussaint-Louverture,* Paris, Firmin-Didot & Cie, 1930; Louis Marceau Lecorps, *La politique extérieure de Toussaint-Louverture, Nos premières relations politiques avec les Etats-Unis. Lettres de Toussaint-Louverture et d'Edward Stevens (1799-1800),* Port-au-Prince, Chéraquit, 1935; Anatoli Vinogradov: *The Black Consul . . . trans. from Russian by Emile Burns, New York, The Viking Press, 1935; Ralph Korngold: Citizen Toussaint,* Boston, Little Brown & Co., 1944; Elie Lescot: *Toussaint précurseur de l'amitié américano-haitienne,* Port-au-Prince, Impr. de l'Etat, n.d. (1944?); Timoléon C. Brutus: *Rançon du génie ou la leçon de Toussaint-Louverture,* Port-au-Prince, N.A. Théodore, 1945; Cyril Lionel Robert James: *Les Jacobins Noirs, Toussaint-Louverture et la révolution de Saint-Domingue* (trans. from English by Pierre Naville), third edition, Paris, Gallimard, 1949; *The Black Jacobins; Toussaint Louverture and the San Domingo revolution,* New York, The Dial Press, 1938; second edition, revised, New York, Vintage Book, 1963; Gérard M. Laurent: *Coup d'oeil sur la politique de Toussaint-Louverture,* Port-au-Prince, Ed. Henri Deschamps, 1949; *Toussaint-Louverture à travers sa correspondance (1794-1798),* Madrid, Industrias Graficas, España, 1953 (Collection du Tricinquantenaire de l'Indépendance d'Haiti); Raphael Tardon: *Toussaint-Louverture, le Napoléon noir,* Paris, Ed. Bellenand, 1951; Luc Dorsinville: *Toussaint-Louverture, général haitien,* Port-au-Prince, Impr. de l'Etat, 1953 (Collection du Sesquicentenaire de l'Indépendance d'Haiti); Gabriel Debien: *Toussaint-Louverture et quelques quartiers de Saint-Domingue vus par des colons* (Oct. 1799-Jan. 1800), Notes d'Histoire Coloniale, No. 33 (1954); Emilio Rodriguez Demorizi: *Invasiones Haitianas de 1801, 1805 y 1822,* Ciudad Trujillo, Ed. del Caribe, 1955 (Academia Dominicana de la Historia); Faine Scharon: *Toussaint-Louverture et la révolution de Saint-Domingue,* 2 vols., Port-au-Prince, Impr. de l'Etat, 1957, and 1959; Aimé Césaire: *Toussaint-Louverture,* preface by Charles-André Julien, Paris, Présence Africaine, 1961; Thomas O. Ott: *The Haitian Revolution 1789-1804,* Knoxville, The University of Tennessee Press, 1973; Ronald Syme: *Toussaint Louverture, the Black Liberator,* New York, Morrow, 1971; George F. Tyson: *Toussaint L'Ouverture,* Englewood Cliffs, N.J., Prentice Hall, 1973.

LUBIN, Maurice Alcibiade

(pseudonym: **MALU**)

b. September 21, 1917, Jacmel, Haiti.
Critic, teacher, demographer, statistician, anthologist, literary historian.

Lubin attended the School of Christian Brothers of Jacmel and then the Lycée Pinchinat of Jacmel and the Lycée Pétion of Port-au-Prince. He graduated from the School of Law.

He was a teacher at different Lycées of Saint-Marc and Port-au-Prince. Recipient of a scholarship, he took his training in the field of Statistics, Housing and Census at Columbia University and the Bureau of Census of Washington, D.C. He contributed to the founding of the Bureau of Census of Port-au-Prince and, afterwards, of the Haitian Statistical Institute. He contributed to the first Haitian technical census in 1950. Lubin studied Economics and Public Administration in Rio de Janeiro, Brazil, and at the Institute of European Studies in Torino, Italy.

As a journalist, he has contributed to many newspapers, including: *Haiti-Journal, Le Nouvelliste, Aya-Bombé, La Revue de la Société d'Histoire et de Géographie d'Haiti, Conjonction, Présence Africaine, Revista de Bibliographia,* and *L'Intermédiaire des Chercheurs et Curieux.*

He fulfilled a one-year mission for the United Nations in the Republic of Mali. At present he is an assistant professor at Howard University for African Literature of French expression. He has published and edited many collections of poetry and written much criticism.

Writings: Anthologies: *Panorama de la Poèsie d'Haiti* (with Carlos Saint-Louis), Port-au-Prince, Ed. Henri Deschamps, 1950; 2nd ed., Nendeln, Liechtenstein, Kraus Reprint, 1970; *Poèsies haitiennes,* Rio de Janeiro, Casa do Estudante, 1956; *Florilège Jacmélien,* Port-au-Prince, Ed. Henri Deschamps, 1962; *L'Afrique dans la poèsie haitienne,* Port-au-Prince, Eds. Panorama, 1965; *Anthologie de la jeune poèsie d'Haiti* (in English and Spanish); *MELE,* International Poetry Letter, Honolulu, Hawaii, 1967.

Census: Du Recensement en Haiti, Port-au-Prince, mimeo., 1950; *Expériences d'Haiti dans le domaine des caractéristiques économiques,* paper delivered at COINS, Washington, D.C., 1951; *De la Démographie en Haiti,* paper delivered in Rio de Janeiro, mimeo., 1955; *Activités Statistiques d'Haiti* (English and Spanish), Washington, D.C., Inter American Statistical Institute (IASI), No. 13 (1959).

Literary Criticisms: *Quelques thèmes haitiens de poèsie,* Port-au-Prince, mimeo., 1959; *De la poèsie haitienne,* Port-au-Prince, Ed. Henri Deschamps, 1962; *Five Haitian Poets,* in *Young Poetry of the Americas,* Vol. 1, Pan American Union, Washington, D.C., pp. 70-81 (1965) in English, Spanish and Portuguese; *Quelques poètes haitiens de la jeune génération,* Port-au-Prince, Ed. Henri Deschamps, 1965; and *Jean F. Brierre and his work* (trans. by Martha K. Cobb) in *Black World,* Vol. XXXI, No. 3 (Jan. 1973), pp. 36-49, *reprinted in English, Spanish and Portuguese in Americas,* (Organization of American States), Vol. 26, No. 10 (Oct. 1974), pp. 34-41.

History: *Les premiers rapports de la nation haitienne avec l'étranger,* extract from *Journal of Inter-American Studies,* Vol. XX, No. 1, pp. 277-306 (April 1968); “La participation des classes populaires au mouvement national d'Indépendance,” in *Mouvements Nationaux d'Indépendance et Classes populaires aux XIXè et XXè siècles en Occident et en Orient,* Vol. II, Paris, Armand Colon, 1971, pp. 652-671; “First Letter from the New World,” in *Americas,* (Organization of American States), Vol. 23, No. 4 (April 1971), pp. 2-13, in English, Spanish, and Portuguese; same text in English in *Manuscripts,* Vol. XXIII, No. 4 (Fall 1971), pp. 244-257.

Culture: *Etape d'une visite culturelle* (under the pseudonym of MALU), Port-au-Prince, Impr. de l'Etat, 1964 (deals with the trip of Léon G. Damas on the latter's cultural mission for UNESCO); *Haiti et Culture,* Paris, Eds. L. Soulanges, 1974.

African Literature: *Afrique et Politique,* Paris, La Pensée Universelle, 1974.

MACOUBA, Auguste

(pseudonym for **Auguste ARMETH**)
b. August 17, 1939, Case-Pilote, Martinique.
Playwright, essayist, poet.

Born near Fort-de-France in a family of limited means, Auguste Armeth studied at the Collège Technique before leaving for France in 1958 to work as a skilled laborer at the Citroen plant. In July 1961 he was drafted to serve in Algeria. In 1965 he entered the University of Paris, where he earned a *licènce* in sociology and a diploma from the Ecole pratique des Hautes Etudes in 1967. In 1970 he earned a *licence* in sociology and a diploma from the Ecole Pratique des Hautes Etudes in 1967. In 1970 he published *Esquisse d'une sociologie politique de la Martinique: de l'assimilation au sentiment national.* He has published a number of articles on Martiniquain politics in Canadian, French and American journals.

titled “Le Cri antillais” in 1964 earned him a series of difficulties with the French government which made it impossible for him to return to the island.

Recently he has served as an instructor in social anthropology at the Ecole Normale Croix-Rivail in Martinique. Currently, he is an inspector with the public health service in Martinique.

He was a political activist and his play *Eia Man maille la!* in three acts and two sections, celebrates and mourns the popular uprising beginning at 7 P.M., December 20, 1959, at Fort-de-France. The author puts it this way:

> *Trois jours de combat de rues qui marquent un tournant historique dans l'itinéraire de ce qu'il convient d'appeler: un peuple transplanté et colonisé à merci.*

Three days of rioting, tear-gassing and shooting by the police ended in the calm of death and shock, and Martinique remained in the orbit of France as a colony called a “département” while other Caribbean islands either had their independence or were on the way to it.

The play was written somewhat closely after the events concerned but was published almost ten years afterwards when civil disorder was sweeping France itself.

René Depestre, the well-known poet from Haiti, wrote the informative introduction to the play.

Writings: Poetry: *Le cri antillais,* Paris, Ed. de l'Etoile, 1964 (confiscated in Fort-de-France); "Boutou Grand Soir" (unpublished).

Play: *Eia! Man-maille-la,* Honfleur, Pierre-Jean Oswald, 1968.

Essays: "La poèsie moderne est révolutionnaire," in *Bulletin de l'étudiant guadeloupéen* (date unknown); *Les problèmes de l'émigration antillaise* (Mémoire E.P.M.E., 1967); *L'enseignement et la formation professionnelle à la Martinique,* Paris, Inst. des Sciences Sociales du Travail, 1968; "Esquisse d'une sociologie politique de la Martinique: de l'assimilation au sentiment national," (unpub. thesis), University of Paris, 1970; "La pratique politique chez Césaire," in *Nouvelle Optique,* Montreal, 1973; "A propos des élections legislatives 1973 à la Martinique: Césaire, Le Parti Progressiste Martiniquais et les électeurs du Centre," in *Cahiers Césairiens* No. 1 (Spring 1974); "Césaire, homme politique," in *Etudes Littéraires* (University of Laval, Special Issue on Césaire, 1974).

MADIOU, Alexandre

b. May 20, 1824, Port-au-Prince, Haiti; d. May 31, 1888, Port-au-Prince.
Biographer.

Madiou attended the Ecole Lancastérienne and the Lycée Pétion of Port-au-Prince and went to France to complete his education.

He was a passionate student of Haitian history and wrote a biography of each President of Haiti from 1804 to the 1880's and other prominent personalities of his country.

Writings: Biography: *Album historique,* unpublished.

MADIOU, Thomas

b. 1814, Port-au-Prince, Haiti; d. May 26, 1884, Port-au-Prince.
Historian, diplomat.

Madiou was educated in France from his tenth year and met in Bordeaux Toussaint Louverture's son, Isaac. Excited by the patriotic events in his far-off homeland, he burned to return and was disappointed at not finding any published work on Haitian history, he resolved to write one himself.

Thomas Madiou (Dessin de Remponeau).

Returning to Haiti, he became a secretary to General Inginac, President Boyer's minister and was active in public affairs. He was named Director of the Lycée Pétion of Port-au-Prince and Director of the official newspaper, *Le Moniteur.* He was appointed Haitian minister to Spain and he later became Minister of Public Instruction and Religion, and of Foreign Affairs, serving for many years.

Madiou published three volumes of his history and he left many works in manuscript.

Writings: History: *Histoire d'Haiti,* 3 vols., Port-au-Prince, Impr. J. Courtois, 1847, 1848;

second edition by the Department of Public Instruction, 1922, printed by Edm. Chenet, and second edition by Impr. Aug. A. Héraux, and third edition by Impr. Chéraquit, and Vol. 4: Port-au-Prince, Impr. J. Verrolot, 1904; *Capitulation du Cap (1803) épisode de l'histoire d'Haiti,* Port-au-Prince, Impr. de la Feuille du Commerce, 1845.

Biographical/Critical Sources: Pradel Pompilus & Frères de l'Instruction Chrétienne, *Manuel illustré d'histoire de la littérature haitienne,* Port-au-Prince, Ed. H. Deschamps, 1961, pp. 51-63; Ghislain Gouraige, *Histoire de la littérature haitienne,* Port-au-Prince, Impr. N.A. Théadore, 1960, pp. 453-456; Dantès Bellegarde, *Ecrivains haitiens,* Port-au-Prince, Ed. H. Deschamps, 1950, pp. 49-59; Arthur Lescouflair, *Thomas Madiou,* Mexico, Instituto Panamericano de Historia e geografia, 1950.

MAGLOIRE, Auguste

(pseudonym: **Jean Le FURETEUR**)
b. August 13, 1872, Port-au-Prince, Haiti; d. June 13, 1948, Port-au-Prince.
Historian, journalist, sociologist.

Magloire was educated in Port-au-Prince at the Petit Séminaire Collège Saint-Martial. Soon he was involved in politics, coming to work closely with several presidents, and in time becoming Minister of Finance, Commerce and Public Education.

He was named Haitian Minister in London, and counsellor of State.

Auguste Magloire campaigned for a deep transformation of the Haitian educational system and suggested the adoption of the Anglo-Saxon education as more practical than the long-followed French system. In the field of sociology, he was definitely a follower of Desmoulin. According to the comments of critics:

> *Les oeuvres historiques d'Auguste Magloire passionnent l'opinion et provoquent beaucoup de discussions par leur souci de remonter aux causes des évènements et de présenter les personnages sous le jour de la vérité.*

He contributed to many Haitian magazines and newspapers, and he was the main contributor of *Le Matin* founded by his brother, Clément Magloire.

Writings: History: *Etude sur le tempérament haitien,* Port-au-Prince, Impr. du "Matin," 1908; *L'erreur révolutionnaire et notre état social,* Port-au-Prince, Impr. Lib. du "Matin," 1909; *Histoire d'Haiti d'aprés un plan nouveau basé sur l'observation des faits (1804-1909); édition spéciale à l'usage des adultes et des gens du monde, première partie; l'ère nouvelle,* Port-au-Prince, Impr. Lib. du "Matin," 1909; *2ème partie: Les insurrections:* tome premier, Port-au-Prince, Impr. Lib. du "Matin," 1909; *deuxième partie; les insurrections,* tome deuxième, Port-au-Prince, Impr. Lib. du "Matin," 1910; tome 3ème, Port-au-Prince, Lib. Impr. du "Matin," 1910; deuxième partie: *les insurrections;* tome quatrième, Port-au-Prince, Impr. Lib. du "Matin," 1911.

Politics: *Louis Borno, son oeuvre et le parti progressiste,* Port-au-Prince, Impr. du "Matin," 1929; *Le parti libéral (1870-1884);* première partie, Port-au-Prince, Impr. du "Matin," 1935.

Chronicles: *La semaine qui finit* (published under the pseudonym Jean Le Fureteur), Port-au-Prince, Impr. du Collège Vertières, 1935.

MAGLOIRE, fils, Clément

(see under **Magloire SAINT-AUDE**)

MAGLOIRE, Francis L.

(see under **Francis L. SEJOUR-MAGLOIRE**)

MAGLOIRE, Jean Auguste

b. May 29, 1909, Port-au-Prince, Haiti.
Essayist, journalist, biographer, public servant.

Jean Magloire received his education in Port-au-Prince. He very early began publishing articles with his uncle, Clément Magloire, and his father, Auguste Maloire, who managed the famous Haitian paper *Le Matin.* Later, Jean Magloire founded his own newspaper, *Oedipe.*

He has served Haiti in various capacities: as Deputy for Port-au-Prince; Director of the National Press; Minister of State of Tourism, Interior or Commerce. He is presently a member of the Council of the National Bank.

Writings: Biography: *Dumarsais Estimé, esquisse de sa vie politique,* Port-au-Prince, Impr. de l'Etat, 1950.

Essays: *Au service de la Patrie,* Port-au-Prince, Impr. Oedipe, 1967; *Remarques,* 2 vols., Tome 1, Port-au-Prince, Impr. de l'Etat, 1938; Tome II, preface by Roger Gaillard, Port-au-Prince, Presses du Quotidien Oedipe, 1966.

MAGLOIRE, Nadine

b. ca. 1932, Port-au-Prince, Haiti.
Novelist, essayist.

Nadine Magloire received her education partly in Port-au-Prince, partly in Paris.

Very committed to the improvement of conditions for women in Haiti, Magloire's works have shocked some for their frankness, description of unusual situations and rawness of expression.

Writings: Novels: *Le Mal de vivre,* Port-au-Prince, Eds. du Verseau, 1967; second edition, Port-au-Prince, Impr. Serge L. Gaston, 1970; *Le sexe Mythique,* Port-au-Prince, Eds. du Verseau, 1975; *Autopsie in vivo,* Port-au-Prince, 1975.

Biographical/Critical Sources: Henriette Saint-Victor, "Le Sexe mythique," by Nadine Magloire, Lakansiel, No. 3, September 1975, p. 29.

MALU

(pseuodnym for **Maurice A. LUBIN**)

MANGONES, Victor Michel Raphaël

b. December 16, 1880, Jérémie, Haiti; d. November 10, 1949, Port-au-Prince.
Poet, storywriter, businessman.

Victor Mangonès studied at the Institution of Saint Louis de Gonzague. He spent some years as an employee at the National Bank, and became chef de division at the Interior Department.

Writings: Poetry: *Menuaïlles d'or et d'argent,* preface by Abel Lacroix, Port-au-Prince, Impr. La Presse, 1933.

Tales: *Dix contes vrais; chroniques parlées,* Port-au-Prince, Impr. de l'Etat, 1934.

MANICOM, Jacqueline

b. 1938, Guadeloupe; d. April or May, 1976.
Novelist.

Manicom, of Indian stock, was educated in Guadeloupe and became a midwife, though she earned both a law and medical degree. With her husband, Yves Letourneur, she founded the Association for Familial Planning, and even led a movement to make abortion legal, as well as being a co-founder of the feminist group, "Choisir." She died in an automobile accident on Guadeloupe, and because of the eruption of Mt. Souffrière and the interruption of communications at that time, it has been hard to establish the details of her death.

Manicom's novel, *Mon examen de blanc,* deals with the perennial problem of white prejudice and island attempts to be accepted. The novel's heroine, Madevie, a Guadeloupienne, tries to pass her "exam" into whiteness by entering into love affairs with Frenchmen Xavier, a bourgeois doctor, and Cyril, and old good friend. She gets to know the hypocrisy of France with regard to both race and colonialist attitudes. The novel concludes with the 1967 shooting by police of striking sugar-cane workers in Pointe-à-Pitre. France cannot, obviously, even imagine the islands of

Guadeloupe and Martinique having indepedence though all around the other islands are free.

Writings: Novels: *Mon examen de blanc,* Paris, Eds. Sarrazin, 1972; *La Graine,* Presses de la Cité, 1974(?).

MANIGAT, Leslie François

b. August 16, 1937, Port-au-Prince, Haiti.
Essayist, historian, teacher, scholar, lecturer.

Leslie F. Manigat was educated at the Institution of Saint Louis de Gonzague, directed by the Christian Brothers. He later studied in Paris at the Sorbonne. When he returned to Haiti, he was a teacher, and later an official of the Department of Foreign Affairs. He in time became Director of the Institut des Hautes Etudes Internationales, but was forced into exile and spent some years in the United States and then in Paris. At present, Manigat is the Director of the Institute of International Relations in Trinidad at the University of the West Indies.

Writings: Literary Essays: *Une date littéraire; un évènement pédogogique; compte-rendu critique de l'ouvrage de Pradel Pompilus et du Frère Raphael, Manuel illustré d'Histoire de la littérature haitienne,* Port-au-Prince, Impr. La Phalange, 1962.

History: *L'avènement à la présidence d'Haiti du général Salomon: essai d'explication d'un point de théorie d'histoire; un fait historique,* Port-au-Prince, Impr. de l'Etat, 1957; *Le délicat problème de la critique historique, un exemple; les sentiments de Pétion et de Boyer vis-à-vis de l'indépendance nationale,* Port-au-Prince, Impr. de l'Etat, 1955; *La politique agraire du gouvernement d'Alexandre Pétion (1807-1818),* Port-au-Prince, Impr. La Phalange, 1962; *La révolution de 1843; essai d'analyse historique d'une conjoncture de crise,* Port-au-Prince, Ed. Le Normalien, 1959; "La crise haitiano-dominicaine de 1963-1964," in *Revue Française de Sciences Politiques* (April 1965), No. 2, pp. 288-296; "Les Etats-Unis et le secteur caraibe de l'Amérique Latine," in *Revue Française de Sciences Politiques* (1969), Vol. XIX, No. 3, pp. 645-682; *Statu Quo en Haiti? D'un Duvalier à l'autre: l'itinéraire d'un fascisme de sous-développement,* Paris, 1977; "La substitution de la prépondérance américaine à la prépondérance française en Haiti, au début du XIXème siècle. La Conjoncture (1910-1911)," in *Revue d'Histoire Moderne et Contemporaine* (Oct-Dec 1967), pp. 321-358.

International Relations: *L'Amérique Latine au XXème siècle (1889-1929),* Paris, Ed. Richelieu, 1973.

Politics: *Ethnicité. Nationalisme et Politique. Le cas d'Haiti,* New York, Editions Connaissance d'Haiti, 1976.

MANIGAT, Thalès

b. December 23, 1860, Cap-Haitien, Haiti; d. June 27, 1927, Cap-Haitien.
Poet, essayist, biographer, teacher.

Manigat received his education in Cap-Haitien where he later was a school teacher and director of his own private college, Grégoire. He contributed to such newspapers as *Les Mousquetaires, Le Vigilant, Le Ralliement, Le Peuple, L'avant-garde.*

Writings: Essay: *Conférence sur le vaudoux,* Cap-Haitien, Impr. "La Conscience," 1897.

Biography: *L'Abbé Grégoire.*

Poetry: "Les Antiléennes" (unpublished).

History: "Le Roi Henry Christophe," "Histoire des campagnes de l'Est," "Vingt années d'histoire contemporaine," all unpublished.

MARAN, René

b. November 5, 1887, Fort-de-France, Martinique; d. May 9, 1960, Paris.
Novelist, poet, biographer, critic, government official.

Son of Leon-Hermenegilde, an official of the French colonial service of Guyanese origin, René Maran lived his first years in Martinique. In 1890 his father was assigned to Gabon, and at age three the young Maran first arrived in Africa. After four years he was sent to school in

Bordeaux because he was having difficulty adjusting to the Gabonese climate. He stayed on in Bordeaux schools until 1909,lonely and discriminated against, but learning to write and becoming saturated with French culture (which he never repudiated though he became a severe critic of colonialism and assumed racial superiority of whites). He graduated from the Lycée de Talence in Bordeaux in 1909 and that same year published his first work, a collection of poems now out of print, *La maison du bonheur.* In his much later novel, *Le coeur serré* (The Oppressed Heart), published in 1931, Maran retells the lonely days in Bordeaux with his family in Africa and recalls the generally cool indifference of the French.

With few personal resources, Maran joined the French Colonial Service in 1909 and was posted to Equatorial Africa where his father had spent most of his career. Remaining until 1923 in the Service, all of it in Africa, Maran felt himself a Frenchman but always also a man of African origin. In his collection of stories, *Le petit roi de chimerie* (1924), Maran probably revealed his own attitude: "For now, with my French heart I yet feel I stand on the soil of my ancestors, ancestors whom I disapprove because of their primitive minds and ways—but, they are ancestors nonetheless." This sentiment reflects the young Maran, new in Africa, and as the years passed in his duty there his feelings of superiority decreased and his identification with the lives and culture of Africans intensified.

During the six years Maran worked on the manuscript of his most famous work, his novel *Batouala* (1921), he saw the peoples of the Oubangi Chari (now the Central African Empire) suffer famines so severe that one sub-nation dropped in population from 10,000 to 1,080 between 1910 and 1918 by official French count. He saw that the heavy taxes either turned the populations into enslaved drudges for whatever employers they could find or drove them into the inhospitable bush to escape. The novel itself was descriptive; but the emotional preface provoked a violent reaction because it "simply pointed out what was so" about the horrors of colonialism.

Batouala is a series of set scenes, each offering in brief compass the predicaments or daily routines of the *mokoudji* (chief) Batouala as he moves from sleep to wakefulness of a chilly morning to a death conceived in the veritist or naturalist

tradition of the Zola novel. Maran's style also consciously employs an extremely rich vocabulary, delights in African terms, and is to some degree exotic, callous, reflecting the African natural world and the cruelty of man and beast in an imperfect world. Ernest Hemingway, covering the story of Maran's winning the coveted Prix Goncourt in 1921 for the *Toronto Star,* wrote:

> *You smell the smells of the village, you eat its food, you see the white man as the black man sees him, and after you have lived in the village you die there. That is all there is to the story, but when*

you have read it, you have been Batouala, and that means that it is a great novel.

Winning the Prix Goncourt made Maran the center of world interest, for he was the first and so far still the only author of African blood ever to be so distinguished. The award also brought the attention of French chauvinists and racists and provoked a debate in the French National Assembly. This led to the despatch of a commission to Africa which chose, however, not to examine Maran's charges and "allowed" itself to be side-tracked into matters which would not force it to discover the evils of the colonial system. Maran, who was on station in Africa during most of the furor, found the hostility aroused by his book was so strong that he shortly took advantage of a minor medical problem to "retire" from the Colonial Service. Thereafter, he became a professional writer, though he was almost always in economic straits. Though *Batouala* became a best seller in France, Russia, and Japan, and proved successful in other countries, the author realized only modest royalties.

Despite these relative misfortunes, black artists everywhere recognized the work, and the award, as a breakthrough. Félix Eboué, fellow Antillan and member of the Colonial Service, and later to be world-famous as the only Governor in the French colonial war to recognize De Gaulle's Free French movement, was the first to write Maran from Paris with news of the novel's success with the Prix Goncourt committee. He himself had provided much information concerning the Banda language and customs Maran had used in the novel, and it was he who encouraged the author to leave the Service to devote himself fully to a life as a writer.

During his writing career, Maran produced numerous works over the next thirty years. *Journal sans date* (1927), originally entitled *Roman d'un noir* (Novel of a Black Man), tells the painful story of the young manhood of Jean Veneuse and his thought-to-be-hopeless love for Andrée, a Parisienne who, despite Veneuse's bitter self-doubts about his race, agrees to marry him. Only veiled autobiography, Maran later expanded this short book into the novel, *Un homme pareil aux autres* (1947) which is quoted extensively in Frantz Fanon's popular study of black psychology, *Black Skin, White Masks.*

Djouma, chien de brousse (Djouma, Dog of the Bush) appeared in 1927, and celebrated the life and trials of Batouala's much abused dog. Stoned as a bad omen after his master's death, Djouma seeks refuge with a new white master. Here he is wonderfully treated, grows fat, and his meals are even brought to him in contrast to the abuse and starvation he suffered at Batouala's heels. He waxes as the Africans he had deserted grow sicker and weaker.

Bêtes de la brousse (Animals of the Bush), published in 1942, and the earlier *Le livre de la brousse* (The Book of the Bush), published in 1934, also have African settings. *Le livre de la brousse,* considered by its author to be his best, dramatizes the love triangle of Kossi and Tougoumali for Yassi. The work ends in violence and tragedy. Throughout, the laws of the jungle are seen as no better—and no worse—than the strictly enforced laws of man. *Bêtes* employs the age-old device of using animals as actors in a moral or, in this case, an amoral world drama. The stories of the rhinoceros (Bessaragba), the buzzard (Doppele), the python (Bokorro), the dog (Boum), and the buffalo (Dog) spell violence—and all are dead at book's end by virtue of the lightning-stick of the white man, except for Bokorro, and he knows his days are numbered.

In all of his fiction Maran employs songs: work, hunting, funeral, lullabies and love songs. There are also dances, proverbs, and other typically African modes of expression. Combined with his graphic descriptions and the naturalist's desire to get all of reality down, these "African" works are among the most documentary and vivid ever written about people from the continent.

Maran's middle years were fulfilling, for he published more novels, several collections of verse, a biography of Livingstone, and other special· studies of Africa. Though restrained in his fiction, Maran actively sought the betterment of blacks everywhere through his journalism and was in close touch with American blacks in the arts and scholarship. In 1942 the French Academy awarded Maran the Grand Prix Broguette-Gonin, an especially significant award, particularly in the light of the Nazi occupation of Paris. Other awards were: Grand Prix de la Société des Gens de Lettres (1949), Prix de la Mer et de l'Outre-Mer (1950), and Prix de Poèsie de l'Académie Française (1959). He was elected a member of the Académie Internationale de Belgique.

Although Maran did some travelling outside France after his resignation from the Colonial Service, he lived most of the time in Paris until his death in May 1960. His widow Camille lived for seventeen years near their former apartment, actively concerned with his works and reputation. (She died in March, 1977).

Maran's work has generated new interest in the 1970's with the publication of the first English translation of the definitive 1938 edition of *Batouala* in 1972 (see *Writings* for details). This new translation by Barbara Beck and Alexander Mboukou has been called "beautifully rendered" by Ezekiel Mphahlele. It was adopted as a Book-of-the-Month Club Alternate in early 1973, and was published by Heinemann in paperback in the distinguished African Writers Series.

Writings: Poetry: *La maison du bonheur,* Paris, Ed. du Beffroi, 1909; *La vie intérieure,* Paris, Ed. de Beffroi, 1912; *Le visage calme,* Paris, Eds. du Monde Noveau, 1922; *Les belles images,* Paris, Delmas, 1935; *Le livre du souvenir: Poèmes* (1909-1957), Paris, Présence Africaine, 1958 (winner of the Grand Prix de Poèsie de l'Académie Française).

Novels: *Batouala,* Paris, Albin Michel, 1921; illustrated with designs by Iacovleff, Paris, Eds. Mornay, 1928; definitive French edition, Paris, Albin Michel, 1938; in "Collection des Prix Goncourt," Monaco, Ed. de l'Impr. Nationale, 1946, 1948; *Batouala* ("Edition définitive"), Paris, Albin Michel, 1938; English language translations of the 1921 edition; *Batouala* by Adele Szold Seltzer, New York, Thomas Seltzer, 1922; *Batouala: a Negro Novel from the French,* London, Jonathan Cape, 1922; *Batouala; a novel,* translated by Alvah C. Bessie, illustrated by Miguel Covarrubias, New York, The Limited Editions Club, 1932; and of the 1938 definitive edition: *Batouala: A True Black Novel,* Washington, D.C., Black Orpheus Press, 1972, and as *Batouala, An African Love Story,* Black Orpheus, 1973, as trans. by Barbara Beck and Alexandre Mboukou; the same publication is also available in paperback in Heinemann's African Writers Series, 1973, and New York, Fawcett paperback, 1975; there were also translations into 50 languages, among them Russian, Japanese, German, Dutch, Polish, Hungarian, Portuguese, Romanian, Swedish, and Arabic; *Djouma, chien de brousse,* Paris, Albin Michel, 1927; *Journal sans date,* Paris, Arthème Fayard et Cie., 1927 (published in *Les Oeuvres Libres,* 1927, No. 73); *Le coeur serré,* Paris, Albin Michel, 1931; *Le livre de la brousse,* Paris, A. Michel, 1934; *Youmba* (novelette), published with definitive edition of *Batouala,* Paris, Albin Michel, 1938; *Bètes de la brousse,* Paris, Albin Michel, 1942; *Mbala, l'eléphant,* Paris, Eds. Arc-en-ciel, 1942; *Un homme pareil aux autres,* Paris, Eds. Arc-en-ciel, 1947, 1962; *Bacouya, le cynocéphale,* Paris, A. Michel, 1953; *Ecrits posthumes (Nouvelle-roman),* Paris, Maspero, 19??.

Stories: *Le petit roi de chimérie; contes,* Paris, A. Michel, 1924; *Peines de coeur,* Paris, S.P.L.E., 1944.

Biographies: *Livingstone et l'exploration de l'Afrique,* Paris, Gallimard, 1938; *Les pionniers de l'Empire,* Paris, Albin Michel, 1943, 1946, 1955; *Savorgnan de Brazza,* Paris, Gallimard, 1941, and definitive edition, Paris, Eds. du Dauphin, 1951; *Félix Eboué: grand commis et loyal serviteur 1885-1944,* Paris, Eds. du Dauphin, 1951, and Paris, Eds. Parisiennes, 1957; *Bertrand du Guesclin; l'épée du roi,*

Paris, Eds. Albin Michel, 1961.

Articles: "French Colonization," in *Opportunity,* Vol. 14 (Feb. 1936); *Asepsie noire!,* Paris, Les Laboratoires Martinet, 1931; "Gandhi," in *Opportunity,* Vol. 3 (Feb. 1925); "The Harriet Beacher Stowe of France," in *Opportunity,* Vol. 3 (Aug. 1925); "Negro Humanism in French Letters," in *Crisis,* Vol. 56 (May 1949). Also: in *Présence Africaine:* "Gide et l'Afrique noire," No. 5 (1948), pp. 739-748 and "Le professeur Alain Leroy Locke," No. 6 (1949), pp. 135-138.

Essays: *Le Tchad de sable et d'or,* Paris, Librairie de la Revue Française, 1931.

Scholarship: *Afrique Equatoriale Française—Terres et Races d'Avenir,* Paris, Ghalandre, 1937.

Biographical/Critical Sources: Mercer Cook, *Five French Negro Authors,* Washington, D. C., The Associated Publishers Inc., 1943; Lilyan Kesteloot, *Les écrivains noirs de la langue française,* Brussels, 1963, and in English translation by Ellen Conroy Kennedy as *Negritude is Born,* Philadelphia, Temple University Press, 1973; Léon G. Damas, "Pour saluer René Maran," in *Les Lettres Françaises,* No. 825 (May 1960); for a recapitulation of the reactions to *Batouala* and its being awarded the Prix Goncourt see René Gillouin, *Le destin de l'occident,* Paris, 1929, pp. 69-84, and D. Herdeck's introduction to the English translation for Black Orpheus Press of the 1938 edition of *Batouala* cited above in "Writings" section, for memorial essays, see *Hommage à René Maran,* Paris, Présence Africaine, 1965; Also see: Brian Weinstein's *Eboué,* New York, Oxford University Press, 1972, for useful and previously unknown material concerning Eboué's aiding of Maran and the life-long friendship of the two men. For as yet unpublished correspondence of Maran's, much of it bearing on *Batouala,* see his 18 letters addressed to the black American scholar Alain Leroi Locke, in holograph in the Moorland-Spingarn Collection, Howard University, Washington, D.C.; Also see: Michel Hauser's *Les Deux 'Batouala' de René Maran,* Sherbrooke, Quebec, Eds. Naaman, 1975; Also see: Randolph Hezekiah, "René Maran and the Search for Identity," in *Black Images,* II, 1, pp. 21-24; René Trautman, *Au pays de Batouala,* Paris, Payot et Cie., 1922; F. Abiola Irele, *Literature and Ideology of Martinique: Maran Cesaire Fanon,* Special Studies Series, Council on International Studies (107 Townsend Hall, SUNYAB, Buffalo, New York 14214); "René Maran and the Racial Question, or the Literature of alienation and frustration," by Femi Ojo-Ade, in *Black Images,* II, 3 & 4 (Autumn-Winter 1973), pp. 17-32; and Ph.D. diss. by M.B. Tolson, Jr., "The Romans et Récits of René Maran," University of Oklahoma, 1964), and "L'Idéologie dans l'oeuvre littéraire de René Maran (1887-1960)," by Femi Ojo-Ade, Ph.D. diss., University of Toronto, 1975; Chidi Ikonné, "René Maran (1887-1960): A Black Francophone Writer Between Two Worlds," in *Research in African Literatures,* No. 5, pp. 5-22; Also see: Femi Ojo-Ade, *René Maran: A Bio-Critical Study,* Washington, D.C., Three Continents Press, (to be pub. 1979); Michel J. Fabre, "Autour de Maran," in *Présence Africaine,* No. 86, Second Quarterly, 1972, pp. 165-172; Michel J. Fabre, "René Maran, trait d'Union entre deux négritudes," in *Négritude Africaine et Négritude Caraïbe,* Collection du Villetaneuse, (Jan. 1973), Brussels, Ed. de la Francité, 1973, pp. 55-62; Femi Ojo Ade, *René Maran,* Paris, Fernand Nathan, 1977.

MARBOT, François Achille

b. May 29, 1817, Fort-Royal, Martinique; d. October 31, 1866.

Creole storywriter, folklorist, translator-adapter.

Marbot attended schools in Martinique and served in the naval administration in Guadeloupe, Guyana and Reunion Island as commissioner.

He won literary consideration for his creole version of La Fontaine's *Fables,* setting the original in "Martinica" and portraying customs, creeds and costumes of these fables in "island" context.

Writings: Creole Fables: *Les bambous: fables de La Fontaine, travesties en patois martiniquais par un vieux commandeur,* Fort-Royal, Martinique, 1846, Aix-en-Provence, Impr. A. Makaire, 1886, new edition: "revue et augmentée d'une notice littéraire et d'une traduction française par Louis Jaham-Desrivaus," Paris, J. Peyronnot, 1931.

MARC, Jules André

b. May 29, 1941, Port-au-Prince, Haiti.
Poet, literary critic, storywriter, essayist.

Marc was educated at the Tertulien Guilbaud School and the Lycée Toussaint Louverture. He afterwards studied surveying at the Faculty of Sciences. He is now teaching at the Lycée Toussaint Louverture and the Lycée of Tri-cinquantenaire for girls.

He has named his generation "la génération du vertige," and has suggested Haitian artists must look for new ways to express the tortuous reality of contemporary Haiti.

Writings: Poetry: *Téberli ou ma nuit,* Port-au-Prince, Impr. Marcel Ewald, 1967; *Les chants de JAM et légendes Sambas,* Port-au-Prince, Presses Port-au-Princiennes, 1969; "Et ku dis que," (unpublished).

Essays: *Le problème des femmes* (unpublished).

Literary Criticism: *Regards sur la littérature haitienne,* mimeo., 1973.

Play: *Flore ou le destin,* drama in 3 acts, unpublished.

MARCELIN, Emile

b. January 16, 1874, Port-au-Prince, Haiti; d. July 24, 1936.
Novelist, literary critic, diplomat.

Marcelin was educated at the Petit Séminaire Collège Saint-Martial. He graduated from the law school.

He was Counsellor of State, then became Minister of Finance and was named Minister plenipotentiary to Cuba.

Writings: Memoirs: *De l'enfance à la jeunesse,* Port-au-Prince, Impr. du Séminaire Adventiste, 1934.

Novel: *La reine Anacaona,* Havana, Pi y Margal, 1934 (roman historique de moeurs indiennes).

Criticism: *Médaillons littéraires; poètes et prosateurs haitiens,* Impr. de l'Abeille, 1906.

MARCELIN, Frédéric

b. January 11, 1848, Port-au-Prince, Haiti; d. 1917, Paris.
Novelist, storywriter, critic, economic and social historian, lawyer, diplomat.

Marcelin was educated in Port-au-Prince and France. He studied law under the guidance of Attorney Valcin. He was extremely active in his public career, for he was a Deputy in 1874 and 1882. He began his diplomatic career as secretary to the Haitian legation in Washington, D. C., and became Minister of Finance and of Commerce during President Florvil Hyppolite's tenure, and later, in 1905 when President Nord Alexis was in office.

Marcelin had the energy and talent to write five novels, a collection of essays and miscellaneous other works. He practiced journalism and founded *La Voix du Peuple* in 1890, and *Haiti Littéraire et Sociale* in 1900 with Edmond Laforest. He contributed works in a variety of genre to many journals and otherwise was an influential writer during a long life.

His prose style was generally smooth, though touched with vivacity and variety at times. He was one of the most convincing users of local color and folkloric material. As he said:

La couleur locale . . . un des éléments constitutifs, en la matière, de toute personnalité et de toute originalité, n'a pas toujours l'estime de nos écrivains. Ils la considèrent à peu près comme une faute de goût, un instinct non dompté de vulgarité banale. S'inspirer de nos vieilles coutumes, présenter le tableau réel, photographique de nos passions, de nos préjugés, de nos vertus, ne leur paraît pas oeuvre sérieuse.

Writings: Novels: *Thémistocle Epaminondas Labasterre; petit récit haitien,* Paris, Soc. D'Editions Littéraires et Artistiques, first and second editions, 1901; third edition, 1902; *La vengeance de Mama; roman haitien,* Paris, Soc. D'Editions Littéraires et Artistiques, first and second editions, 1902; third edition, 1903; *Marilisse, roman haitien,* Paris, Soc. D'Editions Littéraires et Artistiques, first and second editions, 1903; third edition, 1903; *La confession de Bazoutte,* Paris, Soc. D'Editions Littéraires et Artistiques (Lib. Paul Ollendorf), first and second editions, 1909.

Essays: *Autour de deux romans,* Paris, Impr. Kugelmann, 1903; *L'haleine du centenaire,* Paris, Taillefer, 1901; *Propos d'un haitien,* Paris, Impr. Kugelman, 1915; *Le Passé (impressions haitiennes),* Paris, Impr. Kugelmann, 1902.

Biography: *Ducas-Hippolyte, son époque, ses oeuvres,* Le Hâvre, Impr. A. Lemale aîné, 1878.

Politics: *Choses haitiennes; politique et littérature,* Paris, Société Anonyme de l'Impr. Kugelmann, 1896; *La politique; articles de journaux, discours à la chambre,* Paris, Impr. J. Kugelmann, 1887; *Le Département des Finances et du Commerce d'Haiti* (1892-1894), Paris, Impr. Kugelmann, 1895; *Le général Nord Alexis,* 3 vols., (1905-1908), Paris, Soc. Anonyme de l'Impr. Kugelmann, 1909; *Les Chambres Législatives d'Haiti (1892-1894),* Paris, Impr. Kugelmann, 1896.

Memoirs: *Au gré du souvenir,* Paris, Augustin Challamel, 1913; *Bric-à-brac,* Paris, Soc. Anonyme de l'Impr. Kugelmann, 1910.

Economico-Political: *La Banque Nationale d'Haiti; une page d'histoire,* Paris, Impr. Kugelmann, 1890; *Haiti et sa banque nationale,* Paris, Impr. Kugelmann, 1896; *Haiti et l'indemnité française,* Paris, Impr. Kugelmann, 1898; *Nos douanes* (Haiti) . . . Paris, Impr. Kugelmann, 1897; *Questions haitiennes (La Banque du Commerce et de l'Industrie-menus propos),* Paris, Impr. Kugelmann, 1891; *Finances d'Haiti, emprunt nouveau-même banque,* Paris, Impr. Kugelmann, 1911; *Une évolution nécessaire,* Paris, P. Taillefer, 1898.

Travel: *Vingt-quatre heures à Puerto Plata,* Port-au-Prince, Impr. Enélus Robin, 1875.

Biographical/Critical Sources: Ayraud Degeorge, "Un Roman Haitien," in *Intransigeant,* June 20, 1901; Charles Foley, "Le Roman Haitien," in *L'Echo de Paris* (July 1, 1901); Berthe de Nyse, "Autour de deux romans," in *Le National* (June 9, 1902); Ghislain Gouraige, *Frédéric Marcelin, peintre d'une époque,* (thesis), Laval University, Quebec, 1948; "Frédéric Marcelin" in *The Literature of Latin American Writers,* Vol. 1, Washington, D.C., Pan American Union, 1944; Hénock Trouillot, *Les origines sociales de la littérature haitienne,* Port-au-Prince, Impr. N.A. théodore, 1962, pp. 289-313; Ghislain Gouraige, *Histoire de la littérature haitienne,* Port-au-Prince, 1960, pp. 105-121; Pradel Pompilus & Frères de l'Instruction Chrétienne, *Manuel illustré d'Histoire de la littérature haitienne,* Port-au-Prince, Eds. H. Deschamps, 1961, pp. 275-285.

MARCELIN, Pierre

b. August 20, 1908, Port-au-Prince, Haiti. Novelist, storywriter.

Pierre Marcelin is known only as a novelist and storywriter. Unlike his brother Philippe, he is not a poet and has no THOBY in his name, because Philippe, his constant co-worker, had been adopted by their maternal uncle, Perceval Thoby. Pierre was educated at Saint Louis de Gonzague directed by the Christian Brothers, and later he spent many years in Cuba when his father was in that country as a diplomatic representative of Haiti.

He was awarded in 1943 the Latin American first prize for his novel written with Philippe, *Canapé Vert.* Since this international success they have closely collaborated on various new novels.

Writings: Novels: *Canapé Vert,* New York,

Farrar and Rinehart, 1944, trans. into English by Edward Larocque Tinker (work produced in collaboration with his brother Philippe-Thoby Marcelin); *La bête de Musseau,* New York, Ed. de La Maison Française, 1946, trans. as *The Beast of the Haitian Hills* by Peter Rhodes, London, Gollancz, 1951, and New York, 1946 (second Latin American Literary Prize contest); *Le crayon de Dieu* (written with Philippe-Thoby Marcelin), Paris, La Table Ronde, 1952, trans. by Leonard Thomas as *The Pencil of God,* Boston, Houghton Mifflin, 1951, and London, Gollancz, 1951; *All Men are Mad,* trans. into English by Eva Thoby-Marcelin, New York, Farrar, Straus and Giraux, 1970 (the original text in French: *Tous les hommes sont fous* is still unpublished).

Folklore: *Contes et légendes d'Haiti,* (with Philippe-Thoby Marcelin), illus. by Philippe Degrave, Paris, F. Nathan, 1967; in English translation by Eva Thoby Marcelin published as *Singing Turtle and Other Tales from Haiti,* New York, Farrar, Straus and Giraux, 1971; *Sortilèges haitiens (récits folkloriques),* unpublished.

Biographical/Critical Sources: Edmund Wilson, "The Marcelin-Novelists of Haiti" in *The Nation* (Oct. 14, 1950); Vere W. Knight, "Pierre Marcelin and Philippe-Thoby Marcelin, Sensationalism or Realism," in *Black Images,* Vol. II (Spring, 1973), pp. 30-42.

MARIAMOUR, Jean Hubert

(pseudonym for **Hubert PAPAILLER**)

MARIE-SAINTE, Kiki

b. ca. 1941, Martinique.
Novelist.

Marie-Sainte's one novel takes place in Toulon and Paris and onboard a trans-atlantic liner, and Martinique and contrasts "islanders" to the French in the usual ambiguous relationship of colonized and colonizer.

Writings: Novel: *L'Antillaise à l'amour double,* Paris, Soulanges, 1966.

MARRAUD de SIGALONY, Joseph

b. March 24, 1890, Macouba, Martinique.
Novelist, poet, astronomer.

Joseph Marraud de Sigalony attended the Séminaire Collège of Saint-Pierre and also the Lycée Schoelcher of Fort-de-France. He was a practicing astronomer and a member of the Astronomical Society of France. He was a talented "amateur" of poetry, publishing much of his verse in local newspapers.

Writings: Poetry: *Rêves et idéals,* Fort-de-France, Deslandes, 1918; *Madinina, poèmes,* Fort-de-France, Deslandes, 1919.

Novel: *Les Antillaises,* Paris, Ed. Débresse, 1937.

MARRAUD de SIGALONY, Louise

b. ca. 1933, Martinique.
Poet.

Louise Marraud's one creative work to date is her modest 1963 collection of sonnets and lyrics.

Writings: Poetry: *Au jardin du Rêve: sonnets et poèmes,* Fort-de-France, Eds. des Horizons Caraibes, 1963.

MARS, Dr. Jean Price

(see under **Dr. Jean PRICE-MARS**)

MARSOLLE, Edouard

b. June 7, 1921, Saint-Claude, Guadeloupe; d. August 5, 1964.
Poet.

Marsolle attended schools in his community and afterwards in Pointe-à-Pitre. He faced many financial problems but was enabled to study, however, at a lycée in Martinique for his higher education. He has been a driver, a mechanic, and was a professional accountant.

Writings: Poetry: *Au clair de mon âme,* Paris, Grassin, 1960.

MARTINEAU, Fernand

b. June 9, 1910, Jérémie, Haiti; d. January 17, 1945, Cuba.
Poet, teacher.

Martineau was educated in Jérémie and was a schoolmate and close friend of Jean F. Brierre. He taught for a period in Haiti before going to Cuba. He published one volume of verse during his short life.

Writings: Poetry: *Résonances (poèmes),* Jérémie, Impr. du Centenaire, 1936; and Jérémie, Libr. Edmond Laforest, 1947.

MARX, Jean

(see under **Paule Cassius de LINVAL**)

MATHON, Alix

b. October 9, 1908, Port-au-Prince, Haiti.
Novelist, journalist, lawyer.

After his primary studies in Port-au-Prince, Mathon went to Berne, Switzerland, at Gruneau Institute for further education.

When he returned to Haiti, he completed legal training, practicing in the law office of his father. He was later appointed professor at the Law School. Mathon became Secretary of the Council of Secretaries of State and later Undersecretary to the Presidency.

He has contributed prose work to various newspapers and was manager-editor of the magazine, *La Relève.*

In 1970, Mathon was recipient of the France-Haiti Prize for his novel, *La fin des baïonnettes.*

Writings: Novels: *La fin des baïonnettes,* Paris, Eds. de l'Ecole, 1972; *Le drapeau en berne,* Port-au-Prince, details not known.

MATHON, Etienne

b. February 14, 1864, Cap-Haitien, Haiti; d. 1929, Port-au-Prince.
Playwright, essayist, lawyer.

Mathon came to Port-au-Prince to attend the Petit Séminaire Collège Saint-Martial. He was a teacher in Cap-Haitien and he studied law and graduated from the Free Law School of Cap-Haitien.

Mathon was appointed Secretary of the Council of Secretaries of State and became a judge at the commercial court. He was elected Mayor of Port-au-Prince and finally was named Minister of Public Education.

Writings: Conférence (delivered at the Museum of Petit Séminaire, Dec. 27, 1895), Port-au-Prince, Impr. Vve J. Chenet, 1896; *Ogé et Chavanne, conférence historique,* Port-au-Prince, Impr. Mme Smith, 1903.

Politics: *Documents pour l'histoire d'Haiti; révolution de 1888-1889; actes des trois départements du Nord, Nord-Ouest et de l'Artibonite, et du Gouvernement Provisoire du 27 novembre 1888; recueillis et annotés,* Paris, Impr. de la Faculté de Médecine (Henri Jouve), 1890; *Frédéric Marcelin ou l'homme de la petite dîme,* Port-au-Prince, Impr. Vve J. Chenet, 1895.

Essay: *Haiti et Cuba; conséquences de la guerre Américano-Espagnole,* Port-au-Prince, Impr. H. Chauvet, 1898.

Play: *Judas, drame historique en 4 actes, en prose,* Port-au-Prince, Impr. de l'Abeille, 1916.

Law: *Annuaire de législation haitienne, contenant les lois votées en l'année 1904,* Port-au-Prince, Impr. J. Verrollot, 1905; and *années 1905, 1906, 1907, 1908, 1909, 1910, 1911, 1912, 1913, 1914,* Port-au-Prince, Impr. J. Verrollot (yearly, 1906-1915); *années 1915, 1916, 1917,* Port-au-Prince, Impr. de l'Abeille (yearly, 1916-1918); *années 1918,* Port-au-

Prince, Impr. J. Verrollot, 1919; *Année 1919,* Port-au-Prince, Impr. Edm. Chenet, 1920; *Annuaire de législation haitienne, table générale des matières, année 1904 à 1913,* Port-au-Prince, Impr. Edm. Chenet, 1914.

MAUVOIS, Georges

b. ca. 1936, Martinique.
Playwright (in French and creole).

Mauvois' one play, *Agénor Cacoul,* like many recent novels from the islands, deals with the rising clash of social and cultural groups long muted by harsh regimes.

The play is set in the late colonial period and concerns Major Agénor Cacoul who is seen preparing for city elections during a bitter strike of farm workers. Creole is used to provide not only reality to the words of the strikers but psychological-poetic contrast to the standard French of the whites and the well-to-do Antillan bourgeoisies. As one critic noted, " . . . les conflits du langage recoupent et reflètent les contradictions entre les couches sociales.'

Writings: Play: *Agénor Cacoul (Pièce en 3 actes),* introducion by René Ménil, Fort-de-France, Impr. Populaire, 1966 (also published as supplement to the review *Action,* No. 11-12, directed by René Ménil).

MAYARD, Constantin

b. November 27, 1882, Port-au-Prince, Haiti; d. December 27, 1940, Santiago, Chili.
Poet, playwright, journalist, diplomat.

Constantin Mayard was educated at the Petit Séminaire Collège Saint-Martial. He early was engaged in politics. He was elected député in 1911, and became Minister of Interior in 1915. He was senator in the national Parliament and served as Councillor of State, Minister to Paris and Santiago de Chili where he died. His body was brought home for a state funeral by President Sténio Vincent.

From 1901 on he was an active contributor to *La Ronde,* the leading cultural literary journal of its day. Viatte says Mayard's subjects, tropical moons, the beauty of the creole girl, social needs, were of the common sort, but that his "langue se raffine, les tirades se condensent en distiques, le vocabulaire se complique jusqu'au maniérisme," and he quotes these lines from an uncited poem in *Trente poèmes,* 1933.

Gyrovage errant par des venelles
pierreuses,
J'ai rencontré ton coeur; ton coeur est
un couvent,
Couvent de nonnes-angélices,
secoureuses
Au chemineau lassé qui s'égare en
rêvant.

Writings: Poetry: *Trente poèmes,* Milo Rigaud (ed.), Paris, L'Action Intellectuelle, 1933.

Verse Play: *Guacanagaric (opéra lyrique en trois tableaux),* in ms.

Essays: *De la solidarité,* Port-au-Prince, Impr. Aug. A. Héraux, 1918; *Haiti* (conférence prononcée le 28 Janvier 1934 pour inaugurer la session annuelle de l'Oeuvre des Isolés coloniaux), Chatellerault, L'Action Intellectuelle, 1934.

Speeches: *Discours politiques.*

Biographical/Critical Sources: Maurice Laraque, *Constantin Mayard, étude,* Port-au-Prince, Impr. N. Telhomme, 1944.

MAYARD, Pierre

b. November 13, 1912, Pétionville, Haiti.
Poet, playwright, journalist, teacher, diplomat.

Pierre Mayard was educated at the Petit Séminaire Collège Saint-Martial. He published essays in *La Bataille, Le Temps-Revue* and also *Haiti-Journal,* where he was editor-in-chief.

Mayard was a professor of French at the Institut Tippenhauer and Henri Odéide and the Collège de Port-au-Prince.

He was first secretary of the Haitian Legation in Paris and in Washington, D.C.

He also served as Inspecteur des Ambassades et Consulats in Paris and he is presently Ambassador of Haiti to the Holy See.

Writings: Journalism: work in many journals, including *La Bataille* and *Temps-Revue.* His daily chronicle, *Raccourcis,* has not been collected.

Plays: *La Famille des Petite-Caille,* performed at Rex Théâtre.

Poetry: A great deal of his poems in French or in creole appeared in newspapers such as *Haiti-Journal* and *Le Temps-Revue.*

Tourism: *Haiti, la merveille des Antilles,* Port-au-Prince, Impr. de l'Etat, date unknown.

MEDARD, Yves

(pseudonym: **Rassoul LABUCHIN**)

MEGIE, Emile C.

(see under **Emile CELESTIN-MEGIE**)

MELON-DEGRAS, Alfred

b. ca. 1945, Saint Esprit, Martinique.
Poet.

After schooling in Martinique, Melon-Degras went to Paris to earn his Agrégé at the Sorbonne. Since then he has been teaching Latin American literature at the New Sorbonne.

His poetry deals with political and social concerns, reflecting Latin American writers, especially Miguel-Angel Asturias, the Nobel laureate from Guatemala.

Writings: Poetry: *L'Habit d'Arlequin,* 1974; *Le Silence,* 1975; *Avec des Si, avec des mais,* 1976; *Battre le rappel,* 1976, all Paris, Ed. Saint-Germain-des-Près; the poem "L'aide au Tiers-monde" appears in *La Poésie Antillaise,* Maryse Conde, ed., Paris, Fernand Nathan, 1977.

MENIL, René

b. ca. 1902, Martinique.
Essayist, journalist.

After he attended schools in Martinique, René Ménil went to Paris to complete his education. With Etienne Léro and Jules Monnerot, he founded *Légitime défense* (1932), the single issue journal that was the first clarion call for Negritude and a new attitude to Africa and its culture wherever carried and however preserved. He was a collaborator with Aimé Césaire and Suzanne Césaire and others in the first important French language literary journal *Tropiques,* published in the islands of Martinique and Guadeloupe. He criticized harshly the parochial and timid attitudes of his fellow Antillans in his essay published in a 1941 issue of *Tropiques.* He asked:

> *Qui parlent ici? Des Martiniquais vivant sur la ligne des Tropiques, entre les deux Amériques, partageant avec la France les chances de sa culture impériale, et qui s'interrogent aujourd'hui sur leur destin, à l'heure où la civilisation occidentale se révolutionne pour rattraper la vie qui l'avait dépassée. Des gens qui ont derrière eux trois siècles de Récitation et qui toujours vinrent aux assises de la Culture les mains vides, n'ayant jamais rien fait. Nous avons lu la culture des autrees. Les plus sots d'entre nous prennent pour de la culture les textes qu'ils ont appris en classe et croient que la culture est chose qui se passe dans la mémoire. La mécanique récitation des temps passés, l'enfantine manie de collectionner des images d'Epinal, de dire des mots que les autres ont inventés, n'ont pu faire des meilleurs d'entre nous que des sorciers politiques, des comédiens d'estrade, vaticinant avec moins de convictions et de beauté que les faiseurs de pluie australiens. La culture est ailleurs. La vie aussi, du reste. Le vent passe.*

René Ménil wrote the same criticisms in *Légitime Défense:*

> *Cette littérature qui manque de res-*

sort et s'agite vaguement, sans attaches à la chair, s'est en effet, donné pour maîtres tous ceux qui (Heredia, Banville, Samain, de Régnier) n'étaient résolus ni à s'embarquer dans le mouvement de la vie, ni à vivre en plein rêve.

In the 1960's Ménil was the editor-founder of the literary review *Action*, published in Fort-de-France.

Writings: Essay: "Naissance de notre art," in *Tropiques* (April 1941), p. 59.

MENOS, Solon

b. March 9, 1859, Baradères, Haiti; d. October 15, 1918, New York.
Poet, playwright, diplomat, lawyer, statesman.

Menos had his local schooling at the Petit Séminaire Collège Saint-Martial, but took his law degree at the University of Paris. His career was mostly in private law practice and in Haiti's diplomatic services in which he held many important posts, including service in Washington as Haitian Minister, and Minister of Foreign Affairs.

His creative work is by and large Parisian, almost untouched by Haitian culture or events.

Writings: Poetry: *Les Mnémoniennes*, Paris, A. Cotillon & Cie, 1882.

Play: *Les roses perdues*, performed at Bagatelle Theatre.

Anthology: *Morceaux choisis*, 2 vols. (prose & poetry), written with Dantès Bellegarde, Amilcar Duval, and Georges Sylvain, Port-au-Prince, Impr. de Mme F. Smith, 1904.

Law: *La séparation des patrimoines*, Paris, Cotillon, 1881; *L'affaire Luders*, Port-au-Prince, Impr. J. Verrollot, 1898; *Un cas d'arbitrage (France et Haiti)*, Paris, Lib. Générale de Droit et de Jurisprudence, 1906; *Affaire Aboilard*.

Essay: *Haiti et sa première exposition; la statue de Victor Hugo*, Paris, A. Cotillon & Cie, 1882.

Biographical/Critical Sources: Pradel Pompilus & Frères de l'Instruction Chrétienne, *Manuel illustré d'histoire de la littérature haitienne*, Port-au-Prince, Ed. H. Deschamps, 1961, pp. 197-201; Robert Cornevin, *Le théâtre haitien, des origines à nos jours*, Quebec, Ed. Léméac, 1973, p. 103.

MENTOR, Etienne Victor

b. December 26, 1771, Saint-Pierre, Martinique; d. October 18, 1806, Port-au-Prince, Haiti.
Politician, orator.

Born in Martinique, Mentor had the opportunity to receive a fine education in France.

In 1797, he was promoted to adjutant general in the French army, and went with the French commissioner Félicité Sonthonax on a mission to Saint-Domingue (Haiti). Settling in Haiti, he was later elected member at the Council of Five-Hundred, facing many problems to get his seat. He was ousted from this Council after Brumaire 18th and left the island.

When Haiti proclaimed its independence in 1804, Mentor, who knew Saint-Domingue, and many Haitians went back to Haiti. He was welcomed and lived among those close to Emperor Dessalines. Jealous and anxious to reach power, he was a poor advisor to Dessalines, for he was inclined to suggest inappropriate government measures, apparently to make Dessalines unpopular. Historian Thomas records this statement by Etienne Mentor:

> *Est-ce qu'un ignorant tel que Dessalines est fait pour nous commander? Des hommes tels que nous* (talking to a general educated in France) *devaient être à la tête du gouvernement. J'organise un parti contre l'empereur, sois des nôtres, tu acquerras une haute position quand j'aurai réussi. Je veux que Dessalines commette tant d'injustices que le peuple soit obligé de se soulever contre lui.*

Mentor was shot to death in the prison of Port-au-Prince the day after Emperor Dessalines was killed.

Writings: Politics: *Etienne Mentor . . . Au Conseil des Cinq cents,* Paris, n.d.; *Dernier d'Etienne Mentor, représentant du peuple, à Etienne Bruix, Ministre de la Marine et des Colonies,* Paris, n.d.; *Discours prononcé par Etienne Mentor, représentant du Peuple, Député de la colonie de St-Domingue, dans la séance du 12 Prairial, an 6, Paris,* Impr. Nationale, Prairial, an VII; *Motion d'ordre par Etienne Mentor, en faveur des colons patriotes, déportés par les Anglais et des réfugiés de Saint Domingue,* Paris, n.d.; *Observations d'Etienne Mentor et de Louis Auncy, députés de St Domingue, sur l'opinion du citoyen Brothier, membre du Conseil des Anciens,* Paris, Impr. Vantard, 1797; *Opinion d'Etienne Mentor sur les élections de Saint Domingue pour l'an 6 du 8 floréal, an 7,* Paris, Impr. Nat., Prairial, an VIII.

MERCIER, Louis

b. May 5, 1893, Cap-Haitien, Haiti; d. May 18, 1946, Cap-Haitien.

Biographer, scholar, musician, composer, diplomat.

Mercier's father was from Cayes, a southern city, but Mercier was a Cap-Haitien citizen by birth and by virtue of the maternal side of his family, long-time inhabitants of the Cap-Français peninsula. He was educated in his native city. He became a teacher at the Lycée Philippe Guerrier and at the College Notre Dame du Perpétuel Secours, of which he became director.

Mercier was appointed to a diplomatic post to serve as secretary of the Haitian Legation at Washington, D.C., where he spent three years. At home, he was a competent guide to inform visitors about Citadelle Henri and King Henri himself, activities so appreciated that he was called, "Mercier, the champion of guides."

Worth full noting is Mercier's comment about Haiti:

> *Haiti a peiné et souffert pour l'émancipation de toutes les colonies américaines. Il n'y en a pas une seule qui ne lui soit redevable de quelque aide généreusement apportée. Son exemple servira d'ailleurs à fortifier l'opinion des émancipateurs et de leurs amis. Le Ministre des Etats-Unis, en France, écrira le 22 Juillet 1818 au Secrétaire d'Etat John Quincy Adams: "Je m'étonne que vous puissiez douter de la possibilité pour les colonistes espagnols de former un gouvernement capable de diriger les affaires de l'Etat et d'entre tenir des relations avec les pays étrangers, et je cite Santo Domingo (il voulait dire Haiti) comme une preuve que même des esclaves peuvent établir un gouvernement constitué d'hommes tirés de leur race, et totalement indépendants au moins de leurs anciens maîtres." Et, en 1902, c'est un amiral haitien qui montrera au monde comment on répond à une insolence et comment on meurt dans une auréole de fumée, d'honneur et de gloire.*
>
> *Quand on veut trouver un monument qui apparente l'Amérique à l'Egypte, c'est en Haiti qu'on peut l'admirer, et ce monument s'appelle la citadelle.*
>
> *Haiti, la perle des Antilles, Haiti, la douloureuse, la glorieuse, la toute belle, Haiti qui est, au dire de Victor Hugo, une lumière, a une histoire qui ressemble à une fable, qui mérite d'être incorporée à celle de la civilisation, et qui peut être contée par les Haitiens avec plaisir, avec orgueil.*

Writings: History: *La vie au Cap-Français en 1789,* Paris, Ed. de la "Revue de Paris," 1933; *Contribution de l'île d'Haiti à l'histoire de la civilisation,* Cap-Haitien, Les Presses Capoises, n.d.; *La bataille de Vertières continue,* Cap-Haitien, Les Presses Capoises, 1936.

Speech: *Abraham Lincoln (discours prononcé au Lycée Philippe Guerrier, du Cap-Haitien, à l'occasion de l'inauguration du portrait de Lincoln,* Port-au-Prince, Impr. N. Telhomme, 1941.

History: "Histoire de Dessalines; Biographies du Roi, de Pétion, de Boyer," (unpublished).

Biographical/Critical Sources: Lycée National Philippe Guerrier: *Hommage à Louis Mercier (5 Mai 1893-1946),* Port-au-Prince, Société d'Edition et Librairie, 1946.

METRO, Henri

b. ca. 1935, Guyane.
Novelist, storywriter.

After local schooling through the Lycée, Métro went to France to study psychology. Breaking off his studies, he became a mail carrier for the French postal system, and later was a soldier serving in the French forces in Germany. He returned to Paris to a career in journalism. Afterwards, he took assignments in Saint Louis in Senegal, moved to Brazzaville, Congo, and returned to Paris. Finally, he returned to America in 1961 to live in Martinique and Guadeloupe.

Métro's first novel, *K. et M.,* portrays the two allegorically languid and meaningless twin sisters K. (for Karukéra which is Guadeloupe) and M. (for Madinina, a name for Martinique) as they search for some sense in their lives.

Writings: Novels: *K. et M. (Guadeloupe-Martinique), filles de France,* Paris, Louis Soulanges, 1965; *Quand la canne lève; Antilles mes soeurs,* Rodez, Eds. Subervie, 1971.
Story: "Man Baleine, conte."

MILSCENT, Jules Solime

b. 1778, Grande Rivière du Nord, Haiti; d. May 7, 1842, Cap-Haitien.
Poet, playwright.

Son of an old settler family from the Anjou, and of a free African mother, Milscent was educated in France after his father suffered execution in the late years of the French Revolution. He returned to Haiti as a member of President Boyer's group. He lived in Port-au-Prince and had a close relationship with Colombel, President Pétion's secretary. With Colombel, he founded Haiti's first literary review, *L'Abeille Haytienne,* beginning with the issue of August 1, 1817 (the journal lasted until December 31, 1820).

Milscent was *greffier* (chief clerk) at the Tribunal de Cassation, and became Deputy and President of the Haitian Chamber of Deputies in 1832. He died in the earthquake which struck Cap-Haitien, May 7, 1842.

Milscent wrote in a wide variety of forms: the fable, madrigal, love lyric, the ode, the "epitre," and published several plays.

Writings: Poetry: in various journals, including the poems "L'Union," in *L'Abeille Haytienne* (June 15-Oct. 31, 1820), pp. 3-4; "Epîtres à son Excellence le Président d'Haiti" in *L'Abeille Haytienne*(Aug. 1, 1817), pp. 9-12; "Epître à Monsieur Lhérisson, citoyen d'Aquin," in *L'Abeille Haytienne* (June 16, 1818).
Plays: *Le philosophe physicien (prose comedy),* published in *L'Abeille Haytienne* (June 15-Oct. 31, 1820), pp. 5-53; *Le prix de la vertu* (verse comedy after Molière).

Biographical/Critical Sources: Robert Cornevin, *Le théâtre haitien, des origines à nos jours,* Montreal, Ed. Léméac, 1973, pp. 56-57; Auguste Viatte, *Histoire littéraire de l'Amérique française,* Quebec, 1953, pp. 347-350.

MIRAMANT, Yves

(pseudonym for **Irmine ROMANETTE**)

MOISE, Rodolphe

b. February 21, 1914, Port-au-Prince, Haiti; d. December, 1977, Paris.
Poet.

Moïse was educated in Port-au-Prince. He was a member of the generation which considered revolt against government the main subject for poetry. He took part in the bloodless revolt of January 1946 against President Elie Lescot, which led to Lescot's fall. In France he studied sculpture after the 1946 events.

After a short stay in Haiti in the 1950's he left Haiti permanently.

Writings: Poetry: *Gueules de feu (poèmes),* Port-au-Prince, Impr. de l'Etat, 1947; Two of his poems are in *Panorama de la poèsie haitienne,* edited by Carlos Saint Louis and Maurice A. Lubin; also given in English translation are: "Hymne ancestral," and "Crépuscule," which appear in N.R. Shapiro's *Negritude: Black Poetry from Africa and the Caribbean,* New York, October House, 1970; *Aux Armes Guérilleros,* preface by Lélio Basso, Paris, Eds. Pierre Jean Oswald, 1975.

MONNEROT, Jules Marcel

b. ca. 1906, Martinique.
Poet, sociologist.

Founder with Etienne Léro and René Ménil of the now famous one-issue review *Légitime Défense,* in Paris, Monnerot argued for new kinds of poetry in the Antilles and greater pride by Antilleans in their islands heritage. An interest in Marx and Lenin were also major elements in the polemics arguing for a new deal for the Caribbean peoples.

Writings: Poetry: *Ballades du Tricentenaire avec deux ou trois autres,* Fort-de-France, Impr. Illemay, 1936.
Essay: *Anniversaire,* Fort-de-France, Impr. du Gouvernement, 1943.

MONNERVILLE, Gaston Charles François

b. January 2, 1897, Cayenne, Guyane.
Biographer, lawyer, public servant, memorialist.

Monnerville left Guyane very early to live in France where he was educated. After graduating from the Law School in Toulouse, he was admitted to the bar of that city in 1918 and to the Paris bar in 1921. He practiced law, was secretary of the Conference of Lawyers, and worked with the famed French lawyer, César Campinchi for some years.

Monnerville was elected mayor of Cayenne in 1935 and deputy for Guyane in 1938. He was named Undersecretary of State for Colonies (1937-1938). He served in the French navy in the Second World War and won the war cross, "la rosette de la résistance," and the "legion d'honneur."

He became a member of the French Consultant Assembly in 1944 and chairman of the Committee of Overseas France. He was re-elected in Guyane to serve in the Constituent Assembly, and was a delegate of France to the U.N. Assembly.

Named Councillor of the Republic, Monnerville was elected Senator for Lot (France), in 1948, 1955, 1958 and later he became president of the Council of the Republic and president of the Senate of the French Community.

Writings: Law: *L'enrichissement sans cause.*
Politics: *Le Sénat.*
Biography: *Clemenceau, Les grandes études historiques,* Paris, Fayard, 1968.
Memoir: *Témoignage de la France Equinoxiale au Palais du Luxembourg,* Vol. I, Paris, Plon, 1975.

MONPLAISIR, Emma

b. June 18, 1918, Nantes, France (associated with Martinique).
Novelist, storywriter.

Although born in Nantes of a French mother and a Martinican father, Monplaisir came very early to Martinique. She attended the Pensionnat Colonial and then the girls' Lycée of Fort-de-France. In Paris, she attended the Institut Maintenon at Auteuil and the Lycée Victor Duruy, receiving her baccalaureat in France and later her philosophy degree in Martinique.

Her writing at the beginning was primarily for her children but she had always been interested in fiction. Her half-historical novel, *La Fille du Caraïbe* concerns an Indian métisse girl in Martinique.

Writings: Stories: *Cric . . . Crac . . . Martinique,* Paris, Impr. La Productrice.

Juvenile Novels: *La Fille du Caraïbe,* Paris, Société d'Ed. Extérieures et Coloniales, 1960; *Christophe Colomb chez les Indiens.*

Folklore: *La Martinique et ses danses,* (lecture delivered in Ciné-Théâtre, on Dec. 1, 1961), Fort-de-France, Impr. Bezaudin, 1962.

MORAND-CAPASSO, Florette

b. June 20, 1926, Guadeloupe.
Poet, storywriter, novelist.

Florette Morand was educated in Guadeloupe, and resided a long time in France. A teacher at Morne-à-l'Eau, Guadeloupe for many years, she married an Italian writer and moved to Italy.

She began her own writing very early; her "simple" verse is cryptic, gnomic, something akin to the terse poems of the American poet Emily Dickinson.

Florette Morand was an award winner in the contest sponsored by the Association des Etudiants Guadeloupéens de Paris in 1947, and she also won the prize for prose in the competition "Jeux Floraux de Guadeloupe."

Writings: Poetry: *Mon coeur est un oiseau des iles,* Paris, Ed. de la Maison des Intellectuels, 1955; *Chanson pour ma savane,* preface by Pierre Mac Orlan, Paris, Lib. de l'Escalier, 1959; *Feux de brousse,* Montreal, Eds. du Jour, 1967.

Stories: *Biguines,* Paris, Lib. de l'Escalier, 1956.

Novel: *Doudou.*

MORAVIA, Adeline

b. July 9, 1907, Port-au-Prince, Haiti; d. April 10, 1978.
Novelist.

Daughter of Charles Moravia, the noted poet and journalist of Haiti, Adeline was educated in Port-au-Prince and abroad. She served in various diplomatic posts, and she spent a great number of years in France, Italy and the United States.

The Committee France-Haiti awarded the Prix des Caraïbes to her in 1976 for her novel.

Writings: Novel: *Aude et ses fantômes,* Port-au-Prince, Eds. Caraïbes, 1977.

Morand-Capasso with Price-Mars

MORAVIA, Charles

(pseudonym for **René DARLOUZE**)

b. June 17, 1876, Jacmel, Haiti; d. February 11, 1938, Port-au-Prince.

Poet, playwright, journalist, essayist.

Moravia studied at the Petit Séminaire Collège Saint-Martial in Port-au-Prince. He had a broad public and private career: teacher, deputy in the national parliament, councillor of state, senator, minister plenipotentiary to Washington, and he was the director and founder of *La Plume* and *Le Temps,* a daily paper and later a magazine. Moravia was also elected an officer of the Haitian Academy of Arts and Sciences.

These lines from his "Coucher de soleil" illustrate his late symbolist manner:

Les nuages roses pendent en oriflammes,
Ou montent dans l'azur comme d'un encensoir,
Et les cierges du ciel, allumés par les âmes,
Scintillent au plafond du vaste reposoir.

An admirer of Henrich Heine, Moravia translated the German poet's verse, working from the prose translations of Gérard de Nerval. He was even more influenced by Edmond Rostand's Cyrano de Bergerac and his own personality became Cyrano-esque and his verse often seemed the utterances of the big-nosed Provençal.

Writings: Poetry: *Roses et camélias; poèsies,* Port-au-Prince, Impr. Mme F. Smith, 1903; *Ode à la mémoire de Toussaint Louverture,* Port-au-Prince, Impr. Mme F. Smith, 1903; *L'Intermezzo de Henri Heine, mis en vers français d'après la traduction de Gérard de Nerval,* New York, The Haytian Library, 1917; *Autres poèmes de Henri Heine,* New York, The Haytian Library, 1918.

Verse-Plays: *La Crête-à-Pierrot, poème dramatique en trois tableaux et en vers,* Port-au-Prince, Impr. J. Verrollot, 1908; performed at the Petit Séminaire Collège Saint-Martial, April 13, 1907; *Le fils du tapissier; épisode de la vie de Molière; poème dramatique en un acte et en vers,* Port-au-Prince, Impr. de l'Abeille, 1923; performed May 7, 1921; *Au clair de la lune.*

Prose Plays: *L'Amiral Killick, drame historique en trois tableaux* (written with André F. Chevalier), Port-au-Prince, Impr. du Collège Vertières, 1943.

Essays: *Epître à mon confrère Arsène Chevry,* Port-au-Prince, Impr. Mme F. Smith, 1903.

Biographical/Critical Sources: Auguste Viatte, *Histoire littéraire de l'Amérique française,* Quebec, 1953, pp. 411-412; Pradel Pompilus & Frères de l'Instruction Chrétienne, *Manuel illustré d'histoire de la littérature haitienne,* Port-au-Prince, Ed. H. Deschamps, 1961, pp. 263-267; Ghislain Gouraige, *Histoire de la littérature haitienne,* Port-au-Prince, Impr. N.A. Théodore, 1960, pp. 205-208.

MOREAU de SAINT MERY, Médéric Louis Elie

b. January 13, 1750, Fort-Royal, Martinique; d. January 28, 1819, Paris.

Jurist, scholar.

Moreau de Saint Méry was born in the colony of Martinica, of white parents from Poitiers who had settled centuries earlier. He was educated in Martinique and received training in law with his maternal uncle Borde, notary for the admiralty. He went to France in 1769 and entered the faculty of law and was admitted at King's House. He became a lawyer in 1771. He came back to Martinica, October 1774, and went on to Saint Domingue, in Cap-Français, May 1775. He practiced law, married Louis Catherine Milhet, April 18, 1781. At 35 years, he was appointed (October 29, 1785) Counsellor to the Council of Cap-Français. He travelled over all the French islands to collect laws, geographical and social data about them.

Moreau was elected deputy of Martinica to the Constituent Assembly in Paris, and he played an important political role during the historical events in France.

Threatened by Robespierre, he left France with his family and took refuge in New York and then in Philadelphia. He turned stationer, book-seller and printer, becoming one of the best in Philadelphia. He returned to France, August 1798, and served at the Ministry of Navy and Colonies as historiographer. He was named Councellor of State and later General Administrator of the Republic of Parme and Plaisance but was dismissed by Napoleon.

Moreau de St-Méry, a great scholar, was among the twelve founders of the Cercle des Philadelphes which later became "la Société Royale des Arts et des Sciences" du Cap-Français. His works are important sources of research on the past of the Caribbean islands, once or still held by the French.

Elicoma said about him:

> *Par la variété de ses expériences, l'étendue de ses travaux, le charme de sa personnalité, Moreau de St-Méry mérite d'être sauvé de l'oubli historique.*

One of his biographers uttered this statement:

> *Moreau tranche sur le personnel politique de l'époque, il tranche par sa droiture, par sa constance dans ses opinions, par son intégrité, et peut-être ne faut-il pas chercher ailleurs la cause de ses échecs.*

Moreau engraved this exordium on his watch: "Il est toujours l'heure de faire le bien." It was to Moreau de Saint-Méry that Robespierre voiced the famous words: 'Périssent les colonies plutôt qu'un principe."

Writings: Mémoires des procès plaidés par Moreau de Saint-Méry au Cap-Français, Impr. Royale du Cap-Français, 1771-1783, (3 vols. in 4°); *Lois et constitutions des colonies françaises de l'Amerique sous-le-Vent de 1550 à 1785, suivies: 1) d'un tableau raisonné des différentes parties de l'administration; 2) d'observations sur le climat, la population de la partie française de Saint Dominque; 3) d'une description physique, politique et topographique de cette même partie; le tout terminé par l'histoire de cette isle,* Paris, Quillau, Méquignon jeune 1784-1790, (6 vols. in 4°). Also: *Opinion imprimée par ordre de l'Assemblée Nationale, sur la motion de M. de Curt, député de la Guadeloupe, pour l'établissement de l'examen de tous les objets coloniaux, Séance du ler déc. 1789,* Paris, Impr. Nationale, 1789; *Mémoire justificatif contenant plusieurs détails insérés comme utiles pour Saint Domingue, à Paris, le 14 Janvier 1790,* Paris, Baudoin, 1790; *Opinion de Moreau de St-Méry imprimée par ordre de l'Assemblée Nationale du 28 Octobre 1790,* Paris, de l'Impr. Nationale, 1790; *Mémoire sur une éspèce de Coton, nommé à Saint Domingue coton de soie ou coton de Sainte-Marthe; avec le rapport des commissaires de la Société royale d'Agriculture,* Paris, Vve d'Houry et Debure, 1790; *Considérations présentées aux vrais amis du repos et du bonheur de la France à l'occasion des nouveaux mouvements de quelques soidisant amis des noirs, ler Mars, 1790,* Paris, Impr. du Patriote Français, 1791; *Eloges de Turc de Castelveyre et de Dolicules, fondateurs des deux hospices appelés Maison de Providence au Cap-Français, isle de St-Domingue,* Paris, Impr. G.A. Rochette, MDCCXC; *Observations sur le mémoire de l'Abbé Grégoire pour les gens de couleur; Observations d'un habitant des colonies; Idée générale ou abrégé des Sciences et des Arts à l'usage de la jeunesse; Description de la partie espagnole de l'Isle Saint-Domingue, Philadelphie 1796,* 2 vols., *Description topographique, physique, civile, politique et historique de la partie française de l'isle Saint-Domingue. Avec des observations générales sur sa population, sur le caractère et les moeurs de ses divers habitants; sur son climat, sa culture, ses productions, son administration, etc.; accompagnées des détails les plus propres à faire connaître l'étude de cette colonie à l'époque du 18 octobre 1789; et d'une nouvelle carte de la totalité de l'Isle . . A* Philadelphie, chez les principaux libraires, 1797; 2 vols.; second edition by Semexan Rouzier and Laforestrie (only 3 vols.), tome I, tome 2 and tome 3. (incomplete), third edition; *A topographical and political description of the Spanish part of Saint Domingue containing general observations on the climate, population and productions; on the character and manners of the inhabitants; with an account of the several branches of the government . . .*

translated from the French by William Cobbett . . . Philadelphia, printed and sold by the author, printer and bookseller, 1798, 2 vols.; *Observations sur la culture de la canne à sucre dans les Antilles et plus particulièrement de celle d'Otaïti, lues à* la *Société d'Agriculture le 26 messidor an VIII* (1798) Paris, Impr. de la République, an VIII (1799); *Fragment sur les moeurs de Saint Domingue,* n.p. and n.d.; *De la danse,* par Moreau de Saint Méry, conseiller d'Etat, membre de plusieurs sociétés savantes et littéraires, A Parme, Imprimé par Bodoni, 1801; *Voyage aux Etats-Unis de l'Amérique* (1793-1798), New Haven, 1913; and *Descripcion de la parte española de la isla de Santo Domingo,* traduccion del francès por el Licenciado C. Armando Rodriguez, por en cargo del Generalissimo Rafael L. Trujillo Molina, Ciudad Trujillo, Ed. Montalvo, 1944.

MORISSEAU, Roland

b. September 22, 1933, Port-au-Prince, Haiti.

Poet.

After completing his education at the Lycée Toussaint Louverture in the capital, Morisseau joined the "Samba" group of poets and its organ, *Haiti-Littéraire.* His work is generally sad and full of half-concealed personal griefs.

Writings: Poetry: *5 Poèmes de reconnaissance,* Port-au-Prince, 1961; *Germination d'espoir,* Port-au-Prince, 1962; *Clef du Soleil* (pamphlet, reverse side of which bears the poem "Promesse," by René Philoctète), 1963; *Le Chanson de Roland,* Montréal, Nouvelle Optique, 1978.

Biographical/Critical Sources: Maurice Lubin's "Five Haitian Poets" in *Young Poetry of the Americas,* Washington, D.C., Pan American Union, 1968.

MORISSEAU-LEROY, Félix

(see under **Félix Morisseau LEROY**)

MORPEAU, Louis

b. January 28, 1895, Cayes, Haiti; d. August 30, 1929.

Storywriter, poet, anthologist, teacher, journalist.

Morpeau was educated in Cayes and Port-au-Prince at the Lycée Pétion. He was appointed teacher at the Lycée Pétion and was Sous-Inspecteur des Ecoles of Port-au-Prince.

He went to France and was a successful ambassador of Haitian culture, for he delivered a great number of lectures on Haitian writers.

Morpeau was an active journalist and contributed to many newspapers and magazines in Haiti and in France.

Writings: Stories: *L'enterrement de la merlasse; conte,* Paris, Ed. de La Vallée d'Aoste, 1924; others in various journals.

Essays: *Pages de jeunesse et de foi,* Port-au-Prince, Impr. du Sacré-Coeur, 1919; *Une oeuvre de pitié sociale par le Comité de la Caisse des Ecoles de Port au Prince, Impr. du Sacré*-Coeur, 1919.

Anthologies (Editor): *Anthologie haitienne des poètes contemporains (1904-1920),* Port-au-Prince, Impr. Aug. A. Héraux, 1920; *Anthologie d'un siècle de poèsie haitienne (1817-1925), avec une ètude sur la muse haïtienne d'expression créole,* preface by M. Fortunat Strowski, Paris, Bossard, 1925.

Poetry: in various journals and mss., "Le ecueil pour Madelaine" and "Au gré de la antaisie."

NAGO, Jules

. ca. 1944, Lomé, Togo (associated with Guyane).

Playwright, accountant, professor (Economics and Business Administration).

Jules Nago was born to a farming family near Lomé, Togo, where he received his primary and secondary schooling at a Catholic missionary school. In 1964, after the death of his mother, he went to France or further study where he met a young French Guyanese student whom he maried in 1967. After a brief interruption, he finished his studies in accounting. He now esides in Cayenne (Mont Joly), Guyane.

Jules Nago has enjoyed writing since econdary school when he won a number of first prizes for French composition. He has chosen to write for the theatre since, in his opinion, it is the literary genre whose message is most readily accessible to the people. (Nevertheless, he has a couple of novels in progress.) Mr. Nago uses his alent very effectively to confront and expose the injustices of society and to awaken his countrymen to the dangers of cultural subjugation and by so doing, he eels that he is contributing to the building of a free society.

Writings: Plays: *Homo, Qui es?* Cayenne, Paul Laporte, 1973; *Le Mirage,* Cayenne, Paul Laporte, 1973.

NAJAC, Paul E.

. April 26, 1928, Port-de-Paix, Haiti.

Poet, storywriter, essayist.

Najac was educated in Port-au-Prince. His poetry is ironic, whimsical. His one voume, *Amours délices et orgues* (1949), takes its name from a "curiosity of French well known to students of that language," according to some commentators.

Writings: Poetry: *Amours, délices et orgues,* Port-au-Prince, Impr. du Séminaire Adventiste, 1949, 1965.

NAU, Auguste Théodore Eugène

b. 1814, Port-au-Prince; d. 1887, Port-au-Prince.

Playwright, agronomist, economist.

Nau started his schooling in Port-au-Prince and completed his education in France where he studied agronomy.

When he returned to Haiti he was a member of the Committee of Public Education and became chief editor of *La Gazette Agricole.*

Writings: Agronomy: *L'influence de l'agriculture sur la civilisation des peuples,* Port-au-Prince, Impr. J. J. Audain, 1874; *Le Bassin Général, ses canaux et ses annexes,* Port-au-Prince, Impr. Enélus Robin, 1880; *Agronomie et Agriculture en Haiti; suivies de la deuxième édition de "L'influence de l'agriculture sur la civilisation des peuples,"* Paris, A. Guyot, Ed., Janvier, 1880; *"De l'influence de l'agriculture sur la civilisation des peuples,"* précédé de *"Agronomie et Agriculture en Haiti,"* Paris, A. Guyot, 1886.

Play: *La fiancée de Léogâne; drame en cinq actes et en vers,* Port-au-Prince, T. Bouchereau, Imp-Ed., 1857.

Biographical/Critical Sources: Robert Cornevin, *Le théâtre haitien, des origines à nos jours,* Quebec, Ed. Léméac, 1973, pp. 93-94; Un article de *La Revue de la Ligue de la Jeunesse Haitienne,* Nov. 1916, No. 10, p. 166.

NAU, Emile Auguste

(or, frequently, **Baron NAU**)

b. February 26, 1812, Port-au-Prince, Haiti; d. February 27, 1860, Port-au-Prince.

Journalist, historian.

Emile Nau received a good education in Port-au-Prince. He practiced journalism, published articles in *Le Républicain* and *L'Union,* whose editor was his brother, Ignace. He himself founded in 1858 *La République.* Active in public affairs, he was a frequent contributor to many journals and his writings on the Amerindians were almost the earliest in Haiti. He early called for a national literature and wanted the old gods and goddesses of classical poetry outlawed from the Haitian landscape. Though he did not accept the idea of Créole being used as a literary language, he wanted Haitian French to be more natural and spontaneous for:

> *la langue française, dans nos écrits et dans notre conversation, a toujours l'air d'une langue acquise; un des bienfaits de la civilisation sera de la naturaliser chez nous . . . peut-être que la France ne lira pas sans plaisir sa langue quelque peu brunie sous les tropiques.*
> (as reported in *L'Union,* Nov. 16, 1837)

Writings: History: *Histoire des caciques d'Haiti,* Port-au-Prince, Impr. T. Bouchereau, Impr.-Ed. 1855; second edition published by Ducis Viard, Paris, G. Guérin et cie, 1894; third edition with Panorama, 1967; *Réclamation par les affranchis des droits civils et politiques, Ogé et Chavannes,* Port-au-Prince, T. Bouchereau, 1840.

Literary History: *Littérature,* Port-au-Prince, Impr. J. Courtois, n.d.

Biographical/Critical Sources: Pradel Pompilus et Frères de l'Instruction Chrétienne, *Manuel Illustré d'Histoire de la littérature haitienne,* Port-au-Prince, Ed. H. Deschamps, 1961, pp. 80-84; Ghislain Gouraige, *Histoire de la littérature haitienne,* Port-au-Prince, Impr. N. A. Théodore, 1960, pp. 461-462.

NAU, Ignace

b. July 13, 1808, Port-au-Prince, Haiti; d. 1845, Port-au-Prince.

Poet, journalist, storywriter.

Nau's early studies were in Haiti at Institution Jonathas Granville, but he took advanced education in New York at the Institution Catholique, a rare event in his day.

When he went back to Port-au-Prince he spent many years as an employee at the Ministry of Finance. After his wife's death in 1836, he sought relief by a sojourn in Paris which influenced him toward the heady romanticism of the French capital.

He was managing editor of journals such as *Le Républicain* (1836) and *L'Union* (1837) where he published several poems. He was a contributor of *La Revue des Colonies,* an anti-slavery journal which appeared in Paris, his work being the earliest Haitian poetry in the new style. In 1839, depressed, he retired to the country until his death.

Ignace Nau pioneered a national literature and the "1836" group said in *L'Union* (November 6, 1836):

> *La source de l'inspiration pour nous est en nous et chez nous. . . . Célébrer Haiti, ses fastes et ses gloires militaires, évoquer ses nuits intenses et son ciel profond, ses superstitions et ses légendes, le charme ardent de ses femmes et la ruse finaude de ses paysans, le tout en un français le plus possible pittoresque et coloré.*

He paid tribute to the founder of Haiti, writing:

Dessalines . . . à ce nom, ami
découvrons-nous!
Je me sens le coeur battre à fléchir
les genoux
Et jaillir à ce nom un sang chaud dans
mes veines.

His stories, mostly written in 1836, are considered extraordinarily good by Haitian critics.

Poems and stories by Ignace Nau have not been collected or published in book form.

Writings: Poetry: works in *L'Union* (Jan. 18, 1838); *Le Republicain* (Sep. 1, 1836, Sep. 15, 1836) and in various anthologies, *Le livre de Marie,* etc.

Story: "Un histoire de brigands" (a personal narrative of his experience in Santo Domingo); "Celestina" and "Isalina."

Biographical/Critical Sources: Paul Verna, "Ignace Nau," in *Conjonction,* (Oct. 1949), pp. 35-37; See comments on Nau's stories by Liautaud Ethéart in *Miscellanées,* pp. 10f; and Duraciné Vaval in his *Histoire de la littérature haitienne,* pp. 135-141; Frère Raphaël, *Les pionniers,* Port-au-Prince, Impr. ONEC, 1967.

NEMOURS, Alfred Auguste

(usually called **Général NEMOURS**)
b. 1883, Cap-Haitien, Haiti; d. 1955, Paris.
Historian, storywriter, diplomat.

Son of Nemours Auguste, Alfred Nemours began his education at the local primary school of Cap-Haitien, then went to Paris for his secondary studies, certified by a baccalaureate ès-lettres. In 1902, he entered France's great military academy, Saint-Cyr, and was commissioned lieutenant in 1904. As his classmates gained higher ranks, he also received a promotion, finally reaching the rank of general.

When Nemours returned to Haiti he was named Commandant of the Commune of Trou, 1910-1912, and afterwards he was Commandant of the Arrondissement of Grand'Anse in 1914 and Commandant d'Arrondissement du Cap-Haitien in 1915, with the title of General.

In political life, Nemours was appointed Conseiller d'Etat in 1918, becoming Secretary and President du Conseil d'Etat (1922-1925). He served as Minister Plenipotentiary of Haiti to Paris and Delegate of Haiti to the late League of Nations (1926-1930).

Senator of the Republic (1938) and Secretary of State of Interior (1940), Nemours was eventually named Ambassador of Haiti to the Vatican.

Nemours was a passionate lover of France, for he could write: "la plus grande patrie de l'Homme noir, c'est la France" in his *Ma campagne française,* 1925, during the middle years of the long American occupation of Haiti.

As a noted speaker at the League of Nations in Geneva, Nemours pronounced these words soon to become well-known on the question of the invasion of Ethiopia by Mussolini's fascist troops, "Craignez d'être un jour l'Ethiopie de quelqu'un."

All his researches were dedicated to Toussaint Louverture: " For 33 years, he said in 1945, "I have been studying Toussaint Louverture and that famous personality has kept in the center of all my historical research."

In his *Histoire militaire de la guerre de l'Indépendance,* he indicated that

> "*. . . cette guerre n'a pas été seulement une deuxième révolte de Spartacus, plus heureuse que la première, mais une guerre coloniale, conduite avec méthode, plan, décision et rapidité par des hommes dont les généraux se sont révélés de grands chefs.*

Writings: Story: *Princesses créoles . . .* preface by Claude Farrère, Paris, Nancy-Strasbourg, Berger-Levrault, 1927.

Essays: *Bibliothèque du Docteur et du Général Nemours,* Port-au-Prince, Impr. V. Valcin, s.d.; *Ma campagne française,* Port-au-Prince, Impr. du l'Abeille, 1919.

Political: *Les Borno dans l'Histoire d'Haiti,* Port-au-Prince, Impr. Nationale, 1926.

History: *Histoire de la captivité et de la mort de Toussaint Louverture; notre pèlerinage au Fort de Joux; avec des documents inédits,* Paris, Berger-Levrault, 1929; *Histoire de la famille et de la descendance de Toussaint Louverture,* Port-au-Prince, Impr. de l'Etat, 1945; *Histoire des relations internationales de Toussaint Louverture avec des documents inédits,* Port-au-Prince, Impr. du Collège Vertières, 1945; *Histoire militaire de la guerre d'Indépendance de Saint Domingue,* 2 vols., Paris, Ed. Berger-Levrault, 1925, 1928; *Les premiers citoyens et les premiers députés noirs et de couleur; la loi du 4 avril 1792, ses précédents, sa première application,* Port-au-Prince, Impr. de l'Etat, 1941; *Quelques jugements sur Toussaint Louverture,* Port-au-

Prince, Impr. V. Valcin, 1938; *Toussaint Louverture fonde à Saint Domingue la liberté et l'égalité; avec des documents inédits,* Port-au-Prince, Impr. du Collège Vertières, 1945; *Haiti et la guerre de l'Indépendance Américaine,* Port-au-Prince, Impr. H. Deschamps, 1952.

International: *La charte des Nations-Unies,* Port-au-Prince, Impr. H. Deschamps, 1945; *Craignons d'être un jour l'Ethiopie de quelqu'un; conflit Italo-Ethiopien 1935,* Port-au-Prince, Impr. du Collège Vertières, 1945.

NEPTUNE, Louis

b. November 11, 1927, Jacmel, Haiti.
Poet, scientist.

Louis Neptune was educated in Port-au-Prince, after he had studied at the school of the Christian Brothers of Jacmel. He became a teacher, and began to contribute his verse to various journals, including *La Ruche* and its successor *La Nouvelle Ruche.* After the revolution of 1946 he emigrated to Venezuela where he studied agronomy. When the University of Caracas was closed, he went to Brazil where he took a degree. His main interest is in electronics, a subject he studied in Austria. He has settled in Brazil with his Brazilian wife.

Writings: Poetry: *Gouttes de fiel,* preface by Jean F. Brierre, Port-au-Prince, Ed. H. Deschamps, 1947; his poem "Ma vie" appears in N.R. Shapiro's *Negritude: Black Poetry from the Caribbean,* New York, October House, 1970, and several more poems appear in the anthology, *Panorama de la poèsie haitienne,* by C. Saint-Louis and Maurice A. Lubin, Port-au-Prince, Ed. H. Deschamps, 1950.

NIGER, Emilius

(pseudonym for **Emile ROUMER**)

NIGER, Paul

(pseudonym for **Albert BEVILLE**)
b. December 21, 1915, Basse-Terre, Guadeloupe; d. June 22, 1962.
Poet, novelist.

Niger completed his humanities studies at the Lycée Carnot, Pointe-à-Pitre, and then went to Paris for further study at the Ecole de la France d'Outre-Mer where so many colonial officers were trained. There he met Guy Tirolien and other members of the Paris negritude movement in the Latin Quarter. Niger's verse is violent and tender by turns and though he never became a full follower or user of negritudist ideas, Africa is important in much of his work.

Paul Niger
LES GRENOUILLES
DU
MONT KIMBO
Collection: ECRIVAINS NOIRS DU MONDE

For a considerable period he was a French colonial official in Dahomey, West Africa and it was on vacation during a Guadeloupe home visit that he died in a plane crash just outside of Pointe-à-Pitre in Guadeloupe. Earlier, he had taken an active part in the Antillan-Guyane independence movement. For his efforts, he was downgraded in the colonial service to the lowest possible rung despite his long

his heroic actions in the French underground during the Nazi occupation of France. His pseudonym *Niger,* taken from the great African river, may be due to his last poem "Je n'aime pas l'Afrique" having been written and dated "Bamako," October 1944, for Bamako is a great riverine port on the Niger.

Writings: Poetry: *Initiation,* Paris, Seghers, 1954; poems in many anthologies, including Leopold S. Senghor's *Anthologie de la nouvelle poèsie nègre et malgache,* Paris, Presses Universitaires de France, 1948, and 1972; also: in *Black Orpheus,* Ibadan, Nigeria (May 1958); and in *Présence Africaine* (Dec. 1959-Jan. 1960).

Novels: *Les puissants,* Paris, Ed. du Scorpion, 1956; *Les Grenouilles du Mont-Kimbo* (Series: Ecrivains noirs du monde), Lausanne, Switzerland, Eds. de la Cité, *1964, and Paris, Maspéro,* 1964.

Essay: "L'assimilation, forme suprême du colonialisme," in *Esprit,* No. 305 (Apr. 1962), pp. 518-532.

NOUS-TERRE, Jean

(pseudonym for **Gilbert GRATIANT**)

NUMA, Edgar Nérée

b. May 12, 1881, Cayes, Haiti; d. April 17, 1979, New York City.
Novelist, poet, biographer, politician.

Numa attended schools in Cayes and came to Port-au-Prince to study at the Petit Séminaire Collège Saint-Martial. He graduated from the law school in Port-au-Prince. He taught at the secondary school for girls in Cayes and later was appointed to the Lycée Philippe Guerrier of Cayes. He also practiced law and was a professor at the free law school of that city.

Numa was named secretary to the Haitian legation in Washington, D.C. and was later sent to Paris. Elected Député of Cayes, he ran unsuccessfully for the presidency of Haiti in 1946. He is now living in New York.

Writings: Poetry: *La Corbeille, poèmes* (in collaboration with Frédéric Burr-Reynaud, Dominique Hippolyte, Lys Ambroise and Luc Grimard), Port-au-Prince, Impr. du Collège Vertières, 1943.

Biography: *Antoine Simon et la fatalité historique,* New York, 1974.

Novel: *Clercina Destiné,* New York, E. Cabella French Printing, 1975.

ORVILLE, Xavier

b. ca. 1948, Martinique.
Novelist.

Orville began his schooling at home but completed it in France. He has been a teacher and resident in Toulouse since taking his university degree.

Writings: Novel: *Délice et le fromager,* Paris, Grasset, 1977.

OSENAT, Pierre

b. October 20, 1908, Fécamp, France (of Martinican parents).
Poet, novelist, physician.

Born in Fécamp where his family was living temporarily (his father was from Lorrain, a region of Martinique), Osenat attended the Lycée Schoelcher in Fort-de-France and then went to France to study medicine. He became professor of medicine and served also as a physician for the Red Cross.

Despite his medical career, Osenat has long been interested in literature and has published many poems. He won a poetry prize in 1962 and the José Maria Heredia Prize in 1965.

Writings: Poetry: *Passage des vivants,* preface by J. Audiberti, Paris, Sources, 1962 (winner of the prize José-Maria de Hérédia of l'Académie Française, published in very limited edition); *Chants de mer,* 1965; *Chants des Antilles,* Lyon, A. Henneuse, 1968; *Chants des îles,* 1968; *Cantate à l'île de Sein,* 1970; *Cantate à Arcachon,* 1970.

Narrative: *Cahiers de l'H.O.E., chronique,* 1940.
Novels: *L'interne de garde est mort,* 1952; *Eloge de Clavé,* 1958; *La chronique d'un lancer,* 1967.

OTHILY, Georges

b. January 7, 1944, Cayenne, Guyane.
Poet, shortstory writer, essayist, notary, and businessman.

Georges Othily received his secondary schooling at the Lycée Félix Eboué in Cayenne and at the Lycée Pierre d'Ailly in Compiègne, France. Being particularly interested in the world of business, he did further study at the "Ecole de Notariat" in Paris. He presently resides in Cayenne where he is a notary and owns a real estate agency.

Mr. Othily was very active in the anti-colonialist student movement in Paris, and was President of the Paris chapter of "l'Association des Etudiants Guyanais" for three years.

Harmonie d'Ebène, his first volume of poetry, was created for the occasion of the 1975 "Festival Culturel Antilles-Guyane" which was held in Cayenne. The poems of *Harmonie d'Ebène* demonstrate the author's great concern for the Guyanese people, their cultural integrity, and their past and present problems as well as their hoped for future as a sovereign nation.

Writings: Poetry: *Harmonie d'Ebène,* Fort-de-France, Société d'Imprimerie Martiniquaise, 1975.
In Preparation: a series of short stories; a collection of poems; an essay.

PADOLY, Yves

b. June 10, 1937, Fort-de-France, Martinique.
Poet.

Padoly attended the Lycée Schoelcher in Fort-de-France. He is a teacher and has published two collections of his verse.

Writings: Poetry: *Le Missel noir,* Monte-Carlo, Poètes de notre temps, 1965; *Poèmes pour adultes.*

PAILLERE, Madeleine Dominique

(pseudonym: **FRAENIEL**)

b. February 23, 1916, Port-au-Prince, Haiti.
Poet, storywriter, art critic, teacher.

Madeleine Dominique received her education at the Pensionnat-Saint-Rose de Lima. She has served as teacher and then principal at the College Cours Amédée Brun. A member of many art juries, she served on the Esso Committee judging Haitian painting with the American critic Selden Rodman and has published her scholarly and critical pieces in such journals as *Conjonction* and *Le Nouvelliste* under the name of her husband, Pierre Paillère. For many years she has given the program "Feuilles à feuilles" ("Leaves to Leaves"), a daily summary of events on Radio Haiti-Inter.

Writings: Art Criticism: *Hyppolite-Price,* 1976.
General Essay: *Mentalité haitienne et Précatéchese,* Port-au-Prince, 1977.
Stories: (collection in créole): *Inselbadjo* (Stories for Singing), Port-au-Prince, n.d.; *La Phalange,* 1978, n.d.

PAPAILLER, Hubert

(pseudonym: **Jean Hubert MARIAMOUR**)

b. April 24, 1916, Gonaives, Haiti.
Poet, storywriter, teacher, priest.

Hubert Papailler studied at the School of Christian Brothers in Gonaïves. He went to Port-au-Prince to enter the Apostolic School and was ordained a priest. He has been vicar in Petite-Rivière de l'Artibonite, Ferrier, and other localities. He became Minister of National Education and later was named Ambassador of Haiti to Uruguay. At present Papailler is teaching at Kentucky University.

Writings: Poetry: *Fleurs d'ombre et paillettes d'écumes,* Canada, Séminaire des Saints Apôtres, 1954; *Coup d'ailes,* Montreal, Impr. Saint-Joseph, 1956.

Politics: *Le Bicolore, symbole de l'Unité nationale,* Port-au-Prince, 1959.

Novel: *Les laboureurs de la mer,* Canada, 1959.

General: Unpub. Ph.D. diss., "La Poèsie indigène des Caraibes: Une prise de conscience des poètes de langue Française," University of Kentucky, 1973.

PAPILLON, Pierre

b. ca. 1927, Port-au-Prince, Haiti.
Novelist, storywriter.

Papillon was educated in Port-au-Prince and is employed in his family's business.

Writings: Novels: *L'exilé du ciel,* Port-au-Prince, Eds. H. Deschamps, 1949; *L'Ame qui Meurt,* Port-au-Prince, Les Presses Libres, 1950.

PARET, Timothée L.J.

b. April 21, 1887, Jérémie, Haiti; d. September 20, 1942, Port-au-Prince.
Poet, essayist, biographer, teacher, public official.

Paret was educated in Jérémie. After his schooling, he was a teacher, and later Sub-Inspector of Schools. In 1911, he graduated from Law School. He was chief of the division in the department of Interior and was named Commissaire du Gouvernement, près le tribunal Civil de Port-au-Prince. He was also a councillor of State and Minister of Justice.

His essays and verse appeared in many journals and magazines. André Liautaud and Philippe Thoby-Marcelin have criti-

cized Paret's over-facile rhymes (âme-flammes) and banal themes.

Writings: Poetry: *Janine, essai de nouvelle en vers* (a story in verse), Port-au-Prince, n.d.; second edition, Port-au-Prince, H. Amblard, 1906; *L'âme vibrante, amour tragique; lueurs sereines,* Paris, Albert Messein, 1913; second edition, Paris, Jouve, 1929; *Fleurs détachées; poèsies,* Port-au-Prince, Impr. de l'Abeille, 1917; *Lueurs sereines; journal rétrospectif d'un célibataire; Jeanine, essai de nouvelle en vers; précédés d'une préface de Mr Edmond Laforest,* Port-au-Prince, Impr. H. Amblard, 1908; *Nouvelle floraison, poèmes,* Angers, Soc. Française d'Imprimerie, 1927.

Essays: *Dans la mêlee ... pensées, conférences, discours, etc. (1916-1931),* Paris, Jouve et Cie, 1932; *Eden tropical; Tels qu'ils sont* (saynètes), 1913; *Jérémie et ses environs; Le Drapau Haitien; La Ligue du drapeau.*

Critical-biography: "Anthime Merlet et son oeuvre poètique," and "Edmond Laforest."

Biographical/Critical Sources: André Liautaud and Philippe Thoby-Marcelin: "En marge de nos aînés," in *La Nouvelle Ronde,* Port-au-Prince (June 1925); Ghislain Gouraige, *Histoire de la littérature haitienne,* Port-au-Prince, Impr. N.A. Théodore, 1960, pp. 169-171; Pradel Pompilus et les Frères de l'Instruction Chrétienne, *Manuel illustré d'histoire de la littérature haitienne,* 1950.

PATIENT, Serge

b. March 24, 1934, Cayenne, Guyane.
Poet, playwright, teacher.

Serge Patient completed his secondary schooling at the Lycée Félix Eboué in Cayenne. He holds the following academic degrees: "Licence ès-lettres" (Spanish) and the "Diplôme d'Etudes Supérieures," both from the University of Paris. He was named Professor of Spanish at the Lycée Félix Eboué in 1958, "Principal de CES de Kourou" in 1970, and then Headmaster of the Lycée de Kourou in 1973.

Professor Patient is a charter member of the "Union du Peuple Guyanais" political party; and he was elected "Conseiller Général" from the canton of Kourou in 1973.

The poetry of Serge Patient, like that of his countryman Elie Stéphenson, strives to express a specifically Guyanese reality. In this search for identity, Serge Patient's poetry evolves from a defensive assumption of negritude as a counterforce to the assimilative and consequently destructive force of the colonizer, to a realization and acceptance of the fact of his mixed cultural heritage. His verse is often prose/poetry and filled with evocations to local and ancient African deities or powers.

Writings: Poetry: *Le Mal du pays,* Monaco, Eds. Regain, 1968; collection, "Cayenne en mon miroir," in ms.; and individual poems in collections such as *New Writing in the Caribbean,* A.J. Seymour, ed., Georgetown, Guyana, 1972.

Stories: *Le Nègre du gouverneur,* Paris, P. J. Oswald, 1972; and in George I. Brachfeld's *Lumière noire,* New York, Macmillan, 1972.

Biographical/Critical Sources: Bridget Jones, "Serge Patient and Le Mal du Pays," in *French Caribbean Literature,* Black Images, Toronto, 1975, pp. 71-77.

PAUL, Cauvin L.

b. March 3, 1938, Port-de-Paix, Haiti.
Poet, literary critic, storywriter, teacher.

Cauvin L. Paul received his education in his native city, at the School of Christian Brothers and the Lycée Tertulien Guilbaud of Port-de-Paix. A scholarship was granted to him and he went to Paris where he studied Psycho-Pathology. When he returned, he graduated from the Faculty of Law of Port-au-Prince.

Paul taught at the Lycée Tertulien Guilbaud in Port-de-Paix. He came to New York in 1972 and served as French translator and proof-reader at Appleton Century Publishing House. He is now a teacher at Brandeis High School and the managing editor of the magazine *Lakansiel,* edited both in French and creole.

Writings: Poetry: *Cantilènes d'un naufragé,* Port-de-Paix, Atelier Capois-La-Mort, 1962; *Les Nouvelles Cantilènes,* Port-de-Paix, Atelier Capois-La-Mort, 1963; *Futur simple,* Port-de-Paix, Atelier Capois-La-Mort, 1964; *Bourgeon de Soleil,* Port-de-Paix, Atelier Capois-La-Mort, 1965; *En écoutant le Mistral,* Port-de-Paix, Atelier Capois-La-Mort, 1966; *Laetitia (poèmes), Port-de-Paix, 1970.*

Story: *Nuit sans Fond,* New York, printed by Presses Solidaires, 1976.

Essay: *Manuel . . . ! Un Dieu tombé,* New York, n.p., n.d. (1976).

PAUL, Emmanuel Casséus

b. July 28, 1914, Port-au-Prince, Haiti; d. ca. 1967, Port-au-Prince.
Professor, journalist, ethnologist.

Paul received his education in Port-au-Prince where he attended primary schools and the Lycée Pétion. He also was a student at the School of Ethnology where he won his diploma.

He practiced journalism and contributed to many papers such as *Haiti-Journal, Le Nouvelliste, Panorama, Optique, Bulletin d'ethnologie, Le Jour,* and *Le Matin.*

Paul was a teacher in many schools and taught at the Institute of Ethnology; and he served as the head of the Bureau of Ethnology.

Writings: Folklore: *Notes sur le folklore d'Haiti, proverbes et chansons; préface de Kléber Georges Jacob,* Port-au-Prince, Impr. N. Telhomme, 1946; *Essai d'organographie haitienne* (in collaboration with Lorimer Denis), Publication du Bureau d'Ethnologie de la République d'Haiti, Port-au-Prince, Impr. V. Valcin, 1948; *Nos chansons folkloriques et la possibilité de leur exploitation pédagogique;* Collection "Notre terre", Port-au-Prince, Impr. Les Presses Libres, 1951; *Panorama du Folklore Haitien* (Présence Africaine en Haiti), Port-au-Prince, Impr. de l'Etat, 1962.

Ethnology: *L'Ethnographie en Haiti,* Port-au-Prince, Impr. de l'Etat, 1949; *"La gaguère" ou le combat de coqs,* Port-au-Prince, 1952.

Culture: *Culture, Langue, Littérature,* Port-au-Prince, Impr. de l'Etat, 1962.

PAULTRE, Emile

b. October 31, 1910, Saint-Marc, Haiti; d. ca. 1967.
Poet, teacher, lawyer.

Paultre was educated in Port-au-Prince at the Lycée Pétion. He took his degree in the capital also.

Appointed professor at the Lycée Sténio Vincent in Saint-Marc, he later rose to become the Director.

After he served as chef de division at the Department of Interior, Paultre was named judge to the Civil Court of Port-au-Prince.

Writings: Poetry: *Le sel de la terre.*

Literary Criticism: *Essai sur Mr Price-Mars* (Prix de l'Alliance Française), preface by Etzer Vilaire, Port-au-Prince, Impr. de l'Etat, 1933; second edition, " Essai sur Mr Price Mars avec une étude complémentaire sur La vie et l'oeuvre de Mr Price Mars depuis 1930," Port-au-Prince, Ed. des Antilles, 1966.

Law: *Des restrictions de droits dans notre régime successoral; commentaires des articles du code civil qui apportent des restrictions aux droits héréditaires dans la dévolution successorale d'après la jurisprudence haitienne; à l'usage des étudiants en droit, des hommes de loi et de tous ceux qui, sans avoir fait d'études spéciales, désirent, en la matière, se renseigner, sur l'étendue de leurs droits,* Port-au-Prince, Impr. de l'Etat, 1942.

PEREIRA, Roger

b. June 20, 1932, Port-au-Prince, Haiti.
Poet, teacher.

After completing his early schooling in Port-au-Prince, Pereira went to France to study philosophy and geography. He has since taught in Haiti, France, Tunisia, and Zaire and is presently a teacher in Canada. His one collection of poetry was *Les Galops de Dune* (Sherbrooke, Eds. Naaman, 1977).

PEREZ, Jeanne

b. ca. 1918, Port-au-Prince, Haiti; d. October 4, 1957.
Journalist, novelist, playwright.

Perez, sister-in-law of Jean Price-Mars, received her education at the Institution of Mme Auguste Paret and was tutored by many teachers.

An ardent feminist, she helped to build many associations in order to obtain civil and political rights for women. She was a founding member of Ligue Féminine d'Action Sociale with Cléante Desgraves Valcin, Madeleine Sylvain Bouchereau and Amélie Laroche. She was chief editor of *La voix des Femmes* and she later founded the journal, *La Semeuse.*

Writings: Essay: *La femme, ce qu'elle est, son action à travers les âges, son avenir (1ère partie),* Port-au-Prince, 1948.

Tales: *Taina et mes amis; miettes de souvenirs,* Port-au-Prince, Impr. du Collège Vertières, n.d.

Play: *Sanite Belair; drame historique en trois tableaux,* Pétionville, Ed. de La Semeuse, 1942.

Novel: *La mansarde,* Collection La Semeuse, Port-au-Prince, Impr. du Séminaire Adventiste, 1950.

PERRIER, Rose-Marie

(see under married name: **Rose-Marie Perrier CASIAS**)

PERSE, Saint-John

(see under **SAINT-JOHN PERSE**)

PETION, Alexandre Sabès

b. April 2, 1776, Port-au-Prince, Haiti; d. March 29, 1818, Port-au-Prince.
Soldier, statesman, first President of Haiti.

Son of a white father and a light-skinned mother, Pétion was born a free man ("un affranchi" as they said in the colony). His primary education by the teacher Boisgirard was of a modest sort, and he apprenticed to a goldsmith. At 18 years, interested in artillery, he became a soldier. He fought with the class of freed men for their civil and political rights. He was forced to go to France when General André Rigaud, his chief and commander of the South Department, was defeated by Toussaint Louverture during the war in the South. He returned to Saint Domingue with the military expedition led by Victor Emmanuel Leclerc as Commander-in-Chief of the force and Captain-General of the colony. Jean Jacques Dessalines, Alexandre Pétion, Henri Christophe, Clerveaux and all the rebel leaders, negroes and mulattoes were forced to unify their efforts if they were to know victory. The country became independent January 1, 1804, and the name of Saint Domingue was changed to Haiti. General Pétion served as commander of West Department and after Emperor Dessalines' death (October 17, 1806), Pétion was elected President of the Republic of Haiti in 1807 and was reelected in 1811 and 1815. He died in office.

Writings: Letter: *Réponse du Général Pétion au Général Henry Christophe sur les calomnies insérées contre lui dans ses proclamations des 18 et 24 Décembre 1806,* Port-au-Prince, Impr. de Fourcand, n.d.

Biographical/Critical Sources: Pièces relatives à la correspondance de MM. les Commissaires de S.M. très chrétienne, et du président d'Haiti, précédées d'une proclamation au peuple et à l'armée, Port-au-Prince, Impr. du Gouvernement, 1816; Joseph St-Rémy: *Pétion et Haiti. Etude monographique et historique,* Paris, 5 Vols., Chez l'auteur et Auguste Durand, 1854, 1854, 1855, 1857, 1857; second edition, Port-au-Prince, chez François Dalencour, in one volume, 1956; Saladin Lamour, Sénateur de la République, *Justification de la conduite politique d'Alexandre Pétion, de son vivant, Président de la République d'Haiti, et réfutation raisonnée des calomnies atroces lancées contre lui dans l'ouvrage d'un contemporain,* Port-au-Prince, Impr. T. Bouchereau, n.d.; François Dalencour: *Alexandre Pétion devant l'humanité. Alexandre Pétion et Simon Bolivar, Haiti et l'Amérique. Suivis de l'Expédition de Bolivar par le sénateur Marion aîné,* Port-au-Prince, Chez l'auteur, 1928; François Dalencour: *La fondation de la République d'Haiti par Alexandre Pétion,* Port-au-Prince, chez l'auteur, 1944; *Francisco de Miranda et Alexandre Pétion. L'expédition de Miranda, le premier effort de libération hispano-américaine, le premier vagissement du Panaméricanisme,* Port-au-Prince, chez l'auteur, 1955. Also: Louis Emile Elie: *Alexandre Pétion et l'opposition du Sénat;* Ext. Paper "Le Temps" (Jan. 31, Feb. 1, 2, 4, 5, 6, 1929), typed ms. only; Dantès Bellegarde, *Pétion et Bolivar,* Special issue of Pan American Union on Simon Bolivar, 1930, pp. 56-67, Washington, D.C., Union Panaméricaine; Hector Garcia Chuecos: *Páginas de historia nacional: el Capitan General Nord y el Presidente Petion;* Extract from "El Universal," Caracas, (Dec. 30, 1932-Mar. 23, 1933); Luis Augusto Cuervo: *Bolivar y Pétion. Conferencia leida en el Salon de Actos Publicos de la Academia Colombiana de Historia, el dia 9 de Agosto de 1937,* Bogota, Editorial El Grafico, 1937. Also: in *Revista de la Sociedad Bolivariana de Venezuela,* "Pétion," vol. XIII, No. 41, (Dec. 17, 1953), Caracas, pp. 270-274; Paul Verna: *Pétion y Bolivar; Cuarenta anos (1790-1830) de relaciones haitiano-venezolanas y su aporte a la emancipacion de Hispanoamerica,* Caracas, Impr. Nacional, 1969.

PHELPS, Anthony

b. August 25, 1928, Port-au-Prince, Haiti.
Poet, novelist, journalist, storywriter, critic, play director.

After he was educated at the Institution of Saint Louis de Gonzague, Phelps went to the United States where he studied chemistry at Seton Hall College of New Jersey, and ceramics and photography in Montreal, Canada.

Returning to Haiti, he worked with SCTRH (Service of Technical Cooperation of Water Resources) and he founded with four other poets (Davertige, Serge Legagneur, Roland Morisseau and René Philoctète) the group of "Haiti-Littéraire" and its journal, *Semences.*

Working as a journalist and radio commentator, he ran afoul of authorities for his political activity and was expelled, forced to take up residence in Canada.

Phelps' stage work began with the group "Prismes" which he had founded in Haiti before his exile; he has done several radio sketches for Montreal radio and has recorded interviews and plays, and poetry readings with his recording company, "Disques Coumbites."

Writings: Poetry: *Eté,* Collection Haiti-Littéraire, Port-au-Prince, Impr. N.A. Théodore, 1960; *Présence,* Collection Haiti-Littéraire, Port-au-Prince, 1961; *Eclats de silence,* (Collection Haiti-Littéraire), Port-au-Prince, Art Graphique Press, 1962; *Points Cardinaux, (poèmes),* Montreal, Holt, Rinehart, Winston, 1966; *Mon pays que voici,* followed by *Les Dits du fou-aux cailloux,* Honfleur, P.J. Oswald, 1968.

Recording: *Mon pays que voici . . .* recorded on Disque Coumbite label with other poems of Phelps', as read by him; disque entitled *Pierrot le noir,* from poems in various collections and journals, including *Conjonction, Nouvelle Optique,* etc., and *Motifs pour le temps saisonnier* (poems recited by Phelps), Productions Caliban (Montreal, 1976); ed. Paris, P. J. Oswald, 1976.

Stories: *Et moi je suis une île,* Montreal, Ed. Léméac, 1973.

Novels: *Moins l'infini,* Paris, Ed. Français Réunis, 1973; *Mémoire en colin-maillard,* Montreal, Eds. Nouvelle Optique, 1976.

Play: *Le conditionnel,* Montreal, Holt, Rinehart and Winston, 1968.

Biographical/Critical Sources: Maurice A. Lubin, "Quelques poètes haitiens de la jeune génération," in *Americas,* in English, Spanish

and Portuguese (Jan. and Feb., 1965); Robert Cornevin, *Le théâtre haitien, des origines à nos jours,* Montreal, Ed. Léméac, 1973. Also see: Lubin's essay, "Five Haitian Poets," in *Young Poetry of the Americas,* Washington, D.C., Pan American, 1968.

PHILOCTETE, Raymond

b. June 5, 1925, Jérémie, Haiti.
Poet, essayist.

Raymond Philoctète was educated in Jérémie and Port-au-Prince. He teaches in several schools of Port-au-Prince and he is also a regular contributor to *Le Nouvelliste.*

Writings: Poetry: *Voix dans le soir, poèmes,* Port-au-Prince, Impr. La Semeuse, 1945.

Essay: *Minichronique,* Port-au-Prince, Eds. Fardin, 1976.

PHILOCTETE, René

b. November 16, 1932, Jérémie, Haiti.
Poet, novelist, critic, playwright.

René Philoctète was educated in Port-au-Prince. He started teaching at the Collège

Fernand Prosper, and he is now the director of his own college. He began to contribute poetry and criticism to *Semences,* the leading literary journal founded by Anthony Phelps, Davertige, Serge Legagneur (and Philoctète himself) as a voice for the newest generation of Haitian artists. His work is strongly influenced by the French poets Appolinaire, Aragon, Eluard, and the much earlier work of Rimbaud.

Writings: Poetry: *Saison des hommes,* Port-au-Prince, Collection Samba, 1960; *Margha,* Port-au-Prince, Art Graphique Press, 1961; *Les tambours du soleil,* Port-au-Prince, Impr. des Antilles, 1962; *Promesse,* in folding pages, Collection Haiti Littéraire, 1963; *Et Coetera,* 1967; *Ces îles qui marchent,* collection spirale, 1969, and second edition, Port-au-Prince, Ed. Fardin, 1974. Also see: *Les escargots,* (1965), below.

Plays: *Rose morte* (with Gérard Rézil), performed February and March, 1964; *Boukman ou le Rejeté des enfers* (with Gérard Rézil), performed June, 1964; *Les escargots (poetry and theater),* performed in August and September, 1965; *Monsieur de Vastey,* Port-au-Prince, Ateliers Fardin, 1975.

Novel: *Le Huitième Jour* (won the Prize to the literary contest, Visions de l'An 2000), Port-au-Prince, Editions of 2000 Year, 1973.

PIERRE, Claude C.

b. ca. 1942, Corail, Haiti.
Poet.

After schooling in Haiti, Pierre emigrated to Canada where he published three collections of his verse: *A haute voix et à genoux,* 1965; *Coucou rouge,* 1973; and *Tourne ma toupie* (with) *Oeil,* 1974.

PIERRE, Louis Marie Benoît

(see under pseudonym: **Dieudonné FARDIN**)

PIERRE-LOUIS, Ulysse

b. January 20, 1925, San Juan de la Maguana, Dominican Republic.
Poet, storywriter, teacher.

Pierre-Louis studied at the Lycée Pétion. He graduated from the Faculty of Law and was a professor at the Lycée Sténio Vincent of Saint-Marc, and later at the Lycée Pétion and Lycée Toussaint Louverture of Port-au-Prince. He served as Secretary General of the Local Government of Port-au-Prince.

Several of his poems are full of revolutionary ardor, especially "Torches," "Message d'espérance," and "Mendiants," published, however, only in magazines such as *Conjonction. Le Nouvelliste,* or *Le Nouveau Monde.* He is the managing editor of *Le Nouveau Monde.*

Writings: Critical Essays: *Esquisses Littéraires et critiques,* Port-au-Prince, Impr. de l'Etat, 1959.

Tales: *Sortilèges afro-haitiens: contes et légendes,* Port-au-Prince, Impr. de l'Etat, 1961; "Les amours de Thézin et de Zilia" and "Télesfort" in *Contes et Légendes des Antilles,* Paris, Fernand Nathan, 1963, pp. 173-177, 178-181.

Politics: *La Révolution Duvaliériste: Contenu doctrinal-Conquêtes et perspectives* (Prix Lorimer Denis, Eds. Administration Communale de Port-au-Prince), Port-au-Prince, Impr. de l'Etat, 1965.

PIQUION, René

b. October 19, 1908, Saint-Marc, Haiti. Physician, teacher, journalist, biographer, scholar, critic.

René Piquion was educated in Port-au-Prince at the Lycée Pétion and studied medicine. As a young man he started a career in journalism, contributing to many newspapers such as *L'Action Nationale, l'Assaut, Haiti-Journal, Le Nouvelliste, Le Réveil,* and *Le National,* and he was managing editor of *Le Nouveau Monde.*

Piquion completed his education abroad in the United States, at Columbia University and Howard University, and in Paris at the University, specializing in political science. He studied the French archival system in Paris in 1952-1953. He is a teacher and is serving as the Director of the Ecole Normale Supérieure in Port-au-Prince.

Writings: Biographies: *Langston Hughes: un chant nouveau; introduction par Arna Bontemps,* Port-au-Prince, Impr. de l'Etat, n.d. (criticism by *La Relève,* Nov. 1935), pp. 18-20; *Marian Anderson,* Port-au-Prince, Impr. H. Deschamps, 1950, (written with Jean F. Brierre; this volume contains a poem by Brierre.)

Politics: *L'actualité de Paul E. Magloire,* Port-au-Prince, Impr. H. Deschamps, 1950.

Scholarship: *Archives,* Port-au-Prince, Ed. H. Deschamps, 1954; *Crépuscule de mythes,* Port-au-Prince, Impr. de l'Etat, 1962; *Apothéose,* Port-au-Prince, Ed. H. Deschamps, 1967.

Literary-Critical Essays: *Essai sur la culture* (with Jules Blanchet), Port-au-Prince, Impr. V. Valcin, 1935; *Réveil de culture,* Port-au-Prince, Ed. H. Deschamps, 1958 (concerns his thoughts regarding the 1st Congrès des Ecrivains et Artistes Noirs et de l'Association Africaine de Culture); *Négritude,* Port-au-Prince, Impr. de l'Etat, 1961; *Manuel de négritude,* Port-au-Prince, Ed. H. Deschamps, n.d. (but 1965?); *Les "Trois Grands" de la Négritude,* Port-au-Prince, Impr. H. Deschamps, 1964; *Léon Gontran Damas, un poète de la Négritude,* Port-au-Prince, mimeo., 1964; *Ebène,* Port-au-Prince, Impr. H. Deschamps, 1976.

History: *Histoire d'Haiti à l'usage des écoles primaires (1492-1938),* Port-au-Prince, Impr. de l'Abeille, 1938 (with Love Léger).

Polemics: *Masques et portraits (Réponse à une lettre du Dr Jean Price Mars sur la question sociale et politique en Haiti,* Port-au-Prince, Presses Nationales, 1967, second edition (Price-Mars' *Lettre ouverte au Dr René Piquion,* Port-au-Prince, Ed. des Antilles, 1967, had occasioned Piquion's response).

PLACOLY, Vincent

b. January 21, 1946, Martinique. Novelist, poet.

Placoly attended the Lycée of Fort-de-France, and then the Lycée Louis-le-Grand in Paris. He studied at the Sorbonne, and then returned to teach French at Fort-de-France. He contributed articles and poems to local newspapers.

His novel *L'Eau de Mort-guildive* is a poetically expressed but realistic look at daily life in Martinique's capital of Fort-de-France. Poverty and contrasting luxury explains the novel's march to revolt and the conflict of two peoples who, though both employing French, are so different. His broadside-flyer, *La Fin douloureuse et tragique de André Aliker,* is a hybrid form of theatre and polemical leaflet with "press releases," ballads, prose comments, and poems (some of these in creole), all attacking the French colonial regime struggling on in a Martinique hypocritically masked as an "overseas *departement*" of France.

Writings: Novels: *L'Eau-de-Mort-Guildive,* Paris (Les Lettres Nouvelles), Denoel, 1973; *La vie et la mort de Marcel Gonstran,* Paris (Les Lettres Nouvelles), Denoel, 1971.

Broadside: *La Fin douloureuse et tragique de André Aliker: Schéma pour une présentation de la société coloniale* (Edition du Groupe Révolution Socialiste), Fort-de-France, Martinique, 1973.

Biographical/Critical Sources: "D'au-delà des mers: Placoly et le charme des Antilles," in *Le Monde* (Oct. 18, 1973), p. 31; review of *L'Eau-de-Mort-Guildive: Romans français* in *La Quinzaine Littéraire,* (Oct. 16-31, 1973); review of

La vie et la mort de Marcel Gonstran, by M. Charlery and Montjoly in *Acoma,* Nos. 4-5 (April 1973), pp. 193-194.

PLINVAL, Robert

b. ca. 1904, Fort-de-France, Martinique.
Poet.

Sprung from a family of teachers, Plinval wrote and published five collections of his verse from 1934 to 1944.

Writings: Poetry: *Mes poèmes,* Fort-de-France, Impr. des Arts, 1934; *Pastels,* Fort-de-France, Impr. Ferriez Elizabeth, 1935; *Rêves et réalités,* Fort-de-France, Impr. du Gouvernement, 1937; *Pour toi,* Eds. Paris-Nice, 1939; *Gouttes d'âmes,* Paris, Impr. Officielle, 1944.

POIRIE, Jean Aurele Pierre

(see under pseudonym: **Poirie de SAINT-AURELE**)

POLIUS, Joseph

b. December 21, 1942, Lamentin, Martinique.
Poet (in French and creole).

Polius' early schooling was in Lamentin and his first poetry was written at 16. He left school after taking the "Brevet" to work as a bookkeeper's apprentice. He entered military service in the French forces in 1963 and on release went to Paris to continue his studies in night-school and to work.

"Poème pour le guerillero" laments French oppression in Guadeloupe and Martinique as in this third stanza:

Ici un peuple se bat
Contre la France du crime
Contre l'oppression qui broie
Ah! mon peuple! Ah! mon hymne!

This poem comes from his first collection, *Bonheur de poche* (1968), which is dedicated, "A tous mes camarades ouvriers, à mon Pays."

All the poems are in standard French except the first, "Martinique," which is in island creole.

Cé en ti pays
tout sell
en mitan lan mé
Ki ka gadé ciel
en mitan yeux
Sans janmin
capturé soleils
en tout pitit pays
habillé épi feuille mecsihin
épi en chaque yeux-i en sépent
en pays
ki ka boué l'acid
ka mangé piment.

Writings: Poetry: in various journals, including *La Vie Africaine: Grand Ecart,* and his work is represented in *Nouvelle somme de poèsie du monde noir,* Paris, Présence Africaine, No. 57, 1966; and in N.R. Shapiro's *Negritude: Black Poetry from Africa and the Caribbean,* New York, October House, 1970; *Bonheur de poche,* Honfleur, Pierre-Jean Oswald, 1968; *Martinique debout,* Paris, L'Harmattan, 1977.

Biographical/Critical Sources: E.A. Hurley, "The temptation of cliché in the Poetry of Polius," in *French Caribbean Literature,* Toronto, Black Images, 1975, pp. 56-63.

POMMAYRAC, Alcibiade

b. November 22, 1844, Santo Domingo, Dominican Republic; d. December 4, 1908, Port-au-Prince, Haiti.
Poet, verse playwright, tradesman.

Pommayrac was born in Santo Domingo at the time both countries formed a single Republic. After the secession, he came in his childhood with his family to settle in Jacmel where he spent his entire life.

Pommayrac was very fond of poetry. He contributed to many reviews, including *La Ronde,* and *La Revue de la Société de Législation, Haiti Littéraire et Sociale.* His

"Ode à Victor Hugo" won a prize at the "Concours ouvert à Paris pour le Centenaire de la naissance de V. Hugo " (1902).

Writings: Poetry: *La dernière nuit de Toussaint Louverture; monologue en vers,* Jacmel, Typog. M. Augustin, 1877; second edition, Port-au-Prince, 1899; *Les martyrs du génie,* Port-au-Prince, Impr. J. Verrollot, 1899; *Ode à Victor Hugo,* Port-au-Prince, Impr. H. Chauvet, 1902; *Ode à Jacmel,* Port-au-Prince, n.d.; *Ode aux soldats morts pour notre Indépendance,* Jacmel, Impr. de l'Abeille, 1903; *John Brown,* Jacmel, Impr. de l'Abeille, 1904; and following dates unknown: *Ode à la mémoire d'Edmond Paul; Ode de Jacmel* (different from the similarly named ode just cited), and *Souffrir c'est vivre.*

Verse Play: *Abigail la Sunamite.*

Essays: *Réflexions sur la crise agricole, commerciale et financière d'Haiti,* Paris, Impr. Kugelmann, 1882; *Un Conseil à mons Pays,* Paris, Impr. Bernard et Cie, 1894.

Polemics: *De la nécessité absolue et de la possibilité d'abolir en Haiti les droits à l'exportation en donnant en même temps une valeur plus grande à la monnaie nationale,* Port-au-Prince, Impr. de l'Abeille, 1904.

Biographical/Critical Sources: Jean Claude, "Alcibiade Pommayrac," in *Cahiers d'Haiti* (Port-au-Prince, Dec. 1944).

POMPILUS, Pradel

b. August 5, 1914, Arcahaie, Haiti. Professor, scholar.

After primary studies in Arcahaie, Pompilus came to Port-au-Prince for his education at the Petit Séminaire Collège Saint-Martial. He attended the Faculty of Law and graduated in that field. Later, he won his doctorate-ès-lettres at the Faculty of Letters and Human Sciences of the University of Paris.

Pompilus was a teacher for a period at the Petit Séminaire Collège Saint-Martial, and served at the Lycée Pétion.

He was Undersecretary of State of the Ministry of National Education from 1950 to 1952.

Presently, Pompilus teaches at the Superior Normal School and the Military Academy and he is the principal of his own college, the Cours Secondaires.

Writings: Literary Histories: *Pages de littérature haitienne,* Port-au-Prince, Impr. de l'Etat, 1951; second edition, 1953; *Pages et études critiques de littérature haitienne,* Port-au-Prince, Impr. N.A. Théodore, 1956; *Manuel illustré d'histoire de la littérature haitienne* (in collaboration with Brother Raphael), Port-au-Prince, Ed. H. Deschamps, 1961; *Oswald Durand, études critiques et poèsies choisies,* Port-au-Prince, Impr. des Antilles, 1964; *Etzer Vilaire, études critiques et textes choisis,* Port-au-Prince, Impr. ONAAC, 1968; *Histoire de la littérature haitienne illustrée par les textes,* 3 vols. (in collaboration with Brother Raphael Berrou), Port-au-Prince, Eds. Caraïbes, 1975; *Deux Poètes indigénistes: Carl Brouard et Emile Roumer,* (in collaboration with Brother Raphael Berrou), Port-au-Prince, Eds. Caraïbes, 1976; *Louis Joseph Janvier par lui-même,* Port-au-Prince, Eds. Caraïbes, 1976.

Philology: *Destin de la langue française en Haiti,* Port-au-Prince, Impr. Les Presses Libres, 1952; *Quelques particularités grammaticales du Français parlé en Haiti,* Port-au-Prince, Impr. H. Deschamps, 1958; *La Langue Française en Haiti* (thesis for his doctorate at the Sorbonne), published by the Institut des Hautes Etudes de l'Amérique Latine, with the Centre National de la Recherche Scientifique, Paris,

1961; *Contribution à l'étude comparée du créole et du français*, Port-au-Prince, Eds. Caraibes, 1976.

PORTO, Louis

(pseudonym of **Camille ROUSSEAU**)

b. July 24, 1921, Port-Louis, Marie-Galante (part of Guadeloupe group).

Poet, teacher.

Porto was born in Marie-Galante, but his parents are from Guadeloupe. He studied in Guadeloupe and won his baccalaureate. A teacher, he has published much verse in local journals.

Writings: Poetry: *Fleurs de carême et d'hivernage*, Collection "Les Balisiers," Basse-Terre, Impr. Perfect, 1947.

POSY, Bonnard

b. January 28, 1931, Jacmel, Haiti.

Poet, novelist, essayist, lawyer.

Posy attended the Frère Clément School of the Christian Brothers and the Lycée Pinchinat in Jacmel. He later graduated from the Free Law School of Cayes.

Posy has served in many capacities in Jacmel: professor at the Lycée Pinchinat; Substitut Commissaire du Gouvernement and later Commissaire; Dean of the Civil Court of Jacmel. He is presently the Director of the Lycée Pinchinat.

As a student, Bonnard Posy wrote much verse and published, with his schoolmate, Lélio Brun, his first collection of poems, *Bouquets*, in 1948.

Writings: Poetry: *Bouquets*, with Lélio Brun, Jacmel, Atelier l'Abeille, 1948; *Les Chants du silence*, Port-au-Prince, Art Graphique Press, 1962.

Novel: *Jusqu'au bout du chemin*, Port-au-Prince, Impr. des Antilles, 1966.

Essay: *Roussan Camille, le poète d'Assaut à la Nuit* (lecture delivered Dec. 6, 1962, on 102nd anniversary of the Lycée Pinchinat), Port-au-Prince, Impr. des Antilles, 1963.

POUILH, Duraciné

b. December 16, 1826, Port-au-Prince, Haiti; d. February 5, 1902, Port-au-Prince.

Biographer, critic, grammarian.

Pouilh has served as a judge of Tribunal de Commerce, and later as a judge on the Tribunal de Cassation (1892-1902). He has contributed to the paper *L'Opinion Nationale* along with the associate-editor, Exilien Heurtelou.

Writings: Scholarship: *Dictionnaire étymologique et biographique*, published in sections in various issues of the journal *La Ronde*, but never collected in separate volumes, for Pouilh had planned the work "as an historical monument which might perpetuate the memory of all well-known Haitians."

PRADEL, Seymour

b. July 10, 1875, Jacmel, Haiti; d. April 25, 1943, Port-au-Prince.

Poet, journalist, critic, musician, lawyer, public official.

After early schooling in Jamaica under Camille Bruno, Pradel returned to Port-au-Prince to complete his classical studies at the Lycée Pétion where he had as teachers, Jules Moll and Henri Villain, members of the French educational mission. He graduated from the Law School and then became a teacher at the Lycée Pétion.

He also took an active role in political affairs but was exiled in 1902 with Anténor Firmin. He later returned and served as Minister of the Interior in 1912, and as senator in 1915. On October 14, 1930, Pradel was elected senator and just lost the Presidency in an extremely close vote, losing to Vincent Sténio on November 18, 1930.

Pradel was a founder of the literary review, *La Jeune Haiti*, with Justin Lhérisson, and later he helped found *L'Appel*.

The Parnassian verse of Pradel appeared in random journals of the period but the collection of his poems has remained unpublished. A typical stanza is this from "Le Mapou:"

Sous la large tonnelle, autour du gros tambour
Fait de peau de cabri, les nègres, tour à tour
Se livrent aux ébats sensuels et mystiques
Des souples bamboulas. Aux notes fantastiques
D'une âpre mélopée, où passent des accents
de joie et de colère inquiets et puissants.
Ils mènent, tous, des galops frénétiques.

He published in *La Ronde* a literary study, "Les deux tendances."

Biographical/Critical Sources: Auguste Viatte, *Histoire littéraire de l'Amérique française,* Quebec, 1953, pp. 409-411; Ghislain Gouraige, *Histoire de la littérature Haitienne,* 1960, pp. 178-182; article by Léon Laleau, "Pradel," in *Conjonction,* No. 119 (Port-au-Prince, Feb-March 1973), pp. 53-68.

PRESSOIR, Charles Fernand

(or: **Carlo PRESSOIR**)
b. August 13, 1910, Paris; d. May 27, 1973, New York.
Poet (in French and creole), lawyer, essayist.

Pressoir was educated in France, but returned to Haiti for his studies at Port-au-Prince's Faculty of Law. While practicing law, he worked at the General Office of Tax Revenue, eventually becoming Deputy Director General.

Pressoir urged Haitians to be proud of their island French, saying:

Le créole est une langue au même titre que le français et l'anglais; il est sorti du français comme les langues néo-romanes sont sorties du latin.
(from *Débats sur le créole,* p. 10).

He defined Creole as having a French vocabulary and an African grammar or syntax.

His *Au rythme des coumbites* shows the perplexing Haitian mix of Christian and African religions:

Suivant ainsi ces deux religions,
Celle du blanc, la croyance innée,
Les trépassés vont-ils en légion
En Paradis, ou vers la Guinée?

Writings: Poetry: *Au rythme des coumbites,* Port-au-Prince, Ed. La Presse, 1933 (contains 20 poems describing peasants and their lives); *Sèt poè-m ki sot nan mo-n.Sept poèmes qui viennent de la montagne,* Port-au-Prince, Impr. de l'Etat, 1954 (in French and Créole).

Grammar: *Méthode du français oral à l'usage de l'haitien débutant; en 45 leçons (passage du créole au français) Conversation-grammaire-lecture-copie-dictées,* Port-au-Prince, Ed. H. Deschamps, 1954.

Law: *Code fiscal haitien,* Port-au-Prince, Impr. de l'Etat, 1953; *Supplément fiscal et économique,* Port-au-Prince, Impr. de l'Etat, 1954.

Biographical/Critical Sources: Edner Brutus, "Charles F. Pressoir," in *La Relève* (March 1933), pp. 10-19; Emmanuel C. Paul's criticism of *Débats sur le créole et le folklore* in *Haiti-Journal* (ler au 4 mars 1947); Dieudonné Fardin (Benoît Pierre), "La méthode phonétique de Charles Fernand Pressoir," in introduction to Fardin's *Collier La Rosée, poèmes créoles,* Port-de-Paix, Haiti, 1964.

PRICE, Philippe Hannibal

b. April 24, 1841, Jacmel, Haiti; d. January 1, 1893, Brooklyn, New York.
Essayist, historian, diplomat.

Price was educated in Jacmel by a French teacher, Venance Barbeyer, who lived in that city. Very early, he became interested in commerce, agriculture and industry and throughout his life tried to enlarge his knowledge in those subjects. Elected Deputé from Jacmel in 1876, he became the President of the Haitian parliament. In 1890 President Florvil Hippolyte named Price Minister of Haiti to Washington, D.C.

Earlier, he had written in his unpublished study of Haiti's people:

> *Je suis d'Haiti, la Mecque, la Judée de la race noire, le pays où se trouvent les champs sacrés de Vertières, de la Crête-à-Pierrot, de la Ravine-à-Couleuvres, du Tombeau-des-Indigènes, et cent autres où doit aller en pèlerinage, tout homme ayant du sang africain dans les artères; car c'est là que le nègre s'est fait homme: c'est là qu'il a brisé ses fers . . .*

Writings: Finance: *Etudes sur les finances et l'économie des nations*, Paris, Guillaumin et Cie, 1876.

Political-Social History: *De la réhabilitation de la race noire par la république d'Haiti*, Port-au-Prince, Impr. J. Verrollot, 1900. Also in manuscript various articles and histories on Haiti's people.

Various: *Rapport adressé au Gouvernement d'Haiti* (au sujet de la Conférence Internationale Américaine tenue à Washington, Etats-Unis du 2 Octobre 1889 au 19 avril 1890), New York, Impr. Française, L. Weisse et Co., 1890.

PRICE-MARS, Jean

(a.k.a. **Jean Price MARS**)

b. October 15, 1876, Grande Rivière du Nord, Haiti; d. March 1, 1969, Pétion-ville, Haiti.

Scholar, storywriter, physician, teacher, diplomat, senator, ethnologist.

Price-Mars, son of a protestant father and catholic mother, who became Haiti's most famous scholar, studied at Cap-Haitien at the Collège Grégoire and at the Lycée Pétion of Port-au-Prince. He then completed his medical preparation at the University of Haiti and the University of Paris (1895-1900). While in France he also studied the social sciences, especially anthropology, then a young science. Detoured for a period into his country's diplomatic consular service, Price-Mars served at Berlin (1900-1903) and was Chargé d'Affaires at Washington, D.C. (1908-1910). He also was Envoy and Minister Plenipotentiary at Paris (1915).

From 1905 to 1908 he was a Député in the national chamber and was Haitian commissioner at the St. Louis (U.S.A.) World's Fair of 1903. He was often insulted and shocked at American attitudes to blacks and coming to know Booker T. Washington he was influenced to begin a serious examination of racial attitudes.

Price-Mars was a professor of secondary education from 1918 to 1930, became a Senator and was once in line to be considered for the presidency of Haiti in 1930. With Jacques Roumain, he founded l'Institut d'Ethnologie of Haiti and became the Director, but also taught African culture and sociology. His private research and reading had made him a leading student of local African religious practices, especially what was popularly called "Voodoo" and he gradually became the spokesman for enlightened views that such survivals of belief and rituals were important, not only for scholarship and culture, but in and for themselves. His *Ainsi parla l'oncle* (1928) was the fruit of this long and fertile study period.

As leader of the "indigenism" or "negrism" group in the 20's and early 30's, his thinking influenced Philippe Thoby-Marcelin and Jacques Roumain, and many others. Many young men abandoned the city ways of their bourgeois fathers to learn the countryman's culture and speech in the effort to recapture Haiti's true traditions and to eliminate the still all-pervasive uneasiness about the African origins of most Haitians. Price-Mars published his scientific and philosophical articles in such journals as *La Relève, Haiti Littéraire et Scientifique,* and *L'Essor.*

Interested in Oswald Spengler's grand historical-metaphysical works (*The Decline of the West* and others) and the pioneering studies and discoveries of another great German thinker, Leo Frobenius, who had worked in Nigeria, Price-Mars and his younger followers for the first time gave Haiti an intellectual basis for pride in themselves and a connection with a greater and nobler past than the savage

Price-Mars' family

colonial one and the few brief years of revolutionary glory.

His book had a far reaching influence beyond Haiti, especially among the black students in Paris. Léopold S. Senghor paid tribute to the Haitian scholar in these words:

> *Il est des noms qui sonnent comme un manifeste. Tel me fut révélé le nom du Docteur Price-Mars lorsque je l'entendis pour la première fois. Etudiant en Sorbonne, j'avais commencé de réfléchir au problème d'une Renaissance culturelle en Afrique noire, et je me cherchais—nous nous cherchions—un parrainage qui put garantir le succès de l'entreprise.*
>
> *Au bout de ma quête, je devais trouver Alain Locke et Jean Price-Mars. Et je lus* Ainsi parla l'Oncle *d'un trait l'eau de la citerne. . . . au soir, après une longue étape dans le désert. J'étais comblé.* L'Oncle *légitimait les raisons de ma quête, confirmait ce que j'avais pressenti. Car, me montrant les trésors de la Négritude qu'il avait découverts sur et dans la terre haitienne, il m'apprenait à découvrir les mêmes valeurs, mais vierges et plus fortes, sur et dans la terre d'Afrique.*
>
> *Aujourd'hui, tous les ethnologues et écrivains nègres d'expression française doivent beaucoup à Jean Price-Mars; l'essentiel, cette vérité que "nous n'avons de chance d'être nous-mêmes que si nous ne répudions aucune part de l'héritage ancestral. Singulièrement les écrivains. D'abord les Haitiens, Roumain, Dépestre et les autres, mais aussi les Antillais et les Africains; un Damas, un Césaire, un Niger, un Birago Diop et surtout moi-même.*

His ideas, first given expression in lectures on folklore from 1920 on, saw early print as articles in the *Revue Haitienne* (then edited by Emile Elie) in the issues of March 1, and April 1, 1922, and the *Revue Indigène* (1925).

Writings: Ethnographic Essays: *Ainsi parla l'oncle,* France, Impr. de Compiègne, 1928; second edition, New York, Parapsychology Foundation Inc., 1951; *Así habló el tio,* translated by Virgilio Pinera, prologue by René Dépestre, La Habana, Casa de las Américas,

1968; *Une étape de l'évolution haitienne,* Port-au-Prince, Impr. La Presse, 1929; *Formation ethnique, folklore et culture du peuple haitien,* Port-au-Prince, Impr. V. Valcin, 1939; *Folklore et patriotisme,* conférence, Port-au-Prince, Impr. Les Presses Libres, 1951; *De Saint Domingue à Haiti, essai sur la culture, les arts et la littérature,* Paris, Présence Africaine, 1959; *De la préhistoire d'Afrique à l'Histoire d'Haiti,* Port-au-Prince, Impr. de l'Etat, 1962; *L'Afrique noire et ses peuples,* introduction au cours d'Africologie, Port-au-Prince, Impr. V. Valcin, 1942; *Le bilan des études ethnologiques en Haiti et le cycle du nègre,* Port-au-Prince, Impr. de l'Etat, 1954; *Les survivances africaines dans la communauté haitienne,* Dakar, I.F.A.N., 1953; *Le processus d'une culture* (proceedings of the 79th International Congress of Americanists), Chicago, 1952.

Education: *La vocation de l'élite,* Port-au-Prince, Impr. Edm. Chenet, 1919; *Le problème de l'analphabétisme et sa solution,* Port-au-Prince, V. Valcin, 1943.

Biographies: *Silhouettes de nègres et de négrophiles,* Paris, Présence Africaine, 1960 (covers Toussaint Louverture, Dessalines, Christophe, Aggrey of the Gold Coast, George Washington Carver and others); *Jean-Pierre Boyer Bazelais et le drame de Miragoâne* (à propos d'un lot d'autographes), 1883-1884, Port-au-Prince, Impr. de l'Etat, 1948; *Le sentiment de la valeur personnelle chez Henri Christophe en fonction de son rôle de chef,* Port-au-Prince, Impr. V. Valcin, 1934; *Les fêtes du Cormier . . . conférence sur J.J. Dessalines,* Cap-Haitien, Impr. J.J. Manigat, 1904; *Vilbrun Guillaume Sam, ce méconnu (Ebauches),* Port-au-Prince, Impr. de l'Etat, 1961; *Anténor Firmin,* Port-au-Prince, Impr. Séminaire Adventiste, 1978.

Polemics: *Lettre ouverte au Dr René Piquion, directeur de l'Ecole Normale supérieure, sur son "Manuel de la négritude: Le préjugé de couleur est-il la question sociale,"* Port-au-Prince, Ed. des Antilles, 1967.

History: *La République d'Haiti et la république Dominicaine,* 2 vols., Port-au-Prince, L'Impr. Held, 1953; *La contribution haitienne à la lutte des Amériques pour les libertés humaines,* Port-au-Prince, Impr. V. Valcin, 1942; *Le sentiment de la liberté chez les nègres de Saint Domingue* (see "l'homme de couleur," collection published by Daniel Rops, Paris, Plon, 1939, pp. 166-178; *Ultime Hommage d'un nonagénaire à Sainte-Rose ou Grande-Rivière du Nord, à l'occasion de sa fête paroissiale du 30 Aout 1961,* Port-au-Prince, 1961.

Articles: "A propos de la Renaissance nègre aux Etats-Unis," in *La Relève* (July 1, 1932 and August 1932); "L'état social et la production littéraire en Haiti," in *Conjonction,* No. 34 (Aug. 1951), pp. 49-55; "La culture française en Haiti," in *Culture française,* Vol. 6, No. 2 (May 1957), pp. 29-38; "Survivances africaines et dynamisme de la culture noire outre-atlantique," in *Présence Africaine,* Nos. 8, 9, and 10 (June-Nov. 1956), pp. 272-280; "La position d'Haiti et de la culture française en Amérique," in *Culture Française,* Vol. 5, No. 4 (Oct. 1956), pp. 52-64, and Vol. 14, No. 15 (1965), pp. 16-28.

In Manuscript: many stories and novelettes, and other genres.

Introductions: Preface to J.B. Cinéas' *Drame de la terre,* Cap-Haitien, 1933, and to Jacques Roumain's novel *La montagne ensorcelée,* Port-au-Prince, 1931; Preface to *Charmes Créoles* by R. Auffret-Follain, Paris, Ed. Soulanges, 196?; Preface to *Etape d'une visite culturelle* by Malu, Impr. de l'Etat, 1964.

Biographical/Critical Sources: The major recent study, with detailed bibliography, is the special issue of *Conjonction* (no. 132, Dec. 1976-Jan. 1977): entire issue entitled Un Centenaire: "Jean Price Mars 1876-1976;" Hénock Trouillot, "La pensée de Dr Jean-Price Mars" in *Revue de la Société d'Histoire et de Géographie d'Haiti,* Port-au-Prince, Impr. N.A. Théodore, 1956; René Dépestre, "Jean Price-Mars et le mythe de l'Orphée Noir ou les aventures de la Négritude," in Dépestre's *Pour la Révolution, pour la Poèsie,* Quebec, Ed. Léméac, 1974; in Spanish in *Por la Revolución, por la Poesia,* Havana, 1969; Emile Paultre, *Essai sur M. Price Mars depuis 1930,* Port-au-Prince, Impr. de l'Etat, 1933; also published by Eds. des Antilles, 1966; and second edition of the latter, 1967; *Témoignages sur la vie et l'oeuvre du Dr Jean Price-Mars, 1876-1956,* Port-au-Prince, Impr. de l'Etat, 1956 (essays by several authors on his eightieth anniversary); Jean-Price-Mars in *Conjonction,* No. 69; Jean Price-Mars (1876-1976); Léon G. Damas, "Price-Mars, père du Haitianisme," in *Présence Africaine,* Nos. 32-33 (June-Sept. 1960), pp. 166-178; and "Price Mars n'est plus" in *Présence Africaine,* No. 71 (1969), pp. 5-8; Raymond F. Betts, *The Ideology of Blackness,* Lexington, Mass., D. C. Health, 1971; Pradel Pompilus & frères de l'Instruction Chrêtienne: *Manuel illustré d'histoire de la Littérature Haitienne,* Port-au-Prince, Ed. H. Deschamps, 1961, pp. 553-571; Roger Dorsinville, "Jean Price-Mars," in *L'Afrique Littéraire et Artistique,* Paris, No. 34, pp. 58-62; Maurice A. Lubin, "A Giant Dies, leader of the Haitian thought," in *Negro History Bulletin,* Vol. 32, No. 6, (October 1969), pp. 16-19; Robert Cornevin, Introduction sur Dr Jean Price-Mars, third edition of "Ainsi Parla l'Oncle," Montreal, Ed. Léméac, 1976; Jacques Carmeleau Antoine, *Dr. Jean Price-Mars, Patron Saint of Negritude* (to be published by Three Continents Press, 1979).

PULVAR, César

b. ca. 1927, Martinique.
Novelist.

César Pulvar's one novel, *D'Jhebo, Le Léviathan Noir* (1957), is based on the story of an escaped slave who contributes to the revolts in Martinique which forced the application of abolition in May, 1848, on the island. The "creole" hero seeks equality for slaves, but does not identify himself with his African heritage.

Writings: Novel: *D'Jhébo, le Léviathan Noir,* Paris, Eds. Davy, 1957; *Veillées martiniquaises,* details not known.

RAYMOND, Julien

b. 1743, Bainet, Haiti; d. October 7, 1801, Cap-Français (now Cap-Haitien), Haiti.
Lawyer, colonial public servant.

Raymond was born a freed man, of a family of great landowners. He early went to France for his education, including the law. He practiced law in Paris before returning to Saint Domingue (Haiti) to fight for the civil and political rights of the freedmen class. In 1796, he was chosen a member of the third Civil Commission along with Sonthonax, Roume, Giraud and Leblanc, to apply the revolutionary French decrees in Saint Domingue.

He was also a member of the colonial Directory, the Council of Five-Hundred and the Institute of France. Raymond was among the few genuinely learned people in the colony of Saint Domingue, and Dr. Mercer Cook in his book, *Five French Negro Authors,* called him "the Father of French Negro Authors."

He died in Cap-Français at the age of 58 years during Toussaint Louverture's government.

Writings: Essays-Address-Historical Papers: *Réclamations adressées à l'Assemblée Nationale par les personnes de couleur, propriétaires et cultivateurs de la colonie française de Saint Domingue,* Paris, 1789; *Observations adressées à l'Assemblée Nationale par un député des colons Américains,* Paris, 1789; *Première lettre écrite de la partie de l'Ouest,* Paris, le 21 Octobre 1791 (with Perrier Aîné and Lamothe-Aigron); *Réponse aux considérations de M. Moreau, dit Saint-Méry, sur les colonies par Julien Raymond, citoyen de couleur de Saint Domingue,* Paris, Impr. du Patriote Français, 1791; *Pétition nouvelle des citoyens de couleur des Iles Françaises, à l'Assemblée Nationale; précédée d'un avertissement sur les manoeuvres employées pour faire échouer cette pétition et suivie de pièces justificatives,* Paris, Chez Desennée, etc., 1791; Also an "Avertissement," signed by Raimond l'Ainé, Raimond le jeune, Fleury, Honoré St Albert, Desoulchay de Saint Real et Desoulchay, Porsade et Audiger) entitled, *Observations sur l'origine et les progrès du préjugé des colons blancs contre les hommes de couleur, sur les inconvénients de le perpétuer, la nécessité, la facilité de le détruire, sur le projet du comité colonial . . . ,* Paris, Belin, 1791 (with a six-page preface by Brissot); *Adresse des commissaires des citoyens de couleur en France aux troupes françaises destinées à passer à Saint Domingue, rédigée par Julien Raymond, l'un d'eux,* Paris, Impr. du Patriote Français, 1792; *Véritable origine des troubles de Saint Domingue et des différentes causes qui les ont produits,* Paris, Chez Desenné, Bailly et au Bureau du Patriote Français, 1792 (l'an 4è de la liberté); *Adresse des citoyens de couleur des Isles et Colonies françaises; à l'Assemblée Générale des représentants de la Commune de Paris; prononcée le premier février 1790, par Dejoly, avocat aux Conseils; l'un des Représentants de la Commune, en présentant une députation des citoyens de couleur,* Paris, 1790 (with Raimond Aîné, Ogé Jeune, Fleury, Honoré de St-Albert, Du Souchet de St-Real, commissaires et députés des citoyens de couleur, des Iles et colonies françaises); *Lettre au citoyen D . . . Député à la Convention Nationale; par . . . Colon de St-Domingue, sur l'état des divers partis de cette colonie et sur le caractère des déportés, 24 février 1793,* Paris, 1793; *Mémoire sur les causes des troubles et des désastres de la colonie de Saint Domingue, présenté aux comités de marine et des colonie dans les premiers jours de Juin dernier, par les citoyens de couleur, d'après l'invitation qui leur en avait été faite par les comités, rédigé par l'un d'eux,* Paris, Impr. du Cercle Social, 1793. Also: *Réflexions sur les véritables causes des troubles et des désastres de nos colonies, instamment sur ceux de Saint-Domingue, avec les moyens à employer pour préserver cette colonie d'une ruine totale; adressée à la Convention nationale par Raymond, colon de Saint Domingue,* Paris, 1793; *Correspondance de Julien Raymond avec ses frères de Saint-Domingue, et les pièces qui lui ont été adressées par eux,* Paris, Impr. du Cercle Social (l'an deuxième de la République Française), *1790; Lettre de Julien Raymond à ses frères les hommes de couleur, en comparaison des originaux de sa correspondance avec les extraits perfides qu'en ont fait MM. Page et Brulley, dans un libelle intitulé "Développement des causes des troubles et des désastres des colonies françaises,"* Paris, Impr. du Cercle Social, l'an deuxième de la République Française), 1790; *Lettre d'un citoyen, détenu pendant quatorze mois et traduit au tribunal révolutionnaire, au citoyen C.B., représentant du peuple, en réponse sur une question importante,* Paris, Impr. de l'Union, 1791; *Preuves complètes et matérielles du projet des colons pour mener les colonies à l'indépendance, tirées de leurs propres écrits; ouvrage-présenté à la commission des colonies . . . ,* Paris, Impr. de l'Union, 1790; *Rapport de Julien Raymond Commissaire délégué par le Gouvernement français aux isles sous le Vent, au ministre de la Marine,* Cap-Français, Impr. de P. Roux, 1797.

Biographical/Critical Sources: Mercer Cook, *Five French Negro Authors,* Washington, D.C., The Associated Publishers, 1943 (essay on Julien Raymond, pp. 3-37).

RELOUZAT, Claude

b. ca. 1931, Martinique.
Storywriter.

Relouzat's stories cover his sojourn in France and island experiences, all of them published in Martinique.

Writings: Stories: *Mon voyage en France,* Fort-de-France, Impr. Saint Paul, 1961; *En flânant dans le Sud de la Martinique,* Annuaire, Noria, Martinique-Guadeloupe, 1964; *De l'Amour à la Mort,* Fort-de-France, Librairie Relouzat, 1966; "Les Amours de Danica," in *Almanach de la Martinique* (1968), Fort-de-France, Impr. Martiniquaise, 1968; *Marigot. Connaissance de la Martinique,* Fort-de-France, Librairie Relouzat, 1968.

RENAUD, Alix Joseph

b. ca. 1946, Port-au-Prince, Haiti.
Poet.

Alix Renaud received his education in Port-au-Prince. He early left Haiti to go to Canada (1968). There, he has published many poems in the magazine *Poèsie* and he often contributed to *L'Amitié par la Plume.*

Writings: Poetry: *Extase exacte,* Paris, La Pensée Universelle, 1976.

REY, Dantès

b. October 12, 1883, Port-au-Prince, Haiti; d. March 31, 1921.
Poet.

Rey was educated in Port-au-Prince. When the American Forces of Occupation organized the Gendarmerie d'Haiti, hiring many educated men, Dantès Rey became an officer in the new force. He had previously been in the Haitian navy.

Writings: Poetry: *Reliquiae; oeuvres posthumes,* Port-au-Prince, Impr. V. Valcin, n.d.

REY-CHARLIER, Ghislaine

b. January 21, 1918, Jérémie, Haiti.
Novelist, anthologist.

Born in Jérémie, Ghislaine came early to Port-au-Prince where she received her education. She taught at first at the College of Pétionville before residing abroad for many years, mostly in France and Zaire. Since 1969 she has resided in Canada where she published her collection of fiction, *Anthologie du roman haitien de 1859 à 1946* (Sherbrooke, Eds. Naaman, 1978). Her novel, "Julie Maurer (Mèmoire d'une Affranchie)" is unpublished.

RICHER, Clément

b. 1914, Fort-de-France, Martinique; d. ca. 1968.
Novelist, storywriter.

Richer attended school in Fort-de-France and then went to France where he completed his education at the Lycée Théodore de Banville, in Moulins, southern France. Later, he attended courses at the Sorbonne in Paris and at the Ecole des Sciences Politiques. He long resided in Belgium, staying until the late 1960's, after which he returned to Paris.

Richer's literary career began in 1936 when he founded the review *Bocaccio* with the assistance of Paul Léautaud, Rosny aîné, Rosny jeune, and Léo Larguier. Since then, he has published several novels, won several awards, and received much critical attention.

Gérard d'Houville offered these comments about Clément Richer:

> *La poèsie de la nature, un réalisme ingénu, une ironie et un sens inné des dérisions du sort font partie du talent de Clément Richer.*

Writings: Novels: *Ti Coyo et son requin,* Paris, Librairie Plon, 1941 (winner of the Prix Georges Courteline, 1942, and the Prix Humour de la Société des gens de Lettres, 1943), translated as *Ti-Coyo and his shark: an immoral fable* by Gerard Hopkins, first American edition, New York, Knopf, 1951 (named one of the best novels of the year in the United States, 1951); *La Croisière de la Prescilla,* Paris, Plon, 1947; *Les femmes préfèrent les brutes,* 1949 (Prix Paul Flat); *Len Sly,* Paris, Plon, 1951; *L'Homme à la caravelle,* Paris, Plon, 1952; *Le Capital Nel,* 1953; *Le fils de Ti-Coyo,* Paris, Plon, 1954.

Tales: *Le Dernier voyage de "Pembroke,"* Paris, Plon, 1940 (Prix Marianne, 1939, and Prix Paul Flat, 1941); *Les Passagers de Perwyn,* Paris, Ed. Stock, 1947.

Biographical/Critical Sources: Gérard d'Houville, "Lectures Romanesques," in *La Revue des Deux Mondes,* (Nov. 15, 1949), p. 326; Randolph White, "Foreign Negro Authors," *Ebony,* VII (May 1952). Also see: Elizabeth Brooks, "Three Martiniquain Novelists" (Richer, Mayotte Capécia, and Joseph Zobel), unpublished Ph.D. dissertation, Howard University, 1953.

RICOT, Justinien

b. March 15, 1889, Port-au-Prince, Haiti; d. 1967, Port-au-Prince.
Poet, journalist, lawyer.

Ricot served as chef de bureau of the Ministry of Public Instruction. His verse appeared in several magazines and newspapers from which he collected his work for his only collection.

Writings: Poetry: *Pétales et paillons,* Paris, Jouve, 1927.

RICOURT, Volvick

b. October 18, 1893, Cap-Haitien; d. 1962, New York.
Poet, musician.

Ricourt received his education in Cap-Haitien studying under such teachers as Luc Grimard, Louis Mercier, and Christian Werleigh. He was named chef de bureau of the Department of Interior in 1911. In the latter part of his life he also was a minister of the Baptist Church.

Writings: Poetry: *L'invisible orchestre,* Port-au-Prince, Cie. Lithographique, 1933.

RIGAUD, André

b. January 17, 1761, Cayes, Saint Domingue (now Haiti); d. September 18, 1811, Cayes.
Essayist, military officer.

Son of a French father and a black "arada" woman, Rigaud was born a freed man. He was educated in Bordeaux and learned the goldsmith's craft.

He returned to Saint Domingue to take part in the stirring events which reached out from revolutionary France to shake the colony. There were clashes between "little" white men, royalist great landowners, and republican freed men. André Rigaud was soon elected colonel of the confederate armies of freed men and contributed, with Louis Jacques Beauvais, Pierre Pinchinat, and Alexandre Pétion, to force the colonial regime to accept a concordat which recognized civic and political rights of his class.

He was also among the 800 soldiers who went under Count d'Estaing's command in the Battle of Savannah, in which he was wounded. Recovering, Rigaud was ever the leader of the Freed men and became the commander in the South Department when Toussaint Louverture was responsible for the North and West Departments. General Rigaud declared war on Toussaint Louverture but was unsuccessful; defeated he set sail on July 29, 1800, with many of his partisans, who went with him into short exile. Rigaud and his colleagues then accompanied the expeditionary force commanded by French Captain General Victor Emmanuel Leclerc, February 2, 1802, back to Haiti. After Toussaint was taken prisoner, Rigaud was also forced to leave the island. However, in 1810, he came back and Alexandre Pétion, then President of Haiti, welcomed his former chief and charged him with the pacification of the South Department. Rigaud organized a council which then elected him Commander in Chief in the south and he quickly organized a separate state, taking the title of President. He died shortly thereafter and his dreams of power vanished with mortality.

His many addresses and essays offer vivid pictures of men and events in the independence period.

Writings: Speeches and Addresses: *Adresse à mes concitoyens; 14 prairial, 2 Juin,* Les Cayes, Impr. de Lemery, 1789; *Réponse du Général de Brigade André Rigaud à l'écrit calomnieux du Général Toussaint Louverture,* Les Cayes, Impr. de Lemery, 1789; *Aux vrais républicains de Saint Domingue,* Les Cayes, Impr. de Lemery, 1794; *Relation du siège de Tiburon,* Les Cayes, Impr. de Lemery, 1795; *Aux citoyens des mêmes départements, au sujet des assemblées primaires et électorales,* Les Cayes, Impr. de Lemery, 1796 (with Louis Jacques Beauvais); *A tous les citoyens du même département,* Les Cayes, Impr. de Lemery,

1796; *Précis du projet d'attaque contre le quartier de la Grande Anse par l'Armée de la République en activité dans le Sud, commandée par le Général Rigaud,* Les Cayes, Impr. de Lemery, 1797; *Réponse du Général André Rigaud à la proclamation de l'Agent Roume en date du XV Messidor* (l'An VII), Les Cayes, Impr. de Lemery, 1799. Also: *Au colonel Whitelock, commandant pour le Roi d'Angleterre,* Les Cayes, Impr. de Lemery, 1790; *Relation du siège de Léogane pour les anglais et les émigrés français, tracée par les généraux de brigade Rigaud et Beauvais, d'après les détails qui leur ont été donnés par Renaud Desruisseaux, commandant de l'arrondissement du centre et les renseignements qu'ils ont pris sur les lieux . . . ,* Les Cayes, Impr. de Lemery (an IV, with Louis Jacques Beauvais), 1792; *Mémoire du Général de brigade André Rigaud en réfutation des écrits calomnieux contre les citoyens de couleur de Saint Domingue, 18 thermidor, 1793; Au citoyen Roume, agent particulier du Directoire français à Saint Domingue; Quartier général de Miragoâne, le 27 prairial an 7 de la République Française,* Les Cayes, 1795; *Réponse à la proclamation de Toussaint Louverture, datée du Port-Républicain, le 29 brumaire, an VIII,* Les Cayes, Impr. de Lemery, 1796.

RIGAUD, Milo

(or **Emile**)

b. July 16, 1904, Port-au-Prince, Haiti.
Poet, novelist, journalist, folklorist.

Rigaud's work, creative or sociological, is primarily focussed on his studies of African religious practices still very much alive in Haiti.

Writings: Poetry: *Rythmes et rites,* Poitiers, Ed. Les Amis de la Poèsie, 1932, and Fontenay, Impr. Moderne, 1933; *Rites et rythmes,* Poitiers, Ed. des "Amis de la Poèsie," 1933; *Tassos,* Niort, Ed. "Action Intellectuelle," 1933 (in creole). Creole language poems are in *Les Griots,* Vol. 4, No. 4 (Apr-Sep. 1939), pp. 538-540.

Novel: *Jésus ou Legba ou les dieux se battent, école de symbolisme afro-haitien,* Poitiers, "Les amis de la Poèsie," 1933; *Le combat des dieux: Jésus ou Legba,* Montréal, Nouvelle Optique, 1978.

Politics: *Lettre aux haitiens de toutes couleurs,* Port-au-Prince, Impr. du Matin, 1946; *Réponse aux esclaves volontaires,* Port-au-Prince, 1946; *Dossier Sténio Vincent, Attention! C'est à lire,* No. 1, Port-au-Prince (Dec. 1941); *Contre Vincent,* Port-au-Prince, Soc. d'Ed. et de Lib., 1946; *Sténio Vincent révélé par la Justice et par l'opinion publique,* Port-au-Prince, Impr. Deschamps, 1957.

Folklore: *La tradition vaudou et le vaudou haitien,* Paris, Ed. Niclaus, 1953; *Secrets of Voodoo,* New York, Arco, 1969; *Vè-Vè, Diagrammes rituels du Vodou,* trilingual edition (French, English, Spanish), New York, French & European Publications, Inc., 1974.

ROBION, Jean

(pseudonym for **Clement LANIER**)

ROLLE, Christian

(pseudonym: **Auguste LLERO**)

b. October 7, 1929, Mana, Guyane.
Poet.

Rollé was educated in Guyane and attended the Lycée Félix Eboué of Cayenne. He came to France and travelled extensively in Europe. He published his first poems under the pen-name of Auguste Llero in the magazine *Parallèle 5.*

Rollé has been a member of the Federation of Flemish Writers of French Expression since 1954 and the Poetic Society of France since 1957.

Writings: Poetry: *Esprits et échos; Recoins; Nuits* (all unpublished).

Editor of: "Anthologie d'écrits sur la Guyane" (with others but also unpublished).

Essay: Poèsie guyanaise d'expression française et générations, in *Présence Francophone,* Autumn 1974, No. 9.

ROMAIN, Dr. Jean-Baptiste

b. June 10, 1914, Cap-Haitien, Haiti.
Professor, scholar, poet, essayist.

Romain started his education in Cap-Haitien and completed it at the Lycée Pétion of Port-au-Prince. He took a degree in law and also earned a diploma at the Institute of Ethnology chaired by Dr. Jean Price-Mars. Recipient of a scholarship, he went to Paris and obtained his doctorate ès-lettres (Human Sciences) at the Sorbonne.

He is professor, dean of the Faculty of Ethnology, and director of the Centre de Recherches en Sciences Humaines et Sociales (CRESHS). He attended the first Congress of Free States of Africa (Ghana, 1958), and the first Congress of Negro Arts (Accra, 1966).

Writings: Anthropology: *Mémoire sur l'anthropométrie en Haiti,* preface by professor Jacques Butterlin, Port-au-Prince, Impr. du Collège Vertière, 1946; *Quelques moeurs et coutumes des paysans haitiens,* Port-au-Prince, Impr. de l'Etat, 1959; *Introduction à l'Anthropologie Physique des Haitiens,* Port-au-Prince, Impr. N.A. Théodore, 1962; *Répartition des Groupes Sanguins A, B, O et RH en Haiti,* Port-au-Prince, Impr. de l'Etat, 1964; *Recherches sur la Puberté en Haiti,* Port-au-Prince, Les Presses Port-au-Princiennes, 1969; *L'Anthropologie Physique des Haitiens,* Port-au-Prince, Impr. Séminaire Adventiste, 1971.

Sociology: *Noms de lieux d'époque coloniale en Haiti* (essai sur les survivances françaises), Port-au-Prince, Impr. de l'Etat, 1960.

ROMANE, Jean-Baptiste

b. 1807, Port-au-Prince, Haiti; d. September 21, 1858, Port-au-Prince.
Poet, playwright.

Romane is best remembered for his youthful poem on Haitian freedom, "Hymne à l'Indépendance," written after France finally recognized Haiti in 1825. (The United States did not do so until 1862 after the secession of the Confederate States from the Union.) The poet ended each stanza: "Vive Haiti! Vive la France!"

Writings: Poetry: *Epître à Mademoiselle Francès Wright,* Port-au-Prince, Impr. Joseph Courtois, 1830; *Epître à Madame Henriette Beecher Stowe,* Port-au-Prince, 1831; *Profession de foi; dédiée à mes amis,* Port-au-Prince, 1840; *Sur la pacification du Sud par le Président Riché; chant héroique,* Port-au-Prince, n.d.; *Poèsies (sur les traités conclus entre la France et Haiti; mort de Coutilien; stances sur la ville de Santo Domingo),* Port-au-Prince, Pinard, Impr. 1841; and "Hymne héroîque au Président Guerrier," Port-au-Prince, n.d.

Play: *La mort de Christophe,* extracts published in *Le Propagateur Haitien* (Sep. 15, 1823).

Funeral Oration: "Oraison funèbre de Claire-Amélie Alexandrine-Céline Pétion," in *Le Propagateur Haitien* (Nov. 15, 1825).

Biographical/Critical Sources: Sémexant Rouzier's article on Romane and his brother Eugène also a minor poet, in *Haiti Littéraire et Sociale* (Jan. 20, 1908).

ROMANETTE, Irmine

(pseudonym: **Yves MIRAMANT**)
b. ca. 1895, Martinique.
Poet, novelist, teacher.

Romanette attended schools in Martinique and became a teacher at the Pensionnat Colonial of Fort-de-France.

Writings: Essay: *L'enseignement des jeunes filles à la Martinique* (Revue Universitaire du 15 Mars 1925), in book form, 1927; "Le Tricentenaire de la Martinique," in *Le Trésor des Lettres,* (Jan. 1934), pp. 5-25.

Poetry: *Sonate, poème,* Paris, Jouve, 1951.

Novel: *Sonson de la Martinique,* Paris, Société Française d'Editions Littéraires et Techniques, 1932.

ROSARION, Ulrick

b. November 11, 1932, Port-au-Prince.
Poet.

Rosarion received his education at the Collège Henri Christophe and the Lycée Pétion of Port-au-Prince. After taking his degree in law in Port-au-Prince, he was appointed a Justice of the Peace.

Though committed to law, he is a fervent poet and has confessed:

> *Je voudrais chanter les héros nationaux sur le mode sentimental comme on le fait dans certains pays.*

Writings: Poetry: *La muse frivole,* Port-au-Prince, Les Presses Nationales d'Haiti, 1970; *Ma lyre à la Jeunesse,* Port-au-Prince, Les Presses Nationales, 1972; *Les Lamentations,* and "Les Fleurs Héroiques" (unpublished).

ROSE, Samuel Luzincourt

b. March 16, 1854, Port-au-Prince, Haiti; d. June 13, 1888, Port-au-Prince. Poet.

Grandson of an Italian immigrant from Venice, Rose's mother was an Afro-Haitian women who had married his father, Marc Rose. He received his education in Port-au-Prince where he was a merchant, but his first love was always poetry. In one of his poems, he wrote:

> *Je ne suis qu'un enfant des tropiques, poète,*
> *Que brûle le soleil d'Haiti, mon pays.*

To Luzincourt Rose, Oswald Durand dedicated a sonnet, on September 15, 1880:

> *Ephèbe que le peuple honore*
> *Ta harpe saura plaire aux dieux.*

And Paul Lochard, author of a collection of poems, *Les chants du soir,* expressed this feeling about him: "Luzincourt Rose est tout entier un poète de l'amour."

At this time, poetry and music went together. Haitian musicians used to set poems to music, as Mauléart Monton did for *Choucoune,* the famous creole poem by Oswald Durand. Several of Rose's poems were set to music including "La Reine des Nuits ou la fleur de cactus," set by Mauléart Monton, "Lily ou le chant d'amour," set by Edmond Saintonge, "Ce que c'est que l'amour," set by F. Duchatellier, "Thalie," by Vilaire fils, and "Elise" (or Elaiza for the poet), set by Ménos.

Writings: Poetry: *Les soupirs, poèsies,* preface by Solon Ménos, Paris, Grassart, 1884.

ROSEMOND, Jules

b. October 23, 1874, Port-au-Prince, Haiti; d. July 4, 1928, Port-au-Prince. Poet, lawyer.

Rosemond was educated in Port-au-Prince. He became a lawyer and served as Public Prosecutor and finally was named General Inspector of Customs.

Writings: Poetry: *Les voies aériennes, poèsies,* Paris, Ateliers Haitiens, 1901; *Démesvar Delorme, poème dedié à la ville du Cap,* (12 Novembre 1907), Port-au-Prince, Impr. C. Magloire, 1907; *Triomphe, poème dédié à S.E. Le Président François Antoine Simon,* Port-au-Prince, 1909.

Speeches: *A travers l'oeuvre, soirée littéraire et théâtrale donnée au Palais National le 6 Septembre 1896 par le Cercle "La Jeunesse,"* Port-au-Prince, Impr. H. Amblard, 1896; *Conférence historique sur la vie de Jean-Jacques Dessalines, fondateur de l'Independence haitienne, faite le 17 Octobre 1903 à l'association nationale du Centenaire,* Port-au-Prince, Impr. de l'Abeille, 1903; *La crise morale et civique,* conférence faite à l'Association Mixte de l'Oeuvre chrétienne, Port-au-Prince, Impr. de l'Abeille, 1915; *Du principe éthique; déviation et redressement* (conférence), Port-au-Prince, Soc. Internationale de Conférences d'Haiti, 1921.

Essays: *Travail et Instruction pour Haiti,* Port-au-Prince, Impr. de l'Abeille, 1907; *La question d'Alsace-Lorraine, Appréciations et observations sur l'ouvrage d'Ernest Lavisse et Christian Pfister,* Port-au-Prince, Impr. Centrale, 1919.

Law: *De l'abolition de la mort civile; étude sur nos institutions juridiques,* Port-au-Prince, Impr. J.C. Donat, 1891.

History: *La Crête à Pierrot, lutte pour l'indépendance d'Haiti* (fév. et mars 1802), Port-au-Prince, Impr. Bernard, 1913.

Politics: *Vues d'ensemble (politique et littérature),* Port-au-Prince, Impr. de l'Abeille, 1910; *Davilmar Thédore, Président du Sénat de la République (1911-1912), généralissime de l'Armée Révolutionnaire* (Jan. 1914), Port-au-Prince, Impr. de l'Abeille, 1914.

ROSIERS, Comte de

(see under **Juste CHANLATTE**)

ROUIL, Marie-Thérèse

b. Paris, 1929 (of Martinican parents).
Poet, journalist, musician.

Rouil was born in Paris, but she was brought up in Fort-de-France where she was educated.

She returned to Paris and attended the Ecole Normale de Musique.

Rouil has contributed to many journals in Martinique and France. She presently resides in Belgium.

Writings: Poetry: in *Nouvelle somme de poèsie du monde noir,* Paris, Présence Africaine, 1966, and in N.R. Shapiro's *Negritude: Black Poetry from Africa and the Caribbean,* New York, October House, 1970.

ROUMAIN, Jacques (Jean-Baptiste)

b. June 4, 1907, Port-au-Prince, Haiti; d. August 18, 1944, Port-au-Prince.
Poet, novelist, storywriter, journalist, anthropologist.

Roumain, possibly Haiti's most important writer, was the son of well-to-do-parents, and grandson of General Tancrède Auguste who was a President of Haiti. He began his education at Saint Louis de Gonzague in Port-au-Prince, and at 16 years of age went to Switzerland to sudy at the Institut Grunau, then at a school in Zurich where he became deeply interested in the poetry of Heinrich Heine and did verses in German. In Spain to study agriculture, he became an "aficionado" of bullfighting and in France later he got to know the French poet-playwright Montherlant whose *Bestiaires* overwhelmed him. He said of his youth:

> *A 16 ans: la Suisse, Institut Grunau. Puis Zurich. Je m'engoue de Henri Heine. Je fais des vers allemands. Et aussi tous les sports: boxe, course. Plus tard, voyage en Espagne où j'allais continuer mes études d'agronomie. En fait de zootechnie, je m'intéressai surtout aux courses de taureaux. J'aimais surtour le plein soleil des corridas. Cela correspondait à cet excès de vie que je porte. Ce fut aussi à cette époque que je connus Montherlant. Ses "Bestiaires" m'ont frappé à un point que vous ne pourrez supposer. J'y sentis un poète avec lequel j'avais de certaines affinités.*
>
> (from Antonio Vieux, "Entre nous Jacques Roumain," in *La Revue Indigène,* Septembre 1927, p. 105)

JACQUES ROUMAIN

In 1927 Roumain returned to Haiti to take an active part with several other poets in the literature and art of this country looking toward a renascence. He founded *La Revue Indigène* with Normil Sylvain Antonio Vieux, Carl Brouard, Philippe Thoby-Marcelin and Daniel Heurtelou and later *La Trouée 559* which became a leading journal under his leadership.

Roumain said the poet is “un être qui vit” in a special way and that his work should express an excitement of thought, a veritable fever of feeling of his deepest emotions on important themes. Among the Haitian poets of the past, he praised Oswald Durand’s work because his poems reveal Haiti: “Oswald Durand est un précurseur. Il est indigène.” He advised Haitian poets to employ the tried and true French forms but to work for a genuine Haitian sensibility and to read authors from Latin America who shared similar cultural and political experiences with Haiti. He also translated several poets of Mexico (Maples Arce and Carlos Pellicer) for *La Revue Indigène* (Oct. 1927) and began to introduce black poets from the United States to his Haitian audience. His own plans for a volume of collected verse to be entitled “Le Buvard” for 1928 publication never were realized, though *La Revue Indigène* of September 1927 did carry most of the poems concerned under a rubric of that name (Le Buvard).

Roumain was named Chef de Division at the Department of Interior but he resigned some months later. He was strongly engaged in a student strike organized by the youth of schools and faculties against the long American occupation of Haiti, and he was exiled for his actions and writings. He returned in 1934 to Europe after he had founded the Communist party of Haiti. He settled in Paris for research at the Musée de l’homme and also studied and travelled in Martinique, Cuba, the United States and Mexico. Developing an “advanced” position on all the Caribbean islands’ poverty and rebelling against his own coddled origins, Roumain became a convinced Marxist and returned to take up the cause of the peasants. Particularly, he was also interested in exploring the once embarrassing African origins of the Haitian people. With Price-Mars and other anthropoligists, he

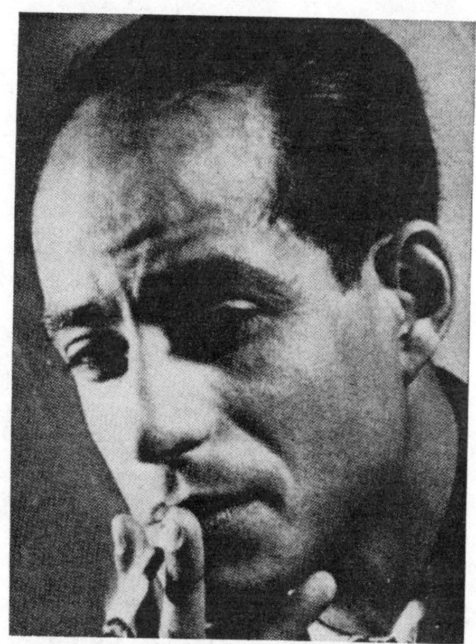

founded the Bureau d’Ethnologie and was named the first director. In this capacity, he published many scientific ethnological studies. He eventually made peace with a new regime which sent Roumain to Mexico as Haiti’s Chargé d’Affaires but he soon fell sick. He returned to die in Port-au-Prince, leaving a wife and two children.

Roumain’s novel, *Gouverneurs de la rosée,* appeared posthumously in Port-au-Prince and Paris in 1944 and thereafter in an early American edition in 1947. In a paperback edition of 1971 it is now easily available and has become a minor classic of Caribbean literature, but it is used in all schools of the Sahelian countries of Africa where drought is the main problem of their national existence. The novel’s peasant hero finds water for his neighbors but dies a victim of envy and jealousy—but the future is seen to be more acceptable since the hero’s martyrdom has pulled his people together.

His earlier novel, *La montagne ensorcelée* (1931), was, however, his first “peasant” novel reflecting his socialist leanings.

The title poem of *Bois d’ébène,* written in Brussels in 1939, has the famous lines:

un silence de 25,000 cadavres nègres
de 25,000 traverses de Bois d'Ebène
Sur les rails du Congo Océan.

Writings: Novels: *La montagne ensorcelée,* Port-au-Prince, Impr. E. Chassaing, 1931; *Gouverneurs de la rosée,* Port-au-Prince, Impr. de l'Etat, 1944; Paris, Editeurs Français Réunis, 1944; translated as *Masters of the Dew* by Mercer Cok and Langston Hughes, New York, Reynal and Hitchcock, 1947, and new paperback edition, New York, Macmillan, Collier Books, 1971; this work has appeared in 17 foreign translations: in Spanish [*Gobernadores del Rocio* (Havana, Imp. Nacional, 1961)], Italian, German [*Herr Uberden Tau,* (Berlin, Ronhelt, 1950)], Portuguese [*Os donos do Orvalho* (Rio de Janeiro, 1955)], Hebrew [*Sarha-talalim,* (Israel, Merhavya, 1948)], Czech among others and in a special French edition, Paris, Bibliothèque française, 1946, and Club français du livre, 1948.

Stories: *La Proie et l'ombre,* preface by Antonio Vieux, Port-au-Prince, Ed. La Presse, 1930; *Les Fantoches,* Port-au-Prince, Impr. de l'Etat, 1931.

Poetry: *Bois d'ébène,* Port-au-Prince, Impr. H. Deschamps, 1945, translated as *Ebony Wood,* New York, Interworld Press, 1972; *Appel,* Port-au-Prince, Impr. V. Pierre-Noel, 1928 (published with Emile Roumer's *La chanson des lambis*); *Oeuvres choisies,* Moscow, Eds. du Progrès, 1964; and poems in many collections and journals such as *La Revue Indigène, La Trouée, La Presse, L'Action Nationale, Anthologie de la poèsie haitienne "indigène,"* preface by Paul Morand, Port-au-Prince, Impr. Modèle, 1928.

Political Essays: *Analyse schématique* (with Christian Beaulieu), Publication du Comité Central du Parti Communiste Haitien, Port-au-Prince, Impr. V. Valcin, 1934; new edition by Idées Nouvelles, Idées Prolétariennes, 1976.

Scholarship: "Griefs de l'homme noir," in *L'Homme de couleur* by S.E. le Cardinal Verdier and others, Paris, Plon, 1939; *L'outillage lithique des Ciboney d'Haiti,* Port-au-Prince, Impr. de l'Etat, 1943, pp. 22-27; *Contribution à l'étude de l'ethnobotanique précolombienne des Grandes Antilles,* Port-au-Prince, Impr. de l'Etat, 1942; *A propos de la campagne anti-superstitieuse; las supersticiones . . .,* Port-au-Prince, Impr. de l'Etat, n.d. (French and Spanish texts); *Le sacrifice du*

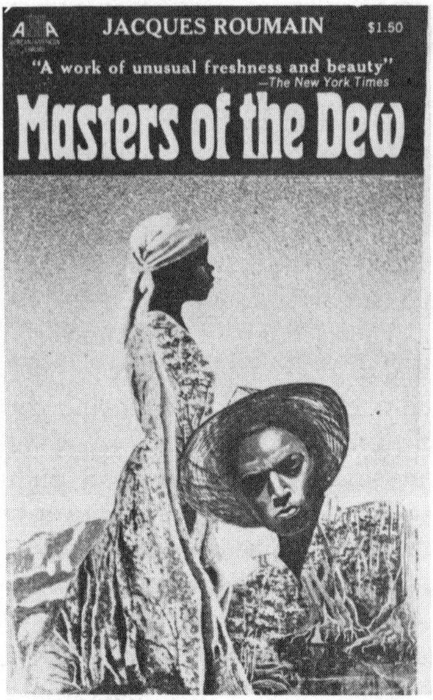

tambour assôtor, Port-au-Prince, Impr. de l'Etat, 1943; and preface to Edris St. Amand's *Essai d'explication de "Dialogue de mes lampes",* Port-au-Prince, Impr. de l'Etat, 1942.

Biographical/Critical Sources: Jacques Stéphen Alexis, "Jacques Roumain vivant" in *Jacques Roumain, Oeuvres choisies,* Moscow, Eds. du Progrès, 1964; Jacques C. Antoine, "Littérature from Toussaint Louverture to Jacques Roumain," in *An introduction to Haiti,* Mercer Cook, ed., Washington, D.C., Pan American Union, 1951; Francine Bradley, "Political Prisoners in Haiti," *New Republic* (March 1935); Jean F. Brierre, *Nous garderons le dieu: en hommage du grand leader haitien de gauche, Jacques Roumain,* Port-au-Prince, Ed. H. Deschamps, 1945; Carl Brouard, review of *La Proie et l'ombre* in *Le Petit Impartial,* No. 9 (Sept. 1930); Edner Brutus, "Jacques Roumain," in *La Relève* (1933), pp. 4-16; A. Dalmas, "Ecrire pour vivre" (Jacques Stéphen Alexis et Jacques Roumain), *Mercure de France,* 338 (1960), pp. 706-708; François Duvalier, review of *Les Fantoches* in *Le Nouvelliste* (Dec. 28, 1931); Roger Gaillard, *L'Univers romanesque de Jacques Roumain* (essai), Port-au-Prince, Ed. H. Deschamps, 1965; Eugénie Galpérina, "Jacques Roumain, Sa vie, son oeuvre," in *Jacques Roumain, Oeuvres choisies,* Moscow, Eds. du Progrès, 1964; Nicolás Guillén, *Elegia à Jacques Roumain e el cielo de Haiti,* Havana, Impr. Ayon, 1948; Maurice Laraque, "En marge des Gouverneurs de la Rosée," in *Optique,* No. 16 (Aug. 1956), pp. 19-27; Antonio Vieux, "Entre nous: Jacques Roumain," *La Revue Indigène,* No. 3 (Sep. 1927), pp. 103-110; Naomi M. Garret, *The Renaissance of Haitian Poetry,* Paris, Présence Africaine, 1963; Alain Locke, "Jacques Roumain," *New Masses,* May 22, 1945; Rémy Bastien, "Jacques Roumain, en el decimo aniversario de su muerte," *Cuadernos americanos,* Julio-Agosto 1954, pp. 243-251; Frère Raphaël, "Gouverneurs de la rosée ou la tragédie de l'eau," *Nouveau Monde,* Port-au-Prince, (Aug. 24, 1970), pp. 1 and 6; Claude Souffrant, "Le fatalisme religieux du paysan haitien," *Europe,* No. 49, No. 501 (Jan. 1971); F. Joachim Roy, "La disgrâce de Stones," *Présence Africaine,* No. 31 (Apr-May 1960), pp. 66-81; Michael Dash, "The Marxist Counterpoint—Jacques Roumain: 1930's to 1940's," in *Black Images,* II, 1 (Spring 1973), pp. 25-29; Edna Worthley Underwood, ed., *The Poets of Haiti,* Portland, Maine, 1934; Ghislain Gouraige, *Histoire de la littérature haitienne,* Port-au-Prince, N.A. Théodore, 1960, pp. 240-244 and 264-269; Pradel Pompilus & Frères de l'Instruction Chrétienne, *Manuel illustré d'histoire de la littérature haitienne,* Port-au-Prince, Ed. H. Deschamps, 1961, pp. 381-384 and 470-476. Also see: Jean-Claude Balmir, "Gouverneurs de la rosée": les chemins de la bonne parole in *Les Littératures d'expression française: négritude africaine, négritude caraïbe,* Paris, Eds. de la Francité, 1972; Marie-Lise Gazarin Gauthier, "Le symbolisme religieux dans *Gouverneurs de la Rosée* de Jacques Roumain, in *Présence Francophone,* No. 7 (Fall, 1973), pp. 19-24; Carolyne Fowler, "Motif Symbolism in Jacques Roumain's *Gouverneurs de la Rosée,*" in *College Language Association Journal,* No. 18, pp. 44-51; Hébert Magloire, "Actualité de Jacques Roumain: le Christ-Noir," Montreal, Ateliers des Sourds, 1975; Carolyn Fowler Gerald, "A Knot in the Thread: The Life and Works of Jacques Roumain," (Ph.D. dissertation, Univ. of Pennsylvania, 1972, to be published); Léon-François Hoffmann, "Langage et rhétorique dans *Gouverneurs de la rosée,*" in *Présence Africaine,* No. 94, second quarterly 1975; Jean Pierre Makouta-Mboukou: "La vision de Dieu chez Jacques Roumain dans *Gouverneurs de la rosée,*" M.A., Paris Faculty of Theology, 1974; Michel Serres, "Christ noir," in *Critique,* No. 39, Jan. 1973, pp. 3-25; Hénock Trouillot: *Dimensions et limites de Jacques Roumain,* Port-au-Prince, Eds. Fardin, 1975; Cauvain L. Paul, *Manuel . . . Un Dieu tombé,* New York, Astoria, 1975; and Martha K. Cobb, *Harlem, Haiti, and Havana: A Comparative-Critical Study of Langston Hughes, Jacques Roumain, and Nicolás Guillén,* Washington, D. C., Three Continents Press, 1979; Fr. Raphael Berrou, "Gouverneurs de la Rosée *ou* le Testament de Jacques Roumain," in *Conjonction,* No. 119 (Port-au-Prince, Feb-March 1973), pp. 53-68.

ROUMER, Emile

(pseudonym: **Emilius NIGER**)
b. February 5, 1903, Jérémie, Haiti.
Poet (in French and creole), critic.

Born into a well-to-do family of the socially elite, Roumer studied in France and England before returning to Haiti as a leading member of *La Revue Indigène* group gathered around Jacques Roumain and Philippe Thoby-Marcelin. On a dare from his fellow lycéans in Paris, he submitted poems to *Les Annales,* a literary journal of the French capital and to his surprise, his work was accepted. The young poet from the Lycée Michelet, under the penname Emilius Niger, had begun his auspicious career.

As a member of the nativist or indigenist group, Roumer exploited local traditions and emphasized vestigial African customs. At the demise of the short-lived *Revue Indigène* which he had directed, he founded his own journal *La Revue Caraibes* which lasted, however, only a few issues.

Roumer's poetry covers numerous aspects of common Haitian life and are often sadly melancholic. He felt that it was better to do a modest work of some personal expressiveness than a refined one of no personal qualities and possible derivative of classical French models. According to Garret, "his verse is full of sensuality, but it is a complex and evocative sensuality with images that stimulate the imagination. When invited to read his poetry for the U. S. Library of Congress in the 1960's he refused, saying he had no copies of his work and didn't think much any longer about Haitian poetry, that he simply had, in short, nothing to offer.

His last years had been busy with the production of works in creole such as *Le Caïman étoilé* (1963) and the creole poems, *Rosaire, Couronne de sonnets,* clearly demonstrating that the poetic form he is most fond of is the sonnet. He uses it, builds the fourteen verses with the facility someone else might exercise with a complex crossword puzzle.

Roumer's poetry early showed the influence of the French poet Jules Laforgue, especially in such works as "Le Thé de Corossol," "Province" and "Bois Verna." An indigenist poem was "Désespoir" from his first collection, *Poèmes d'Haiti et de France* (1925), which offers this strong picture:

Le sang nègre, le sang pourpre de nos vaincus
dit nos plaintes désespérées,
Des "albinos" lancés à l'appât des écus
comme des chiens dans la curée,
ont leur stupre étalé sur les débris d'un mort,
la chair sanglante de Péralte,
les enfants égorgés dans la Plaine du Nord
sans qu'un chrétien ait crié halte,
les coups de poignard au ventre, le poing brutal
sur notre figure meurtrie,
les espoirs vains et nos héros mis à l'étal
après la rouge boucherie.

More light-hearted, almost bizarre was the mixing of terms from creole cookery with strong personal feelings, as in this excerpt from "Marabout de mon coeur:"

Tu es un afiba dedans mon calalou,
le doumboueil de mon pois, mon thé de Z'herbe à clou.
Tu es le boeuf salé dont mon coeur est la couane
L'acassan au sirop qui coule en ma gargane.

This poem set in music is very often sung by all Haitians.

Roumer always felt himself a part of a greater world than Haiti, however, and despite his patriotism and occasional bitterness, could write these lines from "Poèmes en vers":

Que l'on naisse Mondongue ou Peuhl
ce n'est pas mon affaire,
Paul-Jean Toulet est mon grand frère,
et Villon, mon aïeul.

Writings: Poetry: *Poèmes d'Haiti et de France,* Paris, Ed. de la Revue Mondiale, 1925; *Poèmes en vers, Octaves, Contrerimes, Coples,* Special Issue of *Haiti-Journal,* 1948; *Le Caiman étoilé (poèmes),* Port-au-Prince, Ed. Panorama, 1963; *Rosaire, Couronne Sonnets,* Port-au-Prince, Ed. Panorama, 1964, the long poem "La chanson des lambis" was first published in *Poèmes d'Haiti et de France* (1925) and then in a volume with Roumain's "Appel," Port-au-Prince, Impr. Pierre-Noel, 1928, and again in Haiti, Impr. H. Deschamps, 1945; a new edition of *Poèmes d'Haiti et de France,* Port-au-Prince, Ed. Panorama, 1973. Many poems appeared in various journals and collections including *La Revue Indigène, La Presse, L'Action Nationale, Haiti-Journal,* and *Les Griots.*

Essays: "Valéry Larbaud: A-O Barnabooth, son journal et ses poèsies," in *La Revue Indigène,* No. 4 (Oct. 1927), pp. 138-148; and Nos. 5-6 (Jan-Feb. 1928), pp. 189-195.

Biographical/Critical Sources: Edner Brutus, "Emile Roumer," in *La Relève* (Oct. 1932), pp. 13-18; Jay William Smith, "Deux poètes haitiens" (also on St Aude), in *Optique,* No. 1 (March 1954), p. 26; Antoine Vieux, "Entre nous: Emile Roumer," in *La Revue Indigène,* No. 2 (Aug. 1927), pp. 54-58; Naomi M. Garret, *The Renaissance of Haiti Poetry,* Paris, Présence Africaine, 1963, pp. 130-139; Auguste Viatte, *Histoire littéraire de l'Amérique française,* Quebec, Presses Universitaires, 1953, pp. 431-432; Ghislain Gouraige, *Histoire de la littérature haitienne,* Port-au-Prince, Impr. N.A. Théodore, 1960, pp. 238-240; Pradel Pompilus et Frères de l'Instruction Chrétienne, *Manuel illustré d'histoire de la littérature haitienne,* Port-au-Prince, Impr. H. Deschamps, 1961, pp. 366-374.

ROUZIER, Maximilien Louis Sévérin

(also called **SEMEXANT** or **SAINT-MEXANT**)
b. November 26, 1846, Jérémie, Haiti; d. January 29, 1927, Port-au-Prince.
Journalist, novelist, literary historian, essayist, biographer.

Rouzier was educated in Jérémie and Port-au-Prince. He was enlisted in the army, became a second-lieutenant, and aide-de-camp to Major-General Alexandre Carrié. Leaving the military, he spent the rest of his life in wholesale trade.

Rouzier was an eminent collector of the Haitian past: historical documents, pictures, literary works, newspapers, etc. He published a great set of biographical information about the founders of Haitian independence and the prominent figures of the country in *Le Moniteur* and many other magazines such as *Haiti Littéraire et Sociale.*

Rouzier's one novel, *Badio-Popote,* published in 1906, recaptures the Soulouque epoch of Haitian history by following the career of General Badio-Popote in Faustin Soulouque's campaign of 1849-50 in the invasion of the Dominican Republic and the following years of political turmoil. Rouzier's many essays on literature and culture appeared in many journals but never were collected into one volume despite their being in Auguste Viatte's opinion, the finest of Haitian criticism. Viatte states "Rouzier may well be Haiti's greatest literary historian."

Writings: Novel: *Badio-Popote,* published complete in the journal *Le Soir,* Port-au-Prince, 1906.

Scholarship: *Dictionnaire Géographique et administratif universel d'Haiti; illustré ou Guide général en Haiti,* Vol. I, Paris, Impr. de Charles Blot, 1892, Vol. 2, Paris, Impr. de Charles Blot, 1894, Vol. 3, Port-au-Prince, Impr. Aug. A. Héraux, 1927 (published by his son, Charles Rouzier who wrote the preface), Vol. 4, Port-au-Prince, Impr. Aug. A. Héraux, 1928.

Essays: in various journals, no collected edition.

ROY, Francis Joachim

b. 1922, Port-au-Prince, Haiti; d. October, 1969, Paris.
Novelist, translator.

Roy was educated in Port-au-Prince, and spent many years in Paris where he died.

Writings: Novel: *Les chiens, roman,* Paris, Robert Laffont, 1961.

ROY, Hérard L.C.

b. March 18, 1910, Port-au-Prince, Haiti.
Poet, diplomat.

Roy was educated in Port-au-Prince and spent some years in France. After completing a degree in law he worked for the Department of Foreign Affairs, and was named a Haitian Delegate at the Mexico Conference of 1945 and was at the ONU during 1946-47.

Roy in the mid-20th century was still exploiting the Baudelairian approach to shabbiness and despair in such verses as this one from his "Nocturnal crapuleux," published in his one volume to date, *Les variations tropicales et les mandragores* (1945):

Je pourchasse l'oubli dans l'abrutissement,
Remorquant ma douleur dans les bas-fonds du vice.
Et ces filles semblaient d'infernales complices
Distillant dans la nuit un vin d'épuisement,

La lueur d'un quinquet titubait sur la couche
Où se vautrait la chair comme au fond d'un tombeau.

Writings: Poetry: *Les variations tropicales et les mandragores,* Port-au-Prince, Impr. de l'Etat, 1945.

RUPAIRE, Sonny

b. November 7, 1941, Pointe-à-Pitre, Guadeloupe.
Poet.

Rupaire received his education at the Lycée Carnot and then entered the Ecole Normale of Paris.

He began writing poetry as a youth and has been active in intellectual literary circles.

Writings: Poetry: *Choix de Poèmes,* Paris, Ed. Parabole, 1973; *Cette igname brisée qu'est ma terre natale* (???) and four poems in *Littérature antillaise,* Fort-de-France (1971), pp. 227-232.

SABE de, Aristide

(pseudonym for **Lorimer DENIS**)

SAINT-AMAND, Edriss

b. March 26, 1918, Gonaïves, Haiti.
Novelist, journalist, teacher.

Saint-Amand was educated in Port-au-Prince at the Institution of Saint Louis de Gonzague. He left the Ecole des Sciences Appliquées after two years. He practiced journalism and contributed to the journal, *La Nation.* In 1946, he went to Paris where he graduated from l'Ecole des Hautes Etudes Internationales.

He returned to Port-au-Prince in 1958 to teach at the Lycée Pétion, l'Ecole Normale Supérieure and l'Ecole des Hautes Etudes.

Writings: Novel: *Bon dieu rit,* Paris, Domat, 1952 (German translation, *Der flammen Baum,* Buchergilde Gutenberg, Zurich, 1955); *Le Vent de Janvier* (to be published).

Scholarship: *Essai d'explication de "Dialogue de mes lampes"* (a study of the poet Magloire Saint-Aude), Port-au-Prince, Impr. de l'Etat, 1942, with introduction by Jacques Roumain.

Translation (into French from creole original): of *L'Antigone Créole* of Félix Morisseau-Leroy, Paris, Présence Africaine, date not known.

Biographical/Critical Sources: Ghislain Gouraige, *Histoire de la littérature haitienne,* Port-au-Prince, 1960, pp. 299-301.

SAINT-AUDE, Magloire

(born **Clement MAGLOIRE fils**)

b. April 2, 1912, Port-au-Prince, Haiti; d. May 27, 1971, Port-au-Prince.
Poet, storywriter, journalist.

Son of Clément Magloire, director of the famed newspaper, *Le Matin,* Saint-Aude was educated at the Petit Séminaire Collège Saint-Martial, the Institution Saint Louis de Gonzague and at the Tippenhauer Institute. He early entered the field of journalism and began contributing work to *Le Matin, Le Nouvelliste, L'Action Nationale, La Nation, Les Griots,* and *Haiti-Journal.*

The poet legally adopted his name of Magloire Saint-Aude in 1941, taking his father's family name as his first name and the family name of his mother as his new surname, after a disagreement with his father. He thereby also sought to establish a personal identity out from under the shadow of his well-known parent. He has spent most of his life in Port-au-Prince.

Saint-Aude was an extremely pessimistic and hermetic poet. His early, more comprehensible poems were published in *La Relève* in 1933 and in *Les Griots* in the 1938-1939 period. Subsequently, he intensified even further his poems and made them more personal and opaque. In short, Magloire Saint-Aude was a surrealist and his verse is consciously incoherent, dreamlike, as is much of the work of the great French surrealist, Breton.

Writings: Poetry: *Dialogue de mes lampes,* Port-au-Prince, Impr. de l'Etat, 1941; *Tabou,* Port-au-Prince, Impr. du Collège Vertières, 1941, 1949, 1951, 1957; *Déchu,* Port-au-Prince, Impr. Oedipe, 1956; and collected poems: *Dialogue de mes lampes, Tabou, Déchu,* Paris, Première Personne, chez Jacques Veuillet, 1970; and individual poems in various journals, many in *La Relève* and *Les Griots.*
Stories: *Parias,* Port-au-Prince, Impr. de l'Etat, 1949; *Veillée,* Port-au-Prince, Impr. Renelle, 1956; *Ombres et reflets,* Port-au-Prince, Impr. V. Pierre-Noel, 1952.

Biographical/Critical Sources: Gérard Daumec, "Magloire Saint-Aude," in *Optique,* No. 24, (Feb. 1956), pp. 51-56; Edriss Saint-Amand, *Essai d'explication de Dialogue de mes lampes,* preface by Jacques Roumain, Port-au-Prince, Impr. de l'Etat, 1942; William Jay Smith, "Deux poètes haitiens" (Saint-Aude and Roumer) in *Optique,* No. 1 (March 1954), p. 26; Naomi M. Garret, *The Renaissance of Haitian Poetry,* Paris, Présence Africaine, 1963, pp. 184-190; Maurice A. Lubin, "Magloire Saint-Aude, poète surréaliste d'Haiti," in *Présence Francophone,* No. 3 (Autumn 1971), Sherbrooke, Canada, pp. 87-93; Hérard Jadotte, "Idéologie, littérature, dépendance," in *Nouvelle Optique,* No. 4 (Dec 1971), pp. 71-84; Maximilien Laroche, "Magloire Saint-Aude, l'exilé de l'intérieur," in *Présence Francophone,* No. 10 (Spring 1975), pp. 49-57.

SAINT-AURELE, Poirié de

(pseudonym for **Jean-Aurèle Pierre POIRIE**)

b. December 22, 1795, Island of Antigua; d. February 22, 1855, Guadeloupe.
Poet, judge.

Born in a British possession, Antigua, of Guadeloupian parents driven out and exiled by the French Revolution, Saint-Aurèle went to France for his education. He lived in France from 1806 to 1814, and again from 1830 to 1835, and 1848 almost to his death.

In later life, living in Guadeloupe, he was deputy mayor at Sainte-Rose and he became a member of the colonial council of Guadeloupe.

Most of his early poetry, written in France, lamented his lost island paradise, and his work found of interest by the Grand Maître de l'Université, Fontanes, in France.

Back in Guadeloupe, he became a member of a literary association, "l'Athénée," and wrote much verse, mostly published in *La Gazette officielle de la Guadeloupe,* and *Le Courrier de la Guadeloupe.*

He expressed his feelings for his native country, its blue sea, its sun, mountains, blacks, "good colonists" and beautiful Creoles:

J'aime, oh! j'aime avant tout la sensible créole
A la paupière noire, à la taille espagnole,
Doux trésor de pudeur, d'amour et de beauté,
Le front ceint d'un madras plein de coquetterie,
Berçant dans un hamac sa molle rêverie
Et le dolce farniente.

Writings: Poetry: *Le flibustier, poème en 3 chants,* Paris, chez Dupont, 1825; *Veillées françaises,* 1826; *Mussambé, poème en trois chants* (on the Caribs); *Le flibustier* and *Mussambé* appeared in *Cyprès et Palmistes; Poèsies historiques,* Paris, Ed. Gosselin, 1833; *Les veillées des Tropiques,* Paris, Perrotin, 1850.

Politics: *Droit des colonies françaises à une représentation réelle,* 1832; *De la nécessité d'une diminution sur la taxe de sucre des colonies françaises,* 1832; *Loi transitoire sur les sucres; De quelques considérations sur le commerce, l'industrie et les colonies de la France et sur le bill d'affranchissement des colonies anglaises.*

ST-CYR, Mme. Frantz Colbert

(née **MAURASSE**)
b. March 13, 1889, Port-de-Paix, Haiti.
Poet, teacher.

St. Cyr began her studies in Port-de-Paix but completed her education at the University of Paris. Back home in Haiti, she was appointed director of the Port-de-Paix library. Later she was a professor at the Lycée for Girls in the capital.

A strong supporter of the feminist movement, she contributed to its journal and otherwise was in the forefront of better conditions for women. Presently she resides in New York City.

Writings: Poetry: *Gerbe de fleurs (poèmes),* preface by Antoine Poitevien, Port-au-Prince, Impr. V. Valcin, 1949.

SAINT-JEAN, Serge

b. September 3, 1945, Port-au-Prince, Haiti.
Poet, playwright, essayist.

St-Jean received his education at the Lycée Pétion and Toussaint Louverture. He taught in many lycées before being

employed at the Department of Coordination and Information.

Writings: Poetry: *Du Sombre au Clair,* Port-au-Prince, Eds. Panorama, 1964; *Ci-gît, Collection Calfou,* Port-au-Prince, Impr. Centrale, 1966; *Cahier de l'Ile Noire,* Port-au-Prince, mimeo., 1972.

Plays: *Samba Maudit, ballet,* performed at the Institut Français (Dec. 17, 1966); *La Terre aux Fruits d'Or,* Port-au-Prince, Impr. Panorama, 1970.

SAINT-JOHN PERSE

(pseudonym for **Marie René Auguste Alexis Saint-Léger LEGER,** or simply **Alexis LEGER**)

b. May 31, 1887, Pointe-à-Pitre, Guadeloupe; d. September 20, 1975, Presqu'île de Giens, France.
Poet, physician, diplomat.

Saint-John Perse was born on Saint-Léger-les-Feuilles Island across from Point-à-Pitre where his ancestors from Bourgogne came to settle "dans les Isles" in 1682. He spent his first eleven years on the family-owned island where sugar-cane was king. He attended the Lycée of Pointe-à-Pitre, and before the turn of the century, he went to France for study at Pau and Bordeaux. There he became friends with the future writers Francis James, Paul Claudel, Valéry-Larbaud, and Jacques Rivière. He studied medicine and law.

By 1914, he entered the French diplomatic service, eventually serving as secretary at the French Embassy in Pekin, and later in Washington, D.C. as expert on Asian Affairs at the 1923 Arms Limitation Conference. Back in Paris, he worked under the great foreign minister, Aristide Briand, and in 1933 he was named secretary general of the French Foreign Office, remaining until 1940 when he withdrew to Washington, D. C. to escape the Nazi occupation of Paris, remaining through the dark war years.

Saint-John Perse started writing very early. While he was living in Bordeaux André Gide had edited some of his poems published under the title "Eloges" in Gide's *La Nouvelle Revue Française.* When he came back from Pekin with his collection of poems, *Anabase,* André Gide published it under the name of "Saint-John Perse" as the author. Since then, this pen-name became well known in the field of poetry, for he was "a poet of the first rank not only in his own land but in his generation in all lands."

He received for his works, almost always published in limited edition, several prizes and eventually the Nobel Prize for Literature in 1960.

Commenting on Saint Léger, Valery Larbaud said:

> *Il y a quelques années, je demandais aux jeunes poètes de l'Amérique espagnole de renoncer à l'imitation des écoles françaises et castillanes pour créer une poèsie purement américaine. Je ne me doutais guère que mon voeu était en train d'être réalisé, et en langue française par un Français d'Amérique. Car les poèmes que nous donne Mr Saint-Léger Léger ont bien un caractère local et national.*
> (*La Phalange,* Dec. 20, 1911)

One literary critic said of Saint-John Perse:

> *C'est par excellence le poète des profondeurs non tant le poète de l'homme que du monde, des rapports cosmiques de l'humanité et de l'univers, le poète de la grandeur.*

Saint-John Perse's style is often violent, expressive of rapid changes of emotion, often obscure, highly subjective:

Palmes! et la douceur
d'une vieillesse des racines . . .! Les souffles
alizés, les ramiers et la chatte marronne
trouaient l'amer feuillage où, dans la crudité
d'un soir au parfum de Déluge,
les lunes roses et vertes pendaient comme des mangues.

Writings: Poetry: *Eloges,* poèmes, Paris, in *Nouvelle Revue Française,* 1911 (under the name of Saint-Léger Léger); *Eloges* (by Saint-John Perse), Paris, *Nouvelle Revue Française,* 1925 ("Images à Crusoé," Pour fèter une Enfance," "Amitié du Prince" et "Chanson du Présomptif": The last two poems were added to the 1948 edition); *Anabase,* Paris, Nouvelle Revue Française, 1924, second edition, 1925; *Exil,* in *Poetry,* Vol. LIX, No. 6 (March 1942); *Pluies,* Argentina, Lettres françaises, No. 10 Enfance," "Récitation à l'Eloge d'Une Reine," "Histoire du Régent," "Eloges," Amitié du Prince," et "Chanson du Présomtif"; (the last two poems were added to the 1948 edition); *Anabase,* Paris, Nouvelle Revue Française, 1924, 2nd ed., 1925; *Exil,* in *Poetry,* Vol. LIX, No. 6 (March 1942); *Pluies,* Argentine, *Lettres françaises,* No. 10 (Oct. 1943); *Neiges, Sewanee Review,* Vol. LII, No. 4 (Oct. 1944) and Buenos Aires, *Lettres Françaises,* No. 13 (1944); *Vents,* Mesa, Aurora, New York, 1947; *Amers, Poetry,* Vol. 79 (Oct. 1951); *Chronique, Cahiers du Sud* (in 352 copies), Paris, Gallimard, 1960; *Oiseaux,* Paris, Gallimard, 1962; and *Les Oiseaux et l'oeuvre de Saint-John Perse,* Pierre Guerre (comp.), Aix-en-Provence, by La Fondations Saint-John Perse, n.d.; *Chanté par celle qui fut là,* N.R.F., No. 193 (1969); *Oeuvre poètique I: Eloges, La gloire des rois, Anabase, Exil,* (Edition revue et corrigée), Paris, Gallimard, 1960; *Oeuvre poètique II: Vents, Amers, Chronique* (Editions revue et corrigée), Paris, Gallimard, 1960.

Essays: "Briand" (speech delivered at New York University in commemoration of 80th anniversary of Aristide Briand's birth), Aurora, New York, Wells College Press, 1943; "To the Editors of Poetry Review," in *Poetry* (June 1955); "Lettre à Georges Huppert sur l'expression poètique française," *The Berkeley Review* (Winter 1956), bilingual edition, translation by Arthur Knodel; "Tribute to President John F. Kennedy," edited by Pierre Salinger and Sander Vanoccur, in *Encyclopaedia Britannica,* 1964; "Léon-Paul Fargue, poète," *Nouvelle Revue Française* (Aug-Sept 1963), pp. 197-210, 406-422, reprinted in *Poèsies,* Paris, Gallimard, 1963, pp. 7-31; "Pour Dante," Paris, Gallimard, 1965; and in Vol. 257 of *Atti dal Congresso Internazionale di studi danteschi,* pp. 21-29; in English translation by Robert Fitzgerard in *Two Addresses* (of Perse),

New York, Pantheon Books, 1966, pp. 17-31, 45-58.

Address: *Nobel Prize Acceptance Speech,* delivered in Stockholm, Dec. 10, 1960; full text appears as "Saint-John Perse reçoit à Stockholm le Prix Nobel de littérature," in *Le Monde,* 17th year (Dec. 11-12, 1960), p. 16 and other Paris dailies of that period; in separate volume as *Poèsie; Allocution au banquet Nobel du 10 Décembre 1960,* Paris, Gallimard, 1961; English translation by W.H. Auden, "On poetry," New York, Bollingen Foundation, 1961.

Translations of his poetry: *Eloges:* in *Transition,* No. 11 (Feb. 1928), (trans. by Eugène Jolas and Elliot Paul; *Eloges and other Poems,* bilingual edition, introduction by Archibald MacLeish and trans. by Louise Varèse, New York, W.W. Norton, 1944; new edition by Pantheon Books in "Bollingen Series," 1956 (with poem "Berceuse" as *Amitié du Prince,* Milano, All'insegna del pesce d'oro, 1959; *Anabasis:* English translation by T.S. Eliot, London, Faber & Faber, 1930, second edition, 1930, third edition, 1959; *Anabase,* New York, Harcourt Brace, 1938 [dual texts], revised edition by Harcourt, Russian translation by J. Povolzki, 1926; German translation by Bernard G. Groethuysen & Walter Benjamin, 1927; *Exile and other Poems,* bilingual edition, New York, Pantheon Books, Bollingen Series, 1948 (This volume also includes three essays "The Personality of St-John Perse," by Archibald MacLeish, "The Art of St-John Perse," and "The Poet as Guilty Conscience of His Time," (the third article appeared originally in *The Washington Post* (Jan. 22, 1961); "Poem to a Foreign Lady," *Briarcliff Quarterly,* Vol. II, No. 8 (New York, 1946, bilingual edition); "Rains," *Sewanee Review,* Vol. LII, No. 4 (Oct. 1944, trans. by Denis Devlin); "Snows," *Sewanee Review,* Vol. LIII, No. 2 (April 1945, trans. by Denis Devlin); "Winds," New York, Pantheon Books, Bollingen Series, No. XXXIV (trans. by Hugh Chisholm); "Seamarks," *The Yale Review,* Vol. XLIV, No. 3 (Spring 1955, trans. by Wallace Fowlie); also published by Pantheon Books, Bollingen Series, 1961 (bilingual edition); and same text, Harper Torchbooks and Bollingen Series Editions, New York, 1961 (pocket book); *Chronique,* (bilingual edition, Pantheon Books), Bollingen Series, New York, 1961; "Birds," in *Portfolio,* No. 7 (New York, Winter 1963), pp. 24-31, 117-120 (with four illustrations by George Braque), and also Pantheon Books, Bollingen Series, No. LXXXII, 1966 (four of Braque's illustrations but three are different from *Portfolio* edition, trans. by Robert Fitzgerald); *Anabasis y otros poemas,* Havana, Ediciones La Tertulia, 1960.

Recording: *Golden Treasury of Valéry, Claude, Saint-John Perse, Mauriac:* New Rochelle, New York, Spoken Arts (excerpts read by Jean Vilar.

Saint-John Perse: Song for an Equinox, trans. by Richard Howard (Bollingen Series, LXIX, 2, Princeton University, 1977).

Biographical/Critical Sources: The most recent study has been Jacques Robichez' *Sur Saint-John Perse: Eloges, La Gloire des Rois, Anabase, Paris,* CDU et SEDES réunis, 1977. Others are *Hommage à Saint-John Perse; Les Cahiers de la Pléiade* No. X (Summer-Fall, 1950), Paris, Gallimard, (contributions by 32 well-known writers); *Hommage à Saint-John Perse, Combat* (15th Year, May 16, 1957, with contributions by 13 writers); *Hommage à Saint-John Perse,* Paris, Gallimard, 1965 (both collections cited above, *Cahiers de la Pléiade* and *Combat,* together); Maurice Saillet, "Saint John Perse, poète de gloire," followed by a biographical essay on Léger in *Mercure de France,* No. 53 (1952); Alain Bosquet, *Saint John Perse,* first edition, Paris, Pierre Seghers, 1953; revised edition, 1955; later editions, 1959, 1960, 1964, and 1967; Roger Caillois, *Poètique de Saint-John Perse,* Paris, Gallimard, 1954, 1962; Pierre Guerre, *Saint-John Perse et l'homme,* Paris, Gallimard, 1955; Christian Murciaux, *Saint-John Perse,* Paris, Eds. Universitaires, 1960; Jacques Charpier, *Saint-John Perse,* Paris, Bibliothèque Idéale, Gallimard, 1961; Albert Loranquin, *Saint-John Perse,* Paris, Gallimard, 1963; Arthur Knodel, *Saint John Perse, a study of his poetry,* Edinburgh, Edinburgh University Press, 1966; Pierre Emmanuel, *Saint John Perse and Presence* (lecture delivered Dec. 2, 1968, at the Library of Congress), with a bibliography of Perse's writings in the Collections of the Library of Congress by Ruth S. Freitag, Washington, D.C., U.S. Government Printing Office, 1971; Daniel Racine, *La Fortune de Saint-John Perse en Amérique jusqu'en 1970,* Lille, Service de Reproduction des Thèses, Université de Lille, 1973; Emile Yoyo, *Saint John Perse et le conteur,* Paris, Bordas, Collection "Etude," 1971; article: "Aragon et Breton: *Saint-John*

Perse in *"Treize études,"* SIC No. 29 (May 1918); Alain Bosquet, "L'oeuvre de Saint-John Perse," in *Journal des poètes,* No. 10 (Bruselles, Dec. 1949); Luc Estang, "Des poèmes de Saint-John Perse," in *Arts et Lettres* (Dec. 1945); Denis de Rougement, "Saint-John Perse en Amérique," Paris, *Journal des deux mondes* (1948); Claude Roy, "Saint-John Perse," in *Descriptions critiques,* Vol. I, Paris, Gallimard, 1949, pp. 133-145; Maurice E. Coindreau, "Quatre poèmes de Saint-John Perse," in *France-Amérique* (May 15, 1949), p. 4; René Girard, "L'histoire dans l'oeuvre de Saint-John Perse," in *Romantic Review,* Vol. XLIV, No. 1 (Feb. 1953); Emile Henriot, "L'oeuvre poètique de Saint-John Perse," *Le Monde* (Paris, April 8, 1953); René Girard, "Winds and poetic experience," *Berkeley Review,* Vol. I, No. 1 (Winter 1956), pp. 46-52; Wallace Fowlie, "The Poetic of Saint-John Perse," in *Poetry,* Vol. 82 (Sept. 1953); Roger Caillois, "L'image chez Saint-John Perse," *Table Ronde,* No. 72 (Dec. 1953); Pierre Guerre, *Saint-John Perse et l'homme,* Paris, Gallimard, 1955; Pierre de Boisdeffre, "Saint-John Perse l'exilé," in *Histoire vivante de la littérature d'aujourd'hui,* Paris, Le Livre Contemporain, 1958, pp. 470-488; Princesse Bibesco, "Les trois visages du Prix Nobel, 1960," in *Nouvelles Littéraires,* No. 1731 (Nov. 3, 1960); Pierre de Boisdeffre, "Saint-John Perse, Prix Nobel," in *Revue des Deux Mondes,* (Dec. 1, 1960), pp. 455-461; Christian Murciaux, *Saint John Perse,* Paris, Eds. Universitaires, 1961; Dore Ashton, "Saint-John Perse's Guadeloupe," *Kenyon Review,* Vol. 23 (Summer 1961), pp. 520-526; Pieyre de Mandiargues, "A l'honneur de la chair," in *Nouvelle Revue Française,* (May 1, 1962); Léopold Sédar Senghor, "Saint-John Perse ou poèsie du royaume d'enfance," *Table Ronde,* No. 172 (May 1962); Jean Guillou, "Karukéra, Ile natale de Saint-John Perse," in *French Review,* Vol. 39 (Nov. 1965), pp. 281-287; Edouard Eliet, "Honneur à Saint-John Perse," in *Hommages et Témoignages littéraires,* Paris, Gallimard, 1965; Paul Claudel, "Un poème de Saint-John Perse: *Vent*" in *Honneur à Saint-John Perse,* Paris, Gallimard, 1965, p. 44; Katherine Garrison Chapin, "Saint-John Perse chez ses amis d'Amérique," in *Honneur à Saint-John Perse,* Paris, Gallimard, 1965, p. 287; Katherine Garrison Chapin, "Poet of Wide Horizons—A Note on Saint-John Perse," in *The Quarterly Journal of the Library of Congress,* Vol. 27, No. 2 (April 1970), p. 106; Joseph H. McMahon, "A Man Singing of Ambiguities: the Poetry of Saint-John Perse," Stanford University, 1960, p. 7; Pierre M. Van Rutten, "Le Langage poètique de Saint-John Perse," Université d'Ottawa, 1969, p. XIX; Roger Little, "Saint-John Perse et le parler créole," *Revue des Sciences humaines* (July-Sep. 1970), pp. 467-471. Also see: Elizabeth Jackson, *Worlds Apart: Structural Parallels in the poetry of Paul Valéry, Saint-John Perse, Benjamin Péret et René Char,* Paris and The Hague, Mouton, 1976; Christian Doumet, *Les thèmes aériens dans l'oeuvre de Saint-John Perse, Archives des Lettres modernes:* Coll. Etudes de Critique et d'histoire littéraire, No. 165 (1976); Cécile Fournier, "Les thèmes édéniques dans l'oeuvre de Saint-John Perse," *Archives des Lettres modernes,* No. 165, 1976; Eveline Caduc, *Saint-John Perse, Connaissance et création,* Paris, Impr. José Corti, 1977; Henriette Levillain, *Le Rituel poètique de Saint-John Perse* (Collection Idées), Paris, Gallimard, 1977; Yves Alain Favre, *Saint-John Perse: le langage et le sacré,* Paris, José Corti, 1977; Roger Little, *Saint-John Perse: Research Bibliographic and checklists,* London, Grant and Cotler Ltd., 1971; "Hommage à Saint-John Perse," in *La Nouvelle Revue Française,* No. 278 (Feb. 1976); "Lectures de Saint-John Perse," (comp. by Jean Burges and Roger Little), *Cahiers du 20ème siècle,* No. 7, Klincksieck, 1976; Richard Abel, "St-John Perse encounters T.S. Eliot," *Revue de Littérature comparée* (June-Sep. 1975), No. 3, pp. 423-437; Richard Abel, "The Influence of St-John Perse on T.S. Eliot," in *Contemporary Literature,* XIV (Spring 1973), pp. 213-236.

SAINT-LEGER LEGER

(see under **SAINT-JOHN PERSE**)

SAINT-LOUIS, Carlos

b. January 4, 1923, Petit-Goâve, Haiti. Poet, literary editor, journalist, teacher.

Saint-Louis attended the primary school at Petit-Goâve, and the Lycée Sténio Vincent in Saint-Marc. He studied accountancy, but mostly has worked as a schoolteacher. He has published many articles in various newspapers and is now co-editor of *Haiti-Journal.* He has been an active promotor of the Haitiana Association.

Writings: Poetry: *Flammes, poèmes,* Port-au-Prince, Impr. de l'Etat, 1947; *Flots de haine,* preface by Maurice A. Lubin, Port-au-Prince, Impr. Le Réveil, 1949; *Chant du retour* (Collection Haitiana), Port-au-Prince, Impr. H. Deschamps, 1954.

Anthology: *Panorama de la poèsie haitienne* (with Maurice A. Lubin), Port-au-Prince, Impr. H. Deschamps, 1950.

Literary History: *Manifeste de l'école réaliste haitienne,* (with Antoine Dupoux), Port-au-Prince, Impr. H. Deschamps, 1950.

Essay: *Valeurs de civilisation ou propos d'un visiteur,* Port-au-Prince, Impr. N.A. Théodore, 1965.

SAINT-MAURICE, Rémy

b. ca. 1873, Martinique.
Novelist.

Saint-Maurice is known today only for his one fictional study of the volcanic destruction of Guadeloupe's old capital, St. Pierre, in 1902.

Writings: Novel: *Les derniers jours de Saint Pierre,* roman, Paris, A. Lemerre, 1903.

SAINT-PRIX, Rone Eleuthère

b. ca. 1865, Saint-Pierre, Martinique; d. May 8, 1902, Saint-Pierre.
Poet, tradesman.

Although Saint-Prix was engaged in commercial activities, he was always interested in poetry and published most of his works in local newspapers.

Writings: Poetry: *Le triomphe du devoir,* Saint-Pierre, Impr. de la Défense Coloniale, 1895.

SAINT-REMY, Joseph

(or **SAINT-REMY des Cayes**)

b. 1818 or 1819, Sainte-Rose, Guadeloupe; d. September 9, 1858, Paris.
Biographer, poet, journalist, historian.

Coming to Haiti to live in Aux Cayes as a child, Saint-Rémy started his education in Haiti but completed it in France, studying law. Active in the anti-slavery movement, he was one of a group of persons of pure and mixed African blood who offered a specially struck medal to the French député Isambert on November 30, 1838, to honor him for his work in abolishing slavery in the French colonies. Saint-Rémy contributed journalistic pieces to such Paris journals as the anti-slavery paper, *Revue des Colonies,* and his poetry began to see print in French and Haitian journals while he was still a law student.

Inspired by Lamartine's treatment of Christophe, Saint-Rémy set himself to writing a full-scale study of the Haitian hero, publishing his biography in 1850. Although he looked upon Christophe as a tyrant and regretted the excesses of both sides during the Haitian struggle, he remained more French than Afro-Haitian all his life. Nevertheless, he still urged his countrymen to assert their cultural and linguistic independence of France.

Writings: Poetry: in various French and Haitian journals, including *Le Manifeste* (Dec. 23, 1847), which contained the poem "A Monsieur Chenet."

Essays: "Esquisses biographiques sur les hommes de lettres d'Haiti," "Essai sur Henri Christophe," in *Revue des Colonies,* 1839; "Essai sur le préjugé de couleur dans les colonies, 1840.

History: *Mémoires pour servir à l'Histoire d'Haiti par Boisrond Tonnerre,* Proclamation au nom du Peuple Souverain, Paris, 1843.

Biography: *Vie de Toussaint-Louverture,* Paris, Impr. de Moquet, 1850; *Pétion et Haiti: étude monographique et historique,* 5 vols., Paris (Vols. I and II in 1854, Vol. III in 1855, and Vols. IV and V in 1857); *Mémoires du Général Toussaint Louverture écrits par lui-même, pouvant servir à l'histoire de sa vie* (with a fine picture by Choubard), Paris, 1853.

SAINT-ROBERT

(pseudonym for **Félix VIARD**)

SAINVILLE, Léonard

b. March 3, 1910, Lorrain, Martinique; d. May 31, 1977, Paris.
Novelist, biographer, anthologist, teacher.

Sainville attended schools at Basse-Pointe. After a hard childhood, Sainville, the eldest of eight children, went to Paris in 1930 to study for a teaching degree at the Ecole Normale. He later entered the Sorbonne, and overcoming great hardships, finally earned the licence in letters and a diploma in history and geography.

Sainville served in the French army from 1939 to 1941.

Sainville became a professor of literature in Paris in the late 1930's and later was named a head researcher for Senegal. He earned his doctorate with a thesis on the condition of blacks in the colonies.

He was openly active in radical political organizations.

Writings: Novels: *Dominique, nègre esclave,* Paris, Fasquelle, 1950 (Prix des Antilles, 1952); *Au fond du bourg,* Lausanne, Switzerland, Ed. de la Cité, 1964; in progress: "L'Etre prolongé," and "Si la flamme est transmise," and "L'Enfance de Dominique," (to be published).

Editor of Anthology: *Romanciers et conteurs négro-africains,* 2 vols., Paris, Présence Africaine, Vol. 1, 1963, and Vol. II, 1968.

Biography: *Victor Schoelcher,* Paris, Fasquelle, 1950.

History (thesis): *La condition des noirs aux Antilles Françaises durant la première moitié du XIXè siècle,* Paris, Sorbonne, 1971; *Noirs et hommes de couleur du passé; Mer des Caraïbes.*

Essay: "Les fondements négro-africains de la culture dans les Caraïbes et la lutte pour leur sauvegarde," in *Présence Africaine,* Issue Nos. 101-102, pp. 129-157.

SALAVINA

(pseudonym for **Virgile SAVANE**)
b. 1865, Martinique; d. ca. 1920.
Novelist, poet.

Salavina was a survivor of the Mont Pelé eruption of 1902 which destroyed St. Pierre, killing most of its inhabitants. Though he was a follower of the innovative poet, Daniel Thaly, Salavina basically was very conservative in his subject and metrics. He contributed to the early anthology, *Fleurs des Antilles.*

Writings: Poetry: *Fleurs du Soleil (poèsies)* II, *Après Waterloo (poème),* III *Madellina* ("drame en un acte, en vers"), Saint-Pierre, Sainville, 1895-96; also: *Les Tropicales,* Paris, Eds. de la revue des Indépendants, 1921.

Novels: *Trente ans de Saint-Pierre,* preface by J. Monnerot, Fort-de-France, Impr. Deslandes, 1910; *Amours tropicales* ou *Martinique aux siècles des rois,* Paris, 1912; and *Les Volcaniques,* 1921.

SALES, Pierre Marc

b. April 29, 1930, Pétionville, Haiti; d. date unknown.
Poet, storywriter, journalist, essayist.

Salès received his education in Port-au-Prince and was a contributor to many journals.

Writings: Poetry: *Ma Bohème,* Port-au-Prince, Impr. de l'Etat, 1948.

Essays: *Le poison et l'antidote; Préludes,* Port-au-Prince, Impr. N.A. Théodore, 1958; *La révolution capitale,* Port-au-Prince, 1957.

SALGADO, Antoine

b. November 12, 1912, Port-au-Prince, Haiti.
Poet, playwright, lawyer.

Salgado was educated in Port-au-Prince and graduated from the Faculty of Law. His main interest has been in the theater though his career has seen him as cultural attaché in the Ministry of Foreign Affairs and Secretary General at the Ministry of Justice.

He has published poems and articles in *Le Temps Revue, La Gazette des Tribunaux,* and *Le Courrier de l'Education.*

Writings: Plays: *La rivière rouge, pièce en trois actes,* preface by Colbert Bonhomme, Port-au-Prince, Impr. La Gazette du Palais, 1954, and performed Rex Théatre (Oct. 30, 1953); *La route des anonymes, pièce en trois actes,* preface by Pradel Pompilus, Impr. de l'Etat, 1957; *La révolte des femmes; Le triomphe de la terre; La faillite des Raras; Guerre à la nuit; Acaau ou solution paysanne.* (unpublished).

Legal Studies: *L'adultérin devant la société,* Port-au-Prince, Ed. Panorama, 1964; *Problèmes de succession dans l'arrière-pays,* Port-au-Prince, 1967.

SAMPEUR, Marie Angélique Virginie

b. March 28, 1839, Port-au-Prince, Haiti; d. June 8, 1919, Port-au-Prince.
Poet, storywriter, musician, teacher.

Sampeur received a sound education in Port-au-Prince. She was a teacher for a period and then became Directrice of the Pensionnat National des Jeunes Filles. She suffered through an unhappy marriage with Oswald Durand, whom she continued to love even after their separation, and these experiences are the subject of much of her verse. Her only son, Ludovic Lamothe, has become a noted musician.

Virginie Sampeur was the first woman writer in Haiti, publishing her poems and stories in such journals as *La Ronde* and *Haiti Littéraire et Scientifique.*

Her verse was personal and followed the more or less late romantic French style of the period. The third stanza from her poem "L'Abandonnée" illustrates her work and her overwhelming sorrow:

Ah! si vous étiez mort, votre éternel silence,
Moins âpre qu'en ce jour, aurait son éloquence;
Car ce ne serait plus le cruel abandon;
Je dirais: "Il est mort, mais il sait bien m'entendre,
Et peut-être, en mourant, n'a-t-il pu se défendre
De murmurer: "Pardon!"

Some of her poems appeared in Barutey's *Morceaux Choisis,* dedicated to women writers.

In his view on Haitian poetry in the introduction of *Confidences et Mélancolies,* Georges Sylvain wrote about her:

> *Et voici que s'élevant au-dessus du murmure de ces symphonies lointaines une plainte d'une mélancolie et d'une douceur infinies a retenti jusqu'à nous! C'est la cantilène de Sapho, l'immortelle abandonnée qui redit après l'héroïne grecque, mais avec une bien moindre sûreté d'expression, une des rares haitiennes qu'ait tentées la gloire d'Anacaona.*

Writings: Poetry: in various collections and journals, but uncollected.

Stories: *Angèle Dufour; Vierge veuve; Fleur révélatrice; Francine; Le songe d'Estelle,* in miscellaneous journals, but uncollected.

SANNON, Horace Pauléus

b. April 7, 1870, Cayes, Haiti; d. August 27, 1938, Port-au-Prince.
Biographer, political scientist, historian.

After Sannon completed his education in Cayes, he was the recipient of a scholarship to Paris. He studied medicine there for three years but dropped that field for political science. While in Paris, he published his first historical work in 1898. After several years back in Haiti, he lived in Cayes and Jacmel as commissioner of the customs office, and President Nord Alexis named him as his Minister for Foreign Affairs. Later, he became Minister of Haiti to Washington, D.C. (1910).

During the American occupation period, Sannon was a strong supporter of the Haitian Society of History and Geography. After his failure in 1930 to be elected senator and then president, he was named the Minister of Foreign Affairs in the first cabinet of Sténio Vincent (elected President of Haiti, November 18, 1930). Sannon finished his career as Director of the Lycée Pétion.

Writings: Biographies: *Un journaliste sous Boyer,* Port-au-Prince, 1899; *Boisrond-Tonnerre et son temps,* Port-au-Prince, Impr. Aug. A. Héraux, 1904.

History: *Histoire de Toussaint Louverture,* 3 vols., Port-au-Prince, Aug. A. Héraux, 1920, 1932, 1933; *Essai historique sur la révolution de 1843,* Les Cayes, Impr. Bonnefil, 1905; *La guerre de l'Indépendance, études historiques,* Port-au-Prince, Impr. Chéraquit, 1925; *Le Cap-Français vu par une américaine* (Miss Hassal), Port-au-Prince, Impr. Aug. A. Héraux, 1936.

Political Science: *Haiti et le régime parlementaire: examen de la constitution de 1889,* Paris, Albert Fontemoin (Impr. Bussiou, St. Amand), 1898; *Le projet de révision de la constitution: examen des amendements proposés,* Port-au-Prince, Impr. de L'Haitien, 1927.

Biographical/Critical Sources: A. Viatte, *Histoire littéraire de l'Amérique française,* Quebec, Presses Universitaires, 1953, pp. 423-424; Dr. Pradel Pompilus & Frères de l'Instruction Chrétienne, *Manuel illustré d'histoire de la littérature haitienne,* Port-au-Prince, Impr. H. Deschamps, 1961, pp. 502-517; Ghislain Gouraige, *Histoire de la littérature haitienne,* Port-au-Prince, Impr. N.A. Théodore, 1960, pp. 464-466.

SANSARICQ, Walter

b. December 18, 1890, Jérémie, Haiti; d. 1953, Port-au-Prince.
Poet.

Sansaricq was educated in Jérémie and Port-au-Prince and graduated from Law School. He was a teacher and became a Senator.

Sansaricq was of the "old school" of poets and though he published his one volume of poetry, *Le jardin du coeur,* in 1949, he had little in common with the revolutionary poets and novelists of the younger generation who were rebellious under the occupations of the 1920's and early 30's. Nor was he a part of the revolutionary group of the mid 40's. His collection was published in France and won him the Jeux Floraux du Languedoc competition of 1949.

Writings: Poetry: *Le jardin du coeur,* Lamalou-les-Bains (Hérault), France, Ed. de la Revue du Languadoc, 1949. (This collection contains many of Sansaricq's early poems: "Conversion," dated August 29, 1910, "Etat d'âme," dated 1913, "Vaine promesse," dated 1914, and "En face de la nature," of 1914 also.)

Biographical/Critical Sources: Ghislain Gouraige, *Histoire de la littérature haitienne,* Port-au-Prince, Impr. N.A. Théodore, 1960, pp. 331-333.

SAVAIN, Pétion

b. February 15, 1906, Port-au-Prince, Haiti; d. 1973.
Novelist, painter.

Pétion Savain was educated in Port-au-Prince. Very early he became interested in painting and he has become one of the most noted artists of Haiti, though he was not labeled a primitivist as were Hector Hyppolite or Castera Bazile.

In literature, Savain was a part of the "Indigenist" movement which stressed the importance of Haitian realities and the old Haitian traditions still alive in the country. Savain can be grouped among the writers J.B. Cinéas and the Marcelin Brothers.

Writings: Novels: *La Case de Damballah,* Port-au-Prince, Impr. de l'Etat, 1939; second edition, Paris, les Oeuvres Nouvelles, 1943; *Bois-de-Chène,"* unpublished.

Art: *Considérations sur la décoration murale à l'Exposition Internationale de Port-au-Prince,* Port-au-Prince, 1949.

SAVANE, Virgile

(see under pseudonym: **SALAVINA**)

SCHWARZ-BART, Simone

b. January 8, 1938, Guadeloupe.
Novelist.

Simone Schwarz-Bart attended the schools of Pointe-à-Pitre and went abroad to complete her education in Paris and Dakar. She married the established writer André Schwarz-Bart, a German refugee whose novel, *Le Dernier des Justes,* won the Prix Goncourt in 1959.

She has won several prizes with her novels. Regarding her *Pluie et vent sur Télumée Miracle,* one critic wrote:

> *La prose de Simone Schwarz-Bart est nourrie de proverbes, d'images, de tournures arrachées du "fin fond" du terroir qu'il nous plaît de voir victorieusement mis à la sauce du français, nous vengeant ainsi de la nuée de professeurs dits métropolitains qui barraient nos copies de rouge: "Créolisme! Créolisme!"*

This work won *Elle* magazine's Grand Prix 1973 des Lectrices. The novel's heroine, Télumée, is raised by her grandmother, "Reine Sans Nom," an "haute négresse," and the girl struggles for freedom, self-confidence and dignity. When she dies at book's end, she cries: "Je mourrai là comme je suis debout, dans mon petit jardin, quelle joie . . .!"

Un plat de porc aux bananes vertes is set in Paris in the mid-20th century as we follow the life of a very old creole woman from Martinique to her last resting place in a home for old people. She relives her past, almost back to slavery, and the actions of Europe and America are of blood, lust, and cruelty—leaving to the Africans pain, poverty, and isolation.

Writings: Novels: *Pluie et vent sur Télumé Miracle,* Paris, Ed. Seuil, 1972; *Un plat de porc aux bananes vertes* (with André Schwarz-Bart), Paris, Seuil, 1967; *La Mulâtresse solitude* (with André Schwarz-Bart), Paris, Seuil, 1972, and English translations by Ralph Manheim as *A Woman Named Solitude,* New York, Atheneum, 1972.

SEJOUR-MAGLOIRE, Francis L.

(or **Francis L. MAGLOIRE**)
b. January 1, 1940, Jérémie, Haiti.
Poet, storywriter.

Séjour-Magloire was educated in Port-au-Prince at the Lycée Toussaint Louverture.

Writings: Poetry: *Du crépuscule de l'aube à l'aube du crépuscule,* Port-au-Prince, Arts Graphiques Presses, 1962; *Merdicolore,* Port-au-Prince, Eds. Panorama, 1963; *Poème des Cacadeurs,* Port-au-Prince, 1965.

Stories: *La facture du diable,* Printed in Merdovie [sic], 1966.

SIMONISE, Alfred

b. 1822, Port-au-Prince, Haiti; d. 1887, Port-au-Prince.
Playwright, teacher.

Simonise began his studies in Port-au-Prince and completed his education in France. After returning to Haiti, he taught and then became a director of a secondary school in 1853. He was later named Secretary at the Haitian Legation in Paris.

Writings: Religion: *La Croix ou la mort* (religious book written with the French writer, O. de la Countrye).

Plays: *L'Alcade de Zalamea (Calderon), étude dramatique en sept parties,* Port-au-Prince, Impr. de E. Robin, 1873; *Les étrennes de ces dames; comédie en un acte,* Port-au-Prince, Impr. H. Chauvet et Cie, 1896; *Deux lièvres à la fois (comédie en un acte en vers),* unpublished.

DeSOLMS, Melle

(pseudonym for **Thérèse de BETZON**)

STACO, Louis

b. April 4, 1887, Colon, Panama; d. October 31, 1918, Cayes, Haiti.
Poet, lawyer, judge.

Staco was born of Haitian parents in Colon but soon was brought to Haiti where he attended the school of the Christian Brothers and the Lycée Philippe Guerrier, both in Cayes. He later took a law degree.

He was a professor at the Lycée Philippe Guerrier and served as deputy commissioner at the civil court of Cayes. He also served as a judge of the Cayes court.

Writings: Poetry: "Violettes" (poèmes), unpublished; verse in various journals.

STEPHENSON, Elie

b. December 20, 1944, Cayenne, Guyane.
Poet, playwright, musician, government official.

Elie Stéphenson completed his primary and secondary schooling at the Lycée Félix Eboué in Cayenne. He holds the following academic degrees: "Bachelier en Philosophie;" "Diplôme de Second Cycle de Développement Economique et Social" (Paris, 1970); and the "Diplôme de Troisième Cycle de Développement Economique et Social" (Paris, 1975). Stephenson is an official of the Office of Economic and Social Planning, Cayenne.

He has served, or is serving, as President of the Paris chapter of the "Union des Etudiants Guyanais" (1967), Guyanese representative to the "Festival d'Art et de Culture des Caraibes (CARIFESTA) in September of 1972 at Georgetown, Guyana, Assistant Secretary of the "Syndicat des enseignants de l'enseignement technique en Guyane" (1971-1972) and Assistant Secretary of the "Mouvement National Guyanais." He is also a charter member of the theatrical group, "Troupe Angéla Davis." Stéphenson is also a composer and has given recitals in Cayenne, Paramaribo and Georgetown (Guyana).

Elie Stéphenson's poetry strives to express an Afro-Guyanese essence and is concerned with the metaphysics of the ancestral uprooting of his people and the attendant problems of identity between culture and race. However, his poetry is not to be thought of as turned wholly inward, for it also expresses a pervading sentiment of love, in the broadest sense of the word, for all mankind.

Writings: Poetry: *Une flèche pour le pays à l'encan,* Paris, P. J. Oswald, 1975; and work in various collections, including *New Writing in the Caribbean,* A.J. Seymour, ed., Georgetown, Guyana, 1972.

Plays: *O Mayouri* (unpublished, written in Guyanese creole), and *Un rien de pays* (unpublished).

Works in Progress: *Terres Mêlées* (poems); and *Catacombes de soleil* (novel).

SYLVAIN, Georges

b. April 2, 1866, Puerto Plata, Dominican

Republic; d. August 2, 1925, Port-au-Prince.

Poet, translator (in French and creole), travel writer, historian.

Sylvain was born in the Dominican Republic while his family was in exile. After schooling at the school of the Christian Brothers of Port-de-Paix and at the Petit Séminaire Collège Saint-Martial in Port-au-Prince, he went on to Paris for study at the Lycée Stanislas and later earned a law degree at the Université de Paris. Returning to Haiti to take up a professional career at the bar, he quickly became a leading member of the literary group which founded and contributed to *La Ronde* magazine, launched in 1896.

Although the new movement had sought a fresh approach to the writing of verse in French, in fact much of the *La Ronde* poetry was stilted and less than spontaneous, a criticism that for long relegated the group's efforts to scorn by later genuinely liberated poets. Sylvain and his friend, Damoclès Vieux, were particularly refined and rich in their embroidered styles, and subsequently were criticized for it. However, there has been lately some effort to "rehabilitate" the poets of the turn of the century to their rightful place as genuinely concerned artists in the currents of their day.

Sylvain served as Haiti's Minister Plenipoteniary to Paris (1909-1911) and lived into the period of the United States occupation, which began in 1915. He was a leader in the intellectual protest and consequent intellectual ferment which came as a reaction to the sudden loss of independence after 112 years of hard-fought freedom from racism and foreign occupation.

On his death, a grand funeral was provided to honor his combativeness and his great nationalist feeling.

Georges Sylvain's son, Normil Sylvain, became an important poet and critic in his own right.

Writings: Poetry: *Confidences et mélancolies; poèsies (1885-1898),* preface by Justin Dévot, Paris, Ateliers Haitiens, Impr. Lithog., 1901, translation of La Fontaine's *Fables* in a creole version: *Cric? Crac?,* first edition, Paris, Ateliers Haitiens, 1901; and second edition, Paris, Impr. Dussand, 1929, and Port-au-Prince, 1929 (printed for Mme. Georges Sylvain, the poet's widow). His creole poems owe a strong debt to the work and example of the Martiniquais fabulist Marbot, author of *Les Bambous* (Fort-Royale, Martinique, 1846).

Speeches: *La lecture; recueil de causeries faites aux conférences post-scolaires au Comité de l'Alliance Française,* Port-au-Prince, Impr. de l'Abeille, 1908.

Essay: *Le "Thompsonisme,"* with Athanase Laforest, Port-au-Prince, 1889.

History: *Dix années de lutte pour la liberté (1915-1925),* 2 vols., Port-au-Prince, Impr. H. Deschamps, 1959.

Editor: (with Dantès Bellegarde, Solon Ménos and Amilcar Duval), *Morceaux Choisis,* 2 vols. (poèsie and prose), Port-au-Prince, Impr. de Mme. F. Smith, 1904.

Biographical/Critical Sources: Normil Sylvain's article, "Chronique-Program" which includes the particularly interesting "Un rêve de Georges Sylvain," first published in *La Revue Indigène* (July 1927) and given special treatment in the Paris journal, *Nouvelle Revue Française* (Oct.

1927); Jean Price-Mars in *Une étape de l'évolution haitienne,* Port-au-Prince, Impr. La Presse, 1929, pp. 65-66; Ghislain Gouraige, *Histoire de la littérature haitienne,* Port-au-Prince, Impr. N.A. Théodore, 1960, pp. 153-156; Pradel Pompilus & les Frères de l'Instruction Chrétienne, *Manuel illustré d'histoire de la littérature haitienne,* Port-au-Prince, Ed. H. Deschamps, 1961, pp. 220-228; Hénock Trouillot, *Les origines sociales de la littérature haitienne,* Port-au-Prince, Impr. N.A. Théodore, 1962, pp. 350-354; Dantès Bellegarde, *Ecrivains haitiens,* second edition, Port-au-Prince, Ed. H. Deschamps, 1950, pp. 190-200; P. Williams, "La Fontaine in Haitian Creole: A Study of Cric? Crac?" by Georges Sylvain, diss., Fordham University, 1971.

SYLVAIN, Louis François Normil

(a.k.a. **NORMIL-GEORGES**)

b. July 24, 1901, Port-au-Prince, Haiti; d. February 1, 1929, Port-au-Prince.
Poet, essayist, critic.

Son of the important poet of the *La Ronde* group, Georges Sylvain, Normil naturally turned to poetry. He soon became a leading member of the nativist group in Paris in 1926, gathered around Thoby-Marcelin and Jacques Roumain, and the successor movement in Port-au-Prince of the same artists who founded *La Revue Indigène* which appeared in the 1927-29 period. Normil's essay on the dream of his father in *La Revue Indigène* was a bold demand for a specific program for the new poets, because "La poèsie est un instrument de connaissance." He argued, and insisted that literature is the infallible expression of the soul of the people. He accepted the necessity of the poet's studying new poets and opening themselves to new cultural currents, even those imposed upon them by force, but he insisted on the artist's need for an inner integrity and his use only of genuinely needed new elements or formal structures.

Normil Sylvain of course also knew and loved French poetry and was happy in the thought Haiti had poetic allies in Martinique and Guadeloupe in the Caribbean. But, he also wanted a fresh start, and even a return to the deepest current in Haitian life, that of Mother Africa:

> *La vraie poèsie, vous ne la trouverez jamais si vous n'avez pas l'âme d'un petit enfant. La vraie poèsie, je la trouve dans les refrains que nous chantaient le soir les nourrices noires qui bercèrent notre enfance.*
> (from "La jeune littérature haitienne," *Revue Indigène,* Aug., 1927, pp. 51-52)

Dead at 28, Normil published no volume of collected works but he remains an important poet and critic in Haitian literary history.

Writings: Essays: in various journals, including "Léonidas et moi," in *La Trouée* (Aug. 1, 1927); "Chronique-programme," in *La Revue Indigène* (July 1927); "La jeune littérature haitienne," in *La Revue Indigène* (Aug. 1927).

Biographical/Critical Sources: Auguste Viatte, *Histoire littéraire de l'Amérique française,* Laval, Quebec, Presses Universitaires, 1954, pp. 439-441; Naomi M. Garret, *The Renaissance of Haitian poetry,* Paris, Présence Africaine, 1963, pp. 87-93.

SYLVAIN-BOUCHEREAU, Madeleine G.

b. July 5, 1905, Port-au-Prince, Haiti; d. February, 1970, New York.
Sociologist, teacher.

Madeleine Sylvain Bouchereau was educated in Port-au-Prince, and in the United States where she took a degree in sociology and education. She was a teacher at the Technical School of Agriculture and became General Inspector for Rural Education.

Sylvain fought strongly for Haitian women's rights and was for many years the president of La Ligue Féminine d'Action Sociale. She once ran unsuccessfully for the Senate.

Writings: Education: *Education des femmes en Haiti,* Port-au-Prince, Impr. de l'Etat, 1944 (this book won the Susan B. Anthony prize awarded by Bryn Mawr College (Pennsylvania); *Haiti et ses femmes; une étude d'évolution culturelle,* Port-au-Prince, Impr. Les Presses Libres, 1957.

School Text: *Lecture haitienne; la famille Renaud,* Port-au-Prince, Impr. H. Deschamps, 1944.

Scholarship: *Haiti portrait Eines Freien Laudes,* Frankfurt, Verlag Dr Ukldemar Kramer, 1954.

SYLVAIN-COMHAIRE, Suzanne

(née **SYLVAIN**)

b. ca. 1903, Haiti; d. Nigeria, June 20, 1975.

Folklorist, sociologist, linguist, teacher.

Sylvain was educated in France where she followed primary and secondary classes. She later graduated from the University of Paris with her licence in letters in 1936 and her doctorate some years later. On her return to Haiti, Sylvain-Comhaire founded the Ecole des Lettres de Port-au-Prince and taught the history of the French language and French phonetics. She also was an Inspector of Schools in Port-au-Prince.

She spent a great number of years in Ethiopia and Zaire (while on missions for UNESCO) and in Nosakka, Nigeria, where she died.

Writings: Folklore: *Contes haitiens* (extract from *Revue du Folklore Français et du Folklore Colonial*), Paris, 1933; *Creole Tales from Haiti* (extract from *Journal of American Folklore*), New York, 1937-1938; *Les Contes haitiens,* 2 vols., Port-au-Prince, Wetteren, Impr. de Moester, 1937; *Quelques contes du pays d'Haiti,* Port-au-Prince, 1937; *Contes du pays d'Haiti,* Port-au-Prince, 1938; *Tu manges avec une femme (contes populaires),* Bandundu, Zaire, CEEBA, 1973; *Le roman de Bouqui,* Quebec, Eds. Léméac, 1973.

Philology: *Le créole haitien, morphologie et syntaxe,* Port-au-Prince chez l'auteur, 1936 (printed at Wetteren, de Moester).

Sociology: *Loisirs et divertissements dans la région de Kenscoff, Haiti,* Brussells, Impr. des Travaux Publics, 1938; *Etudes haitiennes,* Port-au-Prince, Impr. du Collège Vertières, 1939; *A propos du vocabulaire des croyances paysannes,* Port-au-Prince, 1938; *Making a living in the Marbial Valley* (Haiti), written with Dr. Aldred Métraux & Edouard Berrouet, Paris, 1951; *Food and leisure among the African youth of Leopoldville* (Belgian Congo), University of Cape Town, South Africa, 1950; *Migrations à Addis-Ababa,* Addis-Ababa, Ethiopia, 1962; *Participation des femmes à l'industrie et au commerce en Afrique,* Lagos, 1963; *Les femmes de Kinshasa, Hier et aujourd'hui,* La Haye et Paris, Mouton, 1968; *Le nouveau dossier Afrique* (with Jean Comhaire, Fernand Bézy, Amadou Mahtar M'Bow, and others), Verviers, Belgium, Marabout University, 1971.

Bibliography: *A bibliography with book reviews,* Madison, New Jersey, 1959.

TALBOM, Léon

b. ca. 1891, Bouillante, Guadeloupe.

Novelist, art critic.

Talbom was born of French parents who came to live in Guadeloupe. He attended school on the island, but completed his education in France.

Talbom returned to Guadeloupe for some years, but left to live in Paris where he works as an art critic. His one novel is an early study of Guadeloupe given its old name "Karukéra."

Writings: Novel: *Karukéra,* Paris, Impr. de Vaugirard, 1921.

TARDON, Raphaël

b. October 27, 1911, Fort-de-France, Martinique; d. January 16, 1966.

Novelist, essayist, storywriter, government official.

Raphaël Tardon was born into a wealthy mulatto family in Martinique with large ancestral estates. After studies at the

Lycée Schoelcher in Fort-de-France, he earned *licènces* in law and history in France, served briefly in the French army at the outbreak of World War II, and later in the resistance in southern France. After the war, he worked as a journalist in Paris before setting off to serve the Minister of Information in Madagascar, Dakar and Guadeloupe.

Director of the Information Service in Guadeloupe where he was also Chef de Cabinet of the Prefect of Guadeloupe for three years, he has traveled widely in the United States and throughout the Pacific.

Tardon has not supported the idea of Négritude, and he has failed to publish any paper in *Présence Africaine.* For him, the only important thing, he has said, is the capacity of a person and not his color.

His first work was a collection of stories, *Bleu des Iles* (1946), but he is best known for his novels: *Starkenfirst* (1947), which deals with the slave trade, and *La Caldeira* (1948), centered around the eruption of Mont Pelé. In *La Caldeira* he attacked Caribbean prejudices—white and black. In 1950 he shifted his geographical interest to Polynesia to write *Christ au Poing,* a novel about the alienation of Tahitians from their own values by the influx of Western culture. In 1951 he published a biography entitled *Toussaint Louverture: le Napoleon noir,* and in 1963 a racial study: *Noirs et Blancs.*

Critics have stressed both Tardon's effort to show that the place of mulattoes is in the camp of the Blacks, and his unwillingness to become involved in anything connected with what he has considered Black racism—e.g. *Négritude.* He posthumously won the prize of Literature des Caraïbes.

Writings: Stories: *Bleu des îles: Récits martiniquais,* Paris, Fasquelle, 1946.

Novels: *Starkenfirst,* Paris, Fasquelle, 1947 (Grand Prix des Antilles); *La caldeira,* Paris, Fasquelle, 1948; *Christ au poing,* Paris, Fasquelle, 1950.

Essay: *Le combat de Schoelcher,* Paris, Fasquelle, 1948. Also: articles by Tardon in *Les Cahiers de Quinzaine* (Service d'Information Guadeloupe); *La Martinique depuis sa découverte jusqu'à nos jours.*

History: *Toussaint Louverture, le Napoleon noir,* Paris, Fasquelle, 1951.

Polemics: *Noirs et blancs: Une solution: l'Apartheid?* Paris, Eds. Denoël, 1961.

TAVERNIER, Jeanine

(a.k.a. **Mme Jeanine Tavernier LOUIS**)
b. March 23, 1935, Port-au-Prince, Haiti. Poet.

Tavernier accomplished all her studies at the Ecole des Soeurs du Sacre Coeur at Turgeau. In 1959 she married Gervais Louis and has divided her life between home and poetry since then, her first collection *Ombre Ensoleillée* appearing under the imprint of her husband's publishing house.

In the words of Maurice Lubin she writes

> *. . . with her flesh, her senses, and her nerves. Nevertheless, no matter how closely she is bound to Eros, . . . she suffers from her enslavement. At times*

she feels a distaste for her whole being,
her life as a woman, all that fills the
human universe: Love, friendship,
wealth, religion, and even revolt.

This fragment offers some idea of her despair:

Mon désespoir est en moi
comme une boue stagnante
Je l'ai dans mes entrailles
D'un bout à l'autre de mon corps.

Despair is in my being
like stagnant slime
I have it in my entrails
from one end of my body to another

Writings: Poetry: *Ombre Ensoleillée,* preface by Roland Morisseau, Port-au-Prince, 1962; *Splendeur,* Port-au-Prince, Haiti-Littéraire, 1962.

Biographical/Critical Sources: Maurice Lubin's "Five Haitian Poets," in *Young Poetry of the Americas,* Washington, D.C., Pan American Union, 1968.

THALY, Daniel Désiré Alain

b. December 2, 1879, Dominica Island; d. October 1, 1950, in Dominica.
Poet, physician.

Thaly was born in Dominica, but was educated in Fort-de-France at the Lycée Saint Pierre. He went to France to study medicine at the Faculty of Toulouse and graduated in 1905. When he returned to his island, his family's economic situation had extremely worsened. He became archivist at the Schoelcher Library of Fort-de-France and began to contribute to several magazines (*Les Marges, Le Divan, La Phalange, L'Ile Sonnante* and *Le Beffroi*) what became a flood of verse.

Thaly has been considered the "French" poet of a Dominica controlled by Great Britain for two centuries, and he has written:

Ile mystérieuse, Antille inviolée,
Dominique aux monts bleus, aux soufrières d'or. . . .

As many Caribbean poets have, Thaly felt the nostalgia of Africa, expressed once this way:

Celui qui chante au loin derrière les maïs
Devant la cendre morte au foyer de sa case,
Est un vieux Congolais qui pleure son pays
Et que le clair de lune a remis en extase.

Il n'était rien qu'un mince et dolent négrillon,
Quand, vêtu seulement d'un pagne vermillon,
Sur un blanc négrier il passa l'Atlantique.

Depuis, la nostalgie habite dans son âme;
Rien ne l'a consolé de sa lointaine Afrique
Où sont les fleuves bleus chers à l'hippopotame.

Although Thaly expressed his racial consciousness and his work often reflecting his social situation (his négritude), he profoundly loved France and remained anxious about his final resting place:

Cyprès français, sera-ce vous qui bercerez
Ma tombe en la douceur de l'éternel automne?
Est-ce vous filao, filao monotone,
Qui pour l'éternité sur elle rêverez?

Writings: Poetry: *Les Caraïbes,* Paris, Ollendorf, 1899; *Lucioles et cantharides,* Paris, Ollendorf, 1900 (awarded the Prix de l'Académie des jeux Floraux de Toulouse); *La clarté du Sud,* Toulouse, Société Provinciale, 1905; *Chansons lointaines,* Paris, Le Divan, 1920; *Le Jardin des Tropiques,* Paris, Ed. du Beffroi, 1911; *Chansons de mer et d'outre-mer,* Paris, Ed. de La Phalange, 1911; *Nostalgies françaises,* Paris, Ed. de La Phalange, 1913; *L'Ile et le voyage,* Paris, Ed. de La Phalange, 1923; *Chants de l'Atlantique,* followed by *Sous le ciel des Antilles,* Paris, La Muse Française, Garnier, 1921; *Héliotrope ou les amants inconnus,* Paris, La Muse Française, 1932; Ten of his poems, in French, are in *Poesy: An Anthology of Dominican Verse,* Book Four, edited by Ralph Casimir, Roseau, Dominica, 1948.

Biographical/Critical Sources: Auguste Viatte,

Histoire littéraire de l'Amérique française, Laval and Paris, Presses Universitaires, 1954.

THALY, Fernand

b. 1882, Saint-Marie, Martinique; d. 1947.
Poet.

Younger brother of Daniel Thaly, Fernand attended the Séminaire Collège of Saint-Pierre, and the Lycée Carnot of Pointe-à-Pitre. After his local schooling, he went to France to join his brother and remained there.

Fernand visited Martinique twice in 1906 and 1908. He became the manager of a once popular literary café in Montparnasse, Le Caméléon, with Paul Fort.

Though Fernand was a very minor poet, he published two charming volumes of his miscellaneous verse as memoirs of his homeland.

Writings: Poetry: *Le Poème des îles* (posthumous), Pontvallain, France, 1964; *La leçon des îles*, Paris, Casterman, 1976; and many unpublished poems.

THEARD, Gaston

b. March 19, 1881, Cayes, Haiti; d. April 4, 1955, Port-au-Prince.
Novelist, storywriter.

Gaston Théard received his education in Cayes and came to Port-au-Prince to enter the National School of Law from which he graduated. He studied bookkeeping during the same period.

He has worked for many years as an accountant at the Ministry of Public Works.

Writings: Shortstories: *Le Jacot de Madame Cicéron*, Port-au-Prince, Impr. N. Telhomme, 1944; second edition, Port-au-Prince, Impr. H. Deschamps, 1944; *Grimaces (Contes)*, Port-au-Prince, Compagnie Lithographique, 1948; *Contes Haitiens*, Port-au-Prince, Compagnie Lithographique, 1949.

THEBAUD, Fritz Vély

b. May 9, 1928, Jacmel, Haiti.
Poet.

Thébaud began his primary studies in Jacmel at the Ecole Frère Clément. He later went with his family to Port-au-Prince where he completed his education.

Writings: Poetry: *Raz de Marée*, Port-au-Prince, Les Presses Libres, 1955.

THEVENOT, René Larivière

b. June 13, 1884, Port-de-Paix, Haiti; d. September 27, 1943, Port-de-Paix.
Poet, notary.

Thévenot was a teacher and studied law in a law office and long served as a notary. He contributed many poems to the magazines and newspapers of Cap-Haitien and Port-au-Prince.

Writings: Poetry: *Au pays des ombres; en juillet 1915 (Poème national)*, Port-au-Prince, Impr. Aug. A. Héraux, 1922.

THOBY, Armand

b. 1841, Saint-Marc, Haiti; d. August 9, 1899, Port-au-Prince.
Playwright, politician, lawyer, government official.

Thoby began his studies in Port-au-Prince with Eugène Bourjolly and Liautaud Ethéart and later went to England and France to complete his education. He returned three years later and served as Secretary at the Commission of Public Instruction and also as a member of the local government of Port-au-Prince. He was député of Saint-Marc in 1876. He was then named Minister of Interior, Public Instruction and Agriculture. He became Senator and Minister Plenipotentiary of Haiti to Paris, then to Santo Domingo and, finally to Washington, D.C.

Writings: Play: *Jacques Bonhomme d'Haiti; en sept tableaux,* Port-au-Prince, Impr. de Mme. F. Smith, 1901.

Politics: *De la capacité présidentielle sous le régime parlementaire,* Port-au-Prince, Typog. Athanase Laforest, 1888; *La question agraire en Haiti,* Port-au-Prince, Typog. Athanase Laforest, 1888; *Le Gouvernement de Boisrond-Canal devant l'histoire par un ancien membre du pouvoir,* St-Pierre (Martinique), Impr. du Journal "Les Colonies," 1880; *Les Constitutions haitiennes et leurs metteurs en oeuvre; Les finances d'Haiti sous le gouvernement du Gal Salomon; le budget des recettes et les impôts,* Port-au-Prince, Impr. de la Jeunesse, 1890; *Les finances d'Haiti sous le Président Salomon; la dette flottante du trésor, 27 Octobre 1887; Questions à l'ordre du jour: 1) de l'élection présidentielle; 2) de la durèê et du renouvellement de la charge de Président d'Haiti; 3) responsabilité et irresponsabilité du Président d'Haiti; 4) responsabilité ministèrielle,* all Port-au-Prince, Impr. Athanase Laforest, 1888; *Questions à l'ordre du jour: 1) le Sénat tel qu'il a été; 2) le Sénat tel qu'il pourrait être; 3) la Chambre des Représentants; 4) l'Assemblée Nationale; 5) Le Comité permanent,* all: Port-au-Prince, Impr. Athanase Laforest, 1888; *Questions politiques d'Haiti,* Paris, Impr. M.M. Duval, 1883.

Collected Works: *Oeuvres,* Port-au-Prince, Impr. de la Jeunesse, 1890.

THOBY-MARCELIN, Philippe

b. December 11, 1904, Port-au-Prince, Haiti; d. August 13, 1975, Syracuse, New York.

Poet, novelist, folklorist, critic (wrote in French but some poetry in creole).

Born into a well-to-do family, Thoby-Marcelin started his schooling at the Petit Séminaire Collège Saint-Martial in Port-au-Prince and completed it in Paris. After graduating from law school, he was named secretary general at the Department of Public Works, where he continued for many years.

By 1926 he was a leading member of the "nativist" group with Jacques Roumain which began preaching an anti-European line, wanting a return to sources, particularly African and folk. Along with Normil Sylvain, Carl Brouard and Emile Roumer he returned to Haiti in 1927 to work for a new spirit in poetry and a renewed interest in indigenous Haitian traditions and customs. With Antonio Vieux and Daniel Heurtelou and the others already mentioned Marcelin founded the *Revue Indigène* (1927-1929), which became the most important voice for the new generation.

Despite his aversion to the American occupation he found that American black writers had lessons for the Haitians and through his reading of Franck L. Schoell's *La Renaissance nègre aux Etats-Unis* in the *Revue de Paris* (January 1, 1929 issue), he began to concern himself with new forms and a new way of expressing Haiti's experiences. Valery Larbaud, the French poet and critic, was impressed by Marcelin's work and supported his work in French publications.

In exile for a long period in France, Marcelin became an official of the Pan-American Union in Washington, D. C. in the early 1950's.

Although non-Haitian readers in the U.S. and France (where his work and that of his brother Pierre were best known) were attracted by the exotic, often bizarre aspects of Marcelin's work, recent Haitian and other Caribbean critics have denounced the sensationalist and possible overly imaginative use of Haitian folklore and vestigal African religions, declaring the work to be more commercial than artistic in origin. For discussion of these charges, see Vere Knight's article cited below.

All novels bearing Philippe Thoby Marcelin's name were written with his brother Pierre.

Writings: Poetry: 13 poems in *La Revue Européenne* (Dec. 1928), and in *La Relève, La Revue Indigène, La Trouée,* and *Les Griots;* also: *Dialogue avec la femme endormie,* Port-au-Prince, Impr. C. Beaubrun, 1941; *La négresse adolescenté, poèmes,* Port-au-Prince, Impr. La Presse, 1932; *Lago-Lago, poèmes* published in Christmas issue of *Haiti Journal,* 1943; *A fonds perdu,* Paris, Seghers, 1953 (contains 21 poems of the 1943-49 period).

Novels: *Canapé vert,* New York, Farrar and Rinehart, 1944, translated into English by Edward Larocque Tinker, and in original French text, New York, Eds. de la Maison Française, 1944 (the work won the Latin American fiction prize of 1943 offered by Farrar and Rinehart); Spanish translation, *Canape Verde,* Buenos Aires, Siglo Veinte, 1947; *La bête de Musseau* (written with brother Pierre Marcelin) New York, Eds. de la Maison Française, 1946, translated as *The Beast of the Haitian Hills* by Peter Rhodes, London, Gollancz, 1951 and New York, 1946 (winner of the second Latin American Literary Prize Contest) and published, London, Victor Gollancz, 1951; *Le crayon de Dieu* (written with brother Pierre also), Paris, La Table Ronde, 1952, translated by Leonard Thomas as *The Pencil of God,* Boston, Houghton Mifflin, 1951, and London, Gollancz, 1951, and in Norwegian as *Guds Finger,* Oslo, Den Gule Serie, Oslo, Gylendal Norsk, 1953; *All Men are Mad,* Preface by Edmund Wilson, translated into English by Eva Thoby-Marcelin, New York, Farrar, Straus and Giroux, 1970; original in French, *Tous les hommes sont fous,* Montréal, Nouvelle Optique, 1978; in Spanish as *Todos los hombres estan locos,* Mexico, 1972.

Folklore: *Contes et légendes d'Haiti,* Paris, F. Nathan, 1967, in English translation by Eva Thoby-Marcelin published as *Singing Turtle and Other Tales from Haiti,* New York, Farrar, Straus and Giroux, 1971.

Art History and Criticism: *Panorama de l'art haitien,* Port-au-Prince, Impr. de l'Etat, 1956; *Art in Latin America Today: Haiti,* Washington, D.C., Pan American Union, 1959.

Critical Essays: (with André Liautaud): "En marge de nos aînés," in *La Nouvelle Ronde,* (Port-au-Prince, June 1925); with Antonio Vieux, the article, "La littérature d'hier et celle de demain," in *La Nouvelle Ronde* (July 1, 1925), in which they attacked earlier Haitian poets as imitative of French poets in a slavish manner and as over-doing the landscape and local color treatment of Haiti.

Biographical/Critical Sources: Vere K. Knight, "Pierre Marcelin and Philippe Thoby-Marcelin: Sensationalism or Realism?" in *Black Images,* Vol. II, No. 1 (Spring 1973), pp. 30-42; Valery Larbaud, "Lettres à Philippe Thoby-Marcelin," dated Valbois, July 29, 1925, in *La Relève* (Jan. 1935); Edner Brutus, "Philippe Thoby-Marcelin," in *La Relève* (Sep. 1932), pp. 27-32; poem dedicated to Marcelin, "Pour Philippe Thoby-Marcelin," in *La Revue Indigène,* No. 1 (July 1927), p. 22; Naomi M. Garret, *The Renaissance of Haitian Poetry,* Paris, Présence Africaine, 1963, pp. 93-107; Edmund Wilson, "The Marcelins-Novelists of Haiti," in *The Nation* (Oct. 14, 1950); Auguste Viatte, *Histoire littéraire de l'Amérique française,* Quebec, 1954, pp. 461-462; Ghislain Gouraige, *Histoire de la littérature haitienne,* Port-au-Prince, 1960, pp. 244-248; Pradel Pompilus & Frères de l'Instruction Chrétienne, *Manuel illustré d'histoire de la littérature haitienne,* Port-au-Prince, Ed. H. Deschamps, 1961, pp. 384-387 and 496-497; "In Memoriam: Philippe Thoby Marcelin," in *Présence Haitienne,* No. 2 (Sept. 1975).

THOMAREL, André

b. 1893, Saint-Claude, Guadeloupe; d. ca. 1962.

Teacher, poet, storywriter, novelist.

Thomarel was born in Guadeloupe but his family came from Martinique. He received his education in Guadeloupe. In 1909, he was appointed teacher. After participation in the First World War he returned to become principal of a school.

In the 1930's he served in France on the staff of G. Mandel when the latter was French Minister of Colonies. When pursued by German police during the Nazi occupation, Thomarel fled to Casablanca where he took up residence as Consul of the [French] Antilles.

Writings: Poetry: *Amours et esquisses,* (Paris?), Impr. Prolétarienne, 1927; *Parfums et saveurs des Antilles,* Paris, Ch. Ebener, 1935; *Regrets et tendresses,* preface by Robert Chauvelet, Paris, 1936.

Stories: *Coeurs meurtris* (nouvelle), Paris(?), Impr. Prolétarienne, 1922; *Les Mille et un contes antillais,* Casablanca, Cigefram, 1951; *Contes et paysages de la Martinique,* Fort-de-France, Impr. Antillaise, 1930.

Novels: *Nuits tropicales,* Paris, Les Eds. du Scorpion, 1960; *Zaza,* Paris (?), Impr. Prolétarienne, 1923; *Naïmia, fleur du Maghreb,* 1949.

TIROLIEN, Guy

b. August 13, 1917, Pointe-à-Pitre, Guadeloupe.

Poet, novelist, international civil servant.

Tirolien attended the Lycée of Pointe-à-Pitre, then went on to Paris where he studied at the Lycée Louis le Grand. He later attended the School of Law and the Ecole Coloniale where he was a brilliant student. He was an active member of the Guadeloupe writers' circle and took a leading part in the new movement, "Nègre nouveau." Tirolien entered the wartime conscripted forces of France and was captured, but good fortune placed him in the same compound as occupied by prisoner Léopold S. Senghor, already a published poet and proclaimer of négritude. The two men became friends and his interest in poetry was deepened by this experience.

After the war he began to write seriously while serving in Niger as Commissioner of Information and then as Cultural Adviser to Niger's President. He served five years in the late 1960's as UN representative to Mali living in Bamako, the capital, having earlier worked in the French civil service in Mali (then the Sudan) and the Camerouns, with his final post being in Gabon.

Tirolien's poem, "Marie-Galante," (in the volume *Balles d'or*) is typical of his work; the following lines from that poem are exotic, cruel, recalling some ancient slave uprising on Marie-Galante, an off-shore island to Guadeloupe:

Les soucougnans glissaient dans le
coeur de la nuit.
Des incendies parfois ravageaient les
rhumeries.
D'étranges punchs flambaient,
réchauffant le sang vert des mares
endormies.
Des prêtres sans soutane dansaient
la bamboula;
et les nonnes sanglantes pleuraient
leurs seins coupés.

This stanza from "La prière d'un petit enfant nègre" provides another example of his concern:

Les nègres vous le savez n'ont que
trop travaillé
pourquoi faut-il de plus
apprendre dans des livres
qui nous parlent de choses qui ne sont
point d'ici.

Writings: Poetry: *Balles d'or, poèmes,* Paris, Présence Africaine, 1961; and verse in many journals and anthologies.

Novel: *Feuilles vivantes au matin,* Paris, Présence Africaine, 1977.

Biographical/Critical Sources: Keith Q. Warner's "Redécouverte" de Tirolien: Une Découverte," in *Research in African Literature,* IV, No. 1 (Spring 1973), African and Afro-American Research Institute, The University of Texas, Austin, Texas. Warner discusses striking similarities between some work of Tirolien and that of the earlier and prestigious French poet, Paul Claudel; E.A. Harley, "Guy Tirolien; in search of an attitude" in *Between Negritude and Marvellous Realism,* Black Images, Vol. 3, No. 1 (Spring 1974), pp. 55-64.

TOULANMANCHE, Karl

(pseudonym, legal identity unknown)
b. 1942, Port-au-Prince, Haiti.
Poet, novelist, storywriter, journalist.

Toulanmanche is a pseudonym which hides a poet and a newspaperman. (Toulanmanche is from the creole expression: "trou nan manche" designating someone very clever, who uses tricks to get out of any trouble.)

Writings: Poetry: *Les déshérités,* Paris, Pierre Jean Oswald, 1974.

Novel: *Epaves,* Paris, Pierre-Jean Oswald, 1971.

TROUILLOT, Ernst

b. January 8, 1922, Port-au-Prince, Haiti.
Essayist, biographer, lawyer, historian, teacher, journalist.

Trouillot was educated at the Petit Séminaire Collège Saint-Martial and graduated from the Faculty of Law and the Institute of Ethnology. He taught at the Petit Séminaire Collège Saint-Martial and he has long been a member of the teaching staffs of Fernand Prosper College, Bird College, Saint François d'Assise College, and the Faculty of Law.

He also has been an active journalist and has contributed to *Le Réveil, Le Soir, Haiti-Journal, La National, Le Nouveau Monde, Le Nouvelliste,* and such reviews as *Conjonction, Optique* and the *Revue de la Société d'Histoire et de Géographie.*

He is now the President of the Bar Association of Port-au-Prince.

Writings: Essay: *Symphonie de combat,* Port-au-Prince, Impr. V. Pierre-Noel, 1948.

Biography: *Hommage à Luc Grimard,* Port-au-Prince, Impr. de l'Etat, 1955; *Demesvar Delorme, le journaliste, le diplomate,* Port-au-Prince, Impr. N.A. Théodore, 1958.

History: *Historiographie d'Haiti* (with Dr. Catts Pressoir and Hénock Trouillot), Mexico, Panamerican Institute of Geography and History, 1953; *Prospection d'histoire, Choses de Saint Domingue et d'Haiti,* Port-au-Prince, 1961.

TROUILLOT, Hénock

b. January 19, 1923, Port-au-Prince, Haiti.
Novelist, playwright, historian, scholar.

Hénock Trouillot was educated in Port-au-Prince at the Petit Séminaire Collège Saint-Martial and graduated from the capital's law school. He has taught at the Ecole Normale Supérieure, the Académie Militaire, and the Ecole Normale Rurale. He is presently the Director General of the National Archives of Haiti.

Trouillot has contributed to many papers and was the editor of the *Revue de la Société d'Histoire, de Géographie et de Géologie d'Haiti.*

Writings: Novel: *Chair, Sang et Trahison,* Collection Haitiana, Port-au-Prince, Impr. V. Pierre-Noel, 1947.

Essays: *Le devenir du métissage racial en Haiti,* Port-au-Prince, Impr. V. Pierre-Noel, 1947; *L'intellectuel de couleur et la discrimination raciale,* Port-au-Prince, 1956.

Biography: *Dantès Bellegarde, un écrivain d'autrefois,* Port-au-Prince, 1957; *Démesvar Délorme ou Introduction à une sociologie de la littérature haitienne,* Port-au-Prince, 1968; *La pensée du Dr Jean Price Mars,* Port-au-Prince ("numéro spécial" of the *Revue de la Société Haitienne d'Histoire de Géographie et de Géologie,* Vol. 29, No. 102 (July-Oct. 1956).

Plays: *Retour en Afrique* (performed Nov. 26, 1965, at Institut Français d'Haiti); *Dessalines ou le Sang du Pont-Rouge,* Port-au-Prince, Impr. des Antilles, 1967; *La Vengeance du Mapou,* Port-au-Prince, Impr. des Antilles, 1967; *Patrice Lumumba, cette lumière,* Port-au-Prince, Impr. des Antilles, 1971; *Les Amours de loas; La Révolte des noirs.*

Literary Criticism: *L'Itinéraire d'Aimé Césaire,* Port-au-Prince, Impr. des Antilles, 1968; *Les Origines sociales de la littérature haitienne,* Port-au-Prince, Impr. N.A. Théodore, 1962; *Dimensions et limites de Jacques Roumain,* Fardin, 1975.

History: *Beaubrun Ardouin, l'homme politique et l'historien,* Mexico, Instituto Panamericano de Geografia y Historia, 1950; *Historiographie d'Haiti* (with Dr. Catts Pressoir and Ernst Trouillot), Mexico, Instituto Panamericano de Geografia y Historia, 1952; *La condition des nègres domestiques à Saint Domingue,* Port-au-Prince, 1955; *Le Drapeau bleu et rouge, une mystification historique,* Port-au-Prince, Impr. N.A. Théodore, 1958; *La République de Pétion et le peuple haitien,* Port-au-Prince, 1960, "numero spécial" of the *Revue de la Société d'Histoire, de Géographie et de Géologie; Les anciennes sucreries coloniales et le marché haitien,* Port-au-Prince, Impr. de l'Etat, 1963; *Dessalines ou la tragédie post-coloniale,* Port-au-Prince, Ed. Panorama, 1966; *La condition des travailleurs à Saint-Domingue,* Port-au-Prince, in *Revue de la Société d'Histoire, de Géographie et de Géologie,* Vol. 34, No. 114 (1970); *Le gouvernement du roi Henri Christophe,* Port-au-Prince, Impr. Centrale, 1974; *La guerre de l'Indépendance d'Haiti,* Mexico, Instituto Panamericano de Geografia y Historia, 1971.

Economics: *Economie et Finances de Saint Domingue,* Port-au-Prince, Impr. de l'Etat, 1965.

Religion: *Introduction à une histoire du Vodou,* Port-au-Prince, Impr. Centrale, 1971.

Biographical/Critical Sources: Robert Cornevin, *Le théâtre haitien, des origines à nos jours,* Quebec, Ed. Léméac, 1973, pp. 151-153.

VALCIN, Mme. Virgile

(née **Cléanthe DESGRAVES**)

b. January 13, 1891, Port-au-Prince, Haiti; d. January 27, 1956, Port-au-Prince.

Poet, novelist, editor, critic.

Valcin was educated in Port-au-Prince and was involved very early in cultural activities. She has served as the editor and chief critic of the journal, *La Semeuse,* directed by Mme. Jane Pérez, and has been active in women's rights and the production of a related journal, *Voix des Femmes.*

Writings: Poetry: *Fleurs et pleurs,* Port-au-Prince, Impr. Nationale, 1924.

Novels: *Cruelle destinée,* Paris, Jouve, 1929; *La blanche négresse,* Port-au-Prince, Impr. V. Valcin, 1934.

VALLES, Max

b. April 21, 1939, Port-au-Prince, Haiti.

Poet, playwright, storywriter.

Vallès attended classes at the Petit Séminaire Collège Saint-Martial and the Lycée Pétion in the capital. He later graduated from the Faculty of Ethnology and the Faculty of Law. He is now a Major in the Armed Forces of Haiti. His favorite activity is theater and for him the ceremony of "Bois-Caiman" is the most moving enactment of Haitian history with slaves thirsty for liberty spouting poems of protest during the great days of revolt against the French.

Writings: Poetry: *Confidences du tambour,* Port-au-Prince, Eds. H. Deschamps, 1969; *Yanvalou des premières fleurs,* Port-au-Prince Les Presses Nationales d'Haiti, 1970; *Coumbite des chansons quisqueyennes,* Port-au-Prince, Eds. H. Deschamps, 1972.

Essays: *Pages Choisies,* Port-au-Prince, mimeo., 1974.

Plays: *La Mort de Bouqui,* performed at French Institute (Oct. 28, 1967); *Roi Angole,* performed June 21, 1970; *La Passion du Christ, Malédiction d'Oedipe,* and *La Récolte sera belle, David et Betsabée, Ruth et Noemi,* all performed at the Rex Theatre (April 17, 1971), and prepared in mimeo., Port-au-Prince

VASTEY, Baron de

(originally **Pompée Valentin de VASTEY**)

b. 1745, Cap-Haitien, Haiti; d. October 1820, Cap-Haitien.

Essayist, polemicist.

Brother-in-law of General Dumas and close companion of Christophe, Vastey was a self-made man and through hard intellectual effort reached a high cultural level for his time. He said about himself:

> ... *insulaire qui n'a jamais eu d'autres maîtres que ses livres, d'autres stimulants que la haine des tyrans.*

In 1804, he was chef des bureaux of General André Vernet, Secretary of State for Finance in Dessalines' government. When Dessalines died, Vastey became tutor of Christophe's children and his private secretary, as well as becoming a member of Christophe's private council.

In a time of battle, economic chaos, and the organization from the ruins of colonial Haiti of a new free state, Vastey's writing efforts served much the same purpose Tom Paine's had in the American revolution. Many of his polemical essays attempted to capture the significance of those smoke and blood-drenched days and the splendor and confusion of the Christophe court at Sans-Souci, the Emperor's great capital.

Vastey looked forward to a British connection in Haiti to replace the still hostile French and the ever-menacing white planter threat from the United States. Some of his work even went so far as to urge the British on in their "civilizing" work in Africa.

Regarding Vastey's work, Duracine Vaval made this comment:

> *C'est un écrivain, un grand écrivain dont le style sans être tout à fait pur, possède du mouvement.*

Writings: Political Works: *Le cri de la patrie,* Cap-Henry, P. Roux, 18??; *Le système colonial dévoilé,* Cap-Henry, Impr. Roux, 1814; *Notes à Mr le Baron de V.P. Malouet, Ministre de la Marine et des colonies de Sa Majesté Louis XVIII,* Cap-Henry, chez Pierre Roux, Impr. du Roi, Octobre 1814; *Réflexions sur une lettre de Mazères, ex-colon français adressée à Mr J.C.K. Sismonde de Sismondi sur les noirs et les blancs, la civilisation de l'Afrique, le Royaume d'Haiti,* Cap-Henry, chez Pierre Roux, Impr. du Roi, 1816; *Réflexions adressées aux haitiens de la partie de l'Ouest et du Sud sur l'horrible assassinat du Général Delva, commis au Port au Prince, dans la nuit du 25 décembre 1815, par les ordres de Pétion,* Cap-Henry, Pierre Roux, Impr. du Roi, 1816; *Réflexions politiques sur quelques ouvrages et journaux français concernant Hayti* ..., Sans Souci, de l'Impr. Royale, 1817 and translation in English, London, 1818; *Réflexions politiques sur les noirs et sur les blancs,* Cap-Henry, Chez Pierre Roux, Impr. du Roi, 1817, and translated from the French by W.H.M.B., London, sold by J. Hatchard ... printed by F.B. Wright, 1817; *Essai sur les causes de la révolution et des guerres civiles d'Hayti* ... (with documents), Sans-Souci, de l'Impr. Royale, 1819, and translated from the French by W.H.M.B., Exeter, printed at the Western Luminary Office, 1823.

Biographical/Critical Sources: Auguste Viatte, *Histoire litéraire de l'Amérique française,* Quebec, Presses Universitaires, 1954, pp. 336-340; Pradel Pompilus & Frères de l'Instruction Chrétienne, *Manuel illustré d'histoire de la littérature haitienne,* Port-au-Prince, Ed. H. Deschamps, 1961, pp. 29-31; Hérard Jadotte & Dieudonné Fardin, *Cours d'histoire de la littérature haitienne,* Vol. I, 1965, p. 25.

VAVAL, Duraciné

b. June 1, 1879, Cayes, Haiti; d. October 2, 1952, Port-au-Prince.

Poet, journalist, literary critic, historian, playwright.

Vaval started his schooling in Cayes and Port-au-Prince and completed it at Collège Saint Barbe in Paris where he graduated from the Faculty of Law. He was a teacher at the Lycée Philippe Guerrier of Cayes, and became judge at the civil court of Cayes. He was named head of the Haitian legation in London and afterwards in Havana. On his return to Haiti, he was judge at the Appeals Court of the West Department. He was also a professor at the Lycée Pétion of Port-au-Prince.

Writings: Essay: *Le préjugé des races et Mr Jean Finot; conférence,* Port-au-Prince, Impr. St-Jacques, 1914.

Poetry: *Stances haitiennes,* Paris, Albert Messein, 1922.

Literary History: *La littérature haitienne; essais critiques,* Paris, E. Sansot & Cie., 1911; *Histoire de la littérature haitienne ou "L'Ame Noire,"* Port-au-Prince, Impr. Aug. A. Héraux, 1933.

History: *Conférences historiques: Dessalines devant l'histoire; Toussaint Louverture à travers la littérature nationale,* Port-au-Prince, Impr. de l'Abeille, 1906.

Economics: *Coup d'oeil sur l'état économique et financier de la République d'Haiti de 1872 à nos jours; proposition d'un nouveau plan financier,* Les Cayes, Impr. C. Cassagnol, 1907.

Plays: *L'appel du destin* (1915); *Mademoiselle Michot ou Blanchette Noire* (comedy in 4 acts, performed July 4, 1916); *Le coup d'arrêt, comédie politique en 4 acts* (1917); *Le rachat, comédie en un acte* (1918); *L'apothéose* (1925) verse drama based on life of Pauline Bonaparte; *Mariage haitiano-américain,* published in complete text in Vaval's *Histoire de la littérature,* for which see below.

Biographical/Critical Sources: Oruno Lara, "Duraciné Vaval" in *La Littérature Antillaise,* Paris, 1913, pp. 133-137; Auguste Viatte, *Histoire littéraire de l'Amérique française,* Quebec, 1953, pp. 420-421; Ghislain Gouraige, *Histoire de la littérature haitienne,* Port-au-Prince, Impr. N.A. Théodore, 1960, pp. 220-223; Pradel Pompilus & Frères de l'Instruction Chrétienne, *Manuel illustré d'histoire de la littérature haitienne,* Port-au-Prince, Eds. H. Deschamps, 1961, pp. 463-464; Robert Cornevin, *Le théâtre haitien, des origines à nos jours,* Quebec, Léméac, 1973, pp. 138-139.

VAVAL, Jean-Baptiste F.

b. ca. 1924, Port-au-Prince, Haiti.
Poet, playwright.

Vaval was educated in Port-au-Prince. He has published one play and one collection of verse.

Writings: Poetry: *La sueur de la terre,* second edition, Port-au-Prince, Impr. des Antilles, 1965.

Play: *Tête-à-tête,* Port-au-Prince, Eds. Panorama, 1972.

VERNE, Marc

b. ca. 1902, Saint-Marc, Haiti; d. October 15, 1969, Cap-Haitien.
Novelist, playwright, teacher, notary.

Verne received his education in Cap-Haitien. He was appointed professor at the Lycée Philippe Guerrier. Named Haitian consul in Camagüey, Cuba, he spent several years there. He adapted both of his novels into plays which saw performance but never publication.

Writings: Poetry: *Pour mon plaisir et pour ma peine,* Port-au-Prince, 1932.

Novels: *Marie Villarceaux; roman d'amour,* Port-au-Prince, Ed. H. Deschamps, 1945; "Yoyo" (unpublished).

Plays: (in ms.): *Marie Villarceaux,* performed in 1945; *Yoyo,* performed, details not known.

VIARD, Félix

(pseudonym: **SAINT ROBERT**)
b. August 17, 1882, Port-au-Prince, Haiti; d. 1967, Port-au-Prince.
Essayist, memoirist, journalist, diplomat, farmer.

Viard's family's prominence in Haiti dates back to a signer of the first Constitution of Haiti (1801), promulgated by Toussaint. Viard spent a considerable part of his life in Europe.

He was educated at Saint Louis de Gonzague and became a military officer in an elite unit, "Les Giboziens." Named Secretary of the Haitian Legation to London by President Nord Alexis, Viard served with his uncle Sénèque Viard, head of the mission. After another considerable period in France, he was named Chargé d'Affaires at Rome to the Quirinal by President Borno. During his stay there, he wrote a long poem to Charlemagne Peralte's glory, "Le dernier marron." (Peralte had battled the invading American troops in 1915).

As a journalist, Viard took a strong nationalist position during the long American occupation of Haiti and even was arrested for a period. He was co-editor and director of *Haiti-Intégrale* with Elie Guérin.

He was Inspecteur Général of Public Instruction at the Department of Public Instruction. He became director of *Haiti-Journal,* founded by Sténio Vincent for his campaign for Senator and President of Haiti.

Viard had a strong interest in agriculture, and he did much hunting and otherwise lived the leisured-busied life of the "Grand Seigneur terrien," as well as being elected to the Haitian Society of Arts and Sciences and becoming a Knight of Honneur et Mérite.

Writings: Poetry: *La légende du dernier marron ... poème,* Port-au-Prince, n.d.

Biography: *La dernière étape; Oswald Durand et ses admirateurs,* Montpellier, Ed. des Nouvelles Annales, 1906.

Letters: *Des lettres à Antoine, paysan,* details not known.

Historical Essays: "Monographies historiques sur Christophe Colomb."

Memoirs: "Souvenirs de chasse."

VICTOR, René

b. ca. 1912, Port-au-Prince, Haiti.
Essayist, social scientist, storywriter, teacher.

Victor received his education at the Petit Séminaire Collège Saint-Martial and later graduated from the Faculty of Law. He served many years at the Bureau of Public Health and then at the Ministry of Labor. He was teaching in Haiti and the Congo in the early 1960's when he was hired by UNESCO for its intensive program for the development of education in Zaire.

Writings: Stories: *Les voix de nos rues,* Port-au-Prince, Impr. de l'Etat, 1949; *Choucoune,* Port-au-Prince, Presses Port-au-Princiennes, 1976.

Essays: *Au service d'oeuvres fortes,* Port-au-Prince, Presses Port-au-Princiennes, 1970.

Demography: *Recensement et démographie,* Port-au-Prince, Impr. de l'Etat, 1944; *Configurations culturelles et procréation en Haiti,* Port-au-Prince, Impr. de l'Etat, 1956.

Sociology: *Essais de Sociologie et de Psychologie haitiennes,* Port-au-Prince, Impr. de l'Etat, 1937; *Vues sociologiques,* Port-au-Prince, Impr. de l'Etat, 1940.

VIEUX, Antonio

(also **Antoine**)
b. August 28, 1904, Port-au-Prince, Haiti; d. June 30, 1964.
Poet, critic, lawyer.

Vieux was educated at the Lycée Pétion, and later graduated from the Faculty of Law in Port-au-Prince.

He was professor at several colleges of Port-au-Prince. He later became Undersecretary of State for Justice in 1944, Director of the Toussaint Louverture Lycée in 1948 and later Secretary of State of National Education from 1948-1949.

A member with Jacques Roumain, Philippe Thoby-Marcelin and others of the "indigenist" group, Vieux helped found the *Revue Indigène* (1927-28).

Writings: Poetry: most in *La Revue Indigène.*

Critical Articles and Reviews: most in *La Revue Indigène* and *La Nouvelle Ronde;* with Thoby-Marcelin: "La littérature d'hier et celle de demain," in *La Nouvelle Ronde* (July 1, 1925) in which he attacked earlier poets of Haiti as having followed French poets too slavishly and for having over-done the depiction of the natural beauties of Haiti; and his reviews in the *Revue Indigène* "Entre nous: Emile Roumer" (Aug. 1927), pp. 54-58, and "Entre nous: Jacques Roumain," (Sep. 1927), pp. 103-110.

VIEUX, Damoclès

b. November 14, 1876, Port-au-Prince, Haiti; d. April 23, 1936, Port-au-Prince.
Poet, teacher, public official.

Vieux studied at the National Lycée of

Port-au-Prince where he won the first prize at the Baccalaureate examinations. Vieux was appointed professor of philosophy, Latin, and Greek, and in time became the director of the Lycée Pétion (1922). Later he served as Chef de Division at the Ministry of Public Works, and afterwards Minister of Public Instruction when Eugene Roy was chosen as a provisional President after Louis Borno went out in 1930. He also at one time was director of the Ecole Normale d'Instituteurs.

An important member of the *La Ronde* group centered around the journal of that name founded in 1898, Vieux developed an ornate and highly artificial verse style. Nonetheless, D'Artrey, a French critic and anthologist, considered Vieux as one of the best and most original poets of the French language of his time and further: "Il est le chantre très subtil et lumineux de la vie intime de l'âme . . ."

Vieux at times was bored by the luxury of Haiti's scenery and longed for ice and snow as in these lines from "Satiété" from *L'aile captive:*

Je suis las de couchants de pourpre ensanglantés . . .

Je suis las de subir les mêmes horizons,
L'éternelle splendeur des palmiers hiératiques
Dont le vert est pareil, à toutes les saisons.
La nature est trop belle, ici, sous les Tropiques.

Il faut plus de douceur et d'ombre à mon coeur mort.

Oh! contemplez ailleurs des sites désolés
Et pouvoir être enfin dans un pays de neige,
Un froid pays de brume au ciel morne et glacé,
En Hollande, en Suède, en Islande, en Norvège.

During his lifetime, Vieux published his first collection of poems, *L'aile captive,* and his wife posthumously issued another collection of his.

Writings: Poetry: *L'aile captive,* Paris, Albert Messein, 1913; *Dernières floraisons (poèmes posthumes),* Port-au-Prince, Impr. de l'Etat, 1947.

Biographical/Critical Sources: J.L.L. D'Artrey: *Quinze ans de poèsie française à travers le monde, Anthologie Internationale,* Paris, Eds. de la France Internationale, 1927.

VIEUX, Isnardin

b. September 7, 1865, Port-au-Prince, Haiti; d. September 11, 1941, Port-au-Prince.
Poet, playwright, lawyer.

Vieux studied at the Lycée Pétion of Port-au-Prince, and received his law degree at the Faculty of Law. He was a teacher at the Secondary School for Boys and professor at the Faculty of Law. He subsequently became Commissaire du Gouvernement near the Civil Court of Port-au-Prince and he founded the journal *La Pioche* in 1909.

His writing was confined mostly to his younger days when he published most of his poetry and his plays he wrote for patriotic motives. He said:

> *Notre pays es le jouet des histrions et des joueurs de flûte. On exploite notre peuple et pour lui dessiller les yeux on doit recourir au champ de l'Histoire si fertile en enseignements. C'est là qu'il faut aller chercher tous les grands exemples d'héroisme et de vertu.*

He was a major force in the group of Thoby-Marcelin, Emile Roumer, Normil Sylvain, Carl Brouard and Jacques Roumain, centered around *La Revue Indigène* (July 1927-February 1928).

Writings: Poetry: *Les vibrations; poèsies,* Paris 1895; *Les chants d'automne,* Paris, Impr. Th. S. Spilker, 1911; *Chants et rêves,* Paris, Goupy 1896.

Plays: *Mackandal, drame en 3 actes,* Port-au-Prince, Impr. V. Pierre-Noel, 1925; *Ogé et Chavannes, La fille de Geffrard, La marche à l'Indépendance.*

Essays: *L'Esclavage à travers le monde,* conférence faite à l'Association du Centenaire de l'Indépendance nationale, le 17 Janvier 1894, Paris, Impr. Vve. Victor Goupy, 1894; *Le drame du 6 décembre 1897,* Port-au-Prince, Impr. de l'Abeille, 1903; *Etudes sur la Convention américano-haïtienne,* Port-au-Prince, Impr. Edm. Chenet, 1915.

Biography: *L'amiral Killick,* Port-au-Prince, Impr. L'Abeille, 1909.

Biographical/Critical Sources: Ghislain Gouraige, *Histoire de la littérature haitienne,* Port-au-Prince, Impr. N.A. Théodore, 1960, pp. 74-80; Auguste Viatte, *Histoire littéraire de l'Amérique française,* Quebec, 1953, pp. 395-396; Robert Cornevin, *Le théâtre haitien, des origines à nos jours,* Quebec, Léméac, 1973, pp. 109-110; Dieudonné Fardin and Hérard Jadotte, *Cours d'Histoire de la littéature haitienne,* Vol. II, mimeo., 1965, pp. 33-34.

VIEUX, Marie

(also: **Mme. Aymon CHARLIER** and **Marie Vieux CHAUVET** from her two marriages; pseudonym: **COLIBRI**)

b. September 16, 1917, Port-au-Prince, Haiti; d. 1975, New York City.

Novelist, storywriter, playwright.

Marie Vieux was educated in Port-au-Prince and she was a brilliant student at the Normal School for girls. She was a teacher for many years.

Writings: Play: *La Légende des Fleurs* (folklore in one act, prose), Port-au-Prince, Impr. H. Deschamps, 1949.

Novels: *Fille d'Haiti,* Paris, Ed. Fasquelle, 1954; *La danse sur le volcan,* Paris, Plon, 1957; *Fonds-des-Nègres* (France-Antilles Prize 1960), Port-au-Prince, Impr. Henri Deschamps, 1961; *Amour, Colère et Folie,* Paris, Gallimard, 1968.

Biographical/Critical Sources: Franck Laraque, "Violence et sexualité" in *Amour, Colère et Folie,* New York, Présence Haitienne, No. 2 (Sep. 1975), pp. 53-56.

VILAIRE, Etzer

b. April 7, 1872, Jérémie, Haiti; d. May 22, 1951, Port-au-Prince.

Poet, novelist, lawyer, preacher.

Son of a protestant minister, Vilaire received his first education from his father and then went to Port-au-Prince, where he studied at the Collège Saint-Martial. When he returned to his native city, he became the first director of the new Nord Alexis Lycée of Jérémie in 1905, although most of his career was in law rather than education. He served as judge (Tribunal de Cassation, 1922-1930) and national député (1930-1932). He remained Vice-President of the Tribunal de Cassation from 1932 until 1946.

He made one trip to Paris in 1910 during which he was given a prize by the French Academy and his collected poems were put to press. His early verse was inspired by the new nationalist group gathered around the journal *La Ronde* (1898), but he had a life-long admiration for everything French, particularly the language. He was a poet, but he wrote many novels which have remained unpublished. He was also a preacher and delivered many religiously oriented dis-

courses but Vilaire was subject to religious doubts and hungers all his life.

In his poem "Testament" he wrote:

Où je suis né, mon âme est triste et prisonnière;
Je vis comme une fleur qu'on foule en une ornière . . .

Ces pages, vous verrez qu'elles sont un lambeau
Du linceul palpitant sur mon âme plaintive
Je ne reflète plus que d'horribles images.

Seymour Pradel wrote of his feeling about Vilaire's work when it first appeared: "Il fut pour nous une révélation. C'était le souffle de la grande poèsie." Jean F. Brierre in his *Conjonction* article of 1951 (cited below), considered Vilaire to be Haiti's finest poet ever.

The tone of Vilaire's poetry is that of anguish and pain where the fire of solitude and introspection burns off all but the most spiritual aspects of the artist. Though now dated, his work has the intensity of a genuine talent and he remains an important figure for the turn-of-the-century renaissance of Haitian poets. His nephew, Edmond Laforest (1876-1915), was briefly influenced by Vilaire and became a fine poet in his own right.

Writings: Poetry: *Pages d'amour; les dix hommes noirs,* Port-au-Prince, Impr. Mme. F. Smith, 1901 (a verse novelette); *Le flibustier, essai de roman en vers; Homo, Vision de l'enfer,* Port-au-Prince, Impr. de Mme. F. Smith, 1903; *Poèmes à mon âme,* Port-au-Prince, Impr. Mme. F. Smith, 1905; *Années tendres (1888-1897),* Paris, Librairie Fischbacher, 1907, second edition, Paris, Albert Messein, 1914; *Poèmes de la mort (1898-1905),* Paris, Librairie Fischbacher, 1907; second edition, 1919; *Nouveaux poèmes (1907-1909),* Le Puy-en-Velay, Impr. Peyriller, 1910; *Poèsies complètes,* 3 vols., Paris, Albert Messein, Editeur, (Impr. Bussière), 1914, 1919, 1919.

Autobiography (sketch): in introduction to *Poèmes de la mort,* as "Notice biographique; La vie solitaire pendant l'occupation américaine," Port-au-Prince, Impr. Adventiste, 1972.

Essay: *Quelques mots à M. Texier,* Jérémie, Impr. M. Desquiron, 1891.

Novels: several manuscripts; part of "Thanatophobe" was published in *Haiti Littéraire et Scientifique.*

Biographical/Critical Sources: Seymour Pradel, "Etzer Vilaire," in *Haiti Littéraire et Scientifique* (July 5, Aug. 20, Sept. 20, all 1912); Oruno Lara, "Etzer Vilaire," in *La Littérature Antillaise,* Paris, 1913, pp. 98-101; Jean F. Brierre, "Etzer Vilaire," in *Conjonction* (Aug. 1951); Pradel Pompilus, *Etzer Vilaire: Etudes critiques et textes choisis,* Port-au-Prince, Impr. ONAAC, 1968; and Pompilus' article, "L'Expérience d'Etzer Vilaire, ses risques, ses mérites," in *Conjonction,* No. 119, (Port-au-Prince, Feb-March 1973), pp. 73-90; Jean Claude Fignolé, *Etzer Vilaire, ce méconnu,* Port-au-Prince, Impr. Centrale, 1970; Roger Gaillard, *Etzer Vilaire, témoin de nos malheurs* (Etude suivie de la reproduction intégrale du poème d'Etzer Vilaire, "Les Dix hommes noirs"), 1901, Port-au-Prince, Presses Nationales, 1972; Edmond Laforest, *L'oeuvre poètique de M. Etzer Vilaire,* conférence, Jérémie, Impr. du Centenaire, 1907; "Pétion Gérôme, Etzer Vilaire" in *La Ronde,* No. 8 (Apr. 5, 1901), pp. 130-134, and No. 9 (May 15, 1901), pp. 137-142; Pradel Pompilus & Frères de l'Instruction Chrétienne, *Manuel illustré d'histoire de la littérature haitienne,* 1961, pp. 228-250; Ghislain Gouraige, *Histoire de la littérature haitienne,* pp. 190-205.

VILAIRE, Jean-Joseph

b. August 22, 1881, Jérémie, Haiti; d. March 25, 1967, Port-au-Prince.

Poet, storywriter, essayist, teacher, notary.

Junior brother of Etzer Vilaire, Jean-Joseph studied in Port-au-Prince. He was teacher at the Lycée Nord Alexis of Jérémie. He was engaged for many years in commerce, and he worked as an accountant at the Office of Internal Revenue in Jérémie, and served all his life as a notary.

Writings: Poetry: *Aube-sonnets indiens, poésies,* Paris, Impr. du Progrès, 1914; *Sonnets héroiques sur la mort de Gérin (poèmes),* Port-au-Prince, Chériquit, 1925; *Paysages et paysans,* Paris, Albert Mussein, (Impr. R. Bussière), 1930.

Stories: *Entre maîtres et esclaves, contes,* Port-au-Prince, Impr. N. Telhomme, 1943; *Gens du peuple et gens de la campagne,* Port-au-Prince, Impr. de l'Etat, 1954.

Biography: *Un ami de notre race: le Pasteur E. Eldin,* Port-au-Prince, Les éditions Evangéliques, 1962.

Essays: *Pensées et réflexions,* Port-au-Prince, Impr. de l'Etat, 1942.

Studies: *L'action de l'élite noire à Saint Domingue,* along with "La guerre aux aînés (études)," Port-au-Prince, Impr. N. Telhomme, 1948; *Quatre (4) Causeries (sur Boisrond Tonnerre, Nos duels historiques, Notre créole l'esprit et les moeurs des Affranchis de Saint Domingue* (réunies par Maurice Vilaire), Port-au-Prince, Impr. Adventiste, 1974.

VILLEVALEIX, Charles Séguy

b. September 14, 1835, Port-au-Prince, Haiti; d. 1923, Paris.

Poet, playwright, diplomat.

Charles' father was among the first recipients ever of a French scholarship and graduated from the Ecole Normale Supérieure de Paris and wrote a thesis in 1813 at the Sorbonne: "Les dialogues des orateurs." Charles himself was also educated in Paris. On his return to Haiti, he taught at the Ecole Polymathique and the Caroline Chauveau Institution. President Nissage Saget named him secretary of the Haitian legation in Paris and later in London, and then served as Minister to both Paris and London from 1879-1883. He passed the last fifty years of his long life in France.

Writings: Poetry: *Les primevères,* Paris, Impr. Jouaust, 1866 (includes sonnets, odelettes, etc.).

Play: *La chasse aux émotions* (comedy).

Biographical/Critical Sources: Ghislain Gouraige, *Histoire de la littérature haitienne,* Port-au-Prince, Impr. N.A. Théodore, 1960, pp. 23-25; Pradel Pompilus & Frères de l'Instruction Chrétienne, *Manuel illustré d'histoire de la littérature haitienne,* Port-au-Prince, Eds. H. Deschamps, 1961, pp. 98-102.

VINCENT, Sténio

b. February 22, 1874, Port-au-Prince, Haiti; d. July 19, 1959, Pétionville.
Essayist, journalist, teacher, statesman, orator, President of Haiti.

Born in Port-au-Prince, Sténio Vincent went to live with his mother in Gonaïves where he began his early education which he completed at the Lycée Pétion. He studied law and his wide-ranging private and public career encompassed Secretary of School Inspection in Port-au-Prince (1890), professor of literature at the Collège Louverture (1893-1896), Haitian Secretary of Legation at Paris (1896-1899), and Berlin (1899-1900), Division Chief in the Department of Public Instruction (1902), Communal Magistrate (1907-1908), Haitian Chargé d'affaires at the Hague, Secretary of State of the Ministry of the Interior (1916), Senator, and finally President of the Senate. He was elected Senator, October 14, 1930, and became President of Haiti on November 18, 1930, and was reelected in 1935 for a second term of five years.

As early as 1904 Vincent had expressed Haiti's need to regard "la grande puissante voisine," the United States, as it drew very close to Haiti with its occupation of Cuba and Puerto Rico after the Spanish War of 1898-1900. Haiti, he advised, must add an Anglo-Saxon quality to its Franco-African ones (Speech of Oct. 4, 1904). Ironically, as noted, Vincent was himself President during the last days of the American occupation of Haiti.

Sténio Vincent helped found the Patriotic Union which eventually helped Haiti regain its independence. He was director of the first School of Commerce in Haiti an organized and directed the journal *République-Express* with Auguste Magloire in 1895, *L'Effort* in 1902, and founded *Haiti-Journal,* as voice for his electoral campaign as Senator and President.

Sténio's style is limpid, unadorned, most often direct, both in his frequent political discourses and in his polemical and journalistic pieces.

Writings: Political Essays: *Efforts et résultats,* Port-au-Prince, Impr. de l'Etat, 1938; *En posant les jalons,* 5 vols. (1930-1941), Port-au-Prince, Impr. de l'Etat, 4 vols., 1939, the last volume was 1941.

Speeches: *Les grands jubilés du Barreau Haitien,* Port-au-Prince, Impr. de l'Etat, 1928; *Choses et Autres,* Paris, Vve. Ch. Dunod et P. Vicq, 1895.

History: *La République d'Haiti telle qu'elle est,* Brussels, Société Anonyme Belge d'Impr., 1910.

Law: *La législation de l'Instruction Publique de la République d'Haïti (1804-1895),* with L.C. Lhérisson, Paris, Vve. C. Dunod et P. Vicq, 1898.

Education: *L'écolier haitien,* with Dantès Bellegarde, Namur, A.D. Wesmel-Charlier, 1911; *L'année enfantine d'histoire et de géographie d'Haiti,* with Dantès Bellegarde, Brussels, Société Anonyme Belge d'Impr., 1913; *Petite Histoire d'Haiti,* Paris, Vve. Ch. Dunod & P. Vicq, 1895.

VIXAMAR, Claude

b. January, 1930, Plaisance (near Cap-Haitien), Haiti.
Poet, playwright, teacher.

Vixamar went to Cap-Haitien where he was educated at the College Notre Dame du Perpétuel Secours. He became a lawyer at the Bar of Attorneys of Cap-Haitien.

He has also taught in various secondary schools of this city. Later, he was appointed Deputy-Commissioner of the Government at the Civil Court of Cap-Haitien and recently served as Prefect for the Arrondissement of Cap-Haitien and Grande-Rivière du Nord. Now, he is Undersecretary of State of the Ministry of Information.

Writings: Play: *Les Briseurs de chaînes* (drama in 5 acts), Port-au-Prince, Impr. N.A. Théodore, 1961.

Poetry: *L'Apothéose,* Port-au-Prince, Impr. N.A. Théodore, 1963.

VOLTAIRE fils, Jean-Auguste

b. January 15, 1815, Léogâne, Haiti; d. ca. 1869.
Esssayist.

Son of Jean-Auguste Voltaire, then Adjutant General and Senator, and Mme. Louise Henriette Bazin Voltaire, the young Voltaire became one of the first Haitians to write philosophical works and to seriously model his style on European classical works. He was, then, one of a handful of writers to work in the troubled early years of Haitian independence.

Writings: Essays (and other prose work): *Oeuvres de Voltaire fils,* Port-au-Prince, Pinard, 1841.

WERLEIGH, Christian

b. September 4, 1895, Cap-Haitien, Haiti; d. May 27, 1947, Cap-Haitien.
Poet, playwright, teacher, musician.

After completing his education in Cap-Haitien, Werleigh became a teacher at the Lycée Philippe Guerrier. He published many articles and patriotic verses in the journals of this period and he took a leading part in the intellectual ferment and protest occasioned by the American occupation of Haiti which began in 1915.

He confessed this in the following extraordinary paragraph:

> *A l'aube de la vie, alors que j'écoutais "le Murmure du rêve" ce fut brusquement le glas de l'independence haitienne que j'entendis dans ce qui me semblait le "grondement de la vie." Prisonnier du sort, appuyé* Contre la balustrade, *obligé de chercher des passe-temps pour tromper les fièvres de l'Attente, je pus bien tard "par le sentier qui monte" commencer l'ascension pénible vers le rêve immortel qu'on crut anéantir. Et dans* La Halte au bord des fleuves, *"au son des cloches" comme, plus tard, au souvenir de nos batailles dont j'entendais les canons et les chants endiablés, loin de la tranchée où j'avais vu plus de deux millions de nos frères s'illustrer en vain "sous les drapeaux de la France" j'appris toute la grandeur du Nom haïtien, Emportant partout le souvenir saignant de la Patrie, écrasée sous les bottes d'un Impérialisme plus hypocrite, plus lâche et plus cruel, j'avais délaissé La rampe fleurie pour respirer un peu de l'héroïsme qui soufflait du grand Drame. Je compris ma Race en méditant sur moi-même, mon Pays en contemplant, à côte de mes ancêtres héroïques, mes frères malheureux. Je pris l'Avenir en méditant sur notre histoire.*

Writings: Poetry: *Défilée-la-folle, poème primé,* Port-au-Prince, Impr. Chéraquit, 1927; *Ma ville et mon pays* (collection Capoise), Port-au-Prince, n.d.; *Le palmiste dans la lumière; poèmes* (Collection Capoise), Port-au-Prince, Impr. de l'Etat, 1938; *Le palmiste dans l'ouragan* (Collection Capoise), Cap-Haitien, Impr. du Séminaire, 1943. Details unknown about volumes of verse: "Du sang sur leur croix blanche," "Mes poèmes," "Contre la balustrade," and "La Halte au bord des fleuves."

Plays: *Tout pour le Roi; La Fleur du sacrifice; Le mort couronné.*

WIENER, Jacqueline

b. March 8, ca. 1902, Port-au-Prince, Haiti; d. August 10, 1976, New York.
Poet.

Jacqueline Wiener was educated in Port-au-Prince. She participated in many activities in favor of women's rights, and when she served at the Ministry of Labor and Welfare, she dedicated herself to the protection of abandoned children.

She spent a great number of years in New York, where she died.

Writings: Poetry: *Une femme chante,* Port-au-Prince, Impr. de l'Etat, 1951; *Tumultes,* Port-au-Prince, Impr. de l'Etat, 1958.

WIENER, Wanda Ducoste

b. ca. 1904, Port-au-Prince, Haiti.
Poet, artist.

Wanda Wiener was educated in Port-au-Prince and spent a great number of years in Paris where she was active in cultural and social activities. She has contributed to various papers in Haiti, in France and in the United States.

Writings: Poetry: *Cirque,* Paris, Institut de la Famille, 1961; *Pétales par Pétales,* Paris, Soulanges, 1967 (preface by Charles Vildrac).

WILLIAMS, Charles D.

b. 1849, Port-au-Prince, Haiti; d. March 29, 1895, Port-au-Prince.
Poet, teacher.

Williams was educated in Port-au-Prince. He spent all of his life teaching and eventually became Director of the Lycée Pétion.

A romantic poet, he was strongly influenced by Victor Hugo and Sully-Prudhomme.

Writings: Poetry: *Les voix du coeur; pages de la 20ème année;* followed by *Paris-Souvenirs,* Paris, Impr. Gén. Lahure, 1886.

WOLFF, Carl or Karl

(pseudonym: **CAROLUS**)
b. December 17, 1860, Port-au-Prince, Haiti; d. May 10, 1934, Port-au-Prince.
Verse storywriter, fabulist (in French and creole).

Wolff studied at the Ecole Polymathique of Seguy Villevaleix, and afterwards at the Petit Séminaire Collège Saint-Martial, then went to Paris where he graduated from the Lycée du Prince Impérial.

When he returned to Haiti, he contributed to many reviews under the name of "Carolus." His *Fables locales* was heavily influenced by La Fontaine's *Fables* though his own exploited the originals of the local Haitian folk tradition and employed the rich creole language. Wolff was, however, a strong adherent of French culture. In objecting to contemporaries who urged a closer association with the United States and a greater interest in Anglo-Saxon cultures, Wolff asserted, "French is still our great teacher."

Writings: Tales: *Fables locales sur des proverbes créoles,* Port-au-Prince, Impr. de l'Abeille, 1918.

Essay: "L'évolution intellectuelle," in *L'Essor* (Sep. 1912).

ZEPHYR, Jacques J.

b. ca. 1929, Brooklyn, New York.
Critic, literary historian, teacher.

Zéphyr was born to Haitian parents then residing in New York, but he early went to Port-au-Prince where he attended the Christian Brothers school, Saint Louis de Gonzague. He later taught at the lycées of Jacmel and of Port-au-Prince before returning to the United States to earn a B.A. After winning his doctorate in Canada at Laval University, Zéphyr took a teaching position in New York City.

Writings: Criticism/Biographies: *La Personnalité humaine dans l'oeuvre de Marcel Proust. Essai de psychologie littéraire,* preface by Pierre Henri Simon, Paris, Minard, 1959; *La Névrose de Salavin. Psychologie d'un personnage de Georges Duhamel,* Quebec, Les Presses de l'Université Laval, 1966; *Psychologie de Salavin, de Georges Duhamel,* Paris, Eds. Universitaires, 1970; *Georges Duhamel devant la critique contemporaine. Modernité *de Salavin,* Paris, Lettres Modernes, Minard, 1971; *Bibliographie Duhamélienne. Essai de bibliographie des études en langue française sur l'oeuvre de Georges Duhamel (1907-1970),* préface et complément aux *Ecrits de Georges Duhamel (1951-1966)* by Marcel Saurin, Paris, Nizet, 1972.

ZIZINE, Albert Pierre

b. November 25, 1904, Saint-Esprit, Martinique; d. November, 1976, Paris.

After early schooling at the Lycée Schoelcher in Fort-de-France, then at l'Ecole de la France d'Outre-Mer, Zizine entered the Sorbonne to study the teaching of English. He spent all his life as a teacher in private schools in Paris.

Zizine is a strong Martiniquais nationalist, but serving as editor for a long period of the journal *Les Nouvelles d'Outre-Mer,* he resided in Paris for almost 50 years.

On May 24, 1976, Zizine was awarded the Médaille d'Argent de la Ville de Paris.

Writings: Novels: *Joyaux des Tropiques,* Avignon, Ed. Aubanel Père, 1937; *Théo, le Paladin martiniquais,* Paris, Ed. du Scorpion, 1959.

Essays: "Un hommage à Victor Schoelcher et Félix Eboué;" "L'amiral Robert devant la Haute Cour de Justice."

ZOBEL, Joseph

b. 1915, Petit-Bourg, near Rivière-Salée, Martinique.

Novelist, poet, essayist, storywriter, literary critic.

Zobel attended primary school and the Lycée Schoelcher in Fort-de-France. He started work as a bookkeeper and later became a tutor at the Lycée. In 1938, while supervising at the Lycée Schoelcher, Zobel was able to publish his first short stories in a local newspaper.

His first novel, *Diab'la,* is set in the fishing town, Le Diamant, where in 1937 he was secretary to the Department of Bridges and Highways. The novel was written in 1942 but the Vichy regime ruling Martinique blocked its publication until 1946. During the war, Martinique joined Free France and the new Gaullist Governor of Martinique named Zobel Press Attaché. Meanwhile, he had published the novel *Les Jours immobiles* and the volumes of stories, *Laghia de la Mort ou Qui fait pleurer le tam-tam?*

In 1946, Zobel left for France to attend the Institute of Ethnology of the Sorbonne and to follow a course in dramatic art. He subsequently was appointed assistant-professor at the Lycée François Ier in Fontainebleau. He published at this time *La Rue cases-nègres,* a novel which won the Prix de Lecteurs, awarded by a jury of a thousand readers, and in 1953, *La Fete à Paris,* another novel. He also passed the French Radio Actors' examination and took part in many radio plays. Additionally, he has been successful in persuading many producers to give poetry a greater place on the radio.

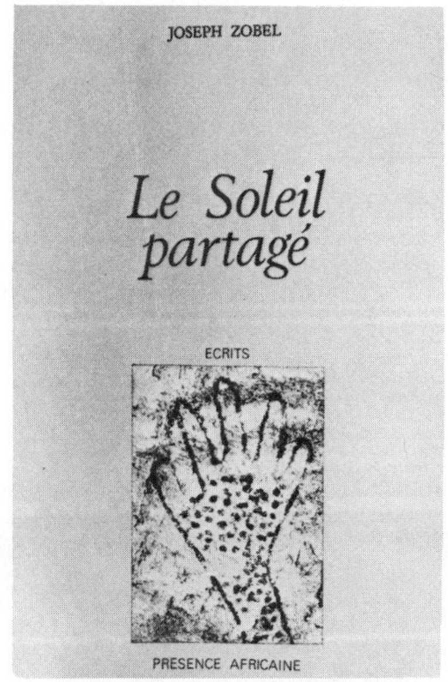

In 1957, Zobel was named director of the Lycée of Ziguinchor in Senegal and later taught at the Lycée of Van Vollenhoven of Dakar. He became cultural adviser to Radio Senegal in 1962 and he has directed the Senegalese Cultural Services which he himself helped organize. In 1964 and 1965, respectively, he published *Le Soleil Partagé* (short stories), and privately in a limited edition, *Incantation pour un retour au pays natal* (poems, 1965).

Zobel is known as Martinique's best regionalist writer. Using a vocabulary limited to that employed by the "petit peuple" he describes the life of the average Martiniquain in great detail.

Writings: Novels: *Diab'la,* Paris, Bellenand, 1946, and Paris, second edition, 1947, with preface by Georges Pillement, Paris, Nouvelles Eds., Latines; *La Rue Cases-Nègres,* Paris, Ed. Jean Froissart, 1950 (Prix des Lecteurs), 1950, 1955; *Les Jours immobiles,* Fort-de-France, 1946; reprinted by Kraus, Liechtenstein, 1969; *La fête à Paris,* Paris, Ed. La Table Ronde, 1953; *Le Journal de Samba Boy,* Paris, Maspero, 19??; and *Intimités avec la terre.*

Stories: *Laghia de la mort ou Qui fait pleurer le tam-tam,* Fort-de-France, Impr. Bezaudin, 1946; new ed., Présence Africaine, 1977; *Le soleil partagé* (eight stories), Paris, Présence Africaine, 1964; *Nouvelles,* Paris, Maspéro 196?.

Poetry: *Incantations pour un retour au pays natal,* Paris, L'Auteur, 1965; and much verse has appeared in various papers and magazines.

Recording: *Joseph Zobel dit trois poèmes de Joseph Zobel.*

Biographical/Critical Sources: Elizabeth Brooks *Three Martinican Novelists* (Clément Richer Mayotte Capécia and Joseph Zobel), Unpub Ph.D. diss., Howard University, 1953.

Supplementary List of Writers from Haiti

JACQUES, Maurice

b. May 15, 1939, Vérettes, Haiti.
Poet, playwright.

After local schooling through a degree in law, Jacques went on to Canada for graduate work in education. He has remained in Canada, publishing in his adopted city of Quebec.

Writings: Poetry: *Le Miroir,* Quebec, Sherbrooke, Eds. Naaman, n.d.; *Le fils Bâtard;* and *Nuit coloniale ou Les cendres des Marrons,* 1968.
Play: *Les Ancêtres du Messie,* 1968.

LAVELANET, François

b. ca. 1877, Port-au-Prince, Haiti; d. d. September 19, 1929.
Novelist, civil servant.

Lavelanet served in the National Bank of Haiti for 35 years after local schooling. He served as chief of the Treasury and his last position was director of the National Archives. In 1907 he published his one known work, the novel *Corinne* (Port-au-Prince, Impr. Aug. A. Héraux).

LEMOINE, Lucien

b. December 19, 1923, Jacmel, Haiti.
Poet, actor.

After local schooling in Jacmel, Lemoine received dramatic training in Paris. He has performed at the Daniel Sorano Theatre in Dakar, Senegal, and is a program announcer and employee of Radio Senegal.

Before emigrating to Africa, Lemoine was active in Haitian theatre and contributed his verse to *Conjonction* and *Haiti-Journal,* the latter issuing a special Christmas issue with much of his work.

Writings: Poetry: *Onze et un poèmes d'amour,* Paris, Seghers, 1966.

METELLUS, Jean

b. April 30, 1937, Jacmel, Haiti.
Poet, physician, teacher.

Metellus began his studies in Jacmel and completed them in Port-au-Prince. For a period he taught mathematics at the Lycée Pinchinat in Jacmel before going on to Paris to study medicine and linguistics, earning doctorates in both subjects. He is presently a physician in Paris.

He has published his verse in *Les Lettres Nouvelles* and *Europe* and in 1978 brought out his first collection, *Au Pipirite Chantant* (The Singing Pirpirite [bird]). Most of his poems are vehement songs dedicated to Haiti's peasants and the country's painful past, as these few lines indicate:

Au pipirite chantant le paysan haitien, debout
aspire la clarté, le parfum des racines, la flèche
des palmiers, la frondaison de l'aube

Il déboute la misère de tous les pores de son corps
et plonge dans la glèbe ses doigts magiques
Le paysan haitien sait se lever matin pour aller
ensevelir un songe, un souhait.

Writings: Poetry: *Au Pipirite Chantant,* Paris, Eds. Robert Laffont, 1978.

ROCHEMONT, Serge

b. May, 19, 1923, Port-de-Paix, Haiti.
Storywriter, essayist, physician.

After his studies in Port-de-Paix at the Lycée Tertulien Guilbaud, Rochemont went to Port-au-Prince to attend the School of Medicine. He received further training in Chicago and Puerto Rico. He is now a member of the medical staff of the Health Ministry in Haiti.

Besides his medical essays, he has published stories in various journals and collected some of them in *Ivraie ou Sénévé* (Wild Wheat and Black Mustard).

Writings: Stories: *Ivraie ou Sénévé,* Port-au-Prince, Les Presses Libres, 1956.

Historical Essay: *Libres propos sur Jacmel et Port-de-Paix,* Port-au-Prince, Presse Nationale d'Haiti, 1967 (3 essays on Jacmel).

FRANCOPHONE LITERATURE: CRITICAL STUDIES/ANTHOLOGIES

Achiriga, Jingiri J. *La révolte des romanciers noirs de langue française.* Quebec: Eds. Naaman, 1972.

Action Poètique. "Peuples opprimés." With Ousmane Sembène, René Dépestre, et al., No. 5, (Mexico, June 1956).

Aguilera, Francisco (comp.) and Georgette Magassy Dorn. *The Archives of Hispanic Literature on Tape: A Descriptive Guide.* Washington, D.C.: Library of Congress, 1974.

Alemeida, Lilian Pestre de. "Rire haitien, rire africain (le comique dans "La Tragédie du Roi Christophe" de Césaire)." *Présence Francophone,* No. 10 (Spring 1975), pp. 59-72.

Anglard, Hervé. *Poètes d'expression francaise* (anthology). Limoges: Hervé Anglard, 1969.

Anthologie de la poèsie haitienne indigène. Port-au-Prince: Impr. Modèle, 1928.

Anthologie des poètes et prosateurs francophones de l'Amerique Septentrionale (Edition des Deux Mondes). Chicago: Adams Press, 1970 (Vol. I), 1971 (Vol. II).

Antilles-Guyane. Special Issue of *Présence Africaine,* New Series, No. 43, 1962.

Antoine, Jacques Carméleau. "Literature from Toussaint Louverture to Jacques Roumain." *Introduction to Haiti,* Mercer Cook, ed., Washington, D. C.: Pan American Union, 1951.

d'Artrey, J.L.L. *Quinze ans de poèsie française à travers le monde (Anthologie internationale).* Paris: Eds. de la France Universelle, 1927.

Aspects de la culture noire (essays). No. 28, in series "Recherches et débats," Paris: Arthème Fayard, 1958.

Aubourg, Gérard. *Haiti: Bibliographie des travaux publiés en France: 1915-1975.* Paris: Eds. C.N.R.S.L.A., 1975.

Auque Lara, Javier. *La poesia Negra* "Los mejores versos de Poesia Negra." (Cuadernillos de Poesia, No. 23), Ed. Simon Latino, Buenos Aires, Editorial Nuestra America, 1958.

Auguste, Yves L. "L'amour dans la littérature haitienne." *Le Nouvelliste,* (December 1963).

Baciu, Stefan. *Antologia de la Poesia Surrealista Latino-americana.* Mexico: Ed. Joaquin Mortiz, 1974.

Ballandier, Georges. "La littérature noire de langue française." *Présence Africaine,* Nos. 8-9 (1950).

____________ . "La littérature de l'Afrique et des Amériques noires." *Histoire des Littératures.* Paris: Encyclopédie de la Pléiade.

Ballagas, Emilio. *Mapa de la poesia negra americana.* Buenos Aires, 1946.

Barudon, Silvio Federico, and Raymond Philoctete. *Poèsie vivante d'Haiti.* Paris:

Ed. Maurice Nadeau, 1978.

Bastide, Roger. *Etat actuel et perspectives d'avenir des recherches afro-américaines: Collection de réimpression du Centre de recherches caraibes.* No. 2, Fonds St-Jacques, Université de Montréal, 1969. An extract is in Special Number "Les Antilles Noires" of the *Journal de la Société des Américanistes,* Vol. LVIII, Paris, 1969.

Bauduy, Robert. "Un second souffle pour le théâtre haitien." *Conjonction,* No. 3 (Fall 1974), pp. 55-71.

Beclard, M. J. *La poèsie noire de langue française et l'évolution de la littérature africaine.* Thesis, Brussels: Institut Universitaire des Territoires d'Outre-mer, 1953.

Bellegarde, Dantès. *Morceaux choisis haitiens.* 2 vols., prose and verse, in collaboration with Amilcar Duval, Solón Ménos and Georges Sylvain. Port-au-Prince: Impr. Mme. F. Smith, 1904. (Awarded prize by the Académie Française in 1904).

__________. *Ecrivains haitiens.* Port-au-Prince: Société d'éditions et de librairie, 1947, and Port-au-Prince, Eds. H. Deschamps, 1950.

Berrien, Albert, and Richard Long. *Negritude: Essays and Studies.* Hampton, Va.: Hampton Institute Press, 1967.

Berrou, F. Raphael, and Pradel Pompilus. *Histoire de la littérature Haitienne illustrée par les textes.* 2 vols., Port-au-Prince: Eds. Caraibes, 1975.

Bibliographic Guide to the Negro World. Yaoundé: Federal University of Cameroun, 1971.

Bibliografia de CentroAmerica y del Caribe. Dirección General de Archivos y Bibliotecas de España, Madrid, 1958.

Bissainthe, Max. *Dictionnaire de Bibliographie Haitienne.* Washington, D. C.: Scarecrow Press, 1951.

__________. *Premier Supplément: Dictionnaire de Bibliographie Haitienne.* Metuchen, N. J.: The Scarecrow Press, 1973.

Blanchet, Jules. *Le destin de la jeune littérature.* Port-au-Prince: Impr. de l'Etat, 1939 and 1943.

__________ and René Piquion. *Essai sur la culture.* Port-au-Prince, 1938.

Bol, V. P., with J. Allary. *Littérateurs et poètes noirs.* Léopoldville (now Kinshasa), Zaire: Librairie de l'Etoile, 1964.

Boly, Joseph. *La voix au coeur multiple.* Paris: Eds. de l'Ecole, 1966.

Bonaventure, Frère. *La littérature haitienne se découvre.* Unpub. M.A. Thesis, University of Ottawa, 1952.

Bonneau, Richard. "Un haitien puise aux sources africaines: El Hadj Omar de Gérard Chenet." *L'Afrique Littéraire et artistique,* No. 31 (1976), pp. 783-790.

Bostick, Herman. "Caribbean French Literature in Proper Perspective." *CLA,* No. 2 (Sept. 1972).

Brachfield, George. *Lumière Noire.* New York, Macmillan, 1972.

Brathwaite, Edward K. "The African Presence in Caribbean Literature." *Daedalus,* No. 103 (1971), pp. 73-109.

Brindeau, Serge. *La poèsie contemporaine de langue française depuis 1945.* (With Jacques Rancourt, Jean Déjeux, Marc Roubaut, Edouard Maunick), Paris: Eds. Saint-Germain-des-Pres, 1973.

Brown, George-Leopold. *Recueil de Morceaux Choisis de Poètes Haitiens.* Port-au-Prince: Thomas-Morris Brown, 1890.

Cameron, J. U. *Pan Africanism and Negritude: A Bibliography.* Ibadan: Institute of African Studies, 1972.

Cartey, Wilfred G. *Black Images.* New York: Teachers' College Press, 1970.

__________ . *Whispers from a Continent: The Literature of Contemporary Black Africa.* New York: Random House, 1969, Vintage Edition, 1970.

Catalogue of Books in the Moorland Foundation Collection. Dorothy Burnett Porter, comp., Washington, D. C.: Howard University Library, 1939.

Charles, Christian. *Dix Nouveaux Poètes et Ecrivains Haitiens.* Port-au-Prince, UNHTI, 1974.

Chevrier, Jacques. *Littérature Nègre: Afrique, Antilles, Madagascar.* Paris: Armand Colin, 1973.

Civil, Jean. "Le roman haitien d'après l'Occupation." *Présence Francophone,* No. 1 (Fall 1970), pp. 121-126.

Collins, Marie. *Black Poets in French: A Collection of Caribbean and African Poets.* New York, Scribners, 1972.

Condé, Maryse. "La littérature féminine de la Guadeloupe: recherche de l'identité." *Présence Africaine,* No. 99-100 (1976), pp. 155-167.

__________ . "Civilisation noire de la Diaspora." *Présence Africaine,* No. 94, pp. 184-195.

Confrontation: A Journal of Third World Literature. Vol. 1, No. 2, 1971, Ohio: Ohio University Press.

Cook, Mercer. *Five French Negro Authors.* Washington, D. C.: The Associated Negro Publishers, 1943.

__________ . "Trends in Recent Haitian Literature." *The Journal of Negro History* (April 1947), pp. 220-231.

__________ . "La littérature française et les Noirs." *Conjonction* (February-April 1950), pp. 74-80.

__________ . "The Poetry of Léon G. Damas." *African Forum,* No. 4 (Spring 1967), pp. 129-132.

Cornevin, Robert. *Le Théâtre haitien, des origines à nos jours.* Montreal: Eds. Léméac, 1973.

Corzani, Jack. "Guadeloupe et Martinique: la difficile voie de la négritude et de l'antillanité." *Présence Africaine,* No. 78 (Fourth Quarter 1970), pp. 16-42.

__________ . *Littérature antillaise (prose and verse).* 2 vols., Emile G. Désormeaux, ed., Fort-de-France, 1971.

Coulthard, G. R. *Race and Color in Caribbean Literature.* London: Oxford University Press, 1962.

Damas, Léon Gontran. *Poètes d'expression française (1900-1945).* Paris, Seuil, 1947.

Daniel, Neptune. *Dissertations de littérature haitienne.* Port-au-Prince: Eds. Panorama, 1964.

Dash, Michael. "Nationalism in Haitian Poetry, 1915-1946." Unpub. Ph.D. Diss., University of West Indies, Cave Hill, Barbados, 1972.

__________. "Marvellous Realism: The Way Out of Negritude." *Black Images,* Vol. 2, Nos. 3-4 (Fall-Winter 1973), 80-95.

Dauty, D. and Potier, M. *Guadeloupe et Martinique: Bibliographie: tendances des recherches en sciences humaines et en médecine, 1945-1975.* Cahiers d'Anthropologie, No. 3 (1975).

Dayan, Joan. *A Rainbow for the Christian West by René Dépestre.* Amherst, University of Massachusetts Press, 1977.

Delmond, S. "Langage et folklore martiniquais." *Mercure de France,* (1935), pp. 83-95.

Denis, Lorimer. *Les tendances d'une génération.* (In collaboration with François Duvalier and Arthur Bonhomme) Port-au-Prince: Impr. Collège Vertières, 1934.

Dictionary Catalog of the Schomburg Collection of Negro Literature and History in the New York Public Library. 9 vols., Boston: Hall, 1962.

Diffusion Haitienne (1804-1954). Lausanne, Switzerland: Impr. Held, 1954.

Duvivier, Ulrick. *Bibliographie générale et méthodique d'Haiti.* 2 vols., Port-au-Prince: Impr. de l'Etat, 1941.

Erdmann, Horst, and Janheinz Jahn. *Modern Erzahler der Welt: Westindien No 13.* fur Internationalen Kultur austausch, 1974.

Esprit. "La Plainte du Noir." (With Frantz Fanon, L. T. Achille, J. Powers), Paris: (May 1951).

Etienne, Gérard V. *Essai sur la Négritude.* Port-au-Prince: Eds. Panorama, 1962.

Etudes Littéraires. Issue devoted to Aimé Césaire. No. 1 (Quebec, April 1973).

Fabre, Michel. "La Revue Indigène et le mouvement noir." *Revue de Littérature comparée,* No. 201 (January), No. 1, pp. 30-39.

Fall, Mahante. *L'âme nègre à travers la poèsie noire d'expression française.* Dakar: D.E.S. Lettres, 1960.

Fardin, Dieudonné, (with Eddy B. Pierre). *Anthologie des poètes et écrivains du Nord-Ouest d'Haiti.* Tome I, mimeo., 1962.

__________. (with Hérard Jadotte). *Cours d'histoire de la littérature haitienne.* 4 vols., Port-de-Paix: Atelier Capois-La-Mort, 1967, 1968.

Fignolé, Jean-Claude. *Les grands écrivains de la littérature haitienne.* Port-au-Prince, 1968.

__________. *Pour une poèsie de l'authentique et du solidaire.* Port-au-Prince, Collection Spirale, 1974.

Fitts, Dudley. *Anthology of Contemporary Latin American Poets.* Norfolk, Conn.: New Directions, 1942.

Fleischmann, Ulrick. *Idéologie und Wirklichkeit in der literature Haitis.* Berlin: Colloquim Verlag, 1963.

__________. *Aspekte der Sozialen und Politischen Entwicklung Haitis.* Stuttgart: PRG Klett, 1971.

__________. *Ecrivain et société en Haiti.* Montreal: Centre de Recherches des Caraibes, Université de Montréal, 1976.

Foisset, J. *Petit recueil de poèsies.* Port-au-Prince: Impr. Telhomme, 1943.

Fouchard, Jean. *Plaisirs de Saint-Domingue. Notes sur sa vie sociale, littéraire et artistique.* Port-au-Prince: Impr. de l'Etat, 1955.

__________. *Le théâtre à Saint-Domingue.* Port-au-Prince: Impr. de l'Etat, 1955.

Fouché, Franck. *Guide pour l'étude de la littérature haitienne.* Port-au-Prince: Eds. Panorama, 1964.

Fowlie, Wallace. "Letter from Haiti." *Poetry,* Vol. 94, No. 6 (Sept. 1959), pp. 398-404. (Covers Roumer, Brierre, M. Leroy).

Frieiro, Eduardo. "Poesia Afro-antillana." *Kriterion,* VIII, (Belo Horizonte, July-Dec. 1955), pp. 339-356.

Gaillard, Roger. *L'univers romanesque de Jacques Roumain.* Port-au-Prince: Eds. Henri Deschamps, 1965.

__________. *La destinée de Carl Brouard.* Port-au-Prince: Eds. Henri Deschamps, 1966.

Galperina, Eugenia. *Vzorvannoe molchanie Sovrem poezia Haiti* [Exploded Silence: Modern Poetry of Haiti]. Trans. from the French. Illus. by A. & P. Borisw, Moscow: Progress, 1968.

Garret, Naomi M. *The Renaissance of Haitian Poetry.* Paris: Présence Africaine, 1963.

González, José Luis and Monica Mansour. *Poesia Negra de America.* Mexico: Ediciones Era, 1976.

Goré, Jeanne Lydie. *Négritude africaine, Négritude caraibe.* Paris: University of Paris, Center of Francophone Studies, 1973.

Gossez, A. M. *Les poètes du XXè siècle.* Paris: Eugène Figuière, 1935.

Gouraige, Ghislain. *Histoire de la littérature haitienne.* Port-au-Prince, Impr. N. A. Théodore, 1961; new ed., 1963.

__________. *Les meilleurs poètes et romanciers haitiens.* Port-au-Prince, Impr. La Phalange, 1963.

__________. *La diaspora d'Haiti et l'Afrique.* Quebec: Eds. Naaman, 1974.

Gourdeau, Jean-Pierre. *La littérature négro-africaine.* Paris: Li. Hatier, 1973.

Grimard, Luc. "Existence historique du théâtre haitien." *World Theatre,* Paris: UNESCO, (Sept-Dec 1967), pp. 534-535.

Guérin, Daniel. *Les Antilles décolonisées.* Introduction by Aimé Césaire). Paris: Présence Africaine, 1957.

Haiti, poètes noirs. Special Issue of *Présence Africaine,* No. 12 (1951).

Handbook of Latin American Studies. One volume each year since 1936-41, vols. to date, Washington, D. C.: Library of Congress.

Hatier. *Poèsie du monde noir.* Paris, 1973.

Haurigot, Georges. "Littérature orale de la Guyane Française in *Revue des Traditions Populaires.*" Vol. 8, Paris, No. 1 (January 1893), pp. 164-173.

Hélène, A. *L'Antillaitisme.* Paris: Eds. Louis Soulanges, 1970.

Hewes, Barbara. *From the Green Antilles.* New York: Macmillan, 1966.

Hoffmann, L. François. "Climats of Haitian Poetry." (in French and Creole). *Phylon,* No. 22 (1961), pp. 59-67.

__________. "L'Image de la femme dans la poèsie haitienne." *Présence Africaine,* XXXIV-XXXV, 1960-1960, pp. 183-206.

__________. "Etat présent des Etudes littéraires haitiennes." *French Review,* (April 1976), pp. 750-759.

Hughes, Langston and Arna Bontemps. *The Poetry of the Negro, 1746-1949.* New York: Doubleday, 1951.

Hyppolite, Michelson Paul. *Une étude sur le folklore haitien.* Port-au-Prince: Impr. de l'Etat, 1954; and English trans. by E. Laforest and Mme. P. Hart, Port-au-Prince, Impr. de l'Etat, 1954.

__________. *Littérature populaire haitienne.* Port-au-Prince, Impr. de l'Etat, 1955.

__________. *Le devenir du créole haitien* (conférence). Port-au-Prince: Impr. de l'Etat, 1962.

Irele, F. Abiola. *Literature and Ideology of Martinique: Maran, Césaire, Fanon.* Special Studies Series, University of Buffalo, New York: Council on International Studies, 19??.

Jahn, Janheinz. *Muntu. An Outline of the Neo-African Culture.* Trans. by Marjorie Greene. New York: Grove Press, 1961.

__________. *A Bibliography of Neo-African Literature from Africa, America and the Caribbean.* London: André Deutsch; New York: Frederick Praeger, 1965.

__________. *Neo-African Literature: A History of Black Writing.* New York: Grove Press, 1969.

Jardal, Pierre. *Bibliographie de la Martinique.* With Maurice Nicolas and Claude Relouzat, eds.; (Les Cahiers du CERAG; Special Issue, 1969).

Jean, Eddy Arnold with Justin Fièvre. *Pour une littérature haitienne nationale et militante.* Lille, Eds. Jacques Soleil, 1975.

__________. *Cahiers de Littérature Haitienne.* 7 vols., mimeo., 1971-1973.

Jones, Edward A. *Voices of Negritude: The Expression of Black Experience in the Poetry of Senghor, Césaire and Damas.* Valley Forge, Pa.: Judson Press, 1971.

Joyau, Auguste. *Anthologie des poètes martiniquais.* Fort-de-France: Eds. des Caraibes, 1961.

__________. *Panorama de la littérature à la Martinique.* Vol. I (XVIII and XIX centuries), Morne Rouge, Martinique: Eds. des Caraibes, 1974.

Kearns, Francis E. *Black Identity.* New York: Holt Rinehart and Winston, 1970.

Kennedy, Ellen Conroy. *The Negritude Poets.* New York: The Viking Press, 1975.

Kesteloot, Lilyan. *Les écrivains noirs de langue française: naissance d'une littérature.* Brussels: Université Libre de Bruxelles, 1963.

__________. *Anthologie Négro-africaine.* Ververs, Belgique: Marabout University, 1967.

Knight, Vere. "French Caribbean Literature: A Literature of Commitment." *Revista Interamericana,* Vol. V, No. 1 (Spring 1975), pp. 67-92.

Koshland, Miriam. "The Creative Writer of African Descent." Second Annual Conference, American Society of African Culture, New York, (June 1959).

__________. "Development of the Literary Idiom in Haiti." *Black Orpheus,* No. 7 (June 1960), pp. 46-60.

Lamothe, Louis. *Los Mayores poetas latinoamericanos.* (Caribbean poetry of Jean Brierre, Léon Laleau, Georges Castera, and Nicolás Guillén), Mexico: Ed. B. Costa Amic, 1959.

Lara, Adolphe. *Contribution de la Guadeloupe à la pensée française (1915-1935).* Paris: Jean Crès, 1936.

Laroche, Maximilien. *Haiti et sa littérature.* Montréal: AGEUM, 1963.

__________. *Le miracle et la métamorphose: essais sur les littératures du Québec et d'Haiti.* Montreal: Eds. du Jour, 1970.

La Selve, Edgard. *Histoire de la littérature haitienne, depuis les origines jusqa'à nos jours.* Versailles, France, 1875.

Lebel, Roland. *Etudes de littérature coloniale.* Paris: Eds. Coloniales J. Peyronnet, 1928.

__________. *Histoire de la littérature coloniale en France.* Paris: Larose, 1931.

Leblond, Marius-Ary. *Anthologie coloniale.* Paris: 1906.

__________. "Rayonnement des Antilles dans la littérature et l'art" in *L'Illustration,* November 23, 1935.

Legendre, Brother Lucien-Jean. *The Catalogue of the Haitian Library of the Brothers of Christian Instruction in Port-au-Prince.* Wincosk, Vermont, U.S.A., mimeo. by St. Michael's College, 1958.

Leiris, Michel. "Martinique, Guadeloupe, Haiti." *Les Temps Modernes,* (February 1950), pp. 1345-1385.

__________. "L'ethnographe devant le colonialisme." *Les Temps Modernes,* (August 1950).

__________. *Contacts de civilisation en Martinique et en Guadeloupe.* Paris: Gallimard, N.R.R. (for UNESCO), 1935.

Lhérisson, Lélia. *Manuel de littérature haitienne.* Port-au-Prince, 1955.

Liautaud, André. "Pour ou contre la culture française." *La voix de la génération de l'Occupation,* Port-au-Prince, 1936.

Lima, Wilson. "Recherches de l'antillanı ɔ." *Présence Africaine,* No. 76 (4th Qtr 1970), pp. 43-63.

Ling, Henry Roth. "Bibliography and Cartography of Hispaniola." *Royal Geographical Society-Supplementary Papers,* Vol. 2, London: 1887, pp. 41-97.

Littératures Ultramarines de langue française: génèse et jeunesse. (Papers from a colloquy, June 13, 1971, at U. S. Vermont: "Les littératures africaine, caraibéenne et canadienne d'expression française: génèse et jeunesse"), Quebec: Naaman, 1974.

Lomax, Alain and Abdul Raoul. *Three Thousand Years of Black Poetry.* New York: Dodd-Mead, 1970.

Louis-Jean, Antonio. *La crise de possession et la possession dramatique.* Ottawa: Eds. Léméac, 1970.

Lubin, Maurice A. (with Carlos Saint-Louis). *Panorama de la poèsie haitienne.* (With poetic map of Haiti), Port-au-Prince: Eds. H. Deschamps, 1950.

Lubin, Maurice A. *L'Afrique dans la poèsie haitienne.* Port-au-Prince: Eds. Panorama, 1965.

__________. *Anthologie de la jeune poèsie d'Haiti.* (Cover with Magloire Saint-Aude's photo.) Honolulu: MELE, 1967.

__________. "Les débuts de la Négritude en Haiti." *Présence Africaine* (Special issue, *Mélanges,* for its 20th anniversary).

__________. "Five Haitian Poets." (J. R. Laforest, René Philoctète, Roland Morisseau, Anthony Phelps, Jeanine Tavernier Louis). *Young Poets of the Americas,* Washington, D. C.: Pan American Union, 1968, pp. 70-81.

__________. *Jacmel et la poèsie haitienne.* Port-au-Prince: Impr. des Antilles, 1967.

__________. "Quelques poètes haitiens de la jeune génération." Reprint from *Journal of Inter American Studies,* Vol. VII, No. 2 (April 1965).

__________. *Poèsies haitiennes.* Rio de Janeiro: Casa de Estudante, 1956.

Lowenthal, Ira and Drexel G. Woodson. *Catalogue de la Collection Mangonęs,* Pétionville, Haiti. New Haven, Yale University Press, 1974.

Manlius, Jack. *Négritude africaine et négritude caraibéenne.* (Colloquy on literature of French Expression), University of Paris, North, Ed. de la Francité, 1973.

Manuel de littérature néo-africaine du XVIème siècle à nos jours, de l'Afrique à l'Amérique. Trans. by Gaston Bailly, Paris: RESMA, Distribution Sedim, 1969.

Marcelin, Emile. *Médaillons littéraires: poètes et prosateurs haitiens.* Port-au-Prince: Impr. de l'Abeille, 1906.

Marcenac, J. "Les littératures noires et la France." *Optique* (December 1956).

Marquez, Robert. *Latin American Revolutionary Poetry* (a bilingual anthology). New York: Monthly Review Press, 1974.

Mbulamwanza, Mudembe-Boyi. *L'oeuvre romanesque de Jacques Stéphen Alexis, écrivain haitien.* Lubumbashi-Kinshasa: Eds. du Mont Noir, 1975.

Ménil, R. "L'évolution de la poèsie antillaise." *Présence Africaine,* No. 22 (Oct-

Nov 1958), pp. 63-73.

Mercier, Roger. "La Poèsie dans les Antilles Françaises: facteurs et caractèristiques de sa transformation." *Etudes Littéraires,* No. 7 (1975), pp. 299-306.

Mirabeau, Roch Lucien. "Contes folkloriques de Port-au-Prince/Etude linguistique et littéraire." Unpub. Ph.D. Diss., University of Illinois, 1967.

Morpeau, Louis. *Anthologie d'un siècle de poèsie haitienne (1817-1925).* Paris: Bossard, 1925.

Naaman, Antoine Y. *Ebauche d'une bibliographie de la littérature nègre d'expression française.* (With J. J. Achiraga), Lagos: University of Ghana, 1966.

Nantet, Jacques. *Panorama de la littérature noire d'expression française.* Paris: Fayard, 1972.

Nicholls, D. "Nationalismes Haitiens (1915-1946)." *Annales-Economie-Sociétés-Civilisations.* No. 4 (July-August 1975).

Nicolas, Maurice. *La Guadeloupe.* Basse-Terre, Librairie Populaire, 1965.

Nouvelle Somme de poèsie du monde noir. (Special issue of *Présence Africaine),* No. 57 (1966).

Nouvelle Critique. "Problèmes de la culture noire." Paris, No. 101 (May 1959).

Ormerod, Beverly. "French Caribbean Literature: The Contemporary Situation." *The Literary Half-Yearly,* XI (July 1973).

Oulié, Marthe. *Les Antilles, filles de la France: Martinique, Guadeloupe.* Paris: Fasquelle, 1935.

Parsons, Elsie Clews. *Folklore of the Antilles.* (French, English). New York: American Folklore Society, Memoir 26, Part I, 1923 (521 pp.); Part II, 1936 (596 pp.).

Patri, A. "Deux poètes noirs en langue française: Aimé Césaire et L. S. Senghor." *Présence Africaine,* (February 1948).

Paul, Emmanuel Casséus. *Nos chansons folkloriques et la possibilité de leurs exploitations pédagogiques.* Port-au-Prince, Les Presses Libres, 1951.

Piérard, Marianne. *Poètes nègres d'Amérique.* Brussels: René Van Sulper, 1930.

Pierre-Louis, Ulysse. *Esquisses littéraires et critiques.* Port-au-Prince, Impr. de l'Etat, 1959.

Piquion, René. *Négritude.* Port-au-Prince: Impr. de l'Etat, 1942.

__________. *Manuel de Négritude* (preface by Bernard B. Dadié). Port-au-Prince: Eds. Henri Deschamps, 1965.

__________. *Les "Trois Grands" de la Négritude.* Port-au-Prince, 1956.

Pompilus, Pradel. *Pages de littérature haitienne.* Port-au-Prince: Impr. de l'Etat, 1951, and Port-au-Prince, Impr. N.A. Théodore, 1956.

__________. *Manuel illustré d'histoire de la littérature haitienne.* (With Brother Raphael Berrou). Port-au-Prince: Eds. Henri Deschamps, 1961.

__________. *Histoire de la littérature haitienne illustrée par les textes.* (With Brother Raphael Berrou) 2 vols., Port-au-Prince: Eds. Caraibes, 1965.

__________. *Louis Joseph Janvier par lui-même.* Port-au-Prince: Eds. Caraibes, 1976.

Prévaudeau, Albert. "Poètes et Romanciers des Antilles." *Les Quatre Samedis des Antilles.* Paris: Impr. Hénon, 1946, (132 pp.).

Price-Mars, Jean. *Une étape de l'évolution haitienne.* Port-au-Prince: Impr. de la Presse, 1929.

__________. *De Saint-Domingue à Haiti.* Paris: Présence Africaine, 1959.

Racine, Daniel L. "French West Indies Poetry from 1900-1970: A Panoramic View (with selected bibliography)." *Black Images,* Vol. 2, Nos. 3-4 (Fall & Winter 1973), pp. 37-43.

__________. "La poèsie des Antilles Françaises face au problème de l'identité." *Présence Francophone,* No. 9 (1974), pp. 72-76.

__________. "Dialectique culturelle et politique en Guadeloupe et Martinique." *Présence Francophone,* No. 13 (Fall 1976), pp. 169-180.

Ramire, Alain. "Idéologie et subversion chez les poètes de la Ronde." (A group of Haitian poets). *Nouvelle Optique,* (January-March 1972), pp. 143-161.

Rémy, Ernest. "Les grands courants littéraires d'Haiti." *Revue des Deux-Mondes.* (December 1972), pp. 608-613.

Rey-Charlier, Ghislaine. *Anthologie du roman haitien (1859-1946).* Quebec, Ed. Naaman, 1978.

Robo, Rodolphe. *La Guyane de fond en comble.* Fort-de-France: Impr. Antillaise Saint-Paul, 1973.

Rogman, Horst J. *Die Thematik der Negerdichtung in Spanischer, franzosischer und portugiesischer, Sprache.* Tubingen: Fotodruck Praziz, 1966.

Rose, M. *La Littérature haitienne.* Brussels: Eds. Conférences et Théâtres, 1938.

Rose-Rosette, Francis. "Aspects de la littérature antillaise de langue anglaise." *ACOMA,* No. 3 (February 1972), pp. 138-141.

Rouzier, Séméxant. *Dictionnaire géographique, administratif universel d'Haiti ou Guide général d'Haiti.* Paris: Impr. Charles Blot, Vols. I and II, 1891; Vols. III and IV, 1928, all Port-au-Prince, Aug. Héraux.

Ruiz del Vizo, Hortensia. *Black Poetry of the Americas (a bilingual Anthology).* Miami, Florida: Ediciones Universal, 1972.

Sainville, Léonard. *Romanciers et conteurs africains.* 2 vols., Paris: Présence Africaine, 1968.

Salandre, H. and R. Cheyssac. *Les Antilles françaises: Histoire et Civilisation.* Paris: F. Nathan, 1962.

Samedy, Jean-Claude. "Literatura e historia en Haiti." *Revista de la Universidad Nacional de Cordoba.* No. 12 (1971), pp. 263-299.

Selected (A) Bibliography on the Caribbean Area: Cuba, Dominican Republic, Haiti and Puerto Rico Including only Islands which are Members of the Organization of American States. Albanelli Norah, Mango Namcy, Conroy Victoria, Kidder Frederick (compilers); Gainesville, Florida: University of Florida, 1956.

Senghor, Léopold Sédar. *Anthologie de la nouvelle poèsie nègre et malgache de langue française.* Paris: Presses Universitaires de France, 1948.

__________. *Liberté I: Négritude et humanisme.* Paris: Seuil, 1946.

__________. "La Négritude comme culture des peuples noirs ne saurait être dépassée." (Lecture delivered in Fort-de-France, February 1976, during Senghor's trip) in *Hommage à Léopold Sédar Senghor, homme de culture,* (Special issue of *Présence Africaine* for the 70th anniversary of the President of Senegal).

Shapiro, Norman R. *Négritude: Black Poetry from Africa and Caribbean.* New York: October House, 1970 (with Rodney E. Harris & Micheline Fort Harris).

__________. *Palabres, contes et poèmes de l'Afrique noire et des Antilles.* Glenview, Illinois: Scott, Foresman, 1973.

Smith, Rowland. *Exile and Traditions: Studies in African and Caribbean Literature.* New York: Africana Publishing Company, 1976.

Souffrant, Claude. "Idéologies religieuses et développement social autour de deux romans: *Gouverneurs de la rosée* de J. Roumain et *Les Arbres Musiciens* de Jacques Alexis." *Memoir,* E.P.H.E., Paris, 1973.

"Textes antillais." *Temps modernes,* No. 52 (1950), Paris.

Theobalde, T. "La littérature engagée et l'écrivain antillais." *Présence Africaine,* No. 27-28 (1959).

Thomas, Peter D. *A Touch of Negritude.* Paris: Présence Africaine, 1969.

Tougas, Gérard. *Les écrivains d'expression française et la France.* Paris: Denoël, 1973.

Trotz, Marilyn. "French Caribbean Literature." *National History and Arts.* Council of Guyana, Georgetown, (August 11, 1973), pp. 85-99.

Trouillot, Hénock. "La pensée du Dr Jean Price-Mars." *Témoignages sur la vie et l'oeuvre du Dr Jean Price-Mars.* Port-au-Prince, Impr. de l'Etat, 1956.

__________. *Dantès Bellegarde, un écrivain d'autrefois.* Port-au-Prince, 1957.

__________. *Les origines sociales de la littérature haitienne.* Port-au-Prince: Impr. N. A. Théodore, 1962.

__________. *L'Itinéraire d'Aimé Césaire.* Port-au-Prince: Impr. des Antilles, 1968.

__________. *Le cas Démesvar Délormé ou introduction à une sociologie de la littérature haitienne.* Port-au-Prince: 1968.

__________. "Les Traditions du théâtre national." *Revue de la Société haitienne d'histoire de géographie et de géologie.* No. 116 (September 1972), pp. 3-39.

__________. *Dimensions et limites de Jacques Roumain.* Port-au-Prince: Eds. Fardin, 1975.

Underwood, Edna Worthley. *The Poets of Haiti (1782-1934).* Portland, Maine: The Mosher Press, 1934.

Valbuena Briones, Angel. "El tema negro en la poesia antillana." *Literatura Hispanoamerica,* Barcelona, 1963.

Valdés, Ildefonso Pareda. *Antologia de la poesia negra americana.* Montevideo. 1956.

Valdés-Cruz, Rosa E. *La Poesia Negroide en America.* New York: Las Americas

Publishing Company, 1970.

Vally, Georges. "Ecrivains et poètes des départements français d'Outre-mer (Paris). *Livre d'Or des Antilles et de Guyane française* (Collection "Notre France:) No. 4.

Valmy-Baisse, J. *La poèsie française chez les noirs d'Haiti.* Paris: Edition Nouvelle Revue Moderne, 1903.

Vaval, Duraciné. *La littérature haitienne: Essais critiques.* Paris: E. Sansot, 1911.

__________ . *Histoire de la littérature haitienne ou l'âme noire.* Port-au-Prince: Aug. Héraux, 1932.

Viatte, Auguste. *Histoire littéraire de l'Amérique française des origines à 1950.* Paris: Presses Universitaires de Frances, 1954.

__________ . "Littérature d'expression française dans la France d'Outre-mer et à l'étranger." *Histoire des littératures,* Vol. II of *Encyclopédie de la Pléiade* (Raymond Quineau, ed.), Paris: Gallimard, 1968.

__________ . *Anthologie littéraire de l'Amérique Francophone.* Quebec: CELEF, 1971.

Vilaire, Maurice. *Prosateurs protestants haitiens.* Port-au-Prince: Impr. des Antilles, 1964.

Wakeman, John and Stanley J. Kunitz. *World Authors (1950-1970).* New York: H. W. Wilson, 1975.

Warner, Keith Q. *Voix françaises du monde noir.* New York: Holt, Rinehart and Winston, 1971.

Watson, Karl S. (comp). *Literature of the English and French Speaking West Indies in the University of Florida, a bibliography.* Center for Latin American Studies, Gainesville, Florida, 1971.

Waters, Harold A. "An aspect of African and Caribbean Theatre in French." in S. O. Mezu's *Modern Black Literature.* Buffalo, New York: Black Academy Press, 1971.

Wauthier, Claude. *L'Afrique des africains: inventaire de la Négritude.* Paris: Eds. du Seuil, 1964.

Whik, Florence E. *Poesia Negra in the Works of Jorge de Lima, Nicolás Guillén Jacques Roumain (1927-1947).* Unpub. Thesis, University of Wisconsin, 1952.

Wolitz, Seth L. *Black Poetry of the French Antilles: Haiti, Martinique, Guadeloupe, Guiana.* Berkeley, Calif.: Fybate Lecture Notes, 1968.

Zell, Hans. "Bibliography." *African Literature Today,* No. 3 (1969).

Zendegui, Guillermo de. "Magical Haiti." *Americas,* Vol. 24, No. 3 (March 1972), S-1 to S-24. (Article covers Haitian culture, religion, and literature).

Zephyr, Jacques. "La Négritude et le problème des langues en Haiti." *Présence Francophone,* No. 5, pp. 15-26.

Zimma, Clarisse. "Patterns of Liberation in Contemporary Women Writers." *L'Esprit Créateur,* Vol. XVII, No. 2 (Summer 1977), pp. 103-114. (Focuses on Guadeloupe and Martinique.)

FRANCOPHONE LITERATURE: SELECTED JOURNALS

L'Abeille Haytienne. fl. August 1817-1820 (Port-au-Prince, Impr. Officielle du Gouvernement).

Acoma. fl. January 1971-March 1972 (published Martinique, printed Paris).

Action. (Fort-de-France).

Afrique Contemporaine. est. April/May 1962 (Paris).

L'Afrique littéraire et artistique. est. October 1968 (Paris).

Annales des Antilles.

L'Avenir. fl. 1859-1861 (Cap-Haitien).

Aya-Bombé. fl. 1947-1949 (Port-au-Prince, Cie. Lithographique).

Black Orpheus. fl. September 1957-August 1967 (London, Heinemann).

Black World. fl. 1969-1976 (Chicago, Johnson Publishing House).

Black Images. est. 1971 (Toronto, Canada, Black Images, Inc.).

La Bluette. fl. April 1924 (Port-au-Prince, Impr. V. Pierre-Noel).

La Bouée. fl. April 1924 (Port-au-Prince, Impr. V. Pierre-Noel).

Le Bronze. fl. 1897 (Port-au-Prince).

Bulletin de la Société des Artistes Antillais.

Cahiers d'Amani-y. fl. June 1953-1957 (Port-au-Prince, Impr. de l'Etat).

Cahiers du CERAG. est. 196? (Fort-de-France).

Cahiers d'Haiti. fl. August 1943-December 1945 (Port-au-Prince, Impr. de l'Etat).

Cahiers de la SNAD. fl. September-December 1951 (Port-au-Prince).

Caravelle. fl. 1945 (Fort-de-France, Impr. Officielle).

Carillon. fl. 1934 (Fort-de-France).

Le Clairon. fl. 1938 (Impr. R. Illeway).

Caribbean Quarterly. fl. 1949-1965 (Kingston).

Conjonction. est. January 1946 (Port-au-Prince, Bulletin of the Institut Français of Haiti).

Coumbite. fl. 1957 (Port-au-Prince, Magazine of the National Society of Dramatic Art).

Culture Française. est. 1951 (Paris, Impr. St. Antoine).

Dialogue. fl. 1957 (Fort-de-France).

Dimanche sportif et culturel. est. 1947 (Martinique).

L'Essor. fl. April 1912-October 1916 (Port-au-Prince).

Esprit. est. 1960 (Paris).

L'Etoile Africaine. fl. 1906-1910 (Paris).

Etudes littéraires. fl. April 1968 (Canada, Laval, Presses de l'Université?).

L'Etudiant Noir. fl. 1934 (Paris).

Femina. fl. December 1923-January 1925 (Port-au-Prince, Impr. Chéraquit).

Les Griots. fl. July 1938-March 1940 (Port-au-Prince, Impr. de l'Etat).

La Guadeloupe littéraire. fl. 1907 (Guadeloupe).

Horizons. fl. 1941-1945 (published Saint Marc, printed Port-au-Prince).

Haiti-Journal. fl. 1929 (Port-au-Prince, yearly Christmas issues dedicated to literature).

Haiti littéraire et scientifique. fl. January 5, 1912-July 5, 1913 (Port-au-Prince).

Haiti littéraire et sociale. fl. January 20, 1905-July 5, 1912 (Port-au-Prince).

Haiti-Rencontres. fl. 1958 (Paris).

Jeune Afrique. est. 1960 (Paris).

La Jeune Haiti. fl. 1893-1896 (Port-au-Prince, Impr. de la Jeunesse).

Junia. fl. May 1924-January 1928 (Port-au-Prince, Impr. V. Pierre-Noel).

Lakansièl (Haiti-Art). fl. 1975-1976 (New York).

La Lanterne. fl. 1940-1947 (Cap-Haitien).

Légitime Défense. fl. 1932 (Paris).

Le Moniteur Haitien. est. February 8, 1845 (Port-au-Prince).

Lucioles. fl. 1927 (Pointe-à-Pitre).

Le National. fl. 1954-1956 (Port-au-Prince, Sunday magazine associated with the daily paper).

La Nouvelle Haiti. fl. March/October 1934 (Port-au-Prince).

Nouvelle Optique. fl. January 1971-1973 (Montreal).

La Nouvelle Revue. fl. November 1907-October 1908 (Cap-Haitien, Impr. du Progrès).

La Nouvelle Ronde. fl. July 1925-November 1928 (Port-au-Prince, Impr. N. Telhomme).

L'Observateur. fl. 1816-182? (Port-au-Prince).

L'Oeuvre. fl. April-October 1927 (Port-au-Prince).

Optique. fl. March 1953-1956 (Port-au-Prince, Impr. Henri Deschamps).

Panorama. est. March 1955 (Port-au-Prince).

Parallèles. fl. 1964 (Fort-de-France).

La Pensée Haitienne. fl. February 1929 (Port-au-Prince, Impr. M. Gachette).

La Petite Revue. fl. 1919-1935 (Port-au-Prince).

Présence Africaine. est. 1947 (Paris).

Présence Francophone. est. Spring 1970 (Sherbrooke, Canada).

Présence Haitienne. fl. 1975-1976 (New York).

Le Petit Samedi Soir. est. 196? (Port-au-Prince).

Projections. fl. 1952 (Port-au-Prince, Magazine of the Haitian American Institute).

Le Printemps. fl. 1954-1956 (Port-au-Prince).

Reflets d'Haiti. fl. 1954 (Port-au-Prince).

La Relève. fl. July 1932-July 1939 (Port-au-Prince, Impr. de l'Etat).

Revue Caraibes. fl. 1965 (Paris, Socipress).

Revue France des Iles. fl. 1965.

Revue Guadeloupéenne. fl. 1946 (Pointe-à-Pitre).

La Revue Haitienne. fl. March/April 1923 (Port-au-Prince).

La Revue Indigène. fl. July 1927-January 1928 (Port-au-Prince).

Revue de la Ligue de la Jeunesse Haitienne. fl. February 20, 1916-June 20, 1917 (Port-au-Prince, Impr. de l'Abeille).

Revue Martiniquaise.

La Revue du Monde Noir. fl. 1931 (Paris, Eds. de la Revue Mondiale).

La Ronde. fl. May 5, 1898-April 15, 1902 (Port-au-Prince).

Rond-Point. fl. 1962 (Port-au-Prince).

Semences. fl. 1962 (Port-au-Prince).

La Semeuse. fl. 1939-1946 (Port-au-Prince).

Stella. fl. March 1926-July 1927 (Cap-Haitien, Impr. Aug. A. Héraux).

Le Télégraphe. fl. January 1821-December 1842 (Port-au-Prince).

Le Temps-Revue. fl. July 1932-June 1941 (Port-au-Prince).

Tropiques. fl. April 1941-October 1943 (Fort-de-France).

La Trouée. fl. July-December 1927 (Port-au-Prince, Impr. Aug. A. Héraux).

L'Union. fl. 1837-1839 (Port-au-Prince).

Les Variétés. fl. December 1904-September 1907 (Port-au-Prince, Impr. C. Magloire).

La Voix des Femmes. fl. 1935-1948 (Port-au-Prince).

Volontés. fl. 1938 (Paris, but also re-edited by Bordas in 1947; also by *Présence Africaine,* 1956; also bilingual edition [French and Spanish] Cuba, 1943).

Volume III

Literature of the Netherlands Antilles and Surinam

ESSAY ON THE LITERATURES OF THE NETHERLANDS ANTILLES AND SURINAM

The writing from the Antilles controlled for several centuries by the Netherlands, is in Dutch, Spanish, and Papiamento (the major dialect of Curacao, Aruba and Bonaire which is predominantly Spanish but touched by Indian and African languages. The populations are a mixture of European and African with some obvious racial characteristics of the Amerindian peoples visible in Aruba and Bonaire. Only recently have locally born writers from the area begun to forge a literature in Papiamento, more than folk, but retaining the vivacity of the local mores and linguistic patterns.

From its beginnings, popular poems and tales have been collected and published and even today such work is an important aspect of Antillean literature. The first relatively sophisticated literature, nonetheless, was by Spanish-speaking emigrés from Venezuela and Colombia, swept there by the vicissitudes of revolution. Founding short-lived journals and literary clubs, this Spanish literature, though ephemeral, did provide a modest base for other writers and offered the first attempts to employ the local customs and atmosphere.

By the 20th century the gradual growth of education and the settlement by a small new colony of Dutch aware of the latest cultural and literary trends of Europe and the Americas, led to the first poetry and fiction of any consequence and the establishment of new island journals and literary groups.

The impulses from the exiled Venezuelans and the new wave of Dutch immigrants could only be helpful in goading speakers of Papiamento to produce works themselves. Henriquez Ureña, the noted Dominican critic and literary historian, considered Papiamento merely a Spanish dialect, but the language is still evolving and seems destined for the major role in the new literature. Whatever the language used, it can be asserted with some confidence that the Papiamento-Spanish flavor of life will dispose the local artists to study the Spanish Caribbean and Latin works of the South American continent with greater attention than Dutch or Anglo-American, or, the French of Martinique or Haiti.

The Spanish-Papiamento literature can be considered in three phases: The colonial (17th and 18th centuries); the romantic (19th century); and the folk-popular and realistic (20th century). Very early in the Spanish period Juan de Castellanos wrote eighteen stanzas celebrating the islands and the beauty of its Indian women and the gentleness of its men. Also in the 1700's Lazaro Bejarano, a Spanish official resident in Curacao (and called "el Señor de Curazao"), wrote satirical poems there and in Santo Domingo which can be considered partially a product of his stay in the islands.

With the arrival of Dutch control, direct contact with Spain, Cuba and Puerto Rico was much more tenuous. In 1880 newspapers in Papiamento began to appear and the important pioneering journal *Civilizado,* edited in Papiamento but often printing Spanish language poems and essays, appeared. Reflecting the late romantic currents of Europe and Spanish America were the writings published in *Notas y Letras* and *Poema,* both weeklies. A. Bethencourt, born in the Canaries, but long resident in Curacao, was the editor of *Notas y Letras* and himself a minor writer. *Poema* concentrated on delicate and brief lyrics under its editors Panchito Arvelo and Ramoncito Ayala. The Spanish poets Gustavo Adolfo Bécquer and Campoamor were the great influences as they were elsewhere in Hispanic areas and Bécquer's poem, supposedly written in a square of Toledo, and containing the immortal lines "pero aquellas no volverán" [swallows that do not return], can be "heard" in the verse of such early poets as A. A. Wolfschoon (*Poesias*, 1894), David M. Chumaceiro (*Crisálidas,* 1898, and *Adelfas,* 1902), and Josef Sickman Corsen (*Poesias,* 1914).

Early prose writers were John de Pool (memoirs: *Del Curazeo que se vas,* 1935) and B.E. Jesurun, an essayist. Also of interest is David Dario Salas, writer of the novels *Raul* and *Josefina,* and of poetry (*In Memoriam* and *Rimas,* both 1911).

Josef Sickman, called a "lucid, melancholy man" by the poet and critic Cola De Brot (a former Governor General of Curacao) was particularly honest in his small sketches of domestic infelicity or personal ennui. In these "contes cruels," he sees defeat lurking behind even the most beguiling beauties.

The realism of John de Pool and Corsen can serve as a bridge to the later writers, and Corsen's poem "Atardi," written in Papiamento, became a classic for all Curaçaons. With W. Kroon and Miguel Suriel the growing realism, one might say a minor naturalism, comes to the fore. Connected with their work is the useful labor of translating plays into Papiamento from leading European drama. May Henriquez adapted Moliere's *L'Avare* and *Le Medècin malgré lui* and the *Pygmalian* of Shaw. René de Rooy's (from Surinam) very free adaptation of *Cyrano de Bergerac* as *Juancho Picaflor* and Raul Romer's adaptation of *Maryken van Nimwegen* (a mystery play from medieval Holland) as *Mari*a de Malpais, provided examples of excellence and linguistic recreation important to later artists. Huber Booi's *Golgatha* (1967), an original play, shows the roots going down deeply and original creation becoming possible.

Pierre Lauffer and Elis Juliana in the more recent period have worked in both English and Spanish, no doubt reaching beyond their island home for audiences. Juliana's poems show him mixing Dutch realism, African folk, and Spanish romanticism in his little versifications of bars, street affairs, life on the wharves, in the "harimentu" (the laugh) form, as he terms them. Lauffer's poetry is full of rhythm in a wide range of tempi and exceptionally sonorous. His volume: *Patria* is Afro-Antillian of the sort popularized by Nicolás Guillén's Afro-Cuban work while his later volumes (*Kumbu, Wiri wiri,* and *Napa*), are very conscious of man in society, and probably reflective of the Puerto Rican poet Luis Palés Matos.

As might be expected in the confinement of island quarters, the satirical exploitation of closely observed idiosyncracies are always popular releases of pressure. Chandi Lagu's "Camind'i Cruz" [At the Crossroads] uses the quick dialogue form to get over the exacerbation of two island politicians with each other. Most well known is Azijn Banana (Oscar van Kampen) whose political satires appeared in the weekly magazine *Lorito Real* between 1948 and 1958, and struck down all island insipidities and pomposities, sparing not the mighty. Tuyuchi (A. Leito) who contributed to *La Cruz,* also deserves mention.

Rounding out a brief enumeration of authors important in the romantic and early realistic period are Mauricio Nouel ("Ode to Ojeda"), Luis H. Daal (*Palabras intimas*), José Ramon Vicioso (*Isla sin bosques*) and Nicolas Piña (b. 1947) who wrote at the age of eleven the fine poem "Poesia." All of these writers employed Spanish primarily, though Nicolas père was an authoritative user of Papiamento as can be seen in his poem "Ban'i paloma."

• • •

The development of a literature in Dutch is a relatively recent phenomenon. Writers in Dutch are either island writers who have spent much of their time in Holland or otherwise identify themselves culturally with Europe and Holland, *or,* Dutchmen who have chosen to become residents of the Antilles and increasingly identify themselves with the Caribbean world though they remain most expressive in their mother tongue. Such poets as Christiaan Engels and the early authors . K. Z. Lampe and S. Krafft who wrote at the turn of the 19th century have long been associated with Curacao or its sister islands. Cola Debrot of Bonaire-Dutch stock, in the 1930-1940 period, also closely identified himself with Curacao, and sought to meld the "sentimiento trágico" of Miguel de Unamuno with the realism of the Papiamento poets and satirists. (Debrot's *Mijn Zuster de negerin* (1935) is still considered the finest of the Dutch Antillean works, and the germ of all developments thereafter in the Dutch-held islands.)

De Stoep [The Porch], founded in 1940 to provide a home to the Dutch writers exiled around the world after the Nazi invasion of Holland, came in time to publish not only the outcasts but the best of the Antillean writers in both Dutch and Papiamento. The surrealistic group associated with the *De Stoep* group were Luc Tournier (C. Engels), Charles Corsen, Tip Marugg (later to become a famous novelist), Oda Glinder (Yolanda Corsen). Most of this work is buried in the pages of *De Stoep,* but Engels made one collection, *Doffe Ore-woed* [Ecstasy in Undertone], published in 1948.

A later prose group associated with *De Stoep* was comprised of Wim van Nuland (Father Michael Mohlmann) and Hendrik de Wit, essayist and critic.

Poets of some importance in the 1950's period and later are Frank Martinus and Alette Beaujon. Martinus' work particularly reflects the reach for African ancestral roots, viz his *Stemmen van Afrika* (Voices from Africa, 1957). Beaujon's *Gedicten aan de Baai en elders* (Poems near the Bay and Elsewhere) are full of her nostalgia for youth and the Antillean shores as felt in foreign lands.

Possibly the most important artists of all are the novelists Tip Marugg and Boeli van Leeuwen whose work is confessional but concerned with social change in the increasing industrialization of the long pastoral, isolated island societies. Marugg's *Weekend Pelgrimage* (Weekend Pilgrimage, 1957) was well received as was the later novel *De Rots der Struikeling* (A Stone of Stumbling, 1960) by van Leeuwen.

The quarterly *Antillian Cahiers,* edited by the Curacaon Henk Dennert and Cola Debrot, offers the best collection of creative and critical work for the 1950 and later periods.

Cola Debrot in summing up his feeling about this new Antillean work, wrote in his essay "Literature of the Netherlands Antilles": ". . . it is not at all surprising that in Curacao the Iberian literature has a Dutch tinge because of its tendency towards intimacy, while the Dutch literature is saturated with the Castillian "Sentimiento Trágico." The main distinction is that the Iberian-Papiamento literature has primarily a communicative character while the Dutch literature must be considered as an expression of individual emotion and existence." Whether Dutch or Papiamento will win out as the true expression of the islanders cannot be answered he concludes, limiting himself to the paradox that "every gain conceals a loss and every loss a gain."

Surinam rides the shoulder of South America between Guyana on the left and Guyane on the right, with giant Brazil and Venezuela for other neighbors. European settlement began in 1651 and by 1667 it became a Dutch possession, producing coffee, cocoa and sugar. Except for the narrow coastal strip Surinam was long a terrifying and dangerous place to the European, for in the eastern portion run-away Africans (the maroons) set up a new-old culture in the so-called "bushnegro" communities Matuari, Saramaccan, Djuka, and others. Further inland yet were the original Indians.

The English were important settlers in the 1650-1667 period and English is still a major ingredient of the local creole. Portuguese also is tracible because many of the Africans brought in during the early days used an Afro-Portuguese pidgin picked up on the slave voyage or in Brazil en route to the new colony. (The 200 Jewish settlers and their descendants who arrived in 1665 may have reinforced Portuguese, though the wide-spread occurence of Portuguese in most of Surinam would show the Jewish connection a slight one.) Because the society was a two-caste one for centuries, a handful of whites and the mass of 90 percent or more of slaves, creole culture in the long run could not but reflect the majority.

The lingua franca, Sranan-Tongo, however, changed from the English, Portuguese, and African parental roots, would grow and reflect the harsh realities of servitude in a vigorous earthy language. By 1844 missionaries, after long having been warned away from plantation workers, were permitted to teach slave children to read in creole but instruction in writing the new language was not allowed until 1856. As early as 1800, however, creole texts had gone into print, but the first creole text specifically intended to be read by the Creole slaves and freed-men did not appear until 1816.

By 1829 the New Testament in creole (with the Psalms from the Old estament) had been published for use in the bushnegro communities and after 844 this work would be widely used all over Surinam. Serving such a purpose vould be the first creole primer (1832) and the long-lived creole monthly *Makzien o Kristen soema zieli* (Magazine for Christian Souls), published from 1852 to 932.

Believed to have been the first creole poem to see print was the half creole oem "De geele vrouw" (The Yellow Woman), written by Hendrik Schouten, a letherlander married to a Creole. The poem has the husband reviling his wife in Dutch and she returning his spite in fluent creole. (*Creole Drum: An Anthology of Creole Literature in Surinam,* J. Voorhoeve and U. M. Lichtveld, eds., offers the omplete text.)

The next important creole works of literature are the *Njoejaari—singi voe esaari* (New Year songs of Cesar), published locally in leaflets in the late 1830's. he deaf-mute Cesaari sold the works in Paramaribo, the capital, and the 1837 ong was reprinted in 1843 in the Dutch periodical *Braga,* with a translation in utch by J.J.L. en Kate, making it possibly the first creole work printed in Holland, nd might have been by the creole lawyer H.C. Focke (1802-1856). Focke ublished his *Neger-Engelsch woordenboek* (Negro-English dictionary) in 1855 hich also has many creole proverbs. Focke also published a study of creole songs nd music in 1858 (posthumously). A few other poems appeared in the mid-entury years and even one issue of a creole weekly, *Krioro Koranti* (Creole Paper) as but little more work saw print until the 20th century because of increasing overnmental pressure to install the Dutch language as the official one in the ountry.

A new factor during this period was the large-scale importation of laborers om China, India and Java on five-year contracts to replace the newly nfranchised Africans who no longer would work on the plantations. Since most of ese people stayed on to become almost half on the present population, their ulture and language became part of the new literary process in time.

Fighting the trend to downgrade creole was J.N. Helstone whose creole rammar *Wan spraakkunst vo taki en skrifi da tongo vo Sranan* (A grammar to lk and write the language of Surinam), published in 1903, had to assert its upposed purpose of teaching Dutch to illiterates to justify its appearance. By the 930's most townspeople knew both creole and Dutch but only with the increased avel and study in Holland after World War II by Surinamese was the creole other-tongue brought back to respectability. God-father of the new turn to creole as J.G.A. Koenders, himself a Creole, who published a monthly journal *Foetoe-oi* (Servant) in creole and Dutch from 1946-1956. Students in Holland (facing ome discrimination, or, sometimes instead, a strong interest in their creole songs nd culture) formed a cultural group "Wie Eegie Sanie" (Our Own Things) in hich both the elites and the working Surinamese could get together. There the arious racial and linguistic groups could begin to evolve a national consciousness. ossibly the most important consequence of this movement was the decided terest in producing a new creole literature, for according to one authority,

Douglas McRae Taylor, creole is known by close to 90 percent of the Surinamese, while Dutch is known by 50 percent or so, Hindi, 30 plus percent, and Javanese, a bit less than 20 percent.

A Netherlands journal joining forces in 1952 was *De Tsjerne* (The Churning Tub) which was the voice for the Frisians in their own attempt to preserve or create a new Frisian language literature. *De Tsjerne* devoted one issue to the creole literature which contained poems and one story, a few items going back to 1949. These were the fore-runners of what was to become a minor flood.

Eddy Bruma, a leading actor in the Wie Eegie Sanie movement, has written verse, short fiction and plays in creole, has helped produce plays on Surinamese historical themes, and is still a major force.

Henri F. de Ziel (Trefossa), born in 1916, is possibly the most important poet in Sranan-Tongo. Arriving in Holland in 1953 he soon joined the Bruma group. By 1957 he had published a small volume of creole poetry, *Trotji,* which was so esthetically successful that it forced the conservative authorities to reconsider their adamant resistance to creole work in the classroom, though Dutch continued to be the language taught and used. Though creole had continued to be used in church services since the 1850's, its stilted, artificial flavor had made it a poor vehicle for literature. Trefossa's gift was to return to the street creole and to forge a supple, sensuous, and intelligent instrument for thought and emotion. The freedom to use what after all was a natural tongue has provoked a veritable passion of writing by the new generation and the process has only just begun.

A brief essay cannot hope to detail all the interesting names and works, but one must start with Johannes King, descendant of runaways who settled in Matuari. Carrying on hit-and-run raids and even outright pitched battles with government forces until 1760, the Matuari and other groups remained ruggedly independent. King, growing up in town because of his mother's need for medical treatment, had been exposed to Christianity and European culture more than was then normal for bushnegroes. In 1855 he was experiencing visions and by 1860 he had founded a church in Maripaston, a village established by his brother, Noah Adrai. Over the next thirty years he was to write four works, or journals, in town creole rather than bush creole, a language as noted rather stiff through its rather stilted usage by the church. King's last book, written in 1893 (but not known to scholarship till 1958), defends his career and focuses on his first missionary work in Djuka in 1864. This work deserves treatment here, for it demonstrates that even in a period just coming out of slavery, a gifted person could, with no known formal schooling, create detailed and lively accounts of more than historical interest in creole.

J.G.A. Koenders, a teacher, has already been mentioned. His work with the women's organization "Pohama hanoe makandra" (Join hands together) led to his writing three booklets in Sranan-Tongo: one deals with the creole language and spelling, the second with elementary hygiene and physiology, and the third, of special interest here, was a collection of sixty well-known songs, *Sieksie tintier moi en bekentie,* all published in 1943. His journal *Foetoe-boi* for ten years, as already noted, fought for the dignity and utility of Sranan-Tongo.

Such writers as Bernardo Ashetu (b. 1929) with his poetry collection *Yanacuna* (1962); J. Ph. A. Defares (b. 1931), poet and playwright; Thea Doelwijt (b. 1942 in the Netherlands of a Surinamese father and a Dutch mother), poet, novelist, film scenarioist; L.H. Ferrier (b. ca. 1938), novelist; Paul Nijbroek (b. 1938), author of the interestingly titled verse collection *PH-7* (1969); Emanuels Orlando (b. 1927), poet; the well-known Robin Ravales (b. 1935), who calls himself Dobru; René de Rooy (1917-1974), critic, novelist, poet, and literary historian; and Asjantenu Sangodare (Michael Slory), poet, are all part of the proud list of new and mature authors.

Very active have also been the poets Martinus Haridat Lutchman (Shrinivasi, born in 1926); Jozef H. Slagveer (b. 1940); van Polanen (Kwami Danilo, born in 1936); and Rudy van Bedacht (Verlooghen). The novelists Bea Vianen (b. 1935) and Edgar Cairo (b. 1948) also call for attention.

Because literature in both creole and a freer local Dutch have been so successful, workers in other areas such as radio, the stage, education, and society in general have felt liberated to be more creative and, particularly with creole, able to express daily reality with a new vigor. Surinamese creole is possibly the most prestigious of all the Caribbean creoles: whether it truly becomes a national language or a second, popular language only time will tell, but certainly many writers have come into print who might forever have remained silent without its being acceptable to use "the people's" language.*

Johanna Schouten-Elsenhout's little poem "Kodyo," given its name by the name of the male child born on a Monday, ends with words appropriate to a young literature:

Mi wan' opodron
lek friman borgu.

Kondre,
dat' ede
m' e dorfu tide.

I want the drumming in the open
like a citizen who is free.

People!
For this
do I dare today

*We have sought to be consistent in using "creole" (rather than Creole) for the popular language and Sranan (rather than Sranen) though both sets of spellings are found in the literature studied. Persons speaking "creole" we call in some cases Creoles.

LIST OF WRITERS FROM THE NETHERLANDS ANTILLES

Alberto, D. M.

Antonio Martes, José (pseudonym: Pierre Lauffer)

Arion, F. M. (see under Frank Martinus Arion)

Armand, S.

Bartolome, Johan (pseudonym for Edward A. de Jongh)

Beaujon, Alette

Berg, H. van den

Blinder, Oda (pseudonym for Yolanda Corsen)

Bogan, Pedro

Bonofacio, Stanley

Booi, Elisabeth (née Hart)

Booi, Jubert (or Hubert)

Brenneker, Paul H. F. (a.k.a. Vitus Brenneker)

Brion, Andres G. en Hernandez Victor

Cardoze, Carlos Jacobus

Chobil (pseudonym for Arturo Leito)

Chumaceiro, David Mendes

Corsen, Charles Sickman

Corsen, Joseph (Jozef) Sickman

Corsen, Yolanda (pseudonym: Oda Blinder)

Daal, Luis Henrique

Debrot, Cola

de Pool, John

Doelwijt, Thea

Domacasse, Pacheco

Engels, Christiaan J. H. (pseudonym: Luc Tournier)

Fraai, Manuel Antonio

Garmers, Sonja

Geerdink-Jesurun Pinto, Nilda Maria (née Jesurun Pinto)

Habiba, Henry

Henriquez, Julio, Sr.

Henriquez Alvarez Correa, May

Hernandez, Victor P. (pseudonym for Cornelius [Nechi] Raphaela)

Heyliger (pseudonym for Eddie Pieters)

Hoyer, Willem Manuel

Jesurun, Pablo Alex

Jongh, Edward A. de (pseudonym: Johan Bartolome)

Juliana, Elis

Keuls, H.

Kroon, José

Kroon, Willem Eligio

Kweirs, G. Th. Pieters (a.k.a. G. Th. Pieters Kwiers)

Lagun, Chandi

Lampe, J. K. Z.

Lauffer, Pierre (pseudonym for José Antonio Martes)

Leito, Arturo (pseudonyms: Chobil Tuyuchi)

Maduro, Antoine J.

Martes, José Antonio (pseudonym: Pierre Lauffer)

Martina, Ornelio

Martina, Sjon Chr.

Martinus Arion, Frank (a.k.a. F. M. Arion)

Marugg, Silvio A. (pseudonym: Tip)

Mohlmann, Father Michael (pseudonym: Wim van Nuland)

van Nuland, Wim (pseudonym for Father Michael Mohlmann)

Pieters, Eddie (pseudonym: Heyliger)

Pieters Kwiers, G. Th. (see Kwiers, G. Th.)

Pina Lampe, Nicolás Antonio

Poiesz, Paulus J.

Raphaela, Cornelius (pseudonym: Victor P. Hernandez)

Reyes, Lupe Maria

Romer, Raul G.

Rosario, Guillerimo A.

Rozenstand, Ernesto E.

Salas, David Dario

Suriel, Simon Miguel

Tip (pseudonym for Silvio A. Marugg)

Tournier, Luc (pseudonym for Christiaan J. H. Engels)

Tuyuchi (pseudonym for Arturo Leito)

van Leeuwen, Boeli

Walle, Johan van de

Wolfschoon, Adolfo A.

LIST OF WRITERS FROM SURINAM

Ashetu, Benardo

Banana, Azijn (pseudonym for Oscar van Kampen)

Bruma, Eddy J.

Cairo, Edgar

Cyrana (pseudonym for Emanuels Orlando)

Dandilo, Kwame (pseudonym for Van P. Polanen)

Defares, J. Ph. A.

de Ziel, Henri Frans (pseudonym: Trefossa)

Dobru, R. (pseudonym for Robin Ravales)

Ferrier, L. H.

Foeng, J. A. Chin A. (pseudonym: Juanchi)

Helman, Albert (pseudonym for Dr. L. A. M. Lichtveld)

Hooi, Richard (pseudonym: Yerba Seku)

Juanchi (pseudonym for J. A. Chin A. Foeng)

Kampen, Oscar van (pseudonym: Azijn Banana)

King, Johannes

Koenders, J. G. A.

Kross, Rudy (pseudonym for Rico Vogelland)

Lutchman, Martinus Haridat (pseudonym: Asjantenu Shrinivasi)

Marlee, Paul (pseudonym for Paul Armand Nijbroek)

Nijbroek, Paul Armand (pseudonym: Paul Marlee)

Orlando (pseudonym for Emanuels Orlando)

Orlando, Emanuels (pseudonyms: Orlando and Cyrano)

Ravales, Robin (pseudonym: R. Dobru)

Rellum, Eugene W.

Rooy, René André de

Sangodare, Asjantenu (pseudonym Michael Slory)

Schouten-Elsenhout, Johanna

Seku, Yerba (pseudonym for Richard Hooi)

Shrinivasi, Asjantenu (pseudonym for Martinus Haridat Lutchman)

Slagveer, Jozef H.

Slory, Michael (pseudonym: Asjantenu Sangodare)

Trefossa (pseudonym for Henri Frans de Ziel)

van Bedacht, Rudy (pseudonym: Corly Verlooghen)

van P. Polanen (pseudonym: Kwame Dandilo)

van Roemer, A. (pseudonym: Zamani)

Verlooghen, Corly (pseudonym for Rudy van Bedacht)

Vianen, Bea

Vogelland, Rico (pseudonym: Rudy Kross)

Wols, Frits (pseudonym for Eugene Wilfred Wong-Loi-Sing)

Wong-loi-Sing, Eugene Wilfred (pseudonym: Frits Wols)

Zamani (pseudonym for A. van Roemer)

Volume III Entries: A to Z

ALBERTO, D.M.

b. ca. 1930, Curacao.
Storywriter, folklorist.

Alberto's published works are in Papiamento.

Writings: Folktales: *Jabi di Union,* Curacao, no date; *Een gesprek met Tula* (19 pp.).
Stories: *Amor di un burace,* Aruba, n.d. (2 vols.); *A venturanan di Adamson.*

ARION, F. M.

(see Martinus Arion, Frank)

ARMAND, S.

b. ca. 1930, Aruba.
Novelist.

Armand writes and has published in both English and Papiamento. His one known work is *Moonlight over Basi-Ruti* (Aruba, Chuchubi, 1960: 150 pp.).

ASHETU, Benardo

b. 1929, Paramaribo, Surinam.
Poet.

Ashetu's work exhibits the general characteristics of Antillean writing, particularly the existentialism of the 1940's and early 1950's brought in by writers influenced by Jean-Paul Sartre in the early post-war years.

His collection of verse *Yanacuna* (1962) takes its title from the plebian-serf caste of Incans of that name—his use of the term being, as Cola Debrot points out, "symbolic" and referring to "the estrangement and displacement" of the ever-increasing number of disoriented persons in the twentieth century.

Writings: Poetry: *Yanacuna,* 1962, published in *Antillaanse Cahiers,* 5th year, No. 2/3 (Amsterdam. Poem "Litteken" in *Nouvelle somme de poésie* du monde noir, Paris, 1966).

Biographical/Critical Sources: Cola Debrot, *Literature of the Netherlands Antilles,* p. 27.

BANANA, Azijn

(pseudonym for **Oscar van KAMPEN**)

BARTOLOME, Johan

(pseudonym for **Edward A. de JONGH**)

BEAUJON, Alette

b. ca. 1927, Curacao.
Poet, biographer.

Beaujon's poetry reflects her exile from her childhood home in Curacao and is full of local sights and sounds. Her poetry is usually cast in Papiamento.

Writings: Poetry: "Gedichten aan de baai en elders [Poems Near the Bay and Others]," in *Antilliaanse Cahiers,* Vol. 2, No. 3-4 (1957).

Biography: *Boeli van Leeuwen, persknipsels met kritieken en biographische gegevens,* Amsterdam, Sticusa, 1967.

BERG, H. van den

b. 1937, Aruba.
Storywriter, mariner.

Berg served as an officer on the sailship *Gladys.*

Writings: Story (autobiographical): *Solo Sed y hamber abordo di Gladys,* Aruba, 1961 (51 pp.), and second edition published by Scherpenheuvel, in a 39 page text, place unknown.

BLINDER, Oda

(pseudonym for **Yolanda CORSEN**)

Oda Blinder, as painted by Lucile Engels

BOGAN, Pedro

b. ca. 1940, Aruba.
Novelist.

His one known work is a juvenile novel, *Rey de Contrabanda.*

Writings: Novel: *Rey de Contrabanda,* Aruba, Aruba Boekhandel (Gebroeders de Wit), no date, 198 pp.

BONOFACIO, Stanley

b. ca. 1933, Curacao.
Playwright.

Bonofacio has written at least six known plays, all in Papiamento.

Writings: Radio Play: *El diablo invisible,* Curacao, 1963.

Plays: *Amor na Jan Kok,* Curacao, 1966; others published but no publishing data: *Carlos, de Jongewachter; Pedritu, dos webu hereba; Condena pa morto; E spoki di Jan Kok.*

BOOI, Elisabeth

(née **HART**)
b. ca. 1892, Curacao (?).
Playwright.

Booi was possibly the earliest Papiamento playwright to be published. Some ten of her plays are known.

Writings: Plays: *Adam i Eva den Paradijs,* Curacao, 1922; *E criar moderno,* n.p., n.d.; *E tanta for di Merca,* n.p., n.d.; *E tanta surdoe,* n.p., n.d.; *St. Cecilia,* 1943; *Navidad,* n.p., 1949; *Ruth,* 1949; *E perla,* n.p., 1950; *Ketty no sa ganja nunca,* Curacao, 1952; *Nos Senora,* 1955.

BOOI, Jubert (or Hubert)

b. July 25, 1919, Bonaire.
Papiamento poet, storywriter, playwright.

Booi has passed most of his life in Aruba and has concentrated his work in the area of folktales and dramas for radio based on island traditions.

Writings: Folkstories and Verse: *Muchila,* Aruba, de wit n. v., 1969 (includes the stories: "Un pal'i kwihi ta konta su storya," and "Kwentanan Kortiko pa Tempu di Pasku," and verse and translation of "Les Mots Pérdús" of Catulle Mendès into Papiamento), and extract of "Un pal'i" is in P. Lauffer's *Di Nos,* along with two poems: "Si mi por," and "I Ora."

Radio Story: *Mala lenga,* Aruba.

Plays: *Golgotha, un drama religioso,"* in *Antilliaanse Cahiers* (1967); *Aurora de salbacion; Dialogo; Carga pasenski; Cuminda galina; Diario di un estudiante; E angelitu malucu; E boto cu buracu; E Perla de Caribe; Futuru esposo; Orjunchi; Triunfodi un piscadó; Un Storia de Pascu:* all in Aruba.

BRENNEKER, Paul H.F.

[Brenneker, Vitus]

b. May 7, 1912, Venlo, Curacao.
Folklorist, storywriter, Dutch priest.

Brenneker, a student of island speech, has a long list of works on Papiamento and published many works in that language.

Writings: Scholarship: *Proverbionan Papiamentu,* Willemstad, 1945, second edition, 1951; *Papiamentse Visnamen afgeleid van het Nederlands,* Willemstad, 1954; *Proverbio,* in *Spreekwoorden,* Nijmegen, Netherlands, 1963; *Proverbio* (in Papiamento), 1963.

Folklore-stories: *Lekete Minawa. Liederen vit de goede oude tijd,* Curacao, 1958; *Benta, zoo liederen uit de goede oude tijd,* Curacao, 1959; "Curacaoensia," in *Folkloristische Aantekieningen,* (Nijmegen, Netherlands, 1960); "Jerba," in *Kruidenboek,* Curacao, 1961; *Pekele cu pikel,* Curacao, 1962 (44 pp.); "Chella un bon mucha," in *De Curacaose Courant,* 1951; "Un bunita Senjorita," Curacao, Paulusdrukkerij, 1963; "Brua," in *Woordenboekje over zwarte kunst,* Curacao, 1966. Also, by "Vitus": *No tin wea pa stoba jiu malucu,* Willemstad, 1951; *Benta. Dos cien cantica dje dushi tempu bieuw,* Curacao, Boekhandel St. Augustinus, 1959, (120 pp.).

BRION, Andres G. en Hernandez Victor

b. ca. 1940, Curacao.
Novelist, storywriter.

Brion has published many stories and one novel, all in Papiamento.

Writings: Novel: *Sombra de Bida,* 4 vols., Curacao, no date.

Stories: *Flor di mi ideal,* Curacao, Casa Editorial Emile, n.d. (14 pp.); *Antonio y Antonietta,* Curacao, Case Editorial Emile, n.d. (12 pp.).

BRUMA, Eddy J.

b. 1925, Surinam.
Playwright, poet, storywriter, lawyer.

After local studies, including training in the law in the late 1940's, Bruma began his efforts to encourage a greater independence of spirit and pride in the local

Sranan-Tongo language. Though influenced by the example of J.G.A. Koenders, Bruma wanted a complete psychological and even political evolution in the local attitudes. In Holland he joined many of his compatriots studying at various universities and developed even more decided ideas about the necessity and cultural independence, a development highly akin to the early negritude ideas of Damas (Guyane) and Césaire (Martinique) in Paris during the 1930's. A founder in Amsterdam of the group "Wie Eegie Sanie" (Our Own Thing) which comprised day laborers as well as students from Surinam (the students learning Sranan from the better creole speaking workers), Bruma returned to Surinam with a powerful wish to disseminate the by-now nationalistic ideas.

Beyond his rather relaxed political efforts (recorded in V.S. Naipaul's *The Middle Passage,* London, Penguin, 1962, p. 178), he wrote poems (published in *Foetoe-boi*) and at least one short story (appearing in *Tongoni*).

His most significant literary efforts, however, have been his annual playwriting, produced for the July first-Emancipation Day celebrations. Though he continued to exploit the by-then traditional theme of slavery, he introduced more complex dramatic scenes and structures which have pushed the still "popular" plays of the street to more interesting expressions of the culture, past and present. Though none of his work performed by his own play group have yet been published in entirety, part of *Basra Pataka* (produced 1958 in Paramaribo) has been published.

"Mi braka mama," one of Bruma's creole poems, begins:

Mi braka mama
natap'hen bangi e dyonko,
ala piken go sribi kaba.
Mi owru mama, kon, opo go sribi,
mi sab fa yu weri mama.

My black mother
dozes on her bench,
all the children have gone to bed.
Old mother, come rise, go to sleep,
I know how weary you are, mother.

Writings: Plays: in ms. except for first act of *Basra Pataka* in Voorhoeve and Lichtveld's *Creole Drum* (1975), pp. 168-181 (in Sranan and English trans.); Dutch language play *De geboorte van Boni,* produced in the Netherlands, 1952; and in Sranan adaptation produced in Surinam, probably 1957.

Poetry: in various journals and collections, including *De Tsjerne* (Sept. 1952) and poems "Mi braka mama," and "Waren-neti dren," in Voorhoeve and Lichtveld's *Creole Drum.*

CAIRO, Edgar

b. 1948, Paramaribo, Surinam.
Novelist, poet.

Cairo completed his studies in Amsterdam. Cairo is known primarily as a novelist though he has written some poetry. His Sranan-language novelette *Temekoe* (1969) of thirty-nine pages is almost obsessively concerned with the central character's father and other close friends and relatives in an obviously highly autobiographical work. The novel ends on the note of a half yearning assertion of independence.

Writings: Novel: *Temekoe,* Paramaribo, Uitgave Bureau Volkslectuur, 1969; in progress: "Sjoeroerwe." The chapter "Wan pisi fu libi (Life) from *Temekoe,* is given in Sranen and English in *Creole Drum,* edited by J. Voorhoeve and Ursy M. Lichtveld, pp. 252-271. The work will have two major parts: *Brokoston* and *Koprokanoe.*

Poetry: *Oroskopoe* (Horoscope), in mimeograph, Paramaribo, 1969; *Kra. Wan bondroe powema,* Paramaribo, Bureau Volkslectuur, N.V. Drukkerij Eldorado, 1970.

CARDOZE, Carlos Jacobus

b. ca. 1935, Curacao.
Storywriter, biographer.

Cardoze's best work is his study of Cola Debrot, long-time governor-general of Curacao, Aruba and Bonaire, and student of literature.

Writings: Story: *Amor Eterno, una emocionante novela.* (Dedicada a Curazao, Aruba y Bonaire), Barranquilla, Colombia, 1965 (17 pp.).
Biography: *Cola Debrot. persknipsels met kritieken en biografische gegevens,* Amsterdam, Sticusa, 1967.

CHOBIL

(pseudonym for **Arturo LEITO**)

CHUMACEIRO, David Mendes

b. March 10, 1877, Curacao; d. Bogotá, April 30, 1922.
Poet.

A member of the pioneering group publishing in *Notas y Letras* and *Poema* in the 1880's and 1890's, Chumaceiro was influenced by Becquer and Campoamor.

Writings: Poetry: *Crisálidas,* 1898; *Adelfas,* 1902, both edited by A. Bethencourt.

Biographical/Critical Sources: B.E. Jesurun's introduction to Chumaceiro's work: *In leiding tot het werk van D.M. Chumaceiro,* details not known.

CORSEN, Charles Sickman

b. March 13, 1927, Curacao.
Poet, storywriter.

Grandson of Joseph Sickman Corsen, a leading poet of the last decades of the

19th century, Charles Corsen is primarily an avant-guard writer of the highest quality. Most of his work appeared first in *De Stoep* magazine edited by Chris Engels in the 1940's, and is mostly metaphysical

and full of concern for his own inner nature. The American poet Kenneth Patchen has influenced his work.

Writings: Poetry: "Eersta gedichten," in *De Stoep,* (Sept. 1948).

Prose: "De wrat op de wang van de duivel," in *De Stoep* (Sept. 1950); "Carmina de Aurora y sus 15 lágrimas," *De Stoep* (May 1951); "Con Sordino," in *De Stoep* (1949).

CORSEN, Joseph (Jozef) Sickman

b. December 13, 1855, Curacao; d. October 9, 1911.
Poet, storywriter.

Corsen, one of a literary family, is considered the best of the group who contributed to *Notas y Letras* and *Poema.* Cola Debrot called him a "lucid, melancholy man," and said he saw ". . . the defeat behind the outward appearance of beauty." His Papiamento poem "Atardi" is a classic poem now known to most

Curacaoans (it is, however, his Papiamento version of the Spanish version of Heine's famous poem which begins "Ich weiss nicht was sol es bedeuten . . .").

These lines from "Atardi" offer a sample of his work:

Ta pakiko, mi no sa;
ma esta tristu mi ta bira,
tur atardi ku mi mira
solo baha den laman.

Writings: Poetry: *Poesias,* Curacao, 1914 (112 pp.), Nijmegan, Netherlands, Kloosterman, foreword by B. A. Jesurun; *Un poko poesia,* details not known; individual poems in P. Lauffer's *Di Nos: Antologia de Nos Literatura,* Curaçao, 1971.

Scholarship: "Practica heneral. Fragment van een spellings voorstel, reeds geschrevenrond 1890," in *Ruku,* Nos. 2 and 3 (J. 2) (1970); "Apuntes sobre la conjugación en papiamento (Los auxiliares simples)." Part I, De Vrijmoedige, No. 48; Part II, De Vrijmoedige, Part III, De Vrijmoedige (all 1899).

Biographical/Critical Sources: B.A. Jesurun's *Inleiding tot het werk van J.S. Corsen,* 1914. Cola Debrot, *Literature of the Netherlands Antilles,* Willemstad, 1964, pp. 9-11.

CORSEN, Yolanda

(pseudonym: **Oda BLINDER**)
b. November 10, 1918, Curacao; d. July 30, 1969, Curacao.
Poet.

Sister of C.S. Corsen and granddaughter of Joseph S. Corsen, both poets, Oda Corsen lived a secluded life of intense inner raptures and lonely pain. Her poetry is tense, enigmatic, gnomic, akin to the verse of Emily Dickinson of the U.S. and Alfonsina Storni of Argentina. Most of her work appeared in Dr. Engels' *De Stoep* magazine of the 1940's and early 1950's.

Corsen's first published volume offers dual Dutch and Papiamento texts.

Corsen's one published volume offers dual Dutch and Papiamento texts.

Writings: Poetry: *Brieven van een Curacaose blinde, en andere gedichten.* Heerlen, Netherlands, 1968 (49 pp.), *Incognito flamboyant,* 1973 (6 pp.).

CYRANO
(pseudonym for **Emanuels ORLANDO**)

DAAL, Luis Henrique
b. October 5, 1919, Curacao.
Poet, storywriter.

Daal writes and publishes his stories and poems in both Spanish and Papiamento. He has also done several studies of old Papiamento texts.

Writings: Prose: "Alta Maya" (written in Madrid, 1962), in Pierre Lauffer's *Di Nos.*

Poetry: *Palabars intimas,* 1952; *Estampas españolas,* Curacao, 1951; *Kosecha di Maloa (Poesia),* Willemstad, Boekhandel Van Dorp, 1963. (76 pp.); "Firmesa" (from *Kosecha,* details not known), in P. Lauffer's *Di Nos; Ku awa na wowo,* Curacao, Editorial Lusafé, 1971 (76 pp.); *Mi so ku bjentu; Mi so ku Awa; Mi so ku Lus;* Individual poems: "Na Unda, Bientu?" from *Mi So ku bjentu* and "Awa di wowo" from *Mi so ku Awa,* and "Dunami" from *Mi so lu Lus,* all in P. Lauffer's *Di Nos.*

Story: "Premjo Majo" in Lauffer's *Di Nos.*

Scholarship: "Glosa di un dokumentu na papjamentu di ana 1863," in *La Union* (Nov. 1965), I; (April 6, 1966) II; (April 13, 1966) III.

DANDILO, Kwame
(pseudonym for **VAN P. POLANEN**)

b. ca. 1936, Surinam.
Poet.

Dandilo writes and publishes in English, Dutch and Sranan-Tongo.

Writings: Poetry: *Palito* (poems in Dutch, English and Sranan-Tongo), introduction by van J.E. Haakmat, Amsterdam, J. Haakmat, 1962, and Paramaribo, Drukkerij Paramaribo, 1970; poems in *9 Surinaamse gedichten in het Nederlands en Sranan-Tongo;* poems: "Bedankt" and "Niets mear" in *Nouvelle somme de poésie du monde noir,* Paris, Présence Africaine, 1966.

DEBROT, Cola
b. May, 1902, Bonaire.

Novelist, storywriter, playwright, critic, editor, lawyer, physician, government official.

Cola Debrot was Governor of the Netherlands Antilles in the 1960's. He edited the literary magazine *Criteriom.* Most of his work first saw print in the 1930-1940 period. It is to some degree Spanish in its feeling for tragedy and is nativist, and realistic, in that its Papiamento aspects reflect the islanders' direct and satirical bent. He worked in a wide range of genres and is one of the leading historians of the Dutch Antillean literature.

His novel *Mijn zuster de negerin* has seen many printings and was one of the first to bring attention to writing in Papiamento.

Writings: Play: *Kelki na boka,* translated from *Bokaal aan de lippen* by Max Henriquez, with poetry by Pierre Lauffer, Amsterdam 1973.

Essays and Literary History: *De polylinguale literatuur van de Nederlandse Antillen,* Amsterdam, Sticusa, 1967 (10 pp. in mimeo), translated by Estelle Debrot and published as *Literature of the Netherlands Antilles,* first in Vol. IV of *Panorama das Literaturas das Americas* (edited by Dr. Joaquim de Montezuma de Carvalho, Nova Lisboa, Angola, Edicao do Municipio, 1965), and then in separate English-language volume in Willemstad, Curacao, Departementram Cultuur en Opvoeding, 1964 (28 pp.); "Bokaal aan de lippen; blijspel in zeven bedrijven (mimeo), 1951, appeared in *Nieuw Vlaams Tijdschrift,* Vol. 5 (1951); article in *Encyclopedia of the Netherlands Antilles,* Amsterdam, edited by Elsevier, 1974; "Het existentialisme; drie voordractiten met discussie," Gravenhage, Leopoldville, 1947 (99 pp.): this is "Roundtable" with R.F. Beerling and J. De Kadt, the first symposium of the Sociëteit voor Culturele Samenwerking).

Stories: *My Sister the Negro,* 1935 as *Mijn zuster de negerin,* first edition, Rotterdam, Nijgh en van Ditmar, 1935, paper edition, Amsterdam Bij, 1935 and Rotterdam: second edition, Amsterdam, Muellenhoff, 1961; Also: *Dagboekbladen uit Genève,* Amsterdam, 1963; *Bid voor Camille Willocq,* Amsterdam, 1947 (86 pp.); *De afwezigen,* Amsterdam, Meulenhoff, 1952 (29 pp.).

Poetry: *Bekentenis in Toledo. Gedichten,* Amsterdam, Balkema, 1945 (18 pp.), and second edition, 's Gravenhage, 1946; *Navrante Somer; gedichten,* Amsterdam, Muelenhoff, 1945 (24 pp.).

Biographical/Critical Sources: C.J. Cardoze: *Cola Debrot persknipsels met kritieken en biographische gegevens,* Amsterdam, Sticusa, 1967; Johan v.d. Walle, *Beneden de Wind,* Amsterdam, Querido, 1974 (deals with Debrot, C. Engels, and politician Da Costa Gomez).

DEFARES, J. Ph. A.

b. ca. 1931, Surinam.
Poet, folklorist, playwright.

Defares is a specialist in Sranan and casts his work in that language.

Writings: Poetry: *Fajabro. Gedichten in het Sranen Tongo,* 1970.

Play: *Minnaar in de duisternis* (play in two acts based on Anancy tales), 1961 (54 pp.).

Scholarship: *Den toe boikoe de Lucas skrifi* (Lucas en Hendelingen in oude en nieuwe Surinaamse vertaling), 1966.

DE POOL, John

b. 1873, Curacao; d. 1947, Panama.
Autobiographer, historian.

A member of the group of Curacao literati contributing to the weeklies *Notas y Letras* and *Poema* in the 1880's and 90's, de Pool's memoirs *Del Curazao que se va,* published in 1935 long after it was written, is considered by Cola Debrot to be one of the most important literary works in modern Curacao literature. Along with J.C. Corsen, de Pool is considered a major realist of the turn of the century period.

Writings: memoirs: *Del Curazao que se va,* Santiago, Chile, Editorial Ercilla, 1935.

Biographical/Critical Sources: Cola Debrot: *Literature of the Netherlands Antilles,* pp. 11-12.

de ZIEL, Henri Frans

(see under pseudonym: **TREFOSSA**)

DOBRU, R.

(pseudonym for **Robin RAVALES**)

DOELWIJT, Thea

b. ca. 1942, Den Helder, Netherlands (associated with Surinam).
Poet, novelist, film scenarioist.

Daughter of a Surinamese father and a Dutch mother, Doelwijt studied journalism in Holland and practices that profession in Surinam. She began publishing her poems in 1967 in local journals in Paramaribo.

Writings: Poetry: *De Speelse Revolutue,* Paramaribo, Drukkerij Moderna, 1967 (contains some prose); *Met weinig worden,* Paramaribo, Moderna, 1968. Her work appears in the collection, *De Vlucht,* Paramaribo, H.v.d. Boomen, 1969, and two of her poems, "Zwarte regen" [Black Rain] and "Opeenszie ik" [Suddenly I See] are in dual Dutch-English text in A.J. Seymour's *New Writing in the Caribbean,* Georgetown, Guyana, 1972.

Novel: *Wajono,* Paramaribo, Eldorado, 1969 (second printing).

In progress: film scenario "Mario."

DOMACASSE, Pacheco

b. ca. 1941, Curacao.
Playwright.

Domacasse has written two mysteriously named plays, both published in Curacao.

Writings: Plays: *Opus I,* n.d.; and *Opus 1795* (Tula), Tone Brulin, 1971.

ENGELS, Christiaan J. H.
(pseudonym: Luc TOURNIER)

b. 1907, Netherlands (associated with Curacao).
Poet, storywriter, art critic, editor, painter, translator, physician.

Born and bred in the Netherlands where he became a medical doctor, Engels removed permanently to Curacao in the 1930's. During the Second World War his magazine *De Stoep* was the only journal open to Dutch language writers outside of German-occupied Holland. Modeled on the earlier literary review *Notas y Letras,* published in Spanish in Curacao in the late decades of the 19th century, *De Stoep* appeared at irregular intervals for some ten years. Its first purpose was to offer a home to exiled writers but it soon became a renewed stimulus to local writing in both Dutch and Papiamento, particularly to the Antillean surrealist group led by Charles Corsen (grandson of the fine early writer Joseph Sickman Corsen), Tip Marugg and Yolanda Corsen (Charles Corsen's sister), a writer akin to the American poet Emily Dickinson or Alfonsina of Argentina.

These writers were not protest poets but mainly introspective and were still attached to European and specifically Dutch themes. Only with the *De Stoep* writers of the later years did there emerge a more locally engagé group led by poets Frank Martinus (a frankly Afro-Antilles writer), and Alette Beaujon, and the novelist Boeli

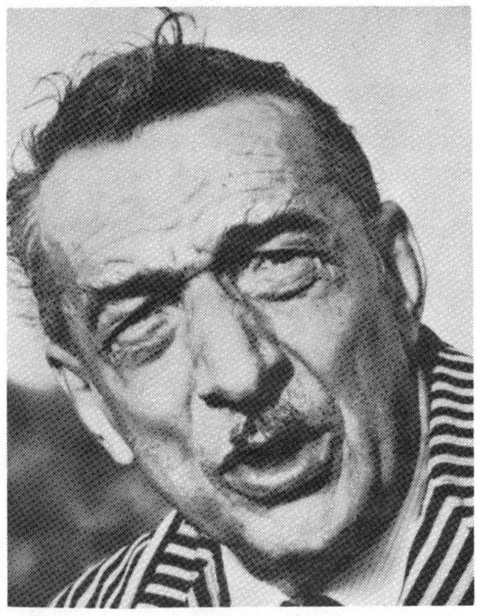

van Leeuwen. They were influenced by the work of Kenneth Patchen (U.S.A.), Garcia Lorca and Luc Tournier—and became the harbinger of the "Experimental poetry developing in Holland in the early 1950's.

Engels has had a long and valuable career as a public health official, (he is now the Director of the Medical Service in Curacao), and with his painter-wife has been a prime mover in the artistic life of the island. Engels established and has continued as director of the first museum of folklore and fine arts of Curacao. His own home, a renovated spacious 18th century mansion with an exotic garden, houses giant paintings and sculptures by himself, his wife and Latin American artists. There, with his three sons and one daughter, Engels offers a major bridge between the older Dutch traditions and the ever more self confident group of locally born islanders who increasingly express themselves in Papiamento in literature and journalism as well as in radio and television dramas and readings.

The poetic persona of Engels has long been "Luc Tournier," who is almost a separate person even to the medical officer himself. The name is borrowed from his mother's family.

Writings: Poetry: In Dutch: *Verzen en penitentie,* 1936; *Kleine Curacao Verzen,* Curacao, 1941; *Doffe Orewoed* (Ecstasy in Undertone); 1941; *Doffe Orewoed* (Ecstasy in Undertone), Amsterdam, J. M. Meulenhoff, 1948; *Conversatie voor de prauw,* 1954; *Don Juan de dupe,* 1956; poem "Bloemlezing uit gedicten," in *De Stoep* (1940) and also in *Antilliaanse Cahiers,* Vol. I, No. 2 (1956), pp. 1-72; *Corpulent en minuscuul,* 1972; *De man van Tortuga,* 1973; and collection: *Geen droom, maar eeuwige verte,* Amsterdam, Meulenhoff, 1977; *Kunst en Vliegwerk,* 1964; *Bij de brand van Willemstad aan het werk aan . . . brandvrijheid,* 1969.

Stories: *De papegaaien sterven en andere verhalen,* Amsterdam, Meulenhoff, 1977.

Criticism-Biography: *Dicter in New York,* Heynis, Zaandijk, 1959, (114 pp.), translated into Spanish as *Federico Garcia Lorca, Poeta en Nueva York.*

Scholarship: *Damas van de eilenden,* 1976 (history); *Papiamento en Portugees, in Amigoe de Curacao* (Willemstad, April 19, 1944); *Opgravingen te Malmok op Aruba,* Aruba, 1970; "Origen del Papiamento" (essay), in *Boletin de Anthropologia,* Bogota, 1971; *Mama di joe chikitoe scucha doktor su consejo (advice to mothers of young children), three printings in Willemstad, La Cruz, no date (16 pp.).*

Editor of Literary Review: *De Stoep,* 26 numbers, some double, September 1940 to May 1951.

Letters: *Brieven aan een Koerantier,* Willemstad, 1977.

Biographical/Critical Sources: Cola Debrot, *Literature of the Netherlands Antilles,* Willemstad, 1964, and in earlier Dutch edition, details not known; Johan v. d. Walle, *Beneden de Wind,*

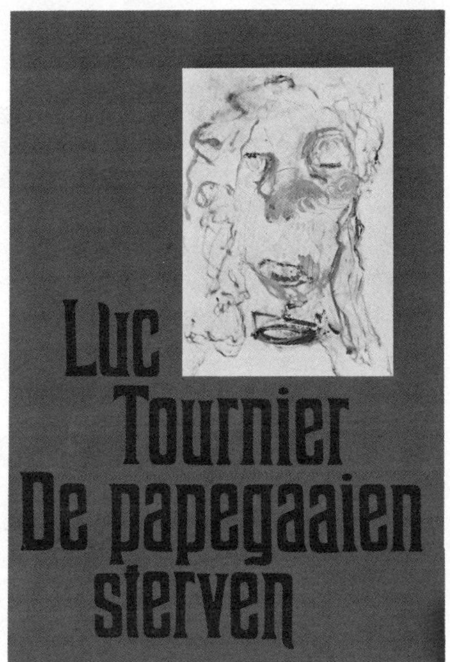

Amsterdam, Querido, 1974; also see special work honoring Engel's 70th year, in the richly illustrated book, Liber Amicorum: Luc Tournier 70, Amsterdam, Meulenhoff, 1977.

FERRIER, L.H.

b. ca. 1938, Surinam.
Novelist.

Ferrier has published two novels, both in Amsterdam.

Writings: Novels: *Atman,* De Bezige Bij, 1968; *El Sisilobi of het basisonderzoek,* De Bezige Bij, 1969.

FOENG, J. A. Chin A.

(see under pseudonym: **JUANCHI**)

FRAAI, Manuel Antonio

b. December 1, 1897, Curacao; d. December 3, 1967, Curacao.
Novelist.

Fraai published all his stories and novels in Papiamento.

Writings: Novels: *Un sacrificio,* n.p., n.d. (180 pp.), second edition, Willemstad, n.d. (188 pp.); *Un huerfano;* novelo original, Curacao, 1954, in 2 vols.; *Mal Aguero,* Curacao, 1959, extract in *Di Nos* by P. Lauffer (ed.); *Nobleza di coerazon,* Curacao, n.d. (111 pp.); and *Polidor,* Curacao, n.d.

GARMERS, Sonja

b. ca. 1925, Curacao.
Storywriter.

Garmers has collected her children's stories in four volumes. She has also done two books on cooking and one on applying cosmetics.

Writings: Juvenile Stories: *Tantan Nini. . . . ta conta,* Curacao, 1955; *Cuentanan pa mucha,* Curacao, 1959; *Conta cuenta,* Curacao, Boekhandel v. Dorp., 1960; *Un macutu jen di cuenta,* Curacao, Boekhandel v. Dorp., 1960.
Cookbooks: *Cu Marina den cushina,* Curacao, 1960, 3 printings; *Recetas,* no publication data.

Cosmetology: *Papiando riba nos bunitesa,* Curacao, 1961.

GEERDINK-JESURUN PINTO, Nilda Maria

(née **JESURUN-PINTO**)
b. December 12, 1918, Curacao; d. April 17, 1954, Hengelo, Netherlands.
Storywriter, folklorist.

Nilda Jesurun Pinto's work and interests were always in Papiamento and island culture.

Writings: Stories: *Cuentanan de Nanzi,* first edition, Curacao, 1952 (99 pp.), second edition, Curacao, Stichting Jeugdcentrale, 1965 (76 pp.); *Bam Canta,* first edition, Curacao, 1944 (112 pp.), second printing, 1948; *Corsouw ta conta,* first edition, Curacao, 1944, second edition, Hengelo, Netherlands, 1954 (103 pp.).

HABIBA, Henry

b. May 6, 1940, Aruba.
Poet.

Habiba published his verse in Papiamento.

Writings: Poetry: *Aurora: Poesie prohibi,* The Hague, Netherlands, Edit. Watapana, 1968 (23 pp.); four poems from unpublished manuscript and extract from *Aurora* are in Lauffer's *Di Nos.*

Scholarship: "Spelling Romer of Daal," in Watapana, Jg. II, No. 7 (July 1970).

HELMAN, Albert

(pseudonym for **Dr. L.A.M. Lichtveld**)

b. 1906, Paramaribo, Surinam.
Novelist, critic, translator, poet, playwright, critic.

Helman is one of the most active of Surinam's writers and has served as Minister Plenipotentiary of the Royal Netherlands Embassy in Washington. He has written in many genres. His first publication is believed to have been the collection of verse: *De glorende dag* (1923) when he was but 17 years old.

Writings: Play: *Caraibisch Passiespel* (5 acts), with prologue and epilogue: Paramaribo, 1960 (98 pp.).

Poetry: *De glorende dag. Verzen,* Amsterdam, Uitgeversmaatschappij Joost van den Vondel, 1923 (67 pp.), under his true name (Lichtveld).

Various: *Surinam. Jang tak terkenal,* Amsterdam, van der Peet, 1951; *Omnibus* (selections from *Mijn aap schreit, Hart zonderland Ratten, Het euvels Gods,* ("Menschen heen-en terugweg . . .), Amsterdam, Amsterdamische Boek-en Courant Mij, 1947 (605 pp.); *Kleine Kosmologie,* Amsterdam, Amsterdamsche Boek-en Courant Mij, 1947 (257 pp.); *Mijn aap schreit; Het euvel Gods,* first edition, 1928, second edition, Amsterdam, Querido, 1966 (192 pp.); *Serenitas,* Utrecht, de Gemeenschap uitgevers, 1930; *De stille plantage,* 1931, 11th printing: 's-Gravenhage-Rotterdam, Nijgh en Van Ditmar, 1962; *De laaiende stilte* (omwerking van De stille plantage), Amsterdam, 1952, second edition, Amsterdam, Querido (192 pp.); Also: *Mijn aap lacht,* Amsterdam Boek-en Courant Mij, 1953 (270 pp.); and *Spokendans,* 1954, same publisher, (123 pp.).

Translations: "Ballad of Canga" by Eric Roach, as "Taki-Taki" in Surinamese rural creole," in *Caribbean Quarterly,* Vol. 4, No. 2, pp. 167-168; Marc Connelly's *Green Pastures,* into play form and published in Paramaribo, Radhakishun, 1954 (56 pp.); *Tam-Tam* from English to Dutch of J.W. van der Cook's novel, Amsterdam, 1935.

Critical Essays: introductory essay to Trotji Aanhef (18 poems of Van Trefossa [Henny de Ziel]), in mimeo, 1957, published later in 1957 in Amsterdam with support of Bureau of Linguistic Research in Surinam, at University of Amsterdam; "Op zoek naar despin," in *De West-Ind Gids,* Vol. 12, pp. 209-230, 305-324.

Novel: *Zuid Zuid-West,* 1926, second edition, Amsterdam, Salamanderpocket, Querida's Uitgeverij, 196?; extract as "My Monkey Weeps," in *From the Green Antilles,* B. Howe, ed., London, Souvenir Press, 1967; and London, Panther Books, 1971, translation by Alex Brotherton.

Biographical/Critical Sources: M. Nord, *Albert Helman; een inleiding tot zijn werk* (with texts, holographs, photos, curiosities and bibliography), 's-Gravenhage, Daamen, 1949 (168 pp.); *Lou Lichtveld/Albert Helman; een representatiev bibliografie,* Paramaribo, 1962, produced by Bureau Volkslectuur.

HENRIQUEZ, Julio, Sr.

b. ca. 1921, Curacao.
Playwright, translator.

Henriquez has written at least ten plays in Papiamento and several translations of his into Papiamento are known.

Writings: Plays: all Curacao: *E tanto a rek e cabuja te e cabuja a rementa p'e; E tia surdoe; Famia Ortiguera; Mama; Prendanan di familia* (two acts); *Sjon Panchita; Tres lomba de baul; Un bruhamentu di demonio; Un plan fracasá; Un trastorno pa motivo de codighi.*

Translation: *Martha y su Silencio,* Curacao, 1951 (from unknown text).

HENRIQUEZ-ALVAREZ CORREA, May

b. May 6, 1915, Curacao.
Translator.

The work of the translator in new languages can be as valuable sometimes as new work and May Henriquez' renderings into Papiamento of one classic of G.B. Shaw and two of Moliere show the flexibility of the language.

Writings: Translations: *Pygmalion,* as *Laiza porko sushi toneelstuk gebaseerd,* Willemstad, Scherpenheuvel, 1954 (139 pp.); of Moliere's *L'Avare,* as *Sjon Pichiri,* in *Antilliaanse Cahiers,* 1967 and *Medecin malgre lui,* as *Ami dokter, lubida.*

HERNANDEZ, Victor P.

(pseudonym for **Cornelius [Nechi] RAPHAELA**)
b. ca. 1914, Curacao.
Storywriter, historian, poet, novelist, essayist.

Raphaela is one of the most prolific and widely published of the writers from Curacao, employing Papiamento and Spanish.

Writings: History: *Historia i sucesonan mundial,* Curacao, 1944 (32 pp.).

Stories: "Nos lo casa toch cu otro," Curacao, eigenbeheer, n.d., in three parts, each 15 pp. (in mimeo); "Ambicion Fatal," Curacao, Casa Editorial La Fe, n.d., five parts, each 12 pp.; "Herman y Maria," Curacao, n.d. (109 pp.); "Amor pa homber casá," Curacao, Casa Edit. La Fe, three parts, each 16 pp.; "Amor di Paganini," Curacao, n.d. (13 pp., a translation); "Un muhe mundana," Casa Edit. La Fe, n.d., ten parts, each 12 pp.

Stories published by "Raphaela": *Alicia de Hasmin Carmin de Luz,* 1955; *Princesa Claverina Albertina de Violetas de Valle,* 1959; *Beatrix,* 1960; *Aventura de don Enrique,* 1961; *E Triunfo de un Reinada* (in *Evolucion* magazine); *Relampage Cientifico* (detective story), 1963; *Julio y Julieta,* 1964, 1965.

Novels: *Herman y Maria,* Curacao, n.d. (109 pp.); *Loretta,* Curacao, Casa Ed. Emile (64 pp.), second edition, Sticusa, 1953; *Felipe y Margaritha,* Curacao, Casa Ed. Emile, n.d. (83 pp.).

Poetry: *Brindonan na papiamentu,* Curacao, 1955 (51 pp.); second printing, n.d. (58 pp.); verse often published in *La Union* and in *Evolucion.*

HEYLIGER

(pseudonym for **Eddie PIETERS**)

HOOI, Richard

(pseudonym: **Yerba SEKU**)
b. ca. 1944, Surinam.
Poet.

Hooi's little collection of poetry (in Dutch) is dedicated to the independence movement of the Dutch Antilles. The poems are composed mostly of one or two word lines and their staccato effect seem to reflect the verse of Leon Gontran Damas, major negritude poet from Cayenne, Guyane. The title poem of the collection is "Mis Eiland" (given in full below) and is a mélange of several languages:

mijn
eiland
is een
mis-eiland
mis-teenage
mis-teensmile
mis-teenprincess
mis-Curacao
mis-press
mis-sport
mis-popular
mis-bon bini
mis-amity
mis-boka chika
mis-vakashon primera
mis-vakashon segunda
mis-haagd
mis-noegd
mis-gund
mis-kend
mis-rekend
mis-deeld
mid-leid
mis-lukt
mis-vormd
mis-handeld
mis-bruikt

HOYER, Willem Manuel

b. June 17, 1862, Curacao; d. July 30, 1953.
Poet.

Hoyer was one of the earliest island poets to be published in Papiamento.

Writings: Poetry: *Canto de Pueblo na ocasion di jubileo di oro di Emancipacion 1863* (Compuesta por Willem III), Curacao, 1913; and three poems in Lauffer's *Di Nos*, Curacao, 1971.

JESURUN, Pablo Alex

b. January 15, 1912, Curacao.
Poet, biographer.

A member of the many-talented Jesurun family, Pablo Max published a modest collection of Dutch-language verse and one study of the poet J.S. Corsen. He also frequently wrote in Papiamento.

Writings: Biography: *Inleiding tot het werk van J.S. Corsen,* 1914.
Poetry: *Gedicten,* preface by René de Rooy, and poems in various collections, including P. Lauffer's *Di Nos.*

JONGH, Edward A. de

(pseudonym: **Johan BARTOLOME**)
b. November 18, 1923, Ambon (associated with Curacao).
Papiamento poet, novelist.

One of the most prolific of Curacaon writers, Jongh's work spans three decades in several genres.

Writings: Poetry: *Tras de e cortina,* Curacao, 1948 (under pseudonym Bartolomé); *Capricho, poëmas,* Curacao, Centro Cultural de Corsouw, 1955; *Quietud, poëmas,* Curacao, eigen baheer, 1957 (24 pp., Premia concurso literario); poems "Den Pobresa" (from *Quietud*) and "Eterno Poesia" (from *Capricho*) in P. Lauffer's anthology, *Di Nos.*
Stories: *Den Mondi di Jan Thiel,* Curacao, Casa Editorial Emile, 1952; *Morto na Seru Fortuna,* Curacao, Casa Editorial Revista, n.d.; *Refleho ·Amorose,* Curacao, Casa Editorial Emile, n.d.; *Bon biaha, novela corticu (y tres Short stories)* [sic], Willemstad, Solas, 1955 (38 pp.); and *Guillermo, novela,* Curacao, 1953 (12 pp.). Extracts from "Shrrrr" and "No tabata sina" from *Bon biaha,* are in Lauffer's *Di Nos.*
Novelettes: *Derecho de Nace,* Curacao, Casa Editorial Emile, 1952 (25 pp.), made into a film: *El derecho de nacer;* Also: *Nan tabata ruman,* Curacao, Casa Editorial Emile, 1954; *Morto de Enid La Cruz,* Curacao, eigen beheer, 1969 (102 pp.).

Article: "Twee letters on der de mikroskoop," in *Ruku,* Nos. 2 and 3, (July 2, 1970).
Essay: "Dos plaka de palabra," Curacao, 1971.

JUANCHI

(pseudonym for **J.A. Chin A. FOENG**)
b. ca. 1941, Surinam.
Poet.

Juanchi is one of the first writers of Chinese origin to published in Surinam.

Writings: Poetry: *Wanneer de rukwind komt; poema's* (in Dutch), Paramaribo, Juanchi Drukkerij Atlas, Paramaribo, 1971 (37 pp.).

JULIANA, Elis

b. August 8, 1927, Curacao.
Poet, playwright for radio (writes in Papiamento, Dutch and Spanish).

Juliana has entitled several of his collections of verse after flowers, and Cola Debrot writes: "Poetry begins for him where a metamorphosis takes place from the things of daily life into flowers. Daphne does not allow Apollo to embrace her, but changes into trembling foliage. He is not the poet of 'passion' but of 'tenura'."

Writings: Radio Play: *Na rudia dilanti Pesebre,* Curacao, n.d.

Folk Stories: *Aventura di un kriki; conta pa e mes,* Curacao, 1960 (46 pp.).

Poetry: *Canta Clara,* Curacao, n.d. (16 pp.); *Dame di Anochi,* Curacao, Van Engelen, 1959 (19 pp.); *Dede pikiña, dedica na nos muchanan* (27 gedichten), Willemstad, Scherpenheuvel, 1964 (poems for children); *Flor di Anglo,* poësia u sketch, Curacao; Scherpenheuvel, 1961 (80 pp.).

Stories: *Maka taka,* Curacao, Boekhandel Van Dorp, 1961 (111 pp.).

Stories and Poetry: *Wazo riba rondo,* Willemstad, Curacao, 1967 (80 pp.); Extracts or poems from *Flor di Anglo, Maka Taka, Canta Clara,* and *Dame di Anochi* in P. Lauffer's *Di Nos.*

Poetry: "Trois minutes," in *Nouvelle somme de poesie du monde noir,* Paris, Presence Africaine, 1966; *Flor di Datu; poesias,* Willemstad, 1956 (77 pp.), second edition, Boekhandel Sakas, 1958; Scharpenheuvel, 1961 (111 pp.).

Folksongs: "Echa Cuenta. Du de papiamentse verhalen," Amsterdam, De Bezige Bij, 1971.

Biographical/Critical Sources: Cola Debrot: *Literature of the Netherlands Antilles,* p. 13.

KAMPEN, Oscar van

(pseudonym: **Azijn BANANA**)
b. ca. 1928, Surinam.
Essayist.

van Kampen contributed satirical pieces to the journal *Lirito Real* in the 1948-1958 period which were some of the earliest of their sort in Papiamento prose.

Biographical/Critical Sources: Cola Debrot, *Literature of the Netherlands Antilles,* p. 15.

KEULS, H.

b. 1927, Holland, for a period resident in Curacao.
Playwright, film-producer.

Keuls is known to have published one play in Papiamento.

Writings: Play: *Plantage Tamarinde* (toneespel in drie bedrijven, bekroond en uitgegeven door Bond van Nederl. Toneeluitgevers), Amsterdam, 1957 (88 pp.).

KING, Johannes

b. ca. 1830, Surinam; d. 1899.
Folklorist, autobiographer, preacher.

Born into the Matuari group descended from Africans fled from the coastal plantations, King lived a long and turbulent life as a Moravian preacher. Having taught himself to read, he moved around Surinam's Para district from 1860 on, when he was baptised, and where, after receiving visions, he began to build a church in 1861. Eight members of his family underwent baptism the next year and he gradually became accepted as a prophet, his reputation even advancing to Europe. In 1868 his first known book was written, dealing with religion and customs of his people. In 1886, he wrote down his visions in his *skrekibuku* [Book of Terror].

Expelled from his home village of Matuari in 1892 by his brother the chief, King composed his third book, telling the story of his first missionary visit to Djuka in 1864 which also included the making of a peace treaty between the Matuari and Djuka groups.

The language employed by King was the "town" variety of Sranan-Tongo, not the "Bushnegro" creole, and generally the Dutch bible style of language was his preferred vehicle.

A fourth work of King's, probably written in 1893, concerning charms and medical potions, is never shown to eyes other than local ones.

Writings: Prose Writings: Some manuscripts have been printed in *Vox Guyane,* Vol. 3, No. 1 (1958), pp. 41-45 (the first vision) and in Lichtveld and Voorhoeve, *Surinam: spiegel der vaderlanse kooplieden,* Zwolle, 1958 (King's history of the bush negroes). Also see Lichtveld-Voorhoeve *Creole Drum* (1955) for examples of his work in the town creole and in English translation: pp. 120-133; *Life at Maripaston,* H.F. de Ziel, editor, The Hague, 1973.

Biographical/Critical Sources: Gottfried A. Freytag, *Johannes King der Buschland-Prophet Ein Lebensbild aus der Brudergemeine in Surinam. Nach seinem eigener Aufzeichnungen dargestellt.* Herrnhut, Netherlands, 1927. For a complete discussion of the entire corpus of King's writings, see Voorhoeve and Donicie, "Johannes King, 1830-1900. Een mens met grote overtuiging," in *Biografieën Emancipatie 1863-1963,* Paramaribo, 1964.

KOENDERS, J.G.A.

b. ca. 1906, Surinam.
Teacher, anthologist, folklorist, poet.

Koenders, a teacher, was one of the earliest to urge the use in schools of readers written in Sranan-Tongo, the "creole" of Surinam, rather than the formal Dutch from Europe. "Ever since my early thirties," he wrote in *Foetoe-boi* (July 1946), "I have known what sort of knowledge parrot knowledge is, to wit, many words, only words, instead of comprehension." Urged on by the activist women in the Pohama Club (Potie hanse makandra—Join Hands Together), Koenders wrote and published three small works in Sranan and Dutch: *Foe memre wi afo* (In Memory of Our Forefathers) which deals with Creole grammar and spelling; *Aksie mie, mie sa piekie joe foe wie skien* (Ask Me, I Shall Answer You About Our Body), dealing with elementary facts of physiology; and *Sieksie tintien moi en bekentie siengie* (Sixty Beautiful and Well Known Songs).

Though Koenders was a very modestly endowed poet and never himself had many poetic pretensions, his poem "Mama Africa e krey fu en pikin" [Mother Africa Weeps for her child] appeared in Janheinz Jahn's pioneering *Schwarzer Orpheus* (1954). His journal *Foetoe-boi* (Paramaribo, 1946-1956) published most of his work, including his occasional original poems and translations from Dutch into Sranan-Tongo.

His poem "Mama Africa . . ." begins:

Pe den alamala go?
Amba, Kwami èn Kodyo.
Farawe fu oso, farawe na abra se
den opo ay e suku pe den oso de.

Whither are they, all of them?
Amba, Kwami, and Kodyo—
So far from home, way across the sea
They stare out—looking for their huts.

Though Koenders struggled hard and long to remove the stigma from Sranan Tonga and the African heritage of most of Surinam's people, his own language at times was over-close to Dutch and not entirely free of self-conscious mannerisms.

Writings: Poetry: mostly in his journal *Foetoe-boi;* one poem "Mama Africa e krey fu en piken" in *Foetoe-boi* (March 1955) and *Schwarzer Orpheus,* 1954, edited by Janheinz Jahn. This poem also in Voorhoeve and Lichtveld's *Creole Drum* along with "Sranen" (Surinam), published originally in *Foetoe-boi* (June 1955).

Prose: *Foe memre wi afo* (grammar), Paramaribo, 1943; *Aksie mie, mie sa piekie joe foe wie skien* (physiology), Paramaribo, 1944; *Sieksie tintien moi en bekentie siengie* (songs), Paramaribo, no date; and various selections in *Creole Drum,* edited by Jan Voorhoeve and Ursy M. Lichtveld.

KROON, José

b. ca. 1921, Curacao.

Biographer, translator, sociologist, journalist.

Kroon's work is in Papiamento.

Writings: Biography: *Angel Obia, un jonge wachter di Cursouw,* Curacao, 1951 (60 pp.).

Translation of novel: *Mi casita den splendor di solo,* Curacao, n.d. (143 pp.).

Sociology: *Zie Algun Nocion de Sociologia.*

Essay: Introduction to Willem Kroon's *Algun Poesia,* Curacao, 1966.

KROON, Willem Eligio

b. December 1, 1886, Curacao; d. January 26, 1949.

Poet, novelist, storywriter.

Kroon has been one of the most published Papiamento writers with six novels, two volumes of verse, and much miscellaneously published tales and stories.

Writings: Novels: *Dos novela,* Curacao, 1927 (140 pp.): I: *E no por casa* (1-75) and II: *Mester a deré prome el a drenta na case* (75-140); *Giambo bieuw a bolbe na wea: Novela intima Curazolenja,* Curacao, 1928; *Etiquette: Lo que nos mester i no mester hasi pa nos tin bon manera,* Curacao, 1941; *Su unico amor. Novela original di . . . ,* Curacao, n.d., n.p., but second edition, Curacao, 1954 (104 pp.); *Yiu di su mama, o castigo di un abuso,* Curacao, 1947, 2 Parts in 1948.

Stories and Poetry: "Preparashon pa e gran dia," and poem "Na memoria di mi mama difuntu," both in Lauffer's anthology: *Di Nos;* Also story: "Mientras solo no a baha, careda di bina no a casa, n.p. and n.d.

Poetry: *Algun poesia,* Curacao, Drukkerij Scherpenheuvel, 1966 (64 pp.), foreword by José Kroon; *Venganz di Amor* (122 pp.).

KROSS, Rudy

(pseudonym for **Rico VOGELLAND**)

b. ca. 1936, Surinam.

Poet, critic, editor.

Kross edited with J. Slagveer, *Njoen moesoede* (poetry in Dutch and Sranan), Paramaribo, Het National Comite voor de Vermievwing, 1970. He also edited a study of the poetry of Michael Slory, John Muller, J.H. Slagveer and his own work: "Surinaams perspektief" in *Contour,* Leiden, Sijhoff, (Sept. 1966).

KWIERS, Guillermo Tharcisio Pieters

(a.k.a. **G. Th. PIETERS KWIERS**)

b. February 10, 1931, Curacao.

Poet, playwright.

Kwiers writes in both Dutch and Papiamento and has thus far published three volumes of his verse and one play.

Writings: Poetry: *Alpha,* Curacao, 1960 (35 pp.); *Nederlands een Papiamentse gedichten,* Curacao, 1960; *De nachtgodin; 30 gedichten,* Willemstad, 1963 (34 pp.); and six poems in P. Lauffer's anthology: *Di Nos.*

Play: *Amor sin pasaporte,* performed on Curacao TV by Eligio Melfors group, 1968.

LAGUN, Chandi

b. ca. 1918, Curacao.
Folklorist.

Lagun employs the folkloric "dialogues" to catch the spirit of the island folk.

Writings: Dialogue-Stories: *Camind'i Cruz* [At the Crossroads], 1948.

Biographical/Critical Sources: Cola Debrot, *Literature of the Netherlands Antilles,* p. 15.

LAMPE, J.K.Z.

b. ca. 1870, Curacao.
Poet (in Dutch).

An early important Dutch Writer of Antilles birth whose work was of the late romantic sort, reflecting Dutch models of the mid-19th century but which bore the stamp of the fin-de siecle weariness.

Writings: Poetry: *Gedichten;* Aruba, 1956 and 's-Gravenhage, Netherlands, 1956 (64 pp.).

LAUFFER, Pierre

(pseudonym for **José Antonio MARTES**)
b. August 22, 1920, Curacao.
Poet, storywriter, anthologist.

Cola Debrot states Lauffer's poetry "owes its attractiveness to its exceptional sonority and variety of rhythm." Lauffer's collection *Patria* is romantic; his *Kumbu, Wiri-wiri,* and *Niapa* are reflective of African themes and probably influenced by the Cuban poet Nicolás Guillén and the work of the Puerto Rican, Luis Palés Matos. Through all of his work runs a vein of realism and an eye for social considerations.

Lauffer founded the Papiamento literary magazine *Simadón* with Nicolás Piña, Raphael Martinez, and Andres Grimar.

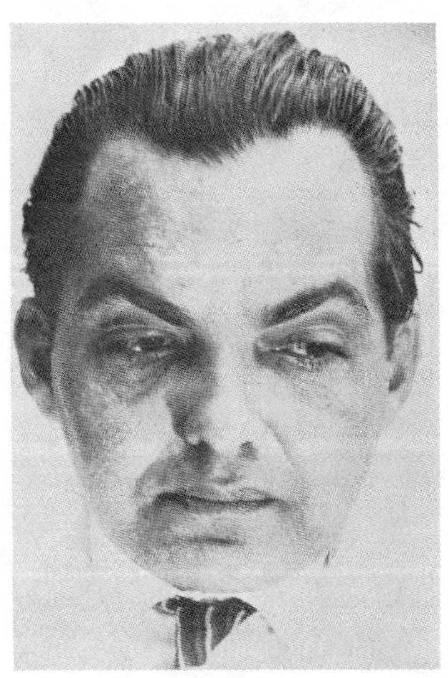

Writings: Poetry: *Patria,* Curacao, 1947; *Kumbu,* Willemstad, Centro Cultural Corsou, 1955; *Kantika pa Bjentu, bundel met 19 gedichten,* Oranjestad, Aruba, De Wit, 1963 (26 pp.) which won first prize in the 1963 competition of the Culturaeel Centrum Curacao; *Lagrima i sourisa* (12 poems), Curacao, 1973; In his anthology *Di Nos* are "Mi ke tumabo" from *Kumbu,* "Wirii-wiri," and "E Pieda de Anakklaca" from *Kwentu pa Kaminda,* "Dolo di Tata" from *Raspá,* and "Kwadro na Shinishi" from *Njapa.*

General: *"Zie: Antillano,"* in *De Stoep* and *Sinadán* I and II.

Stories and Poetry: *Njapa; 30 korte verhalen en 6 gedichten,* Curacao.

Anthology: *Di Nos, Antologia di Nos Literatura,* Willemstad, Libreria Salas, 1971 (241 pp.).

Stories: *Seis anja kaska berde,* Curacao/Aruba, Boekhandel van Dorp, 1968 (54 pp.); *Kwenta pa kaminda,* Curacao, De Wit N.V., 1969; *Carmen Molina,* Curacao, n.d.; *Martirio di Amor,* Curacao, n.d.; *Philomela,* Curacao; *Raspá. 19 korte verhalen en 9 gedichten,* Curacao, Imprent de Skèrpène, 1961; *Wiriwiri,* Willemstad, Curacao, Scherpenheuvel, 1961 (64 pp.).

Biographical/Critical Sources: Cola Debrot, *Literature of the Netherlands Antilles,* pp. 13-14.

LEITO, Arturo

(pseudonyms: **TUYUCHI** and **CHOBIL**)
b. 1910, Curacao.
Storywriter, translator.

Leito published most of his many stories under one of his two pen-names. He contributed satirical pieces to the Curacao journal *La Cruz.*

Writings: Stories (by "Chobil"): "Hacibo ciegoe-pa bo por biba riba mundu," Curacao, Imprenta di Vicariato, 1935 (131 pp.), with first story by van Leito, others by "Tuyuchi" or "Chobil" as authors in: *Mi biblioteca papiamentu,* 6, was translation of story "Un lugar de calamidad," by Tom Richardson, Curacao, 1940; "E misterio di su nacemento," in *Mi biblioteca papiamentu,* 10, 1940 (36 pp.); and translation of story: "Un hecho di desesperacion," from T. Richardsor in *Mi biblioteca papiamentu,* No. 3.

Stories (by "Tuyuchi"): "Un bagatel atrevido, Curacao, n.d.; "Un baga tel coe consecuenc anan fatal," Curacao, 1946; "Un cas de terror, Curacao, Casa Edit. Leon, n.d., (31 pp.); "U conspiracion den lamar gancho," Curacao, n.d (60 pp.); "Un criminal sin consenshi," (60 pp. "Un crimen horrible" (25 pp.); "Un inocent condena; secreto de tres amigo," (40 pp.); "U invento particular" (32 pp.); "Un malbad peligroso"; "Un mensahe tragica," Casa Edi Leon; "Secreto di un recuerdo desagradable, and many others translated into Papiamentc listed in *Di Nos,* edited by P. Lauffer.

Novel: *Noche Buena* (139 pp.).

Folktales: "Amor pa dos ruman;" "Amor si limite;" "Azucena;" "Colmo di barbarism, 1946; "E tirano di Juggerton," Casa Edit. Leor "Investigacion;" "Mira aki bo victima;" "Secret dje cobado di morto," Curacao, Casa Edi Emile, n.d.; "Conta Cuenta," Curacao, n.d. (3 pp.).

LICHTVELD, Dr. L.A.M.

(see under pseudonym: **Albert HELMAN**

LUTCHMAN, Martinus Haridat

(see pseudonym: **Asjantenu SHRINI VASI**)

MADURO, Antoine J.

b. August 20, 1909, Aruba.
Poet, historian, linguistic scholar.

Maduro's one Papiamento verse collectio appeared in 1969. He has published tw works of history and several technic essays on the Papiamento language.

Writings: Poetry: *Pa Distrai, Lorandanan bida,* Curacao, eigen beheer, 1969 (72 pp.)

History: *Paginanan pret u di nos histori*

Curacao, 1961 (72 pp.); *Documentacion pa nos historia,* Curacao, 1962 (46 pp.).

Grammar-Orthography (of Sranen-Tongo): "Ensayo pa yega na un ortografia uniforme pa nos papiamentu," (1953), other details of publication, if any, not known; "Un coto di dicho, refran, proverbio i expresionnan papiamentu i nan nificacion na ulandes," (1959); "Papiamentu, origenif ormacion," 1965); and "Di Dos edison, mehorá i owmentá di 'Proverbio, refran ets'," (1969).

MARLEE, Paul

(pseudonym for **Paul Armand NIJBROEK**)

MARTES, José Antonio

(see under pseudonym: **Pierre LAUFFER**)

MARTINA, Ornelio

b. November 14, 1930, Curacao.
Poet, storywriter.

Martina writes in both Spanish and Papiamento.

Writings: Poetry: *Alivio,* details unknown; three poems from *Alivio* and the stories "E Shap de Frans" and "E Karta Fatal" from collection *Ban* are in P. Lauffer's *Di Nos.* The poem "Serenade" is in *Nouvelle somme de poésie du monde noir,* Paris, 1966.

Stories: *Ban, ban pasa un rondu,* Curacao, Boekhandel Salas, 1954 (35 pp.); and see above for stories in *Di Nos.*

MARTINA, Sjon Chr.

b. ca. 1930, Curacao.
Storywriter.

Martina has one known collection of Papiamento stories, including "Cinco y Seis" and "Amor di un pober schutter."

Writings: Stories: *Desconocida,* Curacao, R.J. Dovale Advertising, n.d. (51 pp.).

MARTINUS ARION, Frank

(a.k.a. **F.M. ARION**)

b. December 17, 1936, Curacao.
Papiamento poet, playwright.

Influenced by the currents of negritude, Frank Martinus seeks a return to mother Africa.

Writings: Poetry: "Stemmen uit Afrika," in *Antilliaanse Cahiers,* 3de jaargang, no. 1, Amsterdam, 1957, separately published as *Stemmen van Africa* [Voices from Africa], 1967. Poems in *Nouvelle somme de poésie du monde noir,* Paris, Présence Africaine, 1966; *In der welken; een gedicht, uitgegeven door Ruku met medewerking van de K.L.M.,* 32 pp., Curacao, 1970. Also see: *Ta amor so por,* Curacao, Boekhandel Salas, 1961; *Ilusion di un anoche,* Curacao, 1968 (20 pp.); *Ser Betris,* Curacao, 1968 (36 pp.); Poems from *Ta amor . . .* and *Ilusion . . .* in P. Lauffer's *Di Nos.*

Play: *Tres perla Antilliana* [Three Antillean Pearls: allegorical play in Papiamento], Nijmegen, Netherlands (31 pp.), 1956.

Scholarship: "De identiteit van het papiamentu-Deel I," in *Ruku* 2 & 3, Jg 2 (1970); "De identiteit van het papiamentu-Deel II," in *Ruku* 4 & 5, Jg 2 (1970).

Biographical/Critical Sources: Cola Debrot, *Literature of the Netherlands Antilles,* pp. 23-24.

MARUGG, Silvio A.

(pseudonym: **TIP**)
b. December 16, 1923, Curacao.
Poet, novelist.

Marugg has been an editor of *De Passaat* a monthly magazine in Curacao. Much of his early work appeared in Dr. Christian Engels' review *De Stoep* in the 1940-50 period. There is a tough-skinned but vivid quality in his poetry seemingly akin to the early imagists Hume, Pound, Flint and others working in London during the period 1910-15 period. His work is generally cerebral and even analytical.

His novel translated as *Weekend Pilgrimage* portrays the pain and anxiety which come to a community moving too rapidly from the stable and traditional ways of a rural society to the egotistic industrial tempo of modern times.

Writings: Novel: *Weekend Pilgrimage,* trans. by Roy Edwards, London, Hutchinson, 1960, 1966, original published in Amsterdam: *Vitgeverig de besige bij* (paperback), 1958, 1966. An extract appears in *From the Green Antilles,* B. Howe, ed., London, Panther Books, 1967.

Biographical/Critical Sources: Cola Debrot, Literature of the Netherlands Antilles, pp. 25-26.

MOHLMANN, Father Michael

(see under pseudonym: **Wim van NULAND**)

NIJBROEK, Paul Armand

(pseudonym: **Paul MARLEE**)
b. 1938, Paramaribo, Surinam.
Poet.

Nijbroek has travelled widely in the United States and Europe. He took his degree from Rijks Hogere Landsbouwschool in Deventer.

Writings: Poetry: *PH-7,* Paramaribo, 1969; poems in the anthology: *Fluidum,* 1969.

van NULAND, Wim

(pseudonym for **Father Michael MOHLMANN**)
b. ca. 1920, Curacao.
Storywriter, poet, priest.

Strongly influenced by Spanish impressionism ("modernismo"), van Nuland, in the words of Cola Debrot, is still "not free" of the literary mannerisms of a past era. His stories are sad tales of sick and maimed men and garrulous old ladies recalling the pain but no longer the details of a long lost love. Much of his work first appeared in Christian Engels' *De Stoep* in Curacao in the 1950's.

Writings: Reistanes in Niemandsland (War-time prose-poetry), Scherpenheuvel.

ORLANDO, Emanuels

(pseudonym: **ORLANDO** and **CYRANO**)
b. 1927, Paramaribo, Surinam.
Poet.

Orlando works as a public relations officer for a Paramaribo bank. His first work appeared in 1964 in Soela under his first pen-name of Cyrano. His themes are generally Afro-Surinamese and full of protest.

Writings: Poetry: *Onze misdaad van zwijgen,* Paramaribo, 1969 (23 pp.); two poems: "Moedernaakt" [Mother Naked] and "Vuist" [Clenched Fist] appear in A.J. Seymour's *New Writing in the Caribbean,* Georgetown, Guyana, 1972.

PIETERS, Eddie

(pseudonym: **HEYLIGER**)
b. ca. 1936, Curacao.
Storywriter, radio broadcaster, lawyer.

Pieters has been very active in pushing the performance on radio of Papiamento

language plays and readings of poetry and stories. He has also sought to encourage more writing by local artists and the awarding of prizes for the best work.

Writings: Story: "Despedida di un sonrisa" and others in various journals.

Plays: *Ata 'ki Mai* and *Un regalu di pascu,* both in one volume, published in Curacao, Sociedad pro arte escenico, 1971.

Biographical/Critical Sources: Newspaper article on Pieters' work in second story and playwriting competition, in *Beurs* (Willemstad, Curacao, May 6, 1974): "Georganiseerd door Echa Palabra: Gilberto Doran winnaar van verhalen-wedstrijd."

PIETERS KWIERS, J. Th.

(see **G. Th. PIETERS KWIERS**)

PINA LAMPE, Nicolás Antonio

b. December 6, 1921, Tocopero, Venezuela; d. June 1, 1967, Aruba.
Poet.

Piña founded the important Papiamento periodical *Simadán* along with
Piña founded the important Papiamento periodical *Simadán* along with Lauffer, Rooy, and others, and published much of his Spanish and Papiamento poems there. His poems also appear in P. Lauffer's *Di Nos*.

POIESZ, Paulus J.

b. October 20, 1875, Sneek, Netherlands; d. September 29, 1919, Curacao.
Poet, scholar, travel-writer.

Poiesz long identified himself with his new home in Curacao and published in Papiamento both verse and travel, besides several studies of the language.

Writings: Poetry: *Shon Fia,* Curacao, A. Bethencourt e Hijos, 1907 (32 pp.).

Travel: *De Corsouw pa Amsterdam,* Nijmegen, Netherlands, 1914.

Linguistics: "Het papiamentu als cultuurtaal" in *Amigoe di Curacao* (Oct. 16, 1915); "Nog eens het papiamentu als cultuurtaal" in *Amigoe* (Oct. 30, 1915).

RAVALES, Robin

(pseudonym: **R. DOBRU**)
b. 1935, Paramaribo, Surinam.
Poet, playwright, critic, civil servant.

After local schooling in Paramaribo, Ravales became a civil servant and an active nationalist. Becoming Vice Chairman of one of Surinam's official opposition political parties, The Party of the National Republic, he was involved in many struggles. He has widely traveled throughout the Caribbean and is one of the best known of his country's poets, being a leader of the group centered around the journal *Moetete*.

Writings: Poetry: *Matapi,* Paramaribo, 1965, second edition, Paramaribo, N.V. Drukkerij Eldorado, 1970; *Mina Afoe Sensi,* Paramaribo, Drukkerij Paramaribo, 1966; (in Dutch and Sranan) Paramaribo, Lionarons, 1967; *Wan monki fri 1969,* Paramaribo, Eldorado, 1969 (76 pp.); Five of his poems appear in original Dutch text and English prose translation in *New Writing in the Caribbean,* A.J. Seymour, ed., 1972.

Plays: *Wasoema, A Prasi foe Bigi Dorsi,* produced 1969; *Bronfoto* (philosophical-political work in progress).

Prose: *Bos mi esesi I en II,* Paramaribo, 1967 (two editions), and Drukkerij Eldorado, 1968; *2 Februari,* Paramaribo, Drukkerij Paramaribo, 1969.

RAPHAELA, Cornelius (Nechi)

(See under pseudonym: **Victor P. HERNANDEZ**)

RELLUM, Eugene W.

b. 1896, Paramaribo, Surinam.
Poet.

Rellum, a Dutch and Sranan poet, lived for long periods in Holland and Indonesia where he trained and then worked as a surveyor. In 1951 he returned to Surinam to work for the local government.

In 1962, back in Holland, he edited the journal *Djogo.* From the beginning of his career he had pushed for a vigorous and local Sranan-Tongo literature for his homeland and has himself published two collections of his work in Sranan.

Writings: Poetry: *Moesoedé,* Paramaribo, 1959 (Sranan); *Kren-Klim,* Paramaribo, Varekamp, 1961 (in dual Sranan-Dutch texts). In the Seymour-edited *New Writings in the Caribbean* appear his "Sranen na mi" [Surinam is me], and "Onderschatting [Underestimation] in both Sranan and English texts. The latter poem and "Groei" are in *Nouvelle somme de poésie noir,* Paris, 1966.

ROOY, René Andre de

b. October 1, 1917, Paramaribo, Surinam; d. 1974.
Novelist, poet, storywriter, translator, literary historian, playwright, sculptor.

René de Rooy was one of the greatest of scholars from Surinam and an acknowledged figure in literature and criticism. His death of a cardiac failure while teaching in Mexico was a signal loss to his country, for he was engaged in new researches and writing on Surinamese literature. He was one of the founders of the literary review, *Simadan,* which was briefly an important voice for Dutch Antillean writers.

He studied Spanish and English in Surinam and worked in the Dutch Embassy in Mexico for a period. He also lectured widely.

Writings: Play: *Juancho Picafor* (a tragicomedy), first edition, with foreword by Cola Debrot, Curacao, 1954, second edition, Curacao, 1958; extract from Act 5 is in P. Lauffer's *Di Nos.* (The play is a very free adaptation of Cyrano de Bergerac.) The play was produced on TV by Henk van Ulsen.

Novel: *Tongoni;* extract as "The Precious Stones of Uncle Brink" appears in *From the Green Antilles,* London, Souvenir Press, 1967, and London, Panther, 1971.

Poetry: *Di Andrés Grimar;* and three poems which are in P. Lauffer's *Di Nos.*

Stories and Poetry: in various journals such as *De Stoep, Simadán, Tongoni,* and *Moetete.*

Critical Essays: in various journals, including: "De letterkunde in Suriname," in *Tijdschrift Wikor* (May 1959), pp. 101-103.

REYES, Lupe Maria

b. March 8, 1953, Bonaire.
Poet.

Reyes attended the Princess Beatrix Girls' School in Kralen, Bonaire. Her Papiamento verse has been influenced by Pierre Lauffer and Calito Nicolaas. In 1973 she began her studies in drama at the Escuela Juana Sujo in Caracas, Venezuela.

Her four-line poem "Preto" is characteristic of her verse:

Tin be min tin horor di pretu,
e ta 'nami miedu ketu ketu
Butami pensa tur momentu,
i strobami di ta kontentu.

Writings: Poetry: *Desahogo,* Curacao, 1974 (contains 17 poems).

ROMER, Raul G.

b. June 19, 1923, Curacao.
Playwright-translator.

Römer's free adaptation of a medieval Dutch mystery play *Maryken van Nimwegen* as *Maria di Malpais* (Malpais being the name of an old plantation in Curacao) became an important text for local theatrical productions.

Writings: Play: *Maria di Malpais,* Curacao, 1954; Curacao, La Cruz, n.d. (32 pp.), TV production by Henk van Ulsen.

Articles: "Papiamento," in *Encyclopedie va de Nederlandsche Antillen,* Amsterdam, p 440-445; and "Geheimen van het papi mento," in *De Nederlandse Antillen in d Actualiteit,* Amsterdam, J. v.d. Walle, ed., 195

ROSARIO, Guillerimo A.

b. January 6, 1917, Porto Cabell Curacao.
Poet, storywriter.

Rosario is one of the most prolific of th Papiamento writers, publishing in mar genres over several decades.

Writings: Poetry: *Legria,* Curacao, 1969 (2 pp.); *E. Korsow ku mi ta korda. Anto Dyos t bo kolo,* 1969 (15 pp.); *Kadushii,* Curaca 1969 (15 pp.).
1969 (15 pp.); Two poems (from *Anto Dyos . .* are in P. Lauffer's *Di Nos; Algun bista di r tena,* Curacao, 1969 (61 pp.).

Historical Novel: *E raiz ku no ke muri, nove original,* Amsterdam, Cadushireeks, 1970.

Stories: all published in Curacao: *Tamb* n.d.; *E Rosa di mas bunita,* 1963; *Kwater A* 1964; Two stories from *Kwater prenda* are Lauffer's *Di Nos;* Also: "Su rival," Curaca

944 (16 pp.); "Un drama den hanchi Punda," uracao, 1946; "Dos bida," Curacao, 1959 (49 ›.); "Mi Casita," Curacao, 1959 (40 pp.); Orkaan," Curacao, 1955 (30 pp.); "E Trahador den Klip," Curacao, 1959 (41 pp.); "E ju di ó," Curacao, 1959 (24 pp.); "Pa motibo di mi ›lo," (1958-59).

ROZENSTAND, Ernesto E.

. ca. 1931, Aruba.
torywriter, folklorist.

ozenstand, after a brief spurt of creativity ith several works published, has lapsed to silence.

'ritings: Story: *Tar cos a keda atras.*
Folktale Collections: *Cuentanan pa un i tur,* ruba, General Printing, n.d. (54 pp.); *Cuentaın Rubiano,* Aruba, General Printing, 1961 3 pp.).

SALAS, David Dario

July 22, 1873, Curacao; d. August, 1937, Curacao.
ovelist, poet.

alas was a member of the literary group the 1880's and 90's who contributed to e weekly journals *Notas y Letras* and *oemas* in Curacao, and who were followers of Gustavo Adolfo Bécquer and ampobetto.

'ritings: Novel: *Raul; Josefina,* (early publicaon in Curacao, 1910-15 period), fourth inting, Spain, 1952.
Poetry: *In Memoriam,* Curacao, Tipografia La oderna, 1911; *Rimas,* Curacao, Tipografia La oderna, also 1911.

SANGODARE, Asjantenu

seudonym for **Michael SLORY**)
1935, Coronie, Surinam.
oet (mostly in Sranan-Tongo).

After schooling in Holland, Sangodare began writing poetry in Dutch, and only turned to Sranan after an illuminating but upsetting close contact with African culture. Though he still occasionally composed a Dutch-language work, he generally works with national Afro-Surinamese themes and in local dialects.

His first collection of verse was *Sarka Bittere Strijd* [Bitter Struggle], published in 1961, which is highly political. His next collection, *Fraga mit wortoe* (Listen to What I Say), is more subjective, often dealing with his youth. This volume and later ones were published at author's expense.

Writings: Poetry: *Sarka Bittere Strijd* (26 poems in Sranen-Tongo), Amsterdam, Uitgeverij Pegasos, 1961; *Frage mi wortoe* (25 poems in Sranan), Paramaribo, Drukkerij Atlas, 1970; *Nengre-oema* [Black Woman], 1971; *Bonifoto* [Fortress], Paramaribo, Drukkerij Atlas, 1971; *Vietnam,* 1972; *Lobisingi* [Love Songs], 1972; *Memri den de* [Remember Those Days], Paramaribo, 1973(?); Also sonnets in Sranan-Tongo: *Firi joesrifi,* Paramaribo, Drukkerij Atlas, 1971; Poems in many collections, including: *Nouvelle somme de poésie noir,* ["Orfeu, negro," and "Kawina-ritman"], Paris, 1966; early Dutch poems in *Tongoni 1* (1960); *Brievan aan de Guerilla* [Letters to the Guerrillas], Amsterdam, Pegasus, 1968; *Brieven aan Ho Tsji Minh* [Letters to Ho Chi Minh], Amsterdam, Pegasus, 1969.

Biographical/Critical Sources: R.F. Kross' "Surinaams perspektief," an essay on Slory, John Muller, J.H. Slagveer, and himself, in *Contour* (Leiden, Sitjhoff, Sept. 1966), pp. 115-139.

SCHOUTEN-ELSENHOUT, Johanna

b. 1910, Paramaribo, Surinam.
Poet (in Sranan).

Schouten began writing scraps of her thoughts in occasional notebooks and only because friends told her what she had "done" was poetry did she begin seriously to reorganize her work. Her verse is deemed obscure, for it often employs very local idiomatic and/or colloquial terms, referring to Creole life and experiences not normally reflected in more cosmopolitan works. Further, her work expresses the deep-seated anguishes and pain of common life only a little removed from the angers and frustrations of slavery—still so alive in the subconscious of most of the people.

Her "Duman" [Man of Action], provides some ideas of her work:

Mi no wani/wan ati
di n'abi kra,
mi wani/wan yeye d'e libi.

Mi n'e wer/susu
di n'e fit mi,
m'e wer/mi eygi krompu.

Mi n'e sdon/luku
a fesi fu sma,
m'e luku ini/mi eygi spikri

I will no heart
without a soul,
I want a living spirit.

I wear no shoes
which do not fit,
I wear my very own clogs.

I do not look
at another's face
but in my very own mirror.

Writings: Poetry: *Tide ete. Fo sren singi* (32 poems in Sranan-Tongo), Paramaribo, Drukk-Lionarons, 1963; *Awese* (62 poems in Sranen-Tongo), Paramaribo, 1965. Many of her poems are in *Creole Drum,* Jan Voorhoeve and Ursy M. Lichtveld, eds., 1975. Her first poetry appeared in review *Soela.*

Editor of: *Sranen Pangi* (1000 plus proverbs in Creole), Paramaribo, Bureau Volkslectuur, 1974.

SEKU, Yerba

(pseudonym for **Richard HOOI**)

SHRINIVASI, Asjantenu

(pseudonym for **Martinus Harida LUTCHMAN**)

b. 1926, Beneden, Surinam District, Surinam.

Poet, teacher.

One of the best-known of Surinam's artists, Shrinivasi has been a teacher in Holland and in Curacao. Since 1964 he has left off his academic career for publishing. His own work (in Hindi, Dutch and Sranen) often appears in the journal *Tongoni, Soela, Nieuwe Stemmen, Caraibisch Venster, Moetete,* and *Fri.*

Writings: early poetry in collection of various authors: *Wortoe d'e tan abra. Bloemlezing uit de Surinaamse Poezie,* Paramaribo, Bureau Vanaf, 1957. His collections are: *Pratikshâ* Paramaribo, Eldorado, 1968, with second printing that year; *Dilâkâr* (in Hindi, Dutch, and English), 1970, by Eldorado; *Katern I, 1 minuut stilte* (Dutch and Hindi poems), Paramaribo Eldorado, 1970 (16 pp.); *Katern II, Phagwâ* 1971, also by Eldorado. Two poems "Kinderen" and "Onschuldigen" appear in dual Dutch-English texts in A.J. Seymour's *New Writing in the Caribbean,* 1972.

SLAGVEER, Jozef H.

b. 1940, Totness, Coronie District Surinam.

Poet, novelist, journalist.

Slagveer, considered a major Sranen poet and fiction writer, studied journalism in Holland in the 1960's and thereafter ran a press agency. He has four collections of his verse in print and one novel.

Writings: Poetry: *Kosoe Dron,* Paramaribo D.A.G., 1967; *Sibi boesi* (28 Sranen poems Paramaribo, Eldorado, 1967; *Kankantri,* Paramaribo, Eldorado, 1968; *Tigri Fadon o en Wik* 1969. His poem "Revolutie" appears in Seymour's *New Writing in the Caribbean,* 197?

Novel: *De Verpletterde Droom* (in Dutch text with eight short additional sketches in Sranen Paramaribo, Eldorado, 1968.

Biographical/Critical Sources: R.F. Kross' "Surinaams perspektief" in *Contour* (Leiden, Sijhoff, Sept. 1966), pp. 115-139.

SLORY, Michael

(see under pseudonym: **Asjantenu SANGODARE**)

SURIEL, Simon Miguel

b. March 24, 1890, Curacao; d. November 27, 1963, Curacao.
Storywriter.

One of the earliest published novelists and storywriters of Curacao, Suriel has one novel, *Muhé Culpabel* [The Guilty Woman], and at least one novelette, *Boeki de quadrilla,* in his bibliography.

Writings: Novel: *Muhé Culpabel,* first edition, 1931; and second edition, Curacao, Drukkerij De Stad N.V., 1948 (182 pp.); *Boeki di quadrilla,* second edition, Curacao, Bethencourt e Hijos, 1910, and third edition, Curacao, Paulusdrukkerij (date unknown but 30 pp.).

TIP

(pseudonym for **Silvio A. MARUGG**)

TREFOSSA

(pseudonym for **Henri Frans DE ZIEL**)
b. 1916, Paramaribo, Surinam.
Poet, storywriter, teacher.

After earning a teacher's certificate in Paramaribo where he has lived most of his life, Trefossa could find no school position. After service in the Dutch army, de Ziel worked as a male nurse and then as a teacher in a leprosarium. After his own relatively protected early life and education in the capital, including schooling in a Moravian mission, his later experiences made him seriously study ordinary life and speech.

After four years in Holland (1952-56), studying for a degree in library science and where he did much reading of archival materials on Surinam culture and history, de Ziel returned home to be librarian of the Cultural Center of Paramaribo, later to serve as director. Discouraged by the "politics" of culture he soon resigned but continued his writing of creole poems and edited Johannes King's pioneering creole works for the press (*Life at Maripaston,* 1973).

Henri de Ziel's first collection of Sranen poems appeared in 1957 under his pen name of Trefossa, apparently a creole version of Tryphosa, mentioned in the Bible (Romans 16:12). His poem "Bro," written in 1949 in the traditional sonnet form (but linguistically in the popular street creole rather than the more Dutch-influenced church or upperclass "town" creole), was a striking success and begetter of followers.

"Way!" provides a short example of his poetry:

d'e opo den srefi gi son,
den grun wiwiri,
te angri fu gro
priti buba fu siri.

na mi?
piki . . . piki!
apinti, na mi?
san de lufru so,
san wiki?

Leave off!

They open up themselves to the sun,
the verdant plants,
when their hunger to grow forth
has torn apart the seedling's coat.

Am I that?
Answer . . . answer!
Apinti [large drum], am I that?
What is it that rumbles so,
what that awakens here?

Writings: Poetry (and Linguistics): *Trotji, Puëma. Met een stilistische studie over het gedicht Kopenhage, vertalingen en verklarende aantekeningen door J. Voorhoeve,* Amsterdam, Noord-Holl., Uitg. Mij, 1957 (this collection contains 19 of his poems—published as part of a study by the Bureau for Linguistic Research in Surinam (U. of Amsterdam), and the volume was dedicated to J.G.A. Koenders, with introduction by A. Helman (L.A.M. Lichtveld); "Sranen" in *Nouvelle somme de poésie du monde noir,* Paris, Présence Africaine, 1966; poem "Bro," in *Creole Drum,* edited by Voorhoeve and Lichtveld (1975), pp. 192-193, first published in *Foetoe-boi* (1951) and seven other poems are in the same collection, pp. 198-215. Various poems appeared in *Foetoe-boi* (1955 and 1956), in *De Gids* 9 (1970).

Stories: "Owrukuku ben kari," in *Tongoni 2* (*Vox Guyane* 3, 1959), and in *Creole Drum,* op. cit.

Biographical/Critical Sources: J. Voorhoeve's analysis of some of Trefossa's poems in *Trotji* collection (1957) and in Voorhoeve's essay "Het vertalen van poezie" in *Vox Guyane 3,* Vol. 6, pp. 8-14; and "The Art of Reading Creole Poetry," in *Pidginization and Creolization of Languages,* Dell Hymes, ed., Cambridge, Mass., 1971, pp. 323-326. Also see *Creole Drum,* pp. 195-197.

TUYUCHI

(pseudonym for **Arturo LEITO**)

VAN BEDACHT, Rudy

(see under pseudonym: **Corly VERLOOGHEN**)

VAN LEEUWEN, Boeli

b. ca. 1930, Curacao.
Dutch-language novelist.

The name of his well-received novel *De Rots der Struikeling* (1960) comes from Isaiah 8:14: "And he shall be a stone of stumbling and a rock of offence" and concerns the fragmentary notes of a violently-killed last member of a crumbling family in Curacao. Very loosely constructed, the work is a Kierkegaardian drama of pursuit by the hero of reality and the mystery of human motivations. Cola Debrot comments, "The use of language is characteristic of our island, it varies between the formal style of the official and the crudity of the soldier. The book is haunted by biblical texts and blasphemous curses."

Writings: Novels: *De Rots der Struikeling* [A Stone of Stumbling], Willemstad, Curacao, 1959; and Amsterdam: P.N. van Kampen and Zoon N.V., 1960; extract in *From the Green Antilles,* B. Howe, ed., London, Souvenir Press, 1967; and London, Panther Books, 1971; *Een vreemdeling op aarde,* Amsterdam, 1963; *De eerste Adam,* Amsterdam, van Kampen, 1966.

Biographical/Critical Sources: A. Beaujon, *Boeli van Leeuwen, persknipsels met kritieken en biografische gegevens,* Amsterdam, Sticusa, 1967; Cola Debrot, *Literature of the Netherlands Antilles,* pp. 26-27.

VAN P. POLANEN

(see under pseudonym: **Kwame DANDILO**)

VAN ROEMER, A.

(see under pseudonym: **ZAMANI**)

VERLOOGHEN, Corly

(pseudonym for **Rudy VAN BEDACHT**)
b. 1932, Paramaribo, Surinam.
Poet, critic, journalist.

Verlooghen studied journalism in Holland, 1954-1959, after which he travelled widely in Latin America and the Caribbean. In 1962 he was back in Europe, first in Spain and the Netherlands, and then in Sweden where he studied Swedish language and literature. During these and subsequent years he contributed many articles and much verse to Surinamese journals.

Writings: Poetry: *Kans op Onweer* (poems in Dutch and Sranen), Paramaribo Srenang, 1960; *Dans op de Vourgrens,* Paramaribo, Eldorado, 1961; *Jachtgebied,* Paramaribo, Eldorado, 1961; *Oe,* Paramaribo, Lionarons, 1962; *De held van Guyana* (22 revolutionary poems, with author's discussion of Surinamese culture), Amsterdam, 1965; *De Glinsterende Revolutie,* Amsterdam, author, 1970. His poems "Mijn Geheim," and "De Wolven" are in *Nouvelle somme de poésie du monde noir,* Paris, 1966; and three poems in *New Writing in the Caribbean,* A.J. Seymour (ed.), 1972.

VIANEN, Bea

b. ca. 1935, Surinam.
Poet, novelist.

Vianen has published one modest collection of verse and three novels, and has miscellaneous work in Sranen in various journals and anthologies.

Writings: Poetry: *Cautal* (24 poems), Paramaribo, Lionarons, 1965 (32 pp.).
Novels: *Surnami, hai,* Amsterdam, Querido's Uitgeverij, 1969; *Strafhok,* Amsterdam, Querido's, 1971 (203 pp.); *Ik eet, ik eet, tot ik niet meer kan,* Amsterdam, Querido's, 1972.

VOGELLAND, Rico

(see under pseudonym: **Rudy KROSS**)

WALLE, Johan van de

b. ca. 1926, Curacao.
Novelist, journalist.

Walle has published four novels, full of historical and local color details. His *Een vlek op de rug* (1963) is set in Surinam in the period 1842-1863 and his earliest work, *De slavenopstand* (1956) is of course concerned with the institution of slavery and its social consequences.

Cola Debrot remarks that "van de Walle's novels are permeated with a Caribbean atmosphere, by a 'mark on the back,' as he has called one of his books, the echo between sentences, or by the elusive peculiarities in the use of words and composition."

Writings: Novels: *De slavenopstand* (186 pp.), 1956; *Achter de spiegel* (180 pp.), 1959; *De overtocht* (186 pp.), 1960?; *Een vlek op de rug* (336 pp.), 1963: all in Amsterdam, by van Kampen en Zoon.

Kampen en Zoon; *Beneden de Wind: Herinneringen aan Curacao,* Amsterdam, Querito (179 pp.).

Biographical/Critical Sources: Cola Debrot, *Literature of the Netherlands Antilles,* p. 27.

WOLFSCHOON, Adolfo A.

b. June 12, 1889; d. March 12, 1963, Curacao.
Poet.

Wolfschoon was one of the pioneering generation of island writers whose work appeared in the *Notas y Letras* and *Poemas* journals of the 1880's and early 1890's in Curacao. He was influenced by Gustavo Adolf Bécquer and Campoamor

Writings: Poetry: *Poesias,* Curacao, 1894.

WOLS, Frits

(pseudonym for **Eugene Wilfred WONG-LOI-SING**)
b. Post Groningen (Saramaca), Surinam.
Poet, novelist.

Wols' first poems appeared in the journals *Omhoog* (1961) and *Opbouw* (both Paramaribo). One collection, published in 1967, offers the best access to his work to date.

Writings: Poetry: *Beeldhouwer van het Abstrakte,* Rotterdam, 1967.
Novel: in progress.

ZAMANI

(pseudonym for **A. VAN ROEMER**)
b. ca. 1940, Surinam.
Poet.

Zamani writes and publishes in Dutch and Sranen.

Writings: Poetry: *Sasa. Mijn actuele zijn,* Paramaribo, Eldorado, 1970.

NETHERLANDS ANTILLES AND SURINAM: CRITICAL STUDIES AND BIBLIOGRAPHIES

(Curacao, Bonaire, Aruba and Surinam)

Adhin, J.H. *Beginnend Surinaams-Hindostaanse literature,* Paramaribo Bureau Volksliteratuur, 1963.

Comvalius, Th. A.C. "Oud-Surinaamsche rhythmische dansen in dienst van de lichamelijke opvoepding," in *De West-Indische Gids,* Vol. 27 (1946), pp. 97-100.

Daelaman, Jan. "Kongo Elements in Saramacca Tongo," *Journal of African Languages,* Vol. 11 (1972), pp. 1-44.

Debrot, Cola. *Literature of the Netherlands Antilles.* (translated from Dutch by Estelle Reed Debrot). Willemstad: Bureau voor Cultuur en Opvoeding, 1964.

Donicie, A. "Iets over de taal en de sprookjes van Suriname," *De West-Ind. Gids,* Vol. 33 (1952-53), pp. 153-173.

Felhoen Kraal, J. "Caraibische letteran." *West-Ind. Gids,* XXXV (1955), 192-218.

Helstone, J.N. *Wan spraakkunst va taki en skrifi da tongo va Sranen.* Paramaribo, 1903.

Herskovitz, M.J. *Rebel Destiny.* New York, 1934.

__________. *Surinam Folklore.* New York: Columbia University Press, 1936.

Klooster, W.S.B. *"Roman literatuur over Surinam en de Nedelandse Antillen."* OKW Meded, Vol. 25 (1961).

__________. *Poesie uit Suriname.* OKW Meded, Vol. 26 (1962).

Moor, W. de. "De poezie van Surinam." *De Tijd* (July 24, 1971).

Rens, Lucien L.E. *The Historical and Social Background of Surinam's Negro-English* (thesis). Amsterdam: North Holland Publishing Company, 1953.

Rooy, R. de. "De letterkunde in Surinam." *Tijdschrift Wikor* (May 1959), 101-103.

Soons, Alan. "Patterns of Imagery in Two Novels in Curacao," in *Caribbean Quarterly,* Vol. XIII, No. 2.

Smit, C.G.M. and W.F. Heuvel. *Autonoon. Nederlandstalige literatuur op de Antillen.* Rotterdam: Flamboyant, 1976.

Sonja. "Surinaams perspectief. Beschouwing over Surinaamse literatuur met 15 gedichten." in *Contour* (Leiden, September 4, 1966), 115-139.

Teylingen, H. van. "De Surinaamse letteren (behandelt o.m. de social positie van Surinaamse letterkundigen)" in *Avenue* (December 1971), 16, 18.

De Tsjerne (Special Surinam literature issue, September 1952).

Voorhoeve, Jan. "Fictief verleden. De slaventijd in de Surinaamse belletrie," De Nwe West-Indische Gids, Vol. 45 (1966), 32-37.

__________. Varieties of Creole in Surinam. the Art of Reading Creole Poetry. Article in *Pidginization and Creolization of Languages,* Dell Hymes, ed., Cambridge: Cambridge University Press, 1971.

NETHERLANDS ANTILLES AND SURINAM: ANTHOLOGIES

(In Dutch, Sranan, or English Translation from Dutch)

Afanti. Lobi Ten. *Gedichten in Sranan-Tongo en Nederlands.* 1970.

Breinburg, Petronella. *Legends of Suriname.* London; Port of Spain, Trinidad New Beacon Books, 1971.

Blau Kepanki (van O.L. Kemble). *Poewema foe blaw-kepanki. Surinaamse gedichten met Nederlandse vertalen.* 1971.

Capelle, H. Van. "Surinaamsche Negervertellingen" (Negro Tales from Surinam) in *Bijdragen tot de taal-land-en Volkenkunde van Nederlandsch-Indie,* Vol. 72, 1916.

Dandillo, Kwame. "9 Surinaamse gedichten in het Nederlands en Sranan Tongo," in *Nouvelle somme de poesie du monde noir.* Paris: Présence Africaine 1966.

Doelwijt, T. *De Vlucht. (Opstellen* van thea Doelwijt, Benny Ch. Ooft, Henk F. Herrenberg, Henny F. de Zielen R. Dobru). Paramaribo: Boomen, 1968.

Felhoen Kraal, J. "Caraibische letteren." *West-Indische Gids,* XXXC (1955).

Hartman, A. and W.J.P.J. Schalker and W.C. Muller. *Repertorium op de literatuur betreffende de Nederlandse Kolonien voorzover zij verspreid is in tijdschriften, periodieken, serie-en mengelwerken.* s'Gravenhage, 1895-1925.

Herskovits, M.J. and F.S. Herskovits. *Suriname Folk-lore; with Transcriptions of Surinam Songs and Musicological Analysis by M. Kolinski.* New York Columbia University Press, 1936.

Oudschans, Dentz. "De Plaats Van de Creeol in der Literatuur van Suriname (The Place of Creole in the Literature of Surinam)," in *De West-Indische Gids.* 19:208-211 (1937).

Shrinivasi [Martinus Lutchman]. *Wortoe d'e tan abra Bloenlazing vit de Surinaames poëzie vanaf* [Words that Remain], Paramaribo, 1957.

De Tsjerne (Special Surinam [Sranan-Tongo] poetry number, Frisian Islands, September 1952).

Voorhoeve, Jan and Ursy M. Lichtveld (eds.). *Creole Drum: An Anthology of Creole Literature in Surinam.* Princeton, N.J.: Princeton University Press 1975. (English translations by Vernie A. February).

__________. *Suriname: spiegel der vaderlandse kooplieden. Een historisch leesboek* [Mirror of the Dutch Traders. A Historical Reader]. Zwolle Netherlands, 1958.

(In Papiamento or from Papiamento)

Lauffer, Pierre. *Di Nos: Antologia de Nos Literatura.* Willemstad; Curacao: Libreria Solas, 1971.

Latour, M.D. "Cuenta di Nanzi [Stories of Anansi]" in *De West-Indische Gids.* Vol. 19-20, 1937-38.

Pavert, Stephanus. *Trenza litteraria ofreci na pueblo Curazoleno.* Curacao: Cooperative Vereniging en Nijverheid, 1916. (58 pp.).

Pinto, N.M. Geerdink-Jesurun (translated into English by Richard E. Wood). *Nanzi Stories: Curacao Folklore.* Willemstad; Curacao: Stichting Wetenschappelijke Bibliotheek, 1972.

Roach, Eric. "Ballad of Canga," in *Caribbean Quarterly,* 4 (2): 167-168, 1955.

Volume IV

Spanish Language Literature from the Caribbean

G. G. de Avellaneda

ESSAY ON THE LITERATURE OF CUBA

Cuban literature, like the other literatures of the Caribbean, was for long but a provincial part of the colonial world, subspecies of Spanish, French or English. But also, local variations of emphasis, a growing body of experiences, and the concomitant growth of self-awareness and national identity, would slowly be reflected in the writings of the more sensitive souls of the island. Even today foreign cultural influences and literary currents will affect Cuban literature, but the local author will react on a more personal level, choosing what he wishes, and combining, rejecting, re-creating in a particular voice and style the experiences which must be Cuban.

Literary historians have divided Cuban literature into these general periods: the earliest colonial days through the 18th century (1492-1790); the long middle period, mostly romantic in tendency, when the Cuban soul crystalized (1790-1902), and the modern period of independence (1902-present).

The early period would offer the usual explorers journals fragments or reports still extant of a few casual poets and essayists, and a smattering of island histories common to any settlement. A few records of the Amerindian peoples, including their legends, would also find their way into print. Here and there, letters and newspaper accounts of unusual events would also be preserved. In 1608, Silvestre de Balboa Troya wrote *Espejo de paciencia,* a canto on the struggles between Bishop Juan de las Cabezas y Altamirano and the French pirate-merchant Gilbert Girón. Born in the Canaries in 1563, Balboa's psuedo-epic had two major sections, the first of 70 and the second of 75 royal octavas, making it the most considerable literary effort of the early period though it was a pedestrian effort in every other way.

A few church fathers wrote ecclesiastical verse and occasionally one celebrated the island as in these lines by Lorenzo Lasso (Laso?) de la Vega:

Dorado isla de Cuba o Fernandina,
de cuyas altas cumbrs eminentes
bajan a los arroyos, rios y fuentes,
el acendrado oro y plata fina . . .

The chronicler Manuel Dionisio González mentions in his *Memoria histórica de la villa de Santa Clara* (1858) a few of the earliest writers whose work is mostly not extant: José Surí y Aquila (1696-1762), Martínez Avileira (1722-1782), and Mariano José de Alva y Monteagudo (1761-1800), all from the Villa Clara or Santa Clara area which may be said to have had the first Cuban "school" of writers.

Believed to have been the first Cuban born dramatist was Francisco de Mojica (b. 1558) whose Corpus Christi drama was performed August 20, 1588. A much more important theatrical work (and much later) was *El Principe Jardinero* by Santiago Pita (ca. 1700-1755) whose play was published in Seville in 1730.

Possibly the first genuinely interesting writers of the early period were Fray José Rodríguez Ucares (Padre Capacho), born ca. 1725, whose décimas were popular in his day though his work was not collected and published until 1823.

In the first half of the 19th century one could cite Manuel de Zequeira y Arrango (1764-1846), a poet of rhetorical tendencies; Manuel Justo Rubalcava (1769-1805) whose poems *La muerte de Judas* (1830) and *La vida del avaro* (1847) are of some interest, showing he was a better poet than Zequeiro but still of a minor order; Manuel María Pérez y Ramírez (1781-1853), author of elegant sonnets after the manner of Sully Prudhomme, and whose dialogue *El Pastor y el Eco* is of interest, and Pedro José del Sol (1777-1858), a minor poetic voice.

Author of the first collection of verse published in Cuba by a native was Ignacio Valdés Machuca (1792-1851) whose *Ocios poeticos* of 76 pages appeared in 1819.

A much more talented poet than these mentioned above was José María Heredia y Heredia (1803-1839) whose *En el Teocalli de Chobula* is a landmark of early Cuban romantic poetry and whose collected works appeared in 1940-41. Heredia, long resident in Mexico and the United States, was a singer of political freedom too, as typified by "¡Espana libre!" at the start of the liberal movement in 1820. His "El himno del desterrado" has these lines which show the emotion of the long-exiled:

¡Tierra! claman: ansiosas miramas
al cofin del sereno horizonte,
y a lo lejos descubrese un monte . . .
¡Lo conozco! . . . ¡Ojos tristes llorad!

His poetry was continental as well as Cuban, for he sang of freedom, of a new spirit, of an urbane civilized humanity, as much as of any one time or place. For him, the one goal was "la sublime dignidad del hombre."

Francisco Iturrondo (1800-1860), one of the earliest of the romantic writers, dedicated his *Rasgos descriptivos de la naturaleza cubana* (1831) to Valdes Machuca and his work is strongly influenced by Chateaubriand.

Important intellectuals of the first part of the 19th century were José Cipriano de Luz y Caballero (1800-1862), philosopher, and teacher; José Zacharias González del Valle (1820-1851), novelist, poet, critic and philosopher; and

Domingo del Monte y Aponte (1804-1853), primarily a critical historical writer who published many little romances under a variety of pseudonyms in the journals of the day. Other important authors of this period were Cirilo Villaverde (1812-1894), author of the important early treatment of slavery in his novel *Cecilia Valdés* (1882); Ramón de Palma (1812-1860); Anselmo Suárez y Romero (1818-1878), and José Antonio Echeverría (1811-1855).

One of the most historically interesting writers was the once famous Plácido (Gabriel de la Concepcion Valdes, 1809-1844), son of a slave, whose street songs were once wildly popular. Seized and imprisoned during a rebellion of Afro-Cubans in 1842, Plácido died before a firing squad.

Students of folklore, increasingly important as the romantic period matured and regional local-color was exploited, were José Maria de Cárdenas (1812-1882); José Victoriano Betancourt (1813-1875); Manuel González del Valle (1802-1884), and Ramón Zambrana (1817-1866).

This movement, to be called "Criolismo" in time, also included Francisco Poveda y Armenteros (1796-1881), who was known popularly as "El Trovador Cubano" and is scorned more as a vulgar writer than a "popular" one by Max Henriquez Ureña, but whose many published volumes are among the earliest to exploit Cuban themes. Ramón Vélez Herrera (1808-1886), and José Fornaris (1827-1890), of the *Cantos del Siboney* (1855), marked the vigorous arrival of Indian themes in Cuban romantic writings, though José María Heredia's many poems on Indians and Plácido's romances *Cora* and *Jicotencal* had earlier entered this terrain. Other "cibonistas" were Juan Cristóbal Nápoles Fajardo (1829-1862) and Miguel Teurbe Tolón (1820-1857).

One of the earliest playwrights of this period was Francisco Javier Foxá (1816-1865?), born in Santo Domingo but early brought to Cuba where at least five of his plays saw production in the 1830's. His work, now of interest only historically, is extant mostly in fragments.

Possibly the major romantic poet of the first ground-swell of romanticism in Cuba was José Jacinto Milanes (1814-1863) who exploited more organically than the criollistas had the Indian and folkloric elements in such works of his as *Triste amor de un guajiro* and his antislavery romance *El negro alzado.* He published many verse legends, patriotic poems, and some work for the theatre as well, including *El Conde Alarcos* (1838).

Writing in many genres, poetry, drama, long fiction particularly, was Cuba's most productive woman writer, Gertrudis Gómez de Avellaneda (1814-1873) who twice widowed, lived much of her life in Europe and most of whose many plays (at least 21 are known) were produced on the stages of Madrid and other Spanish and Cuban cities. Her play *Baltasar,* a four-act Biblical drama (1858) was her best received play. Her first of several goodbys to Cuba was in 1836 when she left the islands for Spain:

¡Adios, patria feliz, edén querido!
¡Doquier que el hado en su furor me impela,

tu dulce nombre halagará mi oido.

Avellaneda's novel *Sab* (1841) is probably the first antislavery tract novel to be published anywhere in Latin America. Set in Cuba, *Sab* predated the vastly more famous *Uncle Tom's Cabin* by Harriet Beecher Stowe (1811-1896) by ten years, and is a realistic, non-propagandistic picture of the institution in Cuba. (Félix Tanco's *Petrona y Rosalia,* not published until 1925, *Francisco* by Anselmo Suárez y Romero, written in 1839 but not published until 1880, and the above-cited *Cecilia Valdés,* published in 1882, were other early novelistic treatments of Cuban slavery.)

Avellaneda wrote some seven novels and four "legends" in all, most of them in the full current of the romanticism of the day, and most of them historical fiction. Her *Guatimozin-Ultimo experador de México* (1846) is claimed by Max Henriquez Ureña to be the finest early novel with an "indianista" or "indigenista" theme, far surpassing the pedestrian efforts of the "criollistas" and others mentioned above and other writers from Latin America not mentioned here. Her last legend, *El aura blanca* (1861), is the only of her four to be based on Cuban folklore.

Great romantic contemporaries of Avellaneda were the already cited Cirilo Villaverde who published six romances, many short stories, and six novels; Ramón de Palma y Romay, distinguished author of many collections of verse and stories and two plays. Always published in French were the works of Maria de las Mercedes Santa Cruz y Montalvo (1789-1852) who called herself La Condesa de Merlin and was an interesting memoirist and storywriter.

The literature of the "costumbrist" group of local colorists was led by Gaspar Betancourt Cisneros (1803-1866); Joaquin Lorenzo Luaces (1826-1867); Rafael Maria de Mendive (1821-1886); and Juan Clemente Zenea (1832-1871). José Victoriano Betancourt (1813-1875), was the major playwright of this movement, with Luaces, who was considered the finest lyric poet since Avellaneda by Menéndez y Pelayo in his introduction to his *Antologia de poetas hispano-americanos* (1893).

Luisa Pérez de Zambrano (born Pérez y Montes de Oca, 1835-1922) was an important lyric poet whose long life of 86 years ended in great national honors in 1918 from the Havana Atheneum and a new collected edition of her poetry in 1920. Luisa's sister, Julia Pérez y Montes de Oca (1839-1875), was also a fine poet, as were the brothers, Francisco Sellén (1836-1907), Antonio Sellén (1838-1889), and Alfredo Torroella (1845-1879) who followed in the steps of Mendive. Of historical interest today is Torroella's three-act prose play *El Mulato* (1870).

A late group of romantics called "El Laúd del Desterrado" were named for the poets published in the collection of that name (1858) who went into exile in the United States after the dismal failure of Narciso López' sea invasion of Cuba against Spanish control. José Augustín Quintero y Woodville (1829-1885), Pedro Santacilia y Palacios (1826-1910), Leopoldo Turla (1818-1877), and Juan

Clemente Zenea were the most important.

With the maturation of Cuban literature, critics and literary historians were becoming important figures, and we note such writers as: Rafael Maria Merchán (1844-1905); Ricardo del Monte y Rocio (1838-1909), and Raimundo Cabrera y Bosch (1852-1923), all of whom were also good poets.

The most important figure of the century's last years was José Marti (1853-1895), and Cuba's great martyr, killed in one of the battles of the next to last revolt which finally ended in Cuban independence in 1902. No Cuban writer has stimulated more study, biographical or critical, and his own work continues to see new edition after edition.

With the advent of independence, many new cultural journals and newspapers sprang up, and the "Arpas Cubanas" group named after a collection of poets published in 1904, would display the work of José Manuel Carbonell (1880-), Francisco Díaz Silveira (1871-1924), Enrique Hernández Miyares (1859-1915), and Dulce María Borrero (1883-1945) who went on to do important work in many other genres.

Two fine poets of the new century not of the "Arpas Cubanos" group were Francisco Javier Pichardo (1873-1941) and Agustín Acosta y Bello (b. 1886), leader of the regional group in Matanzas. José Manuel Poveda (1888-1926) and Sócrates Nolasco (b. 1884), with Regino Boti (1878-1958), one of the Oriente group of poets, exploited the new currents of "modernismo," "postmodernismo" and "neo-modernismo."

The "Cenáculo" group included such writers as poet Fernándo Torralva Navarro (1885-1913), playwright Enrique Gay Calbó (b. 1889), and the Manzanillo regional group contributed such good writers as Manuel Navarro Luna (b. 1894) who published many volumes of verse, and Luis Felipe Rodriguez (1888-1947).

Important writers of the new century were the realists José Antonio Ramos (1885-1946), also a playwright and critic; Alfonso Hernández Catá (1885-1940); Mariano Brull (1891-1956); Jésus Castellanos (1879-1912), one of the most vigorous of the new novelists and storywriters; and Carlos Loveira (1882-1928), and, possibly the most celebrated, Miguel de Marcos Suárez (1894-1954), a humorist whose "cuentos pantuflares" [slipper-stories] were published in the volume *Fábulas de la vida apacible* (1943).

The theatre had an active period after independence and has remained a lively force in Cuban culture right into the recent Castro period with such writers as: José A. Ramos, a leader of the realistic movement, Ramón Sánchez Varona (b. 1883), Marcelo Salinas (b. 1889), Hernandez Catá and Mariano Brull already mentioned, and Luis Felipe Rodriguez (1888-1947).

Major poets whose work continued into the mid-century period were José Zacharias Tallet (b. 1893), Federico de Ibarzábal (1894-1954), Rubén Martinez Villena (1899-1934), who took part in the successful revolt against dictator Machado and whose work bespeaks his fervent communism, and Emilio Ballagas (1910-1954).

Coming in from Haiti, Paris and Harlem were new revolutionary currents including négritude, and with the growing strength of socialism and communism, the Afro-Cuban poets such as Alejo Carpentier (b. 1904), also of course a major novelist and folklorist, and the world-famous Nicolás Guillén.

The African theme might be said first to have entered Cuban verse in "Bailadora de rumba" by Ramón Guirao in his volume *Diario de la Marino* (1928), and *La Rumba* (1928) of José Z. Tallet, mentioned above. Of course earlier interest in black Cubans had been manifested in earlier cited works such as *La mulata* (1845) by Muñoz del Monte, and the later *El grito abuela* (1915) by José M. Poveda. The new work tried much more seriously to employ genuine Afro-Cuban speech and mannerisms, however, and with the advent of Guillén's more genuine knowledge of the black Cuban culture, this influence made for a positive contribution to the nation's literature.

Guillén (b. 1902), author of scores of works, and still busy as poet, cultural and diplomatic ambassador, and prime stimulus of the post-Castro writers in many ways, began with the seminal *Sóngoro cosongo* (1931), *West Indies, Ltd.* (1934), and *Cantos para soldados y Sonas para turistas* (1937). Though poets and novelists have now moved beyond Afro-Cubanism, no writer henceforth would care to reflect only European or Hispanic culture: the total population of Cuba would be reflected in the new literature and an ever harsher, often polemical realism would predominate.

Playwrights such as Pichardo Moya (1892-1957); Rafael Suárez Solis (b. 1882); Flora Diaz Parrado (b. 1902); Renée Potts (b. 1908); and César Rodriguez Expósito (b. 1904) wrote through the 1930's into the recent era; but José Antonio Ramos (1885-1946); José Montes López (b. 1901), Carlos Felipe (b. 1914), author of the experimental *Esta noche en el bosque* (1939), might also be mentioned here. Felipe's later plays deal with the slums of Havana, including his important works *El travieso Jimmy* (1949) and the early *Tambores* (1943), set in Africa and the popular quarters of Havana, which show his social orientation. Virgilio Piñera (b. 1914), José Luis de la Torre (b. 1911), satirical commentator on the modern scene, also call for particular mention, though many more of equal merit might be added to the roll.

As realism and social protest became ever more important, novelists such as Enrique Serpa (b. 1899); Lina Novás Calvo (b. 1905); Enrique Labrador Ruiz (b. 1902), and Marcello Pogolotti (b. 1902) worked successfully in long fiction, as did the storywriters: Lydia Cabrera (b. 1900) who often employed Afro-Cuban themes, Ramón Guirao, and Carlos Fernández Cabrera (b. 1899).

Major figures of the late pre-Castro period were Juan Marinello (b. 1898), poet and statesman, Francisco Ichaso (1900-1962); and José Maria Chacón y Calvo (b. 1893), critics and cultural leaders as well as creative artists. José Lezama Lima (b. 1937) whose journal *Verbum* gave voice to a new generation of writers called the "transcendentalists," is a major figure. Other journals established or supported by Lezama Lima were *Nadie parecia* (1942) and *Origenes* (1944-1956). *Ciclón,* founded by Rodriguez Feo in 1955; *Grafos, Clarileño,* established by Gaston Baquero in 1943, and *Poeta,* Virgilio Piñera's review; all served as lively sounding boards for the revolutionary new tendencies in literature and politics.

A few names of the writers coming to the fore in the last decade or so before Fidel Castro are Fina García Maruz (b. 1923), wife of the critic Cintio Vitier, herself a leading member of the *Origenes* group of "transcendentalists," Samuel Feijoo (b. 1914), author of an overpowering long list of works; Aldo Menéndez (b. 1918); Fernández Retamar (b. 1930), and Fayad Jamis (b. 1930).

With the advent of Castro, great changes would come about in Cuban writing. Many of the older established figures would flee or be pushed into exile and a new group of Marxist-oriented artists would find newly established presses and cultural journals open to their work. Of course, such old revolutionary reliables as Guillén would achieve the prosperous acceptance of their long-held beliefs and party loyalty, and refugee writers from elsewhere in the Caribbean such as the Haitian poet, René Depestre, would find a welcome. Close to two decades have gone by since Castro took over Cuba from Battista and many new names are now important to students of Cuban literature.

Signal contributions to literary history of the recent period are Seymour Menton's *Prose Fiction of the Cuban Revolution* (1975); José M. Bonald Caballero's *Narrativa cubana de la revolución* (1968); Jacques Ehrmann's *Literature and Revolución* (1967); and José O. Jiménez's *Estudios sobre poesia cubano contemporaneo* (1967). It would seem fruitless to attempt any synopsis of this brief, hectic and still confused era. The citation of the works above may serve to lead the scholar to the important figures and detailed discussions of the preoccupations of the very contemporary writer. This present volume has included a few of the seemingly more interesting writers who work in exile or, in some measure of peace, with the new government and philosophy in Havana.

It might be fitting to end this brief essay on Cuban literature by quoting a few lines from Heberto Padilla (b. 1932) as translated by J.M. Cohen, noted student of Latin-American writing. Padilla served the Castro regime well for some years into the late 1960's after a ten-year exile during Battista's government, serving as an official in London and Moscow. He published his poetry in state supported journals, even winning the Julian del Casal prize for his *Fuera del Juego* (Sent off the Field) in 1968 after a vicious battle within the prize committee. But in 1971 he, his wife, and a friend, were arrested and he appears to have been severely treated in prison, being freed only after an abject ritualistic self-confession. His "New looks through old locks," written earlier, now reads nostalgically:

> *I see once more through the keyhole*
> *the sad ideologist with the nylon tongue,*
> *the overwhelming dullness of the* Manual of Marxism
> *that shines like a missal,*
> *the impatient glances of the executioners*
> *and the tiny, sharp flower*

of happiness in the poems.
And then comes the most difficult task:
to devise a strategy, a tactic
for pushing the door ajar.

ESSAY ON THE LITERATURE OF THE DOMINICAN REPUBLIC

Spanish is the official language of the Dominican Republic and in its European and local varieties the speech of most of the inhabitants, but a French créole along the Haitian border is common. Only 35% of the people are literate. In 1960 there were 4900 primary schools, 600 intermediate, secondary, technical and night schools. Some 7800 students attended the five teacher-training colleges and the University of Santo Domingo, founded in 1538, the oldest university in the Western Hemisphere.

In 1539 Pope Paul III, through the papal bull, "In apostalatus culmine," authorized the institutionalization of Santo Tomás de Aquino University; and in 1550, the School of Gorjón was raised to the category of University with the name "Santiago de la Paz University." Both of them functioned and prospered for several centuries.

In the literary field, the first works were histories, ships' logs, diaries, and the chronicals of travellers and missionaries. Among the most important were *Historia Natural y General de Indias* by Gonzalo Fernández de Oviedo, *Doctrina Cristiana* by Brother Pedro de Córdoba, and *Historia de las Indias* by Brother Bartolomé de las Casas. This plain writing spoke of the customs of the aborigines, the events of the conquest, and the painful process of colonization. Only after the first half of the 16th century did the first poets and playwrights appear, but as might be expected it was of an inferior sort. Elvira de Mendoza, Leonor de Ovanda, and Francisco Tostado de la Peña are a few of those obscure poets. In drama, Cristobal de Llerena, a canon of the Cathedral and a university professor, wrote plays for the church.

The 17th and 18th centuries were of little cultural importance, a consequence of the loss of population in the northwest section of the island, the subsequent deterioration of the island's economy and the relaxing pattern of life as the link to Spain was attenuated. The French and English invaded the country and poverty became common as the sugar cane plantations declined. As social and cultural

Spain was attenuated. The French and English invaded the country and poverty became common as the sugar cane plantations declined. As social and cultural activity suffered, the once pre-eminence of Hispaniola was lost for centuries, and the country became just another island nation in the Caribbean.

A popular singer and poet of this period was Manuel Monica (b. ca. 1731) whose father had been manumitted. His ballads first appeared in a regular collection in 1884, but he was widely known in his own times and he may well be the first artist of African origin to be published from the Caribbean area.

An important event for the entire country and one marked in much of the 19th century writings was the declaration of independence from Spain of 1844 by the group gathered around Juan Pablo Duarte (1813-1876). Most stimulated was Félix Maria del Monte (1819-1899) whose patriotic verse, especially his "Canción Dominicana" which has been set to music as a national hymn, make him remembered.

José Joaquin Pérez (1845-1900) has been called the "poet of the Indian race," for his poems were inspired by the memories of the original inhabitants now sadly all vanished. His *Fantasias Indigenas* (1877) contain descriptive poems particularly influenced by the Tainos, a name given these people by the Spaniards. Joaquin Pérez' poetry, nationalistic in sentiment, is historically important, but derivative romantic verse for the most part.

In contrast, the work of Salomé Ureña (1850-1897), daughter, wife and mother of poets and scholars, taking her concern for women's improvement and culture for her themes, wrote works of a power more related to the neoclassic Spanish tradition of the previous century. Influenced particularly by the thinking and example of Eugenio Maria de Hostos (1839-1903), the most important of Caribbean educators, Salomé Ureña channeled her energies more into education for women than into literature.

A few other important writers of the 19th century may be cited. César Nicolás Penson (1855-1901) whose *Cosas Añejas* (1892) was once a popular collection of folk stories, though, read today, its underlying anti-Haitian (racist) bias and elitism ring poorly. A very romantic work was *Bani, o Engracia y Antoñita* (1892) by Francisco Gregorio Billini (1844-1898), sketches and tales. The most important work of the folkloric sort was, however, *Enriquillo* by Manuel de Jesús Galván (1834-1910). New editions are issued frequently and the work is still widely popular. Openly pro-indian, the Spanish strengths as felt by the author, valor, physical prowess, and courtesy, are also prominent features of his work.

Dominican criticism and literary history were becoming practiced arts in the latter part of the century. Most important are the names of the two famous sons of Salomé Ureña: Max Henriquez Ureña (1885-1968) and Pedro Henriques Ureña (b. 1884), and Federico Garcia Godoy (1857-1924).

The 20th century was to continue the nation's travail, for in the first twelve years two presidents would be assassinated and the year 1916 would bring the U.S. marines in for an occupation to last almost a decade. This was soon followed by the Trujillo dictatorship (1931-1961) that would even persist after its fall for the next decade at least as a destabilizing element in the new governments.

During the pre-occupation period three names are the most important: Gastón Fernando Deligne (1861-1913), a conservative poet whose works are psychologically developed and whose pure diction and elegant lines make him worth attention; Federico Garcia Godoy, referred to above, wrote a powerful trilogy of novels dealing with the arrival of independence in the 1880's: *Rufinito* (1908), *Alma Dominicana* (1911), and *Guanuma* (1914). A writer more in touch with the new literary currents of Europe was Federico Bermúdez (1884-1921) whose collection *Los Humildes* (1916) focuses on the suffering and humiliations of the Dominican masses.

A leavening influence in the strongly conservative island culture was the literary movement "Posthumanismo" which called for a more sincere search for folk and popular values in a peasant life and the more authentic use of the local creole. Domingo Moreno Jiménes (b. 1894) became the leading poet of this group. Unfortunately, the posthumanists overdid their insular approach and generally ignored other new ideas, including dadaism and futurism and rejected any influences which in the long run might have been beneficial from British and American literature. What could have been a major development became an escape to a re-evoked (and safer past), for even the all pervasive U.S. presence failed to provoke a reaction.

After the sleepy days of the 1920's and 1930's, a renovating literary movement called "Surprised Poetry" arose in 1943. Finally outside influences were openly received and the new intellectual currents opened up the island imagination. Jorge Guillén, Juan Ramón Jiménez and André Bréton were foreign artists whose work was particularly stimulating. The dictatorship of Trujillo still made caution necessary so the work of such as Manuel Rueda (b. 1921) and Lupo Hernández Rueda (b. 1930) used symbols and opaque metaphors to say what had to be said. Surrealism was both style and mask for the new poets.

Considered the father of the movement was Franklin Mieses Burgos (b. 1907) whose rather ethereal constellation of angels, loneliness, and roses are lyrical clusters in his hermetic verse. His *Clima de Eternidad* (1944) is a telling denunciation of the climate of terror and its impact on the sensitive poet and citizen. Manuel Rueda's verse, particularly his sonnets, make him one of the most harmonious and delightful of poets. His *Trinitaria Blanca* won the National Literature Prize in 1957 and his highly imaginative plays show a verbal dexterity unusual in the Republic. Recently the originator of a movement called "Pluralism", he and his friends have sought to take advantage of the best of the literary vanguards and to integrate into their work a multiple expression that permits a wide-range of interpretations or readings.

Antonio Fernández Spencer (b. 1922) won two important poetry prizes in Spain and has written important literary criticism. His collection, *Nueva poesia dominicana* (1953), has brought to light a group of poets that have reached a discerning public as valuable voices for the new currents.

Other important figures were Aida Cartagena Portalatin (b. 1918), Freddy Gatón Arce (b. 1920) whose poem "Vlia" (1944) was Dominica's first "automatic" poem; Mariano Lebrón Saviñón (b. 1922); Manuel Valerio (b. 1918), and Rafael Américo Henriquez (b. 1899).

Suffering exile were many poets of the so-called "independent writers" group who more openly than most attacked the Trujillo regime. Though author of only one work, the epic poem "Yelidá" (1942), Tomás Hernández Franco (b. 1904) is considered one of the foremost poets. Yelidá, daughter of an African woman and a Spanish father, lives through the vicissitudes of the créole mulato, and represents the conflict and worry of the vast majority of the country's population. The poet Manuel del Cabral (b. 1912) also deals with the Afro-Caribbean in his work; his *Compadre Mon* (1943) and *Antologia Tierra* (1949) offer erotic and ritualistic scenes which also outspokenly protest social conditions. Yet, despite genuine talent and feeling, he is somewhat outside his subject matter, never reaching the power of Cuba's Nicolás Guillén, for instance. Another poet exploiting the African theme is Pedro Mir (b. 1913) in his volume *Poema del Llanto Trigueño* (1949). His Marxist ideas are expressed in *Apertura a la estética.*

Héctor Incháustegui Cabral (b. 1912), though favored by the Trujillo regime, yet was able to maintain a psychic independence. His work attacked poverty and injustice and his pioneering "Canto triste a la patria bien amada" in the collection *Poemas de una sola angustia* (1940) presents a nation racked by hunger and unemployment. After a weak middle period, he recovered his powers and his *Diario de la Guerra y Los dioses ametrallados* (1967) is a significant work. Incháustegui's three plays, written in the old Greek vein, could also be cited, especially *Prometeo* (1964) which was a parable on the violence and corruption of the government.

Novelists whose work should be cited are Tulio N. Cestero (1877-1955) whose *La sangre* (1914) deals with the repressive regime of General Ulises Heureaux and whose sketches of the customs and common life of the last decades of the 19th century are of great interest. Andrés Requena (b. 1908), assassinated in New York City in 1952, violently attacked Trujillo in his *Camino del Fuego* (published in Chile, 1941), *Cementerio sin Cruces* (Mexico, 1949), and *Los enemigos de la tierra* (1963, posthumous). His works are primarily propagandistic and consequently fail, unfortunately, of being well structured intellectually.

Much more important is and was Juan Bosch (b. 1909) whose stories particularly are his best work. Of special interest is his novel *La Mañosa* (1936), subtitled "the novel of revolutions," which covers the tumultuous years which culminated in the U.S. of occupation of 1916. All of his work treats of the peasant and are heavily imbued with the feel and pulse of common life. For a brief period, after the fall of Trujillo, Bosch served as his country's president, and he has since 1964, by then out of politics, been mostly occupied with editing and seeing through the press his complete works.

Joaquín Balaguer (b. 1907), president of the Dominican Republic from 1960-1961, 1966-1967, and 1970 to 1978, is primarily a literary historian. However, his historic novels *El Centinela de la frontera* (1962) and the earlier *El Cristo de la Libertad* (1950) are of some interest.

Other prose writers of the "independista" group were Sócrates Nolasco (b. 1884); Néstor Caro (b. 1917); Hilma Contreras (b. 1913) (the only woman prose writer of the group); Virgilio Díaz Grullón (b. 1924) who has written three novels, two of which were science fiction, a relatively unusual local form, *Crónicas de Altocerro* (1966) and *Más Allá del Espejo* (1975).

As the tyranny of Trujillo dragged on, new writers often turned to a severe abstract vein in a development to be called "The Promotion of '48" as 1948 marked the first publication of the works of the poet Abelardo Vicioso (b. 1929). His later *La Lumbre Sacudida* (1958), and his poem "Canto de amor a la ciudad herida," written in 1965 on the occasion of a new U.S. invasion, are important works. Ramón Francisco (b. 1929), poet, critic; and Máximo Aviles Blonda (b. 1931), poet and playwright, are two equally important writers. Francisco's "Patria Montonera" exploits every poetic and unpoetic technique and subject he can to throw a net over the broadest possible area to express his ideas about contemporary Dominican society. Blonda was an innovator with his plays *Yo, Bertolt Brecht* and *Pirainide 179.*

Juan Sánchez Lamouth (b. 1929) also exploited every available resource to break the traditional modes of European poetry and to find the way back to the African spirit so long scorned. His strain often makes for poor poetry but his theme is eloquently expressed at times.

With the death of Trujillo in 1961, new things at long last seemed possible. New writers rushed to publish and older ones now felt free to do so after long silence or cryptic expression. Foreign books and ideas also poured in and though each artist appeared to be going his own way the heady atmosphere could only make for the most intensive questioning of Dominican institutions and traditions. The ever greater poverty of both city and rural masses, however, and the growth of a fairly large middle class, fearful of too quick a sharing of their fragile prosperity, would provoke new revolts and new repressions.

Marcio Veloz Maggiolo (b. 1936) would deal dramatically with such themes in his short stories and novels. His short novel *Los angeles de hueso* (1967) uses the interior monologue, often scatologically, and his *De Abril en Adelante* (1975), called a "protonovel" by the author, deals with the Trujillo period and its first exciting, then agonizingly disappointing aftermath.

New writers of importance in the most recent decade are: the dramatist Iván Garcia Guerra (b. 1939); the poets Miguel Alfonseca (b. 1942); and Jeannette Miller (b. 1945); Norberto James (b. 1945); Héctor Díaz Polanco (b. 1944), author of *Los enemigos intimos* (1969); José Goudy Pratt (1936), author of *Vórtice* (1962), and Federico Jóvine Bermúdez (b. 1944), author of *Huellas de la Ira.* Interesting new prose writers are Armando Almánzar Rodriguez (b. 1935), author of *Limite* (1967); Manuel Mora Serrano (b. 1933), author of *Juego de Domino* (1973); Roberto Marcalle Abreu (b. 1948), author of *Las dos muertos de José Inirio* (1972) and *El minusculo infierno del Sr. Lucas* (1973); and José

Alcántara Almánzar (b. 1946). [Some of these new writers have not been covered in this volume.]

Many influences have played on the Dominican soul. The present and future generations probably will be more international than previous ones—more able and willing to experiment in theme, style, and subject. Marxist or anti-marxist, the writers also probably will be forced to deal with the country's many social and political problems both as professional persons and as artists.

The recent decades have permitted little escapism and writings are all too heavily immersed in the struggle to survive spiritually as well as physically. Realism, experimentalism, protest—these seem to be the modes of Dominican expression, now as in the past.

ESSAY ON THE LITERATURE OF PUERTO RICO

Puerto Rican literature, like that of Cuba and the Dominican Republic, followed the European currents coming primarily from Spain but occasionally from France and England. Obviously in the past seven decades, North American writing has also changed the course of the island's writing.

The nation's literature may be said to have begun with the re-cast Indian tales of the early Spanish explorers and settlers. Juan de Castellanos (1522-1607) and Father Damián López de Haro (1581-1648) were two such writers. One authority, Tomás Navarro, believes the one area remaining with vestigal Indian (Taino) stories which have been absorbed into the local legends is the San Germán mountains of the district of Maricao. The revolt of Caoigue (chief) Agüeybana is recorded in the first Spanish-language poems celebrating the islands, in Juan de Castellanos' *Elegies of Illustrious Men of the Indies*, believed the longest epic poem of Spanish Latin America.

Today, Puerto Ricans at home, scattered throughout the islands, or forging new lives in the mainland United States, are conscious of their long Spanish heritage, but must, somehow, come to terms with the all intrusive Anglo-Saxon culture established in the island since 1900.

Three of the earliest writers of Puerto Rican connection, were Francisco de Ayerra y Santamaria (1630-1708), a Gongorist poet; Bishop Bernardo de Balbueno (1568-1627), a Spanish-born poet whose library was the first major resource for the new colony before it was destroyed in a Dutch attack on San Juan in 1625; and José Campeche (1752-1809) who captured the local scene in his sketches. Also of interest is Abbad y Lasierra (1745-1815) who composed the first history of the island. The early centuries of Puerto Rico were the particular province of poet and playwright Tapia y Rivera (1826-1882) whose *Biblioteca Histórica de Puerto Rico* (1854) is an important document.

As elsewhere in the Caribbean, the European literary movements determined the new literary styles and/or subjects. Several of the more important romantics were the poets Santiago Vidarte (1827-1848) and Manuel Alonso y Pacheco (1822-1889) who while studying in Spain felt the nostalgia for their island. They would be important figures in the establishment of the Atheneum in 1876, an organization that would long stimulate the island's intellectuals. Alonso's tales were published in his important journals, *Album Puertorriqueño* (1844) and *El Jibarro: Cuadro de costumbres de la Isla de Puerto Rico* (1849) which had both prose and verse sections. It was one of the most successful works to deal with both town and country life, employing the popular language of both sectors.

One of the most interesting mid-19th century figures was Francisco J. Amy (1837-1912) whose long residence in North America ended with his taking American citizenship. He translated many of the classic American and British poets into Spanish and, conversely, Latin-Caribbean poets into English. His efforts are believed to have sped up the modernization of island literature.

Baldorioty de Castro (1822-1890), a journalist and writer of travel books, was a prime organizer of the Autonomist Party which, though punished by the Spanish authorities, looked toward the November 1897 royal decree from Madrid granting autonomy to Puerto Rico (later ignored completely by the United States). Many of the late romantic writers joined their Cuban brethren in the anti-colonial struggle, among them the poet Pachín Marín, born in 1863 and dead on a battlefield in Cuba in 1897. Prominent intellectuals who were patriots and writers were Eugenio Maria de Hostos (1839-1903), an important figure also in Cuban and Dominican affairs and literature; Ramón Emeterio Betances (1827-1898) who wrote the romantic novel *La Vierge de Borinquen* (1859); and Lola Rodríguez de Tio (1843-1924), nationalist poet whose "La Borinqueña" became the text of the Puerto Rican national anthem. Mariano Abril y Ostalo (1861-1935), a polemical writer whose opinions expressed in strongly worded editorials earned him a stay in Spanish prisons, was a biographer, historian, and poet of a modest level. Hostos' novel, *La Peregrinación Bayoán* [The Pilgrimage of Bayaón] of 1863, was possibly the best fictional work of the period.

As the romantic movement broadened to include not only the folkloric ballads and the special Spanish forms, the *aguinaldos, coplas,* and the *décimas* of the jíbaros (peasants), Tapia, Meléndez Muñoz, Salvador Brau, Hostos, and José Mercado would contribute important work. The increasing use of the local creole was especially noted in the Indian legends of Cayetano Coll y Toste (1850-1930), and the *Historical Bulletin of Puerto Rico,* edited by Coll from 1914-1927, would become the repository of a valuable collection of such dialectal and folkloric work.

Two of the finest late romantic poets were José Gautier Benítez (1851-1880) whose one lovely little collection of 1880, *Poesia,* is a national treasure, and

Francisco Alvarez Marrero (1847-1881) whose verse collection *Flores de un retamal* and play *Dios en todas partes* were both published in 1881.

The end of the romantic century saw an increasing concern for the depressed and oppressed. One of the great naturalist novelists exploiting the Emile Zola ideas of the "roman experimental" was Manuel Zeno Gandia (1855-1930). His quatrology, unfortunately not yet translated out of Spanish into any other language, was composed of *La charca* (1894), *Garduña* (1896), *El Negocio* (1922) and *Los Redentores* (1925), the last being a study of the traumatic early years of American occupation.

Virgilio Dávila (1869-1943) exploited regionalist and folkloric themes and is one of the best "costombrista" poets with his *Aromas del terruño* (1916) and *Pueblito de antes* (1917). Davila's "Cofre de Sandalo" exudes the fin-de-siècle pseudo-oriental atmosphere so popular then:

En un tallado cofre de sándalo de Oriente
conservo los recuerdos más dulces y queridos:
amarillentas cartas, retratos desteñidos
y rosas que aún escuchan las cuitas de la fuente.

As Puerto Rican artists sought to digest to some degree the American presence and the inculcation of the English language in preserves long guarded by Spain, such writers as Tomás Blanco (b. 1900), poet and novelist, and Luis Palés Matos (1899-1959), exploiter of African themes and inventor of the term and stimulator of the movement called "Diepalismo," and probably the island's best known author in Latin America, excelled in literary expression.

One of the artists most hostile to the U.S. occupation was Juan Antonio Corretjer (b. 1908) who often employed extremely idiomatic street vernacular in his 13 collections. Another of the very nationalist authors is Enrique A. Laguerre (b. 1906) whose nine novels and other works deal with colonialism and often are concerned with the brutalities of life in New York City.

Luis Muñoz Marin (b. 1898), long a leader of the Popular Democratic Party and head of the government, was a polished writer and orator. He was also a thoughtful poet deeply committed to social themes. Other important writers were Félix Franco Oppenheimer (b. 1912); Evaristo Ribera Chevremont (b. 1908); and Francisco Manrique Cabrera (b. 1908), one of the finest poets of the first third of the present century. With the publication of his pioneering studies of the nation's writers in his *Historia de la literatura puertorriqueña* (1947) and *Apuntes para la historia literaria de Puerto Rico* (1957), the nation's writing had come of age.

Writers of the 1920-1950 "Middle Period" were many. Here we can mention Amelia Ceide (b. 1908), poet of intimacy; Carmen Maria Collon Pellot (b. 1911), author of the verse collection *Ambar mulato* (1938), Miguel Meléndez Muñoz (1884-1966); Nemesio R. Canales (1878-1923); Concha Meléndez (b. 1904); and José A. Balseiro (b. 1900).

Of the generation coming into artistic maturity in the 1940-1970 period might be mentioned Andrés Castro Rios (b. 1942); Francisco Lluch Mora (b. 1924), member of the "Transcendentalismo" school, Violeta López Suria (b. 1926); Hugo Margenat (b. 1934); Juan Martinez Capó (b. 1923); and Francisco Matos Paoli (b. 1915), author of a score of volumes of verse. One of the grea prolific is Pedro Juan Soto (b. 1928).

Increasingly, Puerto Rican writers born in, or early brought to, the United States, have written in English. Piri Thomas (b. 1928) whose three autobiographical novels *Down these Main Streets* (1967), *Savior, Savior, Hold My Hand* (1973), and *Seven Long Times* (1975); and Victor Hernandez Cruz (b. 1949), author of *Snaps* (1969), have been in the vanguard of what no doubt will become an important stream of "neo-rican" writing. Carmen Puigdollers (b. 1925?), though writing in Spanish, was born in New York City and has published one volume of poetry to date, *Dominio entre alas* (1955), in a strongly Americanized verse-experience though in her mother tongue.

Some of the most important critics and/or literary historians are Margot Arce de Vázquez (b. 1901); Maria Teresa Babin (b. 1910), and the already mentioned Concha Meléndez. René Márques (b. 1919) has continued also to produce important studies of Puerto Rican literature.

Among Puerto Rico's many playwrights, we can name Francisco Arrivi (b. 1915) who has been one of the most influential. Not only have his many plays been widely performed, but he has been the leading promotor of the island theatre. He has also seriously treated of the Afro-Antillean theme, particularly in *Vejigantes* (1958), a three-act play. He has also published two histories of the island's drama and four collections of the nation's verse.

Emilio Belaval (b. 1903), a storywriter, has six plays, several performed in the drama festivals in San Juan. Salvador Brau y Asencio (1842-1912) was one of the earliest and most successful island playwrights. René Márques has also written and produced many plays and founded the Teatro Experimental del Ateneo in 195 and has served as its secretary since 1954.

Manuel Méndez Ballester (b. 1909) has written six plays performed at the Drama Festival of San Juan and published his historical novel, *Isla cerrera,* in 1970.

Another critic who is also an important playwright is Cesáreo Rosa-Nieve who has also published many volumes of poetry and stories.

One of the younger playwrights is the prolific Luis Rafael Sánchez (b. 1936) with seven plays.

Many Puerto Rican poets have sought to capture the liquidity of sky and sea in their verse. One of the most successful was Tomás Blanco, whose "Unicorn en la isla" is as musical as any:

Isla de la palmera y la guajana
con cinto de bullentes arrecifes
y corola de soles.
Isla de amor y mar enamorado,

Bajo el viento:
Los caballos azules con sus sueltas melenas,
y con desnuda piel de ascuas doradas,
. . . .

and this may be the glory and curse of Puerto Rican writing. Everywhere there is the tropical world of nature and the fading romance of the old Spanish world—and everywhere the smog and roar of modern industrialism. The Cubans and Dominicans have their land to run, badly or well; the Puerto Ricans can only go home from a sojourn in the United States to a brittle culture not really theirs to cure or control.

Other literatures have survived in a dual linguistic-cultural ambiance and the vividness and power of so much island verse and fiction can tell us the island's artists are coming to grips with their inner and outer worlds. One might even hypothecate that the pain of the past several generations, the extreme shock suffered by the Puerto Rican soul at the end of the 19th century, the vicissitudes of travel and work in North America, will forge the strongest voice of all the Caribbean peoples.

But almost certainly that voice will speak more quickly—and more universally—in a renovated Spanish, than in American English.

Migdalia Rivera, a young social worker in Chicago, began her English-language poem "The Straight-Jacket"* with these words:

When one is damaged by a
society as cruel as this, one
must bandage the wounds, But a
sore without air doesn't heal;
it rots and spreads.

and she worries about the suppuration under the cloth:

In my short but painful moments of reflections
I see my sore becoming a cancer.
You ask if it is malignant—

give me freedom today
and you shall have your answer tomorrow.

The private anguish is the national sorrow.

*from *The Rican* (Chicago, Vol. I, No. 1, Fall 1971), p. 18.

LIST OF WRITERS FROM CUBA

Acosta y Bello, Augustin
Aguirre, Mirta
Albaladejo, Mariano
Alfonso, Domingo
Alfonso, Paco
Alonso, Dora
Alvárez Rios, María
Amado Blanco, Luis
Arcocha, Juan
Arenal, Humberto
Arenas, Reinaldo
Areu, Manuel
Argüero, Luis
Armas y Cárdenas, José de (pseudonym: Justo de Lara)
Armas y Cespedes, José de
Arozarena, Marcelino
Arrufat, Antón
Arrugado (pseudonym for Juan Roquero Dominguez)
Augier, Angel I.
Avellaneda, Gertrudis Gómez de (also Gertrudis Gomez de Avellaneda)

Bacardi Moreau, Emilio
Bachiller y Morales, Antonio
Badia, Nora
Balboa Troya y Quesada, Silvestre de
Ballagas, Emilio
Balmaseda, Francisco Javier
Baquero, Gastón
Baragano, José Alvarez
Baralt y Zachariae, Luis A.
Barbera, José Domingo
Barral, Mario
Barreiro, José R.

Benitez Rojo, Antonio
Bernal, Emilia
Betancourt, José Ramón
Betancourt, José Victoriano
Betancourt, Luis
Betancourt Cisneros, Gaspar
Blanchet, Emilio
Blanchie, Francisco Javier
Bobadilla y Lunar, Emilio (pseudonym: Fray Candil and Dagoberto Marmora)
Boissier, Pedro Alejandro
Bolanos, José
Bonnin Armstrong, Ana Inés
Borrero, Dulce María
Borrero, Juana
Borrero Echeverria, Esteban
Boti y Barreiro, Regina Eladio
Bourbakis, Roberto
Bozello y Guzman, Carmen
Brull y Caballero, Mariano
Buch, René
Buesa, José Angel
Busto, Jorge del
Buzzi, David
Byrne, Bonifacio

Caballero, José Agustin
Cabrera, Lydia
Cabrera y Bosch, Raimundo
Cabrera Infante, Guillermo
Cabrisas, Hilarión
Calcagno, Francisco
Camin, Alfonso
Camors, Conde D. E. (pseudonym for Julian del Casal)
Campins, Rolando

Cárdenas y Rodriguez, Nicolás (pseudonym: Teodomofilo)
Cardoso, Onelio Jorge
Carpentier, Alejo
Carreno, Pedro
Carrillo y O'Farril, Isaac
Carrion, Miguel de
Casal, Julian del (pseudonym: Paul Vasili and Conde D. E. Camors)
Casey, Calvert
Castellanos, Jesús
Castillo de Gonzalez, Aurelia
Casuso, Teté
Cepeda, Josefina de
Céspedes de Escanaverino, Ursula
Cid Pérez, José
Clara Lair (pseudonym for Mercedes Negron Muñoz)
Clarens, Angel
Clavijo Tisseur, Arturo
Concepción Valdés, Gabriel de la (pseudonym: Plácido)
Cordova, Armando
Costa, Fernando
Costales, Manuel
Costi y Erro, Cándido
Covarrubias, Francisco
Crespo y Borbon, Bartolomé José
Costi y Erro, Cándido (pseudonym: C. Sicto)
Cruz y Fernandez, Manuel de la

Delmonte y Mena, Jesús M.
Del Monte y Aponte, Domingo
Del Monte y Portillo, Casimiro
Desnoes, Edmundo
Desval (pseudonym for Ignacio Valdes Machuca)
Diaz González, Olallo
Diaz Parrado, Flora
Diaz Rodriguez, Ernesto
Diaz Rodriguez, Jesús
Diaz de la Ronde, Silverio
Diego, Eliseo
Dominguez Arbelo, Juan
Dominguez y Santi, Jacobo

Echeverria, José Antonio
Edo, Enrique
Eguren, Gustavo
Entenza, Pedro
Escobedo Urra, Antonio
Estenger y Neuling, Rafael
Estevez, Sofia
Estorino, Abelardo
Estrada y Zenea, Ildefonso

Feijoo, Samuel
Felipe, Carlos
Fernández, Pablo Armando
Fernández Arrondo, Ernesto
Fernández Retamar, Roberto
Fernández Vilato, Francisco
Fernández de Amado, Isabel
Ferrer, Rolando
Filolezes (pseudonym for José Cipriano de la Luz y Caballero)
Florit, Eugenio
Fornet, Ambrosio
Fornaris, José
Fornaris y Joaquin, Lorenzo (see under Joaquin Lorenzo Luaces)
Fort, Gustavo (assoc. with Puerto Rico)
Frau Marsal, Lorenzo
Fray Candil (pseudonym for Emilio Bobadilla y Lunar)
Fuentes, José Lorenzo
Furé, Rogelio Martinez

Galliano Cancio, Miguel
Garcia Alzola, Ernesto
Garcia Bárcena, Rafael

Garcia Godoy, Federico (assoc. with Dominican Republic)
Garcia Marruz, Fina
Garcia Pérez, Luis
Garcia Vega, Lorenzo
Garcia Tudurí de Coya, Mercedes
Garmendia, Miguel
Gay Calbo, Enrique
Gaztelu, Angel
Gomez de Avellaneda, Gertrudis (see under Gertrudis Avellaneda Gomez)
González, Ana H.
González, Jorge Antonio
González, Manuel Dionisio
González, Nicanor Aristides
González, Reynaldo
González del Valle, José Zacharias
González de Cascorro, Raúl
Govantes, José Joaquín
Granados, Manuel
Güell y Rente, José
Guerrero, Teodoro
Guillén, Nicolás
Guira, Dysis
Guirao, Ramón
Guiteras, Eusebio
Gutierrez, García

Heredia y Heredia, José María de
Hernández, José
Hernández Cata, Alfonso
Hernández Crespo, Manuel
Hernández Miyares, Enrique
Herrera, Ramón Vélez
Hurtado del Valle, Antonio

Ibarzabal, Federico de
Ichaso, León
Iglesia y Santos, Alvaro de la
Insua, Alberto
Irizarri, Francisco
Iturrondo, Francisco
Iznaga, Alcides

Jamís, Fayad
Jesús Medina, Tristan de
Jorrín, José Silverio
Jústiz y del Valle, Tomás Juan de
Justo le Lara (pseudonym for José de Armas y Cárdenas)

Kemp, Vicente Gómez

Labrador Ruiz, Enrique
Lair, Clara (pseudonym for Mercede Negron Muñoz)
Leal, Rine
Leante, César
Leyva y Balaguer, Armando
Lezama Lima, José María
Lizaso, Félix
Lles y Berdayes, Fernando
Lles y Berdayes, Francisco
Llopis, Rogelio
López, César
López, René
López Consuegra, Andrés
López de Briñas, Felipe
Loveira y Chirino, Carlos
Loynaz, Dulce María
Lozano Casado, Miguel
Luaces, Joaquin Lorenzo (also Lorenz Fornaris y Joaquín)
Luz y Caballero, José Cipriano de l (pseudonym: Filolezes)

Macau García, Miguel Angel
Madan y García, Augusto E.
Malpica y Labarca, Domingo
Manet, Eduardo
Manzano, Juan Francisco

Marcos Suarez, Miguel de
Marinello Vidaurreta, Juan
Marmora, Dagoberto (pseudonym for Emilio Bobadilla y Lunar)
Marquéz y Gispert, Matías Felipe
Marre, Luis
Martí Pérez, José Julián (Pepe)
Martínez, Vicente
Martínez Avileira y Perez de Corcho, Lorenzo
Martínez Villena, Rubén
Matamoros, Mercedes
Matas, Julio
Maury, José W.
Mayol Martínez, Jaime
Medina y Cespedes, Antonio
Meireles, Eduardo
Mellado y Montana, Manuel
Mendive, Rafael María de
Menéndez, Aldo
Merchan, Rafael María
Mercedes Santa Cruz y Montalvo, María de las (Condesa de Merlin)
Merchan, Rafael María
Meza y Suarez Inclan, Ramón
Milanes, Federico
Milanes, José Jacinto
Millan, José Agustín
Miro Argentier, José
Mitjans y Alvarez, Aurelio
Miyares, Enriques Hernández
Mojica, Francisco
Monge, José María
Monte, Laureano del
Monte y Rocio, Ricardo del
Montenegro, Carlos
Montes Huidobro, Matías
Montes López, José
Montoro Agüero, José A.
Morales Alvárez, Ramón
Morejon, Nancy
Moret Pérez, Francisco
Morua Delgado, Martín
Muñoz Bustamente, Mario
Muñoz del Monte, Francisco (b. Dom. Rep.)

Napoles Fajardo, Juan Cristobal
Navarrete y Romay, Carlos
Navarro Correa, Noel
Navarro Luna, Manuel
Negron Muñoz, Mercedes (pseudonym: Clara Lair)
Novas Calvo, Lino
Núñez, Ana Rosa
Núñez, Serafina

O'Farril, Alberto
Orgaz, Francisco
Ortega de la Flor, Luis
Ortero, Rafael
Ortiz, Fernando
Otero Gonzalez, Lisandro

Padilla, Heberto
Palma, José Joaquín
Palma y Romay, Ramón de
Palomino, Rafael Leopoldo
Pedroso, Regino
Pequeño, Pedro Néstor
Pérez Tellez, Emma
Pérez y Montes de Oca, Julia
Pérez y Montes de Oca (De Zambrana), Luisa
Pérez y Ramirez, Manuel María
Pichardo, Francisco Javier
Pichardo, Manuel Serafín
Pichardo Moya, Felipe
Pildain, Pablo
Piña, Ramon

Piñera, Virgilio
Piñeyro, Enrique
Pita Rodriguez, Félix
Pita, Santiago
Plácido (pseudonym for Gabriel de la Concepción Valdés)
Planas y Sainz, Juan Manuel
Poey y Aguire, Andrés
Pogolotti, Marcelo
Poo, José de
Portuondo, José Antonio
Potts, Renée
Pous, Arquimedes
Poveda y Armenteros, Francisco
Poveda y Calderón, José Manuel
Prado, Pura del
Puig y de la Puente, Francisco (pseudonym: Julio Rosas)

Quintana, José Maria de
Quintero y Woodville, José Agustin

Ramos, José Antonio
Remos Rubio, Juan José
Rigali, Rolando
Rivas, Duque de
Rivera, Raul
Robreño Puente, Gustavo
Rodriguez, Agustin
Rodriguez, Emilio Gaspar
Rodriguez, Luis Felipe
Rodriguez Acosta, Ofelia
Rodriguez Embil, Luis
Rodriguez Exposito, César
Rodriguez Mendez, José
Rodriguez Santos, Justo
Rodriguez Ucares, Fray José
Rodriguez Velez, Benicio
Roldán, José Gonzalo
Roquero Dominguez, Juan (pseudonym: Arrugado)
Rosas, Julio (pseudonym for Francisco Puig y de la Puente)
Rubalcava, Manuel Justo de

Salazar y Roig, Salvador
Sales, Miguel
Salinas, Marcelo
Sánchez, Carlos E.
Sánchez, René
Sánchez Boudy, José
Sánchez Galarraga, Gustavo
Sáncehz Varona, Ramón
Sánchez de Fuentes y Pelaez, Eugenio (b. Dom. Rep.)
Santacilla, Pedro A.
Sanz y Garcia, Julián
Sarachaga, Ignacio
Sarduy, Severo
Sarusky Miller, Jaime
Sellén, Antonio
Sellén, Francisco
Serra, Narciso
Serpa, Enrique
Sicto, C. (pseudonym for Cándido Costi y Erro)
Simo, Ana Maria
Smith, Octavo
Socorro de León, José
Soloni, Félix
Solorzano y Correoso, Antonio
Soravila, Lesbia
Súarez Solis, Rafael
Súarez y Romero, Anselmo
Suri y Aguila, José

Tallet, José Zacharias
Tejera, Diego Vicente

Teodomofilo (pseudonym for Nicolás Cárdenas y Rodriguez)
Teurbe Tolón, Miguel
Torre, José Luis de la
Torrens de Garmendia, Mercedes
Torres y Feria, Manuel de
Torriente y Brau, Pablo de la
Torroella, Alfredo
Triana, José
Triay, José E.
Turla, Leopoldo

Ugarte, Lucas Arcadio de
Uhrbach y Campuzano, Carlos
Uhrbach y Campuzano, Federico Pio
Urzáis, Fernándo

Valdés, Carlos Genero
Valdés, Ramón Francisco
Valdés Codina, Leopoldo
Valdés Hernández, Oscar
Valdés Machuca, Ignacio (pseudonym: Desval)
Valdés Mendoza, Mercedes
Valdivia y Sisay, Aniceto
Valerio, Juan Francisco (a.k.a. Narciso Valor y Fe)
Valladares, Armando
Valor y Fe, Narciso (see under Juan Francisco Valerio)
Varela Zequira, Eduardo
Varela Zequiera, José
Varona y Pera, Enrique José
Vasconcelos Maragliano, Ramón
Vasili, Paul (pseudonym for Julian del Casal)
Vásquez, Andrés Clemente
Vásquez Gallo, Antonio
Vázquez Pérez, Gregorio
Veléz Herrera, Ramón
Vidaurreta y Alvárez, Antonio
Villa, Ignacio
Villar Buceta, María
Villaronda, Guillermo
Villaverde y De La Paz, Cirilo
Villoch, Federico
Vinajeras, Antonio
Vitier, Cintio (or Cynthio)
Vitier, Medardo

Xenes, Nieves

Zafra, Antonio Enrique de
Zanonet, Félix
Zamacois, Eduardo
Zambrana y Valdes, Ramón
Zambrana y Vasquez, Antonio
Zamora, José Narciso
Zayas, Fernándo de
Zenea, Juan Clemente (pseudonym: Adolfo de la Azucena)
Zequiera y Arango, Manuel (pseudonyms: Izmael Raquenue and Ezequiel Armuna)

LIST OF WRITERS FROM THE DOMINICAN REPUBLIC

Aguiar, Enrique

Alcántara Almánzar, José

Alfonseca, Miguel

Alfonseca, Ricardo Pérez

Alix, Juan Antonio (a.k.a. Papa Toño)

Almánzar, Armando

Amiama, Francisco Javier

Angulo Guridi, Alejandro

Angulo Guridi, Francisco Xavier (or Javier)

Avelino Garcia, Andrés

Aybar, Emiliano I.

Aybar y Delgado, Andrejulio (Andrés Julio)

Aybar o Rodriguez, Manuela (a.k.a. "La Deana")

Auyso, Juan José

Azar Garcia, Aquiles

Balaguer, Joaquin

Bazil Leyva, Osvaldo

Bejarano, Lázaro

Bermúdez, Luis Arturo

Bermúdez y Ortega, Federico Ramón

Berroa y Canelo, Quitero

Billini y Aristy, Francisco Gregorio

Blonda Acosta, Máximo Avilés

Bonó, Pedro F.

Bosch, Juan

Buscón, Juan (pseudonym for Manuel de Jesús Troncoso de la Concha)

Cabral, Eulogio

Cabral, Manuel del

Cándido, Pepe (pseudonym for Rafael Alfredo Deligne y Figueroa)

Cartagena Portalatin, Aïda

Cestero, Tulio Manuel Florentino

Cestero y Sarda, Manuel Florentino

Contreras, Hilma

Cuello, Julio Alberto

Damirón y Sánchez, Rafael

Deive, Carlos Esteban

Deligne, Gastón Fernando

Deligne y Figueroa, Rafael Alfredo (pseudonym: Pepe Cándido)

Del Monte, Félix Maria (pseudonym: Delio)

Del Risco Bermúdez, René

De Peña de Bordas, Virginia

Deschamps, Eugenio (a.k.a. "El Tribuno Popular")

Diaz, Otilio Vigil

Diaz Grullón, Virgilio

Diaz Ordóñez, Virgilio

Dominguez Hernández, Franklin

Duarte y Diez, Rosa

Echavarria, Colón

Fernández Spencer, Antonio

Fiallo y Cabral, Fabio

Foxá y Lecanda, Francisco Javier de

Foxá y Lecanda, Narciso

Francasi, Amelia (pseudonym for Amelia Francisca Marchena de Leyba)

Francisco, Ramón

Franck, Dr. (pseudonym for Francisco Carlos Ortea)

Franco Bidó, Augusto

Galván, Manuel de Jesús

Galván y Velázquez, Rafael Octavio

Garcia Godoy, Federico (b. Cuba)
Garcia Guerra, Ivan
Garrido, Victor
Gatón Arce, Freddy
Ginés, Teodora
Giro, Valentin
Glass Mejia, José Manuel
Goico Alix, Juan
Gómes de Read, Ernestina
González, José Luis (assoc. with Puerto Rico)
González, José Maria

Henriquez, Rafael Américo (a.k.a. "Puchungo")
Henriquez Ureña, Max

Henriquez Ureña, Pedro
Henriquez y Alfau, Enrique
Henriquez y Carvajal, Federico
Heredia y Mota, Nicolás
Hernández Franco, Tomás Rafael
Hernández Rueda, Lupo
Heureaux, Ulises, Jr.
Hungria Lovelace, Luis

Ibarra de Victoria, Maria
Incháustegui Cabral, Héctor

James, Norberto
Jiménez, José Maria
Jiménez, Miguel Angel
Jiménez, Ramón Emilio
Jiménes Grullón, Juan Isidro
Justino Castillo, Rafael

Kennedy, Elena (pseudonym for Virginia Elena Ortea)

Lamarche, Juan Bautista
Lebrón Saviñón, Mariano
Llanes, Manuel
Llenas, Alejandro
López y Lora, José Ramón
Lugo, Américo
Luperón, Gregorio

Marchena de Leyba, Amelia Francisca (pseudonym: Amelia Francasi or Francasci)
Marrero Aristy, Ramón
Mateo, Andrés L.
Matos, Alfredo
Mejia de Fernández, Abigail
Mieses Burgos, Franklin (or Franklyn)
Miller, Jeannette
Mir, Pedro
Mónica, Manuel (a.k.a. Meso Mónica, as Maestro Mónico, and also as Antonio Mónica)
Morales, Gabino Alfredo (b. Puerto Rico)
Morel, Emilio A.
Moreno Jiménes, Domingo
Morillo, Gabriel Angel
Moya, Casimiro N. de
Muñoz del Monte, Francisco (assoc. with Cuba)

Nivar de Pittaluga, Amada
Nouel y Bobadilla, Bienvenido Salvador
Núñes de Cáceres, José (a.k.a. "El fabulista principiante")

Ortea, Francisco Carlos (pseudonym: Dr. Franck)
Ortea, Virginia Elena (pseudonym:

Elena Kennedy)
Osorio, Ana de

Pacheco, Armando Oscar
Peguero, Luis José
Pellerano Amechazurra, Fernando
Pellerano Castro, Arturo Bautista (pseudonym: Byron)
Peña y Reinoso, Manuel de Jesús de
Pensón, César Nicolás
Perdoma y Heredia, Josefa Antonia (pseudonym: "Laura")
Perdomo y Sosa, Apolinar
Pérez, José Joaquin
Pérez Alfonseca, Ricardo
Pérez Cabral, Pedro Andrés
Pérez Licairac, Horacio
Pérez y Pérez, Carlos Federico
Pichardo y Tapia, Esteban
Prud'homme, y Maduro, Emilio
"Puchungo" (see Rafael Américo Henriquez)
Pumarol, Pablo

Read, Horacio
Requena Francisco, Andrés
Reyes, Juan de Jesús
Rodriguez Fernández, Arturo
Rodriguez Objio, Manuel Nemesio
Rueda, Manuel

Sánchez Lamouth, Juan
Saviñón, Altagracia
Sola, José Narciso
Soler y Meriño, Mariano Antonio
Suncar Chevalier, Manuel E.
Suro, Rubén

Tejera y Pensón, Apolinar
Troncoso de la Concha, Manuel de Jesús (pseudonym: Juan Buscón)

Ureña de Henriquez, Salomé (pseudonym: Herminia)
Ureña de Mendoza, Nicolás (pseudonym: "Nisidas" and "Cástulo")
Valencia, Manuel Maria
Valerio, Manuel
Veloz Maggiolo, Marcio
Vicioso, Abelardo

Weber, Delia

Zacarias Espinal, Manuel
Zorrila, Rafael Augusto

LIST OF WRITERS FROM PUERTO RICO

Abril y Ostalo, Mariano
Adsuar Boneta, Jorge
Alegria, José S.
Algarin, Miguel
Alonso y Pacheco, Manuel
Amadeo Antomarchi, Jesús Maria
Amador, Américo (pseudonym for Manuel De Elzaburu)
Amy, Francisco J.
Aponte, José Agustin
A. R. (pseudonym for Enrique Jiménez Solá)
Arana, Felipe N.
Arce, José de (pseudonym for Manuel Martinez Dávila)
Arce de Vázquez, Margot
Arrillaga, Maria
Arrivi, Francisco
Arzola, Marina
Astol, Eugenio
Aviles, Juan

Babin, Maria Teresa
Baldorioty de Castro, Román
Balseiro, José Augustin
Bauza y González, Obdulio
Belaval, Emilio S.
Bibiana Benitez, Maria
Blanco, Antonio Nicolás
Blanco y Géigel, Tomás
Bonafoux y Quintero, Mario Luis
Bonnin Armstrong, Ana Inés
Brau y Ascencio, Salvador
De Burgos, Julia (Julia Constancia Burgos Garcia)

Cabanillas, Isabel
Cadilla de Ruibal, Carmen Alicia
Cadilla de Martinez, Maria (Liana)
Calderón Escobar, Juan
Canales, Nemesio R.
Carreras, Carlos N.
Carrión Madura, Tomás
Castro Quesada, Luis
Ceida, Amelia
Cestero, Ferdinand R.
Coll y Toste, Cayetano
Coll y Vidal, Antonio
Collado Martell, Alfredo
Colón Pellot, Carmen Maria
Corchado y Juarbe, Manuel
Corretjer, Juan Antonio
Cortón, Antonio
Cotto Thorner, Guillermo
Cuchi Coll, Isabel

Dalmau Canet, Sebastián
Daubon, José Antonio
Dávila, José Antonio
Dávila, Virgilio
Degetau y González, Federico
Delgado, Emilio R.
Del Valle, Rafael
Del Valle Atiles, Francisco
Demar, Carmen (pseudonym for Carmen Porrata Doria de Aponte)
Dessus, Luis Felipe
Diaz Alfaro, Abelardo
Diaz Valcarcel, Emilio
De Diego, José
De Diego Padro, José I.
Dominguez, José de Jesús
Duran, Ana Luisa
De Elzaburu, Manuel (pseudonyms:

Fabián Montes and Américo Amador)
Esteves, José de Jesús

Felices, Jorge
Feliciano Mendoza, Esther
Fernández Juncos, Manuel
Fernández Méndez, Eugenio
Fernández Sánchez, Angel (pseudonym: Guido de Ariel)
Ferrer Hernández, Gabriel
Ferrer Otero, Rafael
Figueroa, Edwin
Fonfrias, Ernesto Juan
Fort, Gustavo (b. Cuba)
Foxá y Lecanda, Narciso
Franco Oppenheimer, Félix

Gallego, Laura Matilda
Garrastegui, Anagilda
Gautier Benítez, José
Geigel Polanco, Vicente
Gerena Bras, Gaspar
Gómez Costa, Arturo
Gómez Piñero, Manuel
González, José Emilio (or Josemilio)
González, José Luis (b. Dom. Rep.)
González Alberty, Fernándo
González Carbo, Alfonso
González Garcia, Matias
González (or Gonzalo) Marin, Francisco (pseudonym: Pachin Marin)
Grau Archilla, Raúl
Guerra Mondragon, Miguel

Hernández, José P.H. (sometimes called Peache)
Hernández Alba, Rafael
Hernández Aquino, Luis
Hernández Cruz, Victor
Hernández Vargas, Francisco
Hernández de Araujo, Carmen
De Hostos, Eugenio Mario

De Jesús, Salvador M. de
Jiménez, Francisco P.
Jiménez Malaret, René
Jiminez Sola, Enrique (pseudonym: [?] A.R.)
Joglar Cacho, Manuel
Julia Marin, Ramón
Juvenal Rosa, Pedro

Kadosh, A. (pseudonym for Francisco Mariano Quiñones)

Labarthe López de Victoria, Pedro Juan
Lago, Jesús Maria
Laguerre, Enrique Arturo
Limón de Arce, José
Llorens Torres, Luis
Lluch Mora, Francisco
López, Magda (pseudonym for Magdalena López de Victoria y Fernández)
López López, Joaquin
López Suria, Violeta
López de Victoria y Fernández, Magdalena (pseudonym: Magda López)
Lugo, Samuel

Manrique Cabrera, Francisco
Margenat, Hugo
Marin Francisco, Gonzálo or González (see under pseudonym: Pachin Marin)
Marin, Ramón
Marqués, René
Marrero, Diego O.
Marrero Núñez, Julio
Marrero de Figueroa, Carmen

Martin Montes, José Luis
Martinez Alvarez, Rafael (a.k.a. Martin Alva)
Martinez Capo, Juan
Martinez Dávila, Manuel (pseudonym: José de Arce)
Matos Bernier, Félix
Matos Paoli, Francisco
Matta, Enrique G.
Meléndez, Concha
Meléndez Múñoz, Miguel
Méndez Ballester, Manuel
Mendoza, Ester Feliciano
Mercado, José Ramón (a.k.a. Momo)
Mergal, Angel M.
Mirabal, Antonio
Miranda Archilla, Graciany
Miranda, Luis Antonio
Molina, Francisco
Moll Boscana, Aristides
Momo (pseudonym for José Ramón Mercado)
Montes, Fabián (pseudonym for Manuel De Elzaburu)
Morales Gabino Alfredo (assoc. with Dom. Rep.)
Morales, Jorge Luis
Muñoz, Manuel
Muñoz Igartua, Angel
Muñoz Marin, Luis
Muñoz Rivera, Luis

Negrón Flores, Ramón
Negrón Sanjuro, José A.
Núñez, Guillermo

Oliver Frau, Antonio
Ortiz Stella, Cruz

Pachin Marin (pseudonym for Francisco González [or Gonzalo] Marin)
Padilla, José Gualberto (a.k.a. "El Caribe")
Padilla de Sanz, Trina (a.k.a. La Hija del Caribe)
Padro, Humberto
Palés Matos, Gustavo
Palés Matos, Luis
Palés Matos, Vicente
Palma, Marigloria (pseudonym for Gloria Maria Palma)
Parilla, Joaquin R.
Peach (pseudonym for José P.H. Hernández)
Pedreira, Antonio S.
Pérez Losada, José
Pérez Pierret, Antonio
Porrata Doria de Aponte, Carmen (pseudonym: Carmen Demar)
Porrata Doria de Rincón, Providencia (pseudonym: Alma Rubens)
Puigdollers, Carmen

Quiles, Luis A. Rosario
Quiñones, Francisco Mariano (pseudonym: A. Kadosh)
Quiñones Vizcarrondo, Samuel René

Rafael, Juan Vicente (pseudonym for (Padre) Juan Rivera Viera)
Ramirez Santibanes, José
Ramirez de Arellano, Haydée
Ramirez de Arellano Rechani, Diana
Rechani Agrait, Luis
Rentas Lucas, Eugenio
Riancho Escobales, Providencia
Ribera Chevremont, Evaristo
Ribera Chevremont, José Joaquin
Rigau, Angel

Rivera Landrón, Francisco
Rivera-Otero, Rafael
Rivera Viera, (Padre) Juan (pseudonym: Juan Vicente Rafael)
Rodriguez Cabrero, Luis
Rodriguez Calderon, Juan
Rodriguez de Tio, Lola
Rojas Tollinchi, Francisco
Rosa-Nieves, Cesáreo
Rubens, Alma (pseudonym for Providencia Porrata Doria de Rincón)

Sama, Manuel Maria
Samela Iglesias, Luis
Sánchez, Luis Rafael
Sanchez de Fuente y Pelaez, Eugenio (assoc. with Cuba)
Siaca Rivera, Manuel
Sierra Berdecia, Fernándo
Soto, Pedro Juan
Soto Ramos, Julio
Soto Vélez, Clemente
Sulsona de Cadilla, Elia

Tapia y Rivera, Alejandro
Thomas, Piri

Vassallo y Cabrera, Francisco
Vicens, Nimia
Vicente Rafael, Juan (pseudonym for Padre Juan Rivera Viera)
Vidarte, Santiago
Villaronga Charriez, Luis
Vivas Maldonado, José Luis
Vizcarrondo, Carmelina
Vizcarrondo, Fortunato

Yumet Méndez, José

Zapata Acosta, Ramón
Zavala, Iris M.
Zeno Gandia, Manuel

Volume IV Entries: A to Z

ABRIL Y OSTALO, Mariano

. 1861, San Juan, Puerto Rico; d. 1935.
'oet, journalist, biographer, historian, statesman.

:ditor of *El Clamor* and later of *La)emocracia,* Abril was a polemical writer f powerful opinions which led to his ıcarceration in Spain after a military trial s a politically dangerous person. In his almer later years he served as a deputy nd as a senator in the local legislature epresenting Guayama and at his death 'as the official historian of Puerto Rico.

Vritings: Poetry: *Amorosas,* 1906, introduction y Luis Lloréns Torres.
History: *El socialismo moderno,* 1911.
Biography: *Antonio Valera de Bernabe.*

iographical/Critical Sources: Félix Matos ernier, *Isla de arte,* San Juan, Impr. La rimavera, 1907 (essays on various cultural gures including Zeno Gandia, Luis Muñoz ivera and Abril); Ana Margarita Silva, *Mariano bril y Ostalo: su vida y su obra (1861-1935),* an Juan, Edit. Club de la Prensa, 1966, 174 p. with bibliography.

ACOSTA Y BELLO, Agustin

. 1886, Cuba.
oet, lawyer, politician.

n active "modernista," Acosta produced any poem's but usually collected them nly years later in very modestly sized ollections. Only the tiny *Ultimos inantes* volumes of 1941 returns to the te 19th century themes and tones of ubén Dario.

'ritings: Ala, 1915, 1958; *Hermanita,* 1923; *os camellos distantes,* 1936; *Ultimos instantes,* 1941; *Las islas desoladas,* 1943, all Havana.

ADSUAR BONETA, Jorge

b. 1883, Bayamón, Puerto Rico; d. 1926, San Juan.
Critic, essayist, journalist.

After local schooling, Adsuar travelled in Europe and South America and became, on establishing himself at home, a member of the "modernista" group. He contributed to *El Carnaval* in 1911 and was a regular writer for *Puerto Rico Ilustrado* for many years. His prose style was direct but of a certain light liricism. Antonio S. Pedreira called him the "creador de la entrevista literaria, apicarada, sencilla, fina y elegante."

His best scattered journalistic pieces were published in 1916 and 1925.

Writings: Essays: *Allá va eso,* 1916; *Pico a Pico,* 1925; "¡Blanca!" from *Pico a Pico* appears in L. Hernández Aquino's *El Modernismo en Puerto Rico,* San Juan, 1967.

AGUIAR, Enrique

b. 1887, Dominican Republic; d. 1947.
Poet, novelist.

Aguiar wrote his early poetry under the influence of the French poet Alfred de Musset. His verse is erotic, descriptive, and often religious.

Writings: Poetry: *Desfile de penumbras,* 1913, second edition 1927; *Exaltación a la América Española,* 1921; *Jardines de Psiquis,* Paris, 1926; *Gritos de la sangre,* Paris, 1927; *Gesto de prócer,* 1937.

Literary Criticism: *La ciudad intelectual,* Bogota, 1938.

Novels: *Eusebio Sapote, novela,* Bogota, 1938; *Don Cristobal,* Bogota, 1939; "Fray Bartolomé de Las Casas," unpublished.

AGUIRRE, Mirta

b. 1912, Cuba.
Poet, critic.

Aguirre was educated in Cuba and earned a law degree. Her work is cerebral and often hermetic. Nevertheless, she is a "social" poet and writer whose work balances the highly personal with the harsh daily world "outside." She was interested in metrical experiments and was active in the vanguardista movement. Portuondo called her a poet of sadness and of hope.

She has published important essays on Cervantes and Romain Roland, the French novelist, and has done much theatre criticism.

Writings: Poetry: *Presencia interior,* Havana, 1938; *Poemas de la mujer del preso,* Havana, Talleres Tipográficos Carasa, 1932; *El rio con sed,* Havana, Cuadernos 'Isla,' 1956; and some of her work is in *Ofrenda Lirica de Cuba a la Unión Soviética,* Havana, by Frente Nacional Antifacista, 1942 (during Batista's first full term 1940-1944); and *Isla con Sol* (poems for children).

Biographical/Critical Sources: Polly F. Harrison, "Images and Exile: The Cuban Woman and Her Poetry," in *Revista Interamericana,* Vol. IV, No. 2 (Summer 1974), esp. pp. 204-208.

ALBALADEJO, Mariano

b. 1884, Matanzas, Cuba; d. 1955.
Poet.

Albaladejo's verse generally touched upon the sea.

Writings: Poetry: *Poesias,* Havana, 1957; much verse appeared in miscellaneous journals.

ALCANTARA ALMANZAR, José

b. May 2, 1946, Santo Domingo, Dominican Republic.
Storywriter, sociologist, teacher.

Alcántara's stories are "psychological" and usually deal with exotic and difficult situations. He has studied in the United States and knows North American literature well. He took special American literature courses at the Instituto Cultural Dominico-Americano and in Guadeloupe took franco-phone and French literature courses at the Centre International d'Etudes Françaises at Pointe-à-Pitre. His

doctorate was in sociology at the Universidad Autónoma de Santo Domingo, and after teaching there he took a position at the Free University Pedro Henriquez Ureña in Santo Domingo. In 1977 Alcántara was elected president of the Dominican Association of Sociology.

His second collection of stories, *Callejón sin salida* (1975) are varied in technique and point of view but most are concerned with the urban world which is both a hostile and compelling arena of activity. The characters despair and struggle in an anxious, often political and esthetic jungle and the feeling is that the entire culture is rapidly moving to "descomposición total."

Writings: Stories: *Viaje al otro mundo,* S.D., Taller, 1973; *Callejón sin salida,* S.D., Taller, 1975.

Editor and Author of Critical Essays (as introduction): *Antologia de la literatura dominicana,* S. Domingo, Edit. Cultural Dominicana, 1972; in progress are several other anthologies of Dominican writers.

Sociological Essays: in various sociological reviews beginning in 1970.

ALEGRIA, José S.

b. 1887, Dorado, Puerto Rico; d. 1965.
Storywriter, poet, journalist.

After taking a degree in law, Alegria entered a career of journalism, becoming the publisher of the *Revista Puerto Rico Ilustrado.* He joined the "costumbrismo" movement with his verse collection *Retablo de la Aldea,* published in 1949.

In public affairs he was active most of his life and was a founder of the Nationalist Party of Puerto Rico.

Writings: Poetry: *Retablo de la Aldea,* 1949; his "Romeria de recuerdos" is in the *Antologia de la poesia puertorriqueña,* E. Fernández Méndez, ed., San Juan, 1968.

Political Essays: *Pancho Ibero encadenado,* 1918.

ALFONSECA, Miguel

b. 1942, Santo Domingo, Dominican Republic.
Poet, storywriter, journalist, actor, educator.

Alfonseca is closely identified with the War of April, 1965, and his angry verses against the American occupation are both stark and vehement. His stories, too, are the harshest of any written during the period in their treatment of the American presence. His collection *El Enemigo* (1970) continues his assault and broadens to an almost epical power.

Then, as if saddened and weakened by the passage of ineffectual years, his work takes a turn to a subtle and almost evasive style, and becomes highly individualistic and opaque.

One of his stories won the "Concurso de Cuentos" awarded by *La Máscara* in 1966, and other stories earned prizes in 1967, 1969 and 1971.

Writings: Stories: *El Enemigo,* Santo Domingo, Talleres de la UASD, 1970; and in various collections including the story "La Boca" in José Alcántara Almánzar's *Antologia de la literatura dominicana.*

ALFONSECA, Ricardo Pérez

b. 1892, Dominican Republic; d. 1950.
Poet.

Alfonseca's "Canto a la independencia" was a stirring call to patriotism and helped establish his country's interest in his work.

Writings: Poetry: *Mármoles y lirios,* 1909; *Oda de un Yo,* 1913; *Finis Patria,* 1914; *Canto a la independencia,* 1920; *Palabras de mi madre y otros poemas,* 1925.

Prose: *El último evangelio,* Havana, 1927; *Juan de Nueva York o El Antinarciso,* 1930.

History: *Los diez mil de Trujillo,* 1936.

ALFONSO, Domingo

b. 1925, Jovellanos (Province of Matanzas), Cuba.
Poet, architect.

Alfonso completed his schooling in Matanzas where he was active in youth groups. His first publication was in 1958 and from then on he contributed to many journals and his work began to appear in anthologies, both Cuban and foreign. In 1970 he began studies in architecture at the University of Havana and prepared a new volume of poetry for the press, *Historia de una persona.* His style is harsh and direct.

Writings: Poetry: *Sueño en el papel,* Havana, Organización Nacional de Bibliotecas Ambulantes y Populares, 1959; *Poemas del hombre común,* Havana, Unión, 1964; *Historia de una persona,* Havana, Unión, 1968. His "Arte poética" is in *Writers in the New Cuba,* J.M. Cohen, ed., Harmondsworth, England, Penguin, 1967.

ALFONSO, Paco

b. 1906, Cuba.
Playwright, actor, stage director.

Alfonso, long time member of the Partido Socialista Popular (Communist Party) of Cuba, composed many plays with stark propagandistic intent. Using generally the free burlesque form of the Italian *commedia dell'arte,* he wrote numerous plays exploiting rural and proletariat themes, characters and idiom.

His *Hierba hedionda* (1951) attacks racism and is an example of the new uses of Afro-Cuban folklore and vestigal African religious briefs as were his earlier *Yari-yari, mamá Olúa* where he uses drums, dances, massed groups, etc., to set the "African" scene. His *Mambises y guerrilleros* and *Dos madres* permit him to compare the life of the revolutionary past of the independence period with the corrupt present. His *Voces en la trinchera* (1936) shows the anti-fascist point of view on the Spanish civil war.

Writings: Plays: *Mambises y guerrilleros; Dos madres; Voces en la trinchera; Yari-yari, mamá Olúa; Y vinieron las tiñosas,* 1940; *Seguimos comiendo harina,* 1941; *El caso del dia,* 1946; *Demandas del pueblo,* 1939; *Era un hombre del pueblo; Toros en la Habana* (Afro-cuban farce); *Sabanimar,* 1943; *Hierba hedionda,* 1951, as *Yerba hedionda* (tres actes), Havana, Pagrán, 1959.

ALGARIN, Miguel

b. ca. 1940, Santurce, Puerto Rico.
Playwright, poet, critic, translator, director and producer, teacher.

Algarin teaches English literature at Livingston College, Rutgers University. Translator of Pablo Neruda's *Canción de Gesta* (A Song of Protest), he has been deeply involved with the Nuyorican Playwrights'/Actors' Workshop in New York City which aims to develop both actors and playwrights. He has published three volumes of poetry and is completing a novel.

Writings: Play: *Olú Clemente,* performed at the Delacorte Theater, New York, 1973.

Translation: *Canción de Gesta,* by Pablo Neruda, New York, William Morrow and Co., 1977.

Editor (with Miguel Gómez Piñero) of anthology: *Nuyorican Poetry: An Anthology of Puerto Rican Words and Feelings,* New York, William Morrow and Co., 1975.

ALIX, Juan Antonio

(a.k.a. **Papa Toño**)
b. 1833, Moca, Dominican Republic; d. 1918.
Poet.

Born into a wealthy family, Alix began writing poetry in his 16th year, mostly the ten line décimas. His home was Santiago but his interests embraced the entire life of his nation.

Considered the most important of Dominica's "popular" poets for his originality, force, and drive, Alix was one of the broadest of the "folk" poets for subject matter and treatment of his themes. Other writers were limited to one locality or were to some degree reflective of imported influences as was the case with Nicolás Ureña and his Cuban "local color" songs, but Alix wandered over the entire country and was always fresh in his approach to nativist material, and a gifted user of the local creole. Most of his work appeared in ephemeral broadsides and journals. Many of his works had political purposes, but his dialogue "El dominicano y el haitiano" is considered a landmark in Dominican poetry and has been closely studied by later generations of local poets.

Alix lived by his broadsides and according to one authority, in his home area of Santiago he was idolized by the country men and each citizen looked forward to the newest of his political or ribald décimas. Although the edition of 1927 of his works was poorly organized, an orderly reading of his works therein presents the proof of his artless art full of a sunny panorama of daily life and the events of the larger political world, yet with its harsh storms and cruelties too.

Writings: Poetry: *Décimas de Juan Antonio Alix,* Dominican Republic, 1927, prologue by José Ramón López; republished and edited by Joaquín Balaguer in Vols. 8 and 9 of the Colección Pensamiento Dominicano, Ciudad Trujillo, Libreria Dominicana (Postigo), 1961. This edition has an introduction by Balaguer.

Poetry: in various collections, including Rodriguez Demorizi's *Poesia popular dominicana,* in which appears "Diálogo entre la paz y la guerra," first published in *El Nacional,* No. 52 (Jan. 2, 1875); "Un Pasaporte dado en tiempo de la España vieja," and "Diálogo Cantada: entre un Guajiro dominicano y un Papá boco haitiano en un fandango en Dajabón," were first reported in the journal *La Nueva Era,* Cibao (Apr. 18, 1874), but were not included in the 1927 collection of his work; the latter poem was first published in *El Anunciador,* Nos. 112 and 113 (Nov. 14 and Dec. 10, 1934), printed in Santiago de los Caballeros, with original notes by Alix. This poem also employs the peculiar constructions of the peasants of the Cibao region and the Haitian, a bizarre mixture—half the patois of the Haiti border area and half folk-Spanish. Also the décima "Un testigo ocular," and "Jatuai con le puela pueta," written in 1890, appear in the Rodriguez Demorizi collection.)

Biographical/Critical Sources: J. Balaguer's *Juan Antonio Alix* (décimas), 2 vols, S. Dom., Postigo, 1961.

ALMANZAR, Armando

b. ca. 1933, Santo Domingo, Dominican Republic, 1935.

Storywriter, cinema critic, journalist/public relations.

Almánzar won a first prize in the La Máscara competition of 1966 for one of his stories.

Writings: Story: *Limite,* 1967.

ALONSO, Dora

b. December 22, 1910, Máximo Gómez (Matanzas), Cuba.

Storywriter, novelist, playwright, journalist, poet.

After broken studies in a Cárdenas high school, Dora Alonso did much writing on her own, winning in 1931 a prize offered by the journal *Bohemia* for her story "Humildad." Moving to Havana in 1935, she became an active contributor to many Latin American journals. Her later stories have won prizes from the Ministry of Education and she has written several plays.

Her first novel, *Tierra adentro* (1944), won the Premio Nacional de la Dirección de Cultura and the novel *Tierra inerme* won a prize in the Concurso de la Casa de las Américas, 1961. Her earliest work, the play *Cain* (1955), attacked racism.

Writings: Plays: *Cain o La hora de estar ciegos,* 1955; *La casa de los sueños,* 19??.

Novels: *Tierra adentro,* Havana, 1944; *Tierra inerme,* Havana, Casa de las Américas, 1961, second edition, Havana, Unión, 1964; and Russian translation: *Bezzaschitnaia zemlia; roman,* Moscow, Izdvo inostr. lit., 1963; *Ponolani,* Havana, Granma, 1966.

Stories and Articles: in many journals and anthologies.

Stories: *Aventura de Guille, en busca de la gaviota negra,* Havana, Juvenil, 1966; *Ponolani,* Havana, Granma, 1966; *Once caballos,* Havana, Unión, 1970.

ALONSO Y PACHECO, Manuel

b. 1822, Caguas, Puerto Rico; d. 1889.
Storywriter, poet, anecdotist.

Son of a professional military man, Alonso studied at the Seminary of San Juan del Padre Rufo Manuel Fernández. After receiving his doctorate in medicine from the University of Barcelona, he traveled to his father's home town in Galicia and then to Madrid, where he practiced his profession with great success. There he collaborated with Juan Bautista, Santiago Vidarte, Francisco Vasallo and Pablo Saez on the *Album Puertorriqueño* (1844), the first manifestation of the literature of his homeland. The work is a collection of prose and verse and is the foundation stone of subsequent developments in island writing.

Alonso was a master of common speech and a close observer of rural ways, all reflected in his *El Jibaro* (1849), a collection of essays on 19th century Puerto Rico, also the first of its kind by a native Puerto Rican, and rich with the patois of the countryman as well as of the urban creole.

When Spanish intellectuals were persecuted during the aftermath of the abortive 1868 revolution in Spain, Alonso was forced to flee to Lisbon whence he soon returned to Puerto Rico. Establishing a new practice, he turned with re-invigorated interest to his study of local manners but evading political identification in his quiet way.

Manuel Fernández Juncos said of him:

> *Escriba con sencillez y gracia, era ingenioso yagudo en el decir, tenia una facundia admirable para improvisar y contrar cuentos y anédotas, y nadie dió en su tiempo tan exacto colorido como él a la pintura de costumbres campesinas puertorriqueños* (from the *Antologia Puertorriqueña*).

Alonso was editor of a periodical, *El Agente,* and in his later years he was director of the Asilo de Beneficencia, which evolved into the contemporary insane asylum of San Juan.

Writings: Folk Stories: in journal *Album Puertorriqueño,* 1844 and 1882; *El cancionero de Borinquen,* 1846; *El Jibaro: cuadro de costumbres de la Isla de Puerto Rico,* modern edition, San Juan, 1970 [21 scenes], but Tomo I, Barcelona, Spain, 1849, augmented edition, Tomo II, 1882, *Perico Paciencia,* 1865, new edition with discussion and notes by F. Manrique Cabrera and José Antonio Torres Morales, Rio Piedras, Ed. Colegio Hostos, 1949; *Agapito Avellaneda,* 1880.

Autobiographical Essay: *1833-1883, ¿Perdemos o ganamos?* His story "El sueño de mi compadre" is in the *Antologia puertorriqueña,* M. Fernández Juncos, ed., New York, 1907, pp. 20-29.

Biographical/Critical Sources: Ernesto Juan Fonfrias, *Presencia jibara desde Manuel Alonso hasta Don Florito,* San Juan, 1957; F. Manrique Cabrera, *Historia de la literatura puertorriqueña,* San Juan, 1969, pp. 82-103; Modesto Rivera Rivera, *Concepto y expresión del costumbrismo en Manuel A. Alonso Pacheco, El Gibaro,* published, Mexico, 1952 (217 pp.); Modesto Rivera, *Manuel A. Alonso: su vida y su obra,* San Juan, Edit. Coqui, 1966 (144 pp. with bibliography).

ALVAREZ RIOS, Maria

b. 1919, Cuba.
Playwright, painter.

Alvárez' best work is the comic vein,

though she had some success with the serious dramas, *La hiena* and *La victima.* Her best comedy is thought to be *Marti 9.* All of her work takes a jaundiced eye at the foibles of the present.

Writings: Plays: *El maridito de Beba Fraga,* 1948; *No quiero llamarme Juana,* 1948; *La Habana y un millón; Lila se decide; Marti 9,* 1949; *La hiena; La victima,* (tres actos), Havana, Pagrán, 1959.

AMADEO ANTOMARCHI, Jesús Maria

b. May 4, 1856, Salinas, Puerto Rico; d. June 27, 1927, Bayomón.

Storywriter, novelist, essayist, playwright.

Amadeo was one of the most prolific of Puerto Rico's writers, author of six novels and at least five plays.

Writings: Essays: *Una plaga social y La plegaria de una virgen,* San Juan, Tip. La Correspondencia, 1894, winner of bronze medal as scientific essay from the Esposición de Puerto Rico; second part of *Una plaga: Un pétalo de una rosa blanca,* San Juan, La Correspondencia, 1894 [314 pp.].

Novels and Novelettes: *Olga Duroc,* San Juan, Heraldo Español, 1907 (105 pp.); *Olimpio,* Bayamón, Tip. El Progresso, 1912, (132 pp.); *Mademoiselle de Monmari,* Bayamón, Imp. Variedades, 1919, (346 pp.); *El profeta,* San Juan, La Correspondencia, 1920, (301 pp.); *Maria Duplessis,* San Juan, Imp. Venezuela, 1926, (250 pp.); *Marengo,* details unknown, but unpublished.

Plays: *Avendamor,* [fantasy]; *Don Pepe* [comedy]; *La Capa azul; Maldita Venus; Verdún.*

AMADO BLANCO, Luis

b. April 4, 1903, Asturias, Spain.

Playwright, storywriter, novelist, poet.

Amado arrived in Cuba in 1933 and became a citizen in 1936. His first poetry saw print as early as 1928.

Amado won the Premio Hernández Catá in 1951 for his story "Sola" and won recognition for other pieces of his short fiction. His one novel, *Ciudad rebelde,* appeared in 1967, and was written in Rome where he was serving as Cuban ambassador to the Vatican (since 1961). It deals with the last years of the Batista regime. He wrote one play, *Suicidio.* Amado's wife Isabel Fernández authored two works for the theatre in collaboration with Cuqui Ponce.

Writings: Play: *Suicidio.*

Stories: *Un pueblo y dos agonias,* 19??; stories appeared in various journals and collections. *Doña Velorio (nueve cuentos y una nivola),* Santa Clara, Universidad Central de Las Vilas, 1960, and Barcelona, Nova Terra, 1970.

Novel: *Ciudad rebelde,* Barcelona, Nova Terra, 1967.

AMADOR, Amérigo

(pseudonym: **Manuel De Elzaburu**)

AMIAMA, Francisco Javier

b. March 29, 1849, Dominican Republic; d. July 3, 1914, Santo Domingo.

Novelist.

Amiama's one novel was one of the earliest "local color" works of fiction to be written in the Dominican Republic.

Writings: Novelette: *Adela o Angel del consuelo,* S. Domingo, Edit. Garcia Hermanos, 1872.

AMY, Francisco J.

b. August 2, 1837, Arroyo, Puerto Rico; d. November 30, 1912.

Poet, translator, journalist.

At 14 years, Amy moved to the United States where he entered Episcopal Academy, Cheshire, Connecticut, and at 17 was contributing essays and verse in English to *Waverley Magazine* and other

New England reviews. After seven years in the U.S. he returned to Puerto Rico in 1858 with a richer knowledge of the Anglo-Saxon power to the north than any Puerto Rican of the mid-century. Although offered interesting positions with foreign trading firms he found the colonial atmosphere stifling and soon returned to the United States and became a naturalized citizen of that country.

Tempted once again to work in Ponce, Puerto Rico, in the mid-1880's, he joined Dr. Zeno Gandia in founding the literary-scientific journal *El Estudio* and during this period published a volume of poems, most of them his translations of foreign verse, in *Ecos y notas* (1884).

Back in the United States once more, he published *Letras de Molde,* mixed prose and verse, and a translation into English of Alarcón's *El sombrero de tres picos* called *The Cocked Hat.* In New York he helped edit *La Gaceta Ilustrada* and contributed articles to both English and Spanish language journals. The one collected volume of these journalistic pieces produced during this period was *Predicar en desierto.* Possibly his most valuable work was in rendering the classic American and British poets into Spanish and Spanish and Latin-Caribbean poets into English in the bi-lingual anthology *Musa Bilingüe* (1903). This work and his earlier pieces and verse may well have contributed to modernizing and simplifying Puerto Rican verse techniques. Manuel Fernández Junco wrote "Su estilo, como su carácter, era sobrio, preciso, austero a veces, pero siempre decoroso y correcto."

Writings: Poetry (with some prose): *Ecos y notas,* 1884; *Letras de Molde,* details not known.

Collection of Journalistic Pieces: *Predicar en desierto,* San Juan, Tip. El Alba, 1907.

Translations: *El sombrero de tres picos* by Alarcón, translated into English as *The Cocked Hat; Musa bilingüe* [bi-lingual Spanish language poems into English and American and British poems into Spanish], 1903.

ANGULO GURIDI, Alejandro

b. May 3, 1822, Santo Domingo, Dominican Republic; d. 1906.

Novelist, storywriter.

Angulo's *Los amores...* was the first Dominican novel or prose treatment of the Indians though the Indians treated were natives of Cuba (where the Angulo family had fled after the Haitian invasion of the Spanish portion of Hispaniola) rather than of the natives of his own country. The work owes something to the Chateaubriand novels *René* and *Atala.* He lived in Cuba only during his youth but published one novelette, *La Venganza de un hijo,* on a Cuban theme [the work was co-authored by Blanchie, a Cuban].

Writings: Novelettes: *Los amores de los indios,* Cuba, 1843; *La venganza de un hijo,* 1842 (written with Francisco Javier Blanchie of Cuba); *La joven Carmela,* La Clara, 1841.

Story: "Cecilia," in *El Progreso,* Santo Domingo, 1853.

Literary Criticism: in various journals, including *El Prisma,* Havana, 1846.

Politics: *Temas politicos,* 2 vols., Santiago de Chile, 1891.

Essays: *¿Quién es Modesto Molina? Azotaina biográfica,* Arica, Chile, 1896; *Observaciones criticas acerca de un libro de D. F. Burton,* Managua, Nicaragua, 1902.

ANGULO GURIDI, Francisco Xavier (or Javier)

b. December 3, 1816, Santo Domingo, Dominican Republic; d. San Pedro de Macoris, December 7, 1884.

Poet, novelist, playwright, folklorist, journalist, statesman.

Francisco Xavier Angulo Guridi was the first son of S. Domingo to publish a volume of verse with Dominican themes, *Ensayos Poéticos* (1843). Fleeing his homeland in 1822 with his family because of the Haitian invasion, he grew up in

Puerto Rico, but as a young writer was an active contributor to the Cuban journals *La Prensa, Brisas de Cuba, Alborada de Villa Clara,* and the *Revista de la Habana.* It was during this time he published his volume dedicated to his long lost home, *A la vista de Santo Domingo* (1853).

On returing to S. Domingo he became active in journalism and politics, and for a period was a senator. He founded several journals which took strong political stands and he consequently often suffered exile. He remained outspoken, however, and took an energetic role in restoring independence by expelling the Spanish occupation and he was a signatory of the "Acta de Independencia" in 1863.

Throughout his life he was also busy writing on many subjects other than politics and today is seen as one of the great Dominican patriots and humanists. Nevertheless, he is best remembered as an exploiter of the Amerindian motif, particularly for his stories "Maguanas" (1840), and "La Cuita" (1842). His one published play, *Iguaniona,* is his best known work for the stage.

Writings: Poetry: *Ensayos Poéticos,* Puerto Principe, Camagüey, Cuba, 1843; *A la vista de Santo Domingo,* 1853; "Talebard," in ms. only.

Folklore: *La fantasma de Higüey,* 1857.

Legends, Stories: *La imprudencia de un marido,* 1869; *Una situación poco envidiable,* 1869; *El Panorama* (Part I published in *El Universal,* 1872, and Part II, "Paulino," in same journal, 1873, and again in Rodriguez Demorizi's *Tradiciones y cuentos dominicanos,* 1969.

Novelettes: "La campaña del Higo," "La ciguapa," 1868; "Silvao": all in *El Tiempo,* 1866, and then in a single volume, S. Domingo, 1866. The legend "La ciguapa" was republished in 1876.

Plays: *Los apuros de un destierro* (one act); *El Conde de Leos,* performed to great applause, May 3, 1868, S. Domingo. *Los apuros* is written in the dialect of Curacao called Papiamento, and was read in a "concert" version in 1868; *Cacharros y manigüeros* (a three-act comedy), unpublished, but performed Oct. 11, 1867, in S. Domingo; *Don Junipero,* performed 1868; *Iguaniona,* written in 1867, but published in 1881.

Geography: *Geografia de la Isla,* 1866; *Elementos de geografia fisico-histórica antigua y moderna de la Isla de Santo Domingo,* 1866.

Articles: "Un episodio de la Restauración," in *El Sol* (S. Domingo, Feb. 1870); "Un dolor mata" [historical legends of the Spanish restorati period 1861 and after], in *El Dominicano,* (Feb. 1874); and "Recuerdos de Palo Hincado," in *Clio,* No. 89 (1951), edited by Alfau Durán with notes by Angulu Guridi attached.

Biographical/Critical Sources: Rafael A. Deligne's "Javier Angulo Guridi, estudio critico," in *Letras y Ciencias* (S. Domingo, Nov. 30, 1894); José Castellanos' *Lira de Quisqueya;* Max Henriques Ureña's *Panorama Histórico de la Literatura Dominicana;* A. Cometta Manzoni's *El Indio en la Poesia de la América Española,* Buenos Aires, 1939 (see esp. p. 185); J. Balaguer's *Los Próceseres escritores,* Buenos Aires, 1947, p. 204; E. Rodriguez Demorizi's *Próceseres de la Restauración,* (S. Domingo, 1963) has extensive biographic information on Angulo Guridi.

APONTE, José Agustin

b. ca. 1857, Aguadilla, Puerto Rico;
d. after 1905.
Poet.

Aponte's poetry is influenced by Salvador Diaz Mirón and is considered the most original follower of the popular poet at the end of the long romantic movement. *Flores y nubes* (1887), his first volume, is redolent of Diaz Mirón, and even his second collection, *Ecos del nuevo mundo* (1905), is touched by Mirón, as can be seen in these lines from "Sur la breche," published in that volume:

Rompe tu inmuda cárcel; desafia
los dardos de la envidia, que te abruma;
abre tus blancas alas, en el dia,
y lo mismo que el sándalo: ¡perfuma!

Writings: Poetry: *Flores y nubes,* Mayagüez, Puerto Rico, Tip. Comercial, 1887; *Ecos del nuevo mundo,* Mayagüez, Puerto Rico, Imp. El Progreso, 1905.

Biographical/Critical Sources: "Poesia Mironiana," by Enrique A. Laguerre, in *La poesia modernista en Puerto Rico,* San Juan, Edit. Coqui, 1969, pp. 29-33; Félix Matos Bernier, *Isla de arte,* San Juan, Imp. La Primavera, 1907, pp. 181-184.

A. R.

(pseudonym for **Enrique JIMENEZ SOLA**)

ARANA, Felipe N.

b. 1902, Hatillo, Puerto Rico.
Poet, journalist.

A late follower of the "costumbrista" movement led by Virgilio Dávila, Arana has been living in the United States since the 1960's. C. Rosa-Nieves said of his poetry that it demonstrates:

> *. . . una temática variada, tesoro de emociones intimas, de acercamientos cordiales; jibarismo poético, amor, paisaje narcista, beatus ille, carpe diem, festivismo epigramático . . .*

His "Armonia" begins:

Vida es lucha. Mirad le piedra amiga
de la playa como soporta a solas
los azotes del mar que la castiga
con el foete de espumas de las olas.

Writings: Poetry: *Florecillas silvestres,* 1927; *Retoños liricos,* 1933; *Música aldeana,* 1934; *Antena,* 1937; and *Sementera,* 1945.

ARCE, José de

(pseudonym for **Manuel MARTINEZ DAVILA**)

ARCE DE VAZQUEZ, Margot

b. March 10, 1892, Caguas, Puerto Rico.
Critic, literary historian, teacher.

After taking the B.A. at the University of Puerto Rico and the doctorate in philosophy and letters at the Universidad Central de Madrid, Margot Arce de Vázquez became a professor in the Department of Hispanic Studies at her home university, and, in time, Director of the department.

Writings: Literary Histories: *Garcilaso de la Vega,* Madrid, Ed. Hernando, 1931; *Vienticinco años del ensayo puertorriqueño, 1930-1955* (with Mariana Robles de Cardona), 1955; *Impresiones,* San Juan, Ed. Yaurel, 1950 [148 pp.]; *Gabriela Mistral: persona y poesia,* 1958, and awarded the Premio del Instituto de Literatura Puertorriqueña, translated as *The Poet and Her Work* by Helene Masslo Anderson, New York, New York University Press, 1964; *Lecturas puertorriqueñas: poesia* (with Laura Gallego and Luis de Arrigoitia), Sharon, Conn., Troutman Press, 1966, San Juan, 1968; *La obra literaria de José de Diego,* San Juan, Instituto de Cultura puertorriqueña, 1967; extracts of her work as "Puerto Rico en las canciones de Rafael Hernández" and "El paisaje de Puerto Rico," are in Edgar Martinez Masdeu and Esther M. Melon's anthology, *Literatura puertorriqueña,* second edition, Vol. II, Rio Piedras, 1972, pp. 209-223.

Biographical/Critical Sources: José Luis Martin, *Arco y flecha (A puntando a la vida y a las obras): Estudias de critica literaria),* San Juan, Edit. Club de la Prensa, 1961 [chapter on Margot Arce]; Jose Ferrer Canales, *Acentos civicos: Marti, Puerto Rico y otros temas,* San Juan, 1972 [essay devoted to Arce].

ARCOCHA, Juan

b. 1927, Santiago de Cuba, Cuba.
Novelist, journalist.

After serving as editorial assistant to Carlos Franqui on the newspaper *Revolución Lunes,* the important early literary magazine published under Castro, Arcocha was sent to Moscow as a correspondent in 1962. He stayed there but one year, returning with his new Russian wife to Havana to publish a pro-communist novel, *Los muertos andan solos* (1962). Then assigned to Paris in 1963, Arcocha broke amicably with the Castro regime to stay on to work for UNESCO.

His second novel, *A Candle in the Wind,* though not reflective of his more critical view of Castro, does picture the grossly ineffective efforts of the Cuban communists to improve conditions in Cuba. His fourth novel, *La bala perdida* (1973) is another of his non-fiction novels, this one recreating his years of exile.

Writings: Novels: *Los muertos andan solos,* Havana, Revolucion, 1962, second edition, 1963; *A Candle in the Wind* (anon. translator), New York, Lyle Stuart, 1967, one chapter appearing in *Casa de las Américas,* Nos. 22-23 (Jan-Apr 1964); *Por cuento propia, 1970; La bala perdida,* 1973.

Biographical/Critical Sources: See Arcocha's discussion of controversy surrounding first edition of *Los muertos andan solos* in the introduction to second edition of *Los muertos* (1963); also see Seymour Menton's *Prose Fiction of the Cuban Revolution,* Austin, Texas, University of Texas Press, 1975.

ARENAL, Humberto

b. 1927, Havana, Cuba.
Novelist, storywriter, critic, play director.

In exile in the United States and Mexico for some eleven years in the 1940's and 1950's, Arenal returned to Cuba after the advent of Castro. Since his return he has become a director of plays, and written much theatre criticism, and published novels and many short stories. His novel *El sol a plomo* may be considered the earliest of the revolutionary novels predicated on the events of Castro's efforts and final success.

Writings: Novels: *El sol a plomo,* New York, Las Americas Publishing Co., 1958, translated as *The Sun Beats Down, a novella of the Cuban Revolution,* Jos. M. Bernstein, trans., New York, Hill & Wang, 1959, 2nd Cuban ed., Havana, Cruzada Latinoamericana de Difusión Cultural, 1959; *Les animales sagrados,* Mavana, Instituto de Libro, 1967, extract of *Los animales* in *Narrativa cubana de la revolución,* selected by J. M. Caballero Bonald, Madrid, Alianza Editorial, 1968, 1969, 1971.

Stories: *La vuelta en redondo,* Havana, Revolución, 1962; *El tiempo ha descendido,* Havana, Revolución, 1964.

ARENAS, Reinaldo
(or **Reyaldo**)

b. 1943, Holguin (Oriente), Cuba.
Novelist, storywriter.

Arenas studied at the Escuela de Planificación and the University of Havana and worked for many years at the Instituto de Reforma Agraria and the Biblioteca Circulante José Marti. His stories have appeared in such journals as *Unión* and *Casa de las Américas.*

His novel *El mundo alucinante* is a fictionalized biography of the Mexican hero Fray Servando Teresa de Mier. The earlier *Celestino antes del alba,* influenced by William Faulkner and Miguel Angel Asturias, pictures the poverty of rural Cuba.

Writings: Novels: *Celestino antes del alba,* Havana, Ed. Uniones, 1967 and Buenos Aires, Ed. Brújula, 1968; *Le puit,* Paris, 1973; *El mundo alucinante,* Mexico, Ed. Diógenes, 1969 and in French as *Le monde hallucinant,* Paris, 1969, and in English (as *Hallucinations,* trans. by Gordon Brotherston, London, Penguin, 1976), American, German, Dutch, Italian, Portuguese and Argentine editions in languages of those areas; *Le palais des très blanche mouffettes,* translated from Spanish by D. Coste into French, published Paris, Seuil, 1975.

Stories: *Con los ojos cerrados,* Uruguay, 1972; in various journals and collections; "El hijo y la madre," appears in *Narrativa cubana de la revolución,* J.M. Caballero Bonald, ed., Madrid, 1969; "Celestino y yo," in *Unión,* No. 3 (July-Sep. 1967).

Biographical/Critical Sources: Seymour Mentor, *The Cuban Novel of the Revolution,* Austin, Texas, University of Texas Press, 1975; review of *El Mundo Alucinante* in Penguin edition, by Patricia Tobin, "The Author as Escape Artist," in *Review 76* (Winter 1976), pp. 86-87, and earlier review in *Focus* on same novel (Spring 1973).

AREU, Manuel

b. ca. 1871, Cuba.
Playwright.

An all but forgotten playwright, Areu is known to have written at least two plays.

Writings: Plays: *Episodios de la vida de un actor* (cuatro cuadros en prosa y versa), Havana, Imp. La Tipografía, 1901; *Gloria y miseria,* (prose and verse), Havana, Imp. La Tipografia, 1901; performed first time in Albisu Theatre, Havana, June 23, 1900.

ARGUERO, Luis

b. 1937, Consolación del Sur (Pinar del Rio), Cuba.
Storywriter, journalist, critic, novelist.

Forced to abandon his university studies when Batista closed Havana University in 1959, Argüero became a journalist and free-lance writer. After the success of Castro, Argüero began work on radio and television and became chief editor of *La Gaceta de Cuba.* His (still unpublished) second collection of stories won the prize awarded in the Concurso de la Unión de Escritores y Artistas in 1967, the same year as his novel *La vida en dos* appeared.

Writings: Stories: *De aqui para allá,* 1962; "Santa Rita's Holy Water," is in *Writers in the New Cuba,* J. M. Cohen, ed., Harmondsworth, England, Penguin, 1967.

Novel: *La vida en dos,* Havana, 1967.

ARMAS Y CARDENAS, José de

(pseudonym: **"Justo de Lara"**)
b. March 26, 1866, Guanabacoa, Cuba; d. December 28, 1919.
Critic, essayist, biographer, journalist, playwright, lawyer.

One of Cuba's greatest scholars and possibly its purest writer of Castillian, Armas also was a fine linguist and did much critical and appreciative studies of English literature. He was also a leading Cervantes scholar. At 18, he published his first work, "La locura de Sancho" (in *La Nación,* Havana, June 22, 1882). Two years later he published two major studies, one on Vega, the other on his favorite subject, Don Quixote. In the same year he earned his law degree and entered the legal profession.

Armas was a major contributor to the literary pages of the journal *Lunes de la Unión Constitucional* (1888-1892). After his second trip to Spain, Armas founded *Las Avispas* in 1892 which, however, lasted only a few months.

Writings: Plays: *Los triunfadores* (2 acts), by "Justo de Lara," Havana, Imp. El Comercio Tipográfico, 1895, premiered with title *La lucha por la vida* in the Teatro Tacón, Havana, March 27, 1895.

Literary Criticism/Histories: *La Dorotea de Lope de Vega,* Havana, 1884; *El Quijote de Avellaneda y sus criticos,* Havana, 1884; *Cervantes y el Quijote,* Havana, 1905; *Ensayos criticos de literatura inglesa y española,* Madrid, 1910; *Estudios y retratos,* Madrid, 1911; *El Quijote y su época,* Madrid, 1915; *Historia y literatura,* Havana, 1915; *Cervantes en la literatura inglesa* (conference), Madrid, 1916; and other journalistic and historical works, including: "Lo locura de Sancho"; "Los dos Quijotes"; "El error de un ingenio" (J. M. Heredia); "Un precursor de Leopardi, J. Manriques y sus coplas"; "Rubén Dario"; *Treinta y cinco trabajos periodisticos,* Havana, Secretaria de Educación, 1935.

Biographical/Critical Sources: Max Henriquez

Ureña, *Panorama histórico de la literatura cubana,* New York, 1963, pp. 138-143; Antonio L. Villaverde, *Vida y obra de José de Armas y Cárdenas,* Havana, 1923.

ARMAS Y CESPEDES, José de

b. 1834, Guanabacoa, Cuba; d. 1900.
Novelist.

Armas completed his historical novel *Frasquito* in 1864 but was unable to publish it till 30 years later. It deals with the nationalist plot of Frasquito Agüero and Manuel Andrés Sánchez in 1825 and their eventual execution by the colonial government.

Writings: Novels: *Un desafio,* Havana, 1864; *Frasquito,* Havana, 1894, 2nd ed., Havana, 1923.

AROZARENA, Marcelino Esteban Boerrero Echevarria

b. 1912, Havana, Cuba.
Poet.

Arozarena of Cuban-African heritage graduated from the Escuelas Normales de la Habana. He was a founding member of the "Sociedad de Estudios Afrocubanos," and published in *Adelante, Miramar, Revista Bimestre Cubana,* and *El Mundo,* journals interested in the literature of this movement.

The work of José Z. Tallet, Alfonso Camin, Nicolás Guillén, and Alejo Carpentier influenced Arozarena's development and his work is even more full than theirs of African feeling and deals more naturally with such gods as Yemayá, Orumbila, Changó, and Babalú Ayé. Alfonso Camin's poem "La Macoriña" further stimulated Arozarena, he has declared, to create works in the Afro-Cuban mood.

Possibly the most "African" of his poems is "Amelia":

Amalia baila como una llama,
Como una lengua de sed bestial,
Como si fuera su cuerpo crecido arroyo
Como si fuera un jamaqueado majá criollo,
Como si fuera palma en bandera,
Como si fuera
Como si fuera
Como si fuera . . .

In his "Cubandalucia" he mixes rhythms of the rumba and the fandango:

Pacatá
Tacatá
Pacatacataracá
¡Olé! ¡Alsa!

Writings: Poetry: *Canción negra sin color,* Havana, Unión, 1966, contains 18 of his poems written in the 1933-1966 period. His work also appears in many anthologies and appeared in the journals of the day.

Biographical/Critical Sources: Ildefonso Pereda Valdez, *Lo Negro y lo Mulato en la poesia cubana,* Montevideo, Ediciones Ciudadela, 1970.

ARRILLAGA, Maria

b. 1940, Puerto Rico.
Poet, teacher.

After emigrating to New York to study and teach, Arrillaga returned home in 1973 where she now is a professor of Spanish at the University of Puerto Rico. She writes in both English and Spanish and has one collection, "New York in the Sixties," looking for a publisher. Two anthologies in Spanish found print in the past few years.

She has done children's journalism and is completing a novel.

Writings: Poetry: *Vida en el Tiempo,* and *Poemas Supersonic* (1976?): other details not known; in ms., "New York in the Sixties"; The poem "I" appeared in *Melanthika: An Anthology of Pan-Caribbean Writing* (1977).

ARRIVI, Francisco

b. 1915, San Juan, Puerto Rico.
Poet, playwright, literary historian.

Arrivi has devoted most of his adult life to promoting the Puerto Rican theatre and a new concern with local traditions and cultural values. His play *Vejigantes* (1958) is set in two periods, 1910 and 1955, and concerns the Afro-Antillan heroine Clarita and her problems with her North American fiancé. The African roots and folk traditions of Puerto Rico are richly exploited in this three-act play.

Writings: Plays: *Alumbramiento,* 1945; *Maria Soledad,* 1947; early version entitled *Una sombra menos* (the later version of *Maria Soledad* was first performed in 1948); *Caso de muerto en vida,* premiered in 1950; *Bolero y Plena,* 1956; *Vejigantes: comedia en tres actos,* San Juan, 1958, 1968; *Cuento de Hadas,* in *Teatro breve hispanoamerican,* edited by Carlos Solorzano, Madrid, Aguilar, 1970; *Máscara puertorriqueña,* Rio Piedras, Edit. Cultural, 1971; *Cóctel de don Nadie,* in *Teatro puertorriqueño,* septimo festival, San Juan, 1965; *Tres piezas de teatro puertorriqueño,* San Juan, 1968 (contains: *Maria Soledad, Vejigantes; Club de Solteros*) and three works republished as *Teatro hispanoamericano: tres piezas,* New York, Harcourt, Brace, and World, 1969, in edition edited by Frank N. Danster; *Vejigantes* also is in the ninth festival edition of *Teatro puertorriqueño* (San Juan, 1959 and 1960) and *Maria Soledad* is in *Teatro puertorriqueño* in the fourth festival work, 1963.

Essays: *Entrada por las raices: entranamiento en prosa,* San Juan, 1964 (essays written 1940-1961).

Poetry: *Frontera: poemas,* San Juan, 1960; *Isla y nada,* San Juan, 1958; *Ciclo de lo Ausente,* San Juan, 1962; *Escultor de la sombra: poemas,* San Juan, 1965.

Literary Histories (of Puerto Rican theatre): *Areyto Mayor,* San Juan, Instituto de Cultura Puertorriqueña, 1966; *Conciencia puertorriqueña del teatro contemporánea 1937-1956,* San Juan, Instituto de Cultura Puertorriqueña, 1967.

Biographical/Critical Sources: Wilfredo Braschi, "Apuntes para la historia critica del teatro puertorriqueño contemporáneo," unpublished Ph.D. diss., U. of Puerto Rico, 1952; F. Manrique Cabrera, *Historia de la literatura puertorriqueña,* Rio Piedras, 1969, pp. 334-335; "Coctel de Don Nadie," review study by Angelina Morfí in *Temas del teatro,* Santo Domingo, Dom. Republic, 1969.

ARRUFAT, Antón

b. 1935, Santiago, Cuba.
Playwright, poet, storywriter, journalist.

After a considerable period in New York as editorial reader for Las Américas publishing house, Arrufat returned to Cuba in 1959 to take up several editorial positions, including one with *Lunes de Revolución,* a weekly cultural supplement to the now defunct *Revolución.* He is active also as reader for the Teatro de Estudio de la Havana and has had several of his plays performed, among them *El caso se investiga,* premiered 1957, and *Todos los domingos,* performed 1965. Two volumes of his collected verse are now in print as well as one collection of his stories.

Writings: Stories: *Mi antagonista y otras observaciones,* Havana, Revolución, 1964; Story, "The Discovery" in English translation in *Writers in the New Cuba,* J.M. Cohen, ed., Harmondsworth, England, Penguin, 1967.

Plays: *El caso se investiga,* 1957: this play also in *Teatro Cubano en un acta,* ed. by Rine Leal, Havana, Revolución, 1963; *Todos los domingos,* 1965; *Teatro* [with six of his plays], Havana, 1963; also *Cuatro obras* (contains Arrufat's *El vivo al pollo*), Havana, Casa de las Américas, 1961.

Poems: *En claro,* Havana, La Tertulia, 1961; *Repaso final,* Havana, Revolución, 1963.

Editor [with Fauto Maso] of: *Nuevo cuentistas cubanos,* Havana, Casa de las Américas, 1961.

Critical Essays: "Teatro 1959," in *Lunes de Revolución* (Jan. 18, 1960); "Función de critica literaria," Casa de las Américas, Vol. III, Nos. 17-18 (March-June 1963), pp. 78-80; also see Arrufat's "An Interview on the theatre in Cuba and in Latin America," trans. by Duard MacInnoss, *Odyssey Review*, II, 4 (1962).

ARRUGADO

(pseudonym for **Juan ROQUERO DOMINGUEZ**)

ARZOLA, Marina

b. 1939, Puerto Rico.
Poet.

Arzola's poem "El niño de cristal y los olvidados" won first prize in the Ateneo Puertorriqueño competition of 1966. She has published one collection of her verse (1968).

Writings: Poetry: *Palabras vivas,* Barcelona, Edit. Rumbos, 1968; and in many journals, including *Alma Latina, Bayoán, Prometeo, Palestra, Guajana, Asomante, Revista del Instituto de Cultura Puertorriqueña, La Nueva Sangre* (New York City); *Surcos;* and also represented in anthologies: *Cantos a Puerto Rico,* San Juan, Instituto de Cultura Puertorriqueña, 1968; and in *Poesia nueva puertorriqueña,* Luis Rosario Quiles, ed., San Juan, Edit. Edil, Producciones Bondo, 1971.

ASTOL, Eugenio

b. 1868, Caguas, Puerto Rico; d. 1948.
Poet, storywriter, playwright, travel writer, journalist, critic.

Son of parents who were professional actors, Astol from childhood developed an affection for the stage. With his family he travelled to Cuba, the Dominican Republic, and Venezuela. He helped organize *El Libro Azul de Puerto Rico* with Eugenio Fernández Garcia, and was co-editor of it with him. He contributed many articles and essays on literary figures and works to various journals of the day.

Writings: Poetry: in many journals and collections, including the *Antologia de la poesia puertorriqueña,* E.F. Méndez, ed., San Juan, 1968; well-known poems: "Armonia ideal," "Trilogia épica," "Una noche de Nerón," "Sonata simbólica," "Oración de las siete llamas," and "Uranos."

Criticism: article on José A. Negrón Sanjuro and others in *Puerto Rico Ilustrado,* San Juan, No. 69, Year II (June 25, 1911).

Biographies: *Hombres del pasado.*

Play: *Tres banderas,* 1912; monologue, *Noche de fiesta,* 1929.

Stories: *Cuentos y fantasias,* 1904.

Biographical/Critical Sources: A. Collado Martell, "Eugenio Astol: nuestro idealista estóico," in *Indice* (Nov. 13, 1929); S. R. Quinoñes, *Temas y letras,* San Juan, 1941.

AUGIER, Angel I.

b. 1910, Cuba.
Poet, critic.

Augier's poetry was neo-romantic and post-modern and full of social concerns for the Cuba of his day.

Writings: Poetry: *Uno,* Manzanillo, 1932; *Canciones para tu historia,* Havana, 1941; *Breve antologia,* Santa Clara, Dirección de Publicaciones, Universidad Central de Las Villas, 1963; *Isla en el tacto,* Havana, Unión, 1965.

Biographical/Critical Sources: Nicolás Guillén, *Notas para un estudio biográfico critico,* 2 vols, 1965.

AVELINO GARCIA, Andrés

b. 1900, Monte Cristi, Dominican Republic; d. 1974, Santo Domingo.
Poet, philosopher.

Avelino Garcia was one of the major figures of "Postumismo," and the primary theorist of the group as seen in his "Manifesto Postumista" published in *Fantaseos* (1921). He published much of his work in the newspaper columns of *Cuna de América.*

Writings: Poetry: *Fantaseos,* 1921; *Panfleto Postumistico,* 1921, and S. Domingo, La Cuna de America, 1922; *Pequeña Antologia Postumista,* 1922, and S. Domingo, La Cuna de America, 1924; *Del Movimiento Postumista,* 1923; *Raiz Enésima del Postumismo (poesia matemática),* Buenos Aires, Ocampo, 1924; *Cantos a mi Muerta Viva,* S. Domingo, La Cuna de America, 1926; Poems also in Rueda's *Antologia* cited below.

Proclamation: "Manifiesto Postumista," published in the Manuel Rueda's *Antologia Posible,* 1941; *Esencia y Existencia del Ser y de la Nada,* 1942; *El Problema de la Fundamentación del Problema del Cambio y la Identidad,* 1944; *Une lettre à Maritain,* 1945; *Filosofia del Conocimiento 1948-50; El Problema antinómico de la Fundamentación de una Lógica Pura,* 1951; "La relatividad de Einstein y la relatividad de Garcia de la Concha," in *Obras completas,* Santo Domingo, Universidad Autónoma de Santo Domingo, 1970; "Los Problemas antinómicos de la esencia de lo ético," in *Obras Completas,* 1971.

Biographicl/Critical Sources: See Manuel Rueda's *Antologia panoramica de la poesia dominicana (1912-1962),* pp. 89-90 for critical comments; published Madrid, 1972.

AVELLANEDA, Gertrudis Gómez de

b. March 23, 1814, Puerto Principe (Camagüez), Cuba; d. 1873, Madrid.
Novelist, playwright, poet, biographer.

Gómez de Avellaneda emigrated to Spain in 1836 in her 22nd year and spent most of the rest of her life there. She lost her first husband, Pedro Sabater, in 1846, in the first year of their marriage, and she remarried in 1855, becoming the wife of Colonel D. Domingo Verdugo Massieu, a deputy in the Spanish parliament. After a brief period back in Cuba with her spouse who had been exiled to Cuba where he soon died, she returned to Madrid where she flourished as a major romantic poet and a well-considered dramatist. Her fiction was of less interest and she herself wished to drop her first three novels from her collected works (published in 1869-71 and again in 1914, long after her death).

Avellaneda's most famous novel, *Sab* (1841), is strongly against the then still existent slavery of Cuba, and may well be, as Max Henriquez Ureña believes, the very first anti-slavery work of literature to be published in its entirety anywhere in the Americas.

Writer of scores of plays, her most famous was *Báltasar,* most probably influenced by Byron's *Sardanapalus.*

Avellaneda's letters to several writers and to her cousin Eloisa de Arteaga have been published and her collected poetry first appeared in an edition of 1841 and in her later *Obras literarias* (1869).

Writings: Novels: *Sab,* Madrid, 1841, and Havana, Consejo Nacional de Cultura, 1963; *Dos mujeres,* Madrid, 1842-43; *Espatolino,* 1844; *Dolores, páginas de una crónica de familia,* published in *Semanario Pintoresco* (Madrid, 1851); and republished in Havana, 1860; *El artista barquero o Los cuatro cinco de junio* (written in Havana, 1861); and bio-graphic-historical work: *Guatimotzin—Ultimo emperador de México,* Havana, 1846 and a fragment republished as "Un anécdota de la vida de Cortés), in *Obras literarias,* 1869-71.

Legends: *La velada del helecho o El Donativo del diablo,* 1849; *La baronesa de Joux,* 1844; *La ondina del lago azul,* 1859; *La flor del ángel,* 1860; *El cacique de Turmequé; La montaña maldita,* 1851; *La dama de Amboto,* 1860; *La Bella Toda y Los doce jabalies,* 1871; *El aura blanca,* 1861 (this latter the only one based on a Cuban folk-tradition).

Letters: see below for details.

Poetry: *Poesias,* Madrid, 1846, second edition, 1850; most verse collected in *Obras literarias,* Madrid, 1869; her odes "A S. M. la Reina Doña Isabel Segunda . . ." were first published in a Madrid journal in 1843 and republished in *Poesias,* edition of 1850; and see Vol. VI of centenary edition of her work, 1920, for "Tabla de variantes" of her poetry, as discussed by José Maria Chacón y Calvo; also: *Antologia de la poesia religiosa de la Avellaneda,* Florinda Alzaga and Ana Rose Núñez (eds.), Miami, Ediciones Universal, 1975.

Plays: *Leoncia,* written 1840 but refused performance in Havana, published in Madrid, Tip. Revista de Archivos, Bibliotecas y Museos, Olozaga 1, 1917; *Alfonso Munio* (later called *Munio Alfonso*), in 4 acts, published Madrid, Repullés, 1844; *El Principe de Viana* (4 acts, tragedy), Madrid, Repullés, 1844; *Egilona* (3 acts), Madrid, Repullés, 1845; *Saúl* (4 acts), Madrid, Repullés, 1849; *Flavio Recaredo* (3 acts), Madrid, Repullés, 1851; *Errores del corazón* (3 acts), Madrid, Repullés, 1852, premiered Teatro del Drama, Madrid, May 7, 1852; *La verdad vence apariencias* (2 acts, verse), Madrid, Repullés, 1852; *La hija de las flores o Todos están locos* (3-act comedy), Madrid, C. González, 1852, premiered Teatro del Principe, Madrid, Oct. 21, 1852; *El donativo del diablo* (prose), Madrid, Imp. C. González, 1852, and second edition, Mexico, 1858, first performed Teatro de Principe, Madrid, Oct. 4, 1852; *La aventurera* (4 acts, comic verse), Madrid, C. González, 1853; *Oraculosde Talia o Los duendes en palacio* (5 acts, verse comedy), Madrid, J. Rodriguez, 1855, premiered Teatro de La Cruz, 1855; *La hija del rey René* (1 act), Madrid, Rodriguez, 1855, premiered Teatro de La Cruz, Madrid, Feb. 9, 1855; *Simpatia y antipatia* (1-act comedy), Madrid, Rodriguez, 1855; *Los tres amores* (3 acts), Madrid, Rodriguez, 1858, premiered Teatro del Circo, Madrid, March 20, 1858; *Báltasar* (a biblical drama, 4 acts, in verse), first performed Teatro Novedades, Madrid, April 1858, second edition, Madrid, Imp. José Rodriguez, 1858; edited and with notes by Carlos Bransby, New York, American Book Co., 1908, also Havana, Consejo Nacional de Cultura, 1962; *Catalina* (4 acts, verse), Seville, 1867; *El millionari y la maleta* (comedy), unpublished in any separate edition (written in 1860's), but published in *Obras de la Avellaneda,* 1914 (for which see below); and her adaptation of Soulié's play, *Hortensia,* was performed but never published, as was also the case with *Los puntapies,* written with her brother Manuel.

Collected Works: *Obras literarias de la Sra. Doña Gertrudis Gómez de Avellaneda,* 5 vols., Madrid, Rivadeneyra, 1869-1871; *Obras de la Avellaneda,* Edición nacional del centenario, 3 vols., Havana, Miranda, 1914 (second volume contains these dramatic works: *Munio Alfonso; El Principe de Viaña; Recaredo; Saúl; Báltasar; Catilina; Egilona; El donativo del diablo;* third volume contains: *La hija de las flores o Todos están locos; La aventurera; Oráculos de Talia o los duendes en palacio; La hija del rey René; El millionario y la maleta; La verdad vence apariencias;* and *Tres amores.*) Also see: *Teatro,* Havana, Consejo Nacional de Cultura, 1965.

General: *Ensayo de diccionario del pensamiento vivo de la Avellaneda,* Miami, Ediciones Universal, 1975.

Biographical/Critical Sources: Emilio Cotarelo, *La Avellaneda y sus obras: ensayo biográfico y critico,* Madrid, 1930; Max Henriquez Ureña, *Panorama histórico de la literatura cubana,* New York, 1963, pp. 197-225 ff; Mario Méndez Bejarano's *Tassara: nueva biografia critica,* Madrid, 1928, which includes letters of Avellaneda to Tassara; Also see Avellaneda's letters to Ignacio de Cepeda y Alcade, with other letters of hers, in *La Avellaneda: Autobiografia y cartas de la ilustre poetisa, hasta ahora inéditas y con un prólogo y una necrologia por don Lorenzo Cruz de Fuentes,* Huelva, 1907 (a later edition contains forty more letters); Domingo Figarola-Caneda published *Memorias inéditas de la Avellaneda* (letters addressed to Eloisa de Arteaga, her cousin, in 1838), 1914, which offers biographic information. Also: José Chacón y Calvo, "Gertrudis Gómez de Avellaneda. Los influencias castellanas: examen negativo," in *Literatura Cubana* (critical essays), Madrid, 1922; Ignacio Manuel Altamirano's critical analysis of Báltasar in "Ensayo critico sobre Báltasar," Mexico, 1868, in pamphlet, republished in *Revista de Cuba* (March-April 1880); Aurelio Castillo de González, *Biografia de Gertrudis Gómez de Avellaneda y juicio critico de sus obras,* Havana, 1886; Mariano Aramburo, *Personalidad literaria de Doña Gertrudis Gómez de Avellaneda,* Madrid, 1898 (four lectures); Aurelio's Mitjan's "De la Avellaneda y sus obras," in *Estudios literarios,* Havana, 1887; Polly F. Harrison, "Images and Exile: The Cuban Woman and Her Poetry," in *Revista Interamericana,* Vol. IV, No. 2 (Summer 1974), pp. 184-219; Nelly A. Santos, "Las ideas feministas de Gertrudis Gómez de Avellaneda," in *Revista Interamericana,* Vol. IV, No. 2 (Summer 1974), pp. 276-281; Raimundo Lazo, *Gertrudis Gómez de Avellaneda, la mujer y la poetisa lirica,* Mexico, Edit. Porrua, 1972; Carmen Bravo-Villasante, *Una vida romántica, la Avellaneda,* Barcelona Editora y Distribuidora Hispano Americana, 1967; José Antonio Portuondo, "La dramática neutralidad de Gertrudis Gómez de Avellaneda," in *Revolución y Cultura,* No. 11 (no date), pp. 2-17.

AVILES, Juan

b. 1905, San Sebastián del Pepino, Puerto Rico.

Poet, journalist.

Aviles' poetry is post-modernist, though still reflecting the more traditional romanticism of an older Spanish culture than affected by most poets of his own generation. As a practicing journalist he has contributed to *El Imparcial, El Mundo, Prensa, Alma Latina,* and *Puerto Rico Ilustrado.* His poem "El Cafetal," first published in *Prensa* (II, 2, 1956), begins:

Yo soy del cafetal, de monte adentro,
del llano y de la jalda.
A pecho me he subido al varillaje
de la verde sombrilla de las guabas.
Soy el intimo amigo de los cedros,

Writings: Poetry: *Los caminos sin sombras,* New York, 1954 (introduction by Maria Teresa Babin).

Stories: in various journals, in ms.: the collection entitled "Puntuario del Pasado."

Play (in ms.): *Las vacaciones del periodista.*

AYBAR, Emiliano I.

b. ca. 1853, Dominican Republic; d. August 29, 1908.

Folklorist, historian, journalist, magistrate.

Aybar was active in journalism and his paper, *El Montecristeño* (1894-95), was very strong in its support of the Cuban struggle against Spain, led by his good friend José Marti. The journal was closed down by the Heureaux Administration because of official Spanish complaints. Renamed *El Noroeste,* it came out under the editorship of his son Manuel Aybar S.

Writings: History-Folklore: *Breves apuntes históricos de la Restauración,* 1883, republished in E. Rodriguez Demorizi's *Diarios de la guerra dominico-española,* S. Domingo, 1963; *El Tesoro de la familia Alvarez,* Montecristi, Dom. Republic, Tip. La Habana, 1900, preface by Virginia Ortea; and republished in E. Rodriguez Demorizi's *Tradiciones y cuentos dominicanos,* S. Domingo, Postigo, 1969, pp. 141-147.

Biographical/Critical Sources: See discussion of his periodical pieces in M.A. Amiama's *El*

Periodismo en la República Dominicana, S. Domingo, 1933, p. 56; Aybar's relationship with the Cuban revolutionist-poet Marti and Máximo Gómez is in *Marti en Santo Domingo,* Havana, 1953, and in *Papeles dominicanos de Máximo Gómez,* S. Domingo, 1954, both by E. Rodriguez Demorizi.

AYBAR Y DELGADO, Andrejulio (Andrés Julio)

b. 1872, Dominican Republic; d. 1965.
Poet, novelist, critic.

Much of Aybar's life was passed in Europe, most of it in Paris.

Writings: Poetry: *Propos d'amour ou de dépit* [written in French], Paris, 1928; *Margarita de amor,* 1950; *Del Hogar a los caminos,* Paris, 1954; *Mis romances de ternura y de sangre,* 1935.

Criticism: His essay which serves as introduction to *Cancionero de Heine,* entitled "Poeta para poetas," written in French, and translated into Spanish by Pérez Bonalde, Paris, 1910.

Letters: *Epistola al Presidente Bordas,* Paris, 1913; *Epistola a Juan Pablo Duarte,* Paris, 1914.

Translation: *Las confidencias de una abuela* (of a novel by Abel Hermant), Paris, 1906.

AYBAR O RODRIGUEZ, Manuela

(a.k.a. **"La Deana"**)
b. 1790, San Juan de la Maguana, Dominican Republic; d. 1850(?).
Poet, autobiographer.

Manuela Aybar was an activist woman who kept a small hand press in her home on which she printed her own political verse pamphlets. Deeply convinced of the rightness of the cause of General Santana and a fervent enemy of President Manuel Jimenes, she spared no polemical efforts in her work. In 1849 crowds shouted "Viva Jimenez—Death to the traitor Doña Manuel la Deana" at the time of Santana's downfall. She was possibly the first published Dominican woman poet.

Writings: Autobiography: *Historia de una mujer,* S. Domingo, Imprenta Nacional, 1849.

Poetry: one poem, beginning "Vencio al gigante Goliat," was written in Neyba, June 22, 1849, and circulated in a flyer printed in S. Domingo. A copy is conserved in the personal archives of the historian Dr. Alcides Garcia along with much more of her work, most of which was in flyer form and mostly lost.

Biographical/Critical Essay: E. Rodriguez Demorizi's *Poesia popular dominicana,* 1938, second edition, S. Domingo, UCMM, 1973, pp. 205-213.

AYUSO, Juan José

b. ca. 1945, Dominican Republic.
Poet, journalist.

All of Ayuso's poetry is dominated by his constant preoccupation for the "little man" who each day invades the streets and coffee-bars, walking and consuming away his bitter, opaque existence in minute doses—each day, every day. Ayuso has announced two new books: "Bienaventurador los cimarrones" and "Cantotiempo," genres of both unknown but probably poetry.

Writings: Poetry: (details unknown): *Primer Canto Rudimentario; Segundo Canto Rudimentario; Tercer Canto Rudimentario.*

AZAR GARCIA, Aquiles

b. ca. 1930, Dominican Republic.
Poet, painter.

Azar Garcia's poetry is concerned with the peasants, most of them black, and their constant poverty. These lines from "La Tierra y Las voces" reflect his concern:

Cubierto de polvo
pagado a la piedra
mi voz ahogado
en miseria
surge de las entrañas mismas
de la tierra.

Most recently, Azar has devoted himself more to painting than to literature and has had several shows of his work.

Writings: Poetry: *Los pies descalzos.*

Biographical/Critical Sources: F.A. Mota Medrano's comments in his *Relieves Alumbrados,* S. Domingo, 1971, pp. 215-225.

BABIN, Maria Teresa

b. 1910, Ponce, Puerto Rico.
Critic, biographer, poet, essayist.

Maria Babín has been a professor of Hispanic literature of the Graduate Center of the City University of New York and Professor of Puerto Rican Studies at Lehman College, C.U.N.Y., since the early 1960's. From 1968-1972 she was chairman of the first American Department of Puerto Rican Studies, at Lehman College.

Writings: Personal Essays: *Fantasia boricua: estampas de mi tierra,* San Juan, Instituto de Cultura Puertorriqueña, 1966.

Critical Essays: "Apuntes sobre *La Carreta,*" [of René Marquéz] in *Asomante* IV (Oct.-Dec. 1953); *Jornadas literarias: temas de Puerto Rico,* Barcelona, Ediciones Rumbos, 1967.

Critical Biography: *El mundo poético de Federico Garcia Lorca,* San Juan, Biblioteca de Autores Puertorriqueños, 1954 [316 pp.], and essays on Pachín Marín, Clemente Soto Vélez and others.

Poetry: *Las voces de tu voz: poemas,* Santander, Spain, La Isla de los Ratones, 1962.

Cultural History: *Panorama de la Cultura Puertorriqueña* (preface by Andrés Iduarte), San Juan, Inst. de Cultura, 1958.

Other Works: *Introducción a la cultura hispánica,* 1949; *Siluetas literarias,* 1965; *La cultura de Puerto Rico,* 1970; *The Puerto Rican's Spirit,* 1971. She also edited, with Stan Steiner, *Borinquen: An Anthology of Puerto Rican Literature,* New York, Alfred A. Knopf, 1974, and Vintage paperback (Random House), 1974.

BACARDI MOREAU, Emilio

b. 1844, Santiago, Cuba; d. 1922.
Novelist, playwright.

Both of Bacardi's historical novels are set in the early to middle part of the 19th century and are full of local details and customs. *Al abismo* was his only play, apparently never published, and weak in stage effectiveness according to Max Henríquez Ureña.

Writings: Novels: *Via-Crucis,* Havana, 1910, Barcelona, 1914; *Doña Güimar,* Barcelona, 1916, 2 vols.

Play: *Al abismo* (unpublished).

BACHILLER Y MORALES, Antonio

b. 1812, Havana, Cuba; d. January 10, 1889.
Playwright, poet, historian, folklorist, anthropologist, teacher.

Bachiller was one of the broadest and most indefatigable writers and scholars of his day. He taught natural law at the University of Havana and contributed to or otherwise supported such journals as *El Nuevo Reganón* (1830); *El Album* (1830); *La Siempreviva* (1838); *El Faro Industrial* (1841); *Revista de la Habana* (1853); *Brisas de Cuba* (1855); and *Cuba Literaria* (1882). During his exile in the United States, he published in *El Mundo Nueva* and *América Ilustrada,* both of New York, and in other Spanish-language papers and journals.

His *Los negros* (1887) was one of the earliest detailed studies of slavery in Cuba and he authored innumerable works in agriculture, history, law, and anthropology, along with some minor verse.

Writings: Folklore: *Fábulas literarias y morales,* 1839.

Literary History: *Apuntes para la historia de las letras en la isla de Cuba,* Havana, 1862; earlier published as *Apuntes para la Historia de las letras y la instrucción pública en Cuba,* 3 vols., 1859-1860; republished Havana, Imp. de P. Massana, 1959-61 (in three volumes).

Play: *En la confianza está el peligro* (verse, 2 acts), 1841.

History: *Cuba primitiva,* Havana, 1838, rev. ed., 1883; *Cuba, monografía histórica,* 1883.

Anti-slavery Study: *Los negros,* Barcelona, Biblioteca de la Ilustración Cubana, 1887.

Law: *Filosofía del derecho,* Havana, 1857; *Elementos de filosofía del derecho.*

Agriculture: *Memorias* (on exports of raw tobacco), 1835; *Prontuario general de agricultura para el uso de los labradores y hacendados de Cuba,* Havana, 1856; "Disquisición crítico-histórica sobre el aje y las batatas de Cuba," in *Revista de Cuba,* Havana, 1882.

Anthropology: *Antiguedades americanas.*

Biographical/Critical Sources: Max Henríquez Ureña, *Panorama histórico de la literatura cubana,* New York, 1963.

BADIA, Nora

b. 1921, Cuba.
Playwright.

Both of Badia's plays are one character works, really extended monologues.

Writings: Plays: *Mañana es una palabra,* and *La alondra,* both monologues, composed in 1947; the former play is in Teatro cubano en un acto (Rine Leal, ed.), Havana, Revolución, 1963.

BALAGUER, Joaquin

b. 1907, Navarrete, Dominican Republic.
Poet, novelist, essayist, diplomat, lawyer, statesman, teacher.

Balaguer took his B.A. in philosophy and letters from the Escuela Normal de Santiago (1924) and his law degree from the University of Santo Domingo (1929), followed by studies of economics in Paris. He served as professor of law at the University of Santo Domingo for some years, and ambassador to Venezuela (1940), Colombia (1945), and Mexico (1947), and Honduras (1947), and held important posts in the Ministry of Education and served as Vice President of the Dominican Republic in 1957.

During the era of Dictator Trujillo, Balaguer was the most prominant intellectual and writer. From youth he had dedicated himself to literature and Dominican history. Not only a close student of history and politics, he was also a historical novelist and poet, and his bibliography is long and still growing. Four times he served as president of his country (1960-61, 1966-67, 1970-74 and 1974-78).

He is currently interesting himself in a complete edition of his works in Madrid. His most recent work, a modest volume of verse, the first of fifty years since his last, circulates in a private edition among his friends and admirers.

Writings: Poetry: *Psalmos paganos,* Santiago, Dominican Republic, Edit. "La Información," 1922; *Clara de Luna,* "La Información," 1922, and *Tebaida lirica,* Editora "Franco Hermanos," 1924, also Santiago, date unknown; new verse collection, 1970's, details not known.

Critical Essay: *Nociones de Métrica Castellana,* Santiago, Dom. Republic, Imp. "Vila," 1930 (done with Oscar Contreras Marrón); *Apuntes para la historia prosódica de la métrica castellana,* Madrid, 1954.

Literary Criticism: *Azul en los charcos,* Bogotá, Edit. Selecta, 1941; *Letras dominicanas,* Santiago, Edit. "El Diario," 1944; *Guia emocional de la ciudad romántica,* El Diario, 1944; *Los próceres escritores,* Buenos Aires, Imp. Ferrari Hermanos, 1947; *Semblanzas literarias,* Buenos Aires, Ferrari, 1948; *Literatura dominicana,* Buenos Aires, Edit. "Americalee," 1950, second edition, Buenos Aires, Gráfica Guadeloupe, 1971.

Political Essays: *Tratado Trujillo-Hull y la liberación financiera de la República dominicana,* Bogota, Consorcio Editora, 1941; *La politica internacional de Trujillo,* Bogota, Consorcio, 1941; *El principio de la alterna bilidad en la historia dominicana,* S. Domingo, Impresora Dominicana, 1952; *La realidad dominicana,* Buenos Aires, Imp. Ferrari Hermanos, 1941; *Discursos. Panegíricos, Politica y Educación politica international,* Madrid, "Ediciones Acies," 1957.

Literary History: *Colón, Precursor literario,* Buenos Aires, Artes Gráficas," 1958; *Federico Garcia Godoy,* 1951 (Vol. 6 of Col. Pensamiento Dominicano, S. Domingo, Edit. "Libreria Dominicana"); *Historia de la literatura dominicana,* S. Domingo, Libreria Dominicana, 1955, second edition, 1958, third edition, 1965, fifth edition, S. Domingo, Julio D. Postigo & Hijos, 1970 (winner of the National Prize for "Obras Didácticas," 1956).

Speeches: *La marcha hacia el capitolio,* 1974; *Guia emocional de la ciudad romántica,* Santiago, 1944, second edition, Spain, 1972.

Editor of Selected Works: *El Pensamiento vivo de Trujillo,* Vol. I of the collection "La era de Trujillo. 25 años de Historia Dominicana," en conmemoración del 25º aniversario de la era de Trujillo," S. Domingo, Impresora Dominicana, 1958.

Biographical/Critical Studies: Juan Antonio Alix I, II (décimas), S. Domingo, Postigo, 1961; *El Cristo de la libertad. "Viva de Juan Pablo Duarte,"* Buenos Aires, Americalee, second edition, Buenos Aires, Artes Gráficas, 1958; *Federico Garcia Godoy,* S. Domingo, Libreria Dominicana, 1951; *El centinela de la frontera (Vida y hazaña de Antonio Duvergé),* Buenos Aires, 1962.

BALBOA TROYA Y QUESADA, Silvestre de

b. 1563, Puerto Principe, Grand Canaries; d. after 1624.
Poet.

Balboa is believed to have arrived in Cuba as a child and to have lived well into the 17th century. His epic poem "Espejo de paciencia," written in octavas reales in the early 17th century (probably about 1608), is considered the oldest manuscript extant of Cuban literature. It is in the ornate, erudite form, a "literary" epic rather than a "popular" epic. The poem describes the voyage of Bishop Cabezas y Altamirano to Yara (situated between Bayamo and Manzanillo) on a pastoral visit. The pirate Gilberto Girón, who is besieging Manzanilla, seeks to capture the prelate coming in by sea. The ancient sea gods, in the best of traditions, offer the good bishop aid, but he, splendid Christian, refuses. At epic's end the hero Gregorio Ramos rescues Cabezas and destroys the pirate, freeing city, God's man, and country:

Con esta majestad y este aparato
entró Gregorio Ramos en la villa,
. . . .
. . . .
y dio las gracias a la madre chijo
de la nueva victoria y regocijo
(second from last verse)

Writings: Poetry: "Espejo de paciencia," first collected in 1760 in Pedro Agustin Morrell de Santa Cruz's *Historia de la Isla y Catedral de Cuba,* but not completely published until 1929, Havana, Academia de la Historia de Cuba. The original ms. of Morrell's is now destroyed, but the copy made by José Antonio Echeverria in 1837 was first published in second edition of *Bibliografia cubana de los siglos XVII y XVIII* in 1927 and then in Vol. I of *Evolución de la Cultura cubana,* 1928, edited by José Carbonell; later editions were as separate volumes in the *Caudernos de Cultura,* 5th series, Havana, Ministry of Education, No. 4 (1942), and as part of "Textos Cubanos" of the University of Las Villas, 1960. Separate edition by Comisión Nacional de Cuba de la UNESCO, Havana, 1962.

Biographical/Critical Sources: See study of poem and manuscript by Felipe Pichardo Moya as introduction to the Cuadernos de Cultura edition, cited above, and foreword and notes of Cintio Vitier of the Textos Cubanos edition. Also see pp. 35-48 in Max Henriquez Ureña's

Panorama histórico de la literature cubana, New York, 1963.

BALDORIOTY DE CASTRO, Román

b. March 14, 1822, Guaynabo (Bayamón), Puerto Rico.
Journalist, traveloguist, politician, educator.

Baldorioty attended a seminary school in San Juan, and, with three other students, he travelled to Spain on a scholarship to prepare himself for a teaching career. Taking a degree ("Licenciado en Fisico-Matemáticas") equivalent to a doctorate at Madrid University, Baldorioty went on to Paris to study technical arts. He taught technical and scientific subjects in Puerto Rico, including courses for ship-pilots and was named Puerto Rican representative to the Paris World's Exposition in 1867. Two years later Baldorioty was elected deputy to the Cortes Constituyentes in Madrid which resulted in Prince Amadeo being chosen to assume the Spanish throne. Baldorioty was highly visible in Madrid as a proclaimer of Puerto Rican rights, but on returning to his own country he found the political climate unsuitable and he emigrated to Santo Domingo where he soon founded the Colegio Antillano and also served as a professor at the Central School of the capital.

Returning to Puerto Rico, he founded the journal *El Derecho* and in 1880 began a lively political campaign on the need for more liberal Spanish treatment of island affairs, mostly in his new paper, *La Crónica* of Ponce. A result of this work was the organization of a political party seeking independence—or at least autonomy—and Baldorioty became its first president.

Writings: Travel: *América,* written 1867, published in journals of the day, reprinted in the *Antologia puertorriqueña: prosa y verso,* Manuel Fernández Juncos, ed., New York, Hinds, Hayden & Eldredge, 1952, pp. 1-18.

Biographical/Critical Sources: Cesareo Rosa-Nieves' play, *Román Baldorioty de Castro* [Biodrama entres actos y en verso], published 1948, offers much information and comments on the subject's life and career; Sebastián Dalmau Canet, *Román Baldorioty de Castro,* 1910.

BALLAGAS, Emilio

b. 1908, Camagüey, Cuba; d. 1954.
Poet, anthologist, essayist.

Ballagas was an early exploiter of Afro-Cuban forms and rhythms. Two years after Tallet's first Afro-Cuban poems ("La rumba" and "Quintin Barahona") Ballagas wrote "Elegia de Maria Belén." His "Nocturno y elegia" from the collection Sabor eterno (1939) concludes:

No soy el que traiciona a las palomas,
a los niños, a las constelaciones. . . .
Soy una verde voz desamparada
que su inocencia busca y solicita
con dulce silbo de pastor herido.

Ballagas joined the vanguardista movement of social realists in the 1940-1950 period.

Writings: Essays: "Pasión y muerte del Futurismo" (critique of Marinetti's futurist movement), "La herencia viva de Tagore," and "Ronsard ni más ni menos."

Poetry: *Jubilio y fuga,* Havana, 1931, Madrid, Ediciones Héroe, 1939; *Elegia sin nombre,* 1936; *Nocturno y elegia,* 1938; *Cuadernos de poesia negra* (folksongs), Santa Clara (Havana), 1934; *Sabor eterno,* Havana, Imp. Ucar, Garcia, 1939; *Cielo en rehenes* (in *Obra poética*). Edición póstuma, introduction by Cintio Vitier, Havana, Impresores Ucar, Garcia, 1955; *Nuestra Señora del Mar,* 1943; poems in many reviews and anthologies including *Revista-Avance* (1928); *Social* (Havana), *Repertorio Americano* (Costa Rica), *Gaceta Literario* (Madrid); and in E. Ballagas' *Antologia de la poesia negra* (for which see below). Also see his latest collections: *Orbita,* Havana, Unión, 1965 and *Obra poética de Emilio Ballagas,* Miami, Mnemosyne, 1969.

Editor of: *Antologia de la poesia negra hispana-americana,* Madrid, 1935; and Mapa de la poesia negra americana, Buenos Aires, 1946.

Biographical/Critical Sources: Dirección Nacional de Educación General's *Emilio Ballagas,* Havana, Instituto Cubáno del Libro, 1973 (with discussion of works, etc.); Argyll Pryor Rice, *Emilio Ballagas: poeta o poesia,* Mexico, Ediciones de Andrés, 1967; José Olivio Jimenez discussions on Ballagas on pp. 357-358 of A.P. Rice's *Antologia de la poesia hispanoamericana contemporánea: 1919-1970,* Madrid, 1972.

BALMASEDA, Francisco Javier

b. March 31, 1833, Remedios, Cuba; d. March 31, 1907.

Poet, playwright, novelist, journalist, agriculturalist.

Patriot and educator, Balmadeda founded several schools and libraries and took an active part in the separatist movement of 1869, resulting in his being exiled to Fernando Poo off the coast of Equatorial Guinea (Spanish Rio Muni) from whence he later fled to the United States. He published many plays and didactic works and some poetry. Max Henriquez Ureña finds his best work to be in his "original" fables.

Writings: Fables: *Fábulas morales,* 1860.

Plays: *Eduardo el Jugador* (1 act verse comedy), 1861; *Las primas y las montañas de oro* (3 act verse comedy), 1861; *Los montes de oro* (4 act verse comedy), Havana, La Antilla, 1866, second edition, Cartagena, Colombia, 1874; *El dinero no es todo o Un baile de máscaras* (1 act prose comedy), second edition, Cartagena, 1874; *Sin prudencia todo falta* (1 act prose comedy), Cartagena, 1874, second edition, 1888; *Amelio o La vuelta del estudiante* (1 act prose comedy), Cartagena, 1874, and third edition, Havana, La Antilla, 1888; *Amor y riqueza* (zarzuela in 2 acts), Havana, La Antilla, 1888, with music by Rafael Paláu; *Carlos Manuel de Céspedes* (2 acts, historic drama), Havana, 1900 (believed to be by Imp. Compostela but José Rivera Muñoz says Imp. A. Casanova); *Monólogos,* Havana, Imp. de Elias F. Casona, 1889 (contains *Amor y honor* and Edmundo Dantés, both in verse and about five pages long each).

Novels: *Clementina,* Cartagena, 1897; *Los ebrios o La familia de Juana Candaya,* 1903; *Los misterios de una cabaña,* Remedios Franck, 1866, 2 vols.

Poetry: *Rimas cubanas,* Havana, 1846; *Poesias,* 1887.

Memoirs: *Los confinados a Fernando Poo,* New York, 1869 (which includes his *Impresiones de un viaje a Guinea*).

Collections of Various Genres: *El miscelánico,* 1894; *Obras,* Cartagena, 1874; *Los confinados a Fernando Poo,* New York, 1869 (see Memoirs rubric above).

Agriculture: *Tesoro del agricultor cubano,* 3 vols., Havana, 1885-1887; *Enfermedades de las aves,* 1887.

Labor: *El libro de los labradores,* 1891.

BALSEIRO, José Augustin

b. August 23, 1900, Barceloneta, Puerto Rico.

Poet, critic, novelist, storywriter.

Balseiro is considered a major figure in Puerto Rican critical circles and his poetry and fiction are also major contributions to island literature. For many years he taught Spanish literature at various universities in the United States. Alfonso Reyes called him "... caballero de verso y prosa, fino puertorriqueño andante, varón español y universal que ha demostrado pericia en la novela, la critica y la cátedra ..."

Writings: Poetry: *La copa de Anacreonte,* Madrid, 1924; *Música cordial,* Madrid, Tip. Artística Cervantes, 1926; *Flores de primavera,* San Juan, Cantero Fernández, 1919; *Las palomes de Eros,* Madrid, Edit. América, 19??; *Al rumor de la fuente,* San Juan, Edit. Real Hermanos, 1922; *La pureza cautiva,* 1946 *Vispera de sombra,* Mexico, Ediciones de Andre, 1959; nine of his poems are in the *Antologia de la poesia puertorriqueña,* E.

Fernández Méndez, ed., San Juan, 1968, and work in many other collections and journals, including *Saudades de Puerto Rico,* with *La pobreza cautiva* (foreward by Alfonso Reyes), Madrid, Aguilar, 1957.

Stories: *El destino roto,* 1955.

Literary Essays: *El vigia ensayos,* 3 vols., Madrid, Edit. Mundo Latino, 1925-1942; *Cuatro individualistas españoles,* and *Novelistas españoles modernos,* 1933; and his *Expresión de Hispanoamérica,* in *Seis estudios de Rubén Dario.* In English translation by Muna Lee: *The Americas Look at Each Other,* Coral Gables, Fla., U. of Miami Press, 1969.

Novels: *El sueño de Manõn,* Madrid, Rivadeneyra, 1922; *La ruta eterna,* Madrid, Mundo Latino, 1923, 1926; *La maldecida,* Madrid, Edit. Novela de Amor, 1923; *Cuando el amor nace,* Madrid, Mundo Latino, 192? (published with *En vela mientras el mundo duerme,* San Juan, 1953; *La gratitud humana,* Miami, Florida, Mnemosyne, 1969.

Biographical/Critical Sources: Alfonso Reyes, *De viva voz,* Mexico, Ed. Stylo, 1949; Maria Teresa Babin in her *Jornado literarios,* Barcelona, 1967; Juan Enrique Colberg Petrovich, *Cuatro autores clásicos contemporáneos de Puerto Rico,* San Juan, 1966.

BAQUERO, Gastón

b. 1916, Cuba.
Poet, critic, journalist.

An innovator and an adaptor of foreign verse developments reaching from Whitman to T.S. Eliot, Baquero was also an active journalist, serving as director of *Diario de la Marina.* He published many reviews and literary articles which work in time seemed to extinguish the poet in him. His best poetic work first appeared in the review *Clavileño* which he founded with four friends in 1944.

Writings: Poetry: *Poemas,* Havana, Talleres de S. Garcia, 1942; in pamphlet form; *Saúl sobre la espada,* Havana, 1943; *Memorial de un testigo,* Madrid, Rialp, 1966.

BARAGANO, José Alvárez

b. 1932, Cuba; d. 1962.
Poet, journalist, critic.

A strong supporter of Fidel Castro with whom he fought, Baragaño employed surrealistic verse in his revolutionary writing. He died of a heart attack. The last lines of sonnet-like "Illumination" as translated by J.M. Cohen are surprising:

. . .
all you need now is the eyes of a
theologian
to raise upon the hard rind of your
skin
the beliefs of ancient times, like one of
those acids
that revive the letters
and ciphers on ancient mirrors.

Writings: Poetry: in various collections and journals, including *Writers in the New Cuba,* J. M. Cohen, ed., Harmondsworth, England, Penguin, 1967.

BARALT Y ZACHARIAE, Luis A.

b. April 12, 1892, New York City, U.S.A. (of Cuban parents).
Playwright, civil engineer.

Born during his family's exile in the United States, Baralt returned to Cuba after independence to take a doctorate in engineering. For many years he was a professor of English at the Instituto de Segunda Enseñanzo of Havana and professor of philosophy and esthetics at the University of Havana. He also became secretary of Public Education and Fine Arts in 1934 and served as Secretary of the Escuela de Verano of the University of Havana, as president of the Corporación Nacional de Autores (1944-46), and did much teaching at home and abroad.

With José Cid Pérez, José Hurtado de Mendoza and others, Baralt founded the Teatro de Arte La Cueva. He directed many plays, Spanish and European classics, modern American, and of course Cuban, and translated several plays.

Baralt's plays were very innovative. His *Taowami* is an early attack on man's machine civilization and his *Tragedia indiana,* though set in Cuba, is in a highly imaginative world of the 1500's.

Writings: Plays: *Taowami,* written 1920; *Meditación* (1 act), written early in the author's life, was first performed August 11, 1955 in the Lyceum Lawn Tennis, Havana; *La luna en el pantano* (3 acts), published Havana, 1936, performed Teatro Principal de la Comedia under Baralt's direction; *Junto al rio* (1 act); *La mariposa blanca* (1 act), premiered May 26, 1948 in Teatro del la Escuela; *Tragedia indiana* (3 acts) in *Teatro Cubano Contemporáneo,* 1959, 1962 (see below); *Meditaciones en tres por cuatro,* written 1950; *La luna en el rio,* in *Teatro cubano,* Santa Clara, 1960.

Biographical/Critical Sources: José Cid Pérez' introduction to Baralt's *Tragedia indiana,* in *Teatro cubano contemporáneo,* 1959, second edition, Madrid, Aguilar, 1962, coll. and ed. by Dolores Marti de Cid.

BARBERA, José Domingo

b. ca. 1854, Cuba.
Playwright.

Today an all but forgotten playwright, Barberá once was a popular writer for the comic stage.

Writings: Plays: *Los arrancados o En la tea brava* (1 act prose comedy), Havana, Imp. del Batallón Mixto de Ingenieros, 1892, performed Teatro Cervantes, Havana, June 28, 1884; *Los Guanajos* (1 act comic skit), Havana, Imp. del Battalón, 1892, premiered Teatro Albiso, Havana, Dec. 24, 1889; *Margarita o el Traviato* (1 act verse musical), Havana, Imp. del Battalón, 1892 (parody by the opera *La Traviata*), performed Sep. 1, 1880, Havana; *Mazorra reformada* (1 act prose farce), Havana, Imp. del Battalón, 1892, premiered "former" Theatre Cervantes, May 1, 1885.

BARRAL, Mario

b. 1915, Cuba.
Playwright.

Barral's work was generally comic and symbolist.

Writings: Plays: *Retaguardia,* 1943; *Diez años de amor; Aqui es el diablo quien habla,* 1944; *Solarium en el roof,* 1945; *Sonata inconclusa,* 1947; *Lamento de la tierra,* 1948.

BARREIRO, José R.

b. ca. 1869, Cuba.
Playwright.

Barreiro wrote eight known plays, many of them set to music, but none ever was published.

Writings: Plays (all in manuscript): *Al romper la molienda* (1 act farce musical), music by Rafael Palau, premiered Teatro Irijoa (today Teatro Martí), Havana, 1899; *El asistente o Crisante* (1 act, prose), Havana, July 1896; *El briyo* (1 act musical, music by José Maria Varona); *La gran rumba* (1 act, music by Jorge Anckermann), performed Havana, July 1896; *La noche de San Juan* (1 act, music by Rafael Palau), performed June 23, 1897 in Teatro Irijoa, Havana; *La mulatas* (1 act, music by R. Palau); *Los cheverones* (farce, music by R. Palau); *Los tabaqueros* (1 act, music by R. Palau), dated 1897.

BAUZA Y GONZALEZ, Obdulio

b. 1907, Lares, Puerto Rico.
Poet, lawyer.

Bauzá's familiarity with coffee plantation life is exploited in *La casa solariega,* his second volume of verse. These opening lines from "En la noche. En la hacienda" provide a vivid introduction to such life:

En la noche, en la hacienda
Cuando duerme el pitirre

Y las palmas reales son picachos de sombras
y la máquina sueña con café de la aurora:
¡llegas,
Viejo fantasma de los montes lejanos
a sentarte en los muros.
. . .
. . .
aspira los aromas del café de los tanques.

Bauzá has travelled widely in the United States, Mexico, and the Caribbean and has been open to all the new poetic currents of the century. Much of his verse first appeared in *Alma Latina, El Mundo* and *Puerto Rico Ilustrado.*

Writings: Poetry: In trans. by Helen Wohl Patterson, *Selected Poems* (with original Span. text), foreword by Concha Meléndez, Madrid, 1961. *Hogueras de cal,* San Juan, 1947; *La casa solariega,* San Juan, 1955; poems in various journals and anthologies including *Antologia de la poesia puertorriqueña,* Fernández Méndez, ed., San Juan, 1968.

Biographical/Critical Sources: Concha Meléndez, *Poetas hispanoamericanos diversos,* San Juan, 1971.

BAZIL LEYVA, Osvaldo

b. October 9, 1884, Dominican Republic; d. October 5, 1946.
Poet, literary critic and historian.

Bazil was one of the leading "modernist" poets, with many volumes published over five decades.

Writings: Poetry: *Rosales en flor,* S. Domingo, 1906; *Arcos votivos,* Havana, 1907; *Parnaso Dominicano,* Barcelona, 1912; *Parnaso Antillano,* Barcelona, 1913; *Campanas de la tarde,* Havana, 1922; *La Cruz transparente,* Buenos Aires, 1939; *Huerto de inquietud,* Paris, 1926; *Tarea literaria y patricia,* Havana, La Verónica, 1943; *Remos en la sombra,* S. Domingo, Edit. El Diario, 1945.

Conference Papers: *Vidas de iluminación,* Havana, 1932; *Una conferencia del Señor Osvaldo Bazil,* S. Domingo [Publications of the Secretary of State of Foreign Affairs (Relaciones Exteriores)], 1938.

Essays: *Movimiento intelectual dominicano,* Washington, D.C., in *Boletin de la Unión Panamericana* (July 1924); *Cabezas de América,* Havana, 1938.

Speech: *La apoteósis de las lágrimas,* Havana, 1926.

Biography: "Biografía de Rubén Dario" [the Nicaraguan poet], in *Rubén Dario y sus amigos dominicanos,* edited by E.R. Demorizi.

Editor/Compiler: *Parnaso Dominicano. Compilación Completa de los Mejores Poetas de la República de Santo Domingo,* Barcelona, Maucoi, n.d. (but 1915).

Biographical/Critical Sources: F.A. Mota Medrano, *Relieves Alumbrados,* S. Domingo, 1971, pp. 79-.

BEJARANO, Lázaro

b. ca. 1500, Seville, Spain (lived in San Domingo); d. ca. 1560.
Poet.

Bejarano, before emigrating to the New World, was a member of the Seville group of poets gathered around Gutierre de Cetina before he established himself as one of the earliest poets of the Caribbean area. Arriving in Santo Domingo in 1535 he remained for five years before moving to Curaçao to become governor and plantation owner in that island and of Aruba and Bonaire. However, he quickly returned in 1541 and took up residence in the capital where he watched the antics and foibles of his fellows with some dismay.

His poetry was satirical as a consequence and his poem "El purgatorio del amor," for example, deals with most of the important or "self-important" citizens of S. Domingo. This did not make him popular and for these and other reasons he was forced to undergo a trial from the Inquisition in 1549 being charged with heresy and accused of failing to attend mass for three years entire. Even worse, Bejarano had supported Father Bartolomé de las Casas in the latter's efforts to ameliorate the condition of the Indians and had run afoul of the position of Juan Ginés de Sepúlveda who had no such sympathies and had his powerful friends.

Only a few of his works are extant.

Writings: Poetry: a few poems are known to have been circulated in Seville in 1531, 1533, and 1534, and exist in manuscript; some poems are in Rodriguez Demorizi's *Poesia popular dominicana,* pp. 104-107; his poems dedicated to San Pablo and to St. Madeleine are in the *Cancionero General* of Hernando del Castillo; some poetry in J. Balaguer's *Historia de la literatura dominicana.*

Biographical/Critical Sources: Pedro Henriquez Ureña, *La cultura y las letras coloniales en Santo Domingo,* 1936; Emilio Rodriguez Demorizi's *Poesia popular dominicana,* second edition, 1973; J. Balaguer's *Historia,* cited above, fifth edition, 1970; biographic data is in "Discursos medicinales," 1611 by Juan Méndez Nieto, in ms. in the Biblioteca de Palacio, Madrid, and fragments of Nieto have been published in Vol. I, pp. 314-327, of *Historia de la poesia hispanoamericana* by Marcelino Menendez y Pelayo, 2 vols., Madrid, 1911.

BELAVAL, Emilio S.

b. 1903, Farjardo, Puerto Rico.
Storywriter, playwright, autobiographer, essayist, lawyer, judge.

After completing high school at the Escuela Superior Central de San Juan, Belaval went on to the University of Puerto Rico, taking his law degree in 1927. The next four years he was a department head for the Puerto Rico Telephone Company. From 1931-1941 he was in private law practice, leaving for a judgeship in Bayamón and then San Juan, finishing as an associate judge of the Supreme Court of Puerto Rico.

He served as president of the Pro Arte Musical in 1935 and of the Ateneo Puertorriqueño in 1937-1938 and founded, with Leopold Santiago La vandero, the dramatic society Areyto.

Rosa-Nieves considered Belaval's best play to have been *La hacienda de los cuatro vientos.* Belavel has written (in a note in the *Antologia Puertorriqueña,* edited by Rosita Silva (San Juan, Imp. Venezuela, 1928), that he had written 385 short stories, destroying a great number of them.

Writings: Stories: *Cuentos para colegiales 1918-1923; Los cuentos de la Universidad,* San Juan, Edit. de Autores Puertorriqueños (E.A.P.), 1935; *Cuentos para fomentar el turismo,* San Juan, E.A.P., 1946, and Barcelona, Ediciones Rumbos, 1967; these stories are in Concha Meléndez' volume cited below in Biographical/Critical section: "El Verano de Hortensita se Complica," "Santiagua de Santiguero," and "Nuestra Cruz Menchaca."

Essay: *Los problemas de la cultura puertorriqueña,* 1934; *El teatro como vehiculo de expresión de nuestra cultura,* 1940; *El tema futuro de nuestra música,* 1939; *El niño Sanromá, biografia minima,* San Juan, E.P.A., 1953; *La intrigulis puertorriqueña,* 1952.

Plays: *La muerte,* 1935; *La novela de un vida simple,* (comedy, 3 acts), 1935; *La presa de los vencedores* (comedy, one act), 1939; *La hacienda de los cuatros vientos* (drama, three acts), 1949, 1958, also contained in *Teatro puertorriqueño,* San Juan, 1959, 1960; *La muerte, comedia de delirantes* (prose, three acts), 1953, discussed by F. Manrique Cabrera in *Historia de la literatura puertorriqueña,* Rio Piedras, 1969, pp. 315-320; *Circe o el amor,* Teatro puertorriqueño: Quinto festival, *Cielo caido,* in *Teatro puertorriqueño;* tercer festival, San Juan, 1961.

Biographical/Critical Sources: Concha Meléndez, *El arte del cuento en Puerto Rico,* New York, 1961, pp. 86-93; Antonio S. Pedreira, *Los cuentos de la Universidad, Aclaraciones y critica,* Rio Piedras, Edit. Phi Eta Mu, University of Puerto Rico, 1941; Juan Bosch, *Emilio Belaval, cuentista de Puerto Rico,* Havana, 1940, but first published in *Puerto Rico Ilustrado* (July 1940); René Marqués, "Apuntes para una interpretación, un autor, un intringulus y una obra," in *Asomante* (Oct-Dec. 1953), which discusses *La muerte;* Flavia Lugo de Marichal, *Belaval y sus cuentos para fomentar el turismo,* San Juan, 1972.

BENITEZ ROJO, Antonio

b. 1931, Havana, Cuba.
Storywriter, critic.

After study at the University of Havana (business) and American University, Washington, D.C., Benítez travelled widely in Europe and the Americas. His post-university interests, however, have been mostly in the theatre and he is a director of the Casa del Teatro, created by the new Consejo Nacional de Cultura.

His first stories began to appear only in 1966, but his collection *Tute de Reyes,* was awarded the prize by the Casa de las Américas in 1967 in quick recognition.

Writings: Stories: *Tute de Reyes,* Havana, Casa de las Américas, 1967; *El escudo de hojas secas,* Havana, Unión, 1969; and stories in various journals and anthologies, including the poem "La tejera" in *Narrativa cubana de la revolución,* J.M. Caballero Bonald, ed., Madrid, 1969.

Biographical/Critical Sources: Seymour Menton, *Prose Fiction of the Cuban Revolution,* 1975.

BERMUDEZ, Luis Arturo

b. 1854 or 1855, Santo Domingo, Dominican Republic; d. April 9, 1917, San Pedro de Macoris.
Playwright, folklorist, journalist.

Bermúdez graduated from the Colegio San Luis Gonzaga. He became the Public Prosecutor (Defensor Publico) in San Pedro de Macoris, and was licensed to practice law in 1888 by El Instituto Profesional; in 1889 he was Deputy in the parliament for Macoris, and from then on held many important posts or offices.

With Rafael A. Deligne, he founded the important literary review *Prosa y Verso* in 1895 and the newspaper *El Cable* with Antonio F. Soler.

Writings: Plays: *El licenciado Arias,* 1900 (considered one of the best Dominican plays); *Tomás Carite (Las cosas de seño Tomás),* first published in *Prosa y Verso* journal; *El carnaval; Los mellizos; Guadeloupe y Mateo,* all unpublished.

Sketches: "Las cosas de Seño Tomás," May 1895; "El Ojo en la uña de gato," June 1895; "De Gato y Gallina," July 1895: all in *Prosa y Verso,* San Pedro de Macoris.

Article: "Cosas del Tio Perete," in *El Teléfono,* S. Domingo (June 3, 1889).

In Manuscript: many plays and historical sketches.

Biographical/Critical Sources: Essay by Osvaldo A. Rodriguez of "El genio de Seño Tomás," in *Prosa y Verso,* San Pedro de Macoris (Oct. 1895); M. A. Amiama's *El Periodismo en la República dominicana,* S. Domingo, 1933, p. 56.

BERMUDEZ Y ORTEGA, Federico Ramón

b. August 29, 1884, San Pedro de Macoris, Dominican Republic; d. March 3, 1921.
Poet, playwright, critic, journalist.

Federico Bermúdez was the son of playwright and folklorist Luis A. Bermúdez. Much of Federico's work dealt with the poor and lowly and his sympathy for the suffering of the rural Dominicans is very marked.

Writings: Poetry: *Oro Virgen,* 1910; *Los humildes,* 1916, second edition, S. Domingo, Ediciones de la UCMM, with an introduction by J. Balaguer, 1968; *Las liras del silencio,* 1923.

In Manuscript: Plays: *Ele,* and *El Fantasma (monólogo),* the latter was performed; and Criticism: "Juicios criticos."

Biographical/Critical Sources: J. Balaguer's *Historia de la literatura dominicana,* fifth edition, S. Domingo, Postigo, 1970, pp. 250-251.

BERNAL, Emilia

b. 1884, Cuba.
Poet, novelist, translator, biographer, traveloguist.

A fertile poet, Bernal travelled widely and published many volumes of verse and translations in and out of Spanish.

Writings: Poetry: *Alma errante,* Havana, 1916; *Vida,* Madrid, 1925; *Exaltación,* Madrid, 1928; *América,* Santiago, Chile, 1933; *Como los pájaros,* San Jose, Costa Rica, 1921; *Poesiás inéditas,* New York, 1922; *Cuestiones Cubanos,* Madrid, 1928; *Negro,* Havana, 1934.
Autobiographical Novel: *Laika Froika,* Madrid, 1931.
Prose-poems: *Sentido,* Santiago, Chile, 1933.
Biography: *Marti por si mismo,* Havana, 1934.
Travel: *Mallorca,* Santiago, Chile, 1933.
Translations: *Sonetos* (of A. de Quental), Madrid, 1929; *Poesias* (of J. Folguera), Barcelona, 1930; *Saudades* (of Rosalia de Castro), Santiago, Chile, 1938.

BERROA Y CANELO, Quitero

b. 1871, Dominican Republic; d. 1936.
Creole poet, storywriter.

Berroa's poetry was formal, elegant, sometimes extremely artificial.

Writings: Poetry: *Pétalos,* 1910 (mostly prose-poems).
Stories: published in various journals.

BETANCOURT, José Ramón

b. 1823, Cuba; d. 1890.
Novelist, orator, poet, historian, politician.

Betancourt's one novel, *Une feria de la caridad,* is a very successful picture of the mid-19th century life of Matanzas, the so-called "epoca del Lugareño" [after folklorist Gaspar Betancourt Cisneros (El Lugareño)]. As a tract against the vice of gambling, the work has strong didactic purposes but it is still a lively work.

Writings: Novel: *Una feria de la caridad en 183 . . . ,* Puerto Principe, Imp. El Fanal, 1841, 2nd. ed., 1855.
Prose and Poetry: *Prosa de mis versos,* Barcelona, 1887.
Politics/Orations: *Discursos y manifiestos politicos,* Madrid, 1887.
History: *Las dos banderas,* Sevilla, 1870.

BETANCOURT, José Victoriano

b. 1813, Guanajay, Cuba; d. 1875.
Sketchwriter, folklorist, biographer, playwright, lawyer.

Betancourt studied in Havana and practiced law there until 1869 when he fled to Mexico after taking part in the independence movement of that year. He was considered the most popular of the writers employing everyday themes in his sketches and tales, most of which appeared in the daily newspapers and other journals of the day.

Writings: Sketches: *Los curros del Manglar; El dia de Reyes; El velorio; La salida del primer diente.*
Articles: in various journals, collected and published as *Articulos de costumbres* in *Cuadernos de Cultura,* Havana, Dirección de Cultura del Ministerio de Educación, 1941.
Biography: *Descripción de las Cuevas de Bellamar,* Matanzas, 1863 [28 pp.].
Play: *Las apariencias engañan* (one-act verse comedy), Matanzas, Tip. del Gobierno, 1847, performed 1847.

BETANCOURT, Luis Victoriano

b. 1843 (or 1842?), Cuba; d. 1885.
Folklorist, poet.

Brother of José Victoriano Betancourt, Luis took part in the revolt of 1868 against Spain but was primarily a peaceful scholar interested in the customs of the Cuban people. His articles were almost as worked out as tales what with their interest in character, language and atmosphere.

Writings: Folklore: *Articulos de costumbres y poesias,* 1867; the prose part was republished as *Articulos de costumbres,* Havana, Colección de Libros Cubanos, 1929.

Poetry: in various journals and in the collection *Los poetas de la guerra,* edited by José Marti, New York, 1893.

Biographical/Critical Sources: Federico de Córdova, *Luis Victoriano Betancourt,* Havana, 1943.

BETANCOURT CISNEROS, Gaspar (a.k.a. "El Lugareño")

b. 1803, Cuba; d. 1866.
Storywriter, folklorist, patriot.

Betancourt's stories of common life were vastly popular in his day and his pen name "El Lugareño" became a by-word for the epoch. His stories were ironic, playing often on idiosyncracies or the particular social mannerisms of the members of the classes and professions living in his world. There was a benign air, however, and the mixture of local color, the sounds of crowds, the speech of ordinary people of all classes, and his own not always inobtrusive opinions made them educational as well as splendid entertainment.

An early fighter for Cuban independence, he quarreled in print with his friend José A. Saco's ideas that Cuba should seek annexation by the United States. Betancourt argued for pure independence in his *Ideas sobre la incorporación de Cuba en los Estados Unidos, en contraposición a las que ha publicado D. José Antonio Saco.* His address of September 1, 1854 at New Orleans elaborated further on his belief that only in total independence from both Spain and the U.S., could Cuba be free. His property in Cuba was sequestered for his part in several conspiracies and in 1856 he left the U.S. for Europe, returning to Cuba after wide travel in Europe in 1861 when reforms were being permitted to be discussed.

Writings: Stories: *Escenas cotidianas,* published in issues of *Gaceta de Puerto Principe,* 1838-39, collected and published one volume, Havana, Publicaciones del Ministerio de Educación, Dirección de Cultura, Clásicos cubanos: I, 1950.

Politics: *Ideas sobre la incorporación de Cuba en los Estados Unidos,* New York, in the offices of the journal *La Verdad,* 1850; address as published in a leaflet and published in English: *Addresses delivered at the celebration of the third anniversary of the martyrs for Cuban freedom* [by Betancourt and J.S. Thrasher, 8 pp.].

Other Papers: *Cartas del Lugareño,* Vol. I of Colección Epistolarios, Havana, Publicaciones del Ministerio de Educación, 1950.

Biographical/Critical Sources: Federico de Córdova's *Gaspar Betancourt Cisneros, el Lugareño,* Havana, 1938, and Córdova's introductions to the 1950 editions of *Escenas Cotidianas* and *Cartas del Lugareño* are useful; Max Henriquez Ureña, *Panorama histórico de la literatura cubana,* New York, 1963, pp. 239ff, and 320.

BIBIANA BENITEZ, Maria

b. December 1, 1783, Aguadilla, Puerto Rico; d. April, 1873, San Juan, Puerto Rico.
Poet, playwright.

Bibiana's work is impregnated with a universal sense of the tragic, incited by the romantic bards of Europe (i.e. Heine, Goethe, Hugo and Byron). These appear in her profitable "lirica" with the theme of "progreso Humano." Her play, *La cruz del Morro* (1862), celebrates the beating back of the Dutch attack on Morro Castle in 1625. Her niece was the minor poet Alejandrina Benitez.

Writings: Poetry: *Diálogo* (en verso), San Juan, Puerto Rico, 1858; "La Ninfa de Puerto Rico," (an ode), in *Boletin Histórico de Puerto Rico,* Ano XIII, No. 3 (May-June 1926), pp. 147-149; "A La Vejez," ibid, pp. 149-150.

Play: *La Cruz del Morro* (two acts), San Juan, Puerto Rico, 1862.

BILLINI Y ARISTY, Francisco Gregorio

b. May 25, 1844, Santo Domingo; d. November 28, 1898, Santo Domingo.
Novelist, poet, playwright, educator, journalist, statesman.

Billini was president of the Dominican Republic one year, 1884-1885.

In 1869 he disembarked with other patriots at Saint Marco to fight against annexation to the U.S., considered a near possibility in the early years of President Grant's administration. He founded in 1871 the journal *El Pabellón Dominicano,* to support Baez's revolutionary movement. He was named Vice President in 1878 in the Provisional Government of General Cesáreo Guillermo. He was Minister of Guerra y Marino in the Administration of Governor Meriño (1880-82). In 1884 he succeeded Ulises Heureaux as president, a post he resigned on May 16, 1885. In 1893 he was elected president of the Junta Columbina.

His novel *Engracia y Antoñita* was one of the earliest works to employ local color and it was doubly "realistic" for its dramatic use of details and events of the period from the restoration of Spanish control to the independence movement of 1865. Balaguer, critic (and a president himself of the Republic) believes this novel is still the best Dominican fiction of the local color school.

Billini's poetry was occasional verse and set mostly on patriotic themes, as with "A mi patria," and "Al Libertador Máximo Gómez," where his prose is generally late romantic, lush and more lyrical. Often it is a vivid evocation of local customs and the daily lives of the people of the period just passed.

Writings: Novel: *Bani o Engracia y Antoñita,* 1892; new edition as *Engracia y Antoñita,* S. Domingo, Postigo, 1963.

Verse Drama: *Amor y expiación,* 1882 (inspired by the execution of the poet Manuel Rodriguez Objio).

Plays (in prose): *Una flor del Ozama,* written 1867, performed in an amateur production.

Legal Scholarship: "Habeas Corpus," in *El Eco de la Opinion,* 1886.

Biographical/Critical Sources: J. Balaguer's *Historia de la literatura dominicana,* fifth edition, 1970, pp. 194-196; Américo Lugo has a biographic section on Billini in his *A punto largo,* 1901; also see Max Henriquez Ureña's *Panorama histórico de la literatura dominicana,* 2 vols., second edition, S. Domingo, Postigo, 1966.

BLANCHET, Emilio

b. 1829, Matanzas, Cuba; d. 1915.
Poet, playwright, teacher.

Blanchert took part in the 1869 Cuban nationalist movement and was obliged to leave the island for work as a teacher in Barcelona, Spain. His verse works, published in occasional journals were hardly inspired but are considered "expresivos y enérgicos."

Writings: Plays: *Una carta anónima* (verse, two acts), performed Matanzas, 1849; *El unillo de Maria Tudor,* 1858; *La sortija de la reina Isabel* (historical play), 1858; *La fruta del cerdado ajeno,* Matanzas, Imp. Aurora del Yumuri, 1868; *La conjura de Pisón* (3 acts), Matanzas, R.L. Betancourt, 1906; *La verdadura culpable* (3 acts), Matanzas, Betancourt, 1906.

History: *Compendio de la Historia de la Isla de Cuba,* 1849; *Manual de la Historia de España,* 1865; *Manual de Historia Sagrada,* 1865.
Language: *Idiotismos franceses en su traducción.*

BLANCHIE, Francisco Javier

b. 1822, Havana, Cuba; d. 1847, Havana.
Poet, playwright, novelist.

Orphaned at eleven years of both parents, Blanchié was educated in a Dominican Friars' school and seminary. His life was full of troubles and his poetry reflects his deep melancholy.

Writings: Poetry: *Las margaritas,* 1845 or 1846 [16 pp.], foreword by Alejandro Angulo Guridi.
Plays: *No hagáis caso* (verse, farce), Havana, Imp. de Barcina, 1841; *Un tio* (verse, one-act comedy), Havana, 1842; *La seca y el huracán* (one-act comedy), 1845.
Novel: *La venganza de un hijo,* published in *El Eco de Villadera,* 1842 (written with Dominican writer Alejandro Angulo Guridi, while Angulo lived in Cuba).

BLANCO, Antonio Nicolás

b. 1887, San Juan, Puerto Rico; d. Hato Rey, Puerto Rico, 1945.
Poet.

Blanco was a late member of the modernista movement and active supporter of, and contributor to, the movement's leading journal, *Revista de las Antillas.* His poem "A Rubén Dario" expresses the strongly held affection for Dario's work and career:

Porque fue Rubén Dario
corazón hermano nuestro
y fue Rey y fue maestro,
y fue luz, ritmo y rocio . . .
Porque fue sencillo y pio,

He contributed much of his verse to such popular journals as *Puerto Rico Ilustrado* and his verse emphasized landscape and bucolic peasant scenes. Luis Samalea Iglesias said of his work:

> *Su poesia es refinada y alta. Tiene conceptos que detienen e invitan a ahondar. Y es elegante y aristocrático, en su porte y manera. Y es fluido, ritmico y cedoso . . .*

Blanco's poetry provided the basis for the "modernista" literary movement, especially his first collection, *El jardin de Pierrot* (1914). Stylistically, his blending of the melancholic and the intimate, and his accentuation of the gallant, but not the frivolous, remains unmatched. He is to be found at the roots of lyricism in Puerto Rican poetry through his continuing interest and exploration of the sonnet and madrigal structures of his day. He was a formative influence on a latter-day giant, Rubén Dario. In recent days he has been given a deepening scrutiny by scholars and critics of Puerto Rican literature.

Antonio Coll Vical's poem "Mi gran hermano" (in Coll's *Mediodia,* New York, 1919) speaks of Blanco:

El buen don Antonio Nico-
lás Blanco, de ojos de cobre,
que nunca saldrá de pobre
porque no sabe ser rico

tiene en su mirar el premio
de una inocencia divina,
que le dió el Hada Madrina
por consagrada bohemio.

Writings: Poetry: *El jardin de Pierrot, Poesias,* San Juan, Biblioteca Américana, 1914; *Muy sencillo,* San Juan, Standard Printing Works, 1919; *Alas perdidas,* San Juan, Imp. Real Hermanos, 1921, 1926, 1928. Poems in various collections, including *Antologia* (of Blanco's poems), San Juan, Ateneo Puertorriqueño, 1959 (Cuadernos de poesía, 9).

Biographical/Critical Sources: Enrique A. Laguerre, *La poesia modernista en Puerto Rico,* San Juan, 1969, pp. 95-102.

BLANCO Y GEIGEL, Tomás

b. 1900, Santurce, Puerto Rico.
Poet, storywriter, essayist, historian.

Blanco studied medicine in the United States and has lived a considerable period in Europe, mostly in Spain. He is primarily a storywriter but his rare verse is considered of high quality. Blanco's "Unicorno en la isla" shows his musicality, as in these opening lines:

Isla de la palmera y la guajana
con cinto de bullentes arrecifes
y corola de soles.
Isla de amor y mar enamorado.
Bajo el viento:
Los caballos azules con sus sueltas melenas,
y con desnuda piel de ascuas doradas,

Writings: Poetry: *Los cinco sentidos. Cuaderno suelta de un inventario de cosas nuestras,* San Juan, Pan American Book Co., by Imp. Venequela, 1955, and San Juan, Instituto de Cultura Puertorriqueña, 1968; *Letras para música,* San Juan, Ateneo Puertorriqueño, 1964.

Novelette: *Los vates,* San Juan, Asomante, 1950; *Heil de los Caines.*

Stories: in various collections and journals. Published separately were: *The Child's Gifts, A Twelfth Night's Tale,* trans. by Harriet de Onis, San Juan, Pan American Book Co., 1954, and London, Aldus Printers, 1954, and in Spanish as *Los aguinaldos del Infante* (gloss on the Epiphany), San Juan, Pava Prints, 1963; *La Dragonetea. Cuento de Semana Santa,* San Juan, Edit. del Departamento de Intrucción Pública, 1956; and "El Coqui" in *Asomante* (San Juan, Jan-March 1953), and "Los Vates" in *Asomante* (1949).

Social Studies: *El prejuicio racial en Puerto Rico,* San Juan, Biblioteca de Autores Puertorriqueños, 1942, second edition, 1948.

Biographical/Critical Sources: Concha Meléndez, ed., *El arte del cuento en Puerto Rico,* New York, 1961, pp. 55-60; study of *Los cinco sentidos,* in *Asomante,* No. 3 (July-Sep. 1955), p. 105; F. Manrique Cabrera, *Historia de la literatura puertorriqueña,* New York, Las Américas, 1956, pp. 293-296.

BLONDA ACOSTA, Máximo Avilés

b. May 16, 1931, Santo Domingo, Dominican Republic.
Poet, playwright, actor educator, lawyer.

Blonda, a member of the group sometimes called the "Promotion of '48," first published when his collection of poetry, *Aura de Soledad* (1957), came out. His knowledge of Dominican history and his vocation for social justice is visible in the second collection, *Centro del Mundo* (1962). The Greek influences on his thinking and work are evident in *Cantos a Helena* (1971).

His plays have been experimental, and *Yo, Bertolt Brecht* and *Piramide 179,* which deals with the Dominican-Haitian conflicts and history of warfare, are important in Dominican terms, and a highpoint of the vanguardist style. There is a poetic quality in his prose and there is much interspersed verse in his dramatic work as if to express tensions and turmoils too complex and painful for mere prose to utter.

Writings: Plays: *Las manos vacias,* S. Domingo, Arquero, 1959; *Teatro,* S. Domingo, Ed. de la Sociedad de Autores y Compositores Dramáticos, 1968. Unpublished: *Yo, Bertolt Brecht,* and *Pirámide.*

Poetry: *Aura de Soledad,* 1957; *Centro de Mundo,* S. Domingo, Editora del Caribe, 1962; *Cantos a Helena,* S. Domingo, 1971.

Interview: in *Trio*: with Rafael Valera Benitez and Lupo Hernández Rueda, S. Domingo, Col. El silbo vulnerado, 1957 (this work has a preface by P.R. Contin Aybar entitled "La invención poética").

BOBADILLA Y LUNAR, Emilio

(pseudonym: **Fray CANDIL** and **Dagoberto MARMORA**)
b. 1862, Cardenas, Cuba; d. 1921, Biarritz, France.

Poet, novelist, playwright, critic, journalist, storywriter.

Bobadilla was in the center of most of the literary brouhaha of his day, but was mostly known as a journalist and free-wheeling critic and social polemicist. He wrote four novels, four collected books of poetry, and a great deal of travel-memoirs, criticism and journalistic pieces.

Writings: Novels: *Novelas en gèrmen,* Madrid, 1900; *A fuego lento,* Barcelona, 1903, and second edition, Havana, Universidad de Habana, 1965; *En pos de la paz,* Madrid, 1917; *En la noche dormida,* Madrid, 1920.

Poetry: *Relámpagos* (24 poems), published under pseudonym Fray Candil), Havana, 1884; *Fiebres,* Madrid, 1889; *Vórtice,* Madrid, 1902; *Rojeces de Marte* (sonnets), Madrid, 1921.

Epigrams: *SAl y pimienta* (by Dagoberto Mármora), printed in Havana, but marked New York, 1891; *Mostaza,* Havana, 1885.

Play: Don Severo el literato (one act, prose sketch), 1881, in ms.

Travel: *Viajando por España,* Madrid, 1912; *Giromanos de América,* Madrid, 1902.

Journalism: *Reflejos de Fray Candil,* Havana, 1886; and see his articles in *Grandes periodisas cubanos,* Havana, 1952.

Essays: *Escaramuzas,* Madrid, 1888; *Capirotazos,* Madrid, 1890; *Criticas instantáneas:* I: *El Padre Coloma y la aristocracia,* Madrid, 1891; *Triquitraques,* Madrid, 1892; *Solfeo,* Havana, 1894; *La vida intelectual. Folletos criticos:* I: *Baturrillo,* Madrid, 1895; *Al través de mis nervios,* Barcelona, 1903; *Sintiéndome vivir,* Madrid, 1906; *Muecas,* Paris, 1908; *Con la capucha vuelta,* Paris, 1909; *Bulevar arriba, bulevar abajo,* Paris, 1911.

Biographical/Critical Sources: Max Henriquez Ureña, *Panorama histórico de la literatura cubana,* New York, 1963, pp. 127-132.

BOISSIER, Pedro Alejandro

b. 1839, Matanzas, Cuba.
Poet, playwright, engineer.

Boissier spent most of his adult life as an engineer in France where he wrote much occasional verse and the plays performed in his natal city.

Writings: Plays: *Intrigas familiares* (five-act comedy, verse), Matanzas, Folletines de "la Aurora," 1896; *El diamante perdido,* performed in Matanzas; *Los ultimos carbonarios,* performed in Matanzas.

BOLANOS, José

b. ca. 1832, Cuba.
Playwright.

Bolaños' three known plays were published in the 1860's but are today of only historical interest.

Writings: Plays: *Una empresa inesperada* (one act), Havana, Imp. El Vapor, 1862; *A puros de un guajiro* (one-act comedy), Havana, 1865; *El médico y su portera* (one act), Havana, Imp. de Villa, 1867.

BONAFOUX Y QUINTERO, Mario Luis

b. 1855, Puerto Rico; d. 1918, London.
Critic, novelist, storywriter, travelwriter, biographer, journalist.

Bonafoux early removed himself to Europe for study and permanent residence, mostly in Madrid (where he took a law degree) and Paris. Most of his life was spent in a feverish career as a professional writer and his excellent English and French opened intellectual vistas still rare in that period to most of his fellow Puerto Ricans. He often belittled his island comrades and in such works as *El Carnaval en las Antillas* (1879) sneered mightily at the provincial ways of the stay-at-homes. Though he wrote in many genres, his general purposes were polemical-journalistic more than belle-lettrist.

Manrique Cabrera wrote of him:

> *La critica punzante y dura que su pluma produce es hija de una franqueza cruda y sin embargo hidalga.*

Writings: Novels: *El asesinato de Victor Noir,*

Salamanca, 1877; *El avispero,* Madrid, Imp. Popular, 1882; *Betances,* 1901; Bilis, 1908; *Bombos y palos,* 1907.

Essays: *Semblanzas y caricaturas,* 1907; *Casi criticas reguños,* 1910; *Clericanallas,* 1910; *Coba,* 1888; *Yo y el plagiario Clarin,* 1888; *De mi vida y milagros,* 1910; *Emile Zola* (no date); *Esbozos novelescos,* 1894; *Francesas y franceses,* 1913; *Gotas de sangre,* 1910; *Huellas literarias.*

Biographical/Critical Sources: Joaquin Dicenta, "Bonafoux, nota bohemia," in *El Mundo,* San Juan (June 18, 1955); F. Manrique Cabrera, *Historia de la literatura puertorriqueña,* Rio Piedras, 1969, pp. 191-193; José A. Romeu, "Notas para un estudio sobre Luis Bonafoux," in *Asomante,* Vol. I (1950); Also see: *Literatura de Bonafoux,* 1887; *Los españoles en Paris,* 1912; *Melancolia,* 1911; *Mosquetazos de Aramis,* 1887; *Paris al dia,* 1900; *Paños calientes,* 1905; *Por el mundo arriba,* 1909; *Principes y majestades,* 1912; *Risas y lágrimas,* 1900; *Silvetas episcopales,* 1907; *Tiquismiquis,* 1888; *Ultramarinos,* 1882; *España politica, Paris en la guerra: Paris en la paz; Tristes y agrios;* and others.

BONNIN ARMSTRONG, Ana Inés

b. 1902, Ponce, Puerto Rico.
Poet, journalist, playwright.

Ana Bonnin Armstrong has spent most of her life in Barcelona, Spain, but she has published much of her work in Puerto Rican literary reviews. Her work is generally "postmodernist," original in syntax and ideas, and very free in her handling of line and rhythm.

Writings: Poetry: *Fuga,* Barcelona, Montaner y Simon, 1948; *Poema de las tres voces y otros poemas,* 1949; *Luz de blanco,* 1952; and in various journals, including *Asomante* and *Orfeo.*

Plays: *El mendigo y otros dialogos,* first edition, Barcelona, Ediciones Destino, 1960; *La dificil esperanza,* in Teatro puertorriqueño, octavo festival, San Juan, 1966.

BONO, Pedro F.

b. 1828, Dominican Republic; d. 1906.
Storywriter, historian, journalist, sociologist.

Bonó was considered to have been the first fiction writer of the Dominican Republic along with the brothers Alejandro and Javier Angulo Guridi. Bonó is believed one of his nation's outstanding intellectuals, particularly in the realm of sociology. His understanding of and scholarship in 19th century studies is marked and his specialized papers numerous.

Writings: Novelette: *El montero,* preface by Emilio Rodriguez Demorizi, S. Domingo, Postigo, 1968, but original edition was published in journal *El Correo de Ultramar,* Paris, 1851.

Papers and Articles: *Papeles de Pedro F. Bonó,* S. Domingo, Editora del Caribe, 1964 (with introduction by Rodriguez Demorizi).

BORRERO, Dulce Maria

b. 1883, Cuba; d. 1945.
Poet, critic, government official.

Daughter of poet and scientist Esteban Borrero Echeverria, Dulce Maria Borrero published one collection of verse, *Horas de mi vida* (1912) which Max Henriquez Ureña found intimate and refined. Her verse could be highly descriptive and sonorous as in these lines from "el remanso":

Del airón altivo de una palma
enhiesta
oculta en los flecos, con trinos de fiesta
modula un sinsonte sus claras octavas;

Mientras doblegados amorosamente,
con leve murmullo besan la corriente
los penachos liricos de las cañas bravas.

Borrero became director of the Office of Culture in the Ministry of Education a few years before her death.

Writings: Poetry: *Horas de mi vida,* Havana, 1912.

Esthetics: *La poesia a traves del color,* Havana, 1912.
Social Problems: *El matrimonio en Cuba,* Havana, 1912.

BORRERO, Juana

b. May 18, 1877, Cuba; d. March 8, 1896, Cayo Hueso, Cuba.
Poet.

Perished at 19, Juana Borrero still wrote and published some of the best verse of her period according to Max Henriquez Ureña who especially praises "Rimas," published 1895, "Ultimo Mimo," "Sol poniente," "Las hijas de Ran" and "Apolo." "Rimas" begins:

¿Quieres sondear la noche de mi espiritu?
Allá en el fondo oscuro de mi alma
hay un lugar donde jamás penetra
la clara luz del sol de la esperanza.

and "Ultima rima" ends:

Damé el beso soñado en mis noches,
en mis noches tristes de penas y lágrimas,
que me deje una estrella en los labios
y un tenue perfume de nardo en el alma.

Writings: Poetry: *Poesias,* Havana, Academia de Ciencias de Cuba, 1966; some of her work also appears in several volumes of verse, *Grupo de familia,* Havana, 1895 (along with verse of her father, Esteban Borrero Echeverria, and her brother, Manuel).

Biographical/Critical Sources: Max Henriquez Ureña, *Panorama histórico de la literatura cubano,* New York, 1963, pp. 250-252.

BORRERO ECHEVERRIA, Esteban

b. January 29, 1849, Camagüey, Cuba; d. 1906.
Storywriter, poet, physician, teacher.

Born into a very poor family and son of a father who was a fiery nationalist but left his young wife and son as he fled to exile in 1858, Echeverria himself fought against the colonial government. Imprisoned in Havana for a period, he later was able to complete his medical studies in 1879 at Havana University. Moving to Puentes Grandes he took up the position of municipal medical officer. Inthe revolution of 1895 he moved to Cayo Hueso and finally was forced to flee to Costa Rica because of his revolutionary sympathies. Eventually returning to become a professor at the school of Medicine in Havana, he continued his life-long love affair with letters. Enrique José Varona called him the most talented man he had ever known and a fine scientist and writer.

Writings: Stories: "Calófilo," in *Revista de Cuba,* 1879; "Cuestión de monedas," in *Revista Cubana,* 1888; small collection: *Lectura de pascuas,* Havana, 1899 (with three stories): "Una novelita," first published in *Revista de Cayo Hueso;* "Machito pichón," and "Cuestión de monedas"; and "El ciervo encantado," published 1905; and many others.
Poetry: *Poesias,* Havana, 1878; *Grupo de familia* (verse of his own and that of his brother, Manuel, and of his daughter, Juana), Havana, 1895.
Biography/Criticism: *Notas biográficas y criticas sobre el Dr. Joaquin G. Lebredo,* Havana, 1887.
Criticism: *Alrededor del Quixote* (three essays), Havana, 1905.
Fantasy: *El ciervo encantado,* Havana, 1905.
School Reader: *El amigo del niño,* Havana, 1901, and many others.
Science: *La vieja ortodoxia y la moderna* (given as speech), Havana, 1879.
Politics: *27 de Noviembre* (speech), Key West, USA, 1896; *El fusilamiento de los estudiantes y la agonia del poder colonial de España en Cuba,* Key West, 1897.
Agriculture: *El café,* Havana, 1880.

BOSCH, Juan

b. June 30, 1909, La Vega, Dominican Republic.
Storywriter, novelist, essayist, biographer, teacher, historian, statesman.

Bosch is widely known throughout Spain and Latin America, first for his important and wide range of literary and historical works but also for his political and doctrinal studies and essays. His approach to literature is that it ought to contribute to the improvement of mankind, spiritually and socially. His stories generally deal with the problems and psychology of rural people not only at home but everywhere in the Caribbean and Latin world. His style is economic and he frequently employs colloquial language, particularly that of his native region of Cibao.

JUAN BOSCH

He helped organize the Partido de la Liberación Dominicana (PLD) since the demise of the Partido Revolucionario Dominicano of which he was president.

President of the Dominican Republic for seven months (1962-1963), Bosch has published numerous volumes in many fields, most of them outside of his homeland because of his long proscription and exile during the Trujillo era. For a long period he was a professor at the Instituto de Ciencias Politicas de San Isidro, Coronado, Costa Rica during one stretch of early exile, and he also spent nineteen years in Cuba. After being removed from office as president he lived in exile in Puerto Rico for a short period before going on to Spain.

He is possibly the most prolific and wide-ranging of any Dominican writer, for his interests and varied experiences have led him to examine many aspects of the historical and political world and his personal bent has led him to transform some of these personal reactions into stories and novels.

Bosch long maintained he would not publish any more fiction because his interests lay in politics, but he has recently spoken of bringing out an old, previously unpublished novel.

Writings: Stories: *Camino Real—Cuentos,* first edition, limited edition, 1933, second edition, Santiago, Dom. Rep., 1937; *La muchacha de La Guarira,* Santiago, Chile, Nascimiento, 1955; *Cuentos escritos en el exilio,* S. Domingo, 1962; *Mas cuentos escritos en el exilio,* S. Domingo, Libreria Dominicana-Postigo, 1964. His stories are in many collections including *Narradores dominicanos,* Aïda Cartagena, ed., 1969, and *From the Green Antilles,* Barbara Howes, ed., 1971.

Novels: *Hostos el sembrador,* Havana, Edit. Trópico, 1939; *La mañosa: novela de las revoluciones,* Santiago, Edit. "El Diario," 1936, limited edition, and S. Domingo, Postigo, 1966.

Critical Essay: *Emilio Belaval, cuentista de Puerto Rico,* Havana, 1940, first published in *Puerto Rico Ilustrada* (July 1940).

Essays: *Indios—Apuntes históricos y leyendas,* first edition, limited, 1935.

Polemics: *Trujillo: Causas de un tirania sin ejemplo,* Caracas, Libreria Las Novedades," 1959, 1961; *El Pentagonismo, sustituto del imperialismo,* 1967.

Social History: *Composición social dominicana: Historia e interpretación,* S. Domingo, Publicaciones Ahora, 1970; *The Unfinished Experiment. Democracy in the Dominican Republic,* New York, Praeger, 1965.

History: *Judas Iscariote, El Calumniado,* Santiago, Chile, Prensa Latinoamericana, 1955; *Estudios y documentos: Crisis de la democracia de America en la Republica Dominicana,* first edition, Nov. 1964, second edition, Jan. 1965, third edition, Feb. 1965, all Mexico by Centro de Estudios y Documentacion Sociales, A.C.; *Dictadura con respaldo popular,* S. Domingo, 19??; also: *Breve historia de la Oligarquia,* S. Domingo, Imprensa Arte y Cine, 1971; *De Aristobal Colón a Fidel Castro,* Madrid, Alfaguara, 1970 (740 pp.).

Speeches: *Discursos (dispersos en diarios nacionales (1961-1972); El Feudalismo* (three conference papers), S. Domingo, 1971.

Biographies: *Simón Bolivar: Biografia para escolares,* Caracas, Distribuidora Escolar, 1960; *David, Biografia de un rey,* Madrid, Edición Cid, 1967, and S. Domingo, Postigo, 1964.

General: *Cuba, la isla fascinante,* Santiago, Universitaria, 1955.

Biographical/Critical Sources: Stefán Baiu's *Juan Bosch: Del exilio o la presidencia,* Buenos Aires, Bases Ed., 1963; H. Inchaustegui Cabral's *De literatura dominicana siglo veinte,* S. Domingo, UCMM, 1973 (good for its discussion of Mañosa and other fiction), pp. 288-308; Max Henriquez Ureña's *Historia de la literatura dominicana,* fifth edition, S. Domingo, Postigo, 1970, pp. 314-317.

BOTI Y BARREIRO, Regina Eladio

b. 1878, Oriente Province, Cuba; d. 1958.
Poet, biographer, prose narrative writer.

Boti moved from the "modernismo" of her youth to "postmodernismo" in her three collections of verse. She edited some of Rubén Dario's works: *Hipsiplas; El árbol del rey David,* and others.

Writings: Essay: *Marti en Dario,* date unknown.

Biography: *Guillermón,* Guantanamo, 1912.

Prose: *Rumbo a Jauco,* Guantanamo, 1910, and *Prosas emotivas,* Guantanamo, 1910.

Poetry: *Arabescos mentales,* Barcelona, Tobella, 1913; *El mar y la montaña,* Havana, 1921; *La torre del silencio,* Havana, 1926; *Kodak-Ensueño,* Havana, 1929; and prose poems: *Kindergarten,* Havana, 1930.

Literary History: *La nueva poesia en Cuba,* Havana, 1927, and its enlarged version as *Tres temas sobre la nueva poesia,* Havana, 1928.

BOURBAKIS, Roberto

b. 1919, Cuba.
Playwright.

All of Bourbakis' plays are symbolic, employing strange devices and effects. His *La gorgona* has but one character and he addressed the audience through a hearing horn used for the deaf. *Survey* has an angel visiting earth to discover whether mankind realizes angels exist, somewhat like the situation in Sean O'Casey's *Within the Gates. La rana encantada* takes place in the never-never land of Anacronia, and *Las buhardillas de la noche* is set in an old Paris during Carnival.

Writings: Plays: *Survey,* 1950; *La rana encantada,* 1950; *Las buhardillas de la noche,* 1949; *La gorgona,* 1951.

BOZELLO Y GUZMAN, Carmen

b. ca. 1846, Cuba.
Playwright.

Bozello's one known play is of only historic interest.

Writings: Play: *Abnegación y sacrificio* (two-act prose comedy), Arroyo, Cayetano Sánchez y Vegas, 1876.

BRAU Y ASENCIO, Salvador

b. January 11, 1842, Cabo Rojo, Puerto Rico; d. November 5, 1913.
Poet, playwright, storywriter, historian, journalist, statesman.

Son of a Spanish (Catalán) father and a Venezuelan mother who had emigrated to Puerto Rico during a period of civil strife in Venezuela, Brau was considered to be one of the island's finest prose writers. After local schooling under Ramón Marin, Brau completed a play on the revolt of the comunes during the reign of Emperor

Charles V of Spain, the work seeing production in Cabo Rojo, Mayagüez, and other island cities. Well received, the play encouraged him to write others, including *De la superficie* and *La vuelta al hogar.*

An active political talent, the young Brau early entered the journalistic arena where polemics on independence and Spanish rule were the constant topics. He contributed to such journals as *El Agente, El Clamor del Pais, El Asimilista, El Buscapie,* and the short-lived but important *Revista Puertorriqueña* which he himself had helped found in 1887. Though a fighting liberal and nationalist, Brau also loved Spanish culture and the language and by 1894 was doing research with official support on the archival documents concerning Puerto Rico in Spain. After four years of such work he could consider himself a working historian, and, while serving as a customs officer in San Juan, Brau published his *Historia de Puerto Rico* (1904) for school use and two years later his *Historia de los cincuenta primeros años de la conquista y la colonización de Puerto Rico,* the latter sponsored by the Casino Español de San Juan.

In his last years, the legislature named Brau "Official Chronicler" which gave him a dignified and modestly remunerated post.

Writings: Plays: *Héroe y mártir,* performed 1870, published San Juan, Gonzáles, 1871; *De la superficie al fondo* (a three act comedy), San Juan, Tip. Gonzáles, 1874; *La vuelta al hogar,* (three acts, verse), San Juan, Nueva Imp. del Boletin Mercantil, 1877; *Los horrores del triunfo* (three acts, verse), San Juan, Tip. González Font, 1887; *Obra teatral,* 2 vols., Rio Piedras, Edit. Coqui, 1972.

Poetry: *Hojas caidas,* San Juan, La Democracia, 1909; the long poem "¡Patria!" appears in the *Antologia portorriqueña,* edited by M. Fernández Juncos, New York, 1907, pp. 239-254. Poems in many collections and journals.

Journalistic Articles: *Ecos de la batalla,* San Juan, Imp. J. Gonzáles Font, 1886; and individual pieces: "Las clases jornaleras," "La campesina (sociology essays, published 1886); "La herencia devota" (1886); "La danza" (1887); and "La pecadora"; Also see his essay as introduction to second edition of Manuel A. Alonso's *El Gibaro,* San Juan, 1882, pp. xv-xvii; Also: "La danza puertorriqueña," in *Escritos sobre Puerto Rico,* Barcelona, Ed. José Gonzáles Font, 1903.

History: *Puerto Rico y su historia,* 1894; *Historia de Puerto Rico,* New York, Appleton and Co., 1904; *La colonización de Puerto Rico,* 1906; "Los primeros escritores y los primeiros libros puertorriqueños" in *Heraldo Español* (San Juan, Year XIV, No. 170, July 19, 1970); *Dos factores de la colonización de Puerto Rico* (from Conference Papers of the Ateneo de Puerto Rico), San Juan, Imp. de J.J. Acosta, 1896.

Social Studies (pamphlets): *Disquisiciones sociológicas,* 1965.

Novelette: *La pecadora,* first published in *Revista Puertorriqueña,* 1887, and in separate volume, San Juan, 1890.

Biographical/Critical Sources: F. Manrique Cabrera, *Historia de la literatura puertorriqueña,* Rio Piedras, 1969, pp. 169-177; Cristóbal Real, *Salvador Brau,* San Juan, Imp. M. Burillo, 1910; Carmen Gómez Tejera, *La novela en Puerto Rico,* Río Piedras, 1947; Augusto Malaret, *Salvador Brau,* San Juan, Boletin Mercantil, 1910.

BRULL Y CABALLERO, Mariano

b. 1891, Cuba; d. 1956.
Poet.

Brull was a member of the Vanguardist movement of the 1940-1950 period. Influenced by Malarmé and Valery, he tried to realize in his verse similar qualities of purity and refinement. Cintio Vitier defined Brull's poetry as being based on symbols that work throughout the poem: ". . . el desnudo ante el espejo, la rosa desconocida, el fantasma del tiempo inapresable, las vísperas del yo y el mundo . . ."

The third verse of "Granada" is typical of his work:

¡Qué nudo anuda me carne
Raiz de aire que me enlaza
a música de temblores
en parpadeos de alma!

An example of his more eccentric vanguardista poetry are these three stanzas from "Verdehalago" from his collection *Poemas en menguante*:

Por, el verde, verde
verderia de verde mar
Rr con Rr
Viernes, virgula, virgen
enano verde.
Verduleria cantarida
Rr con Rr
...
Vengo de mundo dolido
y en Verdehalago me estoy

Writings: Poetry: *La casa del silencio,* intro. by Pedro Henriquez Ureña, 1916; *Poemas en menguante,* 1928; *Canto redondo,* Havana, 1934; *Sola de rosa,* Havana, 1941; *Temps en peine/Tiempo en pena* (original text and French translation by Mathile Poenés), 1950.
Translations: *Rien que/Nada mas* (Spanish and French text), Havana, 1954.

Biographical/Critical Sources: Max Henriquez Ureña, *Tránsito y poesia de Mariano Brull,* Havana, 1958.

BUCH, René

b. 1926, Cuba.
Playwright.

Buch's dramas portray the life and customs of his natal Santiago de Cuba region and are psychological in emphasis.

Writings: Plays: *Del agua de la vida,* 1948; *Nosotros los muertos* (one act), 1948; and *La caracola vacia* (one act), 1951.

BUESA, José Angel

b. 1910, Cuba.
Poet, playwright.

Buesa, a major poet of his period, and a "postmodernista," wrote a melodic line and became very popular. Max Henriquez Ureña is not overly impressed, however, by his 17 volumes of verse, finding only the sonnet "Yo vi la noche . . ." as being worth remembering. It begins:

Yo vi la noche ardiendo en su tamaño,
y yo crecia hacia la noche pura
en un afan secreto de estatura,
uniendo mi alegria con mi daño.

Writings: Plays: *La mujer del farol,* premiered in London; *Sol de domingo,* 1933.
Poetry: *La fuga de los horas,* 1932; *Misas paganas,* 1933; *Babel,* 1936; *Canto final,* 1938; *Oasis,* 1943, 14th edition, Mexico, Minerva, 1966; *Hyacinthus,* 1943; *Prometeo,* 1943; *La vejas de don Juan,* 1943; *Odas por la Victoria,* 1943; *Muerte divina,* 1943; *Cantos de Proteo,* 1944; *Lamentaciones de Proteo,* 1947; *Canciones de Adán,* 1947; *Alegria de Proteo,* 1948; *Antologia,* 1949; *Poemas en la arena,* 1949; *Nuevo Oasis,* 1949; *Versos de amor,* Havana, 1959; *Poeta enamorado,* Havana, 1960; *Los mejores poemas de José Angel Buesa,* Havana, 1960; *Poemas prohibidos,* Havana, all by Distribuidora Antillana de Libreria, 1959 (in two editions); *Libro secreto,* Havana, 1960.

DE BURGOS, Julia (Julia (or Julia Constancia BURGOS GARCIA)

b. 1914, Carolina, Puerto Rico; d. 1953, New York City.
Poet, journalist, teacher.

Julia De Burgos is considered by most of her countrymen to be the island nation's finest woman poet. Her "Rio Grande de Loiza" is very well known. It opens with these lines:

¡Rio Grande de Loia! . . . Alárgate en mi espiritu
y deja que mi alma se pierda en tus riachuelos,
para buscar la fuente que te robó de niño
y en un impetu loco te devolvio al sendero.

and it ends:

si no fuera más grande el que de mise sale
por los ojos del alma para mi esclavo
pueblo.

Her early style was relatively relaxed, natural, but her later work was more touched by "Superrealismo" or the subconscious, becoming very emotional.

Writings: Poetry: *Poemas exactos a mi misma,* privately published in mimeograph, 1937; *Poema en viente surcos,* San Juan, Imp. Venezuela, 1938; *Canción de la verdad sencilla,* San Juan, Imp. Baldrich, 1939; *El mar y tú otros poemas,* San Juan, Puerto Rico Printing and Publishing Co., 1954; ten of her poems are in the *Antologia de la poesia puertorriqueña,* E. Fernández Méndez, ed., San Juan, 1968, and she is represented in many other collections, including five poems in *Aguinaldo lirico,* edited by C. Rosa-Nieves, 1957, pp. 416-421, and poems in *Antologia poética* [foreword by Yvette Jiménez de Báez], San Juan, Edit. Coqui, 1967; *Poesias,* San Juan, Instituto de Cultura Puertorriqueńa, 1964. Also: *Obra poética,* San Juan, Instituto de Cultura Puertorriqueńa, 1961.

Biographical/Critical Sources: Yvette Jiménez de Báez, *Vida y poesia* [of De Burgos], San Juan, Editorial Coqui, 1966; *Aguinaldo lirico,* C. Rosa-Nieves, Rio Piedras, 1957, pp. 415-416; F. Manrique Cabrera, *Historia de la literatura puertorriqueña,* Rio Piedras, 1969, pp. 354357; Isabel Cuchi Coll, *Dos poetas de América: Clara Lair, Julia de Burgos,* Barcelona, 1970; Tomás Jesús Castro, 2 vols., *Esbozos,* Barcelona, 1957. Also see "Clara Lair y Julia de Burgos: Reminiscencias de Evaristo Ribera Chevremont y Jorge Font Saldaña," by Gladys Neggers, in *Revista Interamericana,* Vol. IV, No. 2 (Summer 1974), pp. 258-263.

BUSCON, Juan

(pseudonym for **Manuel de Jesús TRONCOSO DE LA CONCHA**)

BUSTO, Jorge del

b. 1918, Cuba.
Plawright.

Busto's *La suicida* employs the not completely unusual device of just one character, in this case a woman, but she does not speak herself, but reacts to voices coming from off-stage which are evocations of her past and her problems.

Writings: Plays: *El Cristo,* 1948 (farce); and *La suicida,* 1950 (one-act, one character play).

BUZZI, David

b. 1932, Havana, Cuba.
Novelist, storywriter, lawyer.

Buzzi studied law at the University of Havana and practiced that profession before entering government service in 1959. During the Castro-led movement to establish a new regime, Buzzi served in the Hermanos Sainz brigade. He has published many of his tales in Cuban journals and both of his novels were well recieved.

Writings: Novels: *Los desnudos,* Havana, Unión, 1967 (honorable mention in Concurso de la Casa de las Américas, 1966); *Treinta minutos* (Finalist in the Concurso de la Unión de Escritores, 1967); *La religión de los elegantes,* Havana, Instituto del Libro, 1969; *Mariana,* Havana, Unión, 1970.
Stories: in many journals.

BYRNE, Bonifacio

b. March 3, 1861, Matanzas, Cuba; d. 1936.
Poet, playwright, editor.

Byrne at one time or other served as director to the journals *La Manana, La Juventud Liberal,* and *El Obrero* and as editor to *El Diario de Matanzas,* the last journal suppressed by Spain because of its revolutionary sentiments. After independence Byrne visited the United States and his enthusiasm led him to write the verse collected in "La Nación Maravillosa" but never published.

His plays *El anónimo* and *El lagado* were warmly received. The most famous poem of the revolutionary period leading to Cuban freedom was probably Byrne's "Mi bandera" which begins:

Al volver de distante ribera
con el alma enlutada y sombria,
afanoso busqué mi bandera
y otra he visto, adémas de la mia!

Writings: Poetry: *Eccéntricas,* Matanzas, 1893; *Efigies, sonetos patrióticos,* Philadelphia, 1897; *Lira y espada,* Havana, 1901; *Poemas,* Havana, 1903; *En medio del camino,* Matanzas, 1914; "La nación maravillosa," written in 1915 but remains in manuscript.

Plays: (All performed but unpublished): *El anónimo; El espiritu de Marti; El legado; Rayo de sol; Varón en puerta.*

Biographical/Critical Sources: Unpublished Ph. D. dissertation by Armantina Rodriguez Cáceres has detailed discussion of Byrne's unpublished works.

CABALLERO, José Augustin

b. 1762, Cuba; d. 1835.
Essayist, philosopher, orator, priest.

Taking a doctorate in theology in 1783, Caballero became a teacher at the Seminario de San Carlos of which he became a director and which he reformed with the the ideas of Locke, Condorcet and Newton, all new currents in colonial Cuba. He helped found the journal *El Papel Periódico* and other such cultural organs.

Writings: Philosophy: *Lecciones de filosofia electiva,* written in Latin, but eventually published in Spanish translation, Havana, University of Havana, 1944.

Biographical/Crritical Sources: Articles in *Diario de la Havana* (April 20, 1855); Max Henriquez Ureña, *Panorama histórico de la literatura cubana,* New York, 1963, pp. 95-97.

CABANILLAS, Isabel

b. 1905, Mayagüez, Puerto Rico.
Poet.

Cabanillas' poetry, much of it collected in *Lota* (1954), seems influenced by Alfonsina Storni and Juana de Ibarbourou. Her themes are Hellenic love and the countryside. The last lines from "Alegria" give an idea of her work:

¿Quién me compra me alegria que mis ojos van gritando?
Cómpramela buena niña, cómpramela buen amado,
Alegria, alegria, alegria de mis manos.
Compro esta loca alegria ahora que aun es temprano
ahora que huelo a selva, a pomarrosas y nardos.

Writings: Poetry: *Lota,* Madrid, 1954; "Alegria," first published in *Prensa II,* 2 (1956).

CABRAL, Eulogia

b. 1868, Dominican Republic; d. 1928.
Poet (in creole), storywriter.

Cabral was considered one of the finest of the popular tale writers of his day. His *Cachimbolas,* a collection of creole stories and songs, are artless but in their very naturalness much closer to the folkspirit than are most of the literary "reconstructions" of the more educated poets working the same vein of peasant literature.

Writings: Folk tales and Poetry: *Cachimbolas,* details not known.

CABRAL, Manuel del

b. March 7, 1907, Santiago de los Caballeros, Dominican Republic.
Poet, storywriter, novelist, playwright, editor, autobiographer.

Cabral is one of the finest poets in the Republic. Leaving behind the "Vanguardista" poetry of his early days, Cabral became a vivid realist in his work, seeking a direct encounter with the working people of his island nation. In his autobiography *Historia de mi voz* he explains his poetics and the principles of his work. His 1935 collection of poems, his second, *12 poemas negros,* marked the first leap into "modernism" of a Dominican writer and is also a very important work reflecting Afro-Caribbean culture.

Writings: Poetry: *Pilón; cantos del terruño y otros poemas,* Santiago, D. R., 1931, 2nd ed., Santiago, 1936; *Color de agua,* 1932; *12 poemas negros,* 1935; *8 gritos,* 1937; *Biografia de un silencio,* Buenos Aires, Editorial Tor, 1940; *Trópico negro,* Buenos Aires, Editorial Sopena Argentina, 1941; *Compadre mon,* 1943, 2nd ed., Buenos Aires, Ed. Losada, 1957; *Sangre major,* 1945; *Antologia tierra* (1930-1949), Madrid, Seminario de Problemas Hispanoamericanos, 1949; *Segunda antologia tierra 1930-1951,* Madrid, Gráficas Garcia, 1952 [this volume contains the prose poems of "Chincina" and parts of *Comprade* and some new works]; *Los huéspedes secretos,* 1951; *De este lado del mar,* Ciudad Trujillo, Impresora Dominicana, 1949; *Sexo y alma,* 1956; *Pedrada planetaria,* Buenos Aires, Editorial Alfa, 1958; *14 mudos de amor,* 1962; *La isla ofendida,* 1965; *Los anti-tiempo,* 1967; in ms: "Edad sin tiempo."

Stories: *30 parábolas,* Buenos Aires, Editorial Lucania, 1956; *Dos cantos continentales y unos temas eternos,* 1956; *Carta para un fósforo no usado y otras cartas,* 1958; *Chinchina busca el tiempo,* Buenos Aires, Ed. Perlado, 1945 and Buenos Aires, Editoriale Americalee, 1957 [these are prose-poems]; *Rélampagos lentos,* Buenos Aires, Ed. Suramericana.

Play: *La Carabina Piensa* (one-act), S. Domingo, Taller, 1976, in miniature edition (3 3/4" x 5).

Biographical/Critical Sources: José Olivio Jiménez's comments, pp. 346-47 in *Antologia de la poesia hispanoamericana contemporánea 1914-1970.* Madrid, 1972.

CABRERA, Lydia

b. 1900, Cuba.
Folklorist, anthologist.

After local schooling, Cabrera went to Paris for a long stay, but she maintained an abiding interest in her homeland, particularly the folk-stories of the Afro-Cubans. She published two important collections of Afro-Cuban legends, first in French and later in Spanish. By the 1950's she had removed to Florida where she continued her research and publications on this subject.

Only in 1971 with *Ayapá,* a collection of nineteen Afro-Cuban tales, and *Las piedras preciosas* of the previous year, did she seem to recover her stride in exile.

Writings: Folkstories: *Cuentos negros de Cuba,* Havana, La Verónica, 1940; *Porque . . .Cuentos negros de Cuba,* Havana, 1940, 1948; *Ayapá: Cuentos de Jicotea,* Miami, 1971; *Otan Iyebiye: Las piedras preciosas,* Miami, 1970.

Ethnic Studies: *El Monte, Igbo Finda, Ewe Orisha, Vititinfinda. Notas sobre las religiones, la magia, las supersticiones y el folklore de los negros criollos y del pueblo de Cuba,* Havana, 1954; new edition, Miami, Rema Press, 1968, with new information on Shango cult in Cuba.

Biographical/Critical Sources: Hilda Perera, *Idapo: El sincretismo en los cuentos negros de Lydia Cabrera,* Miami, 1971.

CABRERA Y BOSCH, Raimundo

(a.k.a. **"C. C."** and **Ricardo BUENAMAR**)

b. March 9, 1852, Havana, Cuba; d. May 21, 1923.
Playwright, novelist, poet, memorist, lawyer.

An early and fervent nationalist, Cabrera was imprisoned for a period as a young man for his political activities, and later was a founder of the Liberal Party in Güines, his family's long resident, Cabrera studied law in Spain and carried on a legal career filled with his political efforts, amateur acting, occasional versifying and the writing of four burlesque plays.

Exiled in 1895, he voyaged in Europe and the United States and founded in New

York City the review *Cuba y América* in 1897. Returned to Cuba he was exiled again in 1917 for a short period. In his late years he has been much honored and has served as president of the society Amigas del Pais.

Writings: Novels: *Sombras que pasan,* 1916; *Ideales,* 1918; and *Sombras eternas,* 1919 (a trilogy), all Havana.

Plays: *Viaje a la luna,* Güines, El Democrata, 1885, music by D.M.J Mauri, and shown to be authored by "C.C."; *¿Vapor correo!* (one act, four scenes, comedy), Havana, El Retiro, 1888; *Del parque a la luna* (one act farce, music by D.M.J. Mauri), Havana, El Retiro, 1888; *Intrigas de un secretario* (two act farce), Havana, Soler, Alvarez, 1889.

Poetry: Juveniles, 1907.

Stories: *Cuentos mios,* 1904; *Medio siglo* (novelette).

Memoir: *Mis buenos tiempos,* 1891; *Cartas a Govin,* 2 vols., 1892-93 (based on 1892-93 trip to U. S. and particularly to the Chicago Columbian Exposition); *Cartas a Estévez,* 1906; *Episodios de la guerra: Mi vida en la manigua,* Philadelphia, 1898, semi-biographical; *Borador de viaje,* 1910; *Desde mi sitio,* 1912; *Mis malos tiempos,* 1920.

Polemics: *Cuba y sus jueces,* 1887, six more printings by 1889 and an English translation by Laura Guiteras as *Cuba and the Cubans, Philadelphia, 1896.*

Biographical/Critical Sources: Max Henriquez Ureña, *Panorama histórico de la literatura cubana,* New York, 1963, pp. 93-97.

CABRERA INFANTE, Guillermo

(pseudonym: **G. CAIN**)

b. April 22, 1929, Gibara (Oriente), Cuba. Novelist, storywriter, editor, diplomat, journalist.

A searcher for honesty and no pretense, Cabrera has written (under the pseudonym G. Cain) many critical articles on the cinema, collected in 1963, most of them for the now defunct *Carteles.* In 1959, he established *Lunes de Revolución,* the literary supplement to the paper *Revolución,* but it was banned in 1961 and the editor accepted a post as cultural attache of the Cuban Embassy in Brussels, later being promoted to chargé d'affaires of the Embassy. He resigned in 1965 while home for his mother's funeral and located himself thereafter in London.

He founded the Cinemateca de Cuba in 1951 and in 1956 became director of that organization.

Writings: Novel: *Tres tristes tigres,* 1964, winner of the Premio Biblioteca Breve, published Barcelona, Seix y Barral, 1967; in French trans. by Albert Bensoussan and author, as *Trois tristes tigres,* Paris, Gallimard, 1970, and English trans. by Donald Gardner, Suzanne Jill Levine and author, *Three Trapped Tigers,* New York, Harper and Row, 1971.

Stories: *Asi en la paz como la guerra,* Havana, Revolución, 1960, and many other eds. including Barcelona, Seix y Barral, 1970. Trans. into French as *Dans la paix comme dans la guerre,* Paris, Gallimard, 1964 and into Italian, Polish, Russian, Czech and Chinese. Story, "A Sparrows Nest in the Awning," is in English translation in *Writers in the New Cuba,* J. M. Cohen, ed., Harmondsworth, England, Penguin, 1967. Other work is in *Mundus Artium* journal, III, 3 (1970).

Poetry: *Exorcismos de esti(l)o.* Barcelona, Seix Barral, 1976 (302 pp.)

Collection of Film Criticism: *Un Oficio del Siglo XX,* Havana, Ediciones R, 1963.

Biographical/Critical Sources: William Siemens, "Guillermo Cabrera Infante: Language and Creativity," unpublished Ph.D. dissertation., Univ. of Kansas, 1971; Eligio Garcia, "Los relatos de Cabrera Infante," *Imagen* (August 22-29, 1970), section 2, pp. 4-5; review of *Exorcismos de esti(l)o,* by Klaus Müller-Bergh, in *World Literature Today* (Spring 1977), p. 253.

CABRISAS, Hilarión

B. 1883, Matanzas, Cuba; d. 1939. Poet.

Possibly the most popular poet of his day,

Hilarión had no major collected works. Some of his best-known poems were "La lágrima infinita," "Plegaria del peregrino absurdo;" he published the latter poem in the chapbook, *¿Esperanza?*, in Havana in 1911.

CADILLA DE RUIBAL, Carmen Alicia

b. 1908, Arecibo, Puerto Rico.
Poet, journalist.

Struck by paralysis at seven, Carmen Cadilla has of necessity turned to books and an inner life. She is strongly religious and has been influenced by Gabriela Mistral, Juana de Ibarbourou and Alfonsina Storni.

Rosa-Nieves writes of Cadilla's verse that it has ". . . un suave fluir, una amargura color de hilo de agua, una alegria triste de tarde de oro que espera a su novio en la cascada, un anhelar infinito de horizontas ariscos e inquietos . . ." and her tone is intimate and "piano, pianisimo."

"Arbol muerto" (from *Brújula* 1, 3 & 4, August, 1935 of San Juan) begins:

Aquel árbol tenia
las raices tan hondas
como el mirar de un loco
y tan largas
como su propia sombra

Writings: Poetry: *Los silencios diáfanos,* 1931; *Lo que tú y yo sentimos,* 1933; *Canciones en flautablanca,* 1934; *Raices azules,* 1936; *Zafra amarga,* 1938; *Litoral del sueño,* 1938; *Voz de las islas intimas,* 1939; *Ala y ancla,* 1940; *Antologia poética* (her selected poems), 1941; *Mundo sin geografia,* 1948 (prose poems with introduction by Enrique Laguerre); *Tierras del Alma: Poemas de amor,* San Juan, Ateneo Puertorriqueño, 1969; *Antologia poética,* San Juan, Imp. Venezuela, 1941. Several of her poems are in *Agüinaldo liricos,* C. Rosa-Nieves, ed., 1st ed., Rio Piedras, 1957. Three poems of hers in Spanish original and English translation are in *An Anthology of Contemporary Latin American Poetry,* Dudley Fitts, ed., New York, New Directions, 1942.

CADILLA DE MARTINEZ, Maria (Liana)

b. December 21, 1884, Puerto Rico; d. August 23, 1951, San Juan.
Folklorist, scholar, literary critic, storywriter.

Cadilla has produced some of the most useful studies of island culture in his four volumes of folklore and numerous scholarly articles on Cuban folklore and legends from the Ponce area.

Writings: Stories: *Hitos de la raza (cuentos tradicionales y folklóricas),* San Juan, Imp. Venezuela, 1945.

Folklore: *El tesoro de Don Alonso* [25 pp.], from legend collected in Ponce, *Pictorial Review* (1917), which journal also had Cadilla's "Del sendero florido," pp. 35-47 and "El pródigo," pp. 125-138: all these also in *Editorial Puerto Rico Ilustrado,* 1925 [138 pp.]; *Costumbres y tradicionalismos de mi tierra,* San Juan, Imp. Venezuela, 1938; *Juegos y canciones infantiles de Puerto Rico,* San Juan, Imp. Baldrich, 1940; *Raices de mi tierra,* Arecibo, P.R., Tip. Hernández, 1941.

Critical-Literary History: *La poesia popular en Puerto Rico,* Madrid, Universidad de Madrid, (Imp. Moderna), 1933; "La elegia VI de Juan de Castellanos," unpublished M.A. Thesis, U. of P.R., 1931.

Biographical/Critical Sources: Margot Arce de Vásquez, *Impresiones [essay on Cadilla], San Juan, 1950.*

CALCAGNO, Francisco

b. July 1, 1827, Güines, Cuba; d. Barcelona, Spain, March 22, 1903.
Playwright, poet, critic, biographer, autobiographer.

Son of an Italian-born father, long resident in Cuba, Calcagno became Cuba's earliest and greatest literary historian. His *Diccionario biográfico cubano* (1878) was a milestone in Cuban cultural history and his more specialized work *Poetas de color* (also 1878) provided detailed information on Plácido (Gabriel de la Concepción Valdés), Manzano, Augustin Baldomero

Rodriguez, Ambrosio Echemendia and Antonio Medina.

He wrote several plays and his first novel, *Romualdo* (1881) was a castigating look at Cuba's recently abandoned slavery. His third novel, *S.I.* (1896) was a less polemical work, based as it was on the lives of Bishop Juan de las Cabezas Altamirano and the pirate Gilberto Girón.

Writings: Plays: *Avant de te marier, regarde ce que tu fais* (one act comedy), Havana, S.S. Spencer, 1886 or 1887 (adopted from dramatic piece by Spanish writer Charles Navarrete); *El aprendiz del zapatero* (verse monologue), Havana, Imp. *El Pilar,* 1891; *Torquemada* (three acts), adapted from Victor Hugo's play, published Havana, 1891 and Barcelona, Tip. Moderna, 1900.

Poetry: *Y yo entre ellos,* Havana, 1885.

Novels: Romualdo o Uno de tantos, Havana, 1881; *Los lazos,* Havana, 1893 (in later editions it was entitled *Mina*); S.I. (meaning Su Ilustrisima), Barcelona, 1896; *En busca del eslabón,* Havana, 1888.

Literary History: *Poetas de color,* first published in the journal *La Revolución,* edited in New York by Issac Carrillo y O'Farril, 1868, first book edition, Havana, 1878, and eight further editions at least; *Diccionario biográfico cubana, in Revista de Cuba,* New York, 1878, as a book in Havana, 1878; *Apuntes biográficos del ilustre sabio cubano D. Tranquilino Sandalio de Noda,* Matanzas, 1891.

Memoirs: *Recuerdos de antes de ayer,* Havana, 1893.

Speech: *Zanella,* Barcelona, 1896.

Various Works: *Los crimenes de Concha,* Havana, 1887; *El vaso de agua con panales,* Havana, 1885; *Don Enriquito,* Havana, 1895; *Historia de un muerto y noticias del otro mundo,* Havana, 1895; *El emisario,* Barcelona, 1896; *El catecismo autonómico,* Havana, 1887; *Un casmiento misterioso,* Havana, 1897; *La República,* unica salvación *de la familia cubana,* Barcelona, 1898.

CALDERON ESCOBAR, Juan

b. 1902, San Juan, Puerto Rico; d. 1942. Poet.

Calderón initiated the local poetic movement "Atalayismo" in 1928 which had a strong nationalist political purpose including support of the efforts of the Partido Nacionalista. The influence of Edgar Allen Poe, José Asunción Silva, and Baudelaire are all visible in his verse and Rosa-Nieves writes in his *Aguinaldo lirico:* "Es una poemática sombria, florecida de visiones grises, y de negros presagios . . . La vida de Juan Calderón Escobar fue una encrucijada de misterios, de sombras y de secretas interrogaciones, su misma muerte de espectacularismo tabloide, dejo atónitos a todos sus allegados y amigos."

His "El pájaro negro" (from *Bajo la tapa comba) begins:*

Sobre una torre en ruinas, baja un plomizo cielo
donde espectros de nubes forma la tempestad,
un pájaro negruzco, causado por desvelo
suelta a los aires frios neurótico cantar.

Writings: Poetry: *Baja la tapa comba,* San Juan, 1923; *Saludo a la bandera Atalayista,* San Juan, 1930; *La tierra de en la luna* (also contains stories and articles), 1935; *Los motivos del nuevo Job* (sonnets), San Juan, 1939; verse in various journals and anthologies including C. P. Rosa-Nieves, *Agüinaldo lirico de la poesia puertorriqueña,* 1st ed., 1957, Rio Piedras, 1957.

CAMIN, Alfonso

b. 1890, Roces (Girón), Spain. Poet.

Though born in Spain, Camin emigrated early to Cuba and became one of the earliest and best known of the Afro-Cuban poets. Emilio Marin Pérez said of his work: ". . . los negros de sus poemas son reales y no unos angelitos más o menos morenos." Though most of his work was hurried he has good poems here and there and a careful selection would produce a dignified collection. His "Elogia de la negra" begins:

Negra, carbón celeste, carne de tamarindo
que desprecias al negro barbilindo
que está a la puerta de la barberia
multicolor, viendo morir el dia.

Writings: Poetry: *Carey,* 1945; *Maracas,* 1952, and at least 23 other volumes. Much of his work was first published in newspapers and other journals in Spain, Mexico, and Cuba. Four poems of the hey-day of Afro-Cuban verse are "Negro," "Malaquita," "Macorina," and "Elogia de la negra," and appear in *Poesia negra del caribe,* edited by Hortensia Ruiz del Vizo.

CAMORS, Conde D. E.

(pseudonym for **Julián del CASAL**)

CAMPINS, Rolando

b. 1940, Palma Soriano (Oriente), Cuba. Poet.

Campins came of age during the successful Castro-led revolution and his work is closely tied to the struggles and experiences of the Afro-Cubans of which he is one. His four stanza poem "Mulata" begins:

Ten, ten la negra con pelo,
ten, ten la blanca con bemba
¡pero el que quiera mulata,
que la mantenga!

Writings: Poetry: *Vecindario,* details not known; *Habitante de toda esperanza,* Palencia, Colección de Poesia Hispanoamericana, 1969; *Sonsonero mulato,* New York, Colección Nueva Sangre, 1969; *Arbol sin paraiso (Las tribulaciones y los sueños),* Madrid, Alfaguara, 1971.

CANALES, Nemesio R.

b. December 18, 1878, Jayuya, Puerto Rico; d. New York, September 14, 1923. Storywriter, essayist, critic, playwright, poet, lawyer.

Canales after a brief period of study of medicine in Spain in 1898, transferred to Baltimore School of Law (Baltimore, Maryland, U.S.A.) to study law. Subsequently, he entered legal practice in Puerto Rico in 1903 in Ponce and later in San Juan. At home he was active as a journalist and literary critic and began writing in verse and dramatic forms.

He joined the group supporting the journal *Revista de las Antillas* founded by Luis Lloréns Torres and later founded the weekly, *Juan Bobo* (later called *Idearium* as a monthly) with Lloréns Torres. He also was the editor of *Cuasimodo,* published in Buenos Aires and later in Panama, and *El Dia* in which he first published the essays collected in *Paliques* (1913), a deeply humorous but sympathetic study of the human condition.

Canales served as a representative in the Puerto Rican legislature and traveled widely throughout Latin America.

One of Canales' best friends, Sócrates Nolasco, published a study (*Escritores De Puerto Rico,* 1953) of Canales and his relationships with other Puerto Rican writers such as Antonio Pérez Pierret, Miguel Guerra Mondragón and Luis Lloréns Torres.

Writings: Essays: *Paliques,* 1913, and 2nd ed., Rio Piedras, Ed. Phi Eta Mu [U. of P.R.], 1952; 5th ed. San Juan, Edit. Coqui, 1968.

Novelette: *Hacia un lejano sol,* Buenos Aires, Novela de la juventud, No. 8 (Dec. 23, 1970);*Mi voluntad se ha muerto,* Buenos Aires, 1921 (21 pp.).

Play: *El héroe galopante* (comedy), Caguas, Publicaciones Caguas, Vol. I (1935), pp. 55-86, 1923-1935, 2nd ed., San Juan, Editorial Coqui, 1967.

Criticism: *La leyenda benaventina,* 922 (articles which appeared in *Cuasimodo* journal, edited by Canales).

Biographical/Critical Sources: Patria Dueño, "La satira en la literatura puertorriqueña hasta Nemesio R. Canales," unpublished M.A. Thesis, U. of P.R., 1952, 248 pp.; Antonio De Jesús, "Nemesio R. Canales," in *El héroe galopante,* Caguas, Publicaciones Caguas, Vol. I, 1935; Encarnita Montes de Rodriguez, *Nemesio Canales, vida y obra,* 197?; F. Manrique Cabrera, *Historia de la literatura puertorriqueña,* Rio Piedras, 1969, pp. 265-270. Sócrates Nolasco,

Escritores de Puerto Rico, foreword by Luis Muñoz Marin, Manzanillo, Cuba, Edit. El Arte, 1953 (emphasis on Canales).

CANDIDO, Pepe

(pseudonym for **Rafael Alfredo DELIGNE Y FIGUEROA**)

CAPIRO, Eligio Eulogio

b. 1825, Villaclara, Cuba; d. 1859.
Poet, journalist, teacher.

Capiro's pioneering work has appeared in several collections, including *Cuba poética,* edited by José Fornaris, Havana, 1859.

Biographical/Critical Sources: Ofrenda consagrada a la memoria del distinguido poeta Villaclareno Eligio Eulogio Capiro la noche del 1º de noviembre de 1865 . . ., Villaclara, 1865.

CARBONELL, José Manuel

b. 1880, Cuba.
Poet, critic.

Once an active collaborator of José Marti, Carbonell's work today is only of academic interest. His literary history, *Evolución de la cultura cubana* (1928) is, however, an excellent collection of important cultural-literary documents and useful discussions of them.

Writings: Poetry: Mi libro de amor; Patria; Penachos.

Pamphlet: *La visión del águila,* Havana, 1908.

Criticism: *Alrededor de un gran poeta: Leopoldo Lugones,* Havana, 1912; in *Los poetas de "El Laúd del desterrado"; La critica en la literatura cubana,* Havana, 1930.

Editor of: *Evolución de la cultura cubana,* 18 vols., Havana, 1928.

CARDENAS Y CHAVEZ, Marqués de San Miguel

b. 1802, Cuba; d. 1890.
Poet.

Cárdenas wrote poetry in imitation of the nature poetry of Andrés Bello, Spanish writer á la mode in the mid-1800's.

Writings: Poetry: *Flores cubanos,* 1842; *Poesias,* Madrid, 1854.

CARDENAS Y RODRIGUES, José Maria

b. 1812, Limonar, Cuba; d. 1882.
Poet, playwright, storywriter, journalist, folklorist.

Educated in the Colegio de San Fernando in Havana, Cárdenas went on to the United States for advanced schooling. He was a leading figure in the Cuban journalism of the day, being a contributor and/or editor to such journals as *La Prensa, El Artista, Revista de la Habana, Revista pintoresca* and *El Faro Industrial,* the latter of which he founded.

His collection of folklore (1847) may have been the first such work published in Cuba and his poetry, too, early exploited the regional-folkloric vein.

Writings: Folklore: *Colección de articulos satiricos y de costumbres,* 1847; *Costumbrista, Jeremias de Decaransa,* no known details; he is also represented in *Los cubanos pintados por si mismos,* Havana, 1852.

Stories: "El administrador de un ingenio," "El educado fuera," "Untitulo," and "Colocar al niño."

Poetry: in various journals, uncollected; "La compadre," a romance.

Plays: *No siempre el que escoge acierta* (4 act verse comedy), Havana, 1841; *Un tio sordo* (3 act verse comedy), Havana, Barcina, 1848, first performed at the Liceo Artistico y Literario of Havana by students of the Liceo, May 13, 1848.

CARDENAS Y RODRIGUEZ, Nicolás

(pseudonym: **Teodomófilo**)

b. 1814, Cuba; d. 1868.
Poet, playwright, essayist, novelist, folklorist.

Brother of José Maria Cárdenas y Rodriguez, Nicolás served as editor of *La Prensa* of Havana and under the pen-name of Teodomófilo submitted articles to *El Artista, El Faro Industrial, El siglo* and others, many of these papers also published or directed by his brother. In 1842, Spanish authorities prohibited him from publishing, but his novel *Las dos bodas* did appear in 1844.

Writings: Plays: *Diego Velásquez* (4 acts, prose, historical drama), 1840.
Folklore: *Escenas de la vida de Cuba,* Havana, 1841.
Novel: *Las dos bodas,* 1844.
Essays: *Ensayos poéticos por un cubano ausente de su patria,* New York, 1836.

CARDOSO, Onelio Jorge

b. 1914, Calabazar de Sagua (Las Villas), Cuba.
Storywriter, journalist.

Born of peasant parents, Cardoso had to struggle for his education and has followed many occupations, including photographer's apprentice, drug salesman, rural schoolteacher. In Havana, he caught on in radio work as an author of brief pieces and in 1945 he won the Hernández Catá prize for his story "El carbonero." Cardoso has served as president of the musical section of the Sociedad de Autores and has worked in the Ministry of Culture.

Cardoso's stories spring from the lives of the poor farmers he knows so well. He writes slowly and has published only a small number of his well-crafted stories which are widely translated, most often in Eastern European languages, including Russian, Czech and Bulgarian, but Chinese and German translations have also appeared.

Writings: Stories: *Taita, diga usted cómo,* Mexico, 1945; *El cuentero,* Las Villas, 1958; *El caballo de coral,* Santa Clara, Las Villas, 1960; *La lechuza ambiciosa,* Santa Clara, 1960; *Cuentos completos,* Havana, Unión, 1962, 1965, 4th ed., 1969, in Havana, by Instituto del Libro, 1969; *La otra muerte del gato,* Havana, Unión, 1964; *El perro,* Havana, La Tertulia, 1964; *Iba caminando,* Havana, Granma, 1965; *Abrir y cerrar los ojos,* Havana, Unión, 1966, 1969; *El hilo y la cuerda,* Havana, UNEAC, 1974.
Journalism: *Gente de pueblo,* Las Villas, 1962.
Editor of: *El pueblo cuenta,* Havana, Biblioteca del Capitolio Nacional, 1961.

CARPENTIER, Alejo

b. November 4, 1904, Havana, Cuba.
Novelist, poet, critic, folklorist, musicologist, journalist.

Carpentier is deemed the first Caribbean writer to catch up the entire Caribbean region in his work. In Paris (1928-1939), he associated with the group centered around the journal *Révolution Surrealiste* (Bréton, Aragon, Tzara, Eluard). He visited Haiti in 1943 with his wife and the famous French film actor, Louis Jouvet, and was entranced by his experiences there. His novel, *El reino de este mundo* (1949) celebrates Haiti's gifted but tyrannical king, Henri Christophe.

Several of Carpentier's stories were written in French to enable him to develop a new style, less flat than his original one derived from "nativismo." Though of European ancestry (his father was French), Carpentier was one of the earliest writers to exploit negro themes, though he was later to repudiate his shallow treatment of what he came to realize were more than vestigal quaintnesses derived from Africa. A product of this Afro-cuban period was the novel *Ecué-Yamba-O* (1933).

Having abandoned his university studies to become a journalist, Carpentier early joined the "Grupo Minorista" and was a founder of the cultural organ *Revista de Avance* (1927-1930) with Jorge Manach, Juan Marinello and Francisco Ichaso in which "vanguardista" works appeared and he edited *Carteles.*

In 1945, Carpentier was in Venezuela, staying there until Castro's successful revolution. In Cuba he was named chief of the official publishing house, Editora Nacional, and made a professor of literature at Havana University. In 1966 he was sent to Paris as a diplomat.

His collection of essays *Tientos y diferencias* (1964) includes his important manifesto on "magical realism."

The 93 page novel, *Concierto barroco* (1974) which takes a Mexican of European descent to the Europe of Vivaldi, Scarlatti and Handel during carnival season, 1709, is a tour de force. As the work progresses the style becomes more and more that of Luis de Góngora and the present fades away and the search for a Latin American identity deepens. Maria Gowland reviewing the novel writes: "There is a celebration of the senses in this work, a delight in style, in the precise description of objects, in colors, in sound, in plays on words, in symbiotic relationships, and a heightened sense of perception characteristic of baroque aesthetics. At times one has the sensation of reading a text from the seventeenth century, the Golden Age of Spanish literature, given additional vigor by ingredients from a new era.

His new novel, *El recurso del mètodo* (1974), an obvious play on Descartes' *Discurso del mètodo* to give it a Spanish title, is set in a Mexico-like republic of the 1912-1927 period but events throughout Latin America are woven through this complex work probably influenced by the novel *Viernes de Dolores* (1972) by Manuel Granados which was placed in the same time frame. An early reviewer, T.J. Peaver, found it successful only in spots though were it " . . .by a lesser artist, it could be viewed a success."

Another aspect of Carpentier's interest in history is shown in his *El camino de Santiago* (1967) which deals with Europe's infatuation with the "myth" of America during the 16th century.

Writings: Essays: *Tientos y diferencias,* Mexico, 1946, Havana, 1966, Buenos Aires, Arca, 1967 (in paper).

Poetry: *Poemas des Antilles* (nine poems set to music by Marius François Gaillard), Paris, 19??

Musicology: *La musica en Cuba,* Mexico, 1946, and 1972 edition: "Colección Popular," No. 109, Mexico, Fondo de Cult. Econ.

Novels: *Ecué-Yamba-O,* Madrid, Edit. España, 1933, and Buenos Aires, Xanadú, 1968; *Los pasos perdidos, novela,* Mexico, Ibero-Americana de Publicaciones, 1953, also edition in Mexico by Cia General de Ediciones, 1959, 1966, 5th printing in 1968; and edition in Montevideo, Arca, 1966 and London, Penguin, 1968; and new Cuban edition in Havana, Organización Continental de los Festivales del Libro, 1960, paperback, Barcelona, Barral Editores, 1972; and translated as *The Lost Steps,* New York, Knopf, 1957, 1967, and Gollancz, London, 1956, and fragment published in *New World Writing,* New York, Knopf, 1956, pp. 51-66; and in French translation by Gallimard, Paris, 1954 (winner of Prix du Meilleur Livre Etranger); *El reino de este mundo,* Mexico, Ibero-

Americana de Publicaciones, 1949, and Lima, Imprensa Sr. Valverde, 1958, Havana, Unión, 1964 and Barcelona, 1967 and Havana, Org. Cont. de los Festivales del Libro, 1959, Montevideo, Arca, (paper), 1965, 1966, 1968, and Barcelona, Seix Barral, 1966, 1967, 1969, and Santiago, Chile, Universitas, 1967, and Mexico, Compañia Gral. de Ediciones, 1967, and translated as *The Kingdom of the World* by Harriet de Onis, New York, 1957, and as *The Explosion in a Cathedral,* Boston, Little Brown, and in London, Gollancz, both in 1963, and in paper edition, New York, Collier Books, 1970; *El siglo de los luces,* Mexico, Cia General de Ediciones, 1962, 1965, 1966, 1967, and Havana, Revolución, 1963, 1965 and Barcelona, 1965, and Buenos Aires, Galerna, 1967, and Havana, Instituto del Libro, 1968; *El acoso,* 1st ed., Buenos Aires, Losada, 1956, Mexico, 1958, Buenos Aires, Jorge Alvarez, 1966, Havana, Instituto del Libro, 1969, and translated by H. de Onis as *Manhunt,* in *Noon II* (April 1959), pp. 109-180; *Concierto barroco,* Madrid, Mexico City, and Buenos Aires, all November 4, 1974 (on author's 70th birthday), by Siglo Veintiuno; *El recurso del método,* Mexico, Siglo Veintiuno Editores, 1974.

Novelette: *El camino de Santiago,* Buenos Aires, Edit. Galerna, 1967, 1968 (paper, 106 pp.).

Stories: *Guerra del tiempo; tres relatos y una novela,* Mexico, 1958, 1967, 1968 (contains "El camino de Santiago," "Viaje a la semilla," "Semejante a la noche," and the novelette "El acoso"), volume later published in Havana, Ed. UNEAC, 1963, and Lima, Peru, Populibros Peruanos, 1964 (?) and Buenos Aires, Andina, 1969 ("El camino de Santiago" was separately published in Buenos Aires, Galerna, 1967); many other stories in various journals and collections. Edition of *Guerra del tiempo* in French as *Guerre de temps,* Paris, Gallimard, 1967, and as *War of Time* in English, New York, Knopf, 1970. and as *Tres relatos* by Tauro, Montevideo, 1967. Stories in *Cuentos Cubanos* (with other authors), Barcelona, Laia, 1974.

Biographical/Critical Sources: Klaus Müller-Bergh, *Alejo Carpentier. Estudio Biografico-Critico,* Madrid, Anaya, 1972; Zulma Palermo, et al., *Historia y mito en la obra de Alejo Carpentier,* Buenos Aires, Fernando Garcia Cambeiro, 1972; Marina Atia's *Alejo Carpentier: 45 años de trabajo intelectual, recopilación bibliográfica,* Havana, Biblioteca Nacional José Marti, 1966; Helmy Giacomán, *Homenaje a Alejo Carpentier: Variaciones interpretivas en torno a su obra,* New York, Las Américas, 1970; Edmundo Gómez Mango, *Construcción y lenguaje en Alejo Carpentier,* Cuadernos de Literatura, Vol. 5 Montevideo, Fund. de Cult. Universitaria, 1968; M. Ian Adams, *Three Authors of Alienation* (on Maria Luisa Bombal, Juan Carlos Onetti, and Carpentier), Austin, Texas, U. of Texas, 1975; Juan Manuel Alonso, "The Search for Identity in Alejo Carpentier's Contemporary Urban Novels: An Analysis of *Los pasos perdidos* and *El acoso."* Unpublished Ph.D. diss., Brown University, 1967. Other Ph.D. dissertations: Mercedes Zabala, "Alejo Carpentier: Un mundo en metamórfosis," Columbia, 1971; Eugene R. Skinner, "Archetypal patterns in four novels of Alejo Carpentier," U. of Kansas, 1968; Frank Janney, "Regression in the Early Works of Alejo Carpentier," Harvard, 1972; Janina J. Montero, "La perspectiva histórica en Augusto Roa Bastos, Alejo Carpentier y Gabriel Garciá-Márques,' U. of Pa., 1973; Klaus Müller-Bergh, "La prosa narrativa de Alejo Carpentier en *Los pasos perdidos,"* Yale, 1966; Ricardo R. Fernández, "La novelistica de Alejo Carpentier," Princeton, 1969; Ramón F.J. Garcia-Castro, "Perspectivas temporales en la obra de Alejo Carpentier," U. of Pa., 1972; Maurice R. Assardo, "La técnica narrativa en la obra de Alejo Carpentier; Enfasis; el tiempo," UCLA, 1968.

Articles: James Irish, "Magical Realism: A Search for Caribbean and Latin American Roots," in *The Literary Half-Yearly,* XI, 2 (July 1970), pp. 127-139; José Sánchez-Boudy, *La temática novelistica de Alejo Carpentier,* Miami, 1969; review of *El Reino* (in British trans.) in *Bim,* Vol. 12, No. 46 (Jan-June 1968), pp. 136-137 by Edward Baugh; essay on Carpentier by Edouard Glissant, in the section "Du divers au Commun," in Glissant's collection of essays, *L'Intention Poetique,* Paris, Seuil, 1969, pp. 136-142; review of *Concierto barroco* by Maria Gowland de Gallo, in *Américas,* Vol. 27, No. 9 (Sept 1975), pp. 37-38. Also see review of Carpentier's *El recurso del método* in *Latin American Literary Review,* III, 6 (Spring-Summer, 1975), pp. 31-36, by Terry J. Peaver.

Also: Special Issue of *Casa de las Américas* dedicated to Carpentier (Havana, 15, November-December 1974), pp. 5-72.

CARRENO, Pedro

b. ca. 1822, Cuba.
Playwright.

Today Carreño's work is of only academic interest.

Writings: Plays: *La restauración* (5 acts, verse), Matanzas, Imp. del Gobierno, 1852; *El Industrial de nuevo cuño* (2 act farce), Havana, Soler, 1854; *Pércances de la avaricia* (1 act comedy), Havana, Soler, 1855; *Más quiero que sierren tablas* (5 act comedy), Havana, Soler, 1856; *Pedro Crespo o El Alcade de Zalamea* (reworked tragedy of Pedro Calderón de la Barca), Havana, Soler, 1956.

CARRERAS, Carlos N.

b. ca. 1890, Puerto Rico.
Poet, storywriter, playwright, critic, editor.

Carreras was under the influence of Rubén Darío, Francisco Villaespesa and Emilio Carrera. Most of his verse, first published in journals of the 1920's, was gathered in his one collection, *El Caballero del silencio,* 1940.

Writings: Stories: *Luna verde, y otros cuentos,* 1st ed., Barcelona, Edit. Rumbos, 1958.

Poetry: *El caballero del silencio,* San Juan, Biblioteca de Autores Puertorriqueños, 1940, (176 pp.).

Play: *Juan Ponce de León,* 1932 (written with José Ramírez Santibañez).

Editor of: *Antología de poetas puertorriqueños: Los poetas que fueron,* San Juan, Biblioteca Puerto Rico Ilustrado, 1922; *Antología de poetas puertorriqueños: Los nuevos,* San Juan, Biblioteca Puerto Rico Ilustrado, 1922; *Antología de poetas puertorriqueños: Los contemporáneos,* San Juan, Biblioteca Puerto Rico Ilustrado, 1922.

CARRILLO Y O'FARRIL, Isaac

b. 1844, Havana, Cuba; d. New York City, 1901.
Playwright, poet, novelist.

After study at the Colegio del Salvador and the University of Havana, Carrillo spent most of his adult years in New York. Inspired to write a sonnet addressed to Queen Isabel II and "guilty" of other "ideas exaltadas" he was imprisoned in 1868 for a period and he determined to emigrate to the United States where he practiced law until 1900, returning to Cuba only for what was to be his last year, taking up a judgeship (Audiencia de la Habana).

His once-famous poem with a French title, "Connais-tu le pays?" long appeared in school anthologies after its initial appearance in the Nicolás Heredia poetry collection made for school use, *El lector cubano.*

Writings: Novel: *María,* 1863.

Poetry: *Matilde,* and others.

Plays: *Luchas del alma,* Havana, 1864; *El que con lobos anda* (1 act, verse), Havana, La Antilla, 1867; *Magdalena* (prose), 1868; *El casada por fuerza* (sketch), published, no date, but probably in late 1860's when it was written.

Biographical/Critical Sources: Max Henriquez Ureña, *Panorama histórica de la literatura cubana,* New York, 1963, pp. 322-324.

CARRION, Miguel de

b. April, 1875, Havana, Cuba; d. 1929, Havana.
Novelist, naturalist.

Carrión's fiction was in the absolute mode of Zola's naturalism and his four novels, whether set in the middle class or working class, deal resolutely with the little verities of life and develop highly concrete lives of the characters.

Writings: Novels: *El milagro,* Havana, 1903; *La última voluntad,* Havana, 1903; *Las honrades,* 1918, and Havana, Instituto de Literatura y Lingüística, Academia de Ciencias de Cuba, 1966; *Las impuras,* 1919 and 2nd ed., Havana, Org. Continental de las Festivales del Libro, 1959, in 2 vols.; *La esfinge,* Havana, Comisión Nacional Cubana de la UNESCO, 1961.

CARRION MADURA, Tomás

b. 1870 (1872?), Juana Diaz, Puerto Rico; d. Ponce, Puerto Rico, 1920.
Poet, Playwright.

Carrión is today an all but forgotten figure but he published in a variety of genres and a few of his poems were widely anthologized.

His most liked poem is probably "Misericordia Monólogo del escéptico," published in 1889.

Writings: Poetry: "Alma Latina"; "Ten con ten" in *Cumba,* San Juan (?), 1903; "En voz baja" in *El Carnaval,* San Juan, No. 71 (Year III, 1903).

Essays: Foreward to *Lampos y penumbras* of Angel Marcucci, San Juan, La Correspondencia de Puerto Rico, 1915.

Play: *Verán ustedes la suerte de un jugador,* performed in Ponce, in ms. only.

Religion: *La Idea Católica: Su triunfo definitivo en el mundo,* Ponce, Imp. El Dia, 1919.

CARTAGENA PORTALATIN, Aïda

b. 1918, Moca, Dominican Republic.
Poet, novelist, storywriter, educator.

After taking her degree at the Universidad Autónoma de Santo Domingo, Cartagena studied music and theory at the School of Plastic Arts in Paris. She is currently a teacher at her alma mater.

Cartagena was a valiant supporter of free intellectual life in the harsh times of Trujillo's dictatorship and in December 1961 she founded the press Brigadas Dominicanas which put out ten titles beginning March 1963, as well as publishing local authors' works in book form under the title "Colección Baluarte." She has travelled widely and is an expert decorator and able artist craftsman. In her earlier days she was a member of the poetic group "La Poesia Sorprendida" and had served as director of the Museo de Antropologia in Santo Domingo.

Writings: Poetry: *Visperas del sueño,* 1944; *Del sueño al mundo,* 1945; *Llámale verde,* 1945; all three, S. Domingo, Ed. La Poesia Sorprendida; *Una mujer está sola,* Ciudad Trujillo, Sol. La Isla Necesaria, 1953 and 1955; *Mi mundo el mar,* Ciudad Trujillo, La Isla Necesaria, 1953, 2nd. ed., S. Domingo, Libreria Dominicana, No. 10, 1955; *La voz desatada,* S. Domingo, Brigadas Dominicanas, 1962; *La tierra escrita,* S. Domingo, Brigadas Dominicanas, 1967.

Novelette: *Escalera para Electra,* S. Domingo, Ed. de la Universidad Autónoma de S. Domingo, 1970.

Art Criticism: *José Vela Zanetti,* S. Domingo, La Isla Necesaria, 1954.

Editor of: *Narradores dominicanos,* Venezuela, Monte Editores, 1969.

Socio-Musicology: *El culto sincrético en villa mella, música, canto y danzas de los indios de española,* details not known.

Biographical/Critical Sources: Poems and a brief critical study in Manuel Rueda's *Antologia panorámica de la poesia dominicana contemporánea 1912-1962,* Santiago, D. R., 1972.

CASAL, Julián del

(pseudonyms: **Paul VASILI** and **Conde de CAMORS**)

b. 1863, Cuba; d. 1893.
Poet, essayist, journalist.

A leading "modernist," Casal painted a detailed picture of Havana society in his popular series published in *La Habana Elegante,* though one of them "El General Sabas Marin y su familia" occasioned the banning of the entire work and his being fired from his modest job with the Agriculture Department. Casal's work often reflected Baudelaire and his artificial paradise as well as José Maria de Heredia and Leconte de Lisle, the French poet.

Writings: *Hojas al viento,* Havana, 1890; *Bustas y rimas,* Havana, 1893; *Nieve,* Mexico, 1893; *Poesias completas,* Havana, 1945; *Poesias. Edición del Centenario,* Havana, Consejo Nacional de Cultura, 1963.

Articles: *La sociedad de la Habana* (stories and chronicles first published in *La Habana Elegante* under name of Paul Vasili), Paris, 189? and in *Selected Prose of Julián del Casal,* University of Alabama, 1949, edited by Marshall E. Nunn.

Biographical/Critical Sources: Ramón Meza's critical study: *Julián del Casal, estudio biográfico,* 1910; Max Henriquez Ureña, *Panorama histórico de la literatura,* New York, 1963; pp. 232-250; Julio E. Hernández-Miyares, "Julián del Casal, Escritor," unpublished Ph.D. diss., New York University, 1972 (but see J.E. Hernández-Miyares, *Julián del Casal: Estudios críticos sobre su obra,* Miami, Ediciones Universal, 1974); William Jack, "A Critical Study of Julián del Casal," unpublished Ph.D. diss., Louisiana State, 1935; Marshall Elbert Nunn, "The Life and Works of Julián del Casal," unpublished Ph.D. diss., U. of Illinois, 1939.

CASEY, Calvert

b. 1923, Baltimore, Maryland, U.S.A. (of Cuban mother, American father); d. Rome, May 17, 1969.
Storywriter, novelist, editor, theatre critic, journalist.

Educated in Cuba, Casey lived abroad (1946-1957) for many years, publishing in both English and Spanish, but returned to Cuba during the Castro revolution to work as a magazine editor. His story, "The Execution," is a Kafka-esque one of false arrest and execution in a land and prison that could be almost anywhere. He early won a story contest run by the New York publishing house, Doubleday Doran, and he published widely in Latin American journals and was a member of the *El Puente* review group of young writers.

He lived off and on in the U. S., Canada, France and Switzerland, and in the late 1960's was in Rome working in exile as a translator for an international organization. He committed suicide in 1969 in the Italian capital. Casey had gone to Poland in 1965 to be present at a celebration of publication in Polish of his well-regarded *El regreso.* He then got back to Paris and moved on to Rome by way of Spain.

Writings: Stories: *El regreso,* Havana, Revolución, 1963, 2nd ed., Barcelona, 1967 and *El regreso y otros relatos,* Barcelona, Seix y Barral, 1967; stories in various collections including *Writers in the New Cuba,* edited by E.M. Cohen, Penguin, 1967.

Novel: *Notas de un simulador,* Barcelona, Seix Barral, 1969, which has title novel (of 80 pages) and short stories, including his story "Polacca brillante" which appeared in English in the *Latin American Literary Review* in trans. by Seymour Menton (Vol. IV, No. 7, Fall-Winter 1975).

Essays: *Memorias de una isla,* Havana, 1967.

CASTELLANOS, Jesús

b. 1879, Cuba; d. 1912.
Novelist, storywriter.

Castellanos' career was cut short but he published two novels, part of a third and many stories, collected and uncollected. Max Henriquez Ureña declared that the novel *La manigua sentimental* ". . . es una de las más bellas evocaciones narrativas, si no la más bella que se conoce de la guerra de independencia cubana, por la interesante armazón episódica del relato y por los pintorescos y exactos cuadros de la vida de los cubanos en la manigua."

Writings: Novels: *La conjura,* Madrid, 1909; *La manigua sentimental,* Madrid, 1910; "Los Argonautas" (only first few chapters published in *Obras*).

Stories: *De tierra adentro,* Havana, 1906; *Campanas de boda; Los agüinaldas; En la laguna;* and in various journals.

Collected works: *Obras,* 3 vols., Havana, Academia Nacional de Artes y Letras, 19?? (posthumous) and contains, among other writings, the incomplete novel, "Los Argonautas," and the story "El puente."

Biographical/Critical Sources: Wilburn P. Smith, "Jesús Castellanos, His Life and Works," unpublished Ph.D. diss., Univ. of North Carolina (Chapel Hill), 1935; Wilbur C. Zeigler, "Las obras literarias de Jesús Castellanos," unpublished Ph.D. diss., Middlebury, 1950.

CASTILLO DE GONZALEZ, Aurelia

b. 1842, Camagüez, Cuba; d. 1920.
Poet, storywriter, biographer, travel-memoirist, translator.

Castillo's first works appeared in the local Camagüez journals in 1869. She married the Spanish career soldier Francisco González del Hoyo who was as liberal as a soldier could be in that period and Aurelia's own burning nationalist sentiments were somehow understood by the husband. González was eventually ordered back to Spain and Aurelia accompanied him, returning to Cuba only after his death in 1890. She translated works of D'Annunzio, Ada Negri, Carducci, Lamartine, François Coppée, Byron, and others. Though she was not a major figure she made her contribution and was one of the most sensitive and talented of the Cuban women writers of the nineteenth century.

Writings: Stories: *Fábulas,* Cádiz, 1879 (for children).
Poetry: *Adiós de Victor Hugo a la Francia de 1852,* Havana, 1885; 8 poems at rear of *Un paseo por Europa,* Havana, 1891.
Travel: *Un paseo por Europa,* Havana, 1891; *Un paseo por América,* Havana, 1895.
Biography: *Biografia de Gertrudis Gómez de Avellaneda y juicio critico de sus obras,* Havana, 1887; *Ignacio Agramonte en la vida privada,* Havana, 1912.
Collected Works: *Escritos,* 6 vols., Havana, 1913-1918.
Critical Essay: See her introduction to the poetry of Nieves Xenes, *Poesias,* Havana, 1915.

CASTRO QUESADA, Luis

b. 1928 (?), Ponce, Puerto Rico; d. 195?
Poet.

Castro, a feverish, bohemian soul, perished young. His *Itinerario de Otoño* (1947) and his second volume *El Volantin empurpurado y otras poemas* (1951) were precocious and full of the cosmic sensibility of the late romantics and the European post-war poets.

Writings: Poetry: *Itineario de Otoño,* San Juan, 1947; *El volantin empurpurado y otras poemas,* Ponce, 1951.

CASUSO, Teté

b. 1912, Cuba.
Storywriter, novelist, poet, playwright.

Casuso's verse was delicate and her "Canción frutal" and "Canción de cristal sin motivo," were praised by Max Henriquez Ureña. Her play *Realengo 18* (1939) was based on the report published by her husband Pablo de la Torriente y Brau, in 1934. The dialogue is rapid, natural, and the scenes set vividly. (Rodriguez Vélez had dealt with the same rural uprisings of 1934 in his play *Realengo 20.*)

Her stories are set on revolutionary themes as was her novel *Los ausentes.*

Writings: Play: *Realengo 18,* Havana, 1939.
Novel: *Los ausentes,* Havana, date unknown.
Poetry and Stories: in various journals.

CEIDE, Amelia

b. 1908, Aguadilla, Puerto Rico.
Poet, journalist.

Rosa-Nieves says Ceide's verse " . . . nace florecido en deseos sexuales: naturaleza viva y ardiente, furor de cosas nuevas, maduras a la luz del sol tropical, anhelos mozos en carne eufórica." She has learned from Ibarbourou and Storni as well as Garcia Lorca—but her voice is deeply personal, though somewhat analytical.

Writings: Poetry: *Interior,* San Juan, Imp. Venezuela, 1936; *Mi cantar de cantares,* 1940 (prose poems); *Puertas,* San José, Costa Rica, Edit. Borrasé, 1946; *Cuando el cielo sonrié,* San José, Costa Rica, Edit. Borrasé, 1946.

Biographical/Critical Sources: Tomás Jesús Castro, *Esbozos,* Barcelona, Ediciones, Rumbos, 1957.

CEPEDA, Josefina de

b. 1907, Cuba.
Poet.

Cepeda's poetry is sonorous and modernist.

Writings: Poetry: *Grana y armiño,* 1935; *Versos,* 1936; *Palabras en soledad,* 1938.

CESPEDES DE ESCANAVERINO, Ursula

b. 1832, Bayamano, Cuba; d. 1874.
Poet.

A minor but skillful poet, Céspedes' best work was in such elegies as "¡Está dormida!" "En la muerte de mi padres," and in the decima form, such as "El amor de la serrana," and the romance "Consejos de un guajiro."

Writings: Poetry: *Ecos de la selva,* foreword by Carlos Manuel Céspedes; *Cantos postreros,* private edition, date unknown; *Poesias,* forword by Juan J. Remos, Havana, Cuaderno de Cultura del Ministerio de Educación, 1948.

CESTERO, Ferdinand R.

b. 1868, San Juan, Puerto Rico; d. 1945.
Poet.

Born into a wealthy family on a hacienda in the Valle del Toa, near Dorado, Castero was privately educated, mostly by his father. A close friend of the Mexican poet, Juan de Dios Peza, he published many volumes of verse over almost forty years of his long life.

Writings: Poetry: *Ave populi,* 1904; *Lira y corazón,* 1929; *Sueños y quimeras,* 1939; *Banderas y palmas,* 1940.

CESTERO, Tulio Manuel Florentino

b. 1877, Dominican Republic; d. 1955.
Novelist, playwright, poet, essayist, critic.

Cestero's work was influenced by the Italian poet-novelist Gabriele D'Annunzio and Cestero himself was considered an important figure in the 1900-1940 period.

He wrote critical essays on Gastón F. Deligne and other scholar-artists of his country. His novel *La sangre* is considered one of the best fictional treatments of the regime of President-Dictator Ulise Heureaux (late 19th century), a common theme in Dominican writing.

Writings: Dramatic-Poetry: *Citerea,* (with four

works: *La enemiga; El torrente; La medusa;* and *La medusa y La sangre*), Madrid, 1907; *Sangre de primavera,* Madrid, 1908; *Ciudad romántica,* Paris, 1911.

Poetry: *Por el Cibao,* 1902; *Del amor,* 1901 (verse pamphlet), *Una campaña,* 1903.

Travel: *Hombres y piedras,* 1909, Biblioteca Andrés Bello, with introduction by Rubén Dario, and Madrid, 1915.

Play: *El torrente* and *La enemiga,* both published with other minor works for the theatre in the volume *Citerea,* Madrid, 1907, noted above.

Critical Essays: *Notas y escorzos,* 1898; *El jardin de los sueños,* 1904.

History and Politics: *A propósito de la neutralización en la R.D.* (thesis), 1916; *Rubén Dario,* Havana, 1916; *El problema dominicano,* New York, 1919; *La tragedia haitiana,* New York, 1918; *César Borgia,* Mexico, 1935; *Hostos, hombre representativo de América,* Buenos Aires, 1940; *Los Estados Unidos y las Antillas,* Madrid, 1931; *Colón,* 1933.

Novel: *La sangre,* 1914; 2nd ed., Ciudad Trujillo, Postigo, 1955; 3rd ed., Postigo, 1974.

Biographical/Critical Sources: Max Henriquez Ureña, *Historia de la literatura dominicana,* 5th ed., S. Domingo, Postigo, 1970, pp. 286-288.

CESTERO Y SARDA, Manuel Florentino

b. August 18, 1878, Santo Domingo; d. April 14, 1926, Santiago de Cuba.
Storywriter, novelist, critic, educator.

Cestero lived for a considerable period in the United States and his one novel *El canto del cisne* is set both in the U.S. and in his homeland.

Writings: Stories: *Cuentos a Lila,* 1906.

Novel: *El canto del cisne,* 1915.

Criticism: *Ensayos criticos,* S. Domingo, Gaston F. Deligne, 1911.

Politics: *Estados Unidos por dentro,* Mexico, 1918; *The Dominican Republic and the Military Occupation,* New York, 1920.

Education: *Un documento notable,* 1906; *A propósito de la educación del niño,* 1907; *La politica y la familia,* 1910.

CID PEREZ, José

b. November 12, 1906, Guanabacoa, Cuba.
Playwright, critic, novelist, folklorist, translator.

After local schooling, Cid Pérez attended the University of Havana and Columbia University in New York. He organized the theatre of the Escuelas Municipales of Havana and became Artistic Director of the National Corporation of Tourism, the director of the Cinematographic organization C.M.Q. El Crisol, the director of Teatro Radial and director of many theatrical companies. Cid Pérez has translated works from many languages including Luigi Pirandello's *La amiga de la mujer* and *En las manos de Euridice* by Pedro Block of Brazil (both titles being the translated Spanish ones).

Writings: Closet Dramas: *¡Mamá, tengo miedo!* and *La comedia de los muertos,* performed 1953 in Barcelona, and translated into Danish, English and Italian.

Plays: *Cadenas de amor,* premiered 1927; *Altares de sacrificio,* 1931, first performed Teatro Principal de la Comedia, Havana, 1932; *¡Justicia!* premiered in 1934; *La duda,* performed and published 1932; first prize of the Circulo de Bellas Artes, 1934; *Estampas rojas; A quiso más la vida* (earlier entitled *El doctor*), and premiered in Buenos Aires, 1936 and performed in Havana 1951; *Su primer cliente,* performed Buenos Aires in 1948; *Hombres de dos mundos* (triptico dramático), performed Barcelona, 1953, and published in *Teatro cubano contemporáneo,* D. Marti de Cid, ed., Havana, 1959, 1962; dramatization of *Biajani* (Indian legend); and *Rebeca,* dramatization of novel of that name, performed in New York, 1931.

Children's Plays: *Azucena,* 1934, performed Teatro Nacional de la Habana, 1943, translated into French and English; *Episodios de la historia de Cuba,* performed Anfiteatro Nacional during first International Congress of American Teachers, Havana, 1939;

Legend: *Biajani* (on Cuban Indian tale, written with his wife Dolores Marti de Cid).

Novels: *Secreto de confesión,* winner in 1927 of competition "La Novela Semanal" in Madrid; *Rebeca, la judia,* adapted into play in 1931.

Biographical/Critical Sources: Introduction to his *Hombres de dos mundos* reprinted in *Teatro Cubano contemporáneo,* Dolores Marti de Cid, ed., 2nd ed. Madrid, Aguilar, 1962.

CLARA LAIR

(pseudonym for **Mercedes NEGRON MUNOZ**)

CLARENS, Angel

(pseudonym: **ACACIA**)

b. ca. 1867, Cuba.
Playwright.

Once one of Cuba's most performed dramatists, Clarens is today all but forgotten.

Writings: Plays: *Notas mundanas* (2 act musical), Havana, El Figaro, 1897; *Ilusiones* (comic skit), Santiago, Cuba, El Ateneo, 1916; *Desde Cuba libre* (verse monologue), Santiago, Imp. de Nicolás Pérez, 1902, performed Teatro Oriente, Santiago, Cuba, July 29, 1902; *El buscapié* (1 act comic verse sketch), music by Manuel Mauri, Havana, 1895, in ms.; *El fantasma del hambre o Cuba en la guerra* (1 act verse), Santiago, Morales Roca, 1918; *El hijo del diablo* (1 act, prose and verse), music by Rodolfo Hernández and Tomás Planes, Santiago, Cuba, Imp. de Antonio Torralbas, 1909, performed Teatro Oriente, Santiago, February 12, 1909; *La montaña rusa* (1 act, prose and verse), 1894, by "Acaciais"; *Madre mia* (verse monologue), Havana, Imp. El Pilar, 1893; *Notas mundanas* (2 acts), music by Jorge Anckermann, Havana, El Figaro, 1897 (142 pp.).

CLAVIJO TISSEUR, Arturo

b. ca. 1895, Santiago, Cuba.
Poet, playwright, novelist.

Clavijo's best poetry is in his first collection *Cantos a Elvira* (1925). The critic José Luis Perrier has written of him: "La poesia de Clavijo Tisseur nos recuerda la de los parnasianos franceses por la perfección riparnasianos franceses por la perfección rítmica y el al mismo tiempo sencilla, fluida y cristalina como la de sus ilustres compatriotas Marti y Julián del Casal. Es una poesia tierna, sincera y pura, llena de encanto y de misterio."

Writings: Novel: *La morfinómana de San Pedro,* Madrid, 1926.

Play: *El arte entre sudarios* (one-act comedy), Santiago de Cuba, Imp. Arroyo Hnos, 1922.

Poetry: *Cantos a Elvira,* Santiago, Arroyo, 1925; *A ritmo de tambor. Versos negros,* Santiago de Cuba, 1937; *Albores y penumbras; Consagración eterna.*

Biographical/Critical Sources: Commentary on Clavijo follows text of play *El arte entre sudarios* (see above).

COLL Y TOSTE, Cayetano

b. 1850, Arecibo, Puerto Rico; d. 1930.
Poet, historian, critic, storywriter.

Coll studied medicine in Spain but his main "vocation" was as a historian.

Writings: Poetry: *En el combate; poesias completas,* San Juan, 1969.

Histories: *Historia de la instrucción pública en Puerto Rico hasta el 1898,* San Juan, Imp. El Boletin Mercantil, 1910; *Leyendas y tradiciones puertorriqueñas,* in two series; and "Historia de la poesia en Puerto Rico," both in *Boletin Histórico de Puerto Rico,* San Juan, Tip. Cantero, Fernández, 1914-1927, published in three volumes, complete (I-II-III) and 14 more vols., incomplete. Other Histories: *Crónicas de Arecibo,* 1891; *Colón en Puerto Rico,* 1893; reprinted as *Cristóbal Colón en Puerto Rico primera llegado de los conquistadores,* Sharon, Conn., U.S.A., Troutman Press, 1972; *Repertorial histórico de Puerto Rico,* 1896; *Reseña del estado social, económico y politico de la isla de Puerto Rico al tomar posesión de ella los Estados Unidos,* 1899; *Prehistoria de Puerto Rico,* 1907; *Historias que parecen cuentos,* Rio Piedras, Edit. Universitario, 1972.

Biographies: *Puertorriqueños ilustres.*

Critical Essay: "La poesia," in *Boletin histórico,* San Juan, Tip. Cantero, Fernández, Vol. XIII (1926).

Story: "The Pirate's Treasure" as translated by William E. Colford, in *Colford,* pp. 189-203.

Biographical/Critical Sources: Salvador Arana Soto, *Las poesias del Doctor Cayetano Coll y Toste,* San Juan, 1970.

COLL Y VIDAL, Antonio

b. 1898, Lares, Puerto Rico.
Poet, playwright, journalist.

Coll was an editor of such island journals as *El Imparcial* and *El Mundo,* and contributed his verse to many literary reviews, much of it collected in his three volumes which showed a rapid movement from late romantic to the modernista style and subject matter.

Writings: Poetry: *Trovas de amor,* 1915, Bayamón, Tip. El Progreso, 1916; *Mediodia,* New York, Hispania Press, 1919, introduction by Amado Nervo; and *Rosario,* 1929.

Play: *Un hombre de cuarenta años,* 1929.

Novelette: *Madre haraposa* (written with Evaristo Ribera Chevremont and Luis Muñoz Marin, San Juan, Tip. Barros, 1918 (100 pp.).

COLLADO MARTELL, Alfredo

b. April 23, 1900, Santo Domingo, Dominican Republic.
Storywriter, poet, journalist.

Son of Puerto Rican exiles in the Dominican Republic, Collado first saw his native land in 1908 when his parents returned to Puerto Rico. Most of his life he worked as a chemist for a large sugar firm and as an official in the Office of Public Instruction. He was a transitional figure between "modernismo" and the new realism of the postwar years of the 1920's. Some "modernista" motifs and stylistic mannerisms remain in the stories published in his one volume *Cuentos absurdos,* the stories for the most part being from his earliest period, but influenced by Rubén Dario. Concha Meléndez believes his best writing was in his stories for children.

With Antonio S. Pedreira, Vicente Géigel Polanco, and Samuel R. Quiñones, Collado helped found the cultural review *Indice* which announced a new direction in Puerto Rican letters.

Writings: Stories: *Cuentos absurdos,* San Juan, Libreria y Edit. Campos, 1929, 1931, an extract of which, "El bibelot de mi escritorio," appears in L. Hernández Aquino's *El modernismo en Puerto Rico,* San Juan, 1967, and in *Literatura puertorriqueña,* 2nd ed. Vol. II, E. Martinez Masdeu and Esther M. Melon, eds. Rio Piedras, 1972, pp. 225-235.

Poetry and Journalism: in various journals; uncollected.

Biographical/Critical Sources: Samuel R. Quiñones, "Los cuentos absurdos de Alfredo Collado Martell," in *Temas y letras,* 3rd ed. Biblioteca de Autores Puertorriqueños, 1941, 1955 and see Concha Meléndez' remarks in *Antologia de autores puertorriqueños,* El Cuento, Vol. III, pp. xvii-xix, and Concha Meléndez in *El arte del cuento en Puerto Rico,* New York, Las Américas Publishing Co., 1961, pp. 13-17.

COLON PELLOT, Carmen Maria

b. March 14, 1911, Arecibo, Puerto Rico.
Poet, journalist, teacher.

Colón's poetry strongly expresses African cultural traditions. Though her work reflects the "modernismo" school of poets led by Rubén Dario, she has a very personal voice and a passionate viewpoint to express.

Poetry: Ambar mulato, Arecibo, P.R., Imp. Jusino, 1938; two poems, "Canto a la raza mulata" and "Motivos de envidia mulata," both from her collection, are in *Aguinaldo lirico,* C. Porta-Nieves, ed., Rio Piedras, 1957.

CONCEPCION VALDES, Gabriel de la

(pseudonym: **PLACIDO**)

b. June 27, 1809, Cuba; d. 1844.
Poet.

Son of an Afro-Cuban father, a barber, and a Spanish mother who was a dancer, Plácido composed the romantic lyrics on nature which were the most popular songs of his day. He also extolled Cuba but otherwise had little to say concerning his personal origins nor did he deliver himself on any serious themes. He took his pen-name from the hero of a then well known novel by Madame de Genlis, *Plácido y Blanca,* and received his second family name from Bishop Jerónimo Valdés who had baptized him.

The young Plácido was a good student but soon apprenticed in a workshop in the town of Boloña. He began writing poetry

very early and became friends with Ramón Velez Herrera, Valdéz Machuca and Domingo del Monte. His innocent poem "A los dias de S.M. la Reina Doña Isabel Segunda" was one of two addressed to the queen. His "El juramento" was another matter, for it ended:

Ser enemigo eterno del tirano;
manchar, se me es posible, mis vestidos
con su execrable sangre, por mi mano.

derramarlos con golpes repetidos,
y morir a las manos de un verdugo,
si es necessario, por romper el yugo.

Plácido was arrested in 1842 as an alleged member of a negro-mulato plot and served two months in prison. Rearrested and accused of a part in the so-called "Escalera conspiracy" of 1844, he died before a firing squad.

Writings: Poetry: *Poesias completas,* Paris, Imp. d'Aubusson y Kugelmann, 1856; *Poesias completas de Plácido (Gabriel de la Concepción Valdés),* 2nd. ed., Paris, En casa de Mme. C. Denné Schmitz, Libreria Española, 1857, 3rd ed., Paris, Schmitz e hijo, 1862; *Plácido (Gabriel de la Concepción Valdés). Poesias completas, con doscientas diez composiciones inéditas,* Havana, Libreria y efectos de escritorio, 1886, new ed., Buenos Aires, Casa editorial Maucci Hermano, 1903; and Havana, Cultural, n.d.; *Poesias de Plácido,* Matanzas, Cuba, Imp. de Gobierno y Marino, 1838; *El veguero; poesias cubanos dedicados por Plácido a sus amigos de Villa-Clara,* Matanzas, Imp. de Comercio, 1841; *El hijo de maldición; poema del tiempo de las cruzadas,* Matanzas, Imp. de Gobierno por S.M., 1843; *Poesias de Plácido,* Veracruz, Mexico, Imp. del Censor, 1845; *Poesias escogidas de Plácido,* Matanzas, Cuba, Imp. de Gobierno y Marina, 1842 (but actually published in 1846); *Poesias de Plácido,* New Orleans, Imp. de la Patria, 1847; *Poesias de Gabriel de la Concepción Valdés [Plácido],* Ed. Francisco Javier Vingut, New York, Roe, Lockwood & Son, 1854 and New York, Lockwood & Son, 1855, and Paris, Boudry, 1857 in 2 vols.; *Colección de las mejores poesias de Plácido,* Edición económica, New York, Imp. de Sebástian Falet, 1858; *Poesias completas* (trans. into French by D. Fontaine),

Paris, Sartoricus, 1863; *Poesias,* Matanzas, 1866, and New York, 1885; *Colección escogida de las mejores poesias de Plácido,* new ed., Brussels, 1885 (?); *Poesias de Plácido (Gabriel de la Concepción Valdés),* new ed., Paris, Bouret, 1894 (same as Vingut's edition of 1860); *Poesias selectas de Plácido,* Havana, Cultural, 1930; *Gabriel de la Concepción Valdés (Plácido): Musa cubana,* Paris, Casa Editorial Franco-Ibero-americano, no date; *La siempre viva,* 1832; *El veguero; Jocotencal* (romance); *Cora* (latter two based on Indian legends); and poems written in prison: "La plegaria a Dio," "Adios a mi lira," and "Despedido a mi madre."

Biographical/Critical Sources: Garcia Garófala Mesa, *Plácido, poeta y mártir,* Mexico, Ediciones Botas, 1938; Carlos M. Trelles' biography: *El historiador Antonio José Valdés* has section and comments on Plácido.

See also the play written on Plácido by Diego Vicente Tejera: *La muerte de Plácido,* New York, Imp. N. Ponce de Léon, 1875; concerning Plácido's writing of *La plegaria,* see *¿ Es de Plácido la Plegaria a Dios?* of Francisco Gonzáles del Valle, Havana, 1923. Also see unpublished Ph. D. diss. (Illinois, 1941) by Ben Frederic Carruthers: "The Life, Work and Death of Plácido."

CONTRERAS, Hilma

b. 1913, San Francisco de Macoris, Dominican Republic.
Storywriter.

Contreras passed most of his years abroad. His stories were original and reflective of his experiences beyond the confines of the Caribbean.

Writings: Stories: *Cuatro Cuentos,* 1953; *Doña Endrina de Calatayud,* 1955; *El Ojo de Dios,* details not known.

CORCHADO JUARBE, Manuel

b. September 12, 1840, Isabela, Puerto Rico; d. November, 1884, Madrid.
Poet, storywriter, biographer, playwright, lawyer, orator.

Corchado studied and practiced law in Barcelona and served as a representative of Puerto Rico at the Spanish court. A fervent anti-slavery man, Corchado sought emancipation throughout the remainder of the Spanish empire. His poetry, never collected, was published in the literary journals of the day in Spain and Puerto Rico. The city of Mayagüez elected Corchado its deputy at the Cortes in 1871 (Madrid) and he became a leading spokesman for the liberal group and advocate of greater autonomy for Puerto Rico. On his return to Puerto Rico in 1879 he continued his advocacy of reform and local freedom and served in the island's legislature.

Writings: Stories: *Historias de ultratumba,* Madrid, Alcántara, 1872.

Poetry: in various journals; "Una consulta" appears in the *Antologia de la poesia puertorriqueña,* E. Fernández Méndez, ed., San Juan, 1968; *Páginas sangrientas,* Madrid, 1875.

Biografia *de Lincoln.*

Plays: *Maria Antonieta* (a verse tragedy), first performed in Puerto Rico, 1880, published there by Acosta, 1880 (30 pp.); *Desde la comedia al drama* (comedy, verse, in 3 acts), Puerto Rico, Imp. de El Asimilista, 1885 (104 pp.).

Socio-Political Work: *Las barricadas,* Barcelona, 1870.

Biographical/Critical Sources: See pp. 132-134 in *Antologia puertorriqueña,* Me. Fernández Juncos, ed., 1st ed., New York, Hinds, Noble & Eldredge, 1907, reprinted 1913, 1923, 1952; Carmen Gómez Tejera, *La novela en Puerto Rico,* Rio Piedras, 1947; Ernesto Juan Fonfrias, *Sementera,* San Juan, 1962.

CORDOVA, Armando

b. ca. 1936, Batabanó, Cuba.
Poet, painter.

Primarily a painter, Córdova has published much verse devoted to the travail of Afro-Cubans.

Writings: Poetry: *Poemas dedicados a Macua,* Havana, 1966 (in *Cuadernos del hombre libre*).

CORRETJER, Juan Antonio

b. 1908, Ciales, Puerto Rico.
Poet, essayist, journalist, critic, politician.

One of the most prolific of the island's poets, Corretjer has been strongly hostile to the United States and he has taken a strong stand for Puerto Rican independence, much of this patriotic fervor clearly evident as subject and passion in his poetry. He has worked in many forms including the copla and the sonnet and often employs idiomatic and patois speech.

Writings: Poetry: *Agüeybana,* Ponce, P.R., Tipografia del Llano, 1932; *Ulises,* Ponce, Puerto Rico evangélico, 1933; *Amor de Puerto Rico,* San Juan, Edición La Palabra, 1937; *Cántico de guerra,* 1937; *El leñero (Poema de la revolución de Lares),* New York, 1944; *Los primeros años,* San Juan, Casa Baldrich, 1950; *Tierra nativa,* San Juan, 1951; *Alabanza en la Torre de Ciales,* San José, Costa Rica, Repertorio Américano, 1953, San Juan, 1965; *Don Diego en el cariño,* San Juan, Editorial La Escrita, 1956; *Distancias,* Guaynabo, P.R., Ediciones Vel, 1957; *Yerba Bruja,* San Juan, Imp. Venezuela, 1957, San Juan, Instituto de Cultura Puertorriqueña, 1970; *Genio y figura (Rapsodia criolla),* Guaynabo, P. R., Litografia Guilliani, 1961; *Pausa para el amor,* San Juan, Cooperativa de Artes Gráficas Romualdo Real, 1967; *Canciones de Consuelo, que son canciones de protesta,* mimeographed, Guaynabo, Publicaciones de la Liga Socialista Puertorriqueña, 1971; a fragment of "Distancias," in *Asomante* (April-June 1955).

Politics: *La lucha por la independencia de Puerto Rico,* 1949; *Contestación al miedo,* 1954; *Nuestra bandera,* 1947; *La historia que gritó en Lares,* Guaynabo, 1970.

Critical Biography: *Llorens: juicio histórico,* 1947.

CORTON, Antonio

b. 1854, San Juan, Puerto Rico; d. 1913.
Critic, poet.

Primarily a critic, Cortón left Puerto Rico for Spain in his nineteenth year, writing the poem "Adiós a la patria." Manrique Cabrera states: "Sin la menor duda Cortón representa, en virtud de su imaginación humoristica, penetrante, fina, y a veces mordaz, el más destacado de los criticos puertorriqueños de fines del siglo XIX y comienzos del presente."

Writings: Poetry: "Adiós a la patria," in *Boletin Histórico de Puerto Rico,* Vol. XIII, pp. 241-242.

Critical Studies: Introduction to *La religión del amor* of Abelardo Morales Ferrer, Madrid, 1885; *Folleto a Salvador Brau y Frasquito Oller,* Madrid, 1895 (44 pp.); *Patria y cosmopolitismo,* Madrid, 1881; *El fantasma del separatismo,* Valencia, Spain, 1898 (written as dialogues); *Pandemonium,* Madrid, 1898; *Espronceda,* Madrid, 1906.

Biographical/Critical Sources:José Luis Martín, "Don Cortón, periodista, ensayista y critico de nuestro siglo XIX," in *Revista Historia,* vol. V, no. 1 (April 1955), Universidad de Puerto Rico, p. 113; F. Manrique Cabrera, *Historia de la literatura puertorriqueña, Ri*o Piedras, 1969, pp. 189-191.

COSTA, Fernando

b. ca. 1844, Cuba.
Playwright.

Costa's work is today only of historical interest.

Writings: Plays: *Memorias intimas* (3 act comedy, prose), Havana, La Propaganda literaria, 1877, performed Teatro Payret, Havana, August 4, 1877; *Confidencias,* Havana, La Propaganda literaria, 1877, performed Teatro Payret, December 4, 1877; *Un relámpago de celos* (1 act comic sketch), Havana, La Propaganda literaria, 1877; *El maledetto,* musical, 1880; *¡Mulata santa!,* 1880; *Fruta de verano; El major dolor* (1 act sketch), Havana, Imp. Militar de la Viuda de Soler, 1877, performed Teatro Albisu, Havana, June 7, 1877; *El chiflado* (1 act prose comedy) in ms.

COSTALES, Manuel

b. 1815, Cuba; d. 1866.
Folklorist, storywriter.

One of Cuba's earliest folklorists, Costales published a pioneering little novel, *Florentina.*

Writings: Novelette: *Florentina,* 1856.
Folklore: in many journals and in such collections as *Los cubanos pintados por si mismos,* 1852; and *Tipos y costumbres de la Isla de Cuba.*

COSTI Y ERRO, Cándido
(pseudonym: **C. SICTO**)

b. ca. 1862, Cuba.
Playwright.

Today Costi's work is of historic interest only.

Writings: Plays: *El golondrino de Niña* (1 act prose comedy), written by "Sicto," Havana, La Moderna, 1892; *El marqués de Taco Taco* (1 act prose comedy), by "C. Sicto," 1892, ms.; *El ruiseñor de Inocencia* (1 act prose comedy), Havana, La Moderna, 1892, performed Teatro Alhambra, Havana, August 5, 1892; *Julia Suárez* (1 act prose comic sketch), Havana, La Moderna, 1892, performed Teatro Alhambra, July 29, 1892; *La novia del orangután* (1 act prose comic sketch), Havana, 1892; performed Teatro Alhambra, December, 1892; *Vino de papayina* (1 act prose comedy), Havana, La Moderna, 1892, performed Teatro Alhambra, Havana, June 8, 1892.

COTTO THORNER, Guillermo

b. 1916, Juncos, Puerto Rico.
Novelist.

Cotto Thorner has long been a teacher of Hispanic literature in the New York school system. His one novel, *Trópico en Manhattan,* reflects the author's own sharp experience of the double cultural heritage of the contemporary Puerto Rican adrift in the giant American metropolis.

Writings: Novel: *Trópico en Manhattan,* San Juan, Edit. Occidente, 1951, 2nd ed., San Juan, Edit. Cordillera, 1967.

COVARRUBIAS, Francisco

b. 1775, Cuba; d. 1850.
Playwright, poet, actor.

A famous poet and actor in the early 1820's in Havana, Covarrubias remained an important figure until mid-century. Though modern literary critics find no merit in his work—as they also do not in other popular pieces of "teatro bufo," where obscene or at least licentious allusions were common, the bufo pieces were alive and genuine responses to the times and the needs of the proletariat piling up in the crowded cities.

J. A. Millán wrote a biography on his good friend Covarrubias which appeared in 1850.

Writings: Plays: (unpublished, dates are those of writing): *La tia Catana y el tio Bartolo,* Sainete, 1820; *La virtudes del Zurriago,* Sainete, 1822; *Un montero en el teatro o El cómico de Ceiba Mocha,* performed in Havana, 1835; also the burlesques or sketches, now only extant in fragments; *Los verlorios de la Habana; Las tertulias de la Habana; La feria de Carraguao; La valla de gallos; El foro de catre;* and many others.

Biographical/Critical Sources: José Augustin Millán, *Biografia de don Francisco Covarrubias, primera actor de carácter jocoso de los teatros de la Habana,* Havana, 1851; Max Henriquez Ureña, *Panorama histórico de la literatura cubana,* New York, 1963, pp. 245-46.

CRESPO Y BORBON, Bartolomé José
(pseudonyms: **Creto GANGA** and **EL ANFIBIO**)

b. 1811, Ferrol, Spain; d. Havana, Cuba, 1871.
Playwright, poet.

Crespo came to Cuba in his tenth year and became a leading journalist. He wrote many carnival farces and such pieces as *A Slapstick Comedy, or the Marriage of Pancha Jutia and Cañuto Raspadura* (1947). The characters are Afro-Cubans and employ the local rural dialect, one of the earliest plays to deal with Afro-Cuban speech. He also published a series of satirical articles written in the so-called "bozal" dialect of Africans newly arrived in a Cuba still suffering from slavery. Though he wrote much, Max Henriquez Ureña said his work "vale poco."

Writings: Plays: *El chasco* (1 act), Havana, Palmer, 1837; *Laborintos y trifucas de canavá,* Havana, 1846; *Un ajiaco, o La boda de Pancha Jutia y Cañuta Raspadura,* Havana, Oliva, 1847; *Debajo del tamarindo* (1 act), Havana, Imp. La Honradez, 1864; Los pelones, Havana, n.d. and published under name of "El Anfibio," but there is an edition of 1839, Havana, published by Oliva; *Los apuros de Covarrubias,* and *La muerte de Declos,* both unpublished.

Poetry: *El látigo del Anfibio,* 1836; *Sátiras,* 1838; *Cartas a midifunta Francisca; Las habaneras pintadas por si mismas en miniatura,* 1847; and his work is in several collections including *Mapa de la poesia negra américana,* Buenos Aires, 1946, edited by Emilio Ballagas.

Biographical/Critical Sources: J. Jahn, *Neo-African Literature,* New York, Evergreen, 1968.

CRUZ Y FERNANDEZ, Manuel de la

(pseudonym: **Isais**)

b. 1861, Cuba; d. February 19, 1896.
Storywriter, literary historian, journalist.

An active adherent of Cuban independence, Cruz was a polemicist and journalist particularly interested in the revolt of 1868. He was a foreign correspondent for several journals, notably *Revista Cubana* and *La Nación* of Buenos Aires. His pieces later were collected as *La guerra de Cuba* and he helped found *Patria,* the voice of the Partido Revolucionario Cubano.

Writings: Stories: *El Capitán Córdova,* 1886; *La hija del montero,* Havana, 1895.

Collected Works: *Obras,* edited by Calleza, 6 vols., Havana, 1924-26.

Literary History: *Reseñs histõrico-critica del movimiento literario de la isla de Cuba (1790-1890),* Buenos Aires, F. Lagomaggiore, 1890, reprinted in *Revista Cubana,* 1891.

Biographical-Critical Essays: *Tres caracteres (Cortina, Sanguily and Varona),* Key West, Florida, 1889 (published under pseudonym of Isais).

Journalism: *Episodios de la revolución cubana,* 1890, reprinted Havana, Inst. del Libro, 1967; *Cromitos cubanos,* Havana, 1892; *La revolución cubana y la raza de color,* Key West, Florida, 1895; *La guerra de Cuba,* details unknown.

Biographical/Critical Sources: Max Henriquez Ureña, *Panorama histórico de la literatura cubana,* New York, 1963, pp. 143-147.

CUCHI COLL, Isabel

b. 1904, Arecibo, Puerto Rico.
Storywriter, essayist, critic, playwright.

Cuchi-Coll was one of the earliest woman critics from Puerto Rico and her play set in New York, one of the first dealing with Puerto Ricans in the metropolis.

Writings: Play: *La familia de Justo Malgenio: Puertorriqueños en Nueva York,* Barcelona, Ediciones Rumbos, 1963.

Stories: *13 novelas cotras,* Barcelona, 1965.

Essays and Articles: *Oro nativo,* 1936.

Critical Essays: *Dos poetas de America: Clara Lair, Julia de Burgos,* Barcelona, 1970.

CUELLO, Julio Alberto

b. 1898, Dominican Republic.
Poet.

Beginning as a traditionalist writer of alexandrines, Cuello evolved toward the more innovative group "verso-librismo," or free verse.

Writings: Poetry: *Clamor libertario,* 1926; *Los poemas del instinto,* 1926; *La parábola trunca,* 1935.

DALMAU CANET, Sebastián

b. 1884, Puerto Rico; d. 1937.
Essayist, biographer.

Dalmau arrived in Puerto Rico shortly before Spain lost the island to the United States. He was employed in a minor position in Ponce but slowly took root in his new home and began to contribute articles and essays to local journals. His *Crepúsculos literarios* (1903) provides a panoramic view of literary currents in the island during the change-over period.

Writings: Essays: *Crepúsculos literarios,* 1903.
Biographies: *Emilio Zola,* 1903; *Castelar,* 1907; *Roman Baldorioty de Castro,* 1910; *Luis Muñoz Rivera,* 1917; *Proceres,* 1917; *José de Diego,* 1923.

Biographical/Critical Sources: Nicolás Rivas, "Sebastián Dalmau y Canet," in *Puerto Rico Ilustrado* (March 27, 1937).

DAMIRON Y SANCHEZ, Rafael

b. June 9, 1882, Barahona, Dominican Republic; d. January 6, 1956.
Novelist, poet, playwright, folklorist, essayist.

Damirón's work is now almost forgotten, but his plays were once performed with some success and he also published five novels and many miscellaneous poems and essays.

Writings: Novels: *Del cesarismo,* 1909; *¡Ay de los vencidos!,* 1925; *Revolución,* 940; *La cacica,* 1944; *Monólogo de la locura,* S. Domingo, Montalvo, 1914.

Folklore: *La sonrisa de Concho,* 1921; *Estampas,* 1938.

Plays: *Alma criolla,* performed 1916 and inspired by Pellerano Castro's *Criollas; Mientras los otros rien* performed Teatro Colón de Santo Domingo, 1918; *La trova del recuerdo,* performed 1917; *Tres minutos de otro tiempo; Cómo cae la balanza.*

Poetry: in various journals and anthologies.

Political articles: *Pimentones; De Soslayo.*

DAUBON, José Antonio

b. 1840, San Juan, Puerto Rico; d. 1922.
Poet, folklorist, journalist.

Daubón employed local customs and colloquial language in his prose and verse. The greatest influences on him were those of Espronceda, Zorrilla, and the great French poet of the mid-19th century, Lamartine. Much of his work appeared in *Pais* and *El Buscapié.* His style is very personal, fresh, and usually happy, full of local color.

Writings: Poetry: *Poesias,* San Juan, Imp. de F. J. Marxuach, 1900 (207 pp.).
Folklore: *Cosas de Puerto Rico,* 1904.

DAVILA, José Antonio

b. October 7, 1899, Bayamón, Puerto Rico; d. December 4, 1941.
Poet, critic, physician.

Son of Virgilio Dávila, José Antonio was an active member of the modernista group of the 1920's and is considered a fine lyric poet. *Almacén* contains his juvenile, even puerile verse while *Vendimia* shows his best qualities, never completely realized, however, according to several critics. Love, death and a certain sad religiosity are his themes, his tone, his purposes.

Writings: Poetry: *Vendimia* (1917-1939), 1940, 4th ed., Rio Piedras, Edit. Cultural, 1967; *Almacén de baratijas,* 1941 (contains earliest work); *Motivos de Tristán; Poemas,1930-1934,* San Juan, Ateneo Puertorriqueño, 1957; *Poemas,* San Juan, Edit. Cordilleras, 1964. The English translation of some of his poems appeared in *Un libro para mis nietos,* published by José's father, Virgilio Dávila.

Critical Essays: *El decir y su sombra; La critica como orientadora de nuestra cultura.*

Biographical-Critical Study: *Mariano Feliu Balseiro, Apuntes biográficos,* 1941.

Biographical/Critical Sources: Adriana Ramos Mimoso, *Vida y poesia en José Antonio Dávila,* unpublished M.A. thesis, U. of Puerto Rico, 1948.

DAVILA, Virgilio

b. January 28, 1869, Toa Baja, Puerto Rico; d. August 22, 1943, Bayamón, Puerto Rico.
Poet, teacher, statesman, farmer.

After taking his B.A. in 1885 at the Instituto Civil de Segunda Enseñanza, Dávila entered politics and soon began to contribute poetry to the "modernistas" journal *El Carnaval* and other local reviews. His verse was a mixture of classical, romantic, and the new currents coming from Europe, but his preferred style was clear and unadorned. He did, however, often employ rural and city speech. Along with Llorens Torres and Palés Matos, Dávila became a leader in the modernist developments and with Matias González Garcia and Miguel Meléndez Muñoz he was closely associated with the regional and creole speech movement.

Dávila's "Cofre de Sándalo" reflects the oriental themes then so popular in late romantic poetry:

En un tallado cofre de sándalo de Oriente
conservo los recuerdos más dulces y queridos:
amarillentas cartas, retratos desteñidos
y rosas que aún escuchan las cuitas de la fuente.

Writings: Poetry: *Patria,* 1903; *Viviendo y Amando,* Bayamón, 1912, 2nd ed., 1963; *Aromas del terruño,* 1916, 2nd ed., San Juan, Baldrich, 1939, and San Juan, 1963; *Pueblito de antes,* Bayamón, Imp. Cantero, 1917, 2nd ed., 1930, 3rd ed., 1941 (which included English translation of the poems by his son, José Antonio Dávila), 4th ed., edited by son also, San Juan, Edit. Cordilleras, 1967; *Un libro para mis nietos,* 1928; *Virgilio Dávila—obras completas,* San Juan, Instituto de Cultura Puertorriqueña, 1964; also nine short poems in L. Hernández Aquino's *El Modernismo en Puerto Rico,* San Juan, 1967 (which includes some poems in English translation and the poems: "Patria," "Viviendo y Amando," "Un libro para mis nietos," "Aromas del terruno").

Essays: *Prosa-ensayos-articulos y cartas literarias,* selections and notes by Vicente Géigel Polanco, San Juan, 1971.

Biographical/Critical Sources: C. Rosa-Nieves, *Ensayos escogidas,* San Juan, 1970, pp. 141-159; Maria Arroyo, "Vida y obra de Virgilio Dávila," unpublished M.A. thesis, U. of Puerto Rico, 1946; Carlos Orama Padilla, *Virgilio Dávila, su vida y su obra,* 2nd ed., San Juan, 1963 (copyright, 1964); Ana Margarita Silva, *El jibaro en la literatura de Puerto Rico* (comparado con el campesino de España e Hispanoamérica), 2nd ed., San Juan, Imp. Venezuela, 1957 (with much discussion of Dávila).

DEGETAU Y GONZALEZ, Federico

b. December, 1862, Ponce, Puerto Rico; d. January 20, 1914.
Storywriter, novelist, journalist, editor, statesman.

After primary schooling in Ponce, Degetáu went to Barcelona, Spain, to take his B.A.

In the Catalan capital he was befriended by many writers and artists but pulled himself away for the more vigorous study of law at Madrid University. He widened his circle of friends to scientists and musicians (he was already an excellent violinist). At age nineteen Degetau won his law degree and was elected to the Academia de Ciencias Antropológicas of Madrid. Travelling to Paris to discuss the abolishment of the death penalty with Victor Hugo, he broadened his horizons further and then returned to Spain for further legal studies at Granada, Salamanca, and Valladolid.

Always interested in children, he helped introduce the new ideas of Froebel's *Jardines de la infancia* (in its Spanish version) into Spain and he himself developed many new methods of pedagogy. Degetau's one novel, a "study" of folk customs, was *Juventud.*

His republican sympathies led him to found in Madrid in 1887 with his own money *La Isla de Puerto Rico* as a voice for protests against the growing conservatism of Spain and oppression at home. Elected to the Spanish Cortes by his fellow Puerto Ricans he took an important role in the business of the legislature though still a young man in his thirties. In 1901, after the United States took over the island, Degetau was chosen to serve as Puerto Rican delegate to the Congress in Washington, D. C., staying for four years. He finished his service to his country by helping organize a Panamerican University in Puerto Rico and by making an official trip to Europe (1911-12) to seek out paintings and other art works, ancient and modern, destined to be the core of the new center's collection.

Writings: Stories: *¡Qué Quijote!,* 1883; *El fondo del aljibe,* Madrid, Enrique Teodóro, 1886; *El secreto de la domadora,* 2nd ed., Madrid, Teodóro, 1886; *Silvia,* in *Cuentas para el viejo,* San Juan, 1894; *Cuentos pedagógicos y literarios,* San Juan, Edit. Puerto Rico Ilustrado, 1925; and two collections of children's stories, in ms.

Novel: *Juventud,* Madrid, A. Avrial, 1895.

Essay: *Fé y pensando,* 1915.

Biographical/Critical Sources: Angel Mergal, "Federico Degetau," unpublished M.A. thesis, U. of Puerto Rico, 1940; also Mergal's *Federico Degetau, un orientador de su pueblo,* New York, Hispanic Institute, 1944; Carmen Gómez Tejera, *La novela en Puerto Rico,* San Juan, 1947, pp. 75-76.

DEIVE, Carlos Estéban

b. 1935, Sarriá, Lugo, Spain.

Playwright, storywriter, journalist, essayist, literary critic, teacher, ethnologist.

Deive won a National Prize in Literature in 1963, the first prize for plays in the Concurso de Teatro Popular in 1957, and a prize given by the Banco de Reservas for plays written in 1970. Though he continued to write critical pieces and reviews Deive increasingly devoted himself to his professional work as an ethnologist.

Writings: Novel: *Magdalena,* 1964.

Plays: *Los señores impertinentes,* 1957 (winner of Primer Concurso Teatro Popular, 1957); *El Lider máximo; El antropófago; El hombre que nunca llegaba,* 2S. Domingo, Ed. del Caribe, 1970.

Literary Criticism and History: *Tendencias de la novela contemporánea,* S. Domingo, Col. Arquero, 1963, awarded the Premio Nacional de Literatura in 1963.

Story: "En el pueblo hay guerrilleros, S. Domingo, *Suplemento Cultural de El Nacional* (January 16, 1972), and also appeared in *Antologia de la literatura dominicana* edited by José Alcántara Almánzar, Santo Domingo, Editora Cultural Dominicana, 1972.

DELGADO, Emilio R.

b. 1904, Corozal, Puerto Rico.

Poet, journalist.

Delgado has published in many journals,

including *Faro* (1926), *Vórtice* (1927), *Hostos* (1928), *Puerto Rico Illustrado, El Mundo, El Imparcial* and *Asomante*. He was the editor for a period of *La Correspondencia*. Much of his verse is lightly melancholic, smooth, almost "transparent." Closely associated with Rosa-Nieves, Vicente Palés Matos, Géigel-Polanco and S. R. Quiñones at the University of Puerto Rico in the 1920's, Delgado helped initiate the new movement of vanguardismo called locally "Noismo."

No. "VII" of his "Pequeños poemas" is very attractive as the few lines may indicate of the work's total of twelve:

Si la violeta
palidece en tus manos.
Si el débil junco se dobla
cuando lo toca el viento.
Si el agua mineral de tus ojos
no se detiene.

Manrique Cabrera praises both the prose and verse of Delgado very highly in *Historia de la literatura puertorriqueña* (p. 372).

Writings: Poetry: *Tiempos del amor breve,* N.Y., Las Américas, 1958 and in many journals and collections, including Fernándo Gutierrez, *Las mejores poesias de amor puertorriqueñas,* Barcelona, 1954; and C. Rosa-Nieves, *Aguinaldo lirico de la poesia puertorriqueña,* 1st ed., Rio Piedras, 1957, 2nd ed., 1971; Angel Valbuena Briones and L. Hernández Aquino, *Nueva poesia de Puerto Rico,* Madrid, 1952.

DELGADO, Martin Morúa

(see under **Martin MORUA DELGADO**)

DELIGNE, Gastón Fernando

b. October 23, 1861, Santo Domingo, Dominican Republic; d. January 18, 1913, San Pedro de Macoris, Dominican Republic.
Poet, novelist.

Gastón was considered the finest poet of his day and was patriotic, nationalistic and perfervid in his interests in independence. His interest in character and his own extreme sensitivity led him to inaugurate "psychological" poetry, beginning with "Soledad," and his new work from there on would become more and more analytical. The permutations of thought in a woman facing severe predicaments are caught in such works as "Confidencias de Cristina," "La aparición," and "Angustias."

His earlier and simpler political poetry is reflected in these lines from "Ololoi":

Y pregona su orgullo inaudito,
que es mirar sus delitos, delito:
Y que de ellos murmúrese y hable,
es delito más grande y notable;
Y prepara y acota y advierte
para tales delito, la muerte.
Adulando a aquel idolo falso,
que de veces irguióse el cadalso!
Y a nutrir su homofobia larvada,
¡cuántas veces sinuó la emboscada!

Deligne suffered from the dread disease of leprosy as did his brother Rafael Alfredo, also a poet, and Gastón found his only escape was suicide.

Writings: Novel: *Del patibulo.*

Poetry: *Soledad,* 1887, 1897, republished S. Domingo, Editora Montalvo, 1946; *Galaripsos,* 1908, 2nd ed., S. Domingo., Ed. Libreria Dominicana, 1963; *Romances de la Hispanola, 1931; Páginas olvidadas,* in *Centenario de la República Dominicana, 1844-1944,* S. Domingo, Editora Montalvo, 1944; extracts of "Angustias" are in M. Rodriquez Ureña's *Panorama histórico de la literatura,* 1965, pp. 234-236; and extracts of "En el botado," on pp. 236-239.

Biographical/Critical Sources: Fernando A. Tió Amiama's *Contribución a la bibliografia de Gastón Fernando Deligne,* Ciudad Trujillo, Luis Sánchez Andújar, 1944; Rodriguez Ureña's *Panorama . . .,* S. Domingo, Postigo, 1965; J. Balaguer's *Historia de la literatura dominicana,* 5th ed., S. Domingo, Postigo, 1970, pp. 225-239; F. A. Mota Medrano, *Relieves Alumbrados,* S. Domingo, 1971, pp. 43-76; Gustavo A. Mejia Ricart, *Gastón F. Deligne, Poeta Civil,* details unknown.

DELIGNE Y FIGUEROA, Rafael Alfredo

(pseudonym: **Pepe CANDIDO**)

b. July 25, 1863, Santo Domingo, Dominican Republic; d. April 29, 1902, San Pedro de Macoris.

Poet, critic, playwright, storywriter, lawyer.

Rafael was a better writer of prose than of poetry, but his verse had some of the qualities of that of Gastón, his brother, and was philosophical and psychological. He contributed many essays to *El Cable* of San Pedro under the pseudonym of Pepe Cándido which became a well-known signature. He founded with Fabio Fiallo, the important journal *El Hogar* in 1894 and a year later the literary magazine *Prosa y Versa* with Arturo Bermúdez.

He suffered the agonies of leprosy as had his brother and succumbed to it in his 39th year.

Writings: Verse Play: *La justicia y el azar,* performed 1894.

Prose Play: *Vidas tristes,* 1901 (3 acts).

Verse Narrative: *Milagro,* 1896, San Pedro.

Critical essays and poetry, mixed: *En prosa y en verso,* 1902.

Stories: *Narraciones dominicanas,* El Pobre Cabo, San Pedro, 1895; and in journal *Prosa y Verso,* 1903; and stories in various journals including those collected and published in *Listin Diario,* S. Domingo, under general heading "Cuentos del Lunes," (July 27, 1896), as "Los tres besos," (August 24, 1896), as "Dulce y sabrosa" (September 14, 1896), and as "El corazón de más valor," (October 5, 1896).

In mss: most of his occasional articles in original holograph, including "Estudio sobre la Constitución del Estado," the four-act play, *Montbars el Exterminador,* in prose and verse, and the two-act prose play, *Encarnación.*

Memoirs: "Cosas que fueron y cosas que son; otras recordando reconstruyendo," published various journals.

DEL MONTE, Félix Maria

(pseudonym: **DELIO**)

b. November 20, 1819, Santo Domingo, Dominican Republic; d. April 24, 1899, Santo Domingo.

Poet, playwright, journalist, orator, judge, teacher.

Son of a lawyer, José Joaquin del Monte, Félix studied under his father and then Dr. Moscoso and Padre Gaspar Hernández. Taking a law degree he served as a lieutenant in the Guardia Nacional, but he soon became an active member of the secret revolutionary group "La Trinitaria" which aimed at the establishment of a republic. Del Monte published his poetry in *La Filantrópica,* the journal of the movement headed by Juan Pablo Duarte, himself an occasional writer of patriotic poems. He founded the literary magazine *El Dominicano* in 1845 with Valencio Serra y Bobea.

Considered, with Javier Angulo Guridi, one of the first poets of his country, Del Monte wrote the first patriotic song for

Dominica's independence, proclaimed February 27, 1844, the "Canción Dominicana" which was set to music by Juan Bautista Alfonseca (1810-1875) and which begins:

¡Al arma, españoles!
¡Volad a la lid!
Tomad por divisa:
¡Vencer o morir!

where "españoles" meant the Spanish speaking population of Hispañola. This word was later changed to "patriotas" by

the author but the original term has remained the popular one when the national hymn is sung by the multitudes.

The long poem "Las vírgenes de Galindo" attacked the Haitian occupying army and its outrages. His most popular political verse was "El arpa del proscrito" and he attacked in several poems the Spanish favoring President Santana in the 1840's. The poem "A mi patria" compares the much fought over Dominica to Poland:

¡Alli está la Polonia americana
al poste del oprobio conducida;
alli está lo odalisca prostituida.
Señora ayer y sierva a la mañana!

Del Monte was a member of the legislature from 1852 on and in 1854 founded with Nicolás Ureña de Mendoza, the journal, *El Porvenir,* and the same year was elected a deputy to the Congreso Revisor that established the Constitution of February 25, 1854. From October 9, 1856 to June 13, 1858, he was Minister of Foreign Affairs and of Justice in the second administration of President Baéz, and in May of 1858 he was named Minister of Defense (Guerra y Marino).

In 1852 he had been named a professor of literature at the Colegio de San Buenaventura and in 1875 he took a chaired professorship in literature and jurisprudence at the Instituto Profesional.

In his younger years he was active in the literary group "Amigos del Pais," from 1846, and is one of his country's greatest statesman-writers. His plays also were pioneering efforts and he is called the father of the modern (post colonial) theatre in the Dominican Republic.

Writings: Poetry: *Las vírgenes de Galindo,* 1885 (written in 1860); various poems in *El Dominicano* (1845-46), the first literary magazine of the republic, and include: "El arpa del proscrita," written in Saint Thomas, 1855, and "A mi patria," published in many journals and: in Rodríquez Demorizi's *Poesia popular dominicana* are "El Banilejo y la Jibarita," first published in *El Eco del Pueblo,* No. 25 (January 25, 1857), "Noche buena en San Miguel," and "El Valle de Higüero."

Verse in mss: "Versos Campunos," written in 1864, and "Cantos dominicanos," written in 1875: these poems being in an unpublished collection preserved by the poet's daughter Mercedes at one time.

Play: *El diluvio universal* (sacred tragedy), Madrid, 1834; *Ozema* (light piece), Matanzas, 1834; *Ozema o La virgen Indiana,* Ponce, Puerto Rico, Imp. El Pais, 1867 (only one copy of this publication is extant, it being in the archives of the publishing house El Pais); *El mendigo de la catedral de León; Un vals de Strauss; El último abencerraje* (fragments only extant), written about 1872; *Antonio Duvergé o Las victimas del 11 de abril,* written 1865 (shortly after Duvergé was imprisoned by General Santana); *El artista Antonio Brito* (dramatic legends), ms. is extant; *El premio de los pichones* (comedy based on story of Alexandre Dumas). Most of these works were performed, and some of them read in "concert" versions by the group "La Juventud."

Biographical/Critical Sources: Emilio Rodriguez Demorizi's *Poesia popular dominicana,* 1938, 2nd ed., S. Domingo, 1973, pp. 229-248.

DELMONTE Y MENA, Jesús M.

b. 1824, Santiago, Cuba; d. 1877.
Poet, playwright, mathematician, educator.

Delmonte occupied the chair for mathematics and was Vice-Rector of the Colegio del Salvador.

Writings: Plays: *Una mala vecina* (3 acts, verse comedy), Santiago, Cuba, Martinez, 1846; *Mi suegra otra vez en casa* (1 act fantasy), unpublished.

Poetry: *Declaración joco-seria de amor.*

Mathematics: *Aritmética teorico-práctica,* Santiago, Cuba, 1848.

DEL MONTE Y APONTE, Domingo

(pseudonym: **Sánchez de ALMADOVAR** and **Bachiller Toribo SANCHEZ DE ALMODOVAR**)

b. 1804, Maracaibo, Venezuela; d. 1853, Madrid.
Poet, storywriter, letter writer.

Arrived in Cuba while but six, Del Monte became a leading romantic writer in his new homeland. A student of Félix Varela at the Seminario de San Carlos, Del Monte studied and then practiced law for a period with Nicolás Manuel Escobedo (1795-1840), then a professor and famous orator. He travelled in Europe and on his return in 1829 began to contribute work to a wide range of the journals of the day. He served as secretary of the literary section of the Sociedad Económica de Amigos del Pais and occupied several important government posts. Exiled in 1843, he lived in the U. S. and Paris for a time, and released eventually from sentence of arrest, he went to Spain where he died barely 50 years of age.

Del Monte founded (with J. Vallarino) *La Moda o Recreo Semanal del Bello Sexo* (1829-31) and was associated at various times with *El Puntero Literario* (1830), *El Plantel* (1838), *El Album* (all of Havana), and *La Aurora* of Matanzas (1828-1857). His work may be divided into three major elements: politico-social questions, literary criticism and poetry. His influence was strong indeed on several generations of Cubans, possibly the greatest of any man who was not himself a great poet, original thinker, or martyred patriot. His rather sonorous poetry reflected early "criollo" tendencies and the popular new American note.

Writings: Selected Works: *Escritos de Domingo del Monte,* introduction and notes by José Antonio Fernández de Castro, 2 vols., Havana (?), 1929, as Vols. XII-XIII of *Colección de Libros Cubanos,* edited by Fernándo Ortiz.

Politics: *La Isla de Cuba tal cual esta,* 1836; *Proyecto de Memorial a la Reina a nombre del Ayuntamiento de la Habana . . .,* 1838.

Letter: *Centón epistolario de Domingo del Monte,* Havana, La Academia de la Historia de Cuba, 1924-1956.

Papers: "Cartas de Domingo del Monte," in *Revista de la Biblioteca Nacional* (1909-1910).

Poetic Romances: "El montero de la sabana," "El desterrado del hato," "El llanero correspondido," "Lá patria," and many others in various journals from 1824 and under pseudonyms.

Biographical/Critical Sources: Max Henriquez Ureña, *Panorama histórico de la literatura cubana,* New York, 1963, pp. 153-161; Bill James Karras, "The Literary Life of Domingo Del Monte y Aponte," unpublished Ph.D. dissertation, U. of Colorado, 1969.

DEL MONTE Y PORTILLO, Casimiro

b. 1838, Cimarrones, Cuba; d. 1887.
Poet, playwright, novelist, journalist.

Several of Del Monte's verse works won local prizes and he wrote a novel, unpublished (and title unknown) on the events surrounding the "Escalera" conspiracy.

Writings: Plays: *Rosas y diamantes* (3 acts, verse comedy), Matanzas, Imp. El Ferrocarril, 1865; *El árbol de los Guzmánes,* unpublished.
Poetry: in various journals and ode: "A la muerte de Quintana," and elegy "A la muerte de Don José de la Luz" (awarded the prizes of the Liceo de Matanzas, 1861 and 1863 respectively); the ode "A la América" also won the Liceo award in a later year.

DEL RISCO BERMUDEZ, René

b. 1937, San Pedro de Macoris, Dominican Republic; d. 1972.
Poet, storywriter.

Del Risco's special interest was in penetrating the lives of the lower middle class and expressing the feelings of the younger generation under the Trujillo dictatorship. His poems from *El viento frio* (1967) speak of the disappointments suffered by the young when they saw society and politics moving back to the old harsh realities after the failure of the 1965 revolt. His short stories are usually concerned with the average man, bored by the tedium of lives with few goals and opportunities, and by the consequent infantile dream of the carefree attitudes of childhood. His characterizations are vigorous, his stories usually ending with a twist, and his overall use of language is vivid.

His poetry has been awarded several prizes.

Writings: Poetry: *El viento frio,* S. Domingo, Col. El Puño, 1967; *Del júbilo a la sangre,* 1967.
Stories: *En el Barrio no hay banderas,* details unknown. The story "Ahora que vuelvo" is in *Suplemento Cultural de El Nacional,* S. Domingo, (March 2, 1969).

DEL VALLE, Rafael

b. 1846, Puerto Rico; d. 1917.
Poet.

Del Valle's themes were religion, science and progress. His work, though romantic, had a certain classical coolness as in these lines from "Aguadilla-Mi Nido":

Con los recuerdos de mi edad primera,
Con el cristal urente de estas lágrimas
Que en las recias angustias de la ausencia
De lo más hondo de mi pecho saltan!

Writings: Poetry: *Lucilla* (46 pp.), and *De la forma al fondo,* (232 pp.) both published in 1897 by Imp. Siglo XX; *Poesias completas,* San Juan, Imp. La Primavera, 1921.

DEL VALLE ATILES, Francisco

b. ca. 1854, Puerto Rico.
Novelist.

His *Inocencia* is believed to be the very first realistic (naturalistic) novel published by a Puerto Rican.

Writings: Novel: *Inocencia,* San Juan, El Asimilista, 1884 (201 pp.).

Biographical/Critical Sources: M. Martinez Roselló, "Don Francisco del Valle Atiles, Novelista," in *Puerto Rico Ilustrado* (October 6, 1928), p. 17.

DEMAR, Carmen
(pseudonym for **Carmen PORRATA DORIA DE APONTE**)

b. 1911, Humacao, Puerto Rico.
Poet.

Demar is a neo-romantic poet whose major themes are loneliness and gray anomie where sky and sea are symbols of isolation and hopes deferred. "El mar y yo" from her second volume of verse, *Derrumbe* (1948) begins:

¡Oh mar de mi Borinquen, azul como el ensueño.
tú y yo estamos sujetos a un mismo padecer;
llevamos en la entraña profundidad de duelos,
y sordas resonancias de trémulos desvelos,
cual la inquietud de insomnio que enhebra un gran querer!

Writings: Poetry: *Alas plegadas,* 1941; *Derrumbe,* San Juan, 1948; *Vuelo íntimo* and *Mar Sargazo,* San Juan, Imp. Venezuela, 1954; two poems from *Derrumbe* and "Hijo que fecundó la muerte" from *Vuelo íntimo* are given in *Aguinaldo lírico,* C. Rosa-Nieves, ed., Río Piedras, 1957.

DE PENA DE BORDAS, Virginia

b. ca. 1930, Dominican Republic.
Poet, storywriter.

De Peña's work has exploited local themes often elevated into mythical or fabulous realms.

Writings: Stories: *La Eracra de Ora.*
Novelettes: *Toeya; La princepa de los cabellos platinados; Atardecer en la montaña, La hora del destino; El fulgor de una estrella; Sombra de pasión; Magia de primavera;* and others.

Biographical/Critical Sources: F. A. Mota Medrano, *Relieves Alumbrados,* S. Domingo, 1971, chapter on De Peña, pp. 319-341.

DESCHAMPS, Eugenio
(a.k.a. **"El Tribuno Popular"**)

b. July 15, 1861, Santiago, Dominican Republic; d. August 27, 1919, Santo Domingo.
Poet, journalist.

Deschamps was an active journalist and supporter of popular causes, especially the movement against dictator Ulises Heureaux, and he was a friend of the Cuban poet-revolutionist, José Martí. His speeches were also notable, but he surpassed himself with his now classic welcome to Máximo Gómez, Martí's comrade in arms, pronounced in 1900. It is akin in power and fame to the U. S. revolutionary patriot's speech, that of Patrick Henry: "Give me liberty, or give me death!"

Deschamps served as deputy in parliament, as governor, as secretary of state, vice president of the Republic, and he helped found the Alianza Cibaeña, a "Sociedad de Artes y Oficios," still an important cultural organization.

Much of Eugenio Deschamps' polemical, journalistic pieces appeared in *La Alborada* and *La República* in the years 1883-84, the latter a review founded and directed because of the sharpness of his views, spending some time in Grand Turn island, but more in Puerto Rico. Busy there, too, he contributed to journals in his new home.

As for his style, he was orotunde and sonorous. His spiritual-political mentor was Victor Hugo. His delivery and emphasis was always that of the purposeful and aroused public tribune of the people, trying to warn and to illuminate. In his last years he was still vigorous enough to found, with Luis Amiama *La Hoja Suelta* in San Pedro de Macorís.

Writings: Poetry: *Juramento de amores,* written in Puerto Rico, 1886, published in *El Teléfono,* No. 222, S. Domingo (June 19, 1887).
Folkstories: "Tradiciones Quisqueyanas," in *Letras y Ciencias,* S. Domingo, 1895, republished in *Clio,* S. Domingo, No. 89 (1951) and in extracts in E. Rodriguez Demorizi's *Tradiciones y cuentos dominicanos,* 1969, pp. 163-165.
Autobiography: *Mis destierros,* left incomplete with only a few chapters extant.
Speeches and Articles: widely dispersed in the political pamphlets of the day, and speeches in *Ecos tribunicios,* but collected by E. Rodri-

guez Demorizi's *Discursos históricos,* S. Domingo, 1947.

Biographical/Critical Sources: Rufino Martinez' *Hombres dominicanos,* Vol. I, S. Domingo, 1936 [this work is dedicated to Deschamps and to Heureaux and their rivalries]; also see Max Henriquez Ureña's *Panorama histórico de la literatura dominicana,* Rio de Janeiro, 1945; and J. Balaguer's *Historia de la literatura dominicana,* S. Domingo, 1968.

DESNOES, Edmundo

b. 1930, Havana, Cuba.
Novelist, storywriter, essayist, journalist.

After some years in the United States spent as editor of the Spanish-language journal *Visión,* Desnoes lived for a period in Venezuela and the Bahamas and travelled widely in Europe.

Returning to Cuba after Castro's revolutionary government, including the Instituto del Libro and the editorial board of Casa de las Américas.

Some of his stories have been translated into English, French and Italian. The film treatment of his story "Memorias del subdesarrollo" has been widely acclaimed and among other awards a special plaque and a $2,000 prize by the (U.S.) National Society of Film Critics in 1973 was made to Tomás Gutiérrez Alea, the film's director. (Alea was subsequently barred from visiting the United States, and anyone who might wish to receive the award on his behalf was threatened by the State Department with prosecution under the Trading with the Enemy Act.)

Another story of Desnoes' was rewritten for film treatment, "Una aventura en el tropico."

Writings: Novels: *No hay problema,* Havana, 1961; *Revolución,* 1964; *El cataclismo,* Havana, Ed. Revolución, 1965; *Inconsolable memories,* translated from the Spanish by the author, New York, New American Library, 1967 and London, Deutsch, 1968.

Stories: *Memorias del subdesarrolo,* Havana, Unión, 1965, and Buenos Aires, Galerna, 1968, and as *Memories of Underdevelopment,* London, Penguin, 1973. The story "Una aventura en el trópico," appears in *Narrativa cubana de la revolución,* selected by J. M. Caballero Bonald, Madrid, Alianza Editorial, 1968, 1969, 1971.

Essays: *Puntos de vista,* Havana, Instituto del Libro, 1967.

Biographical/Critical Sources: Roque Dalton, *El intelectual y la sociedad,* Mexico City, Siglo XXI, 1969 (covers Desnoes and four other writers); Julianne Burton, "*Memories of Underdevelopment:* Alienation and Critical Response," review of film made of *Memorias del subdesarrollo,* in *Review 76* (Winter 1976), pp. 51-61.

DESSUS, Luis Felipe

b. 1875, Juana Diaz, Puerto Rico; d. 1920.
Poet.

Dessús, a rebel by birth, was self-taught. His combative nature led him to challenge old poetic practices and he early joined the "modernista" movement in the wake of Rubén Dario, and the Mexican poets Diaz Mirón and Vargas Vila. Dessús' "Toussaint" is a vivid praise-song of the great Haitian liberator as one can see from the opening lines:

Un grito se oyó un dia en una tierra indiana.
Era un desesperado grito de rebelión,
porque, bajo el ramaje de una selva antillana,
un rugido lanzaba african león.
Era "Toussaint" que, al frente de febril caravana,
de su pueblo y su raza combatia la opresión.

Y en el bosque frondoso y en la fértil sabana
el poder derrocaba del Primer Napoléon.

Much of Dessús' work appeared in the review *El Carnaval.*

Writings: Poetry: *Flores y bolas,* Guayama,

Puerto Rico, Tip. Unión Guayamesa, 1916.
Editor of: *Album de Guayama,* San Juan, Cantero Fernández, 1918.

DESVAL

(pseudonym for **Ignacio VALDES MACHUCA**)

DIAZ, Otilio Vigil

b. 1880, Santo Domingo, Dominican Republic; d. 1961.
Poet, storywriter.

Diaz was a bizarre, spirited, humorous writer, influenced by Gabriel D'Anunzio, the Italian poet-novelist-aviator. Originator of "Vedrinismo" and a precursor of the movement called "Postumismo" with his free verse poem "Arabesco," published in 1917 in the review *La Primada de América.* Moreno Jiminez in 1920 said he believed Diaz, along with Argentine poet, Almafuerte, and the Dominican, Gastón Deligne, were the three finest Spanish-American poets then living.

In his *Galeras de Pafos* Diaz said he wanted to create a musical prose-poetry without rhythm or rhyme—free enough to express every nuance of the soul and every quiver of dream and turn of thought. He moved on his work and his Postumismo period was productive of a few important works, but he never really identified with the movement, for his heart was with the vibration of the soul. And he wrote: "Si he escrito algo asimilable ha sido pura gentileza o mero intento de hacer notarque mis cuerdas se emocionan con todas las pulsaciones, que puedo danzar en qualquier tono. Pero, realmente, me case es otra cosa distinta de eso."

The critic Zorrillo wrote in his review of *Galeras de Pafos:*

> *El poeta Vigil Diaz, dotado de una super visión tan poca común, hace danzar sus emociones estéticas dentro de una orquestración tan complicada y sutil que dificilmente seria demostrar si han sido vaciados en prosa o en versos, de ellas puede decirse que viven y paltitan con el ritimico oscilar de la paradoja.*

Writings: Poetry: *Góndolas,* 1912; *Galeras de Pafos,* 1921, 1927; Diaz's preface to *Galeras* and some verse is republished in M. Rueda's *Antologia* (see below); *Miserere patricio,* 1915 (a long prose poem).

Stories: *Orégano (cuentos criollos),* 1949; *Lilis y Alejandrito (anecdotario histórico),* 1956.

Musical History: *Musica de ayer,* 1925, 1952.

Pamphlet: *Del Sena al Ozama,* 1922.

Biographical/Critical Sources: Manuel Rueda's *Antologia panorámica de la poesia dominicana 1912-1962,* Santiago, D. R., UCMM, 1972, pp. 418-426; F. Elio Alcántara's *Vigil Diaz en prosa de caricatura,* 1929; Rafael Augusto Zorrilla's review of *Galera de Pafos,* in the journal *Listin Diario* (March 16, 1921).

DIAZ ALFARO, Abelardo

b. 1920 (?), Caguas, Puerto Rico.
Storywriter, poet, radio broadcaster, educator.

After schooling in Caguas, Tao Alta, Bayamón, and Ponce, Diaz studied painting under Miguel Pau and then took his B.A. at the Instituto Politécnico de San Germán, followed by a degree in social work at the University of Puerto Rico. He worked in the ghettos of Yaurel de Arroyo, Bayamoncito, and Rio Abajo de Comerio and then became a supervisor of labor laws for the Department of Labor.

He has also been a radio broadcaster at radio station W.I.P.R. for the Department of Public Education of Puerto Rico, under the program names of "Teyo Gracia" and "Retablo del Soler."

Son of a director of *Puerto Rico Evangélico,* and influenced by the work of Ricardo Guiraldes, José Fustasio Rivera, and Rómulo Gallegos, Diaz often employs creole in his popular stories, his first collection having been published in 1947. His best tales are believed to be "El Josco" and "Los Perros," and his collection *Terrazo* (1947) won the prize of the Sociedad de Periodistas Universitario y Instituto de Literatura Puertorriqueña. Diaz's one published poem "El Mozambique" appeared in *Jaycoa* magazine in 1959.

In 1950 he married Gladys Meau.

Writings: Stories: *Terrazo,* San Juan, Imp. Venezuela, 1947 and San Juan, Edit. Yaurel, 1948, 1949, 1950, 1954, 1967 (contains four stories and five sketches); *Mi isla sonada,* San Juan, 1967; story "Josco" appears in *From the Green Antilles,* edited by Barbara Howe, 1967; "Los Perros" originally published in *Asomante,* III (1956), appears in English in *The Eye of the Heart,* Barbara Howe, ed., Bobbs-Merrill, 1973.

Biographical/Critical Sources: Margot Arce de Vasquez, *La Lúmbre de la esperanza,* essay on Diaz, in 2nd edition of *Terrazo,* 1948, pp. 107-109; Concha Meléndez, *Abelardo Diaz Alfaro y la expresión puertorriqueña: Figuración de Puerto Rico y otras estudios,* 2nd edition, San Juan, Yaurel, 1948; 3rd edition, San Juan, Instituto de Cultura Puertorriqueña, 1958, pp. 61-64; Monelsa L. Pérez Marchand, "Notas en Torno a Los Perros: Cuento de Abelardo Diaz Alfaro," part 1 in *El Mundo* (San Juan, November 9, 1957); part 2, *El Mundo* (November 16, 1957); Ricardo Gullón, "Abelardo Diaz Alfaro, Narrador de Puerto Rico," in *El Mundo* (April 1959); Mariano Picón Salas's prologue to *Terrazo* contains information, published Caracas, Venezuela, University of Caracas, 1947; Wilfredo Braschi, "Abelardo Diaz Alfaro," *El Mundo* (September 8, 1956); José Emilio González, "Agonia de la Liberación en *Terrazo* de Diaz Alfaro," *El Mundo* (March 24, 1947); Francisco Lluch Mora, "*Terrazo,*" in *El Mundo* (December 25, 1948); Francisco Manrique Cabrera, *Historia de la literatura puertorriqueña,* 1969; *Cuentos puertorriqueños de hoy,* preface and notes by editor René Márques, Mexico, Club del Libro de Puerto Rico, 1959 (and see especially the interview, pp. 46-49).

DIAZ GONZALEZ, Olallo

b. ca. 1858, Cuba.
Playwright.

Certainly one of Cuba's most prolific poets, Diaz González is all but forgotten today.

Writings: Plays: *La Perla de las Antillas* (comic review in 2 acts), Matanzas, Imp. Galeria Literaria, 1888, performed Teatro Habana; *El buen camino* (comic review in 2 acts), Matanzas, Imp. Galeria Literaria, 1890; *Doña Cleta la adivina* (1 act, prose and verse, folkloric, 3 sketches), Havana, Imp. Galiano, 1891, performed Circo Teatro de Jané, March 10, 1882; *Al vivac* (1 act verse comedy), Havana, 1893, in ms.; *Amigas de confianza* (1 act prose comedy-folkloric), Havana, in ms.; *De la muerte a la vida* (1 act comedy), Havana, 1894, in ms.; *Desde Cuba al Paraiso* (2 acts), Matanzas, Imp. Galeria Literaria, 1887, performed Teatro Irijoa, May 14, 1887; *La cana y la remolacha* (in ms.); *La cuestión del pan* (1 act), Havana, Imp. M. Ricoy, 1897, performed Teatro Alhambra, June 11, 1897; *La Nautilus en Havana* (1 act comedy) music by M. Mauri, Havana, El Arte, 1908, performed Teatro Alhambra, July 29, 1908; and seven other listed in José Revero Muñiz, *Bibliografia del teatro cubano,* Havana, 1957.

DIAZ GRULLON, Virgilio

b. 1924, Santiago de los Caballeros, Dominican Republic.
Storywriter, lawyer.

In 1958 Diaz won a first prize for literature for *Un dia cualquiera,* and the Instituto de Cultura Hispánica later gave him a prize for his story "Edipo." His most recent work is *Más allá del espejo,* science fantasy.

Writings: Stories: *Un dia cualquier,* S. Domingo, Editorial Libreria Dominicana, 1958; *Crónica de Altocerro,* 1966; *Más allá del espejo,* 1975.

DIAZ ORDONEZ, Virgilio

(a.k.a. **Ligio VIZARDI**)

b. 1895, Macoris, Dominican Republic; d. 1968.
Poet, novelist, scholar, translator.

Diaz's poetry is extremely personal, tremulous, not brilliant. His style is sensitive, evocative, well within the range of accepted poetic expression for the period of naturalism during which he produced most of his poetry.

Writings: Poetry: *Los nocturnos del olvido, 1925; La sombra iluminada,* 1929; *Figuras de barro,* 1930; *Poemario,* 1947.

Novel: *Archipiélago,* Lima, Peru, Edit. Torres, 1947.

Scholarship: *El más antigua y grave problema antillano,* 1938.

Translation: *Los Rubayat de Omar Khayamm,* 1954.

DIAZ PARRADO, Flora

b. 1902, Cuba.
Playwright.

Diaz's work was symbolic, sometimes humorous, often employing local manners and colloquialisms to get across her social or philosophical points.

Writings: Plays: *El velorio de Pura,* 1941; *Juana Revolico,* 1944 (contains other works besides title play; *El alcalde de Nueva de los Leones,* and *Noche de esperanzas* (both farces), and three dramatic sketches: *El remordimiento; El odre,* and *Drama en un acto.*

DIAZ RODRIGUEZ, Ernesto

b. ca. 1947, Cojimar, Cuba.
Poet.

Though born of fishermen and workers, Ernesto Diaz was imprisoned in 1968 for his actions protesting certain aspects of communism in Cuba. Sentenced to a fifteen year term at first, his period of imprisonment was extended to forty years in 1974 for having "conspired against the state from jail." His recent poems, smug-

gled out of prison, were published in a small volume entitled *Un testimonio urgente* (An Urgent Testimony), Miami, 1977. Two poems in English text: "Incomprehension" and "Leave Me Here with the Orphans (to Fidel Castro, traitor)" appeared in *Of Human Rights* (Fall 1977), published in Washington, D. C.

DIAZ RODRIGUEZ, Jesús

b. 1941, Havana, Cuba.
Storywriter, essayist, cinema critic, editor, teacher.

Expelled from high school for his unseemly revolutionary activities, Diaz continued to agitate for political change in student groups. In time, he became an artillerist in the new revolutionary armed forces and a teacher of dialectical materialism at Havana University. He has published stories, philosophical and political articles in leading Cuban journals, and won a prize in the Concurso de las Casa de las Américas in 1966 for his stories. For a period he edited *El Caiman Barbudo,* a journal for new writers.

Writings: Stories: *Los años duros,* Havana, Casa de las Américas, 1966; and *Muy al principio,* Havana, Casa de las Américas, 1966, and Buenos Aires, J. Alvarez, 1967 which was the winner of the Casa de las Américas prize for 1966. "The Cripple" is in *Writers in the New Cuba,* Harmondsworth, England, Penguin, 1967 and "Amor, La Plata Alta," is in *Narrativa cubana de la revolución,* J. M. Caballero Bonald, ed., Madrid, 1969.

DIAZ VALCARCEL, Emilio

b. October 16, 1929, Trujillo Alto, Puerto Rico.
Storywriter, novelist, radio playwright.

After local schooling through high school, Valcárcel joined the U.S. Army and saw service in Korea. The product of this sad and brutal period was his collection of stories *La sangre inútil,* not published until 1958 in Mexico. He won a Guggenheim Foundation award and has published stories in both English and Spanish language periodicals. He has spent a considerable period in New York since leaving the U.S. Army.

Writings: Stories: *Proceso en diciembre,* Madrid, Taurus Ediciones, 1963; *El hombre que trabajó el lunes,* Mexico, Era, 1966 (146 pp., 5 stories). Individual stories: "Dos Hombres," in *Asomante,* San Juan, Puerto Rico, No. 1, 1951, pp. 84-88; *La sangre inutil,* Biblioteca de Autores Puertorriqueños) 196?; *El Asedio y otros cuentos,* Mexico, Editorial Arrecife, 1958; "Sol negro," and "El sajo en el espejo" appears in R. Marqués' collection *Cuentos Puertorriqueños de hoy* (the latter story also appeared in *El asedio* in 1958, Mexico, Editorial Arrecife).
Radio/Television Play: *Una sola puerta hacia la muerte,* on T.V., Station WIPRTV, in 1957.
Novels: *Panorama,* Rio Piedras, Edit. Cultural, 197?; *Donde se esconde el silencio; Damián Sánchez, G.I.,* originally written in Spanish, translated by Lee Robinson, published in *San Juan Review* (September 1965); also in *Speaking for Ourselves, American Ethnic Writing,* L. Foderman and B. Bradshaw, eds., Glenview, Ill., Scott, Foresman, 1975.

Biographical/Critical Sources: José Luis González, in *El Asedio* as commentator and editor; René Marqués, *Cuentos Puertorriqueños de hoy,* pp. 235-237; Pedro Juan Soto, "El 'si' y el 'no' de Diaz Valcárcel," in *El Mundo,* San Juan, May 9, 1959; Concha Meléndez, ed., *El arte del cuento en Puerto Rico,* New York, 1961, pp. 367-372, and the stories "Dos Hombres" and "La Mente en Blanco" appear there, pp. 372-395. Also see Randolph D. Pope, "Dos noveles, "Album," libro de Manuel de Cortázar y "Figuraciones en El Mes" de Diaz Valcárcel," in *The Bilingual Review,* I, 2 (May-August 1974), pp. 170-184.

DIAZ DE LA RONDE, Silverio

b. 1902, Cuba.
Poet.

Lyric poet, Diaz' work was patriotic and highly personal.

Writings: Poetry: *Eros,* 1935; *Con la espada inocente de la luz,* 1951; *Himno a la virgen,* 1951; all in Havana.

DE DIEGO, José

b. April 16, 1866, Aguadilla, Puerto Rico; d. July 21, 1918, New York City.
Poet, essayist.

Son of an army officer, Felipe de Diego and of Eliza Martinez, the young José soon demonstrated a remarkable intelligence. After local schooling de Diego attended university in Madrid in 1890 and published poetry in *Madrid Cómico* and *La Semana Cómica* under the influence of Rubén Dario, the great Nicaraguan poet.

José de Diego is considered the earliest of the "modernismo" poets with his early poem of 1901 "Genetrix" published in *Madrid Cómico,* and to have quickly reflected the new North American influences in his work after the U. S. takeover of Puerto Rico following the war with Spain. De Diego sought to "renovate" the late romantic verse of his contemporaries but his own practice was indecisive, or hesitating, according to Laguerre. His major theme was patriotism and his style remained that of the 19th century.

Concha Meléndez wrote of his early work: "Si en Jovillos nos vuelve Jano la cara risueña, afirma los pies en lo circundante y vislumbra algunas veces el futuro, en *Pomarrosas* mira el pasado romántico en ecencias y formas, con muy escasos deslices a otro atmósfera." (from *Signos de Iberoamérica,* p. 20).

Diego joined Muñoz Rivera's party and for many years was one of the leading actors in Puerto Rican politics, though he was considered more poetic, even to being a "fantaseador," than was proper for a nationalist politician. His oratory was considered the most sublime and inspiring of all in a nation and period when most statesman were excellent speakers. He founded the Instituto Universitario and established a chair of law in the Instituto among other achievements in a very busy life.

Writings: Poetry: *Obras poéticas: Sor Ana,* 1877, 2nd ed., also, but details unknown; *Los grandes infames* (26 sonnets), n.d. but known to be in 1885; *Pomarrosas,* Barcelona, Imp. Henrich, 1904; *Jovillos,* Barcelona, Editorial Maucci, 1916 (of poems earlier published in Spanish journals *Madrid Cómico* and *La Semana Cómica* between 1887-1890); *Cantos de rebeldia,* Barcelona, Maucci, 1916; *Nuevas campañas,* Barcelona, Soc. General de Publicaciones, Biblioteca de la Unión Antillana, 1950; "Ultima acción," and "En la brecha" in *Antologia de la poesia puertorriqueña,* E. F. Méndez, ed., San Juan, Ateneo Puertorriqueño, 1966, and *El Caballero de la Raza* (6 poesias de Serie), Libros del Pueblo No. 3, San Juan, Inst. Cult., P. R., 1966 (24 pp.).

Law: *La codificación administrativa; Delinquencia y penalidad.*

Critical Essay: Introduction to Antologia de poetas jóvenes de Puerto Rico, E. Ribera Chevremont and José Alegria, San Juan, 1918.

Biographical/Critical Sources: Cesáreo Rosa-Nieves, "Patria, amor y jibarismo en tres poetas puertorriqueños (José de Diego, Luis Llorens Torres and Virgilio Dávila)," in *Ensayos escogidos,* San Juan, 1970, pp. 141-159; Enrique A. Laguerre, *La poesia modernista en Puerto Rico,* San Juan, Editorial Coquí, 1969, pp. 25-29; Concha Meléndez, "Jovillos y volantine," in *Signos de Iberoamerica,* Mexico City, 1936; Sebastián Dalmau Canet, *José de Diego,* 1923; Margot Arce de Vásquez, *La obra literaria de José de Diego,* San Juan, Instituto de cultura puertorriqueña, Rio Piedras, 1969, pp. 219-224; and see Meléndez' essay "José de Diego en mi memoria," in *Obras completas,* San Juan, 1966, 1970, 2 vols. Also see Salvador Arana Soto, *Muñoz Rivera—José de Diego: La disidencia independentista,* San Juan, 1970; Félix Matos Bernier, comments in his *Isla de arte,* San Juan, 1907; the special issue devoted to Diego in *Revista del Instituto de Cultura puertorriqueña,* Vol. 9, No. 31 (San Juan, April-June 1966); José Ferrer Canales, *Acentos civicos: Marti, Puerto Rico y otros temas,* Rio Piedras, Edit. Edil, 1972 (contains essay on Diego).

DE DIEGO PADRO, José I.

b. 1899, Vega Baja, Puerto Rico.
Poet, novelist.

De Diego Padró's *La última lámpara de los dioses* is midway between modernismo and contemporary work.

His poem "Siesta" is calming as even the last five lines will indicate:

Calor, sueño, fastidio. La pereza invasora
roza concedos tenues el sapor afelpado
de mis nervios; la carne se adormece y
afloja;
y la siesta, esa virgen de los trópicos,
pasa
aferrada al calmoso caracol de la hora.

Writings: Poetry: *La última lámpara de los dioses,* and San Juan, Biblioteca de Autores Puertorriqueños, 1950, but first edition was Madrid, Biblioteca Ariel, 1921 with introduction by José Peréz Losada; "Siesta" is in the *Antologia de la poesia puertorriqueña,* E. Fernández Méndez, ed., San Juan, 1968; *Escaparate iluminado (autobiografia),* Barcelona, Ediciones Rumbos, 1959.

Novels: *Sebastián Guenard,* San Juan, Tip. El Compás, 1924; *En babia (El manuscripto de un braquicéfalo),* San Juan Imp. Puerto Rico, 1940, 2nd ed., Mexico, 1961 (641 pp.), 1940, awarded a prize by the Instituto de Literatura Puertorriqueña; *Ocho epistolas mostrencas,* Madrid, 1952; *El tiempo jugó conmigo,* Barcelona, Ediciones Rumbos, 1960; *El minotaur se devora a si mismo,* Edición J. Ponce de León, 1965; *Un cencerro de dos badajos,* San Juan, Ediciones Juan Ponce De León, 1969 (453 pp.).

DIEGO, Eliseo

b. 1920, Havana, Cuba.
Poet, storywriter, critic.

Diego has travelled much in Europe and the United States but is presently living in Cuba. His last collection of poems, *En la calzada de Jesús del Monte* (1947), sketches his own childhood, evoking the fondly remembered streets and neighborhood in sharply drawn portraits. His stories are poetic renderings of intimate scenes and are considered to be of high quality by such critics as Max Henriquez Ureña.

Writings: Stories: *En las oscuras manos del ovido,* Havana, Ediciones "Clavileño, 1942; and individual stories in many journals and collections, including "Something to Everyone," and "How His Excellency Spent the Time," in *From the Green Antilles,* London, Souvenir Press, 1967 and London, Panther, 1971.

Poetry: *Divertimientos,* Havana, Ed. Origines, 1946, and *Divertimientos y versiones,* Montevideo, Arca, 1967; *El oscuro esplendor,* Havana, Belic, 1966; *En la calzada de Jesús del Monte,* Havana, Ucar, Garcia, 1947; *Muestrario del mundo o libro de la maravillas de Boloña,* Havana, Instituto del Libro, 1968, 1969; *Versiones,* Havana, Unión, 1970.

DOMINGUEZ, José de Jesús

b. 1843, Puerto Rico; d. 1898.
Poet, historian, folklorist.

After local schooling, José de Jesús Dominguez studied medicine in France, a period when the Parnassian poets were in full flower. Influenced by the French developments, Jesús (after medical service with the French army fighting Prussia in the Franco-Prussian War) on his return to Puerto Rico became a major innovator in Spanish-Puerto Rican prosody. His work was the precursor to the "modernista" school of the end of the century, particularly his third collection *Las huries blancas* of 1880 which predated Rubén Dario's famous volume *Azul* (1888) and made most clear the esthetic which would be proclaimed by the modernistas: plastic beauty, musicality, color, sophisticated urban themes, exoticism and vague, narcoticized trance-like feelings.

His title poem, "Las huries blancas," is, in the words of Manrique Cabrera, an "extenso poema de fondo oriental en el cual su autor se anticipa a la atmósfero del modernismo con sus vislumbres estéticos." These few lines from that poem are typical of his work:

Y dentro del crepúsculo irizado,
que reina sin cesar en el paraje,
se destaca el verdor apasionado,
la suntuosa esmeralda del paisaje.

Writings: Histories: *Los jibaros de Puerto Rico; Prehistoria de Bunken; Historia del lenguaje y la civilización* (incomplete).

Poetry: *Odas elegiacas,* 1883; *Las huries blancas,* 1886, reprinted in *Asomante* (January-March 1947); F. Manrique Cabrera, *Historia de la literatura puertorriqueña,* Rio Piedras, 1969, pp. 214-217.

DOMINGUEZ ARBELO, Juan

b. 1909, Cuba.
Playwright.

Dominguez was one of the better playwrights working the vein of social protest of rural poverty. Only his *Ignacio Agramonte* dealt with the more common theme of Cuba's great revolutionary past.

Plays: Las humanas miserias of La tragedia guajira, 1931; *Sombras del solar,* 1937; *Agonias conyugales,* 1933; *Política, veneno social,* 1933; *Incesto, El bohío de las pasiones; Ignacio Agramonte, caballero sin tacha.*

DOMINGUEZ HERNANDEZ, Franklin

b. June 5, 1931, Santiago de los Caballeros, Dominican Republic.
Playwright.

Dominguez is a prolific writer with some 39 works in print. He has served as president of the Society of Authors and Composers of the Dominican Republic and was a founder of the first large circulation journal in the Republic—*La Silla.* His plays have generally been political satires, but a few are psychological studies or exploit forms from the Greek classical drama.

Writings: Plays: *Un amigo desconocido nos aguarda,* S. Domingo, Talleres de Gonzalo Dominguez, 1958; *El último instante* and *La broma del Senador,* S. Domingo, Col. El silbo vulnerado, 1958; *La espera,* S. Domingo, Impresora Arte y Cine, 1959; *Se busca un hombre honesto,* 1965, S. Domingo, Ed. Panoramas, 1965; *Teatro,* S. Domingo, Ediciones de la Sociedad de Autores y Compositores Dramáticos, 1968.

DOMINGUEZ Y SANTI, Jacobo

b. ca. 1840, Cuba; d. 1898.
Playwright, poet.

Dominguez is today of only historic interest.

Writings: Plays: *Un lance de crisis* (1 act comedy), parody of original work of Lavapiés, Havana, Imp. Militar de la Viuda de Soler, 1875; *La calle de la Muralla* (dramatic poem), 2nd ed., Havana, Propaganda Literaria, 1878; *Ni ella es ella, ni él es él* (1 act prose and verse), written with Enrique Edo, music by José Mauri, Havana, La Razón, 1882.

DUARTE Y DIEZ, Rosa

b. 1819, Dominican Republic; d. 1888.
Biographer, chronicle-history writer.

Rosa Duarte was the favorite sister of the great patriotic leader Juan Pablo Duarte (1813-1876). She wrote a biography of her brother and his revolutionary movement in "La Trinitaria." Her history is useful and interesting for its vivid picture of men and events she knew and experienced so personally, though stylistically, it is less than skillful.

Writings: History: *Apuntes para la historia de la isla de Santo Domingo,* details unknown.

DURAN, Ana Luisa

b. ca. 1939, Puerto Rico.
Storywriter.

Durán has been living in California for many years and both of her stories in her one published volume (1969) are set in that state.

Writings: Stories: *Prometeo y el estreno,* Mexico, B. Costa-Amic, 1969 (2 stories, 114 pp.).

ECHEVARRIA, Colón

b. ca. 1920, Dominican Republic.
Poet, novelist.

Colón Echevarría is one of the militant new Latin writers who unabashedly proclaims his African ancestry and culture.

Writings: Poetry: *Tambor de negros,* Buenos Aires, 1946.
Novel: *No hay peligro en Siguirlo,* San Juan, Edit. Puerto Rico, 1937.

ECHEVERRIA, José Antonio

b. 1815, Cuba; d. March 11, 1885, New York.
Novelist.

Echeverría is remembered for his one fine

early novel, *Antonelli,* a reconstruction of the life, times and works of the Italian engineer Giovani Battista Antonelli who was sent in the last decades of the sixteenth century by Philip II to put up some of the major works in Havana including the Moro fortresses of the La Punta.

Writings: Novel: *Antonelli,* published in *La Cartela Cubana,* 1839.
Collected Works: *Obras Escogidas,* Havana, Ministry of Education, 1906 (107 pp.).

Biographical/Critical Sources: Juan Miguel Dihigo, *José Antonio Echeverría,* Havana, 1928.

EDO, Enrique

b. ca. 1838, Valencia, Spain; d. Cienfuegos, 1913.
Playwright, journalist.

Edo lived most of his life in Cuba and founded the journal *El Telégrafo.*

Writings: Plays: *Un quid pro quo* (1 act verse comedy), Havana, 1878; *1878 en Cuba* (1 act verse comedy), Havana, 1878; *Ni ella es ella ni él es él* (1 act verse comedy), written with Jacobo Dominguez Santi, music by José Mauri, Havana, Imp. La. Razón, 1882; *Dudas y temores* (1 scene), Havana, La Propaganda Literaria, 1887; *Percances de carnaval* (1 act verse), music by Manuel Mauri Estevez, Havana, La Razón, 1882; *Ardides de amor* (farce); *El loco del valle* (3 acts); *Marieta. Por buscar una mujer; Quien mucho abarca; Un infeliz* (comedies); *Un amigo* (2 acts), Cienfuegos, El Telégrafo, 1863, performed October 10, 1862, in the Sociedad Filarmónica de Cienfuegos.

EGUREN, Gustavo

b. 1925, Isla de Piños (Pinar del Rio), Cuba.
Storywriter, journalist, novelist.

Eguren moved to Havana as a child and after a career as a journalist, was named a Cuban diplomat to India, Finland and West Germany after the Castro revolution. He was in the late 1960's and early 1970's an editor of the *Unión.*

Writings: La robla, Havana, Unión, 1967, first edition, 1925; *En la cal de las paredes,* Havana, Unión, 1971.
Stories: in many journals, and the collection, *Algo para la palidez y una ventana sobre el regreso,* Havana, Unión, 1969.

DE ELZABURU, Manuel

(pseudonyms: **Fabián MONTES** and **Américo AMADOR**)
b. 1852, Puerto Rico; d. 1892.
Critic, poet, journalist.

Much of Elzaburu's work was in the field of translation and criticism. His frequent contributions to journals of articles and literary criticism were under the pen-name, Fabián Montes, and his prose-poems often appeared under the name Américo Amador. He was a long-time president and secretary of the Ateneo Puertorriqueño.

Writings: Prose-ballads: *Balsamias.*
Critical Essays: in many journals; see especially his introduction to the *Poesias* of Gautier Benítez, San Juan, 1929.

Biographical/Critical Sources: M. Fernández Juncos, "Manuel Elzaburu," speech made at the Ateneo Puertorriqueño, September 13, 1892, published in *Revista Puertorriqueña,* Vol. 6, San Juan, 1892.

ENTENZA, Pedro

b. 1932, Cuba; d. 1969.
Novelist.

Entenza's one novel *No hay aceras* won the Spanish prize Villa de Torelló in 1969, the same year he died in a traffic accident.

Writings: Novel: *No hay aceras,* Barcelona, Planeta, 1969.

ESCOBEDO URRA, Antonio

b. ca. 1870, Puerto Principe, Cuba.
Playwright.

Escobedo's play *Bolas de nieve* was one of the first Cuban plays devoted to the new Cuban republic and its problems.

Writings: Plays: *Bolas de nieve* (1 act prose comedy), Puerto Principe, Imp. La Ilustración, 1902, premiered December 23, 1900; *Apagó el Cuba* (1 act prose comic sketch), Puerto Principe, La Ilustración, 1903.

ESTENGER Y NEULING, Rafael

b. October 15, 1899, Santiago, Cuba.
Poet, storwriter, novelist, journalist.

A graduate of Havana University's law school, Esténger never practiced, but instead entered journalism, writing in South America and Cuba. Much of his work appeared in *El Sol, El Heraldo,* and *Diario de la Marina,* all of Havana.

Esténger wrote Afro-Cuban verse in the 1930's and is a continuer of the symbolist movement in Cuban literature. "Caperucita," "Rincón provinciano," and "Poemitas de breviario" are some of his best known poems. Luis Carbonnel, a very influential singer, was particularly fond of Esténger's "Coloquio" and gave it wide popularity. 'Coloquio" begins:

Arrunyémbere—caúa,
arruyémbere—ca.

—No sea vulgá, mi'ja Etreya;
no baile la rumba má.
ya ere toitica una dama;

Writings: Poetry: *Los énfasis antiguos,* Manzanillo, El Arte, 1924; *Retorno: romancero, sonetario estampas criollas, poemas inconexos,* Havana, Imp. Alfa, 1945; *Las máscaras del sueño,* Havana, Ediciones de la Organización Nacional de Bibliotecas Ambulantes y Populares, 1957; *Cuba en la Cruz,* Vol. I of series Circulo de Cultura Hispanoamericana, Troy, New York, 1971.

Novel: *El pulpo de oro,* Mexico, 1954.

Musical Drama: *Caperucita.*

Biographies: *Heredia, la incomprehensión de si mismo,* 1938; *Socopatia américana, Comentarios a Hostos,* Havana, 1939; *Don Pepe, retrato de un maestro de escuela,* 1940 (biography of José Cipriana de la Luz y Caballero); *Vida de Marti,* details unknown; *Marti frente al comunismo,* Miami, Ediciones del Directorio Magisterial Cubano, *Exilio,* No. 27 (1966); *Los amores de cubanos celebres;* and various biographies for children.

Essay: introduction to Poveda's *Premios de cenáculo,* In *Cuadernos,* Havana, Dirreción de Cultura del Ministerio de Educación, 1948, entitled "Evocación de Poveda"; and critical studies of various writers in the anthology edited by Esténger: *Cien de las mejores poesias cubanas,* Havana, 1943, 1948.

ESTEVES, José de Jesús

b. October 15, 1881, Aguadilla, Puerto Rico; d. November 1, 1918, New York.
Poet, critic, lawyer, judge.

A practicing lawyer, Esteves was an important member of the "modernistas" group. Beginning in the late romantic style, he fell under the influence of Julio Herrera Reissig in his second volume, *Crisalidas,* but moved on in his final work, collected in *Rosalde Amor,* to verse affected by the style of Rubén Dario. He contributed both verse and prose to the local journals of his day.

Esteves' "Tono Menor" begins:

Nunca he visto nevar. Pero en mis sueños
dejo a veces las tierras tropicales
y a las árticas voy en los sedeños
lomos de mi pegaso de ideales . . .

Entonces a lo largo de un camino
todo tristeza y soleda y aburo,
peregrino con fé de peregrino
bajo la nieve silenciosa y pura

and ends in the fourth stanza:

Y viajo envuelto en azulados brumos,
mientras descienden de los cielos
plumas
de las muertas palomas de la nieve.

His poetry was sensual, refined, full of local color, and musical. Esteves was often afflicted with a nervous condition and his work is generally mildly melancholic. Much of his traditionalist, non-political verse appeared in *Puerto Rico Ilustrado,* and his subjects were love, the countryside, the nation. Ismael Casalduo called him "el poeta más sensual, más humano, que hemos tenido en Puerto Rico."

Esteves is buried in his natal city, Aguadillo.

Writings: Poetry: *Besos y plumas,* 1901; *Crisálidas,* Humacao, P.R., Imp. F. Otero, 1909; *Rosal de amor,* San Juan, Imp. Real Hermanos, 1917, eight poems in L. Hernández Aquino's *El modernismo en Puerto Rico,* San Juan, 1967, which includes a large extract from the long poem "Alma adentro."

Editor of: *El modernismo en la poesia. Conferencias dominicales de la Biblioteca Insular de Puerto Rico,* San Juan, 1914.

Literary History: "Problemas literarias Puertorriqueños," in *Puerto Rico Ilustrado,* San Juan (August 26, 1916).

Biographical/Critical Sources: Ismael Casalduc de Miranda, "José de Jesús Esteves," unpub. M.A. Thesis, Univ. of P. R., Rio Piedras, 1939-1940; and see Chapter V in Enrique Laguerre's *La poesia modernista en Puerto Rico,* San Juan, 1969, pp. 91-95.

ESTEVEZ, Sofia

b. 1848, Camaguez, Cuba; d. 1901.
Novelist, poet, journalist.

Sofia Estévez was an ardent patriot and early woman journalist, founding the journal *El Céfiro,* in 1866 with Domitila Garcia de Coronado, and writing for and editing other journals. (Domitila Garcia [1847-1937] edited also the *Album poético fotográfico de escritoras cubanas* [1872].)

Writings: Novels: *Alberto el trovador* and *Doce años despues,* both published in *El Céfiro,* 1866.

Poetry: *Lágrimas y sonrisas,* 1875.

ESTORINO, Abelardo

b. 1925, Cuba.
Playwright, producer, actor, dentist.

Estorino, though a practicing dentist, has lived most of his adult life close to the theatre. His two published plays are on revolutionary themes.

Writings: Plays: *El robo del cochino,* Havana, 1961 (3 acts); Havana, Revolución, 1964, this play is also in *Cuatro obras,* Havana, Casa de las Américas, 1961, *La casa vieja,* 1964 (3 acts); this play also in *Teatro,* Havana, Casa de las Américas, 1964; *Cain's Mangoes* (1 act), is in *Writers in the New Cuba,* E. M. Cohen, ed., Harmondsworth, England, Penguin, 1967; several other one-act plays and adaptations of stories for children's theater. Also: *El peine y el espejo* is in *Teatro Cubano en un acto* (Rine Leal, ed.), Havana, Revolución, 1963.

ESTRADA Y ZENEA, Ildefonso

b. ca. 1846, Cuba.
Poet, playwright, journalist.

A leading journalist, Estrada edited such papers as *Periquito* which he founded in Matanzas, *El Iris* in Merida, Yucatán, Mexico, and *La Primavera,* Mexico.

Writings: Plays: *Luisa Sigea (La Minerva de Toledo)* (a historic play, 3 acts, verse), first performed in the Teatro Nacional de México, August 26, 1876, published, Matanzas, Imp. Aurora del Yumuri, 1878; 2nd edition, Mexico, Imp. de Ildefonso Estrada y Zenea, 1906 (8 pp.).

Romance: *El Guajiro,* 1861.

Military Scholarship: *Biblioteca y archivo militar,* 1876.

FEIJOO, Samuel

b. 1912, Cuba.
Poet, playwright, novelist, storywriter, critic, folklorist.

Feijóo has been one of the most active new poets and critics, having organized the notebook-review *Concierto* with Alcides Isnaga and Aldo Menéndez, and having sought a multitude of new styles and subjects. His poetry is usually extremely personal, but there are works of a more general sort following the lines of the Cuban experience ("linea vegetal cubana"), though Max Henríquez Ureña believed the more intimate works were by far his best.

Writings: Poetry: *Cuerda menor,* Santa Clara, 1964; *Ser fiel: 1948-62,* Santa Clara, 1964; *Camarada celeste,* Havana, 1944; *Media imagen,* in a volume of *Concierto,* Havana, 1947; *Beth-el,* Havana, 1949; *Errante asilo,* Havana, 1949; *Cara en otoño: agua de nieblas de oro,* Havana, 1957; *Poemas del bosquezuelo,* 1954; *Poemas del bozquezuelo, Haz de la ceniza, 1958-59,* Havana, 1960; *Sabiduria, guajira,* Havana, Ed. Universitaria, 1965; *El pájaro de las soledades; diario de un joven poeta enfermo, 1937-40,* Santa Clara, Universidad Central de las Villas, 1961; *El girasol sediento, 1937-48, poesias,* Ed. defintiva, Santa Clara, 1963; *Libreta de pasajero,* Santa Clara, 1964, and Havana, Univ. Central de las Villas, 1964; *Caminante montés, 1955-59,* Santa Clara, 1962; *Cuerda menor (1937-1939); versos,* Ed. definitiva, Santa Clara, 1964; *Pleno dia,* Havana, Ediciones Universal, 1974. (Some of his verse also is published in his collections of prose, including the volume *La alcancia del artisano,* 1958.)

Novel: *Juan Quinquin en Pueblo Mocho,* Santa Clara, Consejo Nacional de Universidades, 1964.

Folklore: *Diario abierto; temas folkóricos cubanos,* Santa Clara, 1959; *Refranes, adivinanzas, dicharachos,* . . .2 vols., Santa Clara, 1961, 1962; *Mitos y leyendas en La Villas,* Santa Clara, 1965 (Feijóo selected and edited this collection); *Cuentos populares cubanos,* 2 vols., Santa Clara, 1960-1962.

Criticism: *La décima popular* (selected by Feijóo), Havana, Imp. Nacional de Cuba, 1961; *Azar de lecturas,* Santa Clara, Universidad Central de La Villas, 1961; *La décima culta a Cuba; muestrario,* Santa Clara, Universidad Central de las Villas, 1963; *El movimento de los romances cubanos del siglo XIX* (selected by Feijóo), Santa Clara, 1964; *Colección de poetas de la ciudad de Camagüey,* Havana, Ediciones del Grupo Yarabey, 1958; *Cantos a la naturaleza cubana del siglo XX,* Santa Clara, 1964; *Sobre los movimentos por una poesia cubana hasta 1856,* in *Revista Cubana* (1949), and Havana, 1961; *Sonetos en Cuba,* Santa Clara, 1964; *Los trovadores del pueblo,* Santa Clara, Dirección de Investigaciones Folklóricos, 1960.

Plays: *La alegre noticia,* in *Teatro Cubano,* Santa Clara, Universidad Central de las Villas, 1961.

Stories: *Tumbago,* Santa Clara, Editora del Consejo Nacional de Universidades, 1964.

Travel: *Diarios de viajes; montaneses y llaneros, 1939-46,* Santa Clara, 1958.

Art Sketches: in *Dibujos* (text by Roberto Fernández Retamar), Havana, Consejo Nacional de Cultura, 1961.

Editor of: *Cuentos populares cubanos,* 2 vols., Santa Clara, Universidad de las Villas, 1960, and Havana, Unión, 1965.

Essays: *Libros de apuntes,* Havana, 1954; *La alcancia del artisano,* Havana, 1958.

FELICES, Jorge

b. 1917, Puerto Rico.
Novelist, poet.

Enrique Abril, the hero of Felices' autobiographical novel of that name (1947), is only an anti-hero. Leaving the university for the supposed freedoms of the untrammeled bohemian life, Abril finishes by living a banal middle-class life of utter vacuity through a series of burlesque political misadventures.

Writings: Novel: *Enrique Abril, héroe,* 1947.

Poetry: *Cantares de biafara: poemas,* Madrid, Ediciones Castilla, 1970 (88 pp.).

FELICIANO MENDOZA, Esther

b. 1918, Aguadilla, Puerto Rico.
Poet, storywriter, critic, teacher.

Feliciano's poetry and stories are mostly concerned with country life and its sights and sounds. Rosa-Nieves characterizes her: "Muy breve en su arquitectura estética. Verso de ternuras y diafanidades liricas: sedosamento maternal, sin trivialismos almibarados." Her page-long poem, "Domingo de San Garabito," (from *Nanas,* her first volume of verse) ends:

Estrellas, luceros,
canciones, politos,
!a dormir ligero,
mañana es Domingo
del buen caballero
que es San Gerabito!
¡Adormir, mi nene,
mañana es Domingo!

Writings: Poetry: *Nanas,* Rio Piedras, Junta Editora de la Universidad, 1945; *Nanas de la Navidad,* San Juan, Edit. Campos, 1959; and as *Nanas de la adolescencia,* San Juan, Edit. *Yaurel, 1963; Arco Iris,* Rio Piedras, Consejo Superior de Enseñanza de la Universidad, 1951; *Voz de mi tierra,* San Juan, Biblioteca de Autores Puertorriqueños, 1956; *Coqui,* San Juan, Imp. del Departamento de Instrucción, 1957,

Stories: in various journals; "Reflejos del Saliral," in Concha Meléndez, ed., *El arte del cuento en Puerto Rico,* New York, 1961, pp. 180-183; "La Mancha de Platano," in *Antologia de Autores Puertorriqueños,* III, San Juan, 1957, pp. 273-276.

Articles: *Voz de la tierra mia,* San Juan, El Mundo, 1954-55.

Legends: *Sinfonia borincana,* Rio Piedras, Instituto de Cultura Puertorriqueña, 1962(?).

Critical Biography: *Antonio Perez Pierret: vida y obra,* San Juan, 1968.

Biographical/Critical Sources: F. Manrique Cabrera, "Página Poética, Esther Feliciano Mendoza," in *Revista de la Asociación de Maestras de Puerto Rico,* No. 5 (1945), pp. 191-199; and see *Historia de la literatura puertorriqueña,* New York, Las Américas Publishing Co., 1956, pp. 357-358.

FELIPE, Carlos

b. November 4, 1914, Havana, Cuba.
Playwright.

Born into poverty, Felipe struggled through a modest education and menial jobs to knowledge of English, French, and Italian and a skilled lyrical command of Spanish. One of his first successes was winning second prize in the competition La Hora Múltiple for his play *El divertido viaje de Adelita Cossi,* and in 1939 the Premio Nacional de Teatro for *Esta noche en el bosque.* Though less regarded when it first appeared, his *Tambores* (1943) is by some critics considered a richer and more important work. It has scenes set in Africa and the poor quarters of Havana and in the words of Dolores Marti de Cid: "El motivo del tambor vuelve a oirse cuando ensayan una comparsa, y después, al final de la comedia. . . En *Tambores,* el negro, la mulata y el guajiro perfilan sus capacidades humanes, elevándose sobre el nivel discriminativo común al actual teatro bufo."

Felipe's early plays demand such special effects and staging problems as to have prevented their production thus far.

Writings: Plays: *El divertido viaje de Adelita Cossi; Esta noche en el bosque,* 1939; *Tambores,* 1943; *El Chino,* premiered Teatro ADAD, 1947, and winner of ADAD's first prize; *Capricho en rojo* (3 acts), winner of ADAD's first prize in 1950 and premiered by ADAD company in 1951; published Havana, Pagrán, 1959; *Ladrillos de plata* (comedy); *El travieso Jimmy,* winner of Premio Nacional de Teatro, 1949, performed Patronato del Teatro in 1951, published in complete text in *Teatro Cubano Contemporáneo,* Dolores Marti de Cid, 2nd edition, Madrid, Aguilar, 1962. Also: *La bruja en el obenque (*1 act comedy); *Obras,* Havana,

1959 (contains *Ladrillos de plata; El chino;* and *El travieso Jimmy*); and *Teatro* (contains *Los compadres; El chino; El travieso Jimmy; Requiem pro Yarini*), Havana, UNEAC, 1967 and in *Teatro cubano,* Santa Clara, 1960.

FERNANDEZ, Pablo Armando

b. 1930, Cuba.
Poet, novelist.

After many years in the United States, Fernández returned to Cuba to take part in the revolution led by Castro. He was named cultural attaché to London and has travelled widely, including trips to Russia and China. His early verse was strongly influenced by North American models, but his third collection, *Libro de los héroes* (1964), was far more felt—being Afro-Cuban laments for the fallen in the recent revolution: the Fidelista comrades are shown fighting and dying in the struggle against Batista.

His recent novel, *Los niños se despiden,* was a prize winner (Casas de las Américas) in 1968 and is very experimental in structure and rhythm.

Writings: Poetry: *Toda la poesia,* Havana, Revolución, 1961, 2nd ed., 1962; *Himnos,* Havana, La Tertulia, 1962; *Libro de los héroes,* Casa de las Américas, 1964; *Los niños se despiden,* Havana, Casa de las Américas, 1968; *Un sitio permanente,* Madrid, Rialp, 1970.

FERNANDEZ ARRONDO, Ernesto

b. 1897, Cuba; d. 1956.
Poet.

Fernández' verse is involuted and reflective of a very personal fantasy and love of country at one and the same time, a new but necessary note in a time of harsh political repressions of unsanctified views.

Writings: Poetry: *Bronces de libertad,* 1923; "Canto a la patria" (Cardenas Prize, 1922); *Inquietud,* 1925; *Tránsito,* 1937; *Poemas del amor feliz,* 1944; *Hacia mi mismo,* Madrid, 1950; the others all published in Havana.

FERNANDEZ JUNCOS, Manuel

b. 1846, Asturias, Spain; d. 1928, San Juan.
Poet, folklorist, storywriter, anthologist, critic, poet.

Fernández Juncos early emigrated to Puerto Rico and closely identified himself with the culture and people of the island. His *Antologia puertorriqueña* was long a popular text in the school system and he was editor (and founder) of the journal *La Revista de Literatura, Ciencias y Arte* (1887-1893). His interesting poem "Sursum corda" begins:

No te apenes jamás de haber nacido
en una isla de extensión escasa;
que no se juzga al hombre, por su casa;
ni a las aves cantoras por su nido.

He is a humorous prose artist and has published many diverting collections of tales.

Writings: Editor of: *Antologia puertoriqueña,* 1913, and many later editions.

Folklore: *Tipos y caracteres, puertorriqueños de mi tiempo,* 1882, 4th ed., Tip. Guzmán Diaz, 1919; *Costumbres y tradiciones,* San Juan, Biblioteca El Buscapie, 1883; *Cuentos y narraciones,* 1926; *La última hornada,* 1928.

Poetry: in various journals and collections including *Almanaque de los damas,* 1887, and his "Sursum corda" appears in the *Antologia de la poesia puertorriqueña,* E. F. Méndez, ed., San Juan, 1968.

Novelettes: *Marqués y marquesa,* 1911; *La vida cara,* published in *La Novela Azul,* San Juan, Vol. I, No. I (December 21, 1918), 19 pp.

Literary Criticism: *Lecturas escogidas,* 1910; *Aromas del terruño (Boceto critico),* San Juan, Tip. Germán Diaz Hermano, 1916; and "Literatura y elocuencia" in *Libro de Puerto Rico,* pp. 756-766.

Biographical/Critical Sources: F. Manrique Cabrera, *Historia de la literatura puertorriqueña,* Rio Piedras, 1969, pp. 177-180; Pedro Conde, "La vida y los tiempos de don Manuel Fernández Juncos," unpub. M.A. thesis, U. of Puerto Rico, 1932 (89 pp.); and see Sebastián Dalmau Canet, *Crepúsculos literarios,* San Juan, Imp. Boletin Mercantil, 1904, p. 15.

FERNANDEZ MENDEZ, Eugenio

b. 1924, Cayey, Puerto Rico.
Poet, literary historian, anthologist, historian, teacher.

Fernández is a professor at the University of Puerto Rico. Much of his work has appeared in such journals as *Orfeo* (Yauco-Ponce), *Asomante* and *Pegaso.* He edited (and had published in 1954) a rare historic document on San Juan (see below) written by a Cuban officer Fernando Miyares Gonzáles.

The poetry of Fernández Méndez is philosophical, existentialist, touched by the "common-man" voice of Walt Whitman (USA) and Pablo Neruda (Chile).

He is also disturbed by science and asks in his poem "Biografia Sucinta de la Materia":

Pregunto, pregunto a la materia,
al terra terra de la materia gris,
a lo unánime de la almohada en que ausculto
a la igual
el mil agro de la noche,
precisión de los eritrocitos y las horas:
¿Por cuál fluyente espacio y a qué velocidades
has llegado a integrarme? (1st stanza)

Writings: Poetry: *Tras siglo,* 1959; several poems of his are in *Aguinaldo liricos,* including the poem quoted above in part, C. Rosa Nieves, ed., Rio Piedras, 1957.

History: *Noticias particulares de la Isla y Plaza de San Juan Bautista de Puerto Rico,* 1954.

Editor of: *Antologia de la poesia puertorriqueña,* San Juan, 1968.

FERNANDEZ RETAMAR, Roberto

b. 1930, Cuba.
Poet, teacher, critic, literary historian, biographer.

After local schooling through the university, concluding with his doctorate, Fernández lived much of his life abroad before returning to Cuba after the Castro-led revolution. For a period he studied in Paris and London and at Yale University where he also taught. His "conversational" poetry was a popular success after the difficult hermetic work of Alejo Carpentier and his school, but Fernández' verse on revolutionary themes, according to a few critics, is weak, even sentimental. His *Historia antigua* (1964) shows a more assertive personal vision, and the collection of his work from 1948 to 1966 in *Poesia reunida* (1966) shows his genuine strengths.

Much of his early work was with the transcendentalist group gathered around José Lezama Lima and the journal *Origenes.*

Writings: Poetry: *Vuelta de la antigua esperanza,* Havana, 1959; *En su lugar, la poesia,* Havana, Unión, 1966; *Buena suerte viviendo,* Mexico, Era, 1967; *Algo semejante a los monstruos antediluvianos,* Barcelona, El Bardo, 1970, and republished as *Que Veremos arder,* Havana, Unión, 1970; and *A quien pueda interesar,* Mexico, Siglo XXI, 1970 (included *Vuelta de la antigua esperanza; Buena suerte viviendo; Historia antigua; Que veremos arder; Con las mismas manos;* and previously unpublished *Cuaderno paralelo* [written in 1970]. Two poems, "Adoration of the Kings," and "Of Reality: Those who marry in hired clothes," in English text, appear in *Writers from the New Cuba,* edited by E. M. Cohen (1967). Other major poems of his are: "Elegia como un himno" (published in 1950 in memory of Rubén Martinez Villena); "Patrias" (winner of national poetry prize and published in 1952); and his song for Cuba: "Vuelta a la antigua esperanza," previously cited. Some of his verse is in *Latin American Revolutionary Poetry,* Robert Marquez, ed.

Critical Biography: *Páginas escogidas de José Marti* (as foreword), Havana, Edit. Universitaria, 1965.

Esthetics/Criticism: *Idea de la estilistica,* Havana, 1959; "Hacia una intelectualidad revolucionaria en Cuba," in *Casa de las Américas,* 1967.

Editor of: *Poesia joven de Cuba,* Havana, Organización Continental de los Festivales del Libro, 1959; *La poesia contemporánea de Cuba (1927-1953),* Havana, Origenes, 1954.

Biographical/Critical Sources: Roque Dalton. *El intelectual y la sociedad,* Mexico City, Siglo XXI, 1969 (discusses Fernández, René Depestre, Edmundo Desnoes, Ambrosio Fornet, and Carlos Maria Gutiérrez).

FERNANDEZ SANCHEZ, Angel

(pseudonym: **Guido de ARIEL**)

b. 1903, Manati, Puerto Rico.
Poet, lawyer, judge, farmer.

Rosa-Nieves called Fernández ". . .un espiritu rebelde contra todo (lo humano y lo divino): iconoclasta, de bravos arrestos y de hirientes mostacillas cáusticas," and he adds, "Dos zonas estéticas avizoramos en su poemática inquieta y trashumante: el festivismo satirico (que vedesco), de admonición y de virilismo dinámico, y su poesia serena; . . ." His work is varied, often concerned with Afro-Caribbean subjects, touched by proletariat sympathies, sensual, and nationalistic.

The poem, "Fernández Rubi" (from *El Volantin . . .*) begins:

Gota de sangre que cuajó la suerte
sobre el blanco magnolia de tu mano,
candente gota del dolor humano,
simbolo de crueldades en el fuerte.

Writings: Poetry: *25+ Poemas Diagonales* (private edition, mimeographed), 1930; *El Volatin de los flecos sonoros,* San Juan, 1932; unpublished volumes are: "La honda de David" (covering work done 1915-32); "Veredas de tierra adentro," (work 1932-59); "Las retinas de Tantalo" (1935-55); and "Epitafio en el sol" (1940-55); also: poems in various reviews and collections including *Aguinaldo lirico* (1st ed., 1957, Rio Piedras), C. Rosa-Nieves, ed.

FERNANDEZ SPENCER, Antonio

b. 1922, Santo Domingo, Dominican Republic.
Poet, critic.

Fernández' first verse saw print in the journal *La Poesia Sorprendida* which took its name from the active poetic experimentalists of that name. His work was surrealistic, but eventually took on less specifically localized manifestations of the international surreal art movement. He edited *Entre las Soledades* in 1947, a short-lived successor of *La Poesia Sorprendida,* and soon went on to Spain to study for a diploma at the University of Salamanca in Spanish Philology, having earlier earned a doctorate in philosophy at his home university of Santo Domingo.

While in Spain Fernández married and began serious writing which has led to his being one of the most prolific of his generation.

After returning from Spain he established the publishing house Colección Arquero of which he is director and house editor.

In 1961 he was named undersecretary of state in the Ministry of Education and Fine Arts and he is a member of many professional associations, including the Academia Dominicana de la Lengua. He also has served as a professor at the Universidad Nacional "Pedro Henriquez Ureña," and in the early 1970's became the Dominican Ambassador to Uruguay.

A typical example of his poetry is this extract from his poem CXXVII from the collection "Epigramas a Lesbia" which is not yet published in its entirety, entitled "Lo Que Me Queda de ti". It begins:

Sólo me queda de ti, Lesbia,
claras castas de manzanas,
y al rocio que tocó tus ojos,
y el retrato del pájaro
que aquella noche se posó en tus manos.

Writings: Poetry: *Nueva poesia dominicana,* Madrid, Ed. Cultura Hispanica, 1953; *Bajo la luz del dia,* Madrid, 1953, 2nd ed., Ciudad Trujillo, Col. Arquero, 1958 [this won the Premio Adonais in 1952]; *Los testigos,* S. Domingo, Ediciones Brigadas Dominicanas, 1962; *Vendaval interior,* S. Domingo, La Poesia Sorprendida, 1943; "Noche infinita," S. Domingo, published in *Diario del Mundo* (1969) and at Madrid, Ed. Instituto de Cultura Hispánica, 1970 (winning the Premio Leopoldo Panero, 1969).

Essays: *A orillas del filosofar,* S. Domingo, Colección Arquero, 1960; *Ensayos literarios,* S. Domingo, Ed. Ateneo Dominicano, 1960; *Meditaciones entorno a la Restauración,* 1963; *Caminando por la literatura hispánica,* S. Domingo, Colección Arquero, 1964 [this won the National Prize for Literature in 1964].

Biographical/Critical Sources: Manuel Rueda's comments, pp. 349-352 in his *Antologia panorámica de la poesia contemporánea 1912-1962,* Santiago de los Caballeros, UCMM, 1972.

FERNANDEZ VILATO, Francisco

b. ca. 1838, Cuba.
Playwright, actor.

Fernández was a long-time member of the Compañia de Bufos Habaneros which performed in the Teatro Villaneuva of Havana.

Writings: Plays *Los negros catedráticos* (burlesque farce based on folklore, in prose and verse), 2nd ed., Havana, Lit. del Comercio, 1868: first performed in Teatro Villaneuva, Havana, , May 31, 1868; *El bautizo* (second part of *Los negros catedráticos*), Havana, Imp. Tropical, 1968 and Havana, Imp. de la Real y Imperial Fábrica La Honradez, 1868; *El negro Cheche o veinte años después* (third part of *Los negros catedráticos*), Havana, Imp. La Tropical, 1868, and Havana, Imp. Militar de la Vda. e hijos de Soler, 1868, performed in Teatro Variedades, Havana, July 26, 1868 and written with Pedro Néstor de Pequeño, as was Fernández' *Músico,* Havana, Imp. Militar, 1872, 2nd ed., 1892, first performed in Teatro "familier" of Augustin T. Muro, in Calabazar, 1870; *Coña Caralimpia* (1 act), produced in Villa Clara, 1878, in ms.; *Politicos de Guinea o el restaurant de las moscas* (1 act, prose comedy), performed Havana, 1890, in ms.; *Retórica y poética* (1 act prose and verse), Havana, in ms.; *Un drama viejo* (1 act, prose and verse), Havana, 1880, in ms.; *Una casa de empeño* (1 act comedy, prose and verse), Villa Clara, June 25, 1879 performance, in ms.

FERNANDEZ DE AMADO, Isabel

b. 1910, Cuba.
Playwright.

Isabel Fernández, wife of playwright Luis Amado Blanco, wrote two comedies in the 1940's.

Writings: Plays: *El qué dirán,* 1944; *Lo que no se dice,* 1945; both written with Coqui Ponce.

FERRER, Rolando

b. 1925, Cuba.
Playwright.

Ferrer has lived and produced his work in

Santiago de Cuba, most of it influenced by Garcia Lorca.

Writings: Plays: *Lila la mariposa,* 1950; *Soledad,* 1947; *Otra vez la noche,* 1948; *Cita en el espejo,* 1948; *La fija de Nacho,* 1951; *Teatro* (contains *La hija de Nacho; Lila, la mariposa; La taza de cafe; Los próceres; Función homenaje; A las siete la estrella; Fiquito; El corte; El que mató al responsable*), Havana, UNEAC, 1963. *Los próceres* is also in *Teatro cubano en un acto* (Rine Leal, ed.), Havana, Revolución, 1963.

FERRER HERNANDEZ, Gabriel

b. 1847, San Juan, Puerto Rico.
Poet, playwright, physicist, chemist.

Ferrer took science degrees in physics and chemistry at the Instituto Civil and studied anatomy at the Institución de Estudios Superiores.

Writings: Plays: *Herir en el corazón* (4 acts, prose), Puerto Rico, Imp. del Boletín Mercantil, 1883.

Poetry: in various journals; one volume: *Consecuencias,* published, date unknown, and a collection, unpublished of lyric verse.

Scholarship: *La mujer puertorriqueña; La instrucción pública en Puerto Rico,* 1885.

FERRER OTERO, Rafael

b. August 21, 1885, San Juan, Puerto Rico; d. February 15, 1951, San Juan.
Critic, essayist, journalist, biographer.

Ferrer took his law training at Syracuse University (Syracuse, New York, USA) and practiced law at home while entering into an active public career. He was a frequent contributor to *Revista de las Antillas, Juan Bobo,* and *Puerto Rico Ilustrado* and other journals of the "modernista" school. Most of his pieces were collected by his brother Miguel and published in 1965, some fourteen years after Rafael's death.

Writings: Essays: *Lienzos,* edited by Miguel Ferrer, San Juan, 1965, with introduction by Carlos N. Carreras; the essay "Los jardines de Santurce," first appearing in *Revista de las Antillas* (June 1914), also appears in L. Hernandez Aquino's *El modernismo en Puerto Rico,* San Juan, 1967.

Critical Biographies: "Perfiles: Antonio Pérez Pierret," in *Revista de las Antillas,* San Juan, (September 1914); "Perfiles: Miguel Guerra Mondragón," in *Revista de las Antillas,* San Juan (September 1914).

FIALLO Y CABRAL, Fabio

b. February 3, 1867, Santo Domingo, Dominican Republic; d. August 28, 1942, Havana, Cuba.
Poet, journalist, storywriter, playwright, teacher, diplomat.

Balaguer believes Fiallo to have been the greatest of the "erotic" poets of the Dominican Republic. Fiallo wrote stories and plays but he will be remembered mostly for his sensuous poetry. A director of the important journal *El Hogar,* he founded *La Bandera Libre* in 1899 to fight the government of President Jiménez and was subsequently brought into court several times. With Tulio Cestero, Fiallo in 1905 established *La Campaña* to replace the silenced *La Bandera Libre* which itself reappeared in 1907 as *Libre* and later with close to its original name, *La Bandera.*

In 1920 Fiallo was imprisoned for his attacks on the U. S. occupation of his country which set off protests throughout Latin America. The American authorities saw fit to release him several months later.

Rubén Dario wrote of his friend's work, "En sus versos y en sus cuentos. . . es un puro, un fino, un noble poeta; su lirica es a cortas vuelas, a suspiros, a quejas, a caricias. . ." Pedro Henriquez Ureña stated he was the first initiator in the Dominican Republic of the new European and North American currents.

Writings: Poetry: *Primavera sentimental,* Caracas, 1902; *Cantaba el ruiseñor,* Berlin, 1910; *Canciones de la tarde.* Madrid. 1920: *La*

canción de una vida, Madrid, 1926, 2nd ed., Santiago, D. R., 1942; *Canto a la bandera,* 1925; *El balcón de Psiquis,* Havana, 1935; *Sus mejores versos,* Santiago, Chile, 1938; *Poemas de la niña que está en el cielo,* 1935, 2nd ed., 1936.

Stories: *Cuentos frágiles,* New York, 1908, Madrid, Biblioteca Rubén Darío, 1929; *Las manzanas de Mefisto,* Havana, Ucar, 1934.

Political Essays: *Plan de acción y liberación del pueblo dominicano y Yubr,* 1922; *La Comision Nacionalista Dominicana en Washington (1920-21),* Santiago de los Caballeros, 1939.

Play: *La cita* (1 act), 1924.

Editor of: *Las mejores poesias liricas de los poetas,* Vol. LIX, Barcelona, 1931.

Biographical/Critical Sources: J. Balaguer's *Historia de la literatura dominicana,* 5th ed., S. Domingo, Postigo, 1970; F. A. Mota Medrano, *Relieves Alumbrados,* S. Domingo, 1971, pp. 103-125.

FIGUEROA, Edwin

b. March 26, 1925, Guayama, Puerto Rico. Storywriter, novelist.

After local schooling in Guayama, including training as an engineer, completed in 1942, and some months spent at the Colegio de Agricultura y Artes Mecánicas, Figueroa took his first job in the Department of Public Instruction in San Juan under the playwright Manuel Méndez Ballester. He completed formal university work in 1948 with his B.A. and then an M.A. in Linguistics, meanwhile working for radio station W.I.A.C. In 1955 Figueroa joined the university faculty as a general instructor in the humanities at Ponce and in 1958 he began to teach Spanish Studies, including Spanish literature.

Most of Figueroa's work concerns the rural poor and his peasant characters are always treated sympathetically, if realistically. His story "Aguinaldo Negro," winner of the first prize in the Ateneo Puertorriqueño competition of 1953, exploits the rich folkloric material of the black Puerto Ricans of his natal Guayama district. Other prize-winning stories of his in the Ateneo competition were "Lolo Manco" (third prize, 1956), and "Raiz amarga" (first prize, 1957).

Writings: Stories: *Sobre este suelo: nueve cuentos y una leyenda,* 2nd ed., Rio Piedras, Edit. Cultural, 1971; stories in various journals. Of specific interests is "Aguinaldo Negro" in *Antologia de escritores puertorriqueños,* III and in *El Cuento,* San Juan, pp. 255-58, and in *Revista del Café* (December 1954), pp. 19-22, and *Asomante* (April-June 1954), pp. 48-51; "Lolo Manco," in *Asomante* (San Juan, 1956); "El Rebelde," in *El Mundo* (February 26, 1957); "Raiz Amarga," in *El arte del cuento en Puerto Rico,* C. Meléndez, ed., 1961, pp. 282-290.

Novel: *Salón Boricua,* extracted in Nina Kaiden's *Puerto Rico: The New Life,* New York, Renaissance Editions, 1966.

Biographical/Critical Sources: Concha Meléndez, *El arte del cuento en Puerto Rico,* New York, pp. 256-262.

FILOLEZES

(pseudonym for **José Cipriano de la LUZ Y CABALLERO**)

FLORIT, Eugenio

b. 1903, Madrid, Spain.
Poet, critic, playwright.

Son of a Spanish father and Cuban mother, Florit arrived in Cuba at 15 years from his natal Spain. He completed his schooling in Havana through the university and then entered Cuba's Consular Service, serving first in New York.

Florit's work, covering five decades, spans the changes from the Mallarmé-influenced "vanguardistas" of the 1920's through surrealism, neo-classicism and realistic-testimonial. He has always sought harmonious diction throughout, free of harshness of any sort. Generally, all of his work is flowing, pensive, highly personal. One critic, Cintio Vitier, considered Florit's *Doble acento* (1937) to be his most typical collection, fully representing the poetic-stylistic world of the period between the two great wars. The last lines from the key poem "Doble acento" from the volume of that name are:

Qué sueño sin ensueños torcedores,
abierta el alma a trémulas caricias
y sobre el corazón fijas las manos.

Qué lejana la voz de los amores.
Con qué sabor la boca a las delicias
de todos los serenos oceanos.

Writings: Poetry: 32 poemas brevas, 1927; *Trópico,* 1930; *Doble acento, 1930-36,* preface by Juan Ramón Jiménez, 1937; *Reino,* 1938; *Cuatro poemas,* 1940; *Poema mio,* 1920-1944 (containing all his verse from 1920-1944), 1947: all these published in Havana. Also: *Asonante final,* Bogota, 1950; *Conversación con mi padre,* 1949; *Asonante final y otros poemas,* 1955; *Antologia poética (1930-1955),* preface by Andrés Iduarte, 1956; *Siete poemas,* Montevideo, Cuadernos Julio Herrera y Reissig, 1960; *Hábito de esperanza,* poemas, 1936-1964, Madrid, Insula, 1965; *Antologia penúltima,* Madrid, Plenitud, 1970.

Critical Essays: "Misonéismo," in *Revista de avance,* Vol. III, No. 19 (February 1928); "Regreso a la serenidad" in *Universidad de la Habana,* magazine, Vol. II, Nos. 8-9.

Plays: *La nube gris; La estrella,* both Havana, 1947; *Una mujer sola,* Havana, 1956 (all three works are one-act).

FONFRIAS, Ernesto Juan

b. November 7, 1909, Toa Baja, Puerto Rico.
Poet, storywriter, critic, journalist, statesman.

Fonfrias has served as president of the Sociedad de Periodistas Puertorriqueños and of the Liga Atlética (of Puerto Rico). He has been a senator in the island legislature and a well-known literary critic and story writer. He has particularly been interested in young people's writings and has sought to encourage the formation of new artists to enhance the island's awareness of its long culture and to develop new "expressors" of Puerto Rico's identity.

The poetry of Fonfrias is of the school of Luis Lloréns, José Santos Chocano and Rubén Dario, but he has his own voice and imagery. His common themes are patriotic, rural, the lot of the farmer or countrymen.

Writings: Poetry: *Diadema de lirios,* 1926; *Hebras de sol,* 1934; *Canteras eufóricas,* 197(?); *Bajo la cruz del sur,* 1951, (prose poetry); poems in various journals and anthologies, including *Aguinaldo lirico,* C. Rosa-Nieves, ed., Rio Piedras, 1957.

Stories/Novelettes: *Raúl,* 1927 (novelette); *Al calor de la lumbre,* 1936 (short stories). *Conversao en el batey: historia de un jibaro bragao,* 2nd. ed., San Juan, Edit. Club de la Prensa, 1958 (301 pp.); *Guasima,* San Juan, Club de la Prensa, 1957, *Una voz en la montaña,* San Juan, Club de la Prensa, 1958; *Raiz y espiga,*

Madrid, Colenda, 1962, 3rd ed., San Juan, Club de la Prensa, 1970.

Literary Essays and History: *Presencia jibaro desde Manuel Alonso hasta Don Florito,* foreword by Alberto Maria Carreño, San Juan, 1957; *Sementera: Ensayos breves y biografias minimas,* San Juan, 1962; *Tintillo bravo del que hacer puertorriqueño,* San Juan, 1968.

FORNET, Ambrosio

b. 1932, Veguita (Oriente), Cuba. Storywriter, essayist, novelist, critic.

After several years employed in a modest position in a bank in Bayamo, Fornet was able to study at the University of Havana (philosophy and literature) and has travelled widely in North Africa, Europe and lived for a period in New York City. In Cuba he has contributed his critical articles and reviews to leading journals. He works for the Instituto del Libro and is a member of the board of the review *Casa de las Americas.*

Writings: Stories: "A un paso del diluvio," Barcelona, 1958; the story "Yo no vi ná" appears in *Narrativo cubana de la revolución,* J. M. Caballero, ed., Madrid, 1969.

Essays: *En tres y dos,* Havana, 1964; *En blanco y negro,* Havana, 1967.

Editor of: *Antologia del cuento contemporáneo,* Mexico, Era, 1967.

Biographical/Critical Sources: El intelectual y la sociedad, Mexico City, Siglo XXI, 1969 (covers Fornet and four other writers).

FORNARIS, José

b. 1827, Bayamo, Cuba; d. Havana, 1890. Poet, playwright, translator, scholar, lawyer.

Once one of the most famous of Cuban poets after the epoch of Heredia and Milanés, the reputation of Fornaris has sadly declined and even in his last years his quickly won acclaim had vanished. Critics find he pieced out his lines with false exoticisms and barely understood legends, particularly in his supposed memorial to the Indian past in his *Cantos del Siboney.* Fornaris' use of the term "Siboney," taken from Fray Bartolomé de las Casas' work and referring to the speech of the Cuban Indians was of course common throughout Spanish America as a variety of "criollismo." Casas had written: "Llamábanse en su lengua ciboneyes, la penúltima silaba lengua . . . " (La Casas' work was not published until 1875 but copies of his original manuscript in Madrid were widely made and diffused in Mexico, Cuba and elsewhere.)

Fornaris did much translating, putting into Spanish work by Victor Hugo, Lamartine, Sully Prudhomme, Heine and Goethe.

Writings: Poetry: *Poesias,* 1851, augmented edition, 1857; *Cantos del Siboney,* 1855, with four more editions during his lifetime; *Flores y lagrimas,* 1860; *El libro de los amores,* 1862; *Obras,* volume one. 1862 (no other published); *Cantos tropicales,* Paris, 1874; *El arpa del hogar,* Paris, 1878, published with dramatic poem: "El toque de alarma"; *Poesias,* 1888.

Editor of: *Cuba poética,* Havana, 1855 (with José Socorro de Leon) and a new version with Joaquin Luaces, 1858, with a 2nd edition in 1859 and reprint in 1861 (these latter done with both Luaces and Socorro).

Scholarship: *Elementos de Retórica y poética;* and *Compendio de historia universal.*

Plays: *La hija del pueblo* (3 acts, verse), Havana, La Antila, 1865; *Amor y sacrificio* (3 acts), Havana, G. Cacho-Negrete, 1866.

FORNARIS Y JOAQUIN, Lorenzo

(see under **Joaquin Lorenzo LUACES**)

FORT, Gustavo

b. ca. 1893, Cuba. (assoc. with Puerto Rico)

Fort's poetry was bizarre—a mixture of the supranatural and the halucinatory. José de Jesús Esteves called him "cósmico." His poem, "Aldebarán," begins:

Aldebarán, rojo sol; astro abuelo y milenario,
cristal de un purpúreo duelo,
fantástico, legendario,
tan antiguo como el cielo.

Writings: Poetry: Much of his work appeared in such reviews as the *Revista de la Antillas* and in many critical anthologies since his early death: in the essay, "Poetas modernistas de Puerto Rico," by Manuel Martínez Plée, published in *Libro azul de Puerto Rico,* San Juan, 1923; and in *El modernismo en la poesia;* also "Paisaje nocturno" appeared in *Parnaso antillano,* Enrique Torres Rivera, ed., and "Aldebarán" in *Revista de la Antillas* (March 1914), p. 50.

Literary Criticism: "La cuestión de escuelas rarias y otras cuestiones," in *Revista de la Antillas,* San Juan (May 1913).

FOXA Y LECANDA, Francisco Javier de

b. 1816, Santo Domingo, Dominican Republic; d. 1865(?).
Poet, playwright.

While still a child, he went with his family in exile to Cuba to escape the Haitian invasion of the Dominican portion of Hispaniola. In his new home he grew up to become one of the most active writers and on August 9, 1838, his very romantic-historical drama *Don Pedro de Castilla* was performed. Its new style and subject made it a scandalous success, for not only did it call up the career of "don Pedro el Cruel" but its romantic flavor was shocking to the provincial audience. The excitement was akin to that stirred up by Hugo's *Hernani* in its opening night in Paris a few years earlier. Though Max Henriquez Ureña dismisses all of Foxá's dramatic work as weak, there is little doubt Foxá opened up the Latin American theatre to the new currents from Europe.

Foxá'a brother, Narciso (1822-1883) was an important poet and essayist.

Writings: Plays: *Don Pedro de Castilla,* performed August 9, 1838 in Teatro Principal of Havana; published Havana, Boloña, 1838; *Ellos son* (comedy); *El templario,* performed December 1838, published Havana, Imp. del Comercio, 1839; *¡Ellos son!* (1 act, verse), Havana, 1839; *Enrique Octavo,* 1839, (banned from performance 1839).

Biographical/Critical Sources: The scandal is discussed in J. M. de Andueza's *Isla de Cuba pintoresca,* Madrid, 1841, where he recounts his attendance at the play, and the resulting furor. Also see Max Henriquez Ureña's *Panorama histórico de la literatura dominicana,* 1965, pp. 141-142.

FOXA Y LECANDA, Narciso

b. 1822, San Juan, Puerto Rico; d. 1883, Paris.
Poet, essayist, playwright.

Foxá early left Puerto Rico for Santo Domingo, Cuba, and finally France where he passed his last days. In 1846, he received his first fame as the winner of an award from the Liceo de la Habana for his "Canto épico sobre el descubrimiento de América por Cristóbal Colón." Manrique Cabrera quotes a few lines from that poem, beginning:

La aurora coronada de azucenas
Con sus dedos de rosa descorria
En el Oriente, perezosa, apenas
Las cortinas magnificas del dia;

Writings: Plays: *Don Pedro de Castilla,* premiered in Teatro de Tacón, August 9, 1838 in Havana, and published Havana, Boloña, 1838; *El Templario* (verse), premiered December 25, 1838, Havana and published Havana, Imp. del Comercio, 1839; *¡Ellos son!* (1 act, verse), 1838; *Enrique Octavo,* written in 1838 but banned from production or printing.

Poetry: *Ensayos poéticos,* Madrid, 1849, introduction by Manuel Cañete; *Canto épico sobre el descubrimiento de América por El Cristóbal Colón,* Havana, December 1846 (Ildefonso Estrada y Zenea, Foxá's old friend, had assembled the individual works), (winner of Juegos Florales del Liceo de la Habana).

Biographical/Critical Sources: F. Manrique Cabrera, *Historia de la literatura puertorriqueña,* Rio Piedras, Edit. Cultural, 1969, pp. 88f; Max Henriquez Ureña, *Panorama histórico de la literatura dominicana,* Santo Domingo, 1965, pp. 141-142, and Henriquez' *Panorama, histórico de la literatura cubano,* New York, 1963, pp. 180ff.

FRANCASI, Amelia

(pseudonym for **Amelia Francisca MARCHENA DE LEYBA**)

FRANCISCO, Ramón

b. 1929, Puerto Plata, Dominican Republic.
Poet, critic, storywriter, teacher.

One of the major poets of the Dominican Republic, Francisco has been an original force and made his contemporaries recognize new modes of expression and concepts of beauty. He is also a keen literary critic with a wide cultural-intellectual background.

Writings: Poetry: *Las superficies sórdidas,* Ciudad Trujillo, Revelación, Centro de Publicaciones, 1960.

Critical Study: *Literatura dominicana 60,* Santiago, Dominican Republic, UCMM, 1969.

FRANCK, Dr.

(see under **Francisco Carlos ORTEA**)

FRANCO BIDO, Augusto

b. July 29, 1857, Santiago, Dominican Republic; d. Santiago, July 24, 1929.
Storywriter, judge, government official.

Franco attended local schools in Santiago, including the Colegio de Monsieur Achille Michel and the Escuela de Idiomas of Professor Pedro Bestard. He became a friend of the Cuban poet-patriot José Marti who came to visit Franco in his colonial home in Santiago when both were "senior statesman."

Active in local affairs, named to the bench, and involved in the controversies of the day, Franco was associated with many newspapers. He was co-director of *Unión Nacional* and a frequent contributor to *El Dia, El Santiagués, El Derecho,* the *Revista Cientifica, El Album,* and many others, and founded *La Voz de Santiago.* He also was a leader in the establishment of the Escuela de Bachilleres in Santiago and of other professional and technical schools.

Writings: Stories (in Creole): in many and various journals.

Historical Essays: "Discurso histórico nacional" in *Revista Cientifica,* S. Domingo, No. 15, (September 12, 1883); "Las Máscaras" in same journal, Nos. 28-29 (Jan-Feb 1883). Sketches: "No juegues, magino" (Cuento Serrano) in *El Album,* Santiago (1900) and in *La Opinion,* No. 1603 (March 30, 1932), and republished in extract in E. Rodriguez Demorizi's *Tradiciones y cuentos dominicanos,* S. Domingo, Postigo, 1969, pp. 261-265.

FRANCO OPPENHEIMER, Félix

b. July 10, 1912, Ponce, Puerto Rico.
Poet, essayist, critic, journalist, teacher.

Franco took his B.A. and M.A. (1953) at the University of Puerto Rico (Rio Piedras). Founder of "Transcendentalismo" in 1948 with F. Lluch Mora, Eugenio Rentas Lucas and others, Franco has tried to move away from the over-scientific and dry work of his immediate predecessors toward a warmer, more personal tone. In 1954 he was in the "Ensuenismo" movement led by C. Rosa-Nieves, a grouping called for subtle, psychological expression and nativist themes.

Oppenheimer wrote his M. A. thesis on the verse of Carrera Andrade published in

1953 as *La poesia de Jorge Carrerra Andrade* and is a professor at the University Puerto Rico. He has published much of his work in *El Mundo, Orfeo, Alma Latino,* and *Universidad.*

Writings: Poetry: *El hombre y su angustia,* San Juan, Edit. Yaurel, 1950; *Del tiempo y su figura,* Santurce, 1956, 2nd ed., Rio Piedras, Edit. Edil, 19??; *Estas cosas asi fueron,* 1956; *Imágenes,* 1957; *Los lirios del testimonio,* San Juan, Edit. Yaurel, 1964; *Prosas sin clave,* foreword by E. Ribera Chevremont, San Juan, Edit. Yaurel, 1971; three poems are in the *Antologia de la poesia puertorriqueña,* E. Fernández Méndez, ed., San Juan, 1968, and five are in *Aguinaldo lirico,* C. Rosa-Nieves, ed., Rio Piedras, 1967.

Literary Essays: *Contornos,* 1960.

Critical Biography: "La poesia de Jorge Carrera Andrade," unpublished M. A. thesis, University of Puerto Rico, 1953.

Critical History: *Imagen de Puerto Rico en su poesia,* Mexico, 1964.

Biographical/Critical Sources: José Luis Martin, *Arco y flecha,* San Juan, 1961.

FRAU MARSAL, Lorenzo

b. 1885, Igualada, Cuba.
Poet, playwright, storywriter, journalist.

Now an almost forgotten figure, Frau Marsal was the editor and director of many journals, including *La Ilustración, El Diario de la Marina, La Opinión,* and *El Noticiero.*

Writings: Plays: *Lulu Cancán; La traviesa Mimi; Miss Pagenta; Horas de New York; El Divorcio.*

Stories: *Hombres y mujeres.*

Poetry: *La Babel de hierro; Las tierras ocultas.*

FRAY CANDIL

(see under **Emilio BOBADILLA Y LUNAR**)

FUENTES, José Lorenzo

b. 1928, Santa Clara (Las Villas), Cuba.
Storywriter, novelist, journalist.

Forced to leave school well before he could hope to enter the university because of his family's poverty, Fuentes soon moved from Santa Clara to Havana. In 1952, his early story "El lindero" won an international prize—the Hernández Catá award—and he quickly made a name for himself as a journalist and creative writer. For a period he worked under Ché Guevara, was an assistant editor on the review *Cuba,* and in the 1960's began work as culture page editor for *El Mundo* and *Bohemia.*

Writings: Stories: *Maguaraya arriba,* Santa Clara, Las Villas, 1963; *El vendedor de dias,* Havana, Unión, 1967. *Después de la gaviota,* Havana, Casa de las Américas, 1968.

Novels: *El sol, ese enemigo,* Havana, Revolución, 1962; *Viento de enero,* winner of prize in Concurso de la Unión de Escritores y Artistas de Cuba, 1967, published Havana, Unión, 1968.

Editor of: *Los cuentistas cubanos y la reforma agraria,* Havana, Tierra Nueva, 1960 (done with Francisco Baeza).

FURE, Rogelio Martinez

b. ca. 1938, Cuba.
Folklorist, musician.

Furé has edited the collection *Chants and Yoruba Songs* and was the singer and flautist in the Afro-Cuban musical *Shango de Ima,* performed by Teatro Guiñol, Havana, 1969.

Writings: Editor of: *Chants and Yoruba Songs,* Havana, 1968.

GALLEGO, Laura Matilda

b. 1924, Bayamón, Puerto Rico.
Poet.

Gallego is a professor at the University of Puerto Rico and has published most of her verse in such island journals as *Alma Latina, Bayoán, Orféo,* and *Asomante.* Rosa-Nieves discusses her "Poemas Numerados," published in *Orféo* and says they show " . . . un verismo atormentador, grisáceo: un estado animico que vislumbra lejanias deseadas, ensueños sin playas vecinas."

Her *Poem No. 6,* "Claroscuro de Bayamón" concludes:

Suaves momentos, prisas de tristeza
y el agua que se arroja duramente
como avalancha blanca en mi cabeza.

Writings: Presencia, San Juan, B.A.P., 1952; and "Poemas Numerados" in *Orféo, Yauca-Ponce* (December 4, 1955), and some republished in *Aguinaldo lirico,* C. Rosa-Nieves, ed., Rio Piedras, 1957. *Calajes,* San Juan, Ateneo Puertorriqueña, 1959.

GALLIANO CANCIO, Miguel

b. 1890, Province of Las Villas, Cuba.
Poet.

A modest, often sentimental poet, Galliano published two collections of verse in his 20's, *El rosal . . .* and *Ruiseñors del alma* but has not published since. Most of his life was spent in Manzanilla.

Writings: Poetry: *El rosal de mis sueños,* 1913; *Ruiseñores del alma,* 1915, both in Havana.

GALVAN, Manuel de Jesús

b. January 13, 1834, Santo Domingo, Dominican Republic; d. December 13, 1910, San Juan, Puerto Rico.
Novelist, journalist, lawyer, diplomat.

Galván was the private secretary to President Santana in 1859, was named Chief of Negotiations and Secretary of Government during the discussions with the Spanish during the early period of annexation by Spain of the break-away colony. After independence, a member of the "wrong side," he went into exile in Puerto Rico where the Spanish made him Intendente de la Real Hacienda and he was later named Spanish Consul to the city of Puerto Principe in the Dominican Republic. After the revolution of November 25, 1873, he joined the liberals around Ulises Francisco Espaillat and in 1874 was elected a member of the Constitutional Convention which voted the *Carta Orgánica* of March 9, 1875.

President Espaillat named Galván Foreign Minister in 1876 and in 1883 Galván became head of the Supreme Court, there remaining until 1889.

In 1890, with J. M. Glass and Emiliano Tejera, Galván negotiated long outstanding boundary differences with the Haitians. In 1891 he became the Dominican Minister to the United States, and in 1893 he again became Foreign Minister, this time under President Heureaux. In exile again on the fall of Heureaux's regime, Galván finished his life out in Spain while on a visit.

Galván's historical novel *Enriquillo* deals with the first Spanish settlers in Dominica and their treatment of and relations with the Indians. Joaquin Balaguer writes of this work: "En esa pintura patética de la tragedia del indio reside uno de los toques más punzantes de *Enriquillo,* quizás la más realista y al propio tiempo la más conmovedora de cuantas obras se han escrito en América, inspiradas por el infortunio de la raza aborigen."

Galván contributed many articles to *El Oasis* and *El Eco de la Opinión* and in the latter published a strong defense of General Pedro Santana who had led the Spanish-oriented forces of reoccupation in mid-century and who remains a villain to most Dominicans even today. Galván's style and diction were of the most classical and pure sort—and his career and literary production the the flower of a high personal culture and broad experience with men and ideas.

Writings: Works: *Enriquillo,* 1879, incomplete edition; 1882, first complete edition with preface by José Joaquin Pérez; 1909, Barcelona, foreword by José Marti, 1940, 1944, Buenos Aires, Editorial Americalee; 1956, Santo Domingo, Postigo; and in 1962 another edition by Postigo; French language edition, Paris, Unesco, in translation by Marcelle Auclair and the Unesco English language translation by Robert Graves.

Political Pamphlet: *El General Pedro Santana y la anexión de Santo Domingo a España,* 1862.

Polemics: His articles in a debate with José Gabriel Garcia are in *Controversia histórica sostenida en 1889 entre "El Teléfono" y "El Eco de la Opinión,"* 1891.

Biographical/Critical Sources: Joaquin Balaguer's *Historia de la literatura dominicana,* 1970, pp. 190-194.

GALVAN Y VELAZQUEZ, Rafael Octavio

b. 1877, Dominican Republic.
Novelist, playwright, poet.

Galván was a member of the "Modernist" group. His short play *El principe travieso* won a prize in the year of its publication, 1907, and is based on the Renaissance masque.

Writings: Novel: *Lidia,* 1901.

Dramatic Sketch: *El principe travieso* (1 act), performed in 1907 and published in *La Cuna de América,* 1907.

GARCIA ALZOLA, Ernesto

b. 1914, Cuba.
Poet, storywriter.

Garcia's poetry is sonorous and possibly touched by Neruda and Vallejo. His story "El molino de viento" of 1946 won the Premio Hernández Catá, and the next year "Siete horas" won a mention in the same competition. The later story gave its name to Garcia's collected stories which won the Premio Nacional de Cuentos given by the Dirección de Cultura.

Writings: Poetry: *Rumbo sin brújula,* Havana, 1939; *Diálogo con la vida,* Havana, 1947.

Stories: *Siete horas y otros cuentos.*

GARCIA BARCENA, Rafael

b. 1907, Cuba.
Poet.

Garcia Bárcena combined patriotism with a very personal style and idiom, much like that of E. Fernández Arrondo. His grandeloquent poem, "Rapsodia patria," was a winner in the national competition for patriotic verse.

Writings: Poetry: *Proa,* 1927; *Sed,* 1935 (National Prize for Poetry).

GARCIA GODOY, Federico

b. December 25, 1857, Santiago, Cuba;

d. February 12, 1924, La Vega, Dominican Republic.
Novelist, critic, essayist, biographer, journalist, teacher.

Garcia was one of the broadest and most intelligent of Dominica's great nineteenth century humanists. An advocate of "Literary Americanism" he strove to increase the range of subjects in local writing and to bring a deeper culture to their treatment. He was also one of the earliest writers of the "historical" novel and in his own works exploited relatively contemporary Dominican history and political events.

As was the case with so many artists of the period he was active in public affairs and a busy journalist and advocate of reform. He founded, and directed two journals, *Patria,* 1910 and *El Dia,* 1914.

Writings: Novels: *Cibao y sur;* this volume contains Garcia's three novels, here edited by Henriquez Ureña, publishing details unknown; *Rufinito (Sucedido histórico),* S. Domingo, Imp. La Cuna de América, 1908, 2nd ed., 19??; *Alma dominicana (Novela histórica),* S. Domingo, 1911; *Guanuma,* S. Domingo, Imp. La Cuna, 1914; 2nd ed., S. Domingo, Postigo, 1963.

Novelette: "Margarita," in *Recuerdos y opiniones,* 1888.

Essays: *La hora que pasa,* S. Domingo, 1910; *Perfiles y relieves,* S. Domingo, 1907; *De aqui y de allá* (Notas criticas), S. Domingo, 1916; *Páginas efimeras,* S. Domingo, La Cuna, 1912; *Impresiones,* Moca, 1899; *Recuerdos y opiniones,* 1888; *De la historia,* La Vega, 1920, *El derrumbe,* 1917, republished in *Cuba Contemporánea,* 19??.

Stories: *Narraciones cortas,* details unknown.

Biographies: *El General Luperón (boceto histórico); Vida del General Mellá; Lorenzo Perelló hijo (folleto).*

Literary History: *La literatura dominicana,* Paris, New York, 1916 and separately published in *Revue Hispanique,* Vol. XXXVII, 1916; "Vida intelectual dominicana," in *Nuestra America,* Buenos Aires (July 1919), and translated into English and published in *Inter-América,* New York, 1920, pp. 298-303; *Americanismo literario,* Madrid, 1918 (deals with Pórtico, Marti, José Enrique Rodó, Francisco Garcia Calderón, and Rufino Blanco-Fombona); *La literatura americana de nuestros dias,* Madrid, Biblioteca Andrés Bello, 1916, extract in *Revue Hispanique,* Vol. 37 (Paris).

Political articles: *Del Terruño (Criollism politico); Bajo la dictadura (folleto politico),* 1914; *La patria y el héroe (folleto),* 1911.

Economics: *Al margen del Plan Peynado,* La Vega, 1922.

Biographical/Critical Sources: Abigail Mejia's *História de la literatura dominicana,* S. Domingo, 1929, 1937; Joaquin Balaguer's *Federico Garcia Godoy,* S. Domingo, Postigo, 1951; Joaquin Balaguer's *História de la literatura dominicana,* 5th ed., S. Domingo, Postigo, 1970, pp. 273-275; F. A. Mota Medrano, *Relieves Alumbrados,* S. Domingo, 1971, pp. 155-164 in essay "Garcia Godoy y la poesia de Apolinar Perdomo."

GARCIA GUERRA, Ivan

b. February 26, 1938, San Pedro de Macoris, Dominican Republic.
Playwright, storywriter, actor, director.

Garcia won a prize as the best director of a local play given in 1966 and the first prize in the La Mascara story competition of 1968. The winning play, *Más allá de la búsqueda,* was published in 1967.

Garcia's plays are touched with "vanguardismo" and are nihilistic, focusing only on reality or non-reality and the problem of communication. Drawing on both the classical and absurd theatre, especially on Frisch and Durrenmatt for the latter, his *La fábula de los cinco caminantes,* is a fatal condemnation of the characters to a leaden fate. *Más allá de la búsqueda* (1967) takes the Prometheus theme: Pandora and the hero try to confront the world, to get through to it, to make it "see" what needs to be done. In some ways his work is the best key to the feelings of the present generations of youth in the Republic.

Writings: Plays: *La fábula de los cinco caminantes,* unpublished; *Más allá de la búsqueda,* S. Domingo, 1967.

GARCIA MARRUZ, Fina

b. 1923, Cuba.
Poet, critic.

The one feminine member of the transcendentalist group of poets speaking through the journal *Origenes,* Garcia Marrúz generally wrote free verse and often a very original line though she did not eschew the traditional alexandrine and the pentatonic sonnet. In general she was a neo-classicist, subtile and delicate. Her criticism of poetry was knowing and skillful. She married the critic poet, Cintio Vitier. She has published four volumes of poetry, mostly on religious themes.

Writings: Poetry: *Poemas,* Havana, 1942; *Transfiguración de Jesús en el Monte,* Havana, 1947; *Visitaciones,* Havana, UNEAC, 1970; *Las miradas perdidas,* Havana, 1951, and poetry in various journals and collections, including Nathaniel Tarn, *Con Cuba.*

Critical Essays: "Lo exterior en la poesia," and one on José Marti, among others.

GARCIA PEREZ, Luis

b. 1832, Santiago, Cuba; d. October 2, 1893, Alvarado, State of Veracruz, Mexico.
Playwright.

An ardent patriot, Garcia Pérez lived much of his life in exile, either in the United States or in Mexico.

Writings: Play: *El grito de Yara* (4 acts, verse), New York, Hallet and Breen, 1879; and Vera Cruz, Tip. El Progresso, 1900.

GARCIA VEGA, Lorenzo

b. 1926, Cuba.
Poet, storywriter.

Garcia Vega enjoyed fantasy and these few lines from "Lima" may show his originality:

Conquistadores a zancadas en los almohadones
En Lima
los galápagos jardineros Verlaine las trompetas
lágrimosas
los surburbios de naranja las pirámides de sal
para trinchar la luna
. . . . . .

He is the director of the Centro de Investigaciones Literarias.

Writings: Poetry: *Suite para la espera,* Havana, 1948.

Stories: *Espirales del cuje,* Havana, 1952; *Cetreria del titere,* Santa Clara (Dept. of Cultural Relations), 1969.

Editor of: *Antologia de la novela cubana,* Havana, Dirección General de Cultura, 1960.

GARCIA TUDURI DE COYA, Mercedes

b. 1904, Cuba.
Poet.

Garcia's poetry was intimate, lyrical, often philosophical.

Her poetry, especially in the years before exile are metaphysical, probing searching for her identity, as in "Inquietud":

Y sueño a todas horas con la ignoto,
¡sueño, como sueña la dormida
fuente, con descifrar el gran secreto
del cielo azul que en mi interior se mira!

Since leaving Cuba after the advent of Castro, Garcia's poetry became more metaphorical, more symbolical.

Writings: Poetry: *Alas,* 1935; *Arcano,* 1947, both in Havana; *Ausencia,* Madrid, Progreso, 1968.

Biographical/Critical Sources: Polly F. Harrison, "Images and Exile: The Cuban Woman and Her Poetry," in *Revista Interamericana,* Vol. IV, No. 2 (Summer 1974), esp. pp. 208-211.

GARMENDIA, Miguel

b. 1862, Cuba; d. 19??.
Novelist.

Garmendia's only work of fiction *Sol de otoño* is in beautiful Spanish, delicate and sensitive.

Writings: Novels: *Almas perdidas,* published serially, in *Diario de Matanzas,* 1886; *Sol de otoño,* Havana, 1893.

GARRASTEGUI, Anagilda

b. October 8, 1932, San Sebastián, Puerto Rico.
Poet.

Garrástegui studied journalism at Madrid University (1954-1955) and has worked for the Autoridad Sobre Hogares de Puerto Rico. Much of her work first appeared in *Alma Latina, Universidad,* and *El Mundo.* Rabindranath Tagore and Gabriela Mistral have influenced her work which is short-lined, precise, very personal.

Writings: Poetry: *Desnudez,* 1956.
Essay: "Juan Ramón Jiménez," in *Revista Interamericana,* Vol. IV, No. 4 (Winter 1974/5), pp. 542-544.

GARRIDO, Victor

b. 1886, Dominican Republic.
Poet, storywriter.

Garrido's late romantic poetry, especially "Elegia blanca" and "Aria de Otoño" was extraordinarily popular. His sonnets and romances were also full of the new poetic currents.

Writings: Poetry: *Poesias completas, 1910-1953,* Buenos Aires, 1954.

GATON ARCE, Freddy

b. 1920, San Pedro de Macoris, Dominican Republic.
Poet, journalist, lawyer.

After local schooling, Gatón took a doctorate in Law at the University of Santo Domingo in 1946 and later became director of the School of Science of Public Information, vice-dean of the faculty of humanities at the University of Santo Domingo, and in 1970 became director of the daily paper *El Nacional de Ahora,* staying on until 1974.

In his early years he was one of the founders of the important literary movement finding expression in the review *La Poesia Sorprendida.* Manuel Rueda compares Gatón's long prose-poem *Vlia* to Aimé Cesaire's famous *Retour à mon pay natal* for their similar language, their strong emphases, and the associational leaps from subject to subject which are primarily connected by the emotional motifs. *Vlia* opens with these lines:

Los espacios aquietados, azules de enclavados astros,
dan su violeta a la torre invertida del cielo.
La torre,
extática, muda, salta nerviosa en sus risas y gemidos,
como mama tallada de virginidad. Cantar los gallos
espacia la vigilia y el mundo—noche de todos los donceles—.

Writings: Poetry: *Vlia,* Ciudad Trujillo, Ed. de La Poesia Sorprendida, No. IV, 1944; *La leyenda de la muchacha,* S. Domingo, Ed. El Caribe, 1952; *Poblana,* in *Revista de la USAD,* No. 1, dated May 1964, but published in 1965; and poems in various journals and collections including Gatón's *Antologia,* Ciudad Trujillo, 1952.

Biographical Criticism: *Franklyn Mieses Burgos,* S. Domingo, Postigo, 1952.

Biographical/Critical Sources: See introduction to Gatón's *Antologia,* Ciudad Trujillo, 1952; and critical essay, pp. 253-254, in M. Rueda's *Antologia. . . .,* Santiago de los Caballeros, UCMM, 1972, including his treatment of the Poesia Sorprendida group.

GAUTIER BENITEZ, José

b. November 12, 1851, Caguas, Puerto Rico; d. January 24, 1880.
Poet.

Son of the gifted minor poet Alejandrina Benitez de Gautier (d. 1879), and Don Rodulfo Gautier, Gautier Benitez studied at the Military Academy of Toledo in Spain. He eventually abandoned a military career (1865-1968) for a new one in politics on his return to Puerto Rico in 1869, his association being with the Partido Liberal Reformista. He wrote for the monthly journal *El Progreso* (1871-74) which he founded with Manuel Elzabura under the name "Gustavo" and from 1879 he often published his essays and articles in the *Revista Puertorriqueña* and other journals. Though he published widely in his time and has been of increasing interest to critics, his one collection, *Poesias,* put together the year of his death, was not published until 1929, 49 years later.

Writings: Poetry: *Poesias,* 1929; eight of his poems are in the *Antologia de la poesia puertorriqueña,* edited by Eugenio Fernández Méndez, San Juan, Ediciones "El Cemi," 1968; his popular "¡Puerto Rico!" is in the *Antologia puertorriqueña,* M. Fernández Juncos, New York, 1907. Also see the *Obra poética completa* (of Gautier), edited by Socorro Girón de Segura, Palma de Mallorca, 1960, and *Obras completas,* San Juan, Edit. Coqui, 197? and *José Gautier Benitez, vida y obra poética,* Rio Piedras, 1970; and *Selección: José Gautier Benitez,* San Juan, Inst. de Cultura Puertorriqueña, 1960.

Biographical/Critical Sources: Essay on Gautier by Cesáreo Rosa-Nieves, in *Ensayos escodigos,* San Juan, 1970, pp. 53-65, with good bibliography; Francisco J. Am, "José Gautier Benitez," in *Predicar en desierto,* San Juan, 1907, p. 236; Eugenio Astol, "Hombres del pasado—José Gautier Benitez," in *El libro de Puerto Rico,* San Juan, 1923, pp. 1008-1010; José A. Balseiro, "Gautier Benitez y el espiritu de su época," in *El Vigia,* Madrid, Edit. Mundo Latino, 1925, Vol. I, pp. 143-204; Balseiro'a "Nuevas notas sobre Gautier Benitez," in *Hispania,* California, Vol. XIII, No. 6 (December 1930), pp. 485-496; Alfredo Collado Martell, "José Gautier Benitez, el Gustavo Adolfo Bécquer de la lirica puertorriqueña," in *Gautier Benitez, José, Poesias,* San Juan, 1955, pp. 37-49; Sotero Figueroa, "Jose Gautier Benitez," in *Ensayo biográfico,* Ponce, P.R., Tip. El Vapor, 1888, pp. 253-262; Socorro Girón de Segura, *Epistolas de José Gautier Benitez,* Madrid, 1956; Manuel Siaca Rivera, "José Gautier Benitez," in *Asomante,* Year I, No. 4 (October-December 1945), pp. 79-92; Mario Braschi's "¡En el infinito! A La Memoria del Melogrado Poeta Puertorriqueña D. José Gautier Benitez," in *Antologia puertorriqueña,* M. Fernández Juncos, New York, 1st ed., 1907, pp. 186-191: Miriam Curet Cuevas, "La poesia de José Gautier Benitez," unpublished M.A. thesis, U. of P.R., date unknown; F. Manrique Cabrera, in *Historia de la literatura puertorriqueña,* Rio Piedras, 1909, pp. 127-137. Also see *José*

Gautier Benitez; vida y obra poética, Rio Piedras, Edit. Edil, 1970 (contains the collected poems of Gautier and critical studies on him by Rosa-Nieves, Manuel Giménez, Manuel Elzabura, and Alfredo Collado Martell).

GAY CALBO, Enrique

b. 1889, Holguin, Cuba.
Playwright, lawyer, historian.

Primarily a historian, Gay Calbó wrote two plays and one study of Cuban literature.

Writings: Plays: *El ayer; Era un cazador,* Cienfuegos, 1913.
Literary History: *Origenes de la literatura cubana,* Havana, 1939.
Histories: *La intromisión norteamericano en Centro-America,* 1922; *La América indefensa,* 1925; *El ideario politico de Varela,* 1936; *El Padre Varela en las Cortes españolas de 1822-1823,* 1937; *Ciudadania y extranjeria,* 1937; *Nuestro problema constitucional,* 1936; *El momento constitucional,* 1937; *El cubano, a vestruz del trópico,* 1938; *Arango y Parreño,* 1938; *Isla de Pinos, belga,* 1942, all in Havana.

Biographical/Critical Sources: Max Henriquez Ureña, *Panorama histórico de la literatura cubana,* New York, 1963, pp. 305-306.

GAZTELU, Angel

b. 1914, Navarra, Spain.
Poet, priest.

Arriving in Cuba as an adolescent, Gáztelu studied at the Seminario de San Carlos y San Ambrosio and entered priestly orders in 1938. He was a friend of the leading transcendentalist poet José Lezama Lima from 1932 on. Though he employed a wide range of metrical patterns and line lengths, he often favored the classical alexandrine as in his "Nocturnos," which has such lines as:

Nada se escucha. Oh soledad de siempre.
Oh seguro regazo del patio y de la casa.
Un tañido del aire recorre lo verde
y vibra en la penumbra como una
campaña.

His "Oración y meditación de la noche shows the long swing of his more original lines as this fragment may demonstrate:

Un comienzo de aurora por la luz
de tu rostro rompe el centro del alma,
y me siento invadido todo de una
caudalosa avenida de música,
toda iluminada, oh amor, por las claras
vihuelas de tus infantes de espumas.
Oh divina lumbrarada. Cómo por cantar
tu nombre, madrugan los trinos,
se incendian las fuentes de fanales y de
liricos halos las campañas,
Yo sé que toda la hermosura del campo
sueña a la sombra de tu gracia,
sé que por ti se ilumina el aire y se
esclarece el agua;

Writings: Poetry: *Poemas,* published as one of the *Espuela de Plata* pamphlets of the Lezama Lima group, Havana, 1940; *Gradual de laudes,* Havana, 1955.

Biographical/Critical Sources: Max Henriquez Ureña, *Panorama histórico de la literatura cubana,* New York, 1963, pp. 436-437.

GEIGEL POLANCO, Vicente

b. 1904, Isabela, Puerto Rico.
Poet, biographer, essayist, editor, lawyer.

After local schooling Géigel took a law degree at the University of Puerto Rico. He was active in political and cultural circles, becoming president of the Ateneo Puertorriqueño and occupying the chair of Law and Social Sciences at the University of Puerto Rico. He helped found the seminal review, *Indice* (1929-1931), with Antonio S. Pedreira and Samuel R. Quiñones. His work appeared in such journals as *Asomante, Faro, Vótice, Hostos, Puerto Rico Ilustrado, La Democracia* and *El Mundo.*

He edited several collections of essays

and was for a considerable period Puerto Rico's Procurador General. At the university he founded with Rosa-Nieves and others the movement "Noismo" influenced by Marinetti's "Futurismo" and Tristán Tzara's "Dada." His total literary work was relatively scant because of the pressures of his public and legal careers.

Writings: Poetry: *Palabras de nueva esperanza,* San Juan, 1969 (114 pages); *Baja el signo de Géminis; poemas de ayer y de hoy,* 1963; *Canto de Tierra adentro,* 1965, *Canto del amor infinito,* 1962. Poems in various journals; see especially "Salutación Noísta," dedicated to Pauline Uzcudun of Spain (published in *Gráfico de Puerto Rico*, Valores de Puerto Rico, San Juan, 1943).

Editor of: Essay collections: *El despertar de un pueblo,* 1942 (popular philosophical articles); and *Valores de Puerto Rico,* 1943 (essays and biographies).

Bibliography: *Bibliografia puertorriqueña 1892-1894,* details unknown.

GERENA BRAS, Gaspar

b. March 12, 1909, Puerto Rico.
Poet, journalist, musical composer, lawyer.

Editor from 1926-1929 of the weekly *Excélsior* on his own press, Gerena published his work in that journal and in *Alma Latina, La Revista Blanca* and *Puerto Rico Ilustrado.* His verse is fluent, melodious, often concerned with love.

Writings: Poetry: *Mientras muere la tarde, 1929; Trilogia lirica; Aljibe, Los sonetinos del mar, Las cenizas tienen, alas,* San Juan, 1969.

GINES, Teodora

b. ca. 1550, Santiago de los Caballeros, Dominican Republic.
Folk-singer.

Teodora and her sister Micaela were of African race and their songs became widely popular in the Spanish islands. Accompanying themselves on various instruments and singing in the local creole they adapted and invented new folksongs into their repertoire which quickly and permanently entered the folk literature of both Dominica and Cuba. Both sisters had gone to Santiago, Cuba in 1580 or so and Micaela is known to have gone on to Havana and still to have been living in 1598.

Teodora's "Tonada de la Má Teodora" is one of the earliest, still extant African influenced songs from the Americas and begins:

Dondé está la Má Teodora?
Rajando la leña está.
¿con su palo y su bandola?
Rajando la leña está
¿Dondé está que no la veo?
Rajando la leña está. . .

Writings: Song: "Tonada de la Má Teodora," in Las artes en Santiago de Cuba, collected and edited by Laureano Fuentes y Matons, Santiago de Cuba, 1893, and quoted and discussed in Max Henriquez Ureña's *Panorama histórico de la literatura dominicana,* S. Domingo, Postigo, 1965, pp. 122-123.

GIRO, Valentin

b. 1883, Dominican Republic; d. 1949.
Poet, critic.

Giro was one of the very early modernists, those influenced by the French symbolists whose work had only slowly come to be known in the Caribbean.

Writings: Poetry: *Ecos mundanos,* 1902; *Clemente,* 1908; *Oda a Lindbergh,* 1929; *Al Niágara,* 1939; and *Sinfonia heróica,* 1941: all in Santo Domingo.

Biographical-Critical Study: *Jacinto Dionisio Flores,* 1939.

Biographical/Critical Sources: Max Rodriquez Ureña's *Panorama historico de la literatura dominicana,* 2nd ed., S. Domingo, Postigo, 1965, pp. 249-252; Joaquin Balaguer's *História de la literatura dominicana,* 5th ed., S. Domingo, Postigo, 1970, pp. 250-254.

GLASS MEJIA, José Manuel

b. 1923, Santo Domingo, Dominican Republic.
Poet, journalist, radio show producer, teacher.

After schooling in Santo Domingo, including a degree in philosophy at the University of Santo Domingo, Glass became a teacher of philosophy and logic, and psychology at the National University of Pedro Henriquez Ureña.

One of the youngest members of the "La Poesia Sorprendida" group, Glass's early work was light and sprightly, but he moved away gradually to other kinds of work and began to contribute to Antonio Fernández Spencer's review *Entre las Soledades* in 1947.

Writings: Poetry: in various journals and anthologies, including ten poems in M. Rueda's *Antologia. . . .*, Santiago de los Caballeros, UCMM, 1972, pp. 403-411.

GOICO ALIX, Juan

b. 1891, Dominican Republic; d. 1958.
Poet.

Goico's poetic style is languid, paradisiacal, full of sighs and confessions.

Writings: Poetry: "Diálogo entre un dominicano y un haitiano," and collection, *Los poemas del insomnio,* S. Domingo, 1937.

GOMEZ COSTA, Arturo

b. 1896, Juana Diaz, Puerto Rico.
Poet, critic, editor.

Gómez Costa was a major contributor to the important cultural journal, the *Revista de las Antillas.* In the 1960's he became the Executive Director of the Puerto Rican Academy of Arts and Sciences. In poetry he was a minor figure in the modernismo movement.

One of the earliest modernistas, Gómez Costa's verse, form and style may be seen in tnese lines from "Sonata de amor," published in his 1918 collection *El Alcázar de Ariel:*

El rumor de mi fuente castalia,
el paisaje lunático y
el azur de tu sueño Onfalia:
era todo un motivo de Italia
un motivo muy lejos de aqui.

Although the poet-critic Laguerre finds him limited and his verse too closely derivative of Rubén Dario's work, many anthologies contain his poetry.

Writings: Poetry: *El Alcázar de Ariel,* San Juan, Editorial Cantero, Fernández, 1918; *Las luces en éxtasis (Poemas del Viejo San Juan, Capital de Puerto Rico); San Juan, Ciudad fantástica de América: Poemas, 1950-1956,* Barcelona, Edic. Rumbos, 1957.

Criticism: "Nuestra moderna literatura y la aparición de Oasis," in *Puerto Rico Ilustrado,* San Juan (September 4, 1915).

Biographical/Critical Sources: see Enrique Lefebre, "La poesia" in *Paisejes mentales,* San Juan, Cantero, Fernández, 1918, p. 17; *Almanaque Asenjo,* San Juan, Tip. La Idea, 1913, p. 56 and 60; Enrique Torres Rivera, *Parnaso puertorriqueño,* Barcelona, Spain, Imp. Maucci, 1920, pp. 295-299.

GOMEZ PINERO, Miguel

b. December 19, 1946, Gurabo, Puerto Rico.
Playwright, poet, actor.

Gómez was brought to New York early in life and grew up on the Lower East Side where he still lives and works with his friend and colleague Miguel Algarin. Almost completely self-educated, Gómez has written several plays and published much poetry, winning the New York Drama Critics Circle Award and the Obie (Off-Broadway), and in 1974-75, he was a nominee for the Antoinette Perry (Tony) Award.

An active member of the Actors Equity Association, the Dramatists Guild and the Authors League of America, Gómez' work is gradually drawing attention to his own talent and that of other Puerto Ricans working and writing for the Nuyorican Playwrights'/Actors' Workshop in New York.

GOMEZ DE AVELLANEDA, Gertrudis

(see **Gertrudis AVELLANEDA GOMEZ**)

GOMEZ DE READ, Ernestina

b. 1908, Dominican Republic.
Poet.

Gómez' *Canción de la noche* (1933) is very personal, even intense and sensual, at times sad and sentimental. Mota found this volume's most interesting poems to be "Sacrificio de Amor," "Oyendo la Khowanchina de Moussorgsky," and the best "Canciones de la Noche."

Her second collection, *Figuras de porcelana* (1936), is more harmonious, somewhat freer and more mature, but still passionate.

Writings: Poetry: *Figuras de porcelana,* 1936; *Canción de la noche,* 1933.

Biographical/Critical Sources: Chapter on Gómez in *Relieves alumbrados* by F. A. Mota Medrana, S. Domingo, 1971, pp. 249-260, with extensive quotations.

GONZALEZ, Ana H.

b. ca. 1901, Cuba.
Poet, storywriter, essayist.

As early as 1931 Gonzáles was publishing verse of the Afro-Cuban sort, including the "Romance negro del negro" which begins:

¡La igualidad entre los hombres!
Lenta voz enronquecida
y honda de tus hablares,
quiere morder los lamentos,
quiere tornarse en un grito
donde se guardan rebeldes
ansias de siglos y siglos

Since the early 1960's, González has lived in exile, mostly in the U. S. A. All of her new work continues to be concerned with the civil rights and cause of Afro-Americans.

Writings: Poetry: *Circulo poético,* Troy, 1971; *La sombra inusitado,* 1965.

GONZALEZ, Jorge Antonio

b. 1916, Cuba.
Playwright.

González' plays are generally satirical, especially his *Studio A* which pokes fun at the avant-garde novelists who he believed perverted the good sense of the public.

Writings: Plays: *Novela,* 1916, and *La arena esta entre el mar y las rocas,* 1947, both written with Carlos E. Sánchez; *Una mujer,* 1948; *Rick,* 1948; *Un hombre en un programa,* 1949; *Studio A.*

GONZALEZ, José Emilio

(or **Josemilio**)

b. 1918, Gurabo, Puerto Rico.
Poet, journalist, critic, teacher.

José González is a professor at the University of Puerto Rico. Rosa-Nieves in a review in *El Mundo* of *Profecia de Puerto Rico* (1954) by González wrote: ". . .caminando hacia adentro de la patria te encontrarás tu mismo, desaminando hacia afuera, te extrañarán en todas las latitudes y longitudes de la tierra. . ."

Writings: Poetry: *Profecia de Puerto Rico,* San Juan, 1954; three poems from *Profecia* are found in *Aguinaldo lirico,* C. Rosa-Nieves, ed., Rio Piedras, 1957, most verse is scattered in various journals. Also: *Soledad absoluta,* San Juan, Edit. Universitaria, 1972(?).

Literary Essays and History: *Los poetas puertorriqueños de la decada de 1930,* San Juan, 1960; *La poesia contemporánea de Puerto Rico, 1930-1960,* San Juan, 1972.

GONZALEZ, José Luis

b. March 8, 1926, Santo Domingo, Dominican Republic. (assoc. with Puerto Rico)
Storywriter, novelist.

Son of a Puerto Rican father and a Dominican mother, González lived in Guaynabo, Puerto Rico in his infant years, but removed to San Juan as a child. His schooling was in the Escuela Superior Central and in 1946 he earned a B. A. in modern languages and social sciences at the University of Puerto Rico. At the New School for Social Research in New York he took post-graduate work in social science (Ph.D. 1957). From 1950 to 1952 he was in Europe, much of it in Prague, and in 1953 he took a Masters and then a Ph.D. in Letters at the National University of Mexico. Later González occupied teaching posts at the University of Guanajuato and the National University of Mexico.

A convinced Marxist since 1943, González has sought Puerto Rican independence from the United States. He is considered one of the major reviewers of Puerto Rican short fiction with his sharply stated themes and social realism. His story collection *Cinco cuentos de sangre* won a prize from the Instituto de Literatura Puertorriqueña, 1946.

Writings: Stories: *En la sombra,* San Juan, Imp. Venezuela, 1943; *Cinco cuentos de sangre,* San Juan, Imp. Venezuela, 1945; *El hombre en la calle,* Editorial Bohique, Santurce, P. R., 1948; *El este lado,* Mexico, Los Presentes, 1954; *La galeria y otros cuentos,* Mexico, Biblioteca Era, 1972; "La Carta" from *El hombre en la calle,* and "En el fondo del caño hay un negrito," (translated by Paul Blackburn as "There's a little Negro at the bottom of the caño," *New World Writing,* 1958, pp. 125-128), and "El pasaje," both from *En Este lado,* are in *Cuentos Puertorriqueños de Hoy,* René Marqués, ed.; "Carta a un psiquitra," is in *Antologia del cuento hispanoamericano,* Ricardo Latcham, ed., Santiago de Chile, Zig-Zag, 1958, pp. 122-123.

Novel: *Paisa, un relato de la emigración,* 1st ed., 1950, Mexico, Fondo de Cultura, 2nd ed., rev., Mexico, Los Presentes, 1955.

Biographical/Critical Sources: René Marqués, ed., *Cuentos puertorriqueños de hoy,* Mexico, 1959, pp. 77-80; Carmen Alicia Cadilla, "Puertorriqueñidad del cuento de José Luis González," the introduction to González, *En la sombra;* Francisco Matos Paoli, "José Luis González cuentista del hombre commun," the introduction to *5 cuentos de sangre;* Luis Enrique Délano, "Luis González escritor y combatiente," in *Paisa;* Concha Meléndez, *El arte del cuento en Puerto Rico,* New York, 1961, pp. 291-298; F. Manrique Cabrera, *Historia de la literatura puertorriqueña,* Rio Piedras, 1969, pp. 320-324.

GONZALEZ, José Maria

b. July 6, 1830, Santo Domingo, Dominican Republic; d. August 5, 1863, Santo Domingo.
Poet, journalist, businessman.

Son of Ignacio González Infante and Francisca Santin Bustamante de Gonzáles, and brother of former President General Ignacio Maria González, the poet's liberal ideas were punished by then President Santana. He was forced to flee to St. Thomas where he wrote one of his best known poems "Un isleño desterrado (A su Amada)" in 1855. On return from exile, González entered commerce and was an editor of the anti-Santana journal *El Eco del Pueblo* for a short period ending in March 1857. During his remaining brief years he wrote no further verse.

Writings: Poetry: in various journals and collections including Castellanos' *Lira de Quisqueya* which contained "Un isleño desterrado" which appeared originally in *El Eco del Pueblo,* No. 31, S. Domingo, (March 28, 1857).

Biographical/Critical Sources: E. Rodriguez Demorizi's *Poesia popular dominicana,* 1938, 2nd ed., S. Domingo, UCMM, 1973, pp. 249-254.

GONZALEZ, Manuel Dionisio

b. 1815, Villaclara, Cuba; d. 1883.
Poet, playwright, historian, folklorist.

One of Cuba's earliest folklorists, González also published poetry and wrote at least three plays.

Writings: Folklore: *El indio de Cunabacón o las brujas de Peña Blanca* (legend), 1851.
History: *Memoria histórica de la villa de Santa Clara y su jurisdicción,* 1858.
Poetry: in various journals, including the poems "La infancia," and "Epistola a Miguel Gutiérrez."
Plays: all believed unpublished; *Sobre todo, mi dinero* (1 act, comedy); *Idealismo y realidad* (comedy); *El judio errante* (monologue).

GONZALEZ, Nicanor Aristides

b. 1843, Matanzas, Cuba; d. 1898.
Poet, playwright, journalist.

Gonzalez founded the literary journal *El Pensamiento* and published work in *La Libertad, El Diario de Matanzas,* and the *Revista de Cuba.*

Writings: Poetry: in various journals. One of his best works was "¡Olvidar!"
Play: *El éxito de un drama* (5 acts), Matanzas, Imp. Galeria Literaria, 1883.

GONZALEZ, Reynaldo

b. 1931, Cuba.
Storywriter, novelist.

González' collection of stories published in 1964 celebrates the events and heroes of the Castro-led revolution.

Writings: Stories: *Miel sobre hojuelas,* Havana, Revolución, 1964; "Four in a Jeep" appears in *Writers in the New Cuba,* E. M. Cohen, ed., Harmondsworth, England, Penguin, 1967.
Novel: *Siempre la muerte, su paso breve,* Havana, Casa de las Américas, 1968, 238 pages.

GONZALEZ ALBERTY, Fernándo

b. 1908, Yabucoa, Puerto Rico.
Poet.

A strong-voiced patriot, González announced his work to be ". . .el grito mozo de mi sonido trece en el pentagrama de la moderna estética." A member of the Atalayismo movement launched at the University of Puerto Rico in 1929, he was associated in the efforts to use poetry for the nationalistic purposes with Soto Vélez and others.

Writings: Poetry: *Grito, Polemario de Vanguardia,* San Juan, Editorial Atalaya de los Dioses, 1931.

GONZALEZ CARBO, Alfonso

b. June 28, 1901, Rio Piedras, Puerto Rico.
Poet, government official.

González' one volume of poetry reflects the postmodernist work of the 1920-40 period but bears traces of the early Rubén Dario dominated "modernismo" movement. Generally working in the sonnet form, González is considered by Rosa-Nieves to have created verse of ". . .una sana claridad de alba, y una mansa ondulación lirica." And he adds: "Es una poesia sin grandes pretensiones barrocas, ni brutales rebeldias estilisticas."

Writings: Poetry: *Sonetos de mi reino interior,* Mexico, 1946; poems in various journals and anthologies, including *Antologia de poetas contemporáneos de Puerto Rico,* Pedro Juan Labarthe, ed., Mexico, 1946; *Aguinaldo lirico de la poesia puertorriqueña,* C. Rosa-Nieves, ed., Rio Piedras, 1st ed., 1957; 2nd ed., 1971.

GONZALEZ GARCIA, Matias

b. December 9, 1866, Naguabo (Rio Blanco), Puerto Rico; d. 1938, Gurabo, Puerto Rico.
Storywriter, novelist, playwright, poet, journalist.

González Garcia attended school in Gurabo, Puerto Rico, but went to Spain for his B. A. and two following years of medical studies. Once at home again, he began to write seriously and with Zeno Gandia, he became an early naturalist of the Zola school. *La primera cria* (1892) was his first work, a short novel.

González was an active journalist and editor, associated with such reviews and newspapers as *El Buscapié, Revista Puertorriqueña de Literatura, Ciencias y Arte, La Ilustración Puertorriqueña, La Democracia, El Mundo,* and *Puerto Rico Ilustrado.* He was a leading member of the folklore group, the "costumbristas" and accordingly is known for his common use of Puerto Rican creole and his studies of local customs. His work is mildly naturalistic, occasionally humorous, even satirical in touches.

C. Rosa-Nieves finds these stories among his finest: "La Bruja," "La Semana Santa," "La primera cria,' "Los reyes," "Clavelin," "Las Cosas del Mundo," and "El Cuento de los difuntos."

Writings: Stories: *Mis cuentos,* 1899; *Cosas de Antaño y Cosas de Ogaño,* 2 vols., Caguas, 1918-1922; but most stories are uncollected from original publication in various journals.

Novelettes: *La primera cria,* San Juan, Boletin, 1892; *El escándalo,* San Juan, Tip. A. Córdova, 1894; *Cosas,* San Juan, Tip. A. Córdova, 1898; *Ernesto,* San Juan, Imp. El Buscapié (Special Issue), 1895; *Carmela,* San Juan, Heraldo Español (Special Issue), 1903, 2nd ed., San Juan, Editorial Puerto Rico Ilustrado, 1925, 3rd ed., San Juan, Edit. Coqui, 1938 and 1966; *El tesoro del Ausubal,* Caguas, Imp. Borinquin, 1913.

Critical Biography: *Morel campos,* 1922.

Plays: *Gritos de Angustia; Amor que vence; Por me tierra y por me dama* (performed 1929 at the Ateneo Puertorriqueño: all in ms. only).

Biographical/Critical Sources: Cesáreo Rosa-Nieves, "Matias González Garcia, El costumbrista," in *Ensayos escogidos,* San Juan, 1970, pp. 117-119; Concepción Cuevas de Marcano, *Matias González Garcia: Vida y obra,* San Juan, Edit. Coqui, 1966; F. Manrique Cabrera, in *Historia de la literatura puertorriqueña,* Rio Piedras, 1969, pp. 200-202; and see *Indice* journal, No. 7 (San Juan, October 13, 1929), p. 99, for biographic data.

GONZALEZ (or GONZALO) MARIN, Francisco

(see under pseudonym: **PACHIN MARIN**)

GONZALEZ DEL VALLE, José Zacharias

b. 1820, Cuba; d. 1851.
Novelist, poet, philosopher, essayist, teacher.

A philosopher, González travelled widely and with his brother Manuel, was a member of the most modern and scientific group in Havana. Both were influenced by the French thinker, Victor Cousin.

His poetry was published in miscellaneous journals and collected in *Tropicales* (1842) and his elegy for his lost love and fiancée Adelaida Alonso y Renté (the Alaida of the poem) was *Guirnaldo fúnebre* (1844). His novelettes of no particular distinction appeared in various journals and were works of his youth.

Writings: Stories: in various journals, uncollected: including "Luisa" (novelette), "Recuerdos del colera," "Carmen y Adela," "Amor y dinero."
Travel: *Viajes por Europa,* 1842.
Poetry: *Tropicales,* 1841; *Guirnaldo fúnebre,* 1844.
Philosophy: *Breves explicaciones con motivo de algunos pasajes de Aristóteles,* 1839; *Rasgos históricos de la filosofia,* 1840; "Filosofia en la Habana," in *La Cartera Cubana* (Havana, 1839); *Consideraciones sobre el placer y el dolor,* Havana, 1855; *Elogio,* Havana, 1861.
Science: *Lecciones elementales de meteorologia. . .,* 1849.
Novelettes: *Luisa; Recuerdas del cólera; Carmen y Adela; Amor y desamor; Amor y morir;* and others—all published in various Cuban journals, 1838-42.

Biographical/Critical Sources: Max Henriquez Ureña, *Panorama histórica de la literatura cubana,* New York, 1963; Anselmo Suárez y Romero, *Colección de articulos,* 1859 (has critical essay on González del Valle and others of his near contemporaries); Ramón Meza, *Los González del Valle,* Havana, 1911.

GONZALEZ DE CASCORRO, Raúl

b. June 13, 1922, Cascorro (Province of Camagüez), Cuba.
Storywriter, poet, playwright, novelist.

Educated in Cuba, González' work is well regarded, his story "La Cadena" winning the Premio Nacional de Cuentos Hernández Catá in 1952 and his "Un Centavo de Sol para su Alma" was a winner of a competition organized by *El Nacional* in Mexico in 1954.

Writings: Stories: *Cincuenternario y otros cuentos,* 1952; *Vidas sin Domingo,* 1956; *La Semilla,* Havana, Revolución, 1960; *Gente de Playa Girón,* 1st ed., Havana, Casa de las Américas, 1962 and Havana, Casa de las Américas, 1973.
Poetry: *Motivo,* 1954.
Plays: *Arboles sin raices* (first mention in Concurso Luis de Soto, 1958), Santa Clara, Departamento de Relaciones Culturales, Universidad Central de las Villas, 1960; *El mejor fruto,* premiered 1960; and *Regreso a la raiz; Piezas de museo,* Havana, Ponciano, 1959.
Novel: *Concentración pública,* Havana, Unión, 1962; *La semilla,* Havana, Eds. R., 1965.

Biographical/Critical Sources: Salvador Bueno, *Antologia del Cuento de Cuba (1902-1952),* Havana, 1953, pp. 371-378.

GOVANTES, José Joaquin

b. ca. 1830, Havana; d. 1881, Guanabocoa.
Playwright, journalist, poet, essayist.

Govantes was an editor for *El Aguinaldo Habanero* and *La Aurora* and founded the Spanish-language journal *La Voz de la Patria* in New York City.

Writings: Plays: *Una vieja como hay muchas* (1 act, verse comedy), Havana, La Intrépida, 1865.
Poetry: *Poesias,* date unknown.
Essays: *Horas de amargura,* 1865.

GRANADOS, Manuel

b. 1931, Cuba.
Novelist, poet.

Granados' novel *Adire y el tiempo roto* is one of the new socialist novels written from the Afro-Cuban point of view and with an Afro-Cuban central character.

Writings: Novels: *Adire y el tiempo roto,* Havana, Casa de las Américas, 1967; *El viento en la casa-sol,* Havana, Unión, 1970.
Poetry: *El orden presentido,* Havana, El Puente, 1962.

GRAU ARCHILLA, Raúl

b. October 10, 1910, Toa Alta, Puerto Rico.
Poet.

Grau Archilla took his B. A. at the University of Puerto Rico, and early began to submit verse to local journals. Three volumes of the collected work have appeared so far of this vanguardist poet.

Rosa-Nieves says of his verse, "La suya es poesia neoromántica de sereno fluir, cargado de azules, de sueños, de perfumados nombres de mujer, y de paisaje intimista. . ."

Writings: Poetry: *Noche, Tu Poema,* San Juan, 1952; *Vértigo de la nube,* Mexico, 1954; *Golondrina,* Madrid, 1956.

GUELL Y RENTE, José

b. 1818, Cuba; d. 1884, Madrid.
Poet, playwright, novelist.

Güell's *Anacaona* and *Guacanagari* were, along with J. Joaquin Pérez' *Fantasias indigenas* (1877) and F. M. del Monte's play *Ozema o La virgén indiana* (1867), two of the earliest Latin American works to treat the Indians.

Writings: Poetry: *Guacanagari*; *Anacaona.*

Play: *Don Carlos* (5 acts), Barcelona, López, Rambla del Centro, No. 20, 1883.

Novels and Novelettes: *Gua canajari, rey de Marién,* Madrid, 1855 (44 pp.); *Lágrimas del corazón,* Madrid, Alonso, 1848 (129 pp.); *Leyendas del alma triste,* Paris, M. Lévy, 1860 (278 pp.); *Nieta de rey* [legends], Paris, Impr. de Claye, 1858; *La virgen de las azucenas* [legends], Madrid, Las Novedades, 1858 (136 pp.).

Biographical/Critical Sources: Fermin Peraza, *Diccionario biográfico cubano.*

GUERRA MONDRAGON, Miguel

b. September 29, 1880, San Juan, Puerto Rico; d. April 9, 1947, San Juan, P. R.
Essayist, critic, lawyer.

Considered Puerto Rico's leading critic of the "modernista" school, Guerra studied in Spain and the United States, returning to his island nation to practice law. He early associated himself with Luis Lloréns Torres and Nemesio R. Canales, and though he was thoroughly familiar with Spanish classical prosody he also sought to learn from British and American poets as well. He translated Oscar Wilde and did much critical writing on the newest Anglo-Saxon poets, including Michael Strange, Alan Seeger, and the Anglo-American group of imagists led by Ezra Pound and later by Amy Lowell.

Working on such new journals as *Juan Bobo* (later *Idearium*), and *Revista de las Antillas,* Guerra became the leading spokesman for change and he attacked the overly conservative habits and styles of many of his contemporaries. His own prose is elegant and precise.

Writings: Literary History: "San Juan de Puerto Rico, su movimiento literario," in *Revista de las Antillas,* San Juan (June 1914).

Journalism: in *Indice* (an editorial), San Juan, Vol. I, No. 1 (April 23, 1929); "¿Qué Somos? ¿Cómo somos?" and "Colaboran en este número," San Juan, Vol. I, No. 2 (May 13, 1929).

Critical Biography: *Oscar Wilde,* San Juan, Biblioteca Américana, 1914.

Critical Essays: "Desfile romántico," in *Revista de las Antillas,* San Juan (May 1914); *El critico como artista* (on Oscar Wilde), 1914; "El poeta," his preface to *Bronces* (verse collection of A. Pérez Pierret), 1914; many essays in journals, uncollected; his essay "El lirio de los valles," first appearing in *Revista de las Antillas* (May 1913), was republished in L. Hernández Aquino's *El Modernismo en Puerto Rico,* San Juan, 1967, pp. 145-149.

Biographical/Critical Sources: F. Manrique Cabrera, *Historia de la literatura puertorriqueña,* Rio Piedras, 1969, pp. 264-265; Socrates Nolasco, *Escritores de Puerto Rico,* Manzanilla, Cuba, 1953.

GUERRERO, Teodoro

b. 1820, Havana, Cuba; d. 1905.
Playwright, storywriter, novelist.

Today Guerrero's work is of only historical interest.

Writings: Stories: *Cuentos de salón,* details unknown.

Plays: *Está en duda* (comedy), Havana, 1845; *Siglo XVIII y siglo XIX* (1 act comedy), Madrid, Repullés, 1851; *Carlos Broschi* (3 acts, verse farce, music by Joaquin Espin Guillen), Madrid, Operarios, 1853; *Los jardines del Buen Retiro* (3 acts, verse farce), Madrid, Rodriguez, 1854; *Tales padres tales hijos* (1 act, comedy verse), Madrid, Rodriguez, 1854; *La escala del poder* (3 acts), Madrid, Rodriguez, 1855; *Fea y pobre* (3 acts, comedy), Madrid, T. Fortanet, 1857; *La cabeza y el corazón* (3 acts, verse comedy), Havana, Imp. del Gobierno, 1861; 2nd ed., Madrid, Rodriguez, 1871; *La filosofia del vino* (Fábulas en acción), Madrid, 1874; *Sermon perdido* (1 act), Madrid, Rodriguez, 1874; *Fábulas en acción (Cuadritos dramáticos en verso),* Madrid, Tello, 1887, containing the following works: *La filosofia del vino* (1 act); *El valor del tiempo* (1 act); *Un minuto de olvido* (1 act); *La lógica del duelo* (1 act); *La educación de la mujer* (1 act); *El dinero y la hermosura* (1 act), and others.

Novel: *Entre dos amores,* San Juan, Edit. Boletin Mercantil, 1900.

GUILLEN, Nicolás

b. July 10, 1902, Camagüey, Cuba.
Poet, biographer, folklorist, playwright, journalist.

Son of a father (Nicolás Guillén Urra) murdered by Spanish soldiers, and Argelia Batista Arrieta, the young Guillén lived a childhood of poverty and acute suffering. He finished high school and went onto Havana in 1930 to study law at the university, but his poverty forced him to abandon a legal career. He then worked as a typographer, journalist, editor and state employee. He edited the journal *Mediodia* and was a founder of the Sociedad des Estudios Afrocubanos. As early as 1920-21 he was a contributor of verse to the poetry review *Castalia* and he has published in scores of journals since, including *Suplemento Literario* (of *Diario de la Marina*), *Orbe* and others.

Guillén's pioneering interest in Afro-Cuban culture led him to create many works in the *son,* a particular Cuban popular song form derived from African folklore and music. His long unpublished collection of 46 erotic-mystical poems in many metrical forms "Cerebro y corazón," originally written in 1922, shows more of what was to become his life-long preoccupation—the picturing of common lives and the use of his poetry as a protest against class and race barriers to a decent life. His poem "Capricho" has these typical lines:

> *La barca azul de mi ilusión navega*
> *como si fuera un cisne sobre un lago*

which also reflects a strain of a residual

"European" consciousness.

Possibly Guillén's best known volumes, *Motivos de son* (1930) and *Sóngoro cosongo* (1931) are, with Alejo Carpentier's early work, the major efforts to bring Afro-Cuban culture into the main-stream of Cuba's literature.

Motivos de son appeared to his contemporaries almost as a supernatural event, deeply welling up from the subconscious and with the old rhythms and old memories of the sounds of the rural world. The subjects are not usually political—and were quickly accepted as set to music by Garcia Caturla and Amadeo Roldán.

The popular poem "Yambambo" from *Sóngoro Cosongo* begins:

Repica el congo solongo
repica el negro bien negro;
congo solongo del Songo,
bailá yambó sobre un pie,
Mama tomba
serembe cuserembá

and the poem ends:

Tamba, tamba, tamba, tamba
tamba del negro que tumba
tumba del negro caramba,
caramba que el negro tumba.
Yamba, yambó Yambambé.

In 1936 he was arrested along with other editors and contributors to the anti-fascist journal *Mediodía* (Juan Marinello, José Portuondo, Carlos Rafael Rodriguez, Jorge Rijol, Edith Garcia Buchaca, Aurora Villar Bucata, Carlos Montenegro, and Angel Augier). Only Guillén, however, was imprisoned during the trial but even he was found innocent of the charges of "subversive propaganda and pornography."

In the same year (1936), Guillén was Cuban representative to the First International Congress of Writers for the Defense of Culture, meeting in Barcelona, Valencia, and Madrid, Spain, with Juan Marinello, Félix Pitá Rodriguez and Alejo Carpentier. In Spain, then undergoing the fascist attack of Franco, Guillén met such world famous writers as Hemingway, Malraux, René Maran, Leon Feuchtwanger, Alexis Tolstoy, Langston Hughes, Pablo Neruda, César Vallejo and others. He then visited Venezuela, Colombia, Peru, Chile, Argentina, and Brazil, being warmly received everywhere. Details of this trip are in Augier's second biographic volume on Guillén (1964).

Guillén attended the Congress of the League of Revolutionary Writers and Artists (LEAR) in Mexico in 1937, the Second International Congress of Writers for the Defense of Culture in Valencia and Barcelona, Spain in 1938, and many other international conferences of like nature. Becoming a communist in 1937, he unsuccessfully ran for public office (mayor) of Camagüez in 1942 on the Communist Party ticket. In 1953 he was awarded the Stalin Prize and in 1961 he was laureled as "Poeta Nacional," the year he also became president of UNEAC (the Union of Cuban Writers), an organization of which he remained president as late as 1975.

He has continued to edit many journals, including *La gaceta de Cuba,* UNEAC's organ, and *Unión.* Since Castro's rise to power in 1959, Guillén has represented Cuba at many cultural and diplomatic meetings abroad.

Guillén has written two works for the theatre, *Poema con niños* (1943), an attack on racism in Cuba, and *Floripondito o Los fiteres son personas,* a farce (1951).

Writings: Poetry: *Sóngoro cosongo (poemas mulatos),* Havana 1930; *Motivos de son,* 1st ed., Havana, Rambla y Bouza, 1931, and later as *El son entero,* Buenos Aires, 1947; *West Indies Ltd.,* Havana, Ucar, Garcia y cia, 1934, and in Italian translation by Antonino Tullier, Rome, Cuoma, 1962; *Espagna, poema en cuatro angustias y una esperanza,* Valencia, Spain, 1937, 2nd ed., Mexico, Edit. Mexico Nuevo, 1937; *Sonas por turistas y Cantos para soldados,* Mexico, Masas,

1937; *Sóngoro cosongo y otras poemas de Nicolás Guillén*, Havana, Edit. "La Verónica," 1942, 1943; *El son entero; suma poética, 1929-1946* (musical text by Eliseo y Emilio Grenet, Alejandro Garcia Caturla and Silvestre Revueltas, Buenos Aires, Edit. Pleamar, 1947; *Elegia a Jacques Roumain en el cielo de Haiti*, Havana, Impr. Ayon, 1948; *La paloma de vuelo popular, Elegias*, Buenos Aires, Losada, 1948, 1958, English translation as *Cuba Libre* (selections from *El son entero*), by Langston Hughes and Ben Frederic Carruthers, Los Angeles, The Ward Ritchie Press, 1948, and Buenos Aires, Losada, 1959; *Elegia a Jesús Menéndez*, Havana, Páginas, 1951, and Havana, Imp. Nacional de Cuba, 1962; *Cantos para soldados y sonas para turistas, El son entero*, Buenos Aires, Losada, 1952, 1957; *Chansons cubaines et autres poèmes* (bi-lingual ed.) translated into French by Claude Couffon, Paris, Seghers, 1955; *Elégies et chanson cubaines*, Paris, Seghers, 1959; *Sus mejores poemas*, Lima, Peru, Talleres Gráficos Torres Aguirre, 1959(?); *Antologia poética*, edited and translated by Ary de Andrade, Rio de Janeiro, Leitura, 1961; *Poemas para el Che 196?, Poemas de amor*, preface by Angel Augier, Havana, La Tertulia, 1964; *Antologia major*, 1964; *El gran zoo*, Havana, Unión, 1968, Madrid, El Bardo, 1969; and in René Depestre's French translation as *Le grand zoo*, Paris, Seghers, 1967. *El gran zoo* is also in Robert Márquez' edited and translated *Patria o muerte: The Grand Zoo and Other Poems by Nicolás Guillén*, New York, October House, 1972. Robert Márquez and David Arthur McMurray (translators and editors), *Man-Making Words. Selected Poems of Nicolás Guillén*, Amherst, University of Massachusetts Press, 1972; *Buenos dias, Fidel*, Mexico, Gráfica Horizonte, 1959; *Sus mejores poemas*, Lima, Org. Continental de los Festivales del Libro, 1959; *Antologia poética*, Rio de Janeiro, Leiture, 1961 (in Portuguese); *Canti cubani*, Roma, Rinuiti, 1961, edited by Dario Puccini; *Los mejores versos de Nicolás Guillén*, Buenos Aires, *Nuestra América*, 1961; *¿Puedes?* 2nd ed., Havana, La Tertulia, 1961; *Balada*, Havana, 1962; *Poesias*, Havana, Comisión Nacional Cubana de la UNESCO, 1962; *El son entero, Cantos para soldados y sones para turistas*, 4th ed., Buenos Aires, Losada, 1968. Miscellaneous: *Cerebro y corazón*, written Camagüey, but not published until 1965 as appendix to Angel Augier's biography on Guillén (see below); *Ballad of the Ancestors—Sensemayà*; two poems translated by Sangodare Akanji, in *Black Orpheus* magazine, No. 3, Ibadan (May 1958); *Tengo*, 1st ed., Santa Clara, Cuba, Consejo Nacional de Universidades, 1964; 2nd ed., Montevideo, in *El Siglo Ilustrado*, 1967; "El jarron," "En China," "Primero de Octubre en Pekin," "Voy hasta Ujian," "Wu Sang Kuei," composed after trip to China; "Angels Davis," in Márquez and McMurray, *Man-Making Words*, (op. cit.); and poems in Ramón Guirao's *Orbita de la poesia afrocubana 1928-37*, Havana, 1938. Also see *La poesia de Nicolás Guillén*, Madrid, 1971 and *Summa poética*, edited by Luis Iñigo Madrigal, Madrid, Cátedra, 1976 (299 pp.).

Essays: *Prosa de prisa; crónicas*, Santa Clara, Universidad Central de Las Villas, 1962; and Buenos Aires, Edit. Hernández, 1963.

Biography: *Claudio José Domingo Brindis de Salas. Rey de las Octavas. Apuntes Biográficos*, Havana, Cuadernos de Historia Habanera, Municipio de la Habana, 1935.

Plays: *Poema con niños* (one act), 1943; *Floripondito o Los fiteres son personas*, (farce), 1951.

Collection: *Antologia mayor*, Mexico, Diogénes, 1972.

Biographical/Critical Sources: Dennis Sardinha's *The Poetry of Nicolás Guillén, an Introduction*, London, New Beacon Books, 1976(?) offers a rare English study; Angel Augier, *Nicolás Guillén. Notas para un estudio biográfico critico*, Havana, 1965, 1968, in two vols., 1st ed., Santa Clara, Edición de la Universidad de Las Villas, 1964; Nancy Morejon, ed., *Recopilación de textos sobre Nicolás Guillén*, Havana, Casa de las Américas, 1974; Ildefonso Pereda Valdés, *Lo negro y lo mulato en la poésia cubana*, Montevideo, Uruguay, Edicion Ciudadela, 1970; Cuellar Vizcaino, "El Guillén que usted no conoce," in Pereda Valdes, (op. cit.); Ezequiel Martinez-Estrada, *La poesia afrocubana de Nicolás Guillén*, Montevideo, Edit. ARCA, 1966; Janheinz Jahn, *Neo-African Literature*, New York, Evergreen, 1968; Robert Márquez, "Introducción a Guillén," in *Casa de Las Américas*, XI, 65-66 (March-June 1971), pp. 136-142, originally published as preface to

Patria o muerte: The Great Zoo and Other Poems; also see Márquez' introduction to *Man-Making Words,* New York, 1972. Alfred Melón, "Guillén: poeta de la síntesis," Unión, No. 4, 9th year (December 1970), pp. 96-132. J.A. George Irish's "Nicolás Guillén's Position on Race: A Reappraisal" in *Revista Interamericana,* Vol. VI, No. 3 (Fall, 1976); Claude Couffon's critical-bibliographical study in her *Nicolás Guillén,* Paris, Seghers, 1964; Wilfred Cartey, "Three Antillan Poets: Emilio Ballagas, Luis Palés Matos, and Nicolás Guillén. "Literary Development of the Negro Theme in Relation to the Making of Modern Afro-Antillean Poetry and the Historic Evolution of the Negro," unpublished Ph.D. diss. Columbia University, 1965; other dissertations: Florence E. White, "Poesia negra in the Works of Jorge de Lima, Nicolás Guillén, and Jacques Roumain, 1927-1947," University of Wisconsin, 1952; Joseph R. Farrell, "Nicolás Guillén: Poet in Search of Cubanidad," Univ. of Southern California, 1968; Mary Castan de Pontrelli, "The Criollo Poetry of Nicolás Guillén," Yale, 1958. Also see Alejo Carpentier, *La música en Cuba,* Mexico, Fondo de Cultura Económica, 1946; Angel Augier, "The Cuban Poetry of Nicolás Guillén," in *Phylon,* XII (1951); Fernándo Ortiz, *La africania de la musica folklórica de Cuba,* Havana, Publicaciones del Ministro de Educacción, Dirección de Cultura, 1950; and Max Henriquez Ureña, *Panorama histórico de la literatura cubana,* New York, 1963, pp. 378-382. Also see Frederick S. Stimson's *The New Schools of Spanish American Poetry,* Valencia, 1970, for chapter on Guillén, and E. J. Mullen's "Nicolás Guillén and Carlos Pellicer: A Case of Literary Parallels," in *Latin American Literary Review,* Vol. III (Spring-Summer), pp. 78-87. Also, Carlos Cortinez' review of collection *Summa poetica,* edited by Luis Iñigo Madrigal in *World Literature Today* (Spring 1977), pp. 253-254; Jorge Maria Ruscalleda Barcedóniz, *La poesia de Nicolás Guillén,* Rio Piedras, Edit. Universitaria, 1975 which has a good biographical introduction.

GUIRA, Dysis

b. 1929, Cuba.
Playwright.

Guira's first play, *Liberación de Romeo,* has Shakespeare's eternal lover bored with his role in Verona and seeking a quiet life elsewhere. Her play, *Tierra,* based on the work of Marti's "Los zapaticos de rosa," is set in the country and is felt to be less than a success. The plays are conceived in poetic terms, in structure and diction and represent a turning away from the naturalistic theatre of the past two decades.

Writings: Plays: *Liberación de Romeo,* 1952; *Tierra,* 1955.

GUIRAO, Ramón

b. 1908, Havana, Cuba; d. 1949.
Poet, storywriter.

Guirao was one of the first to employ Afro-Cuban speech in his work. His "Bailadora de rumba" was possible the first of the Afro-Cuban poems ever to be published in Cuba (1928). He contributed to *Revista-Avance 1927,* edited by Jorge Mañach, Juan Marinello and Francisco Ichaso. Guirao's version of a popular poem from folklore, "Canto para Matar Culebras" republished in his *Orbita de la poesia afrocubana* (1938) begins:

— *¡Mamita, mamita!*
Yen, yen, yen.
¡Culebra me pica!
    Yen, yen, yen.
¡Culebra me come!
    Yen, yen, yen.
¡Me pica, me traga!
    Yen, yen, yen.

which is the first of six in a conversation between a "Negrita" and a "Diablito."

Writings: Poetry: *Bongó,* Havana, 1934; *Poemas,* introduction by Alberto Baeza Flores, published San Rafael de Mendoza, Argentina, Ed. Brigadas Liricas, 1947; "Bailadora de rumba," was first published in *Diario de la Marina* (April 1928).

Editor of: *Orbita de la poesia afrocubana, 1928-37,* Havana, 1938.

GUITERAS, Eusebio

b. ca. 1870, Cuba; d. before 1903.
Novelist.

Guiteras' two novels are considered fairly interesting by Max Henriquez Ureña. *Irene Albar* (1895) is still redolent of the 18th century in its obvious reflection of the style and thinking of J. J. Rousseau.

Writings: Novels: *Irene Albar,* Barcelona, 1895; *Gabriel Reyes,* published posthumously in *Cuba y América,* 1903.

GUTIERREZ, Garcia

b. ca. 1806, Cuba.
Playwright.

Gutiérrez was one of the earliest of Cuban playwrights.

Writings: Plays: *El trovador,* 1836; *Don Pedro de Castilla,* 1836.

HENRIQUEZ, Rafael Américo (a.k.a. **"Puchungo"**)

b. 1899, Santo Domingo, Dominican Republic; d. 1968.
Poet.

Originally a member of the"Postumista" group, he was the son of Enrique Henriquez, one of the most romantic of the Dominican poets. Rafael became a leader of the group writing "poesia sorprendida" with Fabio Fiallo and Max Henriquez Ureña. He mixed modern motives with archaic expressions in his later work and was imaginative and sensual, reflecting to some degree Garcia Lorca and Gabriel Miró. Little of his work was published and no volume ever appeared except *Rosa de Tierra* (1949). That prose-poem is given in toto in M. Rueda's *Antologia.*

Writings: Poetry: *Rosa de Tierra (poema).* Santo Domingo, Ediciones de la Poesia Sorprendida, 1944. Some poems also in Manuel Rueda's *Antologia,* Santiago, UCMM, 1972 with critical notes, pp. 131-162, and including "Voz" and "Partes de Biografia," formerly unpublished but offered to Rueda for his collection by Henriquez Américo himself.

HENRIQUEZ URENA, Max

(pseudonym: **Hatüey**)

b. 1885, Santo Domingo, Dominican Republic; d. 1968.

Novelist, critic, historian, journalist, poet, playwright.

An eminent literary scholar, Max Henriquez usually signed his lesser journalistic pieces "Desde mi butaca" in the *Listin Diario* with the pen-name "Hatüey." He was active in many intellectual fields and was a major student of Dominican and Cuban history, politics, and literature. He originated, too, the idea of bringing out the best local works in a "Biblioteca Minima Dominicana" which has indeed been successful in offering important insular works to a receptive circle of aficionados at a low price.

His interest in politics and local history led him to dramatize recent events in four novels, and over all his work, in story form, criticism, or straight history, he throws the net of his wide-ranging mind. Brother of the great scholar and literary historian Pedro Henriquez Ureña, both sons of Francisco Henriquez y Carvahal, physician, statesman, and writer, and Salomé Ureña de Henriquez, Dominica's leading woman poet, Max early was destined for a leading role in literature.

At fifteen he was named drama critic to *La Lucha,* published in Santo Domingo, and during his long life he founded and/or edited many other cultural organs, including *La Discusión, El Figaro,* both in Cuba, and *El Diario* of Mexico, and *La Gaceta* of Guadalajara, Mexico.

Writings: Novels: *La independencia efímera,* Paris, 1938, 2nd ed., S. Domingo, Postigo, 1962; *La conspiración de los Alcarrizos,* Lisbon, 1941; *El Arzobispo Valera,* Rio de Janeiro, 1944; *El ideal de los Trinitarios,* Madrid, 1951.

Stories: *Cuentos insulares,* Buenos Aires, 1949; *Hermano y maestro,* S. Domingo, 1950, 2nd ed., Mexico, 1957

Play: *La combinación diplomática* (farce), Havana, El Siglo XX, 1916.

Poetry: *Anforas,* 1914.

Politics and History: *Los Yanquis en Santo Domingo,* Madrid, 1929; *Reseña histórica sobre Santiago de Cuba,* Santiago, Cuba, 1931; *Panorama de la República Dominicana, Buenos Aires, 1935; La Liga de Naciones Américanas y la Conferencia de Buenos Aires,* New York, 1937; *Homenaje a Sanin Cano,* Havana, 1957; *El continente de la esperanza,* Brussels, 1959.

Literary History and Criticism: *Whistler y Rodin,* Havana, 1906; *La enseñanza de la literatura cubana,* 1915; *Tres poetas de la música,* Havana, 1915; *Rodo y Rubén Dario,* Havana, 1918; *El ocaso del dogmatismo literario,* Havana, 1919; *Heredia,* 1924; *El intercambio de influencias literarias entre España y América,* Havana, 1926; *Programa de gramática castellana,* Santiago de Cuba, 1926; *Tabla cronológica de la literatura cubana,* Santiago de Cuba, 1929; *Historia abrevado de la literatura española,* translated from work of Fitzmaurice Kelly, with notes, Santiago de Cuba, 1929; *Tratado elemental de música* (with Antonio Serret), Santiago de Cuba, 1929; *Antologia cubana de los escuelos,* Santiago de Cuba, 1929; *Fosforencencias,* Santiago de Cuba, 1930; *El retorno de los galeones,* Madrid, 1930; *Los trofeos de J. M. Heredia,* translated by Henriquez, Santiago de Chile, 1930; *Les influences francaises sur la poésie hispanoamericaine,* Paris, 1937, translated into Spanish by Henriquez, Buenos Aires, 1940; *Poetas cubanos de expressión francesa,* Mexico, 1941; *Breve historia del modernismo,* Mexico, 1954, 2nd ed., revised, Mexico, 1957; *Tránsito y poesia de Mariano Brull,* Havana, 1958; *Garra de Luz,* Havana, 1958; *De Rimbaud a Pasternak y Quasimodo,* details unknown; *Panorama histórico de la literatura dominicana,* 2 vols., Rio de Janeiro, 1945, 2nd ed., S. Domingo, Postigo, 1965; *Panorama histórico de la literatura cubana,* 2 vols., New York, Las Américas, 1963.

HENRIQUEZ URENA, Pedro

b. 1884, Santo Domingo, Dominican Republic.

Critic, playwright, literary historian, teacher, scholar.

An eminent scholar and literary historian as were his father, Henriquez Carvajal, his mother, Salomé Ureña, and his brother Max, Pedro was early interested in the theatre and history. His major works were in criticism, literary history, and bibliographical areas. Like his brother, Pedro also had a deep interest in music.

Writings: Criticism: *Obra Critica* (includes *La cultura y las letras coloniales en S. Domingo* and *El Teatro de la América española en la época colonial*), Mexico, Fondo de Cultura Económica, 1960.

Bibliography: "Bibliografia de Sor Juana Inés de la Cruz." *Revue Hispanique,* XL (Paris, 1917); *Tablas cronólogicas de la literatura española,* Boston, Heath, 1920.

Literary Criticism and History: *Horas de estudio,* Paris, 1909; *La cultura y las letras coloniales en Santo Domingo,* Buenos Aires, 1936; *Las corrientes literarias en la América hispaña,* Mexico-Buenos Aires, 1949, translated as *Literary Currents in Hispanic America,* Cambridge, Harvard University Press, 1945.

Anthologies: *Antologia de la versificación ritmica,* San José, Costa Rica, Imp. Alsina, 1918; *Cuadernos de poesia dominicana,* Santo Domingo, Museo Nacional.

Play: *El nacimiento de Dionisos* (5 episodes), New York, Imp. de las Novedades, 1916.

Music: *Música popular en América* (Conferencias del Colegio Nacional de la Universidad de la Plata,)Vol. I, La Plata, 1930.

HENRIQUEZ Y ALFAU, Enrique

(pseudonym: **"Amable Razonador"**)

b. November 30, 1859, Santo Domingo, Dominican Republic; d. June 5, 1940, Santo Domingo.

Poet, journalist, lawyer, diplomat.

Active in law, public affairs, and diplomacy, Enrique Henriquez served as Foreign Secretary at the height of his career.

His poetry, in contrast to his busy, outward-looking life, was dark and introspective. Balaguer termed his verse the "hija de la noche," the daughter of the night, and much of his work shows the influence of the American poet, Edgar Allen Poe, possibly experience through Baudelaire's translations into French.

His romantic qualities can be seen in these lines from the poem "Canto al Dolor" which is a profession of Christian faith and belief in an ascetic ideal:

Por ti, sin tregua el corazón transido
de caida en caida,
de zozobra en zozobra,
esta vida que sin odios he vivido
esta cristiana vida
perennemente llena
de bondad nazareña
es diáfano prodigio de tu obra

Writings: Poetry: *Nocturnos y otros poemas,* 1939.

Criticism: *Sutilez e inexactitudes de Don Hipólito Billini,* 1901, published under name of Amable Razonador.

Legal Study: *Defensa de William L. Bass,* 1906, record of a famous case on which he had worked with other lawyers: the report is unsigned. William Louis Bass' *L'ordre nouveau* (in its French translation from English by René J. Rosemond) was published Port-au-Prince, Imp. de l'Etat, 1945 (44 pp.).

Autobiography: *Memorias,* Vol. I, 1894; Vol. II, 1895. The little volumes are respectively 27 and 24 pages long.

Biographical/Critical Sources: F. A. Mota Medrana, Relieves Alumbrados, S. Domingo, 1971, pp. 29-42.

HENRIQUEZ Y CARVAJAL, Federico

b. 1848, Dominican Republic; d. 1951.
Poet, journalist.

Federico Henriquez produced more than a score of works in many genres during his extremely long life-time and was active in public affairs most of his life and a leading polemicist in the turbulent affairs of the republic.

His "Himno épico" to independence and his "Himno a Duarte," both put to music by José de Jesús Ravelo, were important patriotic efforts in their time. Even at 96 he completed the sonnet "¡Ave, Patria!" to commemorate the 100th anniversary of Dominican independence.

He was a contributor to many journals and the owner-director of the newspaper *Diarias.* For many years he was in exile in Cuba returning home only 1903-1904 in a period of many years, but kept active writing for *Cuba Literaria* on world events. Typical articles or essays were: "El trabajo libre y la tirania de los millones," "Lucha

de razas: rusos y japoneses," "Kruger," and "Tolstoy y la guerra."

Henriquez was the father of Max and Pedro Henriquez Ureña.

Writings: Poetry: *Juvenilia,* 1904; *Dolorosa,* 1909; *Del amor y del dolor, poesias,* 1926, 2nd ed., Barcelona, 1932; *Rosas de la tarde,* Gibrara, 1923; *Mi álbum de sonetos,* 1927; *Marti, El poema de la história,* 1948; and "¡Ave, Patria!" written in 1944.

Verse Play: *La hija del hebreo,* 1883.

Plays (in prose): *El hombre epopeya o De flor en flor,* written 1870 (1 act comedy), unpub.

Novels: *Romances históricos,* 1937; Bani, 1939.

Stories: *Cuentos,* 1950.

Speeches: *Ramón Mella,* 1891; *Discurso pro Duarte,* 1916.

Biography-History: *Duarte,* 1944.

Philosophy: *Etica y estética:* I. *Páginas breves,* 1929; II. *Almas y libros,* 1929.

Journalism: pieces published in *El Mensajero,* conserved in Harvard University Library, 3 vols., first volume published in 1964.

Essays: these were devoted to his first wife, the great poetess Salomé Ureña: *Intima,* 1897; and *Meditación,* 1898.

Political Essays: *Informe del Presidente de la Delegación Dominicana en la Segunda Conferencia Internacional Americana,* 1902; *El derecho público internacional y la guerra,* 1915; *Páginas electas,* La Vega, 1918; *Cuba y Quisqueya, conferencias,* 1920; *Guarocuya: El monólogo de Enriquillo,* 1924; *Todo por Cuba,* 1925; *Nacionalismo,* 1925; *Páginas electas, comentarios sobre temas internacionales,* 1926; *Anales de la Universidad de Santo Domingo: Memoria de la Rectoria,* 1932.

Biographical/Critical Sources: Max Henriquez Ureña's *Panorama histórico de la literatura dominicana,* S. Domingo, 1965, pp. 200-211; Joaquin Balaguer's *História de la literatura dominicana,* 5th ed., S. Domingo, 1970, pp. 184-186.

HEREDIA Y HEREDIA, José Maria de

b. December 31, 1803, Santiago, Cuba; d. 1839, Toluca.
Poet, playwright.

Son of Dominican parents, the young Heredia studied at first in Santo Domingo and then in Havana and early showed intellectual precocity, learning Latin and Greek at three years and translating classical works into Spanish. At ten his poetic essays were well thought of by the critic Muñoz del Monte, especially "El Filósofo y el Buho."

A fervent nationalist from his earliest days, Heredia had to go into exile before he was twenty, and thereby travelled widely in the United States and Mexico. He spent, in fact, less than three months overall in Cuba the rest of his life. His two years in North America were sad ones, however, and he found American English a "horroso lenguaje." Happier in Mexico from 1825 on, he worked for the Office of the Secretary of State and other state bureaus.

Though long absent, Heredia loved Cuba, but he could also criticize it as in these lines from his "El himno del desterrado":

¡Dulce Cuba! en tu seno se miran
en el grado más alto y profundo
las bellesas del fisico mundo,
los horrores del mundo moral.

Heredia's plays were mostly based on the work of others, but were not just facile translations—they were more re-creations in the sensibility of his own time and personal culture.

Max Henriquez Ureña termed Heredia "...el poeta de la democracia republicana: cantó los ideales de todo un continente."

Heredia's best know works were "El Niagara," an ode described as "entre los poemas más perfectos de la literatura española," and "El Teocali de Cholula," a description of a gigantic Aztec ruin.

Writings: Poetry: *Poesias liricas,* 2 vols., Havana,

Municipio de la Habana, 1940-41; (verse and prose): "Prédicas de libertad," in *Cuadernos de Cultura,* 2nd series, No. 4 (Publicaciones de la Secretaria de Educación), Havana, 1936; translation of Heredia's "Los Conquistadores" by Vivian Virtue, in *Caribbean Voices* (selected by John Figueroa), Vol. I, London, Evans, 1966. Also: *Versos: selección,* Havana, Lex, 1960; *Poesias,* Consejos Nacional de Cultura, 1965.

Plays: *Eduardo IV,* written by Heredia at 18 and performed in Matanzas in 1819 (never published); *Ateo,* performed 1822 (5 acts, tragedy, after Crébillon); *El campesino espantado,* Sainete, 1819; *Sila* (5 acts, tragedy), Mexico, Valdés, 1825; *Tiberio* (5 acts, tragedy, after Voltaire), Mexico, Imp. del Supremo Gobierno, 1827; *Los últimos romanos* (3 acts, tragedy), Tlalpan, Imp. del Gobierno, 1829; *Abufar o la familia árabe* (4 acts, tragedy, after Ducis), New York, Lockwood, 1854 (but written in 1826 and performed in 1833); *Cayo Graco* (3 acts, tragedy), based on play of Chénier, written in 1826 but published in *Revista de Cuba,* Vol. VI (1879); *El fanatismo* (5 acts, tragedy, after Voltaire and freely translated), published in *Revista de Cuba* IX (1881); and fragment of *Moctezuma* (tragedy), first act and part of second extant in ms.

Letters: *Del epistolario de Heredia,* Madrid, 1926, edited by José Maria Chacón y Calvo.

Works Translated into English: The Trophies; Sonnets, translated by Frank Sewall, Small, Maynard and Co., Boston, 1900; *Sonnets of José Maria de Heredia,* translated by Edward Robeson Taylor, San Francisco, W. Doxey, 1900; *Sonnets from the Trophies of José Maria de Heredia,* translated by E. R. Taylor, San Francisco, P. Elder and Co., 1906; *Translations from José Maria de Heredia,* translated by Merle St. Croix Wright, New York, Vinal, 1927; *The Trophies with Other Sonnets,* translated by John Myers O'Hara and John Hervey, New York, John Day Co., 1929; *Trophies,* translated by Brian Hill, Philadelphia, Dufour, 1962.

Biographical/Critical Sources: Rafael Esténger's *Heredia, la incomprehensión de si mismo,* 1938; José Maria Chacón y Calvo's *Estudios heredianos,* 1939; Garcia Garáfolo Mesa's *Vida de José Maria Heredia en México 1825-1829,* 1945; Manuel Pedro González del Valle's *Cronologia herediana, 1803-1839,* 1938; Max Henriquez Ureña's *Heredia,* 1924 and discussion in *Panorama histórico de la literatura cubana,* New York, 1963, pp. 101-117; Chacón y Calvo's *Vida universitaria de Heredia,* Havana, 1916 and Chacón's *Nueva vida de Heredia,* Santander, 1930. For a sketch of Heredia's political career, see "Predicas de libertad" by Francisco G. del Valle, in *Cuadernos de Cultura,* 2nd Series, No. 4 (1936). Also see "José Maria Heredia: vida y obras del primer romántico hispano-americano," unpublished Ph.D. dissertation, Florida State University, 1969, by Lomberto Diaz.

HEREDIA Y MOTA, Nicolás

b. 1852, Bani, Dominican Republic (with long residence in Cuba); d. July 12, 1901.

Novelist.

Heredia removed with his family early in his life to Cuba and he spent much of his life there where he became a strong supporter of Cuban independence. Manuel Sanguily, writing in *Hojas Literarias,* declared Heredia's *Un hombre de negocias* was "esencial y absolutamente cubana, de más exacto colorido local. Contemplada bajo ese aspecto es un rico panorama de Cuba y el cuadro completo de la vida social de una de sus comarcas, antes del alzamientos de Céspedes."

Writings: Novels: *Un hombre de negocios,* Matanzas, E. Lavastida, 1883; *Leonela,* Havana, La Moderna, 1893.

Biographical/Critical Sources: Juan J. Reinos, "La personidad de Nicolás Heredia y su obra polémica," speech, Havana, P. Fernández y Cia, 1955 (20 pp.); Edna Coll, *Indice Informativo de la novela hispanoamericana,* Vol. I, San Juan, 1974, pp. 312-313.

HERNANDEZ, José

b. ca. 1855, Cuba.
Playwright.

At least four of the Hernández plays saw performance, but today they are only of academic interest.

Writings: Plays: *Amor sin interés* (1 act prose comedy), Havana, Imp. La Moderna, 1891; *El corazón y la cara* (1 act farce), first performed Teatro Albisu, Havana, November 12, 1885, published Havana, Imp. de Batalón, Mixto, 1891; *Tanto tienes, tanto ales* (1 act farce), premiered Teatro Irijoa, Havana, April 1, 1887; *todo precaución es poca!!!* (1 act prose comedy), Havana, La Moderna, 1898, premiered Teatro Albisu, Madrid, February 5, 1887.

HERNANDEZ, José P. H.

(sometimes called **PEACHE**)

b. 1892, Hatillo, Puerto Rico; d. April 2, 1922, in Rio Grande.
Poet, pharmacist, musician.

Born into a humble and even sorrowful family, Hernández struggled for an education, becoming after great effort a trained musician and pharmacist. Accordingly, his verse reflects the ordinary speech and musicality of the poor and employs highly colloquial language on occasion. Some critics, including Angel Mergal and Carmen Alicia Cadilla, have found Hernández the most touching, the most sincere, of all Puerto Rico's "modernista" poets.

His first work appeared in journals in 1912, being late or post-romantic, but undergoing the influence of the great Rubén Dario, and Julio Herrera Reissig, Hernández became one of his country's most lyrical and purest poets. Possibly his most anthologized work was "A Unos ojos astrales."

Long ill with tuberculosis, from which he died at the age of 30, Hernández sought in melancholic themes some surcease from his pain—some solace to be extracted from his birth in suffering.

The people of Rio Grande erected a statue in his honor.

Hernández' "La última flor" begins:

Tuya es la última flor
de mi huerto de ilusiones
Mis eras son hoy eriales:
pedruscos en vez de flores
los arenales tapizan
di mi huerto de ilusiones

Writings: Poetry: *Coplas de la vereda,* San Juan, Standard Printing Works, 1919; *El último combate,* San Juan, Edit. La Democracia, 1921; *Cantos de la sierra,* San Juan, Edit. Puerto Rico Ilustrado, 1925; *Antologia,* San Juan, Cuadernos del Ateneo Puertorriqueño, 1956; *José P. H. Hernández, poesias,* Vol. I (includes *Coplas de la vereda* and *El último combate*), San Juan, Ediciones Borinquen, 1966; *Poesias,* Vol. II (included *Cantos de la sierra,* plus previously uncollected verse from journals), also Ediciones Borinquen, 1966, seven of his poems appear in Luis Hernández Aquino's *El modernismo en Puerto Rico,* San Juan, 1967; and E. Fernández Méndez' *Antologia de la poesia puertorriqueña,* San Juan, 1968; *Obras poética,* 2nd ed., San Juan, Instituto de Cultura Puertorriqueña, 1966 (includes *Coplas de la vereda; El último combate;* and *Cantor de la sierra,* plus other poems and articles).

Biographical/Critical Sources: S. R. Quiñones, "Sobre P. H. Hernández," in *Alma Latina* (May 1936) as are the next two items: Angel Mergal, "Intento critico-biográfico de Peache [Hernández]," and Carmen Alicia Cadilla, "Peache"; Also see chapter VII in E. A. Laguerre's *La poesia modernista en Puerto Rico,* San Juan, 1969, pp. 139-163. Manuel Siaca Rivera has written an unpublished M. A. thesis, "Vida y obra de José P. H. Hernández," University of Puerto Rico, 1951; published in revised form as *José P. H. Hernández: Vida y obra,* San Juan, Edit. Coqui, 1965, and Siaca has written a detailed introduction to Hernández' *Obra poética,* 1966.

HERNANDEZ ALBA, Rafael

b. ca. 1815, Sancti Spiritu, Puerto Rico.

Poet, playwright, military officer.

Hernández was one of the earliest published Cuban playwrights though he is today an all but forgotten figure.

Writings: Poetry (with drama): *Ensayos poéticos y dramáticos,* Trinidad, Murtra e hijos, 1841.
Plays: *Amoriós de novela* (1 act, verse), Puerto Principe, Imp. del Gobierno, 1844; *Sancho Saldaña* (5 acts, verse), Matanzas, Roquero, 1848; *Una madre como muchas,* (Comedia de costumbres, 3 acts, verse), 1848; *Gato por liebro* (1 act, prose and verse), 1848; *Pasor a tiempo* (1 act, comedy), 1852; *Pablo y Virginia* (3 acts, verse), awarded a prize by the Juegos Florales del Liceo de Matanzas, 1867.

HERNANDEZ AQUINO, Luis

b. 1907, Lares, Puerto Rico.
Poet, novelist, storywriter, essayist, journalist, teacher.

Hernández took his B.A. and M.A. in 1951 from the University of Puerto Rico at Rio Piedras and Doctor of Philosophy and Letters from the Central University at Madrid, Spain, 1952. He is presently professor of literature at the University of Puerto Rico.

He founded *Insula* (1943) and he edited the review *Bayoán,* an organ for the young poets of the day and criticism of the contemporary works, local and foreign. Much of his work has appeared in *El Pais, El Dia Estético, Alma Latina, El Mundo, Bayoán,* and *Puerto Rico Ilustrado.* His work is characterized by an intense exploration of the enigma and travail of the black man within a fictional context.

Beginning as a follower of Luis Lloréns Torres, Herrara Reissig and other "modernistas" of the Rubén Dario school, Hernández Aquino moved on to "Atalayismo" (1929-1936) and since the 1940's his work has become very clear and intense.

The recent collection of his work *Antologia poética* (ed., José Emilio Gonzáles) provides much previously unpublished verse from 1925 to 1968 and three poems as *Tres poemas indigenas* of 1971.

His novel *La muerte anduvo por el Gausio* (1959) deals with the U. S. invasion of the island.

Writings: Poetry: *Entre la elegia y el réquiem, poemas,* Rio Piedras, Edit. Edil, 1968; *Cantos a Puerto Rico* (Hernández was compiler), San Juan, Inst. de Cultura Puertorriqueña, 1967; *Niebla lirica,* San Juan, 1931; *Del Tiempo contidiano,* 1961; *Agua de remanso,* 1933; *Poemas de la vida breve,* 1939; *Isla para la angustia,* San Juan, Ed. Insula, 1943; *Memoria de Castilla,* 1956; *Voz en el tiempo,* 1952, 1957, a collection of his poetical works, 1925-52; poems in various collections including *Literatura puertorriqueña,* 2nd ed., Vol. II, E. Marlinez Masdeu and Esther M. Melon, eds., Rio Piedras, 1972, pp. 239-246; *Antologia poética,* Barcelona, Spain, Edit. Universitaria, Universidad de Puerto Rico, 1974.

Editor of: *El modernismo en Puerto Rico: poesia y prosa,* University of Puerto Rico, San Juan, printed in Spain by M. Pareja, Barcelona, 1967; *Poesia puertorriqueña,* Edit. de la Universidad de Puerto Rico, 1954; *Nueva poesia de Puerto Rico,* in collab. with Angel Valbuena Briones, Madrid, 1952; *Nuestra aventura literaria—Los Ismos en la literatura puertorriqueña, 1913-1948,* (Prize from the Institute of Puerto Rican Literature, 1964, 2nd ed. San Juan, 1966; *Notas sobre la poesia puertorriqueña,* 1956; *Antologia de Antonio Nicolás Blanco* (selection and prologue), 1967; unpub. M. A. thesis by Hernández: "Movimientos literarios del siglo XX en Puerto Rico," University of Puerto Rico, 1951, 163 pp; *Poetas de Lares Antologia,* San Juan, Centro Cultural de Lares, 1966.

Critical Studies: "Rubén Dario en Puerto Rico," *Revista de Instituto de Cultura Puertorriqueña* (January-December, 1960).

Novel: *La muerte anduvo por el Gausio,* Madrid, Ediciones Areyto, 1959, 2nd ed., Santo Domingo, Edit. del Caribe, 3rd and 4th editions also in S. Domingo, 5th rev. ed. in Colección Uprex, Serie Ficción, Universidad de Puerto Rico, 1971; excerpted in *Puerto Rico: The New Life,* Nina Kaiden, ed., New York, Renaissance Editions, 1966 (fragment translated and entitled *Death Roamed the Gausio River*).

Stories: in various journals and collections including "Aire de Guazábara" (second prize in story competition of Instituto de Cultura Puertorriqueña, 1959), and "Un enigma y una clave" in Concha Meléndez, ed., *El arte del cuento en Puerto Rico,* New York, 1961, pp. 146-153.

Literary History: *Nuestra Aventura Literaria,* S. Domingo, Edit. Arte y Cine, 1964.

Linguistics: *Diccionario de Voces Indigenas,* Bilbao, Edit. Vasco Americana, 1969.

Biographical/Critical Sources: José Emilio González, "Reseña sobre nueva poesia de Puerto Rico," (of Hernández and Briones) in *Asomante* (October-December 1953), pp. 94ff; F. Manrique Cabrera, *Historia de la literatura puertorriqueña,* San Juan, 1969; Margot Arce de Vásquez, Introduction to *Voz en el Tiempo,* 1952; Concha Meléndez, *La Isla Ignoranda de Hernández Aquino: Figuración de Puerto Rico y otros estudios,* San Juan, Instituto de Puerto Rico, pp. 77-79, 1958; also by Meléndez, in *El arte del cuentro en Puerto Rico,* New York, 1961, pp. 144-146; Manuel Garcia Blanco, "Salamanca y un poeta de Puerto Rico," in the *Regional Gazette of Salamanca,* (December 12, 1956); Francisco Lluch Mora, "Luis Hernandez Aquino: Evocación de Castillia en su poesia," *El Mundo,* San Juan, Puerto Rico, (May 9-16, 1957); Wilfredo Braschi, "Luis Hernández Aquino—Galeria Literatura," in *El Mundo,* San Juan, (January 26, 1957); Helcias Martán Góngora, *Memoria de Castilla,* Diario Official, Bogotá, Colombia, 1957, article on Hernández Aquino by Josefina Rivera de Alvarez in her *Diccionario de literatura puertorriqueña* (Rio Piedras, Ediciones "La Torre," 1955), pp. 313-315, and see introduction by José Emilio González (dated April 19, 1973) to *Antologia poética* (of Hernández Aquino), above, for 28 page discussion of poet and his work.

HERNANDEZ CATA, Alfonso

b. June 24, 1885, Santiago, Cuba; d. 1940.

Novelist, playwright, storywriter, essayist, poet, diplomat.

Hernández Catá passed most of his life in Spain, much of it as Cuban Consul in Madrid. He also served in diplomatic-consular post in Chile and was Ambassador to Brazil where he died in a plane crash.

He wrote little poetry after his 20's and did most of his work in long and short fiction. His style is pleasant and diverting, but generally his work is not very original or energetic. Though he dabbled in the Afro-Cuban movement his work is not deeply knowledgable of the African roots of his country.

Writings: Stories: *Cuentos pasionales,* Madrid, 1907; *Novela erótica,* Madrid, 1909; *Los frutos ácidos* (novelettes), Madrid, Atenea, 1919; *Cuentos,* Havana, Instituto de Literatura y Lingüistica, Academia de Ciencias de Cuba, 1966.

Criticism: *Mitologia de Marti,* Havana, 1929.

Novels: *La juventud de Aurelio Zaldivar,* Madrid, 1911; *El placer de sufrir,* Madrid, A. Pueyo, 1920; *La voluntad de Dios,* Madrid, A. Pueyo, 1921; *La muerta nueva,* Madrid, Edit. Mundo Latino, 1922; *Piedras preciosas; Fuegos fatuos; El Angel de Sodoma; Manicomio; Pelayo-González: Algunas de sus ideas, algunos de sus hechos, su muerte,* Madrid, Mundo Latino, 1922; *El corazón,* 1924; *El bebedor de lágrimas,* Madrid, Edit. El Mundo Latino, 1926 (318 pp.).

Stories: "Bajo la luz," in *Cuba Contemporánea, Vol. 34 (Feb. 1924), pp. 97-121; Cuentos,* Havana, Instituto de Literatura y Lingüistica, Academia de Ciencias de Cuba, 1966.

Plays: *La culpa ajena,* Barcelona, Biblioteca Teatro Mundial, 1916 (written with Alberto Insua, 2 act prose comedy), and Madrid, Sociedades de Autores Españoles, 1916, premiered Teatro Infanta Isabel, Madrid, April 11, 1916; *Sin pies ni cabeza* (1 act comedy), Madrid, Imp. Moderna, 1904; *En familia* (2 act comedy), Madrid, Pueyo, 1914; also written with Alberto Insúa: *Nunca es tarde* (1 act comedy), Madrid, 1914 and *El amor tardio* (3 act romance), Madrid, Renaciemiento, 1915; *El pasado* (1 act), Havana, in *Cuba Contemporánea,* 1917, and *El bandido* (3 act comedy), Havana, in *Cuba Contemporánea,* 1917; written with Eduardo Marquina: *Don Luis Mejia* (3 act, verse), Madrid, Edit. Reus, 1925; others: *La mujer desnuda* (3 act comedy), trans. from French, in *Cuba y América,* 1915; *Cabecita loca,* details unknown.

Biographical/Critical Sources: Enrique Serpa, *Recordación de Hernández Catá,* 1943; Max Henriquez Ureña, *Panorama histórico de la literatura cubana,* New York, 1963, pp. 413-414; Dorothy S. Gardiner, "Psychological Values in the Work of Alfonso Hernández Catá," unpublished Ph.D. dissertation., UCLA, 1961; Anisia M. González, "Las novelas cortas de Alfonso Hernández Catá, unpublished Ph.D. dissertation, Florida State, 1970; Alberto Gutiérrez de la Solana, "Lino Novás Calvoy Alfonso Hernández Catá: Contraste de vida y obra," unpublished Ph.D. dissertation, New York University, 1967; Pedro N. Trakas, "The Life and Works of Alfonso Hernández Catá," unpublished Ph.D. dissertation, University of North Carolina, 1954.

HERNANDEZ CRESPO, Manuel

b. ca. 1850, Cuba; d. 1886.
Playwright, pharmacist.

A minor playwright, Hernández is today all but forgotten.

Writings: Plays: *Artistas para recreo,* 1880; *Don Crisanto o un cuadro por ocho pesos,* 1880.

HERNANDEZ CRUZ, Victor

b. 1949, Aguas Buenas, Puerto Rico.
Poet, teacher.

Hernández arrived in New York City in 1954 and has lived in East Harlem since. He attended Franklin High School in Harlem until 1967 and the next year opened the East Harlem Gut Theatre on East 104th Street. His first published verse appeared in *Evergreen Review* in 1967, much of it work written during his high school days. Some of this work had appeared earlier in the volume *Papo got his gun* in 1966.

He has worked for the New York City Parks Department as a culture program officer and has participated in Teachers' Writers Collaborative and worked with Herbert Kock in experimental teaching methods.

Hernández has read his poetry before many groups and is at present teaching English at the University of California at Berkeley.

Writings: Poetry: *Papo got his gun,* New York, Calle Once Publications, 1966; *Snaps,* New York, Random House, 1969; *Mainland,* New York, Random House, 1973; and various poems in reviews, including *Journal of Black Poetry; Ramparts;* and *Evergreen Review,* and several anthologies, including *Speaking for Ourselves: American Ethnic Writing,* L. Faderman and B. Bradshaw, eds., Glenview, Ill., Scott, Foresman, 1975, pp. 381-386.

HERNANDEZ FRANCO, Tomás Rafael

b. April 29, 1904, Santiago de los Caballeros, Dominican Republic; d. 1952.
Poet, storywriter, critic.

Joaquin Balaguer considered Hernández Franco "como uno de los poetas y escritores dominicanos que se han señalado por su inconfundible originalidad y por su limpieza de expresión . . ."

Writings: Poetry: *Canciones del litoral alegre,* S. Domingo, 1926; 2nd ed., Ciudad Trujillo, Distribudores de Santo Domingo, Ed. "La Nacion," 1936; 3rd ed., 1953; *Yelidá,* San Salvador, Ediciones Sargazo, 1942; *Cansancio,* details unknown.

Poetic Essays: *Rezos bohemios,* 1921; *Amor, inquietud y cansancio,* 1923 (combined volume).

Stories: *El hombre que habia perdido su Eje; La fuerza espiritual de un pequeño pais; Isla* (stories in ms.); *Cibao,* 1951.

Literary Criticism: *Apuntes sobre poesia popular y poesia negra en las Antillas,* San Salvador, 1942; *Capitulario,* details unknown; *La poesia en la República Dominicana* (lectures).

HERNANDEZ MIYARES, Enrique

b. 1859, Cuba; d. 1915.
Poet, journalist, literary critic.

A transitional poet, moving on to "modernismo" from romanticism, Hernández was closely associated with Julián del Casal, both publishing in *La Habana Elegante.* His sonnets were particularly liked, including "¡Patria!" "In pace," and "Dos Banderas." In general his tone was pessimistic, but almost tranquil, even vaguely sceptical.

Writings: Poetry: *I Poesias, II Prosas,* Havana, Academia Nacional de Artes y Letras, 1915.

HERNANDEZ RUEDA, Lupo

b. July 29, 1930, Santo Domingo, Dominican Republic.
Poet, teacher, lawyer.

Hernández was a director and owner of the literary journal *Testimonio* and co-director of the collection of classical Dominican works, "El silbo vulnerado." He has also been active in public affairs and has served as president of the Dominican Right to Work and Social Security Association. His collection of verse *Muerte y Memoria* won the national prize in the Gastón F. Deligne competition, 1963. He was one of the founding professors of the National University Pedro Henriquez Ureña where he teaches Labor Law.

Writings: Poetry: *Como naciendo Aún,* 1st ed. (8 poems only), S. Domingo, Col. La Isla necesaria, 1953; 2nd ed. (with 5 new groups of poems), S. Domingo, Impresora Arte e Cina, 1960; *Trio* (with Máximo Aviles Blonda and Rafael Valera Benitez), S. Domingo, 1957; *Muerte y Memoria,* S. Domingo, El Silbo Vulnerado, No. 4, 1963; *Santo Domingo vertical,* S. Domingo, Col. Baluarte, Ediciones Brigadas, 1962; *Crónica del sur,* 1964; *Por ahora 1948-1975* (major collection), Santiago, D. R., UCMM, 1975.

Co-editor (with Manuel Rueda): *Antologia panorámica de la poesia dominicana contemporánea (1912-1962),* Santiago, D. R., UCMM, 1972, and editor of many legal manuals and legal studies.

Critical and autobiographical comments: in *Trio* (with Rafael Valera Benitez and Máximo Blonda), S. Domingo, El Silbo Vulnerado, 1957 (this work also has a preface by P. R. Contin Aybar: "La invención poética.") Also see essays by Manuel Valldeperes, Héctor Incháustegui Cabral, Pedro Rene Contin Aybar, Socrates Nolasco, Marcio Veloz Maggiolo and Ramón Emilio Reyes in *Por ahora* (1975).

HERNANDEZ VARGAS, Francisco

b. 1914, Arecibo, Puerto Rico.
Poet, journalist, lawyer.

Hernández took a law degree at the University of Puerto Rico. His poetry generally exalts his home island and/or love and he is a highly social conscious poet. In the words of Rosa-Nieves his work is "duro, sincero, de un terrible verismo . . .la tierra es su angustia preocupación vital." His poem, "Sangre," from *Brazos,* begins:

No es la sangre azul
no es a la sangre noble,
no es a la sangre de los potentados;
es a la sangre roja,
es a la sangre humilde,
es a la sangre del obrero explotado.

Writings: Poetry: *Música criolla,* 1933; *La vereda,* 1937; *Brazos,* San Juan, Imp. Venezuela, 1939.

HERNANDEZ DE ARAUJO, Carmen

b. 1832, Puerto Rico; d. 1877.
Playwright, storywriter, poet.

Antonia Sáez has declared Hernández' play *Los dos rivales* (1846) to be the earliest play written by a Puerto Rican discovered thus far. Her poem "Tres Coronas," was written with a strong religious feeling as were "A la Santa Cruz," and "Agonia de Jesús en el Huerte." She is known to have won a prize in 1847 in a competition given to honor the painter José Campeche (see below).

Writings: Play: *Los deudos rivales* (5 acts) written 1846, published Puerto Rico, 1863 (70 pp.); *Hacer bien al enemigo es imponerle el major castigo,* Puerto Rico, 1866.

Religious: "El catecismo Biblicos," in ms.

Novelette: "Flores o virtudes y abrojos y pasiones," in ms.

Poetry: mostly in ms., but her "Tres Coronas" was published in *Corona poética a José Campeche,* San Juan, *Boletin Mercantil,* 1863.

Biographical/Critical Sources: Antonia Sáez, *El teatro en Puerto Rico,* Rio Piedras, 1950, pp. 20, 41, and elsewhere; Marcelino Menéndez y Pelayo, *Historio de la poesia hispanoamericana.*

HERRERA, Ramón Vélez

b. 1808, Cuba; d. 1886.
Poet, playwright.

A leading poet in the criollismo movement, Herrera often told his "stories" in verse as with his *Romanced cubanos* (1956) and his legend *Elvira de Oquendo* (1840). His poetry was generally prosaic, however, and such titles as "Franklin, inventor del pararrayos" were hardly inspired.

Writings: Poetry: *Poesias,* 1833; *Poesias,* 1837, *Poesias,* 1838 (all different collections); *Elvira de Oquendo,* 1840; *Las flores de otoño,* 1849; *Romances cubanos,* 1856.

Play: *Los dos novios en los Baños de San Diego,* 1843.

HEUREAUX, Ulises, Jr.

b. 1876, Dominican Republic; d. 1938.
Novelist, playwright, storywriter.

Son of a famous general and statesman of the same name, the writer Ulises spent much of his adult years abroad in the pursuit of literature.

Joaquin Balaguer considered Heureaux an exceptionally able playwright for his works' "playability," and his plays are possibly the best written by a Dominican for the national theatre. Heureaux was very familiar with the modern French theatre and the new currents in world theatre, but also knew the classical French theatre well, too, from his long Paris sojourn. Although his own imaginative gifts are of a lower quality, his craftsmanship make his dramas excellent vehicles for his ideas and experiences. Two of his works of fiction have been published, *En la copa de Arbol* and *Amor que emigra,* but none of his plays, though all of them are extant in manuscript and most of them were performed during his lifetime.

Writings: Novels: *En la copa del Arbol,* 1908; *Amor que emigra,* 1910.

Plays: *Consuelo* (3 acts), 1901; *Genoveva* (3 acts), 1903; *Lo Inmutable* (3 acts), 1909; *El articulo 291; El grito de 1844; La muerte de Anacaona; El enredo; Blanca; Entre dos fuegos; La noticia sensacional; En la hora suprema* (3 acts), 1926.

History: *Alfonso XII;* and others.

Biographical/Critical Sources: J. Balaguer's *Historia de la literatura dominicana,* 1970, p. 197.

DE HOSTOS, Eugenio Maria

b. February 11, 1839 (village near Mayagüey), Puerto Rico; d. August 11, 1903.
Novelist, literary critic, teacher, poet, patriot.

De Hostos studied under Jerónimo Gómez at San Juan, then at the Seminario Conciliar de Puerto Rico and he took his B.A. at Bilboa and, much later, a law degree at Madrid University.

An innovator in education, de Hostos was a fervent liberal who life-long sought the independence of Cuba and Puerto Rico. In 1875 he was aboard the steamship *Charles Miller* with General Francisco Vicente Aguilero in 1875 when it wrecked in the revolutionary expedition against Cuba.

De Hostos spent much of his life outside of Puerto Rico, passing the years 1851-1969 in study and travel in Spain and France, the United States (New York City, 1875), Chile (1872-73 and 1888-1898), and his two three-year sojourns in Santo Domingo (June 1875 to 1888) where he served as a special assistant to General Gregorio Luperón of the Dominican Republic and from 1900-1903 as an assistant to Dominican President Horacio Vásquez. In 1877 he married Belinda de Ayalá y Quintana. From 1880-88 he directed the Escuela Normal in Santo Domingo, an institution he had been instrumental in founding.

In 1898 de Hostos founded the "Liga de Patriotas Puertorriqueños" and travelled with Henna and Zendo Gandia in a special mission to President McKinley to Washington to ask for greater freedom for Puerto Rico. In Bayoán, the hero of his *La peregrinación de Bayoán,* de Hostos had an Indian spokesman for his own love of Puerto Rico and his fierce hunger for personal and political freedom. (Copies of the book were seized by the Spanish authorities and it is the second Chilean edition of 1873 that is known today). In contrast, *Inda* is a poetic, late romantic story, lightly fictionalizing the author's new bride Belinda de Ayalá. Both works are considered relatively lightweight, but de Hostos' collection of critical essays *Romeo and Juliet* (1867) and *Hamlet* (1873) on Shakespeare are profound studies.

Writings: Novels: *La peregrinación de Bayoán,* Madrid, Imp. El. Comercio, 1863, 2nd ed., Santiago de Chile, 1873; also in *Obras completos,* Vol. III, Havana, 1939; *Inda,* 1878, San Juan, Instituto de Cultura Puertorriqueña, 1970 (319 pp.).

Poetry: "El nacimiento del Nuevo Mundo," fragment of an epic, in Vol. X of de Hostos' *Obras completas,* 1939.

Literary Criticism: *Romeo and Juliet,* 1867; and *Hamlet,* trans. by M. D. Howland and G. Rivera, *Puerto Rican Bulletin,* Rio Piedras, No. 12 (1940), 1873 and the essays: "Las tradiciones Peruanas," "La cuarterona," "Salomé Ureña de Henriques," and "José Joaquín Perez."

Diary: *Diario,* 2 vols. (?), Havana, 1939.

Social Studies: *Derecho Constitucional,* 1887; *Moral Social,* 1888, 2nd ed., Madrid, 1906; *Moral Social,* Buenos Aires, Universitaria, 1968.

Travel: *Mi viaje al sur,* 18??; *Cartas públicas*

acerca de Cuba, 1887.

Complete works: *Obras completas,* 20 vols., Havana, 1939.

Biographical/Critical Sources: Cesáreo Rosa-Nieves, Chapter "Tres Inquietudes Insignes en la vida de Eugenio Maria de Hostos 1839-1903," in *Ensayos escogidas,* San Juan, 1970, pp. 93-108; Adelaide Lugo Suárez, "Hostos, critico literario," unpub. M.A. thesis, U. of P. R., 1956, 236 pages; Carmen Gómez Tejera, *La novela en Puerto Rico,* Rio Piedras, 1947; F. Manrique Cabrera, *Historia de la literatura puertorriqueño,* Rio Piedras, 1969, pp. 160-169. *América y Hostos, vida y obra,* New York, Hispanic Institute, 1940; Pedro de Alba's introduction to *Hostos* (selection of poems by Hostos), Mexico, Ed. de la Secretaria de Educación Pública, 1944; José A. Franquiz, "Esencia ideológica de Hostos," in *Hostos y América,* Havana, 1939; "Bibliografia de Eugenio Maria de Hostos," in *Boletin de la Biblioteca Iberoamericana y de Bellas Artes,* No. 2 (Mexico, 1939), 8-10; Adelaida Lugo Guernelli, *Eugenio Maria de Hostos: Ensayista y critico literario,* San Juan, Instituto de Cultura Puertorriqueña, 1970 (207 pp. with bibliography); *The Lima Resolution, The Essay on Hamlet, and other Papers,* Cambridge, Mass., Harvard University Press, 1940 (published under auspices of De Hostos Centenary Commission, San Juan).

HUNGRIA LOVELACE, Luis

b. 1897, Dominican Republic; d. 1947.
Poet.

Hungria's verse is generally quiet, non-revolutionary, non-experimental.

Writings: Poetry: *Bajo el último crepúsculo,* 1920; *Rosaleda de ensueños,* 1927; *Mi libro tuyo,* 1938; *Luciérnegas,* 1938; *Misal de amor,* 1940; *Arquimedes,* 1946.

HURTADO DEL VALLE, Antonio

(pseudonym: **El hijo del Damuji**)
b. 1842, Cuba; d. 1875.
Poet.

One of the revolutionary poets called "Los poetas de la guerra" by Cuban literary historians after Marti's collection of that name, Hurtado published only one collection of his work. His verse was musical and romantic in both subject and style.

Writings: Poetry: Six of his poems appeared in the anthology edited by José Martí: *Los poetas de la guerra* which includes Hurtado's well-known "El combate de Atollaosa." His one collection is: *Producciones de Hurtado del Valle,* Guanabacoa, 1864.

IBARRA DE VICTORIA, Maria

b. 1922, Dominican Republic.
Poet.

Ibarra's poems are very personal, simple and clear. Her "Poema Bucolico del desencanto" from the collection *Ondas de emoción* is typical:

Estoy llena de verde
y cansada de azul
Enveulvo mis esperanzas
para tirarlas muy lejos

Es que el mundo se ha caido
sobre mis ojos
he retrocedido tanto,
que ya no absorbo el paisaje,
ni adulo la luna.

Writings: Poetry: *Alma en penumbra,* 19??; *Ondas de emoción de ayer,* 1949; 2nd ed., S. Domingo, Editora Tribuna Hispánica, 1973, with an introduction by Angel Rafael Lamarche.

IBARZABAL, Federico de

b. 1894, Cuba; d. 1954.
Novelist, poet, storywriter.

A much published poet though not considered a major figure, Ibárzabal wrote three novels, the best being *Tam-tam* (1941). Influenced by Joseph Conrad, Ibárzabal's own obsession with the sea made for hallucinatory moral tales such as "Avon" and "Todo bien a bordo."

His poetry was often erotic, and as Max Henriquez Ureña puts it, of 'mediocre inspiración." His later verse turned to city themes where his natural sarcasm found excellent targets. Evaristo Carriego and Luis Carlos López appear reflected in his verse.

Writings: Novels: *La avalancha,* Havana, 1924; *La casa del diablo,* in *El Crisol* (as inserted pamphlet-leaflet), 1934; *Tam-tam,* Havana, 1941.

Stories: *Derelictos y otros cuentos,* Havana, 1937; *La charca,* Havana, 1938.

Poetry: *Huerto lírico,* Havana, 1913; *El balcón de Julieta,* Havana, 1916; *Una ciudad del trópico,* Havana, 1919. As of 1963, Ibárzabal's other poetry in four collections gathered by the author remained unpublished.

Editor of: *Cuentos contemporáneos,* Havana, 1937.

Biographical/Critical Sources: Alberto L. Schweyer, "Federico de Ibárzabal," in *Los Contemporáneos,* Havana, Los Rayos X, 1921.

ICHASO, León

b. 1869, Durango, Viscaya, Spain.
Playwright, poet, journalist.

Ichaso emigrated to Cuba in 1896 in his 27th year. He was a leading playwright in the island and frequently collaborated with Julián Sanz.

Writings: Plays: *La escuela del periodismo* (1 act verse), written with Manuel Piños, Cienfuegos, Imp. Mercantil, 1908, premiered Teatro Terry, Cienfuegos, July 30, 1905; *Los aburridos* (3 act comedy), with M. Piños, Cienfuegos, 1908.

Plays written with Julián Sanz: *Dia de recibo* (1 act comedy), Cienfuegos, 1908; *La reina de los cantares* (1 act), Cienfuegos, 1909; *Premio y castigo* (comedy), Cienfuegos, 1909; *Tragedia feliz* (1 act, prose and verse), Cienfuegos, 1909; *El cacizue* (1 act, 4 scenes), Cienfuegos, 1910; *El Cometa Halley* (1 act), Cienfuegos, 1910; *La real moza* (1 act, music by F. Barbat and C. Bonafoux), Cienfuegos, Valero, 1910; *El amor libre* (1 act), Havana, 1912; *Amar a ciegas* (2 acts), Havana, Imp. Ruiz, 1914; *La flor del camino* (2 acts), Havana, Ruiz, 1914; *Rosalba* (3 acts), Havana, Imp. El Siglo XX, 1916, premiered Teatro de la Comedia, Havana, May 8, 1916.

Poetry: *Fuego y ceniza.*

Criticism: *Notas y vibraciones.*

Folklore-customs: *La comedia feminina; La comedia masculina.*

IGLESIA Y SANTOS, Alvaro de la

b. 1859, La Coruña, Spain; d. 1940, Cuba.
Novelist.

Of Spanish birth, Iglesia early emigrated to Cuba and became part of his new country's literary history. He published several works of Cuban legends and folklore and many stories. His novels were late romantic in tone and subject and highly nuanced.

Writings: Novels: *Adoración,* 1894; *La alondra,* Havana, 1897; *Amalia Batista o El último danzón,* 1900; *Una boda sangrienta o El fantasma de San Lázaro,* 1900; *La bruja de Atarés o Los bandidos de la Habana,* 1901; all published in Havana.

Biographical Novel: *Manuel Garcia,* Havana, 1895 (205 pp.).

Stories and legends: *Pepe Antonio,* 1903; *La factoria y la trata,* 1906; *Tradiciones cubanas,* 1911; *Cuadros viejos,* 1915; *Cosas de antaño,* 1916, all in Havana.

INCHAUSTEGUI CABRAL, Héctor

b. July 25, 1925, Baní, Dominican Republic.
Poet, critic, essayist, playwright, teacher, diplomat.

Incháustegui studied philosophy at the University of Santo Domingo. He became chief of the editorial section and writer for *Listín Diario* and of *La Nación,* and director of *La Opinión.* He became a member of the group issuing the *Cuadernos dominicanos de cultura,* 1943 to 1952.

He served as ambassador to Mexico twice, was ambassador to Venezuela, Ecuador, El Salvador and Brazil. Twice he was Undersecretary of Foreign Relations and of Education and Fine Arts. Other positions he held have been director of Radio Santo Domingo Television y de Radio Caribe; head of Corporación de Fomento Industrial; director of publications for his university, corresponding member

of the Spanish Royal Academy of Speech, president of the National Association of Writers, and vice-president of the Sociedad de Autores Dramáticos Dominicanos.

He has held the chair of Spanish and of History and Literature at the Universidad Católica Madre y Maestra de Santiago de los Caballeros since the early 1970's.

Writings: Poetry: *Poemas de una sola angustia,* 1940; *Rumbo a la otra vigilia,* 1942; *En soledad de amor herido,* 1943; *De vida temporal,* 1944; *Canciones para matar un recuerdo,* 1944; *Versos 1940-1950,* 1950; *Casi de ayer,* 1952; *Las insulas extranas,* 1952 (awarded the Pedro Henriquez Ureña prize of 1952); *Rebelión vegetal,* 1956; *El pozo muerto,* S. Domingo, Postigo, 1960; *Por Copacabana buscando,* 1964; *Diario de la guerra y los dioses ametrallados,* 1967.

Literary Criticism: *De literatura dominicana siglo XX,* 1968 and Santo Domingo, UCMM, 1973, Santiago de los Caballeros, UCMM.

Plays: *Teatro,* 1964, 2nd ed., 1968, Ed. de la Soc. de Autores y Com. Dram. (contains the trilogy: *Miedo en un puñado de polvo* with its three plays: *Prometeo, Filoctetes,* and *Hipólito.*

Novels: *Muerto en el Edén,* 1951.

INSUA, Alberto

b. 1885, Havana, Cuba.
Playwright, novelist, storywriter, travelloguist.

Insúa's many novels and plays are elegant and psychologically probing. Many non-Spanish language critics such as Maurice Barres have been very receptive to his work.

Writings: Plays: (written with A. Hernández Catá): *En familia* (2 act comedy), Madrid, Pueyo, 1914; *Nunca est tarde* (1 act, prose), Madrid, 1914; *Cabecita loca,* Madrid, 1914; *El amor tardio* (3 acts), Madrid, Renacimiento, 1915; *La culpa ajena* (2 act comedy, prose), Barcelona, Biblioteca Teatro Mundial, 1916 (the literary historian Luis Rivera-Muñoz also shows Madrid, Sociedad de Autores Espanoles, 1916, for *La culpa ajena*), premiered Teatro Infanta Isabel, Madrid, April 11, 1916; *El bandido* (3 acts), Havana, *Cuba Contemporánea,* 1917; *El pasado* (1 act, prose), Havana, *Cuba Contemporánea,* 1917. Other plays: *La Madrileña* (comedy), Madrid, 1918 and *La domadora* (comedy written with Sara Insúa), Madrid, 1925.

Travel: *Don Quixote en los Alpes.*

Novel: *En tierra de santos,* 1907, first part of trilogy: "Historia de un esceptico"; *La hora trágica,* 1908, the second part of trilogy; *El triunfo,* 1903, third work of trilogy; *La mujer fácil,* 1909; *Las neuróticas,* 1911; *La mujer desconocida,* 1911; *Las flechas de amor,* 1912; *El demonio de la voluptuosidad,* 1912; *Los hombres,* 1913; *El alma y el cuerpo de Don Juan* (novelettes); *El deseo* (novelettes); *El peligro,* 1915; *De un mundo a otro,* 1916; *Por Francia y por la libertad,* 1917; *Nuevas páginas de la guerra,* 1917; *Las fronteras de la pasión,* 1920; *Maravilla,* 1921; *La batalla sentimental,* 1921; *Un corazón burlado,* 1921; *El negro que tenia el alma blanca,* 1922; *La hiel; La mujer y la muñeca, Un idilio de quince dias* (novelettes); *La mujer que necesita amar,* and the second part: *La mujer que agotó el amor,* 1923; *Un enemigo del matrimonio,* 1925.

IRIZARRI, Francisco

b. ca. 1855, Cuba.
Playwright.

Only one play is known of this all but forgotten playwright.

Writings: Play: *Un matrimonio al vapor* (1 act, verse), performed Teatro de Juncos, June 5, 1885; published Ponce, P. R., Imp. de Manuel López, 1886.

ITURRONDO, Francisco

(pseudonym: **Delio**)

b. 1800, Cadiz, Spain; d. 1868.
Poet, translator.

Arrived in Cuba in his sixth year, Iturrondo loved his new country and celebrated its natural beauties in his *Rasgos descriptivos de la naturaleza cubana* (1831), an ode influenced by the Spanish poet Bello. Its sonorous qualities fail to hide a certain lack of genuine poetic talent according to Max Henriquez Ureña and much of his work was prosy as with the later odes "Colon," "Las ruinas del palacio árabe de la Alhambra," "A Cristina de Borbón," "La peste en la Habana," "Oda en la muerte del Obispo Espada" and "Oda en los funerales del Obispo Espada."

Writings: Poetry: *Rasgos descriptivos de la naturaleza cubana,* 1831; *Ocios poéticos,* Matanzas, 1835 (written by "Delio").

Verse translation: *El paria* (translated into Castillian of Casimir Delavigne's drama), New Orleans, U.S.A., 1847.

IZNAGA, Alcides

b. 1910, Cienfuegos, Cuba.
Novelist, poet.

Iznaga was a founder in 1947 of the journal *Concierto* (along with Feijóo and Menéndez) in which he published much of his early work. His novel *La cercas caminaban* won the UNEAC Writers' Unión Award in 1969 as Cuba's best novel of that year.

Writings: Novels: *Los valedontes,* Havana, 1959; *Las cercas caminaban,* Havana, Unión, 1970 (188 pp.).

Poetry: in various journals and volumes: *Patria imperecedera,* Cienfuegos, Signo, 1959; *La roca y la espuma,* Santa Clara, Editora Universitaria Universidad Central de las Villas, 1965.

Biographical/Critical Sources: Edna Coll, *Indice Informativo de la novela hispanoamericana,* Vol. I., San Juan, 1974, pp. 318-319.

JAMES, Norberto

b. 1945, Dominican Republic.
Poet.

One of the most interesting of the young poets is James whose *Sobre La Marcha* (1969) and *La provincia sublevada* (1972) are of a high order of lyricism.

JAMIS, Fayad

b. 1930, Mexico.
Poet, editor, art teacher.

Of Arabic parentage, Jamis passed most of his youth in Havana where he published at 19 his first collection *Brújula* in 1949. He was a member of the *Origenes* poetry group centered around the transcendentalist José Lezama Lima. For many years Jamis lived in Paris as a housepainter and metal-worker, forced to give up oil painting because of poverty. He published an early collection of verse in 1962 based on his Paris experiences, but he first received recognition for his revolutionary poems in *Por esta libertad,* also 1962, the product of his return to his more lyrical self manifested in his first collection *Los puentes* (1962).

He teaches art and is an editor of the house magazine of the Cuban Writers' Union.

Writings: Poetry: *Brújula,* Havana, 1949; *Vagabundo del alba,* Havana, La Tertulia, 1959; *Cuatro poemas en China,* Havana, Cuadernos de Poesia, 1961; *Los puentes, poesia, 1956-1957,* Havana, Revolución, 1962; *Por esta libertad,* Havana, Casa de las Américas, 1962, winner of the Casa's prize for 1962; *La pedrada,* Havana, La Tertulia, 1962; *La victoria de Playa Girón,* Havana, 1964; *Cuerpas,* Havana, Unión, 1965. Two poems, "On the River Bank," and "Life" in English translation by J. M. Cohen appear in *Writers in the New Cuba* (Cohen, ed.), Harmondsworth, England, Penguin, 1967, and represented in *Con Cuba,* edited by Nathaniel Tarn, New York, 1969.

JESUS, Salvador M. de

b. October, 1927, Palo Seco (near Bayamón), Puerto Rico.
Storywriter.

After local schooling through Bayamón High School, and service with the U. S. Army in the Korean War, de Jesús joined the Division of Finances of the Department of Instruction. Consequently he does a great deal of travelling and has come to know his country extremely well.

Jesús' first stories (including "Lágrimas de Mangle") appeared in *Alma Latina,* and an anthology supported by the journal *Asomante.* He was an editor with M. Rodriguez Román for a period on the review *Educación.* He began a novel in the 1950's.

Writings: Stories: *Esta buena gente.* The stories "La llama del fosforo," and "Vertiente" appear in René Marqués' *Cuentos Puertorriqueños de hoy,* Mexico, 1959, pp. 205-206; "Lágrimas de mangle," in *Asomante, número antológico,* III (1956), San Juan.

Biographical/Critical Sources: René Marqués' *Cuentos puertorriqueños,* Mexico, 1959; Maria Teresa Babín, "El cuento puertorriqueño de hoy," in *El Mundo,* San Juan (April 13, 1957); Concha Meléndez, ed., *El arte del cuento en Puerto Rico,* New York, 1961, pp. 334-377; this anthology includes de Jesús' stories "Lágrimas de Mangle," and "La otra hija de Jairo," pp. 337-350.

JESUS MEDINA, Tristán de

b. 1833, Bayamón, Cuba; d. 1886.
Storywriter.

After studies in Philadelphia, Jesús Medina went on to further work in Madrid and Germany where he completed his work in the humanities, all before his 18th year. Soon married and soon widowed, he entered the priesthood in the Seminary of San Basilio el Magno where he was a professor for a period. He established a reputation as an orator both in Cuba and in Madrid which he visited again in 1955. A fervent nationalist, he supported the insurrection of 1868, was punished by the state and his church. He broke with Catholicism and became a Methodist minister, removing to Germany for a period. Once again back in Cuba, he returned to his original faith but remained a strong nationalist.

Many of Jesús Medina's stories had musical themes: "Mozart ensayando su Réquiem," "El Carnaval de Paganini," "La Sonata y el Sátan de Haydn." José memorial article in *Revista Cubana* (Vol. III, 1886) emphasized his fantasy, intelligence and absolute articulate control of his thoughts in highly sensitive and personal language.

Writings: Story-novelette: *Mozart ensayando su réquiem,* Madrid, Imp. de Fortanet, 1881, and Havana, Biblioteca Nacional José Marti, 1964 (88 pp.), prologue by Cintio Vitier.

JIMENEZ, Francisco P.

b. 1903, Caguas, Puerto Rico.
Poet, journalist, teacher.

Jiménez' first volume, *Hojas de sándalo* (1920), is in full modernista flavor reflecting Luis Lloréns Torres and Virgilio Dávila. His poetry began to change during his study for the M. A. at the University of Puerto Rico, moving him to more social themes in one direction, to more personal ones of love in the other. His second collection, *Las trompetas de Jericho* (1940), according to the judgment of Rosa-Nieves, is ". . .viril, verista, comprometido con los ideales de la justicia social de los humildes."

Writings: Poetry: *Hojas de sándalo,* Caguas, Tip. Morel Campos, 1920; *Las trompetas de Jericho,* Caguas, Tip. El Pueblo, 1939; and poems in various collections including *Aguinado lirico* of Cesáreo Rosa-Nieves, 1st ed., Rio Piedras, 1957, pp. 141-142 (which also offers on pp. 142-148 the poems of "Pétalo azul" and ¡Muchachito." "Humanidad," "No harán falta los ricos. . ." and "Noche buena" (latter three from his group "Sonetos proletarios") and "Los ignorados."

JIMENEZ, José Maria

b. 1868, Santiago de los Caballeros, Dominican Republic; d. 1928.
Poet, playwright.

Jiménez' plays were late romantic in theme and treatment.

Writings: Plays: *Maldito amor* (verse), 1886; *Pedir peras al olmo (comedy),* 1887.
Poetry: *La flor del Jerico,* 1894; *Perfiles,* 1903; *De la vieja lira,* 1911.

JIMENEZ, Miguel Angel

b. 1901, Dominican Republic.
Novelist, storywriter (in creole), playwright.

Jiménez was once strongly interested in employing creole speech and he published several stories exploiting folkloric materials and colloquial language and is known to have written at least five plays.

Writings: Novelette: *La hija de una cualquiera.*
Creole Stories: in various journals.
Plays: *Los amores de Ezequiela; Por la buena or por la mala; Un drama en una comedia; El secreto de las teclas; Orgullo de raza y amor de madre.*

JIMENEZ, Ramón Emilio

b. 1886, Dominican Republic.
Poet, essayist, folklorist.

Once a wide-ranging writer in several genres, Jiménez is today an all but forgotten figure of the early part of this century.

Writings: Poetry: *Lirios del trópico,* Santiago de los Caballeros, 1910; *Espumas en la roca,* 1917; *La patria en la canción,* 1933; *Espigas suetas,* 1938; *Diana lirica,* Santiago, 1920.
Essays: *El Patriotismo y la escuela,* 1917.
Speech: *El Ateneo de Santo Domingo a la memoria de Santos Chocano,* 1935; *Oración panegirica en memoria del Academico fenicido Dr. Adolfo A. Novel. . .,* 1938.

JIMENES GRULLON, Juan Isidro

b. 1903, Dominican Republic.
Critic, essayist, sociologist.

Jiménes was his nation's leading socialist. He was a skilled writer of essays and his prose generally curtly paragraphed and his thought carefully structured. His logic was severe and he pruned out all but the most necessary ideas.

His intellectual interests were broad, reaching from Galileo to Ortega y Gasset, to revolution of the masses.

Writings: Critical Studies: *República Dominicana: una ficción merita,* Venezuela, 1965; *Pedro Henriquez Ureña: realidad y mito; El ser y el deber—ser del escritor,* S. Domingo, Ed. Lib. Domo., 1969; *Anti-Sábato: un escritor dominando por fantasmas,* Maracaibo, Venezuela, 1968; *Al margen de Ortega y Gasset.*

History: *Una Gestapo en America.*

Philosophical Essays: "En torno a Galileo and "Critica a la rebelión de las masas."

Sociology-Politics: *La America Latina y La revolución socialista,* Santo Domingo, Cultural Dominicana, 1971; *Sociologia politica,* Vol. I, S.Domingo, Taller, 1974.

JIMENEZ MALARET, René

b. 1903, Adjuntas, Puerto Rico.
Poet, journalist, playwright, critic.

Jiménez was a journalist for *El Mundo, El Imparcial, Alma Latina, Puerto Rico Ilustrado* and *Brújula.* His poetry is philosophical, often somber, to some degree touched by the alienation of the 1930's or the "postmodernist" esthetic.

Writings: Poetry: *Estados del alma,* 1932; *La palabra al viento,* 1943.

Philosophical Essay: *Meditaciones de un misántropo,* 1939.

Journalism: *Vórtice, temas de crónicas y entrevistas,* 1940.

Play: *Cosas de familia,* 1941.

JIMENEZ SOLA, Enrique

(pseudonym: **A. R.**[?])

b. 1911, Caguas, Puerto Rico.
Poet, pharmacist.

Jiménez published a mysterious little volume with no title but merely citing "A R" as epigraph in 1947. The critic Margot Arce wrote of it: "Los cinco poemas, de A R, tienen la forma del romance heróico: endecasilabos que se agrupan en estrofas de extensión variable, apoyándose en la asonancia de los pares. . .Los versos fáciles, limpios, bien medidos y acentuados le prestan un fluir sereno como de rios o de mares en calma."

Writings: Poetry: five poems, untitled, but carrying epigraph A R, Rio Piedras, 1947; one poem "Miserere" from *A R,* and "Noche Buena," first published in *La Voz de Turabo* (December 24, 1955), are in *Aguinaldo liricos,* C. Rosa-Nieves, ed., Rio Piedras, 1957.

JOGLAR CACHO, Manuel

b. 1898, Morovis, Puerto Rico.
Poet.

Joglar is a mystic, lyrical poet with six volumes of published verse.

Writings: Poetry: *Góndolas de Nacar,* 1925; *En voa baja,* 1945; *Faena intima,* San Juan, Imp. Venezuela, 1955; *Soliloquios de Lázaro,* 1956; *Canto a los ángeles,* 1957; *La sed del agua,* Barcelona, Edit. Rumbos, 1965; *Por los caminos del dia,* 2nd ed., San Juan, Tip. por Will Carter, 1969.

JORRIN, José Silverio

b. 1816, Cuba; d. 1897.
Essayist, critic.

Primarily an art and literary critic, Jorri delivered the most important lecture-speech at the debates organized at the Liceo de Guanabacoa in 1861 which expressed the then strong neo-classical currents of the arts in mid-century.

Writings: Essays: Critical and Literary History: "¿Es la literatura un pasatiempo vano?" *Noches Literarias,* 1865 (journal edited by Nicolas Azcárate); "Italia y la poesia," 1885; "La anatomia y la mitologia en su relaciones con la estatuaria y la pintura," 1886; "Cristóbal Colón y la critica contemporánea," 1883; the latter three all appeared in the *Revista Cubana.* "El descubrimiento de América, delivered October 11, 1892; "Disquisiciones columbinas," in *Revista Cubana.*

Biographical/Critical Sources: Ricardo del Monte, memorial article on Jorrin in *El Pais* (October 8, 1897); Max Henriquez Ureña, *Panorama histórico de la literatura cubana,* New York, 1893; Elias Entralgo, *José Silverio Jorrin o la timidez politica,* Havana, 1937.

JULIA MARIN, Ramón

b. 1878, Utuado, Puerto Rico; d. 1917, Cataño.
Novelist, critic.

Julia was a naturalist and full of knowledge for country ways in his fiction. His first novel has been translated into English and his second deals with Puerto Rican migrant farmers going off to far-away Hawaii for work.

Writings: Novel: *Tierra adentro,* 1911, translated as *In the Hinterland,* extract from which is in Nina Kaiden's *Puerto Rico: The New Life,* New York, Renaissance Editions, 1966; *La gleba,* 1912; San Juan, Tip. Real Hnos., 1912 (155 pp.): both in one vol., Utuado, 1962.

Critical Essay: "Sobre literatura y critica," in *Puerto Rico Ilustrado,* San Juan (October 5, 1912).

JUSTINO CASTILLO, Rafael

b. February 28, 1861, Santo Domingo, Dominican Republic; d. April 24, 1933, Santo Domingo.
Storywriter, journalist, jurist.

Son of José Zoilo Castillo and Maria Francisca del Rosario Contin, Justino was born into an educated and literary family. He became president of the Supreme Court after an active career in law and public service.

He was a major contributor to *El Teléfono,* established in 1898, the leading journal of its day.

Writings: Stories: in *El Hogar* (published 1894-1895): "Un pecado mortal," "Recuerdo de Navidad," "Honda tristeza," "Gotas de agua," "Paisaje," "Los Leña doves," "Alborada," and "Noches de luna." In the *Letras y Ciencias* he published: "La casita verde" (July 31, 1894); "Su carta" No. 87 (December 1895); "Monólogo" No. 94 (March 1896); "Los tres amores" No. 96 (May 1896) and many other tales in *Prosa y Verso* (San Pedro de Macoris), in *Listin Diario,* in *Revista Ilustrada* (S. Domingo), including "Honor Campesino," which also appears in Emilio Henriquez Demorizi's *Tradiciones y cuentos dominicanos,* S. Domingo, Postigo, 1969, pp. 245-257.

Essay: "Acerca de la alimentación y las razas," in *Revista Dominicana de Cultura,* S. Domingo, No. 2.

JUSTO DE LAR

(pseudonym for **José ARMAS Y CARDENAS**)

JUSTIZ Y DEL VALLE, Tomás Juan de

b. 1871, Santiago, Cuba; d. 1959.
Playwright, novelist, critic, journalist, teacher, historian.

Jústiz y del Valle edited several journals, including *La Noche* and taught history and geography at the University of Havana.

His novels and plays are weakly constructed and often the characters are poorly developed. His last novel *Ecos de una guerra a muerte* (1941) is really a series of sketches of the Spanish civil war during the year 1936. His first work was the novel *Carcajadas y solluzos* which deals with the last days of Spanish control and the American occupation.

Writings: Novels: *Carcajadas y sollozos,* Havana, 1906; *El suicida,* Havana, 1912; *Ecos de una guerra a muerta,* Havana, 1941.

Plays: *Ultima esperanza* (3 act comedy), Havana, Cuba intellectual, 1910; *La victima* (3 act comedy), Havana, La Moderna Poesia, 1911; *Terrible sanidad* (comedy), Havana, 1915.

Criticism: *¿Existe una literatura cubana?,* Havana, 1900.

History: *Historia universal,* Havana, 1916.

JUVENAL ROSA, Pedro

b. 1897, Hatillo, Puerto Rico.
Novelist, essayist, lawyer.

Juvenal's 336 page novel *Las masas mandan* is one of the earliest truly "revolutionary" novels of Puerto Rican literature, though its hero dies in an exemplary romantic fashion.

Writings: Novel: *Las masas mandan,* Barcelona, Araluce, 1936.

KADOSH, A.

(pseudonym for **Francisco Mariano QUINONES**)

KEMP, Vicente Gómez

b. 1914, Santiago, Cuba.
Poet, novelist.

Kemp wrote Afro-Cuban influenced verse in the 1930's, employing the popular speech and creole vocabulary. He often recited his poems before white and black audiences in Santiago de Cuba to great applause. Working in Mexican television from 1942-46, he returned to become a leading television producer in Cuba. Exiling himself in 1960, he worked in television in Puerto Rico and Venezuela and in 1965 began teaching at Miami-Dade Junior College.

KENNEDY, Elena

(pseudonym for **Virginia Elena ORTEA**)

LABARTHE LOPEZ DE VICTORIA, Pedro Juan

b. October 20, 1906, Ponce, Puerto Rico; d. March 3, 1966.
Poet, novelist, journalist, teacher.

Labarthe López has travelled widely in the Americas, Europe and the Caribbean and resides in the United States. Some of his work has appeared in the journals *Puerto Rico Ilustrado* and *El Mundo,* but more of his work has been published abroad than in his home island. According to Rosa-Nieves, Labarthe is ". . .un poeta de raiz filosófica y de fuertes avecinamientos religiosos," and his verse reflects his love of the work of Carl Sandburg and Walt Whitman.

Writings: Poetry: *Atalaya,* 1932; *Estrias de sueños,* 1936; *Reclinatorio, Acetre y Corazón,* Mexico, 1944; *Cirios,* 1945; *Yo me voy preguntando,* San Juan, Edit. Campos, 1959; *Interrogatorio a la muerte,* Mexico, Imp. Juan Pablos, 1961.

Novel: *Pueblo Gólgota del espiritu,* San Juan, Edit. Venezuela, 1938.

Editor of: *The Gateway Poets,* (in English dealing with U. S. poets), 1953; *Antologia de poetas contemporáneos de Puerto Rico,* Mexico, 1946.

LABRADOR RUIZ, Enrique

b. May 11, 1902, Sagua la Grande (Las Villas), Cuba.
Novelist, storywriter, journalist.

Labrador Ruiz was influenced by many of the avant-garde currents of the 1920's, particularly that of Paris. The methodologies of Joyce, Kafka, and the American William Faulkner are similar in some ways to his work, but he made his own style and to some degree was an innovator, even a refugee from his own times—seeking new ways to express the painful twentieth century. In his "gaseiformes" trilogy what is happening is intensely vague, and the sequence of events utterly impossible to establish. The reader must perforce produce a new reality from whatever fragments he can seize and hold. His later works were equally irreal, but less dictated by the stylistic devices of the trilogy.

Labrador continued his efforts to strike a new mode of writing in his cubistic stories ("cuenteria cubiche"), collected in *El gallo en el espejo.*

Writings: Novels: Trilogy: *El laberinto de si mismo,* 1947; Separate volumes: *Cresival,* 1936; *Anteo,* 1940; *Carne de quimera,* 1947; *Trailer de sueños; La sangre hambrienta,* Havana, Ayon Impresores, 1950; and by Cruzado Latinoamericana de Difusión Cultural, 1959.

Stories: *El gallo en el espejo,* Havana, 1953; *Conejito Ulán,* Havana, La Tertulia, 1963; *Cuentos,* Havana, UNEAC, 1970.

LAGO, Jesús Maria

b. 1860(?) 1873(?), Utuado, Puerto Rico; d. December 4, 1927(?) Santurce.
Poet, painter.

Lago's only schooling was in the local institutions of Utuando and he was mainly self-taught. He travelled to Europe and the Caribbean and in time became the president of the Ateneo Puertorriqueño. Though Lago polished his verses assiduously his work is considered important mostly because he was an early "modernista."

His poetry is descriptive, sensual, sometimes precious in the Parnassian manner of the early "modernistas," and often exotic. When he employs colloquialisms they are mostly for effect, never intrinsically organic. The sonnet form was his favorite form. *Cofre de sandalo,* his one volume, contains his best work, most of it from the early "modernista" part of the twentieth century. (He became extremely interested in Japan and things Japanese, probably through the influence of Rubén Dario and the French Parnassian poet Charles Cros whose *Le coffre de santal* is obviously reflected in Lago's own *El cofre de sándalo.*)

Much of his work first appeared in the review *El Carnaval.*

Writings: Poems: *La princesa Ita-Lu,* 1904 (in *El Carnaval,* No. 18, year IV); *Melodia blanca,* 1905; *El canto a las rosas,* 1907; *Cetro de amor,* 1912; *La flota de los sueños.*

Poetry: *El cofre de sándalo,* Madrid, 1927; eight of his poems are in Luis Hernández Aquino, *El modernismo en Puerto Rico,* San Juan, 1967; and three poems are in the *Antologia de la poesia puertorriqueña,* San Juan, 1968. *Antologia* (poem of Lago selected with foreword by Angel Luis Morales), San Juan, Ateneo Puertorriqueño, 1959.

LAGUERRE, Enrique Arturo

b. May, 1906, Moca, Puerto Rico.
Novelist, playwright, literary historian, teacher.

After schooling in Isabella and Aguadilla, Laguerre was a teacher for several years before returning to school to take the B. A. in 1937 and the M. A. in 1941, both at the University of Puerto Rico. He then joined the faculty of the University. He has been visiting lecturer at Queens College of the University of New York. He has travelled widely and worked for a period (1951-52) for UNESCO on an education project in Mexico.

Laguerre's *El Laberinto,* translated as *The Labyrinth* appeared in Spanish eight years after the New York edition in English of 1960. In it Porfiro Urebe lives in New York after leaving his godparents in Coama, Puerto Rico to face all the problems of poverty and race prejudice in the brutal city. The novel ends with the hero dead in a revolutionary battle against the tyrant of the "Republic of Santiago."

His novel *Solar Montoya* (1941) deals with the coffee economy in crisis and *La Resaca* (1943) with the island in the years 1870-1898, the period of extreme Spanish repression of independentistic sentiments. *30 de febrero* (1943) concerns Téofilo Sampedro who is "un hombre interino," and his life at the University of Puerto Rico. His one play, *La resentida* (1944) deals with the last few years of Spanish rule of the island.

Writings: Novels: *La llamarada* (novela), Aguadilla, P.R., Talleres Tip. Ruiz, 1935; *Solar Montoya,* San Juan, Imp. Venezuela, 1941; *El 30 de febrero,* San Juan, 1942, 2nd ed., Rio Piedras, 1943; *La Resaca,* San Juan, 1949; *Los dedos de la mano,* 1st ed., San Juan, Biblioteca de Autores Puertorriqueños, 1941, 3rd ed., 1945, 4th ed., 1949, editions in Rio Piedras, 1956, 1968 and 1971, and Barcelona, 1967; *La ceiba en el tiesto,* Rio Piedras, B.A.P., 1956; *Cauce sin rio: diario de mi generación,* Madrid, Nuevas Editoriales Unidas, 1962, reprint Rio Piedras, Edit. Cultural, 1968; *El laberinto,* Rio Piedras, Edit. Cultural, 1968, but first published in English in New York as *The Labyrinth,* Las Américas Publishing Co., (1959), in translation by William Rose; also Barcelona edition, 1967, and Rio Piedras, 1971; *El fuege y su aire,* Buenos Aires, Edit. Lozada, 1970.

Criticism: *La poesia modernista en Puerto Rico,* San Juan, Edit. Coqui, 1969.

Play: *La resentida,* 1944, 1960.

Essays: *Pulso de Puerto Rico,* San Juan, B.A.P., 1956 (covering articles of the 1952-54 period).

Stories: *Cuentos españoles,* 1953; *Antologia de cuentos puertorriqueños,* 1955; *El jibaro de Puerto Rico: Simbolo y figura,* 1968.

Complete works: *Obras completas,* 3 vols., San Juan, Instituto de cultura puertorriqueña, 1962-1964 (Vol. I: *Semblanza; Prológo; La llamarada; Solar Montoya; El 30 de febrero; Vocabulario;* Vol. II: *La resaca; Los dedos de la mano; La ceiba en el tiesto;* Vol. III: *El laberinto; La resentida; Pulso de Puerto Rico; Palabras finales*).

Editor of: (with Esther M. Melón): *El jibaro de Puerto Rico: Simbolo y figura,* Sharon, Conn. (USA), Troutman Press, 1968.

Biographical/Critical Sources: José Juan Beauchamp, *Imagen del puertorriqueño en la novela* (essays on Laguerre, Tapia y Rivera, and Zeno Gandia); Angelina Morfi's *Enrique A. Laguerre y su obra: La resaca, cumbre en su arte de novelar,* San Juan, 1964; Concha Meléndez, *El arte del cuento en Puerto Rico,* New York, 1961, pp. 117-120; also by Meléndez, *El llamado de la montaña, Apuntes sobre la novela de Enrique A. Laguerre,* Mexico, Manuel León Sánchez, 1936, pp. 129-134; Meléndez' "Reseña sobre *La resaca* de Enrique A. Laguerre," in *Asomante* (January-March 1950); José M. Colón, "La naturaleza en Manuel Zeno Gandia y Enrique A. Laguerre," unpublished M. A. thesis, U. of P. R., 1949; José Luis Martin, *Arco y fleche,* San Juan, 1961; "*La resentida* de Enrique A. Laguerre," in Angelina Morfi's *Temas del teatro,* S. Domingo, D. R., 1969; also see Francisco Arrivi's review of

Laguerre's novella *La ceiba en el Tiesto* in Arriví's *Entrada por las raices,* San Juan, 1964.

LAIR, Clara

(pseudonym for **Mercedes NEGRON MUNOZ**)

LAMARCHE, Juan Bautista

b. 1894, Dominican Republic; d. 1957.
Poet, essayist.

Lamarche celebrated the political group of "Los Trinitarios" (who had gathered around Juan Pedro Duarte) in his symbolic "La cruz y la espada" and the heroic period of the liberation struggle in "El delirio sobre el Chimborazo." His work is considered somewhat superficial but sonorous and imaginative. His prose is equally melifluous and poetic, even to being flowing and hyper-fluent.

Writings: Poetry: *Patria recóndita,* 1937; *A la sombra de los olivos,* 1956.

Biographical/Critical Sources: See F. A. Mota Medrano's discussion in *Relieves Alumbrados,* S. Domingo, 1971, pp. 165-174.

LEAL, Rine

b. 1930, Cuba.
Playwright.

Leal has accepted the influence of Garcia Lorca and the plays are heavy with the brooding feeling of doom. Set in contemporary Cuba these works still seek the universal rather than the particular life of the island.

Writings: Plays: *Desde adentro; Jorge ha regresado; El pequeño Miguel,* 1951; all these in one act; *El mar de nuevo* (three acts).

Editor of: *Teatro cubano en un acto,* Havana, Revolución, 1963 (contains one play each by A. Arrufat, Norah Badia, Raul de Cárdenas, Nicolás Dorr, Abelardo Estorino, Rolando Ferrér, Ignacio Gutiérrez, Matias Montes Huidobro, Virgilio Piñera, Manuel Reguera Saunell and José Triana.

LEANTE, César

b. 1928, Matanzas, Cuba.
Novelist, journalist, critic.

After completing high school in his native city, Leante with his family removed to Havana. He was active in the revolutionary movement led by Castro and was appointed cultural attaché of the Revolutionary government of Cuba to Paris. At present he is secretary of public relations of the Unión de Escritores y Artistas.

Long active in journalism Leante is on the board of *Unión* and has published widely in journals and cultural reviews. His first novel *El perseguido* deals with the unsuccessful plot to assassinate Baptista on March 13, 1957.

Writings: Novels: *El perseguido,* Havana, Revolución, 1964; *Padres e hijos,* Havana, Unión, 1967.

LEBRON SAVINON, Mariano

b. 1922, Santo Domingo, Dominican Republic.
Poet, playwright, essayist, medical doctor, teacher.

Lebrón was an early member of the group "La Poesia Sorprendida" and a co-director of the review of the same name. He was also a member of the Academia Dominicana de la Lengua.

His *Triálogos* is a discussion of esthetics held with Alberto Baeza Flores and Domingo Moreno Jiménes, published in three pamphlets. Lebrón's only collection of poetry is *Sonámbulo sin sueño* which is traditional in form but highly original in its imagery and subjects. He has published miscellaneous essays in the Hispanic and Arabic literary areas, and some plays.

Writings: Poetry: *Sonámbulo sin sueño,* S. Domingo, Ed. La Poesia Sorprendida, 1944; poems in various journals and collections including Manuel Rueda's *Antologia* . . ., Madrid, 1972, pp. 343-348.

Critical Essays: *Triálogos,* 1943; *Luces del trópico,* Buenos Aires, Editorial Americalee, 1949.

LEYVA Y BALAGUER, Armando

b. January 14, 1888, Oriente Province, Cuba; d. December 9, 1942, Havana.
Poet, storywriter.

More a chronicler than a storywriter of the modern sort, Leyva's style was old-fashioned and ornate. Most of his work was relaxed and vaguely metaphysical.

Writings: Stories: *Del ensueño y de la vida,* Havana, 1910; *Seroja,* Banes, 1911; *Alma perdida,* Puerta Padre, 1915; *Las horas silenciosas,* Santiago, Cuba, 1920; *La provincia, las aldeas; Estampas del regreso.*

Poetry: *Los pequeños poemas; Museo.*

LEZAMA LIMA, José Maria

b. December 19, 1910, Havana, Cuba; d. August 9, 1976.
Poet, critic, novelist, essayist.

Lezama Lima founded in 1937 the literary journal *Verbum* for the "transcendentalist" group which later was to include Félix Franco Oppenheimer (b. 1913), Eugenio Rentas Lucas (b. 1910), and Francisco Lluch Mora (b. 1925) as major figures. From 1939-1941, Lezama put out the successor review, *Espuela de Plata,* and then for a few months, *Nadie parecia.*

His poetry is hermetic, strongly influenced by Mallarmé, Valéry, Rilke and T. S. Eliot, and though Cuban in content, is very international in tone and style. His complex ideas and involved imagery is particularly striking, but he is also brusque, almost barbaric in his thrust, and often colloquial. His later work may be seen in this fragment from Sonnet XXVII ("Venturas Criollas") from the volume *Dador:*

La noche va a la rana de sus metales,
palpa un buche regalado para el palpo,
el rocio escuece a la piedra en gargantilla
que baja para tiznarse de humedad al Palpo.

La rana de los metales se entreabre en el sillón
y es el sillón el que se hunde en el pozo hablador.
El fragmento aquel sube hasta al farol
y la rana, no en la noche, pega su buche en el respaldo.

Cintio Vitier wrote of his work: "La poesia de José Lezama Lima expresa la realidad como u hecho carnal en el idioma, y a traves de una mirada que no interpreta ni organiza en lineas lógicas ni sentimentales su objeto, sino que prefiere dejarlo en su mistico exterior y reducirlo a sustancia paladeable de lo desconocido."

During the period 1944-1957, Lezama was the center of a group around the journal *Origenes* which included José Rodriguez Feo, Gastón Baquero, Eliseo Diego, Cintio Vitier, and Fina Garcia Marruz. In the 1960's, he edited *Unión,* an important literary and cultural journal.

Max Henriquez Ureña termed Lezama's first volume of poetry *Muerte de Narciso* (1937), a "revelation," and his second, *Enemigo rumor* (1941), a "revolution."

Paradiso, Lezama's one novel (1966) is ornate in style, extremely picturesque verbally, with absurd-sensical metaphors in most every phrase as possibly even the few words from p. 455 of the American edition (1974) may show: "Licario's room was a chamber in the style of Balzac, . . . everything was dusted with a look. There was no lack of thundering irony in the room: the armillary sphere was a replica of one in the Escorial; he caressed its movement of rotation, its somber strolling, with long waxy fingers of a syphilitic monarch who was an amateur guitarist."

Writings: Novel: *Paradiso,* Havana, Unión, 1966, but copyrighted and published by Biblioteca Era, Mexico, 1968, with author's revisions, translated into French (Paris, Seuil, 1971), and into English (by Gregory Rabassa), New York, Farrar, Straus, and Giroux, 1974. Other editions: Mexico, Era, 1968 (rev. ed.), Buenos Aires, De La Flor, 1968.

Poetry: *Muerte de Narciso,* Havana, 1937; *Enemigo rumor,* Havana, 1941; *Aventuras sigilosas,* Havana, 1945; *La fijeza,* Havana, 1949; *Dador,* Havana, 1960; *Orbita de Lezama Lima, Ensayo preliminar, selección y notas,* collected by A. A. Bravo, Havana, Unión, 1966. Also: *Lezama Lima,* Buenos Aires, J. Alvárez, 1968 (prose and poetry); *Poesia completa,* Havana, Arte y Literatura, Instituto del Libro, 1970.

Criticism: *La cantidad hechizada,* Madrid, Ediciones Jucar, 1974.

Other: *Tratados en la Habana,* Buenos Aires, La Flor, 1969, and as *Algunos Tratados en la Habana,* Barcelona, Anagrama, 1971.

Editor of: *Antologia de la poesia cubana,* Havana, Consejo Nacional de Cultura, 1965.

Biographical/Critical Sources: José Augustin Goytisolo, *Polible imagen de José Lezama Lima,* with preface and notes by Goytisolo, Barcelona, Libre de Sinera, 1969; *Armando Alvárez* Bravo's *Orbita de Lezama Lima,* cited above in poetry section; review of *Paradiso* in *Acoma,* No. 3 (February 1972), pp. 132-135; Max Henriquez Ureña, *Panorama histórico de la literatura cubana,* New York, 1963, pp. 433-435; and see *Review 74* (Special issue on Lezama's novel *Paradiso,* New York), No. 12 (Fall 1974, 83 pp.).

LIMON DE ARCE, José

b. 1877, Arecibo, Puerto Rico.
Playwright.

In 1914 Limón de Arce founded the journal *La Voz de la Unión* as a voice for his desire to preach Puerto Rican independence. When the island became a "territory" of the U. S. he, with 287 others, renounced American (U. S.) citizenship, and became "stateless." His play *Después de la Prohibición* satirized the puritanical and (unenforceable law of Liquor Prohibition) imposed on Puerto Rico along with other U. S. territories and was played with great success.

Writings: Plays: *Redención* (4 acts, prose), San Juan, Prats, 1906; *Almas y olas* (farce in 3 acts, verse), unpublished; *Después de la Prohibición* (1 act, "bufo-cómico-satirico," prose and verse), performed Arecibo, Mayagüez and in San Juan, by the Bonoris-Saavedra Company; *El triunfo de la caridad* (1 act dramatization of Masonic Lodge philosophy, in verse), performed in the Teatro Oliver of Arecibo.

Masonic Lore: *Horas de acacia,* San Juan, 1926.

LIZASO, Félix

b. 1891, Cuba.
Playwright, literary critic, biographer, historian, essayist, editor.

Lizaso is pre-eminently a scholar of José Marti. Lizaso's one theatrical work, devoted to Marti's life, is *Estapas martianas,* with its five parts: "El primer discurso [of Marti before the court charged with fraud], "La bandera que nadie conocia," "Reconciliación cubana," "El viajero iluminado," and "La muerte en el campamento."

Lizaso was an active member of the "Grupo Minorista" and contributor to its voice, the journal *Social,* founded by Conrado Walter Massaguer, and later he helped found the *Revista de Avance* with Jorge Mañach, Juan Marinello and others.

Writings: Play: *Estampas martianas,* written with Rafael Marquina (1887-1960).

Literary History: *Panorama de la cultura cubana,* Mexico, 1949.

Editor of: *La poesia moderna en Cuba,* Madrid, 1926 (edited with José Antonio Fernández de Castro); *Ensayistas contemporáneos, 1900-1920,* Havana, 1938.

Works on Marti: *Marti, mistico del deber,* Buenos Aires, 1940; *Mendive, Maestro de*

Marti, 1937; *Pasión de Marti,* 1938; *Marti y la utopia de América,* 1942; *Marti, espiritu de la guerra justa,* 1944; Preface by Lizaso to *José Marti Apuntes, ineditos,* Havana, 1951; *Marti, critico de arte,* 1953; *Marti, precursor de la UNESCO,* 1954; and editor of *Epistolario de José Marti,* 3 vols., 1930-1931; *Articulos desconocidos de Marti,* 1930; and the 20 volumes of the review, *Archivo José Marti,* all published in Havana.

LLANES, Manuel

b. 1899, Santo Domingo, Dominican Republic.
Poet.

Llanes was a leading member of "La Poesia Sorprendida" group with his friend Rafael Américo Henriquez after having passed through a Postumista phase. In his verse he combined lines from various sources with his own in a bizarre jarring fashion, not unlike some of the free-associational experiments of the surrealists. He begins his poem "Rutas Nocturnas":

Duerman. Oid insectos: sabéis algo del ministerio
en la blásfema azul de la oración que fenece . . . ?
Cuando tocan las timidas esquilas del recuerdo,
a veces llora sin saber por qué llora los muertos.
Y se volvieron alegres, mucho más alegres la campanas . . .

and he ends the poem:

El destino de la cuerda tendida sobre un abismo,
un equilibrio de mis ritmos. Tiembla como la primera estrella.

Writings: Poetry: *El fuego,* S. Domingo, Col. La Isla Necessaria, 1953; and poems in various journals and anthologies including Manuel Rueda's *Antologia* . . . , 1972, which has critical comments on some of the works, pp. 163-177.

LLENAS, Alejandro

b. February 14, 1844, Santo Domingo, Dominican Republic; d. May 29, 1902.
Folklorist, historian, medical doctor.

Llenas took a medical degree from the University of Paris in 1874 and returned the next year to Santo Domingo for a career in medicine. He entered politics, however, and served in the national chamber as a Deputy for Santiago de los Caballeros and was a diplomat in Haiti and Rome, Italy. He belonged also to many scientific organizations, national and international.

He published many studies of early Dominican history in such journals as *El Dominicano* ("Invasión de Toussaint Louverture," and Invasión de Dessalines"); and *Minas, El Porvenir.*

Writings: Folklore-history: "Expedición de Penn y Venables," in *El Teléfono,* S. Domingo, No. 295 (1891); "La Isabella," in *El Eco del Pueblo,* Santiago, No. 295 (1891); "Campaña de 1845 y Guerra de Independencia," in *El Eco del Pueblo,* No. 118, and, following numbers of July 1888. Copies of these and other articles are in one ms. collection held by the Sociedad Amantes de la Luz de Santiago; "La Boca del Indio," first published in *La Opinión,* S. Domingo, edición extraordinario (March 30, 1932); republished in Emilio Rodriguez Demorizi's *Tradiciones y cuentos dominicanos,* 1969; pp. 133-138.

Scientific Research: *Descubrimiento del cráneo de un indio ciguayo en Santo Domingo,* published in French translation by C. Armando Rodriguez, Nantes, France; also published in original Spanish, with notes by V. Alfau Durán, in *Clio,* No. 78 (1947).

Biographical/Critical Sources: for study of Llenas' journalistic pieces see M. A. Amiama's *El Periodismo en la República Dominicana,* S. Domingo, 1933, pp. 46, 47, 54; also see *Viejas memorias,* p. 28, by Sócrates Nolasco for brief comment on Llenas's journalism, and see Emilio Cordero Michel's *La revolución haïtiana y Santo Domingo,* S. Domingo, 1968, p. 88.

LLES Y BERDAYES, Fernando

b. 1883, Seiba Mocha, Cuba; d. 1949.
Playwright, essayist, poet.

Lles was strongly influenced by the works of Friedrich Nietzche and his own plays and philosophical essays are pessimistic and anti-religious. His poetry appeared in three collections along with that of his brother's work (for which see Francisco Lles).

Writings: Play: *La bestia* (3 acts, prose: written with Francisco Lles), published in pamphlet form, date unknown.

Philosophical Essays: *La higuera de Timón,* Matanzas, 1921; *La metafisica en el arte,* Matanzas, 1922; *La sombra de Heráclito,* Havana, 1923; *La escudilla de Diógenes,* Havana, 1924; *El individualismo,* Matanzas, 1926; *Individualismo, socialismo y comunismo, Valencia, 1932; El individuo, la Sociedad, y el Estado,* Havana, 1933; and *Conferencias,* Havana, 1944.

Poetry: *Crepúsculos,* 1909; *Sol de invierno,* 1911; and *Limoneros en flor,* 1912, all published in Matanzas.

LLES Y BERDAYES, Francisco

b. 1887, Matanzas, Cuba; d. 1921.
Poet.

An early modernist, Francisco Lles' verse was mildly philosophical. He published three volumes with his brother Fernándo.

Writings: Poetry: *Crepúsculos,* 1909; *Sol de invierno,* 1911; *Limoneros en flor,* 1912, all in Matanzas.

LLOPIS, Rogelio

b. 1926, Cuba (?).
Storywriter.

Educated in New York City, Llopis has a wide experience of life and often writes fantasies ranging from the early models of H. G. Wells to that of Jorge Luis Borges.

Writings: Stories: *La guerra y los basiliscos,* Havana, Unión, 1962; *El fabulista,* Havana, Revolución, 1963; and *El buscador de tesoros,* Havana, Unión, 1971.

"A Horrible Man" appears in English translation by Jean Franco in *Writers from the New Cuba,* E. M. Cohen, ed., Harmondsworth, England, Penguin, 1967.

LLORENS TORRES, Luis

b. May 14, 1878, Collores de Juana Diaz, Puerto Rico; d. June 15, 1944, San Juan.
Poet, essayist-critic, playwright, lawyer, politician.

After local studies, Lloréns took a degree in philosophy and letters at the University of Grenada where he also took his law degree. After a relatively fallow period on returning to Puerto Rico, Lloréns founded the *Revista de las Antillas* (1913) as a showpiece for his fellow modernistas, his own new work therein being entitled "Visiones de mi musa." He also founded "Pancalismo" (todo es bello) and "Panedismo" (todo es verso).

Though one of the earliest Puerto Rican poets influenced by "modernismo," a late 19th century poetic development coming from Spain and itself a result of even earlier French symbolist developments in Paris, Lloréns was politically wary of social changes and otherwise conservative. His political leanings rested more on nostalgia for the mother country, Spain, than a true intellectual conservatism, for he was a member of the upper creole circles.

An admirer of Rubén Dario, Lloréns' verse was always varied and original, often patriotic in a general way, and he considered himself the national poet of the island. Luis Araquistain considered him one of the greatest poets of Latin America.

The first two stanzas (of four) of Lloréns "Oración Criolla" give some idea of his descriptiveness:

Soy higo de las playas tropicales,
donde el palmar al viento se desfleca,
y en el colchón de la hojarasca seca,
adormeci mis brios ancestrales.

La palma hinchó sus pechas maternales
bajo sus alas de amorosa clueca
y el sol ecuatorial hiló en su rueca
el lino de mis cálidos pañales.

Writings: Poetry: *Fragmento, soneto,* and *Adiós,* (in a very small volume), Granada, Spain, 1899; *Al pie de la Alhambra,* Granada, Imprenta Viuda e hijos de Sabatel, 1899; *Sonetos sinfónicos,* San Juan, Antillana, 1914 (in Biblioteca Americana, Vol. I); *La canción de las Antillas y otros poemas* (the title poem "La Canción de los Antilles" was first published in 1913), San Juan, Negociado de Materiales, Imp. y Transporte, 1929; *Voces de la campana mayor,* San Juan (Aguadilla), Edit. Puertorriqueña, 1935; Alturas de América, San Juan, Imp. Baldrich, 1940; *Poesías*, San Juan, Instituto de Cultura Puertorriqueña, 1959; *Obras completas,* Vol. I (Poesia), San Juan, Instituto de Cultura Puertorriqueña, 1967; and verse in various anthologies, including six poems in L. Hernández Aquino's *El modernismo en Puerto Rico,* San Juan, 1967, and *Antologia de la poesia puertorriqueña,* E. Fernández Méndez, ed., San Juan, 1968.

Play: *El gritos de Lares,* 1917; reprinted in *Obras completas,* San Juan, Instituto de Cultura Puertorriqueña, 1967-1969 in 3 vols., with introduction, biographical notes and analysis by Carmen Marrero (in Vol. I). (Also see introduction to Vol. II by Maria Teresa Babin, and Volume III, which contains his journalistic pieces.

Essays: *América,* 1898; but most of occasional essays appeared in journals and are not otherwise collected. A few prose pieces are in Luis Hernández Aquino's *El modernismo en Puerto Rico,* op. cit. (pp. 139-141); "Visiones de mi musa" appeared in *Revista de las Antillas* (June 1913).

Criticism: "Pancalismo," and "Panedismo," both first published in *Revista de las Antillas* (1913), and, in 1914, as the preface to his collection: *Sonetos sinfónicos.*

Biographical/Critical Sources: Pedro Juan Labarthe, "Luis Lloréns Torres, Poeta de la Tierras Antillanas," in Repertorio americano, Vol. 17, No. 24, p. 375 (discusses author and the novel *Voces de la campaña mayor*); Luis Hernández Aquino, *Nuestra aventura literaria,* Puerto Rico, 1966 (Chapter I is entitled "Pancalismo y Panedismo" after Lloréns' essays of 1913); also see Hernández Aquino's "Rubén Dario y Puerto Rico: apuntes para nuestra historia literaria," in *Revista del Instituto de Cultura Puertorriqueña,* No. 9 (October-December 1960), pp. 1-4; C. Rosa-Nieves, chapter in *Ensayos escogidas,* San Juan, 1970, pp. 141-159; A. S. Pedreira and Concha Meléndez, "Luis Lloréns Torres: poeta de Puerto Rico," in *El Mundo* (San Juan, August 20, 1933). Also see Chapter VI in *La poesia modernista en Puerto Rico* (San Juan, 1969), by E. A. Laguerre, pp. 125-138; Lidio Cruz Monclova, "Con el iniciador del modernismo," in *Puerto Rico Ilustrado* (May 31, 1919); Miguel Guerra Mondragón, "El movimiento literario," in the *Revista de las Antillas* (June 1914) which discusses Lloréns Torres on p. 84; Palmira Cabrera de Ibarra, "Luis Lloréns Torres ante el paisaje," unpublished M. A. Thesis, U. of P. R., 1946; Washington Lloréns, *Los grandes amores del poeta Luis Lloréns Torres,* San Juan, Campos, 1959; Carmen Marrero de Figueroa, *Luis Lloréns Torres: Vida y obra (1876-1944),* 2nd ed., San Juan, Ed. Cordillera, 1968 (187 pp. with bibliography); Sócrates Nolasco, *Escritores de Puerto Rico,* Manzanilla, Cuba, 1953.

LLUCH MORA, Francisco

b. 1924, Yauco, Puerto Rico.
Poet, critic.

Lluch is a professor at the University of Puerto Rico at Mayagüez. He has been part of the poetic current called "Transcendentalisino" and has published in *El Mundo, Alma Latina, Orfeo* and Pegaso.

Lluch's décima (called "Décima") is typical of his work:

Blanco rostro de ternura
catado en raros jazmines,
pureza de serafines,
flor exacta de hermosura.
Irradia en la comisura
de tus labios la sonrisa,

simbolo y que se irisa
mientras el cuello de nieve,
si palpita, no se mueve,
aunque lo bese la brisa.

Much of Lluch's later work is religious, reflecting the Catholic Bible and the Spanish mystics.

Writings: Poetry: *Tu presencia,* 1949; *Del asedio y la clausura,* San Juan, Edit. Yaurel, 1950; *Coral de la alegria,* 1953; *Del barro a Dios,* San Juan, Yaurel, 1955; *Canto desesperado o la ceniza,* 1955; *El ruiseñor y el olvido,* Barcelona, Edit. Rumbos, 1960; *Momentos de la alegria,* San Juan, Ediciones Yaurinquen, 1959; *Poemas sin nombre; Canciones,* San Juan, Edit. Club de la Prensa, 1963; three of his poems are in *Antologia de la poesia puertorriqueña,* E. Fernández Méndez, ed., San Juan, 1968.

Criticism: *La huella de cuatro poetas en las coplas de Jorge Maurique,* 1964.

Critical Essays: *Miradero: Ensayas de critica literaria,* San Juan, Editorial Cordillera, 1966.

Biographical/Critical Sources: Cesáreo Rosa-Nieves, his introduction to Lluch's *Del asedio y la clausura,* 1950; F. Manrique Cabrera, *Historia de la literatura puertorriqueña,* Rio Piedras, 1969, pp. 363-364.

LOPEZ, César

b. 1933, Santiago, Cuba.
Poet, storywriter, theatre critic.

After medical studies completed at the Universities of Havana and Salamanca, López was named Cuban Consul in Scotland and later became an official of the Ministry of Foreign Affairs. Ever more interested, however, in a literary career and after 1959 a frequent contributor to leading Cuban journals, he published many poems, critical articles, reviews, and tales. In the 1960's, he became "coordinator" of the Unión de Escritores y Artistas.

Writings: Poetry: *Silencio en voz de muerte,* Havana, UNEAC, 1963; *Apuntes para un pequeño viaje,* Havana, 1966; *Primer libro de la ciudad,* Havana, UNEAC, 1966; poems in many journals and anthologies, including *Con Cuba* (a bi-lingual collection), edited by Nathaniel Tarn, New York, 1966.

Stories: *Circulando al cuadrado,* Havana, Revolución, 1964; story "Pedazos y despedazados" appears in *Narrativa cubana de la revolución,* J. M. Caballero Bonald, ed., Madrid, 1969.

LOPEZ, Magda

(pseudonym for **Magdalena Lopez de VICTORIA Y FERNANDEZ**)

LOPEZ, René

b. 1882, Cuba; d. 1909.
Poet.

López was one of the innovators of Cuban poetry, experimenting with the shorter 12-syllable line, mixed metrical patterns within a verse, and his verse was thoughtful in tone. This stanza from his "Retrato" of 1903 reads:

Anchas espaldas y robustos brazos;
jabón que adorna brilladores lazos;
oscuros botas, toledano acero.

López was most influenced by his fellow Cuban poet Casal and to a lesser extent by Rubén Dario, as were all of the modernistas.

Writings: Poetry: no collection; miscellaneous verses in journals and anthologies. (The doctoral dissertation of Maria Rodriguez (University of Havana) contains most of the work from journals which was brought together by Rodriguez).

Biographical/Critical Sources: Max Henriquez Ureña, *Panorama histórico de la literatura cubana,* New York, 1963, pp. 285-287; also see the above mentioned unpublished Ph. D. dissertation of M. Rodriguez.

LOPEZ CONSUEGRA, Andrés

b. ca. 1808, Cuba.
Playwright.

Once a popular dramatist, López is now all but a forgotten figure of the earliest period of Cuban playwriting.

Writings: Plays: *La Romántico-mania* (1 act comedy), Havana, Boloña, 1838; *Conversación de un clásico cesante con un romántico* (1 act comedy), 1838; *El doncel* (verse), Havana, Imp. de la Real Marina, 1839; *Wenemaro o Las pasiones y el juramento* (5 acts, prose), Havana, Barcina, 1941, premiered Teatro Tacón, Havana, December 15, 1841.

LOPEZ LOPEZ, Joaquin

b. August 19, 1900, Guayama, Puerto Rico; d. 1942, Hato Rey.
Poet, educator.

López was an official of the Department of Hispanic Studies at the University of Puerto Rico under Dr. Antonio S. Pedreira.

His first published verse appeared in *El Carnaval* in 1922 as well as in *El Imparcial, El Mundo,* and *Puerto Rico Ilustrado* and reflected Dario and Julio Herrera Reissig, but his later work has developed away from these romantic-modernista origins to a more Lorcian tone and expression as evidenced in *A plena lumbre* and *Romancero de la luna.*

A "negrista" poem of interest is "La negra Macomba" (from *Brújula,* Vol. III, nos. 9-10):

Zarcillos de tizones penden de sus orejas;
sus ancas de azabache imponen majestad,
al ritmo de la bomba su talle se cimbrea,
y ondula, tiembla, y gima y se vuelve un cantar. (3rd stanza)

and the poem ends:

Cachongos cocoteros de melcocha de luna
a la negra Macomba agua dulce darán,
porque Macomba quiere, porque Macomba manda,
esta noche la noche se ha hecho plata de mar.

Writings: Poetry: *Obra poética,* San Juan, Edit. Coqui, 1972(?). Also volumes: *A plena lumbre,* 1934; *Romancero de la luna,* San Juan, Biblioteca de Autores Puertorriqueños, 1939.

Biographical/Critical Sources: Edgar Martinez Masdeu, *Joaquin López: su vida y su obra,* San Juan, Edit. Coqui, 1972.

LOPEZ SURIA, Violeta

b. 1926, Santurce, Puerto Rico.
Poet, storywriter, teacher.

Violeta López Suria took her B. A. and M. A. at the University of Puerto Rico and her Ph.D. at the Universidad Central de Madrid in 1961. Her work is limpid, almost infantile in its clarity and honesty.

A typical work of López Suria is this 12-line poem "De mano el mundo todo":

No se trata de un rito obedencial
pero iremos
Rota la carátula
de la desigualdad
habra un apretón de espiritu
Oye tú, nacida la esperanza
Caerá un influjo de relámpagos.
Se partirá la tierra
y estaremos tan juntos
que encarnará Dios
y casi por amor
ni lo veremos.

Writings: Poetry: *Gotas en mayo,* Santurce, 1953; *Elegia,* 1953; *Es un trigal de ausencia,* 1954; *Sentimiento de un viaje,* 1955; *Riverside, 1955; Poema de la yerma virgen,* 1956; *Unas cuantras estrellas en mi cuarto,* 1957; *Diluvio,* 1958; *Amorosamente,* 1961; *Hubo unos piños claros,* 1961; *La piel pegado al alma,* San Juan, Imp. Venezuela, 1962 (awarded a prize by the Instituto de Literatura de Puerto Rico); *Poemas al la cántora,* 1963; *La nubes dejan sombras,* San Juan, Imp. Venezuela, 1965; *Me va la vida,* 1965; other verse in various journals and collections, including F. Manrique Cabrera's *Historia de la literatura puertorriqueña,* Rio Piedras, 1969 (contains the poem "Mis manos"), p. 369, originally published in *Orfeo,* (Yauco, P. R., December 1955). Also: *Obsesión de heliotropo,* Rio Piedras, Edit. Edil, 1969;

Antologia poética, selected and ed. by Juan Martinez Copo, Rio Piedras, Edit. Universitaria, 1970.

Stories: in *Gotas en mayo* (along with verse), 1953.

LOPEZ DE BRINAS, Felipe

b. 1822, Cuba; d. 1877.
Poet.

López' poetry is prosaic, unoriginal, though he once had a modest reputation and his "Canto safico" was widely anthologized in the 19th century.

Writings: Poetry: *Poesias,* Havana, 1849, Cuba, 1855; *Al descubrimiento de América por Cristóbal Colón,* 1855; *Fabulas, alegorias y consejas,* 1856.

LOPEZ DE VICTORIA Y FERNANDEZ, Magdalena

(pseudonym: **Magda LOPEZ**)
b. May 25, 1900, Yauco, Puerto Rico.
Poet, painter, teacher.

A member of the post-modernista group of the 1930's, Magda López later followed Luis Hernández Aquino into "Integralismo." Rosa-Nieves said "Su lirica se destaca por la ternura, dulcedumbre, religiosidad sencilla y el pacifico existir hogareño."

These few lines from the first two stanzas of "En secreto de Albas" (from *Amor*) give her beauty:

En secreto de Albas mi cántara fragante
Vuelva sombras. Estamos
frente al mundo, los dos.
Me hallarás en la Esencia de tu amasijo claro
cuando nazcan tus blancos clarines al Amor.

Por los áureos caminos cargan sueños las horas.
Rios de cumbres encienden cordilleras de luz.
Voy dando la voz dulce para el vuelo de un rezo;
¡alas, para tu azul!

Writings: Poetry: *Hijos,* 1930; *De Puerto Rico al Corazón de America,* 1943; *Amor,* 1956.

LOPEZ Y LORA, José Ramón

b. February 3, 1866, Monte Cristi, Dominican Republic; d. August 2, 1922, Santo Domingo.
Storywriter, historian, novelist, playwright.

López was a sagacious, temperate mind and his essay of 1915, *La paz and la República,* sought to examine the reasons for the horrible civil wars of the past several decades in the Republic. His earlier essay, *La alimentación. . .*was a deep look at the structure of Dominican society and the relations between the various groups in it, particularly the problem of the peasants who were poor, black and uneducated. He became the director of many journals, including *El Dominicano* (1909), *El Nacional* (1911) and *Pluma y Espada* (1911, 1921-22).

Writings: Essays: *La alimentación y las razas,* Santiago, Cuba, 1st ed., 1896; 2nd ed., also Santiago, Cuba, 1899, reprinted, No. 1 of *Revista dominicana de cultura* (November 1955) edited by Emilio Rodriguez Demorizi; *La República dominicana (Memoria oficial para la Exposición de Milan),* 1906; *La paz en la República dominicana,* S. Domingo, Contribución al estudio de la sociologia nacional, 1915; *Censo y catastro de la común de Santo Domingo,* 1919; *Manual de agricultura,* 1920.

Folk-stories: *Cuentos puertoplateños,* 1904.

Novelette: *Nisia,* 1898, 1904.

Novel: *Dolores,* published only in fragments in *El Lápiz* (Venezuela, 1892).

History: "Colonización de la frontera occidental," in *Ateneo* (1910) and reprinted by Rodriguez Demorizi in *Cuadernos dominicanos de cultura,* No. 2 (October 1942).

Geography: *Geografia de la América antillana, en particular de la República Dominicana,* 1915.

Play: in ms: with Virginia Elena Ortea, title unknown.

Biographical/Critical Sources: J. Balaguer's *Historia de la literatura dominicana,* 1970, pp. 275-276; Max Henriquez Ureña's *Panorama histórico de la literatura dominicana,* 2 vols., 1966: see especially Vol. II, pp. 344-345.

LOVEIRA Y CHIRINO, Carlos

b. 1882, El Santo (Las Villas), Cuba; d. January 26, 1928.

Novelist.

Loveira was a worker on railroads in Cuba, Mexico, Chile and took part in many strikes. His stories appeared in a wide range of Latin-American journals. In time his work and experience gained him a position in the Cuban Labor Ministry and he often represented his country at international labor conferences.

He helped found *Cuba Contemporánea,* a publishing house which brought out his own work. All of his fiction was in the naturalist mode, but his last work, *Juan Criollo,* was particularly direct in its vigorous portrayal of actions and characters. His work has a strong social-critical tendency.

Writings: Novels: *Los immorales,* Havana, 1919; *Generales y doctores,* Havana, 1920, and Havana, Consejo Nacional de Cultura, 1962; *Los ciegos,* Havana, El Siglo XX, 1922; *Juan Criollo,* Havana, 1927, and Havana, Consejo Nacional de Cultura, 1962 by *Cuba Contemporánea;* American edition: New York, Oxford University Press, 1965.

Editor of: Adrian del Valle: *Escritor y Periodista de Cuba* (Conferencia dada por el Sr. . ., el dia 13 Febrero de 1927 en la Academia Nacional de Artes y Letras. Havana, Siglo XX, 1927 (29 pp.).

Biographical/Critical Sources: Miguel A. Martinez, "Vision cubana de Carlos Loveira," unpublished Ph.D. dissertation, Northwestern University, 1969.

LOYNAZ, Dulce Maria

b. 1901, Havana, Cuba.

Poet, novelist.

A member of a family of many poets (Enrique, b. 1904; Carlos, b. 1906; Flor, b. 1907), Dulce Maria Loynaz dealt with the intimate moments of her life in luminous lines of very personal fantasy, as in these lines from "Premonición":

Alguien exprimio un zumo
de fruita negra en mi alma:
Quedé amarga y sobria
como niebla y retama.
Nadie toque mi pan,
nadie beba mi agua . . .
Dejadme sola todos.
Presiento que una cosa ancha y oscura
Y desolada viene sobre mi,
como la noche sobre la llanura . . .

She had a degree in law.

Writings: Poetry: *Versos, 1920-1938,* Havana, 1938(?); *Obra lirica,* Madrid, 1953; *Juegos de agua,* Madrid, 1947; *Poemas sin nombre,* Madrid, Aguilar, 1953. Her work is in Cintio Vitier's *Cinquenta años de poesia cubana (1902-1952),* Havana, 1952.

Prose-Poems: *Jardin,* Madrid, 1951; *Poemas (1902-1952),* Havana, 1952.

Novel: *Jardin. Novela lirica,* Madrid, Aguilar, 1951.

Biographical/Critical Sources: Polly F. Harrison, "Images and Exile: The Cuban Woman and Her Poetry," in *Revista Interamericana,* Vol. IV, No. 2 (Summer 1974), esp. pp. 200-202.

LOZANO CASADO, Miguel

b. 1873, Medellin, Spain; d. 1939, Cuba.

Poet, journalist.

Though born in Spain, Lozano spent most of his years in Cuba and his work is considered part of the island's literature. He published in *Letras* and *El Figaro* journals and wrote several short novels and two general autobiographical narratives. His verse is generally elegant, often recalling the lost days of the Moorish period in ancestral Spain, and reflecting the influence of Villaespesa. Max Henriquez Ureña (in *Panoramo histórico de la literatura cubana*) finds him capable of the purest and most personal moments, however, especially when dealing with his own strongest feelings, as in these lines, source unidentified:

Corazón, ya somos viejos;
hemos dejado tan lejos
nuestra juventud de ayer,
que ha nevado en mi cabeza . . .

Hoy, corazón, reza, reza
por la vida que ahora empieza
y por la enorme tristeza
de lo que no ha de volver.

Writings: Poetry: *Claros de luna,* 1904; *La canción de los recuerdos,* 1906; *Tiempos de leyenda,* 1909, all Havana.

Short Novels (collection): *Del amor y del recuerdo* (experiences in a hospital), Havana, 1907; *Covadonga* (experiences on a farm), date unknown; *La novela de la vida,* Havana, 1913.

LUACES, Joaquin Lorenzo

(also **Lorenzo Luaces FORNARIS Y JOAQUIN**)

b. July 21, 1826, Havana, Cuba;
d. November 7, 1867.
Poet, playwright, translator, storywriter.

Luaces began the study of philosophy and law, but forced out of university by ill-health and enabled by his family's wealth, he devoted himself to literature, residing mostly in the southern Cuban island of Isla de Pinos until 1852. Returning to Havana, he joined the group around Felipe Poey and published in many reviews, founding *La Piraguo* (lasting 1856-57) with José Fornaris. He edited the second anthology to bear the name *Cuba Poética,* Havana, 1858. His poem on the inventor of the underseas cable "A Cyrus Field" won a prize from the University of Havana in 1858 as did his poem "El trabajo" in 1867, the award coming just a few days after his early death, November 7, 1867.

Max Henriquez Ureña believes Luaces to have produced a few excellent poems, citing particularly "Ultimo amor" of 1853, the elegy "El la muerte de don José de la Luz y Caballero" of 1862 and he quoted extensively from "Oración de Matatias," of 1965 in his study of Luaces.

Luaces' friendship with José Fornaris influenced him to write stories of local color or folkloric tendency—in the criollos-mo or ciboneyismo movement. Such tales or sketches as "El amante indiscreto," "Adiós del montero" were in this mode, and he then moved to more complex romances such as "La flor," of 1856, "La guajira coqueta" of 1856, and others published in the journals of the day.

Writings: Translations: of Mosca's work as "En busca de Cupido" from Italian, published in "Canción de Harmodio y Aristogitan," (1852); an ode of Calistrato; portion of Abate Barthelmy's "Viaje del joven Abacarsis"; and a work of de Beranger's as "El Sello" (1849). Many of his erotic *Anacreonticas* poems are in *Cuba Literaria,* (1862).

Poetry: *Cuba, poema mitológico,* Havana, Comisión Nacional Cubana de la UNESCO, 1964; *Poesias de Joaquin Lorenzo Luaces,* Havana, 1857, poems in many journals and collections, including major poems in *Cuba y América* (1903) and "La oración de Matatias" in *Noches literarias en casa de Nicolas Azcarte,* Havana, 1866, and the *Antologia de poetas hispano-americanos* of Marcelino Menéndez y Pelayo, Madrid, 1911; in *La Moderna Poesia,* 1909; poem "El trabajo" is in 30 page booklet published in 1868; "Cuba" in *Revista de Cuba,* Vols. 10, 11 (1882).

Stories: "La piragua" and "Managua," both published in the review *La Piragua* (directed by Luaces y Fornaris, 1856) and others, some cited above, published in journals but never collected.

Plays: *Teatro,* Havana, Consejo Nacional de Cultura, 1964; *El mendigo rojo* (5 acts, verse), 1859, 2nd ed. published, Havana, Imp. La

Antilla, 1866; *Aristodemo* (5 acts, verse), Havana, Imp. La Antilla, 1867 and others; *Arturo de Osberg,* unpublished (tragedy); *El conde y el capitán,* unpublished (tragedy); *El fantasmón de Aravaca; La escuela de los parientes, Dos amigas; El becerro de oro* (1859), scenes published in *Liceo de Habana* (Havana, 1860); *A tigre y zorra y bull-dog* (5 acts, verse comedy), unpublished.

Letters and Notes: the legend "La cruz de la serviente" in *Cuban Biblioteca* Nacional collection of manuscripts.

Editor of: *Cuba poética,* Havana, 1858; 2nd ed., 1861.

Biographical/Critical Sources: Salvador Salazar's *Milanés, Luaces y la Avellaneda,* Madrid(?), 1916. Aurelio Mitjans discussed the plays, many of them he had read in the original manuscripts now lost, in his *Estudio sobre el movimiento cientifico y literario de Cuba,* Havana, 1890; Marcelino Menéndez y Pelayo, *Antologia de poetas hispano-americanos,* 2 vols., Madrid, Real Academia Española, 1911; Max Henriquez Ureña, *Panorama histórico de la literatura cubana,* New York, 1963, pp. 248-259.

LUGO, Américo

b. 1870, Dominican Republic; d. 1952.
Playwright, critic, essayist, historian, biographer, editor, lawyer.

Lugo took his law degree in 1889 and served a long life in the law and public service. His plays were extravagantly mannered and full of verbal fireworks, but weak theatrically.

Writings: Plays: *Ensayos dramáticos,* S. Domingo, Imp. La Cuna de América, 1906 (contains the monologues: *Elvira, Vispera de boda, En la peña pobre,* and the one act play, *El ávaro*); *Higuenamota* (1 act, folklore theme).

Essay: *A punto largo,* 1901, 2nd ed., Paris, Ollendorff, 1910.

Editor of: selection of works by Cuban poet, Marti: *Flor y lava,* Paris, 1912.

History: *La cuarta conferencia internacional americana,* Seville, 1912; *El estado dominicano ante el derecho público,* 1916; *La intervención americana,* 1916; *Camafeos,* 1919; *El plan de validación Huges-Peynado,* 1922; *Sobre lo que significaria para el pueblo dominicano la ratificación de los actos del gobierno militar norte-américano,* 1921; *El nacionalismo dominicano,* 1923; *Historia de Santo Domingo (desde 1556 hasta 1608),* 1952.

Law thesis: "¡En arreglada a Derecho Natural la prohibición de la investigación de la paternidad!"

Biography: *Jose Marti,* 1909.

LUGO, Samuel

b. 1905, Lares, Puerto Rico.
Poet, journalist.

Lugo's work is full of love of the countryside and his sympathy for the "jibaro" (countryman). One of his creole poems, "¿Y tu agüela, a onde ejta?" begins:

Ayé me diji te negro.
y hoy te boy a contejtá:
Mi mai se sienta en la sala,
¿y tú agüela, a' onde ejta?
. . . . . .

Lugo was an editor (1944-1945) of *Alma Latina* and *Bienestar Público* (1948).

As a fervent supporter of greater independence for Puerto Rico, Lugo joined the patriotic-nationalistic poets of the Ayalayismo movement (1929). Twelve years later (1941) he had joined the "Integralismo" group in Ponce (L. Hernández Aquino, Carmelina Vizcarrondo and Maria Mercedes Garriga).

Writings: Poetry: *Donde caen las claridades,* San Juan, Tip. Florete, 1931; *Yumbra,* San Juan, Imp. Venezuela, 1943; *Ronda de la llama verde,* San Juan, 1949; and much of his work is in *Puerto Rico Ilustrado, Alma Latina, Brújula,* and Asomante. Also see *Antologia poética,* foreword by Luis Hernández Aquino, Rio Piedras, Edit. Edil, 1971.

Biographical/Critical Sources: "El dia estético," in *Revista Bimestre Integralista,* I, 1 (June-July, 1941); Tomás Jesús Castro, *Esbozos,* Barcelona, 1957.

LUPERON, Gregorio

b. September 8, 1839, Puerto Plata, Dominican Republic; d. May 21, 1897. Autobiographer, historian, soldier.

An active soldier and statesman in Dominica's most troubled period, Luperón was a member of the government of President Espaillat and after the outbreak of revolts he was able to re-establish peace for a period in 1879, ruling for one year by the sword and attempting to set the country back on the way to voting and a civil government. He supported the resulting administration of President Meriño who came to power in 1880, but he went into opposition to President Heureaux in the next administration.

He was named Minister to several European governments and helped negotiate an Arbitration Convention between El Salvador and the Dominican Republic, the first of its sort between two Latin American states. In 1889, his effort to secure the presidency was again thwarted (he had made a tentative effort in1879-1880), and went into exile in 1894, remaining at St. Thomas where he composed his *Notas autobiográficas y apuntes históricos,* published the next year, 1895, in Puerto Rico. Severely ill shortly thereafter, he was allowed to come home by his old political enemy, Ulises Heureaux, only to die in his natal Puerto Plata a short while thereafter.

Balaguer says Luperón's *Notas* (beyond their historical worth and their lively picture of the revolutionary period in which he was the country's greatest soldier) is "el mejor libro de recuerdos personales de que se puede enorgullecar hasta hoy la literatura dominicana."

Writings: Autobiography: *Notas autobiográficas y apuntes históricos,* Puerto Rico, 1895.

Biographical/Critical Sources: J. Balaguer's *Historia de la literatura dominicana,* 1970, pp. 208-214, Manuel Rodriguez Objio's *Vida del General Gregorio Luperón e Historia de la Restauración,* 1939.

LUZ Y CABALLERO, José Cipriano de la

(pseudonym: **Filolezes**)
b. 1800, Cuba; d. June 22, 1862.
Essayist, orator, teacher, philosopher.

Graduate of the Seminario de San Carlos (B. A. in philosophy), and taking a law degree in 1823, Luz early travelled in the United States and Europe, including Russia. He was a polyglot and a leading cultural figure in his day. Caballero was also a famed orator and intellectual, serving as director of the Colegio del Salvador for many years. He was a member of the Sociedad Económica de Amigos del Pais, part of the Academia de Literatura. In 1843, he moved to Paris to seek medical treatment, but he returned in 1844 to stand trial, accused of participating in the so-called "Escalera" plot of blacks against whites (eventually to be acquitted).

Writings: Essays: *Aforismos, Elencos y discursos académicos, Escritos sociales y cientificos, Escritos literarios,* with *De la vida intima,* as part of the Biblioteca de autores cubanos, published in five-volume collection by the University of Havana, 1946-1948. This collection of *Obras* also includes "Impugnación a las doctrinas filosóficas de Victor Cousin (Primera parte, en que se refuta su análisis del 'Ensayo sobre el entendimiento humano' de Locke,' " written 1840 under pen-name "Filolezes"), part of vast manuscript of which only 140 pages were actually published in Luz y Caballero's own time.

Biographical/Critical Sources: Ramón Zambrano y Valdés, "Elogio de José de la Luz y Caballero"; Francisco Zayas, "Palabras ante el cadaver de don José de la Luz y Caballero," in *Libros de lectura,* edited by Luis Felipe Mantilla (1833-1878); Max Henriquez Ureña, *Panorama histórico de la literatura cubana,* New York, 1963, pp. 144-152; Manuel I. Mesa Rodriguez has a biography on José de la Luz, details unknown.

MACAU GARCIA, Miguel Angel

b. 1886, Matanzas, Cuba.
Playwright, poet, novelist.

Macau was primarily a writer for the stage, but he did publish two modest volumes of late romantic verse in 1912.

Writings: Plays: *La justicia en la inconsciencia* (3 acts), Matanzas, Betancourt, 1909, premiered Teatro Santo de Matanzas, August 26, 1909 by Compañia Evangelina Adams; *Julián* (verse monologue), Matanzas, El Radium, 1910; *El triunfo de la vida* (2 act comedy), winner of Juegos Florales de Oriente prize, 1914; *Obras dramaticas,* Matanzas, Imp. González, 1913, which includes: *La justicia en la inconsciencia* (first published 1910); *Julián, La partida* (prose "duodrama"); *Teatro,* 1924, which includes: *La herencia maldita; La fuerza incontrastable; La encina; El triunfo de la vida.*

Novels: *Clotilde Tejidor. Novela cubana,* Havana, Edit. Lex, 1958; *Y es salvaba el amor,* Havana, P. Fernández, 1959.

Poetry: *Lirica saturnal,* Havana, 1912; *Flores del trópico,* Barcelona, 1912; *Véspero radiante,* Havana, 1961; *Poema a mi valle, canto en espineles,* Havana, 1962.

Novel: *Y es salvaba el amor,* Havana, P. Fernández, 1959.

MADAN Y GARCIA, Augusto E.

b. 1853, Matanzas, Cuba; d. 1915.
Playwright, poet.

Though considered at best only a mediocre writer, Madan probably was one of Cuba's most prolific playwrights. His very extensive library on the theatre, available to all amateurs and professionals of the stage, became an important intellectual source for his generation of playwrights.

Writings: Plays: *La piel del tigre* (2 act comedy, verse), Madrid, 1872, and Madrid, J. Rodriguez, 1877; *La lucha de la codicia* (1 act), Madrid, 1873, 2nd ed., Matanzas, Imp. La Nacional, 1880; *Galileo* (3 acts, historical drama, verse), Madrid, López, 1873; 2nd ed., Madrid, Indicador de los caminos de hierro, 1875; *El anillo de Fernando IV* (4 acts, historical drama, verse), Madrid, 1874, 2nd ed., Madrid, Rodriguez, 1877; *El puñal de los celos* (2 acts, verse),

Madrid, 3rd ed., Madrid, Rodriguez, 1877; *Bermudo* (3 acts, verse), Madrid, Rodriguez, 1875, 2nd ed., 1877; *El gran suplicio* (2 acts, verse), Madrid, Rodriguez, 1875; *Las redes de amor* (1 act farce, verse), Madrid, Hernández, 1875; *Este coche se vende* (1 act, verse), Madrid, Moliner, 1875, 2nd ed., Matanzas, La Nacional, 1880; *Los cómicos en camisa* (1 act, verse), Madrid, Moliner, 1875; *Genio y figura hasta la sepultura* (1 act farce, verse), Madrid, Indicador de los caminos de hierro, 1875; 2nd ed., Madrid, J. Rodriguez, 1876; *Asdrúbal* (5 act historical drama, verse), Madrid, Indicador, 1875; *Rosa* (3 acts, verse), Madrid, Rodriguez, 1876; *Matrimonio al vapor* (2 act comedy, verse), Madrid, 1876; *Percances matrimoniales* (1 act, verse), Madrid, Rodriguez, 1876; *El talismán conjugal* (1 act, verse), Madrid, Rodriguez, 1876; *Robar con honra* (4 acts, verse), Madrid, Moliner, 1877; *Viaje en globo* (1 act satire), Madrid, Rodriguez, 1877; *Artistas para la Habana* (1 act, verse), Madrid, Rodriguez, 1877; *La escuela del crimen* (3 act melodrama), Madrid, Rodriguez, 1877; *El rival de un rey* (2 acts, verse), Madrid, Rodriguez, 1877; *Cuidado con los estudiantes* (1 act, verse), Madrid, Rodriguez, 1877; *Novio, padre y suegro* (2 acts, verse), Madrid, Rodriguez, 1877; *Deber y afecto en contienda* (3 acts, verse), Madrid, Rodriguez, 1877; *Fiebre de amor* (2 act prose farce), Matanzas, 1878; *Un besugo cantante* (4 acts, prose), Matanzas, 1878; *Curarse sin botica* (1 act, verse), Matanzas, 1878; *¡Es pariente de!!!* (macarronic verse), Matanzas, Imp. El Ferrocarril, 1879; *Consecuencias de un matrimonio* (2 acts, prose), Matanzas, El Ferrocarril, 1879; *Jugar al alza* (1 act, prose), Matanzas, El Ferrocarril, 1879; *El Capitán Amores* (2 acts, operatta, verse), Matanzas, El Ferrocarril, 1879; *La mujer del porvenir* (2 acts, verse), Matanzas, El Ferrocarril, 1879; *¡El Can Can!, Matanzas, El Ferrocarril, 1879; Percances del periodismo* (1 act, verse), Matanzas, E. Ferrocarril); *Dos torturas* (4 acts, verse), Matanzas, El Ferrocarril, 1879; *Todos hermanos* (1 act, verse), 3rd ed., Havana, La Propaganda Literaria, 1879, 5th ed., Matanzas, El Ferrocarril, 1880; *La Pimienta* (1 act comedy, verse), Havana, La Propaganda Literaria, 1879; *Contratiempos de la noche de bodas* (1 act prose), Matanzas, El Ferrocarril, 1879; *¡El!* (1 act, verse), Matanzas, El Ferrocarril, 1879; *El Capitán Centellas* (3 act prose melodrama), Matanzas, El Ferrocarril, 1879; *El Calvario de la deshonra* (3 acts, verse), Matanzas, Imp. del Diario, 1879, 2nd ed., Havana, Nuevo Ideal, 1906; *El cáncer social* (3 act comedy, verse), Havana, La Propaganda Literaria, 1879, 5th ed., Havana, Tip. Nuevo Ideal, 1905; *El Olimpo a la española* (2 acts, verse), Matanzas, El Ferrocarril, 1880; *La esposa de Putifar* (1 act verse), Matanzas, La Nacional, 1880; *Llueven huéspedes* (1 act, verse), Matanzas, El Ferrocarril, 1880; *La reina Moda,* 1880; *Un* El Ferrocarril, 1880; *La reina Moda,* 1880; *Un amadis por fuerza* (1 act comedy, verse), 1880; *Pablo y Virginia* (3 acts, verse), Matanzas, 1880; *Peraltilla* (4 act comedy, verse), 1880; *Cuerpo y alma* (1 act, verse), 1880; *El Calvario de los alma* (1 act, verse), 1880; all Matanzas, El Ferrocarril; *El Calvario de los tontos,* (2 acts, prose), Matanzas, La Nacional, 1880; *La Perla de Portugal,* (3 acts, verse), Matanzas, El Ferrocarril, 1880; *El Padrino universal* (1 act, verse and prose), Matanzas, El Ferrocarril, 1880; *Cleopatra* (3 act comedy, verse), Matanzas, La Nacional, 1881; *El rey mártir* (3 acts, verse), Matanzas, La Propaganda, 1894; *Obras dramáticas. Primera serie,* Havana, La Propaganda Literaria, 1879; *Obras completas,* Matanzas, El Ferrocarril, 2 vols., 1880-1881.

Biographical/Critical Sources: Rafael Maria Liern's "Dos palabres sobre las obras dramáticas de Augusto E. Madán y Garcia," which is foreword to *Obras dramáticas* (see above), 1879.

MALPICA Y LABARCA, Domingo

b. ca. 1860, Cuba; d. 1910.
Novelist.

Malpica's socio-historical novel *En el cafetal* (1890) is a weak work with poorly realized characters, though gracefully written.

Writings: Novel: *En el cafetal,* Havana, 1890.

MANET, Eduardo

b. 1927, Cuba.
Playwright, novelist, film writer, photographer.

Manet's work is poetic and very imagistic, though still full of the newest currents in Spanish and international theatre. His two novels, both in French, were published in Paris. He is of Cuban-French extraction.

Writings: Plays: *Scherzo,* published 1948; *Presagio,* 1950; *La infanta que quiso tener los ojos verdes,* 1951.

Novels: *Les étrangers dans la ville,* Paris, Juillard, 1960; *Un cri sur le rivage,* Paris, Juillard, 1963.

MANRIQUE CABRERA, Francisco

b. 1908, Bayamón, Puerto Rico.
Poet, literary historian, essayist, teacher.

Manrique's *Poemas de mi tierra-tierra* (1936) was received as a major collection of Puerto Rican poetry. Rosa-Nieves said of him, "El jibarismo poético de Cabrera, apares de abundante de acrobacias lingüísticas y de juegos malabares de abolengo barroco." José Emilio Gonzáles said of him: " . . .tambien la adhesión a nuestra naturaleza se siente sen Huella-Sombra y Cantar. . ." and "Un credo socialista de aliento a la visión de un orden justiciero."

Manrique frequently published in such journals as *El Imparcial, El Mundos, Puerto Rico Ilustrado, Asomante, Brújula, Alma Latina,* and *El Diluvio.* His "Los piladores" from *Mi tierra-tierra* goes:

Los piladores pilan
pan pon
pun pon
pon pon.

Y las recias manos
callosas de dolor y tierra.
atadas a tan finas cinturas de macetas,
lluevan sobre la tosca
copana de madera.

Writings: Poetry: *Huella, sombra y cantar,* San Juan, Imp. Venezuela, 1934 (awarded a prize by the Instituto de Literatura Puertorriqueña); *Poemas de mi tierra-tierra,* San Juan, Puerto Rico Progress, 1936; *Antologia de poesia infantil,* 1943; *Décimas de mi tierra,* San Juan, Edit. del Departamiento de Instrucción Pública, 1967.

Editor and Collector of: *Historia de la literatura puertorriqueña,* 1947, 2nd ed., Mexico, Brevarios del Fondo de Cultura Económica, 1957, 3rd ed., Rio Piedras, Edit. Cultural, 1969, 4th ed., Rio Piedras, Edit. Cultural, 1971; *Apuntes para la historia literaria de Puerto Rico,* San Juan, 1957.

Essays and Talks: "Décima ¿vehiculo de nuestro queja?" in *Puerto Rico Ilustrado* (July 3, 1943); "Notas sobre la novela puertorriqueña en los ultimos veintecinco años," *Asomante;* radio-talks "Puntos de partida" on Station WIPR, quoted in part in F. Manrique's *Historia de la literatura puertorriqueña,* pp. 341-342.

Biographical/Critical Sources: José A. Franquiz' *Los tiempos poéticos de Manrique Cabrera y la metafisica del tiempo en su poesia,* Mexico, Cuadernos Luminar series, 1944, with bibliography.

MANZANO, Juan Francisco

b. 1797, Cuba; d. 1854, Havana.
Poet, autobiographer, playwright.

Manzano was born in slavery but won his freedom through his poetry. His autobiography (not published until 1937) relates his loss of a kind mistress at 11 and how he was beaten by his next for daring to write. At 25 he fled his country origins by taking refuge in Havana. Able to establish himself there after some bad times, he eventually married and began to write in earnest.

His sonnet "Mis treinta años" earned him many friends who helped him obtain freedom legally in 1837. Unfortunately in 1844-45 he was sent to prison for joining "La Escalera," a conspiracy, and upon release decided to write no longer. His limited education precluded his ever being a skilled poet but his was the first black voice raised in Cuban literature.

Instrumental in his purchase of freedom

was the liberal Domingo del Monte y Valdés Machuca who sought out subscriptions among the intellectual community of Havana. Though Manzano showed little interest in African themes in his poetry, the fact that he was an African writer who contributed to such literary reviews as *La Moda o Recreo Semanal del Bello Sexo* (1831), *El Pasatiempo* (Matanzas, 1838) and *El Aguinaldo Habanero* (1837) and had many published volumes of verse and one play, *Zafira* (1842), in print, was an important matter for persons of race. He suffered imprisonment on an apparently wildly false accusation of complicity in the "Escalera" conspiracy which in Plácido's case resulted in death by firing squad.

Writings: Poetry: *Cantos a Lesbia, poesias liricas,* 4th ed., Havana, 1821; *Flores pasageras,* Havana, 1830 (Max Henriquez Ureña doubts this work exists or ever existed); seven poems in Ramón Guirao's *Orbita de la poesia afrocubana,* Havana, 1938; poem "Mis treinta años" in Jahn's *Neo-African Literature* (see below); *Poems by a slave in the islands of Cuba recently liberated,* translated by Richard Robert Madden, "with the history of the early life of the Negro poet, written by himself," to which are prefixed two pieces descriptive of Cuban slavery and the slave trade, by R. R. Madden," London, Ward, 1840 (188 pages); various of his poems appear in José Fornaris' *Cuba Poética;* José Domingo Cortés' *América poética;* Cal cagno's *Poetas de color;* Antonio López Prieto's *Parnaso cubano;* and Ramón Guirao's *Poetas negros y mestizos de la época esclavista;* and his poems "Al cerro de Quintana," "A la Ciudad de Matanzas," and "Mis treinta años" are in French translation by Victor Schoelcher and published in Schoelcher's pioneering work, *Abolition de l'esclavage; examen de prejugé contre la couleur des africains et des sangmelés,* Paris, 1840.

Play: *Zafira, tragedia en cinco actos,* Havana, Imp. de L. Mier, 1842, and Havana, Consejo Nacional de Cultura, 1962.

Autobiography: *Autobiografia, cartas y versos,* Havana, Administración del Alcalde, 1937 (includes the same materials as the London publication of 1840 *Poems by a slave*... which included Manzano's autobiographical writings, published in *Cuadernos de Historia Habanera,* Havana, Oficina del Historiador de la Ciudad, 1937 [original text edited by Emilio Roig de Leuchsenring, with introduction by José Luciano Franco] and then as 1937 Administración del Alcalde edition).

Biographical/Critical Sources: José L. Franco, "Juan Francisco Manzano, el poeta esclavo y su tiempo," in same volume as Manzano's *Autobiografia,* 1937; Janheinz Jahn, *Neo-African Literature,* New York, Evergreen, 1969, pp. 131-133 for brief biography and text in Spanish of "Mis treinta años" with English translation and Ildefonso Pereda Valdez, *Lo negro y lo mulato en la poesia cubana,* Montevideo, Uruguay, Ediciones Ciudadela, 1970, pp. 29 ff.

MARCHENA DE LEYBA, Amelia Francisca

(pseudonym: **Amelia FRANCASI** or **FRANCASCI**)

b. October 4, 1850, Dominican Republic; d. February 27, 1941.

Novelist, storywriter, biographer, autobiographer.

Marchena's work, most of it in the short fiction forms of tales and novelettes, is lively in scene and well realized in characterization.

She wrote her biography *Monseñor de Meriño intimo* in her eighties after a long period of silence.

Writings: Novelettes: *Madre Culpable,* S. Domingo, 1893; *Francisca Martinoff,* S. Domingo, 1901; *Lo Impenetrable,* published only in *Panfilia* magazine; *Duelos del Corazón,* S. Domingo, 1901.

Short Stories: *Cierza en primavera* (which contains "Pepa, Pepe y José," "La confesión de un joven timido," "Mi pretendiente," all with a Cuban setting), S. Domingo, 1902.

Biography: *Monseñor de Meriño intimo,* S. Domingo, 1926.

Memoir: *Recuerdos e impresiones (historia de una novela),* S. Domingo, 1901.

Biographical/Critical Sources: Max Rodriguez Ureña's *Panorama histórico de la literatura,* 2 vols, 1966, see esp. pp. 334 of Vol. II.

MARCOS SUAREZ, Miguel de

b. 1894, Cuba; D. 1954.
Storywriter, novelist.

One of Cuba's finest humorists, Marcos' "Cuentos pantuflores" appeared in his best collection of stories, *Fábulas de la vida apacible* (1943) which offer relaxed and intimate scenes of domestic life. He improvised and never went back over his work which is accordingly refreshing, capricious, but at times unable to make its points effectively.

Writings: Stories: *Cuentos nefandos,* Havana, 1914; *Fábulas de la vida apacible,* Havana, 1943.
Novel: *Fotuto, Papaito Mayari.*

MARGENAT, Hugo

b. 1934, San Juan, Puerto Rico; d. 1957.
Poet.

Son of Alfredo Margenat, poet and journalist, Hugo quickly began to publish his verse in such journals as *Orféo* and *Guajana.* Manrique has written: "La poesia de Hugo Margenat va perfilándose con un decir acerado, sobrio y audaz. Laten alli aunque con tono seco, cortante, a veces, hondas ansias que andan pugnando por salir."

Writings: Poetry: *Lámpara apagada,* San Juan, 1954; *Interperie,* San Juan, Imp. Baldrich, 1955; *Mundo abierto,* San Juan, Imp. Balrich, 1958; *Ventana hacia lo último,* San Juan, Imp. Venezuela, 1960; and in various journals, including *Orfeo* and *Guajana* which latter dedicated an entire issue to his work (Vol. I, No. 4, 1963), and *Aguinaldo Lirico,* C. Rosa-Nieves, ed., Rio Piedras, 1957, 1971.

MARIN FRANCISCO, Gonzalo or González

(see **PACHIN MARIN**)

MARIN, Ramón

b. 1832, Arecibo, Puerto Rico; d. 1902.
Playwright, journalist, teacher.

After local schooling, Marin became a teacher at 18 years at Cabo Rojo and later founded a college in Yabucoa. After 25 as an educator he entered journalism, founding and editing *Al Avisador, La Crónica, El Pueblo, El Popular,* and *El Cronista,* all in Ponce, Puerto Rico. In 1897, he was appointed director of the Asilo de Beneficiencia de San Juan.

Writings: Plays: *El hijo del amor* (3 act comedy, verse), Ponce, Francisco Vidal, 1972; *Lazos de amor, second part of El hijo del amor* (2 act comedy, verse), Ponce, Establecimiento tipográfico El Vapor, 1878.

MARINELLO VIDAURRETA, Juan

b. 1898, Cuba.
Poet, essayist, literary critic, historian, statesman.

Marinello's very personal verse appeared in the Havana journal *Revista de Avance* which was published 1927-39 as an organ of the younger poets and writers of the "Grupo Minorista." His career was mostly in politics and his writing in the critical essay form since the 1920's. His style and tone can be seen in these lines from "Ya esta eterna nostalgia":

Ya esta eterna nostalgia de las
alturas, y este
atalayar eterno de cumbres intocadas
e inaccesibles, ¿cuándo
morirán en el alma?
¿Por que, si no podemos volar, sueñan
un vuelo
las alas ideales que se aferran al suelo
sangrando el vencimiento? . . .

Marinello was a president of the Socialist Party (Socialista Popular), served in the legislature from 1940, had several high posts in the government, including Minister without portfolio in the administration of President Batista (1942).

Writings: Poetry: *Liberación,* Madrid, 1927; and verse in various journals including *Revista de Avance.*

Essays: *Juventud y vejez,* Havana, 1928; *Americanismo y cubanismo literarios,* 1932; *Poética: ensayos en entusiasmo,* Mexico, 1933; *La cultura y la paz: homenaje a Enrique González Martinez y a Baldomero Sanin Cano,* Havana, 1952. Many essays on José Marti: "El poeta José Marti," introduction to verse collection of Marti's published Havana, Collección de Libros Cubanos; "Españolidad literaria de José Marti, 1942; "Actualidad americana de José Marti," 1945; "El caso literario de José Marti: Motivos de centenario," 1945; "José Marti, escritor americano," Mexico, 1958.

Literary History and Criticism: *Sobre el modernismo: polémica y definición,* Havana, 1958.

Politics: *Viaje a la Unión Sovietica y a las democracias populares,* Havana, 1950.

MARMORA, Dagoberto

(pseudonym for **Emilio BOBADILLA Y LUNAR**)

MARQUES, René

b. October 4, 1919, Arecibo, Puerto Rico; d. March 22, 1979.

Playwright, critic, storywriter.

Marqués studied at the Colegio de Agricultura y Artes Mecánicas in Mayagüez, taking a degree in agronomy. He married Serena Velasco in 1946. He worked for the Department of Agriculture for two years, but after the birth of his second son, he moved his family to Madrid for one year so that he could study literature at the Universidad Central. His early sketches appeared in *El Mundo* and *Asomante,* leading Madrid journals of the day.

Marqués founded the Pro Arte de Arecibo and was its first president after his return to Puerto Rico. In 1949 he studied theatre at Columbia University in New York, thanks to a Rockefeller Grant, after he had served for a year as editor for *El Diario de Puerto Rico.*

In 1951 he founded the Teatro Experimental del Ateneo of which he has been secretary since 1954. In 1954 he won a Guggenheim grant but only in 1957 could he accept it, using it to write his first novel, *La vispera del hombre* (published 1959).

After a brief visit to Madrid to participate in the premiere performance of his play *La carreta* (1957), he visited his father's relatives in ancestral Palma de Mallorca, and in 1958 he was a member of the official Puerto Rican Delegation to the first Interamerican Biennial of Painting.

Marqués believes literature is "the result of the writer's becoming an ethical person, a moralist in spite of himself." His many essays are accordingly directed to analyzing his own Puerto Rican society. Most recently available, at least in English, are his essays in *The Docile Puerto Rican* (1976).

Writings: Plays: *Carnaval afuera, carnaval adentro,* Rio Piedras, Edit. Antillana, 1971; *El hombre y sus sueños,* 1948; *La carreta; drama en tres actos,* first published at Teatro Nacional Maria, Madrid, but published first in *Asomante,* Vol. IV (1951), pp. 67-87, I (1952), 54-85, III (1952) 66-92, then in Rio Piedras, Puerto Rico, 1968, (*The Oxcart [of La Carreta,* now in 5th ed.] translated into English by Charles Pilditch, New York, Scribner, 1969); *El sol y los MacDonald,* written in Spain, first performed at the Teatro Universitario in San Juan; *Palm Sunday,* written in New York, 1949, premiered at Teatro Tapia, San Juan, 1956, first published in 1952; *Los solos truncos,* performed Teatro Tapia, 1958, Edit. Antiallana, 1971, and Teatro puertorriqueño, primer festival, San Juan, 1959, 1960 and 1968; *Un niño azul para esa sombra,* in *Teatro Puertorriqueño, tercer festival,* San Juan, 1961; *La carreta* in *Teatro Puertorriqueño, cuarto festival,* San Juan, 1963; *El apartamiento* in *Teatro Puertorriqueño,* San Juan,

1965; *Mariano o el alba* in *Teatro Puertorriqueño,* San Juan 1966; *Un niño azul para esa sombra* (first prize of Teatro del Ateneo Puertorriqueño, 1958); *Teatro* (includes *Los dos truncos, Un niño azul para esa sombra* (first prize of Teatro del Ateneo Puertorriqueño, 1958); *Teatro* (includes *Los dos truncos, Un niño azul para esa sombra* and *La muerte no entrará en palacio*), 1959, and in ms: the tragedy, *La muerte no entrará en palacio* (Honorable Mention in competition of Teatro del Ateneo); *Purificación en la Calle del Cristo,* Rio Piedras, Edit. Cultural, 1970; *Sacrificio en el Monte Moriah* (14 scenes), Rio Piedras, Edit. Antillana, 1969; *Teatro: El hombre y sus sueños; El sol y Los MacDonald,* Rio Piedras, Edit. Cultural, 1970; *La casa sin reloq; El Apartamiento,* Rio Piedras, 1971; *Via crusis del hombre puertorriqueño,* Rio Piedras, Edit. Antillana, 1971.

Stories: *En una ciudad llamada San Juan,* 3rd ed., amplified, Rio Piedras, Edit. Cultural, 1970 (15 stories); "Give US This Day" as translated by Catherine Randolph in *Flakoll,* pp. 158-170; *Otro dia nuestro,* San Juan, Imp. Venezuela, Instituto de Cultura Puertorriqueña, 1955; "En la popa hay un cuerpo reclinado," first prize in the competition *Cuentos del Ateneo Puertorriqueño,* 1956; two stories in *Cuentos puertorriqueños de hoy,* Mexico, 1959; the story "Dos vueltas de llave y un arcángel," "La sala," "El niño en el arbol," and *Tres hombres junto al rio;"* the last won a prize for the historical stories awarded by the Instituto de Cultura Puertorriqueña; the story "Dos vueltas..." appeared in *Antologia de autores puertorriqueños; El Cuento,* San Juan, Edit. del Departamento de Instrucción, 1957, pp. 239-249; "La Muerte," "La Sala" (first prize "Certamen de Cuentas," Festival de Navidad, 1958, Ateneo Puertorriqueño, "Tres hombres junto al rio," are in Meléndez' *El arte del cuento en Puerto Rico,* New York, 1967, pp. 224-249.

Novel: *La vispera del hombre,* Mexico, Talleres de Gráfico Hispanoamericana, 1959, 2nd ed., San Juan, Rio Piedras, Edit. Cultural, 1970.

Essays: *Ensayos (1953-1966),* 2nd ed., rev. and augmented, Rio Piedras, Edit. Antillana, 1966, and with six new ones, in *Ensayos (1953-1971);* "Pesimismo literario y optimismo politico: su coexistencia en el Puerto Rico actual," in *Cuadernos Américanos,* Mexico, 1959; *The Docile Puerto Rican; essays,* translated by Barbara B. Aponte, Phila., Temple University Press, 1973 (eight essays from *Ensayos 1953-1966*).

Pantomime: *Juan Bobo y la Drama de Occidente,* Mexico, 1956, 2nd ed., Rio Piedras, edit. Antillana, 1971, also in *Teatro puertorriqueña,* San Juan, 1959, 1960.

Editor and Collector of: *Cuentos puertorriqueños de hoy,* Mexico, Club del Libro de Puerto Rico, 1959, see especially pp. 97-107; *David y Jonathan, Tito y Berenice: Dos dramas de amor, poder, y desamor,* Rio Piedras, Edit. Antillana, 1970.

Biographical/Critical Sources: Maria Teresa Babin, "Apuntes sobre *La Carreta,*" *Asomante* (San Juan, 1953, No. 4); Concha Meléndez, *Cuentos de René Marqués, Figueración de Puerto Rico y otros estudios,* San Juan, Instituto de Cultura Puertorriqueña, 1958, pp. 65-72, and Meléndez, ed., *El arte del cuento en Puerto Rico,* New York, 1961, pp. 218-223; Victoria Espinosa Torres, *El teatro de René Marqués y la escenificaciones de su obra: Los soles truncos,* Mexico, 1969 (also discusses overall Puerto Rican theatre developments); Angelina Morfi's *Temas del teatro,* S. Domingo, D. R., 1969 for essays "El apartamiento," and "Nueva ruta en el teatro de René M. Marqués"; Angel M. Aguirre's "René Marqués and the Struggle of the Puerto Rican Theatre," in *Revista Interamericana,* Vol. II, No. 4; and review by Julio Marzán, "A Moralist in Spite of Himself," of Marqués' *The Docile Puerto Rican* in *Review 76* (Winter), pp. 88-90.

MARQUEZ Y GISPERT, Matias Felipe

(pseudonym: **Dámaso Gil ACLEA**)

b. 1851, Cuba; d. 1887.
Novelist, storywriter, lawyer.

Marquéz was one of Cuba's earliest naturalist novelists and he also published three "historical" stories in *Bosquejos* in 1878.

Writings: Novels: *Un dia de emociones,* Madrid, 1877; *Juan Pérez,* also Madrid, 1877.

Stories: *Bosquejos,* Madrid, 1878.

MARRE, Luis

b. 1929, Cuba.
Poet, naturalist.

Marré has been a gardener and farmer most of his life and his one volume of verse *Los ojos en el fresco* obviously reflects such experiences.

Writings: Poetry: *Los ojos en el fresco,* Havana, Revolución, 1963; *Canciones,* Havana, La Tertulia, 1964; *Habaneras y otras letras,* Havana, Unión, 1970; and he is represented in several journals and collections, including *Writers in the New Cuba,* E. M. Cohen, ed., Harmondsworth, England, Penguin, 1967, and Nathaniel Tarn's *Con Cuba,* New York, 1969.

MARRERO, Diego O.

b. 1896, Ciales, Puerto Rico.
Poet, journalist, lawyer.

Beginning as a passionate follower of Rubén Dario, José Santos Chocano and Luis Lloréns Torres, Marrero slowly moved away from "modernismo" toward a freer, more subjective poetic—coming under the pull of the great German poet, Rainer Maria Rilke.

These lines from "La tristeza del Yunque" (from *Geografia Poética*) gives his flavor:

Triste pico, tu entraña no sabe
del azufre, la lava y calor,
que a otros picos conmueve y exalta
en arrestos de lucha y pasión;
mas por eso no pierde tu cima
su grandeza y su magna virtud
de ser signo con el cual tú marcas
el camino de la rectitud . . .

Writings: Poetry: *Bronces épicos,* 1943; *El divino puntero; Geografia poética,* 1951.

MARRERO ARISTY, Ramón

b. June 14, 1913, San Rafael del Yuma, Dominican Republic; d. July 17, 1959.
Novelist, storywriter, historian, diplomat.

He was active in public affairs as an editor of the journal *Listin Diario, La Opinión* and *La Nación* and was also editor of the illustrated review *Babeque.* He served as Minister of Education, and held several diplomatic posts. Marrero was assassinated in an attempt to overthrow Trujillo.

Writings: Novelettes: *Pérfiles agrestes,* 1933; *Balsié,* S. Domingo, Editorial Caribes, 1938; (both appeared in the work *La República Dominicana,* 1957); "El Camión Rojo" (unpublished).

Epic: *Over* (prose-poem), 1939, 2nd ed., S. Domingo, Ed. Lib. Hispañola, C. P. D., No. 26, 1970, also in Colección Pensamiento, Postigo, S. Domingo, 1963, the eighth edition (3,000 copies), published S. Domingo, Taller, 1976.

Biography: of Rafael L. Trujillo, details unknown.

Biographical/Critical Sources: H. Incháustegui Cabral, *De literatura dominicana siglo veinte,* S. Domingo, UCMM, 1973, pp. 309-324, concerning *Over* and related matters, including economic and political oppression in the Republic.

MARRERO NUNEZ, Julio

b. 1910, Puerto Rico.
Playwright, play director, historian.

Marrero took his B. A. at the University of Puerto Rico and has done graduate work at Yale University and the Academia de Bellas Artes in Madrid University. He has been active in establishing a Puerto Rican theatre, and has written and directed plays. In the 1960's he was Chief of the Historical Section of the National Park Service of the U. S. Department of Interior.

Writings: Play: *Borinquen,* 1946; *El hombre terrible del '87: versión libre de un episodio histórico en tres actos,* Barcelona, Edic. Rumbos, 1967.

Stories: *Cuentos de San Felipe del Morro;* "El sitiador," in *Insula* (Madrid, September 1952); "El caballito blanco," *Insula* (June 15, 1955);

"Réquiem por un soldado del rey de España," in Concha Meléndez, ed., *El arte del cuento en Puerto Rico,* New York, 1961, pp. 155-159.

Biographical/Critical Sources: Josefina Rivera de Alvárez, *Diccionario de literatura puertorriqueña,* Rio Piedras, Universidad de Puerto Rico, 1955, pp. 355-356; Wilfred Braschi, "Apuntas para la historia del teatro puertorriqueño," unpublished M. A. thesis, U. of P. R., 1952, pp. 110-111; republished in revised version as *Apuntes sobre el teatro puertorriqueño,* San Juan, Edit. Coqui, 1970.

MARRERO DE FIGUEROA, Carmen

b. 1907, Morovis, Puerto Rico.
Playwright, poet, essayist, journalist, teacher.

Marrero has worked for a long period with the daily paper *El Imparcial* and her poetry, influenced by Alfonsina Storni and Juana de Ibarbourou, has appeared in many Puerto Rican journals.

Writings: Play: *¿Por qué no se casa, Señor Senador?,* 1953.
Poetry: *Fémina,* 1930; *Sonetos de la Verdad,* New York, Las Américas, 1964 (introduction by Concha Meléndez).
Critical Biography: *Luis Lloréns Torres: vida y obra,* in *Revista Hispánica Moderna,* New York, (January-December 1953), pp. 1-84, in separate volume, 2nd ed., San Juan, Edit. Cordillera, 1968 (187 pages and bibliography).

Biographical/Critical Sources: Concha Meléndez, *Poetas hispanoamericanos diversos,* San Juan, 1971.

MARTI PEREZ, José Julián (Pepe)

b. January 28, 1853, Havana, Cuba; d. May 19, 1895.
Poet, playwright, critic, essayist, editor, teacher, patriot, lawyer.

A rebel since youth, Marti suffered exile at 16, living in Spain and Mexico, Venezuela and Guatemala. He also spent a considerable period in New York where he published articles in the New York *Sun* and from which he sent articles to the *La Nación* of Buenos Aires. After some 24 years of struggle, he returned to revolutionary Cuba in 1895, only to perish in the battle of Dos Rios. Charles Dana, editor of the *Sun,* eulogized him in the lead editorial of May 23, 1895: ". . .He was a man of genius, of imagination, of hope, and of courage. One of those descendants of the Spanish race whose American birth and instincts seem to have added to the revolutionary tincture which all Spaniards inherit. . ."

Son of a Spanish-born father, Mariano Marti, originally sent to Cuba to put down one of the incessant island insurrections, and of Leonor Pérez, the young Marti was an excellent student at a private school, San Anacleto, located outside of Havana and later at both a public school and a private one, San Pablo, founded by Don Rafael Maria Mendive, a fervent nationalist. Here, Marti and his friend, Fermin Valdés Dominguez, joined the revolt in 1868 led by Carlos Manuel de Céspedes and put out a weekly underground magazine, *La Patria Libre,* which published *Abdala,* an epic poem on freedom by "Pepe." Even earlier he had written a sonnet "The Tenth of October" (English trans. of title), published in an underground paper. Shortly thereafter Marti and Fermin Valdés were imprisoned, Marti sentenced for six years and given forced labor in the Presidio and later in a stone quarry. Eventually deported to Spain in 1871, he was allowed to attend law school at the Central University of Madrid, and began *The Political Prison in Cuba* (English title) which he published at his own expense. Forced to work, he was fortunate to find employment as a teacher to the children of Doña Barbarita Echevarria, Cuban-born widow of a Spanish General. In 1873, reunited with

Fermin, himself newly exiled to Madrid, José addressed his paper, *The Spanish Republic and the Cuban Revolution* (English trans. of title) to the head of the short-lived Spanish revolutionary government. Despite this effort and later oratory, he found republican Spaniards as averse to freeing Cubans as had been the monarchists. Discouraged, he and Fermin removed to the lovely provincial city of Zaragoza in Aragon province—there he earned a B. A. in philosophy and letters and then a doctorate in law.

Joining his father's family in Mexico, he began to write for the leading journals, but soon moved on to Guatemala, there meeting Carmen Zayas Bazán, of the prominent family from Camagüguez, Cuba. They married in 1878. In Guatemala, still only 24 years old, Marti became a teacher of French, Italian and German literature and the history of philosophy, edited a review, and composed a four-act play on an historical theme. After the end of the "Ten-years War" started by Carlos Manuel de Céspedes, Marti returned to Havana to practice law where he found his countrymen bitter and hopeless. He continued to argue for independence and for his pains was soon arrested. After a new exile to Spain, Marti decided to go to the United States. In New York he struggled with poverty, the dislike of his wife for the revolutionary activities he engaged in, and eventually, he found himself alone, his wife having returned to Cuba with their young son.

In Venezuela in 1882, Marti taught at Caracas Normal School and published a volume of poems written for his son, the collection *Ismaelillo* (1882). From 1881 to 1895, Marti again lived in New York city, working as a bookkeeper and secretary for a business firm and teaching literature and French in a private school.

Appleton Publishing Company hired him to do translations of English and French novels into Spanish and it was during this period he contributed to Charles Dana's *New York Sun.* He also was Consul for many Latin American countries and, as always, deeply engaged in planning the independence of Cuba. He became the spokesman for Pan-Americanism and a voice in the U. S. of Latin-American viewpoints. The Cuban exiles of New York organized themselves as "Los Pinos Nuevos" (The New Pines) from the conclusion of a fiery speech by Marti and by 1892, Marti was organizing the new Cuban Revolutionary Party and writing the *Bases and Statutes of the Cuban Party* and founding a voice for it in the newspaper *Patria.* Several years of planning passed and as the Cuban people once again rose against Spain Marti slipped back into Cuba the night of April 11, 1895. A month and four days later he was dead in a charge against a Spanish-held position. His devotion to Cuban freedom, and freedom everywhere, is celebrated on January 28th, his birthdate, as Cuba's national holiday.

Marti did not write much poetry, nor was he free to become a professional writer—so poor and often rushed was he to dash off the latest polemic or to refute someone—or to meet a deadline on an article for a journal. Some critics find his best poetry in his last volume *Versos sencillos* which truly are simple and open precursors of the new tendency to avoid the strained and complex and to seek the heart direct—a movement to be called "modernismo."

The mass of his work is in prose, possibly the best of it in the undated collection *Los Estados Unidos* (Madrid) which shows his selecting good elements from U. S. culture but eyeing suspiciously certain expansionistic American (U. S.) tendencies toward the Caribbean.

The volume of studies on Marti is so vast that we offer below just a portion of the still growing stream.

Writings: Poetry: *Versos, Abdala* (verse play), Havana, 1913; verse volumes: *Ismaelillo,* 1882; *Versos libres,* 1882; *Versos sencillos,* 1891.

Letters: *Epistolario de José Marti* (edited by Lizaso), Havana, 1930; *José Marti apuntes ineditos,* preface by Lizaso, Havana, 1951; *La clara voz de México,* 2 vols. 1933-36 (articles originally published in several Mexican journals); *Los Estados Unidos,* Madrid, in series Biblioteca Andrés Bello, no date; essays collected and edited by Philip S. Foner as *Inside the Monster,* New York, Monthly Review Press, 1975 (rev. in *Revista/Review Interamericana,* Vol. V, No. 1 [by Earl P. Hanson]).

Plays: *Amor con amor se paga,* Mexico, Dublan y Cia, 1876, and Havana, Rambla y Bouza, 1913 (*Amor* was premiered in the Teatro Principal de Méjico, December 19, 1875 and met an excited reception); *Amor* was translated by W. K. Jones as *Love is Repaid by Love,* published in *Archivo de José Marti,* Vol. 11 (January-December 1947), pp. 50-60. Also: *Adúltera,* Havana, Ed., Trópico (in *Teatro Cubano* collection), 1936, edited and with notes by Gonzalo de Quesada y Miranda, but first published in *La Patria Libre* (Semanario democratico-cosmopolita), Vol. I, No. 1 (Havana, January 23, 1869), pp. 7-8 (this play was first noted in *El Federalista,* Vol. VIII, No. 1626 [Mexico, January 28, 1976] as having been prepared for performance, but since no author for the work was cited and only the name *Adúltera* was furnished, some authorities have dismissed this as absolute proof of either performance or that the play conclusively was Marti's).

Collections of Marti's Works: *Antologia critica de José Marti* (Manuel Pedro Gonzáles, ed.), Mexico, Edit. Cultura, 1960; Selected Works: *José Marti: Prosas,* selection, foreword, and notes by Andrés Iduarte, Washington, D. C., Unión Panamericana, 19??; *Obras completas,* 27 vols., Havana, Edit. Lex (contains *Abdala; Adúltera,* and *Amor con amor se paga*); *José Marti. Obras completas,* Havana, Edit. Lex, 1953; *Obras completas,* 74 volume set of works, edited by Gonzálo de Quesada y Miranda, Havana, Trópico, 1936-1949; new collection in two giant volumes, Havana, Lex, 1946 (edited by M. Isidro Méndez and Mariano Sánchez Roca); *Sección constante,* compiler and foreword: Pedro Graces, published Caracas, 1955; *Obras completas,* 8 vols., edited by Néstor Carbonnell, Havana, 1918-1920; and re-edited by Alberto Ghiraldo, 8 vols., Madrid, 1924-1929. Earlier collections were *Flor y lava,* Paris, 1910; and *Páginas escogidas,* Paris, 1919. For journalism and other genres in collected works, see appropriate rubrics above.

Biographical/Critical Sources: Juan J. Remos, *Deslindes de Marti,* Havana, J. Suárez, 1953; Rosario Rexach de Léon, *El caracter de Marti* y otros ensayos, Havana, Com. Nac. Cubana de la UNESCO, 954; Manuel Pedro Gonzáles, *José Marti, Anticlerical, Irreductible,* Mexico, Humanismo, 1954; Jorge Mañach, *Marti, el apóstol,* Madrid, 1933; translated by Coley Taylor as *Marti: Apostle of Freedom,* foreword by Gabriela Mistral, New York, Devin Adair, 1950, and later Spanish-language edition: New York, Las Américas Publishing Co., 1963; Jorge Mañach, *El pensamiento politico y social de Marti,* Havana, Edición Oficial del Senado de la República, 1941; Lyn Smith Manduley, *José Marti,* Washington, D. C., Pan American Union, 1968; *Marti: Documentos para su vida,* preface by M. Isidro Méndez, Havana, 1947; Blanca Zacharie Baralt, *El Marti que yo conoci,* Havana, 1945; Alberto Baeza Flores, *Vida de Marti,* Havana, 1942; also by Baeza Flores: *Pensamiento y acción de José Marti,* Havana, 1953; and *Vida y pensamiento de Marti,* Havana, 1942; Carlos Márquez Sterling, *Marti, maestro y apóstol,* Havana, 1942; Manuel Pedro González, *La revalorización de Marti,* Havana, Cultural, 1942; Félix Lizaso, "La intimidad literario de Marti," in *Revista Cubana,* Vol. 5 (Havana, 1936), pp. 306-328; José Ferrer Canales, *Acentos civicos: Marti, Puerto Rico y otros temas,* Rio Piedras, Edit. Edil, 1972; essay on Marti in *Hombres de Cuba,* Havana, Publicaciones de la Secretaria de Educación, 1936; José Antonio Portuondo, *José Marti: critico literario,* Washington, Unión Panamericana, 1953; Esther Elise Shuler, *José Marti. Su critica de algunos authores norteamericanos,* Minneapolis, Perine Book Store, no date (mimeographed); Félix Lizaso y Gonzáles, *Marti, mistico del deber,* translated by Esther Elise Shuler as *Marti, martyr of Cuban Independence,* Albuquerque, University of New Mexico Press, 1953; also by Lizaso y Gonzáles, the article, "What makes a man great?" in *Am PAU,* II, 2 (December 1950), pp. 16-19 and p. 26; Jo Ann Harrison Boydston, "José Marti en

Oklahoma," in *Archivo José Marti,* Vol. IV, pp. 195-201; Néstor Carbonell, "Marti en la Argentina," in *La Revista Américana de Buenos Aires,* Vol. XXIII (October 1929) and republished in Vol. LXV; Also see Olga Blondet, "José Marti: bibliografia," in *Revista Hispánica Moderna,* XVIII (1952), pp. 151-161; Manuel Pedro Gonzáles, *Fuentes para el estudio de José Marti. Ensayos de bibliografia clasificada,* Havana, Ministerio de Educación, 1950, (517 pp.), and reviewed by Fermin Peraza Sarausa, in *Revista Interamericana de Bibliografia,* I (1951), pp. 110-111; Lizaso, "José Marti," in *Cuba Contemporánea,* XXXV, pp. 281-289; Fermin Peraza, *Bibliografia martiana, 1853-1953,* Havana, Comisión Nacional Organizadora de los Actos y Ediciones del Centenario y del Monumento de Marti, 1954 (692 pp.); Peraza, *Bibliografia martiana, 1942-1943,* Havana, Biblioteca Municipal de la Habana, 1944, in 2 vols., (Serie C. Guias bibliográficas, 8, 9) and *Bibliografi martiana,* 1945, Havana (same publisher as previous, 1946 (Serie C, 13); Américo Lugo, *José Marti,* Havana, 1910; Max Henriquez Ureña, *Panorama histórico de la literatura cubana,* New York, 1963, pp. 210-231; Rafael Esténger, *Marti frente de comunismo,* Miami, Ediciones del Directorio Magisterial Cubano (*Exilio*), No. 27 (1966); Roberto Fernández Retamar, *Páginas escogidas de José Marti (Prologo),* Havana, Origenes, 1954; other articles by Lizaso: "Marti en Nueva York," in *Américas,* Vol. 17, No. 7 (Washington, D. C., July 1965); *Marti, recuento de centenario,* Havana, Ucar Garcia, 1953; "Normas periodisticas de José Marti," in *Revista Iberoamericana,* XXIX, No. 56; "Nuestro Marti," in *Politica,* III, No. 34 (Venezuela, Mary 1964); and many other articles by Lizaso. Also: Juan Marinello, *Actualidad de José Marti,* Havana, Edit. Páginas, 1943; *El caso literario de José Marti* (motivos de Centenario), Havana, Vega, 1954; *Conferencia en la Cátedra Martiana del 11 de abril de 1962,* Havana, Comisión de extensión Universitaria, 1962; *Marti desde ahora,* Havana, Imp. de la Universidad de la Habana, 1962; *Marti, escritor américano,* Havana, Imp. Nacional de Cuba, 1962. Also: Ezequiel Martinez Estrada, *Marti: el héroe y su acción revolucionaria,* Mexico, Siglo XXI Editorial, 1966; Julio Antonio Mella, *Glosando los pensamientos de Marti,* Havana, Imp. Berea, 1941; Humberto Piñera, "Marti, pensador," in *Antologia critica de José Marti,* Mexico, Edit. Cultura, 1960; Fernándo de los Rios, "Reflexiones en torno al sentido de la vida en Marti," in *Mensajes de la Institución Hispanocubana de Cultura,* Vol. I (July 1928); Raúl Roa, "Marti, poeta nuevo," in *Revista de Avance,* I, 10 (August 1927); Carlos Rafael Rodriguez, "José Marti," in *Unión,* Nos. 5 and 6 (January-April 1963); Alfredo A. Roggiano, "Poética y estilo de José Marti," in *Antologia critica de José Marti,* Mexico, 1960 (op. cit.); Medardo Vitier, *Marti: su obra politica y literaria,* Havana, 1911, and *Marti, estudio integral,* Havana, 1954; Rafael G. Argilagos, *Granos de oro* (on Marti), Santiago, Cuba, 1915; Juan Jerez Villareal, *Triptico* (on Céspedes, Maceo and Marti), date unknown; Luis Rodriguez Embil, *José Marti, el Santo de América,* Havana, 1940; Emilio Gaspar Rodriguez, "Marti y la América," in *Los conquistadores,* Havana, 1921; Andrés Iduarte, *Marti Escritor,* 2nd ed., Havana, Ministry of Education, 1951; Francisco Ichaso, *Marti y el Teatro,* Cuadernos de Divulgación Culto de la Comisión Nac. Cubana de la UNESCO, No. 16, Havana, P. Fernández, 1953; Mauricio Magdaleno, *José Marti,* Mexico, Botes, 1941; Ivan A. Schulman, *Simbolo y color en la obra de José Marti,* Madrid, Gredos, 1960; *Estudios Martianos, Seminario José* Marti, Barcelona, for Edit. Universitaria, Univ. de Puerto Rico, 1974; José de la Luz León, *La imagen de cumbre en la prosa de Marti,* Havana, 1950; Wilfredo Fernández, Marti *y la filosofia,* Miami, Ediciones Universal, 1974; Anon: "José Marti en México," in *Nivel Gaceta de Cultura,* No. 148 (Mexico, April 30, 1975); Antonio Martinez Bello, *Notas para un sistema de estética, Ideas sociales y económicas de Marti,* Havana, 1940; Raúl Roa, "Marti y el fascismo," essay, 1937, and José Marti y el destino americano," essay, 1938; Antonio Iraizos, *La estética acrática de José Marti,* Havana, 1924; Roig de Leuchsenring, *Marti en España,* Havana, 1924; Alfonso Hernández Catá, *Mitologia de Marti,* Havana, 1929; *Facetas de Marti,* Havana, 1939; *Marti, hombre,* Havana, 1940; *Marti, periodista,* Havana, 1929 (all 3 works by Gonzaló de Quesada y Miranda); Néstor Carbonell, *Marti: carne y espiritu,* Havana, 1952; A. R. de Carricarte, *Iconografia de José Marti,* Havana, 1926; Guillermo de Zéndegui, *Ambito de Marti,* Havana, 1953; and works by Manuel P. Gonzáles (editor of *Antologia critica de José Marti,* Havana, 1953); *Indagaciones martianas,*

Havana, 1961 (five essays); and with Ivan A. Schulman: *Esquema ideológico martianas de José Marti,* Mexico, 1961, and with somewhat different title: *José Marti: esquema ideológico,* Madrid, 1961; José Angel Ceniceros, *Marti o la tragedia como destino glorioso,* Mexico, Botas, 1947; Raul José Fajardo, *La conciencia universal y Marti,* Havana, Lex, 1952; play: *Marti en Dos Rios,* Mexico, Cosmos, 1954; José Angel Cisneros: *José Marti y las artes plásticas* (anthology of his criticism of art), Madrid, Castilla, 1972.

MARTIN MONTES, José Luis

b. 1921, Vega Baja, Puerto Rico.
Poet, essayist, teacher.

A professor of humanities at the University of Puerto Rico, Martin has learned much from Garcia Lorca and the island poets Luis Lloréns Torres and Virgilio Dávila. He was a signer of the Ensueñismo manifesto of 1954 along with Rosa-Nieves, E. Rentas Lucas and F. Franco Oppenheimer.

Writings: Poetry: *Psiquis* (prose-poems), 1938; *Agonia del silencio,* 1953; "Romancero del Cibuco," reviewed in 1955 but written in 1953 and as yet unpublished; two poems from "Romancero . . ." are in *Aguinaldo lirico,* C. Rosa-Nieves, ed., Rio Piedras, 1957.

Literary Biographies and Histories: *Análisis estilistico de la Sataniada de Tapia,* San Juan, 1958; *Arco y flecha: Estudios de critica literaria,* San Juan, 1961; *La poesia de José Ensebio Caro: contribución estilistica al estudio del romanticismo hispanoamericano,* Bogotá, Instituto Caro y Cuervo, 1966 (510 pages on Columbian poet Caro [1817-1853]).

Biographical/Critical Sources: Review of "Romancero del Cibuco" by C. Rosa-Nieves in *El Mundo* (San Juan, February 14, 1955), p. 16; "Don Antonio Cortón, periodista, ensayista y critico de nuestro siglo XIX," in *Historia,* Vol. V, No. 1, Universidad de Puerto Rico (April 1955).

MARTINEZ, Vicente

b. 1908, Cuba.
Playwright.

Martinez' plays are social tracts on the worker-victims of the large estates and attacks on the politics of exploitation.

Writings: Plays: *El hombre está asegurao,* 1940; *El lanzamiento,* 1951; and *Hombre de negocios,* 1951.

MARTINEZ ALVAREZ, Rafael

(a.k.a. **Martin ALVA**)

b. June 13, 1882, San Juan, Puerto Rico; d. 1959.
Poet, novelist, playwright, teacher, lawyer.

Martinez studied law in Albany, New York (USA), and in time became Dean of the Law School of the University of Puerto Rico and was active in legal and public affairs.

Associated with the "modernista" school of poets in his earlier days, he later turned to realism in his novels and plays. His style was direct but nuanced, occasionally lyrical, and touched by his "modernista" origins. He was awarded many prizes for his poems but none of his verse has been collected in a subsequent single volume except for the early *Del verdin de mis jardines.*

Writings: Poetry: *Del verdin de mis jardines,* 1914, and numerous poems in journals.

Novels: *Don Cati,* San Juan, Real Hnos, 1923 (284 pp.); *El loco del Condado,* San Juan, Cantero Fernández, 1925 (257 pp.); *La ciudad chismosa y calumniante,* San Juan, Imp. Venezuela, 1926, (234 pp.); *Madre, ahi tienes a tu hijo,* San Juan, El Mundo, 1927, (225 pp.); *Pancho Ibero,* 1935; *Novus ordo,* 1938.

Plays: *La convulsiva,* 1917; *Tabaré,* 1919; *Doña Doro,* 1924; *La madreselva enflorecida,* 1927.

History: *un mes en el Norte,* 1919 (on World War I).

Art: *Hilachos: Colección de acuarelos y otros menudencias* (watercolors, and other), 1921.

Essay: *Paz de Altura,* 1923.

MARTINEZ AVILEIRA Y PEREZ DE CORCHO, Lorenzo

b. 1722, Villa Clara, Cuba; d. 1782.
Poet, priest.

Martinez' poetry had a spotaneous quality, particularly in his satirical décimas, the popular ten-line poems of the day. Raimundo Lazo quotes a few lines of his poems in his *La literatura cubana* (p. 31):

Insigne poeta inculto
cuyos conceptos ignaros,
aunque en luces son tan claros,
te obligan a andar oculto.
Sal, pues, y no hables a bulto,
que en la métrica palestra
no falta espada tan diestra
que mida a la tuya el filo,
y dé a tu sátiro estilo,
para que aprenda, una muestra . . .

Biographical/Critical Sources: Raimundo Lazo, *La Literatura cubana,* Mexico, Universidad Nacional Autónomia de México, 1965.

MARTINEZ CAPO, Juan

b. 1923, Aibonito, San Juan, Puerto Rico.
Poet, journalist, essayist.

Martinez was for a long period the editor of the important literary journal *El Mundo* and has published articles and verses in such reviews as *Asomante, Orfeo, Bayoán,* and *Versiones,* and the New York periodical, *La Prensa.* Rosa-Nieves finds that "Su poemática revela una poesia de preocupaciones esnobista en la parte formal: verso intimista y de serios logros metafóricos."

Writings: Poetry: *Viaje,* San Juan, Ediciones Asomante, 1961, Introduction by Maria Teresa Babin; three of his poems first published in *Orfeo* are also in *Aguinaldo lirico,* C. Rosa-Nieves, ed., Rio Piedras, 1957.

Biographical/Critical Sources: Concha Meléndez, *Poetas hispanoamericanos diversos,* San Juan, 1971.

MARTINEZ DAVILA, Manuel

(pseudonym: **José de Arce**)

b. 1883, Puerto Rico; d. 1934.
Poet, essayist, novelist.

Martinez was a "modernista" poet whose work appeared in the important journals of the day. Manrique Cabrera believes the novel *Venus del Patio* (1934) is the best long work of fiction produced by a writer of that literary influence.

Writings: Essays: *Lo azul en el arte,* 1929.
Novel: *Venus del patio,* 1934.
Poetry: uncollected.

MARTINEZ VILLENA, Rubén

b. 1899, Cuba; d. January, 1934.
Poet, storywriter, polemicist.

Sentimentalist-ironist, Martinez, dead so early of tuberculosis, wrote verse dealing with the city in such works as "Sinfonia urbana" and "Andante meridiano." His own mortal struggle shows up in the more personal "Defensa del miocardio inocente" and "Motivos de la angustia indefinida" which ends:

Sufrir el infructuoso cerebralismo insano,
el cruel distanciamiento del espiritu
la maldición de Palas en la gracias de Apolo . . .
Y en el continuo esfuerzo hacia lo inasequible
quedar, al fin, aislado, ¡perpetuamente solo,
igual que un verso de consonancia imposible!

He could write verse of the most classical sort as with "El cazador" and in "Fin de velada" which begins:

Anfora insigne do la fiebre augusta
vertió la miel de su labor divina;
ejerció de brava disciplina,
troquel de bella suavidad robusta;

A fervent communist, Martinez took part in the revolt which finally drove Machado from his dictatorship. His poem

La pupila insomne is a passionate attack on Machado.

Writings: Poetry: *La pupila insomne,* Havana, 1936, 2nd ed., Havana, Organización Continental de los Festivales del Libro, 1960, 3rd ed., Havana, Publicaciones del Gobierno Provincial Revolucionario de la Habana, 1960.
Stories and Polemical Essays: in various journals and newspapers.

Biographical/Critical Sources: see introduction by Raúl Roa to *La pupila insomne* and Roa's same essay in *Orbita de Rubén Martinez,* Villena, UNEAC, 1965, (242 pp.), selection and notes by R. Fernández Retamar.

MATAMOROS, Mercedes

b. March 13, 1851, Cienfuegos, Cuba; d. 1906.
Poet, playwright.

One of Cuba's finest poets of her century, Mercedes Metamoros published much verse and one play.

Metamoros' biographer, Pichardo, published Mercedes' birth certificates showing the March 13, 1851 date, correcting the long believed one of 1858. Max Henriquez Ureña also insists her death year was 1906, not 1907 as most authorities have it.

Her poetry was influenced by Lord Byron and Chenier and much of her work appeared in the journals of the day, including "Al morir el dia," "El triunfo," "El sueño del poeta," "A un águila," and "La muerte del esclavo."

Her highly musical quality may be seen in these last lines from "El himno de la lluvia":

Mi voz canta en las ramas celestes
armonias;
yo pueblo los bascajes
de plácidos rumores;
Y en las oscuras selvas y agrestes
serranias
mis ritmos son gorjeos
de alegres ruiseñores.

Writings: Poetry: *Poesias completas,* Havana, 1892; *Sonetos* (including "El último de Safo"), Havana, 1902.
Play: *El invierno en flor* (1 act), 1882.

Biographical/Critical Sources: Hortensia Pichardo de Portuondo, *Mercedes Matamoros, su vida y su obra,* Havana, 1952.

MATAS, Julio

b. 1931, Cuba.
Storywriter, teacher, actor, director.

After local schooling through a degree in law at the University of Havana, Matas became an actor and later directed a production of Ionesco's *The Bald Soprano.* Breaking off his work toward a doctorate at Harvard in 1959, he returned to Havana to become director of the National Cuban Theatre, remaining in theatre and television work until 1965 when he went into exile. Completing the Ph.D. at Howard, he became a professor at the University of Pittsburgh.

Matas' stories are generally escapist, most influenced by Virgilio Piñera's cruel fantasies, and his novelettes often exploit the aches and agonies of frigid women and impotent men. One story, "Carambola del 57" is vaguely "political" in its treatment of the excesses of Batista's police.

Writings: Stories: *Catálogo de imprevistos,* Havana, 1963; *Erinia,* 1971 (includes the ten stories of Catá*logo* and nine new ones).

MATEO, Andrés L.

b. ca. 1930, Dominican Republic.
Poet.

Mateo's poetry has been marked with strong social feeling and expresses great relief at the overthrow of Trujillo. His tone is pessimistic, almost sour.

Writings: Poetry: *Poemas publicados en diversos*

diarios nacionales, date unknown; some of his verse appears in the *Antologia informal* of Pedro Conde and the *Antologia de la literatura dominicana,* of José Alcántara.

MATOS, Alfredo

b. 1860, Dominican Republic; d. 1935.
Playwright.

Matos was one of the more prolific and popular poets of his day and four of his plays are historically important though none of them has been published.

Writings: Plays: *Rasgos de nobleza; Al fondo de un abismo; Es igual;* all performed, and *Sin padre* (written with Telesforo Alfonseca, 1879-1910).

MATOS BERNIER, Félix

b. 1869, San Blas de Boamo, Puerto Rico; d. Ponce, November 5, 1937.
Critic, essayist, poet.

Matos was a late romantic poet whose work was mostly published by 1914. He did one naturalist novel *Puerta de sol* (1903), but his most interesting work may be *Isla de arte* (1907) which details the literary scene of the island.

Writings: Poetry: *Nieves y lavas,* 1894; *Recuerdos benditos,* 1895; *Notas errantes,* 1885; *Acantos,* 1902; *Cantos rodados,* 1900; *La protesta de Satán,* 1909; *Poema de las islas,* 1914.

Journal Articles and Essays: *Ecos de la propaganda,* 1889; *Cromos ponceños,* 1896; *Pedazos de roca,* 1894; *Páginas sueltas,* 1897; *Muertos y vivos,* 1905; *Isla de arte,* San Juan, Imp. La Primavera, 1907.

Novel: *Puesta de sol,* San Juan, Tip. San Juan News, 1903.

Biographical/Critical Sources: Carmen Rosa Diaz, "Félix Matos Bernier: su vida y su obra," unpub. M. A. thesis, U. of P. R., 1940, 145 pp.; Carmen R. Diaz de Olano, *Félix Matos Bernier: su vida y su obra,* San Juan, 1955.

MATOS PAOLI, Francisco

b. 1915, Lares, Puerto Rico.
Poet, essayist, critic, teacher.

Matos Paoli was for a long period professor of Puerto Rican literature and humanities at the University of Puerto Rico where he did undergraduate studies. He did further work at the University of Paris. Matos is considered one of the great poets of the post-modernista period.

Matos spent time for his separatist efforts in the Princesa and Oso Blanco prisons and his greatest work, one critic has claimed, is his "Canto de la locura" (1962) written with nails and blood on a cell wall. "Canto de la locura (I)" begins:

Ya está transido, pobre de rocio,
este enorme quetzalde la nada.
No bastan los signos
hirvientes,
las manos colmadas, los rios,
las lenguas atadas.

Religion and God are the constant themes of his work. His poem "Democracy" is typical:

A silence of hunger
Where the beggars
eat horrified
a succulent plate of nothingess.
A silence of pus
swung by the war
that decorates heroes
without looks
which turns blood
into dirty coins of the pariahs
. . .
. . .
a silence of slaves:
it is called democracy.
(trans: Digna Sánchez-Méndez)

His "Mar Heróico" begins:

Luchas contra el imposible
de la roce denodada
Derrotas la noche anclada
en el pavor. Indecible
como poema, infalible
como norme, saltarás
al cielo . . .

Writings: Poetry: in various collections including the *Puerto Rican Poets,* Matilla and Silén, eds., New York, Bantam, 1972, and separate volumes: *Signario de lágrimas,* Aguadilla, P. R., Tribuna Libre, 1931; *Cardo labriego y otros poemas,* San Juan, Imp. Venezuela, 1937; *Habitante del eco (1937-1941),* Santurce, Soltero, 1944; *Teoria del olvido,* Rio Piedras, Junta Editora de la Universidad de Puerto Rico, 1944; *Canto a Puerto Rico,* San Juan, Ateneo Puertorriqueño, 1952 (won Ateneo's first prize in 1950); *Luz de los héroes,* San Juan, Casa Baldrich, 1954; *Criatura del rocio,* San Juan, Ateneo Puertorriqueño, 1958; *Canto de la locura,* San Juan, Ediciones Juan Ponce de León, 1962; *El viento y la paloma (1961-1963),* San Juan, Ediciones Juan Ponce de León, 1969; *Cuadernos de poesia,* edited by José R. de la Torre, San Juan, Instituto de Cultura Puertorriqueña, 1971; *Cancionero,* Ediciones Juan Ponce de León, 1971; *Ser en el alba,* San Juan, Ed. Libreria Internacional, 1971; *La mares sube,* San Juan, Edic. Juan Ponce de León, 1971; *La semilla encendida,* 1971; *Cancionero II,* Juan Ponce de León, 1972; *Antologia poética,* edited by José E. Gonzáles, Rio Piedras, Editorial Universitaria, 1972; *Cancionero IV,* San Juan, Ediciones Juan Ponce de León, 1976; and poems in various anthologies, including *Literatura puertorriqueña,* 2nd ed., Vol. II, E. Martinez Masdeu and Esther M. Melon, Rio Piedras, 1972, pp. 249-254, which has "Canto de la locura (I)."

Biographical/Critical Sources: Aguinaldo lirico, C. Rosa-Nieves, ed., Rio Piedras, 1957, pp. 401-402, and see José Emilio González' introduction to *Antologia poética* (1972) with brief bibliography of criticism of Matos Paoli's work, for which see above; Julio César López, "Francisco Matos Paoli y el vanguardismo literario," in *La Patria en dos poetas y un paralelo modernista,* Barcelona, Talleres Gráficos Ariel, 1968, pp. 13-21.

MATTA, Enrique G.

b. ca. 1894, Puerto Rico.
Novelist.

In 1924 Matta was mayor of his village and led a protest against the Sugar Cane Corporation. His novel *The Americano* treats of the island at the time the United States seized Puerto Rico from the Spaniards and the ensuing changes, often rapid and disturbing. The hero is Glenn Sumners who, though an outsider, comes to love the place and tries to fight the still entrenched old Spanish landowners who are only for the old values if they serve to preserve their privileges.

Writings: Novel: *The Americano,* San Juan, Department of Education, 1968.

MAURY, José W.

b. ca. 1879, Santiago, Cuba.
Playwright.

Maury wrote two plays but is otherwise all but forgotten.

Writings: Plays: *El quinto no matar* (comedy), 1909; *La hormiga blanca* (comedy), 1910.

MAYOL MARTINEZ, Jaime

b. 1849, Regla, Cuba.
Playwright.

Mayol published seven of his once popular plays, all in Guanabocoa, Cuba.

Writings: Plays: *Las que resultan* (comic sketch), Imp. de A. Roca, 1909; *Lorenzo* (2 acts, prose), 1910; *Realidad* (1 act comedy, prose), 1910; *El buen amigo* (3 acts), 1911; *Lo previsto* (2 act comedy), with *El réprobo* (comedy) and with *El buen amigo* (3 acts), 1913.

MEDINA Y CESPEDES, Antonio

b. 1824, Havana, Cuba; d. 1886.
Poet, playwright.

Of African race, Medina was one of the earliest Cuban writers. After many struggles he earned a diploma in 1850. Antonio Medina was called by Juan Gualberto Gómez the "José de la Luz y Caballero de la raza de color."

Writings: Poetry: *Lodoiska o La maldición* (5 acts, verse), Havana, Imp. de Torres, 1849, and as *La maldición* (5 acts, verse), 2nd ed., Havana, Imp. de Ejercito, 1882; *D. Canuto Ceibamocha o el Guajiro generoso* (2 act farce of local manners), Havana, 1854, 2nd ed., Havana, Imp. del Ejercito, 1881; *Rogerio el Bandido* (chivalresque drama after the Italian), in ms. only; and *Jacobo Girondi* (3 acts, verse), Havana, Imp. La Lolita, 1881, premiered Teatro Payret, Havana, March 26, 1881.

MEIRELES, Eduardo

b. 1865, Havana, Cuba.
Playwright, educator.

Meireles published three of his known four works for the theatre but is today of academic interest only.

Writings: Plays: *En el juzgado* (1 act verse), Havana, written 1891, in ms.; *Los matrimonios* (1 act, prose), Havana, Imp. La Moderna, 1891; *Matanzas en camisón* (review, 1 act, 3 scenes), Havana, La Moderna, 1894; *La entrega del mando o Fin del siglo* (1 act, verse), Puerto Rico, Lynn e hijos, 1899.

MEJIA DE FERNANDEZ, Abigail

b. 1895, Dominican Republic; d. 1940.
Novelist, critic.

Today almost unknown, Abigail Mejia published two novels and two literary histories, one of which was her *Historia de la literatura dominicana.*

Writings: Novels: *Sueña Pilarin,* Spain, and *Por entre frivolidades,* dates unknown.

Literary Histories: *Historia de la literatura castellana,* 1926; *Historia de la literatura dominicana,* 1937.

MELENDEZ, Concha

b. 1904, Caguas, Puerto Rico.
Poet, critic, literary historian, teacher.

After local schooling Meléndez attended the University of Puerto Rico (B. A. 1924), taking thereafter an M. A. at Columbia University (1926) and a doctorate at the National University of Mexico (1932) in philosophy and letters. For many years (1940-1959) she was a professor of Latin-American literature at the University of Puerto Rico and a leading critic and literary historian.

Writings: Critical Essays: *La inquietud sosegada, poética de Evaristo Ribera Chevremont,* San Juan, Ed. Universidad de Puerto rico, 1946; *Figuración de Puerto Rico y otros estudios,* San Juan, Instituto Alfonso Reyes, 1956; *Palabras para oyentes,* 2 vols., San Juan, Instituto de Cultura Puertorriqueña, 1970.

Literary Histories: *La novela indianista en hispanoamérica,* 1935; *Signos de Iberoamérica,*

Mexico City, Imp. Manuel Sánchez de León, 1936; *Estudios hispanoamericanos,* Asomante, 1939; *La generación del treinta, cuento y novela,* 1960; *El arte del cuento in Puerto Rico,* New York, Las Américas, 1961, and reprint in San Juan, Edit. Cordilleras, 1961; *Literatura hispanoamericana,* San Juan, Edit. Cordilleras, 1967; *Poetas hispanoamericanos diversos,* San Juan, Edit. Cordilleras, 1971; *Literatura de ficción en Puerto Rico: cuento y novela,* San Juan, Edit. Cordilleras, 1971.

Critical Biographies: *Amado Nervo,* New York, Instituto de las Españas, 1926; "Pablo Neruda: vida y obra," in *Revista Hispánica Moderna,* No. 1 (New York, 1936); *De frente al sol, apuntes sobre la poesia de Luis Muñoz Rivera,* 1963.

Poetry: in various journals and anthologies, including "Lo saben las montañas" and "Post Umbra," in *Antologia de la poesia puertorriqueña,* E. Fernández Méndez, San Juan, 1968.

Travel: *Entrada al Perú,* 1941.

Genre unknown: *Psiquis doliente,* 1926.

Editor of: *Cuentos hispanoamericanos,* 1956; *Antologia de autores puertorriquenos,* San Juan, Ediciones del Gobierno, 1957.

Biographical/Critical Sources: Cecilia Arvaldi de Olmeda, *Concha Meléndez: Vida y obra,* Rio Piedras, Edit. Universitaria, 1972; and see essay on Meléndez in Juan Enrique Colbert Petrovitch, *Cuatro autores clásicos contemporáneos de Puerto Rico,* San Juan, 1966.

MELENDEZ MUNOZ, Miguel

b. July 22, 1884, Cayey, Puerto Rico; d. 1966.

Critic, essayist, storywriter, journalist, folklorist, sociologist.

A leading "modernista" critic, Meléndez has passed most of his long life in his natal Cayey. His first essays appeared in 1904 in local journals and he has contributed down the years to many reviews until today he is close to being the major critical voice of the island.

Meléndez' style is usually poetic, even lyrical, full of love for nature and country people. Nevertheless, his esthetic is highly informed and he has always been interested in social and intellectual questions. Rosa-Nieves considers his *Lecturas puertorriqueñas* to have helped "regenerate" Puerto Rico's flagging culture. Many of his stories won prizes, including "Dos Cartas" (1908), "El Novio" (from the journal *América*), and "Tirijala" (1932, prize of Ateneo Puertorriqueño).

His one published novel was *Yuyo* (1913) which is mildly of the naturalist vein and set in the country, but a second novel, "Madre Tierra" remains in manuscript, as do so many of his essays and articles gathered by him under the titles, "Sobre esto y aquello," "Socialismo y la guerra," and the "La cuestión agraria, Discursos."

Writings: Essays: *Retazos,* 1905; *Estado social del campesino puertorriqueño,* 1916; *Lecturas puertorriqueñas,* 1st ed., 1919, 4th ed., San Juan, Edit. Campos, 1959; *Retablo puertorriqueño,* 1941; *Fuga de ideas,* 1942; his essay "Desde la revuelta de la guasima," *Puerto Rico Ilustrado* (May 5, 1917), appears in L. Hernández Aquino's *El modernismo en Puerto Rico,* San Juan, 1967; *Algunos ensayos,* San Juan, Edit. Club de la Prensa, 1958.

Novel: Yuyo, San Juan, Boletin Mercantil, 1913.

Stories: *Cuentos del cedro,* 1936; *Cuentos de la Carretera; Fuerzas contrarias,* in *Retazos,* San Juan, Tip. Boletin Mercantil, 1905 (45 p.).

Play: *Retablo puertorriqueño,* 1941.

Complete Works: *Miguel Meléndez Muñoz: Obras completas,* San Juan, Ediciones Rumbos, 3 vols., 1963.

Editor of: *El cuento, antologia de autores puertorriqueños,* III, San Juan, Ediciones del Gobierno, Estado Libre Asociado de Puerto Rico, 1957.

Biographical/Critical Sources: Cristóbal Real, "La Novela de Meléndez Muñoz," *Puerto Rico Ilustrado,* No. 214 (April 4, 1914); C. Rosa-Nieves, in *Ensayos escogidas,* San Juan, 1970, pp. 161-163; Josefina Lube Droz, "Miguel Meléndez Muñoz: vida y obra," unpub. M. A. thesis, U. of P. R., 1951, (used as an introduction to *Obras Completas,* 1963). Also see J. E. Colberg Petrovich, *Cuatro autores clásicas contemporáneos de Puerto Rico,* San Juan, 1966.

MELLADO Y MONTANA, Manuel

b. 1892, Cuba.
Playwright.

Mellado's prolific works, most of them unpublished, deserve mention because of their number and relative historical importance rather than for their intrinsic esthetic merit.

Writings: Plays: *Perico Masca Vidrio o La Vispera de San Juan,* Havana, Imp. El Correo Militar, 1880, performed 1880 by Compañia de Bufos; *La casa de Taita Andrés* (1 act), 1880, in ms.; *D. Diego y D. Dieguito* (1 act), 1880; *D. Silvestre del Campo* (1 act), 1880; *El 19 de enero* (1 act), 1880; *El hombre de la culebra* (1 act), 1880; *El muerto al hoyo* (1 act), 1880; *Apuros de un figurin* (1 act, prose), Havana, Imp. del Batallón Mixto de Ingenieros, 1891; *Miseria humana* (1 act comedy, prose), Havana, Imp. del Batallón Mixto. . ., 1891, performed 1880 by the Compañia de Bufos; *Buchito en Guanabacoa* (1 act), written 1891, in ms.; *El triunfo de un tabaquero* (melodrama), Havana, 1881, in ms.; *Guebito en Guanabacoa* (1 act), Havana, 1881, in. ms., performed May 30, 1881 by Compañia de Bufos; *La casa de Socorro* (1 act, prose), Havana, 1888, in ms.

MENDEZ BALLESTER, Manuel

b. 1909, Aguadillo, Puerto Rico.
Novelist, playwright, actor, theatrical director.

Méndez' two plays are concerned with social problems of the day and are in a realistic vein. His third play *Hilarión* takes an Oedipan theme in treating of the dictatorship of Bocanegra and the hero's efforts to combat Bocanegra in a tragic conflict so familiar to the area. His novel *Isla cerrera* (1938) deals with the difficult early period of Puerto Rico settlement.

Writings: Novel: *Isla cerrera: Novela basado en la conquista de Puerto Rico,* 1938, Mexico, Edit. Diana, 1949, Barcelona, Imp. M. Pareja, 1970.

Plays: El clamor de los surcos, 1938, and San Juan, Talleres Tip. de la Casa Baldrich, 1940 (109 p.); *Hilarión; Encrucijada,* in *Teatro puertorriqueño: primer festival de teatro,* San Juan, Instituto de Cultura Puertorriqueña, 1959; reprint, Rio Piedras, Edit. Edil, 1960; *El milagro,* in *Teatro puertorriqueño: cuarto festival,* San Juan, Instituto de Cultura Puertorriqueña, 1963; *Tiempo muerto,* San Juan, Colección Areyto and in *Teatro puertorriqueño: quinto festival,* San Juan, Instituto de Cultura Puertorriqueño, 1964; *Bienvenido, Don Goyito,* in *Teatro puertorriqueño: octavo festival,* San Juan, 1966; *La feria o el mono con la lata en el rabo,* In *Teatro puertorriqueño: sexto festival,* San Juan, 1964.

MENDIVE, Rafael Maria de

b. 1821, Havana, Cuba; d. Havana, 1886.
Poet, playwright, drama critic, teacher.

After the study of philosophy in the Seminario de San Carlos in Havana, Mendive studied law at the University of Havana and then lived in the United States and Europe from 1849 to 1852. Back home again, he joined José Gonzaló Roldán in founding *Flores del Siglo* which flourished in 1845-1846 and the *Revista de la Habana* (1853-56) with José de Jesús Quintiliano Garcia.

Mendive served as secretary of the Liceo de la Habana and was a director of the Colegio Superior Municipal de Varones in Havana, and later came into a direct relationship with the young José Marti on whom he had a distinct influence.

Imprisoned in 1869 for his nationalist

sentiments, Mendive was deported to Spain whence he was able to make his way to the United States where he lived most of the next ten years. Allowed to return to Cuba in 1878, Mendive eventually founded the journal *Diario Liberal* in Matanzas.

Mendive's early volume of verse, *Pasionarios* (1847) was well received and his translation of Thomas Moore's poetry as *Melodias irlandesas* (1875) was a late accomplishment of this minor poet. According to Luis Perrier, "No posee Mendive la elocuencia de Luaces o la ternura apasionada de Zenea. Sus poemas de asunto heróico, tales como el "Canto a Juárez," carecen de profundidad y de elevación poética, pero nadie canta los afectos domésticos con más gracia y delicadeza."

Writings: Poetry: *Pasionarias,* 1847; *Poesias,* 1860, 2nd ed., 1883; and translation of Moore's poetry as *Melodias irlandesas,* New York, 1863 (55 p.), 2nd ed., 1875.

Opera: *Gulnara,* premiered in Teatro Tacón, published Havana, both 1848. (Luigi Arditi [1822-1903] later used the libretto for one of his own works).

Drama Criticism: in various journals, but never collected.

Plays: (all unpublished): *La nube negra* (only 8 scenes exist of this fragmented work); *Las immaculadas; Los pobres de espiritu; Por la patria* (dramatic poem); *Un drama en el mar;* and the romances: *Bajo los lirios azules,* and *Yumuri.* (all works no longer extant except *La nube negra*).

Biographical/Critical Sources: Salvador Salazar's *Maria Mendive,* Madrid(?), 1915; and Max Henriquez Ureña, *Panorama histórico de la literatura cubana,* New York, 1963, pp. 260-269.

MENDOZA, Ester Feliciano

b. 1918, Aguadilla, Puerto Rico.
Poet, storywriter (for children), folklorist.

A strong folklorist, Ester Mendoza has devoted her art to reclaiming the island's lore for the new generation. Her "¡A navegar!" demonstrates her usual quick style:

Haré para ti
un barquito
con un pétalo de luna,
con velas de seda pura
y mástiles de cristal
¡A navegar, marinero!
¡A navegar!

Writings: Folklore: *Arco-iris,* 1951.

Poetry: in various journals and collections, including *Antologia de la poesia puertorriqueña,* E. Fernández Méndez, ed., San Juan, 1968.

MENENDEZ, Aldo

b. 1918, Cuba.
Poet.

A founder with Feijóo and Iznaga of the poetry journal *Concierto,* Menéndez published his early work therein in 1947, but his later work published elsewhere has appeared in several collections. His work is often bizarre, recondite, and complex.

Writings: Poetry: *Morada temporal,* in "notebook" of *Concierto,* 1947; *Puerto inmovil,* Havana, 1953; *Ciudad cerrada, Cienfuegos, 1955, Hojas evasivas,* Cienfuegos, 1956; *Patria imperecedera,* Cienfuegos, 19??; *Helena,* Havana, La Tertulia, 1965; *Siempre cantábamos,* Havana, UNEAC, 1969.

MERCADO, José Ramón

(a.k.a. **Momo**)

b. October 7, 1863, Caguas, Puerto Rico; d. March, 1911.
Poet, journalist.

Self-educated, Mercado left school at 12 and first worked as a street vendor in Caguas where he became wise with folk wisdom and as still a very young man took part in a contest of composing poems (the famous décimas). He won the first prize. His life continued in a relaxed, bohemian fashion, his poetry appearing in random local journals. After 17 years in San Juan (1888-1905), he went to Havana where he was well received in literary circles in which he generally moved—always with little or no money. Despite his knockabout life, Mercado is well considered as a minor figure of comic, but noble warmth.

Writings: Poetry: *Virutas,* 1900; *Mi equipaje,* 1901; miscellaneous pieces in Cuban journals: "La lengua castellana" appears in *Antologia puertorriqueña,* edited by M. Fernández Juncos, New York, 1907, pp. 230-235; "Los candelados," in *La Araña,* San Juan (February 1902).

Biographical/Critical Sources: Antologia puertorriqueña, 1st ed., Manuel Fernández Juncos, New York, 1907, pp. 224-229; Providencia Vieta de Miranda, "Vida y obra de José Mercado (Momo)," unpub. M. A. thesis, U. of P. R., 1948, (236 p.); F. Manrique Cabrera, *Historia de la literatura puertorriqueña,* Rio Piedras, 1969, pp. 206-208.

MERCEDES SANTA CRUZ Y MONTALVO, Maria de las (Condesa de Merlin)

b. 1789, Havana, Cuba; d. 1852.
Autobiographer, letter-writer, travel-writer, storywriter.

Mercedes grew up in Madrid and married French General Christophe Antoine. She was the mistress of several famous salons in Paris and Madrid and for a brief period in 1840 in her natal city, Havana. She wrote a frank autobiography and her letters and other writings attacked slavery.

She was also an ardent feminist for her time and is possibly Cuba's first woman literary figure of any consequence. All her writing was in French.

She published a biography of then famous actress Marie Felicité Malibran in Paris (1838) and a strong attack on slavery in 1840. Though there were some aspersions made in her own time that she had not indeed authored some of the works published under her name, Max Henriquez Ureña, for one, states categorically that there is no merit in such a charge.

Writings: Novelettes: *Histoire de Soeur Inés,* Paris, 1838; *Duc d'Athénes,* Paris, 1852; "Una pascua en San Marcos," included in *La Havane* (see below).

Travel: *Viaje a la Habana* (in Spanish translation and with introduction by Gertrudis Avellaneda, Madrid, 1844, and Havana, 1922; also: as *La Havana,* 3 vols., Paris, 1842 (French text throughout).

Sociology-Tract: *L'esclavage aux colonies espagnols,* Paris, 1840.

Memoirs: *Souvenirs et mémoires,* Paris, 1836; *Mes douze premières annés,* Paris, 1838.

Biographical/Critical Sources: Max Henriquez Ureña, *Panorama histórico de la literatura cubana,* Vol. I, New York, 1963, pp. 233-234.

MERCHAN, Rafael Maria

b. 1844, Manzanillo, Cuba; d. 1905, Columbia, South America.
Critic, journalist, essayist, poet.

A student of the Seminario de Santiago de Cuba, Merchán considered entering the priesthood, but instead turned to journalism. After a period in Bayamo, he moved to Havana in 1860 to edit *El Siglo,* then *El Pais* and quickly identified himself with the revolutionary cause.

Merchán took over the editorship of the journal *La Revolución* from Enrique Piñeiro in New York in 1868-69 after the failure of the revolt against Spain led by Carlos Manuel de Céspedes. After a life of struggle, mostly passed in Colombia and the United States, he was finally awarded when the newly independent Cuba sent him as Cuba's first Ambassador to Madrid.

His literary criticism was highly analytical and much concerned with purity of diction and appropriate form. As a poet, Max Henriquez Ureña finds him less than excellent though he said his verse at times had a certain felicity. Merchán was only occasionally able to devote himself to poetry, for his busy life was filled with the need to support the cause of Cuban independence. Moving from one editorial desk to another, including the editorship of the Bogotá journals *El Repertorio Colombiano* and *La Luz* (1881-1884), he should be remembered primarily as an ideologue and journalist than as a creative writer, though his one collection of verse, *Emociones,* had two editions.

Writings: Critical Essays: *Variedades,* Bogotá, 1894; *Carta al Señor Juan Valera sobre asuntos americanos,* Bogotá, 1890; *Un poco de todo,* Bogotá, 1890; *Comentarios,* Bogotá, 1898; also *Estudios criticos,* Bogotá, 1886 (volume includes essay "Juan Clemente Zenea, poeta cubano," first published, Bogotá, 1881);

Poetry: *Emociones,* private edition, 1899, 2nd ed., Bogotá, 1902; translation of Longfellow's poem as *Evangelina, cuento de Acacia,* Bogotá, 1882, 1883, 1887 and Costa Rica, 1919.

Polemics: *Cuba: justificación de su guerra de independencia,* Bogotá, 1896; *La honra de España en Cuba,* New York, 1871; *La autonomia de Cuba,* Bogotá, 1890; *Colombia y Cuba,* Bogotá, 1897; *La redención de un mundo,* Bogotá, 1898; *Un ex liberatador: Gustavo Ortega,* Bogotá, 1898.

Speech: *La educación de la mujer* (given at the Colegio Pestalozziano), Bogotá, 1894.

Biographical/Critical Sources: Max Henriquez Ureña, *Panorama histórico de la literatura cubana,* New York, 1963, pp. 86-90.

MERGAL, Angel M.

b. August 9, 1909, Cayey, Puerto Rico.
Poet, critic, literary historian, teacher.

Mergal is best known for his many studies of Hispanic literature and his political writings. He has published one modest collection of verse *Puente sobre el abismo* (1941). Much of his work has appeared in *Nueva Democracia* (published in New York City), *Luminar* (Mexico), *Carteles* (Cuba) and *Cuadernos Teológicos de Buenos Aires.* His poetry is often religious or philosophical.

Writings: Critical Biographies: *El hidalgo iluminado,* 1939; *El agraz,* 1945; "Federico Degetau" (unpublished doctoral dessertation, University of Puerto Rico, 1945), but see: *Federico Degetan,* New York, Hispanic Institute, 1944, (200 p.); "Intento critico-biográfico de Peache," in *Alma Latina* (May 1936 [of José P. H. Hernández]); and "José A. Negrón Sanjurjo, su tiempo su vida y su obra," unpublished M. A. thesis, U. of P. R., 1940.

Political Essays: *Defensa de la educación democratica; Reformismo Cristiano,* 1949; *Arte cristiana de la predicación; Reformismo y alma español,* Buenos Aires, Ed. La Aurora, 1949.

MEZA Y SUAREZ INCLAN, Ramón

b. January 18, 1861, Havana, Cuba; d. 1911.
Novelist, critic, playwright, teacher, journalist.

Meza's seven novels exploited local customs and folklore. He was once a well-known literary figure in the island and considered a critic worth listening to.

Writings: Novels: *El duelo de mi vecino,* Havana, 1886, and Havana, Comisión Nacional Cubana de la UNESCO, 1961; *Flores y calabazas,* Havana, 1886; *Carmela,* Havana, 1887; *Mi tio el empleado,* Barcelona, 1887, and Havana, Dirección General de la Cultura, 1960; *Don Aniceto el tendero,* Barcelona, 1889; *Ultimas páginas,* Havana, 1891; *En el pueblo de la Florida,* published in *Cuba y América,* 1898-99.

Criticism: in various journals. One of his best studies was "La obra postuma de Mitjans" (on Aurelio Mitjans) and *Estudio histórico-critico de la Iliada y La Odisea y sus influencia en los demás géneros poéticos de Grecia,* Havana,

1894; also: *Don Quijote como tipo ideal,* Havana, 1905.

Play: *Una sesión de hipnotismo* (2 act comedy), Havana, El Pilar, 1891.

Speech: *Discurso en elogio del general Máximo Gómez,* Havana, 1905; and see second item in Education (below).

Education: *Observaciones sobre educación,* Havana, 1905; *La educación en nuestro medio social* (speech), Havana, 1908.

Biographies: *Miguel Melero,* Havana, 1909; *Julián del Casal,* Havana, 1910; *Los González del Valle,* Havana, 1911.

Biographical/Critical Sources: many studies and monographs, among them: Evelio Rodriguez Lendians, *Elogio del Dr. Ramón Meza y Suárez Inclán,* Havana, El Siglo XX, 1915 (68 pp.), and Domingo Figarola-Caneda, "El Dr. Ramón Meza y Suárez Inclan," in *Noticia bio-bibliográfica,* 2nd ed., Havana, 1909 (21 pp.).

MIESES BURGOS, Franklin (or **Franklyn**)

b. 1907, Santo Domingo, Dominican Republic.
Poet, verse playwright, lawyer.

In a busy life of law and public affairs, Mieses has also been a creative innovator in poetry, a co-director of the Isla Necesaria series of Dominican authors, and executive director of the Institute of Hispanic Culture as well as editor of its review. He was also a prime mover in the "Poesia Sorprendida" group.

Mieses' poems "Sin mundo ya y herido por el cielo" and "Clima de eternidad" are considered two of the finest in the nation's literature. Moving past the influences of Rilke and Lorca he has sought his own very particular idiom of symbols. His fervent verse often is pervaded with the image of the angel as the ultimate of human experience and a contrast to man's loss of purity. His many sonnets are very carefully organized yet remain supple instruments of his thought. One critic, Manuel Rueda, points out the poems "Elegia a Tomás Sandoval" and "Paisaje con un merengue al fondo" as being particularly perfumed and colorful, demonstrating "una pureza e idealidad" almost of paradise.

However, social pressures and the disorders of the Trujillo regime are reflected in such poems as "Clima de eternidad" first published in 1944. Ramón Emilio Reyes considered this work the most valiant political denunciation in the years of Trujillo's terror and oppression.

Mieses experimented with complicated verse forms, including the alexandrine and even the fourteener (14 syllabic lines), but always found the musical way to express his feelings, no matter what metrical and syllabic lines and patterns he chose.

Writings: Poetry: *Clima de eternidad,* S. Domingo, Col. La Poesia Sorprendida, 1944; *Sin mundo ya y herido por el cielo,* also in La *Writings:* Poetry: *Clima de eternidad,* S. Domingo, Col. *La Poesia Sorprendida,* 1944; *Sin mundo ya y herido por el cielo,* Col. *La Poesia Sorprendida,* 1944; *Presencia de los dias,* Mendonza, Argentina, 1948, and Montevideo, Uruguay, Ed. Brigadas Liricas, 1951; *Seis cantos para una sola muerte,* S. Domingo, Cuadernos dominicanos de cultura, 1948; *Franklin Mieses Burgos: Antologia Poética,* Ciudad Trujillo, preface and selections by Freddy Gatón Arce, S. Domingo, Postigo, 1952.

Verse Drama: *El héroe: Poema con intención escénica en dos sueños, S. Domingo, Col. La Isla Necesaria, 1954.*

Biographical/Critical Sources: Freddy Gatón Arce's preface to *Franklyn Mieses Burgos,* S. Domingo, Postigo, 1952.

MILANES, Federico

b. 1815, Cuba; d. 1890.
Playwright, poet.

Brother of José Jacinto Milanés, Federico's plays have not been published and the manuscripts seem no longer extant. Domingo del Monte in a letter to José Jacinto stated his high opinion of Federico's plays, *Un baile de ponina* being considered his best work.

Writings: Plays: Un baile de ponina (3 act comedy, folkloric), performed Matanzas; *Mercedes* (4 act comedy), premiered at Liceo de Matanzas, 1861, Juego Mercedes prize 1867, with *La visita del marqués* (3 act comedy), Juegos Florales del Liceo de Matanzas prize 1861; *La cena de don Enrique el Doliente,* apparently never performed.

Poetry: "Oda a la muerta de Quintana," awarded first prize in Juegos Florales, Matanzas, 1861; elegy: "Aniversario," for his brother José; and satires: "Contra los vicios de la sociedad cubana," and "Contra la mania de publicar tomos de poesias con titulos inadecuados y prólogos altisonantes y laudatorios."

MILANES, José Jacinto

b. 1814, Matanzas, Cuba; d. 1863.
Poet, playwright.

Once considered one of Cuba's most famous romantic lyric poets, Milanés

executed works in a wide variety of styles and subjects—and was original though reflecting, even in a new age, the great classics of Spanish literature. Some of his most famous poems were "La madrugada," "La fuga de la tortola," and "La guajarita del Yumuri."

The poet's middle years showed a breakdown of mind and sensibility and he spent his last twenty years in an asylum. His play *El Conde Alarcos* (1838) is a typical work of the period. Once very popular it is now felt to be undistinguished even though it has good verse.

Writings: Poetry: *Poesias,* Havana, Edición Nacional del Centenario de Milanés, 1920.

Centennial Edition of His Works: *Obras completas,* 2 vols., Havana, Editora del Consejo Nacional de Cultura, 1963, (541 p. and 444 p.).

Plays: *El Conde Alarcos* (3 acts, verse), Havana, Imp. del Gobierno, 1838; *A buen hambre no hay pan duro* (1 act, verse), Havana, Imp. del Faro Industrial, 1846; plays in *Obras de José Jacinto Milanés,* Havana, Imp. del Faro Industrial, 4 vols., 1846, 2nd ed., New York, Juan F. Trow, 1 vol., 1865 (Vol. IV of the first edition of *Obras* contained *El Conde Alarcos; Un poeta en la corte* (3 acts, verse, written 1838-1840); *Por el puente o por el rio* (unfinished: first act and part of Act II in ms.); and nine little stage pieces.

Biographical/Critical Sources: Carolina Poncet y de Cárdenas' *José Jacinto Milanés,* Havana, 1923; Max Henriquez Ureña, *Panorama histórico de la literatura cubana,* New York, 1963, pp. 186ff., Salvador Salazar's *Milanés, Luaces y la Avellaneda,* Madrid(?), 1916.

MILLAN, José Agustin

b. ca. 1815, Havana, Cuba; d. ca. 1865.
Playwright, editor, folklorist, biographer.

Millan was one of the most famous playwrights of Cuba and wildly applauded for his 22 works. He was associated with several journals, including *El Muza.*

Writings: Plays: *Apuros del carnaval* (1 act

comedy), Havana, Oliva, 1841; *El médico lo manda* (1 act comedy), Havana, Torres, 1841; *Mi tio el ciego o Un baile en el cerro* (1 act comedy), Havana, Oliva, 1841; *El hombre de la culebra* (1 act), Havana, Oliva, 1841; *Una aventura o el camino más corto* (3 act comedy), Havana, Barcina, 1842; *El novio de mi mujer* (1 act comedy), Havana, Imp. del Faro Industrial, 1842; *El recién nacido* (1 act comic piece), Havana, Soler, 1843; *Amor y travesura o Una tarde en el Bejuca* (1 act comedy), Havana, Imp. El Faro Industrial, 1843; *La Guajira o Una noche en un ingenio* (1 act comedy), Havana, 1844; *Un concurso de acreedores* (1 act comedy), Havana, Barcina, 1845; *La hechicera de Paris* (5 acts), Imp. del Faro Industrial, 1843; *La Guajira o Una noche en un ingenio* (1 act comedy), Havana, 1844; *Un concurso de acreedores* (1 act comedy), Havana, Barcina, 1845; *La hechicera de Paris* (5 acts), Havana, Imp. del Faro Industrial, 1845; *Sota y Caballo o el Andaluz y la Habanera* (1 act comedy), Havana, 1846; *Una mina de oro* (1 act comedy), Havana, 1847; *Miscelánea dramática y critica, o sea Colección completa de las obras dramáticas y articulos de costumbres cubanas,* 2nd ed., Havana, Soler, 1848; *Los sustos del huracán* (1 act comedy), Havana, Soler, 1848; *Un velorio en Jesús Maria* (1 act comedy), Havana, Torres, 1848; *Amor y guagua* (1 act comedy), Havana, Soler, 1848; *Manjar blanco y manjarete,* 1848; *Un californiano* (1 act comedy), Havana, Barcina, 1851; *¿La bendición Papá?* o El viejo enamorado (1 act comedy), Havana, Imp. La Habanera, 1856; *Función de toros sin toros* (1 act comedy), Havana, Barcina, 1857; *El cometa del trece de junio o El fin del mundo* (1 act comedy), Havana, Barcina, 1857; *Don Silvestre del Campo,* 1857; *Obras dramáticas, Edición completa,* 2 vols., Havana, Barcina, 1857.

Folk Sketches: in miscellaneous journals and collections, including *Los cubanos pintados por si mismos,* Havana, 1852.

Biography: *Biografia de don Francisco Covarrubias, primer actor de carácter jocoso de los teatros de la Habana,* Havana, 1851.

MILLER, Jeannette

b. 1945, Dominican Republic.
Poet, teacher.

Miller is considered one of the most important poets of modern Dominican literature. Her verse is highly personal, showing an intense awareness of words, their timbre and most particularly their meanings. The feminine voice, the feminine experience, is at the heart of everything she says—and the loneliness and alienations of modern life.

Writings: Poetry: *Fórmulas para combatir el miedo,* S. Domingo, Taller, 1972.

Editor of: "Poemas del Domingo," S. Domingo, in *Revista Liberación,* No. 3.

MIR, Pedro

b. 1913, Dominican Republic.
Poet, essayist, teacher, lawyer.

Mir has spent most of his adult life in Cuba where he has also published most of his work. As a fervent opponent of dictator Trujillo, he could not enjoy living in his own country and his verse expresses the melancholy of exile at times though he came to feel "at home" in Cuba. He won the "Premio Nacional de Literatura" in the historical section, 1975, for his *Las raices dominicana de la doctrina Monroe.*

Writings: Poetry: *Hay un pais en el mundo y seis momentos de esperanza,* Havana, Talleres de "La Campaña Cubana," 1949, 2nd ed., S. Domingo, Ed. Brigadas Dominicana, 1962; *Poemas de amor; Tres leyendas de colores; ensayo de interpretación de las primeras revoluciones del nuevo mondo* ("Prólogo póstumo" by Rafael Altamira), S. Domingo, Ed. Nacional, 1969; *Viaje a la muchadumbre,* 1971; *Contracanto a Walt Whitman, Guatemala.*

History: *El gran incendio,* S. Domingo, Taller, 1974; *Las raices dominicanas de la doctrina Monroe,* S. Domingo, Taller, 1974.

Philosophy-Esthetics: *Apertura a la Estética,* S. Domingo, Edit. Cultural Dominicana, 1974.

MIRABAL, Antonio

b. ca. 1887, Puerto Rico.
Poet.

Mirabal's poetics are late post-romantic, hardly touched by the new currents of modernismo of his maturity. His verse is elegant, almost classical, though of decided musicality.

Writings: Poetry: *De tu rosal y mi sela,* Ponce, , P. R., Imp. El Dia, 1917, (187 p.); *Alas y olas,* Ponce, P. R., Imp. El Dia, 1922, (120 p.).

Biographical/Critical Sources: Salvador Rueda's introduction to *De tu rosal. . .*(1917).

MIRANDA ARCHILLA, Graciany

b. 1910, Morovis, Puerto Rico.
Poet, journalist, editor.

Miranda served as editor of the important literary journal *Alma Latinas* and *El Mundo* and was a frequent contributor to *Gráfico de Puerto Rico, La Linterna, El Imparcial, El Mundo,* and *Puerto Rico Ilustrado.* Rosa-Nieves finds his third volume, *El oro en la espiga* to be his best collection: "Puñado de poemas sembrado de fuerza poética, de emociones inéditas, de instrumentación virtuosa, y de homenajes paisajistas."

Miranda was one of the lesser poets of modernista movement influenced by Rubén Dario.

His poem "Alguien" ends:

Ojos, labios y manos de una sombra
que para ti nació, pero que en balde
te miran y te besan y te tocan,
gritando que las ames. . .
No has de secar la copa del Olvido;
alguien te adora; *¡alguien!*

Writings: Poetry: *Cadena de sueños,* 1926; *Responsos a mis poemas naúfragos,* 1931; *Si de mi tierra,* 1937; and *El oro en la espiga,* San Juan, Imp. Venezuela, 1941; his poem "Alguien" is in the *Antologia de la poesia puertorriqueña,* E. Fernández Méndez, ed., San Juan, 1968; and four poems from *El oro en la espiga* in *Aguinaldo lirico,* C. Rosa-Nieves, ed., Rio Piedras, 1957, "Canto a la lengua castellana," won first prize in the competition of the Ateneo Ibero-Americano de Buenos Aires.

MIRANDA, Luis Antonio

b. June 13, 1896, Ciales, Puerto Rico.
Poet, novelist, journalist.

Miranda moved from the modernista movement to an even more sensual, private style. Eroticism in his work became more pronounced, bringing him back to the late romantic period where he had begun.

Writings: Poetry: *Abril florido,* San Juan, Tip. Real Hermanos, 1919; *El rosario de doña Inés,* San Juan, 1919; *Albas sentimentales,* San Juan, Edit. Fraguada, 1923; *Música prohibida,* Manati, Puerto Rico, Editorial Harry C. del Pozo, 1925; *El árbol lleno de cantos,* 1946.
Novel: *Prosas ingénuas,* San Juan, Imp. Cantero Fernández, 1922 (206 pp.).

MIRO ARGENTER, José

b. 1857, Cuba; d. 1925.
Playwright, novelist, journalist.

Miro Argenter, active in politics and journalism, produced one novel on the theme of the war of independence (*El Pacifico*), and one play of modest merit.

Writings: Play: *El pacifico,* Havana, 1914.
Novel: *Salvador Roca,* Havana, 1910.

MITJANS Y ALVAREZ, Aurelio

b. 1863, Cuba; d. 1889.
Literary historian, critic, poet.

Most of Mitjan's critical studies appeared in the journals *Estudios Literarios, La Habaña Elegante,* and *Revista Cubana.*

His work was analytical and objective, much concerned with correctness of language, metrics and form. His poetry, in the opinion of Max Henriquez Ureña, was of slight importance.

Writings: Literary Criticism-Biography: "De la Avellaneda y sus obras," (published in *Estudios Literarias,* Havana, 1887).

Literary History: *Carácteres dominantes en la literatura de los últimos cinquenta años,* Havana, 1887; *Estudios sobre el movimento cientifico y literario de Cuba,* Havana, 1890, and re. ed., entitled *Historia de la literatura cubana,* Havana, 1918; "Del teatro bufo y de la necesidad de reemplazarlo fomentando la buena comedia," essay published in *Estudios Literarias* (Havana, 1887) with "De la Avellaneda . . . " and *Carácteres dominantes . . .*

Biographical/Critical Sources: Ramón Meza, "La obra póstuma de Mitjans," in *Revista Cubana* (April-July 1881).

MIYARES, Enriques Hernández

b. 1859, Cuba; d. 1914.
Poet, journalist, literary critic.

A poet of the transition, moving from romanticism to the moderns, Miyares often published in *La Habana Elegante,* a "modernista" journal. His sonnets were especially appreciated.

Writings: Poetry: *Obras completas, (I. Poesias; II. Prosas),* Havana, Academia Nacional de Artes y Letras, 1915-1916.

MOJICA, Francisco

b. ca. 1558, Cuba.
Playwright.

Though Mojica's one known play is no longer extant, he and the drama deserve mention as the first work written by a native Cuban and performed in the island.

Writings: Play: not extant, title unknown; performed Corpus Christi Day, 1588, in Cuba.

Biographical/Critical Sources: Max Henriquez Ureña, *Panorama histórico de la literatura cubana,* New York, Las Américas, 1963, p. 28; José Juan Arrom, *Historia de la literatura dramática cubana,* New Haven, Yale University Press, 1944, pp. 6-9.

MOLINA, Francisco

b. b. 1913, Vega Baja, Puerto Rico.
Poet, protestant minister.

Francisco Molina, a Lutheran minister, has published one collection of his verse (1953) in which his religious feelings and training are apparent but not overly evident. Touched by "postmodernismo" his work is very personal, sometimes even humorous.

Writings: Poetry: *Ciudad allende al mar,* (another source shows title to be *Ciudad allende el alba*), Santurce, 1953, (112 p.); much work in ms., or uncollected from publication in occasional journals; five of his poems are in *Aguinaldo lirico,* C. Rosa-Nieves, ed., Rio Piedras, 1957.

MOLL BOSCANA, Aristides

b. b. 1885, Adjuntas, Puerto Rico;
d. 1964, Berkeley, California (USA).
Poet, medical doctor.

Moll studied widely in Spain, the United States and in France. He practiced medicine in Ponce and was an official in Aduana and Mayagüez and worked in Washington, D. C.

His verse was heavily influenced by Rubén Dario both in form and subject matter and is a precursor or early example of "modernismo," his *Mi misa rosa* being the earliest of the new style in Puerto Rico, that title being taken from the prologue of

Darios' *Prosas Profanas* (1896) which begins "yo he dicho en la *misa rosa* de mi juventud, mis antifonas. . ."

He was an editor for a period of the journal of the American Medical Association and associate editor of the *Boletin de la Oficina Sanitaria Panamericana* while serving as the secretary of the Panamerican Medical Association.

Writings: Poetry: *Mi misa rosa,* San Juan, Tip. El Boletin, 1905; and his work in many reviews and in unpublished mss.; seven of his poems appear in Luis Hernández Aquino, *El modernismo en Puerto Rico,* San Juan, 1967.

Medical Scholarship: *Esculapio en Latinoamerica.*

Biographical/Critical Sources: Pedro Henriquez Ureña, *La corrientes literarias en la América Hispaña,* 1945.

MOMO

(pseudonym for **José Ramón MERCADO**)

MONGE, José Maria

b. 1840, Mayagüez, Cuba.
Playwright, poet, journalist.

One of Cuba's earliest dramatists, Monge is believed to have published but one play.

Writings: Play: *Los apuros del bachillerato* (verse dialogue), Mayagüez, Tip. Comercial, 1886.

MONICA, Manuel

(a.k.a. **Meso MONICA,** as **Maestro MONICA,** and also thought by some authorities to have the Christian name of Antonio, rather than Manuel)

b. ca. 1731, Santiago, Dominican Republic; d. after 1796.
Folk-singer, poet.

Of African race, Manuel Mónica, son of freedmen, was one of the most popular cantadores of the 18th century. He entered verse singing contests, popular at that time, and was so adept he could "speak" in verse. His songs became widely known outside of Dominica and he has been confused in tradition with the Afro-Mexican singer, José Vascóncelos, termed "el Negrito poeta," and even with Lorenzo Música from Chile and Padre López, also from Dominica. However, authorities argue his work is generally recognizable because of its obvious references to northern Dominican towns, especially Santiago de los Caballeros, and to events of his own period. One of his ten-line verses (décima) begins in one version:

Aristoteles decia
(filósofo muy profundo)
que en la redondez del mundo
no existe cosa vacia.
Miente su filosofia
según lo que a mi me pasa,
y él no sentara tal basa
y al punto se convenciera
si hoy al medio dia viera
las cazuelas de mi casa

A poem "Versos dirigidos por un Cabo de Cuba al Maestro Mónica" by a rival gives some details in a somewhat sarcastic vein of Mónica's appearance and career:

Dime, negro como pez
¿quien te ha enseñado a versar,
que en versos sabres llorar
la falta del almirez?

The last years of Mónica are uncertain, but research appears to show he married in 1751 and had a son who married well in his time.

Writings: Folk-songs: in *Revista Cientifica Literaria y de Conocimientos Utiles,* 1884; poetry in E. Rodriguez Demorizi's *Poesia popular dominicana,* 1938, 2nd ed., S. Domingo, UCMM, 1973, 117-175.

Biographical/Critical Sources: Rodriguez' *Poesia popular dominicana,* above referenced, devotes 58 pages to Mónica's career and the work of other popular poets of the period in

Dominica, Mexico and elsewhere in Latin America, and provides many extracts from their poems; Max Henriquez Ureña's *Panorama histórico de la literatura dominicana,* Vol. I, 2nd ed., S. Domingo, Postigo, 1965, pp. 125-127; Nicolás Léon, *El Negrita Poeta Mexicana,* Mexico, 1912; Rubén M. Campos' *El folk-lore literario mexicano,* Mexico, 1929; and article by Nicolás Ureña de Mendoza and Manuel Maria Guatier in *El Oasis,* No. 2, S. Domingo, (December 1854).

MONTE, Laureano del

b. ca. 1872, Cuba.
Playwright.

His *Artilleros y colegialas* (1902) was one of the first post-independence plays to appear in Cuba.

Writings: Play: *Artilleros y colegialas,* music by Rafael Paláu (1 act musical, prose and verse), Havana, Imp. Teniente Rey 38-A, 1902, performed Teatro Alhambro, Madrid, Nov. 21, 1902; *Con Don y sin Don, ayer y hoy* (1 act farce, prose and music by M. F.), Havana, Imp. El Aerolita, 1894, performed at Teatro Alhambra, Feb. 23, 1894; *Tortilla a la francesa* (1 act prose sketch), Havana, 1897, in ms.

MONTE Y ROCIO, Ricardo del

b. 1828, Cuba; d. 1909.
Poet, critic, journalist, essayist.

Monte often contributed to *El Pais, El Nuevo Pais, Cuba,* and the earlier journal *El Triunfo.* His poetry, 28 sonnets and 13 other poems including translations from Horace, came out ten years after del Monte's death. Only in 1926 were many of his critical and journalistic pieces published by the Academia Nacional de Artes y Letras (some 41 separate pieces).

Perhaps his most important critical work was "El efectismo lirico," published in *Revista de Cuba,* which dealt with the excesses of much of nineteenth century verse and tried to point the way to a cleaner, more genuine style and honest subject matter. The work of Saturnino Martinez served as a subject for much of Monte's surgical analysis.

Writings: Poetry: *Poesias,* 1919.
Prose: in *Obras,* 1 vol., 1926.

MONTENEGRO, Carlos

b. 1900, Galicia, Spain.
Playwright, novelist, storywriter, journalist.

Born in Spain of Cuban parents, Carlos Montenegro passed wandering early years in Argentina, Mexico and the United States, working as a mines and textile mill employee. He also spent five years at sea in the merchant marine. Convicted for the death of a man he had quarreled with, Montenegro began to write stories during the long years in prison. Winning a competition sponsored by *Carteles,* he gained favorable attention and some writers joined together to get his sentence halted. Eventually freed, he turned out several plays and four works of fiction, including his first collection of stories (1929) and his one novel, based on the brutal realities of prison life. All of his work was full of protest against class oppression and the grinding poverty of the great number of mankind. Montenegro became a journalist and remained in Cuba the rest of his career.

Writings: Plays: *Tururi ñam ñam,* set to music by the author; *Los perros de Radziwill,* 1939; *En la prisión: asesinato del lider,* 1940.

Novel: *Hombres sin mujer,* 1938, and Mexico, Mundo Nuevo, 1959.

Stories: *El renuevo y otros cuentos,* Havana, 1929; *Dos barcos,* Havana, 1934; *Los héroes* (contains five stories: "Cuentos de la manigua," one of them recalls the period of national liberation), Havana, 1941.

MONTES, Fabian

(pseudonym for **Manuel DE ELZABURU**)

MONTES HUIDOBRO, Matias

b. 1931, Cuba.
Playwright, critic, storywriter, poet.

Most of Montes' plays are universal in theme and set in an undefined time period except for *Las caretas* which celebrates the carnival season in Santiago de Cuba. His work was performed in Cuba in the 1950's, but he has exiled himself since the advent of Castro and now teaches at the University of Hawaii with his work being fiction and poetry. The title story of his short story collection *La anunciación* (1967) and three others are critical of the Castro regime.

Writings: Plays: *Las cuatro brujas* (1 act), 1949; *Sobre las mismas rocas,* 1951; *Sucederá mañana; La puerta perdida; El verano está cerca; Las caretas; Gas en los poros,* in *Teatro* cubano en un acto, Rine Leal, ed., Havana, Revolución, 1963.

Literary History: "Teatro colonial cubana: Desconcierto-trágico-burlesco," in *La Enciclopedia,* Santurce, P. R., Enciclopedia y Clasicos Cubanos, pp. 377-393.

Stories: *La anunciación y otros cuentos cubanos,* Madrid, Gráfica Clemares, 1967.

Poetry: *La vaca de los ojos largos,* Honolulu, Cuadernos Internacionales de poesia, 1967, (28 p.).

MONTES LOPEZ, José

b. 1901, Cuba.
Playwright.

Montes' two plays, *Chano* and *La sequia* are realistic-naturalistic presentations of the lives of share-croppers and day-laborers on the vast estates of Cuba. The plays are not great works of art but are serious and valid pictures of the conditions of the 1930's. Montes won one of the then newly established awards for theater pieces offered by the Ministry of Education.

Writings: Plays: *Chano,* 1937; *La sequia,* 1938.

MONTORO AGUERO, José A.

b. 1930, Cuba.
Playwright.

Montoro's *Cumbre y abismo* returns to the anti-romantic tradition and is less poetic than most of the works of the period.

Writings: Plays: *Cumbre y abismo,* 1950.

MORALES, Gabino Alfredo

b. 1881, Puerto Rico; d. ca. 1963.
Poet.

Morales lived in the Dominican Republic for a long period and wrote his poem "Ante la ocupación militar" to protest the invasion and occupation by U. S. marines (1916-1924).

Writings: Poetry: *Miniaturas,* 1905; *De oportunidad,* 1907; *Monolitos,* 1943.

Politics: *Bosquejo politico-social,* 1907.

MORALES, Jorge Luis

b. 1930, Ciales, Puerto Rico.
Poet, essayist, critic, teacher.

Morales earned his B. A. and M. A. at the University of Puerto Rico and his Ph. D. in philosophy and letters at the University of Madrid. His poetry is "postmodernist" in style and subject matter, often metaphysical, sometimes surrealistic.

Writings: Poetry: *Metal y piedra,* 1949, 1952; *Inspiración del viajé,* 1953; *Mirado en el olvido,* 1953; *Decir del propio ser,* New York, 1954; *La ventana y yo,* 1960; *Jornada precisa,* 1963;

Discurso a los pájaros, 1965 (the title poem of this collection, plus six others are in E. Fernández Méndez *Antologia de la poesia puertorriqueña,* San Juan, 1968; and other poems are in *Aguinaldo lirico,* C. Rosa-Nieves, ed., 1st ed., Rio Piedras, 1957, 2nd ed., 1971; also see *Antologia poética,* San Juan, Edit. Universitaria, 1968.

Biographical/Critical Sources: José Luis Martin, *Arco y fleca,* San Juan, 1961.

MORALES ALVAREZ, Ramón

b. 1852, Santiago de la Vegas, Cuba; d. 1910.
Playwright.

Writer of at least six plays, Morales Alvárez is an all but forgotten figure today.

Writings: Plays: *El paso de la Malanga* (1 act comedy, music by Enrique Guerrero), Havana, Imp. La Nueva Principal, 1882, performed Teatro Torrecillas de la Havana; and *El proceso del oso,* performed January 28, 1882, in Teatro Torrecillas, 1882; *La plancha H.* (1 act), Havana, 1882; *Globos dirigibles,* performed Teatro Alhambra, September 18, 1902, Havana, 1902: all by La Nueva Principal. In ms: *Petra o subir por derecho proprio* (1 act comedy, prose and verse), Havana, written March 1897; *Don Benito Pimentón* (1 act sketch), Havana.

MOREJON, Nancy

b. 1944, Havana, Cuba.
Poet.

After local schooling with major studies in French literature, Morejón began publishing her verse in such journals as *Unión, La Gaceta de Cuba, El caiman barbudo* and *Casa de las Américas.* She is a member of the Council of Collaboration of the journal *Gaceta de Cuba.*

Her work is lyrical, soft, occasionally sentimental.

Writings: Poetry: *Richard trajo su planta y otros argumentos* (Honorable Mention in Unión's poetry competition, later published in *Poésie cubanne* (a bi-lingual Spanish-French anthology); *Mutismos y amor; Amor, ciudad atribuida,* Havana, El Puente, 1964; *Richard trajo su flauta y otros argumentos,* Havana, Instituto del Libro, 1967; poem "Los heraldos negros," in *Présence Africaine,* New Series, No. 57 (1966), pp. 536-539.

MOREL, Emilio A.

b. 1887, Dominican Republic; d. 1953 (or 1958).
Poet, journalist, playwright.

Morel was director of the journal *El Diario* of Santiago de los Caballeros in which he ran a series of editorials entitled "¿A qué viene ese hombre?" which demonstrated his passionate nature and combative spirit. His verse, too, is usually the product of an intensely felt moment rather than of a totally poetically controlled mood and structured expression.

Writings: Poetry: *Lucernulas,* Ponce, P. R., 1911; *Puñado de simientes,* 1915; *Romance heroico,* 1916; *A las abiertas,* Santiago de los Caballeros, 1925; *Pequeños poemas,* 1937.

Plays: *La copla triste; El demador; El pésame; Entre nubes; El trino errante,* 1917.

Speeches: *En vos alta,* 1936.

Politics: *Desde mi sector,* 1936; *Elementos de aportación para una história de la politica dominicana,* 1939; *Armas dominicanas,* 1939.

MORENO JIMENES, Domingo

b. 1894, Santiago de los Caballeros, Dominican Republic.
Poet.

Moreno was one of the principal creators of the movement "Postumismo" and was considered the "Sumo Pontéfice" of the group, being "dethroned" only briefly by Rafael Zorrilla (1892-1937).

Moreno Jiménes' work initiated a new period in Dominican poetry. As the Spanish tradition diminished, new writers could experiment as did Morena with free verse, new subjects, and no rhymes. For many years he travelled widely throughout the republic, selling his own books. Moreno recently won the "Premio Nacional de Poesia," demonstrating that his reputation is at its peak.

A typical poem of the "Postumismo" style is this, "Hora azul," given in its entirety:

Ondas.
Vuelos.
Romanzas lejanas.
Media luz.
Bisbiseos de sombras en el puerto.
Gasas que cubren el horizonte reverberante.
Crujir de jarcias recias
Ay Dios! ¡Qué será de las lilas
con medio cuerpo bajo el cieno, y medio cuerpo sobre la vida!

Writings: Poetry: in many collections including Flérida de Nolasco's *Domingo Moreno Jiménes,* Ciudad Trujillo, Lib. Dom., 1949; and in José Alcántara Almánzar's *Antologia de la literatura dominicana,* S. Domingo, E.C.D., 1972; *Obra poética,* S. Domingo, Taller, 1975.

Biographical/Critical Sources: See above works cited for his poetry and Manuel Mora Serrano's "Defense de Moreno Jiménes," in *Suplemento Cultural de El Nacional* (July 16, 1972); and pp. 65-67 in M. Ruedo's *Antologia panorámica . . . ,"* Madrid, 1972, for critical comments.

MORET PEREZ, Francisco

b. 1863, Bolondron, Cuba.
Playwright, pharmacist.

Moret Pérez wrote and produced at least one known play.

Writings: Play: *Perdón que redime* (2 acts), Matanzas, Quirós y Estrada, 1905, 2nd ed., Unión de Reyes, Imp. La Central, 1914, premiered December 18, 1904 in Matanzas.

MORILLO, Gabriel Angel

b. 1884, Dominican Republic; d. 1961.
Poet.

Morillo's work was generally mildly touched by "modernismo," but it was less experimental than other verse by his contemporaries in both subject and style.

Writings: Poetry: *Mirthos,* 1910; *Dulces enigmas, poemas en prose,* La Vega, 19??; *Dios y Libertad,* Santiago, D. R., 1927.
Talks: *Conferencias,* Moca, 1926.

MORUA DELGADO, Martin

b. April 28, 1857, Matanzas, Cuba; d. 1910.
Storywriter, biographer, critic, autobiographer, journalist.

Son of slaves freed before his birth, Morúa founded in Matanzas the important journal *El Pueblo* in 1879. Thrown into prison in 1880 for a few days because of his editorial policies, Morúa went into exile in the United States. A member of the revolutionary group in New York City, Morúa later travelled to Panama, Mexico and Jamaica to seek out support for Cuban independence.

By 1890 he was back in Cuba, founding the paper *El Tribuno* and soon to write the novels *Sofia* (1891) and later *La familia Unzúazu* (1901), both in the new naturalistic mode of Zola. His criticism was important during the years 1890-1896, especially for his work embodied in *Las novelas del Señor Villaverde* (1892), Villaverde at that time being the most respected Cuban novelist, and for his studies of Turgenieff, Dostoievski, Tolstoy and Gogol in his two-part "Rusia contemporánea."

Still the active journalist, Morúa also founded *La Nueva Era* in 1892 and pushed for the acceptance of Ibsen in many critical articles.

In 1898 he joined the revolutionists and in 1900 helped found the Cuban Republican Party, becoming a senator. In 1909 Morúa was named Minister of Agriculture by President José Miguel Gómez.

Morúa projected a series of naturalistic novels as the "Cosas de mi tierra" series along the lines of Balzac's "La Comédie Humaine" and Zola's "Los Rougon Macquart" novels, but completed only two in his over-busy journalistic life.

Writings: Novels: *Cosas de mi tierra: Sofia,* Havana, Alvárez, 1891; *La familia Unzúazu, novela cubana,* Havana, Imp. La Prosperidad, 1901.

Literary Criticism: *Impresiones literarias: Las novelas del Señor Villaverde,* 1892.

Journalism: *Colección de articulos,* Key West, Florida, 1881.

Complete Works: *Obras completas* (Edición de la Comisión del Centenario de Martín Morúa Delgado), Havana, Impresores Nosotros, 1957. *Obras* has six parts in five volumes: I: *Sofia, novela cubana;* II: *La familia Unzúazu;* III: *Integración cubana y otros ensayos;* IV: *Traducciones de Martin Morúa Delgado* [of] John R. Beard's biography of Toussaint L'Ouverture, and Beard's translation of *The Life of Toussaint L'Ouverture* (Ouverture's autobiography); V: *Impresiones literarias y otras páginas.*

Translation: *Recordación* (of H. Conroy's *Called Back*).

Prose Satire: *Dos apuntes,* New York, 1882 (biographies of lobsters who "seemed" to be men).

Biographical/Critical Sources: Manuel Isias, Mesa Rodriguez, *Martin Morúa Delgado,* Havana, Imp. "El Siglo XX," 1956; Rufino Pérez Landa, *Vida Publica de Martin Morúa Delgado* (written with Maria Rosell Pérez), Havana, 1957; Leopoldo Horrego Estuch, *Martin Morúa Delgado, vida y mensaje,* Havana, 1957.

MOYA, Casimiro N. de

b. December 19, 1849, Santo Domingo, Dominican Republic; d. May 27, 1915. Novelist, poet, cartographer, historian.

Moya was active in public affairs and served as Vice President of the Republic. In several administrations Moya was a cabinet minister. His career as a cartographer was a distinguished one and he also was a skilled amateur historian.

Writings: Novels: fragments of "Páginas de una novela nacional histórica inconcluida," in *La Cuna de América,* S. Domingo, No. 101 (December 13, 1908); "Dramas dominicanos," in *El Progreso;* in ms., the novel "Episodas dominicanos," in part represented by the sections published in *El Progreso.*

History: "Historia de Santo Domingo," 7 ms. vols., as *Archivo General de la Nación;* 1st vol. only published, and entitled *Bosquejo histórico del descubrimiento y conquista de la Isla de Santo Domingo;* sketch: "Historia del Comegente," in E. Rodriguez Demorizi's *Tradiciones y cuentos dominicanos,* S. Domingo, Postigo, 1969, pp. 175-195.

Biographical/Critical Sources: Alfáu Durán's "Centenario del historiador y geógrafo D. Casimiro N. De Moya," in *Clio,* S. Domingo, No. 86 (1950), p. 18.

MUNOZ, Manuel

b. ca. 1932, Puerto Rico. Novelist.

Muñoz' one novel *Guarionex* is a sympathetic study of the 1511 effort of the Indian chief, Guarionex, to push the Spaniards out of Puerto Rico.

Writings: Novel: *Guarionex, la historia de un indio rebelde, simbolo heróico de un pueblo y de una raza,* San Juan, 1962; *Gloria en llamas,* San Juan, 1964; *Los mil otoños de una primavera,* Hato Rey, n.d.

MUNOZ BUSTAMENTE, Mario

b. 1881, Cuba; d. 1921.
Poet, journalist, novelist.

Primarily a journalist and writer of humorous sketches, Muñoz published one short work of fiction and a collection of his breezy, sarcastic verse.

Writings: Poetry: *Rimas de gozo,* Havana, 1915. Novelette: *El pantano,* Havana, 1905. Journalistic Articles: *Crónicas humanas,* Havana, 1905; *Ideas y colores,* Havana, 1907.

MUNOZ IGARTUA, Angel

b. 1905, Quebradillas, Puerto Rico.
Poet, teacher, lawyer.

Angel Muñoz studied law at the University of Puerto Rico and has published three volumes of verse. The long poem, "Savia intima," is under the influence of Rubén Dario and Herrera Reissig. In the 1960's Muñoz Igartua was mayor (alcalde) of Manati.

Writings: Poetry: *Savia intima,* Arecibo, Edit. del Pozo, 1927; *Escaparate polifónico,* 1933; *Versos de ayer y de hoy,* 1946; and *Por el Sendero,* Monati, 1954; *Vibraciones: poemas,* San Juan, 1960. "Invocación a Dios" is in the *Antologia de la poesia puertorriqueña,* E. Fernández Méndez, ed., San Juan, 1968.

MUNOZ MARIN, Luis

b. 1898, Puerto Rico.
Poet, novelist, storywriter, statesman.

Son of the great journalist and statesman Luis Muñoz Rivera, Muñoz has resided in the United States for many years and took degrees at Georgetown University, Washington, D. C., and Columbia University in New York City, the latter granting him a graduate degree in journalism.

Influenced by Vachel Lindsey and other U. S. poets of the 1920's, Muñoz brought a new voice to the verse of Puerto Rico. He helped found *La Revista de Indios,* a bilingual literary journal in New York and published in U. S. and Puerto Rican magazines before he became a leader of the Popular Democratic Party and the President of the Puerto Rican Senate. Consequently his political career rapidly diminished his time for poetry, particularly his long service (1948-1964), as elected Governor of Puerto Rico (1948-1964).

Writings: Novelette: *Madre haraposa* (written with Antonio Coll y Vidal and Evaristo Ribera Chevremont), San Juan, Tip. Barros, 1918. Poetry: *Barrones,* San Juan, Impr. La Democracia, 1917; and verse in various journals and collections, including the *Antologia de la poesia puertorriqueña,* San Juan, 1968, which offers five of his works: "Cantos de la humanidad forcejeanco," "Proletarios," "Primavera," "La canción de los cinco perros flacos," and "Panfleto."

Biographical/Critical Sources: César Andrew Iglesias, *Luis Muñoz Marin, un hombre acordelado por la historia,* Rio Piedras, Ediciones Puerto Rico, 1972.

MUNOZ RIVERA, Luis

b. July 17, 1859, Barranquitas, Puerto Rico; d. November 15, 1916.
Poet, playwright, journalist, statesman.

Largely self-educated, Muñoz was called the "Bible of our nation" by poet-critic Luis Lloréns Torres. F. Manrique Cabrera wrote of him: " . . . la maestria verdadera de Muñoz literato habria de completarse referencia a su rotundo manejo de las prosa. . ." and his great pieces of journalism further made him a most important figure.

Active in island politics, and a leader in the nationalist movement both before and after the arrival of U. S. authorities, Muñoz' printing press was destroyed in 1900 by a republican anti-American group protesting Muñoz' apparent call for reconciliation and acceptance of the U. S. presence. Muñoz was the editor of *El Pueblo* and founded *La Democracia* in Ponce, *El Territorio* in San Juan, and *The Puerto Rico Herald* in New York.

His early collection of verse, *Tropicales* (1902) was a late neo-classical reflection of Parnassian verse, long moribund in France and elsewhere.

Writings: Poetry: *Tropicales,* 1st ed., New York, Imp. H. M Coll, 1902, 2nd ed., Madrid, Ed. Puerto Rico, 1925; *Poesias,* San Juan, Inst. de Cultura Puertorriqueña, 1961; *Poemas y pensamientos,* San Juan, 1963; three of his most important poems: "Retamas," "La flor de la dicha," and "Vendimiaria," are in the *Antologia de la poesia puertorriqueña,* E. F. Méndez, ed., San Juan, 1968. "Retamas" was first published in *El Vapor* in 1891.

Collected Works: *Obras completas,* San Juan, Inst. de Cultura Puertorriqueña, 1968, in 8 vols., but see also the earlier *Obras completas,* Madrid, Ed. Puerto Rico, 1925.

Play: *Las dos musas,* Puerto Rico, Imp. de José González Font, 1886.

Biographical/Critical Sources: Concha Meléndez, *De frente al sol; apuntes sobre la poesia de Luis Muñoz Rivera,* San Juan, 1960; also see Concha Meléndez in her *Poetas hispanoamericanos diversos,* San Juan, 1971; Félix Matos Bernier's *La isla arte,* San Juan, 1907; Manuel Fernández Juncos, *Antologia puertorriqueña,* 1st ed., New York, 1907, pp. 307-311; Sebastián Dalmau Canet, *Luis Muñoz Rivera,* 1917; Salvador Arana Soto, "La disidencia independentista," San Juan, 1970; essay on Muñoz in Arturo Morales Carrión's *Ojeada al proceso histórico y otros ensayos,* San Juan, 1971; José Agustin Balseiro's essay, "Luis Muñoz Rivera, Civil Poet of Puerto Rico," in *The Americas Look at Each Other,* by Balseiro, translation by Muna Lee, Coral Gables, Fla., Univ. of Miami Press, 1969; Ramón Lebron Rodriguez, *La Vida del Procer,* San Juan, Soltero, 1954; Arturo Morales Carrión, *The Loneliness of Luis Muñoz Rivera,* Puerto Rico Booklets Series, No. 1, Washington, D. C., Office of the Commonwealth Puerto Rico, 1965; Rafael Torres Mazzoranna, *Luis Muñoz Rivera y el pacto con Sagasta,* San Juan, Inst. de Cultura Puertorriqueña, 1969 (30 pp.).

MUNOZ DEL MONTE, Francisco

b. 1800, Santiago de los Caballeros, Dominican Republic; d. 1865, Madrid. Poet, journalist.

Muñoz was taken to Cuba by his family after the Haitian invasion and disturbances of war between Spanish and French revolutionary forces. His father, Andrés Muñoz Caballeros, was a writer of verses. Returning to Santo Domingo with his parents after Spanish rule was re-established, Muñoz wrote the poem "A la muerte de mi amigo y condiscipulo Don José Maria Heredia" which recalled Heredia's stay in 1810 in Santo Domingo when Muñoz himself was only ten years old. Muñoz returned to Cuba in the 1820's and was quick to take a liberal position in the politics of that colony.

A friend of Manuel Lorenzo, Governor of Santiago de Cuba, a proponent of liberal constitutional reforms, Muñoz composed the "Himno a la Milicia Nacional de Cuba" and when Lorenzo proclaimed Cuba independent, Muñoz was elected a member of the Constitutional Assembly which met in Santiago, October 29, 1836, to work out a new government. When this effort failed, Lorenzo was forced into exile, and Muñoz went to Spain where he established the journal *La Epoca* with José Antonio Saco and there began to argue for political liberty for the Cubans. For his troubles he was asked to spend some time in prison and Saco was forced to flee to Portugal.

In Cuba, Muñoz had founded *La Minerva* which lasted from 1820 to 1823 and was one of the earliest literary magazines of the island. Later, in Spain, his *Revista Español de Ambos Mundos* and *La América* were both devoted to literary and political subjects.

Muñoz finished his career by becoming a lawyer and he practiced this profession from 1840 to 1848 in Cuba, but then, still relatively young, returned to Spain, eventually perishing in a cholera outbreak the spring of 1865.

Writings: Poetry: in various reviews and anthologies; *Poesias,* Madrid, 1880, compiled and edited by the author's son; this volume also included two brief prose works: "La literatura contemporánea," and "La elocuencia en el foro."

Critical Essays: "El orgullo literario," in *La América;* " Dios es lo bello absoluto," Havana, Biblioteca del Liceo, 1858; and "La literatura contemporánea," in *Poesias,"* see above.

Cultural History: *La mulata,* Havana, 1845; reprinted in *La evolución de la cultura cubana,* edited by José Manuel Carbonel, Havana, 1928; *El verano en la Habana* and *La habanera,* details unknown.

NAPOLES FAJARDO, Juan Cristobal

(a.k.a. **"El Cucalambé"**)

b. 1829, Victorias de las Tunas, Cuba; d. 1862.
Poet, playwright.

Born in the country, Nápoles wrote poetry usually concerned with Cuba's natural beauties and culture. His verse was spontaneous and his work once widely known throughout the island. His most nativist colloquial works (criollist) were "Hatuey y Guarina," "Al cacique de Maniabón," "El bohique de Yariguá," "Narey y Coalina," "Los indios de Cueiba," and "Caonaba," all employing Indian themes or dealing with the simple Cuban peasants. His "Hatuey y Guarina" begins:

Con un cocuyo en la mano
y un grau tabaco en la boca,
un indio desde una roca
miraba el cielo cubano.

Though Nápoles reflected, sometimes too closely, the work of Poveda y Armenteros, his verse is genuinely more popular (in the good sense) according to Max Henriquez Ureña.

He took part in the 1848 and 1852 nationalist (separatist) movements, but later accepted a colonial post. Though apparently happily married with loving children, Nápoles one day disappeared never to be seen again, possibly a suicide by a plunge into the nearby sea.

Writings: Poetry: *Rumores del Hormigo,* Havana, 1857, 2nd ed., 1859, 3rd ed., Holguin, Cuba, 1867, 4th ed., Paris, 1878, and reissue: Havana, Imp. Nacional, 1960; six poems are in *Tipos costumbras de la Isla de Cuba,* Havana, 1881.

Plays: *Consecuencias de una falta* (4 act comedy, verse), Santiago, Martínez, 1859, performed Teatro de la Reina, Santiago, December 18, 1858.

NAVARRETE Y ROMAY, Carlos

b. ca. 1830, Cuba.
Poet, critic.

A member of the literary circle in Havana which included Rafael Maria Mendive and Nicolás Azcárate, Navarrete tried his hand at many forms of literature without great success. His best work was in criticism and for some years he was a contributor to the *Revista de Cuba.*

Writings: Poetry: *Romances cubanos,* 1856; *Poesias,* Paris, 1866.

Novelette: *Margarita,* in *La Habana* journal, 1859-60.

Play: *Antes que te cases, mira lo que haces,* in *Noches literarias,* ed., by Nicolás Azcarate.

NAVARRO CORREA, Noel

b. 1931, Matanzas, Cuba.
Novelist, journalist.

Navarro studied at the Escuela Normal in Holguin and then at the Segundo Enseñanza of Santa Clara. He early joined the literary circle in Camagüey centered around Rolando Escardó. An active participant in political activities aimed at Batista, he published in such reviews as *Revolución, Lunes de Revolución, Diario Libre, Carteles, Casa de las Américas, Unión, Hoy-Domingo, Pueblo y Cultura, Cuba,* and he served as director of *Culturales* in 1967.

His fiction was recognized by several prizes offered by publishing houses: the Concursos de Ediciones R (1961) and Ediciones Granma (1967).

Writings: Novels: *Los dias de nuestra angustia,* Havana, Ediciones R, 1962 (first prize in Ediciones R, competition of 1961); *El plano inclinado,* Havana, Instituto del Libro, 1968; *Los cammos de la noche,* Havana, Granma, 1967.

Biographical/Critical Sources: Reviews of *Los dias de nuestra angustia,* in *Casa des las Américas* (Havana), IV, 26 (Oct-Nov 1964), pp. 164-165 and in *Pueblo y Cultura* (Havana, 1963), pp. 15-16, article by Reynaldo González, and in *Unión* (Havana), II, 5-6 (Jan-Apr 1963), pp. 119-123), article by Luis Suadiaz.

NAVARRO LUNA, Manuel

b. 1894, Province of Matanzas, Cuba.
Poet.

A member of the Matanzas poets group, Navarro published a great deal of verse and prose. His poetry was intimate, lyrical, simple, eschewing the excesses of late romanticism. As a "vanguardista" his work also at times reflected social problems or attacked abuses in his society.

His "¡Adelante!" concludes:

Aunque nada en las sombras de despierte
Sobre la llama inerte,
Siempre se escuchará su clamor delirante
sobre los proprios hierros de la muerte:
¡Adelante. . . .! ¡Adelante. . . .!

Writings: Poetry: *Ritmos dolientes,* 1919; *Corazón adentro,* 1920; *Refugio,* 1927; *Surco,* 1928, all in Manzanillo; *Pulso y onda,* 1932, 2nd ed., Havana, La Tertulia, 1962; *Doña Martina, elegia,* 2nd ed., Havana, Patronato del Libro Popular, 1961; *Odas mambises, Havana, Imprenta Nacional de Cuba, 1961; Obra poética,* Havana, Unión, 1962 (collected poems); *Poemas,* Havana, Unión, 1963; *La tierra herida,* 1936; *Los poemas mambises,* 1944, Havana, Ucar Garcia, 1959, 2nd ed., 1961; *La tierra herida* was republished in Havana, Empresa Consolidada de Artes Gráficas, Ministerio de Industrias, 1962, (50 p.).

Prose Works: *Silvetas aldeanas,* 1924; *Cartas de la ciénaga,* 1930; *Los pasos del hombre,* 1948; *Las ideas de Manuel Jibacoa,* 1949.

Biographical/Critical Sources: Max Henriquez Ureña, *Panorama histórico de la literatura cubana,* New York, 1963, pp. 307-309; and see critical biographical essays by Juan Marinello and José Portogallo in the 1962 reissue of *La tierra herida* (op. cit.) and forewords by Heberto Padilla and Juan Marinello to *Obra poética,* 1962 (op. cit.).

NEGRON MUNOZ, Mercedes

(pseudonym: **Clara LAIR**)
b. 1895, Cuba; d. 1973.
Poet.

Negrón's poetry was deeply melancholic, even bitter, and strongly touched by "postmodernismo." These lines from "Fantasia del olvido" show her limpid strain of sadness:

¡Ya no viene. . .! solloza la sombra que te aguarde,
vagabunda en la tarde, donde por fin te pierdes. . .
¡y lloran los almendros sobre la tierra parda,
dos grandes hojas verdes!

Writings: Poetry: *Arras de cristal,* Havana, Bibliografia de Autores Puertorriqueños, 1937; *Tropico amargo,* Havana, 1950; *Poesias,* San Juan, Instituto de Cultura Puertorriqueña, 1961. Collection of works: *Trópico amargo, Arras de cristal,* and *Más allá del poniente,*

San Juan, Biblioteca de Autores Puertorriqueños, 1950.

Biographical/Critical Sources: See "Clara Lair y Julia de Burgos: Reminiscencias de Evaristo Ribera Chevremont y Jorge Font Saldaña," by Gladys Neggers, in *Revista Interamericana,* Vol. IV, No. 2 (Summer 1974), pp. 258-263.

NEGRON FLORES, Ramón

b. 1867, Trujillo Alto, Puerto Rico; d. 1945.
Storywriter, poet, essayist, biographer.

A contributor to many literary journals with works in a variety of genres, Negrón served as mayor of Rio Piedras and published a political biography and one collection of his verse.

Writings: Poetry: *Siempre vivas,* 1940.
Biography: *Don José Pablo Morales,* 1938.

NEGRON SANJURO, José A.

b. 1864, Puerto Rico; d. 1927.
Poet.

Negrón Sanjuro was a Parnassian, but more, according to Eugenio Astol, he was "francés en la manera y el gusto . . . sus sonetos tienen la blancura mate de los mármoles de Heredia . . . apolinea elegancia de Proudhome [sic] . . .recuerda a Gutiérrez Nájera, pero su sitio está más próxima a Julián del Casal." Félix Matos Bernier, however, felt Negrón "no es modernista ni en los temas ni en las formas."

Writings: Poetry: *Poesias,* San Juan, Tip. Boletin Mercantil, 1905; *Mensajeros,* Ponce, Tip. La Democracia, 1909, (99 p.).

Biographical/Critical Sources: Angel M. Mergal's "José A. Negrón Sanjuro: su tiempo, su vida y su obra," unpublished M. A. thesis, U. of P. R., Ri Piedras, 1940 (176 pp.); Eugenio Astol's article in *Puerto Rico Ilustrado,* San Juan, No. 69, Year II (June 25, 1911); Félix Matos Bernier, *Isla de arte,* San Juan, Imp. La Primavera, 1907.

NIVAR DE PITTALUGA, Amada

b. ca. 1908, Dominican Republic.
Poet.

Amada Nivar has been a president of the Consejo Nacional de Mujeres. Her work is Christian, pietistic, almost resigned in its tone and much of its subject matter. Jorge Ribas said of her work that the musical arrangement of her images and the overall temperament of her sensibility kept her above any triviality and "El suceso humano tras ciende su animado acento de realidad conmovedora."

Writings: Poetry: *Palma real,* 1938; *Rosa de América,* 1957; *El Amado Immortal; Los tres tiempos de la Rosa; Poemas del atardecer.*

Biographical/Critical Sources: See F. A. Mota Medrano's comments in *Relieves alumbrados,* S. Domingo, 1971, pp. 261-283.

NOUEL Y BOBADILLA, Bienvenido Salvador

b. 1874, Santo Domingo, Dominican Republic; d. 1934.
Poet.

An early poet, Nouel is all but forgotten today, and little is known of his life or works.

Writings: Poetry: *Pincelados,* Moca, 1904.

NOVAS CALVO, Lino

b. 1905, Galicia, Spain (long resident in Cuba).
Storywriter, novelist, teacher, translator.

Novas-Calvo arrived as a child with his Spanish parents in Cuba but spent most of his life in New York City. His stories are well known and he has done much translating from Spanish to English and vice versa. His wide knowledge of American literature helped popularize much American work in the Spanish-reading world.

An outstanding storyteller of the Hemingway tradition, Novas-Calvo used repetitions, curt lines, detailed descriptions (for ultimate effect and not for itself as mere documentation). Max Henriquez Ureña found the stories "La noche de Ramón Yendia" (from the 1942 collection) and "La visión de Tamariz" (from *Cayo Canas*) masterpieces. Novas-Calvo's *El negrero* is the "biography" of a once well-known pirate who has been "recreated" to serve his new role in the author's story.

In 1934 Novas-Calvo translated work of William Faulkner, the earliest ever in Spanish. After teaching in Havana in 1939-40, he went to New York City where he remained for seven years working for a period on the journal *Vanidades*. Since 1967, he has been a professor of Latin American literature at Syracuse University (New York State).

Writings: Novelette: *Pedro Blanco, El negrero,* Madrid, 1933.

Stories: Collections: *La luna nona y otras cuentos,* Buenos Aires, 1942; *Cayo Canas,* Havana, 1946; *No sé quién soy,* Mexico, 1945; *En los traspatios,* Havana, 1946; *El otro cayo,* 2nd ed., Havana, Cruzado Latinoamericano de Difusión Cultural, 1959; *Maneras de contar,* New York, Las Américas, 1970. Individual stories: "Esperimento en el barrio chino" (1936), "Un dedo encina," (1946), and "En los traspatios," (1946). One of his stories, translated into English by Myron I. Lichtbau as "The Cow on the Rooftop" appears in *Latin American Literary Review, IV,* 7(Fall-Winter 1975), pp. 111ff., originally published in *Papeles de San Armadans* (Spain, March 1973). The story "Allies and Germans" (English version), is in *From the Green Antilles,* B. Howe, ed., London, 1967.

Biographical/Critical Sources: Salvador Bueno, "Un cuentista cubano," in *Américas* (Washington, D. C.), III, 3 (March 1951), pp. 10-12; and S. Bueno, "Semblanza biográfica y critica de Lino Novás Calvo," in *Lyceum,* Havana, VII, 28 (1951), pp. 36-49; Sergio Fernández, "Lino Novás Calvos hechizador de negros," in journal of Universidad de Nuevo León (Mexico), nos. 14-15 (April 1957), pp. 47-55; Agustin de Saz, "Lino Novás Calvo y la novela de protesta social," in *Revista Cubana* (Havana), Vol. 26 (Jan-June 1950), pp. 320-323.

NUNES DE CACERES, José

(a.k.a. **"El fabulista principiante"**)

b. March 14, 1772, Santo Domingo, Dominican Republic; d. September 12, 1846, Ciudad Victoria.

Storywriter, poet, statesman.

After local schooling, including a doctorate of laws degree at the University of Santo Domingo in 1795, Núñes moved to Camagüey, Cuba for a period. Returned from Cuba, he became an active supporter of nationalism and on November 30, 1821 called for the independence of the state of "Haiti Español" and asked Colombia to protect the new state. He

wrote a *Declaration of Independence* based on his reading of Rousseau's *The Social Contract* and *De los colonias y de la revolución actual de la América* (Paris, 1817) by the Abbot of Pradt.

Max Henriquez Ureña states Núñes de Cáceras was only a modest versifier but a graceful and ingenious fabulist. Núñes published many of his fables in his lively, nationalist journal *El Duende,* along with documents, essays, polemics and poems in 1821.

Driven out of the island shortly after his efforts at independence were disastrously aborted, he fled to Venezuela where he hoped to enlist support for a Colombian-Venezuelan invasion and counter-attack on the Haitians who had taken over Dominica. He founded new journals *El Cometa* (1824) and *El Constitucional Caraqueño* (1824-25), *El Relámpago* (1826) and *El Cometa Extraordinario* (1827), all full of his enthusiastic, often violent diatribes. His articles were sarcastic, ironic, combative. One authority, Juan Vicente González, called him "erudición irreligiosa y gracia satirica." Núñes' very vehemence and independence, however, was too much for Bolivar and Núñes had to leave for Mexico in 1828. There he practiced law in Puebla for a period, before moving on to San Luis de Potosí, and finally to Ciudad Victoria, the capital of the state of Tamaulipas.

In Mexico he was well regarded and even elected in 1833 to the local legislature. In 1848, after his death, the local legislature put his name in gold plated letters on its great chamber door.

Just before his death, he learned of his homeland's independence from Haiti and he was moved to write two articles about the long-awaited moment, though he had not been intransigent on the question as might have been expected.

Writings: Poetry: "A los vencedores de Palo Hincado," published in *El Duende.*

Folktales: mostly published in the journal *El Duende;* available issues of the journal have the tales "La lechuza y la ciguena," "El paloma, la paloma y la lechuza," "El camello y el dromedario," "El conejo, los corderos y el pastor," "El mulo y la acémila," and many others; "El camello y el dromedario" was republished in *Analectas* by Eduardo Matos Días (June 1937).

Speech: Discourse of Núñes concerning the necessity of accepting the Haitian occupation with as good grace as possible, written after Haitian General Boyar's successful invasion of February 9, 1822. Speech was published in French, in the bi-lingual journal *L'Etoile Haytienne* of March 17, 1822. Max Henriquez Ureña's copy, which may be the only extant one, is reproduced in *Clio,* No. 32 (1938).

Document: "Declaratoria de Independencia del pueblo dominicana," in *El Duende* (December 1821).

Biographical/Critical Sources: Max Henriquez Ureña's *La Independencia efimera,* Paris, 1938 (which provides much bibliographic material for the period of the first Dominican Republic and the career of Núñes and others). Also see Henriquez' *Panorama histórico de la literatura dominicana,* 2 vols., S. Domingo, Postigo, 1965, pp. 112-120; J. Balaguer's *Los proceres escritores,* 2nd ed., Buenos Aires, Gráfica Guadelupe, 1971; and Balaguer's *Historia de la literatura dominicana,* 1970; and Carlos V. Sanchéz y Sanchéz' *La independencia boba de Núñes de Cáceres ante la historia y el derecho público,* details unknown.

NUNEZ, Ana Rosa

b. July 11, 1926, Havana, Cuba.
Poet.

Núñez received her doctorate in philosophy and letters from the University of Havana in 1954. Since that time she has been a librarian at the University. Much of her work is touched by her love of nature absorbed from her earliest years on her family's farm darkened by a strain of personal melancholy. She was a founder of the review *Alacrán Azul* and has published in such journals as *Punto Cardinal, Exile, Resumen* and *Las Américas.* She left Cuba in the early 1960's and has since published in Miami, Florida, U. S. A.

Writings: Poetry: *Un dia en el verso 59,* Havana, 1959; *Gabriela Mistral, amor que hirio,* Havana, Atabex, 1961; *Las siete lunas de enero,* Miami, 1967; *Loores a la palma real,* Miami, Universal, 1970; *Réquiem para una isla,* Miami, Universal, 1970; *Viaje al casabe,* Miami, 1970; *Escamas del Caribe* (Háikus de Cuba), Miami, Universal, 1971. Also see her poem "Gotas de Ebano" in *Poesia Negra del Caribe,* Hortensia Ruiz del Vizo, Miami, 1971, pp. 90-94.

Editor of: *Poesia en éxodo,* Miami, Universal, 1970.

Critical Study: *Nuestro Gustavo Adolfo Bécquer.*

NUNEZ, Guillermo

b. ca. 1936, Puerto Rico.
Poet.

Self-taught, Núñez, a mechanic by trade, has won a prestigious award for his first collected poems, *Esta voz primera* of 1964, and is considered one of the most promising of the young generation.

His poem "El mar" is original, curt:

El mar
es un hombre triste
Un hombre encadenado
al mundo.
Un hombre
con las manos en los bolsillos
Y la es puma rozando las estrellas.
Un hombre borracho
. . . .

Writings: Poetry: *Esta voz primera,* 1964 (won a prize in the competition of the Puerto Rican Institute of Literature); *Esta otra voz,* 1966.

NUNEZ, Serafina

b. 1913, Cuba.
Poet.

Núñez' poetry is extremely vibrant, almost tense, and has developed to ever more mature expression. Max Henriquez Ureña cites for especial praise her sonnet "A un ruiseñor amaneciendo."

Writings: Poetry: *Mar cautivo,* 1937; *Isla en sueño,* 1938; *Vigilia y secreto,* 1941, with introduction by Juan Ramón Jiménez.

O'FARRIL, Alberto

b. 1899, Santa Clara, Cuba.
Playwright, actor, editor.

O'Farril was editor of *Profeo,* a literary journal, and author of many plays including the musical melodrama, *Un negro misterioso,* performed in 1921, and *Los misterios de chango* (performed 1926), two of the earliest Cuban works devoted to Cuban themes.

Writings: Plays: (all unpublished) *Un negro misterioso* (1 act musical), premiered at the Teatro Esmeralda, Havana, 1921; *Las pamplinas de Agapito* (1 act musical comedy), premiered Apollo Theatre, New York City, August 1, 1926; *Un negro en Andalucia* (musical comedy), premiered Apollo Theatre, New York City, August 22, 1926; *Un doctor accidental* (1 act farce), performed Apollo Theatre, New York City, August 29, 1926.

OLIVER FRAU, Antonio

b. April 4, 1902, Lares, Puerto Rico;
d. 1945, Ponce, Puerto Rico.
Storywriter, critic, lawyer.

Oliver did his studies at the Escuela Superior of Lares near his father's coffee plantation and took a law degree at the University of Puerto Rico. He served as a judge in Carolina, Juana Diaz, Yanco and Ponce. He early began to contribute to journals in San Juan, a collection of which pieces he hoped to published in 1922 in one collection, "Crónicas. . . ,"but which he never did.

Exercising the profession of law in association with his fellow-writing lawyer Emiliano Martínez Avilés with whom he founded the literary review *La Torrecilla,* Oliver was active in public affairs as well, serving as a judge for his last years in the cities of Yanco and Ponce. Most of his work is in the folkloric vein and his interest in the traditions and customs of the village and countryside are evident in his one collection *Cuentos y leyendas del cafetal* (1938), the stories being mainly from his more active literary period of the 1920's.

With Alfredo Collado Martell, Oliver Frau was an important transitional figure between the major literary movement of "modernismo" of the 1890-1915 period and the later, harsher, more realistic writings of the 1930's and later.

Writings: Stories: *Cuentos y leyendas del cafetal,* Yanco, 1938, 2nd ed., San Juan, Instituto de Cultura Puertorriqueña, 1967; unpublished collection, "Crónicas de juventud, de vida y de fantasía"; one fragment of *Cuentos y leyendas* is entitled "La Lama Rubia de los ojos color de mar" and appears in L. Hernández Aquilo's *El modernismo en Puerto Rico,* San Juan, 1967, pp. 209-212, and in *Literatura puertorriqueña,* Martínez Masden and Melon, eds., Rio Piedras, 1972, pp. 265-274; the stories "Cheman, el Correcostas," "La Simiente Roja," and "Juan Perdio," are in Concha Meléndez' *El Arte del Cuento en Puerto Rico,* New York, 1961.

Biographical/Critical Sources: Concha Meléndez, *El arte del cuento en Puerto Rico,* New York, 1961, pp. 32-38; Margarita Vázquez has bio-critical study of Oliver in *Cuentos y leyendas,* 1967; Enrique A. Laguerre, "Resumen histórico del relato en Puerto Rico," in *Revista del Instituto del Cultura Puertorriqueña,* San Juan, 1958.

ORGAZ, Francisco

b. 1810, Havana, Cuba; d. 1873, Madrid, Spain.
Poet, playwright.

Orgaz passed much of his life in Spain, but he remained a battler for Cuban freedom and rights while serving as editor of such Spanish journals as *El Contemporáneo* and *El Espectador.* For a period he had also been a teacher and governmental official.

His poetry was full of the romantic exuberances of the day, sonorous and over-energetic. Menéndez y Pelayo wrote of his work: "Sus poemas pertenecen a un género de efectismo rimbombante que deja fatigados con su estrépito los oidos vacio de formas el entendimiento."

Preludios del arpa, his first collection of poetry, was banned in Cuba. The poem "Los tropicales" celebrating the life of the Indians was one of the then popular efforts to recall the lost inhabitants of the islands in the movement often called "Ciboneyismo" after the term first used by Las Casas, the reformer.

Writings: Poetry: *Preludios del arpa,* Madrid, Boix, 1841; *Poesias,* Madrid, 1850.

Plays: *El pescador* (4 act comedy, verse), unpublished, written in 1839; *Consecuencias de un disfraz* (1 act comedy), published Madrid, Lalame, 1852.

ORTEA, Francisco Carlos

(pseudonym: **Dr. Franck**)

b. 1845, Dominican Republic; d. 1899.
Storywriter.

Ortea did most of his writing in Puerto Rico. A fine stylist, his sentimental, romantic stories were popular in their usual magazine appearances between 1887 and 1880 in Puerto Rico.

Writings: Novelettes: *El tesoro de Cofresi,* Mayagüez, Tip. Commercial, 1889 (a continuation of *La enlutada del tranvia* for which details are unknown); *Un novela al vapor,* Santiago de Cuba, Ravel, 1882; *Madame Belliard* (in three parts), details unknown; *Escenos de la vida intima; Margarita,* Mayagüey, Imp. Arecco, 1889, 2nd ed., Santiago, Cuba, 18??; *Maria,* details unknown.

ORTEA, Virginia Elena

(pseudonym: **Elena KENNEDY**)

b. June 17, 1866, Santo Domingo, Dominican Republic; d. January 30, 1903, Puerto Plata, Dominican Republic. Storywriter, novelist, playwright.

In 1879 the family of Virginia Ortea removed to Puerto Rico for political reasons and remained in exile for many years. Her first stories began to appear soon after her return to her natal island in such journals as *Letras y Ciencias* and *El Listin Diario.* Joaquin Balaguer considers her the most gifted of any of the women prose writers of the nineteenth century in Domincan letters: "Jamás se ha visto en la literatura nacional, imaginación más resueña, inteligencia más ágil, pluma más abundantemente dotada del don de narrar, en páginas encantadoras, las pequeñeces del vivir cotidiano."

Balaguer finds her novel *Mi hermana Carolina* an immature, if sensitive work, but finds her story collection *Risas y lágrimas* "de profunda cadencia subjetiva."

Ortea's poetry, including "A Puerto Plata," and "Nostalgia" which appeared in journals but never in separate volumes, was very delicate, yet sure, but not as pure and original as the prose of her tales.

Writings: Stories: *Risas y lágrimas,* 1901; the stories "Los diamantes," and "En tu glorieta" appeared in various journals.

Novels: *Mi hermana Carolina,* completed in 1897, but never published, and most of the ms. has now been lost; *Crónica Puertoplateña,* which deals with the life of Emilia Michel.

Plays: *La feministas* (3 acts), music set by José Maria Rodriguez Arrezón and José Ramón López was a collaborator; López also collaborated with her on the play *Dolores,* never performed or published.

Biographical/Critical Sources: Joaquin Balaguer's *Historia de la literatura dominicana,* 5th ed., S. Domingo, Postigo, 1970, pp. 176-179.

ORTEGA DE LA FLOR, Luis

b. 1814, Cádiz, Spain; d. 1894, Cuba. Playwright.

Ortega emigrated early to Cuba and identified himself with his new land. Settling in Matanzas, he joined the nationalist party movement. All of his published works saw print in just three years (1856-58), the midpoint of his long life of 80 years.

Writings: Plays: *Una fiesta en un ingenio o Los dias del mayoral* (1 act comedy, verse), Puerto Principe, 1856; *Felipe o el hijo de maldición* (5 acts, verse), Santiago, Cuba, Martinez, 1857; *La válida y el válido* (3 act comedy, verse), Santiago, Martinez, 1857; *El viejo enamorado* (1 act musical comedy, verse), Havana, Imp. La Charanga, 1858; *Herminia de Albarracini* (3 acts), Puerto Principe, 1858.

ORTERO, Rafael

b. 1827, Havana, Cuba; d. 1876, Matanzas. Poet, playwright.

Ortero's lighthearted poem, "El tio Miguel en la Habana," was very popular. Some of his best individual poetic works were "Cosas de las máscaras," "Las bombillas Jabón," Parece mal parece bien," and "Poco importa."

Writings: Poetry: "El tio Miguel en la Habana" and others, published in newspapers and literary journals.

Plays: *Un novio para la isleña* (1 act comedy), Havana, Imp. Soler, 1847; *Mi hijo el francés* (comedy), Havana, 1847; *Un bobo del dia* (1 act comedy, verse), premiered Teatro Tacón, Havana, August 23, 1848, published, Havana, Torres, 1848, 2nd ed., Cárdenas, 1857, 3rd ed., Matanzas, Imp. del Gobierno, 1857; *El muerto lo manda* (2 act comedy), Havana, Barcina, 1850; *Quien tiene tienda, que atienda* (3 act comedy), Havana, Barcina, 1851; *Ambición y castigo* (1 act comedy, verse), Havana, 1855; *Un Coburgo* (comic folkloric play), Matanzas, Imp. Aurora del Yumuri, 1857; *Cuatro a una*

(2 act farce, verse), Matanzas, Imp. El Ferrocarril, 1865; *Del agua mansa nos libre Dios* (1 act, verse), performed Teatro del Instituto de Matanzas, Aurora del Yumuri, 1867.

Folklore: in various journals and in *Los cubanos pintados par si mismos,* Havana, 1852.

ORTIZ, Fernándo

b. ca. 1897, Cuba; d. ca. 1963.
Folklorist, musicologist, sociologist, criminologist.

Ortiz is wide ranging in his many interests and has edited *Ultra* and *Archivos del folklore cubano.* He has published some 75 different works.

Writings: Folklore: *Los negros brujos,* Madrid, 1905; *Los negros esclavos,* 1916; *El huracán, su mitologia y sus simbolos,* 1947; *Los bailes el teatro de los negros en el folklore de Cuba,* Havana, 1951.

Articles: "Los últimos versos mulatos," in *Revista Bimestre Cubana,* VI (1953); "Más acerca de la poesia mulata," *Revista Bimestre Cubana,* I-II (1936).

ORTIZ STELLA, Cruz

b. July 10, 1900, Maunabo, Puerto Rico.
Poet, lawyer, politician.

Ortiz has spent most of his life in Humacao and he early published his verse volumes *Los oros se vislumbran* (1918) and *La caravana oscura* (1921), much of it under the influence of José de Diego, Virgilio Dávila, Rubén Dario and others of the "modernismo" school. Later he became a close associate of Padre Juan Rivera and has become religious and introspective.

Ortiz Stella's "Bajo la luna" shows the poet's moodiness as can be seen in even a few lines reflective of Herrera Reissig:

Bajo esta luna fea,
canallesca y burlona,
mi trágica persona
su miseria pasea

Writings: Poetry: *Los oros se vislumbran,* Humacao, P. R., Tip. Victoria, 1918; *La caravana oscura,* San Juan, Tip. Real Hermanos, 1921; and poems in *Almanaque de Humacao,* Humacao (directed by Padre Juan Rivera Viera), 1935, and other years.

OSORIO, Ana de

b. ca. 1795, Santo Domingo, Dominican Republic; d. 1851.
Folk-singer, poet.

Ana de Osorio was a wandering folk-singer and folk-poet. She was a good friend of Nicolás Ureña and his wife, Doña Gregorio Díaz, parents of the famous poetess Salomé Ureña, who recalled Osorio's life and wrote down some of her verse, including an eight-line poem dedicated to their new-born daughter, Ramona, in 1848.

Writings: Songs: in *Cuadernos de poesias y apuntes,* a ms. collection of popular verse edited and collected by Pedro Henriquez Ureña, now in the custody of the Museo Nacional, and two poems in E. Rodriguez Demorizi's *Poesia popular dominicana,* for which see below.

Biographical/Critical Sources: Emilio Rodriguez Demorizi, *Poesia popular dominicana,* 1938, 2nd ed., S. Domingo, UCMM, 1973, pp. 177-179.

OTERO GONZALEZ, Lisandro

b. 1932, Havana, Cuba.
Novelist, journalist, storywriter.

Otero has travelled widely, served as foreign correspondent in Paris, and won in 1955 the Juan Gualberto Gómez prize for his articles on the Algerian war of independence. After Castro's own successful struggle, Otero returned to Cuba where he had several important posts, including vice-president of the National Council of Culture and director of the reviews *Cuba* and *RC.*

His novel *La situación* won the first prize of the *Casa de las Américas* in 1963.

Writings: Novels: *La situación,* Havana, Casas de las Américas, 1963; *Pasión de urbino,* Buenos Aires, J. Alvárez, 1966, and Havana, Instituto del Libro, 1967; *En ciudad semejante,* Havana, Unión, 1970.

Stories: *Tobaco para un jueves santo,* Paris, 1955.

Journalism: *Cuba, zona de desarrollo agrario,* Havana, 1960.

Biographical/Critical Sources: Anon., "Lisandro Otero," in *Europe. Literatura de Cuba* (Paris), Vol. 41 (May-June 1963), pp. 409-410.

PACHECO, Armando Oscar

b. 1902, Dominican Republic.
Poet, novelist, playwright.

Primarily a playwright, Pacheco has published two novels and miscellaneous poetry.

Writings: Poetry: first two collections unpublished): "Via Láctea"; "Derelicta"; "Canto a la patria que ha llegado a un siglo," 1944.

Novels: *El fuego entre la nieve,* Lima, Peru, Edit. Runac, 1951; *El hombre de los pies en el agua,* S. Domingo, Edit. Dominicana, 1959.

Plays: *La gondola azul,* music by Alfredo Max Soler; *Como las demás; Amatista; En la boca del lobo; El amor se va de vaciones; El pez dorado en la pecera de cristal;* and a comedy performed in 1963, written as an angry reply to the existentialist ideas of J. P. Sartre.

PACHIN MARIN

(a.k.a. **Francisco GONZALEZ (or Gonzaló) MARIN**)

b. March 9, 1863, Arecibo, Puerto Rico; d. November, 1897.
Poet, storywriter, journalist, playwright.

After local schooling the fiery Pachin Marin founded the political journal *El Postillón* which quickly ran into censorship by the Spanish authorities. Forced to leave Puerto Rico, Francisco emigrated to Santo Domingo but found even more repression so he went to Venezuela. By 1890 he was back in Puerto Rico and the next year revived his old journal which was quickly suppressed once more by the Spanish authorities. Once again he felt he could not stay and he went to New York City where he wrote for the *Gaceta de Puerto Rico,* directed by Vélez Alvarado and for a third time his renewed *El Postillón.*

Pachin Marin died in the Cuban struggle for independence from Spain in the 1896-1897 revolt, of a fever while on a campaign in serving as a special official for Máximo Gómez.

His poem "Mariposas" ends:

II

Cuando me encorve el peso de los años,
cuando la senda del dolor recorra
y, cuando viajero, sin un triunfo
me tienda a descansar sobre una fosa,
¡quierra Dios que en la noche de mi cráneo,
asi como en el hueco de la alcoba,
Vengan a fabricar, madre del alma.
nido de luz aquellas mariposas!

Writings: Poetry: *Flores nacientas,* 1884; *Mi óbolo,* 1887; *Romances,* Imp. Modesto A. Tirado, 1892; *En la arena,* New York, S. I., 1898; two poems, "Corte de caja" and "Mariposas" appear in *Antologia de la poesia puertorriqueña,* E. F. Méndez, ed., San Juan, 1968; "A la estatua de Bolivar, Las botas y Judas," Venezuela.

Complete Works: *Obras completas del poeta-mártir, Francisco Gonzalo Marin,* Manzanillo, Cuba, Ed. El Arte, 1944; *Antologia* (selections of Pachin's poetry by Maria Teresa Babin), San Juan, Ateneo Puertorriqueño, 1958.

Play: *27 de febrero* (dramatic allegory), performed in Dominican Republic.

Biographical/Critical Sources: See play by

Cesáreo Rosa-Nieves: *Pachin Marin;* F. Manrique Cabrera, *Historia de la literatura,* Rio Piedras, 1969, pp. 217-219; Juan Braschi, *Biografia de Francisco Gonzálo Marin,* Arecibo, Tip. El Machete, 1909; Patria Figueroa de Cifredo, *Pachin Marin, héroe y poeta 1863-1897,* foreword by C. Rosa-Nieves, San Juan, 1967.

PADILLA, Heberto

b. 1932, Cuba.
Poet, journalist.

Padilla emigrated to the United States in 1948 but returned to Cuba the very next year. But he then spent the next decade in the United States teaching and writing as a journalist. Soon he restlessly moved on to London, Western Europe and to Moscow as a journalist. He returned to Cuba in 1958 with great enthusiasm and by the mid 1960's he had become head of the state export agency and travelled widely in this post, particularly in the USSR and Eastern Europe. His first collection of verse, *El justo tiempo humano,* offers work written and/or published between 1953 and 1961. Much of his early work is influenced by contemporary American and English poets.

As his experiences of political and artistic repression widened and deepened, his work changed and he began to be considered a "counter-revolutionary." As late as 1968, however, he was awarded the Julián del Casal prize for his *Fuera del juego* after great pressures on the award jury to refuse the prize to him. After the award the Cuban Army paper *Verde Olivo* made a scurrilous attack on him and the foreign trip which was part of the prize was cancelled. After a brief respite as professor at the University of Havana, he was arrested at Havana Airport March 20, 1971 with his wife Belkis Cuza Malé for "conspiracy against the regime." (Cuza's Malé's own poetry is in *Cartas a Ana Frank,* Havana, Unión, 1966). By late April he was out of prison, having signed a long "self-criticism" circulated by the state's press agency, his "crimes" being of all sorts, including "work" for the C.I.A. In the late 1960's and 1970's he and his wife were confined to a little village with only rare visits to Havana permitted. They are translating and otherwise vaguely employed by the State Publishing House.

J. M. Cohen's selected translations of Padilla's work as *Sent Off the Field* gives a modest portion of *El justo tiempo humano,* almost all of *Fuero del juego,* and all but a few of the later poems, most of which are still in manuscript.

Writings: Poetry: *El justo tiempo humano,* Havana, La Tertulia, 1962, 2nd ed., 1964; *La marca de la soga,* 196?; *La hora,* Havana, La Tertulia, 1964; *Fuera del juego,* Havana, Unión, 1968, and Buenos Aires, Aditor, 1969, and Rio Piedras, San Juan, P. R., 1971 (118 p.); and represented in Nathaniel Tarn's *Con Cuba,* New York, 1969; a selection of Padilla's verse, in English translation by J. M. Cohen, is *Sent Off the Field,* London, Andre Deutsch, 1972; *Subversive Poetry: The Padilla Affair,* Washington, D. C. Georgetown University Cuban Students Association, 1974, (44 p.); *Poetry and Politics,* Four poems in English text ("Sometimes those Bad Thoughts"; "Instructions for Entering A New Society"; "The Old Bards Say"; and "To Write in the Scrapbook of a Tyrant") appeared in *Of Human Rights* Georgetown University, Washington, D. C., Fall 1977), p. 20.

PADILLA, José Gualberto

(a.k.a. **"El Caribe"**)

b. July 12, 1829, San Juan, Puerto Rico; d. 1886.
Poet, physician.

After local schooling, Padilla studied at Santiago de Galicia for his B. A. and his first year of medicine. Padilla studied medicine further in Spain at Barcelona and returned in 1857 to practice his profession in Arecibo and Vega Baja. His daughter Trina became a well-known poet whose verse, however, is deemed of little genuine merit. His life was divided between medicine, farming and poetry. Possibly his best-known single poem is "Puerto Rico." Padilla employed verse polemically and with his daughter entered word-combat with Spanish critic Manuel del Calacio.

Writings: Poetry: *Horas de prisión,* 1913; two poems, "La flor silvestre," and "El Maestro Rafael" are in Manuel Fernández Juncos' *Antologia puertorriqueña,* New York, 1952, pp. 74-71; *En el combate: Poesias completas,* San Juan, Instituto de Cultura Puertorriqueña, 1969; *Antologia,* San Juan, Ateneo Puertorriqueño, 1961.

PADILLA DE SANZ, Trina

(a.k.a. **"La Hija del Caribe"**)

b. ca. 1880, Puerto Rico.
Poet.

Daughter of the well-known physician and poet, José Gualberto Padilla, Trina Padilla is considered an unoriginal, overly romantic poet. Her fame was due in some part to her father's and her polemics against the Spanish poet, Manuel del Palacio. Much of her work was published in the various journals of the period and gathered late in her only collection *De mi collar* (1926).

Writings: Poetry: *De mi collar,* Paris, Ed. París-América, 1926.

Biographical/Critical Sources: See sketch on Padilla in Ernesto Juan Fonfrias' *Sementera: Ensayos breves y biografias minimas,* San Juan, 1962.

PADRO, Humberto

b. 1906, Ciales, Puerto Rico.
Poet, storywriter.

Humberto Padró has published much of his work in *El Imparcial, Florete, El Mundo, Alma Latina* and *Puerto Rico Ilustrado.* His stories are stirring and colorful and his poetry, influenced by Garcia Lorca's work, but also reflecting the earlier influence of Guy de Maupassant.

Writings: Stories: *Diez cuentos,* San Juan, Imp. Venezuela, 1929, (64 p.).
Poetry: *Los Cármenes de Oro Malva,* San Juan, 1947.

PALES MATOS, Gustavo

b. 1907, Guayama, Puerto Rico.
Playwright, poet, journalist.

Brother of Puerto Rico's finest poet Luis Palés Matos, Gustavo is generally a cautious follower in the wake of the great "post modernista" poets of the 1930's and has been influenced by Garcia Lorca.

Writings: Poetry: *Romancero de Cofresi,* 1942.
Play: *Cofresi,* 1949.
Editor of: *Antologia de poetas contemporáneos de Puerto Rico,* Mexico, 1946.

PALES MATOS, Luis

b. March 20, 1898, Ciudad Bruja (Guayama), Puerto Rico; d. February 23, 1959.
Poet, novelist.

Luis Palés Matos is considered the greatest of the Puerto Rican poets and one of the artists most interested in employing African themes and styles in his work. Born in Guayana, a small, mostly black-occupied village, his poetry constantly moves toward a difficult synthesis of his black social and personal experiences and the white cultural values of the United States and its imposed values on the island. At times he seems defensive, or over-exotic, about African qualities but he has dealt with the black experience where many other writers have not. His latest poetry is so obscure, however, as he moved to an ever more personal idiom, that he has left even his fondest critics puzzled.

He contributed to *El Pueblo* which was edited and directed in Fajardo by F. Sárraga Figueroa. By the 1920's, Palés Matos was in San Juan where he was active as a journalist and where he was to write most of his prose and verse thereafter. With J. T. de Diego Padró, he initiated the new esthetic "Diepalismo" (an anagram on the first syllables of their names) which called for greater musicality, onomatopeia and a greater flow between lines. The first poem written under the "new regime" was Palés Matos' "Orquestación Deipálica" published in *El Imparcial* (November 7, 1921). His first Afro-Antillan verse was "Pueblo Negro" (1925) although he had written in 1918 the merely external picture of black life in "Danzarina Africana."

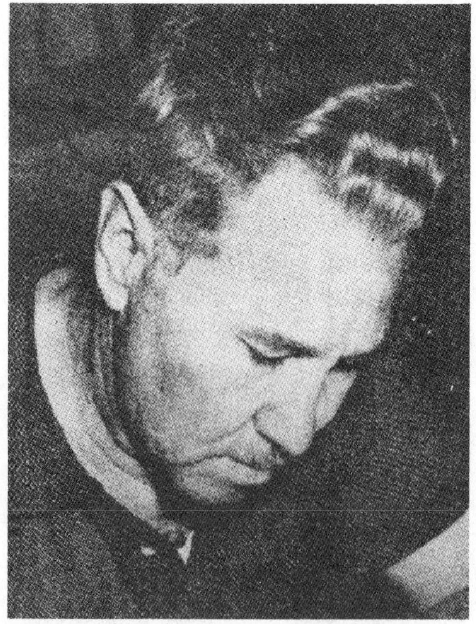

His first collection, *Azáleas. Poesias,* appeared in 1915, reflecting his belief that onomatopeia was most important for initiating a new verse (the so-called "Diepalismo" movement). His *Tuntún de pasa y griferia* of 1937 most strongly shows his development of interest in the African themes popular in Cuba and Haiti in the 1930's or somewhat earlier.

Much of his work has been anthologized and translated and his poem "Danza negra" was popularized by the Spanish actor José González Marin in his many recitations. Edna Underwood's translation of "Nanigo to Heaven" in its English title offers an approach to his work of the middle period:

A fiesta in Heaven, Sweetness
Of meringues and caratos.
Marmalade of prayer.
Genuine milkshake of psalmody.
With bronze and golden fingers
The trumpet of heralds
On the balconies of Heaven
Hang festoons of song.
(from third verse)

Palés Matos often moves from a prosaic to a richly embroidered style, often vivid and overblown in a baroque orchestration of his complex themes.

The poem "Tic-tac" expresses his lifelong ennui with the routines and horrors of daily city living as even these final lines may illustrate:

Y estrujar en la cama la neurosis de avispa
con los nervios crispados cual bruscas sabandijas,
y buscar en un sueño de alcanfor y fatiga
el canto de la alondra que anuncia el nueva dia.

Writings: Poetry: *Azáleas. Poesias,* Guayama, Edit. Rodriguez, P. R., 1915; *Túntun de pasa y griferia, Poemas afroantillanos,* preface by Angel Valbuena Prat, San Juan, Biblioteca de Autores Puertorriqueños, 1937; new edition, 1950, with preface by Jaime Benitez, 3rd ed., 1960; *Poesia 1915-1956,* Rio Piedras, introduction by Federico de Onis, San Juan, University of Puerto Rico, 1957, later editions, 1964, 1968, 1971, 1974; *Poesias,* illustrations by Rafael Tufiño, San Juan, Cuadernos del Instituto de Cultura Puertorriqueña, 1959; "Danza negra" and seven other poems are in Vol. II of *Literatura Puertorriqueña,* E. Martinez Masden and Esther M. Melón, eds., Rio Piedras, Edit. Edil, 1972, pp. 97-115. Also: *Poesias, 1915-1956,* 3rd ed., San Juan, Ediciones de la Universidad de Puerto Rico, 1968; also poetry in ms., "El palacio en sobras," 1919, 1920, "Canciones de la vida media," 1925; other verse, *Obra completa,* Margot Arce-Vásquez, ed., Rio Piedras, Editorial Universitaria, 1971; group of poems entitled "Poemas negros" in *Ateneo puertorriqueños,* Vol. I (1935), pp. 53-66; "Danza negra" and "Nañigo to Heaven" in *New Writing in the Caribbean,* Georgetown, Guyana, 1972.

Autobiographical Novel (incomplete): "Memorias de un hombre insignificante," as "Litoral (Reseña de una vida inútil)," published in *El Diario de Puerto Rico* (San Juan, 1949, from February 5 to April 25, each Saturday), then completely published in the periodical *Universidad* (University of Puerto Rico, November 9, 1951-May 15, 1952).

Biographical/Critical Sources: Margot Arce-Vásquez, "Más sobre los poemas negros de Luis Palés Matos" in *Ateneo Puertorriqueño* (San Juan), Vol. II (1934), pp. 35-45; Tomás Blanco's "Una critica al poeta Palés Matos," in *Revista bimestre cubana,* (Havana), Vol. 38 (1936), pp. 286-287; and other essays on Palés Matos in same issue, pp. 24-45; also Miguel Enguidanos, *La poesia de Luis Palés Matos,* Rio Piedras, 1961; and see discussion of Palés Matos by José Olivio Jiménez in his *Antologia de la poesia hispanoamericana contemporánea: 1914-1970,* Madrid, 1971, 1973; also, Federico de Onis, *Luis Palés Matos, vida y obra,* Santa Clara, Cuba, 1959; Federico Onís' introduction to *Luis Palés Matos poesia (1915-1956),* Rio Piedras, 1964, offers many critical insights into Palés' work and bibliography of criticism (pp. 287-298); and *Nuestra aventura literaria* by Luis Hernández Aquino in Chapter 2: "Diepalismo y euforismo," gives special treatment to Palés' "membership" in the "diepalismo" movement which heavily emphasized "onomatopeia" initiated by him and José I. de Diego Pedró; also see "Luis Palés Matos: Poeta de Hastio, el Pesimismo y la Ironia" in C. Rosa-Nieves' *Ensayos escogidas,* San Juan, 1970, pp. 165-176; and section by Enrique A. Laguerre in his *La poesia modernista en Puerto Rico,* San Juan, 1969, pp. 116-123; Hector Barrera, "Renovación poética de Luis Palés Matos," in *Asomante,* No. 2 (San Juan, 55-67); F. Manrique Cabrera, *Historia de la literatura puertorriqueña,* Rio Piedras, 1969, pp. 255-260; Concha Meléndez, Poetas hispanoamericanos diversos, San Juan, 1971.

PALES MATOS, Vicente

b. 1903, Guayama, Puerto Rico.
Poet, storywriter, lawyer.

Brother of the well-known Luis and Gustavo Palés Matos, Vincente has followed a career in the law. His one published volume of verse and stories was *Viento y espuma.* With Tomás L. Batista he founded in 1922 the vanguardist movement they termed "Enforismo" influenced by Marinetti's "Futurismo" (1909-1914). With Quiñones, Delgado, Rosa-Nieves and others Palés Matos organized a second literary effort, this one called "Noismo" attempting to do in Spanish verse what Apollinaire in Franca, e. e. cummings in the United States, and others elsewhere, with bizarre typographical handlings of the poetic line, including breaks in words, eccentric punctuation among other techniques.

Writings: Poetry and Stories: *Viente y espuma,* Mayagüez, 1945; *La fuente de Juan Ponce de León y otros poemas,* San Juan, Edit. Cordillero, 1967; his poem "Hoy me he echado a reir," is in the *Antologia de la poesia puertorriqueña,* E. Fernández Méndez, ed., San Juan, 1968.

PALMA, José Joaquin

b. 1844, Cuba; d. 1911, Guatemala.
Poet.

One of the "last" romantics, Palma was a participant in the great revolt of 1868 and in his long exile was adopted by Honduras and Guatemala as their son. His most famous poem was probably "Tinieblas del alma," dedicated to his friend Antonio

Zambrano. He wrote the national hymn of Guatemala. His verse is facile, melodious, natural.

Writings: Poetry: *Poesias,* Guatemala, Tip. Nacional de Guatemala, 1901.

PALMA, Marigloria

(pseudonym for **Gloria Maria PALMA**)

b. 1920, Puerto Rico.
Poet.

Gloria Maria Palma published her first and only volume of verse in 1942, a work of clarity, almost of transparent feeling, particularly of her own African origins as in her "Raiz Negra" which begins:

La raiz de mi cepa la traigo yo de lejos,
de allá de caños limpios y de riscos morenos. . .
De la sequia del blanco y la invasión del negro
que vino con sus tigres y músculos de hierro
a exprimirle a mis aguas el sol cuajado dentro,
. . . .

Rosa-Nieves wrote of her work: "La liromática de Marigloria Palma es un verso inesperando, vibrante, colorista y desnudo: dice llanamente lo que quiere."

Writings: Poetry: *Agua mansa; La razón del cuadrante; Agua suelta,* San Juan, B.A.P., 1942; *Entre dos azules: poemas,* Barcelona, Edicionas Rumbos, 1965.

PALMA Y ROMAY, Ramón de

(pseudonym: **"El Bachiller Alfonso de Maldonado"**)

b. 1812, Havana, Cuba; d. 1860.
Poet, playwright, storywriter.

Palma y Romay's earliest poetry appeared in 1833 and the next year, under his penname, his second collection. A "criollo" poet, his *Matanzas y Yumuri* of 1837 was the first prose work written on an Indian theme by a Cuban. His romances "El combate de las piraguas," and "El cacique de Ornofay" were other works in this then exotic and "naturist" vein. His earliest prose tales, including "Los amores del cocuyo y la maravilla" (1845), also an Indian story, were published in *El Aguinaldo Habanero,* the pioneering work gathering together such work.

Writings: Poetry: *Atributos de la hermosura* (octavas), 1833; *Poesias del Bachiller Alfonso de Maldonado,* 1834; "Una pascua en San Marcos" in *El Album,* 1838; *Aves de paso,* 1841; *Melodias poéticas,* 1843; *Hojas caidas,* 1844; collected edition of his major verse, edited by Anselmo Suarez y Romero, published as *Obras de D. Ramón de Palma: Poesias liricas,* 1861; and symphonic ode: "Una escena del descubrimiento del Nuevo Mundo por Colón," music by Bottesini, 1848; "Una pascua en San Marcos" and "El Cólera en la Habana" first appeared in *El Album* (1838), and the former poem was translated into French by La Condesa de Merlin (b. Havana, 1789) and placed in her book, *La Havane,* 3 vols., Paris, 1842.

Novelette: *El Ermitaño del Niágara,* 1845.

Stories: "Matanzas y Yumuri" in *El Aguinaldo Habanero,* 1837; and *El Cólera en La Habaña,* in *El Album,* 1838, and one volume: *Cuentos cubanos,* 1928.

Plays: *La prueba o La vuelta del Cruzado* (1 act), Havana, Palmer, 1837; *La pena de los enamorados* (3 acts, based on legend), Havana, Imp. Literaria, 1839.

Editor of: *Cantares de Cuba,* 1854.

Biographical/Critical Sources: see forward by Anselmo Suárez y Romero to *Obras de Ramón de Palma,* 1861.

PALOMINO, Rafael Leopoldo

b. ca. 1830, Spain; d. Cuba.
Playwright, journalist, novelist.

Palomino early emigrated to Cuba where he became a leading journalist as editor of

Eco del Comercio and *La Prensa,* both in Havana.

Writings: Novel: *Mi siglo y mi corazón.*
Plays: *Flor del desierto* (3 act comedy), Cádiz, 1857; *Omunda* (5 scenes), Havana, La Charanga, 1859, 2nd ed., 1875; *Un sevillano en la Habana* (1 act comedy), 1860.

PARILLA, Joaquin R.

b. 1900, Naguaba, Puerto Rico.
Poet, teacher.

Parilla's work is precise, almost enamelled. Early influenced as most young men of his day by Herrera Reissig and the local poets Luis Lloréns Torres and Antonio Nicolás Blanco, Parilla sought out a minor key to make his own. "Aromas" from his only volume of verse *Plumón de Cisne* (1930) begins:

Echarnos sobre el hombro toda la carga
de los seres tristes qua no tienen fe:
repartir migajas de amor a la amarga
procasión de almas que la luz no ven. . .

Writings: Poetry: *Plumón de Cisne,* Humacao, 1930.

PEACHE

(pseudonym for **José P.H. HERNANDEZ**)

PEDREIRA, Antonio S.

b. 1898, San Juan, Puerto Rico; d. 1939.
Critic, biographer, bibliographer, scholar, essayist.

Pedreira took his Normal School degree in 1920 in teaching and his B. A. in 1923, both at the University of Puerto Rico, and an M. A. at Columbia University in New York City in 1926. Six years later he earned a doctorate in philosophy and letters at Madrid University. He founded the Cultural journal *Indice* with Vicente Geigel Polanco, Samuel R. Quiñnones, and Alfredo Collago Martell.

Writings: Obras completas, 2 vols., (749 p. and 718 p.), San Juan, 1969.
Bibliography: *Bibliografia puertorriqueña* (1493-1930), Madrid, Hernándo, 1932; *De los nombres de Puerto Rico,* 1927; *El periodismo en Puerto Rico,* Havana, Garcia, 1941.
Histories: *El año terrible del 87,* San Juan, Biblioteca de Autores Puertorriqueños, 1937.
Biographies: *Un hombre del pueblo: José Celso Barbosa,* San Juan, Imp. Venezuela, 1937; *Hostos, ciudadano de América* (about Eugenio Maria de Hostos), Madrid, Espasa-Calpe, 1932 (Ph.D. dissertation at Madrid).
Essays: *Insularismo: ensayos de interpretación puertorriqueña,* Madrid, Tip. Artistica, 1934; 2nd ed. San Juan, Biblioteca de Autores Puertorriqueños, 1942; *Tres ensayos,* Rio Piedras, Edit. Edil, 1969; *La actualidad del Jibaro,* Rio Piedras, Universidad de Puerto Rico, 1935; *Aristas: Ensayos,* Rio Piedras, Edit. Edil, 1969 (and again his *Obras Completas*); *Aclaraciones y critica,* Rio Piedras, Universidad de Puerto Rico, Edit. Phi Eta Mu, 1941, 1969; also "Ensayo cromático," in *Aristas,* San Juan, Libreria y Editorial Campos, 1930, pp. 43-75; five essays are in Martinez Masdeu and Esther M. Melon, *Literatura puertorriqueña,* Vol. II, 2nd ed. (Rio Piedras, 1972), pp. 145-207.
Sociology: *La acutalidad del jibaro,* Rio Piedras, Universidad de Puerto Rico, 1935; *Insularismo,* Madrid, Tip. Artistica, 1934.
Criticism: "Luis Lloréns Torres: poeta de Puerto Rico," in *El Mundo,* San Juan (August 20, 1933), written with Concha Meléndez.

Biographical/Critical Sources: Fernándo Sierra Berdecia, Antonio S. Pedreira (a critical biography), 1940; Margot Arce de Vásquez, "Reflexiones en torno a Insularismo," in *Impressiones,* San Juan (1950); S. R. Quiñones, *Temas y letras,* San Juan, 1941 (essay on 15 writers including Pedreira).

PEDROSO, Regino

b. 1898, Unión de Reyes, Matanzas Province, Cuba.
Poet, storywriter.

Of Chinese-African ancestry, Pedroso could remain in school only until his thirteenth year when he had to seek work as a field laborer, carnival helper, and after migrating to Havana, to earn his living as a mechanic and carpenter. He began writing poetry in 1918 and became active in workers' politics, this new interest quickly becoming reflected in his poetry. Pedroso composed some Afro-cuban verse, including the poem "Hermano Negro." His first published verse on social themes saw print in the journal *Avance* (1927) and bore the title: "Salutación fraterna al taller mecánico."

His first "Chinese" poems were published in the volume *Nosotros* (1933) as "Dos poemas chinos." In 1935 he spent six months in jail as a political prisoner along with his offending colleagues of the journal *Masas,* Juan Marinello and J. M. Valdés Rodriguez. The tide turned briefly, however, in the early 1940's when he was named Minister of Education.

Honored by many and specifically praised by Guillén as one of the most solid and serious poets of America, Pedroso was enabled to visit China in 1964 and became recognized as one of the leading worker-poets of the new Cuba.

The last lines of Pedroso's "Opinions of the New Student" offer an example of his work:

En la llama de ahora
cocciono impaciente la droga de manaña;
quiero profundamente aspirar la nueva
época
en mi ancha pipa de jade.
Una inquietud curiosa ha insomnizado
mis ojos oblicuos.
Y para otear más hondo el horizonte,
salto sobre la vieja muralla del pasado. . .

Yo fui hasta ayer ceremonioso y pacifico

Writings: Poetry: *La ruta de Bagdad y otros poemas,* Havana, 1918; *Las canciones de ayer (1924-1926),* 1926; *Nosotros. Poemas.* Havana, 1938; *Antologia poética (1918-1938),* Havana, Municipio de la Habana, 1939; *Más allá canta el mar. Poema de Regino Pedroso* (first prize: Premio Nacional de poesia, 1938), Havana, En la Verónica, Imp. de Manuel Altolaguirre, 1939; *Bolivar; sinfonia de libertad, poema,* Havana, P. Fernández, 1945; *Los dias tumultuosos,* 1950; *El ciruelo de Yan Pei Fu; poemas chinos,* Havana, 1955; *Poemas, antologia,* Havana, Unión Nacional de Escritores y Artistas de Cuba, 1966.

Biographical/Critical Sources: Ildefonso Pereda Valdéz, *Lo negro y lo mulato en la poesia cubana,* Montevideo, Ediciones Ciudadela, 1970.

PEGUERO, Luis José

b. ca. 1732, Bani, Dominican Republic;
d. ca. 1792.
Poet, autobiographer, historian.

Peguero was one of the founders of Bani in the valley of Peravia, the natal city of the beloved nineteenth century nationalist General Máximo Gómez, great companion of the Cuban poet-revolutionist José Marti. Though Peguero's creative works are few they have a strength and directness which makes them worth preserving.

Writings: all in ms: Autobiography: "Borradores autógrafos de Luis José Peguero, residente en el valle de Bani, en su hato de San Francisco y el Rosario de la Isla Española de Santo Domingo, Año 1763."

Prose and Verse: "Notas, apuntes y versos." (Some of the poetry is given in Rodriguez Demorizi's *Poesia popular dominicana,* pp. 110-116.

History: "Historia de la conquista de la Isla Española," written 1762-63.

Biographical/Critical Sources: E. Rodriguez Demorizi's "El primer escritor de Bani," in *Bahoruco,* No. 274 (November 1935); Fr. Cipriano de Utrera's *La familia de Máximo Gómez,* S. Domingo, 1929, p. 58; E. Rodriguez Demorizi's *Poesia popular dominicana,* 1938, 2nd ed., S. Domingo, UCMM, 1973.

PELLERANO AMECHAZURRA, Fernando

b. 1899, Dominican Republic; d. 1933.
Playwright.

Fernando was the son of the poet Arturo Pellerano Castro.

Writings: Plays: *El más fuerte* (comedy of social manners); *Grandeza efimera; En la casa del loco; Los defensores del pueblo;* and *Un cobarde;* all performed but unpublished except *El más fuerte* which saw print in 1928.

PELLERANO CASTRO, Arturo Bautista

(pseudonym: **Byron**)

b. March 13, 1865, Curacao; d. May 5, 1916, Santo Domingo, Dominican Republic.
Poet, autobiographer, playwright.

Pellarano studied under Padre Billini at the Colegio de San Luis Gonzaga, and in 1880 entered the Escuela Normal founded by Eugenio Maria de Hostos. Pellerano's plays reflected much of the new "realism" of the European theatre of Ibsen and others.

Writings: Plays: *Fuerzas contrarias,* first performed, 1892, at the National Theatre; *La Repúblicana; Antonia,* performed, 1895, by the Roncoroni Company; *De mala entraña,* 1902; *De la vida,* performed, 1912, by Virginia Fabregas Company, and major scenes published in review *Ateneo.*

Poetry: *La última cruzada,* 1888; *Criollas,* 1907, 2nd ed., as *Criollas de casa,* 1927; *Fuerzas, corrida de sortijas* (verse romance).

Autobiography: *Autobiografia.*

Biographical/Critical Sources: Max Henriquez Ureña's *Panorama histórico de la literatura dominicana,* 2nd ed., S. Domingo, Postigo, 1965, pp. 239-240; J. Balaguer's *Historia de la literatura dominicana,* 5th ed., S. Domingo, Postigo, 1970, pp. 242-243.

PENA Y REINOSO, Manuel de Jesús de

b. December 2, 1834, Licey, Dominican Republic; d. August 2, 1915, Havana, Cuba.
Poet, storywriter, critic, journalist, teacher.

Manuel Peña took an active part in the revolt at Santiago of July 7, 1857 against President Buenaventura Báez. He was a very good friend of the liberal poet Félix Maria del Monte and Peña published most of his poetry in the patriotic journals of the day. He was still a fervent supporter of liberal positions in 1876 and worked for the government of Ulises Francisco Espaillat as the Minister of Interior. He also took a personal military part in the Cuban revolt "de los diez años," beginning in 1868.

Peña's poetry reflects his arduous, combative nature, but it increasingly reflected thought rather than inspiration. His *Rasgos épicos,* composed in 1892 to commemorate the 400 years since Columbus' first voyage, is an "obra de reflexion más que de inspiración; de maestro, antes que de poeta," in the worlds of critic Max Henriquez Ureña.

Peña helped found the journal *El*

Dominicano and was head of many educational institutions, including the Colegio Central of Santo Domingo, and in 1902 he was named head of the Escuela Normal de Santiago de los Caballeros. His critical essays on Galván's "Enriquillo" and the "Fantasias Indigenas" of José Joaquin Pérez are considered of very high quality.

After many exiles because of his political beliefs and actions, Peña in 1904 entered permanent exile in Cuba.

Writings: Stories: "El calorico y la luz," "El tocoloro," "Las dos palmas," "El color azul" and others in various journals along with his miscellaneous poetry.

Rhetoric: *Lecciones de análisis lógico y puntuación,* Santiago, Cuba, 1883.

Criticism: *Estudio critico sobre "Enriquillo,"* 1897.

General: *Espiritu de la masoneria simbólica,* Santiago, Cuba, 1882; and *Lectura hecha en la primera investidura de maestros del Colegio Central de Santo Domingo,* 1896.

Biographical/Critical Sources: J. Balaguer's *Historia de la literatura dominicana,* 1970, pp. 156-164.

PENSON, César Nicolás

b. January 22, 1855, Santo Domingo, Dominican Republic; d. October 29, 1901, Santo Domingo.
Poet, storywriter, essayist, journalist.

Penson was the prime mover in establishing the study of Dominican folklore and popular speech and he also was an early student of colonial architecture in the islands. He founded the first daily newspaper in the Republic, *El Telegrama,* August 7, 1882. In January, 1883 he founded another journal, *El Diario del Ozama,* and earlier the publishing house or press, El Pueblo.

He was a strong supporter of Salomé Ureña and her efforts to establish the first high school for women in the country, the Instituto de Señoritas, November 3, 1881, and he also taught there. As a major poet of the group "Los Amigos del Pais" he helped organize many literary conferences and supported the review *El Estudio,* and put out editions of various poets, including Salomé Ureña (*Poesias*), Manuel Rodriguez Objio (also entitled *Poesias*) and the *Historia de Santo Domingo* of Antonio del Monte y Tejada.

Penson also helped found the "Amigos del Adelanto," a popular education group and for a time he edited its journal *La Idea,* beginning June 3, 1875.

Writings: Play: *Los viejos verdes* (comedy), unpublished, but composed in 1875; original in Rodriguez Demorizi's personal library.

Folktales: *Cosas añejas: La hermandad de las ánimas y el juego de San Andrés,* 1891, in book form, but first published in *El Telegrama,* 1889, and in 1972 edition, Santo Domingo, Taller, with introduction by José Alcántara Almánzar (with two printings in 1974 and one more in 1976).

Criticism: *Reseña histórico-critica de la poesia en Santo Domingo,* 1892.

Scholarship: *Compendio de las partes de la*

oración francesa; "Anotaciones al Tapado," published in the review, *Letras y Ciencias,* Santo Domingo, 1892, pp. 218-227.

In ms: stories in groups entitled: "Costumbres antiguas y modernas," "Costumbras nacionales y tradiciones," and "Costumbres y episodios de Santo Domingo"; "Biografías de dominicanos ilustres"; "La Escuela de Antaño."

Biographical/Critical Sources: Eugenio Polanco y Velásquez, "Penson," in *El Lápiz,* S. Domingo (May 4, 1891); a review of *Cosas Añejas,* in *Letras y Ciencias,* S. Domingo, (1893), p. 374; article by Raphael A. Deligne about Penson's poetry, "La víspera del combate," in *Letras y Ciencias* (1896), p. 906; another review of *Cosas Añejas* in *El Cable,* San Pedro de Macorís (March 28 and 29, 1940); review of *Cosas Añejas* by Federigo García Godoy in *Letras y Ciencias,* No. 48 (March 1894); M. A. Machado's "C. N. Penson" in *La Cuna de América,* S. Domingo, No. 42 (1904); E. R. D.'s "Penson, traductor de Manzoni," in *Cuadernos dominicanos de cultura,* S. Domingo, No. 25 (1945); Gustavo Penson's "Licenciado César Nicolás Penson, rasgos biográficos," in *La Nación,* S. Domingo, (August 16 and 19, 1940), based on autobiographical notes left behind by C. N. Penson; J. Balaguer's *Historia de la literatura dominicana,* 5th ed., S. Domingo, Postigo, 1970, pp. 164-167.

PEQUENO, Pedro Néstor

b. ca. 1838, Cuba.
Playwright.

Pequeño's work is of importance historically, for it dealt with Afro-Cubans in a period just beginning to be interested in the folk and African ingredients of Cuban culture.

Writings: Plays: (written with Francisco Fernández): *El negro Cheche o veinto años después,* Tercerea parte de *Los negros catedráticos* (1 act musical), Havana, Imp. La Tropical, 1868, premiered Teatro Variedades de la Habana, July 26, 1868, by the Compañia de Bufos Habaneros; *Músico, poeta y loco* (1 act verse musical), Havana, Imp. Militar, 1872, 2nd ed., 1892 (see entry for Francisco Fernández for details on *Los negros catedráticos*).

PERDOMO Y HEREDIA, Josefa Antonia

(pseudonym: **"Laura"**)
b. June 13, 1834, Santo Domingo, Dominican Republic; d. May 25, 1896.
Poet.

Josefa Perdomo was influenced by her uncle Manuel de Jesús Heredia, also a poet, most of her verse was originally published in *El Oasis,* a journal of the Sociedad "Amantes de las Letras" and a few other literary periodicals of her day, and usually signed "Laura." Balaguer said she was a soul overwhelmed with feeling and her religious poems are full of the ecstasy of emotion and dedication to the love of God as in "A Dios, soneto."

A una débil mujer, ¡Oh Dios clemente!
a quien el hado con furor oprime,
hasta tu solio espléndido y sublime
alzar le es dado su clamor ardiente.

Biographical/Critical Sources: J. Balaguer's *História de la literatura dominicana,* S. Domingo, Postigo, 1970, pp. 137-141; José Dubeau, *Liceo de Puerto Plata,* 1896 (Dubeau comments on Perdomo's work).

PERDOMO Y SOSA, Apolinar

b. 1882, Dominican Republic; d. 1918.
Poet, playwright.

Perdomo's work was extremely sensuous and, like Fabio Fiallo, he is considered one of the finest of the Dominican poets. But, Perdomo is natural, simple, whereas Fiallo is courtly, refined. Generally his work is lyrical love poetry, and only occasionally does the civil strife of his troubled homeland intrude in his verse.

Writings: Poetry: *Cantos a Apolo,* S. Domingo, Rafael V. Montalvo, editor, 1923; 2nd ed., 1941.

Plays: *Cuento de amor,* performed 1917; *En la hora del dolor,* parts published but play was never performed.

Biographical/Critical Sources: J. Balaguer's *Historia de la literatura dominicana,* 5th ed., S. Domingo, Postigo, 1970, pp. 247-249.

PEREZ, José Joaquin

b. April 27, 1845, Santo Domingo, Dominican Republic; d. April 6, 1900. Poet, journalist, lawyer, diplomat.

Although not of a combative nature, Pérez wrote poetry always nationalistic and calling for independence. Forced into exile, he continued to plea his country's cause for a brief period, and on returning to Dominica he served as Minister of Justicia, Fomento e Instrucción Pública in the short-lived administration of his old friend and fellow poet, Francisco Gregorio Billini, President of the Republic, 1884-1885.

Pérez' *Fantasias indigenas* was one of the earliest poems to treat of the Indian theme and possibly the finest, with its "set" poems on various topics and/or focussed on individual Indian leaders.

Writings: Poetry: *Obra poética,* S. Domingo, UNPHU, 1972,; and prose poems: *Fantasias indigenas,* 1877, 1937; *La industria agricola (Oda),* 1882; *La lira de J. J. Pérez* (most of his verse), S. Domingo, Imp. de J. R. Vda. Garcia, sucesores, 1928; *J. J. Pérez,* S. Domingo, Publicación de la UNPHU., 1970; *Poesias varias* (1896-1900), and verse in various reviews and newspapers.

Translation: *Versiones del poeta inglés Thomas Moore (1871-1896).*

Biographical/Critical Sources: Max Henriquez Ureña's *Panorama histórico de la literatura dominicana,* 2 vols., S. Domingo, Libreria Dominicana, 1965; pp. 181-184, which included extracts of Pérez's "La vuelta al hogar," written in 1874, and some discussion of *Fantasias indigenas,* pp. 284-286 in Vol. II; J. Balaguer's *Historia de la literatura dominicana,* 5th ed., S. Domingo, Postigo, 1970, pp. 111-119.

PEREZ ALFONSECA, Ricardo

b. 1892, Dominican Republic; d. 1950. Poet.

Pérez was a member of the "Postumista" group and ever elegant, sceptical, searching in his poetry, seeking the telling phrase, the singing line. One of his best works, *Mármoles y lirios* (1909), saw publication when Pérez was only 17 years old, and is the first known "free verse" in Dominican poetry. He was a close friend of Rubén Darío, of Fabio Fiallo and of Gastón Deligne.

Rubén Darío, the great Nicaraguan poet, ended his "A Ricardo Pérez Alfonseca" written in Paris, 1914:

Haz tus versos de noche, haz tus versos
de nieve
y, meditando en lo que la vida te inspira,
deluida en la aurora y en la tarde suspira,
con el dáctil y con la danza leve.

Writings: Poetry: *Mármoles y lirios,* 1909; *Ritmos y aspectos,* 1925; *Nueva infancia,* 1930; *Palabras de mi madre y otros poemas* (selected poems from earlier volumes and new works by the author), date unknown.

Essays: "El último Evangelio" and 'Juan de Nueva York o el Antinarcismo."

Biographical/Critical Sources: F. A. Mota Medrano, *Relieves alumbrados,* S. Domingo, 1971, pp. 127-149.

PEREZ CABRAL, Pedro Andrés

b. ca. 1910, Dominican Republic.
Novelist.

Pérez was a member of the La Cueva group whose senior members were Juan Bosch, Ramón Marrero Aristy and Andrés Francisco Requeña. His one published novel, *Jengibre,* attacked the Trujillo tyranny in guarded terms.

Writings: Novel: *Jenjibre,* San Pedro de Macoris, 1940; "Del suelo" (72 pp.), unpub.

PEREZ LICAIRAC, Horacio

b. 1895, Dominican Republic; d. 1958.
Playwright, economist, teacher.

Horacio Pérez has been a professor of economics and a director of economic research in the Central Bank of his country. His one play, *La isla de la leyenda,* 1939, was a very refined and highly personal expression and his poetry similarly very lyrical and subjective.

Writings: Play: *La isla de la leyenda,* 1939.

Poetry: *Trazos en la arena y otros poemas,* date unknown; and poetry in various journals.

Finance: *Aspectos de la libertad financiera,* 1946; *La heredad reintegrada,* 1953; *Sintesis de legislación mercantil y aduanera,* 1958.

PEREZ LOSADA, José

b. 1879, Cádiz, Spain; d. September 24, 1937, San Juan.
Novelist, storywriter, playwright, editor.

Pérez Losado emigrated permanently to Puerto Rico in 1895 and was for a considerable period editor of *El Imparcial,* and was an active writer of criticism, reviews, novels and plays. He is remembered especially as a leader of the Spanish emigré group in Puerto Rico and for the generous encouragement he gave to young writers.

Writings: Novels: *La Patulea,* San Juan, Boletin, 1908, (308 p.); *El Manglar,* 1909, San Juan, Boletin Mercantil, (313 p., second part of *La patulea); La feria del luzo,* details unknown; *Trazos de Sombra,* San Juan, 1903; *Alma negra* (novela relámpago), in *Trazos de sombra,* San Juan, Tip. Boletin Mercantil, 1903.

Plays: *Sangre mora* (1 act, 4 scenes, written with Luis Díaz Caneja), performed San Juan, 1906; *La Cantaora* (1 act farce, prose and verse), performed 1907; *La crisis del amor* (3 act comedy), performed April 23, 1912; *La Rabia* (1 act), performed 1912; *Los primeros frios* (3 acts, awarded first prize in the Ateneo Puertorriqueño competition), performed, 1914; *La vida rota* (3 acts comedy), performed in the Teatro Robledo de Gijón (Spain, 1918); *El año de la guerra o Los sobrinos del Tio Sam* (satire, written with Luis Díaz Caneja), performed January 24, 1919; *El viaje de los congresistas* (3 acts, written with Díaz Caneja), performed 1919; *La vida es ácida o Las industrias de la*

Prohibición (3 act comedy), performed 1920; *Teatro Puertorriqueño. Tomo primero* (with) *La crisis del amor. La vida es ácida, La Rabia,* San Juan, Tip. Real Hermanos, 1925, (264 p.).

Biographical/Critical Sources: Alfonso Camin, "José Pérez Lozado," in *Indice,* No. 19 (San Juan, October 1930); Rafael Martinez Nadal, review of *La Patulea* in *Tempraneras,* San Juan, 1908, pp. 83-85.

PEREZ PIERRET, Antonio

b. 1885, San Juan, Puerto Rico; d. 1937, San Juan.
Poet.

Pérez, the son of a Spanish father and a Dominican mother, studied in Puerto Rico and Spain (taking a law degree at the University of Oviedo). Pérez spent some time in England in travel and further study. There he became somewhat acquainted with British poetry, something relatively rare in that period, and his work obviously reflected some of this broader experience. After more travel on the continent, Pérez returned home for a career, first in the law and then in finance, but he kept alive his love for literature and was a close friend of the poet Luis Lloréns Torres. He was an active member of the circle supporting the *Revista de las Antillas.*

Though primarily a symbolist, Pérez sought a formal beauty—almost an objective treatment of emotions, but also a highly musical verse. His major subjects were love, death and solitude, but much of his work also concerned local or Hispanic-American themes and pre-occupations. His long, prose-like lines appeared to some as hardly poetic, not at all verse. Guerra Mondragón finds him ". . .poeta fuerte y sano, que gasta coche, . . . marcha francamente hacia la energia poética." And Ferrer says he is surely no madrigal singer—rather "un gimnasta de prodigioso impulso. . ."

"Me Pegaso" begins:

Y monto un anglo-árabe de recia contextura,
de finas cañas ágiles y de alongado cuello.
La rama de los nervios rubrica su figura
y es ridiculo y raro a fuerza de ser bello.

And the poem goes on in an energetic struggle of man against horse and word against word which images the action.

Writings: Poetry: *Bronces,* San Juan, Biblioteca Américana, Edit. Antillana, 1914, San Juan, Edit. Coqui, 1968, foreword by Miguel Guerra Mondragón; *El modernismo en Puerto Rico,* San Juan, 1967; *Antologia,* San Juan, Ateneo Puertorriqueño, 1959.

Biographical/Critical Sources: See foreword by M. Guerra Mondragón to *Bronces,* 1914; Rafael Ferrer, "Perfiles: Antonio Pérez-Pierret," in *Revista de las Antillas* (August 1914); Enrique A. Laguerre, *La poesia modernista en Puerto Rico,* San Juan, 1969, pp. 109-116; Esther Feliciano de Mendoza, *Antonio Pérez Pierret: vida y obra,* San Juan, 1968; Sócrates Nolasco, *Escritores de Puerto Rico,* Manzanillo, Cuba, 1953 (emphasis on Canales).

PEREZ TELLEZ, Emma

b. 1901, Cartagena, Spain.
Poet.

Pérez arrived in Cuba as a child and lived there the rest of her life. A "postmodernista," she has written much for children, her work filled with social concern.

Writings: Autobiographical Poetry: *Elegia por Luisa Téllez,* Havana, 1944; *Haz en la niebla,* Havana, 1946.

Poetry: *Poemas de la mujer del preso,* 1932; *Nina y el viento de manaña,* 1937; *Una mujer canta en su isla,* 1937; *Para otra madre de mis isla,* 1944; *Canciones a Stalin,* 1944; *Isla con sol,* 1945.

PEREZ Y MONTES DE OCA, Julia

b. 1839, Cobre District, Cuba; d. 1875, Artemisa, Cuba.
Poet.

Sister of the more famous poet Luisa de Zambrana (Pérez y Montes de Oca), Julia was quiet with a fine sensibility and melancholic view which soon manifested itself in such poems as "Abril" and "Al campo," "La tarde" and "A un lego." Her constant battle against tuberculosis made her a sceptic about life and her late poem "Desesperación" has these lines:

¡O tiempo, tiempo amarga de la vida!
¡Qué lento te deslizas para mi!
No me des a beber más desengaños;
corre veloz, que es hora de morir. . .

She moved to Havana in 1860, but after a brief period in the intellectual world in which her sister Luisa was already a major figure, she withdrew, to die in her 35th year in 1875.

Writings: Poetry: *Poesias,* Barcelona, 1887, edited by Domingo Figarola-Caneda (included by him in the series "Biblioteca de la Ilustración Cubana"; *Poesias* was republished in Vol. XIV of the collection *Los Zambranos,* edited by Malleén Zambrana, Havana, 1958.

PEREZ Y MONTES DE OCA (De Zambrana), Luisa

b. 1835, Cobre District, Cuba; d. May 25, 1922.
Poet, novelist, essayist.

Raised in an isolated, rural home with only lower schooling, Luisa Pérez still manifested genuine poetic gifts as early as her sixteenth year. Her work naturally was based on rural themes and experiences as well as the intimate interiors of the heart and the family. Of a melancholic disposition, her loss of several children and of her husband, professor and critic Ramón Zambrana, after just eight years of marriage, led to an elegiac tone in all of her work.

At the death of her father, Joaquin Pérez Naranjo (in November, 1952), her mother and her children, including Luisa, removed to Santiago where the young poet came into contact with the lively spirits of the major metropolis. Her first published verses soon appeared in *El Orden* of Santiago and their favorable reception encouraged her to greater efforts. Her poetry appealed to the man who was soon to fall in love with her and would take her off as his wife to Havana. In the capital, Luisa flourished, and she soon published two novels, a new collection of poetry, and many miscellaneous essays and articles.

Widowed, she remained in Havana for a long period but closed her days in Regla. New poets and journalists and events followed in slow course and Luisa's work was gradually almost forgotten. But in 1918, the Ateneo de la Habana offered homage to "la poetisa olvidada" and many leading poets of the day were present at a special ceremony honoring her. A new edition of her works with many, many items dating after 1860, appeared in the 1920 edition. Two years later, she died, aged 87.

Writings: Poetry: *Poesias,* Santiago, Cuba, 1856 (but not circulated until 1857); *Poesias,* preface by Gertrudis de Avellaneda, Havana, 1860 (contains 22 of the original 50 of the first collection, plus many new ones on her married life, her young daughter, and other topics); *Poesias,* Havana, Imp. Siglo XX, 1920; and *Poesias,* edition "definitiva," edited and with notes by Malleén Zambrana, Havana, 1957, Vol. XI of the collection, *La Zambrana.*

Essay (Foreword) by Luisa Zambrana: to *Anatomia del corazón* of Teodoro Guerrero, Havana, 1867.

Novels: *Angélica y Estrella,* Havana, 1864; *La hija del verdugo,* in the collection *La Zambrana,* Vol. V, Havana, 1955; and *Angélica y Estrella* was republished in *La Zambrana,* Vol. XII, 1957. *La hija . . .* was first published in serial form in *Revista del Pueblo* (1865).

Biographical/Critical Sources: Max Henriquez Ureña, *Panorama histórico de la literatura cubana,* New York, 1963, pp. 307-318; *Luisa Pérez de Zambrana,* Conference papers and essays by Elias José Entralgo (editor), Havana, 1921 in *Sintesis Biografica,* Tomo II, Havana, P. Fernández, 1956; and foreword by Federico Garcia Copley (1829(?)-1894) to Pérez' first verse collection, *Poesias,* 1856. Also see Polly F. Harrison's "Images and Exile: The Cuban Woman and her Poetry," in *Revista Interamericana,* Vol. IV, No. 2, pp. 191-195.

PEREZ Y PEREZ, Carlos Federico

b. 1913, Dominican Republic; d. 1965.
Critic, novelist, teacher.

Pérez' *Evolución poética dominicana* won the Premio Nacional de Literatura Patria Nueva, 1956. (Sources disagree on birth year: Max Henríquez Ureña gives 1913, others 1900.)

Writings: Novel: *Juan Mientras la ciudad crecia,* Ciudad Trujillo, Imp. Arte y Cine, 1960, first published in *Quaderno Dominicanos de Cultura,* Vol. II, No. 15 (Nov. 1944).

Literary History: *Evolución poética dominicana,* 1956, Buenos Aires, Ed. Poblet, 1956; *La naturaleza en la novela hispanoamericana,* 1943.

Essay: *Experiencias de Martin Fierro,* 1957.

PEREZ Y RAMIREZ, Manuel Maria

b. 1781, Santiago, Cuba; 1853.
Poet.

Serving in the military forces fighting in Santo Domingo in 1796, Pérez came to know Zequiera and Rubalcava, but lacking the vocation quickly retired to an active life as a journalist, founding many journals. His poetry is generally considered inferior to that of his two friends. Known poems, some only in fragments, are "Emanuel," "El amigo reconciliado," and "El Pastor y al Eco."

PICHARDO, Francisco Javier

b. 1873, Cuba; d. 1941.
Poet.

Pichardo was conservative in his metrics and rhymes, essaying little, but clearly describing the common realities of life. His sonnet "Angelus" has a construction worker saying:

> *Señor, he trabajado durante todo el dia;*
> *aqui, sobre este andamio de pié, me halló la aurora,*
> *y aqui, bajo el incendio del sol, hora tras hora,*
> *en vano ha consumido me cuerpo su energia.*

Writings: Poetry: *Voces nómadas,* Havana, 1908.

Biographical/Critical Sources: Max Henriquez Ureña, *Panorama histórico de la literature cubana,* New York, 1963, pp. 288-289.

PICHARDO, Manuel Serafin

b. 1869, Cuba; d. 1937.
Poet, translator, editor, journalist.

Longtime director of the journal, *El Figaro,* Pichardo welcomed new currents of writing in his journal. Named diplomat to Spain in 1910, Pichardo gave up writing and his long announced volume "Credos y visiones" never appeared. (Sources disagree on birth year; Max Henriquez Ureña gives 1863.)

Writings: Poetry: *Canto a Villaclara,* Havana, Ruiz y Hno, 1907; *Cuba a la república, poema en dos cantos,* Havana, Tip. "El Figaro," 1902.

Journalism: *La ciudad blanca,* Havana, 1894 (about Washington, D. C.).

PICHARDO MOYA, Felipe

b. 1892, Cuba; d. 1957.
Poet, playwright, essayist.

Leading member of the Evasionist School led by Regino Boti y Barriero, Pichardo was an early user of Afro-Cuban color and rhythms. His "Poema de los cañaverales" is possibly his best of that period and reflects the slavist past. Both his verse dramas were published only in reviews. His three act play *Agüeybana* treats the Indian tragedy of Cuba and Cuban colonization, but his last play, *Esteros del Sur,* is set in the sugar plantations and mills of modern times.

Writings: Essays: "La comparsa," in *Gráfico,* 1916; "Filosofia del bronce."

Poetry: *Poema de los cañaverales* and *La zafra,* both Havana, 1926, in periodicals; *La ciudad de los espejos,* Camagüez, 1925.

Plays: *Alas que nacen. Farsa que quiere ser trágica,* Havana, in *Cuba Contemporánea,* Vol. 32 (1923), pp. 50-65; *La oración,* in *Revista Cubana* (2 act farce), written probably mid to late 1920's; *Agüeybana* (3 act tragedy), 1941; *Esteros del Sur.*

PICHARDO Y TAPIA, Esteban

b. 1799, Santiago de los Caballeros, Dominican Republic; d. 1879.
Poet, amateur historian, geographer and naturalist, lawyer.

Son of Lucas Pichardo y Zereceda and Rosa de Tapia y Saviñón, both from Santiago de los Caballeros, Esteban Picharda lived most of his life in Cuba where his parents had fled early in the nineteenth century.

Pichardo's novel *El fatalista* was the first considerable work of long fiction to be published in the Dominican Republic probably in the 1850's, and recalled the Cuban world of the early nineteenth century when he first arrived there as a member of a family fleeing the Haitian invasion of Santo Domingo. After portraying life in a genuine fashion, Pichardo ends his novel by turning his hero into a pirate and otherwise reducing the work to a decadent romantic piece.

Writings: Novel: *El fatalista,* Dominican Republic, 185?, and in Havana, Soler, 1866.

Poetry: *Miscelánea poética,* Havana, 1822, 1828 (includes an essay on the poetic arts).

History: *Notas cronológicas sobre la isla de Cuba,* Havana, 1828.

Geography: *Geografia de la Isla de Cuba,* Havana, 1854; *Gran carta geotopográfica de Cuba,* with a *Memoria justificativa,* completed in 1874, unpublished.

Religious History: *Autos acordados de la Audiencia de Puerto Principe (Camagüey),* Havana, 1834; new ed., Havana, 1840.

Dictionary: *Diccionario provincial casi razonado de voces cubanas,* 4 editions, 1836, 1849, 1862, 1875; the 1875 edition, with additions, notes, and an introduction—all by Esteban Rodriguez Herrera, with *Picarda novisimo,* published in Havana, 1957, as 5th ed.

PILDAIN, Pablo

b. 1848, Cuba; d. date unknown.
Playwright, critic, actor.

Pildain was a very popular actor, especially in roles in plays by Avellaneda and Luaces as well as the classic Calderón de la Barca and José Echegaray. He recited in the formal old school as he stood tall and impressive. Despite his early successes he died poor and forgotten.

Writings: Plays: *Maria* (3 acts, verse), Havana, Imp. La Tropical, 1866; *Tres contra una* (1 act musical), Havana, Villa, 1866, premiered October 21, 1866, in the Sociedad del Pilar, Havana.

PINA, Ramón

b. 1819, Havana, Cuba; d. 1861, Madrid.
Playwright, novelist.

Piña modeled his work carefully on the national and internationally famous romantic writers but had little genuine flair. His several plays, however, were well received in their first performances.

Writings: Novels: *Jerónimo el honrado,* Madrid, 1857; *Historia de un bribón dichoso,* Madrid, M. Tello, 1860.

Plays: *No quiero ser Conde* (2 act comedy), Havana, Palmer, 1838; *Una sobrina en España* (3 act comedy), Havana, 1838; *Las equivocaciones* (3 act comedy), Havana, Torres, 1848; *Dios los cria y ellos se estorban* (comedy), Havana, 1848.

Biographical/Critical Sources: Eusebio Guiteras, "Historia de un bribón dichoso," review, in *Revista Habanera* (Havana), I (1861), pp. 27-30; Juan J. Remos, "Notas sobre Ramón Piña," in *Micrófono* (Havana), 1937, pp. 218-221.

PINERA, Virgilio

b. 1914, Cárdenas (Matanzas), Cuba.
Poet, critic, novelist, playwright, storywriter.

After early residence in Guanabacoa and Camagüez, Piñera moved to Havana where he took a degree in philosophy at the University of Havana. In 1942 he founded the brief-lived journal *Poeta.* After many years in Argentina, Piñera returned to Cuba after the Castro revolution to write for the stage and to be an editor for the journal *Ciclón.* In 1963 he published his first work in Havana, the novel *Pequeñas maniobras* (his second novel). He is presently a director of the publishing house Ediciones R. and has published many articles in Latin American journals. Some of his work has been translated into French, English and Italian.

Piñera's collection of stories, *Cuentos frios,* published in Buenos Aires in 1956 are Kafkaesque, disturbing, circular—and the narrator is an eventual victim of inexplicable plots.

Writings: Novels: *La carne de René,* Buenos Aires, 1952; *Pequeñas maniobras,* Havana, *(Revolución),* 1963; *Presiones y diamantes,* Havana, Unión, 1969; *La vida entera,* Havana, Unión, 1969.

Stories: *Cuentos frios,* Buenos Aires, Edit. Losada, 1956; translations into French (Paris, Gallimard), and into Italian (Milan, Feltrinelli); and stories in several anthologies, including *Writers in the New Cuba,* E. M. Cohen, ed., 1967 and *Poesia y prosa,* 1944; *La isla en peso,* Havana, 1943; *Poesia y prosa,* Havana, 1944; *Cuentos,* Havana, Unión, 1964; *El que vino a salvarme,* Buenos Aires, Sudamericana, 1970.

Poetry: *Las furias,* Havana, 1941.

Essays: *Presiones y diamantes,* Havana, 1967.

Plays: *Electra Garrigó,* performed in Havana, 1945, published in *Teatro completo,* Havana, 1960, 2nd ed., Havana, Revolución, 1962; as was *Falsa alarma,* which had a Havana production in 1949, and first published in *Origenes,* Nos. 21, 22 (1949), and published in *Teatro Cubano en un acto* (Rine Leal, ed.), Havana, Revolución, 1963; *Jesús,* performed 1948; *Los siervos* (about Communist party), details not known; *Aire frio,* Havana, *La Milagrosa,* 1959; *Dos viejos pánicos,* 1st ed., Havana, Casa de las Américas, 1968 and 2nd ed., Buenos Aires, Centro Editor de América Latina, 1968.

Biographical/Critical Sources: Luis F. González-Cruz' "Virgilio Piñera y el teatro del absurdo en Cuba," *Mester* No. 5, (Los Angeles November 1974), pp. 51-57.

PINEYRO, Enrique

b. 1839, Cuba; d. 1911.
Critic, biographer, literary historian.

Piñeyro studied at the Colegio del Salvador, Havana, under the famous José Luz y Caballero.

Writings: Biography: *Morales Lemus y la revolución de Cuba,* New York, 1871; republished in *Biografias Americanas,* Paris, 1907.

PITA RODRIGUEZ, Félix

b. 1909, Bejúcal, Cuba.
Poet, storywriter, journalist.

Pita's childhood was mostly spent in France, Italy and Spain and he only took up residence in Cuba in 1939, becoming an active participant in various literary movements and a co-founder of the "vanguardista" journal *Atuei.* A contributor of radio pieces and editor of the Havana Sunday supplement *Hoy,* Pita has served as president of the literature section of the *Unión,* the organization's organ of expression. After the advent of Castro, Pita travelled to China, North Vietnam and prepared a volume of his journalistic pieces on his travels for the press. His work has appeared in many journals and collections.

Pita's poetry is often surrealistic but also most often deeply concerned with Cuba's social and political problems. He fought on the loyalist-republican side during the Spanish Civil War in 1936. He deliberately eschewed an elegant or poetic diction and sought a colloquial, low-toned, conversational effect of his work. He declared he wanted "De piedra pura, limpia, desnuda, el poema," and his "Balada para la alegria de un poeta muerto" [Paul Fort] is an example of his extreme sensitivity to nuance and sincerity of emotion."

Pita has written one play, *El relievo,* showing the Chinese battling against the Japanese in the Second World War, and has published two collections of stories. The second, *Tobias,* contains neo-realistic tales.

Writings: Poetry: *Cárcel de fuego,* Havana, 1948; *Las crónicas, poesia bajo consigna,* first published by La Tertulia, 1961, with 3rd ed., Havana, Empresa Consolidada de Artes Gráficas, 1963; and verse in many journals and anthologies, including Nathaniel Tarn's *Con Cuba,* New York, 1969; also, his verse appears in the mixed collection: *Poemas y cuentos,* Havana, 1965.

Play: *El relievo,* details of publication or performance now known.

Genre(?): *Elogio de Marco Polo,* Havana, UNEAC, 1974.

Stories: *San Abul de Montecallado,* Mexico, 1946; *Tobias,* Havana, 1954 (translated by Zoila Nelken was the title story "Tobias" in *SSLA,* pp. 95-110; *La noches,* Havana, La Tertulia, 1964; *Poemas y cuentos,* Havana, Unión, 1965; *Historia tan natural,* Havana, Unión, 1971; also, *Esta larga tarea de aprendar a morir y otros cuentos,* Godfrey, Illinois, Monticello College Press, 1960 and *Cuentos completos,* Havana, Unión, 1963.

Biographical/Critical Sources: Max Henriquez Ureña, *Panorama histórico de la literatura cubana,* New York, 1963, pp. 383-384, and others.

PITA, Santiago (Capitan)

b. early 18th century, Cuba; d. 1755.
Playwright, military officer.

Pita's once very popular play, *El Principe jardinero y fingido Cloridano,* a three act comedy, was first performed in 1791. Though apparently published in Havana, it was stamped as being printed and published in Valencia, Spain, and written by a "Santiago Pita," despite which it long was considered to be the work of Fray José Rodriguez Ucares. Max Henriquez Ureña summarized the case for Pita's authorship which now appears unarguable. Pita's play, Cuba's first known, is loosely adopted from the Italian original of Giacinto Andrea Cicognini's Florentine one. (Cicognini flourished 1606-1660.)

Writings: Play: *El principe jardinero y fingido Cloridano* ("comedia en tres actos por un ingegnio de la Habana"), Valencia, Oficina de José Ferrer de Orga, 1820; also other editions: Barcelona, 1840; Havana, Imp. Cubana, 1842, and revised edition edited by J. J. Ramos and Enrique Larrondo for "Edición de la revista Ideas," Havana, Imp. Molina, 1929, (37 p.); 1951 edition edited by José Juan Arrom, Havana, Sociedad Económica de Amigos del

Pais, and recent edition by Consejo Nacional de Cultura, Havana, 1963. For brief summary of this play and its nine known editions, see Max Henriquez Ureña's *Panorama histórico de la literatura cubana,* New York, 1963, pp. 61-65.

PLACIDO

(pseudonym for **Gabriel de la CONCEPCION VALDES**)

PLANAS Y SAINZ, Juan Manuel

b. 1877, Cienfuegos (Las Villas), Cuba; d. 1963, Havana.

After schooling in Santa Clara, Planas took an engineering degree at the University of Liège (Belgium) in 1906 and a second degree at the University of Havana, 1913. He founded the (Cuban) Oceanographic Society and the (Cuban) Geographical Society and was a member of many technical learned societies in Cuba and elsewhere.

Planas wrote two science fiction works influenced by then popular Jules Verne, and one vaguely historical novel, *La cruz de Lieja* (1923), and one recent work *El sargazo de oro.*

Writings: Novels: *La corriente del golfo,* 1922; *Flor de manigua,* 1926; and *La cruz de Lieja,* 1923; *El sargazo de oro (El vellocino verde),* 1959: all published in Havana.

POEY Y AGUIRE, Andrés

b. 1826, Cuba; d. 1911.
Novelist, humanist, scientist, philosopher.

Son of the eminent scientist-scholar Felipe y Aloy (1799-1891), Andrés himself was a leading Cuban naturalist and philosopher and writer of one undistinguished novel. He spent much of his life in the United States and Europe and wrote French as well as he did Spanish.

Writings: Novel: *La folie amoreuse,* 1889, republished with title *La crise,* 1890.

Philosophy: *Le Positivisme,* 1876; *Catálogo metódico de las aves de la Isla de Cuba,* 1848; *Bibliographie positiviste et critique,* 1871; *M. Littré et Auguste Comte,* 1879.

POGOLOTTI, Marcelo

b. 1902, Cuba.,
Novelist, storywriter, essayist, painter.

A fine stylist, Pogolotti's painterly background is obvious in his distinct dramatic scenes.

Writings: Novels: *La ventana de mármol,* 1941; *Estrella Molina,* 1946; *Los apuntes de Juan Pinto,* 1951, all Havana; *El caserón de Cerro,* Santa Clara, Universidad de las Villas, 1961 (never published before, though written in 1940).

Stories: *Segundo remanso,* Havana, 1948; and stories in a combined volume with *Los apuntes de Juan Pinto,* 1951; also *Detrás del muro; cuentos-novela,* Mexico, Costa-Amic, 1963.

Essays: in various periodicals, and in *Los apuntes de Juan Pinto,* along with the novel and stories.

POO, José de

b. 1831 or 1833, Havana, Cuba; d. 1898.
Playwright.

Poo's work is historically important, but not of serious merit otherwise.

Writings: Plays: *El huérfano de Lucca* (3 act comedy, verse), Havana, Villa, 1864; *Casarse con la familia* (3 act comedy, verse), Havana, Imp. Villa y Hno, 1864, premiered Teatro Tacón, 1864; unpublished: *Luchas del corazón; Corona de león; Dios lo ha querido; En nombre del rey; La daga del rey.*

PORRATA DORIA DE APONTE, Carmen
(pseudonym: **Carmen DEMAR**)

PORRATA DORIA DE RINCO, Providencia
(pseudonym for **Alma RUBENS**)

PORTUONDO, José Antonio
b. 1911, Santiago, Cuba.
Essayist, critic, poet, literary historian.

Portuondo wrote Afro-Cuban poetry in the 1930's, most of it based on traditional negro folksongs, but he is primarily considered a historian and critic of literature.

Writings: Literary Histories: *Proceso de la cultura cubana,* Havana, 1939; *El contenido social de la literatura cubana,* Mexico, El Colegio de Mexico, 1944; *La historia y las generaciones,* Santiago de Cuba, 1958; *Bosquejo histórico de las letras cubanas,* Havana, Edit. Nacional de Cuba, 1960; *El pensamiento vivo de Maceo,* Havana, Lex., n.d.

Poetry: in various journals: some poems published were "Rumba de la negra Pancha," "Mari Sabel," "Lance de Juruminga,' and "Firulitico." Collection: *Astrolabio,* Havana, Instituto Cubano del Libro, 1973.

Critical Essay: "La dramática neutralidad de Gertrudis Gómez de Avellaneda," *Revolución y Cultura,* No. 11 (no date), pp. 2-17.

PRUD'HOMME Y MADURO, Emilio
b. August 20, 1856, Puerta Plata, Dominican Republic; d. July 21, 1932.
Poet, lawyer, educator.

Prud'homme studied law at the Instituto Profesional and though he practiced his major interest was education. He was an innovator and reformer in the latter field and helped establish in Azua the "Escuela Perseverancia" and in 1895 in the capital, Santo Domingo, he founded the Liceo Dominicano. In 1902 he was named director of the Escuela Normal in his natal city of Puerto Plata.

Active in public affairs, Prud'homme was elected deputy from 1899 and served for three years and in 1916 for a period he was Secretary of State for Justice and Public Instruction under President Henriquez y Carvahal. In 1931 he became a judge on the Supreme Court.

His poetry was part of the revolutionary ferment, post-romantic in some ways, and influenced by the example and verse of Salomé Ureña. Prud'homme's work was never collected until after his death. His most important patriotic poems were: "A la juventud dominicana" (1878), "A mi patria" (1878), "El 16 de agosto" (1879), "A la patria" (1879), "Dejame soñar" (1883), "Gloria a la idea" (1884), "Salve" (1887), "La madre del porvenir" (1887), "Invocación y mensaje" (1923). His "American" poems were: "A Bolivar" (1883) and "Canto a América" (1889).

Writings: Poetry: some of his major psychological verse: "Canción" (1877); "La mariposa" (1879), "Hortensia y Fileno" (1879), "Flor del

campo y flores del alma" (1885), "Contrastes" (1894), "En la playa" (1908), "Mediodia" (1908), "En el campo" (1908), "Campestre" (1913), "Paisaje" (1914); and see above for patriotic verse; posthumous volume edited by his daughter Ana Emilia Prud'homme: *Mi libro azul* (Vol. I was his verse, Vol. II was miscellaneous prose), 19??.

Speech: *Discurso de inauguración del monumento que el I. Ayuntamiento de la Capital consagra al Maestro Reyes, autor del Himno Nacional,* 1911.

Biographical/Critical Sources: J. Balaguer's *Los proceres escritores,* Buenos Aires, 1971; Balaguer's *Historia de la literatura dominicana,* 5th ed., S. Domingo, Postigo, 1970, pp. 239-242.

POTTS, Renée

b. February 19, 1908, Havana, Cuba. Playwright, poet.

After local schooling concluding with a certificate as a teacher, Potts worked as a journalist on many reviews, including *La Mujer, Ellas, Grafos, Recortes* and dailies such as *Diario de la Marina, El Pais* and *El Mundo.* Her artistic bent has been critical and directed to the theatre and film for the most part, but she has published poetry, collected in *El Romancero de la Maestrilla,* which was awarded a prize by the Lyceum Femenino in 1936, and the more mature work of Fiesta Mayor, published in 1937.

She is also a well considered short-story writer, winning the first mention of the Premio Internacional Hernández Catá in 1953 with "La ventana y el puente" and the Premio Nacional Hernández Catá in 1955 with "Camino de herradura." Short pieces of hers have also appeared on television, including "Reina de diamante," and "Adelaida."

Her play *El amor del diablo,* winner of the Circulo de Bellas Artes in 1931, and *La Hopalandas* were early plays of hers to win esteem. Her *El Conquistador* won mention in the Concurso Nacional del Circulo de Belles Artes in 1935 and radiobroadcast by the Compañia de Pedro Boquet, and her farce *Una historieta de muñecos* the same year. *Cena de Navidad* had its premier in 1935. Plays about women were *Buen tiempo de amor,* 3 acts, written in 1934, and *Camila o la muñeca de cartón,* and *Imaginame infinita.*

Writings: Plays: *El amor del diablo; Las Hopalandas; El conquistador; Habrá guerra de nuevo; Habrá guerra mañana; Cocoa en el Paraiso,* 1951; *Domingo de Quasimodo* (3 acts), 1952 or 1953; *Los umbrales del arte* (3 act comedy); *Una historieta de muñecos; Cena de Navidad; Buen tiempo de amor; Camila o la muñeca de cartón; Imaginame infinita,* in *Teatro cubano contemporáneo,* Madrid, Aguilar, 1959, 1962.

Poetry: *El Romancero de la Maestrilla,* Havana, 1936; *Fiesta Mayor,* Havana, 1937.

Stories: in many journals.

Criticism: uncollected, published in various journals.

Biographical/Critical Sources: Introduction to her play, *Imaginame infinita,* published in *Teatro cubano contemporáneo,* Dolores Marti de Cid, editor, 2nd ed., Madrid, Aguilar, 1962.

POUS, Arquimedes

b. Cienfuegos, Cuba; d. 1925, Puerto Rico. Playwright.

Pous' literary works are in the farce genre and were widely popular in the island.

Writings: Plays: *Locuras europeas* (1 act musical comedy); *Dinora* (1 act farce); *Habana Barcelona Habana* (farce).

POVEDA Y ARMENTEROS, Francisco

(a.k.a. **"El Trovador Cubano"**)

b. 1796, Havana, Cuba; d. 1879 (or 1881).
Poet, playwright.

Poveda was born poor and remained poor, struggling against a poor education and the hardships of the uneducated at any time and of any place. Despite his handicaps, however, he wrote and published a great deal of verse in the popular journals of the day and saw into print at least five modest volumes of his spontaneous if "incorrect" and un-modish verse during his own lifetime. His one known play remains unpublished.

Once a very popular singer of Cuba's natural beauties, Poveda employed the romantic and popular modes and verse forms he learned on the street. Max Henriquez Ureña says, "Su poesia no es poesia genuinamente popular, sino poesia vulgar. Sus versos son desmañados." Despite these strictures, Poveda's use of colloquial terms and his at least partial concern with daily life did make him an early figure of some importance in the loose movement called "criollismo." ("Aplicarse a cosa o costumbre propia de los paises americanos: manjar criollo.") He was a genuine man of the people with only a rudimentary training in any area—which only bespeaks the more his crude but lively talent.

Writings: Poetry: *La guirnalda habanera,* 1830; *Las rosas de amor,* 1831; *El ramillete cubano; Tiple campesino; Poesias del Trovador Cubanao,* 1879; *Premios de cenáculo,* Havana, Ministerio de Educación, 1948.

Play: *El Peón de Bayamo* (comedy), unpublished.

Biographical/Critical Sources: Max Henriquez Ureña, *Panorama histórico de la literatura cubana,* New York, 1963.

POVEDA Y CALDERON, José Manuel

b. February 23, 1888, Santiago, Cuba; d. January 2, 1926, Manzanillo.
Poet, storywriter, essayist, translator, journalist, lawyer.

Poveda was the leader of the "modernist" school and director of the important Havana review *El Figaro* and of the journals *Heraldo de Cuba* and *La Nación.*

Juan Marinello said of him, "En el momento modernista fué lo negro juego entre preciosita y erudito. En nuestros dias ha servido para caracterizar, decorándolo, el trópico criollo y para decir—después de Frobenius el primitivismo deliciosa de la selva africana." His novel in manuscript, "Senderos de montana" and other unpublished works were burned by his widow, including a translation of Henri de Regnier's work and of the *Rimas byzantines* by Augusto de Armas.

Writings: Poetry: *Versos precursores,* Manzanillo, Cuba, Biblioteca Marti, Imp. "El Arte," 1917; and Havana, Organización Nacional de Bibliotecas Ambulantes y Populares, 1958.

Stories and Essays: *Proemios de cenáculo. Evocación de Poveda por Rafael Esténger,* Havana, Ministerio de Educación, Dirección de Cultura, 1948; collection of his prose in Francisco R. Argilagos *Prosas selectas* (estudios americanistas), Havana, Imp. "El Siglo XX," 1918.

Lecture: "La Musica en el Verso," address given at a literature conference, published by and in *Cuba Contemporánea* (Havana, November 1914).

Biographical/Critical Sources: Rafael Esténger, *Poveda y su doble mundo, Cuadernos de la Embajada de Cuba,* No. 6 (November-Decembe 1957), Mexico; Regino E. Boti and Hector Poveda, *Notas acerca de José Manuel Poveda,* 1928; Max Henriquez Ureña, *Panorama histórico de la literatura cubana,* New York, 1963, pp. 300-303; Juan Marinello, discussion on Poveda in *Poética,* 19??.

PRADO, Pura del

b. 1931, Santiago, Cuba.
Poet.

After publishing four volumes in Cuba while still in her twenties, Pura del Prado has been less visible since going into exile in the U. S. in the 1960's. Influenced, however, by the energy and example of Lydia Cabrera, Prado continues to seek out publishers for her occasional poems. Her poem "Abuela" celebrates the ubiquitous negro washer-woman:

Leonor, la dulce negra lavandera,
pura mujer de soledad sencilla,
me enseño a deletrear en la cartilla
y a respirar profundo en primada
(first stanza)

Writings: Poetry: *De codas en el arcoiris,* Havana, 1953; *Los sábados y Juan,* Havana, 1953; *Canto a Marti,* Havana, 1956; *El rio con sed,* Havana, 1956.

PUCHUNGO

(pseudonym for **Rafael Americo HENRIQUEZ**)

PUIG Y DE LA PUENTE, Francisco

(pseudonym: **Julio ROSAS**)

b. 1839, San Antonio de los Baños, Cuba; d. 1917, Havana.
Novelist.

After study of philosophy at the University of Havana, he took a degree in medicine. In 1856 he emigrated to Spain where he was very active in both political and literary circles. In 1886 he edited *La Joven Cuba* (Los Baños).

A strong nationalist, Puig was associated with Narciso López in 1868. His *El cafetal azul,* a somewhat "modernista" work, is more romantic and historical than his later work which is considered of inferior quality by Max Henriquez Ureña.

Writings: Novels: *El cafetal azul,* Havana, date unknown of 1st ed. (published by Tipografia El Figar, Havana), but later eds. in Guana-Baoca, 1909, two different publishers, Antonio Roca del Monte and Imp. de Aymerich; *Julia, la hija del pescador,* Spain, 1856, 2nd ed., Havana, 1859; *La tumba de las azucenas,* Cadiz, 1956, other eds., Havana, 1859, 1860; *Lágrimas de un ángel,* Havana, 1859, 1860; *Flor del corazón,* Cadiz, 1857, 1858, 1859, 1860; *Graziela,* Guanajay, Imp. El Destello, 1863; *La campaña de la tarde o Vivir muriendo,* Havana, 1873 (3 vols.); *La campaña del ingenio,* Havana, 1883 or 1884.

PUIGDOLLERS, Carmen

b. 1925 (?), New York City, U.S.A. (of Puerto Rican parents).
Poet.

A long-time resident of the United States, Carmen Puigdollers has one published volume of verse *Dominio entre alas* (1955). Her poetry is of exile and suffering. The poetry of Garcia Lorca and Miguel Hernández have shaped her work.

Writings: Poetry: *Dominio entre alas,* New York, Las Américas, 1955, introduction by Puerto Rican poet Josemilio González.

Biographical/Critical Sources: See Francisco Lluch Mora's *Miradero: Ensayos de critica literaria,* San Juan, 1966, for section on Puigdollers.

PUMAROL, Pablo

b. November 6, 1857, Dominican Republic; d. April, 1889.
Poet.

A splendid satirist, Pumarol wrote in various genres, including the novela and comedy. Although he had hoped to publish some of his verse in a volume of 1876, his plans aborted and his work is only now easily available in the *Antologia de la literatura dominicana.* Much of his holograph manuscripts are conserved, however, by his descendents in the family archives.

Writings: Poetry: in *Antologia de la literatura dominicana,* S. Domingo, Edit. del Gobierno Dominicano, 1944, pp. 183-186.

QUILES, Luis A. Rosario

b. 1936, Puerto Rico.
Poet.

Quiles has been the director of the cultural review *Versiones*.

Writings: Poetry: *La vida que pedi*, San Juan, 1958; *El juicio de Victor Campolo*, San Juan, Ediciones Bondo, 1970; and in *Poesia Española, (Madrid), Mester, Versiones,* and other journals.

QUINONES, Francisco Mariano

(pseudonym: **A. KADOSH**)
b. February 15, 1830, Puerto Rico; d. 1903.
Novelist.

Quiñones' all but forgotten novels were published in Europe and are genuine literary curiosities.

Writings: Novel: *Nadir Shah* (announced as a Persian novel in three parts, but Part III never published), Brussels, Hermanos Gottlieben, 1875: I. *Kalila;* II. *Fátima;* III: "Rizakouli"; *La magofonia,* Brussels, Gottlieben, 1875.

Biographical/Critical Sources: Ismael Reyes Garcia, *Francisco Mariano Quiño*nes: vida y obra, San Juan, Edit. Coqui, 1963, (128 p. with bibliography).

QUINONES VIZCARRONDO, Samuel René

b. 1904, San German, Puerto Rico.
Poet, lawyer, critic, journalist, statesman.

After taking a law degree at the University of Puerto Rico, Quiñones entered public life and for a period served as President of the Senate of Puerto Rico. Although only a minor poet, he took an active part in literary circles, and with Antonio L. Pedreira and Vicente Géigel Polanco founded the cultural review *Indice* (1929-1931). From 1935 to 1940 he served as president of the Ateneo Puertorriqueño and as editor of its publication of the same name. Much of his work was published in *El Imparcial, El Mundo, Puerto Rico Ilustrado, Faro, Vórtice,* and *Hostos.* His harmonious verse is strong and has deep feeling and with Delgado, Vicente, Palés Matos and Rosa-Nieves helped found the Puerto Rican University poetic movement called "Noismo" (1925-1926).

Quiñones' "Motivo del mirar intenso" is one of his better known poems. Stanza two of that work reads:

Ser más sentimental, más soñador, más bueno;
Mirarte largamente. . .
tener más oro en mi oro de idealidad;
no estar triste, ni alegre, ni indiferente, sino
sentir yo no sé qué mansa serenidad. . .

Writings: Essays: *Temas y Letras,* San Juan, Biblioteca de Autores Puertorriqueños, 1941.
Biography: *Manuel Zeno Gandia; Nemesio R. Canales,* 19??.
Poetry: in various collections, including "Motivo del Mirar Intenso" in the *Antologia de la poesia puertorriqueña,* E. Fernández Méndez, ed., San Juan, 1968, and in separate volume *¡Vamos Platero!* (foreword by Evaristo Ribera Chevremont), San Juan, Biblioteca de Autores Puertorriqueños, 1966.
Critical Biography: "Sobre José P. H. Hernández," in *Alma Latina,* San Juan (May 1936).

QUINTANA, José Maria de

b. ca. 1857, Cuba.
Playwright, storywriter.

Quintana wrote 22 plays, most of them performed and published, something unusual for the playwrights of his period.

Writings: Plays: *El gran proyecto* (1 act musical), performed November 9, 1887, at Teatro Cervantes, and then banned by Civil Authorities (Governor), but published Havana, Imp. La

Verdad, 1887; and following, all published Havana,1891, Imp. La Moderna: *Enredos y trapisondas o La mar de lios* (1 act comedy, prose); *¡Pun! ¡Plan!; M. de M. o Una posada en Madruga* (1 act farce, prose); *Juego prohibido* (1 act, prose), premiered Teatro Havana, December 17, 1888; *Viva esta tierra* (1 act farce); *Conflicto municipal* (1 act farce, prose), *El otro* (1 act farce, prose); *Por una carboneria o Politico, rey y nada; Trincheras contra el amor o La vieja y el andaluz; ¿Quién quiere a mi mujer? O Regalo mi mujer* (1 act comedy, prose); *¡El demonio es la guaracha! o Felipe Ginebrita* (1 act prose); *En el Vivac* (1 act farce, prose); *Caneca torero* (1 act farce, prose), premiered Teatro Albisu, Havana, March 1, 1887; *Disputado a Cortes* (1 act), premiered T. Albisu, Havana, August 22, 1886; *La mulata de rango* (2 acts, prose), music by Valenzuela, premiered T. Albisu, Havana, October 3, 1885; *Llueven bufos* (1 act, prose) and *El bicho colgado; Adan y Eva* (2 acts, prose) these three, Havana, Imp. La Moderna, 1892; and these plays by other presses: *Como muchos o una fortuna en Cuba* (1 act), Havana, Imp. La Constancia, 1885, performed Teatro Torrecillas, Havana, August 29, 1885; *Danzon y gallos* (1 act), performed Havana, 1885; *La trinchina* (1 act, prose), performed Havana, 1885, in ms.

QUINTERO Y WOODVILLE, José Augustin

b. 1829, Cuba; d. December, 1885, New Orleans.
Poet, translator.

Son of a Cuban father and English mother, Quintero grew up bi-lingual. After study in the Colegio de San Cristóbal, he went to the United States for further schooling at Harvard University. He became a good friend of the American poet Longfellow and later translated much of his work and that of such poets as Tennyson and the Germans, Schiller, Uhland and others. Returned to Cuba in 1848, just in time to take part in a revolt, he was captured and imprisoned, but succeeded in escaping, and fled to the U. S. An American citizen, by 1861, Quintero lived in Louisiana and Texas, and having become a friend of Jefferson Davis, President of the Southern Confederacy, he accepted a mission to Mexico for the South. In Mexico he fought for Benito Juárez and married a local woman. Once again in Havana in 1868, Quintero edited the *Boletin Comercial* for a short period. When Carlos Manuel de Céspedes led a new revolt, Quintero's revolutionary past made him suspect to the authorities and he decided to leave for the U. S., this time never to return.

Writings: Poetry: in many journals and anthologies: some of his major or best known poems were "¡Adelante!" "Retorno al delirio," "Memorias del alma," "Esperanza," "El tiro," and "El banquete del desterrado," the last his famous call to continue the fight for independence.

Translations: *Deutsche Gedichte* of Friedrich Rückert as *Poemas alemanas.* Quinter's best loved translations were his "Sonetos acorazados," his versions of Rückert's "Geharnischte Sonette" in that collection.

Biographical/Critical Sources: Max Henriquez Ureña, *Panorama histórico de la literatura cubana,* New York, 1963, pp. 326-330.

RAFAEL, Juan Vincente

(pseudonym for **(Padre) Juan RIVERA VIERA**)

RAMIREZ SANTIBANES, José

b. 1895, Cabo Rojo, Puerto Rico; d. 1950.
Poet, biographer, politician.

Ramirez studied law at the University of Puerto Rico and was a minor poet of the "modernista" movement.

Writings: Biography: *Cartilla biografia de Eugenio Maria de Hostos,* 1912.

Historical Play: *Juan Ponce de León,* 1932 [written with Carlos N. Carreras (b.1895)].

RAMIREZ DE ARELLANO, Haydée

b. 1912, San German, Puerto Rico.
Poet.

Influenced by Alfonsina Storni and Juana de Ibarbourou, Haydée Ramirez writes love poetry of a soft sensualism, full of color, both psychological and natural. Typical of her work is "Persecución" which begins:

> *Sol de rubias cuchillas, sol de blonda melena,*
> *toca el aire y reparte tu cariño a la brisa,*
> *mas, no enlaces mi talle, blondo sol, tengo prisa,*
> *voy al árbol de mayo y a la sombra serena.*

Her work has appeared in such journals as *Orfeo* and *Asomante.*

Writings: Poetry: *Poemas,* Santiago de Chile, Mar del sur, 1951, (58 p.); poems in *Antologia de poetas contemporáneos de Puerto Rico,* Pedro Juan Labarthe, ed., Mexico, 1946; and in *Aguinaldo liricos,* C. Rosa-Nieves, ed., Rio Piedras, 1957.

RAMIREZ DE ARELLANO RECHANI, Diana

b. June 3, 1919, New York City, U.S.A. (of Puerto Rican parents).
Poet, critic, teacher.

Diana Ramirez, daughter of the poet Enrique Ramirez Brau, has published two volumes of verse since her first one came out in 1947, *Yo soy Ariel.* She has been a professor of Spanish literature at several universities in the United States. Much of her work first saw print in *El Nacional* (Mexico), *El Mundo* (San Juan), *Ya* (Madrid), *Aturuxo* (Galicia, Spain) and *Alma Latina* (San Juan). She moves between her homes in the United States where she may be teaching to La Rábida in Spain.

Though she has accordingly lived outside of Puerto Rico, she is still much concerned with the island's beauty and culture. As a woman she is much concerned with the new roles for women and she is concerned with both the old and the new in poetry as well as in societies on both sides of the Atlantic Ocean.

Her poem "A Ponce en Puerto Rico" begins:

> *He repetido tu nombre*
> *siete veces siete*
> *en mi soledad*
> *Al timido roce del sueño*
> *el mundo se duerme.*

and it ends:

> *y dime, Ponce mio,*
> *¿me reconocerás?*

Writings: Poetry: *Yo soy Ariel,* Mexico, 1947; *Albatrós sobre el alma,* Madrid, 1955; *Caminos de la creación en Pedro Salinas,* Madrid, 1956; *Angeles de ceniza,* Madrid, Edicionas J. Romo Arragui, 1958; *Un vuelo casi humano,* Madrid, Ediciones J. Romo Arregui, 1961; *Privilegio,* New York, Ateneo Puertorriqueño de Nueva York, 1965.

Critical Biography: *Los ramirez de Arellano de Lope de Vega: Estudio critico y notas,* Madrid, 1954.

RAMOS, José Antonio

b. April 4, 1885, Cuba; d. August 27, 1946, Cuba.
Playwright, journalist, novelist, critic, social historian.

Ramos served as Cuban Consul in Philadelphia during the 1920's and at other consular posts in Europe and South America. He also served as secretary general of the Sixth Panamerican Conference held in Havana. Opposed to the dictatorship of Machado, Ramos went into exile in Mexico in 1932. Trained in library science in the United States, Ramos did much to regularize library holdings and records in the Havana collections once he did return to Cuba.

His novel *Coabey* (1927) deals with a mythical Latin republic and its large neighbor Norlandia in a thinly disguised treatment of Latin American-U. S. relations and conflict. His most interesting novel is believed by some critics to be *Caniqui,* published in 1936.

Ramos' plays were influenced by Ibsen and Hauptmann and brought Cuban theatre into the main current of Western playwriting. Writing in the foreword to one of his plays (*FY-3001*), Ramos stated: "A mi me importa el teatro como arte social en acción, como creación, como expresión en diálogo—forma platónica universal insuperable—de todo loque siente y piensa un pueblo, a través de sus más amoros os y profundos exegetas."

Writings: Plays: *Almas rebeldes,* Barcelona, Spain, A. López, 1906; *Una bala perdida* (3 acts), Barcelona, López, 1907; *La hidra* (3 acts), Havana, Imp. de la Cia Cinematográfica Cubana, 1908; *Nanda* (3 act comedy), Havana, Imp. del la Cia Cinematográfica Cubana, 1908; *Hacia el ideal; De las villas a la Habana* (farce), (later called *A la Habana me voy,* a satirical farce, 1910; *Liberta,* Madrid, Casa Vidal, 1911; *Satanás* (2 acts), premiered in 1913 in both Madrid and Havana, published Madrid, Imp. Helénica, 1913; *Cuando el amor muere* (1 act comedy), published at rear of play *Liberta,* 1911; *En las manos de Dios,* Mexico, 1933; *Calibán Rex* (3 acts), premiered Havana, in *Cuba Contemporánea,* Vol. 5 (Havana, 1914), pp. 341-394; *La recurva, Liberta* and *La leyenda de las estrellas,* Havana, 1911; *El Traidor* (first prize of Academia Nacional de Artes y Letras, premiered in 1917, based on a poem of José Marti, published in *Cuba Contemporánea,* Vol. 7 (1915), pp. 254-271; *El hombre fuerte* (3 acts), Madrid, Imp. Artistica, 1915; *Trembladera* (3 acts), awarded prize by Academia Nacional de Artes y Letras in 1916-1917 and published in Havana, Imp. Siglo XX, 1918, and reprinted in *Teatro Cuban Contemporáneo,* Dolores Marti de Cid, ed., Madrid, 1959, 1962; *When Love Dies,* translated version of *Satanás,* by Isaac Goldberg, in *Twenty-five Short Plays International,* New York, F. Shay, ed., 1925, pp. 123-146; and *FV-3001.*

Novels: *Humberto Fabra,* 2 vols., Paris, 1909, and Havana, 1919; *Coabay,* Havana, 1927; *Las Impurezas de la realidad,* Barcelona, Spain, 1929, and Havana, 1931; *Trinidad,* 1930; *Caniqui,* Havana, 1936, and Havana, Consejo Nacional de Cultura, 1963.

Bio-Critical Studies: *Francisco Javier Balmaseda,* Havana, 1928; *Pasos dulces, el inútil vidente,* Havana, 1937.

Political Studies: *La senaduria corporativa,* Havana, 1914; *La primera comunión civica,* Havana, 1916; *Ensayo de una nueva justificación de la República de Cuba,* Havana, 1921; *Manifesto de la acción civica Cubana* (written with Miguel de Marcos); *El sentido económico de la emancipación de la mujer.*

Biographical/Critical Sources: Introduction to *Trembladera* in *Teatro cubano contemporáneo,* edited by Dolores Marti de Cid, Madrid, 1962; Jorge Mañach, "Duelo de José Antonio Ramos," in *Cuadernos de Cultura Hispánica* (Costa Rica, 1946); Max Henriquez Ureña, *Panorama histórico de la literatura cubana,* New York, 1963, pp. 347-349.

READ, Horacio

b. 1899, Dominican Republic.
Novelist.

Read's fictional treatment of the U. S. occupation of the Dominican Republic in the period 1916-1924 in his *Los civilizadores* may be one of the few novels dealing with this still traumatic interlude in the nation's history. His one play, *Sueño de amor etéreo* had to wait forty years to be published after its initial production.

Writings: Novels: *Filtros,* 1918; *Los civilizadores,* 1924; *Venus andrógina,* 1932; *La absurda,* 1936; *Aislados,* 1936; *De la sombra,* 1959; *Cerca de la noche,* 1965; *Vidas rotas,* S. Domingo, Edit. Marrero, 1975, and *La fuga,* S. Domingo, Edit. Marrero, also 1975.

Play: *Sueño de amor etéreo,* performed 1936 at the Teatro "Campoamor de la Habana," and published S. Domingo, 1975.

RECHANI AGRAIT, Luis

b. 1902, Aguas Buenas, Puerto Rico.
Poet, playwright, journalist.

Rechani spent much of his life in journalism, serving for many years as editor of *El Mundo,* one of San Juan's great journals. His play *Mi señoria* was performed in 1940 by the Sociedad de Teatro Areyto in San Juan. Rechani is a scholarly, rather hermetically closed personality, gifted in languages and a humanist of the old classical type. His poetry, uncollected, is very warm, however, romantic, yet modern.

"La vida es un extraña ciudad" provides an idea of his style and imagery as the first verse here may show:

La vida es una extraña Ciudad, donde yo llego
a entretenerme un poco, y a matar este esplin.
Sé el idioma de este gente que me rodea
y entiendo cuando hablan de gozar a sufrir.

Writings: Plays: *Mi señoria,* 1940 (also in *Teatro puertorriqueño, segundo festival,* San Juan, Inst. de Cultura Puertorriqueña, 1960, and reprint, San Juan, 1960, Rio Piedras, Edit. Edil, 1960); *Todos los ruiseñores cantan,* 1964, and in *Teatro puertorriqueño, Séptimo-festival,* San Juan, 1965; *¿Cómo se llama esta flor?* in *Teatro puertorriqueño, noveno festival,* San Juan, 1968.

Poetry: in various journals and anthologies, including the *Antologia de la poesia puertorriqueña,* E. Fernández Méndez, ed., San Juan, 1968; and *Aguinaldo lirico de la poesia puertorriqueño,* C. Rosa-Nieves, ed., Rio Piedras, 1st ed., 1957, 2nd ed., 1971; also *Poems for Children: Nube en el viento,* 1929 (written with Rafael Rivera Otero).

REMOS RUBIO, Juan José

b. 1896, Santiago, Cuba.
Playwright, teacher, literary historian, essayist.

A noted teacher and scholar, Remos founded the review *Arte* and two cultural groups, the Sociedad de Conferencias Demósthenes and the Sociedad de Estudios Artisticos. He was a professor of Spanish literature at the Colegio Inglés de Mariano (1915) and later at the Instituto de la Havana. His plays are romantic or sentimental, relatively untouched by the new "verismo" of the Ibsen variety.

Writings: Plays: *El histrión* (farce), in *Arte,* 1916; *Adaris* (3 act romantic comedy), Havana, Pérez Hnos, 1916 (*Adacia* is the name according to L. Rivera Muñoz, but Max Henriquez Ureña say *Adaris*); *Pedro el grande,* unpublished; *El destino de Israel,* 1929; *La corriente del siglo,* 1930.

Literary Studies: *Curso de historia de la literatura castellana,* 1918, 1919; *Introducción al teatro de Schiller; Deslindes de Marti,* Havana, J. Suárez, 1953; *Movimiento intelectual de Cuba en el siglo XX; Historia de la literatura cubana,* 3 vols., Havana, 1945; *Proceso histórico de las letras cubanas,* Madrid, 1958; *La obra literaria; Micrófono; Hombres de Cuba; Espiritu de América; Panorama literario de Cuba en nuestro siglo,* Havana, 1942;

Tendencias de la narración imaginativa en Cuba, Havana, 1935.
Essays: *Ensayos literarios.*

REQUENA FRANCISCO, Andrés

b. 1908, Dominican Republic; d. 1952, New York.
Novelist.

Requeña passed much of his life in South America in exile from the Trujillo-dominated homeland. Much of his work attacks tyranny and testifies to the ever-constant need of social justice, not only in the Dominican Republic but wherever mankind is not unfree of thought-control, physical coercion, and socio-economic oppression.

Writings: Novels: *Camino de fuego,* Santiago, Chile, Ediciones Ercilla, 1941; *Los enemigos de la tierra,* Santiago de Chile, Edit. Ercilla, 1942, S. Domingo, La Nación, 1963 (a short story published in *Listin Diario* in 1961 was the nucleus of the novel); *Cementerio sin cruces,* Mexico, 1949.

Biographical/Critical Sources: H. Incháustegui Cabral's *De literatura domincana siglo veinte,* 2nd ed., Santiago de los Caballeros, UCMM, 1973, pp. 278-287; Luis Alberto Sánchez, *Proceso y contenido de la novela hispano-americana,* Madrid, Credo, 1968.

RENTAS LUCAS, Eugenio

b. 1910, Ponce, Puerto Rico.
Poet, journalist.

Rentas Lucas wrote poetry keyed to the ideas of the "Transcendentalista" group of Félix Franco Oppenheimer and Francisco Lluch Mora (1948) and in 1954 joined with Rosa-Nieves and others in the "Ensueñista" movement.

Margot Arce says of his work, " . . . una niñez dolorosa e insatisfecha, una juventud inquisidora en lucha consigno mismo y con todas las realidades, una búsqueda apremiante de la última verdad como la única perfección, la que puede aquietar e iluminar la esperanza. . ." Cesário Rosa-Nieves adds "Rentas Lucas es un poeta de saudádicos tonos menores, de penumbras intimistas en poéticas añoranzas."

Writings: Poetry: *Mañana en el alba,* San Juan, 1949; *Salmos en la aurora, autobiografia espiritual: poemas,* San Juan, Edit. Yaurel, 1963.

Biographical/Critical Sources: see Margot Arce's introduction to *Mañana en la alba* and her essay on Rentas in *Impresiones: Notas puertorriqueñas* (ensayos), San Juan, Edit. Yaurel, 1950.

REYES, Juan de Jesús

b. 1872, Dominican Republic; d. 1930's(?).
Poet, playwright.

Reyes was a bitter protester against the U. S. occupation of the Dominican Republic (1916-1924) and his ironic poem, "Romance de la ocupación" was aimed at the marine takeover of his country.

Writings: Poetry: *De tierras cálidas,* Santiago, Dominican Republic, 1922; *Canto a la Fé, Canto a Moca, Romance de la ocupación,* 1928 (combined volume); *Vuelo de mariposas,* Santiago, 1929.
Plays: *El silfo y el rosal; El montuno que se espantó con un avión; Naci cuando el terremoto; El corifeo del arrabal; Una hombra que se alaba.*

RIANCHO ESCOBALES, Providencia

b. August 10, 1901, San Juan, Puerto Rico.
Poet, musician, teacher.

Riancho Escobales, after musical study in Europe and North and South America, particularly in Argentina where she spent many years, has been a teacher, composer, and professional pianist. Her interests also have been literary and for eight years

(1939-1946 and again in 1952), she served as editor of *Horizontes,* a review which has 13 issues in its total life. Rosa-Nieves presents Riancho's "Epistola IV" d "¿A dónde vas?" in his *Aguinaldo lirico* from the second of Riancho's many draft volumes.

Writings: Poetry: *Crucero lirico,* San Juan, 1939; eight other collections remain in ms., two poems in *Aguinaldo lirico de la poesia puertorriqueña,* C. Rosa-Nieves, ed., Rio Piedras, 1st ed., 1957, 2nd ed., 1971.

RIBERA CHEVREMONT, Evaristo

b. 1896, San Juan, Puerto Rico.
Poet, novelist, journalist, storywriter, critic.

Ribera Chrevremont was a "modernist" and influential in bringing Puerto Rican poetry into the contemporary currents of European, especially French developments. He said of poetry that it was ". . .la suprema verdad, ha de ser forma y espiritu. . .y ambas han de quedar libres del instinto de la humanidad." His verse sought absolute clarity and light but was in form fairly conservative, often employing the sonnet form in original ways.

As an early modernista he contributed to *El Carnaval,* established in 1911 to express the new poetry. With José Pérez Losade, Ribera edited also the daily journal *El Imparcial* in 1918, but from 1919-1924, he lived in Spain. Returning, he brought back a renewed interest in poetry and exhorted the island's youth in his column "Página de Vanguardia" in the *Puerto Rico Ilustrado.* His *El sentimiento de la naturaleza en "Color"* (1943) expresses the critical and poetic ideas exposed in his original verse published in *Color* (1938).

His "La Garza" begins:

Es la mañana azul, y hay una grata
pincelada de rosa en la ribera.
La garza, melancólica y austera,
hunde en las ondas su inflexible pata.
En aquel semicirculo de plata.
frente a los cielos, bebe el sol y espera
al pez de ópalo y oro. Se dijera
que su pico se tiñe de escarlata.

While in Spain, Ribera published a very few copies of a verse collection, *La copa de Hebe,* which were given to friends and the author himself conserved no copy of it and it is believed the work is no longer extant.

Writings: Poetry: *Desfile romántico,* San Juan, Real Hermanos, 1912; *El templo de los alabas tros,* Madrid, Ambos Mundos, 1919; *La copa de Hebe,* 1922; *Los almendros del paseo de Covadonga,* San Juan, Puerto Rico Ilustrado, 1928; *La hora del orifice,* Madrid, 1929; *Pajarera,* San Juan, Romero, 1938; *Tonos y formas,* San Juan, Biblioteca de Autores Puertorriqueño, 1940, *Anclas de oro,* San Juan, Imp. Venezuela, 1945; *Barro,* San Juan, Imp. Venezuela, 1945; *Tú, mar y yo y ella,* Rio Piedras, Junta Editora de la Universidad de Puerto Rico, 1946; *Verbo,* San Juan, Imp. Venezuela, 1947; *Antologia poética (1924-1950) y La llama pensativa,* Madrid, Cultura Hispánica, 1954; *Antologia poética (1929-1965),* San Juan, Editorial del Departamento de Instrucción Pública, 1967; *Creación,* San Juan, Imp. Venezuela, 1951; *Los sonetos de Dios, del Amor y de la Muerte,* 1955; *La llama pensativa,* San Juan, Imp. Venezuela, 1950, 1955; *Antologia poética, 1924-1950,* introduction by Federico de Onis, Rio Piedras, Universidad de Puerto Rico, 1957; *Cuadernos de poesia,* VI, San Juan, Instituto de Cultura Puertorriqueña, 1960; *Inefable orilla,* San Juan, Imp. Venezuela, 1961; *Memorial de Arena,* 1962; *Punto final: Poemas del sueño y de la muerte,* 1963; *El semblante,* Rio Piedras, Universidad de Puerto Rico (preface by Concha Meléndez), 1964; *Principio de canto,* San Juan, Imp. Venezuela, 1965; *Nueva antologia,* San Juan, Edit. Cordillera, 1966; *Rio volcado,* 1968; also unpublished collections: "El hondero lanzo la piedra," verse 1921-1924"; "Vitrales góticos," collected 1921-1924 work; "Yo sé de uno que tiene una canción," also work of 1921-1924 period and "Velas negras," of same period. Also see *Poesias,* San Juan, Instituto de Cultura Puertorriqueña, 1960.

Novelette: *Madre haraposa* (written with Luis Muñoz Marin and Antonio Coll y Vidal), San Juan, Tip. Barros, 1918.

Editor of: (With José S. Alegria of: *Antologia de poeta jóvenes de Puerto Rico,* San Juan, Tip. Real Hermanos, 1918.

Criticism-Esthetics: *El sentimiento de la naturaleza en "Color,"* San Juan, 1943.

Novel: *El niño de Arcilla,* San Juan, Biblioteca de Autores Puertorriqueños, 1950.

Journalistic Essays: "San Juan en mi sueño," in *Revista de las Antillas* (1914).

Biographical/Critical Sources: Concha Meléndez, *La inquietud sosegado: Poética de Evaristo Ribera Chevremont,* San Juan, Junta Editora Universidad de Puerto Rico, 1946; José Olivio Jiménez' comments on Ribera in *Antologia de la poesia hispanoamericana contemporánea 1914-1970,* Madrid, El Libro de Bolsilla, 1971; 1973, pp. 153-154; José de Diego, "Entrevista con Evaristo Ribera Chevremont," in *Disquisiciones literarias,* San Juan, Puerto Rico Ilustrado, Year IX (January 19, 1918); Enrique A. Laguerre's *La poesia modernista de Puerto Rico,* San Juan, 1969, pp. 102-109; Antonio S. Pedreira, *Insularismo,* Madrid, Tip. Artistica, 1934, p. 72; Interview with (and by) Rafael Rivera Santiago, "Un poeta de la raza," in *Compresión y análisis,* San Juan, Imp. Venezuela, 1938, but first in *El Mundo,* San Juan (July 23, 1933); F. Manrique Cabrera, *Historia de la literatura puertorriqueña,* Rio Piedras, 1969, pp. 252-255; F. Lluch Mora, *Miradero: Ensayos de critica literaria,* San Juan, 1966.

RIBERA CHEVREMONT, José Joaquin

b. 1897, Puerto Rico.
Poet.

Brother of Evaristo Ribera, José was a romantic, decorative poet, with his best work probably *La lámpara azul* (1933) which, though his third volume, contains much of his juvenile work and, all in all, was written before *Breviario de vanguardia* (1930).

Writings: Poetry: *Elegias románticas,* San Juan, Tip. Mystic Star, 1918; *Breviario de vanguardia,* San Juan, Tip. San Juan, 1930; *La lámpara azul,* San Juan, Tip. Real Hermanos, 1933; *Poemas,* San Juan, Tip. Real Hermanos, 1934.

RIGALI, Rolando

b. 1941, Cuba.
Poet.

Rigali's forte is the evocation of childhood and the feeling of sympathy he evokes for the poor.

Writings: Poetry: *De pie frente a mi, yo,* Havana, Arquimbau, 1963; *El octavo dia,* Havana, Revolución, 1964.

RIGAU, Angel

b. 1916, Sabana Grande, Puerto Rico.
Poet, journalist.

Rigau's poetry is very warm, touched mostly by the examples of Garcia Lorca and Samuel Lugo. Much of his work has appeared in *La Correspondencia, El Mundo,* and *Alma Latina.*

Writings: Los clamores sin rumbo, San Juan, 1949.

DE RIVAS, Duque

b. ca. 1805, Cuba.
Playwright.

One of the earliest Cuban romantic playwrights, along with Martinez de la Rosa, Garcia Gutiérrez and the Dominican, long resident in Cuba, Francisco Javier Foxá y Lecanda.

Writings: Play: *Don Alvaro,* 1835.

RIVERA, Raúl

b. 1945, Cuba.
Poet.

Rivera took a journalism degree in 1973 from Havana University and has won several poetry prizes. His one collection is *Poesia sobre la tierra* (Havana, Instituto Cubano del Libro, 1973). An English version of his poem, called "To the Saddest Dance-Tune," appears in the *Melanthika* anthology (Birmingham, England, 1977).

RIVERA LANDRON, Francisco

b. April 30, 1907, Vega Baja, Puerto Rico.
Poet, novelist, agricultural engineer.

Much of Rivera Landrón's work has appeared in *El Mundo, Puerto Rico Ilustrado, Gráfico de Puerto Rico,* and *La Democracia.*

Writings: Novels: *El alma de la huerta,* 1945, and Barcelona, Edit. Rumbos, 1962; *Mi terruño en el surco,* Barcelona, Rumbos, 1962; *Tierras de Dios,* Rumbos, 1962; *El refugio,* Barcelona, Rumbos, 1963.

Poetry: *Flor de cinco pétalos,* 1951; *Sementaras de lumbre,* San Juan, 1956; *Las tejas húmedas,* 1956.

RIVERA-OTERO, Rafael

b. 1903, Cayey, Puerto Rico.
Poet, journalist (in English and Spanish), editor.

On Columbus Day, October 12, 1930, Rivera-Otero received the Roosevelt Medal for his English language volume of poems, *For All the Days That Were Not Beautiful.* His Spanish language verse has not been collected but for the children's poems in the collection *Una nube en el viento.*

Beginning as a "modernista" poet following the lead of Rubén Dario and Herrera Reissig, Rivera-Otero matured and expressed in his humane, even jovial verse, the newest currents of "post-modernismo." He has served for a long period as editor of *El Mundo* after losing his university post for his part in nationalist manifests and protests.

Writings: Children's Verse: *Una nube en el viento,* 1929.

Poetry: in various collections. English language poems: *For All the Days That Were Not Beautiful.*

RIVERA VIERA, (Padre) Juan

(pseudonym: **Juan Vicente RAFAEL**)

b. 1885, Yauco, Puerto Rico; d. 1953.
Poet, priest.

A romantic poet devoted as might be expected to religious themes, Rivera Viera was strongly touched by French Parnassian poetic subjects and style but later turned to the newer current of modernismo and the use of criollisms. His "El Girasol" begins:

El girasol en la enramada da
miente lozanos surtidores
cuando se quiebra en los alcoves
la tibia luz de la alborada.

Writings: Poetry: *Carmina sacra,* Barcelona, Imp. Luis Gili, 1925; *Carmina amaritudinis;* and poems in various collections and reviews, including "Los contemporáneos," in *Antologia de poetas puertorriqueños,* San Juan, Biblioteca Puerto Rico Ilustrado, Vol. II, 1922.

ROBRENO PUENTE, Gustavo

b. 1873, Pinar del Rio, Cuba; d. 1957.
Playwright, novelist, actor.

Robreño wrote some 200 works for the theatre but none of them was printed. He wrote for the Teatro Alhambra which staged small pieces, farces, burlesques of less than literary quality if of popular and rude vigor. Some of Robreño's works were: *Pachencho, capitalista; Tin-Tan; La madre de los tomates; Entre cubanos no vamos a andar con boberias.* With his brother, Francisco, he wrote *Napoleón,* and *Ciclón.* Max Henriquez Ureña laments the fact that as of 1963 no publication of any of the many extant manuscripts of Robreño had been made. (His son Carlos, however, has a collection of the original manuscripts.)

Henriquez compares Robreño to his equally pioneering colleague, Federico Villoch, and cites some of his plays, also unpublished: "La casita criolla," "La isla de las cotorras;" "La danza de los millones;" and "La mulata Maria."

Writings: Novel: *La acerca de Louvre,* Havana, Rambla, 1925.

RODRIGUEZ, Agustin

b. ca. 1860, Cuba.
Playwright.

Rodriguez is best known for his adaptation of the famous novel *Cecilia Valdés* of Cirilo Villaverde.

Writings: Play: *Cecilia Valdés* (one act, music by Gonzalo Roig, play text by José Sánchez Arcilla), Havana, Edit. Hermes, 1932, premiered Teatro Marti, adapted from novel of Cirilo Villaverde: *Cecilia Valdés o La Loma del Angel,* 1882.

RODRIGUEZ, Emilio Gaspar

b. 1889, Matanzas, Cuba; d. 1939.
Essayist, historian, diplomat.

Educated in the United States, Rodriguez served abroad as Cuban consul in several European and Asian poets. Most of his literary work was devoted to his Quixote studies, but he also wrote historical and political works. Rodriguez finished his official life serving the government on labor matters.

Writings: Critical Essays: *El retablo de Maese Pedro,* Havana, 1916; *Puntos sútiles del Quijote,* Havana, 1922; *Los conquistadores,* Havana, 1921 (which includes a new collection of essays, the "Cervantes y el siglo XVI español" and "Marti y la América"); *Hércules en Yolcos,* Havana, 1923; *Dos maestros del humorismo en el siglo XIX: Larra y Eça de Queiroz,* Havana, 1926; *Plática novisima,* Havana, 1929.

Politics: *La crisis cubana* (only one volume published of intended series), Havana, date unknown.

RODRIGUEZ, Luis Felipe

b. July 30, 1888, Matanzas Province, Cuba; d. August 6, 1947.
Novelist, poet, storywriter, playwright.

Rodriguez was one of the earliest Cuban writers to initiate the quasi-Marxist use of rural life, the so-called "criollism" or folkloric stories which became increasingly important in Cuban literature. His plays are light affairs but his largely autobiographical *Contra la corriente* (1943) is not without interest.

Writings: Novels: *La conjura de la Ciénaga,* Madrid, 1923, and Havana, Org. Continental Madrid, Edit. Calleja, 1923, and Havana, Org. Continental de los Festivales del Libro, 196?; *Marcos Antilla,* Havana, 1932; *La copa vacia,* Havana, Tip. Yagüez, 1926; *Don Quijote en Hollywood,* Havana, La Habana, 1936.

Poetry: *La ilusión de la vida* (prose-poem), Valencia, 1912; *Poemas del corazón amoroso,* Manzanillo, 1924.

Prose: *Gente de Oriente,* Manzanillo, 1915; *Cómo opinaba Damián Paredes,* published for the first time under the title *Memorias de Dámaso Paredes* in Valencia, 1916.

Stories: *Pascua de la tierra natal,* Madrid, 1923; *Marcus Antilla,* Havana, La Tertulia, 1963, (29 p.), first published in 1932 (novelette);

Plays: *Contra la corriente,* 1943, published in *Orto* magazine; *La comedia del matrimonio* and *La turbonada,* last two works remain unpublished.

Biographical/Critical Sources: Salvador Bueno's comments on Rodriguez in Bueno's *Antologia del cuento en Cuba,* Havana, 1953;

Max Henriquez Ureña, *Panorama histórico de la literatura cubana,* New York, 1923, pp. 309-311.

RODRIGUEZ ACOSTA, Ofelia

b. 1912, Artemisa, Pinar del Rio, Cuba.
Novelist, journalist.

Ardent fighter for the civil rights of women and generally more civilized treatment of women, Ofelia Rodriguez wrote many novels full of the emotional tumult of her cause.

Writings: Novels: *El triunfo de la débil presa,* Havana, 1926; *La vida manda,* Havana, 1929; *Dolientes,* Havana, 1931; *La dama del arcón, En la noche del mundo,* Havana, 1940 and Mexico, Estela, 1949; *Hágase la luz: la novela de un filósofo existencialista,* Mexico, Estela, 1953.

Biographical/Critical Sources: Enrique Gay-Calbo, "Ofelia Rodriguez Acosta," in *Revista de la Habana,* I, 3 (March 1930), pp. 347-360.

RODRIGUEZ CABRERO, Luis

b. 1864, Puerto Rico; d. 1915.
Poet, journalist.

Rodriguez spent a considerable period in Spain taking his university studies during which he contributed articles to *El Madrid Cómico, La Revista Cómica,* and *La Camisa,* the latter founded by him in Zaragoza. His journalistic pieces were often jovial, but sometimes acerbic, and his eye quickly caught hypocracies in the U. S. position and attitudes in its new island possession.

Writings: Poetry: *Mangas y capirotes,* San Juan, Imp. de Francisco Marxuach, 1900.

Biographical/Critical Sources: Lydia Fiol Bigas, "Luis Rodriguez Cabrero: vida y obra," unpublished M. A. Thesis, U. of P. R., 1944.

RODRIGUEZ CALDERON, Juan

b. late 18th century, Galicia, Spain.
Poet, autobiographer, historian.

Descendant of the noble family of the Marquis of Santa Cruz, Rodriguez imported a printing press from the United States in the early nineteenth century and his *Poesias* (180?) and *Ocios de la juventud* (1806), printed thereon, are believed the very first books ever published in Puerto Rico.

Rodriguez is a poet expressing "spiritual romanticism" through the lips of neoclassicism and "descuidada." His style was of the "Canto" school, his "Canto Enjusto" being the first song descriptive of the Puerto Rican landscape along with "Sueño poética" and "Canción fúnebre."

Writings: Poetry: *Poesias,* Puerto Rico, 180?; *Ocios de la juventud,* Puerto Rico, 1806; *Cántico a Puerto Rico,* Madrid, 1816, republished as *Canto en Justo Elogio de la Isla de Puerto Rico,* in *Memorias Geographicas, Historicas, Economicas y Estadisticas de la Isla de Puerto Rico,* edited by Pedro Tomás de Córdoba, Puerto Rico Oficina del Gobierno, 1831-1833, 6 vols.

Biographical/Critical Sources: Sra. Eloisa Rivera de Garcia, "La lirica en Puerto Rico durante el siglo XIX" unpub. Ph.D. dissertation, U. of P. R.. (The early history of printing in the island is also discussed in footnote 5, p. 104 in F. Manrique Cabrera's *História de la literatura puertorriqueña,* Rio Piedras, Edit. Cultural, 1969, and also see Cabrera's discussion of Rodriguez in same work, pp. 67-70.)

RODRIGUEZ EMBIL, Luis

b. August 30, 1879, Havana, Cuba; d. April 29, 1954, Havana.
Storywriter, novelist, journalist.

Rodriguez' best work, possibly , is his novel of the war of independence *La insurrección* (1910) which has much local color and is full of life, if tinged with a sentimental melancholy.

Writings: Novel: *La insurrección,* Paris, 1910; *De paso por la vida,* Paris, L. Michaud, 191?.
Story: "Almas de aves," in *El Mundo,* 1903; collection: *Gil Luna, artista,* Madrid, 1908; *La mentira vital,* Madrid, 1920.

RODRIGUEZ EXPOSITO, César

b. 1904, Cuba.
Playwright.

Rodriguez' many plays always have a strong central theme and each play develops the author's own bent and preoccupation to a powerful degree.

Writings: Plays: *Huyendo de la verdad,* 1932; *Humano antes que moral,* 1933; *El poder del sexo,* 1933; *Los muertos viven,* 1934; *La superproducción humana,* 1937; *Los que tienen la culpa,* 1937; *Adulterio ocasional,* 1938; *Violación,* 1943; *Multitudes,* 1944.

RODRIGUEZ FERNANDEZ, Arturo

b. 1947, Dominican Republic.
Novelist.

Winner of several literary prizes, Arturo Rodriguez has written a psychological-social novel, *La Búsqueda de los Desencuentros,* published in 1974. His work is cosmopolitan and devoid of some of the narrow range of interests often noticed in young Dominican writers.

RODRIGUEZ MENDEZ, José

b. 1914, Cuba.
Poet.

Rodriguez' poetry was full of social and racial considerations and a minor part of the Afro-Cuban movement of the 1930's.

Writings: Poetry: in *La Palabra,* journal directed by Juan Marinello. He is represented in E. Ballegas' *Antologia de poesia negra* and in other collections.

RODRIGUEZ OBJIO, Manuel Nemesio

b. December 19, 1838, Santo Domingo, Dominican Republic; d. 1871.
Poet, biographer, historian.

Rodriguez' early studies were at the Colegio de San Buenaventura. Losing his father, Andrés Rodriguez y Rodriguez, in 1855, Manuel went to the United States with his family that year, but he returned in 1856 to live in Azua. He soon enlisted in the army of General Santana who was attacking President Báez. Under Santana, Rodriguez served as Minister of Interior and of Police, but was obliged to go into exile to Saint Thomas on Santana's fall. In 1863 he returned once more to Azua.

His subsequent career was equally vicarious: exile to Venezuela, return to join a revolutionary army and being designated Plenipotentiary del Gobierno Dominicano, and with several generals being asked to negotiate terms at Monte Cristy with General La Gándara. For a period Rodriguez was jailed by La Gándara but he was soon freed and eventually was named once again Minister, this time as Foreign Secretary in Protector Cabral's Provisional Government. Again, in great difficulty, he was saved from execution by a noble and beautiful woman's plea on his behalf and the generosity of President Báez. Rodriguez then entered the army again and died in the subsequent fighting with Spanish troops.

A follower of Félix Maria Del Monte's poetic style, Rodriguez wrote hymns and odes such as his cantos "A los heroes de Febrero" and "Al 27 de Febrero," celebrating the heroic city of Santo Domingo, bombarded in February 1863. His "Acto de fé" is a romantic defiance of pessimism and atheism:

Creo en los altos destinos
de la humanidad proscrita
y en la piedad infinita
del que los mundos formó.
Creo en la verdad que encierra
el misterio de la muerte;
creo en la gracia del Fuerte;
¡creo en la ciencia de Dios!

Balaguer has written: ". . .Rodriguez Objio . . . fue ante todo un poeta de sentimiento y un espiritu excelso que no obstante haber vivido en plena tormenta politica, envuelto en un furioso torbellino formando de broncas pasiones y de intereses contradictorios, halló en su corazón fuerza y entusiasmo para levantar, cual alto pudo el cetro de la poesia en medio de una sociedad anarquisada."

Writings: Poetry: *Poesias,* 1888; and various poems in reviews.

Biography: *Vida del General Gregorio Lupéron e Historia de la Restauración,* (posthumous), 1939; *Relaciones históricas,* 1951.

Biographical/Critical Sources: R. Lugo Lovatón's *Manuel Rodriguez Objio,* 1951; Max Rodriguez Ureña's *Panorama histórico de la literatura dominicana,* S. Domingo, Postigo, 1965, pp. 186-189; J. Balaguer's *Historia de la literatura dominicana,* S. Domingo, Postigo, 1970, pp. 132-137.

RODRIGUEZ SANTOS, Justo

b. 1915, Santiago, Cuba.
Poet.

One of the poets of the *Origenes* group centered around José Lezama Lima, Rodriguez Santos preferred the traditional forms of the sonnet, song, and romance-ballad. He did essay more modern forms and metrical patterns as in his "Elegia":

Sobre tus ojos de perdida luna
gira la lluvia delicadamente
y su rumor de dulce trébol siento
atravesar me frente desolada.

Literary influences quietly reflected in his work are Garcia Lorca, Juan Ramón Jiménez and Francisco Luis Bernárdez.

Writings: Poetry: *F. G. L. 1899-1936. Elegia por la muerte de Federico Garcia Lorca, Havana, 1936; Luz cautiva,* Havana, 1938; *La belleza que el cielo no amortaja,* Havana, 1951; "Profecia de Dos Rios," is only part published of planned *Canto a José Marti; La epopeya del Moncada; poesia de la historia, 1953-1963,* Havana, Unión, 1963.

Editor of: *Antologia del soneto en Cuba,* Havana, 1942.

RODRIGUEZ UCARES, Fray José

(a.k.a. **"El Capacho"** or **Padre CAPACHO,** or **Rodriguez UCRES,** or **UCARES,** or **USCARRES**)

b. ca. 1725, Cuba.
Poet, playwright, priest.

Rodriguez published his poetry in various journals and collections, the most famous poem being "Véjamen a la Universidad," a mixture of Spanish and Latin designed to mock the pseudo-erudite professors.

His several plays (no longer extant) were the first to be written in Cuba, but the play *El principe jardinero y fingido Cloridano,* once thought to be his, now apparently must be ascribed to Santiago Pita (b. 1742). Max Henriquez Ureña cites the scholarship which in the past few decades demonstrates that Fray José Rodriguez Ucares was clearly not the author of *El principe jardiniero.*

Writings: Poetry: *Poesias,* Havana, 1823, edited by José Boloña.

Biographical/Critical Sources: Max Henriquez Ureña, *Panorama histórico de la literatura cubana,* Vol. I, New York, 1963, pp. 61-63.

RODRIGUEZ VELEZ, Benicio

b. 1910, Cuba.
Playwright.

Rodriguez' plays dealt with rural oppression and in the case of *Vida subterránea,* with the lives of miners.

Writings: Plays: *Vida subterránea,* 1943; *Realengo 20; el drama del campesino cubano y los ladrones de tierras,* Havana, La Milagrosa, 1959.

RODRIGUEZ DE TIO, Lola

b. 1843, San German, Puerto Rico; d. November 10, 1924, Havana, Cuba.
Poet, critic.

Daughter of the lawyer Sebastián Rodriguez de Astudillo, Lola married on February 13, 1865 Bonocio Tió Segarra (1840-1905). She and her journalist-businessman husband were forced into exile in 1877, settling for a period in Venezuela from 1877-79.

Although not a very original poet, Lola Rodriguez de Tió was one of the earliest published women poets in the Spanish Caribbean. Her verse was often on patriotic themes, her most famous poem probably being "Cuba y Puerto Rico son," published in her collection *Mi libro de Cuba* (1893). The long poem "A Cuba" has this characteristic stanza:

Cuba y Puerto Rico son
De un pájaro las dos alas,
Reciben flores o balas
Sobre el mismo corazón. . .
¡Que mucho si en la ilusión
Que mil tintes arrelola,
Sueña la musa de Lola
Con ferviente fantasia,
De esta tierra y de la mia
Hacer una patria sola!

She lived in Cuba from the 1890's on and was elected a member of the Cuban Academy of Arts and Letters in 1910.

Writings: Poetry: *Mis cantares,* Mayagüez, 1876, introd. by Bonocio Tió Segarra; *Claros y nieblas,* Puerto Rico, 1865, Mayagüez, 1885; Velada a Beneficio de la Sociedad Protectora de los Pobres," (in honor of Benitez), June 11, 1882; *A mi patria en la muerte de Corchado,* Mayagüez, Tip. Comercial, 1885, (8 p.); *Noche buena,* Mayagüez, Tip. Comercial, 1887, (15 p.); "A Cuba" and "Betances inmortal," in the *Antologia de la poesia puertorriqueña,* E. F. Méndez, ed., San Juan, 1968; *Claros y nieblas,* Mayagüez, 1885; *Obras completas poesias,* San Juan, Instituto de Cultura Puertorriqueña, 1968.

Biographic-Critical Studies: *Velada literaria en honor de Gautier Benitez,* April 17, 1880; *Mi ofrenda,* San German, P. R., Imp. J. Ramón González, 1880, (14 p.).

Editor of: annual review: *Compontes La Almjoabana,* 1881.

Biographical/Critical Sources: Cesáreo Rosa-Nieves, chapter in *Ensayos Escogidos,* Barcelona, Tip. Miguza, 1970, for Academia de Artes y Ciencias de Puerto Rico, Cuaderno No. 5, pp. 67-91; "La poesia patriótica de Lola Rodriguez de Tio," by Coloma Pardo de Casablanca in *Puerto Rico Ilustrado,* San Juan (July 13, 1946); Maria Luisa Angeles, in "Lola Rodriguez de Tio," in *Mujeres Puertorriqueñas,* San Juan, 1909, pp. 71-81; Concha Meléndez, "Nuevo verdor florece," in *La Torre,* Rio Piedras, 1969, pp. 121-215; Carmen Leila Cuevas, *Lola de América,* Hato Rey, P. R., Talleres Ramallo, 1969; Max Henriquez Ureña, *Panorama histórico de la literatura cubana,* New York, 1963.

ROJAS TOLLINCHI, Francisco

b. May 30, 1911, Tauco, Puerto Rico; d. February 13, 1965, Ponce.
Poet, priest.

With Padre Juan Rivera and Francisco Lluch Mora, Rojas made a trilogy of Yaucan poets, religious and pensive in tendency. He published mostly in *La Revista Blanca, Puerto Rico Ilustrado, El Mundo,* and *Pegaso.* His style is severe, classically cool.

Writings: Poetry: *Fronda virgen,* 1940; *Cien*

sonetos en cuatro panfletos, 1944; *Relicario sonoros,* 1945; *Soneto de la vida, el amor y la muerte,* Yauco, Edit. Yaurel, 1955; *Silencio de Dios,* 1956; three poems in *Aguinaldo lirico,* C. Rosa-Nieves, ed., Rio Piedras, 1957.

ROLDAN, José Gonzalo

b. b. 1822, Havana, Cuba; d. 1856.
Playwright, poet, editor.

Roldán was a leading editor of his day, directing such journals as *Las Flores del Siglo, El Faro industrial, La Prensa, El Diario de la Habana, La Revista de la Havana,* and *El Aguinaldo.* His best-known poems were "La Concepción de Maria," "A Heredia," and "El Aguacero."

Writings: Play: *Amores de temporado* (1 act comedy), Havana, 1846.

Poetry: in various journals and collections, and one collection, *El trabajo,* Matanzas, 1856, (19 p.).

ROQUERO DOMINGUEZ, Juan

(pseudonym: **ARRUGADO**)
b. 1825, Cuba; d. 1885.
Playwright.

Important only historically, Roquero published five plays, most of them brief farces.

Writings: Plays: *El efecto de un engaño* (comic farce), Havana, del Faro, 1847; *La cigueña* (1 act comedy), Havana, 1853; *Sufrimiento y gloria,* Matanzas, Imp. La Nacional, 1873; *¡Estaba de Dios!* (1 act verse comedy), 1874; *Poetas hambrientos y agentes industriales* (verse and prose comedy for Vate Arrugado), Matanzas, El Ferrocarril, 1877.

ROSA-NIEVES, Cesáreo

b. July 17, 1901, Juana Diaz, Puerto Rico.
Poet, playwright, critic, literary historian.

Rosa-Nieves served as a professor of Spanish and Puerto Rican literature at the University of Puerto Rico. His first volume of verse *Las veredas olvidadas* (1922) was one of the first collections of "modernista" verse. Later, his work with that of the so-called university poets announced the local "vanguardista" movement called by Rosa-Nieves "Noismo." He then moved on to the "post-modernismo" of *La feria de las burbujas* (1930) and in time his verse reflected the new influences from Europe and the United States in what came to be called "ultramodernismo" or in 1954 "Ensueñismo" by Rosa-Nieves. In this period (1950's) such poets as Eugenio Rentas Lucas, José Luis Martin and Félix Franco Oppenheimer joined the group.

His double-volumed literary histories (cited below) are extremely detailed studies of the entire range of Puerto Rican writers from 1589 to the present (*Historia panoramica*) and in even greater detail the last two centuries (in *Plumas estelares*).

Rosa-Nieves' study of an obscure poet, Francisco de Ayerra de Santa Maria (1630-1708), a Puerto Rican priest long resident in Mexico, was an act of poetic and historic justice and also includes some of Ayerra's verse.

Writings: Literary Histories: *La poesia en Puerto Rico,* Mexico, Ed. Tesis, 1943; *Cinco generaciones estéticas en la poesia puertorriqueña,* Spain, 1956; *Consideraciones sobre literatura puertorriqueña,* Santurce, 1955; *Historia panoramica de la literatura puertorriqueña,* San Juan, Editorial Campos, 1963; *Plumas estelares en las letras de Puerto Rico,* 2 vols., San Juan, Ediciones de la Torre, Universidad de Puerto Rico, 1967-1970; *Aguinaldo lirico de la poesia puertorriqueña,* Rio Piedras, P. R., Edit. Edil, 1957, 1971, 3 vols.

Biographical-Critical Studies: *Francisco de Ayerra Santa Maria: Poeta Puertorriqueño 1630-1708,* 2 vols., 1st ed., 1943, and 2nd ed., San Juan, Editorial Universitaria, Universidad de Puerto Rico, 1948, 1963; *La lámpara del Faro,* 2 vols., San Juan, Edit. Club de la Prensa, 1957-1960; *Tierra y lamento: Rodeos de con-*

torno para una tellurica interpretación poética de lo puertorriqueño, San Juan, 1958; *La poesia en Puerto Rico,* 1943, San Juan, Edit. Campos, 1958, 1969; *Voz folklórica de Puerto Rico,* 1967; *Biografias puertorriqueñas* (with Esther Melón Portalatin), 1970; *Ensayos escogidos,* San Juan, Publicaciones de la Academia de Arte y Ciencias de Puerto Rico, Cuaderno No. 5, 1970.

Editor of: (with Félix Franco Oppenheimer): *Antologia del cuento puertorriqueño,* 2 vols., 2nd ed., San Juan, Edit. Edil, 1970; *Calambreñas: decimario boricua (Motivos de la montaña y la ciudad,* San Juan, Edit. Coquí, 1964.

Poetry: in various anthologies, including the *Antologia de la poesia puertorriqueña,* E. Fernández Méndez, ed., San Juan, 1968; volumes: *La veredas olvidadas,* Caguas, Tip. Morel Campos, 1922; *La feria de la burbujas,* Humacao, P. R., Tip. Comercial, 1930; *Paracaidas,* 1930; *Tú en los pinos,* 1940; *Urdumbre,* 1953; *Siete caminos en luna de sueños,* Santurce, 1951; *Los visperos del Alba Madurarón,* 1959, and San Juan, Edit. Coqui, 1970; *Diapsaón Negro,* San Juan, Edit. Campos, 1960; *Girasol,* San Juan, Campos, 1960, 1964, 1968; *Plenamar de las Garzas de ambar,* 1964; *Calambreñas,* 1964; *La emoción divertida,* 1967.

Plays: *Román Baldorioty de Castro* ("Biodrama" in 3 acts in verse), Santurce, Imp. Soltero, 1948; *Trilogia lirica: El huésped del mar, Flor de Areyto* and *La Otra,* Santurce, 1950; *Pachin Marin; Brazo de Ora.*

Stories: *El mar bajó de la montaña,* San Juan, 1963; *Mañana será la esperanza,* San Juan, Edit. Cordillera, 1964; *El sol pintó de ora los bohios,* Barcelona, Rumbos, 1965; *Mi vocación por el vispero,* 1966; *La canción de los luceros,* San Juan, Edit. Morivivi, 1972; *Los espejos de sol bajó la luna,* San Juan, Morivivi, 1972.

Biographical/Critical Sources: Patria Figueroa de Cifredo, *Apuntes biograficos en torno a la vida y obra de Cesáreo Rosa-Nieves,* San Juan, 1965; also by Figueroa: *Nuevo encuentro con la estética de Rosa-Nieves,* San Juan, 1969; José Luis Martin, *Arco y flecha: Estudios de critica literaria,* San Juan, 1961.

ROSAS, Julio

(pseudonym for **Francisco PUIG Y DE LA PUENTE**)

RUBALCAVA, Manuel Justo de

b. August 9, 1769, Santiago, Cuba; d. 1805. Poet.

Close friend of the poet Zequiera, Rubalcava studied at the Colegio de San Basilio el Magno headed by his brother José Angel de Rubalcava (b. 1752). He became a good Latinist, translating Virgil. As a young man, Rubalcava fought the Spanish troops occupying Santo Domingo where he came to know Zequiera in 1796. Highly gifted, he painted and did sculptures, and sent off verses to all sides. Max Henriquez Ureña found his little pieces the best of his work, citing particularly several of his "Anacronticas" poems, some of his odes and the popular sonnet "A Nise bordando un ramillete" which had these lines:

No es la necesidad tan solamente
inventora suprema de las cosas
cuando de entre tus manos primorosas
nace una primavera floreciente.

Writings: Poetry: *Poesias,* Santiago de Cuba, 1848 (work edited by Luis Alejandro Baralt); *Poesias, por Zequiera y Rubalcava,* Havana, Comisión Nacional Cubana de la UNESCO, 1964, (444 p.); "La muerte de Judas" (in 91 royal octaves), 1st ed., 1830, edited by Manuel Maria Pérez y Ramirez, 2nd ed. of 1847 was edited by Pedro Santacilia; 3rd ed. by José Manuel Pérez Cabrera, 1927, the latter included in Volume I of José Manuel Carbonell's *Evolución de la cultura cubana,* 1928.

Biographical/Critical Sources: Max Henriquez Ureña, *Panorama histórico de la literatura cubana,* New York, 1963, pp. 81-83.

RUBENS, Alma

(pseudonym for **Providencia PORRATA DORIA DE RINCON**)

b. 1910, Caguas, Puerto Rico;
d. June 2, 1968, Santurce.

Poet.

Alma Rubéns was a postmodernist poet whose first collection *Nieblas* (1939) demonstrated a strong lyrical intelligence, both tender and musical. Her "Yo fui una sonámbula," from what some critics consider her best volume, *Corazón* (1953), begins:

Yo vivi en Oriente en algun vida,
vida muy remota, de siglos tal vez
fui lumbre apagada de hoguera
encendida . . .
Fui una perla muerta que adornó un
harén. . .
Fui la nota triste de lenta agonia. . .
Flor de invernadero sin rayo de sol,
. . . .
. . . .

Writings: Poetry: *Nieblas,* 1939; *Puesta de sol,* 1948; *Corazón,* 1953.

RUEDA, Manuel

b. August 27, 1921, Monte Cristi, Dominican Republic.

Poet, playwright, critic, folklorist, pianist, teacher.

Rueda has won the National Prize for Literature (1957) and has served as director of the National Conservatory of Music and of the Institute of Folklore Studies of the U.N.P.H.U. He is a member of the Academia Dominicana de la Lengua and is one of the most active and original collectors and propagators of Dominican folklore. In 1939, he went to Chile as a young man to study music, returning in 1944 to give concerts throughout the country.

He published his first verses in the journal *La Poesia Sorprendida* and became an important member of the group supporting the journal and its kind of poetry. His collection of sonnets, *Las Noches,* was well received and Herman Diaz Arrieta, a leading critic, remarked: "Al par que la música, digamos, audible, sonoro, instrumental, Manuel Rueda ha ido cultivando otra, verbal, imaginaria, de puro aire poético. . ."

In 1951 Rueda founded with other poets the press, La Isla Necesaria, to publish the increasingly active writers of the island. His own poetry has influenced younger writers and his use of the landscape from his natal northern part of the country in a tragic-philosophical fashion has opened new ways of expression as well as inspiring an ever greater use of indigenous folklore, magic and similar matter in Dominican prose and poetry.

Rueda's plays, too, have changed Dominican theatre, beginning with his *La Trinitaria Blanca* which won, as noted above, the first prize in the National Literature competition of 1957.

Rueda's recent work, *Con el tambor de las islas*(1975), is full of orthographic surprises and is straining toward musical expression. The poems have such titles as "Claves para una poesia plural," "Permutaciones," and "Canon ex única" and such appendes essays as "Conexiones de la música de vanguardia con el pluralism" (by Margarita Luna de Espaillat).

Writings: Poetry: *Las noches,* 1949, preface by Pedro Selva-Alone, Santiago, Chile, 1949; later republished in *Atenea* (published by the University of the Concepción, Santiago, Chile); new edition: S. Domingo, La Isla Necesaria, 1951 (this is the only *complete* edition of the sonnets); *Triptico,* Santiago, Chile 1949 (preface by Augusto D'Halmar); poems in *Antologias. . .,* coll. and ed. by Rueda, Santiago de los Caballeros, UCMM, 1972.

Tales: *Adivinanzas dominicanas,* in volume *Teatro,* 1968, see below.

Plays: *La trinitaria blanca,* S. Domingo, Col. Pensamiento Dominicana, 1957; Comp. Dram., 1968, both in S. Domingo; *Teatro* (includes *La Trinitaria blanca, La tia Beatriz hace un milagro,*

Vacaciones en el cielo, Entre alambradas, and *Adivinanzas dominicanas,* S. Domingo, Ed. de la Universidad Nacional "Pedro Henriquez Ureña, 1968; *Con el tambor de las islas: Pluralemas,* S. Domingo, Taller, 1975.

SALAZAR Y ROIG, Salvador

b. 1892, Colon, Panama; d. 1950, Cuba.
Playwright, poet, novelist, literary historian, critic, teacher, editor.

Salazar was a professor of Spanish literature and history of philosophy at the University of Havana. He founded the review *La Novela Cubana* and was a prime mover in the "Circulo Cubano de Bellas Artes" which began to offer prizes to plays in competitions beginning in 1931.

Earlier, Salazar had organized the Institución Cubana Pro Arte Dramático (1929) and the journal *Alma Cubana* which he edited to push playwrighting and production. Today his importance is historical, but his criticism and plays pointed the way to better Cuban theatre.

His fiction is not considered to be of high quality.

Writings: Literary Criticism-History: *Lope de Rueda y su teatro,* 1911; *Literatura cubana: El clasicismo de Cuba,* 1913; *Rafael Maria Mendive,* 1915; *Milanés, Luaces y la Avellaneda,* 1916; *José Marti,* 1918; *Elogio de Raimundo Cabrero,* 1925; *El elemento patriótico en la lirica cubana,* Havana, 1935; *Historia de la literatura cubana,* Havana, 1939.

Novels: *Por las nubes,* 1912; *El vampiro,* 1917; *Epistorlario de un madre.*

Verse: *Ternuras,* 1912.

General: *El porvenir de las pequeñas nacionalidades,* 1918; *La mujer en la guerra,* 1918.

Plays: *Por la fuerza del amor* (2 act comedy), Havana, La Novela Cubana, 1914; *La verdadera aristocracia* (2 act comedy), Havana, La Novela Cubana, 1914; *La caricia de la tarde* (1 act comedy), performed Teatro Cubano, Havana, 1914; *Asi es la vida* (2 act comedy), 1914; *El amor detectiva,* written 1918, published in *Alma Cubana,* Havana (1923-24) in Vol. I, pp. 25-34, 61-74, and in Vol. II (1924), pp. 110-120; *El precio* (3 acts, prose), in *Alma Cubana,* Vol. II (1924), pp. 160-164, 202-208, 240-252; *La torpe realidad,* 1920; *La otra, La canción de la tarde; La gallina ciega* (verse-burlesque); *Caballeresca,* 1925.

SALES, Miguel

b. ca. 1949, Cuba.
Poet.

Sales sought to flee Cuba when he was 16 years old but failed and served a term in prison for five years. After release he effected a successful flight from the island, but on returning in 1975 for his wife and infant child, he was apprehended and was sentenced to a twenty-five year period in jail. His one volume of poetry, created from work smuggled out to the United States, was *Desde las rejas* (From Behind Bars), Miami, 1976. Three poems from that collection, "Credo in Paréntesis" and "To the Murderable Corpse of Pedro Luis Boitel" later appeared in *Of Human Rights* (Fall 1977), published in Washington, D. C., along with "Poem No. 1" which first appeared in *Worldview* (January-February 1977).

SALINAS, Marcelo

b. October 30, 1889, Batabanó, Havana Province, Cuba.
Playwright, novelist.

Keenly devoted to agrarian reform and social improvement of the lot of farm workers, Salinas quickly ran afoul of the authorities and went into exile in the United States where he founded the journal *Liberación,* and during the first world war the journal *El Corsario* (with Puerto Rican and Cuban refugees). Later, he spent four months in prison in Cádiz, Spain. After founding the journal *Nueva Aurora* in Havana, Salinas was arrested but this time found innocent of the charge (of terrorism). He helped form the Cuba Soviética association and continued to battle for his ideas. Breaking with the Third International rather soon thereafter, however, he went on to form a theatre group in the country and took up other jobs, including that of librarian for the Escuela Técnica Industrial and as secretary of Culture of the Confederación de Trabajadores de Cuba (C.T.C.).

His play *Alma guajira* won the Camila Quiroga prize to his great shock. *Gente de La Habana* won the main award in another competition and his novel was given the first prize by the Ministry of Education (*Un aprendiz de revolucionario).* Left in manuscript is "Mi pueblo y el tuyo" (novel) and all his plays except *Alma guajira.* Salinas has written and published a little poetry.

Writings: Plays: *Cimarrón,* music by Gonzalo Roig (2 acts), and *La rosa de la vega,* music by Eliseo Grenet; *El mulato,* Havana, 1940; *Las almas buenas o La santa caridad,* performed Gran Teatro, 1948; *Ráfaga,* prize winner in 1939 of award of the Ministry of Education; *El Poder* (3 act farce); *El vagón de tercera* (surrealistic farce); *Secuestro* (3 act comedy); details of plays unknown; *La tierra . . . , la tierra . . .* (3 acts), premiered Teatro Nacional, 1928; *Las horas de un pueblo viejo,* 1939, details unknown; *Charito* (or) *Alma guajira,* first published, 1928, republished in *Teatro cubano contemporáneo,* 2nd ed., Dolores Martí de Cid, ed., Madrid, 1959, 1962, and exists in other collections.

Novel: *Un aprendiz de revolucionario,* Havana, 1937; and "Mi pueblo y el tuyo" (in ms.).

SAMA, Manuel Maria

b. May 22, 1850, Mayagüey, Puerto Rico; d. April 5, 1907, San Juan (or Miramar, 1913?)

Playwright, journalist, poet, bibliographer, historian.

At fifteen years of age, Sama had already begun to submit verse to the ephemeral journals of Mayagüez supported by the many local literati and the many resident Dominican exiles. This rubbing shoulders with the liberals of the day made Sama a political activist and romantic seeker of reform. With José Maria Monge, he collected and published *Poetas puertorriqueños* and began the scholarship leading to his bibliographical and historical work, *Bibliografia puertorriqueña.*

In his fifties, Sama moved to San Juan where he was elected president of the Ateneo, the leading cultural organization of the island. He published one play, *Inocente y Culpable,* and some poetry in random journals of the day.

Writings: Plays: *Inocente y Culpable* (3 acts, verse), performed in a Mayagüez theatre, 1877, published Madrid, Imp. de José Sol Torrens y Diego Garcia Navarro, 1877; *La victima de su falta* (3 acts, verse), performed in a Santo Domingo theatre, 1878.

Scholarship: *Bibliografia puertorriqueña,* Mayagüez, Tip. Comercial, 1887.

Histories: one on Christopher Columbus' voyages, details unknown; and one on Columbus' discovery of Puerto Rico, details unknown.

Poetry: in various journals and collections, including "Desde el mar" in *Antologia puertorriqueña,* Manuel Fernández Juncos, ed., New York, 1907, 1st ed., pp. 263-267.

SAMELA IGLESIAS, Luis

b. 1888, Ponce, Puerto Rico; d. 1938, San Juan.

Literary critic, journalist.

A leading critic of the "modernista" school, Samela wrote for *El Carnaval* (1911), *El Heraldo Español, Puerto Rico Ilustrado,* and *Revista de las Antillas.* Much of his work was aimed at examining social problems and other matters of public interest. His style was concise, sometimes touched by the elegant refinement of the "modernista" poets he appreciated so much. His journalistic pieces and other essays have not been published in any separate volume.

Writings: Essays: in many journals. His essay "Por el ojo de la historia" from *Puerto Rico Ilustrado* (September 12, 1914), appears in Luis Hernández Aquino's *El modernismo en Puerto Rico,* San Juan, 1967, pp. 171-173.

SANCHEZ, Carlos E.

b. ca. 1916, Cuba.
Playwright.

Sánchez' plays are psychological. His second work *La arena esta entre el mar y las rocas* (1947) is set in the United States and exploits the classical Oedipus pattern in a modern setting.

Writings: Plays: *Novela,* 1946, and *La arena esta entre el mar y las rocas,* 1947 (both written with Jorge Antonio González).

SANCHEZ, Luis Rafael

b. 1936, Humacao, Puerto Rico.
Storywriter, playwright, novelist.

Sánchez took his Ph.D. at the Central University of Madrid after an A.B. at the University of Puerto Rico and M. A. at Columbia University, New York City. He is a professor of literature at the University of Puerto Rico.

In 1976, Sánchez' novel about the new middle classes, *La Guarcha del macho Camacho* appeared. José Alcantará's description is interesting. The work, he states ". . .posee un ritmo ondulatorio, zigsagueante que encaja perfectamente con las situaciones. El lenguaje produce una sencación de borrachera colosal que domina a todos personajes."

Writings: Novel: *La guaracha del macho Camacho,* Buenos Aires, Ediciones de la Flor, 2nd ed., 1976.

Plays: *La espera,* 1959; *Sol 13 interior* (which includes *La hiel nuestra de cada dia* and *Los ángeles se han fatigado*), 1962; *Farsa del amor compradito, o casi el alma* and *La pasión según Antigona Pérez* as well as the title play *Sol 13 Interior; Sol 13 Interior* in complete form found in *Literatura puertorriqueña,* 2nd ed., Vol. II, E. Martinez Masdeu and Esther M. Melón, Rio Piedras, 1972, and also in *Teatro puertorriqueño, cuarto festival,* San Juan, 1963; *Los ángeles se han fatigado: farsa del amor compradido,* republished Hato Rey, P. R., Ediciones Lugar, 1960, (131 p.); *La pasión según Antigona Pérez,* premiered in 1969, published Hato Rey, Ediciones Lugar, 1968 (presented in English, 1972, during tour by Puerto Rican Traveling Company in New York City), republished Puerto Rico, Editorial Cultural, 1973; *O casi el alma,* in *Teatro puertorriqueño, séptimo festival,* San Juan, 1965.

Biographical/Critical Sources: José Alcántara Almánzar's general essay, "*La Guaracha: Del Macho Camacho*—Y El Puerto Rico De Hoy," in *Impacto Socialista, (*Santo Domingo, D. R.) III, Nos. 35-36 (June-July 1977), pp. 41-45; Lorraine Elena Ben-Ur, "Myth Montage in a Contemporary Puerto Rican Tragedy: La pasión según Antigona Pérez: crónica americana en actos," in *Latin American Literary Review,* IV, 7 (Fall-Winter, 1975), pp. 15-21; for a discussion of Sánchez' seven plays, see Angelina Morfi, "El teatro de Luis Rafael Sánchez," in *Revista del Instituto de Cultura Puertorriqueña,* 52 (July-September 1971), pp. 39-49; also see Alyce de Keuhne, "The Antigona Theme in Anouilh, Marechal, and Luis Rafael Sánchez, in papers *French-Brazilian-Spanish-American Literary Relations,* MLA Seminar 17 (Evanston, Illinois: Northwestern University, Department of Spanish & Portuguese, 1970); Review of *La Guaracha del Macho Camacho,* by Manuel Maldonado Denis, in *¡Ahora!* No. 693 (February 21, 1977), p. 40.

SANCHEZ, René

b. 1927, Cuba.
Playwright, actor.

Anade, Sánchez' first play is an intimate picture of a woman who hopes to become a mother and his second work, *Liberación,* a study of the glorious period of Cuban struggle for independence.

Writings: Plays: *Anade,* 1948; *Liberación.*

SANCHEZ BOUDY, José

b. 1927, Havana, Cuba.
Poet, folklórist, storywriter, novelist, lawyer.

Sánchez Boudy has passed most of his adult life abroad but his extensive creative work, mostly in verse and short stories, deals with Cuban life, particularly its Afro-Cuban folkloric aspects. His characteristic poem "Saoca" begins:

Los negros tienan saoco.
Los negros tienen bembé.
Los negros le dan al cuero.
Los negros echan le pie.

La mulata contorsiona.
—¡Echa pa'lante varona!

Writings: Poetry: *Poemas de otoño e invierno,* Barcelona, Bosch, 1967; *Ritmo de solá*, Barcelona, Bosch, 1970; in progress: "Crocante de maní"; *Poemas del silencio,* Barcelona, Bosch, 1968; poems in various journals and collections, including *Poesia negra del caribe,* Miami, Hortensia Ruiz del Vizo, 1971 (which offers "Saoco," "La Escalera" and "Esa Negra Fuló."

Novel: *Lilayando (antinovela),* Miami, Universal, 1971.

Stories: *Cuentos grises,* Barcelona, Bosch, 1966; *Cuentos del hombre,* Barcelona, Bosch, 1969; *Cuentos a luna llena,* Miami, Universal, 1971, foreword by Ana Rosa Núñez.

Biographical/Critical Sources: See Ana Rosa Núñez' foreword to *Cuentos a luna llena,* op.cit.

SANCHEZ GALARRAGA, Gustavo

b. 1893, Havana, Cuba; d. 1934.
Poet, playwright, critic.

Sánchez was one of the most prolific of Cuban poets and dramatists, publishing some thirty volumes of verse and fourteen plays. One of his most "Gongorist" collections is *Glosas del Camino* (1920), full of complex melancholy and romantic, highly polished lines. His work resolutely sought to recapture the past but he often was facile, instead of original. Many of his theatre pieces were set to music by Ernesto Lecuona. Much of his poetry celebrated the Afro-Cuban and his culture as in such works as "La Mulata."

Writings: Plays: *Drama de esclavos* (3 acts); *Soy innocente* (3 acts), performed Teatro Avellaneda, Camaguey, March 10, 1897; and *La expulsada; Los hijos de Herakles* (tragedy); *La sacrificada; Un veterano de Baire* (monologue); and in the five-volume collected plays: Vol. I: *La verdad de la vida* (2 act comedy); *La máscara de anoche* (1 act comedy); *La vida falsa* (2 act comedy), Havana, 1918, but written in 1912; Vol II: *El héroe* (3 acts); *El mundo de los muñecos* (2 act comedy); *La princesa buena* (1 act), originally Imp. Mestre y Martinica, 1918, and Havana, 1920; Vol. III: *El buen camino* (2 act comedy); *Compuesta, y sin novio; Conferencia contra el hombre* (monologue), Havana, 1920; Vol. IV: *La última corrida* (monologue); *Carmen* (4 acts); *Dos de mayo* (monologue), Havana, 1923; Vol. V: *El último areito; El filibústero* (3 acts); *Sangre Mambisa,* Havana, 1923.

Poetry: *La fuente matinal,* 1915; *Lámpara votivo,* 1916; *La barca sonora,* 1917; *El jardin de Margarita,* Havana, 1917; *Copos de sueño,* 1918; *Excelsior,* 1919; *Motivos sentimentales,* 1919; *Cancionero de la vida,* 1920; *La copa amarga,* 1920; *Cromos callejeros,* 1920; *Glosas del camino,* 1920; *Momentos liricos,* 1920; *Música triste,* 1920; *Recogimiento,* 1920; *Flores de agua,* 1921; *El nemanso de las lágrimas,* 1922; *Cancionero de la vida,* (2nd ed. published with *Oblación,* 1922; *Triptico heróica,* 1923; *Mira ardiente,* 1923; *Cancionera española,* 1923; *Humo azul,* 1923; *Tono menor; Senderos de luna; Canto a la mujer cubana; Horas grises; Huerto cerrado; Canto a la Anunciata; La ciudad maga; Palabras dolientes.*

SANCHEZ LAMOUTH, Juan

b. 1929, Dominican Republic; d. 1968.
Poet.

Sánchez won the Gastón F. Deligne National Poetry Prize for 1963-64. He is one of the leading writers employing Afro-Caribbean themes in his work. His verse is elegant and highly thoughtful.

Writings: Poetry: *19 poemas sin importancia,* 1955; *Sinfonia vegetal a Juan Pablo Duarte,* S. Domingo, Ed. del Caribe, 1966; *Brumas; Elegia a las hojas caidas y 19 poemas sin importancia; Cuaderno para una muerte en primavera; Otoño y poesia; Introducción a la tristeza; Memorial de los bosques; El pueblo y la sangre.*

Biographical/Critical Sources: F. A. Mota Medrano, *Relieves Alumbrados,* S. Domingo, 1971, pp. 227-245.

SANCHEZ VARONA, Ramón

b. 1883, Sancti Spiritus, Cuba.
Playwright, journalist.

Sánchez' plays were staged usually long after having been written and consequently almost seemed revivals rather than contemporary works when reviewed. Their tone and verse form were nineteenth century and post-romantic in tone. Nonetheless, both Augustin Acosta and Enrique José Varona found his characters well realized and his scenes dramatic. Max Henriquez Ureña, however, found his work too imitative of the century past and demanding too superannuated attitudes and sentiment to be appreciated.

Writings: Plays: *Las piedras de Judea* (3 act comedy, prose), Havana, Imp. Militar, 1915; *El Ogro* (3 act comedy), 1915; *Marta* (comedy), 1916; *La Asechanza* (2 act prose comedy), Havana, Mestre y Martinica, 1918; *Con todos y para todos* (3 acts historical drama), Havana, Mestre y Martinica, 1918; *La cita* (1 act comedy), published in *Revista Universal* (August 1920); *La sombra,* Havana, 1938; *El amor perfecto,* Havana, 1948.

Sketches: *La hipoteca;* and *El pequeño tirano.*

Biographical/Critical Sources: Augustin Acosta's introduction to *El amor perfecto,* Havana, 1948.

SANCHEZ DE FUENTES Y PELAEZ, Eugenio

b. 1865, Puerto Rico.
Playwright, storywriter.

Sánchez arrived as a child in Cuba and passed his professional life there. His many theatrical works today are of only historical interest.

Writings: Plays: *Un ardid feminil* (1 act, prose), Matanzas, Imp. Galeria Literaria, 1887; *Sacrifici* (3 act prose comedy), Tenerife, Canaries, Imp. Sucesores de M. Curbelo, 188?; *¡Cuatro siglos después!* (1 act, verse), written for four centuries' celebration of Columbus' arrival in Cuba, published Havana, La Especial, 1892; *Entre una mujer y Dios* (3 acts, prose), Havana, La Especial, 1895, premiered March 22, 1895 at Teatro Tacón, Havana; *El primo Basilo* (4 acts, prose), Havana, Fernández, 1901, premiered January 1, 1901, in Teatro Payret, Havana (known to have been based on novel of same name by Portuguese writer José Maria Eça de Quiroz; *Colón y el Judio errante* (2 act verse fantasy), Havana, La Propaganda Literaria, 1877.

Novelette: *Acuarelas,* Havana, 1890 (200 pp.).

SANTACILLA, Pedro A.

b. 1826, Santiago, Cuba; d. 1910.
Poet.

Arrested in 1851 in Santiago for, among other things, having circulated in manuscript his own poem "Himnoa guerra," Santacilla remained incarcerated in Havana's Castillo del Principe until January 25, 1852, and then was sent to forced exile in Spain. He wrote poems while in jail, including "A una nube" and "Adios" and was able to study. After more than seven years in provincial Spanish towns, he escaped to Gibralter and then got to the United States where he joined the Junta Revolucionaria Cubana de Nueva York.

For a period Santacilla worked in New Orleans for Domingo Goicuria y Compañia and then, ever active, he went on to Mexico to support Benito Juárez in his successful campaign against the French troops installed there by Louis Napoleon. He married President Juárez' eldest daughter and performed tasks for the Cuban exiles in 1868 and thereafter. He lived to see Cuban independence, but never returned to the island though he lived until 1910.

In his earlier days, Santacilla founded, with Francisco Baralt, the review *Ensayos literarios* (1847) and was associated with refugee journals such as *La Verdad* and *El Cubano* of New York, and *La Verda* of New Orleans. He had also been an editor of *Diario Oficial* with Guillermo Prieto, and with Prieto and others, he edited *La Chinaca* and *El Nuevo Mundo.*

The most critically acclaimed work of Santacilla is probably his translation "Salmo de David" (Psalm 137). However, his name in literature will be remembered primarily for his editorship of the collection of patriotic poems gathered in the volume *El laúd del desterrado,* published in New York City and including José Marti and other early heroes of Cuban nationalism.

Writings: Poetry: *El arpa del proscritta,* New York, 1856.

Speech-Essay: *Lecciones orales sobre historia de Cuba,* New Orleans, 1859 (eight lectures delivered at the Ateneo Democrático Cubano of New York).

Legends: "El genio del mal," and "La clava del indio," both published in Mexico, Impr. El. Heraldo, 1862.

Translation: *El Papa en el siglo XIX* (of Giuseppe Mazzini's Italian work), New Orleans, 1854.

Editor of: *El laúd del desterrado,* New York, 1858 (contains poems of many of the Cuban fighters for independence: Marti, Miguel Teurbe Tolón, José Agustin Quintero, Pedro Angel Castellón, Leopoldo Turla, Juan Clemente Zenea and Santacilla himself).

Biographical/Critical Sources: Max Henriquez Ureña, *Panorama histórico de la literatura cubana,* New York, 1963, pp. 330-332, 335, 337, 378.

SANZ Y GARCIA, Julián

b. 1886, Cienfuegos, Cuba; d. 1924, Cienfuegos.
Poet, playwright.

Sanz y Garcia, a prolific writer of comic farces at the early part of the 20th century, is almost an unknown figure in Cuban literature today.

Writings: Poetry: in various journals.

Plays: *Dar de comer al hambriento* (verse monologue), premiered July 30, 1905, Teatro Terry, Cienfuegos, and published Cienfuegos, Martin, 1905; *Los lios del entresuelo* (1 act comedy, prose), Cienfuegos, Martin, 1907, premiered Teatro Terry, Cienfuegos, May 16, 1907, and in Teatro Payret, Havana, August 23, 1907; *El abuelito* (1 act), Cienfuegos, Martin, 1907; *Los hermanos Quintero* (1 act prose farce), Santa Cruz de Tenerife, Imp. Benitez, 1909; *Premio y castigo* (comedy), Cienfuegos, 1909; *Por Primo* (1 act, prose), 1910; *La real moza* (1 act musical), Cienfuegos, Imp. Valero, 1910; and written with León Ichazo: *Amar a ciegas* (2 act comedy, prose), Havana, Imp. ruiz, 1914; *La flor del camino* (2 act comedy), Havana, Ruiz, 1914; *Rosalba* (3 act comedy), Havana, Imp. El Siglo, XX, 1916.

SARACHAGA, Ignacio

b. ca. 1850, Havana, Cuba; d. 1900.
Playwright.

Sarachaga was one of the more popular writers for the baudy burlesque stage of Havana in the late decades of the 19th century.

Writings: Plays: *Un baile por fuera* (1 act farce), Havana, Imp. La Habanera, 1880; *Habana y*

Almendares; Los efectos del Base Ball Apropósito (1 act, 5 scenes, prose comedy) with music by Rafael Paláu, Havana, La Moderna, 1892; plays in ms: *El doctor Machete,* performed in the Salon "Trotcha," Havana; *En la cocina* (1 act), Havana, 1881; *En un cachimbo* (1 act farce), Havana, 1880; *Esta noche si. . .*(1 act), Havana, 1881; *Lo que pasa en la cocina* (1 act prose), Havana, 1886.

SARDUY, Severo

b. 1937, Camaguëy, Cuba.
Novelist, editor, journalist, poet, storywriter, painter.

After completing high school in Camagüey, Sarduy moved to Havana where he soon joined the group associated with the journal *Ciclón* and published poems, stories, and a few journalistic articles. For a period after Castro's triumph, Sarduy edited the literary page of *Diario Libre* and was an editor of *Lunes de Revolución.* He exhibited his paintings in showings in New York City, Caracas and Tokyo. He has traveled widely in Europe and in 1962, breaking with Castro, he decided to settle down in Paris where he still lives, working there for a publishing house.

Sarduy's work is experimental, heavily influenced by James Joyce. His first works done through 1969 dealt with a timeless Cuba, but *Cobra* (1972) and *Big Bang para situar en órbita cinco máquinas de Román Alejandro* (1973) move on to more contemporary dreams, bizarre and tinsel-filled with images of disparate cultures and epochs. Speaking of the theme of India as a transvestite of the West in the European imagination, Sarduy explained:

> *. . .we're not talking about a transcendental, metaphysical or profound India, but on the contrary, about an exaltation of the surface and I would say costume jewelry India. I believe. . .that the only unneurotic reading that is possible from our logocentric point of view, is that which India's surface offers. The rest is Christianizing translation, syncretism, real superficiality.*

The novel *Big Bang* is if anything more weird thematically and stylistically and yet the picaresque beginnings of the romance-novel in Spain is evident in these innovative works.

Writings: Novels: *Gestos,* Barcelona, Seix y Barral, 1963, and excerpt in *Narrativo cubano de la revolución,* M. J. Cabballero Bonald, ed., Madrid, 1969; *De donde son los cantantes,* Mexico, Joaquin Mortiz, 1967, and French language version by C. Esteban and author as *Ecrit en dansant,* Paris, Seuil, 1967; *Cobra,* Buenos Aires, Sudamericana, 1972, in French, Paris, Seuil, 1972 (winner of Prix Médicis), and in English translation by Suzanne Jill Levine, New York, E. P. Dutton, 1975, and Toronto, Clarke Inwin, 1975, all entitled *Cobra; From Cuba with a Song,* in English translation by Suzanne Jill Levine and Hallie D. Taylor in book entitled *Triple Cross* (contains also two other works), New York, Dutton, 1972; *Big Bang para situar órbita cinco máquinas de*

Román Alejandro, Paris, Editions Fata Morgana, 1973; *Pasión de Urbino,* Argentina, n.d.

Essays: *Escrito sobre un cuerpo,* 1969; and a collection of essays, interviews, biographical notes, bibliographies, as *Severo Sarduy,* edited by Jorge Aguilar Mora, Roland Barthes, Jean-Michel Fossey, et. al., Madrid, Fundamentos, 1976.

Biographical/Critical Sources: Seymour Menton, *Prose Fiction of the Cuban Revolution,* 1975; Emir Rodriguez Monegal, *El arte de narrar,* Caracas, Monte Avile, 1968 (for interview with Sarduy, see pp. 269-292); Roberto Gonzáles Echevarria, "Para una bibliografia de y sobre Severo Sarduy," *Revista Iberoamericana,* 38, No. 79 (April-June 1972), pp. 333-343; and "Son de la Habana: La ruta de Severo Sarduy," in *Revista Iberoamericana,* 37 Nos. 76-77 (July-December 1972), pp. 725-740. Also see the article, "Homenaje a Lezama," in *Mundo Nuevo,* No. 24 (June 1968), pp. 4-17; and many essays on *Cobra* in *Review 74.*

SARUSKY MILLER, Jaime

b. 1931, Havana, Cuba.
Novelist, journalist.

Active in the revolutionary movement led by Castro, Sarusky has been an editor of several literary journals and works for the Instituto del Libro and contributed many critical articles to major reviews. His first novel, existentialistic, appeared in 1961 (*La búsqueda*) and the second (*Rebelión en la Octavo Casa*), reflecting "magical realism," was a finalist in the Casa de las Américas competition.

Writings: Novels: *La búsqueda,* Havana, Revolución, 1961; *Rebelión en la octava casa,* Havana, Instituto del Libro, 1967, fragment published in *Narrativa cubana de la revolución,* J. M. Caballero Bonald, Madrid, Alianza Editorial, 1968, 1969, 1971.

SAVINON, Altagracia

b. September 28, 1886, Santo Domingo, Dominican Republic; d. December 23, 1942, Santo Domingo.
Poet.

Saviñón's famous "Mi vaso verde" is considered one of the earliest and most perfect of the modernist poems which introduced French impressionistic themes and verse techniques into the Dominican poetic consciousness.

Her major works appeared in the review *La Cuna de América* during its issuance from 1903-13.

Writings: No separate volumes, but her work is in various collections and "Mi vaso verde" can be found in Contin Aybar's *Antologia poética dominicana,* Santiago, D. R., 1943; in *Nuestras mejores poetisas,* edited by R. A. Sonabia, published S. Domingo, 1928; and *Antologia de de la literatura dominicana,* Ciudad Trujillo, 1944.

SELLEN, Antonio

b. 1838, Santiago, Cuba; d. 1889.
Poet, translator.

Brother of Francisco Sellén, Antonio was a skilled and asiduous translator from many languages, including English, German, French and Danish. He was also a minor poet. His major work might well have been *Cuatro poemas de Lord Byron* which added to the growing collection of works in Spanish of the English romantic hero-poet.

Writings: Poetry: *Poesias,* Havana, 1864.

Translations: *Estudios poéticos,* Havana, 1863; *Cuatro poemas de Lord Byron* ("Parisina," "El prisionero de Chillón,"); *Los lamentos del Tasso; La novia de Abydos,* 1877; *Joyas del Norte de Europa,* 1879 (verse of Isaias Tégner, and eight other Danish and German poets); *Ecos del Sena,* 1883 (French romantic poets); "La esperanza en Dios" (Musset's poetry), first appeared in *Revista Cubana,* later in separate booklet, 1883; Lytton Bulwer's poem as "Amor y orgullo," 1886; and translations of Adam Mickiewicz' poem as *Conrado Wallenrod;* both in *Revista Cubana,* 1885.

Biographical/Critical Sources: Max Henriquez Ureña, *Panorama histórico de la literatura cubana,* New York, 1963, pp. 319-322.

SELLEN, Francisco

b. October 10, 1836, Santiago, Cuba; d. 1907.
Poet, playwright, translator.

A strong nationalist, Francisco Sellén was imprisoned in 1868 for supporting the 1868 revolt led by Carlos Manuel de Céspedes. After time in forced exile in Spain, he moved to the United States whence he refused to move until he could return to an independent Cuba, something he did in 1902, five years before his death.

With his brother Antonio, Francisco was an ardent admirer of Lord Byron and translated much of the English poet's work into Spanish. He also did translations from German, French and Scandinavian poets as well.

Writings: Poetry: *Libro intimo,* Havana, 1865; *Poesias,* New York, 1890; *Cantos de la patria,* New York, 1900.

Plays: *Hatuey* (5 acts, verse), New York, A. De Costa Gómez, 1891; *La muerte de Demóstenes* (5 acts), long unpublished, but eventually published in 1911 with preface by Max Henriquez Ureña, and a new Henriquez Ureña edition, Havana, 1926; *Las apuestas de Zuleika* (1 act), New York, Hernández, 1901, performed only once in English translation by Enrique Lincoln de Zayas at Berkeley, Lyceum, April 28, 1893.

Translation of: Heinrich Heine's work as *Intermezzo lirico; Ecos del Rin* (163 poems of 38 different German poets, including nine poems translated by Antonio Sellén); and Byron's poem as "El Giaour" in *Revista Cubana,* 1887; also four novels from English including Nathaniel Hawthorne's *Scarlet Letter,* 1895, Wilkie Collins' *The Moonstone,* 1892, and R. L. Stevenson's *Kidnapped,* 1896; also Zacaria Werner's one act play as *El 24 de Febrero,* Havana, 1864; Moliere's play as *El amor pintor* (1 act prose comedy), Matanzas, 1856; and collection of translations (made by him and his brother Antonio): *Estudios poéticos,* Havana, 1863.

Biographical/Critical Sources: Max Henriquez Ureña, *Panorama histórico de la literatura cubana,* New York, 1963, pp. 319-322.

SERRA, Narciso

b. ca. 1831, Cuba (?).
Playwright.

Both of Serra's plays concern Don Quixote and both works, "bocetas escénicos," were among the earliest by a Cuban playwright.

Writings: Plays: *El loco de la guardilla,* 1861; *El bien tardio,* 1867.

SERPA, Enrique

b. 1899, Havana, Cuba.
Poet, novelist, critic, storywriter.

A poet only in his younger days, Serpa moved on to prose and criticism. His verse was less formal and self-conscious than that of his contemporaries though still highly subjective and intimate in tone. His stories and two novels are in the Zola "naturalismo" mode and highly descriptive of both the physical and emotional worlds of their characters. "Aletas de Tiburón" is felt to be possibly his finest work of naturalism.

Writings: Poetry: *La miel de las horas,* Havana, 1925; *Vitrina,* Havana, 1940 (contains much of his work done from 1923-1925).

Criticism: (of Alfonso H. Catá) in *Recordación de Hernández Catá,* 1943.

Stories: *Aletas de tiburón,* Havana, La Tertulia, 1963 (one story, written 1928); *Felisa y no,* 1937; *Noche de fiesta,* Havana, 1951, and in translation, represented in *Classic Tales from Spanish America,* Great Neck, N. Y., Barron's Educational Series, 1962.

Novels: *Contrabando,* 1938; *La trampa,* 1956.

Genre unknown: *Dias de Trinidad,* Havana, Alvarez-Pita, 1939.

C. SICTO

(pseudonym for **Cándido COSTI Y ERRO**)

SIACA RIVERA, Manuel

b. 1906, Loiza, Puerto Rico.
Poet, essayist, critic.

Siaca Rivera took an A.B. and M.A. at the University of Puerto Rico. His first collection of verse *Gotas liricas* (1931) reflects Rubén Dario and Herrera Reissig and others, but his second volume, *Sombres paralelas* (1936), shows a decided movement forward toward the subject and style of Garcia Lorca, Jorge Guillén and others. His study of José P. H. Hernández places emphasis on his style and major themes—love, death and nature.

Writings: Poetry: *Gotas liricas,* 1931; *Sombras paralelas,* 1936.

Critical Biography: "José P. H. Hernández, su vida y su obra," (M.A. thesis), published as *José P. H. Hernández: vida y obra,* San Juan, 1965.

SIERRA BERDECIA, Fernándo

b. 1903, Ciales, Puerto Rico.
Playwright, storywriter, poet, journalist.

An active journalist, Sierra Berdecia published articles in or worked for such journals as *El Imparcial, El Mundo, Puerto Rico Ilustrado* and *Alma Latina.* His one play, *Esta noche juega el Jóker,* reflects the work of Ibsen and Ramón del Valle Inclán, and had an enthusiastic reception when performed in San Juan and elsewhere in the island. The play's theme was the ever popular one of the trials and joys of Puerto Rican experience in New York City. His second play, *La escuela del buen amor,* is felt to be less successful than the earlier one. He has not collected his verse which is 'profundo, grises . . . " according to C. Rosa-Nieves in his *Aguinaldo lirico.*

Writings: Plays: *Esta noche juega el Jóker,* (3 act comedy, prose), 1939, 2nd ed., Biblioteca de Autores Puertorriqueños, 1948; *La escuela del buen amor,* San Juan, Edit., Coqui, 1963.

Critical Biography: *Antonio S. Pedreira, Buceador de la personalidad puertorriqueña,* 1940, 2nd ed., rev., San Juan, Biblioteca de Autores Puertorriqueños, 1942, (55 p.).

Poetry: in various journals and collections, including *Aguinaldo lirico,* C. Rosa-Nieves, ed., 1st ed., Rio Piedras, 1957, 2nd ed., 1971, pp. 172-176; and *Nueva poesia de Puerto Rico,* Angel Balbuena Briones and Hernández Aquino, eds., Madrid, 1952.

Story: *Aguafuerte,* San Juan, Edit. Coquí, 1963, (21 p.).

SIMO, Ana Maria

b. 1943, Cuba.
Storywriter.

Simó published her first collection at 19 and has remained a dark-imagined fantasist even after the break-up of her once "Beat" group, the "el puente." Her weird story "Growth of the Plant" has a seedling sprouting in a bathroom eventually reaching monstrous and man-eating size and appetite.

Writings: Tales: *Las fábulas,* Havana, El Puente, 1962; stories in various publications, including "Growth of the Plant" in *Writings from the New Cuba,* E. M. Cohen, ed., Harmondsworth, England, Penguin, 1967.

SMITH, Octavo

b. 1921, Cuba.
Poet.

An adherent of the "transcendentalist" group around José Lezama Lima, Smith generally employed the 12-syllable line as in the poem "La casa que la muerte ha visitado":

Con pulcro, translúcido redoble
los cristales
se abrian festoneados de salinos envios,
mojados del tresco encaje onirico asestado
por el mar en diálogo brioso.

Writings: Poetry: *Del furtivo destierro,* Havana, 1946; *Estos barrios,* Havana, La Tertulia, 1966.

SOCORRO DE LEON, José

b. b. 1831, Cuba; d. 1869.
Poet, playwright.

A minor poet, Socorro supported the arts and helped publish the pioneering volumes *Cuba poética* selected by José Fornaris.

Writings: Poetry: *Ensayos poéticos,* 1852; *Flores silvestres,* 1853; *Colección de versos,* 1857.
Play: *Garrotazo y tente tieso* (1 act comedy), Havana, Imp. Barcina, 1863.

SOLA, José Narciso

b. 1890, Dominican Republic; d. 1944.
Playwright.

One of Dominica's earliest and most prolific playwrights, Sola is only briefly mentioned in literary histories today though he helped pioneer use of creole in his plays, eleven of which are known.

Writings: Plays: *El intruso; Temblor politico; Llegó el hombre; El fracaso de Napoléon; Perico se casó; No más yes o Un matrimonio a lo yanqui; El pirata;* the following works flavored with creole expressions: *El gran secretario; Chismes de barrio; El dia de San Pedro; Los ángeles del bien.*

SOLER Y MERINO, Mariano Antonio

b. 1877, Dominican Republic; d. 1899.
Poet.

Soler was considered by Max Rodriguez Ureña to have been an excellent talent, delicate, lyrical, original—but, dead at twenty, his work is more "promising" than realized. His three main topics were liberty, motherhood and woman—good subjects for any young man, and reflecting the obvious influences of the Dominican poets Diaz Mirón and Gastón F. Deligne.

Writings: Poetry: in various journals and collections; one collection, *Flores tropicales,* 1909.

Biographical/Critical Sources: Joaquín Balaguer's *Historia de la literatura dominicana,* 1970, pp. 142-144.

SOLONI, Félix

b. 1900, Cuba.
Novelist, storywriter, folklorist, journalist.

Soloni introduced much local color and colloquial speech into his stories and novels. His story "La ponina" is considered one of his most vivid pictures of common life in Havana, and the dramatization for television of his story "Tina Morejón" was an outstanding success.

Writings: Novels: *Mersé,* Havana, 1924; 2nd ed. (rev.), Havana, 1926; *Virulilla,* Havana, 1927; *Pachin,* Havana, n.d.
Stories: *El alma de las casas; Humo de vida; Parrafitos.*
Essays: "Lógico del absurdo," and others published in various journals.

SOLORZANO Y CORREOSO, Antonio

b. ca. 1817, Cuba.
Playwright.

Solorzano was one of the most widely published early playwrights of Cuba, but is of only historical interest today.

Writings: Plays: *El Conde Don Enrique o La victima del amor* (3 acts), Puerto Principe, Imp. del Gobierno, 1847, 2nd ed., Havana, Imp. El Iris, 1857; *Don Fernando en el siglo XIV* (4 acts), 1848; *Don Pedro de Castilla* (5 acts, verse), Santiago, Imp. de la R. Sociedad Económica, 1852, 2nd ed., 1855; *El triunfo de la virtud o La lealtad de una esposa* (1 act, verse), Havana, Imp. La Cubana, 1857; *El sacrificio y la victima* (3 acts, verse), Havana, Imp. del Vapor, 1858; *El Arturo* (1 act, verse), Havana, Imp. del Vapor, 1858; *Esposa, virgen y mártir* (3 acts, verse), Havana, Imp. del Vapor, 1859.

SORAVILA, Lesbia

b. 1907, Cuba.
Novelist, storywriter.

Soravila was an ardent struggler for women's rights and presented her side of this issue in her novels and stories, the latter, however, never collected in a volume.

Writings: Novels: *El dolor de vivir,* 1932; *Cuando libertan las esclavas,* 1935.

SOTO, Pedro Juan

b. July 11, 1928, Cataño, Puerto Rico.
Novelist, storywriter, playwright, critic.

After primary and secondary education at local schools in Cataño and Bayamón, Soto took his B.A. from the University of Long Island, New York State University, in 1950. In 1953 he earned his M.A. in journalism at Columbia University. Since 1954 he has lived in Puerto Rico and has been the editor of the *San Juan Review.* He has prepared film scripts and educational booklets for the Puerto Rican Division of Community Education.

In his 1961 novel, *Ardiente suelo, fria estación,* the hero Ardiente experiences what any 18-year old Puerto Rican student might in a move to New York City. Here, he constantly feels an outsider—but, on returning to Puerto Rico, he has changed enough to be an outsider there, too. *El francotirador* of 1969 looks at student life in more detail this time in the Puerto Rican ambiance. *Temporada de duendes* of 1970 puts the central character, Baldomero Linares, against his own sloth and unease in a decaying island culture and the forceful, alien ways of a foreign film company arrived in Baldomero's home village of Barrizales. *Usmail* is probably Soto's most noted work, dealing as it does with the impact of U. S. troops on the island of Vieques, an island much like Puerto Rico.

Much of his writing seems strongly under the influences of Faulkner and Hemingway.

Soto is married to the former Rosina Arrivi and they have two sons.

Writings: Novels: *Los perros anónimos* (unpublished but written in 1950); *Usmail,* first published in 1939, reprinted by Book Club of Puerto Rico, 1959, new edition Rio Piedras, Edit. Cultura, 1970; *Ardiente suelo fria estación,* Xalapa, Mexico, Universidad Veracruzana, 1961, trans., *Hot Land, Cold Season,* New York, Dell, 1973; *El francotirador,* Mexico, Joaquin Mortiz, 1969; *Temporada de duendes,* Mexico, Edit. Diógenes, 1970.

Plays: *El huésped,* performed Teatro Experimental, San Juan, 1956, published San Juan, Artes y Letras, 1958; *Las máscaras* (unpublished but written in 1958).

Autobiography: in René Marqués' introduction to *Cuentos puertorriqueños de hoy,* pp. 149-158.

Literary Criticism: in *Asomante* and *El Mundo* and other journals.

Stories: in various periodicals and collections; "Los Inocentes" won first prize in the competition of the Ateneo, 1957, and appears in René Marqués' *Cuentos puertorriqueños de hoy,* with Soto's story "La Cantiva"; one collection of his works is *Spiks,* Mexico, Los Presentes, 1956, 3rd ed., Rio Piedras, Edit. Cultural,

1970; English trans. New York and London, Monthly Review Press, 1974; an extract entitled "The Innocents" appeared in *From the Green Antilles,* London, Panther Books, 1967 (edited by Barbara Howe); and "Garabatos" and "Campeones" are in *Literatura puertorriqueña,* 2nd ed., Vol. II, E. Martinez Masdeu and Esther M. Melón, eds., Rio Piedras, 1972, pp. 341-354.

Biographical/Critical Sources: Nilita Vientós Gastón, "El Primer Libro de Pedro Juan Soto: *Spiks,*" in *El Mundo,* San Juan (February 2, 1957); Hugo Rodriquez Alcala, "*Spiks:* Una Orba de Pedro Juan Soto," in *El Mundo* (December 16, 1957); Concha Meléndez,ed., *El arte del cuento en Puerto Rico,* New York, 1961, pp. 351-354, with the stories "Garabatos" and "Los Inocentes," pp. 354-366; also review of *Temporado de duendes* by Maria Inez Lagos de Pope, "Una alegoria del neocolonialismo," in *The Bilingual Review,* I, 2(May-August 1974), pp. 208-211; Eugene Mohr's review of *Spiks* (English-language edition), in *Revista Interamericana,* Vol. IV, No. 4 (Winter 1974/75), pp. 557-58; and see Victoria Ortiz' introduction to her translation of *Spiks;* essay by Eduardo Seda Bonnila, as "On the Vicissitudes of Being 'Puerto Rican': An Exploration of Pedro Juan Soto's *Hot Land, Cold Season," in Revista Interamericana* VIII, No. 1 (Spr. 1978), pp. 116-128.

SOTO RAMOS, Julio

b. April 20, 1903, Coamo, Puerto Rico.
Poet, critic, journalist.

Soto Ramos introduced his blend of E. E. Cummings (U.S.A.) and Mallarmé (France) in verse he called "Cumarisotismo," which sought a "lirovisuografia" with strong color imagery and bizarre typographic presentations of his poetic ideas. "Cumarisotismo," explained Soto, "es una palabra compuesta de *Cu* (Edward Estlin Cummings), *Ma* (Esteban Mallarmé), *Ri* (Arturo Rivas Sainz) y *Sotismo* (un ismo más, formado de mi apellido paterno)."

His experimentalism in typographical eccentricities in the manner of the U. S. poet e. e. cummings can be seen in "Trapecio." Its title is:

T
U
E *UNA*
N
ESTRELLA

and "El baño" which, though regular, is highly original.

La tarde va denuda a vestirse de olas

Los siglos cantan

la candión de la espuma
Los buzos luminosos hacen señales
en el profondo cien de escama
. . .
Por los dedos abiertos de las palmas
una nube maromera pasa zumbando.

Writings: Poetry: *Cortina de sueños,* 1923: *Relicario azul,* 1933; *Soledades en sol,* 1952; *Trapecio,* San Juan, 1955.

Literary Histories: *Fé de erratas de la antologia nueva poesia de Puerto Rico,* San Juan, 1953; *Panorama literario y periodistico Puerto Rico,* San Juan, Publicaciones del Ateneo Universitario, 1955.

Critical Biography: *Por caminos ajenos,* 1942.

Essays: *Cumbre y remanso: ensayos de apreciación literaria y otros articulos,* San Juan, Edit. Cordillera, 1963; *Una pica enflandes,* San Juan, Edit. Club de la Prensa, 1959.

SOTO VELEZ, Clemente

b. 1905, Lares, Puerto Rico.
Poet, journalist.

A post-modernist, Soto Vélez also for a time joined the "Atalayismo" movement (1929) and he remained a fervent nationalist. His poetry is vigorous, often ideological, and cast in free verse forms.

Writings: Poetry: *Abrazo interno,* New York, Las Américas, 1955; poetry in various journals and collections including *Aguinaldo lirico,* C. Rosa-Nieves, ed., Rio Piedras, 1957, 2nd ed., 1971.

Critical Essay: "Maria Teresa Babin, Poeta de sintesis," in *El Mundo*, San Juan (December 10, 1955).

SUAREZ SOLIS, Rafael

b. 1882, Aviles, Spain (long resident in Cuba).
Playwright, critic, essayist, novelist.

Súarez is considered an important figure in Cuba's theatrical record. His early plays are set in Aviles: *Barrabás; El Camino del cementero; El loco del año* and *Las tocineras*. His later plays are set in Cuba and are replete with island customs. *El hombre es un adorno* (1947) is beyond time and place.

His second collection of essays, gathered from periodicals, *La resonancia del silencio,* Max Henriquez Ureña finds extremely good and believes they will long merit careful reading.

Writings: Plays: *Barrabás,* 1938; *El camino de cementero,* 1945; *El loco del año,* 1946; *Las tocineras,* 1952; *La rebelión de las canas,* 1948; *El señor Milimetro,* 1954; *El hombre es un adorno,* 1947.

Essays: *Molde Imagen; La resonancia del silencio,* Havana, 1941.

Novel: *Un pueblo donde no pasaba nada; novela del tiempo quieto,* Santa Clara, Dirección de Publicaciones, 1962.

SUAREZ Y ROMERO, Anselmo

b. April 20, 1818, Havana, Cuba; d. January 7, 1878, Havana.
Novelist, folklorist, critic, teacher.

Suárez' *Francisco,* intentionally a grim picture of slavery in Cuba, is one of the earliest fictional works from the Americas, co-eval with Félix Tanco's *Petrona y Rosalia,* and Villaverde's early sketch of Cecilia Valdés, later elaborated into the long novel of that name. Domingo del Monte gave a copy in manuscript of Suarez' work to the English abolitionist, Richard R. Madden, who was visiting Cuba in 1837-39 to survey slave conditions in the island. Madden published in London (1840) the autobiography of Juan Francisco Manzano, but not the fictional but equally important and skilled picture of slavery by Suarez' which had this sarcastic phrase as its subtitle: "El Ingenio o las delicias del campo."

Suárez wrote criticism on the works of Milanés, Ramón de Palma, José Zacharias González del Valle and others. His nature essays were weaker, however, than his other prose because of its (to modern tastes at least) excessive, lyrical romantic style and lush vocabulary.

Most of Suárez' works remain in manuscript in the Cuban Biblioteca Nacional ("Costumbres habaneras," "Jurisprudencia y otras materias análogas," "Educación," and "Juicios sobre sus obras.")

Writings: Novel: *Francisco* (written in 1838-39), published in New York, 1880, ms. in Biblioteca Nacional de Cuba; first Cuban printing of *Francisco,* Havana, Instituto del Libro, 1970; *Carlota Valdéz,* n.p., 1838.

Essays: "Cuadros de la naturaleza cubana," in ma.

Literary Criticism: *Colección de articulos,* 1859.

Biographical/Critical Sources: Max Henriquez Ureña, *Panorama histórico de la literatura cubana,* New York, 1963.

SULSONA DE CADILLA, Elia

b. November 18, 1928, Rio Piedras, Puerto Rico.
Poet.

Sulsona took her B.A. at the University of Puerto Rico, Rio Piedras. Her verse, first in *Alma Latina* or *El Mundo* has been collected in one volume. *Hija del árbol*

(1949). It is quiet, very private. Miniatures are her especial distinction, as in "Motivos I" which has these seven lines only:

El cielo es mio.
(Se aquietaron los rios
en su cristal).
El cielo es mio
Un lucero que canta
por las aguas clarisimas
me ha visto suspirar

Writings: Poetry: *Hija del árbol,* Santurce, 1949.

SUNCAR CHEVALIER, Manuel E.

b. 1895, Dominican Republic; d. 1959. Poet.

Suncar was sensual, erotic, subjective for the most part, but he also did some patriotic verse as in his *Sinfonia del nuevo amanecer* which was awarded the Premio Nacional de Poesia "Fernando Gastón Deligne."

Writings: Poetry: *Los poemas del viandante,* 1928; *Sinfonia del nuevo amanecar,* 1956; *Canciones del viandante;* long quotations of his poetry in Mota's *Relieves Alumbrados.*

Biographical/Critical Sources: F. A. Mota Medrano, *Relieves Alumbrados,* S. Domingo, 1971, pp. 175-191.

SURI Y AGUILA, José

b. 1696, Santa Clara, Cuba; d. 1762. Poet, farmer.

Most of Suri's work is not extant, but his poems "A San José," "A la Virgen del Carmen," and various extant fragments concerning the feast day of Corpus Christi, and a few slight works of gallantry, are known to be his. It is known he had studied Latin and that he was possessed of an easy style.

Biographical/Critical Sources: Raimundo Lazo, *La literatura cubano,* Mexico, 1965, pp. 31-32; Menéndez y Pelayo, *Historia de la poesia hispanoamericana,* Vol. I, Madrid, 1911, p. 217; Salvador Salazar, *Historia de la literatura cubana,* 1929, p. 15; Max Henriquez Ureña, *Panorama histórico de la literatura cubana,* 1963, pp. 59-61.

SURO, Rubén

b. 1916, La Vega, Dominican Republic. Poet, lawyer, professor, diplomat.

Suro was an important member of the group "Los Nuevos" and often employed "criollisms" and other popular forms of speech in his work. His poem "La Rabiaca del Haitiano que espanta mosquitos" and other creole verse was found startling in its day. When "Los Nuevos" as a group melted away, Suro lost his own direction and stimulation and he did little thereafter. Busy as a professor of law at the Universidad Autonoma de Santo Domingo and serving as a Deputy in the national parliament, he also took several diplomatic posts, and never published his work in any collected volume.

He is still remembered for his prophetic "Proletario" which shocked some of his readers and his originality can be seen in this extract of the first two stanzas of the ten stanza poem "Rabiaca":

¡Madite
moquite!
me tiene fuñie
con ese sunbie
que no pue aguanté

Yo quema oja seque,
a be si se ba,
yo quema papel
yo quema de to. . .
y él paso mu cerque
de mi negra piel,
juega con el hume,
hace culiñique
y bube a sunbá.

Writings: Poetry: in various collections, and a good selection of his verse is in the Rueda *Antologia* cited below.

Biographical/Critical Sources: Manuel Rueda and Lupa Hernández Rueda's *Antologia panoramica de la poesia dominicana contemporánea (1912-1962),* Madrid, 1972, pp. 111-122, which included critical comments and eight poems.

TALLET, José Zacharias

b. 1893, Matanzas, Cuba.
Poet.

Though of pure European descent, Tallet's work were early manifestations of what came to be called Afro-Cuban poetry. His "Quintin Barahona" and "Rumba" exploit the Caribbean-Afro rhythms in a jazzy way. The latter poem began the very popular vogue when sung by Bertha Singerman in 1934. His verse mixes the vulgar, if vivid commonness of life, with heavy sentiment. His "Estrofas azules" ends:

. . .Y para mí. . .la noche sin alba,
y dando tumbos, andar, andar. . .
don un trozo de hielo en el pecho
que. . .¿más nunca se derretirá?

Writings: Poetry: "La rhumba," first published in *Atuei* (August 1928), later, with most of his other work, in his collection, *La semilla estéril,* Havana, Ministerio de Educación, 1951; "La rhumba" and "Negro Ripiera" appear in *Poesia negra del Caribe y otras áreas,* Hortensia Ruiz del Vizo, Miami, Florida, Ediciones Universal, 1971; also *Orbita de José Z. Tallet,* Havana, Unión, 1969, selection and notes by Helio Orovio.

TAPIA Y RIVERA, Alejandro

b. November 12, 1826, San Juan, Puerto Rico; d. July 19, 1882.
Poet, playwright, biographer, novelist, folklorist, critic, philosopher.

Tapia's first schooling was in the Colegio del Conde de Carpegna in San Juan, but his university studies were in Madrid. Becoming a friend of the great Cuban scholar-bibliographer, Domingo del Monte, Tapia was stimulated to search out, describe and to list important Spanish documents concerned with Puerto Rico. This effort resulted in the publication in 1854 of the *Biblioteca histórica puertorriqueña.* For a period Tapia worked for a leading cigar manufacturer in Havana in the 1950's and early 1960's during which period he began to contribute prose and verse pieces to journals, many of them subsequently collected in *El Bardo de Guamani* (1862) which also included his plays *Roberto D'Evreux* and *Bernardo de Palissy* and the legend *La antigua sirena.* He later published other plays, a collection of folk pieces, novels and the *Estética y Literatura,* as well as a volume of poetry, *La sataniada,* which many critics believe to be his best work though it seeks to gather up *all* human history.

Tapia was founder and editor of the important literary-cultural journal *La Azucena* (est. 1870). His play *Bernardo de Palissy* was performed in San Juan on April 12, 1857, one of the earliest by a Puerto Rican ever to be staged in the island. His *Mis memorias,* according to F. Manrique Cabrera, is as much a spiritual "biography" of Puerto Rico as it is of the author himself.

Writings: Poetry: *La sataniada: Grandiosa epopeya dedicada al principe de las tineblas por crisófilo sardanápalo,* 1st ed., Madrid, Imp. de Aurelio S. Alaria, 1878, 2nd ed., San Juan, Imp. Venezuela, 1945, verse in *El Bardo del Guamani,* Havana, Imp. Venezuela, 1862.

Legends: *La antigua sirena,* in *El Bardo del Guamani,* Havana, Imp. del Tiempo, 1862, and also published as individual work, Barcelona, Ediciones Rumbos, 1966; *La palma del Cacique. Leyenda histórica de Puerto Rico,* Madrid, 1852, and published as "La Palma del cacique,

La leyenda de los veinta años," 2nd [book] ed., Edit. Orión (Mexico), 1952.

Autobiography: *Mis memorias o Puerto Rico como lo encontré y como lo dejo,* 2nd ed., San Juan, Imp. Venezuela, 1946, 1st ed., New York, De Laisne and Rossboro, 1928.

Biography: of the painter Campeche, in *El Bardo de Guamani,* 1862.

Critical Essays: *Estética y Literatura,* Puerto Rico, González, 1881.

History: *Biblioteca histórica de Puerto Rico que contiene varios documentos de los siglos XV, XVI, XVII, XVIII,* Puerto Rico, Imp. de Marquéz, 1854.

Plays: *Roberto D'Evreaux* (written in 1848, performed in 1856), published in Puerto Rico, 1857; *Bernardo de Palissy o El heroismo del trabajo* (performed in 1856), published in *El Bardo de Gaumani,* 1862; *Camóens,* Madrid, 1868; *Vasco Núñez de Balboa* (performed November 11, 1872) (3 acts), published in 1873, Imp. González; *La Cuarterona,* Madrid, T. Fortanet, 1867; *La parte del León* (written 1878, performed San Juan, April 8, 1880); *Hero y Leandro* (monologue), Puerto Rico, *Acosta,* 1878.

Folktales: *Misceláneas,* 1880; "A Orillas del Rhin" and Enardo y Rosael" are in *Misceláneas,* the latter translated as *Enardo and Rosael; an allegorical novella,* by Alejandro Tapia, Jr., 3rd ed., San Juan, Imp. Venezuela, 1944, and New York, Philosophical Library, 1952.

Novels: *Cofresi,* San Juan, Tip. González y Cia., 1876, 3rd ed., San Juan, Imp. Venezuela, 1944; *La leyenda de los veinte años,* San Juan, Imp. González y Cia., 1874; *Postumo el transmigrado,* Puerto Rico, Imp. González, 1882; *El heliotropo,* in *Almanaque-Aguinaldo (de la Isla de Puerto Rico),* 1860 (the work was written in 1848); *La palma del Cacique,* Madrid, in *El Bardo del Guamani,* Havana, Imp. del Tiempo, 1862, and Mexico, Edit. Orión, 1962; *Postumo envirginiado o Historia de un hombre que se coló en el cuerpo de una mujer,* Puerto Rico, Imp. González, 1882; *Historia de un hombre que resucito en el cuerpo de su enemigo,* Madrid, Imp. de J. Aguado, 1872, 2nd ed., San Juan, Imp. Venezuela, 1945; *Cofresi, La antigua sirena,* and *Postumo el transmigrado* appear in *Obras completas: Novela,* San Juan, Instituto de Cultura Puertorriqueña, 1968.

Biographical/Critical Sources: José Juan Beauchamp, *Imagen del puertorriqueño en la novela,* San Juan, 1976 (essays on Tapia y Rivera, Laguerre, and Zeno Gandia); Manuel Garcia Díaz, *Alejandro Tapia y Rivera: su vida y su obra,* San Juan, Edit. Coquí, 1964; José Luis Martin, "Analisis estilistico de la Sataniada de Tapia," unpublished M.A. Thesis, U. of P. R., 1953, but revision published in San Juan, Instituto de Cultura Puertorriqueña, 1958; Carmen Gómez Tejera, *La novela en Puerto Rico,* Rio Piedras, 1947, see esp. pp. 33-50; Magdalena Serrano de Matos, "El teatro de Alejandro Tapia y Rivera," unpublished M.A. thesis, U. of P. R., 1953; F. Manrique Cabrera, *Historia de la literatura puertorriqueña,* Rio Piedras, Edit. Cultural, 1969, pp. 113 ff.; Antonia Sáez, *El teatro en Puerto Rico,* Rio Piedras, 1950; also see José Luis Martin, *Arco y flecha (Apuntando a la vida y las obras): Estudios de critica literaria,* San Juan, Edit. Club de Prensa, 1961; "Alexandro Tapia y *La Cuarterona,*" in Angelina Morfi's *Temas del teatro,* S. Domingo, D. R., Edit. del Caribe C. Por A, 1969; Antonio Sáez, *El teatro en Puerto Rico (Notas para su historia),* Rio Piedras, Edit. Universitaria, 1950; and Elsa Castro Pérez, *Tapia: Señalador de caminos,* San Juan, Edit. Coquí, 1964.

TEJERA, Diego Vicente

b. 1848, Cuba; d. 1903.

Poet, playwright, journalist, translator, critic, essayist.

Tejera was probably the most popular poet of his generation. Varona called him "el paisajista de los climas tropicales, en cuyos versos todo es relieve y colorido." His work was lyrical, highly personal, often set in ballad-like songs of the sort written by Heine. Tejera's work never quite was of the "criollismo" sort but his use of vernacular and of old Indian names made for certain affinities.

Tejera contributed many literary articles to *El Figaro,* later collected in his two volumes of essays. His political and labor interests led him to write many essays on pre-independence Cuban society looking toward the organization of the Cuban Socialist Party.

Writings: La muerte de Plácido, New York, Imp. Ponce de Leon, 1875.

Poetry: *Un ramo de violetas,* Paris, 1877; *Desencanto, 1876-1878.*

Poetry/Essays/Criticism: (mixed) *Un poco de prosa,* Havana, 1895; *Prosa literaria,* Havana, 1935.

Political Essays: "Los futuros partidos politicos de la República Cubana," "La sociedad cubana," "La capacidad cubana," "Blancos y negros," "La educación en las sociedades democráticas," and "Autonomistas y anexionistas" (all originally addresses delivered at conferences at Cayo Huesos, 1897, and published in pamphlet form in 1897 it is believed).

Translation: of works in *Libro de los cantares,* edited by Juan Antonio Pérez Bonalde, of many poems of Heine's *Das Buch der Lieder.*

TEJERA Y PENSON, Apolinar

b. January 6, 1855, Santo Domingo, Dominican Republic; d. July 10, 1922, Santo Domingo.

Poet, indian folklorist, historian, journalist, priest, lawyer.

Tejera studied philosophy and Latin in the Seminary Colegio San Luis Gonzaga. He entered the priesthood in 1879 and was for a long period the Curator of Higüey and then of Santiago de los Caballeros. Leaving religious orders after some two decades he was named Rector of the University of Santo Domingo in 1902, was elected Deputy in the national parliament in 1903, and was a diplomat accredited to The Hague in 1907. He also served on the Supreme Court of Justice, 1908-1913, at which time he was appointed Secretary of State for a brief period and that same year moved to the Ministry of Justice where he stayed for one year. From 1919-1922 he was Procurator of the Republic.

Tejera was the youngest member of the literary group published in *Lira de Quisqueya* in 1874, his work being the Indian legend "La bella Catalina." Though Joaquin Balaguer finds him an uninspired poet, he does praise his translations of French poetry and cites particularly "Extasis," taken from Victor Hugo's "Ecstase."

Writings: Poetry: in miscellaneous journals; poem "La bella Catalina," in *Lira de Quisqueya,* 1874, and later in *El Pais,* Nos. 2-4, S. Domingo, (February-March 1877); and in *Boletin del Archivo General de la Nación,* No. 60 (1949); and again in *Tradiciones y cuentos dominicanos,* S. Domingo, Postigo, 1969, edited by Emilio Rodriguez Demorizi. 115-130.

History: *Rectificaciones históricas,* 1907, in *La Cuna de América,* and in *Blanco y Negro,* 1910; *La República Dominicana en la conferencia internacional de la Haye (memoria de la delegación dominicana),* 1908, written with Francisco Henriquez y Carvajal.

Criticism and Literary History: many miscellaneous articles and some items in *Literatura dominicana, comentario critico-histórico,* 1922; then all his work in Alfaú Durán's "Indice de una vida ilustre, Doctor Don Apolinar Tejera," in *Clio,* No. 102 (1955), (this contains biographic and bibliographic information and a list of his verse and all of his writings, including all of his literary history, *Literatura. . .; Mi homenaje a Cólon,* 1892.

Biographical/Critical Sources: Joaquin Balaguer, *Historia de la literatura dominicana,* 1970, pp. 206-208.

TEODOMOFILO

(pseudonym for **Nicolás CARDENAS Y RODRIGUEZ**)

TEURBE TOLON, Miguel

b. September 29, 1820, Pensacola, Florida, U.S.A.; d. October 16, 1857, Cuba.

Poet, playwright, novelist.

A fiery Cuban nationalist, Teurbe fled to New York after the failure of a plot to overthrow Spanish authority and lived a poverty-filled life in exile for the several years left to him before death of tuberculosis. Yet, his poetry pictures the magical beauty of Cuban scenes and is full of folkloric detail. He returned to Cuba in 1857 to publish his last volume of verse, *Flores y espinas.*

He took part in the 1850 and 1851 disembarkments of Narciso López against the Spanish colonial authorities, having been in exile in the U. S. since 1848. He helped form the Consejo de la Junta revolucionaria cubana and edited or directed such polemical journals as *La verdad* (1848), *El Cubano* (1852), *El Papagayo* (1855) and *El Cometa* (1856). Twenty of his very popular patriotic poems *El laúd del desterrado* (1858), an historically important collection of nationalist verse.

Teurbe taught literature in Matanzas and Spanish in New York where he also published a Spanish grammar.

There is some disagreement about his birthplace, Max Henriquez Ureña citing Matanzas and other authorities stating it to have been Pensacola.

Writings: Poetry: *Los preludios,* Matanzas, 1841; *Preludios,* Havana, 1849; *Luz y sombra,* Havana, 1856; *Leyendas cubanas,* Havana, New York, 1856 (with a second part of lyric poetry from the earlier published *Luz y Sombra*); *Flores y espinas,* Havana, 1857(?) and/or Matanzas, 1858; 20 poems in *El Laúd del desterrado,* New York, 1858.

Plays: *¡Una noticia!* (1 act comedy), Matanzas, Tip. de Gobierno y Marina, 1847; *¡A Yumuri!* (2 acts), 1847; and comic sketches: *El casorio; Ojo al Cristo, que es de plata.*

Novel: *Lola Guara,* Matanzas, 1846.

Translation: *Common Sense* (of Thomas Paine) as *El sentido común* and Emma Willard's history as *Compedio de la historia de los Estados Unidos,* New York, 1954.

Grammar: *The Elementary Spanish Reader and Translator,* New York, 1852.

THOMAS, Piri

b. 1928, New York, U. S. A.
Novelist.

The eldest of seven children of Puerto Rican parents, Piri Thomas' work reflects the mixture of his U. S. and Latin heritage. His first novel, *Down These Main Streets,* deals with a second-generation Puerto Rican in New York City and is based on his own experiences in growing up on the tough streets of Spanish Harlem. In prison at age 22, he began to read and to seriously consider his life. Finding writing helped him regain his courage and spiritual equilibrium, he wrote the first draft of *Down These Main Streets* and began to smuggle portions out. Thomas, released in 1956, worked as a social worker with drug addicts. He then went to his ancestral Puerto Rico to attend the University of Puerto Rico after helping set up a drug rehabilitation center there. The darkest of four brothers and one sister, the hero of Piri's first novel, slowly, if at first reluctantly, comes to identify with American blacks.

His second novel was *Savior, Savior, Hold My Hand,* and his third *Seven Long Times.* A documentary film on Spanish Harlem, "Narration for Petey and Johny," won first prize at the 1964 Festival Dei Popoli, Florence, Italy.

Writings: Autobiographical Novels: *Down These Main Streets,* New York, Knopf, 1967, portions anthologized often, including section "Alien Turf" in *A Gathering of Ghetto Writers,* Wayne Miller (ed.), New York, New York University Press, 1972; *Savior, Savior, Hold My Hand,* New York, 1973; *Seven Long Times,* New York, Praeger, 1974.

Biographical/Critical Sources: Interview with Diane Green and Bill Thompson, June 8, 1974, in *Metropoli,* Vol. I (Summer, 1974), and portion reprinted in *Revista Interamericana,* Vol. IV, No. 4 (Winter 1974-5), pp. 547-549; Reviews of *Down These Main Streets* and *Savior, Savior,* and *Seven Long Times,* in *Revista/Review Interamericana,* in Vol. I, No. 2, in Vol. III, No. 1, No. 2, and in Vol. V, No. 3, respectively.

TORRE, José Luis de la

b. 1911, Cuba.
Playwright.

De la Torre's work was influenced by Pirandello's and his three plays are important historically in Cuban theatre.

Writings: Plays: *Con los pies en el suelo* (1 act comedy); *Azul, rojo y blanco* (1 act comedy); *Henequén.*

TORRENS DE GARMENDIA, Mercedes

b. 1886, Cuba.
Poet.

Mercedes Torrens' intimate and delicate poetry written primarily in her youth, appeared in collected volumes long after her generation's work became generally known.

Writings: Poetry: *Fragua de estrellas,* Havana, 1935; *Jazmines en la sombra,* 1942; *La flauta del silencio,* 1946; *Jardines del crepúsculo,* 1948; *Esquila en el poniente,* 1951.

TORRES Y FERIA, Manuel de

(pseudonym: **SERAFIN DE LA FLOR**)
b. 1833, Havana, Cuba; d. 1892.
Playwright.

Of historic importance only, Torres y Feria wrote seven known plays.

Writings: Plays: *La elección de un novio o Juzgar por las apariencias* (1 act verse comedy); the verse text is by "Serafín de la Flor," Havana, 1857, 2nd ed., Havana, La Prueba, 1883; *El padrino inesperado* (1 act comedy), Havana, Imp. El Telégrafo, 1860, and Havana, Imp. La Prueba, 1882; *El drama del mundo* (3 acts, verse), Havana, La Prueba, 1881; all the following also published by La Prueba: *Azares de la vida* (3 acts, verse), 1882; *El corazón en la mano* (4 acts, verse), 1884; *La mujer fragil* (1 act), 1884; *Miserias humanas* (3 act verse comedy), Havana, 1884; and, in *Mi pasado y mi presente (Obras literarias de M. Torres): Vol. I: Obras dramáticas, (El drama del mundo; El padrino inesperado; Azares de la vida; La elección de un novio),* 1889, also by La Prueba.

TORRIENTE Y BRAU, Pablo de la

b. 1901, Cuba; d. 1936.
Novelist, storywriter, journalist.

Torriente was a talented fiction writer and journalist, killed in his mid-thirties fighting on the Republican side during the Spanish Civil War. His early stories appearing in *Batey* (1930) were influenced by the American, O'Henry, but his later war-time experiences turned him to a graver and more important style and subject matter. The work of his last few years, most of it placed in Spain or influenced by the war, appeared posthumously. His novel, *Historia del soldado desconocido cubano,* despite its theme, or possibly because of it, is humorous.

Writings: Stories: in the collection *Batey,* Havana, 1930, and as *Cuentos de Batey,* Havana, Nuevo Mundo, 1962; *Batey* also contains stories of Gonzálo Mazas Garbayo (b. 1904); *Preleando con los milicianos,* Mexico, 1938.
Novels: *Historia del soldado desconocido cubano,* Havana, 1940; as *Aventuras del soldado desconocido cubano,* Havana, Nuevo Mundo, 1962, with introduction by Raúl Roa; and Havana, Gobierno Provincial Revolucionario de la Habana, 196?.

Biographical/Critical Sources: Pablo de la Torriente y Brau y la Revolución Española, Havana, 1937.

TORROELLA, Alfredo

b. 1845, Cuba; d. 1879.
Poet, playwright.

A member of the Havana group led by

Rafael Maria Mendive and Nicolás Azcárate, Torroella wrote several plays of the "bufo" sort for the popular vaudeville circuit and published two volumes of poetry.

Writings: Poetry: *Poesias,* 1864, and a second *Poesias,* 1866.

Plays: *Amor y probeza,* (3 acts, verse), Havana, Imp. La Antilla, 1864, performed June 9, 1864 in Teatro Tacón, Havana; *Laureles de oro* (3 act comedy), Havana, 1867; *El ensayo de D. Juan Tenorio,* performed by the company of the Teatro de Variedades at its theatre, June 30, 1868, and published, Havana, Imp. del Comercio, 1868; *Un minué,* Havana, Imp. del Comercio, 1868; *El mulato* (3 act social drama, prose), Mexico, Chávez, 1870; *El istmo de Suez,* Mexico, 1870.

TRIANA, José

b. ca. 1932, Cuba.
Playwright.

Once a fervent supporter of Castro, Triana was imprisoned in the late 1960's. His play *La noche de los asesinos* (1965) won the Casa de las Américas, the Gallo de la Habana award at the VI Latin American Theatre Festival and many other awards and received many foreign premieres (Budapest, Paris, Washington, D. C.). This play was the first Latin American play performed on an English stage by a professional company (Terry Hand, Director, Aldwych Theatre, London).

TRIAY, José E.

b. ca. 1862, Cuba.
Playwright.

Once a very popular writer, Triay is today of only historical importance.

Writings: Plays: *A las puertas de la gloria* (1 act), Havana, La Propaganda Literaria, 1892 (third part of his trilogy *España en América; Cervantes* (1 act), Havana, La Propaganda Literaria, 1877, performed April 23, 1877 in Teatro Albisu, Havana; *El cautivo de Argel* (1 act sketch), Havana, Imp. Militar, 1905; performed Teatro Albisu, Havana, May 26, 1905; *El Lazo de Unión,* Havana, La Propaganda Literaria, 1873, performed Teatro Habanera, November 27, 1873; Irez de Paz, 2nd ed., La Propaganda Literaria, 1878, performed in Teatro Tacón, Havana, June 20, 1878; *La vuelta de Andrés* (1 act), Havana, Imp. La Constancia, 1896, performed Teatro Alhambra, Havana, September 11, 1896. Written with Augusto E. Mádan y Garcia: *Cleopatra* (3 act verse comedy), Matanzas, Imp. La Nacional, 1881, performed February, 1881, in Teatro Albisu, Havana.

Translation: *Giroflé y Girofiá,* Spanish version of work by Albert Dauloo and Eugenio Leterrir, music set by Carlos Lecocq, for the Compañia Infantil Mexicana, published Havana, La Propaganda Literaria, 1876, performed Teatro Tacón, February 12, 1876.

TRONCOSO DE LA CONCHA, Manuel de Jesús

(pseudonym: **Juan BUSCON**)

b. 1878, Dominican Republic; d. 1955.

Storywriter, folklorist, law scholar, historian, teacher.

Troncoso considered, with César Nicolás Penson, to have been one of the leading folktale tellers and collectors, was a serious student of the law and amateur historian. Though he was not an original mind and did not seek to re-mold or otherwise exploit the folktales he collected, he showed their nature and caught the genuine spirit of the originals, producing subtle and dramatic effects.

Writings: Traditional Tales: published in various journals under title "Anecdotario dominicano de tiempos pasados" and pen-name of Juan Buscón, with *La Nación* during the period 1943-44 being the usual publisher; *Narraciones dominicanas,* 1946, his one collection which includes his best known stories: "El misterio de Don Marcelino," "La Virgen de las Mercedes y los dominicanos," "Un ahijado del Santismo," and "El secreto de Catatey."

Law: *Elementos de derecho administrativo con aplicación a las leyes de la República Dominicana,* 1939.

History: *La Génesis de la Convención Dominico-americana,* 1941; *La ocupación de Santo Domingo por Haiti,* 1942; *El Brigadier don Juan Sánchez Ramirez,* 1944.

Editor of: *Narraciones dominicanas,* Santiago, D. R., 1946.

TURLA, Leopoldo
(pseudonym: **"Un Quidam"**)

b. 1818, Havana, Cuba; d. March 20, 1877, New Orleans.
Playwright, poet.

Son of an Italian father and mother from New Orleans, Turlo was an excellent student and highly regarded by leading members of literary and cultural circles in Cuba. He early began writing verse in the manner of Milanés, his first collection appearing in 1848. Some months earlier he had been forced to flee to New Orleans because of his nationalistic sentiments. There he joined the exile group around Narciso López. It is believed Turla served as a colonel in López' unsuccessful invasion forces of 1851.

Turla published five poems in the exile inspired volume *El laúd del desterrado,* (1858): "¡Perseverancia!" "Oro," "A Narciso López," "Dos mártires," "Degradación."

After a fallow period, Turla was agitated to new work by the revolution of 1868 and the execution of medical students in 1871, this latter event reflected in his poem "El crimen del siglo."

Writings: Poetry: *Ráfagas del Trópico,* 1848.

Play: *El Padre Jaruata en la Habana* (1 act comedy), Havana, Barcina, 1848 (escrita en pocas horas por "Un Quidam").

UGARTE, Lucas Arcadio de

b. 1807, Havana, Cuba; d. 1868.
Playwright.

One of Cuba's earliest published playwrights, Ugarte wrote three known plays.

Writings: Plays: *El articulo y los autos* (2 acts, folkloric verse), Havana, Imp. del Gobierno, 1839; *Dos para tres* (1 act comedy), Havana, Barcina, 1844; *Dos palabras* (1 act), Havana, Barcina, 1844.

UHRBACH Y CAMPUZANO, Carlos

b. 1872, Cuba; d. 1897.
Poet.

Brother of Federico Uhrbach y Campuzano (b. 1873), Carlos lived in the United States for a period and died at 25 in the revolt which finally led to Cuban independence. All of his work in verse is included in Federico's volume *Oro, versos,* published in 1907.

Writings: Poetry: *Rimas,* date unknown;

Gemelas, Havana, 1894 (done with brother Federico). His work done after 1894 along with work in *Gemelas* is published in *Oro, versos,* Havana, 1907.

UHRBACH Y CAMPUZANO, Federico Pio

b. 1873, Cuba; d. 1931.
Poet, playwright.

Federico's *Amor de ensueño* is a collection of melancholic and delicately sensitive sonnets of the last breath of romanticism. He and his brother Carlos jointly published an early collection, *Gemelas,* in 1894.

Writings: Poetry: *Gemelas, primeras poesias,* Havana, 1894; *Oro, versos,* Havana, 1907; *Amor de ensueño y de romanticismo,* Havana, 1908; *Resurrección, nuevos poemas,* Havana, 1916. The volume *Oro* of 1907 includes the entire poetic production of brother Carlos and his own work to that date, but the author of any particular piece is nowhere indicated.

Play: *Dolorosa* (2 acts), performed at the Gran Teatro Nacional, April 23, 1910; published, Havana, P. Fernández, 1910.

URENA DE HENRIQUEZ, Salomé

(pseudonym: **HERMINIA**)

b. October 21, 1850, Santo Domingo, Dominican Republic; d. March 6, 1897, Santo Domingo.
Poet, teacher.

A leading figure and member of the literary Ureña family, Salomé began to write early and used the name "Herminia" in publishing her verse up to 1874. She married the medical doctor, Francisco Henriquez y Carvajal. With the well-known education innovator Eugenio Maria de Hostos, she founded in 1881 the Instituto de Señoritas, the first high school for women in the Dominican Republic.

As the daughter of Nicolás Ureña de Mendoza, one of the earliest poets in the island, she lived with verse all her life.

Because of the unsettled times and the effort to re-establish a republic her work naturally was of a fervent patriotism, earning her the epithet voiced by the critic, Max Rodriquez Ureña: "Salomé es la nacionalidad misma" (Salomé is the very spirit of nationhood itself). A brief extract from one of her "aciertos parciales" may serve to indicate her vere and verse:

Se estremece el alcázar opulento
de bien, de gloria, de grandeza suma,
que fábrica tenaz el pensamiento;
¡bajo el peso se rinde que le abruma!

In 1884, her son Camila was born but she became ill and suffered extremely from tuberculosis, being forced to leave the capital for the more salubrious climate of Puerto Plata where she remained until her early death at 47. Her sons Max and Pedro Henriquez Ureña became the Republic's leading scholars in their generation.

Writings: Poetry: *Poesías de Salomé Ureña de Henriquez,* 1880; *Poesias,* Madrid, 1920, 2nd ed., S. Domingo, Postigo, 196?; *Poesias completas,* with an introduction by Joaquin Balaguer, S. Domingo, Biblioteca Dominicana: Serie 1, Vol. IV, Impresora Dominicana, 1950; *Poesias escogidas,* S. Domingo, Postigo, 1960; and *Poesias selectas,* 1959.

Biographical/Critical Sources: Silvera R. de Rodriguez Demorizi's *Salomé Ureña de Henriquez,* Buenos Aires, 1944, but first published in a different version in *Cuadernos Dominicanos de Cultura* (December 1943); Max Rodriguez Ureña's *Panorama histórico de la literatura dominicana,* 1965; pp. 189-197; E. Rodriguez Demorizi's *Salomé Ureña y el Instituto de Señoritas,* 1960; J. Balaguer's *Historia de la literatura dominicana,* 5th ed., 1970, pp. 119-131; F. Henriquez y Carvajal's two essays on Salomé: *Intima,* 1897, and *Meditación,* 1898.

URENA DE MENDOZA, Nicolás

(pseudonym: **"Nisidas"** for poetry; **"Cástulo"** for folklore articles)

b. March 25, 1822, Santo Domingo, Dominican Republic; d. April 3, 1875.
Poet, journalist, storywriter, judge, statesman, teacher.

Ureña is considered to have been the introducer of a conscious "local color" technique into Dominican poetry along with Félix Maria Del Monte. He was a teacher and then director of the Escuela Pública de Santo Domingo in 1852. He served as Public Defender for many years, beginning in 1860, and was also magistrate and senator (being elected in 1869 for Puerto Plata). His frankness and liberal opinions forced his exile several times.

His writing was mostly in the fields of popular fiction, novelettes, pastoral verse, the informal essay and epigrams. His best-known poem is "El Guajiro predilecto."

Salomé Ureña, his daughter, came to be a far more important poet than Nicolás, but his influence is evident in some of her early work.

Writings: Poetry: *Nicolás Ureña de Mendoza, Poesias,* Pedro Henriquez Ureña, ed., S. Domingo, 1933 (in mimeograph); most of his work never collected except in manuscript compilation conserved in the Museo Nacional from the personal collection of Max Henriquez Ureña, called "Paciflores, Cuaderno de poesias," and in such other anthologies as *Lira de Quisqueya* of Castellanos, and *Cantos dominicanos* and *Poesia popular dominicana,* pp. 99-103.

Stories: in various journals.

Biographical/Critical Sources: Max Henriquez Ureña's *Panorama histórico de la literatura dominicana,* 2nd ed., S. Domingo, 1965, pp. 217ff; E. Rodriguez Demorizi's *Salomé Ureña y el Instituto de Señoritas,* S. Domingo, 1960, and his *Poesia popular dominicana,* 1938, 2nd ed., S. Domingo, 1960, and his *Poesia popular dominicana,* 1938, 2nd ed., S. Domingo, 1973, pp. 215-227, which offers the texts of tales "Un Guajiro predilicto" and "Un Guajiro en Bayagüana," the former originally published in *El Dominicano,* No. 25 (December 22, 1855) and the latter in *El Eco del Pueblo,* No. 18, S. Domingo (November 23, 1856). Also see José Castellanos' *Lira de Quisqueya,* S. Domingo, 1874; and C. N. Penson's *Reseña histórico-critica de la poesia en Santo Domingo,* S. Domingo, 1892, p. 29.

URZAIS, Fernándo

b. 1840, Cuba; d. 1900.
Playwright, folklorist.

Urzáis was one of the earliest writers for the Cuban stage and based his work on popular, folkloric themes.

Writings: Folklore: in various journals, and represented in *Tipos y costumbres de la Isla de Cuba,* Havana, 1882.

Plays: *Venganza contra venganza* (3 acts, verse), Havana, Imp. La Antilla, 1866; *El hacer bien nunca se pierde,* Guanabacoa, Imp. Revista de Almancenes, 1872; *Nubes en cielo azul* (2 act comedy, verse), Guanabacoa, Imp. Revista de Almacenes, 1882; *La prosa de la vejez* (1 act comedy), Havana, La Antilla, 1866, performed in the Liceo de Guanaboacoa.

VALDES, Carlos Genero

b. 1843, Villa Clara, Cuba; d. 1890.
Poet, journalist, essayist, biographer.

Valdés exploited popular material and subjects in his verse and he collected and published a two-volume collection of Cuban folksongs.

Writings: Poetry: *Vergonzosas,* Havana, 1867; *Un ramo de acacias,* 1879.

Anthology: (of Cuban songs): *Tesoro popular,* 2 vols., 1879-1883, Havana, 1883.

Biography: *Rasgos de Emilio Castelar,* 1872.

VALDES, Ramón Francisco

b. 1810, Cuba; d. 1866.
Playwright.

Little is known of Valdés except that he wrote many plays for the romantic stage of his day.

Writings: Plays: *El doncél* (4 scenes, verse), Havana, Boloña, 1838; *Cora* (4 acts, verse), Madrid, Sánchez, 1839, 2nd ed., Havana, 1841, 3rd ed., Havana, Barcina, 1848; *Ginebra* (5 acts), Madrid, Sánchez, 1839; *Leonor o el Pirata,* Havana, Barcina, 1841; *Ivanhoe o la Judia* (5 acts, prose), Havana, 1842, banned in 1858; *Altea,* 1843; *Pascual Bruno* (5 acts), written in 1843, but never published; *Sustos y apuros* (1 act), Havana; *Doña Sol* (verse), Mexico, 1847, 2nd ed., 1852, Mexico, and Havana, Barcina, 1852; *Enrico* (5 acts), Mexico, 1849, and Havana, 1856; *Querer más de la cuenta* (1 act, verse), Havana, Barcina, 1865.

VALDES CODINA, Leopoldo

b. 1868, Havana, Cuba.
Playwright.

Valdés Codina is generally forgotten today though his two known plays were both performed to some popular applause.

Writings: Plays: *Las mujeres Fin del Siglo* (1 act), Havana, Imp. Las Guásimas, 1905 (music by Ramón Julián); *Se solicita un novio* (1 act), Havana, Las Guásimas, 1905, premiered Teatro Irijoa, Havana, October 27, 1897.

VALDES HERNANDEZ, Oscar

b. 1915, Cuba.
Playwright.

Valdés' work is mostly in the school of rural protest though a few were set in civil war Spain: *La crisis, El hermano de Marcos* and *A puertas cerradas* are set in the Spain of the period of the second world war.

Writings: Plays: *La crisis,* 1939; *El hermano de Marcos,* 1939; *A puertas cerradas,* 1944; *Las guerrillas del pueblo,* 1944 (1 act, set in Europe during World War II); *Corazón atormentado; La feria de las vanidades; Los malhechores del bien; Sin nombre; Al final del camino; Un caballero de frac* (satiric comedy, set in London).

VALDES MACHUCA, Ignacio

(pseudonym: **DESVAL**)

b. 1792, Havana, Cuba; d. 1851.
Poet, playwright, journalist.

Valdés was a contributor and editor to several journals, including *Diario de la Habana* and *Aureola Poética, El Mosquito* (which he founded), and later *La Lira de Apolo.* His *Ocios poéticas* (1819) is the first published volume of poetry by a native Cuban.

Writings: Poetry: *Ocios poéticos,* 1819; *Diálogo entre Teresa y Falconi,* 1821; *Tres dias en Santiago;* and dramatic sketches: *Cantatas,* 1829 (with such names as Diana, Adonis, Tetis, Circe, Céfalo, Baco and others).

Play: *La muerte de Adonis,* Havana, Imp. Palmer, 1819; *El Correnton burlado,* Havana, Imp. Teran, 1831.

Biographical/Critical Sources: Max Henríquez

Ureña, *Panorama histórico de la literatura cubana,* New York, 1963, pp. 162-163.

VALDES MENDOZA, Mercedes

b. 1820, Cuba; d. 1896.
Poet.

Of modest reputation, Valdés published two collections of her poetry, three of her poems were widely anthologized in the 19th century: "La esperanza," "La rosa blanca" and the sonnet "A Scévola."

Writings: Poetry: *Cantos perdidos,* 1847; *Poesias,* 1854.

VALDIVIA Y SISAY, Aniceto

(a.k.a. **Conde KOSTIA**)

b. 1859, Cuba; d. 1927.
Playwright, poet, lawyer.

Valdivia took his law degree in Spain. His prose was clear, unadorned, his criticism balanced and judicious.

Writings: Poetry: *Ultratumba* and *Rimas,* Madrid, 1879; *Melancolia,* Havana, 1904; *Pequenos poemas: Les vendedores del templo,* Havana, 1904.

Verse Plays: *Senda de abrojos,* Havana, 1880; *La ley suprema,* Madrid, 1882.

Journalistic articles: "Mi linterna mágica," in *Grandes periodistas cubanos,* Havana, 1958.

Translations: *Lazáro and Yambos* (of August Barbier's poetry), Madrid, 1884; Hugo's *El grupo de los Idilios,* Madrid, 1886; and *Poemas de Victor Hugo* (done with others), Madrid, 1883.

VALENCIA, Manuel Maria

b. 1810, Dominican Republic; d. 1870, Cuba.
Poet, lawyer, priest.

Valencia is given credit for being one of the first "romantic" poets of Dominica. An early patriot and strong protestor against the Haitian occupation of his country, his political leaflet *La verdad y nada más* of 1843 and *Homenaje a la razón,* 1845, were almost unique in their day as acts of "printed" courage. He took an active part in the abortive Constitutional Assembly of 1844.

The loss of his first betrothed affected him gravely and his fiery poetry became melancholic. "La vispera del suicidio" and "Una noche en el templo" are effusions from this dark period. Recovering enough to marry in time, he rose only to fall, for his wife soon perished and he gave up his civil law career and entered religious orders. He finally emigrated to Cuba where he remained until his death.

Max Henriquez Ureña finds his poetry "defectuosa y declamatoria," but he also states that Valencia's romantic verse stimulated the better work of such poets as Javier Angulo Guridi (as with "En el cementerio y fastidio") and Félix Mota (and his "El blásfemo" and Nicolás Ureña (and his "El quejido de la adversidad").

Writings: Poetry: in various collections and journals.

Political leaflets: *La verdad y nada más,* 1843; *Momenaje a la razón,* 1845.

Biographical/Critical Sources: Max Henriquez Ureña's *Panorama histórico de la literatura dominicana,* 1965, pp. 216-217.

VALERIO, Juan Francisco

(a.k.a. **Narciso VALOR Y FE**)

b. 1829(?), Havana, Cuba; d. 1878.
Sketch-writer, folklorist, playwright.

Valerio's stories and folk sketches were popular with the common reader, but of little merit as literature. His play *Perro huevero,* in a performance of January 22,

1869, in the Teatro Villanueva, led to a riot and shooting because certain ideas of the most recent uprising of October 10, 1868, seemed to be at issue.

Writings: Sketches-Folklore: *Cuadros sociales, Colección de articulos de costumbres,* 1865, 2nd ed., 1876, and others.

Play: *Perro huevero, aunque le quemen el hocico* (1 act, prose), Havana, Imp. La Intrepida, 1868, and Havana, El Profesorado de Cuba, no date, premiered 1868.

VALERIO, Manuel

b. 1918, Moca, Dominican Republic.
Poet.

Valerio was an important member of the group "La Poesia Sorprendida" and contributed much of his work to the journal of that name. He eventually moved on to join the circle "Los Juglares" which identified itself with the poorest quarters of the capital and included the young poets Rafael Astacio, Rafael Lara Cintrón, Ramón Francisco and Juan Sánchez Lamouth. Valerio became the director of the review *Revalación.*

He emigrated to Puerto Rico during the worst days of the dictatorship of Trujillo and still resides there.

Writings: Poetry: *Coral de sombras,* S. Domingo, Ed. La Poesia Sorprendida, 1944; *Sitio para el amor,* 1952; *Canto a Zarah,* 1958; poems in various collections, including Rueda's *Antologia,* referenced below.

Critical Essay: *La soledad y el espiritu creador o lo estra-existente,* S. Domingo, Centro de Publicaciones Revalación, 1960.

Biographical/Critical Sources: Manuel Rueda's *Antologia. . .,* Santiago de los Caballeros, UCMM, 1972, pp. 241-242.

VALLADARES, Armando

b. ca. 1942, Cuba.
Poet, painter.

Sentenced to thirty years in prison in 1960, Valladares was especially harshly treated in an insanitary and lightless cell and has been left a paralyzed invalid. His poems smuggled out of Cuba, appeared in

print as *Desde mi silla de ruedas* (From My Wheel Chair), Florida, 1977. The major poems concern the slaughter and beating of prisoners in Boniato Jail on September 1, 1975. The English text of that work, "Boniato Jail: Account of a Massacre" appeared in *Of Human Rights* (Fall 1977), published by a group of Cuban exiles at Georgetown University, Washington, D. C.

VALOR Y FE, Narciso

(pseudonym for **Juan Francisco VALERIO**)

VARELA ZEQUIRA, Eduardo

b. ca. 1877, Camagüez, Cuba.
Playwright, journalist.

Varela's plays are reflective of the success and mannerisms of Echegareyo.

Writings: *¡Expiación!* (3 acts), Havana, Rambla y Bouza, 1907; *Hogar y patria,* 1908; *La reconquista* (3 act comedy), 1910, premiered by the Sociedad de Fomento del Teatro in the Teatro Nacional, May 21, 1910.

VARELA ZEQUIERA, José

b. 1859, Cuba; d. 1940.

Critic, storywriter, journalist, scientist, anthropologist, anatomist.

For many years professor of anatomy at the University of Havana, Varela contributed many critical articles to the *Revista de Cuba.* His first good work appeared in the collection *Arpasamigas,* edited by Enrique José Varona and appearing in the journal *Revista de Cuba* in 1879.

Writings: Articles and Reviews: critical essays on Nicolás Azcárate's *Idealismo y realismo en el arte,* Havana, 1882, and the novel *El Amigo Manso* of Pérez Galdós, and other pieces in various journals.

Essays: *Bocetos académicos,* Havana, 1913, which includes "Cuba y los Estados Unidos," and "El ritmo psiquico."

Stories: "El Doctor Muller, historia de una loco," in *Revista Contemporánea* (Madrid, April 1879); *El libro de los epilogos,* Havana, Ed. Unión, 1963.

VARONA Y PERA, Enrique José

b. April 13, 1849, Cuba; d. November 19, 1933.

Poet, critic, journalist, orator, philosopher, teacher.

Varona wrote and published poetry in his mid-teens and all through his busy political life he remained a poet and critic of the arts. His major work was in journalism, however, and the *Revista Cubana* and the journal *La Caridad del Cerro* (of the Anthropological Society which he served as president) were two of his forums. He was an important figure also in moving for reforms in the educational system. Though he served as his country's Vice President (1912-1917), he did not ally himself with much of the work of his party, El Partido Conservador, and he remained a free voice much respected for his broad general humanistic concerns.

Varona's manifesto, *Cuba Contra España,* was taken by the Cuban Revolutionary Party as its central argument, and Varona edited José Marti's *Patria* journal in New York during their common exile in the United States in the early 1890's.

Writings: Poetry: *Odas anacréonticas,* Puerto Principe, 1868; *Paisajes cubanos,* Havana, 1879; *La hija prodiga,* Puerta Principe, 1879; *Poesias,* Havana, 1878; *Paisajes cubanos,* Havana, 1879; *Arpas amigas,* Havana, 1879; *De mis recuerdos; Arpas cubanas,* Havana, 1904; *Poemitas en prosa,* Havana, 1921.

Journalism: "Articulos" (in *Grandes periodistas cubanos*), Havana, 1951; and see especially the articles "La politica cubana de los Estados Unidos," and "El fracaso colonial de España."

Essays: *Desde me Belvedere,* Havana, 1907, republished in 1936 as part of *Obras de Enrique José Varona,* and *Obras completas,* Madrid, Aguilar, 1957; *Violetas y ortigas,* Madrid, 1917 and 1936; *Con el eslabón,* Costa Rica, 1918, and 2nd ed., amplified, Manzanilla, Cuba, Edit. El Arte, 1927.

Philosophy: *Conferencias filosóficas: Logica,* 1880; *Seis conferencias,* Barcelona, 1887; *Conferencias filosóficas; Psicologia,* Havana, 1888; *Conferencias filosóficas: Moral,* Havana, 1888; *Nociones de lógica,* Havana, 1902; *Conferencias sobre el fundamento de la moral,* New York, 1903; *Curso de psicologia,* Havana, 1905.

Criticism/Esthetics: *Estudios literarios y filosóficos,* Havana, 1880.

Orations: *Discursos* (by Varona and D. Rafael Montoro, delivered in Teatro Payret, January 21, 1883). This work contains Varona's "Importancia social del arte," first published in pamphlet form with the cited title, Havana, 1883;

Articulos y discursos, Havana, 1891.
Complete Works: see above under rubric of "Essays."

Biographical/Critical Sources: Max Henriquez Ureña, *Panorama histórico de la literatura cubana,* 1492-1952, Vol. II, New York, Las Américas Publishing Co., 1963, pp. 65-85; José de la Luis León, *Enrique José Varona: su olvidada doctrina,* La Coruña, 1934; Carlos Ripoll, in *La generación del 23 en Cuba,* New York, 1968, pp. 57ff; Raúl Roa, "Enrique José Varona y nuestra generación," in *Homanaje a Enrique José Varona y nuestra generación en el centenario de su natalicio,* Havana, 1951; Félix Lizaso, "Varona y la juventud," in *Revista de la Habana,* VI, 39 (1946); Edwin Elmore, "Carta a Enrique José Varona," in *Repertorio Américano,* Vol. LX, No. 20 (January 1920); Gastón Baquero, "Enrique José Varona," in *Revista de la Habana,* Vol. IV, No. 19 (March 1944); Ferrer Canales' *Imagen de Varona,* Havana, 1964; Medardo Vitier's *Enrique José Varona, maestro de Juventudes,* 2 vols., 1937; M. A. Carbonell, "El Varona que yo conoci," in *Homenaje* (see below); Fermin Peraza Sarausa, *Econografia de Enrique José Varona,* Havana, 1942; Elias Entralgo, *El ideario de Varona en la filósofia social,* Havana, 1934; and Entralgo's *Enrique José Varona, su vida, su obra y su influencia,* Havana, 1936 (written with Roberto Agramonte); Oscar Martinez, "Vida y obra de Enrique José Varona, ensayista cubano," unpublished Ph.D. dissertation, Florida State University, U.S.A., 1972; and the already cited *Homenaje a Enrique José Varona en el centenario de su natalicio,* Havana, Ministero de Educación, Dirección de Cultura, 1951; also: Miguel Angel Carbonell, *El Varona que yo conoci,* Havana (Acad. Nac. de Artes y Letras, Serie de Pub. Especiales No. 3), 1950.

VASCONCELOS MARAGLIANO, Ramón

b. 1890, Alacranes, Cuba; d. 1965, Havana.
Novelist, travel-writer, journalist.

Primarily a journalist, Vasconcelos wrote three sturdy works on his residence abroad full of his acute observations, and in 1936 his novel *La letra de molde.*

Writings: Novel: *La letra de molde; novela,* Havana, Culturalo, 1936.
Travel: *U.S.S.R. y el ensayo ruso,* Havana, 1937; *Montparnasse,* 1938; *París bien vale una misa,* 1938; *República Española número dos.*

VASILI, Paul

(pseudonym for **Julián del CASAL**)

VASSALLO Y CABRERA, Francisco

b. November 19, 1823, San Juan, Puerto Rico; d. September 4, 1867.
Novelist.

His one known published work, *Amor y Generosidad* is a romantic picture of long-parted lovers who at book's end, are re-united happily, something rare for the agony-filled works of the day.

Writings: Novel: *Amor y Generosidad,* review in *El Cancionero de Boriquen,* No. 15 (1846), Riera de San Juan, Imp. de Martin Carle, (242 p.).

VAZQUEZ, Andrés Clemente

b. ca. 1870, Havana, Cuba.
Novelist, biographer, folklorist, lawyer.

Vásquez' *Enriqueta Faber* (1884) was a disordered, sensational treatment of a woman who lived and dressed as a man, based on the actual "Monja Alférez," who dared to practice medicine and to "marry" another woman. His life of Beatrice Cenci (best known to English readers through Shelley's play, *The Cenci,* completed in 1819) is treated very freely, though the work was termed a biography rather than a novel.

Writings: Novel: *Enriqueta Faber,* Havana, 1894.
Biography: *Beatriz Cena,* Havana, 1890.

VAZQUEZ GALLO, Antonio

b. 1918, Cuba.
Playwright.

Vásquez' two known plays were both published in the mid to late 1940's.

Writings: Plays: *Camorra,* 1946; *El ladrón* (1 act, set in rural Cuba); *El niño inválido,* 1949 (1 act, Christmas play).

VAZQUEZ PEREZ, Gregorio

b. ca. 1917, Cuba.
Playwright.

Vásquez' one play, *Tierra mambisa,* like so many others of its period, dealt with the harsh exploitation of the field workers.

Writings: Play: *Tierra mambisa,* 1947.

VELEZ HERRERA, Ramón

b. 1808, Havana, Cuba; d. 1886.
Poet, playwright.

An early criollist, Veléz wrote mostly a prosaic verse on such subjects as bread ("El pan de Matanzas") and lightning rods ("A Franklin, inventor del pararrayos"). Most of his work was in the then popular form of verse romances, as with "Elvira de Oquenda" and "La flor de la pitahaya."

Writings: Poetry: *Poesias,* 1833; augmented editions in 1837 and 1838; *Elvira de Oquenda o los amores de un guajira,* 1840; *Flores de Otoño,* 1849; and *Romances cubanos,* 1856.
Plays: *Los dos novios en los baños de San Diego* (3 act comedy), Havana, Imp. del Gobierno, 1843; *Napoleón en Berlin* (5 act verse tragedy), unpublished, written in 1839, and banned by Spanish authorities.

VELOZ MAGGIOLO, Marcio

b. August 13, 1936, Santo Domingo, Dominican Republic.
Novelist, storywriter, playwright, journalist, teacher, diplomat, archeologist.

Velos has won many of his country's literary prizes, including that for Poetry and Literature in 1962 and the William Faulkner Foundation Award for his novel *El Buen Ladrón.*

Much of his work is socio-political in theme. *De Abril en Adelante* (1967), considered one of his best works, treats vividly of the long Trujillo nightmare, of the "War of April" of 1965 and the days ensuing.

Writings: Novels: *El Buen Ladrón* and *Judas,* both in one volume, S. Domingo, Pensamiento Dominicano, 1962; *Judas,* S. Domingo, Col. Testimonio, 1965; *Los ángeles de hueso,* S. Domingo, Col. El Puño (Ed. Arte y Cine), 1967 (a long novelette); and *De Abril en adelante,* S. Domingo, Taller, 1975.
Stories: *Nosotros los suicidas,* 1965; *La vida no tiene nombre,* 1965.
Plays: *El prófugo,* Ediciones Brigadas Dominicanas, 1962; *El sol y las cosas,* Arquero, 1963; *Intus; Creonte,* Arquer, 1963; *El cáncer nuestro de cada dia; Y después las cenizas* (all in S. Domingo).
Critical Essays: *Cultura, teatro y relatos en Santo Domingo,* Ediciones de la UCMM, 1972.
Journalism: most of his work appeared in the Santo Domingo review, *Ahora,* mostly dealing with pre-Columbian Indian culture.

VICENS, Nimia

b. 1914, Caguas, Puerto Rico.
Poet, educationist.

Vicéns' collection of verse, *Anémona nemorosa,* won a prize in the Ateneo Puertorriqueño competition of 1950. Her work is often nationalistic, but her themes are usually of love, of silence, of personal feeling. Some of her work has appeared in *Orféo* (Yauco, P. R.) and other journals, but much of it remains still "in the drawer."

Her poem "Crecida del Silencio" ends:

Verdes ángeles tropicales levantan
sus custodias contra el liquido nimbo
donde se pierden de morise
las estrellas. . .
Yo es como un florecerse
a flor de ser

Writings: Poetry: *Anémona nemorosa,* 1950; *Canciones al mundo,* San Juan, Ateneo Puertorriqueño, 1957; and two poems, including "Crecida del Silencio," are in *Aguinaldo lirico,* C. Rosa-Nieves, ed., Rio Piedras, 1957.

VICENTE RAFAEL, Juan

(pseudonym for **Padre Juan RIVERA VIERA**)

VICIOSO, Abelardo

b. 1930, Dominican Republic.
Poet.

Vicioso was a member of the so-called "Generación del 48" or "Generación de la post-guerra" y "La Generación integradora" which felt radical political and esthetic stirrings.

Writings: Poetry: *La lumbre sacudida,* Ciudad Trujillo, Col. E. Silbo Vulnerado, 1958.

Biographical/Critical Sources: The introduction to *La lumbre sacudido* provided by Rafael Valera Benitez gives details on Viciosa's career and writings and the other writers of the "Generación integradora"; also see F. A. Mota Medardo, *Relieves Alumbrados,* S. Domingo, 1971, pp. 193-213.

VIDARTE, Santiago

b. July 25, 1828, Yabucoa, Puerto Rico; d. 1848, Barcelona, Spain.
Poet, critic.

Vidarte, who used the name of his protector, Rafael Vidarte, died at 20, a student of science in Madrid.

With Manuel Alonso, Francisco Vasallo and Carlos Saez Santiago, Vidarte composed and edited one of Puerto Rico's first collections of literature: *Aguinaldo Puertorriqueño* (1844). His "Insomnio (Fragmento)" ends:

Boguemos, Boguemos
al son de los remos
la noche convida.
¡que hermosa es la vida
la vida del mar!

Another similar version of these simple lines are in "Insomnio," published in M. Fernández Juncos' *Antologia puertorriqueña* (New York, 1952), begins:

Voguemos, voguemos
Al son de los remos;
La noche convida.
¡Qué bella es la vida
Que corre en la mar!

Writings: Poetry: in various journals and collections, including the poem "Insomnio (Fragmento)" in *Antologia de la poesia puertorriqueña,* San Juan, 1968; *Santiago Vidarte: Poesias,* San Juan, Instituto de Cultura Puertorriqueña, 1965; *Obra poética,* San Juan, Edit. Coqui, 1972(?).

Biographical/Critical Sources: See Eduardo Neuman's *Benefactores y hombres notables de Puerto Rico* which ascribes Santiago Vidarte's pen-name to the veiled connection between the young poet and his benefactor Rafael Vidarte who sponsored Santiago's study in Spain. Neuman also states poet was born in Yabucoa, not Humacao which is more often cited as his birthplace).

VIDAURRETA Y ALVAREZ, Antonio

b. 1832, Villaclara, Cuba; d. 1899.
Poet.

A fervent admirer of Núñez de Arce,

Vidaurreta was a minor poet of the school of Villaclara.

Writings: in various journals and in the collections *Céfiros y flores,* Villaclara(?), 1860, and in *Guirnalda villaclareña,* Villaclara, 1894.

VILLA, Ignacio

b. 1902, Guanabacoa, Havana, Cuba.
Poet.

Villa employed Afro-Cuban works and exploited rural settings and manners in his verse in a natural, even naive style. Of pure African race according to one authority, Ballagas has asserted he was a "negro macizo." Though graduated from the Escuelas Normales de la Habana, he never taught, preferring work as a pianist, composer and "disseur." He traveled widely in the United States, Mexico and Central and South America. His verse has never appeared in a collected volume.

Writings: Poetry: in various journals and collections, including R. Guirao's *Orbita de la poesia afrocubana,* 1928-37, Havana, 1939 (with poems: "Drumi, Mobila," and "Calota Ta Mori"); and Ballagas' *Antologia de la poesia negraamericana,* Madrid, 1935.

VILLAR BUCETA, Maria

b. 1898, Cuba.
Poet.

Villar was an ironic, even acerbic poet as these few lines taken from her collection *Unanimismo* can show:

¡En casa todos vamos a morir de silencio!
Yo señalo el fenómeno; pero me diferencio
apenas del conjunto. . . ¡Tengo que ser lo mismo!
. . .
. . .
¡Y asi pasan los dias, los meses y los años!

Harrison says Villar avoided ". . .the straightforward metaphor, preferring the more oblique approach,. . .using cyncism and paradox as a total metaphor for life's complexity and inherent irony."

Raimundo Lazo allowed himself to say of her that she is an unusual case of humor in a woman, "combinado con notas de honda y austera melancolia, en forma de exemplar transparencia y eficaz sencillez."

Writings: Poetry: *Unanimismo,* Havana, 1927.

Biographical/Critical Sources: Polly F. Harrison, "Images and Exile: The Cuban Woman and Her Poetry," in *Revista Interamericana,* Vol. IV, No. 2 (Summer 1974), pp. 203-204; R. Lazo, *La literatura cubana,* p. 191.

VILLARONDA, Guillermo

b. 1912, Cuba.
Poet.

A post-modernist, Villaronda's poetry was satirical and full of social commentary.

Writings: Poetry: *Hontanar* (winner of "Premio Nacional de Poesia"); *Mástil,* 1935; *Poemas a Walt Disney,* 1943, all in Havana.

VILLARONGA CHARRIEZ, Luis

b. June 13, 1891, Barranquitas, Puerto Rico; d. 1964, Hato Rey.
Essayist, novelist, biographer, critic.

A lawyer, Villaronga traveled and studied in Europe and the United States and spent most of his career as a teacher and practicing lawyer. A youthful follower of the Colómbian José Maria Vargar Vila, Villaronga later fell under the influence of Azorin and developed a clearer, more direct, even precise, prose style but always maintaining a rhythmical musical cadence. His work appeared in many journals of the day and some twelve volumes of his work have appeared in published collections.

Writings: Essays: *Alas victoriosos* (includes journalistic pieces), 1925; *Carmencita,* 1933; *Dios* (philosophical essays), 1942; *Los motivos eternos,* 1945; *Contemplación,* 949; *El peregrino de la senda del sol,* 1950; *La torre de marfil,* 1952; and *Paisaje y alma,* 1954.

Biographic-Literary Criticism: *Azorin: su obra, su espiritu,* 1931; *Constancio C. Vigil-El sembrador,* 1939.

Novels: *Banderas rojas,* 1933; *La república sentimental,* 1933; *Carmencita,* Madrid, 1933.

VILLAVERDE Y DE LA PAZ, Cirilo

b. October 12, 1812, San Diego de Nuñez (Pinar del Rio), Cuba; d. October 20, 1894, New York City.

Novelist, storywriter, biographer, teacher.

Villaverde lived an active, even turbulent life, and was arrested in the 1848 revolt against Spanish control, spending many months in prison, but he never was sentenced to death as some have believed. He served as secretary to General Narciso

López who led two invasions (1850 and 1851), but was captured and executed after the second one. Villaverde wrote of the episodes in 1851 in a sixteen page booklet.

Villaverde remained in the U. S. during the 1850's and married in 1855 the active conspirator against Spanish authority, Emilia Casanova (1832-1897). The young couple founded a school near New York City. In 1858, allowed to return to Cuba, Villaverde founded with Francisco Calcagno the review *La Habana,* but in 1861 he returned to the U. S. Again active in revolutionary work, he joined the plot of 1868 established in New York, and wrote *La revolución de Cuba vista desde Nueva York.* Once again in Cuba in 1888, Villaverde remained there until shortly before his death during a trip to New York City in 1894.

Villaverde's earliest stories appeared in local reviews, such tales as "La cueva de Taganana," "La pena blanca," "El ave muerta," and "El perjurio." These stories are full of cruelty, seduction, and often incest. "El espetón de oro" ends, in Max Henriquez Ureña's words: ". . .en un asesinato, monstruosa venganza de un vesánico, que la misma noche de sus bodas clava un espetón en el pecho de la mujer que acaba de unirse a él." Though Villaverde claims to have given up his lurid subjects and style, his later stories remained more than casually bizarre and violent, and his greatest success, the novel *Cecilia Valdes,* centers around an incestuous relationship and ends with "actos de violencia y de muerte," again in the words of Max Henriquez Ureña.

Henriquez praised Cecilia Valdez, however, saying that no historian has been equal to Villaverde's picturing of an entire epoch . . . " Nadie ha descrito con mayor seguridad ni mas honda emoción humana la vida del esclavo en el ingenio, ni las diferencias sociales entre la privilegiada clase de los amos y la de los desheredados libertas. . .La novela de Villaverde es un alegato antiesclavista, aunque ese no fuera el propósito deliberado de su autor."

Sir Walter Scott and Charles Dickens were the strongest influences, Villaverde's *Dos amores* being obviously touched by many of Dickens' stories and his *Cuentos di mi abuelo* (the series of that name) by Scott's "Tales of a Grandfather."

Writings: Novels: *Cecilia Valdés, o La Loma del Angel,* Madrid, 1882 (completed in 1879), new ed., Havana, Consejo Nacional de Cultura, 1964, also Mexico Editorial Porrúa, 1972; the first sketch of what became the novel published in the journal *La Siempreviva* (1839) was republished in *Cuba Intelectual* (1910); translated by Sydney G. Gestas as *Cecilia Valdes or Angel's Hill; a novel of Cuban customs,* New York, Vantage Press, 1962, (546 p.), and in an earlier version as *The Quadroon, or Cecilia Valdes, a romance of old Havana,* Boston, L. C. Page & Co., 1935 (399 p.); *Dos Amores,* 1858; *El quajiro,* (written 1842), published in *Comunidad de nombres y apellidos,* published in one issue of *Biblioteca del Faro Industrial,* 1846, but no copies extant; *El penitente* (written in 1844); *La joven de la flecha de oro,* Havana, Comisión Nacional Cubana de la UNESCO, 1962, (384 p.), and *La peineta calada y la tejerdora de sombreros de yarey,* Havana, C.N. C. de la UNESCO, 1962, (262 p.).

Folklore: various essays, including "La Habana en 1841," "Reloj de repetición," "Máscaras," and "Una mudada."

General: *To the Public: General López, the Cuban Patriot,* New York, 1851.

Biography: *Apuntes biográficos de Emilia Casanova de Villaverde, con parte de su larga correspondencia politica* (the first 24 pp. are Villaverde's general biography of Casanova; the rest of the large volume consists of Casanova's papers).

Stories: "El ciego y su perro," 1842; "Generosidad fraternal," 1846, both published in *El Faro Industrial,* "La joven de la flecha de oro," 1840; "La cruz negra," "Engañar con la verdad," "Lola y su periquito," "Teresa," 1839; and "La tejedora de sombreros de yarey," (fragment of a novel), 1843; "La peineta calada," (on an episode in the life of Plácido); "El penitente," 1844; *Cuentos di mi abuela;* "Diario del Rancheador," (introduction and notes by Roberto Friol), *Revista de la Biblioteca Nacional José Marti* (Havana, January-April 1973), pp. 47-149.

Description of Author's Home Region: *Excursión a la Vuelta Abajo,* Havana, 1891, but in various sections in journals much earlier: first part in *El Album,* 1838-39, the second part in *El Faro Industrial,* 1843.

Romances: "La cueva de Taganana"; "La pena blanca"; "El ave muerte"; "El perjurio"; and "El espetón de oro."

School Texts: *Compendio geográfico de la Isla de Cuba,* (30 p.); *El librito de los cuentos y las conversaciones,* 1847.

Biographical/Critical Sources: Max Henriquez Ureña, *Panorama histórico de la literatura cubana,* New York, 1963, pp. 226-232; and see introduction to *Cecilia Valdés* in Mexico, 1972 edition by Raimundo Lazo, pp. ix-xxxvii. Notes and comments by Esteban Rodriguez Herrera in *Critical Edition of Cecilia Valdés,* Havana, Edit. LEX, 1953; Enrique José Varona, "El autor de *Cecilia Valdés,*" in *El Figaro* (Havana, November 4, 1894); Diego Vicente Tejera, "Una novela cubana," in *Un poco de prosa,* Havana, 1895; Manuel de la Cruz, articles on *Cecilia Valdés,* in *La Ilustración Cubana,* Barcelona, Vol. 3, Year 2, No. 7 (June 20, 1887); and also by Cruz, "Cirilo Villaverde," in *Cromitos Cubanos,* Vol. V, of *Obras* (of Cruz), Madrid, 1926; Martín Morúa Delgado, *Impresiones literarias. Las novelas del señor Villaverde,* Havana, 1892, José A. Rodriguez Garcia, "Sobre Villaverde y su *Cecilia Valdés,*" in *Cuba Intelectual,* Havana, (June 1909); Antonio Maria Eligio de la Puente, introduction to *Dos Amores,* Havana, Ed. Cultural, 1930, edited by Eligio; and also Eligio's introduction to *Cuentos Cubanos* of Ramón de Palma, also edited by Eligio, Havana, 1928; Javier Baraona (pseudonym), *Itinerio de Cecilia Valdés,* in *Carteles,* Nos. 18 and 19, Havana, 1950; and Raimundo Lazo, *Historia de la literatura cubana,* Havana, Edit. Universitaria, 1967.

VILLOCH, Federico

b. 1868, Cuba; d. 1953(?).
Playwright, poet, storywriter.

Villoch, primarily a writer of burlesques and farces performed at the Teatro Alhambra, was a founding father of Cuban theatre along with Gustavo Villoch. He wrote more than a hundred works for the stage, none of them apparently ever published. His "bohemian" free-spirited poetry was once quite popular. Such verse as "Otra Mimi," "Los dias del bohemio," "¡Se alquila!" and "Desde el hospital" bespeak the influence of Murger's famous *La vie bohême.*

Writings: Stories: *Cuentos a Juana.*
Travel: *Por esos mundos,* Havana, 1892.

VINAJERAS, Antonio

b. 1833, Cuba; d. 1905.
Poet, novelist, critic, biographer.

Born into a wealthy family, Vinajeras removed to Madrid in his twenty-first year and after 1858 lived in Paris. Max Henriquez Ureña called him a vain and talentless writer, making even such poor contemporaries as López de Briñas, Roldán, and Blanchie appear decent verse writers. Nevertheless, Vinajeras published much, including his novel, *Enriqueta* (1868), which Henriquez termed detestable.

Writings: Plays: *Virtud o crimen* (3 act verse tragedy), Matanzas, Imp. del Diario, 1879; *Por todas partes se va a Roma* (3 act verse comedy), performed Teatro Esteban, September, 1879; *Maria Antonieta* (3 acts), 1879.
Poetry: *A la memoria de mi padre,* Madrid, 1879.
Novel: *Enriqueta,* 1868.
Critical Essays: *Elogio de Poey,* Paris, 1858; *André Piquier et ses oeuvres,* Montpellier, 1861; *Ideas,* Paris, 1868; *Los elementos jovenes de la Unión Liberal,* Madrid, 1865; *El pan del pueblo,* Madrid, 1866; *Bosquejo critico de la vida de Lord Byron de D. Emilio Castelar,* details not known.
Biography: *Discurso* (given at time he was awarded a law degree at Salamanca).
Collected Works: *Obras,* 2 vols., 1855-58.

VITIER, Cintio (or Cynthio)

b. 1921, Cuba.
Poet, critic, essayist, literary historian.

Published in his sixteenth year, Vitier has been a prolific and innovative poet all his life and a discerning critic and literary historian. He has edited two anthologies, one on the poets of the Origenes group gathered around José Lezama Lima, and the second, which covers the poets from independence to 1952, *Cinquenta años de poesia cubano.*

Writings: Poetry: *Poemas,* Havana, 1938; *Sediente cita,* Havana, 1943; *Estrañeza de estar,* 1943; *De mi provincia,* 1945; *Poética; Temas martianos; Capricho y homenaje,* 1947; *El hogar y el olirdo,* 1949; *Sustancia,* 1950; *Conjetoros,* 1951; *Visperas,* 1953; *Canta llano,* 1956; *Testimonios;* and verse in many journals and collections.
Editor of: *Cinquenta años de poesia cubana,* 1952; *Lo cubano en la poesia,* Havana, 1958; and *Las mejores poesias cubanas,* Lima, Organización Continental de Los Festivales del Libro, 1959; *Los grandes románticos cubanos,* Havana, Organización Continental. . ., 1960; *Los poetas románticos cubanos,* Havana, Consejo Nacional de Cultura, 1962.

VITIER, Medardo

b. 1886, Matanzas, Cuba; d. 1960.
Critic, literary historian, novelist, teacher.

After taking a doctorate in education, Vitier became the director of the Escuela Normal of Matanzas and later helped found the regional university of Central de las Villas. He taught philosophy and held several high posts in the national educational offices of the government. He published almost a score of works in many genres and was one of his period's outstanding scholars.

Writings: Literary Biographies: *Marti: su obra poliitica y literaria,* 1911; *Marti, estudio integral,* Havana, Com. Nac. Org. de los Actos y Edic.

del Centenario y del Monumento de Martí, 1954; *Don José de la Luz y Caballero,* 1914, amplified to *José de la Luz y Caballero como educador,* 1956; *Enrique José Varona, maestro de juventudes,* 2 vols, 1937; *La lección de Varona,* 1945, all Havana; *José Ortega y Gasset,* Havana, 1936; *Arturo Echemendia,* Matanzas, 1932.

Literary History: *Apuntaciones literarias,* Havana, 1935; *Las ideas en Cuba,* 2 vols., Havana, 1938; *Del ensayo americano* (on U. S. literary criticism), Mexico, 1945.

Philosophy: *La filosofia en Cuba,* Havana, Fondo de Cult. Econ., 1948; *Iniciación en su filosofia* (of Kant), Havana, 1959; *La fundamental* (on pedagogy), Havana, 1926; *Las doctrinas filosóficas en Cuba* (conference papers), date unknown; *Las ideas y la filosofia en Cuba,* Havana, Ciencias Sociales, 1970 (reprint of "Las ideas en Cuba" (1938) and "La filosofia en Cuba" (1948).

Journalistic articles: *Valoraciones,* Havana, 1960.

Novel: *La ruta del sembrador,* Havana, 1912.

VIVAS MALDONADO, José Luis

b. 1926, Aguadilla, Puerto Rico.
Storywriter.

After local schooling until 1942, Vivas attended the University of Puerto Rico and later began teaching in Lares and Camuy (1945-1948). For a period he worked in New York (1945) and during that year wrote his first novel, *Destellos umbrios,* and the next two years, back home once more, he began and completed a collection of sketches of his impressions of the local landscapes, *Bocetos* (1947). Returning to the University to finish his degree (1956), Vivas accepted a teaching position at the Colegio San José de Rio Piedras. In the late 1950's he attended Columbia University (New York) to earn an M. A.

His collection *Luces en sombra* won a prize in the Instituto de Literatura (1955).

Vivas is married to Mirta Felipe y José Manuel.

Writings: Stories: *Luces en sombra,* San Juan, Editorial Yaurel, 1955; "El fósforo quemado" and "Interludio" are in R. Márquez' *Cuentos puertorriqueños de hoy;* Concha Meléndez, *El arte del cuento en Puerto Rico,* New York, 1971, pp. 311-316, which also offers "El héroe" and "Interludio," "Cinco cuentos del miedo" and "El niño y su mundo" published in *Almanaque* (1953); "El de los cabos blancos," in *Asomante,* No. 3, 1956, pp. 97-134.

VIZCARRONDO, Carmelina

b. January 9, 1906, Fajardo, Puerto Rico.
Poet, storywriter.

Vizcarrondo has written much verse in the "postmodernista" period (1930-40's) and has been influenced by Federico García Lorca and Gabriela Mistral. Much of her work first appeared in *Alma Latina, Asomante, El Imparcial, El Mundo, Brújula* and *Puerto Rico Ilustrado.* Her "Pregón en llamas" ends:

Los plumones alarmados
cejan sus timbres de plata.
Como pañuelos al viento
brillan en la noche pálida.
Parece un cortejo fúnebre
el adiós de las guajanas.

Writings: Poetry: *Prégon en llamas,* San Juan, 1935; *Poemas para mi niño,* 1937, San Juan, Imp. Venezuela (children's verse); her "El parque Muñoz Rivera" is in the *Antologia de la poesia puertorriqueña,* E. Fernández Méndez, ed., San Juan, 1968.

Stories: *Minutero en sombras,* San Juan, Imp. Venezuela, 1941.

Preface to: *Canciones de ruta y sueño,* by Ramón Zapata Acosta, 1954.

VIZCARRONDO, Fortunato

b. 1896, Carolina, Puerto Rico.
Poet.

Largely self-taught, Fortunato Vizcarrondo wrote a popular, easy, emotional verse, full of the flavor of the black peasants and their humor and music.

Vizcarrondo exploited Afro-Puerto Rican speech and local color in his work which is mostly lyrical and highly subjective. Rosa-Nieves called him a "Poeta de tono ligero en pentagrama populista; verso rico a veces de gracia y humor, y otras de descarnado naturalismo escenico." The influence of Nicolás Guillén's *Motivos del son* (1930) and *Songoro Cosongo,* both "negrista," is evident in Vizcarrondo's work.

"El Cangrejero" (Canto negroide para coger cangrejos) begins:

Candén, cabú, macafú. . .
Sale, juy, que ejtá encuebao.
Titabó, macarabao.
Ambulé, macarabú.

Writings: Poetry: *Dinga y mandinga,* 1942, foreword by José Antonio Dávila, 2nd ed., San Juan, Edit. del Departamento de Instrucción Pública, 1968.

WEBER, Delia

b. 1902, Dominican Republic.
Poet, storywriter.

Writings: Poetry: *Encuentro,* 1939; *Ascuas vivas,* 1939; *Los viajeros,* 1944 (a dramatic poem).
Tales: *Dora y otros cuentos,* 1952.

XENES, Nieves

b. 1859, near Quivicán, Havana Province, Cuba; d. 1915.
Poet.

Xenes' work was astringent, anti-melifluous, but popular just the same. Early come to the capital, Xenes met José Antonio Cortina, José Maria Céspedes and other literati. Aurelia Castillo de Gonzáles said Xenes sought the impossible purity of virtue and perfect love. His poetry appeared in occasional journals but only after his death did the National Academy of Arts and Letters publish Xenes' work in a volume edited by Aurelia Castillo (1915).

Writings: Poetry: *Poesias,* Havana, Imp. Siglo XX de Aurelio Miranda, 1915.

YUMET MENDEZ, José

b. ca. 1890, Puerto Rico.
Poet.

Yumet's verse is late "modernista" with tendencies to express feelings perhaps more prosaic than lyrical.

Writings: Poetry: *Caminos de sol,* San Juan, Tip. Cantero, Fernández, 1920; *Anfora azul,* San Juan, Tip. Venezuela, 1925; *Ala y trino,* San Juan, Tip. Venezuela, 1931.

ZACARIAS ESPINAL, Manuel

b. 1901, San Cristobal, Dominican Republic; d. 1933, Santo Domingo.
Poet.

Zacarias, one of the tragic young poets every nation mourns, died of an overdose of morphine. He strained to surpass the ordinary limits or words, and sought for new sonorities. A modernist of the most unqualified sort, his poetry was akin to "Jitanjáforas" by Alfonso Reyes and many poems of Mariano Brull's. Zacarias reacted against the over-realism and prosaicness of the "Postumistas" and declared himself to be a staunch "Vedrinista." Much of his work was in the sonnet form, but he did some prose-poems and free verse.

The bizarre qualities of his original verse can be seen in this octavo from his sonnet No. 5:

Junto al bárako euforio que apelista
la diapesis narcótica de Hicrea

responza su emperámico Hitorbea
la funcia de Kra-Zoma panevista.

Zigia-20,-Zelé, -Kranimia Hitea
Karma Ozoramia de akelión panista
que frunge su aponema panteista
en zakos de ankoroma y Galilea.

Writings: Poetry: *Poemas* (transcribed and edited by Ligia Espinal de Hoetink), Edición póstuma, Holland, 1961.

Biographical/Critical Sources: Ligia Espinal de Hoeting's introduction to *Poemas,* Holland, 1961, in a privately published edition of 88 p. and illustrated by Eligio Pichardo; and see Manuel Rueda's introduction to the works of Espinal presented in *Antologia panoramica de la poesia dominicana contemporánea (1912-1962),* 1972, pp. 39-40.

ZAFRA, Antonio Enrique de

b. ca. 1826, Seville, Spain; d. 1875.
Playwright, journalist.

Long a resident of Cuba and a leading playwright, Zafra also edited the journal *La Voz de Cuba* and was otherwise active as a journalist.

Writings: Plays: *Las trompas de mi tio* (comedy), 1856; *Un huésped a media noche* (1 act comedy), performed 1856, unpublished; *Isabel de Bossián* (4 acts), performed 1856, unpublished; *Amor contra nobleza* (3 acts, verse), Havana, Soler, 1858; *El lego de San Fardel* (4 acts), written in 1858, but banned from the stage or press by the Spanish authorities, unpublished; *El hombre negro o El carnaval de Sevilla* (3 acts), Havana, Imp. Militar, 1859; *La toma de Tetuan* (3 acts, verse), Havana, Imp. Militar, 1860; *El alcalde Don Rodrigo o La justicia de Dios* (3 acts), Havana, La Cubana, 1862; *Tres parados* (1 act), Havana; *La intrépeda,* 1865; *Un golpe de fortuna* (1 act verse comedy), Havana, Imp. El Iris, 1867; *Dios los cria* (1 act, verse), 1868; *La fiesta del mayoral* (1 act, folkloric), Havana, Imp. El Iris, 1868, and Havana, Imp. OSES, 1924; *Un cuadro de Rafael* (3 acts, verse), Havana, El Iris, 1868; *Colón en Cuba* (1 act, verse), Havana, Imp. Militar, 1869; *Por España y su bandera* (1 act), Havana, Imp. Militar, 1872.

ZAHONET, Félix

b. ca. 1860, Cuba.
Playwright.

Zahonet took an active part in the 1899 rebellion against Spain, serving as a captain in the Ejército Libertador.

Writings: Plays: *Los amores de Eloisa o Heroicidad de una madre* (2 act musical), Key West, Tip. de la Revista Popular, 1890; *Los fosos, Weyler o La reconcentración* (3 acts, verse), Havana, El Figaro, 1899; *Patria o tumba* (3 acts, verse), Havana, El Figaro, 1900; *Delirios de una pasión* (3 acts, verse), Havana, Swan, 1911; *La princesa Noemi* (3 acts, prose), Havana, Flores y Espinas, 1912.

ZAMACOIS, Eduardo

b. 1873, San Luis, Pinar del Río, Cuba.
Novelist, playwright.

Zamacois spent most of his life in Spain and published all of his known works in Madrid or Barcelona. He is one of the earliest novelists to work frankly in the erotic vein in Spanish and was extremely popular.

Writings: Novels: *El Seductor,* 1902; *La enferma,* Barcelona, R. Sospena, 1896; *Duelo a muerte,* Barcelona, Sospena, 1902; *La serpiente sonrié,* Barcelona, Maucci, 2nd ed., 1913; *La opinión ajena,* Madrid, Renacimiento, 1913; *La cita,* Madrid, Renacimiento, 1913; *Memorias de un cortesana,* Barcelona, Sospena, 1918.

Plays: *El pasado vuelve* (1 act comedy), Madrid, R. Velasco, 1909; *Teatro galante: Nochebuena, El pasado vuelve; Frio,* Madrid, A. Garrido, 1910; *El aderzo* (1 act verse comedy), Barcelona, Casa Editorial Maucci, 1913 (published at rear of novel *La Serpiente sonrie,* 1913); *La vida se repite* (comedy), in *Por esos mundos,* Vol. 14 (Madrid 1913), pp. 156-175; *Presentimiento* (1 act), Madrid, Biblioteca Hispania, 1916.

ZAMBRANA Y VALDES, Ramón

b. 1817, Cuba; d. 1866.
Essayist, literary historian, philosopher, teacher, scientist.

Zambrana y Valdés was one of Cuba's earliest literary critics, though today he is given only brief mention in histories of Cuban writings.

Writings: Combined Works: *Obras literarias, filosóficas y cientificas,* 1858.
Literary history: *Diferentes épocas de la poesia en Cuba,* details unknown.
Essays: *Soliloquios,* 1865; *Trabajos académicos,* 1863.
Articles: in *El Kaleidescopio* journal, 1859, most uncollected.
Critical Biography: *Elogio de José de la Luz y Caballero.*

ZAMBRANA Y VAZQUEZ, Antonio

b. 1846, Havana, Cuba; d. March 27, 1922, Havana.
Novelist, critic, journalist, lawyer.

While a youth of seventeen, Zambrana was greatly impressed by his reading of Suárez' anti-slavery novel *Francisco.* He later launched his own attack on slavery in his own novel *El negro Francisco* (1875), written while he was in Chile. Though his work to some degree reflects the earlier novel, he did re-create his own fictional world in a telling drama.

Zambrana served as an envoy to Cuban exile and revolutionary groups in New York, Mexico and Santiago, Chile. He secured Victor Hugo's support for Cuban independence, worked as a lawyer in Costa Rica where he gradually became a leading political and intellectual figure in his new home, even to being named Minister Plenipotentiary of Costa Rica to Nicaragua. After many years he returned to Cuba where he established the journal *El Cubano* in 1886, and was elected to parliament (the Cortes).

He was caught in the middle of the separatist politics of the late 1880's and after publishing *Una visita a la Metrópoli* (1888), which offered his view of Spanish affairs gained from his visit to Madrid in 1888, he returned to an increasingly uncomfortable life in Cuba. In 1891 he returned to Costa Rica where he was again warmly received and where he wrote and published several works on esthetics and politics.

After the independence of Cuba, Zambrana hesitated to return from exile until 1906, but was then hailed as one of the old fighters and named ambassador to Colombia and Ecuador. His years of retirement were spent in Havana on a modest state pension.

Writings: Novel: *El negro Francisco,* written in 1875.
Critical-Esthetic Essays: *Ideas de estética, literatura y elocuencia,* 1896; *La poesia de la historia,* 1900.
Journalism and Politics: *La República de Cuba,* New York, 1873; *La cuestion de Cuba,* Valparaiso, Chile, 1874; *Una visita a la Metrópoli,* 1888; *La administración,* 1897; *Estudios juridicos,* Costa Rica, 1907; *Prensa y tribuna,* Quito, 1912.

Biographical/Critical Sources: Rafael Rodriguez Altunaga, *Antonio Zambrana* ("Reminiscencias de su vida"), in *La Discusión* (May 7, 1922), reprinted in Vol. XIV of *Los Zambrana,* edited by Malleén Zambrana de Fernández, 1958; Max Henriquez Ureña, *Panorama histórico de la literatura cubana,* New York, 1963, pp. 353-357.

ZAMORA, José Narciso

b. ca. 1810, Cuba.
Playwright.

Zamora, now almost forgotten, is known to have published four plays.

Writings: Plays: *Leopoldo* (4 scenes, verse and

prose), Imp. Literaria, 1840; *El Cruzado en Palestina* (3 scenes, prose and verse), 1841; *A los sesenta un rosario* (1 act, verse), Barcina, 1847; *El hacendado ridiculo* (3 act verse comedy), Imp. del Tiempo, 1863, all in Havana.

ZAPATA ACOSTA, Ramón

b. 1917, Cabo Rojo, Puerto Rico.
Poet, essayist, teacher.

A professor at the University of Puerto Rico, Zapata has been the editor of the important poetry reviews, *Pegaso* and *Orfeo* in which many younger island poets were first published. His work is touched by late currents of French "surrealism," and is very personal and carefully worked.

Writings: Poetry: *Canciones de ruta y sueño,* Yauco, Edit. Yaurel, 1954, foreword by Carmelina Vizcarrondo.

Biographical/Critical Sources: F. Lluch Mora, *Miradero, Ensayos de critica literaria,* San Juan, 1966.

ZAYAS, Fernándo de

b. 1876, Cuba; d. 1932.
Poet.

A member of the Arpas group (the anthology *Arpes Cubanas,* 1878), Zayas generally employed the "sixteener" as in "Estival":

¡Parda nube de julio, ve al horizonte;
no oscurezcas el cielo con tu mortaja:
trisca alegre el ganado por la pradera
y al sol tienden los buitres sus negras alas!

Writings: Poetry: *Amorosas,* Havana, 1902; *Sueños de rosa,* Havana, 1906.

Poetry and Prose: *Prosa y verso,* Havana, 1909.

War Chronicle: *Hojas sueltas* (with Orestes Ferrara), Havana, 191?.

ZAVALA, Iris M.

b. 1936, Puerto Rico.
Poet, critic, anthologist.

Zavalá has published his poetry and criticism mostly in journals, but he has two collections of his verse in print.

Writings: Poetry: *Barro doliente,* Santander, Publicaciones La Isla de los Ratones, 1964 (winner of first prize in Puerto Rican Literature competition); *Poemas prescindibles,* New York-Buenos Aires, La Libreria, 1971, and poems in such reviews as *Asomante, Revista del Instituto de Cultura Puertorriqueña, Pájaro Cascabel* (Mexico), and *Sur* (Argentina).

Editor of: (with Rafael Rodriguez): *Libertad y critica: Antologia del ensayo puertorriqueño,* San Juan, Ediciones puertorriqueño, (Edit. Libreria Internacional), 1972.

ZENEA, Juan Clemente

(pseudonyms: **Adolfo de la AZUCENA**; **"Ego-queque"** and **"un amigo de la juventud."**)

b. February 24, 1832, Bayamo, Cuba; d. August 25, 1871, Havana.
Poet, novelist, translator, editor, playwright.

Son of the soldier, Lt. Rafael Zenea y Luz and of Celestina Fornaris y Luque, Zenea moved to Havana to study under his uncle Evaristo Zenea and then went to Spain when his father was sent there on a military transfer.

A fervent nationalist, Zenea took part in many revolts against Spanish control and often fled to exile in the United States or Mexico. Condemned to death in 1853, Zenea escaped to live a tumultuous life—only to return to Cuba in 1868 as a representative of a Cuban revolutionary group in New York whereupon he was incarcerated despite his safe-conduct pass signed by the Spanish ambassador to the U. S. On August 25, 1871, Zenea died before a firing squad.

The Spanish colonial records of Zenea's trial were published in *Cuba Contemporá-*

nea XLII (1926). Though the records indicate Zenea sought to bargain his way out of his predicament by serving the Spanish, Max Henriquez Ureña argues Zenea was obviously not himself after long solitary confinement.

In Mexico in the 60's, he was appointed director of the *Diario Oficial,* staying in that post until 1868 with the support of his father-in-law, President Benito Juárez.

Zenea was felt to be much more French than Spanish in his poetic culture and closer to Alfred de Musset than to any Spanish-language poet.

José Lezama Lima concludes his chapter-long treatment of Zenea by writing: "Aquellas ondas errantes de su poesia se han transformando en un nuevo cuerpo de gloria: su cristal ha sudado la sangre. En la heráldica de la poesia cubana, Zenea es un principe de la sangre."

Writings: Poetry: *Cantos de la tarde,* 1st ed., 1860, 2nd ed., augmented, 1874, republished in *Poesias,* 1936 by Publicaciones de la Secretaria de Educación in Havana (contains *Cantos de la tarde, Poemas varias, Traducciones, En Dias de esclavitud, Diario de un mártir* (which itself is 18 poems composed and memorized in prison and put on paper during his last hours, 15 of them for his wife and daughter and one for his old love, Adah Menken, the American actress); also: *La moderna poesia* (Nueva colección de poemas de Juan Clemente Zenea), 1909; *Poesia,* Havana, Academia de Ciencias de Cuba, 1966.

Criticism: Much of it published in *Revista Habanera,* including "Mis contemporáneos," essays on Cuban writers.

Novels: *Fidelia,* published at end of *Lejos de la patria* (memoirs) of Adolfo de la Azucena, Havana, "La Charanga," 1859; *El Almendares,* Vol. I, 1852 contains part of *El primer amor,* and Vol. II contains the three-page portion entitled "El pájaro errante."

Translations: Play: *Andrés del Sarto* (of Musset), in *Revista Habanera,* 1861; Stories: *Cuentos de niños,* "traducidos por un amigo de la juventud," Havana, 1864 (stories of Edouard Laboulaye's *Contes bleus*).

Literary History: *Sobre la literatura en los Estados Unidos,* Havana, 1861 (but shown to have been actually published in New York to avoid Spanish censorship of Cuban books).

Biographical/Critical Sources: M. Cabrera y Saquí's biography and notes in *Poesias,* Havana, 1936, pp. 5-21; José Lezama Lima's essay on Zenea in *La cantidad hechizado,* Madrid, 1974, pp. 184-213; Rafael Merchán, *Estudios criticos,* 1886, p. 157; Enrique Piñeyro, *Vida y escritos de Zenea,* Paris, 1901 (the appendices contain several of his otherwise un-republished work which first had appeared in journals such as *Lagrimas*; Antonio L. Valverde, *Juan Clemente Zenea,* details unknown; Max Henriquez Ureña, *Panorama histórico de la literatura cubana,* New York, 1963, pp. 280-305.

ZENO GANDIA, Manuel

b. January 10, 1855, Arecibo, Puerto Rico;
d. January 30, 1930, San Juan.
Novelist, playwright, poet, storywriter, journalist, physician.

After local schooling, Zeno moved to Barcelona, Spain for his high school studies and to Madrid for his university degree in medicine and surgery at the University of San Carlo in 1875. He later studied internal medicine and worked at the Hospital San Andrés in Burdeos, Spain and then at various hospitals in Paris.

In France, Zeno came to know the work of Flaubert, Honoré Balzac and Emile Zola. While completing his medical studies at Madrid, Zeno had begun to submit articles and stories to local reviews and after his return to Puerto Rico in 1876 he was active in literature, medicine, journalism and politics. His major work in fiction was the four novel group entitled "Crónicas de un Mundo Enfermo," beginning with what is considered his finest work, *La charca,* 1894. The novel is a relatively mild dose of naturalism, for the hard look at life of a Zola is replaced by a more religiously oriented scrutiny of man's troubles in a world in which God *does* exist.

Writings: Novels: *La charca,* San Juan, Campos, 1894, 2nd ed., 1895, in Ponce, by Imp. y Libreria de Manuel Lopez, and Mexico, D. F. Orión, 1955; *Garduña,* Ponce, in *El Telégrafo,* 1896, completed version was made in November, 1890, and first published in Ponce, Tip. El Telégrafo, 1896, and Mexico, D. F. Orión, 1955; *El negocio,* New York, The Geo. A. Powers Printing Co., Vol. 1922, Vol. III of *Obras Completas,* San Juan, 1955; *Los redentores,* San Juan, El Imparcial, 1922; as Vol. IV of *Obras completas,* San Juan, 1960; a chapter of *Los redentores* is in the review, *Asomante,* No. 4 (October-December 1955).

Novelettes: "Rosa de Marmól" in *Revista Puertorriqueña,* 1889, pp. 17-30; "Piccola" in *Revista Puertorriqueña,* 1890, pp. 385-415.

Stories: *Cuentos,* New York, Las Américas, 1958; and "Un caso inverosimil," "La dicha en el pecado," "De buena cepa," "La trenza," "El sofisma," "Aquella nube," "Los cinco sentidos," and "Teorias de Jonathón," and "Los perros de Bernard" (this last written with his son Antón Giorgi), all published in various journals.

Plays: *Federico Trenk,* written 1875-76 in Arecibo; *Un matrimonio a oscuras o El demonio son los celos,* Madrid, 1873; *Entre las diez y las doce,* dated Arecibo, November, 1876, all unpublished and in the possession of Doña Eleńa Zeno, the author's daughter.

Poetry: *Poesias,* collected and edited by Margarita Gardón, San Juan, Edit. Coqui, 1969.

Medical Scholarship: *Influencia del clima en la enfermadades del hombre,* Madrid, 1873.

Collected Works: *Obras completas,* 3 vols., Rio Piedras, Ediciones del Instituto de Literatura Puertorriqueña, 1958 (Vol. I. contains his first three novels).

Biographical/Critical Sources: José Juan Beauchamp, *Imagen del puertorriqueño en la novela,* Rio Piedras, 1976 (essays on Zeno, Laguerre and Tapia y Rivera); Cesáreo Rosa-Nieves' chapter "Una gran novela de America: *La charca,*" in *Ensayos escogidos,* San Juan, 1970, pp. 109-116; Samuel R. Quiñones, *Temas y Letras,* 3rd ed., San Juan, Biblioteca de Autores Puertorriqueños (but printed in Madrid, Spain, 1955), pp. 11-38; and Quiñones' biography *Manuel Gandia Zeno,* details unknown; Eleńa de Matos, *Manuel Zeno Gandia,* San Juan, Documentos Biográficos y Críticas, 1955; and articles on Zeno by Cabrera Rosa-Nieves and Héctor Barrera with a bibliography by Margot Arce de Vásquez in *Asomante* (October-December 1955); José M. Colón, "La naturaleza en Manuel Zeno Gandia y Enrique A. Laguerre, unpublished M. A. thesis, U. of P. R., 1949; Rosa-Nieves' essay "Presencia de Manuel Zeno Gandia," in former's *La Lámpera del Faro,* Vol. I, San Juan, 1957, pp. 67-73; F. Manrique Cabrera, *Historia de la literatura puertorriqueña,* Rio Piedras, 1969, pp. 180-189; Margarita Gardón Franceschi, *Manuel Zeno Gandia: vida y poesia,* San Juan, Edit. Coqui, 1969; Carmen Tejera, *La novela en Puerto Rico,* Rio Piedras, 1947; Félix Matos Bernier, *Isla de Arte,* San Juan, 1907 (with essay on Zeno); Venus Lidia Soto, *El arte de novelar en Garduña de Manuel Zeno Gandia,* introduction by Margót Arce, San Juan, Edit. de Departamento de Instrucción Pública, 1967.

ZEQUIERA Y ARANGO, Manuel de

(pseudonyms: **Izmael RAQUENUE** and **Ezequiel ARMUNA**)

b. August 28, 1764, Havana, Cuba; d. April 19, 1846.

Poet.

After studies in the Seminario de San Carlos, Zequiera took up arms in military operations against the French in Santo Domingo. At home in 1796 as a "subteniente," he married Doña Maria de Belén Caro Oviedo y Campuzano. In 1810, Zequiera was in the operation against Cuban nationalists at América del Sur, becoming Military Commander of Coro in 1810, Governor of Rio Hacha in 1814, and Santa Marta in 1815, and finally Royal Lieutenant of Cartagena in 1816.

Despite these activities, Zequiera continued to write a good deal of poetry until 1821 when he lost his reason. Much of his work saw print in *Papel Periódica.* Modern literary historians find his work fatiguing and uninspired. Typical of his work for subject and style are "A Daoiz y Velarde," "Batalle naval de Cortés en la Laguna,"

"Al primer sitio de Zaragoza," "La nave de vapor," "A la invención de la imprenta," and "La vida del campo." Only his pseudo-classical ode "A la piña" (republished 1962) shows genuine talent.

Writings: Poetry: *Poesias,* New York, 1829, Havana, 1852; various poems in collections such as José Manuel Carbonell's *La evolución de la cultura Cubana;* and "Albano y Galatea" is in introduction to *Parnaso cubano* of López Prieto, originally published in *Papel Periodica* (December 22, 1792). His eclogue "Albano y Galatea" appears in both editions of *Poesias* and in José M. Carbonnell's *La evolución de la cultura cubano,* Vol. I (1928) ; *Oda a la piña,* Havana, La Tertulia, 1962, and *Poesias, por Zequiera y Rubacava,* Havana, Comisión Nacional Cubana de la UNESCO, 1964 (444 p.).

Biographical/Critical Sources: Max Henriquez Ureña's *Panorama histórico de la literatura cubana,* New York, 1963, pp. 78ff.

ZORRILA, Rafael Augusto

b. 1892, Seybo, Dominican Republic; d. 1937.
Poet, critic.

Zorrila became one of the major figures in the "Postumismo" movement along with Andrés Avelino and Moreno Jiménes. He never published a collection of his work, but Manuel Rueda has collected most of his poems in his *Antologia* . . . A good example of his work is the little poem "Momento," here given in its entirety:

Timido despertar de rosas blancas;
espigas que se inician
a veces tristes,
a ratos pródigas;
rutas de epopeyas por salvaje senda;
en la noche una mueca
que transmutan los astros,
y luego. . .
el eco de una sombra!

Biographical/Critical Sources: Manuel Rueda and Lupo Hernández Rueda, *Antologia panorámica de la poesia dominicana contemporánea (1912-1962),* S. Domingo, UCMM, 1972, pp. 436-438: this work has also a brief discussion of Zorrila's life and work as well as of 23 of his poems, including "Ausencia," dictated just a few days before the poet's death to his son Rafael Mieses.

CRITICAL STUDIES (GENERAL) OF SPANISH-LANGUAGE LITERATURES IN THE CARIBBEAN

Ayala [See P.R. list]

Bascom, W. "Two Forms of Afro-Cuban Divination," in *Acculturation in the Americas* (Sol Tax, ed.), Chicago, University of Chicago Press, 1952.

Barrera, Isaac. *Historia de la Literatura Hispano Americana,* Quito, 1935.

Bellini, Giuseppe. *Poeti delle Antille,* Parma, Italy, 1963.

Blanco Fanbona, Rufino. *El Modernismo y los poetas modernistas,* Madrid, 1929.

Buzo Gómez, Sinforiano. *Caballo de Fuego: La poesia del siglo veinte en America y España,* Buenos Aires, 1952.

Coester, Alfred. *The Literary History of Spanish America,* New York, 1916.

Comette, Manzoni A. *El india en la poesia de la America espanolo,* Buenos Aires, 1939.

Corvalán, Octavio. *Modernismo y Vanguardia. Coordenadas de la literatura hispanoamericana del siglo XX,* New York, 1967.

Coulthard, G.R. *La literatura de las Antillas Inglesas Conferencia,* July 6, 1954, Santiago de Cuba, Universidad de Oriente, Departmento de Extension y relaciones culturales 34, 1954.

Craig, J. Dundas. *The Modernist Trend in Spanish American Poetry,* Berkeley, California, 1934.

Franco, Jean. *The Modern Culture of Latin America: Society and the Artist,* Harmondsworth, Middlesex, England, Penguin, 19??.

Franco, José Luciano. *Afroamerica,* Havana, 1961.

__________. *La presencia negra en el Nuevo Mundo,* Havana, Casa de las Américas, 1968.

Garcia Calderón, Ventura. *Del Romanticismo el Modernismo,* Paris, 1910.

Goldberg, Issac. *Studies in Spanish-American Literature,* New York, 1920.

Gutiérrez, Juan Maria. *Estudias biográficos y criticos sobre algunos poetas anteriores al Siglo XIX,* Buenos Aires, 1865.

Henriquez Ureña, Max. *El intercambio de influencias literarias entre España y América,* Havana, 1926.

Henriquez Ureña, Pedro. *El Teatro de la América Española en la Epoca Colonial,* Buenos Aires, 1936. [And see P.R. list for Pedro Ureña.]

__________. *Literary Currents in Hispanic America,* Cambridge, Mass., Harvard University Press, 1945, trans. by Joaquin Diaz Canedo, into Spanish and published as *Las corrientes literarias en la América Hispanica,* Buenos Aires, 1945, Mexico, 1949.

__________. *Les influences trancaises sur la poésie hispanoamericaine,*

Paris, 1937; Spanish language version, Buenos Aires, 1940.

———. *Apuntaciones sobre la novela en America,* Buenos Aires, by "Humanidades," 1927.

Imbert, E. Anderson. *Historia de la literatura hispanoamericana,* Mexico, Fondo de Cultura Economica, 1961.

Menéndez y Pelayo, Marcelino. *Historia de la poesia hispanoamericano,* Madrid, 1911.

Moses, Bernard. *Spanish Colonial Literature in South America,* New York, 1922.

Moran, Fernando. *Nación y alienación en la literatura negro-africana,* Madrid, Ed. Taunus, 1964.

Olivera, Oto. *Breve historia de la literatura antillana,* Mexico, Manuales Stadium, 1957.

Oliver, D.L.M. *Africa en la literatura española,* Madrid, Ed. *Consejo de Investigaciones Cientificas,* 1964.

Onis, Federico de. "La poesia iberoamericana," in *España en America,* Rio Piedras, Puerto Rico, 1955.

Perotto, Armando. *La Literatura en América: El Coloniaje,* Montevideo, 1937.

Pereda Valdes, Ildefonso. *Linea de color,* Santiago de Chile, Ed. Ercilla, 1936.

———. "El negro en la literatura iberoamericana," in *Caudernos por la Libertad de la Cultura,* Paris, 1956.

Serra, Edelweiss. *Poesia hispanoamericana: Ensayos de approximación interpretiva,* Sante Fe, Argentina, 1964.

Sánchez, Luis Alberto. *América, novels sin novelistas,* Lima, 1935.

———. *Historia de la literatura américana,* Santiago, Chile, 1940.

Torre, Guillermo de. *Tres conceptos de la literatura hispanoamericana,* Buenos Aires, 1961.

———. *Historia de las literaturas de vanguardia,* Madrid, 1965.

Torres-Rioseco, Arturo, *La Novela en la América Hispaña,* Berkeley, California, 1939.

———. *The Epic of Latin American Literature,* Berkeley, University of California Press, 19??.

Toruno, Juan Filipe (ed.). *Poesia negra: ensayo y antologia,* Mexico, 1953.

Uribe Ferrer, René. *Modernismo y poesia contemporánea,* Medellin, Colombia, 1962.

Varios. *Movimiento literarios de vanguardia.* University of Texas at Austin, 1965.

Videla, Gloria. *El ultraismo,* Madrid, 1963.

Underwood, Edna W. "Negro Poets. Negro writers of Jamaica and Cuba; negro poets of Martinique; writers of Haiti," in *West Indian Review* (1935): Sept., 38-39; Oct., 35-36; Nov., 33-36; Dec., 34-37.

White, Florence. "Poesia Negra in Latin America," unpublished Ph.D. diss.,

University of Wisconsin, 1951.

Williams, Eric. "Four Poets of the Greater Antilles," in *Caribbean Quarterly*, Vol. 2, No. 4 (1952).

CUBA: CRITICAL STUDIES AND BIBLIOGRAPHIES

Abella, Rosa. "Bibliografía de la novela publicada en Cuba, en el extranjero por cubanos, desde 1959 hasta 1965," in *Revista iberoamericana,* Vol. 32, No. 62 (July-Dec. 1966), pp. 307-318.

__________. "Cinco años de la novela cubana," in *Cuadernos del Hombre Libre,* No. 1 (July-Sep. 1966), pp. 9-14; and trans. into English, *The Carrel* (Univ. of Miami Library) 7, No. 1 (June 1966), pp. 17-21.

Adams, Michael Ian. "Alienation in Selected Works of the Contemporary Spanish American Authors," unpublished Ph.D. diss., Univ. of Texas, Austin, 1972. (Alejo Carpentier is a major figure treated.)

Amor, Sister Rosa Teresa. "Afro-Cuban Folklore Tales as Incorporated into the Literary Tradition of Cuba," unpublished Ph.D. diss., Columbia Univ., 1969.

Andueza, J.M. de. *Isla de Cuba pintoresca, histórico politica, literaria mercantil e industrial,* Madrid, 1841.

Arrom, José. *Historia de la literatura dramática cubana.* New Haven, Yale University Press, 1944.

__________. "La poesia afrocubana," in *Estudios de Literatura Hispano-américana* (1950).

__________. "Research in Latin American Literature: The State of the Art (A Round Table)." *Latin American Research Review,* 6, No. 2 (Summer 1971), pp. 85-124.

Ayala Duarte, Crispin. "Historia de la literatura cubana," in *Annales de la Universidad Central de Venezuela,* Caracas, Vol. 24 (1935), pp. 154-183; Vol. 24 (1936), pp. 195-216.

Bachiller y Morales, Antonio. *Apuntes para la historia de las letras y de la Instrucción Publica.* 3 vols., Havana, 1859-1861; second edition, 1936.

Ballagas, Emilio. *Mapa de la poesia negra américana.* Havana, 1946.

Barreda, Pedro. "La caracterización del protagonista negro en la novela cubana," unpublished Ph.D. diss., State University of New York, Buffalo.

Blanca García, Francisco. *La literatura española en el siglo XIX,* 3 vols., Madrid, 1894 (Cuban section, Vol. III, pp. 290-304).

Boti, Regina E. *La nueva poesia en Cuba.* Havana, 1927.

__________. *Tres temas sobre la nueva poesia.* Havana, 1928.

Boydston, Jo Ann Harrison. "The Cuban Novel: A Study of Its Range and Characteristics," unpublished Ph.D. diss., Columbia University, 1950.

Bueno, Salvador. *Historia de la literatura cubana (1902-1952),* 1954, third edition, Havana, Ministero de Educación, 1963.

__________. *Medio siglo de literatura cubana (1902-1952).* Havana, Comisión Nacional Cubano de UNESCO, 1953.

__________. "Cuba hoy: novela," in *Insula,* (Havana, July-Aug. 1968), pp. 1, 21, 24 (Criticism of novels since Castro).

__________. *Temas y Personajes de la Literatura Cubana.* Havana, Empresa Consolidada de Artes Gráficas, 1964.

Bustamante y Montor, Antonio S. de. *Las generaciones literarias.* Havana, Molina, 1937.

Caballero Bonald, José Manuel. *Narrativa cubana de la revolución.* Madrid, Alianza Editorial, 1968.

Carbonell, José Manuel. *Evolución de la cultura cubana.* 18 vols., Havana, 1928.

__________. *La critica en la literatura cubana.* Havana, Imp. Avisador Comercial, 1930.

Cartey, Wilfred. "Three Antillan Poets: Emilio Ballagas, Luis Palés Matos, and Nicolás Guillén. Literary Development of the Negro Theme in Relation to the Making of Modern Afro-Antillean Poetry and the Historic Evolution of the Negro." unpublished Ph.D. diss., Columbia University, 1965.

Casal, Lourdes. "A Bibliography of Cuban Creative Literature: 1958-1971." *Cuban Studies Newsletter,* Vol. 2, No. 2 (June 1972).

__________. "The Cuban Novel, 1959-1969: An Annotated Bibliography," in *Abraxas,* 1 (Fall 1970), pp. 77-92.

Casanovas, Marti. *Orbita de la Revista Avance.* Havana, Collección Orbita, 1965.

Chacón y Calvo, José Maria. *Ensayos de literatura cubana.* Madrid, Calleja, 1922.

__________. *Los origenes de la poesia en Cuba.* Havana, 1913.

__________. *Romances tradicionales en Cuba.* Havana, 1914.

Cid Pérez, José. "El teatro en Cuba Republicana." [introduction to] *Teatro Cubano Contemporáneo,* second edition, Dolores Marti de Cid, ed., Madrid, Aguilar, 1962.

Clinkscales, Orline. *Becquer in Mexico, Central America, and the Caribbean Countries.* Madrid, Edit. Hispanoamericana, 1970.

Collazos, Oscar, Julio Cortázar, and Mario Vargas Llosa. *Literatura en la revolució y revolución en la literatura.* Mexico City, Siglo XXI, 1970.

Coulthard, G. R. "Emergence of Afro-Cuban Poetry," in *Caribbean Quarterly,* Vol. 2, No. 3 (1962), pp. 14-17.

Cruz, Manuel de la. *Reseña histórico-critica del movimiento literario de la isla de Cuba (1790-1890).* Buenos Aires, F. Lagomaggiore, 1890; reprinted in *Revista Cubana,* 1891.

Dalton, Rogue. "Diez años de revolución," in *Casa de las Américas,* X, 5 (Sept-Oct. 1969), pp. 7-52 (discusses absurd theatre of the Castro period).

Ehrmann, Jacques, ed. *Literature and Revolución.* First edition, 1967, second edition, Boston, Beacon Press, 1970.

Escoto, José Augusto. "Estado intelectual de los cubanos en el siglo XVI," in *Revista histórica,* critica y bibliografica de la literatura cubana, Vol. 1,

No. 1 (Matanzas, 1916).

Esténger, Rafael. *Caracteres constantes en las letras cubanas.* Havana, 1958.

Feijóo, Samuel. *Azar de lecturas: critica.* Havana, 1961.

__________. *Sobre los movimientos por una poesia cubana hasta 1856.* Havana, 1961 (originally published in *Revista Cubana,* 1949).

Feldman Harth, Dorothy. "La poesia afrocubana, sus raices e influencias." *Miscelanea de Estudios dedicados a Fernándo Ortiz,* Havana, 1935.

Fernández de la Vega and Juan F. Carvajal Bello. *Literatura cubana.* Havana, 1950, and in many later editions.

Fernández de Castro, José A. "El aporto negro en las letras de Cuba en el siglo XIX." *Revista Bimestre Cubana,* Vol. 38 (1936), pp. 46-66.

__________. *Esquema histórico de las letras en Cuba, 1548-1902.* Havana, 1949.

__________. *Tema negro en las letras de Cuba 1608-1935.* Havana, 1943.

Fernández Retamar, Roberto. *La poesia contemporánea en Cuba (1927-1953).* Havana, Origenes, 1954.

Fornaris, José and José Cocorro de León. *Cuba poética.* Havana, 1855; new version, done with Joaquin Luaces, Havana, 1858, second edition, 1859, 1861.

Ford, Jeremiah and Maxwell I. Raphael. *A Bibliography of Cuban Belles-lettres.* Cambridge, Mass., Harvard University Press, 1931.

Fuentes y Matons, Laureano. *Las artes en Santiago de Cuba.* Havana, 1893.

Gallegher, David. "The Literary Life in Cuba." *New York Review of Books* (May 23, 1968), pp. 37-41 (covers Cabrera Infanta's *Tres tristes tigres;* Lezama Lima's *Paradiso;* Carpentier's *Explosion in the Cathedral;* J.M. Cohen's anthology: *Writers in the New Cuba;* Desnoes' *Inconsolable Memories;* Arcocha's *A Candle in the Wind;* and Carlo Franquis' *The Twelve*).

Garcés Larrea, Cristóbal. *Narradores cubanos contemporanéos.* Guayaquil, Edit. Ariel, 1973.

Garcia, Calixto. "El negro en la narrativa cubana." Unpublished Ph.D. diss., City University of New York, 1973.

Garófalo Mesa, Manuel Garcia. *Diccionario de seudónimos de escritores, poetas y periodistas villaclareños.* Mexico, 1938.

Gay-Calbo, Enrique. *Origenes de la literatura cubana.* Havana, 1939.

Godoy, Gustavo J. "La generación cubana de poetas postmodernistas." Unpublished Ph.D. diss., University of Miami, Coral Gables, Florida, 1967.

Gonzáles Curquejo, Antonio. *Breve ojeada sobre el teatro cubano al traves de un siglo (1820-1920).* Havana, 1923.

González Curquelo, Antonio. *Florilegio de Escritoras Cubanas.* 3 vols. Havana, Libreria e Imprenta La Moderna Poesia, 1910. [Contains 99 women poets.]

González y Contreras, Gilberto, "La poesia negra." *Revista Bimestre Cubana,* Vol. 37 (1937), pp. 40-45.

González Freire, Natividad. *Teatro cubano contemporáneo.* Havana, Sociedad Colombista Panamericana, 1958.

Guerra, Armando. "La mujer vuelta-bahera en la poesia cubana." *Revista Bimestre Cubana,* Vol. 37, pp. 249-267.

Guiral Moreno, Mario. *Auge y decadencia del vanguardismo literario en Cuba.* Havana, Edit. Molina, 1942.

Guirao, Ramon. *Orbita de la poesia afrocubana.,* Havana, 1939.

Hansen, Terence Leslie. "The Types of Folklore in Cuba, Puerto Rico, the Dominican Republic, and Spanish South America." Unpublished Ph.D. diss., Stanford University, 1951.

Harrison, Polly F. "Images and Exile: The Cuban Woman and Her Poetry." *Revista Review Interamericana,* Vol. 4 (Summer 1974), pp. 184-219.

Henriquez Ureña, Max. *Panorama histórico de la literatura cubana.* 2 vols., New York, Las Américas, 1963.

__________. *Tabla cronológica de la literatura cubana.* Santiago, Cuba, 1929.

__________. *Les influences françaises sur la poésie hispano-americaine.* Paris, 1937; translated into Spanish, published Buenos Aires, 1940.

__________. *La enseñanza de la literatura cubana.* Havana, 1915.

__________. *Poetas cubanos de expressión francese.* Mexico, 1941.

Hernández-Miyares, Julio. "The Cuban Short Story in Exile: A Selected Bibliography." *Hispánia,* 54 (May 1971), pp. 384-385.

Hollingsworth, Charles. "The Development of Literary Theory in Cuba, 1959-1968," Unpublished Ph.D. Diss., University of California (Berkeley), 1972.

Ichaso, Francisco. *Ideas y aspiraciones de la primera generación republicana. Historia de la nación cubana.* Vol. VII, Havana, Edit. Historia de la Nación Cubana, 1952.

Iraizos, Antonio. *La decima cubana,* Havana, 1928.

__________. *La poesia civil en Cuba.* Havana, 1928.

__________. *La critica en la literatura cubana.* Havana, 1930.

__________. *Raices y justificación de las tertulias y salones literarios.* Havana, 19??.

Jiménez, José O. *Estudios sobre poesia cubano contemporáneo.* New York, Las Américas, 1967.

Kirby, Marjorie Tarleton. "A Literary History of the Cuban Short Story (1797-1959)." Unpublished Ph.D. diss., University of North Carolina, 1971.

Lavandero, Ramón, "Negrismo poético y Eusebia Cosme." *Ateneo Puertorriqueño* (S. Juan), Vol. 2, pp. 46-53.

Lax, Judith Heckelman. "Themes and Techniques in the Socially Oriented Cuban Novel: 1933-1952." Unpublished Ph.D. diss., Syracuse University, 1961.

Lazo, Raimundo. *La literatura cubana.* Mexico, Universidad Nacional Autónoma de México, 1965.

__________. *Historia de la literatura cubana.* Havana, Edit. Universitaria, 1967.

__________. "Literatura cubana en el siglo XX." *Historia de la Nación Cubana,* (Havana, 1952).

__________. "La teoria de las generaciones y su aplicación al estudio histórico de la literatura cubana." *Universidad de la Habana,* XIX, Nos. 112-114 (Jan-June 1954).

Levine, Suzanne Jill. *Latin America: Fiction and Poetry in Translations.* (excludes Puerto Ricans), New York, Center for Inter-American Relations, 1970.

El Libro de Cuba. Havana, 1925. (Among contributors: Chacón y Calvo; J.A. Fernández de Castro; González del Valle.)

Lizaso, Félix and José A. Fernández de Castro. *La poesia moderna en Cuba 1882-1925.* Madrid, Edit. Hernando, 1926.

__________. *Ensayistas contemporáneos, 1900-1920.* Havana, 1938.

__________. *Panorama de la cultura cubana.* Mexico, Fondo de cultura Economica, 1949.

López Barrero, Olga L. "Cronologia de la novela cubana: 1850-1900." *Islas,* No. 4 (Havana, n.d.), pp. 187-212.

López Prieto, Antonio. *Introducción histórico-critica a su obra Parnaso Cubano.* Vol. I (only one published), Havana, 1881.

López-Silvery, Jesús. *De los ritmos libres prosas atrabiliarias.* Havana, Fernández, 1926.

Mañach, Jorge. *La crisis de la alta cultura cubana.* Havana, La Universal, 1925.

__________. *Historia y estilo.* Havana, 1945.

Marchan, Rafael. *Estudios criticos.* Havana, 1886.

Marinello, Juan. *Americanismo y cubanismo literarios.* Havana, 1932.

__________. *Contemporáneos: Noticia y memoria.* Havana, 1964.

__________. *Veinticinco anos de poesia cubana in literatura hispano-americana.* Mexico, 1937.

Martin Llorente, Francisco. *La mujer vuelta bajera en la poesia cubana.* Havana, Molina, 1941.

Megenney, William W. "The Black in Hispanic-Caribbean and Brazilian Poetry: A Comparative Perspective." *Revista Interamericana,* Vol. V, No. 1 (Spring 1975), pp. 47-66.

Melon, Alfred. *Sobre poesia cubana: Realidad, poesia, e ideologia.* Havana, 1973.

Menton, Seymour. *Prose Fiction of the Cuban Revolution.* Austin, University of Texas Press, 1975.

__________. *La novela y el cuento de la revolución cubana: 1959-1969. Bibliografia,* Cuernavaca, mimeo., 1969 (10 pp.).

__________. "The Short Story of the Cuban Revolution, 1959-1969." *Studies in Short Fiction,* 8 (Winter 1971), pp. 32-43.

Miranda, Julio E. *Nueva literatura cubana.* Madrid, Taurus, 1971.

Mitjan, Aurelio. *Estudios sobre el movimiento cientifico y literario de Cuba.* Havana, Alvárez, 1890, and revised edition, retitled *Historia de la literatura cubana,* Madrid, 1918.

Norman, Isabel Hernández. "La novela romantica en las Antillas." Unpublished Ph.D. diss., Yale University, 1966.

Olchyk, Marta K. "Historical Approach to Afro-Cuban Poetry." Unpublished Ph.D. diss., Texas Christian University, 1972.

Olivera, Otto. *Cuba en su poesia.* Mexico, Ediciones Andrea, 1965.

Orlando, Felipe. *Panorámica actual de la literatura cubana.* Mexico, 1956.

Ortega, Julio. *Relato de la utopia: Notas sobre narrativa cubana de la Revolución.* Barcelona, La Gaya Ciencia, 1973.

Ortiz, Fernando. "Los ultimos versos mulatos," in *Revista Bimestre Cubana,* V-VI (1935).

__________. *La decadencia cubana.* Havana, La Universal, 1924.

__________. "Mas acerca de la poesia mulata." *Revista Bimestre Cubana,* Vol. 37 (1936), pp. 23-39, 218-227, 439-443.

__________. *La africania en la música folklórica de Cuba.* Havana, 1950.

Otera, Lisandro. "Cuba: literatura y revolución (Carta a Emmanuel Carballo)." *Siempre* (Mexico, June 15, 1966).

Palls, Terry L. "The Theatre of the Absurd in Cuba After 1959." *Latin American Literary Review,* IV, 7 (Fall-Winter 1975), pp. 67-72.

Pattee, Richard. "La América latina presta atención al negro." *Revista Bimestre Cubana,* Vol. 38 (1937), pp. 17-23 (deals with Cuba, Haiti, Brazil).

Péreda Valdez, Ildefonso. *Lo negro y lo mulato en la poesia cubana.* Montevideo, Uruguay, Ciudadela, 1970.

Pérez Beato, Manuel. "Los primeros dias del teatro cubano." *El Curioso Américano* (July-August, 1927).

Perrier, José Luis. *Bibliografia dramática cubana.* New York, The Phos Press, 1926.

Piedra-Bueno, Andrés de. *Literatura cubana: sintesis histórica.* Havana, 1945.

Poncet y de Cardenas, Carolina. *El romance en Cuba.* Havana, 1915, and Havana, Instituto Cubano del Libro, 1972.

Portuondo, José Antonio. *Bosquejo histórico de las letras cubana.* Havana, Edit. Nacional de Cuba, 1960.

__________. *El contenido social de la literatura cubana.* Mexico, El Colegio de México, 1944.

__________. *Critica de la época y otros ensayos.* Santa Clara, Universidad Central de las Villas, 1965.

Ramirez, Serafin. *La Habana artistica.* Havana, 1891 (mostly on music).

Remos y Rubio, Juan J. *Historia de la literatura cubana.* 2 vols., 1925, and in 3 vols., 1945 (Havana, Cárdenas).

__________. *Curso de historia de la literatura cubana,* 2 vols., 1918-19.

__________. *Proceso histórico de las letras cubanas.* Madrid, Guadarrama, 1958.

__________. *Panorama literario de Cuba en nuestro siglo.* Havana, 1942.

__________. *Resúmen de historia de la literatura cubana.* Havana, 1930, 1938.

__________. *Tendencias de la narración imaginativa en Cuba.* Havana, Casa Montalvo-Cárdenas, 1935.

Ripoll, Carlos. *La generación del 23 en Cuba y otros apuntes sobre el vanguardismo.* New York, Las Américas Publishing Co., 1968.

__________. *La revista de avance (1927-1930): episodo de la literatura cubana.* New York, Las Américas, 1969.

Rodrigues Sardiñas, Orlando. *La ultima poesia cubana.* Madrid, Hispanova de Ediciones, 1973.

__________. "Cuba: Poesia entre revolución y exilio." *Revista/Review Interamericana,* 4 (Fall 1974), pp. 359-369.

Salazar y Roig, Salvador. *El elemento patriótico en la lirica cubana.* Havana, 1935.

__________. *Historia de la literatura cubana.* Havana, 1929.

__________. *Literatura cubana: El clacismo de Cuba.* Havana, 1913.

Sánchez, Julio C. "Bibliografía de la novela cubana." *Islas,* 3 (Sept.-Dec. 1960), pp. 321-356.

Sánchez Gallarraga, Gustavo. *El arte teatral en cuba.* Havana, 1916 (conference papers).

Sanguily, Manuel. *Oradores de Cuba.* Havana, Revista Havana, 1886.

Shaw, Bradley A. *Latin American Literature in English Translation: An Annotated Bibliography.* New York, New York University Press, 1976.

Staudinger, Mabel K. "The Use of the Supernatural in Modern Spanish-American Fiction." Unpublished Ph.D. diss., University of Chicago, 1946 (covers Cuban writers Jesús Castellanos; Gertrudis Gómez de Avellaneda; Enrique Hernández Miyares; Carlos Loveira; Carlos Montenegro; Luis Felipe Rodriguez).

Suárez-Murias, Marguerite C. "La novela romántica en Hispanoamérica." Unpublished Ph.D. diss., Columbia University, 1957 (Part I covers Cuba, Puerto Rico, and Santo Domingo).

Tapia y Rivera, Alejandro. *El bardo del Guamani.* Havana, Imp. del Tiempo, 1862.

Torre, Guillermo de. "Literatura de color." *Revista Bimestre Cubana,* Vol. 38 (1938), pp. 5-11 (study of black writers in U.S. and Antilles).

Torriente, Lola de la. "La revolución y la cultura cubana." *Cuadernos Americano,* Vol. CXI, No. 4 (July-August 1960).

Varela, José Luis. *Ensayos de poesia indigena en Cuba.* Madrid, 1951.

Vitier, Cintio. *Lo cubano en la poesia.* Santa Clara, Universidad Central de Las Villas, 1958.

__________. *Diez poetas cubanos (1937-1947).* Havana, 1948.

__________. *Lo cubano en la poesia.* Las Villas, Cuba, Universidad Central de Las Villas, 1958.

__________. *Cincuenta años de poesia cubana (1902-1952).* Havana, Dirección de Cultura del Ministro de Educación, 1952.

__________. *Apuntaciones literarias,* Havana, 1935.

CUBA: ANTHOLOGIES

Agostini, Victor, and others. *Nuevos cuentos cubanos.* Havana, Ed. Uniones, 1964.

Alonso, Dora, Salvador Bueno, Calvert Casey, and José Rodríguez Feo. *Nuevos cuentos cubanos.* Havana, Unión, 1964.

Arozarena, Marcelino. *Canción negra sin color.* Havana, Ediciones Unión, 1966.

Aparicio Laurencio, Angel. *Cinco poetisas cubanas: 1935-1969.* Miami, Ediciones Universal, 1970.

Arpaz amigos (by six poets). Havana, 1879.

Arpaz cubanos (29 poets). Havana, 1904.

Arrufat, Antón and Fausto Masó. *Nuevos cuentistas cubanos.* Havana, Casa de las Américas, 1961.

Ballagas, Manuel, and others. *Cuentos antologia.* Havana, Ed. Unión, 1967.

Bardas cubanos (selected by Elijah Hills). Boston, 1901.

Benítez, Antonio. *Tute de Reyes.* Havana, Casa de las Américas, 1967.

Berenguer, Antonio. "Ensaladillas villaclereñas." *Archivos del Folklore Cubana,* Vol. IV, No. 3 (1929).

Bueno, Salvador (ed.). *Antologia del cuento en Cuba.* Havana, Dirección de Cultura del Ministerio de Educación, 1953.

__________. (comp.). *Los mejores cuentos cubanos.*, 2 vols., Havana, Organización Continental de los Festivales del Libro, 1959.

Cabada, Carbos, Juan Luis Herrero and Agenor Marti. *Cuentos de ciencia ficción.* Havana, Revolución, 1964.

Caballero Bonald, José Manuel. *Narrativa cubana de la revolución.* Madrid, Alianza, 1968.

Cabrera, Lydia (ed.). *Cuentos negros de Cuba.* Havana, La Veronica, 1940, 1946, and Havana, Nuevo Mundo, 1961.

__________. *Por qué. Cuentos negros de Cuba.* Havana, Ediciones C.R., 1948.

__________. *Pourquoi . . . Nouveaux contes nègres de Cuba.* Paris, Gallimard, 1954.

Calcagno, Francisco. *Poetas de color.,* Havana, 1878.

Caranza, Sylvia and Maria Juana Cazabon. *Cuban Short Stories, 1959-1966.* Havana, Book Institute, 1967.

Carbonell, José Manuel. *Evolución de la cultura cubana.* 18 vols., Havana, 1928.

Cardoso, Onelio Jorge. *El puebla cuenta.* Havana, Biblioteca del Capitolio Nacional, 1961.

Chacón y Calvo, J.M. *Las cien mejores poesias cubanas.* Madrid, 1922.

Cinco poets jovenes. Havana, Belic, 1965.

Cohen, J.M. *Writers in the New Cuba.* Harmondsworth, England, and Baltimore, Penguin, 1967.

Colección de poesias arregladas por un aficionado a las musas. 2 Vols., Havana, Boloña, 1833.

Comités de Defensa de la Revolución. *Teatro.* Havana, Con la Guardia en Alto, 1965.

Congrains Martin, Eduardo. *Narrativa cubana.* Lima, ECOMA, 1972.

Consejo Nacional de Cultura. *Obras de repertorio.* Havana, Talleres de la CTC-R, 1961.

Cronicas de Cuba. Buenos Aires, J. Alvárez, 1969.

Cuba poética. 4 vols., Havana, 1855, 1857, 1859, 1861.

Cuban poetry, 1959-1966. Havana, Instituto del Libro, 1967.

Cuban Short Stories, 1959-1966. Havana, Book Institute, 1967.

Contes cubains, 1959-1966. Havana, Institut du Livre, 1967.

Cuentos; antologia. Havana, Unión, 1967.

Cuentos cubanos de lo fantástico y lo extraordinario. Havana, Unión, 1968.

Cuentos y legendas negras de Cuba 1928-1937. Havana, Ediciones "Mirador," 1942.

Esténger Neuling, Rafael (ed.). *Cien de las mejores poesias cubanas.* Havana, Ediciones "Mirador," 1943, second edition, 1948.

Feijóo, Samuel. *Cuentos populares cubanos.* 2 vols, Santa Clara, Universidad Central de Las Villas, 1960, and Havana, Unión, 1965.

Fernández de Castro, José and Félix Lizaso. *La poesia moderna en Cuba (1882-1925).* Madrid, 1926.

Fernández Retamar, Robert. *La poesia contemporánea en Cuba (1927-1953).* Havana, 1954.

__________ and Fayad Jamis. *Poesia joven de Cuba.* Havana, Organización Continental de los Festivales del Libro, 1959.

Ferrand Latoison, Angel. *Antologia; poetas de Guantánamo,* Havana, n.p., 1962.

Fitts, Dudley. *An Anthology of Contemporary Latin American Poetry.* (Bilingual edition), Norfolk, Conn., New Directions, 1942.

Fornaris, José and José Socorro de León. *Cuba poética.* Havana, 1855.

Fornaris, José and Joaquin Lorenzo Luaces. *Cuba poetica.* Havana, 1858, 1859, 1861.

Fornet, Ambrosio. *Antologia del cuento cubano contemporáneo.* Mexico, Era, 1967.

__________. *Cuentos de la revolución cubana.* Santiago, Chile, Universitaria, 1971.

Garcia de Coronado, Domitila. *Album poético fotográfico de escritoras cubanas.* Havana, 1872, and Havana, Imprenta de 'El Figaro,' 1926.

Garcés Larrea, Cristóbal. *Narradores cubanos contemporáneos.* Guayaquil, Colección Ariel, 1973.

Garcia Garófalo Mesa, Manuel. *Los poetas villaclareños.* Havana, 1927.

Garcia Vega, Lorenzo. *Antologia de la novela en Cuba.* Havana, Dirección General de Cultura, 1960.

Goldberg, Isaac. *Some Spanish American Poets.* New York, Greenwood Press, 1968.

Guirao, Ramón. *Orbita de la poesia afrocubana, 1928-37.* Havana, Ucar, Garcia, 1928, 1938.

__________. *Poetas negros y mestizos de la epoca esclavistas.* Havana, *Revista Bohemia* (August 26, 1934).

Henriquez Ureña, Max. *Antologia cubana de los escuelos.* Santiago, Cuba, 1929.

__________. *Poetas cubanos de expressión francesa.* Mexico, 1941.

Heredia, Nicolás. *El lector cubano.* Havana, 1900, and many later editions.

Hernández-Miyares, Julio. *Antillana rotunda* [poetry]. Barcelona, Edit. Vosgos/ Plaza Mayor, 1974.

__________, (ed.). *Narradores cubanos de hoy.* Miami, Ediciones Universal, 1975.

__________. *Cuentestas cubanos del destierro: Una antologia, 1959-1975.* Miami, Ediciones Universal, 1976.

Ibarzábal, Federico de. *Cuentos contemporáneos.* Havana, 1937.

Javier Amy, Francisco. *Musa bilingue.* San Juan, Boletin Mercantil, 1903.

Jiménez, Juan Ramón, José Maria Chacón y Calvo, and Camilia Henriquez Ureña. *La poesia cubana en 1936.* Havana, Colección, 1937.

El Laud del Desterrado (compilación de poesias patrioticas). New York, 1858.

Lezama Lima, José (ed.). *Antologia de la poesia cubana,.* 3 vols., Havana, Consejo Nacional de Cultura, 1965.

Lizaso, Félix and José Antonio Fernández. *La poesia moderna en Cuba (1882-1925).* Madrid, Hernando, 1926.

Llopis, Rogelio. *Cuentos cubanos de lo fantástico y lo extraordinario.* Havana, Unión, 1968.

López Morales, Humbert (ed.). *Poesia cubana contemporanea; un ensayo de antologia.* New York, Las Américas, 1967.

López Prieto, Antonio. *Parnaso cubano.* Havana, 1881.

Lorenzo Fuentes, José. *Los cuentistas cubanos y la reforma agraria.* Havana, Tierra Nueva, 1960.

Luaces, Joaquin Lorenzo. *Cuba poética.* Havana, 1858, second edition, 1861.

Marti de Cid, Dolores. *Teatro cubano contemporáneo.* Introduction by José Cid Pérez (whose essay on Cuban theatre before Castro is in this volume), Madrid, Aguilar, 1959, second edition, 1962.

Marti, José. *Los poetas de la guerra.* New York, 1893.

Miranda, Julio E. *Antologia del nuevo cuento cubano.* Caracas, Domingo Fuentes, 1969.

Núñez, Ana Rosa (ed.). *Poesia en éxodo (el exilio cubano en su poesia, 1959-1969).* Miami, Universal, 1970.

Ortiz, Fernando. *Los bailes el teatro de los negros em al folclore de Cuba.* Havana, 1951.

Oviedo, José Miguel (selector). *Antologia del cuento cubano.* Lima, Paradiso, 1968.

Pérez, Emma. *Cuentos cubanos.* Havana, 1945.

Piniella, Germán and Raúl Rivero. *Punto de partida.* Havana, Instituto del Libro, 1970.

Los poetas de la guerra (poesia del campamento). New York, 1893.

Portuondo, José Antonio. *Cuentos cubanos contemporaneos.* Mexico, 1946.

Prieto, López. *Parnaso cubano.* Havana, 1881.

Ripoll, Carlos. *La generación de 1923 en Cuba y otros apuntes sobre el vanguardismo.* New York, 1968.

Riva Abreu, Valentin. *Parnaso cubano.* Barcelona, 1926.

Rodriguez Feo, J. (ed. and foreword). *Aqui 11 cubanos cuentan.* Montevideo, Arca, 1967.

__________. *Cuentos: Antologia.* Havana, Unión, 1967.

Rodriguez Santos, Justo. *Antologia del soneto.* Havana, 1942.

Rodriquez Embil, Luis. *La poesia negra en Cuba.* Havana, 1939.

Rodriquez Ucrés, Fray José. *Evolución de la Cultura cubana.* Havana, 1928.

Ruiz del Vizo, Hortensio. *Poesia negra del caribe y otras áreas.* Miami, Ediciones Universal, 1972.

Selección de cuentos cubanos. Havana, Ministerio de Educación, 1962.

Subercaseaux, Bernardo. *Narrativa de la joven Cuba.* Santiago, Chile, Nascimento, 1971.

Tarn, Nathaniel. *Con Cuba: An Anthology of Cuban Poetry of the Last Sixty Years* (bilingual edition). New York, Grossman, 1969.

Teatro bufo, 1890-1899; siete obras. Santa Clara, Universidad Central de La Villas, Dirección de Publicaciones, 1961.

Teatro cubano. Santa Clara, Universidad Central de Las Villas, 1960.

Tres obras dramáticas de Cuba Revolucionaria. Havana, Instituto de Cultura de Marianao, 1961.

UNEAC. *Exposición de Poemas Murales.,* Havana, Unión, 1962.

UNEAC. "Literatura cubana '67." *Unión* 6, No. 4 (December 1967).

Valle, Adrián del. *Parnaso cubano.* Barcelona.

Varios. *Cinco poemas a Lenin.* Havana, Instituto del Libro, Arte y Literatura, 1970.

Varios. *Nueve cuentistas.* Havana, Casa de las Américas, 1970.

Varios. *Ocho poetas.* Havana, Casa de las Américas, 1969.

Varios. *Poemas al Ché.* Havana, Instituto del Libro, Arte y Literatura, 1969.

Varios. *Poemas David 69.* Havana, Unión, 1970.

Vitier, Cintio (ed.). *Cincuenta años de poesia cubano (1902-1952).* Havana, Dirección de Cultura del Ministerio de Educación, 1952.

————. *Las mejores poesias cubanas.* Lima, Organización Continental de los Festivales del Libro, 1959.

————. *Los grandes románticos cubanos.* Havana, Organización Continental de los Festivales del Libro, 1960.

————. *Los poetas románticos cubanos.* Havana, Consejo Nacional de Cultura, 1962.

————. *Diez poetas cubanos (1937-1947).* Havana, 1948.

Walsh, Rodolfo. *Crónicas de Cuba.* Buenos Aires, Jorge Alvarez, 1969.

Walsh, Thomas. *Hispanic Anthology: Poems Translated From the Spanish by English and North American Poets* (bilingual edition). New York, Putnam, 1920.

THE DOMINICAN REPUBLIC: CRITICAL STUDIES AND BIBLIOGRAPHIES

Aguiar, Enrique. *La ciudad intelectual,* Bogota, 1938.

Alfonseca, Iván. *Antologia biográfica. La juventud de Santo Domingo en la poesia contemporanea, 1924-1942,* Buenos Aires, Ed. Claridad, 1942.

Amiama, Manuel A. *El periodismo en en la Republica Dominicana,* 1933.

Ayala Duarte, Crispin. "Tratado antólogico-critico de la literatura dominicana," *Boletin de la Academia Venezolana,* Caracas, 1934.

Baeza Flores, Alberto. "Testimonio sobre 'La Poesia Sorprendida,'" in *Antologia Panoramica de la Poesia Dominicana Contemporánea (1912-1962),* Santiago de los Caballeros, Dominican Republic, UCMM, 1972, pp. 473-479. [The essay is dated by the author: "Paris, otono 1964."]

Balaguer, Joaquin. *Azul en los Charcos,* Bogotá, Edit. Selecta, 1941.

__________. *Federico Garcia Godoy,* (Anthology), Santo Domingo, Colección Pensamiento Dominicano, Libreria Dominicana, 1951.

__________. *Historia de la literatura dominicana,* 5th ed., Santo Domingo, Julio D. Postigo Hijos, 1970.

__________. *Letras Dominicanas,* Santiago, Dominican Republic, Editorial El Diario, 1944.

__________. *Literatura dominicana,* Buenos Aires, Edit. Americalee, 1950.

__________. *Los Próceres escritores,* 1st ed., Buenos Aires, Imprenta Ferrari, 1947; 2nd ed., Buenos Aires, Gráfica Guadeloupe, 1971.

Brazil, Osvaldo. *Movimento intelectual dominicano,* Washington, D.C., 1924. [Separately published in *Boletin de la Union Panamericana* (July, 1924).]

__________. *Parnaso dominicano: Compilación completa de los majores poetos de la República de Santo Domingo,* Barcelona, Maucci, 1915.

Castellanos, José. *Lira de Quisqueya,* Santo Domingo, Imprenta Garcia Hermanos, 1894.

Castellanos y Ortega, Nina. *Breve historia de la literatura dominicana,* Santo Domingo, 1968.

Contin, Aybar, Pedro René. *Notas acerca de la poesia dominicana,* Santo Domingo, Publicaciones de la Secretaria de Estado de Educación y Bellas Artes, 1947.

__________. "Acerca de la novela dominicana," in *El Caribe* (Santo Domingo, Nov. 12, 14, 15, 1957).

Deive, Carlos Esteban. *Tendencias de la novela contemporánea,* Santo Domingo, Col. Arquero, 1963.

Deschamps, Enrique. "Movimento literario y artistico" in his *La Republica Dominicana,* Barcelona, 1907.

Duarte, Crispin Ayala. *Resumen histórico-critico de la literatura hispano-*

americana, Caracas, 1927. [Section covering Dominican literature, pp. 81-92.]

__________. "Tratado antológica-crítico de la literatura dominicana," in *Boletín de la Academia Venezolana,* Caracas, 1934, Vol. I, pp. 66-69, 179-208.

Francisco, Ramón. *Literatura dominicana* 60, Santiago de los Caballeros, UCMM, 1969.

Frías, Fernando. "Teatro nacional: una realidad," in *La Nación* (May 26, 1946).

Fuentes, Carlos. "La nueva novela latinoamericana," in Suplemento de Siempre of *La cultura de Mexico,* No. 128 (July 29, 1964).

García Godoy, Federico. *La literatura dominicana,* Paris, New York, 1916; separately published in the *Revue Hispanique,* 1916, XXXVII.

__________. "Vida intelectual dominicana," in *Nuestra America,* (July, 1919), trans. into English in *Inter-America,* New York, 1920, pp. 298-303.

Garrido, Puello, E.O. *Narraciones y Tradiciones Sureñas,* Santo Domingo, Postigo, No. 18 of Col. Pensamiento Dominicano, 1962.

Goico Castro, Manuel de Jesús. *Literatura dramática dominicana,* [covers Dominican theatre, 1558-1944].

__________. *Raiz y trayectoria del teatro en la literatura nacional,* in *Anales de la Universidad de Santo Domingo,* Nos. 33-36 (1945), Nos. 37-38 (1946).

Hernández de Norman, Isabel. *La novela romántica en las Antillas,* New York, Ateneo puertorriqueño de New York, 1969.

Henríquez Ureña, Max. *Breve historia del modernismo,* 1st ed., Mexico, 1954; 2nd ed., Mexico, 1957, Mexico, F.C.E., 3rd. ed., 1962.

__________. *Panorama histórico de la literatura dominicana,* 2 vols., 1st. ed., Rio de Janeiro, 1945; 2nd ed., Santo Domingo, 1965; 3rd ed., Santo Domingo, Col. Pensamiento Dominicano, 1966.

__________. Chapter XIV in *Panorama Histórico de la Republica Dominicana,* Santo Domingo, 1966.

Henríquez Ureña, Pedro. Chapter on Dominican literature, in *Historia Universal de la literatura,* edited by Santiago Prampolini, Vol. XII, Buenos Aires, 1941.

__________. "Las antologías dominicanas," in *Analectas,* Vol. VII, No. 5, Santo Domingo, February 10, 1935.

__________. Bibliografía literaria de Santo Domingo," in *Repertoria Américano,* San José, Costa Rica (September 7, 14, 21, 1929).

__________. *La cultura y las letras coloniales en Santo Domingo,* Buenos Aires, 1936.

__________. *Literatura dominicana,* Paris, Revue Hispanique, 1917.

__________. *Literary Currents in Hispanic America,* Cambridge, Harvard University Press, 1945, and in original Spanish as *Las corrientes literarias en la América hispaña,* Mexico-Buenos Aires, Fondo de Cultura Economica, 1945; Mexico, 1949.

__________. *Música popular en América* (Conferencias del Colegio Nacional de la Universidad de la Plata), Vol. I (1930). La Plata.

__________. *Obra Critica* (includes *La cultura y las letras coloniales en Santo Domingo* and *El teatro de la America española en la epoca colonial*), Mexico, Fondo de Cultura Economica, 1960.

__________. "Romances en America," in *Cuba Contemporánea,* Havana, 1913.

__________. *Vida intelectual de Santo Domingo,* Santo Domingo, Imp. "Horas de estudio," 1910.

Hernández, Franco Tomas. *La poésie a la Rèpublique Dominicaine,* Paris, 1923; later republished in *Cuadernos dominicanos de cultura* (1952), pp. 109-110.

__________. *Apuntes sobre poesia popular y poesia negra en las Antillas,* San Salvador, Publicaciones Ateneo El Salvador, 1942.

Imbert, E. Anderson. *Historia de la literatura hispanoamericana,* Mexico, Fondo de Cultura Economica, 1961.

Incháustegui Cabral, Hector. *De literatura dominicana siglo XX,* Santiago, UCMM, Copyright, 1968, published 1969; 2nd ed., 1973.

__________. "La poesia de tema negro en Santo Domingo," in *Eme-Eme. Estudios Dominicanos,* 1, 2 (1972); and 1, 5 (1973).

Lebron Saviñon, Mariano. *Luces del trópico,* Buenos Aires, Americalee, 1949.

Lockward, Jaime A. *Teatro dominicano, pasado y presente,* Ciudad Trujillo (Santo Domingo), Editora *La Nación,* 1959.

Lugo, Américo. "Notas sobre nuestro movimento literario," chapter in his *Bibliografia,* 1906. [His preface to the novel *Pinares a dentro* by Pedro Archimbault (Barcelona, 1929), also gives a panorama of then current Dominican writing, with bibliographies].

Martinez, Rufino. *Diccionario biográfico-historico dominicano 1821-1930,* Santo Domingo, UASD, 1971.

Matos, Esthervina. *Estudios de la literatura dominicana,* Ciudad Trujillo, 1955.

Mejia, Abigail. *Historia de la literatura dominicana,* 1st ed., 1929; 2nd ed., Santo Domingo, Editorial "Caribes," 1937.

Menéndez y Pelayo, Marcelino. *Historia de la poesia hispanoamericana,* 2 volumes, Madrid, 1911-1931. [Chapter IV is devoted to Santo Domingo writers.]

Miller, Elizabeth Ann. *Some of the types of Novels in the Dominican Republic* (mimeograph), cited in the Universidad Católica Madre y Maestra journal, *EME-EME,* III, 14 (Sept.-Oct. 1974), p. 1.

Mota Medrano, Fabio Amable. *Relives alumbrados: 14 Poetas (Microensayos),* Santo Domingo, Imprensora "La Isabella," 1971.

Pacheco, Armando Oscar. "La novela dominicana," *Actualidad,* 1, 1 (1947); pp. 1, 4-6, 8, 12 (1947), 3 and 6.

Penson, César Nicolas (ed.). *Reseña historico-critica de la poesia en Santo Domingo,* Santo Domingo, 1892.

Pérez y Pérez, Carlos Federico. *Evolución poetica dominicana,* Buenos Aires, Ed. Poblet, 1956.

__________. *La naturaleza en la novela hispanoamericana,* 1943.

"Poesia Negra en Santo Domingo," in "Suplemento Cultural" of *Nacional de Ahora* (April 30, 1972).

Quiros, Emilio J. *Curso de literatura,* Santo Domingo De la Salle, Dominican Republic, 1970. [High school level.]

Rodriguez Demorizi, Emilio. "De la poesia francesa en Santo Domingo," *Cuadernos Dominicanos de Cultura,* 11, 16 (1944).

__________. *La imprenta y los primeros periodicos en S.D.,* Ciudad Trujillo, Imprenta San Francisco, 1944.

__________. "La poesia patriotica en Santo Domingo," *Cuadernos Dominicanos de Cultura,* 1, 6 (1944).

__________. *Rubén Dario y sus amigos dominicanos,* Bogotá, Ediciones Espiral, 1948.

__________. *Seudónimos dominicanos,* Ciudad Trujillo, Editora Montalvo, 1956.

__________. *Tradiciones y cuentos dominicanos,* Santo Domingo, Julio D. Postigo e hijos Editores, 1969.

Rosario Candelier, Bruno. "Poesia negra en Santo Domingo," in Suplemento to *El Nacional* (April 30, 1972).

Rueda, Manuel. *Compositores dramaticos,* 1968.

__________. *Conocimiento y poesia en el folklore,* Santo Domingo, Arte y Cine, 1971.

__________. "Vigil Diaz: Vedrinismo y versolibrismo en la Republica Dominicana," in Rueda's *Antologia panoramica de la poesia dominicana contemporánea* (1912-1962), Santiago de los Caballeros, Dominican Republic, UCMM, 1972, pp. 418-426.

Serra, V. José Maria. *Apuntes para la historia de los Trinitarios,* Santo Domingo, 1887.

Tejera, Apolinar. *Literatura dominicana. Comentarios critico-históricos,* Santo Domingo, 1922.

Trelles, Carlos Manuel. "Apuntes par la bibliografia dominicana," in *Ensayo de bibliografia cubana de los siglos XVII y XVIII,* Matanzas, 1907, pp. 195-224, new printing in Havana, 1927. [This treatment of the two earliest centuries is supplemented by extracts from *Biblioteca Hispanoamericana Septentrional* by José Mariano Beristain y Sousa, Mexico, 1816-1821, published by Pedro Henriquez Ureña in the review *Ateneo,* 1910-11, and in *La Cultura y las letras coloniales en Santo Domingo,* Buenos Aires, 1936.

Underwood, Edna W. "Literature of Dominica" in *West Indian Review* (October, 1936), pp. 47-48.

____________. "Poets and Prose Writers of Santo Domingo," in *W.I. Review* (January, 1936), pp. 32-35; (February), pp. 33-35; (March), pp. 21-25.

Valldeperes, Manuel. "Evolución de la novela en la República Dominicana," in *Cuadernos Hispanoamericanos* (1967).

Valverde, Sebastián Emilio. "El cuento tradicional en la Republica Dominicana," in *Cuadernos Dominicanos de Cultura,* IX, 108 (1952).

Veloz Maggiolo, Marcio. *Cultura, teatro y relatos en Santo Domingo,* Santiago, Talleres de la Informacion, 1972.

DOMINICAN REPUBLIC: ANTHOLOGIES

Alcántara Almánzar, José. *Antologia de la literatura dominicana,* Santo Domingo, E.C.D., 1972.

Alfau Duran, Vililio. *Apuntes para la historia de la poesia en S.D.,* Ciudad Trujillo, Imprenta Garcia, 1953.

__________. "Apuntes para la bibliografia poética dominicana," in *Clio,* XXXIII (1965), and XXXVI (1968).

__________. "Apuntes para la bibliografia de la novela en S.D.," in *El Caribe* (February 18, April 30, May 2, 3, 5, 7, 8, 11, 16 and 21; all 1959).

Alfonseca, Iván. *Antologia biográfica,* Buenos Aires, Edit. Claridad, 1942. (Poets born since 1900).

Almanaque de "El Album." Santiago de los Caballeros, 1905.

Almanaque de "El Album." Santiago de los Caballeros, 1908.

Almanaque Dominicano. Santiago, Dominican Republic, 1911.

Antologia de la literatura dominicana, Vols. IV and V of Colección Trujillo, Santo Domingo, Edición del Gobierno Dominicano, 1944.

Antologia de la literatura dominicana, Verse, Vol. I; Prose, Vol. II, Santiago, Ed. El Diario, 1944.

Andrade, Manuel J. *Folk-lore from the Dominican Republic,* New York, Publicaciones of the American Folk-lore Society, 19??.

Arango, Rubén C. and Figueroa, Wilfredo. *Poesia antillana,* Santo Domingo, Edit. Cultural Dominicana, 1972.

Arzeno, Julio. *Del Folklore musical dominicano,* 1927.

Avelino, Andrés. *Pequeña antologia postumista,* Santo Domingo, 1924.

__________. "Del movimiento postumista hispanoamericano," in *Repertorio Americano,* VI, 1 (1923).

Bazil, Osvaldo. *Parnaso Dominicano: Compilación completa de los mejores poetas de la República de Santo Domingo,* Barcelona, Maucci, 1915.

Caillet Bois, Julio. *Antologia de la poesia hispanoamericana,* Madrid, Aguilar, 1965.

Cartagena, Aida. *Narradores dominicanos,* Santo Domingo, Monte Avila Editores, 1969.

Castellanos, José. *Lira de Quisqueya. Poesias Dominicanas,* [con notas biograficas de sus autores], Santo Domingo, 1874. [This was the very first first Dominican anthology.]

Castro Noboa, H.B. de. *Antologia poética trujillista,* Santiago de los Caballeros, Edit. El Diario, 1946.

Conde, Pedro. *Antologia informal,* Santo Domingo, Edit. Nacional, 1970.

Contin Aybar, Pedro René. *Antologia poética dominicana,* Santiago, Editorial

El Diario, Dominican Republic, 1943, 1945, 1951. [Each year included new works by new poets.]

__________. *Poesia dominicana,* Santo Domingo, Postigo, 1969.

__________. Vicente Llorens Castillo, and H. Incháustagui Cabral, *Antologia de la literatura dominicana* (Vol. I: Verse, Vol. II: Prose) Cuidad Trujillo, Edición del Gobierno Dominicano, 1944.

Fernández Spencer, Antonio. *Nueva poesia dominicana,* Madrid, Ed. Cultura Hispanica, 1953.

Fiallo y Cabral, Fabio (ed.). *Las mejores poesias liricas de los mejores poetas,* Vol. LIX, Barcelona, 1931.

Franco, José Ulises. *Cuentos y cosas de mi tierra,* Santiago, D.R., 1969.

Fuentos y Matons, Laureano, (coll. & ed.). *Las artes en Santiago de Cuba,* Santiago, Cuba, 1893.

Garcia, José Gabriel. *El lector dominicano* [school anthology], Santo Domingo, 1894.

Garrido, Edna. *Versiones dominicanos de románces españoles,* Ciudad Trujillo, Pol. Hermanos Editores, 1946.

Garrido Puello, E.O. *Narraciones y tradiciones sureñas,* Santo Domingo, Postigo, 19??.

Henriques Ureña, Pedro. *Cuadernos de poesia dominicana,* Santo Domingo, Museo Nacional, n.d.

__________. "Bibliografía literaria de Santo Domingo," in *Repertorio Americana* (San Jose, C.R.), XIX (1929), pp. 138-140; 149-150; 174-175.

__________. *La cultura y las letras coloniales en Santo Domingo,* Buenos Aires, Imprenta de la Universidad, 1936. [criticism and anthology].

Jiménez, José Olivio. *Antologia de la poesia hispanoamericana contemporánea 1914-1970,* Madrid, 1972.

"Las bellas letras en la República Dominicana" [pp. 308-374; an anthology] in the general directory, *La República Dominicana,* Santiago de los Caballeros [but printed in Barcelona, Spain, 1907].

Matos, Esthervina. *Estudios de literatura dominicana,* Ciudad Trujillo, Dominican Republic, 1955.

Mejia Ricart, Gustavo Adolfo. *Antologia de poetas dominicanos,* Cuidad Trujillo, La palabora de S.D., 1954.

Mieses Burgos, Franklin. *Antologia,* Cuidad Trujillo, 1952.

Morel, Tomás E. *Del llano y de la loma,* 1937. [A collection of folklore and of works created by poets in the folk tradition.]

Movimiento Cultural. *La Mascara, Concurso dominicano de cuentos 1966,* S.D. Talleres de Arte y Cine, 1968.

__________. *Concurso dominicano de cuentos 1967,* S.D. Imprenta Amigo del Hogar, 1969.

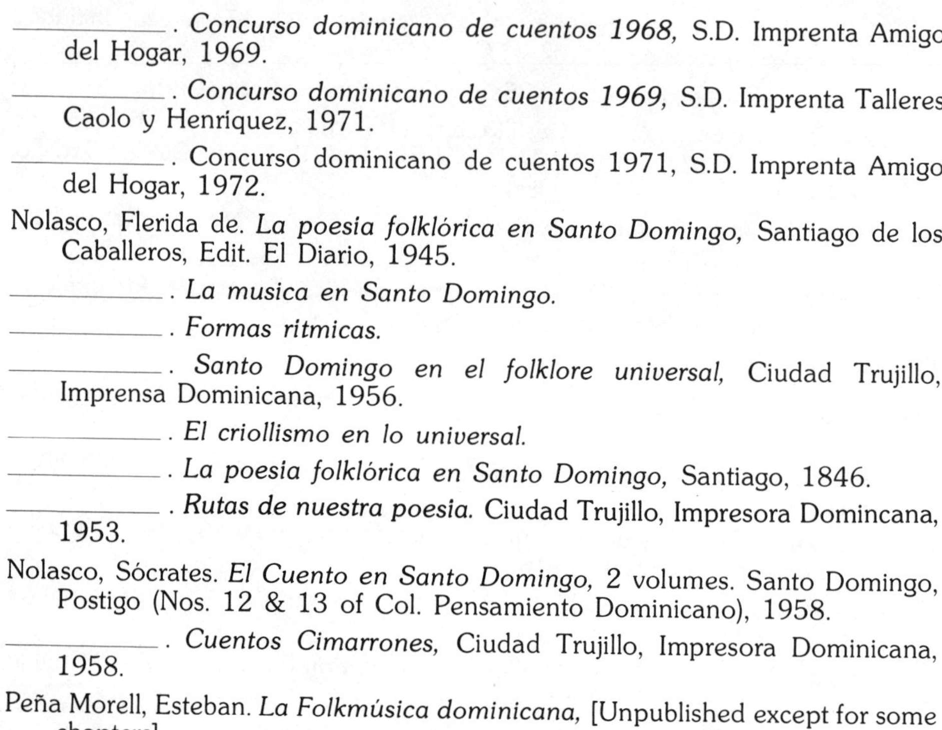

———. *Concurso dominicano de cuentos 1968,* S.D. Imprenta Amigo del Hogar, 1969.

———. *Concurso dominicano de cuentos 1969,* S.D. Imprenta Talleres Caolo y Henriquez, 1971.

———. Concurso dominicano de cuentos 1971, S.D. Imprenta Amigo del Hogar, 1972.

Nolasco, Flerida de. *La poesia folklórica en Santo Domingo,* Santiago de los Caballeros, Edit. El Diario, 1945.

———. *La musica en Santo Domingo.*

———. *Formas ritmicas.*

———. *Santo Domingo en el folklore universal,* Ciudad Trujillo, Imprensa Dominicana, 1956.

———. *El criollismo en lo universal.*

———. *La poesia folklórica en Santo Domingo,* Santiago, 1846.

———. *Rutas de nuestra poesia.* Ciudad Trujillo, Impresora Domincana, 1953.

Nolasco, Sócrates. *El Cuento en Santo Domingo,* 2 volumes. Santo Domingo, Postigo (Nos. 12 & 13 of Col. Pensamiento Dominicano), 1958.

———. *Cuentos Cimarrones,* Ciudad Trujillo, Impresora Dominicana, 1958.

Peña Morell, Esteban. *La Folkmúsica dominicana,* [Unpublished except for some chapters].

Pérez, Echavarria, Miguel Román. *Seis cuentistas dominicanos,* Buenos Aires, Imprenta Ferrari Hermanos, 1948.

Penson, César Nicolás (ed.). *Colección de poesias dominicanos,* collected by the Real Academia Española in 1892 for the Dominican Commission encharged with contributing materials to the *Antologia de poetas hispanoamericanos.*

———, (ed.). *Reseña histórico critica de la poesia en Santo Domingo,* 1892.

Pérez, Carlos Federico. *Evolución poética dominicana,* Buenos Aires, Ed. Poblet, 1956.

Pueblo Sangre y Canto. *Publicaciones del Frente Cultural,* Santo Domingo, 1965.

Quiros, Emilio J. *Antologia dominicana,* Santo Domingo, De La Salle, 1969.

Ravelo, José de Jesús. *Historia de los himnos dominicanos,* 1934.

Rodriguez Demorizi, Emilio. *Cuentos de politica criolla,* Santo Domingo, Postigo, 1963.

———. *Del romancero dominicano,* Santiago, Dominican Republic, Col. Martinez Boog, 1943.

__________. *Fábulas dominicanas,* Ciudad Trujillo, Editora Montalvo, 1946.

__________. *Poesia popular dominicana,* 1st ed., Ciudad Trujillo, 1938; 2nd ed., Santo Domingo, UCMM, 1973.

__________. *Refranero dominicano,* Roma, Stab. Tipografico G. Menaglia, 1950.

__________. *Rutas de nuestra poesia,* Ciudad Trujillo, Impresora Dominicana, 1953.

Rosario Candelier, Bruno. "Poesia negra en Santo Domingo," Santo Domingo, Suplemento Cultural in *El Nacional* (April 30, 1972).

Rueda, Manuel and Lupo Hernández Rueda. *Antologia Panorámica de la Poesia Dominicana Contemporánea 1912-1962,* 2 volumes, Santiago de los Caballeros, Ediciones de la UCMM, Dominican Republic, 1972 [but second volume not yet issued as of 1975].

Sanabia, Rafael Emilio. *Cultura dominicana.* I. *Nuestros jóvenes poetas,* Santo Domingo, 1927; Vol. II. *Nuestras mejores poetisas,* 1928. III. *Nuestra poesia,* Santiago, 1944.

__________. *Nuestros jóvenes poetas,* Santo Domingo, Roques Román Hermanos Editores, 1927.

__________. *Nuestros mejores poetisas,* S.D., Roques Román Hermanos Editores, 1928.

__________. *Nuestra poesia,* Santiago, D.R., Edit. La Información, 1943.

Townsend, Francis E. *Quisquaya, a panoramic Anthology of Dominican Verse,* 1st ed., U.S.A., 1947; 2nd ed., Ciudad Trujillo, Edit. El Caribe, 1954.

Troncoso de la Concha, Manuel de Jesús. *Narraciones dominicanas,* Santiago, Dominican Republic, Edit. El Diario, 1946.

PUERTO RICO: CRITICAL STUDIES AND BIBLIOGRAPHIES

Agridulce, Anticuado. "Parodia modernista," *Puerto Rico Ilustrado,* No. 182, (August 23, 1913).

Alegria, Ricardo E. *El tema del cafe en la literatura puertorriqueña,* San Juan, 19??.

Arana Soto, Salvador. *Diccionario de temas regionalistas en la poesia puertorriqueña,* San Juan, Edit. Club de la Prensa, 1961.

Arce de Vásquez, Margot. *Impresiones: Notas puertorriqueñas,* San Juan, Edit. Yaurel, 1950.

__________. *Los temas fundamentales de la novela puertorriqueña durante la primera decada de Puerto Rico como Estado Libre Asociado a Los Estados Unidos* (1952-1962), Washington, D.C., 1969.

Arrivi, Francisco. *Areyto mayor,* San Juan, Instituto de Cultura Puertorriqueña, 1966 (on Puerto Rican theatre).

__________. *Conciencia puertorriqueña del teatro contemporáneo, 1937-1956,* San Juan, Instituto de Cultura Puertorriqueño, 1967.

Asomante. San Juan, Nos. 1 and 2, 1955. (Issues on Puerto Rican writing).

Asomante. Número antológico, III (1956), San Juan, Puerto Rico.

El autor dramatico: Primer seminario de dramaturgia. San Juan, Instituto de Cultura puertorriqueña, 1963. (Papers read at seminar).

Ayala, D.C. *Resumen histórico-critico de la literatura hispanoamericana,* Caracas, 1927.

Babin, Maria Teresa. *Jornadas literarias: temas de Puerto Rico,* Barcelona, Edic. Rumbos, 1967.

Balseiro, José A. *El Vigia: ensayos,* 3 Vols., Madrid, Edit. Mundo Latino, 1925-1942.

Berenguer, Wilfredo. "Ensaladillos Villaclareñas," in *Archivos del Folklore cubano,* Havana, 1929.

Braschi, Wilfredo. *Apuntes sobre el teatro puertorriqueño,* San Juan, Edit. Coqui, 1970.

Cadilla de Martinez, Maria. *La poesia popular en Puerto Rico,* Madrid, Imp. Moderna, 1933.

Camejo, Raphael W. "El desenvolvimiento de la poesia modernista en Puerto Rico y sus iniciadores," in *Puerto Rico Ilustrado,* No. 365 (February 24, 1917).

Canino Salgado, Marcelino. *La copla y el romance populares en la tradición oral de Puerto Rico,* San Juan, Instituto de Cultura Puertorriqueña, 1968.

Colberg Petrovich, Juan Enrique. *Cuatro autores clasicos contemporáneos de Puerto Rico,* San Juan, Edit. Cordillera, 1966.

Critica y antologia de la poesia puertorriqueña. Trabajos Presentados o leidos en el primer congreso de poesia puertorriqueña celebrado en Yauco, Puerto Rico, el 25 de agosto de 1957, San Juan, Instituto de Cultural Puertorriqueña, 1958.

Cruz Monclova, Lidio. *Curiosidades literarias. Folios,* San Juan, Publicaciones de la Biblioteca de Autores Puertorriqueños, April 1957.

El cuento puertorriqueño en el siglo XX. Rio Piedras, Edit. Universitaria, Universidad de Puerto Rico, 1963.

Dávila, José Antonio. *Prosa. Ensayos, Articulos y cartas literarias,* San Juan, 1971.

Esteves, José de Jesús. *El modernismo en la poesia,* Conferencias Dominicales de la Biblioteca Insular de Puerto Rico, San Juan, Bureau of Supplies-Printing and Transportation, 1914.

Ferrer Canales, José. *Acentos civicos: Marti, Puerto Rico y otros temas,* Rio Piedras, Edit. Edil, 1972.

Fonfrias, Ernesto Juan. *Presencia jibara desde Manuel Alonso hasta Don Florito,* San Juan, Edit. Club de la Prensa, 1957.

__________. *Sementera: ensayos breves y biografias minimas,* San Juan, Edit. Club de la Prensa, 1962.

Franco Oppenheimer, Félix. *Imagen de Puerto Rico en su poesia,* Mexico, Universidad Nacional Autónoma, 1964; and reprint: San Juan, Editorial Universitaria, Universidad de Puerto Rico, 1972 (?).

Geigel y Zenón, José. *Bibliografia puertorriqueña 1892-1894.*

Gómez Tejera, Carmen. *La novela en Puerto Rico: apuntes para su historia,* Rio Piedras, Junta Editora, Universidad de Puerto Rico, copyright 1947, published 1948.

Gonzáles, José Emilio. *Los poetas puertorriqueños de la decada de 1930,* San Juan, 1960.

__________. *La poesia contemporánea de Puerto Rico, 1930-1960,* San Juan, Instituto de Cultura Puertorriqueña, 1972.

Henriquez Ureña, Max. *El intercambio de influencias literarios entre Estre y América,* Havana, 1926.

Hernández Aquino, Luis (comp.). *El modernismo en Puerto Rico: Poesia y Prosa,* San Juan, Edic. de la Torre, 1967. (Basically an anthology but with biographical and critical information.)

__________, (comp). *Nuestra aventura literaria (Los ismos en la poesia puertorriqueña), 1913-1948,* 2nd ed., San Juan, Edic. de la Torre, 1966.

__________. *Poesia puertorriqueña,* San Juan, Edit. de la Universidad de Puerto Rico, 1954.

Jesús Castro, Tomás de. *Esbozos,* Barcelona, Edic. Rumbos, Vol. 1: 1945; Vol. II: 1957.

Jiménez de Báez, Yvette. *La décima popular en Puerto Rico,* Xalapa, Mexico, Universidad Veracruzana, 1964.

————. *Lirica cortesana y lirica popular,* Mexico, El Colegio de Mexico, 1969. (Antecedents of Puerto Rico's popular poetry.)

Laguerre, Enrique A. *La poesia modernista en Puerto Rico,* San Juan, Edit. Coqui, 1969.

Literatura puertorriqueña: 21 conferencias. San Juan, Instituto de Cultura Puertorriqueña, 1969.

Lluch Mora, Francisco. *Miradero: ensayos de critica literaria,* San Juan, Edit. Cordillera, 1966.

Love, Francisca Arana de. *Los temas fundamentales de la novela puertorriqueña durante la primera decada de Puerto Rico como Estado Libre Associado de los Estados Unidos,* Barcelona, Tip. Miguza, 1969. [1st ed. was 1956.]

Manrique, Cabrera, Francisco. *História de la literatura puertorriqueña,* Mexico, 2nd ed., Brevarios del Fondo de Cultura Economica, 1957; 4th ed., Rio Piedras, Edit. Cultural, 1971.

Márques, René. *Ensayos (1953-1966),* 2nd ed., revised, Rio Piedras, Edit. Antillana, 1966.

Martin, José Luis. *Arco y flecha (Apuntado a la vida y a las obras): Estudios de critica literaria,* San Juan, Edit. Club de la Prensa, 1961.

————, and Esther M. Melón. *Literaria puertorriqueña: antologia general,* Rio Piedras, Edit. Edil, 1970.

Martinez Plee, Manuel. "Poetas modernista de Puerto Rico" in *Libro azul de Puerto Rico,* San Juan, El Libro Azul Publishing Co., 1923.

Matilla, Alfredo and Iván Silen. *The Puerto Rican Poets,* New York, Bantam, 1972. [An anthology with some background information.]

Matos Bernier, Félix. *Isla de arte,* San Juan, Imp. La Primavera, 1907.

Meléndez, Concha. *Figuración de Puerto Rico y otros estudios,* San Juan, Instituto de Cultura Puertorriqueña, 1958.

————. *Obras completas,* 2 Vols., San Juan, Instituto de Cultura Puertorriqueña, 1970.

————. *Poetas hispanoamericanos diversos,* San Juan, Edit. Cordillera, 1971. (Covers Rubén Dario, Pablo Neruda and six Puerto Rican poets.)

Morales Carrion, Arturo. *Ojeada al proceso histórico y otros ensayos,* San Juan, Edit. Cordillera, 1971.

Morfi, Angelina. *Temas del teatro,* Santo Domingo, Dominican Republic, Editora del Caribe, 1969.

Nolasco, Sócrates. *Escritores de Puerto Rico,* Manzanillo, Cuba, Edit. El Arte, 1953, 1958.

Pasarell, Emilio Julio. *Crigenes y desarrollo de la afición teatral en Puerto Rico,* Rio Piedras, Edit. Universitaria, Universidad de Puerto Rico, 1951.

Pedreira, Antonio S. *Aclaraciones y critica,* Rio Piedras, Edit. Edil, 1969.

__________. *Tres ensayos,* Rio Piedras, Edit. Edil, 1969.

Primer Congreso de poesia puertorriqueña. Critica y antologia de la poesia puertorriqueña, San Juan, Puerto Rico, 1958.

__________. "Los primeros escritores y los primeros libros puertorriqueños," in *Summer School Review* (July 14, 1933, U. of P.R.).

Primicias de las letras puertorriqueñas, San Juan, Instituto de Cultura Puertorriqueña, 1970.

Quiles de la Luz, Lillian. *El cuento en la literatura puertorriqueña,* Rio Piedras, Edit. Universidad de Puerto Rico, 1968.

Quiñones, Samuel R. *Temas y letras,* San Juan, Biblioteca de Autores puertorriqueños, 1941.

Rivera de Alvarez, Josefina. *Diccionario de literatura puertorriqueña,* 1st ed., San Juan, Ediciones de la Torre, Universidad de Puerto Rico, 1955; 2nd ed., revised and augmented, San Juan, Instituto de Cultura Puertorriqueña, 1970.

__________. *Historia de la literatura puertorriqueña,* Santurce, Edit. del Departamiento de Instrucción Pública, 1969.

Rivera, Modesto. *El modernismo—La Prosa (Literatura Puertorriqueña, 21 Conferencias),* San Juan, Instituto de Cultura Puertorriqueña, 1960.

Rivera Rivera, Eloisa. *La poesia en Puerto Rico antes de 1843,* San Juan, Instituto de Cultura Puertorriqueña, 1965.

Robles de Cardona, Mariana. *Búsqueda y plasmación de nuestra personalidad: antologia critica del ensayo puertorriqueño desde sus origenes hasta la generación del 30,* San Juan, Edit. Club de la Prensa, 1958.

Rodriguez Escudero, Nestor A. *El mar en la literatura puertorriqueña y otros ensayos,* Barcelona, Edic. Rumbos, 1967.

Rodriguez Velázquez, Jaime Luis. *La poesia del romanticismo al modernismo en Puerto Rico,* Mexico, Universidad Nacional Autónoma de Mexico, 1965.

Rosa-Nieves, Cesáreo. *Historia panoramica de la literatura puertorriqueña (1589-1959),* 2 Vols., San Juan, Edit. Campos, 1963.

__________. *Plumas estelares en las letras de Puerto Rico,* 2 Vols., San Juan, Edic. de la Torre, 1967-1971.

__________. *La poesia en Puerto Rico: historia de los temas poéticos en la literatura puertorriqueña,* Mexico, Edit. Tésis, 1943, 1958, 3rd ed., San Juan, Edit. Edil, 1969.

__________. *Voz folklórica de Puerto Rico,* San Juan, 1967.

__________. *Ensayos escogidos (apuntaciones de critica literaria sobre algunos temas puertorriqueños),* San Juan, Publicaciones de la Academia de Artes y Ciencias de Puerto Rico, Cuaderno n. 5, 1970.

__________. *La lámpara del faro: variaciones criticas sobre temas puertorriqueños,* 2 Vols., San Juan, Edit. Club de la Prensa, 1957-1960.

———. *Tierra y lamento: rodeos de contorno para una telurica interpretación poética de la puertorriqueño,* San Juan, Edit. Club de la Prensa, 1958.

———. *Cinco generaciones estéticas en la poesia puertorriqueña,* Spain, 1956.

Sáez, Antonia. *El teatro en Puerto Rico (Notas para suhistória),* Rio Piedras, Universidad de Puerto Rico, 1950.

Sales, Maria de. *El sentimiento religioso en la lirica puertorriqueña,* Cuernavaca, Mexico, Centro Intercultural de Documentación, 1966.

Silva, Ana Margarita. *El jibaro en la literatura de Puerto Rico (comparado con el campesino de españa e hispanoamerica),* 2nd ed., San Juan, Imp. Venezuela, 1957.

Soto Ramos, Julio. *Cumbre y remanso: ensayos de apreciación literaria y otros articulos,* San Juan, Edit. Cordillera, 1963.

———. *Una pica en Flandes (ensayos y otros articulos),* San Juan, Edit. Club de la Prensa, 1959.

Valbuena Briones, Angel, and Luis Hernández Aquino. *Nueva poesia de Puerto Rico,* Madrid, 1952.

PUERTO RICO: ANTHOLOGIES

Aguinaldo Puerto-Riqueño: Coleccion de producciones originales en verso y prosa. Puerto Rico, Imp. de Gimbernet y Dalmau, 1843; facsimile edition: San Juan, Edit. Coquí, 1968.

Algarin, Miguel and Miguel Piñero (eds.), *Nuyorican Poetry. An Anthology of Puerto Rican Words and Feeling,* New York, William Morrow, 1975 (contains Spanish and American English texts of New York poets of P.R. descent or origin).

Alonso, Manuel A. *El Jibaro: cuadro de costumbres de la Isla de Puerto Rico,* San Juan, Instituto de Cultura Puertorriqueña, 1970. (First published as El Gibaro, Barcelona, 1849).

Antologia de jovenes poetas. San Juan, Instituto de Cultura Puertorriqueña, 1965.

Antologia de la poesia puertorriqueña. San Juan, El Cemí, 1968.

Antologia de cuentos puertorriqueños. Foreword and selection by Enrique A. Laguerre, Mexico, Edit. Orión, 1954.

Antologia poética de Asomante, 1945-1959. San Juan, Ateneo Puertorriqueño, 1962.

Anthology of Puerto Rican Poetry in New York. New York, Monthly Review Press, 1972.

Arce y Vásquez, Margot, Laura Gallego, and Luis de Arrigoitia. *Lecturas puertorriqueñas: Poesia,* Sharon, Conn., Troutman Press, 1968.

Cabrera, J.F. (ed.). *Poetas de Puerto Rico,* Mexico, Edit. Orbre, 1950.

Cancel Negrón, Ramon (comp.). *Antologia de la joven poesia universitaria de Puerto Rico,* San Juan, Edit. Campos, 1959.

Chevremont y Alegria. *Antologia de poetas jóvenes de Puerto Rico,* San Juan, Real Hermanos, 1918.

Cooke, Paul J. *Antologia de cuentos puertorriqueños,* Godfrey, Ill., Monticello College, 1956.

Critica y antologia de la poesia puertorriqueña. San Juan, Instituto de Cultura Puertorriqueña, 1958.

Cuentos puertorriqueños de hoy. 3rd ed., Selection and foreword by René Marqués, Rio Piedras, Edit. Cultural, 1971.

Fernández Juncos, Manuel. *Antologia puertorriqueña: prosa y verso para lectura escolar,* 1st ed., San Juan, 1913; and New York, Hinds, Noble and Eldridge, 1913.

Fernández-Mendez, Eugenio. *Antologia de la poesia puertorriqueña,* San Juan, Edic. "El Cemi," 1968.

Ferrer, Canales, José. *Acentos civicos: Marti, Puerto Rico y otros temas,* Rio Piedras, Edit. Edil, 1972.

Hernández Aquino, Luis (comp.). *El modernismo en Puerto Rico: poesia y prosa,* San Juan, Edicones de la Torre, Universidad de Puerto Rico, 1967.

__________. *Poesia puertorriqueña,* San Juan, Edit. de la Universidad de Puerto Rico, 1954.

__________. *Poetas Aguadillandos: antologia poética,* San Juan, 1967.

__________. *Poetas de Lares: antologia,* San Juan, Instituto de Cultural de Lares, 1966.

Jordan, June and Terri Busk. *The Voice of the Children,* New York, Washington Square Press, 1974; first published, New York, Holt, Rinehart, 1970.

Labarthe López, Pedro Juan. *Antologia de poetas contemporáneos de Puerto Rico,* Mexico, 1946.

Laguerre, Enrique A. *La poesia modernista en Puerto Rico,* San Juan, Edit. Coquí, 1969.

Lluch Mora, Francisco. *Miradero: ensayos de critica literaria,* San Juan, Edit. Cordillera, 1966.

López de Vega, Maximiliano. *Las cien mejores poesias de Puerto Rico,* Rio Piedras, Edit. Edil, 1970.

Martinez Masdeu, Edgar, and Esther M. Melon. *Literatura puertorriqueña: antologia general,* Rio Piedras, Edit. Edil, 1970.

Matilla, Alfredo and Ivan Silén. *The Puerto Rican Poets (Los poetas puertorriqueños),* New York, Bantam, 1972.

Matos Bernier, Félix. *Isla de arte,* San Juan, Imp. La Primavera, 1907.

Meléndez, Concha (ed.). *El cuento, antologia de autores puertorriqueños,* San Juan, Ediciones del Gobierno, Estado Libre Asociado de Puerto Rico, 1957.

__________. *El arte del cuento en Puerto Rico,* New York, Las Américas, 1961.

__________. *Literatura de ficción en Puerto Rico: cuento y novela,* San Juan, Edit. Cordillera, 1971.

Miller, Wayne Charles. *Gathering of Ghetto Writers: Irish, Jewish, Black, and Puerto Rican,* New York, N.Y.U. Press, 19??.

Monteagudo, Escámez, Antonio M. *Album de oro de Puerto Rico,* details unknown, translated as *Golden Album of Puerto Rico,* Havana, Ores Gráficas, 1939.

Morfi, Angelina. *Antologia de teatro puertorriqueño,* San Juan, Edic. Juan Ponce de Leon, 1970.

Pedreira, Antonio S. *Aclaraciones y critica,* Rio Piedras, Edit. Edil, 1969.

Poesia puertorriqueña. Selected and foreword by Luis Hernández Aquino, Rio Piedras, Universidad de Puerto Rico, 1954.

Primer Congreso de Poesia Puertorriqueña. Critica y antologia de la poesia puertorriqueña, San Juan, Puerto Rico, 1958.

Ramirez, Raphael W. *Folklore puertorriqueño. Cuentos y adavivanzas recodides de la tradición oral,* Madrid, 1926.

Robles de Cardona, Mariana. *Búsqueda y plasmación de nuestra personalidad: antologia critica del ensayo puertorriqueño desde sus origenes hasta la generación del 30,* San Juan, Edit. Club de la Prensa, 1958.

Rodriguez, Rafael, and Iris Zayala (eds.). *Libertad y critica: Antologia des ensayo puertorriqueño,* San Juan, Edic. Libreria International, 1972.

Rosa-Nieves, Cesáreo. *Aguinaldo lirico de la poesia puertorriqueña,* San Juan, 1957, Rio Piedras, Edit. Edil, 1971.

__________. *La poesia en Puerto Rico, 1943,* San Juan, Edit. Campos, 1958, 1969.

__________, and Félix Franco Oppenheimer. *Antologia del cuento puertorriqueño,* 2 Vols., 2nd ed., San Juan, Edit. Edil, 1970.

__________. *Calambreñas: Decimario boricua (Motivos de la montaña y la ciudad),* San Juan, Edit. Cordillera, 1964.

Rosario Quiles, Luis Antonio (comp.). *Poesia nueva puertorriqueña: antologia,* San Juan, Producciones Bondo, 1971.

Soto Ramos, Julio. *Una pica en flandes (ensayos y otros articulos),* San Juan, Edit. Club de la Prensa, 1959.

Teatro puertorriqueño: Primer festival de teatro. San Juan, Instituto de Cultura puertorriqueña, 1959. [Eight more volumes: 1960, 1961, 1963, 1964 (2), 1965, 1966 and 1968—for next seven festivals.]

Torres Rivera, Enrique. *Parnaso puertorriqueño,* Barcelona, Imp. Maucci, 1920.

Valbuena Briones, Angel, and Luis Hernández Aquino (eds.). *Nueva poesia de Puerto Rico,* Madrid, Edic. Cultural Hispanica, 1952.